From the author

I never started out to become a sociologist. I actually started out as an engineering student. After my first year, I realized I had lost interest in engineering (due in part to my grade point average), which caused me to look at other fields of study. My first sociology course turned out to be the course that truly changed my life. I found that sociology helped me make sense of the world and that it was an interesting, exciting, and fun discipline. I want to share this excitement with you, so I invite you to open this book, enjoy it, and think about the issues and questions it raises. I hope you will find a new and useful way of looking at the world and seeing sociology in everyday life!

John Macionis

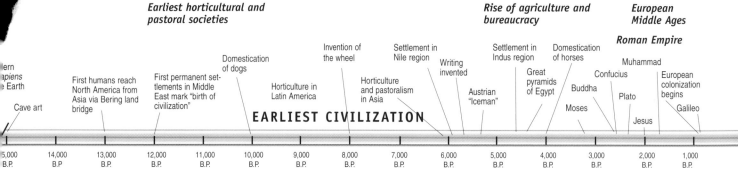

Earliest horticultural and
pastoral societies

Rise of agriculture and
bureaucracy

European
Middle Ages

Roman Empire

Invention of
the wheel

Settlement in
Nile region

Settlement in
Indus region

Domestication
of horses

Domestication
of dogs

Writing
invented

Muhammad

Confucius

First permanent set-
tlements in Middle
East mark "birth of
civilization"

Horticulture in
Latin America

Horticulture
and pastoralism
in Asia

Great
pyramids
of Egypt

Buddha

Plato

European
colonization
begins

First humans reach
North America from
Asia via Bering land
bridge

Austrian
"Iceman"

Moses

Jesus

Galileo

Cave art

EARLIEST CIVILIZATION

| 15,000 B.P. | 14,000 B.P | 13,000 B.P. | 12,000 B.P. | 11,000 B.P. | 10,000 B.P. | 9,000 B.P. | 8,000 B.P. | 7,000 B.P. | 6,000 B.P. | 5,000 B.P. | 4,000 B.P. | 3,000 B.P. | 2,000 B.P. | 1,000 B.P. |

"Baby bust"

Women's movement intensifies

U.S. life
expectancy
77 years

Civil Rights Movement

1974 Punk begins

1960 Rise of folk era and Motown

1997 Backstreet Boys lead
revival of pop

1981 MTV debuts

1999 Eminem merges musical
styles

1979 SugarHill Gang popularizes rap

1969 Woodstock

1991 Nirvana takes
grunge mainstream

1977 Disco peaks

1964 British music invasion
(The Beatles)

Rise of
nd Roll

2000
60% of U.S. women
in labor force

1965
Foreign-born
Japanese eligible
for citizenship

1970 First Earth Day

gregate

1968
First interracial
kiss on TV *(Star Trek)*

1980
Women earn majority
of college degrees

1987
Rhode Island enacts
statewide recycling law

1975
First women's
shelter

1955
First McDonald's
restaurant

1968
Dr. Martin Luther King Jr.
assassinated

1988
Last U.S. Playboy
Club closes

1981
First AIDS cases
reported

Sept. 11, 2001
Terrorist attacks

breaks

1961 European
colonization
of Africa ends

1969
Stonewall riot begins
gay rights movement

2001
War on Terrorism

1954 *Brown v. Board
of Education*

1977
First gay TV character

1973 *Roe v. Wade*

Revolutions in
USSR and
Eastern Europe
1989–1990

Persian
Gulf War
1991

Iraq War
2003–

50–1953

Vietnam War 1963–1975

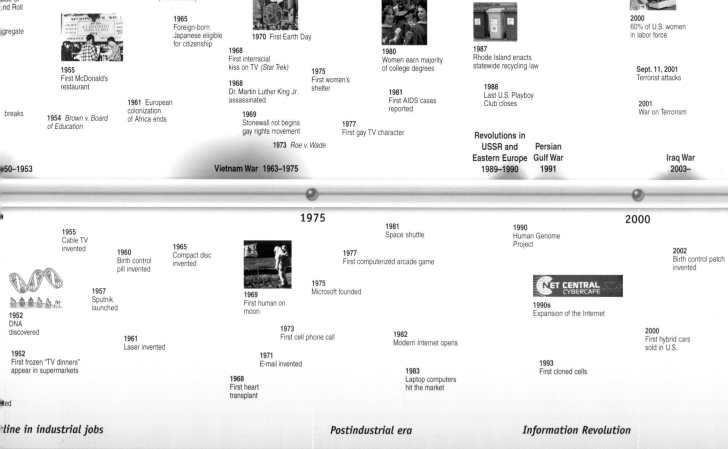

1975

2000

1955
Cable TV
invented

1981
Space shuttle

1990
Human Genome
Project

1965
Compact disc
invented

1960
Birth control
pill invented

2002
Birth control patch
invented

1977
First computerized arcade game

1957
Sputnik
launched

1969
First human on
moon

1975
Microsoft founded

1990s
Expansion of the Internet

1952
DNA
discovered

1961
Laser invented

1973
First cell phone call

1982
Modern Internet opens

2000
First hybrid cars
sold in U.S.

1952
First frozen "TV dinners"
appear in supermarkets

1971
E-mail invented

1983
Laptop computers
hit the market

1993
First cloned cells

1968
First heart
transplant

ted

line in industrial jobs

Postindustrial era

Information Revolution

| 3 billion | 4 billion | 5 billion | 6 billion |

| 150.7 million | | | 292.2 million |

*1959 Goffman debuts
"dramaturgical analysis"*

*1981 Bernard nurtures
gender studies*

Piaget probes how we learn

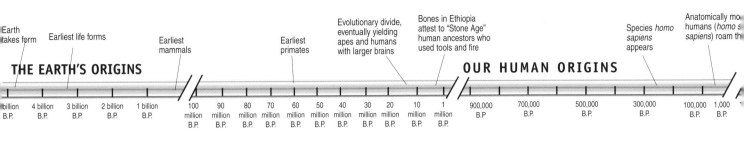

Earth
takes form

Earliest life forms

Earliest
mammals

Earliest
primates

Evolutionary divide,
eventually yielding
apes and humans
with larger brains

Bones in Ethiopia
attest to "Stone Age"
human ancestors who
used tools and fire

Species *homo
sapiens* appears

Anatomically mo
humans (*homo s
sapiens*) roam th

THE EARTH'S ORIGINS

OUR HUMAN ORIGINS

billion B.P. | 4 billion B.P. | 3 billion B.P. | 2 billion B.P. | 1 billion B.P. | 100 million B.P. | 90 million B.P. | 80 million B.P. | 70 million B.P. | 60 million B.P. | 50 million B.P. | 40 million B.P. | 30 million B.P. | 20 million B.P. | 10 million B.P. | 1 million B.P. | 900,000 B.P | 700,000 B.P. | 500,000 B.P. | 300,000 B.P. | 100,000 B.P. | 1,000 B.P.

Birth rates fall in Europe and U.S.

"Baby boom"

U.S. life
expectancy
47 years

U.S. majority in cities

Northward migration
of African Americans

Immigration to U.S.
restricted

Great Depression

1938 Rise of bluegrass

1935 Swing era begins

THE MODERN ERA

1910 Jazz era begins

1950
Rock

1916
First birth control
clinic

1932
First woman
cabinet member

1942 Chemist Albert
Hoffman takes first
LSD "trip"

1948
Armed forces des

1916
First sanitary landfill

1921
First Miss America pageant

1938
Word "teenager"
coined

0
% of U.S. women
abor force

1909
NAACP
founded

1912 Sinking of Titanic

1917
Russian Revolution

1924
Native Americans eligible
for citizenship

1931
First woman governor

1947 Jackie Robinson
baseball "color line"

1920
Women win
right to vote

1925
First College Board tests

1933
First Major League baseball
game under lights

1949
First NASCAR rac

1924
First woman senator

World War I 1914–1918

World War II 1938–1945

Korean War 1

1925

1950

1927
Lindbergh flies
across Atlantic

1947
Aerosol spray
can invented

1914
First coast-to-coast telephone call

1914
First stop sign (Detroit)

1926
Middle East starts pumping oil

1945
First atomic
explosion

1948 Record
debuts

1903 Airplane invented

1931 First electric guitar

02
conditioner invented

1920
First commercial
radio station

1927
Television invented

1940 First inter-
state road (PA
Tpke)

1946
Computer invented

1913
Ford assembly line

1947 Transistor inve

De

2 billion

1902–1931 Cooley and Mead reflect on the self

1902 Simmel analyzes small groups

*1931 W.I. Thomas discusses
defining situations as real*

*1903 Du Bois describes
acial consciousness*

c.1915 Weber sees expanding bureaucracy

This book is offered to teachers of sociology
in the hope that it will help our students understand
their place in today's society and in tomorrow's world.

John J. Macionis

JOHN J. MACIONIS | # SOCIOLOGY

**CUSTOM EDITION FOR
HOUSTON COMMUNITY COLLEGE SYSTEM**

Taken from:

Sociology, Eleventh Edition
by John J. Macionis

Taken from:

Sociology, Eleventh Edition
by John J. Macionis
Copyright © 2007, 2005, 2003, 2001, 1999, 1997, 1995, 1993, 1991, 1989, 1987 by Pearson Education, Inc.
Published by Prentice Hall
Upper Saddle River, New Jersey 07458

Printed in the United States of America

10 9 8 7 6 5 4 3 2 1

ISBN 0-536-25519-9

2006540071

KC/RG

Please visit our web site at *www.pearsoncustom.com*

PEARSON CUSTOM PUBLISHING
75 Arlington Street, Suite 300, Boston, MA 02116
A Pearson Education Company

BRIEF CONTENTS

CONTENTS

Social Class in the United States 278

Global Stratification 304

CHAPTER 15

Aging and the Elderly 392

PART IV
Social Institutions

CHAPTER 16

The Economy and Work 416

Politics and Government   442

Families   468

CHAPTER

Religion 496

CHAPTER

Education 524

Health and Medicine 550

Social Change: Traditional, Modern, and Postmodern Societies   636

BOXES

APPLYING SOCIOLOGY

THINKING CRITICALLY

THINKING ABOUT DIVERSITY: RACE, CLASS, & GENDER

THINKING IT THROUGH

MAPS

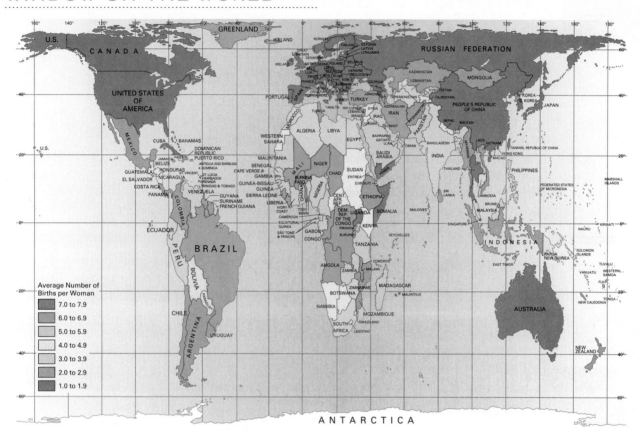

Average Number of Births per Woman
- 7.0 to 7.9
- 6.0 to 6.9
- 5.0 to 5.9
- 4.0 to 4.9
- 3.0 to 3.9
- 2.0 to 2.9
- 1.0 to 1.9

NATIONAL MAPS:
SEEING OURSELVES

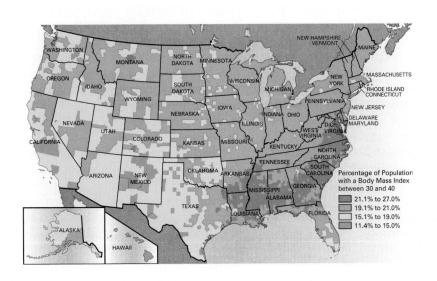

Percentage of Population with a Body Mass Index between 30 and 40
- 21.1% to 27.0%
- 19.1% to 21.0%
- 15.1% to 19.0%
- 11.4% to 15.0%

PREFACE

An Invitation to Students; A Welcome to Instructors

I did not start out to become a sociologist. Like many teenagers, I had almost no idea of what I wanted to do when I grew up. But I did do pretty well in school, especially in mathematics and physics, which got some of my teachers thinking that I ought to go on to study science or engineering. Not able to recognize bad advice when it was staring me in the face, I did what I was told, and enrolled in engineering school.

The first year went well enough, although I remember feeling in a little over my head. Early in my sophomore year, however, I had to face the fact that I simply had lost whatever interest I had in engineering. More to the point, after I posted a 1.3 grade point average the following fall, my college lost interest in me, and my engineering career came to a crashing halt when my advisor called to say that it was time for me to try something else.

Sometimes a personal crisis can help you see other possibilities that you never knew were there. Once the idea of becoming an engineer was out of the way, I had the chance to look around at other fields of study, and as part of my classes for the spring of 1968, I signed up for the introductory sociology course. This one course would truly change my life. From the very beginning, sociology helped me make sense of the world, and, just as important, sociology was *fun*. Thirty-seven years later, I can still say the same thing.

The importance of one person's story lies in the fact that countless people have been turned on to sociology in much the same way. Every semester, all across the United States, hundreds of thousands of students discover the excitement of sociology in an introductory class, and many go on to make sociology their life's work.

If you are a student, I invite you to open this book, to enjoy what you read, and to learn about a new and very useful way of looking at the world. To instructors, I stand with you in knowing the deep satisfaction that comes from making a difference in the lives of our students. There is surely no greater reward for our work than the thanks that comes from the people whose lives we touch and, in my case, no better reason for striving for ever-better revisions of *Sociology*, which, along with the brief, paperback version, *Society: The Basics*, stand out as the discipline's most popular texts.

The new eleventh edition of *Sociology* is exciting, covers it all, and—as students' e-mail messages make clear—is plain fun to read. This major revision elevates sociology's most popular text to a still higher standard of excellence and offers instructors an unparalleled resource to help our students learn about our diverse and changing world.

Organization of This Text

Part I of the textbook introduces the foundations of sociology. Underlying the discipline is the *sociological perspective*—the focus of Chapter 1, which explains how this exciting point of view brings the world to life in a new and instructive way. Chapter 2 spotlights *sociological investigation*, or the "doing of sociology." This chapter explains the methodological diversity of the discipline, presenting the scientific, interpretive, and critical orientations, and illustrating major research strategies with actual, well-known sociological work.

Part II surveys the foundations of social life. Chapter 3 focuses on the central concept of *culture*, emphasizing the cultural diversity that makes up our society and our world. The focus of Chapter 4 is the concept of *society*, presenting four time-honored models for understanding the structure and dynamics of social organization. This unique chapter provides introductory students with the background to understand the ideas of important thinkers—including Karl Marx, Max Weber, and Emile Durkheim, as well as Gerhard Lenski—that appear in subsequent chapters. Chapter 5 turns to *socialization*, exploring how we gain our humanity as we learn to participate in society. Chapter 6 provides a micro-level look at the patterns of *social interaction* that make up our everyday lives. Chapter 7 offers full-chapter coverage of *groups and organizations*, explaining the importance of group life and investigating how and why large organizations have come to dominate our way of life. Chapter 8 explains the social foundations of human sexuality. This chapter surveys sexual patterns in the United States and also explores variations in ideas and sexual practices through history and around the world today. Chapter 9 explains how the operation of society generates both *deviance and conformity* and also surveys the operation of the criminal justice system.

Part III offers unparalleled discussion of social inequality, beginning with three chapters on *social stratification*. Chapter 10 introduces major concepts and presents theoretical explanations of social inequality. This chapter richly illustrates historical changes in stratification and how patterns of inequality vary in today's world. Chapter 11 surveys *social class in the United States*, confronting common perceptions of inequality and assessing how well they square with research findings. Chapter 12 extends the analysis with a look at *global stratification*, revealing the disparities in wealth and power that separate rich and poor nations. Both Chapters 11 and 12 pay special attention to how global developments affect stratification in the United States as they explore our nation's role in patterns of global inequality. Chapter 13, *gender stratification*, explains how gender is a central element in social stratification in the United States as it is worldwide. *Race and ethnicity*, additional important dimensions of social inequality that often intersect differences based on class and gender, are detailed in Chapter 14. *Aging and the elderly*, a topic of increasing concern to "graying" societies such as our own, is addressed in Chapter 15.

Part IV includes a full chapter on each social institution. Leading off is Chapter 16, *the economy and work*, because most sociologists recognize the economy as having the greatest impact on all other institutions. This chapter traces the rise and fall of industrial production in the United States and the emergence of a global economy, and it explains what such transformations mean for the U.S. labor force. Chapter 17, *politics and government*, analyzes the distribution of power in U.S. society and surveys political systems around the world. In addition, this chapter includes discussion of the U.S. military, the threat of war, and terrorism as a new form of war. Chapter 18, *families*, explains the central importance of families to social organization and underscores the diversity of family life both here and in other societies. Chapter 19, *religion*, addresses the timeless human search for ultimate purpose and meaning, introduces major world religions, and explains how religious beliefs are linked to other dimensions of social life. Chapter 20, *education*, analyzes the expansion of schooling in industrial and postindustrial societies. Here again, schooling in the United States comes to life through contrasts with educational patterns in other countries. Chapter 21, *health and medicine*, reveals health to be a social issue just as much as it is a matter of biological processes. This chapter traces the historical development of scientific medicine, analyzes today's medical establishment as well as alternative approaches to health, and compares patterns of health and medical policy in the United States to those in other countries.

Part V examines important dimensions of global social change. Chapter 22 highlights the powerful impact of *population growth* and *urbanization* in the United States and throughout the world, with special attention to the *natural environment*. Chapter 23 explores forms of *collective behavior* and explains how people seek or resist social change by joining *social movements*. Chapter 24 concludes the text with an overview of *social change* that contrasts *traditional, modern, and postmodern societies*. This chapter rounds out the text by explaining how and why world societies change,

and by critically analyzing the advantages and disadvantages sociologists see in traditional, modern, and postmodern ways of life.

Continuity: Established Features of *Sociology*

Sociology is no ordinary textbook: In the discipline, it represents *the* standard of excellence, which explains why this book, and the paperback version, *Society: The Basics*, are chosen by far more faculty than any other text. The extraordinary popularity of *Sociology* over twenty years results from a combination of the following features.

The best writing style   Most important, this text offers a writing style widely praised by students and faculty alike as clear and engaging. *Sociology* is an enjoyable text that encourages students to read—even beyond their assignments. No one says it better than the students themselves, whose recent e-mails include testimonials such as these:

> I live in a small town and I am taking sociology at the University of Texas at Brownsville and it has changed my whole life! I take eighteen hours of classes a week and there are three that I enjoy, and this is based on the textbook you have written. Maybe you have read this a million times, but I just wanted to let you know that your words and actions have changed someone's life.

> I want to thank you for providing us with such a comprehensive, easy-to-read, and engaging book. In fact, my instructor thought it was so interesting and well done, she read the book from cover to cover. Your work has been a great service to us all. My sociology book is the only textbook that I currently own that I actually enjoy reading. Thank you!

> Hi, Professor Macionis. I am taking my first sociology class and I love it. I 'm enjoying your book so much that I have a hard time putting it down.

> I am a student at U-Mass Boston taking Sociology 101 and using your *Sociology* book. I think it is extremely well-written and informative, and the set up is great. I find the book to be so helpful!

> I am taking a Sociology 101 class using your text, a book that I have told my professor is the best textbook that I have ever seen, bar none. I've told her as well that I will be more than happy to take more sociology classes as long as there is a Macionis text to go with them.

> I am fascinated by the contents of this textbook. In contrast to texts in my other classes, I actually enjoy the reading. Thank you for such a thought-provoking, well-written textbook.

> This text is a keeper.

> Dude, your book *rocks!*

Race, class, and gender: A celebration of social diversity *Sociology* invites students from all social backgrounds to discover a fresh and exciting way to see themselves within the larger social world. Readers will discover in this text the diversity of U.S. society—people of African, Asian, European, and Latino ancestry, as well as women and men of various class positions and at all points in the life course. Just as important, without ignoring the problems that marginalized people face, this text does not treat minorities as social problems but notes their achievements. A scholarly analysis of sociology texts published in the American Sociological Association's journal *Teaching Sociology* evaluated Macionis's *Sociology* as the best of all the leading texts in terms of integrating racial and ethnic material throughout (Stone, 1996).

A global perspective *Sociology* has taken a leading role in expanding the horizons of our discipline beyond the United States. It was the first text to mainstream global content, the first to introduce global maps, global "snapshot" figures, and the first to offer comprehensive coverage of global topics such as stratification and the natural environment. It is no wonder that *Sociology* and *Society: The Basics* have been adapted and translated into half a dozen languages for use around the world. Each chapter explores the world's social diversity and explains why social trends in the United States—from musical tastes to the price of wheat to increasing income inequality—are influenced by what happens elsewhere. Just as important, students will learn ways in which social patterns and policies in the United States affect poor nations around the world.

Emphasis on critical thinking Critical-thinking skills include the ability to challenge common assumptions by formulating questions, to identify and weigh appropriate evidence, and to reach reasoned conclusions. This text not only teaches but encourages students to discover on their own. Notice, for example, the "Your Turn" questions throughout each chapter, and the fact that many of the captions for photographs and maps are in the form of questions that require students to think for themselves.

The broadest coverage No other text matches *Sociology*'s twenty-four-chapter coverage of the field. We offer such breadth—at no greater cost—expecting that few instructors will assign every chapter but with the goal of supporting instructors as they choose exactly what they wish to teach.

Engaging and instructive chapter openings One of the most popular features of earlier editions of *Sociology* has been the engaging vignettes that begin each chapter. These openings—for instance, using the tragic sinking of the *Titanic* to illustrate the life and death consequences of social inequality, telling the story of an isolated child to reveal the critical contribution of social experience to personality development, or beginning the discussion of global inequality by describing how a fire in a Pakistani sweatshop that manufactures clothing for sale in the United States left dozens of low-paid workers dead—spark the interest of readers as they introduce important themes. While keeping thirteen of the best chapter-opening vignettes from earlier editions, this revision offers eleven that are new.

Inclusive focus on women and men Beyond devoting two full chapters to the important concepts of sex and gender, *Sociology* mainstreams gender into *every* chapter, showing how the topic at hand affects women and men differently and explaining how gender operates as a basic part of social organization.

Theoretically clear and balanced This text makes theory easy. The discipline's major theoretical approaches are introduced in Chapter 1 and are carried through later chapters. The text highlights the social-conflict, feminist, structural-functional, and symbolic-interaction approaches, and also introduces social-exchange analysis, ethnomethodology, cultural ecology, and sociobiology. Applying Theory tables ensure that students learn the theoretical material in each chapter.

Recent research and the latest data *Sociology, Eleventh Edition,* blends classic sociological statements with the latest research as reported in the leading publications in the field. While some texts ignore new work published in sociology journals, *Sociology* selectively includes recent research from a dozen of the discipline's top publications. Almost 1,500 research citations support this revision, with most published since 2000, twice the share found in some competing texts. Using the latest sources ensures that the text's content and statistical data are the most recent available.

Outstanding images: Photography and fine art *Sociology, Eleventh Edition,* offers the best and most extensive program of photography and artwork available in any sociology textbook. The author searches extensively to obtain the finest images of the human condition and presents them with insightful captions, often in the form of thought-provoking questions to help students see sociology at work in their everyday lives. Just as important, both photographs and artwork present people of various social backgrounds and historical periods. For example, alongside art by well-known Europeans such as Vincent Van Gogh and U.S. artists including George Tooker, this edition has paintings by celebrated African American artists Henry Ossawa Tanner and Jonathan Green, outstanding Latino artist Carmen Lomas Garza, and the engaging Australian painter and feminist Sally Swain.

Thought-provoking theme boxes Although boxed material is common to introductory texts, *Sociology, Eleventh Edition,* provides a wealth of uncommonly good boxes. Each chapter typically contains three or four boxes, which fall into six types that amplify central themes of the text. **Applying Sociology** boxes, which now appear in every chapter, show readers how to apply the perspective, theory, and methods of sociology to greatest advantage. **In the Times** features, also found in every chapter, are recent stories from *The New York Times* that were selected by the author to encourage students to think about current events in sociological terms. **Thinking About Diversity: Race, Class, and Gender** boxes focus on multicultural issues and present the voices of women and people of color. **Thinking Critically** boxes teach students to ask sociological questions about their surroundings and help them evaluate important, controversial issues. **Thinking It Through** boxes present several points of view on hotly debated issues. **Thinking Globally** boxes provoke readers to think about their own way of life by examining the fascinating social diversity that characterizes our world. All boxes are followed by three "What do you think?" questions.

An unparalleled program of forty-eight global and national maps Another popular feature of *Sociology* is the series of global and national maps. Window on the World global maps—twenty-six in all and many updated for this edition—are truly sociological maps offering a comparative look at income disparity, favored languages, the extent of prostitution, permitted marriage forms, the degree of political freedom, the incidence of HIV/AIDS infection, and a host of other issues. The global maps use the non-Eurocentric projection devised by cartographer Arno Peters that accurately portrays the relative size of all the continents.

Seeing Ourselves national maps—twenty-two in all with two new and many more updated for this edition—help to illuminate the social diversity of the United States. Most of these maps offer a close-up look at all 3,141 U.S. counties, highlighting suicide rates, teen pregnancy, risk of violent crime, poverty, interracial marriage, the most widespread religious affiliation, and the extent of obesity. Each national map includes an explanatory caption that poses a question to stimulate students' thinking about social forces. A complete listing of the Seeing Ourselves national maps as well as the Window on the World global maps follows the table of contents.

Graphic "Snapshots" Among the most useful features of *Sociology* are the various "snapshot" figures, which are colorful graphs that convey important data and highlight major themes of the text. These snapshots are of three types. **Global Snapshots** compare social patterns in the United States with those in other nations. **Diversity Snapshots** reveal important differences within the U.S. population along the lines of race, ethnicity, class, or gender. **Student Snapshots** document trends in the behavior and opinions of college students based on surveys conducted by the Higher Education Research Institute at the University of California at Los Angeles since 1966.

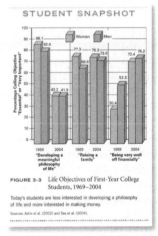

FIGURE 3-3 Life Objectives of First-Year College Students, 1969–2004

Today's students are less interested in developing a philosophy of life and more interested in making money.

Sources: Astin et al. (2002) and Sax et al. (2004).

An annotated instructor's edition This is the only text available in an instructor's edition with a full program of helpful annotations—written by the author—on every page. These annotations provide additional data, notable quotations, and suggestions about teaching the material.

Innovation: Changes in the Eleventh Edition

Each new edition of *Sociology* has broken new ground, one reason that the popularity of this text and its brief version keep rising. Now, having reached the eleventh edition, we energize the book once again, with many fresh ideas, new

SEEING OURSELVES

NATIONAL MAP 9-1
The Risk of Violent Crime
across the United States

This map shows the risk of becoming a victim of violent crime. In general, the risk is highest in low-income, rural counties that have a large population of men between the ages of fifteen and twenty-four. After reading through this section of the text, see whether you can explain this pattern.

Source: American Demographics magazine, December 2000. Reprinted with permission of American Demographics. © 2000 to Intertec Publishing, a Primedia Company.

WINDOW ON THE WORLD

GLOBAL MAP 13-1 Women's Power in Global Perspective

Women's social standing in relation to men's varies around the world. In general, women live better in rich countries than in poor countries. Even so, some nations stand out: In the nations of Norway, Sweden, and Australia, women come closest to social equality with men.

12 CHAPTER TWELVE

Global Stratification

What share of the world's people
live in absolute poverty?

Why are some of the world's countries
so rich and others so poor?

Are rich nations making global poverty
better or worse?

features, and innovative teaching tools. *Sociology* never stands still—one important reason that this book has been the best-seller for more than fifteen years. Two years in the making, this eleventh edition is, quite simply, the best revision yet. Here is a brief overview of what's new in *Sociology, Eleventh Edition.*

A new look As instructors understand, today's students are very visually oriented—in a world of rapid-fire images, they respond to what they see. Just as important, the photographs that we see in newspapers, on television, and online are more sociological than ever before. As a result, this new edition of *Sociology* offers more and better images, and the text has an exciting new look that is clear, attractive, and sure to boost student interest.

Sociology encourages students to use images to learn. Bold, vibrant, and colorful photos on the chapter-opening spreads pull students into the chapter material and become teaching opportunities. Together with the chapter-opening stories that follow, these images will inspire students to want to learn.

A new feel A new look also calls for a new feel to the text. Our goal in this edition can be stated in the form of a promise: Every student in every class will be able to immediately understand the material on every page of the text. This promise does not come at the cost of any of the content you expect. What it means is that the author has prepared this revision with the greatest care and with an eye toward making language and arguments as clear as they can be. Student tested—student friendly!

New chapter-opening questions Each chapter of this edition begins with three questions—a "what," a "how," and a "why" question—that alert students to key themes discussed in the chapter.

Interactive "Your Turn" questions To make this edition of *Sociology* more engaging and interactive, we have placed

at least four or five "Your Turn" questions at different points in every chapter. "Your Turn" questions ask the student to apply the ideas being discussed to some other issue or link the ideas to their personal lives.

A greater focus on careers Most students who enroll in a sociology course hope to find something useful for their future careers. Students using *Sociology, Eleventh Edition,* surely will. This text reflects the discipline's *career relevance* more than ever before. Chapter 1 ("The Sociological Perspective") includes a major new discussion of sociology and student careers. Many of the chapters that follow apply sociological insights to careers, for example, by explaining how today's corporate marketing is becoming more multicultural (Chapter 3, "Culture") and why physicians need to understand the social dynamics of an office visit or a medical examination (Chapter 6, "Social Interaction in Everyday Life"). In addition, there is greatly expanded coverage of the criminal justice system (Chapter 9, "Deviance"), as well as a discussion of the medical establishment, including the work of both physicians and nurses (Chapter 21, "Health and Medicine").

For additional connections between sociology and careers, look for the Sociology@Work icon. Found in all

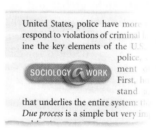

chapters, these icons draw student attention to discussions that have particular importance to the world of work. These icons help students to apply what they read to their consideration of future careers.

Applying sociology to students' everyday lives The value of sociology depends on students' ability to apply what they learn to their own lives. This revision illustrates concepts in ways that encourage students to see these connections. In addition, the Applying Sociology series of boxes—one found in every chapter of the text—shows how to put sociology to work in people's everyday lives, on the job, at home, and on the campus.

Encouraging active reading This book encourages students to be active readers. Of course, the lively, easy-to-understand writing style and use of current examples are important. In addition, all of the boxes in this revision now include three follow-up questions that invite students to think critically and to apply what they have learned to new situations.

A better way to teach theory Sociological theory is important, but it is sometimes challenging to students. To ensure that students learn the important lessons, all

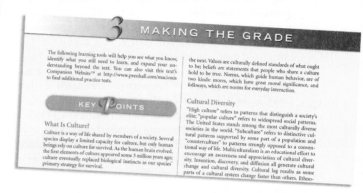

APPLYING THEORY
CULTURE

	Structural-Functional Approach	Social-Conflict Approach	Sociobiology Approach
What is the level of analysis?	Macro-level	Macro-level	Macro-level
What is culture?	Culture is a system of behavior by which members of societies cooperate to meet their needs.	Culture is a system that benefits some people and disadvantages others.	Culture is a system of behavior that is partly shaped by human biology.
What is the foundation of culture?	Cultural patterns are rooted in a society's core values and beliefs.	Cultural patterns are rooted in a society's system of economic production.	Cultural patterns are rooted in humanity's biological evolution.
What core questions does the approach ask?	How does a cultural pattern help society to operate? What cultural patterns are found in all societies?	How does a cultural pattern benefit some people and harm others? How does a cultural pattern help a species adapt to its environment?	How does a cultural pattern support social inequality?

theoretical discussions are followed by "Critical review" sections. In this revision, we have added new Applying Theory tables, which summarize, at a glance, how the various theoretical approaches view the topic at hand.

More popular culture   Today's students live in a world largely defined by the popular culture of the United States. To more directly link the content of *Sociology* to the lives of readers, this revision integrates more popular culture into topic discussions. In particular, we draw many examples of important issues from the mass media, including popular films and television programming.

"In the *Times*" readings   What better way to bring sociology to life than to provide students with brief, well-written news articles that apply sociology to today's world! In every chapter of *Sociology, Eleventh Edition,* you will find an article concerning some aspect of society that recently appeared in *The New York Times.* These readings, carefully selected by the author, all present important and current issues that are sure to engage student readers.

Making the Grade   At the end of each chapter of this text, students will find **Making the Grade,** a new five-part active learning system designed to help students succeed in this course. A **Key Points** summary covers all the important issues, and a **Key Concepts** section provides *precise, italicized definitions of glossary terms.* **Sample Test Questions**—written by John Macionis—include ten multiple-choice questions with answers and two essay questions. Three **Applications & Exercises** help students move beyond the text

to learn on their own on or near the campus, and a suggestion for how to use the **Research Navigator**™ database helps students pursue further research online.

Both students and faculty benefit from the following innovations:

New and updated maps   The only way to improve on our colorful, sociological maps is to ensure that they are as up-to-date as possible. This edition features forty-eight global and national maps, many updated and two new to this edition.

New chapter-opening vignettes   This revision keeps the best of the popular chapter-opening vignettes and adds eleven that are new to this edition.

New and updated boxes   A total of seventy-eight boxes represent five themes of the text: Thinking About Diversity: Race, Class, and Gender; Thinking Critically; Thinking Globally; Thinking It Through; and Applying Sociology. A number of these boxes are new, and many more have been revised and updated for this revision.

A small change in chapter ordering   In this revision, "Sexuality and Society" is moved up one spot to fall before, rather than after, the chapter on "Deviance." This small change results in a more logical flow of topics.

The latest statistical data   Instructors who don't have time to check the latest data should use a textbook that has them all! The eleventh edition comes through, making use of the latest data from various government agencies and private organizations. The author, together with Amy Marsh Macionis and Carol Singer, government documents specialist at Bowling Green State University in Ohio, have made sure the newest statistics are used throughout the text—in most cases for 2004 or even 2005. In addition, readers will find hundreds of new research citations as well as many familiar current events that raise the interest of students.

New topics   The eleventh edition of *Sociology* is thoroughly updated with new and expanded discussions in every chapter. Here is a listing, by chapter, of just some of the new material:

- **Chapter 1: The Sociological Perspective** This chapter includes much more discussion of how to apply the discipline of sociology to our lives, including a new section on the value of sociology to various careers; there is more discussion of sociology and public policy and an expanded discussion of sociology and personal growth; a new Applying Sociology box documents the struggles of low-wage workers; a new "In the *Times*" looks at the social causes of suicide in rural communities; greater attention is given to feminist analysis and race-conflict analysis; a new Summing Up table helps clarify sociology's various theoretical approaches; new end-of-chapter material includes test questions that are similar to those found in the test bank that accompanies this text.

- **Chapter 2: Sociological Investigation** The chapter now gives greater attention to how students can apply sociological methods to their everyday lives; a number of new examples and illustrations speak directly to the experiences of students; a new "In the *Times*" highlights some of the changes in the U.S. population revealed by the latest census; a new Summing Up table provides an easy way to understand the link between methodological approaches and sociological theory; many "Your Turn" questions encourage students to become more active readers.

- **Chapter 3: Culture** The chapter includes an update on languages nearing extinction; a new Applying Sociology box examines the emerging world of Internet communication and cyber-symbols; there is a new discussion of cultural values around the world, including a new figure based on the World Values Survey; a new Applying Theory table makes theoretical analysis of culture even clearer; a new end-of-chapter "Application & Exercise" asks students to think about when and why specific new words came into the English language.

- **Chapter 4: Society** A new journal entry describes the traditional use of horses and plows among farming families in the Andes highlands of Peru; a new Summing Up table offers a more student-friendly summary of how technology shapes society; there is an update on Durkheim's analysis of suicide in modern societies; "What do you think?" questions follow all the boxes in the chapter; a new "In the *Times*" focuses on the lives of pastoral people living in Africa and the Middle East today.

- **Chapter 5: Socialization** This chapter includes an expanded discussion of how families pass along racial and class standing to their children, including a new national map showing where racially mixed children are most and least likely to be born; a new journal entry describes the introduction of the mass media to a remote Scottish isle; find an update on the political controversy surrounding television; a new "In the *Times*" looks at the lives of young adults who are still dependent on their parents; a new Applying Sociology box shows that there are many dimensions to being truly "grown up."

- **Chapter 6: Social Interaction in Everyday Life** This chapter contains a new global map showing how the responsibility for doing housework differs among women and men; "In the *Times*" describes how the mass media have affected public awareness of people with disabilities; the end-of-chapter material includes new exercises as well as new test questions.

- **Chapter 7: Groups and Organizations** Two new Summing Up tables sharpen the contrast between primary and secondary groups and also between social groups and large organizations; there is new discussion on the differences between organizations in Japan and the United States; a new "In the *Times*" analyzes how bureaucratic organizations often fail when faced with the challenge of innovating in order to combat global terrorism; find updates on McDonaldization and the threat posed by organizations to personal privacy.

- **Chapter 8: Sexuality and Society** A new chapter opening points to greater sexual openness in Iraq since the U.S.-led invasion, and some of the resulting controversy; find a new section concerning sexual activity over the life course; there are updates to the discussion of prostitution and pornography; a new Applying Theory table helps students understand theoretical analysis of human sexuality; a new Student Snapshot shows the trend toward greater acceptance of homosexual relationships by U.S. college students; the chapter includes the latest on changing gay marriage laws in the United States.

- **Chapter 9: Deviance** A new chapter opening uses Martha Stewart's stint in federal prison to point out that people convicted of crimes often do not fit the stereotype of the "street criminal"; there is an updated review of the role of biological factors in explaining serious crime; a new journal entry documents the difference between the high-crime city of Lima, Peru, and low-crime villages high in the Andes mountains; find updates on all crime statistics; a new "In the *Times*" examines the rising population of U.S. prisons—even as crime rates have gone down; a new Applying Theory table provides sociological analysis of crime; the chapter includes the latest court ruling about the death penalty.

- **Chapter 10: Social Stratification** A new "In the *Times*" examines how people in the United States and people in Europe have different ideas about making money and living well; there is new symbolic-interaction analysis of social stratification, including a new Applying Sociology box explaining how we can take social position very personally; a new Applying Theory table summarizes and contrasts theoretical approaches to inequality.

- **Chapter 11: Social Class in the United States** A new chapter opening describes the different worlds of wealthy New Yorkers and the people who earn a living cleaning their apartments and houses; the statistical profile of income and wealth in the United States is updated; find all new data concerning U.S. poverty; a new "In the *Times*" takes a look at the increasing problem of homelessness in the United States.

- **Chapter 12: Global Stratification** This chapter now includes a global map identifying the low-, middle-, and high-income nations of the world using the latest economic indicators; find an update on the world's richest person, whose wealth equals the economic output of the world's forty-five poorest countries; "What do you think?" questions have been added to all boxes in the chapter; a new "In the *Times*" takes a look at efforts by the United Nations to define global poverty; there is expanded discussion of the benefits and dangers of the expanding global economy; there is new research and discussion of recent trends in global inequality.

- **Chapter 13: Gender Stratification** This chapter contains updates for all the statistics on women's and men's work, including jobs held, income, and housework; there is expanded discussion of the corporate "glass ceiling"; a new section discusses violence against men, expanding the focus on men and masculinity in this chapter; there is a new Applying Theory table summarizing the two macro-level approaches to understanding gender; there is an update on the attitudes of college men and women toward feminism; a new "In the *Times*" highlights the recent trend in the mass media of depicting men in unfavorable ways.

- **Chapter 14: Race and Ethnicity** A new chapter opening describes multiracial students at Bronx Community College; find an update on school desegregation; the latest data on the social standing of all racial and ethnic categories of the U.S. population are included; a new "In the *Times*" describes the social diversity that is found today in New York, a city with almost 3 million foreign-born residents.

- **Chapter 15: Aging and the Elderly** A new chapter opening highlights the increasing problem of age discrimination, illustrating how age is a dimension of social stratification; a new Thinking Globally box focuses on the aging population of Japan and the problems this change will bring; there are updates on all the statistics concerning poverty for older women and men; a new "In the *Times*" describes the social isolation experienced by people living in one of the best assisted-living facilities in the country; find the latest on the right-to-die debate, including the Terri Schiavo case.

- **Chapter 16: The Economy and Work** A new "In the *Times*" describes how computer technology is resulting in "outsourcing" of work here in the United States; there is expanded discussion of the global economy; find more material on the effects of new information technology on the workplace; find the latest statistics describing the U.S. workforce, including the types of jobs people hold and the racial makeup of today's workplace; there is new discussion of the harmful aspects of economic globalization to workers in the United States and elsewhere.

- **Chapter 17: Politics and Government** A new chapter opening describes the 2005 elections in Iraq and points out that a larger share of people there voted than did so in the U.S. 2004 presidential race; the chapter includes updates on the size of government, the results of the 2004 national election, and the extent of political freedoms in the world; there are new data describing campaign spending for the 2004 elections, as well as the latest figures for voter participation for women and men and various racial and ethnic categories; there is much new material in the Applying Sociology box describing the "rural-urban divide" in U.S. politics; a new Applying Theory table helps students use theory to understand political power; a new section looks at the social-class background of people joining the military; a new "In the *Times*" explains some of the ways the armed forces are trying to keep recruitment high.

- **Chapter 18: Families** A new chapter opening describes the decreasing size of families headed by Latinas who want more freedom to work; the chapter has a stronger emphasis on the diversity of today's family life; find expanded discussion of American Indian families; new research concerning women shows how abuse is linked to reduced ability to form stable relationships; a new Applying Theory table sharpens sociological analysis of families; there are statistical updates for divorce, one-parent families, cohabitation, and the economic standing of families by race and ethnicity; more attention is given to the divorce of parents with young children; find the latest information on the rapidly changing laws on gay marriage around the world and in the United States; a new "In the *Times*" describes the crisis of American Indian children being raised in poor families.

- **Chapter 19: Religion** A new Applying Theory table helps students understand the three theoretical approaches to religion; there is an update on the new pope's opposition to liberation theology; a new journal entry describes a "New Age" religious experience high in the Andes mountains of Peru among descendants of the Inca people; the chapter provides expanded discussion of religious fundamentalism; a new "In the *Times*" suggests that a high level of religiosity in the United States is due to competition among many religious organizations.

- **Chapter 20: Education** A new chapter opening points to the widespread desire to go to college, noting low-income people's limited opportunity to enroll; there is a new journal entry about schooling of poor children; find the latest statistical data on U.S. schooling, including the share of the population that has completed college, how much college graduates earn, and the dropout rate among various racial and ethnic categories; new research-based discussion assesses the effects of the school and the home on children's educational performance; there is new symbolic-interaction analysis of education; a new Applying Theory table sums up the contribution of sociology's major theoretical approaches to our understanding of education; a new "In the *Times*" looks at why people drop out of college.

- **Chapter 21: Health and Medicine** Find an updated chapter opening on the obesity epidemic in the United States; a new journal entry describes the link between low income and poor health; a new section provides supersized discussion of obesity; there is a new national map on the rates of clinical obesity across the United States; an update on the controversies surrounding death and dying includes the Terri Schiavo case; find the latest statistical data on longevity by race and gender, the link between income and health, and the extent to which people lack health insurance in the United States.

- **Chapter 22: Population, Urbanization, and Environment** A new chapter opening describes offers made by dying towns in the Great Plains to attract new residents; the chapter has statistical updates on all demographic measures, including birth rates, death rates, population increase, and infant mortality; a new "In the *Times*" highlights the efforts of three U.S. organizations to assist people in low-income nations by recycling items from the United States.
- **Chapter 23: Collective Behavior and Social Movements** A new chapter opening highlights the tsunami disaster that killed some 300,000 people in Asia and Africa at the end of 2004; in the wake of the hurricanes that hit the United States in 2005, the chapter now has a major new discussion of disasters, including a new Thinking Critically box that explains the ongoing social consequences of the atomic testing by the United States that took place in the South Pacific in 1954; a new "In the *Times*" investigates how two New Orleans families—one poor and one more affluent—were coping in the weeks following Hurricane Katrina.
- **Chapter 24: Social Change: Traditional, Modern, and Postmodern Societies** All boxes now include "What do you think?" questions to spark student reaction; a number of new "Your Turn" questions ask students to apply text material to their own lives; there is new discussion of why measures of happiness have dropped in high-income nations during recent decades; a new "In the *Times*" explores how modernity is slipping into the life of a traditional village high in the mountains of Tibet.

A Word about Language

This text's commitment to describing the social diversity of the United States as well as the world carries with it the responsibility to use language thoughtfully. In most cases, we prefer the terms *African American* and *person of color* to the word *black*. We use the terms *Latino* or *Hispanic* to refer to people of Spanish descent. Most tables and figures refer to "Hispanics" because this is the term the Census Bureau uses when collecting statistical data about our population.

Students should realize, however, that many individuals do not describe themselves using these terms. Although the word "Hispanic" is commonly used in the eastern part of the United States, and "Latino" and the feminine form "Latina" are widely heard in the West, across the United States people of Spanish descent identify with a particular ancestral nation, whether it be Argentina, Mexico, some other Latin American country, or Spain or Portugal in Europe.

The same diversity is found among Asian Americans. Although this term is a useful shorthand in sociological analysis, most people of Asian descent think of themselves in terms of a specific country of origin (say, Japan, the Philippines, Taiwan, or Vietnam).

In this text, the term "Native American" refers to all the inhabitants of North America, including Alaska and the Hawaiian Islands, whose ancestors lived here prior to the arrival of Europeans. Here again, however, most people in this broad category identify with their historical society (for example, Cherokee, Hopi, Seneca, or Zuni). The term "American Indian" refers to only those Native Americans who live in the continental United States, not including Native peoples living in Alaska or Hawaii.

On a global level, we avoid the word "American"—which literally designates two continents—to refer to just the United States. For example, referring to this country, the term "U.S. economy" is more correct than the "American economy." This convention may seem a small point, but it implies the significant recognition that we in this country represent only one society (albeit a very important one) in the Americas.

A Word about Web Sites

Because of the increasing importance of the Internet, each

 Read more about the lives of street children at http://www.hrw.org/children/street.htm

chapter includes Media icons that recommend sites that are current, informative, and, above all, relevant to the topic at hand.

However, students should be mindful of several potential problems. First, Web sites change all the time. Prior to publication, we make every effort to ensure that the sites listed meet our high standards. But readers may find that sites have changed, and some may have gone away entirely.

Second, sites have been selected in order to provide different points of view on various issues. The listing of a site does not imply that the author or publisher agrees with everything—or even anything—on the site. For this reason, we urge students to examine all sites with a critical eye.

Supplements

Sociology, Eleventh Edition, is the heart of an unprecedented multimedia learning package that includes a wide range of proven instructional aids as well as several new ones. As the author of the text, I maintain a keen interest in all the supplements to ensure their quality and integration with the text. The supplements for this revision have been thoroughly updated, improved, and expanded.

INSTRUCTOR PRESENTATION AND ASSESSMENT SUPPLEMENTS

Annotated Instructor's Edition (0-13-195136-X) The AIE is a complete student text annotated on every page by the author. Margin notes include summaries of research findings, examples involving popular culture, statistics from the United States or other nations, insightful quotations, information highlighting patterns of social diversity in the United States, and high-quality survey data from the National Opinion Research Center's (NORC) *General Social Survey* and the *World Values Survey* data from the Interuniversity Consortium for Political and Social Research (ICPSR).

Instructor's Manual (0-13-195135-1) This is the instructor's manual that is of interest even to those who have never used one before. It provides far more than detailed chapter outlines and discussion questions; it contains statistical profiles of the United States and other nations, summaries of important developments, recent articles from *Teaching Sociology* that are relevant to the classroom, and supplemental lecture material for every chapter of the text.

Test Item File (0-13-195137-8) Written by the text author, John Macionis, this key supplement better reflects the material in the textbook—both in content and in language—than the test item file available with any other introductory sociology textbook. The file contains over 2500 items—more than 100 per chapter—in multiple-choice, true/false, and essay formats. New questions based on *TIME* Magazine and the *Socological Classics* reader also allow you to assess students' use of these important tools.

TestGEN-EQ (0-13-195138-6) This computerized software allows instructors to create their own personalized exams, to edit any or all of the existing test questions, and to add new questions. Other special features of this program include random generation of test questions, creation of alternate versions of the same test, scrambling of question sequence, and test preview before printing.

Faculty Resources on CD (0-13-195142-4) Pulling together all of the media assets available to instructors, this CD allows instructors to insert media—video, PowerPoint, graphs, charts, maps—into their classroom presentations. This CD also offers electronic versions of the Instructor's Manual and Test Item File.

Note: The following resources are available only to college adopters.

Prentice Hall Film and Video Guide: Introductory Sociology, Seventh Edition (0-13-191807-9) Newly updated by Peter Remender of the University of Wisconsin-Oshkosh, this guide links important concepts in the text directly to compelling, student-focused feature films and documentaries. Each film is summarized, and critical-thinking questions allow the instructor to highlight the relevance of each film or video to concepts in sociology.

ABCNEWS /Prentice Hall Video Library for Sociology Few will dispute that video is the most dynamic supplement you can use to enhance a class. Prentice Hall and *ABC News* are working together to bring to you the best and most comprehensive video material available in the college market. Through its wide variety of award-winning programs—*Nightline, This Week, World News Tonight,* and *20/20—ABC News* offers a resource for feature and documentary-style videos related to the chapters in *Sociology, Eleventh Edition.* An excellent instructor's guide carefully and completely integrates the videos into your lecture. The guide has a synopsis of each video showing its relevance to the chapter and discussion questions to help students focus on how concepts and theories apply to real-life situations. The videos are available in both DVD and VHS formats.

Prentice Hall Introductory Sociology PowerPoint™ These PowerPoint slides combine graphics and text for each chapter in a colorful format to help you convey sociological principles in a new and exciting way. For easy access, they are available on the Faculty Resources CD, within the instructor portion of the OneKey for *Sociology, Eleventh Edition,* or at www.prenhall.com

OneKey To accompany *Sociology, Eleventh Edition,* this innovative, passcode-protected resource pulls together the teaching and learning materials associated with the text and integrates them into a single location. For students, OneKey offers video, animations, interactive exercises, assignments, and a customized study plan with supporting e-book. For instructors, OneKey automatically grades students' performance on the chapter test and logs results into a gradebook. In addition, instructors can see a snapshot of their entire class performance on every major chapter topic in order to more effectively tailor lectures or offer better test preparation for students. Instructors can access all presentation materials, assessment materials, and communication tools tied to *Sociology, Eleventh Edition.* For a preview of OneKey or for more on ordering information, please visit http://www.prenhall.com/onekey

Classroom Response System (CRS) In-Class Questions Get instant, class-wide responses to chapter-specific questions during a lecture to gauge student comprehension—and keep students engaged. Contact your local Prentice Hall sales representative for details.

SUPPLEMENTS FOR STUDENTS

Study Guide (0-13-195134-3) This guide helps students review and reflect on the material presented in *Sociology, Eleventh Edition*. Each of the twenty-four chapters in the *Study Guide* provides an overview of the corresponding chapter in the student text, summarizes its major topics and concepts, offers applied exercises, and features end-of-chapter tests with solutions.

Interactive Student CD-ROM (0-13-195141-6) Using video as a window to the world outside of the classroom, this innovative CD-ROM offers students videos and animations, arranged by the themes of the book within each chapter, to reinforce the material covered in each chapter. Students can watch relevant *ABC News* clips, view author tip videos, interact with the global and national maps, and apply sociological concepts through the many assignments available to instructors. The CD-ROM can be packaged at no additional cost with all new copies of *Sociology, Eleventh Edition*.

Census Interactive CD-ROM (0-13-191902-4) Capturing the rich picture of our nation drawn by Census2000, this CD-ROM brings related census data into your classroom in a rich, multimedia format. It uses files taken directly from the Census Bureau Web site—even recently released Census Briefs—organizes them around your course, and offers teaching aids to support student learning. This updated CD-ROM can be packaged at no additional cost with *Sociology, Eleventh Edition*.

Companion Website™ Students and professors using *Sociology, Eleventh Edition,* can now take full advantage of the Internet to enrich their study of sociology. The Macionis Companion Website™ continues to provide students with opportunities to explore the topics covered in the text. Features of the Companion Website include chapter objectives and study questions, as well as links to interesting material and information from other sites on the Web that will reinforce and enhance the content of each chapter. Go to http://www.prenhall.com/macionis and click on the cover of *Sociology, Eleventh Edition*.

 **Research Navigator™** Research Navigator™ can help students complete research assignments efficiently and with confidence by providing three exclusive databases of high-quality scholarly and popular press articles accessed by easy-to-use search engines.

- **EBSCO's ContentSelect™ Academic Journal Database**, organized by subject, contains 50–100 of the leading academic journals for sociology. Instructors and students can search the online journals by keyword, topic, or multiple topics. Articles include abstract and citation information and can be cut, pasted, e-mailed, or saved for later use.
- *The New York Times* **Search by Subject™ Archive** provides articles specific to sociology and is searchable by keyword or multiple keywords. Instructors and students can view full-text articles from the world's leading journalists writing for *The New York Times*.
- **Link Library** offers editorially selected "Best of the Web" sites for sociology. Link Libraries are continually scanned and kept up to date, providing the most relevant and accurate links for research assignments.

Gain access to Research Navigator by using the access code found in the front of the brief guide called *OneSearch with Research Navigator™*. The access code for Research Navigator is included with every guide and can be packaged at no extra charge with *Sociology, Eleventh Edition*. Please contact your Prentice Hall representative for more information.

DISTANCE LEARNING SOLUTIONS

Prentice Hall is committed to providing our leading content to the growing number of courses being delivered over the Internet by developing relationships with the leading vendors—Blackboard™, Web CT™, and CourseCompass™, Prentice Hall's own easy-to-use course management system powered by Blackboard™. Please visit our technology solutions site at http://www.prenhall.com/demo

Telecourse The Macionis text *Sociology* has been selected for use in the new telecourse, "The Way We Live," available on DVD from IN-TELECOM. To find out more about this truly outstanding course, go to www.intellecom.org and, under the Alphabetical Listing of Courses, click on "The Way We Live" or call 1-800-576-2988.

TIME: **Sociology, Special Edition, '06 (0-13-154734-8)** Showing how the popular media write with a sociological eye, this special edition of *TIME* magazine, updated for 2006, pulls together the best articles of the past two years dealing with sociological topics. It can be packaged at no additional cost with all new copies of *Sociology, Eleventh Edition*.

"10 Ways to Fight Hate" brochure (0-13-028146-8) Produced by the Southern Poverty Law Center, the leading hate-crime and crime-watch organization in the United States, this free supplement walks students through ten steps they can take on their own campus or in their own neighborhood to fight hate every day. It can be packaged at no additional cost with all new copies of *Sociology, Eleventh Edition.*

Sociological Classics: A Prentice Hall Pocket Reader **(0-13-191806-0)** Compiled by sociologist David Kauzlarich, this edited volume features fourteen selections from classical sociological theorists. It can be packaged at no additional cost with all new copies of *Sociology, Eleventh Edition.*

In Appreciation

The usual practice of listing a single author hides the efforts of dozens of women and men that have resulted in *Sociology, Eleventh Edition.* I would like to express my thanks to the Prentice Hall editorial team, including Yolanda de Rooy, division president, Leah Jewell, editorial director, and Nancy Roberts, publisher, for their steady enthusiasm and for pursuing both innovation and excellence. Day-to-day work on the book is shared by the author and the production team. Barbara Reilly, production editor at Prentice Hall, is a key member of the team who is responsible for the attractive page layout of the book; indeed, if anyone "sweats the details" more than the author, it is Barbara! Amy Marsh Macionis, the text's "in house" editor, checks virtually everything, untangling awkward phrases and catching errors and inconsistencies in all the statistical data. Amy is a most talented editor who is relentless in her pursuit of quality. My debt to her is great, indeed. Karen Trost served as development editor on this revision, making countless suggestions that improved the book. She also had a hand in planning the photo program and editing the "In the *Times*" features. Thanks, Karen, for all your good work!

I also have a large debt to the members of the Prentice Hall sales staff, the men and women who have given this text such remarkable support over the years. Thanks, especially, to Marissa Feliberty and Brandy Dawson, who direct our marketing campaign.

Thanks, too, to Kathie Foote for providing the interior design of the book, and to Kathy Mrozek for managing all aspects of design through the production process. Copy editing of the manuscript was provided by Bruce Emmer and Amy Marsh Macionis.

Tammy L. Anderson, University of Delaware, provided suggestions for including more popular culture that have greatly enhanced this revision. I am truly in her debt.

It goes without saying that every colleague knows more about some topics covered in this book than the author does. For that reason, I am grateful to the hundreds of faculty and also to many students who have written to me to offer comments and suggestions. More formally, I am grateful to the following people who have reviewed some or all of this manuscript:

William Beaver, Robert Morris University
Kimberly H. Boyd, Germanna Community College
Evandro Camara, Emporia State University
Francis N. Catano, Saint Anselm College
Allison Cotton, Prairie View A&M University
Thomas Dowdy, Oklahoma Baptist University
Patricia L. Gibbs, Foothill College
Chad Hanson, Casper College
Michael Hart, Broward Community College
Howard Kurtz, Oklahoma City University
Rodney A. McDanel, Benedictine University
Ronald McGriff, College of the Sequoias
Lisa McMinn, Wheaton College
Marla A. Perry, Iowa State University
Frederick Roth, Marshall University
Mark Rubinfeld, Westminster College-Salt Lake City
Paulina Ruf, University of Tampa
Sylvia Kenig Snyder, Coastal Carolina University
Jin-kun Wei, Brevard Community College
Amy Wong, San Diego State University

I also wish to thank the following colleagues for sharing their wisdom in ways that have improved this book: Kip Armstrong (Bloomsburg University), Rose Arnault (Fort Hays State University), Scott Beck (Eastern Tennessee State University), Lois Benjamin (Hampton University), Philip Berg (University of Wisconsin, La Crosse), John R. Brouillette (Colorado State University), Cathryn Brubaker (DeKalb College), Brent Bruton (Iowa State University), Richard Bucher (Baltimore City Community College), Evandro Camara (Emporia State University), Bill Camp (Luzerne County Community College), Karen Campbell (Vanderbilt University), Harold Conway (Blinn College), Gerry Cox (Fort Hays State University), Lovberta Cross (Shelby State Community College), James A. Davis (Harvard University), Sumati Devadutt (Monroe Community College), Keith Doubt (Northeast Missouri State University), William Dowell (Heartland Community College), Doug Downey (The Ohio State University), Denny Dubbs (Harrisburg Area Community College), Travis Eaton (Northeast Louisiana State University), Helen Rose Fuchs Ebaugh (University of Houston), John Ehle (Northern Virginia Community College), Roger Eich (Hawkeye Community College), Heather Fitz Gibbon (The College of Wooster), Kevin Fitzpatrick (University of Alabama-Birmingham), Dona C.

Fletcher (Sinclair Community College), Charles Frazier (University of Florida), Karen Lynch Frederick (St. Anselm College), Pam Gaiter (Collin County Community College), Jarvis Gamble (Owen's Technical College), Patricia L. Gibbs (Foothill College), Steven Goldberg (City College, City University of New York), Charlotte Gotwald (York College of Pennsylvania), Norma B. Gray (Bishop State Community College), Rhoda Greenstone (DeVry Institute), Jeffrey Hahn (Mount Union College), Harry Hale (Northeast Louisiana State University), Dean Haledjian (Northern Virginia Community College), Dick Haltin (Jefferson Community College), Marvin Hannah (Milwaukee Area Technical College), Charles Harper (Creighton University), Gary Hodge (Collin County Community College), Elizabeth A. Hoisington (Heartland Community College), Sara Horsfall (Stephen F. Austin State University), Peter Hruschka (Ohio Northern University), Glenna Huls (Camden County College), Jeanne Humble (Lexington Community College), Cynthia Imanaka (Seattle Central Community College), Craig Jenkins (The Ohio State University), Patricia Johnson (Houston Community College), Sam Joseph (Luzerne County Community College), Ed Kain (Southwestern University), Audra Kallimanis (Mt. Olive College), Paul Kamolnick (East Tennessee State University), Irwin Kantor (Middlesex County College), Thomas Korllos (Kent State University), Rita Krasnow (Virginia Western Community College), Donald Kraybill (Elizabethtown College), Michael Lacy (Colorado State University), George Lowe (Texas Tech University), Don Luidens (Hope College), Larry Lyon (Baylor University), Li-Chen Ma (Lamar University), Karen E. B. McCue (University of New Mexico, Albuquerque), Doug McDowell (Rider University), Meredith McGuire (Trinity College), Setma Maddox (Texas Wesleyan University), Errol Magidson (Richard J. Daley College), Kooros Mahmoudi (Northern Arizona University), Mehrdad Mashayekhi (Georgetown University), Allan Mazur (Syracuse University), Jack Melhorn (Emporia State University), Will Melick (Kenyon College), Ken Miller (Drake University), Linda Miller (Queens University of Charlotte), Richard Miller (Navarro College), Verónica Montecinos (Pennsylvania State University, McKeesport), Joe Morolla (Virginia Commonwealth University), Peter B. Morrill (Bronx Community College), Craig Nauman (Madison Area Technical College), Dina B. Neal (Vernon College), Therese Nemec (Fox Valley Technical College), Joong-Hwan Oh (Hunter College), Richard Perkins (Houghton College), Anne Peterson (Columbus State Community College), Marvin Pippert (Roanoke College), Lauren Pivnik (Monroe Community College), Michael Polgar (Pennsylvania State University, Hazleton), Nevel Razak (Fort Hays State College), Jim Rebstock (Broward Community College), George Reim (Cheltenham High School), Virginia Reynolds (Indiana University of Pennsylvania), Keith Roberts (Hanover College), Ellen Rosengarten (late, of Sinclair Community College), Michael Ryan (Dodge City Community College), Marvin Scott (Butler University), Ray Scupin (Linderwood College), Steve Severin (Kellogg Community College), Harry Sherer (Irvine Valley College), Walt Shirley (Sinclair Community College), Anson Shupe (Indiana University-Purdue University at Fort Wayne), Brenda Silverman (Onondaga Community College), Ree Simpkins (Missouri Southern State University), Scott Simpson (Arkansas Northeastern College), Glen Sims (Glendale Community College), Toni Sims (University of Louisiana, Lafayette), Thomas Soltis (Westmoreland Community College), Nancy Sonleitner (University of Oklahoma), Larry Stern (Collin County Community College), Randy Ston (Oakland Community College), Verta Taylor (University of California, Santa Barbara), Vickie H. Taylor (Danville Community College), Don Thomas (The Ohio State University), Mark J. Thomas (Madison Area Technical College), Len Tompos (Lorain County Community College), Christopher Vanderpool (Michigan State University), Phyllis Watts (Tiffin University), Murray Webster (University of North Carolina, Charlotte), Debbie White (Collin County Community College), Marilyn Wilmeth (Iowa University), Stuart Wright (Lamar University), William Yoels (University of Alabama, Birmingham), Dan Yutze (Taylor University), Wayne Zapatek (Tarrant County Community College), Frank Zulke (Harold Washington College), and Anthony Zumpetta (West Chester University).

Finally, I am completing this revision at my camp in the Adirondack Mountains, surely one of the most beautiful places in the world. It is one testament to the value of new information technology that writing in such remote places is even possible! But, like many other natural treasures in the United States, this area is now under unprecedented pressure from developers. I would like to dedicate this edition of the book to the many people who love these mountains and lakes, and places like this across our vast country, and who are working generously and tirelessly to save this natural environment so that our children and our children's children may know the natural splendor that we have enjoyed so deeply.

John J. Macionis

ABOUT THE AUTHOR

John J. Macionis (pronounced ma-SHOW-nis) was born and raised in Philadelphia, Pennsylvania. He earned a bachelor's degree from Cornell University and a doctorate in sociology from the University of Pennsylvania.

His publications are wide-ranging, focusing on community life in the United States, interpersonal intimacy in families, effective teaching, humor, new information technology, and the importance of global education. He and Nijole V. Benokraitis have edited the anthology *Seeing Ourselves: Classic, Contemporary, and Cross-Cultural Readings in Sociology*. Macionis has also authored *Society: The Basics*, the leading brief text in the field, and he collaborates on international editions of the texts: *Sociology: Canadian Edition, Society: The Basics, Canadian Edition, Seeing Ourselves, Canadian Edition, and Sociology: A Global Introduction* (published by Prentice Hall Europe). *Sociology* is also available for high school students and in various foreign language editions. In addition, Macionis and Vincent Parrillo have written the urban studies text: *Cities and Urban Life* (Prentice Hall). Finally, Macionis has authored *Social Problems* (Prentice Hall), which is now the leading text in that course. The latest on all the Macionis textbooks, as well as information and dozens of Internet links of interest to students and faculty in sociology, are found at the author's personal Web site: http://www. macionis.com or http://www.TheSociologyPage.com Additional information, instructor resources, and on-line student study guides for the texts are found at the Prentice Hall site, http://www.prenhall.com/macionis

John Macionis is Professor and Distinguished Scholar of Sociology at Kenyon College in Gambier, Ohio. In 2003, he received the Philander Chase Medal for completing twenty-five years of teaching at Kenyon. During that time, he has chaired the Sociology Department, directed the college's multidisciplinary program in humane studies, presided over the campus senate and the college's

faculty, and, most importantly, taught sociology to thousands of students.

In 2002, the American Sociological Association named Macionis recipient of the Award for Distinguished Contributions to Teaching, citing his innovative use of global material as well as introduction of new teaching technology in the development of his textbooks.

Professor Macionis has been active in academic programs in other countries, having traveled to some fifty nations. During his last study tour, he directed the global education course for the University of Pittsburgh's Semester at Sea program, teaching 400 students on a floating campus that visited twelve countries as it circled the globe.

Macionis writes, "I am an ambitious traveler, eager to learn and, through the texts, to share much of what I discover with students, many of whom know little about the rest of the world. For me, traveling and writing are all dimensions of teaching. First, and foremost, I am a teacher—a passion for teaching animates everything I do." At Kenyon, Macionis offers a wide range of upper-level courses, but his favorite course is Introduction to Sociology, which he teaches every year. He enjoys extensive contact with students and each term invites members of his classes to enjoy a home-cooked meal.

The Macionis family—John, Amy, and children McLean and Whitney (along with Braveheart the dog and six very independent cats)—live on a farm in rural Ohio. In his free time, John plays tennis, swims, and bicycles through the Ohio countryside. During the summer, he is a competitive sailor and, year-round, he enjoys performing oldies rock and roll and playing the Scottish bagpipes.

Professor Macionis welcomes (and responds to) comments and suggestions about this book from faculty and students. Write to the Sociology Department, Palme House, Kenyon College, Gambier, Ohio 43022, or direct e-mail to macionis@kenyon.edu.

1

CHAPTER ONE

The Sociological Perspective

How is the sociological perspective a new
and exciting way of seeing the world?

What is a global perspective?

Why is sociology an important tool
for your future career?

I f you were to ask 100 people in the United States, "Why do couples marry?" it is a safe bet that at least 90 would reply, "People marry because they fall in love." Most of us find it hard to imagine a marriage being happy without love; for the same reason, when people fall in love, we expect them to think about marriage.

But is the decision about whom to marry really just a matter of personal feelings? There is plenty of evidence to show that if love is the key to marriage, Cupid's arrow is carefully aimed by the society around us.

Society has many "rules" about whom we should and should not marry. In all states but Massachusetts, the law rules out half the population, banning people from marrying someone of the same sex, even if a couple is deeply in love. But there are other rules as well. Sociologists have found that people, especially when they are young, are very likely to marry someone close in age, and people of all ages typically marry others in the same racial category, of similar social class background, with about the same level of education, and with the same degree of physical attractiveness (Chapter 18, "Family," gives details). People end up making choices about whom to marry, but society certainly narrows the field long before they do (Gardyn, 2002; Zipp, 2002).

When it comes to love, the decisions people make do not simply result from the process philosophers call "free will." Sociology teaches us that the social world guides all our life choices in much the same way that the seasons influence our clothing and activities.

The author's Web site is a great resource for new sociologists: http://www.TheSociologyPage. com (or www.macionis.com).

The Sociological Perspective

Sociology is *the systematic study of human society*. At the heart of sociology is a special point of view called the *sociological perspective*.

SEEING THE GENERAL IN THE PARTICULAR

Years ago, Peter Berger (1963) described the **sociological perspective** as *seeing the general in the particular*. By this he meant that sociologists look for general patterns in the behavior of particular people. Although every individual is unique, a society shapes the lives of its members. Here in the United States, for example, people expect to be in love with the person they marry, an idea almost unknown among, say, people living in a traditional village in rural Pakistan.

In addition, any society shapes the lives of people in various *categories* (such as children and adults, women and men, the rich and the poor). In a classic study of women's hopes for their marriages, for example, Lillian Rubin (1976) found that higher-income women typically expected the men they married to be sensitive to others, to talk readily, and to share feelings and experiences. Lower-income women, she found, had very different expectations and were looking for men who did not drink too much, were not violent, and held steady jobs.

Obviously, what women think they can expect in a marriage partner has a lot to do with social class position. In general, people who come from more privileged social backgrounds tend to be more confident and optimistic about their lives. This is not surprising when we realize that they have more opportunities as well as the training and skills to take advantage of them. We begin to think sociologically by realizing how the society we live in—as well as the general categories into which we fall within that society—shapes our particular life experiences.

We can easily see the power of society over the individual by imagining how different our lives would be had we been born in place of any of these children from, respectively, Bolivia, Ethiopia, Thailand, Botswana, South Korea, and El Salvador.

↔ **YOUR TURN** ↔

How do you think your social class background shapes the kind of job you expect to have after you graduate? What effect did your background have on your decision to go to college?

SEEING THE STRANGE IN THE FAMILIAR

At first, using the sociological perspective is *seeing the strange in the familiar*. Imagine a young woman walking up to a young male friend and saying, "You fit all the right social categories, which means you would make a wonderful husband!" We are used to thinking that people fall in love and decide to marry based on personal feelings. But the sociological perspective reveals the initially strange idea that society shapes what we think and do.

Because we live in an individualistic society, learning to see how society affects us may take a bit of practice. If someone asked you why you "chose" to enroll at your particular college, you might offer one of the following reasons:

"I wanted to stay close to home."

"I got a basketball scholarship."

"With a journalism degree from this university, I can get a good job."

"My girlfriend goes to school here."

"I didn't get into the school I *really* wanted to attend."

Such responses may well be true. But do they tell the whole story?

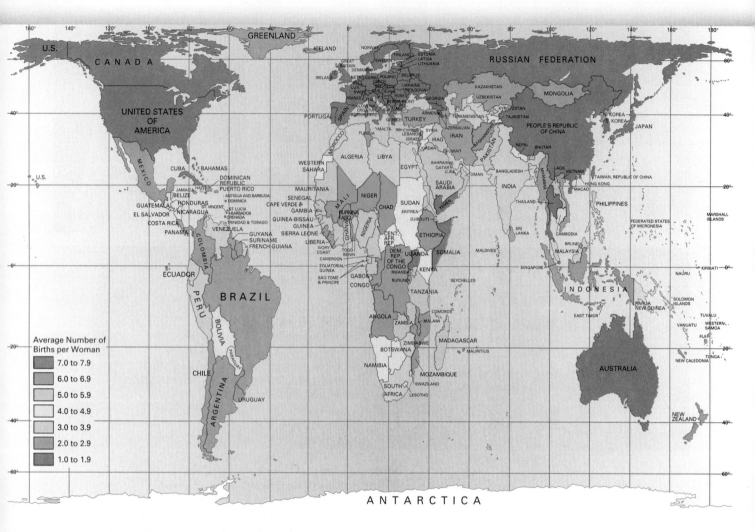

WINDOW ON THE WORLD

GLOBAL MAP 1-1   Women's Childbearing in Global Perspective

Is childbearing simply a matter of personal choice? A look around the world shows that it is not. In general, women living in poor countries have many more children than women in rich nations. Can you point to some of the reasons for this global disparity? In simple terms, such differences mean that if you had been born into another society (whether you are female or male), your life might be quite different from what it is now.

Source: Data from United Nations (2000) and U.S. Census Bureau (2003). Map projection from *Peters Atlas of the World* (1990).

Thinking sociologically about going to college, it's important to realize that only about 5 out of every 100 people in the world earn a college degree. Even in the United States a century ago, going to college was not an option for most people. Today, going to college is within the reach of far more people. But a look around the classroom shows that social forces still have much to do with who goes to college. Most U.S. college students are young, generally between eighteen and about thirty. Why? Because in our society, attending college is linked to this

For a look at how society has shaped celebrity names, click on the "Play 'The Name Game'" link at http://www.TheSociologyPage.com

period of life. But more than age is involved, because fewer than half of all young men and women actually end up on campus.

Another factor is cost. Because higher education is so expensive, college students tend to come from families with above-average incomes. As Chapter 20 ("Education") explains, if you are lucky enough to belong to a family earning more than $75,000 a year, you are almost three times as likely to go to college as someone whose family earns less than $20,000. Is it reasonable, in light of these facts, to say that attending college is simply a matter of personal choice?

SEEING PERSONAL CHOICE IN SOCIAL CONTEXT

To see how society shapes personal choices, consider the number of children women have. In the United States, as shown in Global Map 1–1, the average woman has slightly fewer than two children during her lifetime. In India, however, the average is about three; in Cambodia, about four; in Saudi Arabia, about five; in Niger, about six; and in Yemen, about seven.

Why these striking differences? As later chapters explain, women in poor countries have less schooling and fewer economic opportunities, are more likely to remain in the home, and are less likely to use contraception. Clearly, society has much to do with the decisions women and men make about childbearing.

Another illustration of the power of society to shape even our most private choices comes from the study of suicide. What could be a more personal choice than the decision to end your own life? But Emile Durkheim (1858–1917), one of sociology's pioneers, showed that even here, social forces are at work.

Examining official records in France, his own country, Durkheim found that some categories of people were more likely than others to take their own lives. Men, Protestants, wealthy people, and the unmarried had much higher suicide rates than women, Catholics and Jews, the poor, and married people. Durkheim explained the differences in terms of *social integration:* Categories of people with strong social ties had low suicide rates, and more individualistic categories of people had high suicide rates.

In Durkheim's time, men had much more freedom than women. But despite its advantages, freedom weakens social ties and thus increases the risk of suicide. Likewise, more individualistic Protestants were more likely to commit suicide than more tradition-bound Catholics and Jews, whose rituals encourage stronger social ties. The wealthy have much more freedom than the poor, but once again, at the cost of a higher suicide rate.

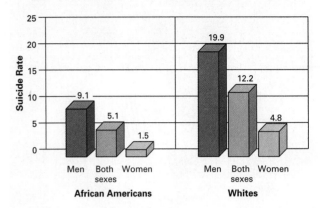

DIVERSITY SNAPSHOT

FIGURE 1–1   Rate of Death by Suicide, by Race and Sex, for the United States

Suicide rates are higher for white people than for black people and higher for men than for women. Rates indicate the number of deaths by suicide for every 100,000 people in each category for 2002.

Source: Kochanek et al. (2004).

A century later, Durkheim's analysis still holds true (Thorlindsson & Bjarnason, 1998). Figure 1–1 shows suicide rates for various categories of people in the United States. Keep in mind that suicide is very rare—a rate of 10 suicides for every 100,000 people is about the same as 6 inches in a mile. Even so, we can see some interesting patterns. In 2002, there were 12.2 recorded suicides for every 100,000 white people, more than twice the rate for African Americans (5.1). For both races, suicide was more common among men than among women. White men (19.9) were more than four times as likely as white women (4.8) to take their own lives. Among African Americans, the rate for men (9.1) was more than six times higher than for women (1.5). Applying Durkheim's logic helps us understand why this is the case: The higher suicide rate among white people and men reflects their greater wealth and freedom; the lower rate among women and African Americans reflects their limited social choices. Just as Durkheim did a century ago, we can see general patterns in the personal actions of particular individuals.

YOUR TURN

Single people are at greater risk of suicide than married people. Can you explain why?

People with the greatest privileges tend to see individuals as responsible for their own lives. Those at the margins of society, by contrast, are quick to see how race, class, and gender can create disadvantages. Before his death in 1996, Tupac Shakur expressed in his music the frustration felt by many African Americans living in this country's inner cities.

SEEING SOCIOLOGICALLY: MARGINALITY AND CRISIS

Anyone can learn to see the world using the sociological perspective. But two situations help people see clearly how society shapes individual lives: living on the margins of society and living through a social crisis.

From time to time, everyone feels like an "outsider." For some categories of people, however, being an *outsider*—not part of the dominant group—is an everyday experience. The greater people's social marginality, the better able they are to use the sociological perspective.

For example, no African American grows up in the United States without understanding the importance of race in shaping people's lives. Songs such as "Trapped" by Tupac Shakur, in which he says he sometimes feels worked "like a slave," show that some people of color—especially African

Americans living in the inner city—feel like their hopes and dreams are crushed by society. But white people, as the dominant majority, think less often about race and the privileges it provides, believing that race affects only people of color and not themselves as well. People at the margins of social life, including women, gay people, people with disabilities, and the very old, are aware of social patterns that others rarely think about. To become better at using the sociological perspective, we must step back from our familiar routines and look at our lives with a new curiosity.

Periods of change or crisis make everyone feel a little off balance, encouraging us to use the sociological perspective. The sociologist C. Wright Mills (1959) illustrated this idea using the Great Depression of the 1930s. As the unemployment rate soared to 25 percent, people out of work could not help but see general social forces at work in their particular lives. Rather than saying, "Something is wrong with me; I can't find a job," they took a sociological approach and realized, "The economy has collapsed; there are no jobs to be found!" Mills believed that using what he called the "sociological imagination" in this way helps people understand not only their society but their own lives, because the two are closely related. The Thinking Critically box takes a closer look.

Just as social change encourages sociological thinking, sociological thinking can bring about social change. The more we learn about how "the system" operates, the more we may want to change it in some way. Becoming aware of the power of gender, for example, has caused many women and men to try to reduce gender inequality.

The Importance of a Global Perspective

December 10, Fez, Morocco. This medieval city—a web of narrow streets and alleyways—is alive with the laughter of playing children, the silence of veiled women, and the steady gaze of men leading donkeys loaded with goods. Fez seems to have changed little over the centuries. Here, in northwest Africa, we are just a few hundred miles from the more familiar rhythms of Europe. Yet this place seems a thousand years away. Never have we had such an adventure! Never have we thought so much about home!

As new information technology draws even the farthest reaches of the Earth closer to one another, many academic

THINKING CRITICALLY

The Sociological Imagination: Turning Personal Problems into Public Issues

The power of the sociological perspective lies not just in changing individual lives but in transforming society. As C. Wright Mills saw it, society, not people's personal failings, is the cause of poverty and other social problems. The sociological imagination brings people together to create change by transforming personal *problems* into public *issues*.

In the following excerpt* Mills (1959:3–5) explains the need for a sociological imagination:

> When a society becomes industrialized, a peasant becomes a worker; a feudal lord is liquidated or becomes a businessman. When classes rise or fall, a man is employed or unemployed; when the rate of investment

---

*In this excerpt, Mills uses "man" and male pronouns to apply to all people. Note that even an outspoken critic of society such as Mills reflected the conventional writing practices of his time as far as gender was concerned.

goes up or down, a man takes new heart or goes broke. When wars happen, an insurance salesman becomes a rocket launcher; a store clerk, a radar man; a wife lives alone; a child

To find out more about C. Wright Mills, visit the Gallery of Sociologists at http://www. TheSociologyPage.com

grows up without a father. Neither the life of an individual nor the history of a society can be understood without understanding both.

Yet men do not usually define the troubles they endure in terms of historical change. . . . The well-being they enjoy, they do not usually impute to the big ups and downs of the society in which they live. Seldom aware of the intricate connection between the patterns of their own lives and the course of world history, ordinary men do not usually know what this connection means for the kind of men they are becoming and for the kinds of

history-making in which they might take part. They do not possess the quality of mind essential to grasp the interplay of men and society, of biography and history, of self and world. . . .

What they need . . . is a quality of mind that will help them to [see] what is going on in the world and . . . what may be happening within themselves. It is this quality . . . that . . . may be called the sociological imagination.

WHAT DO YOU THINK?

1. As Mills sees it, how are personal troubles different from public issues?
2. Living in the United States, why do we often blame ourselves for the personal problems we face?
3. By using the sociological imagination, how do we gain power over our world?

---

disciplines are taking a **global perspective,** *the study of the larger world and our society's place in it.* What is the importance of a global perspective for sociology?

First, global awareness is a logical extension of the sociological perspective. Sociology shows us that our place in society shapes our life experiences. It stands to reason, then, that the position of our society in the larger world system affects everyone in the United States. The Thinking Globally box on page 8 describes a "global village" to show the social shape of the world and the place of the United States within it.

The world's 192 nations can be divided into three broad categories according to their level of economic development (see Global Map 12–1 on page 309). **High-income**

countries are the *nations with the highest overall standards of living.* The roughly fifty countries in this category include the United States and Canada, Argentina, the nations of Western Europe, South Africa, Israel, Saudi Arabia, Japan, and Australia. Taken together, these nations produce most of the world's goods and services, and the people who live there own most of the planet's wealth. Economically speaking, people in these countries are very well off, not because they are smarter or work harder than anyone else, but because they were lucky enough to be born in a rich region of the world.

A second category is **middle-income countries,** *nations with a standard of living about average for the world as a whole.* People in any of these eighty nations—many of

The Global Village: A Social Snapshot of Our World

The Earth is home to 6.5 billion people who live in the cities and villages of 192 nations. To grasp the social shape of the world, imagine shrinking the planet's population to a "global village" of just 1,000 people. In this "village," more than half (610) of the inhabitants are Asian, including 200 citizens of the People's Republic of China. Next, in terms of numbers, we would find 140 Africans, 110 Europeans, 85 people from Latin America and the Caribbean, 5 from Australia and the South Pacific, and just 50 North Americans, including 45 people from the United States.

A close look at this settlement would reveal some startling facts: The village is a rich place, with a spectacular range of goods and services for sale. Yet most of the villagers can only dream about such treasures, because they are so poor: 80 percent of the village's total income is earned by just 200 people.

For most, the greatest problem is getting enough food. Every year, village workers produce more than enough to feed everyone; even so, half the people in the village, including most of the children, do not get enough to eat, and many must go to sleep hungry every night. The worst-off 200 residents (who, together, have less money than the richest person in the village) lack both clean drinking water and safe shelter. Weak and unable to work, their lives are at risk from life-threatening diseases.

The village has many schools, including a fine university. About 50 inhabitants have completed a college degree, but about one-third of the village's people are not even able to read or write.

We in the United States, on average, would be among the village's richest people. Although we may think that our comfortable lives are the result of our own talent and hard work, the sociological perspective reminds us that our achievements also result from our nation's privileged position in the worldwide social system.

WHAT DO YOU THINK?

1. Do any of the statistics presented in this box surprise you? Which ones? Why?

2. How do you think the lives of poor people in a lower-income country differ from those typical of people in the United States?

3. Is your "choice" to attend college affected by the country in which you live? How?

Sources: Calculations by the author based on data from Population Reference Bureau (2005) and United Nations Development Programme (2005).

---

the countries of Eastern Europe, some of Africa, and almost all of Latin America and Asia—are as likely to live in rural villages as in cities and to walk or ride tractors, scooters, bicycles, or animals as to drive automobiles. On average, they receive six to eight years of schooling. Most middle-income countries also have considerable social inequality within their own borders, so that some people are extremely rich (members of the business elite in nations across North Africa, for example), but many more lack safe housing and adequate nutrition (people living in the shanty settlements that surround Mexico City or Lima, Peru).

The remaining sixty nations of the world are **low-income countries,** *nations with a low standard of living in which most people are poor.* Most of the poorest countries in the world are in Africa, and a few are in Asia. Here, again, a few people are very rich, but the majority struggle to get by with poor housing, unsafe water, too little food, and, perhaps most serious of all, little chance to improve their lives.

Chapter 12 ("Global Stratification") explains the causes and consequences of global wealth and poverty. But every chapter of this text makes comparisons between the United States and other nations for four reasons:

1. **Where we live shapes the lives we lead.** As we saw in Global Map 1–1 on page 4, women living in rich and poor countries have very different lives, as suggested by the number of children they have. To understand ourselves and appreciate how others live, we must understand something about how countries differ, which is one good reason to pay attention to the global maps found throughout this text.

2. **Societies throughout the world are increasingly interconnected.** Historically, people in the United States took only passing note of the countries beyond our own borders. In recent decades, however, this country and the rest of the world have become linked as never before. Electronic technology now transmits sounds, pictures, and written documents around the globe in seconds.

One effect of new technology is that people the world over now share many tastes in food, clothing, and music. Rich countries such as the United States influence other nations, whose people are ever more likely to gobble up our Big Macs and Whoppers, dance to the latest hip hop music, and speak the English language.

But the larger world also has an impact on us. We all know the contributions of famous immigrants such as Arnold Schwarzenegger (who came to the United States from Austria) and Gloria Estefan (who came from Cuba). About 1 million immigrants enter the United States each year, bringing their skills and talents, along with their fashions and foods, greatly increasing the racial and cultural diversity of this country.

Trade across national boundaries has also created a global economy. Large corporations make and market goods worldwide. Stock traders in New York pay close attention to the financial markets in Tokyo and Hong Kong even as wheat farmers in Iowa watch the price of grain in the former Soviet republic of Georgia. Because most new U.S. jobs involve international trade, global understanding has never been more important.

3. **Many social problems that we face in the United States are far more serious elsewhere.** Poverty is a serious problem in the United States, but as Chapter 12 ("Global Stratification") explains, poverty in Latin America, Africa, and Asia is both more common and more serious. In the same way, although women have lower social standing than men in the United States, gender inequality is even greater in the world's poor countries.

4. **Thinking globally helps us learn more about ourselves.** We cannot walk the streets of a distant city without thinking about what it means to live in the United States. Comparing life in various settings also leads to unexpected lessons. For instance, in Chapter 12, we visit a squatter settlement in Madras, India. There, despite desperate poverty, people thrive in

One important reason to gain a global understanding is that, living in a high-income nation, we scarcely can appreciate the suffering that goes on in much of the world. This family, living in the African nation of Zambia, has none of the security most of us take for granted. In poor nations, children have only a fifty-fifty chance of surviving to adulthood.

the love and support of family members. Why, then, are so many poor people in our own country angry and alone? Are material things—so central to our definition of a "rich" life—the best way to measure human well-being?

In sum, in an increasingly interconnected world, we can understand ourselves only to the extent that we understand others. Sociology is an invitation to learn a new way of looking at the world around us. But is this invitation worth accepting? What are the benefits of applying the sociological perspective?

YOUR TURN

How would your life be different if you had been born into an impoverished family in an Asian farming village? What might you be doing right now instead of reading this textbook?

Nickel and Dimed: On (Not) Getting By in America

All of us know people who work at low-wage jobs as waitresses at nearby diners, cash register clerks at local drive-throughs, or sales associates at discount stores such as Wal-Mart. We see such people just about every day. Many of us actually *are* such people. In the United States, "common sense" tells us that the jobs people have and the amount of money they make reflect their personal abilities as well as their willingness to work hard.

Barbara Ehrenreich (2001) had her doubts. To find out what the world of low-wage work is really like, the successful journalist and author decided to leave her comfortable middle-class life to live and work in the world of low-wage jobs. She began in Key West, Florida, taking a job as a waitress for $2.43 an hour plus tips. Right away, she found out that she had to work much harder than she ever imagined. By the end of a shift, she was exhausted, but after sharing tips with the kitchen staff, she averaged less than $6 an hour. This is barely above the minimum wage and was just enough to pay the rent on her tiny apartment, buy food, and cover other basic expenses. She had to hope that

she didn't get sick, because the job did not provide health insurance and she couldn't afford to pay for a visit to a doctor's office.

After working for more than a year at a number of other low-wage jobs, including cleaning motels in Maine and working on the floor of a Wal-Mart in Minnesota, she had rejected quite a bit of "common sense." First, she now knew that tens of millions of people with low-wage jobs work very hard every day. If you don't think so, Ehrenreich says, try one of these jobs for yourself. Second, these jobs require not just hard work (imagine completely cleaning three motel rooms every hour all day long) but special skills and real intelligence (try waiting on ten tables in a restaurant at the same time and keeping everybody happy). She found that the people she worked with were, on average, just as smart, clever, and funny as those she knew who wrote books for a living or taught at a college.

Why then do we think of low-wage workers as lazy or as people with less ability? It surprised Ehrenreich to learn that many low-wage workers felt this

way about themselves. In a society that teaches us to believe personal ability is everything, we learn to size people up by their jobs. Subject to the constant supervision, random drug tests, and other rigid rules that usually come along with low-wage jobs, Ehrenreich imagined that many people end up feeling unworthy, even to the point of not trying for anything better. Such beliefs, she concludes, help support a society of "extreme inequality," in which some people live better because of the low wages paid to the rest.

WHAT DO YOU THINK?

1. Have you ever held a low-wage job? If so, would you say you worked hard? What was your pay? Were there any benefits?

2. Ehrenreich claims that most well-off people in the United States are dependent on low-wage workers. What do you think she means by this?

3. Do you think most people with jobs at Wendy's or Wal-Mart have a real chance to enroll in college and to work toward a different career? Why or why not?

Applying the Sociological Perspective

Applying the sociological perspective is useful in many ways. First, sociology is at work guiding many of the laws and policies that shape our lives. Second, on an individual level, making use of the sociological perspective leads to important personal growth and expanded awareness. Third, for anyone, studying sociology is excellent preparation for the world of work. We will look briefly at these different ways of putting sociology to work.

SOCIOLOGY AND PUBLIC POLICY

Sociologists have helped shape public policy—the laws and regulations that guide how people in communities live and work—in countless ways, from racial desegregation and school busing to laws regulating divorce. For example, in her study of how divorce affects people's income, the sociologist Lenore Weitzman (1985, 1996) discovered that women who leave marriages typically experience a dramatic loss of income. Recognizing this fact, many states passed laws that have increased women's claims to marital property and enforced fathers' obligations to provide support for women raising their children.

SOCIOLOGY AND PERSONAL GROWTH

By applying the sociological perspective, we are likely to become more active and aware and to think more critically in our daily lives. Using sociology benefits us in four ways:

1. **The sociological perspective helps us assess the truth of "common sense."**
   We all take many things for granted, but that does not make them true. One good example is the idea that we are free individuals who are personally responsible for our own lives. If we think we decide our own fate, we may be quick to praise very successful people as superior and consider others with fewer achievements personally deficient. A sociological approach, by contrast, encourages us to ask whether such common beliefs are actually true and, to the extent that they are not, why they are so widely held. The Applying Sociology box gives an example of how the sociological perspective sometimes makes us rethink commonsense ideas about other people.

2. **The sociological perspective helps us see the opportunities and constraints in our lives.** Sociological thinking leads us to see that in the game of life, we have a say in how to play our cards, but it is society To view maps showing patterns of interest to sociologists, go to http://www.nationalatlas.gov that deals us the hand. The more we understand the game, the better players we will be. Sociology helps us "size up" our world so that we can pursue our goals more effectively.

3. **The sociological perspective empowers us to be active participants in our society.** The more we understand about how society works, the more active citizens we become. As C. Wright Mills (1959) explained in the box on page 7, it is the sociological perspective that turns a "personal problem" (such as being out of work) into a "public issue" (a lack of good jobs). As we come to see how society affects us, we may support society as it is, or we may set out with others to change it.

Living in a society that stresses individual freedom and responsibility, we grow up thinking that people are entirely responsible for their lives. The sociological perspective helps us to see that the operation of society, including the way the economy works, can shape the fate of millions of people.

4. **The sociological perspective helps us live in a diverse world.** North Americans represent just 5 percent of the world's people, and as the remaining chapters of this book explain, many of the other 95 percent live very differently than we do. Still, like people everywhere, we tend to define our own way of life as "right," "natural," and "better." The sociological perspective encourages us to think critically about the relative strengths and weaknesses of all ways of life, including our own.

CAREERS: THE "SOCIOLOGY ADVANTAGE"

Most students at colleges and universities today are very interested in getting a good job. A background in sociology is excellent preparation for the working world. Of course, completing a bachelor's degree in sociology is the right choice for people who decide they would like to go on to graduate work to eventually become a professor or researcher in this field. Throughout the United States, tens of thousands of men and women teach sociology in universities, colleges, and high schools. But just as many professional sociologists work as researchers for government agencies or private foundations and businesses, gathering important information on social behavior and carrying out evaluation research. In today's cost-conscious world, agencies and companies want to be sure that the programs and policies they set in place get the job done at the lowest cost.

 In a short video, the author offers a personal response to the question, "Why would someone want to be a sociologist?" See the Video Gallery at http:// www.TheSociologyPage.com

Sociologists, especially those with advanced research skills, are in high demand for this kind of work (Deutscher, 1999).

In addition, a smaller but increasing number of professional sociologists work as clinical sociologists. These women and men work, much as clinical psychologists do, with the goal of improving the lives of troubled clients. A basic difference is that sociologists focus on difficulties not in the personality but in the individual's web of social relationships.

But sociology is not just for people who want to be sociologists. People who work in criminal justice—including jobs in police departments, probation offices, and corrections facilities—gain the "sociology advantage" by learning which categories of people are most at risk of becoming criminals as well as victims, how effective various policies and programs are at preventing crime, and why people turn to crime in the first place. Similarly, people who work in health care—including doctors, nurses, and technicans—also gain a "sociology advantage" by learning about patterns of health and illness within the population, as well as how factors such as race, gender, and social class affect human health.

The American Sociological Association (2002) reports that sociology is also excellent preparation for jobs in dozens of additional fields, including advertising, banking, business, education, government, journalism, law, public relations, and social work. In almost any type of work, success depends on understanding how various categories of people differ in beliefs, family patterns, and other ways of life. Unless you plan to have a job that never involves dealing with people, you should consider the workplace benefits of learning more about sociology.

YOUR TURN

Write down five jobs that appeal to you, then identify ways in which sociological thinking would increase your chances for success in each one.

The Origins of Sociology

Like the "choices" made by individuals, major historical events rarely just "happen." The birth of sociology was itself the result of powerful social forces.

SOCIAL CHANGE AND SOCIOLOGY

Striking changes took place in Europe during the eighteenth and nineteenth centuries. Three kinds of change were especially important in the development of sociology: the rise of a factory-based industrial economy, the explosive growth of cities, and new ideas about democracy and political rights.

A New Industrial Economy

During the Middle Ages in Europe, most people plowed fields near their homes or worked in small-scale *manufacturing* (a word derived from Latin words meaning "to make by hand"). By the end of the eighteenth century, inventors used new sources of energy—the power of moving water and then steam—to operate large machines in mills and factories. Instead of laboring at home, workers became part of a large and anonymous labor force, under the control of strangers who owned the factories. This change in the system of production took people out of their homes, weakening the traditions that had guided community life for centuries.

The Growth of Cities

Across Europe, landowners took part in what historians call the *enclosure movement*—they fenced off more and more farmland to create grazing areas for sheep, the source of wool for the thriving textile mills. Without land, countless tenant farmers had little choice but to head to the cities in search of work in the new factories.

As cities grew larger, these urban migrants faced many social problems, including pollution, crime, and homelessness. Moving through streets crowded with strangers, they faced a new, impersonal social world.

Political Change

People in the Middle Ages viewed society as an expression of God's will: From the royalty to the serfs, each person up and down the social ladder played a part in the holy plan. This theological view of society is captured in lines from the old Anglican hymn "All Things Bright and Beautiful":

> The rich man in his castle,
> The poor man at his gate,

Here we see Galileo, one of the great pioneers of the scientific revolution, defending himself before church officials, who were greatly threatened by his claims that science could explain the operation of the universe. Just as Galileo challenged the common sense of his day, pioneering sociologists such as Auguste Comte later argued that society is neither rigidly fixed by God's will nor set by human nature. On the contrary, Comte claimed, society is a system we can study scientifically, and based on what we learn, we can act intentionally to improve our lives.

North Wind Picture Archives

God made them high and lowly
And ordered their estate.

But as cities grew, tradition came under spirited attack. In the writings of Thomas Hobbes (1588–1679), John Locke (1632–1704), and Adam Smith (1723–1790), we see a shift in focus from a moral obligation to God and king to the pursuit of self-interest. In the new political climate, philosophers spoke of *individual liberty* and *individual rights.* Echoing these sentiments, our own Declaration of Independence states that every person has "certain unalienable rights," including "life, liberty, and the pursuit of happiness."

The French Revolution, which began in 1789, was an even greater break with political and social tradition. The French social analyst Alexis de Tocqueville (1805–1859) thought the changes in society brought about by the French Revolution were so great that they amounted to "nothing short of the regeneration of the whole human race" (1955:13, orig. 1856).

A New Awareness of Society

Huge factories, exploding cities, a new spirit of individualism—these changes combined to make people aware of their surroundings. The new discipline of sociology was born in England, France, and Germany—precisely where the changes were greatest.

SCIENCE AND SOCIOLOGY

And so it was that the French social thinker Auguste Comte (1798–1857) coined the term *sociology* in 1838 to describe a new way of looking at society. This makes sociology one of the youngest academic disciplines—far newer than history, physics, or economics, for example.

Of course, Comte was not the first person to think about the nature of society. Such questions fascinated the brilliant thinkers of ancient civilizations, including the Chinese philosopher K'ung Fu-tzu, or Confucius (551–479 B.C.E.) and the Greek philosophers Plato (c. 427–347 B.C.E.) and Aristotle (384–322 B.C.E.).[1] Centuries later, the Roman emperor Marcus Aurelius (121–180), the medieval thinkers Saint Thomas Aquinas (c. 1225–1274) and Christine de Pisan (c. 1363–1431), and the English playwright William Shakespeare (1564–1616) wrote about the workings of society.

Yet these thinkers were more interested in imagining the ideal society than in studying society as it really was.

---

[1]The abbreviation B.C.E. means "before the common era." We use this throughout the text instead of the traditional B.C. ("before Christ") to reflect the religious diversity of our society. Similarly, in place of the traditional A.D. (*anno Domini,* or "in the year of our Lord"), we use the abbreviation C.E. ("common era").

Suicide Rates across the United States

This map shows which states have high, average, and low suicide rates. Look for patterns. By and large, high suicide rates occur where people live far apart from one another. More densely populated states have low suicide rates. Do these data support or contradict Durkheim's theory of suicide? Why?

Source: Kochanek et al. (2004).

Number of Suicides per 100,000 People

Above average: 14.1 or more

Average: 10.0 to 14.0

Below average: 9.9 or fewer

Comte and other pioneers of sociology all cared about how society could be improved, but their major goal was to understand how society actually operates.

Comte (1975, orig. 1851–54) saw sociology as the product of a three-stage historical development. During the earliest, the *theological stage,* from the beginning of human history to the end of the European Middle Ages about 1350 C.E., people took a religious view that society expressed God's will.

For a biographical sketch of Comte, visit the Gallery of Sociologists at http://www. TheSociologyPage.com

With the dawn of the Renaissance in the fifteenth century, the theological approach gave way to a *metaphysical stage* of history in which people saw society as a natural rather than a supernatural system. Thomas Hobbes (1588–1679), for example, suggested that society reflected not the perfection of God so much as the failings of a selfish human nature.

What Comte called the *scientific stage* of history began with the work of early scientists such as the Polish astronomer Copernicus (1473–1543), the Italian astronomer and physicist Galileo (1564–1642), and the English physicist and mathematician Isaac Newton (1642–1727). Comte's contribution came in applying the

scientific approach—first used to study the physical world—to the study of society.[2]

Comte's approach is called **positivism,** *a way of understanding based on science.* As a positivist, Comte believed that society operates according to its own laws, much as the physical world operates according to gravity and other laws of nature.

By the beginning of the twentieth century, sociology had spread to the United States and showed the influence of Comte's ideas. Today, most sociologists still consider science a crucial part of sociology. But as Chapter 2 ("Sociological Investigation") explains, we now realize that human behavior is far more complex than the movement of planets or even the actions of other living things. We are creatures of imagination and spontaneity, so human behavior can never fully be explained by rigid "laws of society." In addition, early sociologists such as Karl Marx (1818–1883), whose ideas are discussed in Chapter 4 ("Society"), were troubled by the striking inequality of industrial society. They wanted the new discipline of sociology not just to understand society but to bring about change toward social justice.

Sociological Theory

Weaving observations into understanding brings us to another aspect of sociology: theory. A **theory** is *a statement of how and why specific facts are related.* The job of sociological theory is to explain social behavior in the real world.

---

[2]Illustrating Comte's stages, the ancient Greeks and Romans viewed the planets as gods; Renaissance metaphysical thinkers saw them as astral influences (giving rise to astrology); by the time of Galileo, scientists understood planets as natural objects moving according to natural laws.

For example, recall Emile Durkheim's theory that categories of people with low social integration (men, Protestants, the wealthy, and the unmarried) are at higher risk of suicide.

As the next chapter ("Sociological Investigation") explains, sociologists test their theories by gathering evidence using various research methods. Durkheim did exactly this, finding out which categories of people were more likely to commit suicide, which were less likely, and then devising a theory that best squared with all available evidence. National Map 1–1 displays the suicide rate for each of the fifty states. "In the *Times*" on pages 16–17 helps explain why suicide is higher in some places than in others.

In building theory, sociologists face two fundamental questions: What issues should we study? How should we connect the facts? In the process of answering these questions, sociologists look to one or more theoretical approaches as "road maps." Think of a **theoretical approach** as *a basic image of society that guides thinking and research.* Sociologists make use of three major theoretical approaches: the structural-functional approach, the social-conflict approach, and the symbolic-interaction approach, each of which will be explored in the remainder of this chapter.

THE STRUCTURAL-FUNCTIONAL APPROACH

The **structural-functional approach** is *a framework for building theory that sees society as a complex system whose parts work together to promote solidarity and stability.* As its name suggests, this approach points to **social structure,** *any relatively stable pattern of social behavior.* Social structure gives our lives shape—in families, the workplace, the classroom, and the community. This approach also looks for a structure's **social functions,** *the consequences of any social pattern for the operation of society as a whole.* All social structure, from a simple handshake to complex religious rituals, functions to keep society going, at least in its present form.

The structural-functional approach owes much to Auguste Comte, who pointed out the need to keep society unified when many traditions were breaking down.

 Find biographical sketches of Durkheim and Spencer in the Gallery of Sociologists at http://www.TheSociologyPage.com

Emile Durkheim, who helped establish the study of sociology in French universities, also based his work on this approach. A third structural-functional pioneer was the English sociologist Herbert Spencer (1820–1903). Spencer compared society to the human body. Just as the structural parts of the human body—the skeleton, muscles, and various internal organs —function

Applying the structural-functional approach, we look at the functions of various aspects of social life. From this point of view, higher education helps society to operate by providing young people with the knowledge and skills they will need to perform important work in the economy.

interdependently to help the entire organism survive, social structures work together to preserve society. The structural-functional approach, then, leads sociologists to identify various structures of society and investigate their functions.

Robert K. Merton (1910–2003) expanded our understanding of the concept of social function by pointing out that any social structure probably has many functions, some more obvious than others. He distinguished between **manifest functions,** *the recognized and intended consequences of any social pattern,* and **latent functions,** *the unrecognized and unintended consequences of any social pattern.* For example, the manifest function of the U.S. system

February 13, 2005

Social Isolation, Guns and a "Culture of Suicide"

By FOX BUTTERFIELD

Stevensville, Mont.—Patrick Spaulding, 17, was the star of his basketball team, an honor student and one of the most popular boys in his class. . . .

Bill Tipps, 83, was devoted to his wife of 62 years, Louise. . . .

Ron Malensek, 42, owned several small businesses, collected guns and called his wife "Princess."

All three died of a single gunshot wound to the head in this valley below the snow-covered Bitterroot Mountains. All three pulled the trigger themselves.

"Americans in small towns and rural areas are just as likely to die from gunfire as Americans in major cities," said Charles Branas, an assistant professor of epidemiology at the University of Pennsylvania School of Medicine. "The difference is in who does the shooting." . . .

Suicides occur at a higher rate in rural areas than in cities or suburbs, with the rate rising steadily the more rural the community. With homicides, the trend works in reverse, with higher rates in more urban areas. . . .

Suicide risk factors like depression, economic worries and alcohol use are, of course, prevalent in urban areas. . . . But they are heightened in rural areas by social isolation, lack of mental health care and the easy availability of guns. . . . In addition, people who see themselves as rugged frontiersmen are often reluctant to reach out for help. . . .

Stevensville is in Ravalli County, which has a suicide rate more than twice the national average. Since 1990, the county has had 103 suicides, more than three quarters of which involved a firearm. By comparison, there have been just 13 homicides in the county . . . [of] 36,000 people. . . .

The youngest to commit suicide in the county was 13 and the oldest was 92. Reflecting a national pattern, suicides rise sharply with age among men in the county. . . . Patrick Spaulding, a 6-foot-4-inch senior, . . . "lived for basketball," said his mother, Paulette Spaulding. . . .

On a Friday night in January 1997, Patrick went out and drank a few beers, . . . and on the way home apparently fell asleep at the wheel. . . . A sheriff's deputy gave Patrick a citation for illegal possession of alcohol.

"Under school rules, . . . he would be suspended from the team for the rest of the season," his mother said. "He . . . felt he had let his family and teammates down." He did not discuss the situation with his parents. . . . The next morning, . . . alone in his bedroom, Patrick shot himself. . . .

Bill Tipps and his wife, Louise, moved to Stevensville from a suburb of Las Vegas to be close to their adult son, Dennis. . . .

One of [Dennis's] sons, Dennis Jr., a contractor, built them a simple ranch-style home.

---

of higher education is to provide young people with the information and skills they need to perform jobs after graduation. Perhaps just as important, although less often acknowledged, is college's latent function as a "marriage broker," bringing together people of similar social backgrounds. Another latent function of higher education is to limit unemployment by keeping millions of young people out of the labor market, where many of them may not easily find jobs.

But Merton also recognized that the effects of social structure are not all good, and certainly not good for everybody. Thus a **social dysfunction** is *any social pattern that may disrupt the operation of society*. People often disagree about what is helpful and what is harmful to society as a whole. In addition, what is functional for one category of people (say, high profits for factory owners) may well be dysfunctional for another category of people (say, low wages for factory workers).

Critical review   The main idea of the structural-functional approach is its vision of society as stable and orderly. The main goal of the sociologists who use this approach, then, is to figure out "what makes society tick."

In the mid-1900s, most sociologists favored the structural-functional approach. In recent decades, however, its influence has declined. By focusing on social stability and unity, critics point out, structural-functionalism ignores inequalities of social class, race, and gender, which cause tension and conflict. In general, its focus on stability at the expense of conflict makes this approach somewhat

But Bill Tipps grew depressed. "My dad hated the cold and the winter," Dennis Tipps said.

He was also becoming increasingly concerned about the health of his wife, who was 80. She had undergone several heart surgeries, and the local doctor said her toes might have to be amputated because of diabetes.

Dennis Tipps now surmises that when the doctor pointed with a sweeping gesture to Louise Tipps's foot, and then her knee and hip, Bill Tipps assumed the doctor was suggesting that his wife's leg would also have to be taken off.

His father hated doctors and would not seek their advice, Dennis Tipps said. So his father never clarified his wife's prognosis or sought help for his apparent depression. . . .

One morning in September 1999, at 8:05 a.m., Bill Tipps called his son at his home.

"I just shot and killed your mother so they can't take her leg off," said the elder Mr. Tipps, who was 83. "Now I'm going to shoot myself."

Dennis Tipps jumped in his truck, and as he approached his parents' house, he heard what he thought was his engine backfiring. It was his father shooting himself. . . .

Debbie Miller describes the gentle side of her husband, Ron Malensek. "He called me Princess and treated me like a princess," she said.

But Mr. Malensek had been diagnosed with depression as a child, she said. . . . In the summer of 2003, . . . he started neglecting customers who called for estimates. . . . He became angry and could not sleep, and he had no energy, she said. . . . On August 5 last year, they went to a favorite bar, the Rustic Hut, in the town of Florence. It was the anniversary of his father's death.

When Ms. Miller left to go home, her husband stayed at the bar. Then he walked out back, retrieved a handgun that he had stashed there earlier, and shot himself. . . .

Ms. Miller does not know the statistics about rural suicides, but she knows enough. Her father and her first husband also killed themselves.

WHAT DO YOU THINK?

1. Why do you think suicide rates are generally higher in rural areas than in cities?

2. Do the findings presented in this article support Durkheim's theory of suicide? Why or why not?

3. What steps might be taken to reduce the rate of suicide in rural areas among people who are socially isolated?

Adapted from the original article by Fox Butterfield published in *The New York Times* on February 13, 2005. Copyright © 2005 by The New York Times Company. Reprinted with permission.

---

conservative. As a critical response, sociologists developed the social-conflict approach.

THE SOCIAL-CONFLICT APPROACH

The **social-conflict approach** is *a framework for building theory that sees society as an arena of inequality that generates conflict and change.* Unlike the structural-functional emphasis on solidarity and stability, this approach highlights inequality and change. Guided by this approach, sociologists investigate how factors such as social class, race, ethnicity, gender, sexual orientation, and age are linked to a society's unequal distribution of money, power, education, and social prestige. A conflict analysis rejects the idea that social structure promotes the operation of society as a whole, focusing instead on how social patterns benefit some people while hurting others.

Sociologists using the social-conflict approach look at ongoing conflict between dominant and disadvantaged categories of people—the rich in relation to the poor, white people in relation to people of color, and men in relation to women. Typically, people on top try to protect their privileges while the disadvantaged try to gain more for themselves.

A conflict analysis of our educational system shows how schooling carries class inequality from one generation to the next. For example, secondary schools assign students to either college preparatory or vocational training programs. From a structural-functional point of view, such "tracking" benefits everyone by providing schooling that fits

We can use the sociological perspective to look at sociology itself. All of the most widely recognized pioneers of the discipline were men. This is because, in the nineteenth century, it was all but unheard of for women to be college professors, and few women took a central role in public life. But Harriet Martineau in England, Jane Addams in the United States, and others made contributions to sociology that we now recognize as important and lasting.

students' abilities. But conflict analysis argues that tracking often has less to do with talent than with social background, so that well-to-do students are placed in higher tracks while poor children end up in the lower tracks.

In this way, young people from privileged families get the best schooling, which leads them to college and, later, to high-income careers. The children of poor families, by contrast, are not prepared for college and, like their parents before them, typically get stuck in low-paying jobs. In both cases, the social standing of one generation is passed on to the next, with schools justifying the practice in terms of individual merit (Bowles & Gintis, 1976; Oakes, 1982, 1985).

Many sociologists use the social-conflict approach not just to understand society but to bring about societal change that would reduce inequality. Karl Marx, whose ideas are discussed at length in Chapter 4 ("Society"), championed the cause of the workers in what he saw as their battle against factory owners. In a well-known statement (inscribed on his monument in London's Highgate Cemetery), Marx asserted, "The philosophers have only interpreted the world, in various ways; the point, however, is to change it."

Feminism and the Gender-Conflict Approach

One important type of conflict analysis is the **gender-conflict approach,** *a point of view that focuses on inequality and conflict between women and men.* The gender-conflict approach is closely linked to **feminism,** *the advocacy of social equality for women and men.*

The importance of the gender-conflict approach lies in making us aware of the many ways in which our way of life

places men in positions of power over women: in the home (where men are usually considered the "head of household"), in the workplace (where men earn more income and hold most positions of power), and in the mass media (how many hip hop stars are women?).

Another contribution of the gender-conflict approach is making us aware of the importance of women to the development of sociology. Harriet Martineau (1802–1876) is regarded as the first woman sociologist. Martineau, who was born to a wealthy English family, made her mark in 1853 by translating the writings of Auguste Comte from French into English. In her own published writings, she documented the evils of slavery and argued for laws to protect factory workers, defending workers' right to unionize. She was particularly concerned about the position of women in society and fought for changes in education policy so that women could look forward to more in life than marriage and raising children.

In the United States, Jane Addams (1860–1935) was a sociological pioneer whose contributions began in 1889 when she helped found Hull House, a Chicago settlement house that provided assistance to immigrant families. Although widely published (she wrote eleven books and hundreds of articles), Addams chose the life of a public activist over that of a university sociologist, speaking out on issues involving immigration and the pursuit of peace. Despite the controversy caused by her pacifism during World War I, she was awarded the Nobel Peace Prize in 1931.

All chapters of this book consider the importance of gender and gender inequality. For an in-depth look at

THINKING ABOUT DIVERSITY:
RACE, CLASS, & GENDER
An Early Pioneer: Du Bois on Race

One of sociology's pioneers in the United States, William Edward Burghardt Du Bois, did not see sociology as a dry, academic discipline. Rather, he saw it as the key to solving society's problems, especially racial inequality.

Du Bois spoke out against racial separation and was a founding member of the National Association for the Advancement of Colored People (NAACP). He helped his colleagues in sociology—and people everywhere—see the deep racial divisions in the United States. White people can simply be "Americans," Du Bois pointed out; African Americans, however, have a "double consciousness," reflecting their status as people who are never able to escape identification based on the color of their skin.

In his sociological classic *The Philadelphia Negro: A Social Study,* published in 1899, Du Bois explored Philadelphia's African American community, identifying both the strengths and the weaknesses of people who were dealing with overwhelming social problems on a day-to-day basis. He challenged the belief—widespread at that time—that blacks were inferior to whites, and he blamed white prejudice for creating the problems that African Americans faced. He also criticized successful people of color for being so eager to win white acceptance that they gave up all ties with the black community, which needed their help.

Du Bois described race as the major problem facing the United States in the twentieth century. Early in his career, he was hopeful about overcoming racial divisions. By the end of his life, however, he had grown bitter, believing that little had changed. At the age of ninety-three, Du Bois left the United States for Ghana, where he died two years later.

WHAT DO YOU THINK?

1. If he were alive today, what do you think Du Bois would say about racial inequality in the twenty-first century?
2. How much do you think African Americans today experience a "double consciousness"?
3. In what ways can sociology help us understand and reduce racial conflict?

Sources: Based in part on Baltzell (1967) and Du Bois (1967, orig. 1899).

feminism and the social standing of women and men, see Chapter 13 ("Gender Stratification").

The Race-Conflict Approach

Another important type of social-conflict analysis is the **race-conflict approach,** *a point of view that focuses on inequality and conflict between people of different racial and ethnic categories.* Just as men have power over women, white people have numerous social advantages over people of color including, on average, higher incomes, more schooling, and better health and longer life.

The race-conflict approach also points out the contributions made by people of color to the development of sociology. Ida Wells Barnett (1862–1931) was born to slave parents but rose to become a teacher and then a journalist and newspaper publisher. She campaigned tirelessly for racial equality and, especially, to put an end to the lynching of black people. She wrote and lectured about racial inequality throughout her life (Lengerman & Niebrugge-Brantley, 1998).

An important contribution to understanding race in the United States was made by William Edward Burghardt

The social-conflict approach points out patterns of inequality. In general, students are relatively privileged women and men who routinely come into contact with other people who have far fewer opportunities for success. What patterns of social inequality do you see in your everyday life?

Du Bois (1868–1963). Born to a poor Massachusetts family, Du Bois enrolled at Fisk University in Nashville, Tennessee, and then at Harvard University, where he earned the first doctorate awarded by that university to a person of color. Like most people who follow the social-conflict approach (whether focusing on class, gender, or race), Du Bois believed that sociologists should try to solve society's problems. He therefore studied the black community (1967, orig. 1899), spoke out against racial inequality, and served as a founding member of the National Association for the Advancement of Colored People (NAACP). The Thinking About Diversity box on page 19 takes a closer look at the ideas of W. E. B. Du Bois.

Critical review The various social-conflict approaches have gained a large following in recent decades, but like other approaches, they have met with criticism. Because any conflict analysis focuses on inequality, it largely ignores how shared values and interdependence unify members of a society. In addition, say critics, to the extent that the conflict approaches pursue political goals, they cannot claim scientific objectivity. Supporters of social-conflict approaches respond that *all* theoretical approaches have political consequences.

A final criticism of both the structural-functional and the social-conflict approaches is that they paint society in broad strokes—in terms of "family," "social class," "race," and so on. A third theoretical approach views society less in

general terms and more as the everyday experiences of individual people.

THE SYMBOLIC-INTERACTION APPROACH

The structural-functional and social-conflict approaches share a **macro-level orientation,** *a broad focus on social structures that shape society as a whole.* Macro-level sociology takes in the big picture, rather like observing a city from high above in a helicopter and seeing how highways help people move from place to place or how housing differs from rich to poor neighborhoods. Sociology also uses a **micro-level orientation,** *a close-up focus on social interaction in specific situations.* Exploring urban life in this way occurs at street level, where you might watch how children invent games on a school playground or observe how pedestrians respond to homeless people they pass on the street. The **symbolic-interaction approach,** then, is *a framework for building theory that sees society as the product of the everyday interactions of individuals.*

How does "society" result from the ongoing experiences of tens of millions of people? One answer, explained in Chapter 6 ("Social Interaction in Everyday Life"), is that society is nothing more than the shared reality that people construct as they interact with one another. That is, human beings live in a world of symbols, attaching *meaning* to virtually everything, from the words on this page to the wink of an eye. "Reality," therefore, is simply how we define our surroundings, our obligations toward others, and even our own identities.

The symbolic-interaction approach has roots in the thinking of Max Weber (1864–1920), a German sociologist who emphasized the need to understand a setting from the point of view of the people in it. Weber's approach is discussed in detail in Chapter 4 ("Society").

Since Weber's time, sociologists have taken micro-level sociology in a number of directions. Chapter 5 ("Socialization") discusses the ideas of George Herbert Mead (1863–1931), who explored how our personalities develop as a result of social experience. Chapter 6 ("Social Interaction in Everyday Life") presents the work of Erving Goffman (1922–1982), whose *dramaturgical analysis* describes how we resemble actors on a stage as we play out our various roles. Other contemporary sociologists, including George Homans and Peter Blau, have developed *social-exchange analysis*. In their view, social interaction is guided by what each person stands to gain and lose from others. In the ritual of courtship, for example, people seek mates who offer at least as much—in terms of physical attractiveness, intelligence, and wealth—as they offer in return.

Critical review   Without denying the existence of macro-level social structures such as "the family" and "social class," the symbolic-interaction approach reminds us that society basically amounts to *people interacting*. That is, micro-level sociology tries to show how individuals actually experience society. But on the other side of the coin, by focusing on what is unique in each social scene, this approach risks overlooking the widespread influence of culture, as well as factors such as class, gender, and race.

The Applying Theory table on page 22 summarizes the main characteristics of the structural-functional approach, the social-conflict approach, and the symbolic-interaction approach. Each approach is helpful in answering particular kinds of questions about society. However, the fullest understanding of our social world comes from using all three, as we show with the following analysis of sports in the United States.

Applying the Approaches: The Sociology of Sports

Who among us doesn't enjoy sports? Children as young as six or seven may play as many as two or three organized sports at a time. For adults, weekend television is filled

The basic insight of the symbolic-interaction approach is that people create the reality they experience as they interact. In other words, as these three students engage one another in conversation, they are literally deciding "what's going on?".

with sporting events, and whole sections of our newspapers report the scores. In the United States, top players such as Mark McGwire (baseball), Tiger Woods (golf), and Serena Williams (tennis) are among our most famous celebrities. Sports in the United States are also a multibillion-dollar industry. What sociological insights can the three theoretical approaches give us into this familiar part of everyday life?

THE FUNCTIONS OF SPORTS

A structural-functional approach directs our attention to the ways in which sports help society operate. The manifest functions of sports include providing recreation, a means of getting in physical shape, and a relatively harmless way to let off steam. Sports have important latent functions as well, from building social relationships to creating tens of thousands of jobs. Sports encourage competition and the pursuit of success, both of which are central to our society's way of life.

Sports also have dysfunctional consequences. For example, colleges and universities that try to field winning teams sometimes recruit students for their athletic skill rather than their academic ability. This practice not only lowers the academic standards of a school but also short-changes athletes who spend little time doing the academic work that will prepare them for later careers (Upthegrove, Roscigno, & Charles, 1999).

APPLYING THEORY
MAJOR THEORETICAL APPROACHES

	Structural-Functional Approach	Social-Conflict Approach	Symbolic-Interaction Approach
What is the level of analysis?	Macro-level	Macro-level	Micro-level
What image of society does the approach have?	Society is a system of interrelated parts that is relatively stable. Each part works to keep society operating in an orderly way. Members have general agreement about what is morally right.	Society is a system of social inequality. Society operates to benefit some categories of people and harm others. Social inequality causes conflict that leads to social change.	Society is an ongoing process. People interact in countless settings using symbolic communications. The reality people experience is variable and changing.
What core questions does the approach ask?	How is society held together? What are the major parts of society? How are these parts linked? What does each part do to help society work?	How does society divide a population? How do advantaged people protect their privileges? How do disadvantaged people challenge the system seeking change?	How do people experience society? How do people shape the reality they experience? How do behavior and meaning change from person to person and from one situation to another?

SPORTS AND CONFLICT

A social-conflict analysis of sports begins by pointing out that the games people play reflect their social standing. Some sports—including tennis, swimming, golf, sailing, and skiing—are expensive, so taking part is largely limited to the well-to-do. Football, baseball, and basketball, however, are accessible to people of almost all income levels.

Throughout history, sports have been oriented mostly toward males. For example, the first modern Olympic Games, held in 1896, barred women from competition; in the United States, Little League teams in most parts of the country have only recently let girls play. Traditional ideas that girls and women lack the strength to play sports have now been widely rejected. But our society still encourages men to become athletes while expecting women to be attentive observers and cheerleaders. At the professional level, women also take a back seat to men, particularly in the sports with the most earnings and social prestige.

For decades, big league sports excluded people of color, who were forced to form leagues of their own. Only in 1947 did Major League Baseball admit the first African American player when Jackie Robinson broke the color line and joined the Brooklyn Dodgers. More

 To read the 2004 Racial and Gender Report Card for U.S. sports, go to http://www.bus.ucf.edu/sport/cgi-bin/site/sitew.cgi?page=/news/index.htx

than fifty years later, professional baseball honored Robinson's amazing career by retiring his number 42 on *all* of the teams in the league. In 2004, African Americans (12 percent of the U.S. population) accounted for 9 percent of Major League Baseball players, 69 percent of National Football League (NFL) players, and 76 percent of National Basketball Association (NBA) players (Lapchick, 2005).

One reason for the increasing number of African Americans in professional sports is that athletic performance—in terms of batting average or number of points scored per game—can be precisely measured and is not influenced by racial prejudice. It is also true that some people of color make a particular effort to excel in athletics, where they see greater opportunity than in other careers (Steele, 1990; Hoberman, 1997, 1998; Edwards, 2000; Harrison, 2000). In recent years, in fact, African American athletes have earned higher salaries, on average, than white players.

But racial discrimination still exists in professional sports. For one thing, race is linked to the *positions* athletes play on the field, in a pattern called "stacking." Figure 1–2 shows the results of a study of race in football. Notice that white athletes are much more likely than African American athletes to play offense and to take the central positions on both sides of the line. More broadly, African Americans have a large share of players in only five sports: baseball, basketball, football, boxing, and track. In all professional sports, the vast majority of managers, head coaches, and owners of sports teams are white (Lapchick, 2005).

Although many individual players get supersized salaries and millions of fans enjoy following their teams, sports are a big business that provides big profits for a small number of people (predominantly white men). In sum, sports in the United States are bound up with inequalities based on gender, race, and economic power.

SPORTS AS INTERACTION

At a micro-level, a sporting event is a complex, face-to-face interaction. In part, play is guided by the players' assigned positions and the rules of the game. But players are also spontaneous and unpredictable. Following the symbolic-interaction approach, we see sports less as a system than as an ongoing process.

From this point of view, too, we expect each player to understand the game a little differently. Some players enjoy a setting of stiff competition; for others, love of the game may be greater than the need to win.

In addition, the behavior of any single player may change over time. A rookie in professional baseball, for example, may feel self-conscious during the first few games in the big leagues but go on to develop a comfortable sense of fitting in with the team. Coming to feel at home on the field was slow and painful for Jackie Robinson, who knew that many white players, and millions of white fans, resented his presence. In time, however, his outstanding ability and his confident and cooperative manner won him the respect of the entire nation.

The three theoretical approaches—the structural-functional approach, the social-conflict approach, and the symbolic-interaction approach—provide different insights into sports, and none is more correct than the others. Applied to any issue, each approach generates its own interpretations. To appreciate fully the power of the sociological perspective, you should become familiar with all three.

↪ **YOUR TURN** ↩

Apply the three theoretical approaches to the issues that opened this chapter—love and marriage. Consider questions such as these: What categories of people are you most likely to date? Why? Why are today's younger college students likely to wait many more years to marry than students did fifty years ago?

DIVERSITY SNAPSHOT

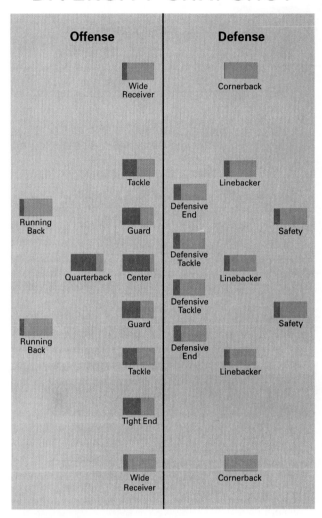

FIGURE 1-2 Race and Sport: "Stacking" in Professional Football

Does race play a part in professional sports? Looking at the various positions in professional football, we see that white players are more likely to play the central and offensive positions. What do you make of this pattern?

Source: Lapchick (2005).

The Thinking It Through box on page 24 discusses the use of the sociological perspective and reviews many of the ideas presented in this chapter. This box raises a number of questions that will help you understand how sociological generalizations differ from the common stereotypes we encounter every day.

THINKING IT THROUGH

Is Sociology Nothing More than Stereotypes?

"Protestants are the ones who kill themselves!"

"People in the United States? They're rich, they love to marry, and they love to divorce!"

"Everybody knows that you have to be black to play professional basketball!"

Everyone, including the sociologist, loves to generalize. Recognizing social patterns is, of course, nothing more than making generalizations about people. However, beginning students of sociology may wonder how generalizations differ from stereotypes. For example, are the preceding statements valid generalizations or false stereotypes?

These three statements are all examples of a **stereotype,** *an exaggerated description applied to every person in some category.* First, rather than describing averages, each statement describes every person in some category in exactly the same way; second, each ignores facts and distorts reality (even though many stereotypes do contain an element of truth); third, a stereotype is often motivated by bias and can sound more like a "put-down" than a fair-minded observation.

Good sociology makes generalizations, which must meet three important conditions. First, *sociologists do not carelessly apply any generalization to everyone.* Second, *sociologists make sure that a generalization squares with available facts.* Third, *sociologists offer generalizations*

fair-mindedly, with an interest in getting at the truth.

Earlier in this chapter, we noted that the suicide rate among Protestants is higher than among Catholics or Jews. However, the statement "Protestants are the ones who kill themselves" is not a valid generalization because the vast majority of Protestants do no such thing. It would be just as wrong to jump to the conclusion that a particular friend, because he is a Protestant male, is about to end his own life. (Imagine refusing to lend money to a roommate who happens to be a Baptist, explaining, "Well, given your risk of suicide, I might never get paid back!")

Second, sociologists shape their generalizations to available facts. A more factual version of the second statement at the beginning of this box is that, on average, the U.S. population has a very high standard of living. It is also true that our marriage rate is one

of the highest in the world. And, although few people take pleasure in divorcing, our divorce rate is also among the world's highest.

Third, sociologists try to be fair-minded and want to get at the truth. The third statement, about African Americans and basketball, is not good sociology for two reasons. First, it is simply not true, and, second, it seems motivated by bias rather than truth-seeking.

Good sociological analysis stands apart from harmful stereotyping. A college sociology course is an excellent setting for getting at the truth behind common stereotypes. The classroom encourages discussion and offers the factual information you need to decide whether a particular statement is a valid sociological generalization or just a stereotype.

A sociology classroom is a great place to get at the truth behind common stereotypes.

WHAT DO YOU THINK?

1. Can you think of a common stereotype of sociologists? What is it? After reading this box, do you still think it is valid?
2. Do you think taking a sociology course can help correct people's stereotypes? Why or why not?
3. Can you think of a stereotype of your own that might be challenged by sociological analysis?

The following learning tools will help you see what you know, identify what you still need to learn, and expand your understanding beyond the text. You can also visit this text's Companion Website™ at http://www.prenhall.com/macionis to find additional practice tests.

The Sociological Perspective

The sociological perspective shows "the general in the particular," or the effect of society on individual lives. Because U.S. culture emphasizes individual choice, recognizing the power of society in our lives may seem, at first, like "seeing the strange in the familiar." C. Wright Mills called this point of view the "sociological imagination," claiming it turns private troubles into public issues that people, working together, can solve. The chapter explained that differences in the number of children born to women around the world, as well as Emile Durkheim's research on suicide rates among some categories of people, show that society affects even our most personal choices and actions. Categories of people who experience social marginality—for example, African Americans or people with disabilities—are more likely to see the world sociologically. For everyone, periods of social crisis encourage sociological thinking.

The Importance of a Global Perspective

Global awareness is an important part of the sociological perspective for four major reasons. First, people (especially in high-income compared to low-income countries) live very differently. Second, all the world's societies are becoming more closely linked. Third, many social problems are most serious in countries other than our own. Fourth, global awareness helps us better understand ourselves.

Applying the Sociological Perspective

Sociology has an impact on our everyday lives because it plays an important part in shaping public policy. On an individual level, sociology promotes personal growth in four major ways. First, it helps us assess common beliefs. Second, it helps us

appreciate the opportunities and limits in our lives. Third, sociology encourages more active participation in society. Fourth, it increases our awareness of social diversity in the world around us. In addition, sociology is excellent preparation for a number of important careers and increases the chances for success in almost any job.

The Origins of Sociology

Sociology was born in response to wide-reaching changes in Europe during the eighteenth and nineteenth centuries. Three changes—the rise of an industrial economy, the explosive growth of cities, and the emergence of new political ideas—made people pay attention to how society operates. Auguste Comte gave sociology its name in 1838. Earlier social thinkers had focused on what society ought to be, but Comte's new discipline used scientific methods to understand society as it is.

Sociological Theory

A theory states how facts are related, weaving observations into insight and understanding. Sociologists use three major theoretical approaches to create theories about the operation of society. The structural-functional approach, which focuses on how patterns of behavior help society operate, highlights society's stability and integration. The social-conflict approach, which emphasizes social inequality, sees conflict as a cause of change. The gender-conflict approach (feminism) highlights how men have power over women. The race-conflict approach focuses on how white people have power over people of color. In contrast to these broad, macro-level approaches, the symbolic-interaction approach is a micro-level framework that focuses on people's face-to-face interaction in specific settings.

Applying the Approaches: The Sociology of Sports

Applied to sports, the structural-functional approach looks at how sports contribute to the operation of U.S. society. The social-conflict approach examines the links between sports and social inequality. The symbolic-interaction approach highlights the different meanings and understandings people have of sports.

KEY CONCEPTS

sociology (p. 2) the systematic study of human society

sociological perspective (p. 2) the special point of view of sociology that sees general patterns of society in the lives of particular people

global perspective (p. 7) the study of the larger world and our society's place in it

high-income countries (p. 7) nations with the highest overall standards of living

middle-income countries (p. 7) nations with a standard of living about average for the world as a whole

low-income countries (p. 8) nations with a low standard of living in which most people are poor

positivism (p. 14) a way of understanding based on science

theory (p. 14) a statement of how and why specific facts are related

theoretical approach (p. 15) a basic image of society that guides thinking and research

structural-functional approach (p. 15) a framework for building theory that sees society as a complex system whose parts work together to promote solidarity and stability

social structure (p. 15) any relatively stable pattern of social behavior

social functions (p. 15) the consequences of any social pattern for the operation of society as a whole

manifest functions (p. 15) the recognized and intended consequences of any social pattern

latent functions (p. 15) the unrecognized and unintended consequences of any social pattern

social dysfunction (p. 16) any social pattern that may disrupt the operation of society

social-conflict approach (p. 17) a framework for building theory that sees society as an arena of inequality that generates conflict and change

gender-conflict approach (p. 18) a point of view that focuses on inequality and conflict between women and men

feminism (p. 18) the advocacy of social equality for women and men

race-conflict approach (p. 19) a point of view that focuses on inequality and conflict between people of different racial and ethnic categories

macro-level orientation (p. 20) a broad focus on social structures that shape society as a whole

micro-level orientation (p. 20) a close-up focus on social interaction in specific situations

symbolic-interaction approach (p. 20) a framework for building theory that sees society as the product of the everyday interactions of individuals

stereotype (p. 24) an exaggerated description applied to every person in some category

---

SAMPLE TEST QUESTIONS

These questions are similar to those found in the test bank that accompanies this textbook.

Multiple-Choice Questions

1. **What does the sociological perspective show us about whom any individual chooses to marry?**
   a. There is no explaining personal feelings like love.
   b. People's actions reflect human free will.
   c. The operation of society guides many of our personal choices.
   d. In the case of love, opposites attract.

2. **Which early sociologist studied patterns of suicide?**
   a. Peter Berger
   b. Emile Durkheim
   c. Auguste Comte
   d. Karl Marx

3. Sociology contributes to personal growth by helping us
   a. see the opportunities in our lives.
   b. see the constraints in our lives.
   c. be more active participants in society.
   d. all of the above.

4. The discipline of sociology first developed in
   a. countries experiencing rapid social change.
   b. countries with little social change.
   c. countries with a history of warfare.
   d. the world's poorest countries.

5. Which early sociologist coined the term *sociology* in 1838?
   a. Karl Marx
   b. Herbert Spencer
   c. Adam Smith
   d. Auguste Comte

6. Which theoretical approach is closest to that taken by early sociologists Auguste Comte and Emile Durkheim?
   a. symbolic-interaction approach

b. structural-functional approach

c. social-conflict approach

d. none of the above

7. **Which term refers to the recognized and intended consequences of a social pattern?**

a. manifest functions

b. latent functions

c. eufunctions

d. dysfunctions

8. **Sociology's social-conflict approach draws attention to**

a. how structure contributes to the overall operation of society.

b. how people construct meaning through interaction.

c. patterns of social inequality.

d. the stable aspects of society.

9. **Which woman, among the first sociologists, studied the evils of slavery and also translated the writings of Auguste Comte?**

a. Elizabeth Cady Stanton

b. Jane Addams

c. Harriet Martineau

d. Margaret Mead

10. **Which of the following illustrates a micro-level focus?**

a. the operation of the U.S. political system

b. patterns of global terrorism

c. class inequality in the armed forces

d. two new dormitory roommates getting to know one another

ANSWERS: 1(c); 2(b); 3(d); 4(a); 5(d); 6(b); 7(a); 8(c); 9(c); 10(d).

Essay Questions

1. Explain why applying the sociological perspective can make us seem less in control of our lives. In what ways does it actually give us greater power over our lives?

2. Guided by the discipline's three major theoretical approaches, create sociological questions about (a) television, (b) war, and (c) colleges and universities.

APPLICATIONS & EXERCISES

1. Explore your local area, and draw a sociological map of the community. Include the types of buildings (for example, "big single-family homes," "rundown business area," "new office buildings," "student apartments") found in various places, and guess at the categories of people who live or work there. What patterns do you see?

2. Figure 18–2 on page 485 shows the U.S. divorce rate over the past century. Using the sociological perspective and with an eye on the timeline inside the front cover of this book, try to identify societal factors that pushed the divorce rate down after 1930, up again after 1940, down in the 1950s, up after 1960, and down again after 1980.

3. Observe male-female couples holding hands. In almost every case, the male will hold hands with his wrist to the front, and the female will do so with her wrist to the rear. Thinking sociologically, what general societal pattern do you see in this particular situation?

NVESTIGATE *with* Research Navigator

Research Navigator.com
RESOURCES FOR COLLEGE RESEARCH ASSIGNMENTS

To access the full resources of **Research Navigator**™, please find the access code printed on the inside cover of *The Prentice Hall Guide to Evaluating Online Resources with Research Navigator: Sociology, 2004.* You may have received this booklet if your instructor recommended this guide be packaged with new textbooks. (If your book did not come with this printed guide, you can purchase one through your college bookstore.) Visit our **Research Navigator** site at **http://www.researchnavigator.com** Once at this site, click on "Register" under "New Users" and enter your access code to create a personal Login Name and Password. (When revisiting the site, use the same Login Name and Password to enter.) Browse the features of the Research Navigator Web site, and search the databases of academic journals, newspapers, magazines, and Web links using keywords such as "sociology," "suicide," and "sports."

2

Sociological Investigation

How does sociological research challenge
common sense?

Why do sociologists use different methods
to do research?

What part do gender and cultural differences
play in sociological research?

While on a visit to Atlanta during the winter holiday season, the sociologist Lois Benjamin (1991) called up the mother of an old college friend. Benjamin was eager to learn about her friend, Sheba; the two women both had dreamed about earning a graduate degree, landing a teaching job, and writing books. Now a successful university professor, Benjamin had seen her dream come true. But as she soon found out, this was not the case with Sheba.

Benjamin recalled early signs of trouble. After college, Sheba had begun graduate work at a Canadian university. But in letters to Benjamin, Sheba became more and more critical of the world and seemed to be cutting herself off from others. Some wondered if she was suffering from a personality disorder. But as Sheba saw it, the problem was racism. As an African American woman, she felt she was the target of racial hostility. Before long, she flunked out of school, blaming the failure on her white professors. At this point, she left North America, earning a Ph.D. in England and then settling in Nigeria. In the years since, Benjamin had not heard from her longtime friend.

Benjamin was happy to hear that Sheba had returned to Atlanta. But her delight dissolved into shock when she saw Sheba and realized that her friend had suffered a mental breakdown and was barely responsive to anyone.

For months, Sheba's emotional collapse troubled Benjamin. Obviously, Sheba was suffering from serious psychological problems. Having felt the sting of racism herself, Benjamin wondered if this might have played a part in Sheba's story. Partly as a tribute to her old friend, Benjamin set out to explore the effects of race in the lives of bright, well-educated African Americans in the United States.

Benjamin knew she was calling into question the common belief that race is less of a barrier today than it used to be, especially to talented African Americans (W. J. Wilson, 1978). But her own experiences—and, she believed, Sheba's too—seemed to contradict such thinking.

To test her ideas, Benjamin spent the next two years asking 100 successful African Americans across the country how race affected their lives. In the words of these "Talented One Hundred"[1] men and women, she found evidence that even among privileged African Americans, racism remains a heavy burden. ◼

Later in this chapter, we will take a closer look at Lois Benjamin's research. For now, notice how the sociological perspective helped her spot broad social patterns in the lives of individuals. Just as important, Benjamin's work shows us the *doing* of sociology, the process of *sociological investigation.*

Many people think that scientists work only in laboratories, carefully taking measurements using complex equipment. But as this chapter explains, although some

---

[1]W. E. B. Du Bois used the term "Talented Tenth" to describe African American leaders.

sociologists do conduct scientific research in laboratories, most work on neighborhood streets, in homes and work-places, in schools and hospitals, in bars and prisons—in short, wherever people can be found.

This chapter examines the methods that sociologists use to conduct research. Along the way, we shall see that research involves not just ways of gathering information but contro-versies about values: Should researchers strive to be objec-tive? Or should they point to the need for change? Certainly Lois Benjamin did not begin her study just to show that racism exists; she wanted to bring racism out in the open as a way to challenge it. We shall tackle questions of values after presenting the basics of sociological investigation.

Basics of Sociological Investigation

Sociological investigation starts with two simple require-ments. The first was the focus of Chapter 1: *Apply the socio-logical perspective.* This point of view reveals curious patterns of behavior all around us that call for further study. It was Lois Benjamin's sociological imagination that prompted her to wonder how race affects the lives of talent-ed African Americans.

This brings us to the second requirement: *Be curious and ask questions.* Benjamin wanted to learn more about how race affects people who are high achievers. She began by asking, Who are the leaders of this nation's black community? What effect does being part of a racial minori-ty have on their view of themselves? On the way white peo-ple perceive them and their work?

Seeing the world sociologically and asking questions are basic to sociological investigation. But where do we look for answers? To answer this question, we need to realize that there are various kinds of "truth."

SCIENCE AS ONE FORM OF TRUTH

Saying that we "know" something can mean many things. Most people in the United States, for instance, say they be-lieve in God. Few claim to have direct contact with God, but they say they believe all the same. We call this kind of know-ing "belief" or "faith."

A second kind of truth comes from recognized experts. Students with a health problem, for example, may consult a campus physician or search the Internet for articles written by experts in the field.

A third type of truth is based on simple agreement among ordinary people. Most of us in the United States would probably say we "know" that sexual intercourse

In a culturally diverse country, there are many different "truths." Our society offers opportunities to learn about people whose lives differ from our own. For example, the Teach for America program is a wonderful way to investigate different ways of life and also to enrich the lives of others.

among ten-year-old children is wrong. But why? Mostly be-cause just about everyone says it is.

People's "truths" differ the world over, and we often en-counter "facts" at odds with our own. Imagine being a Peace Corps volunteer who has just arrived in a small, traditional village in Latin America. Your job is to help local people grow more crops. On your first day in the fields, you observe a strange practice: After planting the seeds, the farmers lay a dead fish on top of the soil. When you ask about this, they explain that the fish is a gift to the god of the harvest. A vil-lage elder adds sternly that the harvest was poor one year when no fish were offered.

From that society's point of view, using fish as gifts to the harvest god makes sense. The people believe in it, their experts endorse it, and everyone seems to agree that the system works. But with scientific training in agriculture, you have to shake your head and wonder. The scientific "truth" in this situation is something entirely different: The decomposing fish fertilize the ground, producing a better crop.

Science represents a fourth way of knowing. **Science** is *a logical system that bases knowledge on direct, systematic ob-servation.* Standing apart from faith, the wisdom of "ex-perts," and general agreement, scientific knowledge rests on **empirical evidence,** that is, *information we can verify with our senses.*

Common sense suggests that, in a world of possibilities, people fall in love with that "special someone." Sociological research reveals that the vast majority of people select partners who are very similar in social background to themselves.

Our Peace Corps example does not mean that people in traditional villages ignore what their senses tell them or that members of technologically advanced societies use only science to know things. A medical researcher using science to develop a new drug for treating cancer, for example, may still practice her religion as a matter of faith, turn to financial experts when making decisions about money, and pay attention to the political opinions of her family and friends. In short, we all hold various kinds of truths at the same time.

COMMON SENSE VERSUS SCIENTIFIC EVIDENCE

Like the sociological perspective, scientific evidence sometimes challenges our common sense. Here are six statements that many North Americans assume are true:

1. **"Poor people are far more likely than rich people to break the law."** Not true. If you regularly watch television shows like *Cops*, you might think that police arrest only people from "bad" neighborhoods. Chapter 9 ("Deviance") explains that poor people do stand out in the official arrest statistics. But research also shows that police and prosecutors are more likely to treat well-to-do people more leniently, as when a Hollywood celebrity is accused of shoplifting or drunk driving. Some laws are even written in a way that criminalizes poor people more and affluent people less.

2. **"The United States is a middle-class society in which most people are more or less equal."** False. Data presented in Chapter 11 ("Social Class in the United States") show that the richest 5 percent of U.S. families control more than half the nation's total wealth, but almost half of all families have scarcely any wealth at all.

3. **"Most poor people don't want to work."** Wrong. Research described in Chapter 11 indicates that this statement is true of some but not most poor people. In fact, about half of poor individuals in the United States are children and elderly people who are not expected to work.

4. **"Differences in the behavior of females and males are just 'human nature'."** Wrong again. Much of what we call "human nature" is constructed by the society in which we live, as Chapter 3 ("Culture") explains. Further, as Chapter 13 ("Gender Stratification") argues, some societies define "feminine" and "masculine" very differently from the way we do.

5. **"People change as they grow old, losing many interests as they focus on their health."** Not really. Chapter 15 ("Aging and the Elderly") reports that aging changes our personalities very little. Problems of health increase in old age, but by and large, elderly people keep the distinctive personalities they have had throughout their adult lives.

6. **"Most people marry because they are in love."** Not always. To members of our society, few statements are so obvious. Surprisingly, however, in many societies marriage has little to do with love. Chapter 18 ("Families") explains why.

These examples confirm the old saying "It's not what we don't know that gets us into trouble as much as things we *do* know that *just aren't so.*" We all have been brought up believing widely accepted truths, being bombarded by expert advice, and feeling pressure to accept the opinions of people around us. As adults, we need to evaluate more critically what we see, read, and hear. Sociology can help us do just that.

YOUR TURN

Think of several "commonsense" ideas you were brought up to believe that you later learned were not true.

Three Ways to Do Sociology

"Doing" sociology means learning more about the social world. There is more than one way to do this. Just as sociologists can use one or more theoretical approaches (described in Chapter 1, "The Sociological Perspective"), they may also use different methodological orientations. The following sections describe three ways to do research: scientific sociology, interpretive sociology, and critical sociology.

SCIENTIFIC SOCIOLOGY

In Chapter 1, we explained how early sociologists such as Auguste Comte and Emile Durkheim applied science to the study of society just as natural scientists investigate the physical world. **Scientific sociology,** then, is *the study of society based on systematic observation of social behavior.* The scientific orientation to knowing, called *positivism,* assumes that an objective reality exists "out there." The job of the scientist is to discover this reality by gathering empirical evidence, facts we can verify with our senses, say, by "seeing," "hearing," or "touching."

Concepts, Variables, and Measurement

A basic element of science is the **concept,** *a mental construct that represents some part of the world in a simplified form.* "Society" is a concept, as are the structural parts of societies, such as "the family" and "the economy." Sociologists also use concepts to describe people, as when we speak of someone's "race" or "social class."

A **variable** is *a concept whose value changes from case to case.* The familiar variable "price," for example, changes from item to item in a supermarket. Similarly, we use the concept "social class" to identify people as "upper-class," "middle-class," "working-class," or "lower-class."

The use of variables depends on **measurement,** *a procedure for determining the value of a variable in a specific case.* Some variables are easy to measure, as when you step on a scale to see how much you weigh. But measuring sociological variables can be far more difficult. For example, how would you measure a person's "social class"? You might look at clothing, listen to patterns of speech, or note a home address. Or trying to be more precise, you might ask about income, occupation, and education.

Because almost any variable can be measured in more than one way, sociologists often have to decide which factors to consider. For example, having a very high income might qualify a person as "upper-class." But what if the income comes from selling automobiles, an occupation most people think of as "middle-class"? Would having only an eighth-grade education make the person "lower-class"? In a case like this, sociologists usually combine these three measures—income, occupation, and education—to assign social class, as described in Chapter 10 ("Social Stratification") and Chapter 11 ("Social Class in the United States").

Sociologists face another interesting problem in measuring variables: dealing with huge numbers of people. How, for instance, do you describe the income of millions of U.S. families? Reporting millions of numbers carries little meaning and tells us nothing about the people as a whole. Thus sociologists use *statistical measures* to describe people. The Applying Sociology box on page 34 explains how.

Defining concepts Measurement is always somewhat arbitrary because the value of any variable partly depends on how it is defined. In addition, deciding how to measure abstract concepts such as "love," "family," or "intelligence" can lead to lengthy debates.

Good research, therefore, requires that sociologists **operationalize a variable,** which means *specifying exactly what is to be measured before assigning a value to a variable.* Before measuring the concept of social class, for example, you would have to decide exactly what you were going to measure: say, income level, years of schooling, or occupational prestige. Sometimes sociologists measure several of these things; in such cases, they need to specify exactly how they plan to combine these variables into one overall score. The next time you read the results of a study, notice the way the researchers operationalize each variable. How they define terms can greatly affect the results.

When deciding how to operationalize variables, sociologists often take into account the opinions of the people they study. Since 1977, for example, researchers at the U.S. Census Bureau have defined race and ethnicity as white, black, Hispanic, Asian or Pacific Islander, and American Indian or Alaska Native. One problem with this system is that someone can be *both* Hispanic and white or black; similarly, people of Arab ancestry might not identify with *any* of these choices. Just as important, an increasing number of people in the United States are *multiracial.* Because of the changing face of the U.S. population, the 2000 census was the first one to allow people to describe their race and ethnicity by selecting more than one category, resulting in a more accurate description of the true diversity of the population.

Reliability and validity For a measurement to be useful, it must be reliable and valid. **Reliability** refers to *consistency in measurement.* A measurement is reliable if repeated measurements give the same result time after time. But consistency does not guarantee **validity,** which means *actually measuring exactly what you intend to measure.*

Getting a valid measurement is sometimes tricky. For example, if you want to study how "religious" people are,

Three Useful (and Simple) Statistical Measures

The admissions office at your school is preparing a new brochure, and as part of your work-study job in that office, your supervisor asks you to determine the average salary received by last year's graduating class. To keep matters simple, assume that you talk to only seven members of the class (a real study would require contacting many more) and gather the following data on their present incomes:

$30,000	$42,000
$22,000	$165,000
$22,000	$35,000
$34,000	

Sociologists use three different statistical measures to describe averages. The simplest statistical measure is the *mode,* the value that occurs most often in a series of numbers. In this example, the mode is $22,000, since that value occurs two times and each of the others occurs only once. If all the values were to occur only once, there would be no mode; if two different values each occurred two or three times, there would be two modes. Although it is easy to identify, sociologists rarely use the mode because it reflects only some of the numbers and is therefore a crude measure of the "average."

A more common statistical measure, the *mean,* refers to the arithmetic average of a series of numbers, calculated by adding all the values together and dividing by the number of cases. The sum of the seven incomes is $350,000. Dividing by 7 yields a mean income of $50,000. But notice that the mean is not a very good "average" because it is higher than six of the seven incomes and is not particularly close to any of the actual numbers. Because the mean is "pulled" up or down by an especially high or low value (in this case, the $165,000 paid to one graduate, an athlete who signed as a rookie with the Cincinnati Reds farm team), it can give a distorted picture of any data that include one or more extreme scores.

The *median* is the middle case: the value that occurs midway in a series of numbers arranged from lowest to highest. Here the median income for the seven graduates is $34,000, because when the numbers are placed in order from lowest to highest, this value divides the series exactly in half, with three incomes higher and three lower. (With an even number of cases, the median is halfway between the two middle cases.) If there should be any extreme scores, the median (unlike the mean) is not affected by them. In such cases, the median gives a better picture of what is "average" than the mean.

WHAT DO YOU THINK?

1. Your grade point average (GPA) is an example of an average. Is it a mode, a median, or a mean? Explain.
2. Sociologists generally use the median instead of the mean when they study people's incomes. Can you see why?
3. Do a quick calculation of the mean, median, and mode for these simple numbers: 1, 2, 5, 6, 6.

Answers: mode = 6, median = 5, mean = 4.

---

you might ask the people you are studying how often they attend religious services. But is going to a church, temple, or mosque really the same thing as being religious? People may attend religious services because of deep personal beliefs, but they may also do so out of habit or because others pressure them to go. And what about spiritual people who avoid organized religion altogether? Even when a measurement yields consistent results (making it reliable), it still may not measure what we want it to (and therefore lack validity). In Chapter 19 ("Religion"), we suggest that measuring religiosity should take account of not only church attendance but also a person's beliefs and the degree to which a person lives by religious convictions. In sum, careful measurement is important, but it is also often a challenge.

YOUR TURN

What specific questions would you ask in order to measure a person's social class position?

Relationships among variables Once measurements are made, investigators can pursue the real payoff: seeing how variables are related. The scientific ideal is **cause and effect,** *a relationship in which change in one variable causes change in another.* Cause-and-effect relationships occur around us every day, such as when studying hard for an exam results in a high grade. *The variable that causes the change* (in this

Cigarette smoking is more common among people of lower social position. But knowing this correlation does not establish cause and effect. In your opinion, why would factory workers be more likely to smoke than people working as corporate executives?

case, how much you study) is called the **independent variable.** *The variable that changes* (the exam grade) is called the **dependent variable.** The value of one variable, in other words, depends on the value of another. Why is linking variables in terms of cause and effect important? Because this kind of relationship allows us to *predict* the outcome of future events—if we know one thing, we can accurately predict another. For example, knowing that studying hard results in a better exam grade, we can predict with confidence that if you do study hard for the next exam, you will receive a high grade, and if you do not study hard, your grade will suffer.

But just because two variables change together does not mean that they are linked by a cause-and-effect relationship. For example, sociologists have long recognized that juvenile delinquency is more common among young people who live in crowded housing. Say we operationalize the variable "juvenile delinquency" as the number of times a person under the age of eighteen has been arrested, and we define "crowded housing" by a home's number of square feet of living space per person. It turns out that these variables are related: Delinquency rates are high in densely populated neighborhoods. But should we conclude that crowding in the home (in this case, the independent variable) is what causes delinquency (the dependent variable)?

Not necessarily. **Correlation** is *a relationship in which two (or more) variables change together.* We know that density and delinquency are correlated because they change together, as shown in part (a) of Figure 2–1 on page 36. This relationship *may* mean that crowding causes more arrests, but it could also mean that some third factor is at work causing change in *both* of the variables under observation.

To identify a third variable, think what kind of people live in crowded housing: people with less money and few choices—the poor. Poor children are also more likely to end up with police records. In reality, crowded housing and juvenile delinquency are found together because *both* are caused by a third factor—poverty—as shown in part (b) of Figure 2–1. In short, the apparent connection between crowding and delinquency is "explained away" by a third variable—low income—that causes them both to change. So our original connection turns out to be a **spurious correlation,** *an apparent but false relationship between two (or more) variables that is caused by some other variable.*

Exposing a correlation as spurious requires a bit of detective work, assisted by a technique called **control,** *holding constant all variables except one in order to see clearly the effect of that variable.* In our example, we suspect that income level may be causing a spurious link between housing density and delinquency. To check whether the correlation between delinquency and crowding is spurious, we control for income—that is, we hold income constant by looking at only young people of one income level. If the correlation between density and delinquency remains, that is, if young people of the same income level living in more crowded housing show higher rates of arrest than young people in less crowded housing, we have more reason to think that crowding does, in fact, cause delinquency. But if the relationship disappears when we control for income, as shown in part (c) of Figure 2–1, then we know we were dealing with a spurious correlation. In fact, research shows that the correlation between crowding and delinquency just about disappears if income is controlled (Fischer, 1984). So we have now sorted out the relationship among the three variables, as illustrated in part (d) of the figure. Housing density and juvenile delinquency

FIGURE 2–1 Correlation and Cause: An Example

Correlation is not the same as cause. Here's why.

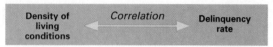

(a) If two variables vary together, they are said to be correlated. In this example, density of living conditions and juvenile delinquency increase and decrease together.

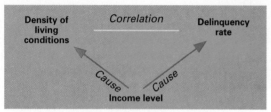

(b) Here we consider the effect of a third variable: income level. Low income level may cause *both* high-density living conditions *and* a high delinquency rate. In other words, as income level decreases, both the density of living conditions and the delinquency rate increase.

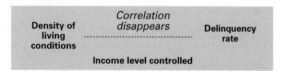

(c) If we control income level—that is, examine only cases with the same income level—do those with higher-density living conditions still have a higher delinquency rate? The answer is no. There is no longer a correlation between these two variables.

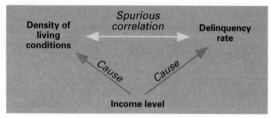

(d) This finding leads us to conclude that income level is a cause of both density of living conditions and delinquency rate. The original two variables (density of living conditions and delinquency rate) are thus correlated, but neither one causes the other. Their correlation is therefore *spurious*.

have a spurious correlation; evidence shows that both variables rise or fall according to income.

To sum up, correlation means only that two (or more) variables change together. To establish cause and effect, three requirements must be met: (1) a demonstrated correlation, (2) an independent (or causal) variable that happens before the dependent variable, and (3) no evidence that a third variable could be causing a spurious correlation between the two.

Natural scientists usually have an easier time than social scientists in identifying cause-and-effect relationships because natural scientists usually work in laboratories, where they can control other variables. Carrying out research in a workplace or on the streets, however, makes control very difficult, so sociologists often have to settle for demonstrating only correlation. Also, human behavior is highly complex, involving dozens of causal variables at any one time, so establishing all the cause-and-effect relationships in any situation is extremely difficult.

The Ideal of Objectivity

Ten students are sitting around a dorm lounge discussing the dream vacation spot for the upcoming spring break. Do you think one place will end up being everyone's clear favorite? That hardly seems likely.

In scientific terms, each of the ten people probably operationalizes the concept "dream vacation" differently. For one, it might be a deserted, sunny beach in Mexico; for another, the choice might be New Orleans, a lively city with a very active social scene; for still another, hiking the Rocky Mountains below snow-capped peaks may be the choice. Like so many other "bests" in life, the best vacations turn out to be mostly a matter of individual taste.

Personal values are fine when it comes to choosing travel destinations, but they pose a challenge to scientific research. Remember, science assumes that reality is "out there." Scientists need to study this reality without changing it in any way, and so they strive for **objectivity,** *personal neutrality in conducting research.* Objectivity means that researchers carefully hold to scientific procedures and do not let their own attitudes and beliefs influence the results.

Scientific objectivity is an ideal rather than a reality, of course, because no one can be completely neutral. Even the topic someone chooses to study reflects a personal interest of one sort or another, as Lois Benjamin showed us in the reasons for her decision to investigate race. But the scientific ideal is to keep a professional sense of distance or detachment from how the results turn out. With this ideal in mind, when conducting research you should do your best to see that conscious or unconscious biases do not distort your findings. As an extra precaution, many researchers openly state their personal leanings in their research reports so that readers can interpret conclusions with them in mind.

The influential German sociologist Max Weber expected that people would select their research topics according to their personal beliefs and interests. Why else, after all, would one person study world hunger, another investigate the effects of racism, and still another examine how children manage in one-parent families? Knowing that people select topics that are *value-relevant,* Weber cautioned researchers to be *value-free* in their investigations. Only by controlling their personal feelings and opinions (as we expect any professionals to do) can researchers study the world *as it is* rather than tell us *how they think it should be.* This detachment, for Weber, is a crucial element of science that sets it apart from politics. Politicians are committed to particular outcomes; scientists try to maintain an open mind about the results of their investigations, whatever they may turn out to be.

Weber's argument still carries much weight in sociology, although most sociologists admit that we can never be completely value-free or even aware of all our biases. Keep in mind, however, that sociologists are not "average" people: Most are white, highly educated, and more politically liberal than the population as a whole (Klein & Stern, 2004). Remember that sociologists, like everyone else, are influenced by their social backgrounds.

One way to limit distortion caused by personal values is **replication,** *repetition of research by other investigators.* If other researchers repeat a study using the same procedures and obtain the same results, we gain confidence that the results are accurate (both reliable and valid). The need for replication in scientific investigation probably explains why the search for knowledge is called "*re*-search" in the first place.

Keep in mind that the logic of science does not guarantee objective, absolute truth. What science offers is an approach to knowledge that is *self-correcting* so that in the long run, researchers stand a good chance of limiting their biases. Objectivity and truth lie, then, not in any one study but in the scientific process itself as it continues over time.

One principle of scientific research is that sociologists and other investigators should try to be objective in their work, so that their personal values and beliefs do not distort their findings. But such a detached attitude may discourage the relationship needed in order for people to open up and share information. Thus, as sociologists study human relationships, they have to be especially mindful of their own—when it comes to their subjects.

Why do you think many doctors, teachers, and police officers avoid working professionally with their own children?

Some Limitations of Scientific Sociology

Science is one important way of knowing. Yet, applied to social life, science has several important limitations.

1. **Human behavior is too complex for sociologists to predict any individual's actions precisely.**
    Astronomers calculate the movement of objects in the skies with remarkable precision, but comets and planets are unthinking objects. Humans, by contrast, have minds of their own, so no two people react to any event (whether it be a sports victory or a natural disaster) in exactly the same way. Sociologists, therefore, must be satisfied with showing that *categories* of people *typically* act in one way or another. This is not a failing of sociology. It simply reflects the fact that we study creative, spontaneous people.

2. **Because humans respond to their surroundings, the mere presence of a researcher may affect the behavior being studied.** An astronomer's gaze has no effect

A basic lesson of social research is that being observed affects how people behave. Researchers can never be certain precisely how this will occur; some people resent public attention, but others become highly animated when they think they have an audience.

whatever on a distant comet. But most people react to being observed. Try staring at someone for a few minutes and see for yourself. People being watched may become anxious, angry, or defensive; others may be especially friendly or helpful. We can change people just by studying them.

3. **Social patterns change; what is true in one time or place may not hold true in another.** The same laws of physics will apply tomorrow as today, and they hold true all around the world. But human behavior is so variable that there are no universal sociological laws.

4. **Because sociologists are part of the social world they study, being value-free when conducting social research is difficult.** Barring a laboratory mishap, chemists are rarely personally affected by what goes on in test tubes. But sociologists live in their "test tube," the society they study. Therefore, social scientists may find it difficult to control—or even to recognize— personal values that may distort their work.

INTERPRETIVE SOCIOLOGY

All sociologists agree that studying social behavior scientifically presents some real challenges. But some sociologists go further, suggesting that science as it is used to study the natural world misses a vital part of the social world: *meaning.*

As humans, we do not simply act; we act for a reason. Max Weber, who pioneered this orientation, argued that the proper focus of sociology must go beyond just observing behavior to include *interpretation*—learning what meaning people find in what they do. **Interpretive sociology** is *the study of society that focuses on the meanings people attach to their social world.*

The Importance of Meaning

Interpretive sociology differs from scientific, or positivist, sociology in three ways. First, scientific sociology focuses on actions, what people do; interpretive sociology, by contrast, focuses on the meaning people attach to their actions. Second, scientific sociology sees an objective reality "out there," but interpretive sociology sees reality constructed by people themselves in the course of their everyday lives. Third, scientific sociology tends to favor *quantitative* data—numerical measurements of people's behavior—and interpretive sociology favors *qualitative* data, or how people understand their surroundings.

The scientific orientation is well suited to research in a laboratory, where investigators stand back and take careful measurements. The interpretive orientation is better suited to research in a natural setting, where investigators interact with people, learning how they make sense of their everyday lives.

Weber's Concept of *Verstehen*

Weber believed the key to interpretive sociology lay in *Verstehen,* the German word for "understanding." The interpretive sociologist does not just observe *what* people do but also tries to understand *why* they do it. The thoughts and feelings of subjects—which scientists tend to dismiss because they are difficult to measure—are the focus of the interpretive sociologist's attention.

CRITICAL SOCIOLOGY

There is a third methodological orientation in sociology. Like the interpretive orientation, critical sociology developed in reaction to the limitations of scientific sociology. This time, however, the problem was the foremost principle of scientific research: objectivity.

Scientific sociology holds that reality is "out there" and the researcher's task is to study and document this reality. But Karl Marx, who founded the critical orientation, rejected the idea that society exists as a "natural" system with a fixed order. To assume this, he claimed, is the same as saying that society cannot be changed. Scientific sociology, from this point of view, ends up supporting the status quo. **Critical sociology,** by contrast, is *the study of society that focuses on the need for social change.*

The Importance of Change

Rather than asking the scientific question "How does society work?" critical sociologists ask moral and political questions, such as "Should society exist in its present form?" Their answer to this question, typically, is that it should not. One recent account of this orientation, echoing Marx, claims that the point of sociology is "not just to research the social world but to change it in the direction of democracy and social justice" (Feagin & Hernán, 2001:1). In making value judgments about how society should be improved, critical sociology rejects Weber's goal that researchers be value-free and emphasizes instead that they should be social activists in pursuit of desirable change.

Sociologists using the critical orientation seek to change not just society but the character of research itself. They often identify personally with their research subjects and encourage them to help decide what to study and how to do the work. Typically, researchers and subjects use their findings to provide a voice for less powerful people and to advance the political goal of a more equal society (B. B. Hess, 1999; Feagin & Hernán, 2001; Perrucci, 2001).

Sociology as Politics

Scientific sociologists object to taking sides in this way, charging that critical sociology (whether feminist, Marxist, or some other critical orientation) becomes political, lacks objectivity, and cannot correct for its own biases. Critical sociologists reply that *all* research is political or biased—

either it calls for change or it does not. Sociologists, they continue, have no choice about their work being political, but they can choose *which* positions to support.

Critical sociology is an activist orientation tying knowledge to action, seeking not just to understand the world but also to improve it. Generally speaking, scientific sociology tends to appeal to researchers with nonpolitical or conservative political views; critical sociology appeals to those whose politics range from liberal to radical left.

METHODS AND THEORY

Is there a link between methodological orientations and sociological theory? There is no precise connection, but each of the three methodological orientations—scientific, interpretive, and critical—does stand closer to one of the theoretical approaches presented in Chapter 1 ("The Sociological Perspective"). Scientific sociology corresponds to the structural-functional approach, interpretive sociology is related to the symbolic-interaction approach, and critical sociology is linked to the social-conflict approach. The Summing Up table on page 40 provides a quick review of the differences among the three methodological orientations. Many sociologists favor one orientation over another; however, because each provides useful insights, it is a good idea to become familiar with all three (Gamson, 1999).

GENDER AND RESEARCH

In recent years, sociologists have become aware that research is affected by **gender,** *the personal traits and social positions that members of a society attach to being female or male.* Margrit Eichler (1988) identifies five ways in which gender can shape research:

1. **Androcentricity.** Androcentricity (*andro-* in Greek means "male"; *centricity* means "being centered on") refers to approaching an issue from a male perspective. Sometimes researchers act as if only men's activities are important, ignoring what women do. For years, researchers studying occupations focused on the paid work of men and overlooked the housework and child care traditionally performed by women. Clearly, research that seeks to understand human behavior cannot ignore half of humanity.

   Gynocentricity—seeing the world from a female perspective—can also limit good sociological investigation. However, in our male-dominated society, this problem arises less often.

2. **Overgeneralizing.** This problem occurs when researchers use data drawn from people of only one sex

SUMMING UP

Three Methodological Orientations in Sociology

	Scientific	Interpretive	Critical
What is reality?	Society is an orderly system. There is an objective reality "out there."	Society is ongoing interaction. People construct reality as they attach meanings to their behavior.	Society is patterns of inequality. Reality is that some categories of people dominate others.
How do we conduct research?	Researcher gathers empirical, ideally quantitative, data. Researcher tries to be a neutral observer.	Researcher develops a qualitative account of the subjective sense people make of their world. Researcher is a participant.	Research is a strategy to bring about desired social change. Researcher is an activist.
Corresponding theoretical approach	Structural-functional approach	Symbolic-interaction approach	Social-conflict approach

to support conclusions about "humanity" or "society." Gathering information by talking to only male students and then drawing conclusions about an entire campus would be an example of overgeneralizing.

3. **Gender blindness.** Failing to consider the variable of gender at all is called "gender blindness." As is evident throughout this book, the lives of men and women differ in countless ways. A study of growing old in the United States might suffer from gender blindness if it overlooked the fact that most elderly men live with their wives but elderly women typically live alone.

4. **Double standards.** Researchers must be careful not to distort what they study by judging men and women differently. For example, a family researcher who labels a couple as "man and wife" may define the man as the "head of household" and treat him accordingly and assume that the woman simply engages in family "support work."

5. **Interference.** Another way gender can distort a study is if a subject reacts to the sex of the researcher, interfering with the research operation. While studying a small community in Sicily, for instance, Maureen Giovannini (1992) found that many men treated her as a woman rather than as a researcher. Some thought it was wrong for any single woman to speak privately with a man. Others denied Giovannini access to places they considered off-limits to women.

There is nothing wrong with focusing research on one sex or the other. But all sociologists, as well as people who

read their work, should be aware of the importance of gender in any investigation.

YOUR TURN

Think of three research topics in U.S. society that might be affected by the gender of the researcher. In each case, explain why.

RESEARCH ETHICS

Like all researchers, sociologists must be aware that research can harm as well as help subjects or communities. For this reason, the American Sociological Association (ASA)—the major professional association of sociologists in North America—has established formal guidelines for conducting research (1997).

Sociologists must strive to be both skillful and fair-minded in their work. Sociologists must disclose all research

 Read the professional Code of Ethics at the Web site of the American Sociological Association: http://www.asanet.org/members/ecointro.html

findings, without omitting significant data. They should make their results available to other sociologists, especially those who want to replicate a study.

Sociologists must also make sure that the subjects taking part in a research project are not harmed. Should research develop in a manner that threatens any participants, investigators must stop their work immediately. Researchers must also protect the privacy of anyone involved in a research project. This last promise can be difficult to keep, since researchers sometimes come under pressure (even from the police or courts) to disclose information. Today, ethical research requires the *informed consent* of participants, which means that subjects understand the responsibilities and risks that the research involves and agree—before the work begins—to take part.

Another important guideline concerns funding. Sociologists must include in their published results the sources of all financial support. They must also avoid taking money that raises concerns of conflicts of interest. For example, researchers must never accept funding from an organization that seeks to influence the research results for its own purposes.

The federal government also plays a part in research ethics. Every college and university that seeks federal funding for research involving human subjects must have an *institutional review board* (IRB) to review grant applications and ensure that research will not violate ethical standards.

Finally, there are global dimensions to research ethics. Before beginning research in another country, an investigator must become familiar enough with that society to understand what people *there* are likely to see as a violation of privacy or a source of personal danger. In a multicultural society such as the United States, the same rule applies to studying people whose cultural background differs from your own. The Thinking About Diversity box on page 42 offers some tips about how outsiders can effectively and sensitively study Hispanic communities.

Methods of Sociological Research

A **research method** is *a systematic plan for doing research.* The remainder of this chapter introduces four commonly used methods of sociological investigation: experiments, surveys, participant observation, and the use of existing data. None is better or worse than any other. Rather, in the same way that a carpenter selects a particular tool for a specific task, researchers choose a method—or mix several methods—according to whom they plan to study and what they wish to learn.

TESTING A HYPOTHESIS: THE EXPERIMENT

The logic of science is most clearly found in the **experiment,** *a research method for investigating cause and effect under highly controlled conditions.* Experimental research is *explanatory;* that is, it asks not just what happens

but why. Typically, researchers devise an experiment to test a **hypothesis,** *a statement of a possible relationship between two (or more) variables.* A hypothesis typically takes the form of an *if-then* statement: *If* one thing were to happen, *then* something else will result.

The ideal experiment consists of four steps. First, the researcher specifies the variable that is assumed to cause the change (the independent variable, or the "cause") as well as the variable that is changed (the dependent variable, or the "effect"). Second, the researcher measures the initial value of the dependent variable. Third, the researcher exposes the dependent variable to the independent variable (the "treatment"). Fourth, the researcher again measures the dependent variable to see what change took place. If the expected change did occur, the experiment supports the hypothesis; if not, the hypothesis must be modified.

But a change in the dependent variable could be due to something other than the supposed cause. (Think back to our discussion of spurious correlations.) To be certain that they identify the correct cause, researchers carefully control other factors that might affect the outcome of the experiment. Such control is easiest in a laboratory, a setting specially constructed to neutralize outside influences.

Another strategy to gain control is dividing subjects into an *experimental group* and a *control group.* Early in the study, the researcher measures the dependent variable for subjects in both groups but later exposes only the experimental group to the independent variable or treatment. (The control group typically gets a "placebo," a treatment that the members of the group think is the same but really has no effect on the experiment.) Then the investigator measures the subjects in both groups again. Any factor occurring during the course of the research that influences people in the experimental group (say, a news event) would do the same to those in the control group, thus controlling or "washing out" the factor. By comparing the before and after measurements of the two groups, a researcher can learn how much of the change is due to the independent variable.

The Hawthorne Effect

Researchers need to be aware that subjects' behavior may change simply because they are getting special attention, as one classic experiment revealed. In the late 1930s, the Western Electric Company hired researchers to investigate worker productivity in its Hawthorne factory near Chicago (Roethlisberger & Dickson, 1939). One experiment tested the hypothesis that increasing the available lighting would raise worker output. First, researchers measured worker productivity (the dependent variable). Then they increased the lighting (the independent variable) and measured

THINKING ABOUT DIVERSITY:
RACE, CLASS, & GENDER

Studying the Lives of Hispanics

Because U.S. society is racially, ethnically, and religiously diverse, all of us have to work with people who differ from ourselves. The same is **SOCIOLOGY** *@* **WORK** true of sociologists. Learning—in advance—the ways of life of any category of people can ease the research process and ensure that there will be no hard feelings when the work is finished.

Gerardo Marín and Barbara Van Oss Marín (1991) have identified five areas of concern in conducting research with Hispanic people:

1. **Be careful with terms.** The Maríns point out that the term "Hispanic" is a label of convenience used by the U.S. Census Bureau. Few people of Spanish descent think of themselves as "Hispanic" or "Latino"; most identify with a particular country (generally, with a Latin American nation, such as Mexico or Argentina, or with Spain).

2. **Be culturally aware.** By and large, the United States is a nation of individualistic, competitive people. Many Hispanics, by contrast, place more value on cooperation and community. An outsider, then, may judge the behavior of a Hispanic subject as conformist or overly trusting when in fact the person is simply trying to be helpful. Researchers should also realize that

Hispanic respondents might agree with a particular statement merely out of politeness.

3. **Anticipate family dynamics.** Generally speaking, Hispanic cultures have strong family loyalties. Asking subjects to reveal information about another family member may make them uncomfortable or even angry. The Maríns add that in the home, a researcher's request to speak privately with a Hispanic woman may provoke suspicion or outright disapproval from her husband or father.

4. **Take your time.** Spanish cultures, the Maríns explain, tend to place the quality of relationships above simply getting a job done. A non-Hispanic researcher who tries to hurry an interview with a Hispanic family, perhaps wishing not to delay the family's dinner, may be consid-

ered rude for not proceeding at a more sociable and relaxed pace.

5. **Think about personal space.** Finally, people of Spanish descent typically maintain closer physical contact than many non-Hispanics. As a result, researchers who seat themselves across the room from their subjects may appear standoffish. Researchers might also wrongly label Hispanics "pushy" when they move closer than non-Hispanic people find comfortable.

Of course, Hispanics differ among themselves, just like people in every other category, and these generalizations apply to some more than to others. But we need to be aware of them. The challenge of being culturally aware is especially great in the United States, where hundreds of categories of people make up our multicultural society.

WHAT DO YOU THINK?

1. Give a specific example of damage to a study that might take place if researchers are not sensitive to the culture of their subjects.
2. What do researchers need to do to avoid the kinds of problems noted in this box?
3. Discuss the research process with classmates from various cultural backgrounds. How are the concerns raised by people of different cultural backgrounds similar? How do they differ?

output a second time. The resulting increased productivity supported the hypothesis. But when the research team later turned the lighting back down, productivity increased again. What was going on? In time, the researchers

realized that the employees were working harder (even if they could not see as well) simply because people were paying attention to them and measuring their output. From this research, social scientists coined the term **Hawthorne**

effect to refer to *a change in a subject's behavior caused simply by the awareness of being studied.*

Illustration of an Experiment: The Stanford County Prison

Prisons can be violent settings, but is this due simply to the "bad" people who end up there? Or as Philip Zimbardo suspected, does the prison itself somehow generate violent behavior? This question led Zimbardo to devise a fascinating experiment, which he called the "Stanford County Prison" (Zimbardo, 1972; Haney, Banks, & Zimbardo, 1973).

Zimbardo thought that once inside a prison, even emotionally healthy people are prone to violence. Thus Zimbardo treated the *prison setting* as the independent variable capable of causing *violence,* the dependent variable.

To test this hypothesis, Zimbardo's research team constructed a realistic-looking "prison" in the basement of the psychology building on the campus of California's Stanford University. Then they placed an ad in the local newspaper, offering to pay young men to help with a two-week research project. To each of the seventy who responded they administered a series of physical and psychological tests and then selected the healthiest twenty-four.

The next step was to assign randomly half the men to be "prisoners" and half to be "guards." The plan called for the guards and prisoners to spend the next two weeks in the mock prison. The prisoners began their part of the experiment soon afterward when the city police "arrested" them at their homes. After searching and handcuffing the men, the police drove them to the local police station, where they were fingerprinted. Then police transported their captives to the Stanford prison, where the guards locked them up. Zimbardo started his video camera rolling and watched to see what would happen next.

The experiment turned into more than anyone had bargained for. Both guards and prisoners soon became embittered and hostile toward one another. Guards humiliated the prisoners by assigning them tasks such as cleaning out toilets with their bare hands. The prisoners, for their part, resisted and insulted the guards. Within four days, the researchers removed five prisoners who displayed "extreme emotional depression, crying, rage and acute anxiety" (Haney, Banks, & Zimbardo, 1973:81). Before the end of the first week, the situation had become so bad that the researchers had to cancel the experiment. Zimbardo explains:

> The ugliest, most base, pathological side of human nature surfaced. We were horrified because we saw some boys (guards) treat others as if they were despicable animals, taking pleasure in cruelty, while other boys (prisoners) became servile, dehumanized robots who thought only of escape, of their own individual survival and of their mounting hatred for the guards. (Zimbardo, 1972:4)

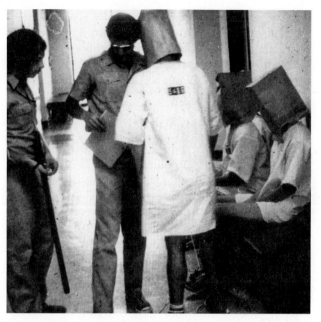

Philip Zimbardo's research helps to explain why violence is a common element in our society's prisons. At the same time, his work demonstrates the dangers that sociological investigation poses for subjects and the need for investigators to observe ethical standards that protect the welfare of people who participate in research.

The events that unfolded at the "Stanford County Prison" supported Zimbardo's hypothesis that prison violence is rooted in the social character of jails themselves, not in the personalities of guards and prisoners. This finding raises questions about our society's prisons, suggesting the need for basic reform. Notice, too, that this experiment shows the potential of research to threaten the physical and mental well-being of subjects. Such dangers are not always as obvious as they were in this case. Therefore, researchers must consider carefully the potential harm to subjects at all stages of their work and end any study, as Zimbardo did, if subjects may suffer harm of any kind.

↦ **YOUR TURN** ↤

How might Zimbardo's findings help explain the abuse of Iraqi prisoners by U.S. soldiers in the Abu Ghraib prison?

ASKING QUESTIONS: SURVEY RESEARCH

A **survey** is *a research method in which subjects respond to a series of statements or questions in a questionnaire or an interview.* The most widely used of all research methods, surveys are especially good for studying attitudes—such as beliefs about politics, religion, or race—since there is no way to observe directly what people think. Sometimes surveys provide clues about cause and effect, but typically they yield *descriptive* findings, painting a picture of people's views on some issue.

Population and Sample

A survey targets some **population,** *the people who are the focus of research.* Lois Benjamin, in her study of racism described at the beginning of this chapter, studied a select population—talented African Americans. Other surveys such as political polls that predict election results treat every adult in the country as the population.

Obviously, contacting millions of people is impossible for even the best-funded and most patient researcher. Fortunately, there is an easier way that yields accurate results: Researchers collect data from a **sample,** *a part of a population that represents the whole.* Benjamin chose 100 talented African Americans as her sample. National political polls typically survey a sample of about 1,000 people.

Everyone uses the logic of sampling all the time. If you look at students sitting near you and notice five or six heads nodding off, you might conclude that the class finds the day's lecture dull. In reaching this conclusion, you are making a judgment about *all* the people in the class (the "population") from observing *some* of your classmates (the "sample").

But how can we be sure a sample really represents the entire population? One way is *random sampling,* in which researchers draw a sample from the population randomly so that every person in the population has an equal chance to be selected. The mathematical laws of probability dictate that a random sample is likely to represent the population as a whole. Selecting a random sample usually means listing everyone in the population and using a computer to make a random selection.

Beginning researchers sometimes make the mistake of assuming that "randomly" walking up to people on a street produces a sample that is representative of the entire city. Unfortunately, this technique does not give every person an equal chance to be included in the sample. For one thing, any street, whether in a rich neighborhood or on a college campus, contains more of some kinds of people than others. The fact that some people are more approachable than others is another source of bias.

Although good sampling is no simple task, it offers a considerable savings in time and expense. We are spared the tedious work of contacting everyone in a population, yet we can obtain essentially the same results.

 To better understand the use of polls in political campaigns, go to http://faculty.vassar.edu/lowry/polls.html

Using Questionnaires

Selecting subjects is just the first step in carrying out a survey. Also needed is a plan for asking questions and recording answers. Most surveys use a questionnaire for this purpose.

A **questionnaire** is *a series of written questions a researcher presents to subjects.* One type of questionnaire provides not only the questions but also a selection of fixed responses (similar to a multiple-choice examination). This *closed-ended format* makes it fairly easy to analyze the results, but by narrowing the range of responses, it can also distort the findings. For example, Frederick Lorenz and Brent Bruton (1996) found that the number of hours per week students say they study for a college course depends on the options offered to them. When the researchers presented students with options ranging from one hour or less to nine hours or more, 75 percent said that they studied four hours or less per week. But when subjects in a comparable group were given choices ranging from four hours or less to twelve hours or longer (a higher figure that suggests students should study more), they suddenly became more studious; only 34 percent reported that they studied four hours or less each week.

A second type of questionnaire, using an *open-ended format,* allows subjects to respond freely, expressing various shades of opinion. The drawback of this approach is that the researcher has to make sense out of what can be a very wide range of answers.

The researcher must also decide how to present questions to subjects. Most often, researchers use a *self-administered survey,* mailing or e-mailing questionnaires to respondents and asking them to complete the form and send it back. Since no researcher is present when subjects read the questionnaire, it must be both inviting and clearly written. *Pretesting* a self-administered questionnaire with a small number of people before sending it to the entire sample can prevent the costly problem of finding out—too late—that instructions or questions were confusing.

Using the mail or e-mail allows a researcher to contact a large number of people over a wide geographic area at minimal expense. But many people treat such questionnaires as junk mail, so typically no more than half are completed and returned (in 2000, just two-thirds of people returned U.S. Census Bureau forms). Researchers must send follow-up mailings (or, as the Census Bureau does, visit people's homes) to urge reluctant subjects to respond.

Finally, keep in mind that many people are not capable of completing a questionnaire on their own. Young children obviously cannot, nor can many hospital patients or a surprising number of adults who simply lack the required reading and writing skills.

Conducting Interviews

An **interview** is *a series of questions a researcher asks respondents in person.* In a closed-format design, researchers read a question or statement and then ask the subject to select a response from several that are presented. More commonly, however, interviews are open-ended so that subjects can respond as they choose and researchers can probe with follow-up questions. In either case, the researcher must guard against influencing a subject, which is as easy as raising an eyebrow when a person begins to answer.

Although subjects are more likely to complete a survey if contacted personally by the researcher, interviews have some disadvantages: Tracking people down is costly and takes time, especially if subjects do not live in the same area. Telephone interviews allow far greater "reach," but the impersonality of cold calls by telephone (and reaching answering machines) can lower the response rate.

In both questionnaires and interviews, how a question is worded greatly affects how people answer. For example, when asked if they objected to gays serving in the military, most adults in the United States said yes. Yet when asked if the government should exempt homosexuals from military service, most said no (NORC, 1991). Emotionally loaded language can also sway subjects. For instance, using the expression "welfare mothers" rather than "women who receive public assistance" adds an emotional element to a question that encourages people to answer negatively.

Another problem is that researchers may confuse respondents by asking a double question, like "Do you think that the government should reduce the deficit by cutting spending and raising taxes?" The issue here is that a subject could very well agree with one part of the question but not the other, so that forcing a subject to say yes or no distorts the opinion the researcher is trying to measure.

Conducting a good interview means standardizing the technique—treating all subjects in the same way. But this, too, can lead to problems. Drawing people out requires establishing rapport, which in turn depends on responding naturally to the particular person being interviewed, as you would in a normal conversation. In the end, researchers have to decide where to strike the balance between uniformity and rapport (Lavin & Maynard, 2001).

Illustration of Survey Research: Studying the African American Elite

We opened this chapter by explaining how Lois Benjamin came to investigate the effects of racism on talented African American men and women. Benjamin suspected

Focus groups are a type of survey in which a small number of people representing a target population are asked for their opinions about some issue or product. Here, an organization opposed to cigarette smoking asks teens to judge which cigarette commercials seem most and least likely to get young people to light up.

that personal achievement did not prevent hostility based on color. She based this view on her own experiences after becom-ing the first black professor in the history of the University of Tampa. But was she the exception or the rule? To answer this question, Benjamin set out to discover whether—and if so, how—racism affected a number of the most successful African Americans.

Opting to conduct a survey, Benjamin chose to interview subjects rather than distribute a questionnaire because, first, she wanted to enter into a conversation with her subjects, to ask follow-up questions, and to pursue topics that she could not anticipate. A second reason Benjamin favored interviews over questionnaires is that racism is a sensitive topic. A supportive investigator can make it easier for subjects to respond to painful questions (Bergen, 1993).

YOUR TURN

Do you think this research could have been carried out by a white sociologist? Why or why not?

Choosing to conduct interviews made it necessary to limit the number of people in the study. Benjamin settled for a sample of 100 men and women. Even this small number kept Benjamin busy for more than two years as she scheduled interviews, traveled all over the country, and met with her respondents. She spent two more years analyzing the tapes of her interviews, deciding what the hours of talk told her about racism, and writing up her results.

In selecting her sample, Benjamin first considered using all the people listed in *Who's Who in Black America.* But she rejected this idea in favor of starting out with people she knew and asking them to suggest others. This strategy is called *snowball sampling* because the number of individuals included grows rapidly over time.

Snowball sampling is an easy way to do research—we begin with familiar people who introduce us to their friends and colleagues. But snowball sampling rarely produces a sample that is representative of the larger population. Benjamin's sample probably contained many like-minded individuals, and it was certainly biased toward people willing to talk openly about race. She understood these problems, and she did what she could to make her sample diverse in terms of sex, age, and region of the country. The Thinking Critically box presents a statistical profile of Benjamin's respondents and some tips on how to read tables.

Benjamin based all her interviews on a series of questions with an open-ended format so that her subjects could say whatever they wished. As usually happens, the interviews took place in a wide range of settings. She met subjects in offices (hers or theirs), in hotel rooms, and in cars. In each case, Benjamin tape-recorded the conversation, which lasted from two-and-one-half to three hours, so that she would not be distracted by taking notes.

As research ethics demand, Benjamin offered full anonymity to participants. Even so, many—including notables such as Vernon E. Jordan Jr. (former president of the National Urban League) and Yvonne Walker-Taylor (first woman president of Wilberforce University)—were used to being in the public eye and allowed Benjamin to use their names.

What surprised Benjamin most about her research was how eager many people were to be interviewed. These normally busy men and women seemed to go out of their way to contribute to her project. Benjamin reports, too, that once the interviews were under way, many became very emotional—at some point in the conversation, about 40 of her 100 subjects cried. For them, apparently, the research provided a chance to release feelings long kept inside. How did Benjamin respond? She reports that she cried right along with them.

Of the research orientations described earlier in the chapter, you will see that Benjamin's study fits best under interpretive sociology (she explored what race meant to her subjects) and critical sociology (she undertook the study partly to document that racial prejudice still exists). Many of her subjects reported fearing that race might someday undermine their success, and others spoke of a race-based "glass ceiling" preventing them from reaching the highest positions in our society. Benjamin concluded that despite the improving social standing of African Americans, black people in the United States still feel the sting of racial hostility.

IN THE FIELD: PARTICIPANT OBSERVATION

Lois Benjamin's research demonstrates that sociological investigation takes place not only in laboratories but also "in the field," that is, where people carry on their everyday lives. The most widely used strategy for field study is **participant observation,** *a research method in which investigators systematically observe people while joining them in their routine activities.*

Participant observation allows researchers an inside look at social life in settings ranging from nightclubs to religious seminaries. Cultural anthropologists commonly use participant observation (which they call *fieldwork*) to study communities in other societies. They term their descriptions of unfamiliar cultures *ethnographies.* Sociologists prefer to call their accounts of people in particular settings *case studies.*

At the beginning of a field study, most investigators do not have a specific hypothesis in mind. In fact, they may not yet realize what the important questions will turn out to be. Thus most field research is *exploratory* and *descriptive.*

As its name suggests, participant observation has two sides. On one hand, getting an "insider's" look depends on becoming a participant in the setting—"hanging out" with the research subjects, trying to act, think, and even feel the way they do. Compared to experiments and survey research, participant observation has fewer hard-and-fast rules. But it is precisely this flexibility that allows investigators to explore the unfamiliar and adapt to the unexpected.

Unlike other research methods, participant observation may require that the researcher enter the setting not just for a week or two but for months or even years. At the same time, however, the researcher must maintain some distance as an "observer," mentally stepping back to record field notes and later to interpret them. Because the investigator must both "play the participant" to win acceptance and gain access to people's lives and "play the observer" to maintain the distance needed for thoughtful analysis, there is an inherent tension in this method. Carrying out the twin roles of insider participant and outsider observer often comes down to a series of careful compromises.

THINKING CRITICALLY
Reading Tables: An Important Skill

A table provides a lot of information in a small amount of space, so learning to read tables can increase your reading efficiency. When you spot a table, look first at the title to see what information it contains. The title of the table below tells you that it presents a profile of the 100 subjects participating in Lois Benjamin's research. Across the top of the table, you see eight variables that describe these men and women. Reading down each column, note the different categories, with the percentages adding up to 100.

Starting at the top left, we see that Benjamin's sample was mostly men (63 percent men, 37 percent women). In terms of age, most of the respondents (68 percent) were in the middle stage of life, and most had grown up in a predominantly black community in the South, North, or Central regions of the United States.

Most of these individuals have a lot of schooling. Half earned either a doctorate (32 percent) or a medical or law degree (17 percent). Given their extensive education (and Benjamin's own job as a professor), we should not be surprised that the largest share (35 percent) worked in academic institutions. In terms of income, these people were pretty well off, and most (64 percent) earned more than $50,000 a year back in the 1980s (a salary that only 33 percent of full-time workers make even today).

Finally, we see that these 100 individuals were generally left-of-center in their political views. In part, this reflects their extensive schooling (which encourages progressive thinking) and the tendency of academics to fall on the liberal side of the political spectrum.

WHAT DO YOU THINK?

1. Why are statistical data, such as those in this table, an efficient way to convey lots of information?
2. Looking at the table, can you determine how long it took most people to become part of this elite? Explain your answer.
3. Do you see any ways in which this African American elite might differ from a comparable white elite? If so, what are they?

The Talented One Hundred: Lois Benjamin's African American Elite

Sex	Age	Childhood Racial Setting	Childhood Region	Highest Educational Degree	Job Sector	Income	Political Orientation
Male 63%	35 or younger 6%	Mostly black 71%	West 6%	Doctorate 32%	College or university 35%	More than $50,000 64%	Radical left 13%
Female 37%	36 to 54 68%	Mostly white 15%	North or Central 32%	Medical or law 17%	Private for-profit 17%	$35,00 to $50,000 18%	Liberal 38%
	55 or older 26%	Racially mixed 14%	South 38%	Master's 27%	Private nonprofit 9%	$20,000 to $34,999 12%	Moderate 28%
			Northeast 12%	Bachelor's 13%	Government 22%	Less than $20,000 6%	Conservative 5%
			Other 12%	Less 11%	Self-employed 14%		Depends on issue 14%
					Retired 3%		Unknown 2%
100%	100%	100%	100%	100%	100%	100%	100%

Source: Adapted from Lois Benjamin, *The Black Elite: Facing the Color Line in the Twilight of the Twentieth Century* (Chicago: Nelson-Hall, 1991), p. 276.

Sociologists can carry out research in almost any setting. Tammy Anderson of the University of Delaware visited many night spots in order to understand how and why young people participate in "raves."

Tammy L. Anderson, Ph.D.

Most sociologists carry out participant observation alone, so they—and readers, too—must remember that the results depend on the work of a single person. Participant observation usually falls within interpretive sociology, yielding mostly qualitative data—the researcher's accounts of people's lives and what they think of themselves and the world around them—although researchers sometimes collect some quantitative (numerical) data. From a scientific point of view, participant observation is a "soft" method that relies heavily on personal judgment and lacks scientific rigor. Yet its personal approach is also a strength: A highly visible team of sociologists attempting to administer formal surveys would disrupt many social settings, but a single skillful participant-observer can often gain a lot of insight into people's natural behavior.

Illustration of Participant Observation:
Street Corner Society

In the late 1930s, a young graduate student at Harvard University named William Foote Whyte (1914–2000) was fascinated by the lively street life of a nearby, rather rundown section of Boston. His curiosity led him to carry out four years of participant observation in this neighborhood, which he called "Cornerville," and in the process to produce a sociological classic.

At the time, Cornerville was home to first- and second-generation Italian immigrants. Many were poor, and many people living in the rest of Boston considered Cornerville a place to avoid: a poor slum that was home to racketeers. Unwilling to accept easy stereotypes, Whyte set out to discover for himself exactly what kind of life went on in this community. His celebrated book, *Street Corner Society* (1981, orig. 1943), describes Cornerville as a complex community with a distinctive code of values and its own social conflicts.

In beginning his investigation, Whyte considered a range of research methods. Should he take questionnaires to one of Cornerville's community centers and ask local people to fill them out? Should he invite members of the community to come to his Harvard office for interviews? It is easy to see that such formal strategies would have gained little cooperation from the local people. Whyte decided, therefore, to set out on his own, working his way into Cornerville life in the hope of coming to understand this rather mysterious place.

Right away, Whyte discovered the challenges of even getting started in field research. After all, an upper-middle-class WASP graduate student from Harvard did not exactly fit into Cornerville life. Even a friendly overture from an outsider could seem pushy and rude. One night, Whyte dropped in at a local bar, hoping to buy a woman a drink and encourage her to talk about Cornerville. Looking around the room, he could find no woman alone. But then he saw a man sitting down with two women. He walked up to them and asked, "Pardon me. Would you mind if I joined you?" Instantly, he realized his mistake:

> There was a moment of silence while the man stared at me. Then he offered to throw me down the stairs. I assured him that this would not be necessary, and demonstrated as much by walking right out of there without any assistance. (1981:289)

As this incident suggests, gaining entry to a community is the difficult (and sometimes hazardous) first step in field research. "Breaking in" requires patience, quick thinking, and a little luck. Whyte's big break came when he met a young man named "Doc" at a local social service agency. Whyte explained to Doc how hard it was to make friends in Cornerville. Doc responded by taking Whyte under his wing and introducing him to others in the community. With Doc's help, Whyte soon became a neighborhood regular.

Whyte's friendship with Doc illustrates the importance of a *key informant* in field research. Such people not only introduce a researcher to a community but often remain a source of information and help. But using a key informant also has its risks. Because any person has a particular circle of friends, a key informant's guidance is certain to "spin" or bias the study in one way or another. In addition, in the eyes of others, the reputation of the key informant—good or bad—usually rubs off on the investigator. So although a key informant is helpful early on, a participant-observer must soon seek a broader range of contacts.

Having entered the Cornerville world, Whyte quickly learned another lesson: A field researcher needs to know when to speak up and when to shut up. One evening, he joined a group discussing neighborhood gambling. Wanting to get the facts straight, Whyte asked innocently, "I suppose the cops were all paid off?" In a heartbeat, "the gambler's jaw dropped. He glared at me. Then he denied vehemently that any policeman had been paid off and immediately switched the conversation to another subject. For the rest of that evening I felt very uncomfortable." The next day, Doc offered some sound advice:

> "Go easy on that 'who,' 'what,' 'why,' 'when,' 'where' stuff, Bill. You ask those questions and people will clam up on you. If people accept you, you can just hang around, and you'll learn the answers in the long run without even having to ask the questions." (1981:303)

In the months and years that followed, Whyte became familiar with life in Cornerville and even married a local woman with whom he would spend the rest of his life. In the process, he learned that the common stereotypes were wrong. In Cornerville, most people worked hard, many were quite successful, and some even boasted of sending children to college. Even today, Whyte's book is a fascinating story of the deeds, dreams, and disappointments of immigrants and their children living in one ethnic community, and it contains the kind of rich details that come only from years of participant observation.

USING AVAILABLE DATA: EXISTING SOURCES

Not all research requires investigators to collect their own data. Sometimes sociologists analyze existing sources, data collected by others.

The most widely used statistics in social science are gathered by government agencies. The U.S. Census Bureau continuously updates a wide range of data about the U.S. population. Comparable data on Canada are available from Statistics Canada, a branch of that nation's government. For international data, there are various publications of the United Nations and the World Bank. In short, data about the whole world are as close as your

 For statistical data about the U.S., your own state, and your own county, go to http:// quickfacts.census.gov/qfd/

library or the Internet. "In the *Times*" on pages 50–51 offers a look at some of the changes to the U.S. population revealed by the most recent census.

Using available data—whether government statistics or the findings of individual researchers—saves time and money. This approach has special appeal to sociologists with low budgets. Even more important, government data are generally better than what most researchers could obtain on their own.

Still, using existing data has some problems of its own. For one thing, available data may not exist in exactly the form needed. You may be able to find the average salary paid to professors at your school but not separate figures for the amounts paid to women and to men. Further, there are always questions about the meaning and accuracy of work done by others. For example, in his classic study of suicide, Emile Durkheim soon discovered that there was no way to know whether a death classified as a suicide was really an accident or vice versa. In addition, various agencies use different procedures and categories in collecting data, so comparisons may be difficult. In the end, then, using existing data is a little like shopping for a used car: There are plenty of bargains out there, but you have to shop carefully.

Illustration of the Use of Existing Sources: A Tale of Two Cities

To people stuck in the present, existing data can be used as a key to unlock secrets of the past. The award-winning study *Puritan Boston and Quaker Philadelphia*, by E. Digby Baltzell (1979b), is a good example of how a researcher can use available data to do historical research.

This story starts with Baltzell making a chance visit to Bowdoin College in Maine. As he walked into the college library, he saw up on the wall three large portraits—of the celebrated author Nathaniel Hawthorne, the famous poet Henry Wadsworth Longfellow, and Franklin Pierce, the fourteenth president of the United States. He soon learned that all three great men had been members of the same class at Bowdoin, graduating in 1825. How could it be, Baltzell wondered, that this small college had graduated more famous people in a single year than his own, much bigger University of Pennsylvania had graduated in its entire history? To answer this question, Baltzell was soon paging through historical documents to see whether New England had really produced more famous people than his native Pennsylvania.

What were Baltzell's data? He turned to the *Dictionary of American Biography*, twenty volumes profiling more than 13,000 outstanding men and women in fields such as politics, law, and the arts. The *Dictionary* told Baltzell *who* was

October 13, 2004

Images of a Growing Nation, From Census to Census

By DAVID J. GARROW

The 2000 United States census was "a snapshot of a moving target," Sam Roberts reports in [a] fascinatingly fact-filled picture of today's America [titled *Who We Are Now*]. . . .

During the 1990s, the nation's population grew to an estimated high of more than 292 million, an increase of 32.7 million people. This is "the largest 10-year numerical increase ever," Mr. Roberts writes. . . . Immigration from abroad was the major reason. In the 1990s, Mr. Roberts writes, "America's foreign-born population increased by 57 percent, to more than 31 million, a record high, making America now the least 'American' it has ever been." . . . Fifty-two percent of those born abroad come from Latin America, and by 2002, Hispanics were a larger proportion of the population

than blacks: 13.4 percent versus 13.1 percent. . . . Changes in the composition of American households are also notable. Since 1950, households of married couples have dropped "from nearly four in five to barely one in two," Mr. Roberts writes. People living alone now constitute 26 percent of households, a greater proportion than married couples with children, who make up only 23.5 percent. Fewer than one-third of those families, just 7 percent of the total, include a working father and a stay-at-home mother.

[On a troubling note], ... in 1960 only 9 percent of children lived with a single parent, while by 2000, 28 percent did, including 53 percent of black children. Indeed, "the number of families headed by a woman grew five times faster in the 1990s than the number of married couples with children," Mr.

Roberts observes. Statistics from 2001–2002 show that one out of three babies, and "nearly two in three black babies," were born out of wedlock. Those developments, Mr. Roberts says, suggest "a further erosion of marriage as a social convention." *Who We Are Now* also paints an interesting picture of what can be called a locally transient country: "Almost two-thirds of Americans still live in the state where they were born," Mr. Roberts reports, but "in the 15 months before the 2000 census, nearly one in five of the nation's 105 million households changed residences." That image of mobility, however, has some limitations, he adds, for "among young adults 18 to 24, 57 percent of men and 47 percent of women are still living with their parents." One large segment of the population is not free to move. At the end of 2002, Mr. Roberts writes, 2,166,260

---

great, and he realized that the longer the biography in the *Dictionary,* the more important the person is thought to be.

By the time Baltzell had identified the seventy-five individuals with the longest biographies, he saw a striking pattern. Massachusetts had the most by far, with twenty-one of the seventy-five top achievers. The New England states, combined, claimed thirty-one of the entries. By contrast, Pennsylvania could boast of only two, and all the states in the Middle Atlantic region had just twelve. Looking more closely, Baltzell discovered that most of New England's great achievers had grown up in and around the city of Boston. Again, in stark contrast, almost no one of comparable standing came from his own Philadelphia, a city with many more people than Boston.

What could explain this remarkable pattern? Baltzell drew inspiration from the German sociologist Max Weber (1958, orig. 1904–5), who argued that a region's record of achievement was influenced by its major religious beliefs

(see Chapter 4, "Society"). In the religious differences between Boston and Philadelphia, Baltzell found the answer to his puzzle. Boston was originally a Puritan settlement, founded by people who highly valued the pursuit of excellence and public achievement. Philadelphia, by contrast, was settled by Quakers, who believed in equality and avoided public notice.

Both the Puritans and the Quakers were fleeing religious persecution in England, but the two religions produced quite different cultural patterns. Boston's Puritans saw humans as innately sinful, so they built a rigid society in which family, church, and school regulated people's behavior. The Puritans celebrated hard work as a means of glorifying God and viewed public success as a reassuring sign of God's blessing. In short, Puritanism fostered a disciplined life in which people both sought and respected achievement.

Philadelphia's Quakers, by contrast, built their way of life on the belief that all human beings are basically good.

people were incarcerated as criminals. Statistics from that year, he says, showed that there were 701 prisoners for every 100,000 United States residents, a notable increase from the rate of 601 just seven years earlier, in 1995. . . .

Growing imprisonment is not the only stark negative. . . . The 2001 poverty rate of 11.7 percent was "about half of what it was in 1959," he states, but "children in poverty included fully 30.2 percent of black children and 28 percent of Hispanic children." In 2001, the poorest fifth of all United States households received only 3.5 percent of the country's aggregate income, the smallest share ever. In contrast, the top fifth of households received 50.1 percent of all income, a record high. . . .

And the population will continue to grow. The current number, more than double the 1950 figure, will grow "to 300 million in 2010, 338 million in 2025, 404 million in 2050, and 571 million" by the end of this century, Mr. Roberts reports. Spurring that increase is a continuing rise in Americans' life expectancy. A century ago, the average person lived to 47. By 1950 that figure had risen to 68, and in 2000 it reached 76.9 years. The pronounced aging of America is already close at hand. . . . From 2000 to 2025, Mr. Roberts warns, "the number of elderly will more than double to 70 million," and "by 2050, the number of Americans 65 and older is expected to be more than 80 million, or more than double what it is today." This will place what Mr. Roberts correctly calls an "unprecedented drain" on entitlement programs for the elderly. . . . Estimates show "a gap of $51 trillion between payroll taxes and costs of medical care and Social Security" by 2030. . . . The question of "Who's going to make up the difference?" may not be one that [we] are eager to address, but *Who We Are Now* convincingly demonstrates that it is a question that Americans will be forced to wrestle with in the years ahead.

WHAT DO YOU THINK?

1. What social effects do you think the 57 percent increase in foreign-born people will have?
2. Why do you think so many young people are still living with their parents?
3. What change mentioned in the article is most important from your point of view? Why?

Adapted from the original article by David J. Garrow published in *The New York Times* on October 13, 2004. Copyright © 2004 by The New York Times Company. Reprinted with permission.

They saw little need for strong social institutions to "save" people from sinfulness. They believed in equality, so that even those who became rich considered themselves no better than anyone else. Thus rich and poor alike lived modestly and discouraged one another from standing out by seeking fame or even running for public office.

In Baltzell's sociological imagination, Boston and Philadelphia took the form of two social "test tubes": Puritanism was poured into one, Quakerism into the other. Centuries later, we can see that different "chemical reactions" occurred in each case. The two belief systems led to different attitudes toward personal achievement, which in turn shaped the history of each region. Today, we can see that Boston's Kennedys (despite being Catholic) are only one of that city's many families who exemplify the Puritan pursuit of recognition and leadership. By contrast, there has never been even one family with such public stature in the entire history of Philadelphia.

Baltzell's study uses scientific logic, but it also illustrates the interpretive approach by showing how people understood their world. His research reminds us that sociological investigation often involves mixing methodological orientations to fit a particular problem.

The Summing Up table on page 52 provides a quick review of the four major methods of sociological investigation. We now turn to our final consideration: the link between research results and sociological theory.

THE INTERPLAY OF THEORY AND METHOD

No matter how sociologists collect their data, they have to turn facts into meaning by building theory. They do this in two ways: inductive logical thought and deductive logical thought.

Inductive logical thought is *reasoning that transforms specific observations into general theory*. In this mode, a

Four Research Methods

	Experiment	Survey	Participant Observation	Existing Sources
Application	For explanatory research that specifies relationships between variables Generates quantitative data	For gathering information about issues that cannot be directly observed, such as attitudes and values Useful for descriptive and explanatory research Generates quantitative or qualitative data	For exploratory and descriptive study of people in a "natural" setting Generates qualitative data	For exploratory, descriptive, or explanatory research whenever suitable data are available
Advantages	Provides the greatest opportunity to specify cause-and-effect relationships Replication of research is relatively easy	Sampling, using questionnaires, allows surveys of large populations Interviews provide in-depth responses	Allows study of "natural" behavior Usually inexpensive	Saves time and expense of data collection Makes historical research possible
Limitations	Laboratory settings have an artificial quality Unless the research environment is carefully controlled, results may be biased	Questionnaires must be carefully prepared and may yield a low return rate Interviews are expensive and time-consuming	Time-consuming Replication of research is difficult Researcher must balance roles of participant and observer	Researcher has no control over possible biases in data Data may only partially fit current research needs

researcher's thinking runs from the specific to the general and goes something like this: "I have some interesting data here; I wonder what they mean?" E. Digby Baltzell's research illustrates the inductive logical model. His data showed that one region of the country (the Boston area) had produced many more high achievers than another (the Philadelphia region). He worked "upward" from ground-level observations to the high-flying theory that religious values were a key factor in shaping people's attitudes toward achievement.

A second type of logical thought moves "downward," in the opposite direction: **Deductive logical thought** is *reasoning that transforms general theory into specific hypotheses suitable for testing*. The researcher's thinking runs from the general to the specific: "I have this hunch about human behavior; let's collect some data and put it to the test." Working deductively, the researcher first states the theory in the form of a hypothesis and then selects a method by which to test it. To the extent that the data support the hypothesis, we conclude that the theory is correct; if the data refute the hypothesis, we know that the theory needs to be revised or maybe rejected entirely.

Philip Zimbardo's Stanford County Prison experiment illustrates deductive logic. Zimbardo began with the general

theory that a social environment can change human behavior. He then developed a specific, testable hypothesis: Placed in a prison setting, even emotionally well-balanced young men will behave violently. The violence that erupted soon after his experiment began supported Zimbardo's hypothesis. Had his experiment produced friendly behavior between prisoners and guards, his hypothesis clearly would have been wrong.

Just as researchers often employ several methods over the course of one study, they typically use *both* kinds of logical thought. Figure 2–2 illustrates both types of reasoning: inductively building theory from observations and deductively making observations to test a theory.

Finally, turning facts into meaning usually involves organizing and presenting statistical data. Precisely how sociologists arrange their numbers affects the conclusions they reach. In short, preparing your results amounts to spinning reality in one way or another.

Often we conclude that an argument must be true simply because there are statistics to back it up. However, we must look at statistics with a cautious eye. After all, researchers choose what data to present, they interpret their statistics, and they may use tables and graphs to steer readers toward particular conclusions. The Thinking It Through box on pages 54–55 takes a closer look at this important issue.

Putting It All Together: Ten Steps in Sociological Investigation

We can summarize this chapter by outlining ten steps in the process of carrying out sociological investigation. Each step takes the form of an important question.

1. **What is your topic?** Being curious and applying the sociological perspective can generate ideas for social research at any time and in any place. Pick a topic you find important to study.

2. **What have others already learned?** You are probably not the first person with an interest in the issue you have selected. Visit the library to see what theories and methods other researchers have applied to your topic. In reviewing the existing research, note problems that have come up to avoid repeating past mistakes.

3. **What, exactly, are your questions?** Are you seeking to explore an unfamiliar social setting? To describe some category of people? To investigate cause and effect among variables? If your study is exploratory or descriptive, identify *whom* you wish to study, *where* the research will take place, and *what* kinds of issues you want to explore. If it is explanatory, you also must formulate the hypothesis to be tested and operationalize each variable.

4. **What will you need to carry out research?** How much time and money are available to you? Is special equipment or training necessary? Can you do the work yourself? You should answer all these questions as you plan the research project.

5. **Are there ethical concerns?** Not all research raises serious ethical questions, but you must be sensitive to this possibility. Can the research cause harm or threaten anyone's privacy? How might you design the study to minimize the chances for injury? Will you promise anonymity to the subjects? If so, how will you ensure that anonymity is maintained?

6. **What method will you use?** Consider all major research strategies, as well as combinations of approaches. Keep in mind that the best method depends on the kinds of questions you are asking as well as the resources available to you.

7. **How will you record the data?** Your research method is a plan for data collection. Record all information

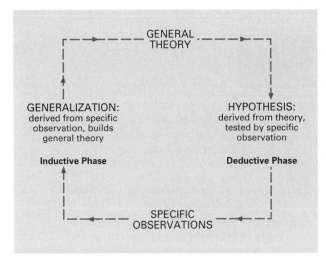

FIGURE 2-2 Deductive and Inductive Logical Thought

Sociologists link theory and method through both inductive and deductive logic.

accurately and in a way that will make sense later (it may be some time before you actually write up the results of your work). Be alert for any bias that may creep into the research.

8. **What do the data tell you?** Study the data in terms of your initial questions and decide how to interpret the data you have collected. If your study involves a specific hypothesis, you must decide whether to confirm, reject, or modify the hypothesis. Keep in mind that there may be several ways to look at your data, depending on which theoretical approach you use, and you should consider all interpretations.

9. **What are your conclusions?** Prepare a final report stating your conclusions. How does your work advance sociological theory? Does it suggest ways to improve research methods? Does your study have policy implications? What would the general public find interesting in your work? Finally, evaluate your own work, noting problems that arose and questions that were left unanswered.

10. **How can you share what you've learned?** Consider sending your research paper to a campus newspaper or magazine or making a presentation to a class, a campus gathering, or perhaps a meeting of professional sociologists. The point is to share what you have learned with others and to let them respond to your work.

THINKING IT THROUGH

Can People Lie with Statistics?

When someone presents you with "data," do you assume the numbers are the same as "truth"? One person who did not think so was an English politician named Benjamin Disraeli, who once remarked, "There are three kinds of lies: lies, damned lies, and statistics!"

In a world that bombards us with numbers—often described as "scientific data" or "official figures"—it is worth remembering that "statistical evidence" is not necessarily the same as truth. For one thing, any researcher can make mistakes. More important, because data do not speak for themselves, someone has to decide what they mean. Sometimes people (even sociologists) "dress up" their data almost the way politicians deliver campaign speeches—with an eye more to winning you over than to getting at the truth.

The best way to avoid being fooled is to understand how people can mislead with statistics.

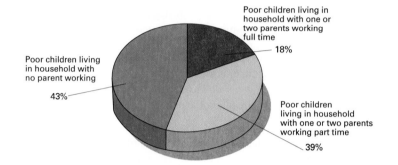

Poor children living in household with one or two parents working full time 18%

Poor children living in household with no parent working 43%

Poor children living in household with one or two parents working part time 39%

1. **People select their data.** Many times, the data presented are not wrong, but they are not the whole story. Let's say someone who thinks that television is ruining our way of life presents statistics indicating that we watch more TV today than a generation ago. It also turns out that during the same period, College Board scores have fallen. Both sets of data may be correct, but the suggestion that there is a cause-and-effect link here—that television viewing is lowering test scores—is not proved. A person more favorable to television might counter with the additional "fact" that the U.S. population spends much more money buying books today than it did a generation ago, suggesting that television creates new intellectual interests. It is possible to find statistics that seem to support just about any argument.

2. **People interpret their data.** People can also "package" their data with a

---

MAKING THE GRADE

The following learning tools will help you see what you know, identify what you still need to learn, and expand your understanding beyond the text. You can also visit this text's Companion Website™ at http://www.prenhall.com/macionis to find additional practice tests.

KEY POINTS

Basics of Sociological Investigation

There are two basic requirements for sociological investigation. First, we should know how to apply the sociological perspective.

Second, we should be curious and ready to ask questions about the world around us.

Three Ways to Do Sociology

Scientific sociology studies society by systematically observing social behavior. This methodological orientation requires carefully operationalizing concepts and ensuring that measurement is both reliable and valid. A goal of science is to discover how variables are related. Correlation means that two or more variables change value together. A cause-and-effect relationship means that change in one variable actually causes change in another variable. When a cause-and-effect relationship exists, a researcher who knows the value of an independent

ready-made interpretation, as if numbers can mean only one thing. Take a look at the figure at the left, which shows the results of one study of U.S. children living in poverty (National Center for Children in Poverty, cited in *Population Today,* 1995). The researchers reported that 43 percent of these children lived in a household with no working parent, 39 percent lived in a household with one or two parents employed part time, and 18 percent lived in a household with one or two parents working full time. The researchers labeled this figure "Majority of Children in Poverty Live with Parents Who Work." Do you think this interpretation is accurate or misleading?

3. **People use graphs to spin the truth.** Especially in newspapers and other popular media, we find statistics in the form of charts and graphs. Graphs, which often show an upward or downward trend over time, are a good way to present data. But using graphs also gives people the opportunity to "spin" data in various ways. The trend depends in part on the time frame used. During the past ten years, for instance, the U.S. crime rate has fallen. But if we were to look at the past fifty years, we would see an opposite trend: The crime rate pushed sharply upward.

The scale used to draw a graph is also important because it lets a researcher "inflate" or "deflate" a trend. Both graphs shown here present identical data for College Board SAT verbal scores between 1967 and 2004. But the left-hand graph stretches the scale to show a downward trend; the right-hand graph compresses the scale, showing a steady trend. So understanding what statistics mean—or don't mean—depends on being a careful reader!

WHAT DO YOU THINK?

1. Why do you think people are so quick to accept "statistics" as true?

2. From a scientific point of view, is spinning the truth acceptable? Is this practice OK from a critical approach, in which someone is trying to advance social change?

3. Find a news story on some social issue that you think presents biased data or conclusions. What are the biases?

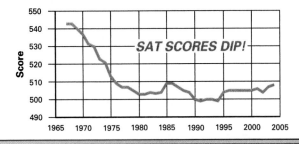

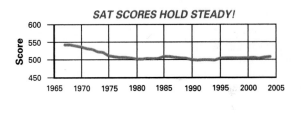

variable can predict the value of some dependent variable. Researchers typically select topics according to their personal interests. But the scientific ideal of objectivity demands that they try to suspend personal values and biases as they conduct research.

Interpretive sociology is a methodological orientation that focuses on the meaning people attach to their behavior. Reality is not "out there" but is constructed by people in their everyday interactions.

Critical sociology is a methodological orientation that uses research as a means of bringing about social change. Critical sociology rejects the scientific principle of objectivity; those who follow this orientation claim that all research has a political character.

Scientific sociology stands closest to the structural-functional approach, interpretive sociology is closest to the symbolic-interaction approach, and critical sociology is linked to the social-conflict approach.

Because research has the ability to harm subjects and communities, sociologists must remain aware of research ethics.

Methods of Sociological Research

The logic of science is most clearly expressed in the experiment, which is performed under controlled conditions and tries to specify causal relationships between two (or more) variables. Surveys measure people's attitudes or behavior using questionnaires or interviews. Participant observation is a method in which a researcher directly observes a social setting while participating in it for an extended period of time. Sociologists often use existing data; using available data is easier and often more efficient than collecting data at first hand, and it allows the study of historical issues.

Theory and research are linked in two ways. Deductive logical thought starts with general theories and generates specific hypotheses suitable for testing. Inductive logical thought starts with specific observations and builds general theories.

KEY CONCEPTS

science (p. 31) a logical system that bases knowledge on direct, systematic observation

empirical evidence (p. 31) information we can verify with our senses

scientific sociology (p. 33) the study of society based on systematic observation of social behavior

concept (p. 33) a mental construct that represents some part of the world in a simplified form

variable (p. 33) a concept whose value changes from case to case

measurement (p. 33) a procedure for determining the value of a variable in a specific case

operationalize a variable (p. 33) specifying exactly what is to be measured before assigning a value to a variable

reliability (p. 33) consistency in measurement

validity (p. 33) actually measuring exactly what you intend to measure

cause and effect (p. 34) a relationship in which change in one variable (the independent variable) causes change in another (the dependent variable)

independent variable (p. 35) a variable that causes change in another (dependent) variable

dependent variable (p. 35) a variable that is changed by another (independent) variable

correlation (p. 35) a relationship in which two (or more) variables change together

spurious correlation (p. 35) an apparent but false relationship between two (or more) variables that is caused by some other variable

control (p. 35) holding constant all variables except one in order to see clearly the effect of that variable

objectivity (p. 36) personal neutrality in conducting research

replication (p. 37) repetition of research by other investigators

interpretive sociology (p. 38) the study of society that focuses on the meanings people attach to their social world

critical sociology (p. 39) the study of society that focuses on the need for social change

gender (p. 39) the personal traits and social positions that members of a society attach to being female or male

research method (p. 41) a systematic plan for doing research

experiment (p. 41) a research method for investigating cause and effect under highly controlled conditions

hypothesis (p. 41) a statement of a possible relationship between two (or more) variables

Hawthorne effect (p. 42) a change in a subject's behavior caused simply by the awareness of being studied

survey (p. 43) a research method in which subjects respond to a series of statements or questions in a questionnaire or an interview

population (p. 44) the people who are the focus of research

sample (p. 44) a part of a population that represents the whole

questionnaire (p. 44) a series of written questions a researcher presents to subjects

interview (p. 45) a series of questions a researcher asks respondents in person

participant observation (p. 47) a research method in which investigators systematically observe people while joining them in their routine activities

inductive logical thought (p. 51) reasoning that transforms specific observations into general theory

deductive logical thought (p. 52) reasoning that transforms general theory into specific hypotheses suitable for testing

---

SAMPLE TEST QUESTIONS

These questions are similar to those found in the test bank that accompanies this textbook.

Multiple-Choice Questions

1. *Science* is defined as
   a. a logical system that bases knowledge on direct, systematic observation.
   b. belief based on faith in some ultimate truth.
   c. knowledge based on a society's traditions.
   d. information that comes from recognized "experts."

2. *Empirical evidence* refers to
   a. quantitative rather than qualitative data.
   b. what people consider "common sense."
   c. information people can verify with their senses.
   d. patterns found in every known society.

3. When trying to measure people's "social class," you would have to keep in mind that
   a. your measurement can never be both reliable and valid.
   b. there are many ways to operationalize this variable.
   c. there is no way to measure "social class."
   d. in the United States, everyone agrees on what "social class" means.

4. What is the term for the value that occurs most often in a series of numbers?
   a. the mode
   b. the median
   c. the mean
   d. all of the above

5. When measuring any variable, *reliability* refers to
   a. whether you are really measuring what you want to measure.
   b. how dependable the researcher is.
   c. results that everyone would agree with.
   d. whether repeating the measurement yields consistent results.

6. We can correctly say that two variables are *correlated* if
   a. change in one causes no change in the other.
   b. one occurs before the other.
   c. their values vary together.
   d. both measure the same thing.

7. Which of the following is *not* one of the defining traits of a cause-and-effect relationship?
   a. The independent variable must happen before the dependent variable.
   b. Each variable must be shown to be independent of the other.
   c. The two variables must display correlation.
   d. There must be no evidence that the correlation is spurious.

8. Interpretive sociology is sociology that
   a. focuses on action.
   b. sees an objective reality "out there."
   c. focuses on the meanings people attach to behavior.
   d. seeks to increase social justice.

9. To study the effects on test performance of playing soft music during an exam, a researcher conducts an experiment in which one test-taking class hears music and another does not. According to the chapter discussion of the experiment, the class hearing the music is called
   a. the placebo.   b. the control group.
   c. the dependent variable.   d. the experimental group.

10. In participant observation, the problem of "breaking in" to a setting is often solved with the help of a
    a. key informant.
    b. research assistant.
    c. bigger budget.
    d. all of the above.

Answers: 1(a); 2(c); 3(b); 4(a); 5(d); 6(c); 7(b); 8(c); 9(d); 10(a).

Essay Questions

1. Explain the idea that there are various types of truth. What are the advantages and limitations of science as a way of discovering truth?

2. Compare and contrast scientific sociology, interpretive sociology, and critical sociology. Which of these approaches best describes the work of Durkheim, Weber, and Marx?

APPLICATIONS & EXERCISES

1. Observe your instructor in class one day to grade his or her teaching skills. Operationalize the concept "good teaching" in terms of specific traits you can measure. How easy is it to measure "good teaching"?

2. Visit three sociology instructors (or other social science instructors) during their office hours. Ask each whether they think sociology is an objective science. Do they agree? Why or why not?

3. Select a number of primetime television shows, and note the race of major characters. You will have to decide what "primetime" means, what a "major" character is, how to gauge someone's "race," and other issues before you begin. Sketch out a research plan to evaluate the hypothesis that African Americans are not very visible on primetime television.

INVESTIGATE *with* Research Navigator

Follow the instructions on page 27 of this text to access the features of **Research Navigator**™. Once at the Web site, enter your Login Name and Password. Then, to use the **ContentSelect**™ database, enter keywords such as "science," "questionnaire," and "participant observation," and the search engine will supply relevant and recent scholarly and popular press publications. Use the *New York Times* **Search-by-Subject Archive** to find recent news articles related to sociology and the **Link Library** feature to find relevant Web links organized by the key terms associated with this chapter.

3

Culture

What is culture?

Why is it so important to understand people's
cultural differences?

How does culture support social inequality?

ack in 1990, executives of Charles Schwab & Co., a large investment brokerage corporation, gathered at the company's headquarters in San Francisco to discuss ways they could expand their business. One idea was that the company would profit by giving greater attention to the increasing racial and ethnic diversity of the United States. In particular, they pointed to Census Bureau data showing the rising number of Asian Americans, not just in San Francisco but throughout the country. The data showed (then as now) that Asian Americans are also, on average, wealthy, with more than one-third of households earning more than $75,000 a year (in today's dollars).

This meeting led Schwab to launch a diversity initiative, assigning three executives to work just on building awareness of the company among Asian Americans. In the years since then, the scope of the program has grown so that today, Schwab employs more than 300 people who speak Chinese, Japanese, Korean, Vietnamese, or another Asian language. Knowing these languages is important because research shows that most Asian Americans who come to the United States prefer to communicate in their first language. In addition, the company has launched Web sites using Chinese and other Asian languages. Finally, the company has opened branch offices in many mostly Asian American neighborhoods in cities on the East and West Coasts.

Has this diversity program worked? Schwab has gained a much larger share of investments made by Asian Americans. Because Asian Americans spend more than $300 billion a year, any company would be smart to follow Schwab's lead. Other ethnic and racial

categories that represent even larger markets in the United States are Hispanics (who spend $580 billion each year) and African Americans ($600 billion) (Fattah, 2002; Karrfalt, 2003). ■

Businesses like Schwab are taking note of the fact that the United States is the most *multicultural* of all the world's nations. This cultural diversity reflects the country's long history of receiving immigrants from all over the world. The ways of life found around the world differ, not only in forms of dress, preferred foods, and musical tastes but also in family patterns and beliefs about right and wrong. Some of the world's people have many children, while others have few; some honor the elderly, while others seem to glorify youth. Some societies are peaceful, while others are warlike; and segments of humanity embrace a thousand different religious beliefs as well as particular ideas about what is polite and rude, beautiful and ugly, pleasant and repulsive. This amazing human capacity for so many different ways of life is a matter of human culture.

What Is Culture?

Culture is *the values, beliefs, behavior, and material objects that together form a people's way of life.* Culture includes what we think, how we act, and what we own. Culture is both our link to the past and our guide to the future.

To understand all that culture is, we must consider both thoughts and things. **Nonmaterial culture** is *the ideas created by members of a society,* ideas that range from art to Zen. **Material culture,** by contrast, is *the physical things created by members of a society,* everything from armchairs to zippers.

Culture shapes not only what we do but also what we think and how we feel—elements of what we commonly, but wrongly, describe as "human nature." The warlike Yąnomamö of the Brazilian rain forest think aggression is

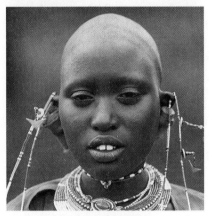

Human beings around the globe create diverse ways of life. Such differences begin with outward appearance: Contrast the women shown here from Brazil, Kenya, New Guinea, and South Yemen, and the men from Taiwan (Republic of China), India, Canada, and New Guinea. Less obvious, but of even greater importance, are internal differences, since culture also shapes our goals in life, our sense of justice, and even our innermost personal feelings.

natural, but halfway around the world, the Semai of Malaysia live quite peacefully. The cultures of the United States and Japan both stress achievement and hard work, but members of our society typically put a higher value on individualism than do the Japanese, who value collective harmony.

Given the extent of cultural differences in the world and people's tendency to view their own way of life as "natural," it is no wonder that travelers often find themselves feeling uneasy as they enter an unfamiliar culture. This uneasiness is **culture shock,** *personal disorientation when experiencing an unfamiliar way of life.* People can experience culture shock right here in the United States when, say, African Americans explore an Iranian neighborhood in Los Angeles, college students venture into the Amish countryside in Ohio, or New Yorkers travel through small towns in the

All societies contain cultural differences that can provoke a mild case of culture shock. This woman traveling on a French bus looks with disapproval at another woman wearing the Muslim hijab head covering. France recently debated banning such apparel.

Deep South. But culture shock is most intense when we travel abroad: The Thinking Globally box tells the story of a U.S. researcher making his first visit to the home of the Yąnomamö people living in the Amazon region of South America.

⟶ **YOUR TURN** ⟵

Can you describe specific practices or social patterns familiar to us in the United States that would shock people from another society?

January 2, high in the Andes Mountains of Peru. In the rural highlands, people are poor and depend on one another. The culture is built on cooperation among family members and neighbors who have lived nearby for generations. Today, we spent an hour watching a new house being built. A young couple invited their families and friends, who arrived at about 6:30 in the morning, and right away they began building. By midafternoon, most of the work was done, and the couple then provided a large meal, drinks, and music that continued for the rest of the day.

No way of life is "natural" to humanity, even though most people around the world view their own behavior that way. The cooperation that comes naturally to people in the Andes Mountains of Peru is very different from the competitive living that comes naturally to many people in, say, Chicago or New York City. Such variations come from the fact that as human beings, we join together to create our own way of life. Every other animal—from ants to zebras—behaves very much the same all around the world because behavior is guided by *instincts*, biological programming over which the species has no control. A few animals—notably chimpanzees and related primates—have the capacity for limited culture, as researchers have noted by observing them use tools and teach simple skills to their offspring. But the creative power of humans is far greater than that of any other form of life and has resulted in countless ways of being "human." In short, *only humans rely on culture rather than instinct to create a way of life and ensure our survival* (M. Harris, 1987). To understand how human culture came to be, we need to look back at the history of our species.

CULTURE AND HUMAN INTELLIGENCE

Scientists tell us that our planet is 4.5 billion years old (see the timeline inside the front cover of this text). Life appeared about 1 billion years later. Fast-forward another 2 to 3 billion years and we find dinosaurs ruling the Earth. It was when these giant creatures disappeared—some 65 million years ago—that our history took a crucial turn with the appearance of the animals we call primates.

The importance of primates is that they have the largest brains relative to body size of all living creatures. About 12 million years ago, primates began to evolve along two different lines, setting humans apart from the great apes, our closest relatives. Then, some 3 million years ago, our distant human ancestors climbed down from the trees of Central

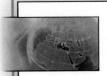

Confronting the Yąnomamö: The Experience of Culture Shock

A small aluminum motorboat chugged steadily along the muddy Orinoco River, deep within South America's vast tropical rain forest. The anthropologist Napoleon Chagnon was nearing the end of a three-day journey to the home territory of the Yąnomamö, one of the most technologically simple societies on Earth.

Some 12,000 Yąnomamö live in villages scattered along the border of Venezuela and Brazil. Their way of life could not be more different from our own. The Yąnomamö wear little clothing and live without electricity, automobiles, or other familiar conveniences. Their traditional weapon, used for hunting and warfare, is the bow and arrow. Most of the Yąnomamö knew little about the outside world, so Chagnon would be as strange to them as they would be to him.

By 2:00 in the afternoon, Chagnon had almost reached his destination. The heat and humidity were almost unbearable. He was soaked with perspiration, and his face and hands swelled from the bites of gnats swarming around him. But he hardly noticed, so excited was he that in just a few moments he would be face to face with people unlike any he had ever known.

Chagnon's heart pounded as the boat slid onto the riverbank. He and his guide climbed from the boat and headed toward the sounds of a nearby village, pushing their way through the dense undergrowth. Chagnon describes what happened next:

> I looked up and gasped when I saw a dozen burly, naked, sweaty, hideous men staring at us down the shafts of their drawn arrows! Immense wads of green tobacco were stuck between their lower teeth and lips, making them look even more hideous, and strands of dark green slime dripped or hung from their nostrils—strands so long that they clung to their [chests] or drizzled down their chins.
> My next discovery was that there were a dozen or so vicious, underfed dogs snapping at my legs, circling me as if I were to be their next meal. I just stood there holding my notebook, helpless and pathetic. Then the stench of the decaying vegetation and filth hit me and I almost got sick. I was horrified. What kind of welcome was this for the person who came here to live with you and learn your way of life, to become friends with you? (1992:11–12)

Fortunately for Chagnon, the Yąnomamö villagers recognized his guide and lowered their weapons. Though reassured that he would survive the afternoon, Chagnon was still shaken by his inability to make any sense of the people surrounding him. And this was to be his home for a year and a half! He wondered why he had given up physics to study human culture in the first place.

WHAT DO YOU THINK?

1. As they came to know Chagnon, might the Yąnomanö, too, have experienced culture shock? Why?
2. Can you think of an experience you had that is similar to the one described here?
3. How can studying sociology help reduce the experience of culture shock?

Source: Based on Chagnon (1992).

Africa to move about in the tall grasses. There, walking upright, they learned the advantages of hunting in groups and made use of fire, tools, and weapons, built simple shelters, and fashioned basic clothing. These Stone Age achievements may seem modest, but they mark the point at which our ancestors set off on a distinct evolutionary course, making culture their primary strategy for survival. By about 250,000 years ago, our own species—*Homo sapiens* (derived from the Latin meaning "thinking person")—finally emerged. Humans continued to evolve so that by about 40,000 years ago, people who looked more or less like ourselves roamed the Earth. With larger brains, these

People throughout the world communicate not just with spoken words but also with bodily gestures. Because gestures vary from culture to culture, they can occasionally be the cause for misunderstandings. For instance, the commonplace "thumbs up" gesture we use to express "Good job!" can get a person from the United States into trouble in Australia, where people take it to mean "Up yours!"

"modern" *Homo sapiens* developed culture rapidly, as the wide range of tools and cave art from this period suggests.

By about 12,000 years ago, the founding of permanent settlements and the creation of specialized occupations in the Middle East (in what today is Iraq and Egypt) marked the "birth of civilization." At this point, the biological forces we call instincts had disappeared, replaced by a more efficient survival scheme: *fashioning the natural environment for ourselves.* Ever since, humans have made and remade their world in countless ways, resulting in today's fascinating cultural diversity.

CULTURE, NATION, AND SOCIETY

The term "culture" calls to mind other similar terms, such as "nation" and "society," although each has a slightly different meaning. *Culture* refers to a shared way of life. A *nation* is a political entity, a territory with designated borders, such as the United States, Canada, Peru, or Zimbabwe. *Society,* the topic of Chapter 4, is the organized interaction of people who typically live in a nation or some other specific territory.

The United States, then, is both a nation and a society. But many nations, including the United States, are *multicultural;* that is, their people follow various ways of life that blend (and sometimes clash).

HOW MANY CULTURES?

In the United States, how many cultures are there? One indicator of culture is language; the Census Bureau lists more than 200 languages spoken in this country, most of which were brought by immigrants from nations around the world.

Globally, experts document almost 7,000 languages, suggesting the existence of as many distinct cultures. Yet the number of languages spoken around the world is declining, and roughly half now are spoken by fewer than 10,000 people. Experts expect that the coming decades may see the disappearance of hundreds of these languages, from Gullah,

 To learn more about how anthropologists study other cultures, go to http://www.aaanet.org

Pennsylvania German, and Pawnee (all spoken in the United States) to Han (spoken in northwest Canada), Oro (in the Amazon region of Brazil), Sardinian (spoken on the European island of Sardinia), Aramaic (the language of Jesus of Nazareth still spoken in the Middle East), Nu Shu (a language spoken in southern China that is the only one known to be used exclusively by women), and Wakka Wakka and several other Aboriginal tongues spoken in Australia. What accounts for the decline? Likely causes include high-technology communication, increasing international migration, and an expanding global economy (UNESCO, 2001; Barovick, 2002; Hayden, 2003).

The Elements of Culture

Although cultures vary greatly, they all have common elements, including symbols, language, values, and norms. We begin with the one that is the basis for all the others: symbols.

SYMBOLS

Like all creatures, humans use their senses to experience the surrounding world, but unlike others, we also try to give the world *meaning.* Humans transform elements of the world into *symbols.* A **symbol** is *anything that carries a particular meaning recognized by people who share a culture.* A word, a whistle, a wall of graffiti, a flashing red light, a raised fist— all serve as symbols. We can see the human capacity to create and manipulate symbols reflected in the very different meanings associated with the simple act of winking an eye, which can convey interest, understanding, or insult.

Societies create new symbols all the time. The Applying Sociology box describes some of the cyber-symbols that have developed along with our increasing use of computers for communication.

APPLYING SOCIOLOGY
New Symbols in the World of Instant Messaging

Soc was Gr8!

  What happened?

I was :'-D

  Y?

The prof looks like =(_8^(1)

  Maybe his wife looks like
  >@@@@8^)

GMTA

  See you B4 class. B4N

BCNU

The world of symbols changes all the time. One reason that people create new symbols is that we develop new ways to communicate. Today, almost 50 million people in the United States (most of them young and many of them students) communicate using an instant messaging (IM) program. All you need to have is a computer and a connection to the Internet. About 100 million people also stay connected away from home using a cellular phone.

The exchange above starts with one friend telling the other how much she enjoyed her new sociology class. It makes use of some of the new "shorthand" symbols that have emerged in the IM world. Here is a sampling of IM symbols. (To appreciate the "emoticon" faces, rotate the page 90° to the right.)

:'-D laughing so hard I cried

:-(I am sad.

:-() I am shocked.

:-) I am smiling.

:-)8 I am smiling and wearing a bow tie.

:-O Wow!

:-ll I am angry with you.

:- P I'm sticking my tongue out at you!

%-} I think I've had too much to drink.

:-x My lips are sealed!

-:(Somebody cut my hair into a mohawk!

@}——>—— Here's a rose for you!

=(_8^(1) Homer Simpson

>@@@@8^) Marge Simpson

AFAIK As far as I know

AWHFY Are we having fun yet?

B4 Before

B4N Bye for now!

BBL Be back later!

BCNU Be seeing you!

CU See you!

GAL Get a life!

GMTA Great minds think alike.

Gr8 Great!

HAGN Have a good night.

H&K Hugs and kisses

IMBL It must be love.

J4F Just for fun

KC Keep cool.

L8r Later

LTNC Long time no see

MYOB Mind your own business.

PCM Please call me.

QPSA? Que pasa?

U You

UR You are

Wan2 Want to

X! Typical woman!

Y! Typical man!

Y Why

2bctd To be continued

2g4u Too good for you

2L8 Too late

WHAT DO YOU THINK?

1. What does the creation of symbols such as these suggest about culture?
2. Do you think that using such symbols is a good way to communicate? Does it lead to confusion or misunderstanding? Why or why not?
3. What other kinds of symbols can you think of that are new to your generation?

Sources: J. Rubin (2003) and Berteau (2005).

We are so dependent on our culture's symbols that we take them for granted. However, we become keenly aware of the importance of a symbol when someone uses it in an unconventional way, as when a person burns a U.S. flag during a political demonstration. Entering an unfamiliar culture also reminds us of the power of symbols; culture shock is really the inability to "read" meaning in new surroundings. Not understanding the symbols of a culture leaves a person feeling lost and isolated, unsure of how to act, and sometimes frightened.

Culture shock is a two-way process. On one hand, travelers *experience* culture shock when encountering people whose way of life is different. For example, North Americans who consider dogs beloved household pets might be put off by the Masai of eastern Africa, who ignore dogs and never feed them. The same travelers might be horrified to find that

إقرأو	**Read**	독서
Arabic	English	Korean
Ꮞꭟꮁꭲꮄ	διαβαζω	بخوانيد.
Armenian	Greek	Persian
ᲠᲛᲐᲜᲔ	אֶקְרָא:	читать
Cambodian	Hebrew	Russian
閱讀	पढ़नाⁿ	¡Ven a leer!
Chinese	Hindi	Spanish

FIGURE 3-1 Human Languages: A Variety of Symbols

Here the single English word "Read" is written in twelve of the hundreds of languages humans use to communicate with one another.

in parts of Indonesia and the northern regions of the People's Republic of China, people roast dogs for dinner.

On the other hand, a traveler may *inflict* culture shock on local people by acting in ways that offend them. A North American who asks for a cheeseburger in an Indian restaurant may unknowingly offend Hindus, who consider cows sacred and never to be eaten. Global travel provides almost endless opportunities for this kind of misunderstanding.

Symbolic meanings also vary within a single society. To some people in the United States, a fur coat represents a prized symbol of success, but to others, it represents the inhumane treatment of animals. In the recent debate about flying the Confederate flag over the South Carolina state house, some people saw the flag as a symbol of regional pride, but others saw it as a symbol of racial oppression.

LANGUAGE

In infancy, an illness left Helen Keller (1880–1968) blind and deaf. Without these two senses, she was cut off from the symbolic world, and her social development was greatly limited. Only when her teacher, Anne Mansfield Sullivan, broke through Keller's isolation using sign language did Helen Keller begin to realize her human potential. This remarkable woman, who later became a famous educator herself, recalls the moment she first understood the concept of language:

> We walked down the path to the well-house, attracted by the smell of honeysuckle with which it was covered. Someone was drawing water, and my teacher placed my hand under the spout. As the cool stream gushed over one hand, she spelled into the other the word *water*, first

slowly, then rapidly. I stood still, my whole attention fixed upon the motions of her fingers. Suddenly I felt a misty consciousness as of something forgotten—a thrill of returning thought; and somehow the mystery of language was revealed to me. I knew then that "w-a-t-e-r" meant the wonderful cool something that was flowing over my hand. That living word awakened my soul; gave it light, hope, joy, set it free! (1903:24)

Language, the key to the world of culture, is *a system of symbols that allows people to communicate with one another.*

 To learn more about the life of Helen Keller, go to http://www.helen-keller.freeservers.com

Humans have created many alphabets to express the hundreds of languages we speak. Several examples are shown in Figure 3–1. Even rules for writing differ: Most people in Western societies write from left to right, but people in northern Africa and western Asia write from right to left, and people in eastern Asia write from top to bottom. Global Map 3–1 shows where we find the world's three most widely spoken languages.

Language not only allows communication but is also the key to **cultural transmission,** *the process by which one generation passes culture to the next.* Just as our bodies contain the genes of our ancestors, our culture contains countless symbols of those who came before us. Language is the key that unlocks centuries of accumulated wisdom.

YOUR TURN

List three cultural elements that were passed on to you from earlier generations; list three (obviously different) elements that have emerged in your own generation. Are these likely to be passed on to your children and grandchildren?

Throughout human history, every society has transmitted culture through speech, a process sociologists call the "oral cultural tradition." Some 5,000 years ago, humans invented writing, although at that time only a privileged few learned to read and write. Not until the twentieth century did high-income nations boast of nearly universal literacy. Still, at least 10 percent of U.S. adults (more than 20 million people) are functionally illiterate, unable to read and write in a society that increasingly demands such skills. In low-income countries of the world, about one-third of men and one-half of women are illiterate (World Bank, 2005).

Language skills may link us with the past, but they also spark the human imagination to connect symbols in new ways, creating an almost limitless range of future possibilities.

WINDOW ON THE WORLD

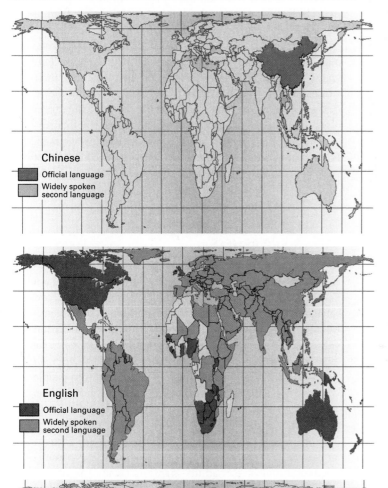

Chinese
- Official language
- Widely spoken second language

English
- Official language
- Widely spoken second language

Spanish
- Official language
- Widely spoken second language

Source: *Peters Atlas of the World* (1990); updated by the author.

GLOBAL MAP 3-1

Language in Global Perspective

Chinese (including Mandarin, Cantonese, and dozens of other dialects) is the native tongue of one-fifth of the world's people, almost all of whom live in Asia. Although all Chinese people read and write with the same characters, they use several dozen dialects. The "official" dialect, taught in schools throughout the People's Republic of China and the Republic of Taiwan, is Mandarin (the dialect of Beijing, China's historic capital city). Cantonese, the language of Canton, is the second most common Chinese dialect; it differs in sound from Mandarin roughly the way French differs from Spanish.

English is the native tongue or official language in several world regions (spoken by one-tenth of humanity) and has become the preferred second language in most of the world.

The largest concentration of Spanish speakers is in Latin America and, of course, Spain. Spanish is also the second most widely spoken language in the United States.

Australian artist and feminist Sally Swain alters famous artists' paintings to make fun of our culture's tendency to ignore the everyday lives of women. This spoof is entitled *Mrs. Matisse Polishes the Goldfish*.

Mrs. Matisse Polishes the Goldfish from *Great Housewives of Art* by Sally Swain, copyright © 1988, 1989 by Sally Swain. Used by permission of Viking Penguin, a division of Penguin Group (USA) Inc.

Language sets humans apart as the only creatures who are self-conscious, aware of our limitations and ultimate mortality, yet able to dream and to hope for a future better than the present.

Does Language Shape Reality?

Does someone who speaks Cherokee, an American Indian language, experience the world differently from other North Americans who think in, say, English or Spanish? Edward Sapir and Benjamin Whorf claimed the answer is yes, since each language has its own distinctive symbols that serve as the building blocks of reality (Sapir, 1929, 1949; Whorf, 1956, orig. 1941). Further, they noted that each language

has words or expressions not found in any other symbolic system. Finally, all languages fuse symbols with distinctive emotions so that, as multilingual people know, a single idea may "feel" different when spoken in Spanish rather than in English or Chinese (Falk, 1987).

Formally, the **Sapir-Whorf thesis** states that *people see and understand the world through the cultural lens of language.* In the decades since Sapir and Whorf published their work, however, scholars have taken issue with this thesis. Current thinking is that although we do fashion reality from our symbols, evidence does not support the notion that language *determines* reality the way Sapir and Whorf claimed. For example, we know that children understand the idea of "family" long before they learn that word; similarly, adults can imagine new ideas or things before inventing a name for them (Kay & Kempton, 1984; Pinker, 1994).

VALUES AND BELIEFS

What accounts for the popularity of Hollywood film characters such as James Bond, Neo, Erin Brockovich, and Lara Croft? Each is ruggedly individualistic, going it alone and relying on personal skill and savvy to challenge "the system." In admiring such characters, we are supporting certain **values,** *culturally defined standards that people use to decide what is desirable, good, and beautiful, and that serve as broad guidelines for social living.* Values are standards that people who share a culture use to make choices about how to live.

Values are broad principles that support **beliefs,** *specific statements that people hold to be true.* In other words, values are abstract standards of goodness, and beliefs are particular matters that individuals consider true or false. For example, because most U.S. adults share the *value* of providing equal opportunities for all, they believe that a qualified woman could serve as president of the United States (NORC, 2003).

Cultural values and beliefs not only affect how we see our surroundings but also help form our personalities. We learn from families, friends, schools, and religious organizations to think and act according to particular principles, to believe certain "truths," and to pursue worthwhile goals. Even so, in a nation as large and diverse as the United States, few cultural values and beliefs are shared by everyone. Our long history of immigration has made the United States a cultural mosaic. In this regard, this country differs from many nations, such as China and Japan, that are more culturally homogeneous.

Key Values of U.S. Culture

Because U.S. culture is a mix of ways of life from other countries all around the world, it is highly diverse. In addition, due to the nation's high level of immigration and the creativity of the population, U.S. culture is always changing. Even so, the sociologist Robin Williams (1970) has identified ten values that are widespread in the United States and viewed by many people as central to our way of life:

1. **Equal opportunity.** Most people in the United States favor not *equality of condition* but *equality of opportunity*. We believe that our society should provide everyone with the chance to get ahead according to individual talents and efforts.

2. **Achievement and success.** Our way of life encourages competition so that each person's rewards should reflect personal merit. A successful person is given the respect due a "winner."

3. **Material comfort.** Success in the United States generally means making money and enjoying what it will buy. Although we sometimes say that "money won't buy happiness," most of us pursue wealth all the same.

4. **Activity and work.** Popular U.S. heroes, from television's Buffy, the vampire slayer, to golf champion Tiger Woods, are "doers" who get the job done. Our culture values *action* over *reflection* and controlling events over passively accepting fate.

5. **Practicality and efficiency.** We value the practical over the theoretical, "doing" over "dreaming." Activity has value to the extent that it earns money. "Major in something that will help you get a job!" parents say to their college-age children.

6. **Progress.** We are an optimistic people who, despite waves of nostalgia, believe that the present is better than the past. We celebrate progress, viewing "the very latest" as "the very best."

7. **Science.** We expect scientists to solve problems and improve the quality of our lives. We believe we are rational, logical people, which probably explains our cultural tendency (especially among men) to look down on emotion and intuition as sources of knowledge.

8. **Democracy and free enterprise.** Members of our society believe that individuals have rights that governments should not take away. We believe that a just political system is based on free elections in

What does the popularity of the television show *The Apprentice* tell you about the values at the heart of U.S. culture?

which adults select government leaders and on an economy that responds to the choices of individual consumers.

9. **Freedom.** We favor individual initiative over collective conformity. While we know that everyone has responsibilities to others, we believe that people should be free to pursue their personal goals.

10. **Racism and group superiority.** Despite strong ideas about equal opportunity and freedom, most people in the United States judge individuals according to gender, race, ethnicity, and social class. In general, U.S. culture values males above females, whites above people of color, rich above poor, and people with northwestern European backgrounds above those whose ancestors came from other parts of the world. Although we like to describe ourselves as a nation of equals, there is little doubt that some of us are "more equal" than others.

YOUR TURN

Think about the games you played when you were growing up, like foursquare or Capture the Flag, or board games, like Monopoly. What cultural values do the games teach? How do they differ from the values taught by today's video games?

Don't Blame Me! The "Culture of Victimization"

A University of North Carolina law student walked down the street, took aim with an M-1 rifle, and killed two men he had never met. Later, from a psychiatric hospital, he sued his therapist for not doing enough to prevent his actions. A jury awarded him $500,000.

A New York man leaped in front of a subway train; lucky enough to survive, he sued the city, claiming that the train had failed to stop in time to prevent his serious injuries. His award: $650,000.

In Washington, D.C., after realizing that he had been videotaped smoking crack cocaine in a hotel room, the city's mayor blamed his woman companion for "setting him up" and suggested that the police had been racially motivated in arresting him.

After more than a dozen women accused an Oregon senator of sexual harassment, he claimed that his behavior had been caused by his problem with alcohol.

In the most celebrated case of its kind, a former city politician gunned down the mayor of San Francisco and a city council member, blaming his violence on insanity caused by eating too much junk food (the so-called "Twinkie defense").

In each of these cases, someone denied personal responsibility for an action, claiming instead to be a victim. More and more, members of our society are pointing the finger elsewhere, which prompted Irving Horowitz (1993) to declare that our way of life is becoming a "culture of victimization" in which "everyone is a victim" and

"no one accepts responsibility for anything."

Further evidence of this culture of victimization is the tendency to blame our faults on "addictions," a term once associated only with uncontrollable drug use. We now hear about gambling addicts, compulsive overeaters, sex addicts, and even people who excuse runaway credit card debt as a "shopping addiction." Bookstores overflow with manuals to help people deal with numerous new medical or psychological conditions ranging from the "Cinderella complex" to the "Casanova complex" and even "soap opera syndrome." And U.S. courts are clogged by lawsuits blaming other people for misfortunes that we used to accept as part of life.

What's going on here? Is U.S. culture changing? Historically, our cultural ideal was "rugged individualism," the

Values: Sometimes in Conflict

Looking over Williams's list on page 69, we see that some values are inconsistent and even opposed to one another. Take numbers 1 and 10, for example: People in the United States believe in equality of opportunity, yet they may also look down on others because of their sex or race.

Conflict between values reflects the cultural diversity of U.S. society. It also sparks cultural change, by which new trends develop alongside older traditions. Recently, for example, what some observers call a "culture of victimization" has arisen to challenge our society's longtime belief in individual responsibility (J. Best, 1997; Furedi, 1998). The Thinking Critically box takes a closer look.

Value conflict causes strain and often leads to awkward balancing acts in our beliefs. Sometimes we decide one value is more important than another by, for example, supporting equal opportunity while opposing the acceptance

of homosexual people in the U.S. military. In such cases, we simply learn to live with the contradictions.

Values: A Global Perspective

Each of the thousands of cultures in the world has its own values. In general, the values that are important in higher-income countries differ somewhat from those in lower-income countries.

Lower-income nations have cultures that value survival. This means that people who are desperately poor have little choice but to place a great deal of importance on physical safety and economic security. They worry about having enough to eat and a safe place to sleep at night. In addition, lower-income nations tend to be traditional, with values that celebrate the past and emphasize the importance of family and religious beliefs, obedience to authority, and conformity. These nations, which are dominated by

idea that people are responsible for their own triumphs or tragedies. But this value has weakened for several reasons. First, everyone is more aware (partly through the work of sociologists) of how society shapes our lives. We now recognize that categories of people (such as Native Americans, African Americans, and women) have suffered real historical disadvantages. But more and more people these days are saying they are victims, including white males, who claim that "everybody gets special treatment but us."

Second, especially since they began advertising their services in 1977, many lawyers looking for new clients encourage people to see themselves as victims of injustice. The number of million-dollar lawsuit awards has risen more than twenty-five-fold in the past twenty-five years.

Finally, the appearance of many new "rights groups" promotes what Amitai Etzioni (1991) calls "rights inflation." Today, we have organizations to protect the rights of hunters (as well as animals), the rights of smokers (and nonsmokers), the right of women to control their bodies (and the rights of the unborn), the right to own a gun (and the right to be safe from violence). As people claim more rights, they are more likely to see themselves as victims (and their opponents as victimizers).

Does this new popularity of being a victim signal a fundamental shift in our individualistic culture? Perhaps, but it also springs from some established cultural forces. For example, a person's claim to victimization depends on a long-standing belief that everyone has the right to life, liberty, and the pursuit of happiness. What is new, however, is that the explosion of "rights" now does more than alert us to clear cases of injustice: It lessens our responsibility for our own lives.

WHAT DO YOU THINK?

1. Do you think our cultural emphasis on individualism is less strong today than in the past? Why?
2. Do you think the United States has experienced "rights inflation"? Why or why not?
3. Does the sociological perspective encourage us to view people as victims? Explain your answer.

men, typically discourage or forbid practices such as divorce and abortion.

Higher-income countries have cultures that value individualism and self-expression. These countries are rich enough that most of their people take survival for granted, focusing their attention instead on developing a high quality of life. People in these countries think about which "lifestyle" they prefer and how to achieve the greatest personal happiness. In addition, these countries tend to be secular-rational, placing less emphasis on family ties and religious beliefs and more on people thinking for themselves and being tolerant of others who differ from them. In higher-income countries, women have social standing more equal to men, and there is widespread support for practices such as divorce and abortion (World Values Survey, 2004). Figure 3–2 on page 72 shows how selected countries of the world compare in terms of their cultural values.

↔ YOUR TURN ↔

Figure 3–2 shows that as a rich nation, the United States ranks high in terms of self-expression but is more traditional than many other high-income nations, such as those in Europe. Can you point to specific beliefs or practices that set us apart from Europeans as more traditional?

NORMS

Most people in the United States are eager to gossip about "who's hot" and "who's not." Members of American Indian societies, however, typically condemn such behavior as rude and divisive. Both patterns illustrate the operation of

GLOBAL SNAPSHOT

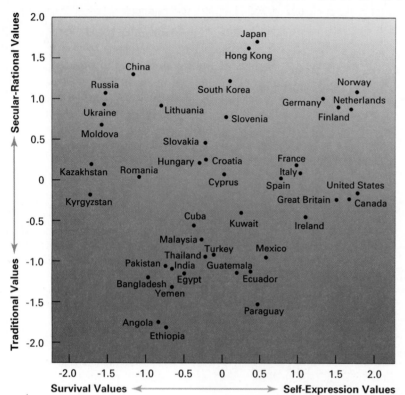

FIGURE 3-2 Cultural Values of Selected Countries

Higher-income countries are secular-rational and favor self-expression. The cultures of lower-income countries are more traditional and concerned with economic survival.

Source: *Modernization, Cultural Change and Democracy* by Ronald Inglehart and Christian Welzel, New York: Cambridge University Press, 2005.

norms, *rules and expectations by which a society guides the behavior of its members.* Some norms are *proscriptive,* stating what we *should not* do, as when health officials warn us to avoid casual sex. *Prescriptive* norms, on the other hand, state what we *should* do, as when U.S. schools teach "safe sex" practices.

The most important norms in a culture apply everywhere and at all times. For example, parents expect obedience from young children regardless of the setting. Other norms depend on the situation. In the United States, we expect the audience to applaud after a musical performance; we may applaud (although it is not expected) at the end of a classroom lecture; we do not applaud at the end of a religious sermon.

Mores and Folkways

William Graham Sumner (1959, orig. 1906), an early U.S. sociologist, recognized that some norms are more important to our lives than others. Sumner coined the term **mores** (pronounced "more-rays") to refer to *norms that are widely*

observed and have great moral significance. Mores, or *taboos,* include our society's insistence that adults not engage in sexual relations with children.

People pay less attention to **folkways,** *norms for routine or casual interaction.* Examples include ideas about appropriate greetings and proper dress. In short, mores distinguish between right and wrong, and folkways draw a line between right and *rude.* A man who does not wear a tie to a formal dinner party may raise eyebrows for violating folkways. If, however, he were to arrive at the party wearing *only* a tie, he would violate cultural mores and invite a more serious response.

YOUR TURN

Give two examples of violating campus folkways and two examples of violating campus mores. What are the likely consequences of each type of violation?

Social Control

Mores and folkways are the basic rules of everyday life. Although we sometimes resist pressure to conform, we can see that norms make our dealings with others more orderly and predictable. Observing or breaking the rules of social life prompts a response from others, in the form of reward or punishment. Sanctions—whether an approving smile or a raised eyebrow—operate as a system of **social control,** *attempts by society to regulate people's thoughts and behavior.*

As we learn cultural norms, we gain the capacity to evaluate our own behavior. Doing wrong (say, downloading a term paper from the Internet) can cause both *shame* (the painful sense that others disapprove of our actions) and *guilt* (a negative judgment we make of ourselves). Only cultural creatures can experience shame and guilt. This is probably what Mark Twain had in mind when he remarked that people "are the only animals that blush—or need to."

IDEAL AND REAL CULTURE

Values and norms do not describe actual behavior so much as they suggest how we *should* behave. We must remember that *ideal* culture always differs from *real* culture—what actually occurs in everyday life. For example, most women and men agree on the importance of sexual faithfulness in marriage. Even so, in one study, about 25 percent of married men and 10 percent of married women reported having been sexually unfaithful to their spouses at some point in their marriage (Laumann et al., 1994). But a culture's moral standards are important all the same, calling to mind the old saying, "Do as I say, not as I do."

MATERIAL CULTURE AND TECHNOLOGY

In addition to symbolic elements such as values and norms, every culture includes a wide range of physical human creations, which sociologists call *artifacts.* The Chinese eat with chopsticks rather than knives and forks, the Japanese put mats rather than rugs on the floor, and many men and women in India prefer flowing robes to the close-fitting clothing common in the United States. The material culture of a people may seem as strange to outsiders as their language, values, and norms.

A society's artifacts partly reflect underlying cultural values. The warlike Ŷanomamö carefully craft their weapons and prize the poison tips on their arrows. By contrast, our society's emphasis on individualism and independence goes a long way toward explaining our high regard for the automobile: We own 230 million motor vehicles—more than one for every licensed driver—and in recent years, half of all cars sold in the United States have been the large sports utility vehicles that we might expect rugged, individualistic people to like.

Standards of beauty—including the color and design of everyday surroundings—vary significantly from one culture to another. These two Nankani women put the finishing touches on their lavishly decorated homes. Members of North American and European societies, by contrast, make far less use of bright colors and intricate detail, so their housing appears much more subdued.

YOUR TURN

If archaeologists dig up our civilization 50,000 years from now, based on the artifacts they find, what kind of people will they think we were? Point to specific "artifacts" (such as SUVs, cell phones, and credit cards) and what they say about us.

In addition to reflecting values, material culture also reflects a society's **technology,** *knowledge that people use to make a way of life in their surroundings.* The more complex a society's technology, the more its members are able (for better or worse) to shape the world for themselves. Advanced technology has allowed us to crisscross the

Any society is actually made up of countless different cultural patterns, some of which may seem strange, indeed, to most people. What cultural values are evident in the pierced noses and tattoos of these two men? Are these values completely at odds with our individualistic way of life?

country with superhighways and to fill them with automobiles. At the same time, the internal-combustion engines in those cars release carbon dioxide into the atmosphere, which contributes to air pollution and global warming.

Because we attach great importance to science and praise sophisticated technology, people in our society tend to judge cultures with simpler technology as less advanced than our own. Some facts support such an assessment. For example, life expectancy for children born in the United States is more than seventy-seven years; the life span of the Yąnomamö is only about forty years.

However, we must be careful not to make self-serving judgments about other cultures. Although many Yąnomamö are eager to acquire modern technology (such as steel tools and shotguns), they are generally well fed by world standards, and most are very satisfied with their lives (Chagnon, 1992). Remember too that while our powerful and complex technology has produced work-reducing

devices and seemingly miraculous medical treatments, it has also contributed to unhealthy levels of stress and created weapons capable of destroying in a blinding flash everything that humankind has achieved.

Finally, technology is not equally distributed within our population. Although many of us cannot imagine life without personal computers, televisions, and CD players, many members of U.S. society cannot afford these luxuries. Others reject them on principle. The Amish, who live in small farming communities across Pennsylvania, Ohio, and Indiana, reject most modern conveniences on religious grounds. With their traditional black clothing and horse-drawn buggies, the Amish may seem like a curious relic of the past. Yet their communities flourish, grounded in strong families that give everyone a sense of identity and purpose. Some researchers who have studied the Amish have concluded that these communities are "islands of sanity in a culture gripped by commercialism and technology run wild" (Hostetler, 1980:4; Kraybill, 1994:28).

NEW INFORMATION TECHNOLOGY AND CULTURE

Many rich nations, including the United States, have entered a postindustrial phase based on computers and new information technology. Industrial production is centered on factories and machinery that generate material goods. By contrast, postindustrial production is based on computers and other electronic devices that create, process, store, and apply information.

In this new information economy, workers need symbolic skills in place of the mechanical skills of the industrial age. Symbolic skills include the ability to speak, write, compute, design, and create images in fields such as art, advertising, and entertainment. In today's computer-based economy, people with creative jobs are generating new cultural ideas, images, and products all the time.

Cultural Diversity: Many Ways of Life in One World

In the United States, we are aware of our cultural diversity when we hear the distinctive accents of people from New England, the Midwest, or the Deep South. Ours is also a nation of religious pluralism, a land of class differences, and a home to individualists who try to be like no one else. Over the centuries, heavy immigration has made the United States the most *multicultural* of all high-income countries. By contrast, historic isolation has made Japan the most *monocultural* of all high-income nations.

Between 1820 (when the government began keeping track of immigration) and 2003, some 69 million people came to our shores. Our cultural mix continues to increase as almost 1 million more people arrive each year. A century ago, almost all immigrants hailed from Europe; today, most newcomers are from Latin America and Asia. To understand the reality of life in the United States, we must move beyond broad cultural patterns and shared values to consider cultural diversity.

HIGH CULTURE AND POPULAR CULTURE

Cultural diversity can involve social class. In fact, in everyday talk, we usually use the term "culture" to mean art forms such as classical literature, music, dance, and painting. We describe people who regularly go to the opera or the theater as "cultured," because we think they appreciate the "finer things in life."

We speak less generously of ordinary people, assuming that everyday culture is somehow less worthy. We are tempted to judge the music of Haydn as "more cultured" than hip-hop, couscous as better than cornbread, and polo as more polished than Ping-Pong.

Such judgments imply that many cultural patterns are readily available to only some members of a society (Hall & Neitz, 1993). Sociologists use the term **high culture** to refer to *cultural patterns that distinguish a society's elite* and **popular culture** to designate *cultural patterns that are widespread among a society's population.*

Common sense may suggest that high culture is superior to popular culture, but sociologists are uneasy with such judgments, for two reasons. First, neither elites nor ordinary people share all the same tastes and interests; people in both categories differ in many ways. Second, do we praise high culture because it is inherently better than popular culture or simply because its supporters have more money, power, and prestige? For example, there is no difference between a violin and a fiddle; however, we name the instrument a violin when it is used to produce classical music typically enjoyed by a person of higher position and a fiddle when the musician plays country tunes appreciated by people with lower social standing.

SUBCULTURE

The term **subculture** refers to *cultural patterns that set apart some segment of a society's population.* People who ride "chopper" motorcycles, Polish Americans, New England

Many subcultures that develop involve young people. One recent example is the skateboarding subculture that includes not only the sport but a distinctive style of dress.

"Yankees," Colorado "cowboys," the southern California "beach crowd," Elvis impersonators, and wilderness campers all display subcultural patterns.

YOUR TURN

Make a list of five subcultures that are part of your life. Which are the most important?

It is easy, but often inaccurate, to place people in some subcultural category because almost everyone participates in many subcultures without necessarily having much commitment to any of them. In some cases, however, cultural differences can set people apart from one another with tragic results. Consider the former nation of Yugoslavia in southeastern Europe. The 1990s civil war there was fueled by extreme cultural diversity. This *one* small country used *two* alphabets, embraced *three* religions, spoke *four* languages, was home to *five* major nationalities, was divided

May 29, 2002

Cultural Divide Over Parental Discipline

By YILU ZHAO

When a Chinese immigrant mother beat her 8-year-old son with a broomstick last month because he had not been doing his homework, she thought she was acting within the bounds of traditional Chinese disciplinary practices. . . .

The next day, when the boy's reddish welts were seen by his teachers, his school in Rego Park, Queens, reported the incident to the Administration for Children's Services, the city agency that protects children. That evening, the police went to the home in Rego Park, and her three children, 6 to 8, were put in foster care. The parents were investigated for child abuse.

. . . The handling of the case touched a nerve in immigrant communities, where many parents have disciplinary ideas that differ from mainstream American views.

"It's something cultural," said David Chen, the executive director of the Chinese-American Planning Council, a non-profit organization, referring to corporal punishment among Chinese immigrants. "The Chinese believe I hit you because I love you. The harder I hit you, the more I love you."

As more such incidents involving immigrant families occur and are reported in New York's ethnic media, from Korean newspapers to Spanish TV, advocacy groups are joining with public schools to educate immigrants about America's child welfare laws. . . .

When the Coalition for Asian American Children and Families, an advocacy group, printed a brochure to advise parents on child abuse issues, it addressed fundamental cultural beliefs.

"In the Chinese culture, the family is most important," it said. "A Chinese family might expect their child to support the family by doing well in school and obeying his parents.

"In America, the individual is the most important. American society might consider the family's discipline to be too strong, especially if the child is hurt physically or emotionally."

The clash about how to discipline a child is not new in New York City, where half of the population are immigrants and their children. Many immigrant parents have said for years that American parents are too permissive, and that children are disrespectful to elders. . . .

Well-meaning advice can put parents in a predicament, said social workers, since many parents know no other way to discipline children.

Mrs. Liu, a Chinatown resident who would give only her last name, said she had been at a loss after she learned about

---

into *six* political republics, and absorbed the cultural influences of *seven* surrounding countries. The cultural conflict that plunged this nation into civil war shows that subcultures are a source not only of pleasing variety but also of tension and outright violence.

Here in the United States, conflict may arise when the cultural patterns of immigrants clash with those of others in their new surroundings. "In the *Times*" takes a closer look at one recent example.

Many people view the United States as a "melting pot" where many nationalities blend into a single new culture; indeed, about eight in ten U.S. adults describe their way of life as "American" (Gardyn, 2002). But given so much cultural diversity, how accurate is the "melting pot" image? For one thing, subcultures involve not just *difference* but *hierarchy*. Too often what we view as "dominant" or "mainstream"

culture are patterns favored by powerful segments of the population, and we view the lives of disadvantaged people as "subculture." But are the cultural patterns of rich skiers in Aspen, Colorado, any less a subculture than the cultural patterns of skateboarders in Los Angeles? Some sociologists, therefore, prefer to level the playing field of society by emphasizing multiculturalism.

MULTICULTURALISM

Multiculturalism is *an educational program recognizing the cultural diversity of the United States and promoting the equality of all cultural traditions.* Multiculturalism is a sharp turn away from the past, when our society downplayed cultural diversity and defined itself primarily in terms of its European (and especially English) immigrants. Today there is a spirited debate about whether we should continue to

local laws. "I don't even dare to touch him," said Mrs. Liu, referring to her mischievous 11-year-old son. "Every time I want to hit him, he threatens to call 911 and have me arrested."

Joe Semidei, a director of the Committee for Hispanic Children and Families, said his organization teaches parents other ways to discipline children.

Mr. Semidei said: "Here are some examples: You are not going to the baseball game this weekend if you do this. But you are going to have a new toy if you do that. You negotiate with the kids and lay the boundaries. Here in America, you reinforce good discipline by rewards."

But many immigrant parents see this as bribery. . . . They grow more antagonistic toward the child welfare system when their children encounter negligent foster parents or guardians.

"Some Chinese kids have become addicted to drugs in foster care, and a few teenage girls got pregnant," said Xue-jun Chi, who was a university professor in China and is now a social worker at the Y.M.C.A. in Chinatown. "When their parents eventually get them back, they are so messed up. The parents ask, 'How has the system cared for them any better than I did?'"

Children's Services is willing to become more sensitive to cultural differences. "Our goal is to keep families together, not to break them up," said Kathleen Walsh, a spokeswoman. "But our ultimate goal is to keep the children safe." The agency has formed an immigrant issues group, which meets once every three months, when officials are briefed by immigrant community leaders about their groups' cultural practices.

WHAT DO YOU THINK?

1. Do you think it is ethnocentric to expect the Chinese families described in this article to discipline their children according to cultural norms common in the United States? Or would you support a culturally relativist approach to letting these parents do what seems right to them?

2. Can you cite other specific cultural patterns brought by immigrants that have come into conflict with established cultural norms?

3. How might such patterns end up changing U.S. culture?

Adapted from the original article by Yilu Zhao published in *The New York Times* on May 29, 2002. Copyright © 2002 by The New York Times Company. Reprinted with permission.

focus on historical traditions or highlight contemporary diversity (Orwin, 1996; Rabkin, 1996).

E pluribus unum, the familiar Latin phrase that appears on all U.S. coins, means "out of many, one." This motto symbolizes not only our national political union but also the idea that immigrants from around the world have come together to form a new way of life.

But from the outset, the many cultures did not melt together as much as harden into a hierarchy. At the top were the English, who formed a majority early in U.S. history and established English as the nation's dominant language. Further down, people of other backgrounds were advised to model themselves after "their betters." In practice, then, "melting" was really a process of Anglicization—adoption of English ways. As multiculturalists see it, early in our history, this society set up the English way of life as an ideal which everyone else should imitate and by which everyone should be judged.

Ever since, historians have reported events from the point of view of the English and other people of European ancestry, paying little attention to the perspectives and accomplishments of Native Americans and people of African and Asian descent. Multiculturalists criticize this as **Eurocentrism,** *the dominance of European (especially English) cultural patterns.* Molefi Kete Asante, a supporter of multiculturalism, argues that "like the fifteenth-century Europeans who could not cease believing that the Earth was the center of the universe, many today find it difficult to cease viewing European culture as the center of the social universe" (1988:7).

One controversial issue involves language. Some people believe that English should be the official language of the

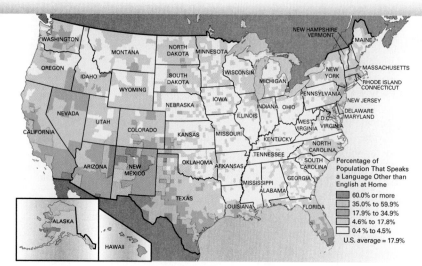

Language Diversity
across the United States

Of more than 262 million people age five or older
in the United States, the 2000 census reports that
47 million (18 percent) speak a language other
than English at home. Of these, 60 percent speak
Spanish and 15 percent use an Asian language (the
Census Bureau lists 29 languages, each of which is
favored by more than 100,000 people). The map
shows that non–English speakers are concentrated
in certain regions of the country. Which ones? What
do you think accounts for this pattern?

Source: U.S. Census Bureau (2003).

Percentage of Population That Speaks a Language Other than English at Home

- 60.0% or more
- 35.0% to 59.9%
- 17.9% to 34.9%
- 4.6% to 17.8%
- 0.4 % to 4.5%

U.S. average = 17.9%

United States. By 2005, legislatures in twenty-seven states
had enacted laws making it the official language. But some
47 million men and women—nearly one in six—speak a
language other than English at home. Spanish is the second
most commonly spoken language, and several hundred
other tongues are also heard across the country, including
Italian, German, French, Filipino, Japanese, Korean, and
Vietnamese, as well as many Native American languages.
National Map 3–1 shows where in the United States large
numbers of people speak a language other than English at
home.

Supporters of multiculturalism say it is a way of coming to terms with our country's increasing social diversity.
With the Asian and Hispanic populations of this country
increasing rapidly, some analysts predict that today's children will live to see people of African, Asian, and Hispanic
ancestry become a *majority* of this country's population.

Moreover, they claim, multiculturalism is a good way
to strengthen the academic achievement of African American children. To counter Eurocentrism, some multicultural
educators call for **Afrocentrism,** *emphasizing and promoting African cultural patterns,* which they see as necessary
after centuries of minimizing or ignoring the cultural
achievements of African societies and African Americans.

Although multiculturalism has found favor in recent
years, it has drawn its share of criticism as well. Opponents
say it encourages divisiveness rather than unity because it
urges people to identify with their own category rather than
with the nation as a whole. Instead of recognizing any common standards of truth, say critics, multiculturalism maintains that we should evaluate ideas according to the race

(and sex) of those who present them. Our common humanity thus dissolves into an "African experience," an "Asian experience," and so on.

But the bottom line, say critics, is that multiculturalism
actually harms minorities themselves. Multicultural policies
(from African American studies to all-black dorms) seem
to support the same racial segregation that our nation has
struggled so long to overcome. Furthermore, in the early
grades, an Afrocentric curriculum may deny children a
wide range of important knowledge and skills by forcing
them to study only certain topics from a single point of
view. The historian Arthur Schlesinger Jr. (1991:21) puts
the matter bluntly: "If a Kleagle of the Ku Klux Klan wanted to use the schools to handicap black Americans, he
could hardly come up with anything more effective than
the 'Afrocentric' curriculum."

Is there any common ground in this debate? Almost
everyone agrees that we need greater appreciation of our
cultural diversity. But precisely where the balance is to be
struck—between the *pluribus* and the *unum*—is likely to remain an issue for some time to come.

COUNTERCULTURE

Cultural diversity also includes outright rejection of conventional ideas or behavior. **Counterculture** refers to
*cultural patterns that strongly oppose those widely accepted
within a society.*

During the 1960s, for example, a youth-oriented counterculture rejected mainstream culture as overly competitive, self-centered, and materialistic. Instead, hippies and

other counterculturalists favored a cooperative lifestyle in which "being" took precedence over "doing" and the capacity for personal growth—or "expanded consciousness"—was prized over material possessions like homes and cars. Such differences led some people to "drop out" of the larger society.

Countercultures are still flourishing. At the extreme, small bands of religious militants exist in the United States, engaging in violence intended to threaten our way of life. Evidence suggests that members of al-Qaeda, the terrorist group led by Osama bin Laden, lived for years in this country before carrying out the attacks on the World Trade Center and the Pentagon in 2001.

CULTURAL CHANGE

Perhaps the most basic human truth of this world is that "all things shall pass." Even the dinosaurs, which thrived on this planet for 160 million years (see the timeline), remain today only as fossils. Will humanity survive for millions of years to come? All we can say with certainty is that given our reliance on culture, for as long as we survive, the human record will show continuous change.

Figure 3–3 shows changes in attitudes among first-year college students between 1969 (the height of the 1960s counterculture) and 2004. Some attitudes have changed only slightly: Today, as a generation ago, most men and women look forward to raising a family. But today's students are less concerned with developing a philosophy of life and much more interested in making money.

Change in one part of a culture usually sparks changes in others. For example, today's college women are much more interested in making money because women are now far more likely to be in the labor force than their mothers or grandmothers were. Working for income may not change their interest in raising a family, but it does increase both the age at first marriage and the divorce rate. Such connections illustrate the principle of **cultural integration,** *the close relationships among various elements of a cultural system.*

Cultural Lag

Some elements of culture change faster than others. William Ogburn (1964) observed that technology moves quickly, generating new elements of material culture (things) faster than nonmaterial culture (ideas) can keep up with them. Ogburn called this inconsistency **cultural lag,** *the fact that some cultural elements change more quickly than others, disrupting a cultural system.* For example, in a world in which a woman can give birth to a child by using another woman's egg, which has been fertilized in a laboratory with the sperm

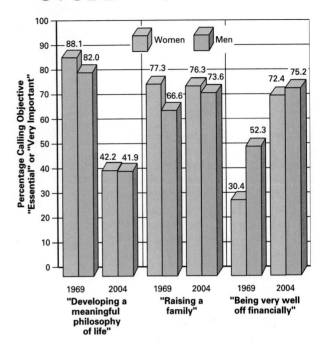

STUDENT SNAPSHOT

FIGURE 3-3   Life Objectives of First-Year College Students, 1969–2004

Today's students are less interested in developing a philosophy of life and more interested in making money.

Sources: Astin et al. (2002) and Sax et al. (2004).

of a total stranger, how are we to apply traditional ideas about motherhood and fatherhood?

Causes of Cultural Change

Cultural changes are set in motion in three ways. The first is *invention,* the process of creating new cultural elements. Invention has given us the telephone (1876), the airplane (1903), and the computer (1947), each of which has had a tremendous impact on our way of life. The process of invention goes on constantly, as indicated by the thousands of applications submitted annually to the U.S. Patent Office. The timeline on the inside cover of this text shows other inventions that have helped change our way of life.

Discovery, a second cause of cultural change, involves recognizing and better understanding something already in existence—perhaps a distant star or the foods of another culture or women's athletic ability. Many discoveries result from painstaking scientific research, and others from a

In the world's low-income countries, most children must work to provide their families with needed income. This young child in Dhaka, Bangladesh, is sorting discarded materials in a factory that makes recycled lead batteries. Is it ethnocentric for people living in high-income nations to condemn the practice of child labor because we think youngsters belong in school? Why or why not?

stroke of luck, as in 1898, when Marie Curie left a rock on a piece of photographic paper, noticed that emissions from the rock had exposed the paper, and thus discovered radium.

The third cause of cultural change is *diffusion,* the spread of cultural traits from one society to another. Because new information technology sends information around the globe in seconds, cultural diffusion has never been greater than it is today.

Certainly our own society has contributed many significant cultural elements to the world, ranging from computers to jazz music. Of course, diffusion works the other way, too, so that much of what we assume to be "American" actually comes from elsewhere. Most of the clothing we wear and the furniture we use, as well as the watch we carry and the money we spend, all had their origin in other cultures (Linton, 1937a).

ETHNOCENTRISM AND CULTURAL RELATIVISM

December 10, a small village in Morocco. Watching many of our fellow travelers browsing through a tiny ceramics factory, we have little doubt that North Americans are among the world's greatest shoppers. We delight in surveying hand-woven carpets in China or India, inspecting finely crafted metals in Turkey, or collecting the beautifully colored porcelain tiles we find here in Morocco. Of course, all these items are wonderful bargains. But one major reason for the low prices is unsettling: Many

products from the world's low- and middle-income countries are produced by children—some as young as five or six—who work long days for pennies per hour.

We think of childhood as a time of innocence and freedom from adult burdens like regular work. In poor countries throughout the world, however, families depend on income earned by children. So what people in one society think of as right and natural, people elsewhere find puzzling and even immoral. Perhaps the Chinese philosopher Confucius had it right when he noted that "all people are the same; it's only their habits that are different."

Just about every imaginable idea or behavior is commonplace somewhere in the world, and this cultural variation causes travelers both excitement and distress. The Australians flip light switches down to turn them on; North Americans flip them up. The Japanese name city blocks; North Americans name streets. Egyptians move very close to others in conversation; North Americans are used to maintaining several feet of "personal space." Bathrooms lack toilet paper in much of rural Morocco, causing considerable discomfort for North Americans, who recoil at the thought of using the left hand for bathroom hygiene, as the locals do.

Given that a particular culture is the basis for each person's reality, it is no wonder that people everywhere exhibit **ethnocentrism,** *the practice of judging another culture by the standards of one's own culture.* Some degree of ethnocentrism is necessary for people to be emotionally attached to their way of life. But ethnocentrism also generates misunderstanding and sometimes conflict.

Even language is culturally biased. Centuries ago, people in Europe and North America referred to China as the "Far East." But this term, unknown to the Chinese, is an ethnocentric expression for a region that is far to the east *of us.* The Chinese name for their country translates as "Central Kingdom," suggesting that they, like us, see their own society as the center of the world. The map challenges our own ethnocentrism by presenting a "down under" view of the Western Hemisphere.

The logical alternative to ethnocentrism is **cultural relativism,** *the practice of judging a culture by its own standards.* Cultural relativism can be difficult for travelers to adopt: It requires not only openness to unfamiliar values and norms but also the ability to put aside cultural standards we have known all our lives. Even so, as people of the world come into increasing contact with one another, the importance of understanding other cultures becomes ever greater.

As the opening to this chapter explained, businesses in the United States are learning the value of marketing to a culturally diverse population. Similarly, businesses are learning that success in the global economy depends on awareness of cultural patterns around the world. IBM, for example, now provides technical support for its products using Web sites in twenty-two languages (Fonda, 2001).

This trend is a change from the past, when many corporations used marketing strategies that lacked sensitivity to cultural diversity. Coors's phrase "Turn It Loose" startled Spanish-speaking customers by proclaiming that the beer would cause diarrhea. Braniff Airlines translated its slogan "Fly in Leather" so carelessly into Spanish that it read "Fly Naked." Similarly, Eastern Airlines' slogan "We Earn Our Wings Daily" became "We Fly Every Day to Heaven." Even poultry giant Frank Purdue fell victim to poor marketing when his pitch "It Takes a Tough Man to Make a Tender Chicken" was transformed into the Spanish words reading "A Sexually Excited Man Will Make a Chicken Affectionate" (Helin, 1992).

But cultural relativism introduces problems of its own. If almost any kind of behavior is the norm *somewhere* in the world, does that mean everything is equally right? Does the fact that some Indian and Moroccan families benefit from having their children work long hours justify child labor?

In two brief videos, the author considers issues of cultural relativism at http://www. TheSociologyPage.com

Since we are all members of a single species, surely there must be some universal standards of proper conduct. But what are they? And in trying to develop them, how can we avoid imposing our own standards on others? There are no simple answers. But when confronting

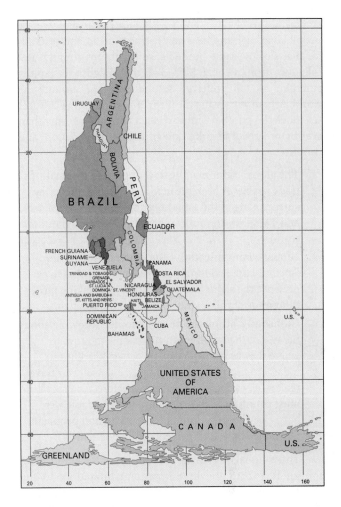

The View from "Down Under"

North America should be "up" and South America "down," or so we think. But because we live on a globe, "up" and "down" have no meaning at all. The reason this map of the Western Hemisphere looks wrong to us is not that it is geographically inaccurate; it simply violates our ethnocentric assumption that the United States should be "above" the rest of the Americas.

an unfamiliar cultural practice, it is best to resist making judgments before grasping what "they" think of the issue. Remember also to think about your own way of life as others might see it. After all, what we gain most from studying others is better insight into ourselves.

A GLOBAL CULTURE?

Today more than ever before, we can observe many of the same cultural practices the world over. Walking the streets of Seoul (South Korea), Kuala Lumpur (Malaysia), Madras

(India), Cairo (Egypt), and Casablanca (Morocco), we see people wearing jeans, hear familiar pop music, and read ads for many of the same products we use in this country. Recall, too, from Global Map 3–1 that English is rapidly emerging as the preferred second language around the world. Are we witnessing the birth of a single global culture?

Societies now have more contact with one another than ever before, involving the flow of goods, information, and people:

1. **The global economy: the flow of goods.** International trade has never been greater. The global economy has spread many of the same consumer goods—from cars and TV shows to music and fashions—throughout the world.

2. **Global communications: the flow of information.** Satellite-based communications enable people to experience the sights and sounds of events taking place thousands of miles away—often as they happen.

3. **Global migration: the flow of people.** Knowing about the rest of the world motivates people to move to where they imagine life will be better. In addition, today's transportation technology, especially air travel, makes relocating easier than ever before. As a result, in most countries, significant numbers of people were born elsewhere (including some 34 million people in the United States, 12 percent of the population).

These global links make the cultures of the world more similar. But there are three important limitations to the global culture thesis. First, the global flow of goods, information, and people is uneven. Generally speaking, urban areas (centers of commerce, communication, and people) have stronger ties to one another, while many rural villages remain isolated. In addition, the greater economic and military power of North America and Western Europe means that these regions influence the rest of the world more than the rest of the world influences them.

Second, the global culture thesis assumes that people everywhere are able to *afford* various new goods and services. As Chapter 12 ("Global Stratification") explains, desperate poverty in much of the world deprives people of even the basic necessities of a safe and secure life.

Third, although many cultural practices are now found throughout the world, people everywhere do not attach the same meanings to them. Do children in Tokyo draw the same lessons from reading the Harry Potter books as their counterparts in New York or London? Similarly, we enjoy foods from around the world while knowing little about the lives of the people who created them. In short, people everywhere still see the world through their own cultural lenses.

Theoretical Analysis of Culture

Sociologists have the special task of understanding how culture helps us make sense of ourselves and the surrounding world. Here we will examine several macro-level theoretical approaches to understanding culture; a micro-level approach to the personal experience of culture is the focus of Chapter 6 ("Social Interaction in Everyday Life").

THE FUNCTIONS OF CULTURE: STRUCTURAL-FUNCTIONAL ANALYSIS

The structural-functional approach explains culture as a complex strategy for meeting human needs. Borrowing from the philosophical doctrine of *idealism*, this approach considers values the core of a culture (Parsons, 1966; R. Williams, 1970). In other words, cultural values direct our lives, give meaning to what we do, and bind people together. Countless other cultural traits have various functions that support the operation of society.

Thinking functionally helps us understand an unfamiliar way of life. Consider the Amish farmer plowing hundreds of acres of an Ohio farm with a team of horses. His farming methods may violate our cultural value of efficiency, but from the Amish point of view, hard work functions to develop the discipline necessary for a highly religious way of life. Long days of working together not only make the Amish self-sufficient but also strengthen family ties and unify local communities.

Of course, Amish practices have dysfunctions as well. The hard work and strict religious discipline are too demanding for some, who end up leaving the community. Then, too, strong religious beliefs sometimes prevent compromise; slight differences in religious practices have caused the Amish to divide into different communities (Kraybill, 1989; Kraybill & Olshan, 1994).

If cultures are strategies for meeting human needs, we would expect to find many common patterns around the world. The term **cultural universals** refers to *traits that are part of every known culture.* Comparing hundreds of cultures, George Murdock (1945) identified dozens of cultural universals. One common element is the family, which functions everywhere to control sexual reproduction and to oversee the care of children. Funeral rites, too, are found everywhere, because all human communities cope with the reality of death. Jokes are another cultural universal, serving as a safe means of releasing social tensions.

Critical review The strength of the structural-functional approach is that it shows how culture operates to meet human needs. Yet by emphasizing a society's dominant cultural patterns, this approach largely ignores cultural diversity.

Following the structural-functional approach, what do you make of the Amish practice of "barn raising," by which everyone in a community joins together to raise a family's new barn in a day? Why is such a ritual almost unknown in rural areas outside of Amish communities?

Also, because this approach emphasizes cultural stability, it downplays the importance of change. In short, cultural systems are not as stable nor a matter of as much agreement as structural functionalism leads us to believe.

INEQUALITY AND CULTURE: SOCIAL-CONFLICT ANALYSIS

The social-conflict approach stresses the link between culture and inequality. Any cultural trait, from this point of view, benefits some members of society at the expense of others.

Why do certain values dominate a society in the first place? Many conflict theorists, especially Marxists, argue that culture is shaped by a society's system of economic production. "It is not the consciousness of men that determines their being," Karl Marx proclaimed; "it is their social being that determines their consciousness" (Marx & Engels, 1978:4, orig. 1859). Social-conflict theory, then, is rooted in the philosophical doctrine of *materialism*, which holds that a society's system of material production (such as our own capitalist economy) has a powerful effect on the rest of a culture. This materialist approach contrasts with the idealist leanings of structural functionalism.

Social-conflict analysis ties our cultural values of competitiveness and material success to our country's capitalist economy, which serves the interests of the nation's wealthy elite. The culture of capitalism further teaches us to think that rich and powerful people work harder or longer than others and therefore deserve their wealth and privileges. It also encourages us to view capitalism as somehow "natural," discouraging us from trying to reduce economic inequality.

Eventually, however, the strains of inequality erupt into movements for social change. Two examples in the United States are the civil rights movement and the women's movement. Both seek greater equality, and both encounter opposition from defenders of the status quo.

Critical review The social-conflict approach suggests that cultural systems do not address human needs equally, allowing some people to dominate others. This inequity in turn generates pressure toward change.

Yet by stressing the divisiveness of culture, this approach understates the ways that cultural patterns integrate members of society. Thus we should consider both social-conflict and structural-functional insights for a fuller understanding of culture.

EVOLUTION AND CULTURE: SOCIOBIOLOGY

We know that culture is a human creation, but does human biology influence how this process unfolds? A third theoretical approach, standing with one leg in biology and one in sociology, is **sociobiology,** *a theoretical approach that explores ways in which human biology affects how we create culture.*

Sociobiology rests on the theory of evolution proposed by Charles Darwin in his book *On the Origin of Species*

Using an evolutionary perspective, sociobiologists explain that different reproductive strategies give rise to a double standard: Men treat women as sexual objects more than women treat men that way. While this may be so, many sociologists counter that behavior—such as that shown in Ruth Orkin's photograph, *American Girl in Italy*—is more correctly understood as resulting from a culture of male domination.

Copyright 1952, 1980 Ruth Orkin.

(1859). Darwin asserted that living organisms change over long periods of time as a result of *natural selection,* a matter of four simple principles. First, all living things live to reproduce themselves. Second, the blueprint for reproduction is in the genes, the basic units of life that carry traits of one generation into the next. Third, some random variation in genes allows a species to "try out" new life patterns in a particular environment. This variation allows some organisms to survive better than others and pass on their advantageous genes to their offspring. Finally, over thousands of generations, the genetic patterns that promote reproduction survive and become dominant. In this way, as biologists say, a species *adapts* to its environment, and dominant traits emerge as the "nature" of the organism.

Sociobiologists claim that the large number of cultural universals reflects the fact that all humans are members of a single biological species. It is our common biology that underlies, for example, the apparently universal "double standard" of sexual behavior. As sex researcher Alfred Kinsey put it, "Among all people everywhere in the world, the male is more likely than the female to desire sex with a variety of partners" (quoted in Barash, 1981:49). But why?

We all know that children result from joining a woman's egg with a man's sperm. But the biological importance of a single sperm and of a single egg are quite different. For healthy men, sperm represent a "renewable resource" produced by the testes throughout most of the life course. A man releases hundreds of millions of sperm in a single ejaculation—technically, enough to fertilize every woman in North America (Barash, 1981:47). A newborn female's ovaries, however, contain her entire lifetime supply

of follicles, or immature eggs. A woman generally releases a single egg cell from her ovaries each month. So although a man is biologically capable of fathering thousands of offspring, a woman is able to bear only a relatively small number of children.

Given this biological difference, men reproduce their genes most efficiently by being promiscuous—readily engaging in sex. This scheme, however, opposes the reproductive interests of women. Each of a woman's relatively few pregnancies demands that she carry the child for nine months, give birth, and provide care for some time afterward. Thus efficient reproduction on the part of the woman depends on carefully selecting a mate whose qualities (beginning with the likelihood that he will simply stay around) will contribute to their child's survival and, later, successful reproduction.

The double standard certainly involves more than biology and is tangled up with the historical domination of women by men. But sociobiology suggests that this cultural pattern, like many others, has an underlying "bio-logic." Simply put, the double standard exists around the world because biological differences lead women and men everywhere to favor distinctive reproductive strategies.

Critical review Sociobiology has generated intriguing theories about the biological roots of some cultural patterns. But the approach remains controversial for two main reasons.

First, some critics fear that sociobiology may revive biological arguments, from a century ago, that claimed the superiority of one race or sex. But defenders counter that

APPLYING THEORY
CULTURE

	Structural-Functional Approach	Social-Conflict Approach	Sociobiology Approach
What is the level of analysis?	Macro-level	Macro-level	Macro-level
What is culture?	Culture is a system of behavior by which members of societies cooperate to meet their needs.	Culture is a system that benefits some people and disadvantages others.	Culture is a system of behavior that is partly shaped by human biology.
What is the foundation of culture?	Cultural patterns are rooted in a society's core values and beliefs.	Cultural patterns are rooted in a society's system of economic production.	Cultural patterns are rooted in humanity's biological evolution.
What core questions does the approach ask?	How does a cultural pattern help society to operate? What cultural patterns are found in all societies?	How does a cultural pattern benefit some people and harm others? How does a cultural pattern support social inequality?	How does a cultural pattern help a species adapt to its environment?

sociobiology rejects the past pseudoscience of racial superiority. In fact, they say, sociobiology unites all of humanity because all people share a single evolutionary history. Sociobiology does assert that men and women differ biologically in some ways that culture cannot overcome. But far from claiming that males are somehow more important than females, sociobiology emphasizes that both sexes are vital to human reproduction.

Second, say the critics, sociobiologists have little evidence to support their theories. Research to date suggests that biological forces do not determine human behavior in any rigid sense. Rather, humans *learn* behavior within a cultural system. The contribution of sociobiology, then, lies in explaining why some cultural patterns seem easier to learn than others (Barash, 1981).

The Applying Theory table summarizes the main lessons of each theoretical approach about culture. Because any analysis of culture requires a broad focus on the workings of society, these are all macro-level approaches. The symbolic-interaction approach, with its micro-level focus on behavior in everyday situations, is explored in Chapter 6, "Social Interaction in Everyday Life."

Culture and Human Freedom

This entire chapter leads us to wonder about an important question: To what extent are human beings, as cultural creatures, free? Does culture bind us to each other and to the past? Or does culture enhance our capacity for individual thought and independent choices?

CULTURE AS CONSTRAINT

As symbolic creatures, humans cannot live without culture. But the capacity for culture does have some drawbacks. We may be the only animals who name ourselves, but living in a symbolic world means that we are also the only creatures who experience alienation. In addition, culture is largely a matter of habit, which limits our choices and drives us to repeat troubling patterns, such as racial prejudice and sex discrimination, in each new generation.

Our society's emphasis on competitive achievement urges us toward excellence, yet this same pattern also isolates us from one another. Material things comfort us in some ways but divert us from the security and satisfaction that come from close relationships and spiritual strength.

CULTURE AS FREEDOM

For better or worse, human beings are cultural creatures, just as ants and bees are prisoners of their biology. But there is a crucial difference. Biological instincts create a ready-made world; culture, by contrast, forces us to choose as we make and remake a world for ourselves. No better evidence of this freedom exists than the cultural diversity of our own society and the even greater human diversity around the world.

Learning more about this cultural diversity is one goal shared by sociologists. The Thinking Globally box on page 86 offers some contrasts between the cultures of the United States and Canada. Wherever we may live, the better we understand the workings of the surrounding culture, the better prepared we are to use the freedom it offers us.

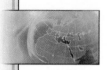
The United States and Canada: Are They Culturally Different?

The United States and Canada are two of the largest high-income countries in the world, and they share a common border of about 4,000 miles. But do the United States and Canada share the same culture?

One important point to make right away is that both nations are *multicultural.* Immigration has brought people from all over the world to both the United States and Canada. In both countries, most early immigrants came from Europe, but in recent decades most have come from nations in Asia and Latin America. The Canadian city of Vancouver, for example, has a Chinese community of about the same size as the Latino community in Los Angeles.

Canada and the United States differ in one important respect—

historically, Canada has had *two* dominant cultures: French (about 25 percent of the population) and British (roughly 40 percent). People of French ancestry are a large majority of the province of Quebec (where French is the official language) and a large minority of New Brunswick (which is officially bilingual).

Are the dominant values of Canada much the same as those we have described for the United States? Seymour Martin Lipset (1985) finds that they differ to some degree. The United States declared its independence from Great Britain in 1776, but Canada did not formally separate from Great Britain until 1982. Thus, Lipset continues, the dominant culture of Canada lies somewhere between the culture of the United States and that of Great Britain.

The culture of the United States is more individualistic, and Canada's is more collective. In the United States, individualism is seen in the historical importance of the cowboy, a self-sufficient loner, and even outlaws such as Jesse James and Billy the Kid are seen as heroes because they challenged authority. In Canada, by contrast, it is the Mountie—Canada's well-known police officer on horseback—who is looked on with great respect.

Politically, people in the United States tend to think individuals ought to do things for themselves. In Canada, however, much as in Great Britain, there is a strong sense that government should look after the interests of everyone. This is one reason, for example, that Canada has a much broader social welfare system (including universal health care) than the United States (the only high-income nation without such a program). It also helps explain the fact that about half of all households in the United States own one or more guns and the idea that individuals are entitled to own a gun is strong, though controversial. In Canada, by contrast, few households have a gun, and the government greatly restricts gun ownership, as in Great Britain.

WHAT DO YOU THINK?

1. Why do you think some Canadians feel that their way of life is overshadowed by that of the United States?

2. Ask your friends to name the capital city of Canada. Are you surprised by how many know the answer? Why or why not?

3. Why do many people in the United States not know very much about either Canada or Mexico, countries with which we share long borders?

Who members of a society celebrate as heroic is a good indication of people's cultural values. In the United States, outlaws such as Jesse James (and, later, Bonnie and Clyde) were regarded as heroes because they represented the strength of the individual standing up against authority. In Canada, by contrast, people have always looked up to the Mountie, who symbolizes society's authority over the individual.

The following learning tools will help you see what you know, identify what you still need to learn, and expand your understanding beyond the text. You can also visit this text's Companion Website™ at http://www.prenhall.com/macionis to find additional practice tests.

What Is Culture?

Culture is a way of life shared by members of a society. Several species display a limited capacity for culture, but only human beings rely on culture for survival. As the human brain evolved, the first elements of culture appeared some 3 million years ago; culture eventually replaced biological instincts as our species' primary strategy for survival.

The Elements of Culture

Culture relies on symbols to express meaning. Language is the symbolic system by which one generation transmits culture to the next. Values are culturally defined standards of what ought to be; beliefs are statements that people who share a culture hold to be true. Norms, which guide human behavior, are of two kinds: mores, which have great moral significance, and folkways, which are norms for everyday interaction.

Cultural Diversity

"High culture" refers to patterns that distinguish a society's elite; "popular culture" refers to widespread social patterns.

The United States stands among the most culturally diverse societies in the world. "Subculture" refers to distinctive cultural patterns supported by some part of a population and "counterculture" to patterns strongly opposed to a conventional way of life. Multiculturalism is an educational effort to encourage an awareness and appreciation of cultural diversity. Invention, discovery, and diffusion all generate cultural change and cultural diversity. Cultural lag results as some parts of a cultural system change faster than others. Ethnocentrism involves judging others by the standards of one's own culture. By contrast, "cultural relativism" means evaluating another culture according to its own standards. Global cultural patterns result from the worldwide flow of goods, information, and people.

Theoretical Analysis of Culture

Structural-functional analysis views culture as a relatively stable system built on core values; all cultural patterns function to maintain the overall system. The social-conflict approach envisions culture as a dynamic arena of inequality and conflict; cultural patterns benefit some categories of people more than others. Sociobiology studies how humanity's evolutionary past shapes cultural patterns.

Culture and Human Freedom

Culture can limit the choices we make; yet as cultural creatures, we have the capacity to shape and reshape our world to meet our needs and pursue our dreams.

KEY CONCEPTS

culture (p. 60) the values, beliefs, behavior, and material objects that together form a people's way of life

nonmaterial culture (p. 60) the ideas created by members of a society

material culture (p. 60) the physical things created by members of a society

culture shock (p. 61) personal disorientation when experiencing an unfamiliar way of life

symbol (p. 64) anything that carries a particular meaning recognized by people who share a culture

language (p. 66) a system of symbols that allows people to communicate with one another

cultural transmission (p. 66) the process by which one generation passes culture to the next

Sapir-Whorf thesis (p. 68) the idea that people see and understand the world through the cultural lens of language

values (p. 68) culturally defined standards that people use to decide what is desirable, good, and beautiful, and that serve as broad guidelines for social living

beliefs (p. 68) specific statements that people hold to be true

norms (p. 72) rules and expectations by which a society guides the behavior of its members

mores (p. 72) norms that are widely observed and have great moral significance

folkways (p. 72) norms for routine or casual interaction

social control (p. 73) attempts by society to regulate people's thoughts and behavior

technology (p. 73) knowledge that people use to make a way of life in their surroundings

high culture (p. 75) cultural patterns that distinguish a society's elite

popular culture (p. 75) cultural patterns that are widespread among a society's population

subculture (p. 75) cultural patterns that set apart some segment of a society's population

multiculturalism (p. 76) an educational program recognizing the cultural diversity of the United States and promoting the equality of all cultural traditions

Eurocentrism (p. 77) the dominance of European (especially English) cultural patterns

Afrocentrism (p. 78) emphasizing and promoting African cultural patterns

counterculture (p. 78) cultural patterns that strongly oppose those widely accepted within a society

cultural integration (p. 79) the close relationships among various elements of a cultural system

cultural lag (p. 79) the fact that some cultural elements change more quickly than others, disrupting a cultural system

ethnocentrism (p. 80) the practice of judging another culture by the standards of one's own culture

cultural relativism (p. 81) the practice of judging a culture by its own standards

cultural universals (p. 82) traits that are part of every known culture

sociobiology (p. 83) a theoretical approach that explores ways in which human biology affects how we create culture

SAMPLE TEST QUESTIONS

These questions are similar to those found in the test bank that accompanies this textbook.

Multiple-Choice Questions

1. **Of all the world's countries, the United States is the most**
   a. multicultural.
   b. culturally uniform.
   c. slowly changing.
   d. resistant to cultural diversity.

2. **Ideas created by members of a society are part of**
   a. high culture.
   b. material culture.
   c. norms.
   d. nonmaterial culture.

3. **Sociologists define a symbol as**
   a. any gesture that insults others.
   b. any element of material culture.
   c. anything that has meaning to people who share a culture.
   d. cultural patterns that cause culture shock.

4. **U.S. culture holds a strong belief in**
   a. the traditions of the past.
   b. individuality.
   c. equality of condition for all.
   d. all of the above.

5. **Cheating on a final examination is an example of violating campus**
   a. folkways.
   b. symbols.
   c. mores.
   d. high culture.

6. *Subculture* **refers to**
   a. a part of the population lacking culture.
   b. elements of popular culture.
   c. people who embrace high culture.
   d. cultural patterns that set apart a segment of a society's population.

7. **Which region of the United States has the largest share of people who speak a language other than English at home?**
   a. the Southwest
   b. the Northeast
   c. the Northwest
   d. the South

8. **Sociologists use the term "cultural lag" to refer to**
   a. the slowing of cultural change in the United States.
   b. the fact that some societies change faster than others do.
   c. that fact that some elements of culture change faster than others.
   d. people who are less cultured than others.

9. *Ethnocentrism* **refers to**
   a. taking pride in your ethnicity.

b. judging another culture using the standards of your own culture.

c. seeing another culture as better than your own.

d. judging another culture by its own standards.

10. **The theoretical approach that focuses on the link between culture and social inequality is the**

a. structural-functional approach.

b. social-conflict approach.

c. symbolic-interaction approach.

d. sociobiology approach.

ANSWERS: 1(a); 2(d); 3(c); 4(b); 5(c); 6(d); 7(a); 8(c); 9(b); 10(b).

Essay Questions

1. In the United States, hot dogs, hamburgers, French fries, and ice cream have long been considered national favorites. What cultural patterns help explain the love of these kinds of foods?

2. From what you have learned in this chapter, do you think that a global culture is emerging? Do you regard the prospect of a global culture as positive or negative? Why?

APPLICATIONS & EXERCISES

1. New words are created all the time. What was going on in the United States that helps explain the creation of the following new words (Herzog, 2004): *sweatshop* (1892), *motel* (1925), *supermarket* (1933), *teenager* (1938), *workaholic* (1971), *couch potato* (1976), and *soccer mom* (1996)?

2. Find someone on campus who has lived in another country, and ask how the culture of that society differs from the way of life here. Look for ways in which the other person sees U.S. culture differently from people who have lived here all their lives.

3. Watch an animated Disney film such as *Finding Nemo, The Lion King, The Little Mermaid, Aladdin,* or *Pocahontas.* One reason for the popularity of these films is that they all share cultural themes. Using the list of key values of U.S. culture on page 69 of this chapter as a guide, what makes the film you selected especially "American"?

 **INVESTIGATE** *with* **Research Navigator**

Follow the instructions on page 27 of this text to access the features of **Research Navigator**™. Once at the Web site, enter your Login Name and Password. Then, to use the **ContentSelect**™ database, enter keywords such as "ethnocentrism," "multiculturalism," and "immigration," and the search engine will supply relevant and recent scholarly and popular press publications. Use the *New York Times* **Search-by-Subject Archive** to find recent news articles related to sociology and the **Link Library** feature to find relevant Web links organized by the key terms associated with this chapter.

4

Society

What factors shape society?

Why do societies change?

How have Karl Marx, Max Weber, and Emile Durkheim increased our understanding of modern societies?

Sididi Ag Inaka has never used instant messaging, logged on to the Internet, or even spoken on a cell phone. Does such a person really exist in today's high-technology world? Well, how about this: Neither Inaka nor anyone in his family has ever been to a movie, watched television, or even read a newspaper.

Are these people visitors from another planet? Prisoners on some remote island? Not at all. They are Tuareg nomads who wander over the vast Sahara Desert in the western African nation of Mali. Known as the "blue men of the desert" for the flowing blue robes worn by both men and women, the Tuareg herd camels, goats, and sheep and live in camps where the sand blows and the daytime temperature often reaches 120 degrees Fahrenheit. Life is hard, but most Tuareg try to hold on to traditional ways. With a stern look, Inaka says, "My father was a nomad. His father was a nomad. I am a nomad. My children will be nomads."

The Tuareg are among the world's poorest people. When the rains fail to come, they and their animals are at risk of their lives. Even in good times, Inaka and his people are a society set apart, with little knowledge of the larger world and its advanced technology. But Inaka does not complain: "This is the life of my ancestors. This is the life that we know" (Buckley, 1996; Matloff, 1997; Lovgren, 1998). ■

The societies that exist around the world can be quite different from our own. But what is a society? What makes societies different? How and why do they change over time?

Society refers to *people who interact in a defined territory and share a culture.* In this chapter, we shall learn more about human societies with the help of four important sociologists. We begin with the approach of **Gerhard Lenski,** who describes how societies have changed over the past 10,000 years. Lenski points to the importance of *technology* in shaping any society. Then we turn to three of sociology's founders. **Karl Marx,** like Lenski, took a long historical view of societies. But Marx's story of society is all about *social conflict* that arises from how people work within an economic system to produce material goods. **Max Weber** tells a different tale, showing that the power of *ideas* shapes society. Weber contrasted the traditional thinking of simple societies with the rational thought that dominates complex societies today. Finally, **Emile Durkheim** helps us see the different ways that traditional and modern societies hang together.

All four visions of society answer a number of important questions: What makes the way of life of people such as the Tuareg of the Sahara so different from your life as a college student in the United States? How and why do all societies change? What forces divide a society? What forces hold a society together? This chapter will provide answers to all of these questions as we look at the work of important sociologists.

Gerhard Lenski:
Society and Technology

Members of our society, who take instant messaging and television, as well as schools and hospitals, for granted, must

 To learn more about Lenski's work, visit http://www.faculty. rsu.edu/~felwell/Theorists/ Lenski/Index.htm

wonder at the nomads of the Sahara, who live the same simple life their ancestors did centuries ago. The work of Gerhard Lenski (Nolan & Lenski, 2004) helps us understand the great differences among societies that have existed throughout human history.

Lenski uses the term **sociocultural evolution** to mean *changes that occur as a society gains new technology.* With only simple technology, societies such as the Tuareg have little control over nature, so they can support just a small number of people. Societies with complex technology such as cars and cell phones, while not necessarily "better," support hundreds of millions of people in far more affluent ways of life.

Inventing or adopting new technology sends ripples of change throughout a society. When our ancestors first discovered how to use wind to move a boat using a sail, they created a device that would take them to new lands, greatly expand their economy, and increase their military power. In addition, the more technology a society has, the faster it changes. Technologically simple societies change very slowly; Sididi Ag Inaka says he lives "the life of my ancestors." How many people in U.S. society can say that they live the way their grandparents or great-grandparents did? Modern, high-technology societies such as our own change so fast that people usually experience major social changes during a single lifetime. Imagine how surprised your great-grandmother would be to hear about beepers and instant messaging, computer matchmaking and phone sex, artificial hearts and test-tube babies, space shuttles and smart bombs.

YOUR TURN

Which of the items just mentioned would most amaze your great-grandmother? Why?

Drawing on Lenski's work, we will describe five types of societies, defined by their technology: hunting and gathering societies, horticultural and pastoral societies, agrarian societies, industrial societies, and postindustrial societies.

HUNTING AND GATHERING SOCIETIES

In the simplest of all societies, people live by **hunting and gathering,** *the use of simple tools to hunt animals and gather vegetation.* From the time that our species appeared 3 million years ago until about 12,000 years ago, *all* humans were hunters and gatherers. Even in 1800, many hunting and gathering societies could be found around the world. But

In technologically simple societies, successful hunting wins men great praise. However, the gathering of vegetation by women is a more dependable and easily available source of nutrition.

today just a few remain, including the Aka and Pygmies of Central Africa, the Bushmen of southwestern Africa, the Aborigines of Australia, the Kaska Indians of northwestern Canada, and the Batek and Semai of Malaysia.

With little ability to control their environment, hunters and gatherers spend most of their time looking for game and collecting plants to eat. Only in lush areas with lots of food do hunters and gatherers have much free time. Because it takes a large amount of land to support even a few people, hunting and gathering societies have just a few dozen members. They must also be nomadic, moving on to find new sources of vegetation or to follow migrating animals. Although they may return to favored sites, they rarely form permanent settlements.

Hunting and gathering societies depend on the family to do many things. The family must get and distribute food, protect its members, and teach the children. Everyone's life is much the same; people spend most of their time getting their next meal. Age and gender have some effect on what individuals do. Healthy adults do most of the work, leaving the very young and the very old to help out as they can. Women gather vegetation—which provides most of the food—while men take on the less certain job of hunting. Although men and women perform different tasks, most hunters and gatherers probably see the sexes as having about the same social importance (Leacock, 1978).

What would it be like to live in a society with simple technology? That's the premise of the television show *Survivor*. What advantages do societies with simple technology afford their members? What disadvantages do you see?

Hunting and gathering societies usually have a *shaman*, or spiritual leader, who enjoys high prestige but has to work to find food like everyone else. In short, people in hunting and gathering societies come close to being socially equal.

Hunters and gatherers use simple weapons—the spear, bow and arrow, and stone knife—but rarely to wage war. Their real enemy is the forces of nature: Storms and droughts can kill off their food supply, and there is little they can do for someone who has a serious accident or illness. Being at risk in this way encourages people to cooperate and share, a strategy that raises everyone's chances of survival. But the truth is that many die in childhood, and no more than half reach the age of twenty (Lenski, Nolan, & Lenski, 1995:104).

During the past century, societies with more powerful technology have closed in on the few remaining hunters and gatherers, reducing their food supply. As a result, hunting and gathering societies are disappearing from Earth.

Fortunately, study of this way of life has given us valuable information about human history and our basic ties to the natural world.

YOUR TURN

What do you think are some of the important lessons we can learn from studying hunting and gathering societies?

HORTICULTURAL AND PASTORAL SOCIETIES

Ten to twelve thousand years ago, as the timeline inside the front cover shows, a new technology began to change the lives of human beings. People discovered **horticulture,** *the use of hand tools to raise crops.* Using a hoe to work the soil and a digging stick to punch holes in the ground to plant seeds may not seem like something that would change the world, but these inventions allowed people to give up gathering in favor of growing their own food. The first humans to plant gardens lived in fertile regions of the Middle East. Soon after, cultural diffusion spread this knowledge to Latin America and Asia and eventually all over the world.

Not all societies were quick to give up hunting and gathering for horticulture. Hunters and gatherers living where food was plentiful probably saw little reason to change their ways. People living in dry regions (such as the Sahara in western Africa or the Middle East) or mountainous areas found little use for horticulture because they could not grow much anyway. Such people (including the Tuareg) were more likely to adopt **pastoralism,** *the domestication of animals.* Today, societies that mix horticulture and pastoralism can be found throughout South America, Africa, and Asia. "In the *Times*" takes a closer look at some of the problems facing pastoral communities that exist in today's world.

Growing plants and raising animals greatly increased food production, so populations expanded from dozens to hundreds of people. Pastoralists remained nomadic, leading their herds to fresh grazing lands. But horticulturalists formed settlements, moving only when the soil gave out. Joined by trade, these settlements formed societies with populations reaching into the thousands.

Once a society is capable of producing a *material surplus*—more resources than are needed to support the population—not everyone has to work at providing food. Greater specialization results: Some make crafts, while others engage in trade, cut hair, apply tattoos, or serve as priests. Compared to hunting and gathering societies, horticultural and pastoral societies are more socially diverse.

But being more productive does not make a society "better" in every sense. As some families produce more than others, they become richer and more powerful. Horticultural and pastoral societies have greater inequality, with elites using government power—and military force—to serve their own interests. But leaders do not have the ability to communicate or to travel over large distances, so they can control only a small number of people, rather than vast empires.

Religion also differs among types of societies. Hunters and gatherers believe that many spirits inhabit the world. Horticulturalists, however, are more likely to think of one God as Creator. Pastoral societies carry this belief further, seeing God as directly involved in the well-being of the entire world. This view of God ("The Lord is my shepherd . . ."—Psalm 23) is common among members of our own society because Christianity, Islam, and Judaism all began in pastoral societies of the Middle East.

AGRARIAN SOCIETIES

About 5,000 years ago, another revolution in technology was taking place in the Middle East, one that would end up changing the entire world. This was the discovery of **agriculture,** *large-scale cultivation using plows harnessed to animals or more powerful energy sources.* So important was the invention of the animal-drawn plow, along with other breakthroughs of the period—including irrigation, the wheel, writing, numbers, and the use of various metals—that this moment in history is often called "the dawn of civilization."

Using animal-drawn plows, farmers could cultivate fields far bigger than the garden-sized plots planted by horticulturalists. Plows have the added advantage of turning and aerating the soil, making it more fertile. As a result, farmers could work the same land for generations, encouraging the development of permanent settlements. With the ability to grow a surplus of food and to transport goods using animal-powered wagons, agrarian societies greatly expanded in size and population. About 100 C.E., for example, the agrarian Roman Empire contained some 70 million people spread over 2 million square miles (Nolan & Lenski, 2004).

Greater production meant even more specialization. Now there were dozens and dozens of distinct occupations, from farmers to builders to metalworkers. With so many people producing so many different things, people invented money as a common standard of exchange, and the old barter system—by which people traded one thing for another—was abandoned.

Of Egypt's 130 pyramids, the Great Pyramids at Giza are the largest. Each of the three major structures stands more than forty stories high and is composed of 3 million massive stone blocks. Some 4,500 years ago, tens of thousands of people labored to construct these pyramids so that one man, the pharaoh, might have a godlike monument for his tomb. Clearly social inequality in this agrarian society was striking.

Agrarian societies have extreme social inequality, typically more than modern societies such as our own. In most cases, a large share of the people are peasants or slaves, who do most of the work. Elites therefore have time for more "refined" activities, including the study of philosophy, art, and literature. This explains the historical link between "high culture" and social privilege noted in Chapter 3.

Among hunters and gatherers and also among horticulturalists, women provide most of the food, which gives them social importance. Agriculture, however, raises men to a position of social dominance. Using the metal plow pulled by large animals, men take charge of food production in agrarian societies. Women are left with the support tasks,

Times

The New York Times

February 5, 2005

Animal Herders of 23 Lands Meet and Swap Stories

By MARC LACEY

ADDIS ABABA, Ethiopia—Bring together pastoralists from 23 countries around the globe and, not surprisingly, the talk will inevitably shift to the sheep, goats, cows and other more exotic animals that play such a central part in their lives.

The Iranian contingent at an international gathering of nomads held this week in the southernmost reaches of Ethiopia amazed others with their descriptions of two-humped camels, which are not known in these parts.

An Indian delegate to the conference, which was convened in the tiny village of Turmi, several hundred miles south of the Ethiopian capital, near the border with Kenya, said fellow herders could not believe that he raised domesticated buffalo.

The herders, from Mauritius to Mongolia, were united on one overriding issue: their common struggle against encroachment on their grazing land.

"Increasing gaps between poor pastoralists and rich others, increasing frustration at erosion of rights and loss of land and increasing destitution, will lead to conflict and migration," the 120 leaders from herder communities said in a statement at the close of the five-day conference.

Pastoralists have gathered in the past to discuss their woes, but this meeting was deemed the first broad international gathering to be staged in a pastoral community. With the nomads' plane fares picked up by the United Nations, the session drew Mongolian camel owners and Spanish shepherds, as well as herders from such far-flung places as Kazakhstan, Chile, Burkino Faso and Switzerland.

"Imagine you're an isolated tribe in the mountains of Iran, or somewhere in Argentina or Kenya, and all of a sudden you realize you're not alone," said Taghi Farvar, who comes from a pastoral tribe in Iran and works at that country's Center for Sustainable Development.

The attendees stayed in tents in a part of Ethiopia so remote that it is considered too harsh for city dwellers. But it was nothing for this lot, some of whom trek hundreds of miles in search of fresh pasture. Making the group feel at home, livestock ambled by as the nomads discussed their threatened existence.

"Globally, pastoralists are on the whole being marginalized by mainstream societies," said Paul Hebert, head of the United Nations Office for Coordination of Humanitarian Affairs, which organized the conference through its Pastoral Communication Initiative. "We're trying to create some political space for them."

With many translators on hand, the pastoralists discussed how education

---

such as weeding and carrying water to the fields (Boulding, 1976; Fisher, 1979).

In agrarian societies, religion reinforces the power of elites by defining both loyalty and hard work as moral obligations. Many of the "Wonders of the Ancient World," such as the Great Wall of China and the Great Pyramids of Egypt, were possible only because emperors and pharaohs had almost absolute power and were able to control a large political system and order their people to work for a lifetime without pay.

To learn more about the seven wonders of the ancient world, go to http://ce.eng.usf.edu/pharos/wonders/list.html

Of the societies described so far, agrarian societies have the most social inequality. Agrarian technology also gives people a greater range of life choices, which is the reason that agrarian societies differ more from one another than horticultural and pastoral societies do.

INDUSTRIAL SOCIETIES

Industrialism, which first took hold in the rich nations of today's world, is *the production of goods using advanced sources of energy to drive large machinery.* Until the industrial era began, the major source of energy had been the muscles of humans and the animals they tended. Around the year 1750, people turned to water power and then steam boilers to operate mills and factories filled with larger and larger machines.

Industrial technology gave people such power over their environment that change took place faster than ever before. It is probably correct to say that the new industrial societies changed more in one century than they had over the course of the previous thousand years. As explained in Chapter 1 ("The Sociological Perspective"), change was so rapid that it sparked the birth of sociology itself. By 1900,

could be provided in mobile schools so that their children could learn without abandoning their culture. They debated the role of women in their cultures, which varied from political leaders to pawns. They motivated each other to keep fighting for nomad rights.

Cattle rustling also popped up in discussions, as well as the use of cattle as payment for brides, and techniques for making milk last longer before spoiling.

There are more than 50 million pastoralists in sub-Saharan Africa, more than any other continent. Ethiopia alone has eight million people—12 percent of its population—who move from place to place with their animals. Experts say their livelihood contributes about a quarter of the country's gross domestic product.

Each person at the conference came away with a different lesson learned. Mr. Farvar, a white-bearded Iranian, said he had learned from Spanish shepherds that the government there protected their migratory routes by law, even if animals must stroll right through cities. Such nomad-friendly policies, he said, might have helped the 300 sheep that were killed in a traffic accident in the southern Iranian city of Shiraz not long ago.

Dolat Ram Guzzar, who raises buffalo, goats and cows in northwest India, said he had picked up new techniques for preserving milk, which is a major part of his diet. The members of the Iranian delegation offered a presentation on how they boiled sour milk and then dried it in the sun, producing milk balls that are nutritious and can be kept for years. Amazed delegates even got to sample some of the balls.

"We're all different, but we share so much," Mr. Farvar said after the conference, as he watched an Ethiopian sheepherder struggle to get a flock to cross a busy street in the capital. "If you take mobility from pastoralists, we're as good as dead. We feel sorry for those of you who live sedentary lives."

WHAT DO YOU THINK?

1. What are some of the problems with living as a pastoralist in today's world?

2. Do you think societies should support such people in their traditional ways or encourage them to modernize? Why?

3. Would you require young people in pastoral societies to attend school? What if that meant that few young people would continue in the pastoral ways of their parents?

railroads crossed the land, steamships traveled the seas, and steel-framed skyscrapers reached far higher than any of the old cathedrals that symbolized the agrarian age.

But that was only the beginning. Soon after, automobiles allowed people to move quickly almost anywhere, and electricity powered homes full of modern "conveniences" such as refrigerators, washing machines, air conditioners, and electronic entertainment centers. Electronic communication, beginning with the telegraph and the telephone and followed by radio and television, gave people the ability to reach others instantly, all over the world.

Work also changed. In agrarian communities, most men and women worked in the home or in the fields nearby. Industrialization drew people away from home to factories situated near energy sources (such as coalfields) that power their machinery. The result is that workers lost close working relationships, strong family ties, and many of the traditional values, beliefs, and customs that guide agrarian life.

December 28, Moray, in the Andes highlands of Peru. We are high in the mountains in a small community of several dozen families, miles from the nearest electric line or paved road. At about 12,000 feet, breathing is hard for people not used to the thin air, so we walk slowly. But hard work is no problem for the man and his son tilling a field near their home with a horse and plow. Too poor to buy a tractor, these people till the land in the same way that their ancestors did 500 years ago.

With industrialization, occupational specialization became greater than ever. Today, the kind of work you do has a

Sociocultural Evolution

Type of Society	Historical Period	Productive Technology	Population Size
Hunting and Gathering Societies	Only type of society until about 12,000 years ago; still common several centuries ago; the few examples remaining today are threatened with extinction	Primitive weapons	25–40 people
Horticultural and Pastoral Societies	From about 12,000 years ago, with decreasing numbers after about 3000 B.C.E.	Horticultural societies use hand tools for cultivating plants; pastoral societies are based on the domestication of animals	Settlements of several hundred people, connected through trading ties to form societies of several thousand people
Agrarian Societies	From about 5,000 years ago, with large but decreasing numbers today	Animal-drawn plow	Millions of people
Industrial Societies	From about 1750 to the present	Advanced sources of energy; mechanized production	Millions of people
Postindustrial Societies	Emerging in recent decades	Computers that support an information-based economy	Millions of people

lot to do with your standard of living, so people now often size up one another in terms of their jobs rather than according to their family ties, as agrarian people do. Rapid change and people's tendency to move from place to place also make social life more anonymous, increase cultural diversity, and promote subcultures and countercultures, as described in Chapter 3 ("Culture").

Industrial technology changes the family, too, reducing its traditional importance as the center of social life. No longer does the family serve as the main setting for work, learning, and religious worship. As Chapter 18 ("Families") explains, technological change also plays a part in making families more diverse, with a greater share of single people, divorced people, single-parent families, and stepfamilies.

Perhaps the greatest effect of industrialization has been to raise living standards, which increased fivefold in the United States over the past century. Although at first it only benefits the elite few, industrial technology is so much more

productive that incomes rise over time and people have longer and more comfortable lives. Even social inequality decreases slightly, as explained in Chapter 10 ("Social Stratification"), because industrial societies provide extended schooling and greater political rights. Around the world, industrialization has had the effect of increasing the demand for a greater political voice, a pattern evident in South Korea, Taiwan, the People's Republic of China, the nations of Eastern Europe, and the former Soviet Union.

POSTINDUSTRIAL SOCIETIES

Many industrial societies, including the United States, have now entered another phase of technological development, and we can extend Lenski's analysis to take account of recent trends. A generation ago, the sociologist Daniel Bell (1973) coined the term **postindustrialism** to refer to *technology that supports an information-based economy.*

Settlement Pattern	Social Organization	Examples
Nomadic	Family-centered; specialization limited to age and sex; little social inequality	Pygmies of Central Africa Bushmen of southwestern Africa Aborigines of Australia Semai of Malaysia Kaska Indians of Canada
Horticulturalists form small permanent settlements; pastoralists are nomadic	Family-centered; religious system begins to develop; moderate specialization; increased social inequality	Middle Eastern societies about 5000 B.C.E. Various societies today in New Guinea and other Pacific islands Ya̧nomamö today in South America
Cities become common, but they generally contain only a small proportion of the population	Family loses significance as distinct religious, political, and economic systems emerge; extensive specialization; increased social inequality	Egypt during construction of the Great Pyramids Medieval Europe Numerous predominantly agrarian societies of the world today
Cities contain most of the population	Distinct religious, political, economic, educational, and family systems; highly specialized; marked social inequality persists, lessening somewhat over time	Most societies today in Europe and North America, Australia, and Japan, which generate most of the world's industrial production
Population remains concentrated in cities	Similar to industrial societies, with information processing and other service work gradually replacing industrial production	Industrial societies noted above are now entering the postindustrial stage

Production in industrial societies centers on factories and machinery generating material goods; today, postindustrial production relies on computers and other electronic devices that create, process, store, and apply information. Just as people in industrial societies learn mechanical skills, people in postindustrial societies such as ours develop information-based skills and carry out their work using computers and other forms of high-technology communication.

As Chapter 16 ("The Economy and Work") explains, a postindustrial society uses less and less of its labor force for industrial production. At the same time, more jobs become available for clerical workers, teachers, writers, sales managers, and marketing representatives, all of whom process information.

The Information Revolution, which is at the heart of postindustrial society, is most evident in rich nations, yet new information technology affects the whole world. As discussed in Chapter 3 ("Culture"), a worldwide flow of goods, people, and information now links societies and has advanced a global culture. In this sense, the postindustrial society is at the heart of globalization.

The Summing Up table reviews how technology shapes societies at different stages of sociocultural evolution.

THE LIMITS OF TECHNOLOGY

More complex technology has made life better by raising productivity, reducing infectious disease, and sometimes just relieving boredom. But technology provides no quick fix for social problems. Poverty, for example, remains a reality for tens of millions of women and men in the United States (detailed in Chapter 11, "Social Class in the United States") and 1 billion people worldwide (see Chapter 12, "Global Stratification").

Technology also creates new problems that our ancestors (and people like Sididi Ag Inaka today) hardly could

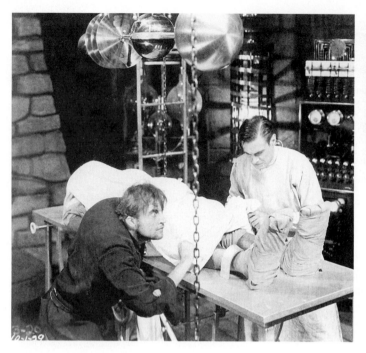

Does advancing technology make society better? In some ways, perhaps. However, many films—as far back as *Frankenstein* (left) in 1931 and as recently as *Minority Report* (above) in 2002—have expressed the concern that new technology not only solves old problems but creates new ones. All the sociological theorists discussed in this chapter shared this ambivalent view of the modern world.

imagine. Industrial and postindustrial societies give us more personal freedom, but often we lack the sense of community that was part of preindustrial life. Further, although technology can be used for good, the most powerful nations in the world today have stockpiles of nuclear weapons that could send the world back to the Stone Age—if we survived at all.

Advancing technology has also threatened the physical environment. Each stage in sociocultural evolution has introduced more powerful sources of energy and increased our appetite for Earth's resources. Ask yourself whether we can continue to pursue material prosperity without permanently damaging our planet (see Chapter 22, "Population, Urbanization, and Environment").

In some ways, technological advances have improved life and brought the world's people closer. But establishing peace, ensuring justice, and protecting the environment are problems that technology alone cannot solve.

YOUR TURN

Why do you think many people are quick to see the advantages of advancing technology but slow to see many of its negative consequences?

Karl Marx: Society and Conflict

The first of our classic visions of society comes from Karl Marx (1818–1883), an early giant in the field of sociology whose influence continues even today. A keen observer of how the Industrial Revolution changed Europe, Marx spent most of his adult life in London, the capital of what was then the vast British Empire. He was awed by the size and productive power of the new factories going up all over Britain. Along with other industrial nations, Great Britain was producing more goods than ever before, drawing resources from around the world and churning out products at a dizzying rate.

 Visit the Dead Sociologists' Society to learn more about Marx: http://www2.pfeiffer.edu/~lridener/DSS/INDEX.HTML

What astounded Marx even more was how the riches produced by this new technology ended up in the hands of only a few people. As he walked around the city of London, he could see for himself how a handful of aristocrats and industrialists lived in fabulous mansions staffed by servants, where they enjoyed both luxury and privilege. At the same time, most people labored long hours for low wages and lived in slums. Some even slept in the streets, where they were likely to die young from diseases brought on by cold and poor nutrition.

Marx saw his society in terms of a basic contradiction: In a country so rich, how could so many people be so poor?

Just as important, he asked, how can this situation be changed? Many people think Karl Marx set out to tear societies apart. But he was motivated by compassion and wanted to help a badly divided society create a new and just social order.

At the heart of Marx's thinking is the idea of **social conflict,** *the struggle between segments of society over valued resources.* Social conflict can, of course, take many forms: Individuals quarrel, colleges have longstanding sports rivalries, and nations go to war. For Marx, however, the most important type of social conflict was *class conflict* arising from the way a society produces material goods.

SOCIETY AND PRODUCTION

Living in the nineteenth century, Marx observed the early decades of industrial capitalism in Europe. This economic system, Marx explained, turned a small part of the population into **capitalists,** *people who own and operate factories and other businesses in pursuit of profits.* A capitalist tries to make a profit by selling a product for more than it costs to produce. Capitalism turns most of the population into industrial workers, whom Marx called **proletarians,** *people who sell their labor for wages.* To Marx, a system of capitalist production always ends up creating conflict between capitalists and workers. To keep profits high, capitalists keep wages low. But workers want higher wages. Since profits and wages come from the same pool of funds, the result is conflict. As Marx saw it, this conflict could end only with the end of capitalism itself.

All societies are composed of **social institutions,** *the major spheres of social life, or societal subsystems, organized to meet human needs.* Examples of social institutions include the economy, political system, family, religion, and education. In his analysis of society, Marx argued that one institution—the economy—dominates all the others and defines the true nature of a society. Drawing on the philosophical approach called *materialism,* which says that how humans produce material goods shapes their experiences, Marx believed that the other social institutions all operate in a way that supports a society's economy. Lenski focused on how technology molds a society, but Marx argued that the economy is a society's "real foundation" (1959:43, orig. 1859).

Marx viewed the economic system as society's *infrastructure* (*infra* is Latin, meaning "below"). Other social institutions, including the family, the political system, and religion, are built on this foundation, form society's *superstructure,* and support the economy. Marx's theory is illustrated in Figure 4–1. For example, under capitalism, the legal system protects capitalists' wealth just as the family

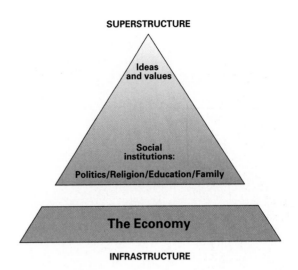

FIGURE 4-1 Karl Marx's Model of Society

This diagram illustrates Marx's materialist view that the system of economic production shapes the entire society. Economic production involves both technology (industry, in the case of capitalism) and social relationships (for capitalism, the relationship between the capitalists, who own the factories and businesses, and the workers, who are the source of labor). On this infrastructure, or foundation, rests society's superstructure, which includes its major social institutions as well as core cultural values and ideas. Marx maintained that every part of a society supports the economic system.

allows capitalists to pass their property from one generation to the next.

Marx was well aware that most people living in industrial-capitalist societies do not see how capitalism shapes the entire operation of their society. Most people, in fact, see the right to own private property or pass it on to children as "natural." In the same way, many of us tend to see rich people as having "earned" their money through long years of schooling and hard work; we see the poor, on the other hand, as lacking skills and the personal drive to make more of themselves. Marx rejected this type of thinking, calling it **false consciousness,** *explanations of social problems as the shortcomings of individuals rather than as the flaws of society.* Marx was saying, in effect, that it is not "people" who make society so unequal, it is the system of capitalist production. False consciousness, he continued, hurts people by hiding the real cause of their problems.

Karl Marx, shown here at work on the *Manifesto of the Communist Party* with his friend, benefactor, and collaborator Friedrich Engels, was surely the pioneering sociologist who had the greatest influence on the world as a whole. Through the second half of the last century, 1 billion people—nearly one-fifth of humanity—lived in societies organized on Marxist principles.

CONFLICT AND HISTORY

For Marx, conflict is the engine that drives social change. Sometimes societies change at a slow, *evolutionary* rate. But they may erupt in rapid, *revolutionary* change.

To Marx, early hunters and gatherers formed primitive communist societies. *Communism* is a system by which people commonly own and equally share the food and other things they produce. People in hunting and gathering societies do not have much, but they share what they have. In addition, because everyone does the same kind of work, there is little chance of social conflict.

With technological advance comes social inequality. Among horticultural, pastoral, and early agrarian societies—which Marx lumped together as the "ancient world"—warfare was frequent, and the victors made their captives slaves.

Agriculture brings still more wealth to a society's elite but does little for most other people, who labor as serfs and are barely better off than slaves. As Marx saw it, the state supported the feudal system (in which the elite or nobility had all the power), assisted by the church, which claimed that this arrangement was God's will. This is why Marx thought that feudalism was simply "exploitation, veiled by religious and political illusions" (Marx & Engels, 1972:337, orig. 1848).

Gradually, new productive forces started to break down the feudal order. As trade steadily increased, cities grew and merchants and skilled craftsworkers formed the new capitalist class or *bourgeoisie* (a French word meaning "people of the town"). After 1800, the bourgeoisie also controlled factories, becoming richer and richer so that they soon rivaled the ancient landowning nobility. For their part, the nobles looked down their noses at this upstart "commercial" class; but in time, these capitalists took control of European societies. To Marx's way of thinking, then, new technology was only part of the Industrial Revolution; it also served as a class revolution in which capitalists overthrew the old agrarian elite.

Industrialization also led to the growth of the proletariat. English landowners converted fields once plowed by serfs into grazing land for sheep to produce wool for the textile mills. Forced from the land, millions of people migrated to cities to work in factories. Marx envisioned these workers one day joining together to form a revolutionary class that would overthrow the capitalist system.

CAPITALISM AND CLASS CONFLICT

"The history of all hitherto existing society is the history of class struggles." With these words, Marx and his collaborator, Friedrich Engels, began their best-known statement, the *Manifesto of the Communist Party* (1972:335, orig. 1848). Industrial capitalism, like earlier types of society, contains two major social classes—the ruling class, whose members (capitalists or bourgeoisie) own productive property, and the oppressed (proletarians), who sell their labor—reflecting the two basic positions in the productive system. Like masters and slaves in the ancient world, and like nobles and serfs in feudal systems, capitalists and proletarians are engaged in class conflict today. Currently, as in the past, one class controls the other as productive property. Marx used the term **class conflict** (and sometimes *class struggle*) to refer to *conflict between entire classes over the distribution of a society's wealth and power.*

Class conflict is nothing new. What distinguishes the conflict in capitalist society, Marx pointed out, is how out in the open it is. Agrarian nobles and serfs, for all their differences, were bound together by traditions and mutual obligations. Industrial capitalism dissolved those ties so that loyalty and honor were replaced by "naked self-interest." Because the proletarians had no personal ties to the capitalists, Marx saw no reason for them to put up with their oppression.

Marx knew that revolution still would not come easily. First, workers must *become aware* of their oppression and see capitalism as its true cause. Second, they must *organize and act* to address their problems. This means that false consciousness must be replaced with **class consciousness,** *workers' recognition of themselves as a class unified in opposition to capitalists and ultimately to capitalism itself.* Because the inhumanity of early capitalism was plain for him to see, Marx concluded that industrial workers would soon rise up to destroy this economic system.

How would the capitalists react? Their wealth made them strong. But Marx saw a weakness in the capitalist armor. Motivated by a desire for personal gain, capitalists feared competition with other capitalists. Marx predicted, therefore, that capitalists would be slow to band together despite their common interests. In addition, he reasoned, capitalists kept employees' wages low in order to maximize profits, which made the workers' misery grow ever greater. In the long run, Marx believed, capitalists would bring about their own undoing.

CAPITALISM AND ALIENATION

Marx also condemned capitalist society for producing **alienation,** *the experience of isolation and misery resulting from powerlessness.* To the capitalists, workers are nothing more than a source of labor, to be hired and fired at will. Dehumanized by their jobs (repetitive factory work in the past and processing orders on a computer today), workers find little satisfaction and feel unable to improve their situation. Here we see another contradiction of capitalist society: As people develop technology to gain power over the world, the capitalist economy gains more control over people.

Marx noted four ways in which capitalism alienates workers:

1. **Alienation from the act of working.** Ideally, people work to meet their needs and to develop their personal potential. Capitalism, however, denies workers a say in
 what they make or how they make it. Further, much of the work is a constant repetition of routine tasks. The fact that today we replace workers with machines

whenever possible would not have surprised Marx. As far as he was concerned, capitalism had turned human beings into machines long ago.

2. **Alienation from the products of work.** The product of work belongs not to workers but to capitalists, who sell it for profit. Thus, Marx reasoned, the more of themselves workers invest in their work, the more they lose.

3. **Alienation from other workers.** Through work, Marx claimed, people build bonds of community. Industrial capitalism, however, makes work competitive rather than cooperative, setting each person apart from everyone else and offering little chance for human companionship.

4. **Alienation from human potential.** Industrial capitalism alienates workers from their human potential. Marx argued that a worker "does not fulfill himself in his work but denies himself, has a feeling of misery rather than well-being, does not freely develop his physical and mental energies, but is physically exhausted and mentally debased. The worker, therefore, feels himself to be at home only during his leisure time, whereas at work he feels homeless" (1964a: 124–25, orig. 1844). In short, industrial capitalism turns an activity that should express the best qualities in human beings into a dull and dehumanizing experience.

Marx viewed alienation, in its various forms, as a barrier to social change. But he hoped that industrial workers would overcome their alienation by uniting into a true social class, aware of the cause of their problems and ready to change society.

Can you think of workplace settings that do not produce alienation? What are they, and what makes them better?

REVOLUTION

The only way out of the trap of capitalism, argued Marx, is to remake society. He imagined a system of production that could provide for the social needs of all. He called this system *socialism*. Although Marx knew that such a dramatic change would not come easily, he must have been disappointed that he did not live to see workers in England

The 2004 film, *The Motorcycle Diaries*, tells the story of the motorcycle journey through South America of Che Guevara. Seeing such desperate poverty inspired Guevara to become a Marxist and fight for revolutionary change. He went on to play an important role in the Cuban Revolution.

rise up. Still, convinced that capitalism was a social evil, he believed that in time the working majority would realize they held the key to a better future. This change would certainly be revolutionary and perhaps even violent. Marx believed a socialist society would bring class conflict to an end.

Chapter 10 ("Social Stratification") explains more about changes in industrial-capitalist societies since Marx's time and why the revolution he wanted never took place. In addition, as Chapter 17 ("Politics and Government") explains, Marx failed to foresee that the revolution he imagined could take the form of repressive regimes—such as Stalin's government in the Soviet Union—that would end up killing tens of millions of people (R. Hamilton, 2001). But in his own time, Marx looked toward the future with hope: "The proletarians have nothing to lose but their chains. They have a world to win" (Marx & Engels, 1972: 362, orig. 1848).

Max Weber:
The Rationalization of Society

With a wide knowledge of law, economics, religion, and history, Max Weber (1864–1920) produced what many experts regard as the greatest individual contribution to sociology. This scholar, born to a prosperous family in Germany, had much to say about how modern society differs from earlier types of social organization.

To learn more about Weber, go to http://www.faculty.rsu.edu/~felwell/Theorists/Weber/Whome.htm

Weber understood the power of technology, and he shared many of Marx's ideas about social conflict. But he disagreed with Marx's philosophy of materialism. Weber's philosophical approach, called *idealism,* emphasized how human ideas—especially beliefs and values—shape society. He argued that societies differ not in terms of how people produce things but in how people think about the world. In Weber's view, modern society was the product of a new way of thinking.

YOUR TURN

Sociologists sometimes say that Weber's work is "a debate with the ghost of Karl Marx." Thinking of their basic approaches, can you explain why?

Weber compared societies in different times and places. To make the comparisons, he relied on the **ideal type,** *an abstract statement of the essential characteristics of any social phenomenon.* Following Weber's approach, for example, we might speak of "preindustrial" and "industrial" societies as ideal types. The use of the word "ideal" does not mean that one or the other is "good" or "the best." Nor does an ideal type refer to any actual society. Rather, think of an ideal type as a way of defining a type of society in its pure form. We have already used ideal types in comparing "hunting and gathering societies" with "industrial societies" and "capitalism" with "socialism."

TWO WORLDVIEWS: TRADITION AND RATIONALITY

Rather than categorizing societies according to their technology or productive systems, Weber focused on ways people think about their world. Members of preindustrial societies are bound by *tradition,* and people in industrial-capitalist societies are guided by *rationality.*

By **tradition,** Weber meant *values and beliefs passed from generation to generation.* In other words, traditional people are guided by the past. They consider particular actions right and proper mostly because they have been accepted for so long.

People in modern societies, however, favor **rationality,** *a way of thinking that emphasizes deliberate, matter-of-fact calculation of the most efficient way to accomplish a particular task.* Sentimental ties to the past have no place in a rational worldview, and tradition becomes simply one kind of information. Typically, modern people think and act on the basis of what they see as the present and future consequences of their choices. They evaluate jobs, schooling, and even relationships in terms of what they put into them and what they expect to receive in return.

Weber viewed both the Industrial Revolution and the development of capitalism as evidence of modern rationality. Such changes are all part of the **rationalization of society,** *the historical change from tradition to rationality as the main mode of human thought.* Weber went on to describe modern society as "disenchanted" because scientific thinking has swept away most of people's sentimental ties to the past.

The willingness to adopt the latest technology is one strong indicator of how rationalized a society is. To illustrate the global pattern of rationalization, Global Map 4–1 on page 106 shows where in the world personal computers are found. In general, the high-income countries of North America and Europe use personal computers the most, but they are rare in low-income nations.

Why are some societies more eager than others to adopt new technology? Those with a more rational worldview might consider new computer or medical technology a breakthrough, but those with a very traditional culture might reject such devices as a threat to their way of life. The Tuareg nomads of northern Mali, described at the beginning of this chapter, shrug off the idea of using telephones: Why would anyone in the desert want a cell phone? Similarly, in the United States, the Amish refuse to have telephones in their homes because it is not part of their traditional way of life.

In Weber's view, the amount of technological innovation depends on how a society's people understand their world. Many people throughout history have had the opportunity to adopt new technology, but only in the rational

A common fear among thinkers in the early industrial era was that people—now slaves to the new machines—would be stripped of their humanity. No one better captured this idea than the comic actor Charlie Chaplin, who starred in the 1936 film *Modern Times.*

cultural climate of Western Europe did people exploit scientific discoveries to spark the Industrial Revolution (Weber, 1958, orig. 1904–05).

IS CAPITALISM RATIONAL?

Is industrial capitalism a rational economic system? Here again, Weber and Marx came down on different sides. Weber considered industrial capitalism to be highly rational, because capitalists try to make money in any way they can. Marx, however, thought capitalism irrational because it fails to meet the basic needs of most of the people (Gerth & Mills, 1946:49).

WEBER'S GREAT THESIS: PROTESTANTISM AND CAPITALISM

Weber spent many years considering how and why industrial capitalism developed in the first place. Why did it emerge in parts of Western Europe during the eighteenth and nineteenth centuries?

Weber claimed that the key to the birth of industrial capitalism lay in the Protestant Reformation. Specifically, he saw industrial capitalism as the major outcome of Calvinism,

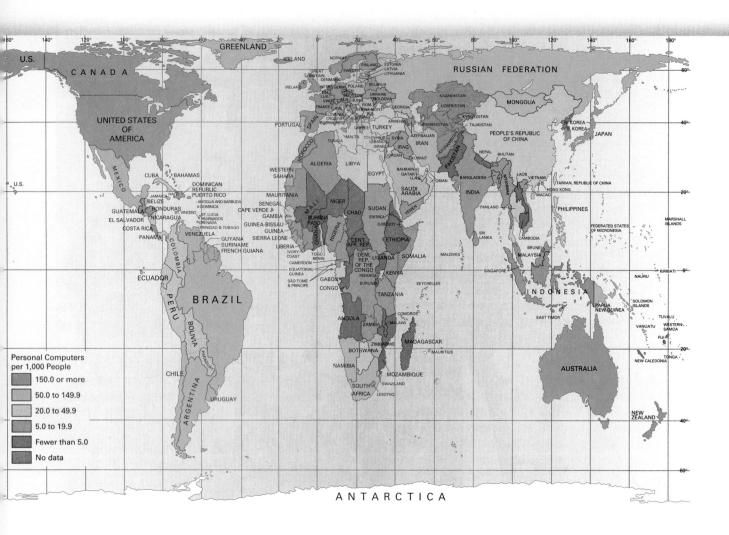

WINDOW ON THE WORLD

GLOBAL MAP 4–1   High Technology in Global Perspective

Countries with traditional cultures cannot afford, ignore, or sometimes even resist new technology, which nations with highly rationalized ways of life quickly embrace. Personal computers, central to today's high technology, are commonplace in high-income countries such as the United States. In low-income nations, by contrast, they are unknown to most people.

Source: International Telecommunication Union (2005).

a Christian religious movement founded by John Calvin (1509–1564). Calvinists approached life in a highly disciplined and rational way. One of Calvin's most important ideas was *predestination,* the belief that an all-knowing and all-powerful God had predestined some people for salvation and others for damnation. Believing that everyone's fate was set before birth, early Calvinists thought people could do

nothing to change their destiny, and even worse, they did not know what their destiny was. So Calvinists swung between hopeful visions of spiritual salvation and anxious fears of eternal damnation.

Not knowing their fate was intolerable, so Calvinists gradually came to a resolution of sorts. Why shouldn't those chosen for glory in the next world, they reasoned, see signs of divine favor in *this* world? In this way, Calvinists came to see worldly prosperity as a sign of God's grace. Eager to gain this reassurance, Calvinists threw themselves into a quest for success, applying rationality, discipline, and hard work to their tasks. They did not pursue wealth for its own sake because spending on themselves would be self-indulgent and sinful. Neither were Calvinists likely to share their wealth with the poor, because they viewed poverty as a sign of God's rejection. Their duty was to press forward in what they saw as their personal *calling* from God, reinvesting profits for still greater success. It is easy to see how such activity—saving money, using wealth to create more wealth, and adopting new technology—became the foundation of capitalism.

Other world religions did not encourage the rational pursuit of wealth the way Calvinism did. Catholicism, the traditional religion in most of Europe, taught a passive, "otherworldly" view: Good deeds performed humbly on Earth would bring rewards in heaven. For Catholics, making money had none of the spiritual significance it had for Calvinists. Weber concluded that this was the reason that industrial capitalism developed primarily in areas of Europe where Calvinism was strong.

Weber's study of Calvinism provides striking evidence of the power of ideas to shape society. Not one to accept simple explanations, Weber knew that industrial capitalism had many causes. But by stressing the importance of ideas, Weber tried to counter Marx's strictly economic explanation of modern society.

As the decades passed, later generations of Calvinists lost much of their early religious enthusiasm. But their drive for success and personal discipline remained, and slowly a *religious* ethic was transformed into a *work* ethic. In this sense, industrial capitalism can be seen as "disenchanted" religion, with wealth now valued for its own sake. This trend is seen in the fact that the practice of "accounting," which to early Calvinists meant keeping a daily record of moral deeds, before long came to mean simply keeping track of money.

RATIONAL SOCIAL ORGANIZATION

According to Weber, rationality is the basis of modern society, giving rise to both the Industrial Revolution and capitalism. He went on to identify seven characteristics of rational social organization:

1. **Distinctive social institutions.** In hunting and gathering societies, the family is the center of all activity. Gradually, however, religious, political, and economic systems develop as separate social institutions. In modern societies, new institutions—including education and health care—also appear. Specialized social institutions are a rational strategy to meet human needs efficiently.

2. **Large-scale organizations.** Modern rationality can be seen in the spread of large-scale organizations. As early as the horticultural era, small groups of political officials made decisions concerning religious observances, public works, and warfare. By the time Europe developed agrarian societies, the Catholic church had grown into a much larger organization with thousands of officials. In today's modern, rational society, almost everyone works for large formal organizations, and federal and state governments employ tens of millions of workers.

3. **Specialized tasks.** Unlike members of traditional societies, people in modern societies are likely to have very specialized jobs. The Yellow Pages of any city's telephone directory suggest just how many different occupations there are today.

4. **Personal discipline.** Modern societies put a premium on self-discipline. Most business and government organizations expect their workers to be disciplined, and discipline is also encouraged by our cultural values of achievement and success.

5. **Awareness of time.** In traditional societies, people measure time according to the rhythm of sun and seasons. Modern people, by contrast, schedule events precisely by the hour and even the minute. Clocks began appearing in European cities some 500 years ago, about the same time commerce began to expand. Soon people began to think (to borrow Benjamin Franklin's phrase) that "time is money."

6. **Technical competence.** Members of traditional societies size up one another on the basis of *who* they are—their family ties. Modern rationality leads us to judge people according to *what* they are, with an eye toward their education, skills, and abilities. Most workers have to keep up with the latest skills and knowledge in their fields in order to be successful.

7. **Impersonality.** In a rational society, technical competence is the basis for hiring, so the world becomes impersonal. People interact as specialists concerned with particular tasks, rather than as individuals concerned with one another as people. Because showing your feelings can threaten personal discipline, modern people tend to devalue emotion.

All these characteristics can be found in one important expression of modern rationality: bureaucracy.

Max Weber agreed with Karl Marx that modern society is alienating to the individual, but they identified different causes of this problem. For Marx, economic inequality is the reason; for Weber, the issue is widespread and dehumanizing bureaucracy. George Tooker's painting *Landscape with Figures* echoes Weber's sentiments.

George Tooker, *Landscape with Figures*, 1963, egg tempera on gesso panel, 26 × 30 in. Private collection. Reproduction courtesy D.C. Moore Gallery, N.Y.C.

Rationality, Bureaucracy, and Science

Weber considered the growth of large, rational organizations to be one of the defining traits of modern societies. Another term for this type of organization is *bureaucracy*. Weber believed that bureaucracy has much in common with capitalism—another key factor in modern social life:

> Today, it is primarily the capitalist market economy which demands that the official business of public administration be discharged precisely, unambiguously, continuously, and with as much speed as possible. Normally, the very large capitalist enterprises are themselves unequaled models of strict bureaucratic organization. (1978:974, orig. 1921)

As Chapter 7 ("Groups and Organizations") explains, we find aspects of bureaucracy in today's businesses, government agencies, labor unions, and universities. Weber considered bureaucracy highly rational because its elements—offices, duties, and policies—help achieve specific goals as efficiently as possible. Weber saw that capitalism,

bureaucracy, and also science—the highly disciplined pursuit of knowledge—are all expressions of the same underlying factor: rationality.

Rationality and Alienation

Max Weber agreed with Karl Marx that industrial capitalism was highly productive. Weber also agreed with Marx that modern society generates widespread alienation, although his reasons were different. Marx thought alienation was caused by economic inequality. Weber blamed alienation on bureaucracy's countless rules and regulations. Bureaucracies, Weber warned, treat a human being as a "number" or a "case" rather than as a unique individual. In addition, working for large organizations demands highly specialized and often tedious routines. In the end, Weber saw modern society as a vast and growing system of rules trying to regulate everything, and he feared that modern society would end up crushing the human spirit.

Like Marx, Weber found it ironic that modern society—meant to serve humanity—turns on its creators and enslaves them. Just as Marx described the dehumanizing effects of industrial capitalism, Weber portrayed the modern individual as "only a small cog in a ceaselessly moving mechanism that prescribes to him an endlessly fixed routine of march" (1978:988, orig. 1921). Although Weber could see the advantages of modern society, he was deeply pessimistic about the future. He feared that in the end, the rationalization of society would reduce human beings to robots.

YOUR TURN

Marx saw revolution as the way to overcome the problems of capitalism. Would the creation of a socialist government solve the problem of excessive rationality that worried Weber? Why or why not?

Emile Durkheim: Society and Function

"To love society is to love something beyond us and something in ourselves." These are the words (1974:55, orig. 1924) of the French For a closer look at the life and work of Durkheim, visit http:// www.hewett.norfolk.sch.uk/ curric/soc/durkheim/durk.htm sociologist Emile Durkheim (1858–1917), another of the discipline's founders. In Durkheim's ideas we find another important vision of human society.

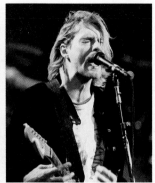

Durkheim's observation that people with weak social bonds are prone to self-destructive behavior stands as stark evidence of the power of society to shape individual lives. When rock-and-roll singers become famous, they are wrenched out of familiar life patterns and existing relationships, sometimes with deadly results. The history of rock and roll contains many tragic stories of this kind, including (from left) Janis Joplin's and Jimi Hendrix's deaths by drug overdose (both 1970) and Jim Morrison's (1971) and Kurt Cobain's (1994) suicides.

STRUCTURE: SOCIETY BEYOND OURSELVES

Emile Durkheim's great insight was recognizing that society exists beyond ourselves. Society is more than the individuals who compose it. Society was here long before we were born, it shapes us while we live, and it will remain long after we are gone. Patterns of human behavior—cultural norms, values, and beliefs—exist as established structures, or *social facts,* that have an objective reality beyond the lives of individuals.

Because society is bigger than any one of us, it has the power to guide our thoughts and actions. This is why studying individuals alone (as psychologists or biologists do) can never capture the heart of the social experience. A classroom of college students taking a math exam, a family gathered around a table sharing a meal, people quietly waiting their turn in a doctor's office—all are examples of the countless situations that have a familiar organization apart from any particular individual who has ever been part of them.

Once created by people, Durkheim claimed, society takes on a life of its own and demands a measure of obedience from its creators. We experience the reality of society in the order of our lives or as we face temptation and feel the tug of morality.

FUNCTION: SOCIETY AS SYSTEM

Having established that society has structure, Durkheim turned to the concept of *function.* The significance of any social fact, he explained, is more than what individuals see in their immediate lives; social facts help society as a whole to operate.

As an illustration, consider crime. Of course, as victims of crime, individuals experience pain and loss. But taking a broader view, Durkheim saw that crime is vital to the ongoing life of society itself. As Chapter 9 ("Deviance") explains, only by defining acts as wrong do people construct and defend morality, which gives direction and meaning to our collective life. For this reason, Durkheim rejected the common view of crime as abnormal. On the contrary, he concluded, crime is "normal" for the most basic of reasons: A society could not exist without it (1964a, orig. 1893; 1964b, orig. 1895).

PERSONALITY: SOCIETY IN OURSELVES

Durkheim said that society is not only "beyond ourselves" but also "in ourselves," helping to form our personalities. How we act, think, and feel is drawn from the society that nurtures us. Society shapes us in another way as well—by providing the moral discipline that guides our behavior and controls our desires. Durkheim believed that human beings need the restraint of society because, as creatures who can want more and more, we are in constant danger of being overpowered by our own desires. As he put it, "The more one has, the more one wants, since satisfactions received only stimulate instead of filling needs" (1966:248, orig. 1897).

Nowhere is the need for societal regulation better illustrated than in Durkheim's study of suicide (1966, orig. 1897), which was described in Chapter 1 ("The Sociological Perspective"). Why is it that rock stars—from Janis Joplin

In traditional societies, such as Amish communities in the United States, everyone does much the same work. These societies are held together by strong moral beliefs. Modern societies, illustrated by urban areas in this country, are held together by a system of production in which people perform specialized work and rely on one another.

and Jim Morrison to Jimi Hendrix and Kurt Cobain—seem so prone to self-destruction? Durkheim had the answer long before the invention of the electric guitar: Now as back then, the *highest* suicide rates are found among categories of people with the *lowest* level of societal integration. In short, the enormous freedom of the young, rich, and famous carries a high price in terms of the risk of suicide.

MODERNITY AND ANOMIE

Compared to traditional societies, modern societies impose fewer restrictions on everyone. Durkheim acknowledged the advantages of modern-day freedom, but he warned of increased **anomie,** *a condition in which society provides little moral guidance to individuals.* The pattern by which many celebrities are "destroyed by fame" well illustrates the destructive effects of anomie. Sudden fame tears people from their families and familiar routines, disrupts established values and norms, and breaks down society's support and regulation of an individual—sometimes with fatal results. Thus, Durkheim explained, an individual's desires must be balanced by the claims and guidance of society—a balance that is sometimes difficult to achieve in the modern world. Durkheim would not have been surprised to see a rising suicide rate in modern societies such as the United States.

EVOLVING SOCIETIES: THE DIVISION OF LABOR

Like Marx and Weber, Durkheim lived through rapid social change in Europe during the nineteenth century. But Durkheim offered different reasons for this change.

In preindustrial societies, he explained, tradition operates as the social cement that binds people together. In fact, what he termed the *collective conscience* is so strong that the community moves quickly to punish anyone who dares to challenge conventional ways of life. Durkheim used the term **mechanical solidarity** to refer to *social bonds, based on common sentiments and shared moral values, that are strong among members of preindustrial societies.* In practice, mechanical solidarity is based on *likeness.* Durkheim called these bonds "mechanical" because people are linked together in lockstep, with a more or less automatic sense of belonging together and acting alike.

With industrialization, Durkheim continued, mechanical solidarity becomes weaker and weaker, and people are much less bound by tradition. But this does not mean that society dissolves. Modern life creates a new type of solidarity. Durkheim called this new social integration **organic solidarity,** defined as *social bonds, based on specialization and interdependence, that are strong among members of industrial societies.* The solidarity that was once rooted in likeness is now based on *differences* among people who find that their specialized work—as plumbers, college students, midwives, or sociology instructors—makes them rely on other people for most of their daily needs.

For Durkheim, then, the key to change in a society is an expanding **division of labor,** or *specialized economic activity.* Weber said that modern societies specialize in order to become more efficient, and Durkheim filled out the picture by showing that members of modern societies count on tens of thousands of others—most of them strangers—for the goods and services needed every day. As members of modern societies, we depend more and more on people we trust less and less. Why do we look to people we hardly know and whose beliefs may well differ from our own? Durkheim's answer was "because we can't live without them."

So modern society rests far less on *moral consensus* and far more on *functional interdependence.* Herein lies what we might call "Durkheim's dilemma": The technological power and greater personal freedom of modern society come at the cost of declining morality and the rising risk of anomie.

Like Marx and Weber, Durkheim worried about the direction society was taking. But of the three, Durkheim was the most optimistic. He saw that large, anonymous societies gave people more freedom and privacy than small towns. Anomie remains a danger, but Durkheim hoped we would be able to create laws and other norms to regulate our behavior.

YOUR TURN

Compare Durkheim's concept of anomie with the two concepts of alienation developed by Marx and Weber.

How can we apply Durkheim's views to the Information Revolution? The Applying Sociology box on page 112 suggests that he and two other theorists we have considered in this chapter would have had much to say about today's new computer technology.

Critical Review: Four Visions of Society

This chapter opened with several important questions about society. We will conclude by summarizing how each of the four visions of society answers these questions.

What Holds Societies Together?

How is something as complex as society possible? Lenski claims that members of a society are united by a shared culture, although cultural patterns become more diverse as a society gains more complex technology. He also points out that as technology becomes more complex, inequality divides a society more and more, although industrialization reduces inequality somewhat.

Marx saw in society not unity but social division based on class position. From his point of view, elites may force an uneasy peace, but true social unity can occur only if production becomes a cooperative process. To Weber, the members of a society share a worldview. Just as tradition joined people together in the past, so modern societies have created rational, large-scale organizations that connect people's lives. Finally, Durkheim made solidarity the focus of his work. He contrasted the mechanical solidarity of preindustrial societies, which is based on shared morality, with modern society's organic solidarity, which is based on specialization.

How Have Societies Changed?

According to Lenski's model of sociocultural evolution, societies differ mostly in terms of changing technology. Modern society stands out from past societies in terms of its enormous productive power. Marx, too, noted historical differences in productivity yet pointed to continuing social conflict (except perhaps among simple hunters and gatherers). For Marx, modern society is distinctive mostly because it brings that conflict out into the open. Weber considered the question of change from the perspective of how people look at the world. Members of preindustrial societies have a traditional outlook; modern people take a rational worldview. Finally, for Durkheim, traditional societies are characterized by mechanical solidarity based on moral likeness. In industrial societies, mechanical solidarity gives way to organic solidarity based on productive specialization.

Why Do Societies Change?

As Lenski sees it, social change comes about through technological innovation that, over time, transforms an entire society. Marx's materialist approach highlights the struggle between classes as the "engine of change," pushing societies toward revolution. Weber, by contrast, pointed out that ideas contribute to social change. He demonstrated how a particular worldview—Calvinism—set in motion the Industrial Revolution, which ended up reshaping all of society. Finally, Durkheim pointed to an expanding division of labor as the key dimension of social change.

The fact that these four approaches are so different does not mean that any one of them is right or wrong in an absolute sense. Society is exceedingly complex, and our understanding of society benefits from applying all four visions.

The Information Revolution:
What Would Durkheim, Weber, and Marx Have Thought?

New technology is changing our society at a dizzying pace. Were they alive today, the founding sociologists discussed in this chapter would be eager observers of the current scene. Imagine for a moment the kinds of questions Emile Durkheim, Max Weber, and Karl Marx might ask about the effects of computer technology on society.

Durkheim, who emphasized the increasing division of labor in modern society, would probably wonder if new information technology is pushing specialization even further. There is good reason to think that it is. Because electronic communication (say, a Web site) gives anyone a vast market (already, several billion people access the Internet), people can specialize far more than if they were trying to make a living in a small geographic area. For example, while most small-town lawyers have a general practice, an information age attorney, living anywhere, can provide specialized guidance on, say, prenuptial agreements or electronic copyright law. As we move into the electronic age, the number of highly specialized small businesses (some of which end up becoming very large) in all fields is increasing rapidly.

Durkheim might also point out that the Internet threatens to increase the problem of anomie. Using computers has a tendency to isolate people from personal relationships with others. In addition, although the Internet offers a flood of information, it provides little in the way of moral guidance about what is wise or good or worth knowing.

Weber believed that modern societies are distinctive because their members share a rational worldview, and nothing illustrates this worldview better than bureaucracy. But will bureaucracy be as important during the twenty-first century? Here is one reason to think it may not: Although organizations will probably continue to regulate workers performing the kinds of routine tasks that were common in the industrial era, much work in the postindustrial era involves imagination. Consider such "new age" work as designing homes, composing music, and writing software. This kind of creative work cannot be regulated in the same way as putting together automobiles as they move down an assembly line. Perhaps this is the reason many high-technology companies have done away with dress codes and time clocks.

Finally, what might Marx make of the Information Revolution? Since Marx considered the earlier Industrial Revolution a *class* revolution that allowed the owners of industry to dominate society, he would probably be concerned about the emergence of a new symbolic elite. Some analysts point out that film and television writers, producers, and performers now enjoy vast wealth, international prestige, and enormous power (Lichter, Rothman, & Lichter, 1990). Just as people without industrial skills stayed at the bottom of the class system in past decades, so people without symbolic skills may well become the "underclass" of the twenty-first century.

Durkheim, Weber, and Marx greatly improved our understanding of industrial societies. As we continue into the postindustrial age, there is plenty of room for new generations of sociologists to carry on.

WHAT DO YOU THINK?

1. Is computer technology likely to continue to increase specialization? Why or why not?
2. Can you think of examples of "creative" businesses that are less bureaucratic than industrial companies used to be? Why would you expect this to be the case?
3. What effect will the increased importance of symbolic skills have on the "earning power" of a college degree?

The following learning tools will help you see what you know, identify what you still need to learn, and expand your understanding beyond the text. You can also visit this text's Companion Website™ at http://www.prenhall.com/macionis to find additional practice tests.

KEY POINTS

Gerhard Lenski: Society and Technology

Lenski's sociocultural evolution explores how technological advances change societies. The earliest societies, which lived by hunting and gathering, were composed of a small number of family-centered nomads. Horticulture began some 12,000 years ago as people used hand tools for cultivation. About the same time, pastoral societies domesticated animals and created networks of trade. Agriculture, large-scale cultivation using animal-drawn plows, developed about 5,000 years ago. This more productive technology allowed societies to expand into vast empires, and it also created more inequality.

Industrialization began just over 250 years ago in Europe as people used new energy sources to operate large machinery. In today's postindustrial societies, production has shifted from heavy machinery making material things to computers and related technology processing information.

Karl Marx: Society and Conflict

Marx's materialist approach claims that societies are defined by their economic systems. He traced conflict between social classes, from "ancient" societies (masters and slaves) to agrarian societies (nobles and serfs) to industrial-capitalist societies (capitalists and proletarians).

Industrial capitalism alienates workers in four ways: from the act of working, from the products of work, from other workers, and from their own potential. Marx believed that once workers overcame their false consciousness, they would overthrow the industrial-capitalist system.

Max Weber:
The Rationalization of Society

Weber's idealist approach claims that ideas have a powerful effect on society. Weber contrasted the tradition of preindustrial societies with the rationality of modern, industrial societies. He traced the origins of capitalism to Calvinist religious beliefs.

Today's rational societies are marked by not only capitalism and science but also by bureaucratic organizations. Weber feared that this rationality would stifle human creativity.

Emile Durkheim:
Society and Function

Durkheim explained that society has an objective existence apart from individuals. He understood that social elements (such as crime) have functions that help society operate. Society also shapes our personalities, guiding how we act, think, and feel. Societies require solidarity. Traditional societies have mechanical solidarity, which is based on moral likeness; modern societies depend on organic solidarity, which is based on specialization, or a division of labor.

KEY CONCEPTS

society (p. 92) people who interact in a defined territory and share a culture

sociocultural evolution (p. 93) Lenski's term for the changes that occur as a society gains new technology

hunting and gathering (p. 93) the use of simple tools to hunt animals and gather vegetation

horticulture (p. 94) the use of hand tools to raise crops

pastoralism (p. 94) the domestication of animals

agriculture (p. 95) large-scale cultivation using plows harnessed to animals or more powerful energy sources

industrialism (p. 96) the production of goods using advanced sources of energy to drive large machinery

postindustrialism (p. 98) technology that supports an information-based economy

social conflict (p. 101) the struggle between segments of society over valued resources

capitalists (p. 101) people who own and operate factories and other businesses in pursuit of profits

proletarians (p. 101) people who sell their labor for wages

social institutions (p. 101) the major spheres of social life, or societal subsystems, organized to meet human needs

false consciousness (p. 101) Marx's term for explanations of social problems as the shortcomings of individuals rather than as the flaws of society

class conflict (p. 102) conflict between entire classes over the distribution of a society's wealth and power

class consciousness (p. 103) Marx's term for workers' recognition of themselves as a class unified in opposition to capitalists and ultimately to capitalism itself

alienation (p. 103) the experience of isolation and misery resulting from powerlessness

ideal type (p. 104) an abstract statement of the essential characteristics of any social phenomenon

tradition (p. 105) values and beliefs passed from generation to generation

rationality (p. 105) a way of thinking that emphasizes deliberate, matter-of-fact calculation of the most efficient way to accomplish a particular task

rationalization of society (p. 105) Weber's term for the historical change from tradition to rationality as the main mode of human thought

anomie (p. 110) Durkheim's term for a condition in which society provides little moral guidance to individuals

mechanical solidarity (p. 110) Durkheim's term for social bonds, based on common sentiments and shared moral values, that are strong among members of preindustrial societies

organic solidarity (p. 110) Durkheim's term for social bonds, based on specialization and interdependence, that are strong among members of industrial societies

division of labor (p. 111) specialized economic activity

SAMPLE TEST QUESTIONS

These questions are similar to those found in the test bank that accompanies this textbook.

Multiple-Choice Questions

1. Which of the following would Lenski highlight as a cause of change in society?
   a. new religious movements
   b. conflict between workers and factory owners
   c. the steam engine
   d. the extent to which people share moral values

2. Horticultural societies are those in which
   a. people hunt animals and gather vegetation.
   b. people are nomadic.
   c. people have learned to raise animals.
   d. people use simple hand tools to raise crops.

3. Lenski claims that the development of more complex technology
   a. has both positive and negative effects.
   b. is entirely positive.
   c. is mostly negative.
   d. has little or no effect on society.

4. Marx believed that the industrial-capitalist economic system
   a. was very productive.
   b. concentrated wealth in the hands of a few.
   c. created conflict between two great classes: capitalists and proletarians.
   d. all of the above.

5. Marx considered which of the following to be the "foundation" of society?
   a. technology
   b. the economy
   c. dominant ideas
   d. type of solidarity

6. Unlike Marx, Weber thought alienation was caused by
   a. social change that is too rapid.
   b. extensive social inequality.
   c. the high level of rationality in modern society.
   d. all of the above.

7. What Lenski called the "industrial" society and Marx called the "capitalist" society, Weber called
   a. the "rational" society.
   b. the "ideal" society.
   c. the "traditional" society.
   d. the "technological" society.

8. Marx's "materialist" analysis contrasts with Weber's
   a. "optimistic" analysis.
   b. "idealist" analysis.
   c. "traditional" analysis.
   d. "technological" analysis.

9. Durkheim thought of society as
   a. existing only in people's minds.
   b. constantly changing.
   c. an objective reality.
   d. having no clear existence at all.

10. Which of the following questions might Durkheim ask about the ongoing war on terror?
    a. Would the war on terror unite people across the United States?

b. Which class benefits most from the war on terror?

c. How does war lead to new kinds of technology?

d. How does war increase the scope of bureaucracy?

Essay Questions

1. How would Marx, Weber, and Durkheim imagine U.S. society a century from now? What kinds of questions or concerns would each thinker have?

2. Link Marx, Weber, and Durkheim to one of sociology's theoretical approaches, and explain your choices.

APPLICATIONS & EXERCISES

1. Hunting and gathering people gazed at the stars and named the constellations in terms that reflected their way of life—mostly the names of animals and hunters. As a way of revealing what is important to *our* way of life, write a short paper imagining the meanings we would give clusters of stars if people in postindustrial societies were naming them and starting from scratch.

2. Spend an hour in your home trying to identify every device that has a computer chip in it. How many did you find? Were you surprised by the number?

3. Do some research on a past civilization such as the Inca society of Peru. Learn about the people's levels of skill in agriculture, weaving, pottery, and architecture. (Some Inca buildings have withstood earthquakes that have destroyed much newer construction.) See if what you learn makes you think twice before assuming that modern societies are always superior to past societies.

INVESTIGATE *with* Research Navigator

Follow the instructions on page 27 of this text to access the features of **Research Navigator™**. Once at the Web site, enter your Login Name and Password. Then, to use the **ContentSelect** database, enter keywords such as "Karl Marx," "technology," and "Max Weber," and the search engine will supply relevant and recent scholarly and popular press publications. Use the *New York Times* **Search-by-Subject Archive** to find recent news articles related to sociology and the **Link Library** feature to find relevant Web links organized by the key terms associated with this chapter.

5

CHAPTER FIVE

Socialization

Why is social experience the key
to human personality?

What familiar social settings have special
importance to human development?

How do people's experiences change
over the life course?

ON A COLD WINTER DAY in 1938, a social worker walked quickly to the door of a rural Pennsylvania farmhouse. Investigating a case of possible child abuse, the social worker entered the home and soon discovered a five-year-old girl hidden in a second-floor storage room. The child, whose name was Anna, was wedged into an old chair with her arms tied above her head so that she couldn't move. She was wearing filthy clothes, and her arms and legs were as thin as matchsticks (K. Davis, 1940).

Anna's situation can only be described as tragic. She had been born in 1932 to an unmarried and mentally impaired woman of twenty-six who lived with her strict father. Angry about his daughter's "illegitimate" motherhood, the grandfather did not even want the child in his house, so for the first six months of her life, Anna was passed among several welfare agencies. But her mother could not afford to pay for her care, and Anna was returned to the hostile home of her grandfather.

To lessen the grandfather's anger, Anna's mother kept Anna in the storage room and gave her just enough milk to keep her alive. There she stayed—day after day, month after month, with almost no human contact—for five long years.

Learning of the discovery of Anna, the sociologist Kingsley Davis immediately went to see her. He found her with local officials at a county home. Davis was stunned by the emaciated child, who could not laugh, speak, or even smile. Anna was completely unresponsive, as if alone in an empty world. ■

Social Experience: The Key to Our Humanity

Socialization is so basic to human development that we sometimes overlook its importance. But here, in the terrible case of an isolated child, we can see what humans would be like without social contact. Although physically alive, Anna hardly seems to have been human. We can see that without social experience, a child is not able to act or communicate in a meaningful way and seems to be as much an *object* as a *person*.

Sociologists use the term **socialization** to refer to *the lifelong social experience by which people develop their human potential and learn culture.* Unlike other living species, whose behavior is biologically set, humans need social experience to learn their culture and to survive. Social experience is also the foundation of **personality,** *a person's fairly consistent patterns of acting, thinking, and feeling.* We

build a personality by internalizing—taking in—our surroundings. But without social experience, as Anna's case shows, personality hardly develops at all.

HUMAN DEVELOPMENT: NATURE AND NURTURE

Anna's case makes clear that humans depend on others to provide the care and nurture needed not only for physical growth but also for personality to develop. A century ago, however, people mistakenly believed that humans were born with instincts that determined their personality and behavior.

The Biological Sciences: The Role of Nature

Charles Darwin's 1859 groundbreaking study of evolution, described in Chapter 3 ("Culture"), led people to think that human behavior was instinctive, simply our "nature." Such ideas led to claims that the U.S. economic system reflects

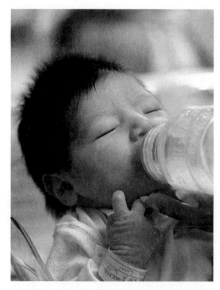 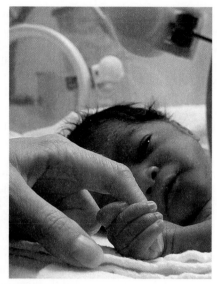 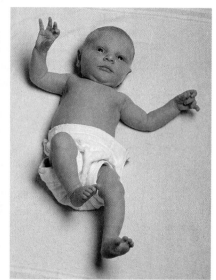

Human infants display various reflexes—biologically based behavior patterns that enhance survival. The sucking reflex, which actually begins before birth, enables the infant to obtain nourishment. The grasping reflex, triggered by placing a finger on the infant's palm causing the hand to close, helps the infant to maintain contact with a parent and, later on, to grasp objects. The Moro reflex, activated by startling the infant, has the infant swinging both arms outward and then bringing them together across the chest. This action, which disappears after several months of life, probably developed among our evolutionary ancestors so that a falling infant could grasp the body hair of a parent.

"instinctive human competitiveness," that some people are "born criminals," or that women are "naturally" emotional while men are "naturally" rational.

People trying to understand cultural diversity also misunderstood Darwin's thinking. From centuries of world exploration, Western Europeans knew that people around the world behaved quite differently from one another. But Europeans linked these differences to biology rather than culture. It was an easy, although incorrect and very damaging, step to claim that members of technologically simple societies were biologically less evolved and therefore "less human." This ethnocentric view helped justify colonialism: Why not take advantage of others if they seem not to be human in the same sense that you are?

The Social Sciences: The Role of Nurture

In the twentieth century, biological explanations of human behavior came under fire. The psychologist John B. Watson (1878–1958) developed a theory called *behaviorism*, which holds that behavior is not instinctive but learned. Thus people everywhere are equally human, differing only in their cultural patterns. In short, Watson rooted human behavior not in nature but in *nurture*.

Today, social scientists are cautious about describing *any* human behavior as instinctive. This does not mean that biology plays no part in human behavior. Human life, after all, depends on the functioning of the body. We also know that children often share biological traits (like height and hair color) with their parents and that heredity plays a part in intelligence, musical and artistic talent, and personality (such as how you react to frustration). However, whether you develop your inherited potential depends on how you are raised. For example, unless children are stimulated to use their brains early in life, the brain does not fully develop. Therefore, the ability to realize any inherited potential depends on having the opportunity to develop it (Goldsmith, 1983; Begley, 1995).

Without denying the importance of nature, then, we can correctly say that nurture matters more in shaping human behavior. More precisely, *nurture is our nature*.

SOCIAL ISOLATION

As the story of Anna shows, cutting people off from the social world is very harmful. For ethical reasons, researchers can never place human beings in total isolation to study what happens. But in the past, they have studied the effects of social isolation on nonhuman primates.

Studies of Nonhuman Primates

In a classic study, the psychologists Harry and Margaret Harlow (1962) placed rhesus monkeys—whose behavior is in some ways surprisingly similar to human behavior—in various conditions of social isolation. They found that complete isolation (with adequate nutrition) for even six months seriously disturbed the monkeys' development. When returned to their group, these monkeys were passive, anxious, and fearful.

The Harlows then placed infant rhesus monkeys in cages with an artificial "mother" made of wire mesh with a wooden head and the nipple of a feeding tube where the breast would be. These monkeys also survived but were unable to interact with others when placed in a group.

But monkeys in a third category, isolated with an artificial wire mesh "mother" covered with soft terry cloth, did better. Each of these monkeys would cling to its mother closely. Because these monkeys showed less developmental damage than earlier groups, the Harlows concluded that the monkeys benefited from this closeness. The experiment confirmed how important it is that adults cradle infants affectionately.

Finally, the Harlows discovered that infant monkeys could recover from about three months of isolation. But by about six months, isolation caused irreversible emotional and behavioral damage.

What new understanding of the ad campaign "Have you hugged your child today?" do you gain from the Harlow studies?

Studies of Isolated Children

Tragic cases of children isolated by abusive family members show the damage caused by depriving human beings of social experience. We will review three such cases.

Anna: The rest of the story   The rest of Anna's story squares with the Harlows' findings. After her discovery, Anna received extensive medical attention and soon showed improvement. When Kingsley Davis visited her after ten days, he found her more alert and even smiling (perhaps for the first time in her life!). Over the next year, Anna made slow but steady progress, showing more interest in other people and gradually learning to walk. After a year and a half, she could feed herself and play with toys.

But as the Harlows might have predicted, five long years of social isolation had caused permanent damage. At age eight, her mental development was less than that of a two-year-old. Not until she was almost ten did she begin to use words. Because Anna's mother was mentally retarded, perhaps Anna was also. The riddle was never solved, because Anna died at age ten from a blood disorder, possibly related to the years of abuse she suffered (K. Davis, 1940, 1947).

Another case: Isabelle   A second case involves another girl found at about the same time as Anna and under similar circumstances. After more than six years of virtual isolation, this girl—named Isabelle—displayed the same lack of responsiveness as Anna. But Isabelle had the benefit of an intensive learning program directed by psychologists. Within a week, Isabelle was trying to speak, and a year and a half later, she knew some 2,000 words. The psychologists concluded that intensive effort had pushed Isabelle through six years of normal development in only two years. By the time she was fourteen, Isabelle was attending sixth-grade classes, damaged by her early ordeal but on her way to a relatively normal life (K. Davis, 1947).

A third case: Genie   A more recent case of childhood isolation involves a California girl abused by her parents (Curtiss, 1977; Rymer, 1994). From the time she was two, Genie was tied to a potty chair in a dark garage. In 1970, when she was rescued at age thirteen, Genie weighed only fifty-nine pounds and had the mental development of a one-year-old. With intensive treatment, she became physically healthy, but her language ability remains that of a young child. Today, Genie lives in a home for developmentally disabled adults.

Learn more about the life of Genie at http://www.pbs.org/wgbh/nova/transcripts/2112gchild.html

Critical review   All evidence points to the crucial importance of social experience in personality development. Human beings can recover from abuse and short-term isolation. But there is a point—precisely when is unclear from the small number of cases studied—at which isolation in childhood causes permanent developmental damage.

What ethical issues prevent the isolation of humans for research purposes? Do these same issues arise when conducting this type of research with animals? Do you think the Harlow studies would be allowed today?

Understanding Socialization

Socialization is a complex, lifelong process. The following discussions highlight the work of six researchers who have made lasting contributions to our understanding of human development.

SIGMUND FREUD'S ELEMENTS OF PERSONALITY

Sigmund Freud (1856–1939) lived in Vienna at a time when most Europeans considered human behavior to be biologically fixed. Trained as a physician, Freud gradually turned to the study of personality and mental disorders and eventually developed the celebrated theory of psychoanalysis.

Visit the Sigmund Freud Museum of Vienna, Austria, at http://www.freud-museum.at/

Basic Human Needs

Freud claimed that biology plays a major part in human development, although not in terms of specific instincts, as is the case in other species. Rather, he theorized that humans have two basic needs or drives that are present at birth. First is a need for sexual and emotional bonding, which he called the "life instinct," or *eros* (from the Greek god of love). Second, we share an aggressive drive he called the "death instinct," or *thanatos* (from the Greek, meaning "death"). These opposing forces, operating at an unconscious level, create deep inner tension.

Freud's Model of Personality

Freud combined basic needs and the influence of society into a model of personality with three parts: id, ego, and superego. The **id** (the Latin word for "it") represents *the human being's basic drives,* which are unconscious and demand immediate satisfaction. Rooted in biology, the id is present at birth, making a newborn a bundle of demands for attention, touching, and food. But society opposes the self-centered id, which is why one of the first words a child typically learns is "no."

To avoid frustration, a child must learn to approach the world realistically. This is done through the **ego** (Latin for "I"), which is *a person's conscious efforts to balance innate pleasure-seeking drives with the demands of society.* The ego develops as we become aware of ourselves and at the same time realize that we cannot have everything we want.

In the human personality, **superego** (Latin meaning "above" or "beyond" the ego) is *the cultural values and norms internalized by an individual.* The superego operates as our conscience, telling us *why* we cannot have everything we want. The superego begins to form as a child becomes aware of parental demands, and it matures as the child

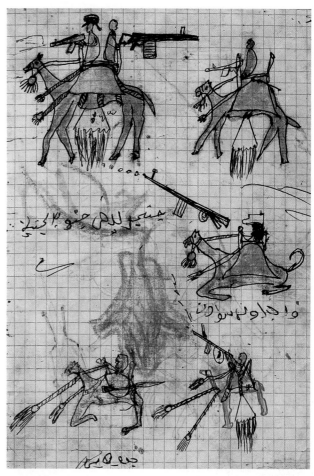

The personalities we develop depend largely on the environment in which we live. When a child's world is shredded by violence, the damage can be profound and lasting. This drawing was made by thirteen-year-old Rahid in the Darfur region of Sudan, where armed militia have killed more than 150,000 people since 2003. What are the likely effects of such experiences on a young person's self-confidence and capacity to form trusting ties with others?

Courtesy of Dr. Annie Sparrow, Human Rights Watch

comes to understand that everyone's behavior should take account of cultural norms.

Personality Development

To the id-centered child, the world is a bewildering assortment of physical sensations that bring either pleasure or pain. As the superego develops, however, the child learns the moral concepts of right and wrong. Initially, in other words, children can feel good only in a physical way (such as by being held and cuddled), but after three or four years, they feel good or bad according to how they judge their behavior against cultural norms (doing "the right thing").

The id and superego remain in conflict, but in a well-adjusted person, the ego manages these two opposing forces. If conflicts are not resolved during childhood, Freud claimed, they may surface as personality disorders later on.

Culture, in the form of the superego, *represses* selfish demands, forcing people to look beyond their own desires. Often the competing demands of self and society result in a compromise that Freud called *sublimation.* Sublimation redirects selfish drives into socially acceptable behavior. For example, marriage makes the satisfaction of sexual urges socially acceptable, and competitive sports are an outlet for aggression.

Critical review   In Freud's time, few people were ready to accept sex as a basic human drive. More recent critics have charged that Freud's work presents humans in male terms and devalues women (Donovan & Littenberg, 1982). Freud's theories are also difficult to test scientifically. But Freud influenced everyone who later studied human personality. Of special importance to sociology are his ideas that we internalize social norms and that childhood experiences have a lasting impact on our personalities.

JEAN PIAGET'S THEORY OF COGNITIVE DEVELOPMENT

The Swiss psychologist Jean Piaget (1896–1980) studied human *cognition,* how people think and understand. As

 To learn more about Piaget and his work, visit http://www. piaget.org

Piaget watched his own three children grow, he wondered not just *what* they knew but *how* they made sense of the world. Piaget went on to identify four stages of cognitive development.

The Sensorimotor Stage

Stage one is the **sensorimotor stage,** *the level of human development at which individuals experience the world only through their senses.* For about the first two years of life, the infant knows the world only through the five senses: touching, tasting, smelling, looking, and listening. "Knowing" to young children amounts to what their senses tell them.

The Preoperational Stage

About age two, children enter the **preoperational stage,** *the level of human development at which individuals first use language and other symbols.* Now children begin to think about the world mentally and use imagination. But "pre-op" children between about two and six still attach meaning only to specific experiences and objects. They can identify a toy as their "favorite" but cannot explain what *kinds* of toys they like.

Lacking abstract concepts, a child also cannot judge size, weight, or volume. In one of his best-known experiments, Piaget placed two identical glasses containing equal amounts of water on a table. He asked several children aged five and six if the amount in each glass was the same. They nodded that it was. The children then watched Piaget take one of the glasses and pour its contents into a taller, narrower glass so that the level of the water in the glass was higher. He asked again if each glass held the same amount. The typical five- or six-year-old now insisted that the taller glass held more water. By about age seven, children are able to think abstractly and realize that the amount of water stays the same.

The Concrete Operational Stage

Next comes the **concrete operational stage,** *the level of human development at which individuals first see causal connections in their surroundings.* Between the ages of seven and eleven, children focus on how and why things happen. In addition, children now attach more than one symbol to a particular event or object. If, for example, you say to a child of five, "Today is Wednesday," she might respond, "No, it's my birthday!" indicating that she can use just one symbol at a time. But a ten-year-old at the concrete operational stage would be able to respond, "Yes, and it's also my birthday!"

The Formal Operational Stage

The last stage in Piaget's model is the **formal operational stage,** *the level of human development at which individuals think abstractly and critically.* At about age twelve, young people begin to reason abstractly rather than thinking only of concrete situations. If, for example, you were to ask a seven-year-old, "What would you like to be when you grow up?" you might receive a concrete response such as "a teacher." But most teenagers can think more abstractly and might reply, "I would like a job that helps others." As they gain the capacity for abstract thought, young people also learn to understand metaphors. Hearing the phrase "A penny for your thoughts" might lead a child to ask for a coin, but a teenager will recognize a gentle invitation to intimacy.

Critical review   Freud saw human beings torn by opposing forces of biology and culture. Piaget saw the mind as active and creative. He saw an ability to engage the world unfolding in stages as the result of both biological maturation and social experience.

But do people in all societies pass through all four of Piaget's stages? Living in a traditional society that changes slowly probably limits a person's capacity for abstract and

Childhood is a time to learn principles of right and wrong. According to Carol Gilligan, however, boys and girls define what is "right" in different ways. After reading about Gilligan's theory, can you suggest what these two might be arguing about?

critical thought. Even in the United States, perhaps 30 percent of people never reach the formal operational stage (Kohlberg & Gilligan, 1971).

LAWRENCE KOHLBERG'S THEORY OF MORAL DEVELOPMENT

Lawrence Kohlberg (1981) built on Piaget's work to study *moral reasoning*, how individuals judge situations as right or wrong. Here again, development occurs in stages.

Young children who experience the world in terms of pain and pleasure (Piaget's sensorimotor stage) are at the *preconventional* level of moral development. At this early stage, in other words, "rightness" amounts to "what feels good to me." For example, a young child may simply reach for something on a table that looks shiny, which is the reason parents of young children have to "childproof" their homes.

The *conventional* level, Kohlberg's second stage, appears by the teen years (corresponding to Piaget's final, formal operational stage). At this point, young people lose some of their selfishness as they learn to define right and wrong in terms of what pleases parents and conforms to cultural norms. Individuals at this stage also begin to assess intention in reaching moral judgments instead of simply looking at what people do. For example, they understand that stealing in order to give food to hungry children is not the same as stealing an iPod to sell for profit.

In Kohlberg's final stage of moral development, the *postconventional* level, people move beyond their society's norms to consider abstract ethical principles. Now they think about liberty, freedom, or justice, perhaps arguing that what is legal still may not be right. When the African American activist Rosa Parks refused to give up her seat on a Montgomery, Alabama, bus in 1955, she violated that city's segregation laws in order to call attention to the racial injustice of the law.

Critical review Like the work of Piaget, Kohlberg's model explains moral development in terms of distinct stages. But whether this model applies to people in all societies remains unclear. Further, many people in the United States apparently never reach the postconventional level of moral reasoning, although exactly why is still an open question.

Another problem with Kohlberg's research is that his subjects were all boys. He committed a common research error, described in Chapter 2 ("Sociological Investigation"), by generalizing the results of male subjects to all people. This problem led a colleague, Carol Gilligan, to investigate how gender affects moral reasoning.

CAROL GILLIGAN'S THEORY OF GENDER AND MORAL DEVELOPMENT

Carol Gilligan, whose approach is highlighted in the Thinking About Diversity box on page 124, compared the moral development of girls and boys and concluded that the two sexes use different standards of rightness.

Gilligan (1982, 1990) claims that boys have a *justice perspective*, relying on formal rules to define right and wrong. Girls, by contrast, have a *care and responsibility perspective*,

The Importance of Gender in Research

Carol Gilligan (1990) has shown how gender guides social behavior. Her early work exposed the gender bias in studies by Kohlberg and others who had used only male subjects. But as her research progressed, Gilligan made a major discovery: Boys and girls actually use different standards in making moral decisions. By ignoring gender, we end up with an incomplete view of human behavior.

Gilligan has also looked at the effect of gender on self-esteem. Her research team interviewed more than 2,000 girls, aged six to eighteen, over a five-year period. She found a clear pattern: Young girls start out eager and confident, but their self-esteem slips

away as they pass through adolescence.

Why? Gilligan claims that the answer lies in our society's socialization of females. In U.S. society, the ideal woman is calm, controlled, and eager to please. Then too, as girls move from the elementary grades to secondary school, they have fewer women teachers and find that most authority figures are men. As a result, by their late teens, girls struggle to regain the personal strength they had a decade earlier.

When their research was finished, Gilligan and her colleagues returned to a private girls' school where they had interviewed their subjects to share the results of their work. As their

conclusions led them to expect, most younger girls who had been interviewed were eager to have their names appear in the forthcoming book. But the older girls were hesitant—many were fearful that they would be talked about.

WHAT DO YOU THINK?

1. How does Gilligan's research show the importance of gender in the socialization process?
2. Do you think boys are subject to some of the same pressures and difficulties as girls? Explain your answer.
3. Can you think of ways in which your gender has shaped the development of your personality?

---

judging a situation with an eye toward personal relationships. For example, as boys see it, stealing is wrong because it breaks the law. Girls are more likely to wonder why someone would steal and to be sympathetic toward a poor person who steals, say, to feed her family.

Kohlberg treats rule-based male reasoning as superior to the person-based female approach. Gilligan notes that impersonal rules dominate men's lives in the workplace, but personal relationships are more relevant to women's lives as mothers and caregivers. Why, then, Gilligan asks, should we set up male standards as the norms by which to judge everyone?

Critical review Gilligan's work sharpens our understanding of both human development and gender issues in research. Yet the question remains: Does nature or nurture account for the differences between females and males? In Gilligan's view, cultural conditioning is at work. If so, the moral reasoning of women and men will probably become more similar as more women organize their lives around the workplace.

GEORGE HERBERT MEAD'S THEORY OF THE SOCIAL SELF

George Herbert Mead (1863–1931) developed a theory of *social behaviorism* to explain how social experience develops an individual's personality (1962, orig. 1934).

The Self

Mead's central concept is the **self,** *the part of an individual's personality composed of self-awareness and self-image.* Mead's genius was in seeing the self as the product of social experience.

First, said Mead, *the self develops only with social experience.* The self is not part of the body, and it does not exist at birth. Mead rejected the idea that personality is guided by biological drives (as Freud asserted) or biological maturation (as Piaget claimed). For Mead, self develops only as the individual interacts with others. Without interaction, as we see from cases of isolated children, the body grows, but no self emerges.

Second, Mead explained, *social experience is the exchange of symbols.* Only people use words, a wave of the

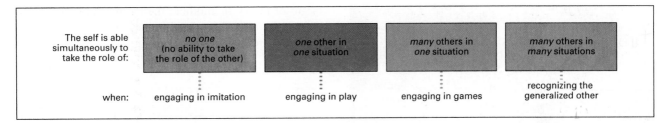

The self is able simultaneously to take the role of:	*no one* (no ability to take the role of the other)	*one* other in *one* situation	*many* others in *one* situation	*many* others in *many* situations
when:	engaging in imitation	engaging in play	engaging in games	recognizing the generalized other

FIGURE 5-1 Building on Social Experience

George Herbert Mead described the development of the self as a process of gaining social experience. That is, the self develops as we expand our capacity to take the role of the other.

hand, or a smile to create meaning. We can train a dog using reward and punishment, but the dog attaches no meaning to its actions. Human beings, by contrast, find meaning in action by imagining people's underlying intentions. In short, a dog responds to *what you do;* a human responds to *what you have in mind* as you do it. You can train a dog to go to the hallway and bring back an umbrella. But because it doesn't understand intention, if the dog cannot find the umbrella, it is incapable of the *human* response: to look for a raincoat instead.

Third, Mead continued, *understanding intention requires imagining the situation from the other's point of view.* Using symbols, we imagine ourselves "in another person's shoes" and see ourselves as that person does. We can therefore anticipate how others will respond to us even before we act. A simple toss of a ball requires stepping outside ourselves to imagine how another will catch our throw. All social interaction involves seeing ourselves as others see us—a process that Mead termed *taking the role of the other.*

The Looking-Glass Self

In effect, others are a mirror (which people used to call a "looking glass") in which we can see ourselves. What we think of ourselves, then, depends on how we think others see us. For example, if we think others see us as clever, we will think of ourselves in the same way. But if we feel they think of us as clumsy, then that is how we will see ourselves. Charles Horton Cooley (1864–1929) used the phrase **looking-glass self** to mean *a self-image based on how we think others see us* (1964, orig. 1902).

The I and the Me

Mead's fourth point is that *by taking the role of the other, we become self-aware.* Another way of saying this is that the self has two parts. One part of the self operates as subject, being active and spontaneous. Mead called the active side of the

self the "I" (the subjective form of the personal pronoun). The other part of the self works as an object, the way we imagine others see us. Mead called the objective side of the self the "me" (the objective form of the personal pronoun). All social experience has both components: We initiate an action (the I-phase, or subject side, of self) and then we continue the action based on how others respond to us (the me-phase, or object side, of self).

Mead is featured in the Gallery of Sociologists at http://www.TheSociologyPage.com

Development of the Self

According to Mead, the key to developing the self is learning to take the role of the other. With limited social experience, infants can do this only through *imitation.* They mimic behavior without understanding underlying intentions, and so at this point, they have no self.

As children learn to use language and other symbols, the self emerges in the form of *play.* Play involves assuming roles modeled on **significant others,** *people, such as parents, who have special importance for socialization.* Playing "mommy and daddy" (often putting themselves, literally, "in the shoes" of a parent) helps young children imagine the world from a parent's point of view.

Gradually, children learn to take the roles of several others at once. This skill lets them move from simple play (say, playing catch) with one other to complex *games* (like baseball) involving many others. By about age seven, most children have the social experience needed to engage in team sports.

Figure 5–1 charts the progression from imitation to play to games. But there is a final stage in the development of the self. A game involves taking the role of specific people in just one situation. Everyday life demands that we see ourselves in terms of cultural norms as *any* member of our society might. Mead used the term **generalized other** to refer

George Herbert Mead wrote: "No hard-and-fast line can be drawn between our own selves and the selves of others." The painting *Manyness* by Rimma Gerlovina and Valeriy Gerlovin conveys this important truth. Although we tend to think of ourselves as unique individuals, each person's characteristics develop in an ongoing process of interaction with others.

Rimma Gerlovina and Valeriy Gerlovin, *Manyness*, 1990. © the artists, New City, N.Y.

to *widespread cultural norms and values we use as a reference in evaluating ourselves.*

As life goes on, the self continues to change along with our social experiences. But no matter how much the world shapes us, we always remain creative beings, able to act back toward the world. Thus, Mead concluded, we play a key role in our own socialization.

Critical review Mead's work explores the character of social experience itself. In the symbolic interaction of human beings, he believed he had found the root of both self and society.

Mead's view is completely social, allowing no biological element at all. This is a problem for critics who stand with Freud (who said our general drives are rooted in the body) and Piaget (whose stages of development are tied to biological maturity).

Be careful not to confuse Mead's concepts of the I and the me with Freud's id and superego. For Freud, the id originates in our biology, but Mead rejected any biological element of the self (although he never clearly spelled out the

origin of the I). In addition, the id and the superego are locked in continual combat, but the I and the me work cooperatively together (Meltzer, 1978).

↔ **YOUR TURN** ↔

Have you ever seen young children put their hands in front of their faces and exclaim, "You can't see me!"? They assume that if they can't see you, you can't see them. What does this suggest about a young child's ability to "take the role of the other"?

ERIK H. ERIKSON'S EIGHT STAGES OF DEVELOPMENT

Although some analysts (including Freud) point to childhood as the crucial time when personality takes shape, Erik H. Erikson (1902–1994) took a broader view of socialization. He explained that we face challenges throughout the life course (1963, orig. 1950).

Stage 1—Infancy: the challenge of trust (versus mistrust). Between birth and about eighteen months, infants face the first of life's challenges: to establish a sense of trust that their world is a safe place. Family members play a key part in how any infant meets this challenge.

Stage 2—Toddlerhood: the challenge of autonomy (versus doubt and shame). The next challenge, up to age three, is to learn skills to cope with the world in a confident way. Failing to gain self-control leads children to doubt their abilities.

Stage 3—Preschool: the challenge of initiative (versus guilt). Four- and five-year-olds must learn to engage their surroundings—including people outside the family—or experience guilt at failing to meet the expectations of parents and others.

Stage 4—Preadolescence: the challenge of industriousness (versus inferiority). Between ages six and thirteen, children enter school, make friends, and strike out on their own more and more. They either feel proud of their accomplishments or fear that they do not measure up.

Stage 5—Adolescence: the challenge of gaining identity (versus confusion). During the teen years, young people struggle to establish their own identity.

In part, teenagers identify with others, but they also want to be unique. Almost all teens experience some confusion as they struggle to establish an identity.

Stage 6—Young adulthood: the challenge of intimacy (versus isolation). The challenge for young adults is to form and maintain intimate relationships with others. Falling in love (as well as making close friends) involves balancing the need to bond with the need to have a separate identity.

Stage 7—Middle adulthood: the challenge of making a difference (versus self-absorption). The challenge of middle age is contributing to the lives of others in the family, at work, and in the larger world. Failing at this, people become self-centered, caught up in their own limited concerns.

Stage 8—Old age: the challenge of integrity (versus despair). Near the end of our lives, Erikson explains, people hope to look back on what they have accomplished with a sense of integrity and satisfaction. For those who have been self-absorbed, old age brings only a sense of despair over missed opportunities.

Critical review Erikson's theory views personality formation as a lifelong process, with success at one stage (say, as an infant gaining trust) preparing us to meet the next challenge. However, not everyone faces these challenges in the exact order presented by Erikson. Nor is it clear that failure to meet the challenge of one stage of life means that a person is doomed to fail later on. A broader question, raised earlier in our discussion of Piaget's ideas, is whether people in other cultures and in other times in history would define a successful life in Erikson's terms.

In sum, Erikson's model points out how many factors—including the family and school—shape our personalities. We now take a close look at these important agents of socialization.

Agents of Socialization

Every social experience we have affects us in at least a small way. However, several familiar settings have special importance in the socialization process.

THE FAMILY

There are many ways in which the family affects socialization. For most people, in fact, the family may be the most important socialization agent of all.

Sociological research indicates that affluent parents tend to encourage creativity in their children while poor parents tend to foster conformity. Although this general difference may be valid, parents at all class levels can and do provide loving support and guidance by simply involving themselves in their children's lives. Henry Ossawa Tanner's painting *The Banjo Lesson* stands as a lasting testament to this process.

Henry Ossawa Tanner, *The Banjo Lesson*, 1893. Oil on canvas. Hampton University Museum, Hampton, Virginia.

Nurture in Early Childhood

Infants are totally dependent on others for care. The responsibility for providing a safe and caring environment typically falls on parents and other family members. For several years—at least until children begin school—the family also has the job of teaching children skills, values, and beliefs. Overall, research suggests, nothing is more likely to produce a happy, well-adjusted child than being in a loving family (Gibbs, 2001).

Not all family learning results from intentional teaching by parents. Children also learn from the type of environment adults create. Whether children learn to see

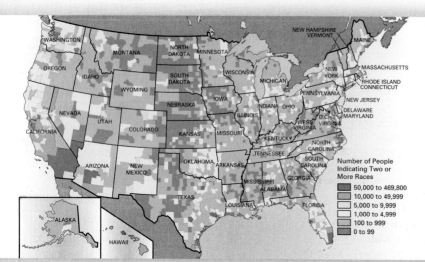

NATIONAL MAP 5–1

Racially Mixed People
across the United States

This map shows the distribution of people who
described themselves as racially mixed in the
2000 census. How do you think growing up in an
area with a high level of racially mixed people
(such as Los Angeles or New York) would be different from growing up in an area with few such
people (for example, the Plains States in the middle of the country)?

Source: U.S. Census Bureau (2001).

Number of People
Indicating Two or
More Races

- 50,000 to 469,800
- 10,000 to 49,999
- 5,000 to 9,999
- 1,000 to 4,999
- 100 to 999
- 0 to 99

themselves as strong or weak, smart or stupid, loved or simply tolerated—and as Erik Erikson suggests, whether they
see the world as trustworthy or dangerous—depends largely on the quality of the surroundings provided by parents
and other caregivers.

Race and Class

Through the family, parents give a social identity to children. In part, social identity involves race. Racial identity
can be complex because, as Chapter 14 ("Race and Ethnicity") explains, societies define race in various ways. In addition, in the 2000 census, more than 7 million people (about
2.5 percent) said they consider themselves to be of two or
more racial categories. This number is rising, and 5 percent
of all births in the United States are now recorded as interracial. National Map 5–1 shows where interracial births are
most and least common.

Social class position, like race, plays a large part in
shaping a child's personality. Whether born into families of
high or low social position, children gradually come to realize that their family's social standing affects how others see
them and, in time, how they come to see themselves.

In addition, research shows that class position affects
not just how much money parents have to spend on their
children but also what parents expect of them (Ellison,
Bartkowski, & Segal, 1996). When people in the United
States were asked to pick from a list of traits that are most
desirable in a child, those with lower social standing favored obedience and conformity. Well-to-do people, by
contrast, chose good judgment and creativity (NORC,
2003).

Why the difference? Melvin Kohn (1977) explains that
people of lower social standing usually have limited education and perform routine jobs under close supervision. Expecting that their children will hold similar positions, they
encourage obedience and may even use physical punishment like spanking to get it. Because well-off parents have
had more schooling, they usually have jobs that demand
imagination and creativity, so they try to inspire the same
qualities in their children. Consciously or not, all parents
act in ways that encourage their children to follow in their
footsteps.

More well-off parents typically provide their children
with an extensive program of leisure activities, including
sports, travel, and music lessons. These enrichment activities—far less available to children growing up in low-
income families—represent important *cultural capital* that
advances learning and creates a sense of confidence in
these children that they will succeed later in life (Lareau,
2002).

Social class also affects how long the process of growing
up takes. The Applying Sociology box explains.

THE SCHOOL

Schooling enlarges children's social world to include people
with backgrounds different from their own. It is only as they
encounter people who differ from themselves that children
come to understand the importance of factors such as race
and social class position. As they do, they are likely to cluster
in playgroups made up of one class, race, and gender (Lever,
1978; Finkelstein & Haskins, 1983).

APPLYING SOCIOLOGY
Are We Grown Up Yet? Defining Adulthood

Are you an adult or still an adolescent? In the United States, when can young people expect to be treated by others as grown up? According to the sociologist Tom Smith (2003), there is no one factor that announces the onset of adulthood. Far from it: The results of his survey—using a representative sample of 1,398 people over the age of eighteen—suggest that many factors play a part in our decision to consider a young person as "grown up."

According to the survey, the single most important transition in claiming adult standing in the United States today is the completion of schooling. But other factors are also important: Smith's respondents linked adult standing to taking on a full-time job, gaining the ability to support a family

financially, no longer living with parents, and finally, marrying and becoming a parent. In other words, almost everyone in the United States thinks a person who has done *all* of these things is fully "grown up."

At what age are these transitions likely to be completed? On average, the answer is about age twenty-six. But such an average masks an important difference based on social class. People who do not attend college (more common among people growing up in lower-income families) typically finish school before age twenty, and a full-time job, independent living, marriage, and parenthood may follow in a year or two. Those from more privileged backgrounds are likely to attend college and may even go on to graduate or professional school,

delaying the process of becoming an adult for as long as ten years, past the age of thirty.

WHAT DO YOU THINK?

1. Do you consider yourself an adult? At what age did your adulthood begin?
2. Consider a woman whose children are grown, who has had a recent divorce, and is now going to college getting a degree so that she can find a job. Is she likely to feel that she is suddenly not quite "grown up," now that she's back in school? Why or why not?
3. How does the research described in this box show that adulthood is a socially defined concept rather than a biological stage of life?

Gender

Schools join with families in socializing children into gender roles. Studies show that at school, boys engage in more physical activities and spend more time outdoors, and girls are more likely to help teachers with various housekeeping chores. Boys also engage in more aggressive behavior in the classroom, while girls are typically quieter and better behaved (R. Best, 1983; Jordan & Cowan, 1995).

YOUR TURN

Point to ways in which life on your campus makes the differences between women and men bigger or smaller.

What Children Learn

Schooling is not the same for children living in rich and poor communities. As Chapter 20 ("Education") explains,

children from well-off families typically have a far better experience in school than those whose families are poor.

For all children, the lessons learned in school include more than the formal lesson plans. Schools informally teach many things, which together might be called the *hidden curriculum*. Activities such as spelling bees teach children not only how to spell but how society divides the population into "winners" and "losers." Sports help students develop their strength and skills and also teach children important lessons in cooperation and competition.

School is also the first experience with bureaucracy for most children. The school day is based on impersonal rules and a strict time schedule. Not surprisingly, these are also the traits of the large organizations that will employ them later in life.

THE PEER GROUP

By the time they enter school, children have discovered the **peer group,** *a social group whose members have interests,*

Concern with violence and the mass media extends to the world of video games, especially those popular with young boys. Among the most controversial games, which include high levels of violence, is *Grand Theft Auto*. Do you think the current rating codes are sufficient to guide parents and children who buy video games, or would you support greater restrictions on game content?

social position, and age in common. Unlike the family and the school, the peer group lets children escape the direct supervision of adults. Among their peers, children learn how to form relationships on their own. Peer groups also offer the chance to discuss interests that adults may not share with their children (such as clothing and popular music) or permit (such as drugs and sex).

It is not surprising, then, that parents express concern about who their children's friends are. In a rapidly changing society, peer groups have great influence, and the attitudes of young and old may differ because of a "generation gap." The importance of peer groups typically peaks during adolescence, when young people begin to break away from their families and think of themselves as adults.

Even during adolescence, however, parental influence on children remains strong. Peers may affect short-term interests such as music or films, but parents have greater influence on long-term goals, such as going to college (Davies & Kandel, 1981).

Finally, any neighborhood or school is made up of many peer groups. As Chapter 7 ("Groups and Organizations") explains, individuals tend to view their own group in positive terms and put down other groups. In addition, people are influenced by peer groups they would like to join, a process sociologists call **anticipatory socialization,** *learning that helps a person achieve a desired position.* In school, for example, young people may copy the styles and slang of a group they hope will accept them. Later in life, a young lawyer who hopes to become a partner in the law firm may conform to the attitudes and behavior of the firm's partners in order to be accepted.

THE MASS MEDIA

August 30, the Isle of Coll, off the west coast of Scotland. The last time we visited this remote island, there was no electricity and most of the people spoke the ancient Gaelic language. Now that a cable comes from the mainland, homes have lights and appliances and— television! Almost with the flip of a switch, this tiny place has been thrust into the modern world. It is no surprise that traditions are fast disappearing and a rising share of the population now consists of mainlanders who come out to their vacation homes.

The **mass media** are *the means for delivering impersonal communications to a vast audience.* The term *media* comes from the Latin word for "middle," suggesting that media serve to connect people. *Mass* media arise as communications technology (first newspapers and then radio, television, films, and the Internet) spreads information on a mass scale.

In the United States today, the mass media have an enormous effect on our attitudes and behavior. Television, introduced in the 1930s, quickly became the dominant medium, and 98 percent of U.S. households now have at least one set (by comparison, just 95 percent have telephones). Two out of three households also have cable  or satellite television. As Figure 5–2 shows, the United States has one of the highest rates of television ownership in the world. In this country, it is people with lower incomes who spend the most time watching TV.

An online chapter on the mass media is available at http://www.prenticehall.ca/macionis/massmedia.html

The Extent of Television Viewing

Just how "glued to the tube" are we? Survey data show that the average household has at least one set turned on for seven hours each day and that people spend almost half their free time watching television. A study by the Kaiser Family Foundation found that youngsters between the ages of two and eighteen average 5 1/2 hours a day "consuming media," including almost three hours of television and the rest watching video movies and playing video games (MacPherson, 1999; Cornell, 2000).

Years before children learn to read, television watching is a regular part of their daily routine. As they grow, children spend as many hours in front of a television as they do in school or interacting with their parents. This is the case despite research suggesting that television makes children more passive and less likely to use their imagination (American Psychological Association, 1993; Fellman, 1995).

Television and Political Bias

The comedian Fred Allen once quipped that we call television a "medium" because it is rarely well done. For a number of reasons, television (as well as other mass media) provokes plenty of criticism. Some liberal critics argue that for most of television's history, racial and ethnic minorities have not been visible or have been included only in stereotypical roles (such as African Americans playing butlers, Asian Americans playing gardeners, or Hispanics playing new immigrants). In recent years, however, minorities have moved closer to center stage on television. There are ten times as many Hispanic actors on primetime television as there were ten years ago, and they play a far larger range of characters (Lichter & Amundson, 1997; Fetto, 2003b).

On the other side of the fence, conservative critics charge that the television and film industries are dominated by a liberal "cultural elite." In recent years, they claim, "politically correct" media have advanced liberal causes, including feminism and gay rights (Rothman, Powers, & Rothman, 1993; B. Goldberg, 2002). On the other hand, the increasing popularity of the Fox Network—home to Sean Hannity, Bill O'Reilly, Brit Hume, and other more conservative commentators—suggests that people can now find

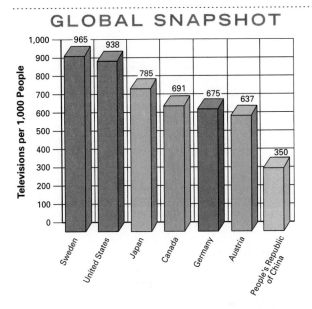

GLOBAL SNAPSHOT

FIGURE 5–2 Television Ownership in Global Perspective

Television is popular in all high-income countries, especially in Sweden and the United States where there is almost one TV set for every person.

Source: International Telecommunication Union (2005).

programming consistent with "spin" from both sides of the political spectrum.

Television and Violence

In 1996, the American Medical Association (AMA) issued the startling statement that violence in television and films had reached such a high level that it posed a hazard to our health. More recently, a study found a strong link between aggressive behavior and the amount of time elementary schoolchildren spend watching television and using video games (Robinson et al., 2001). The public is concerned about this issue: Three-fourths of U.S. adults report having walked out of a movie or turned off the television because of too much violence. Almost two-thirds of television programs contain violence, and in most such scenes, violent characters show no remorse and are not punished (B. Wilson, 1998).

In 1997, the television industry adopted a rating system. But we are left to wonder whether watching sexual or violent programming harms people as much as critics say. More important, why do the mass media contain so much sex and violence in the first place?

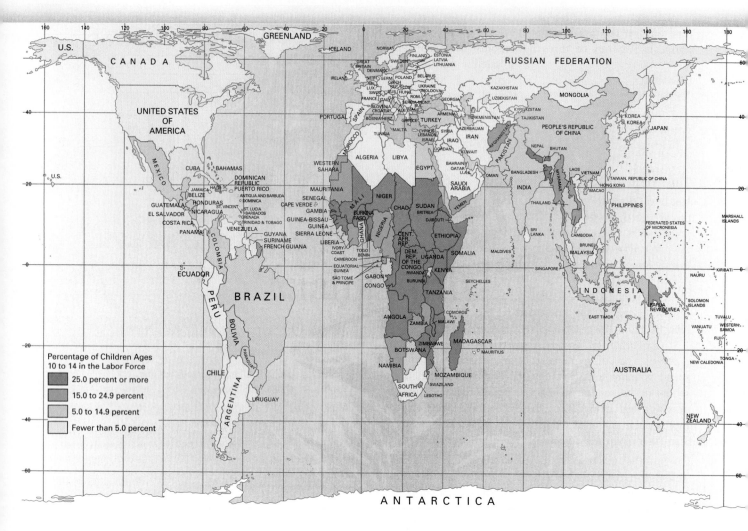

WINDOW ON THE WORLD

GLOBAL MAP 5-1   Child Labor in Global Perspective

Industrialization extends childhood and discourages children from work and other activities considered suitable only for adults. Thus child labor is uncommon in the United States and other high-income countries. In less economically developed nations of the world, however, children are a vital economic asset, and they typically begin working as soon as they are able.

Sources: World Bank (2005) and author estimates; map projection from *Peters Atlas of the World* (1990).

Television and the other mass media enrich our lives with entertaining and educational programming. The media also increase our exposure to diverse cultures and provoke discussion of current issues. At the same time, the power of the media—especially television—to shape how we think remains highly controversial.

Other spheres of life beyond family, school, peer group, and the media also play a part in social learning. For most people in the United States, these include the workplace, religious organizations, the military, and social clubs. In the end, socialization proves to be not a simple matter of learning but a complex balancing act as we absorb information from different sources. In the process of sorting and weighing all the information we receive, we shape our own distinctive personalities.

Socialization and the Life Course

Although childhood has special importance in the socialization process, learning continues throughout our lives. An overview of the life course reveals that our society organizes human experience according to age—childhood, adolescence, adulthood, and, finally, old age.

CHILDHOOD

A few years ago, the Nike Corporation, maker of popular athletic shoes, came under attack. Their shoes are made in Taiwan and Indonesia, in many cases by children who work in factories instead of going to school. Some 250 million of the world's children work, half of them full time, earning about fifty cents an hour (Human Rights Watch, 2004). Global Map 5–1 shows that child labor is most common in the nations of Africa and Asia.

Criticism of Nike springs from the fact that most North Americans think of *childhood*—roughly the first twelve years of life—as a carefree time for learning and play. Yet as the historian Philippe Ariès (1965) explains, the whole idea of "childhood" is fairly new. During the Middle Ages, children of four or five were treated like adults and expected to fend for themselves.

We defend our idea of childhood because children are biologically immature. But a look back in time and around the world shows that the concept of childhood is grounded not in biology but in culture (LaRossa & Reitzes, 2001). In

Human Rights Watch reports on child soldiers around the world at http://www.hrw.org/campaigns/crp/index.htm

rich countries, not everyone has to work, so childhood can be extended to allow time for young people to learn the skills they will need in a high-technology workplace.

Because childhood in the United States lasts such a long time, some people worry when children seem to be growing up too fast. In part, this "hurried child" syndrome results from changes in the family—including high divorce rates and both parents in the labor force—that leave children with less supervision. In addition, "adult" programming on television (not to mention in films and on the Internet) carries grown-up concerns such as sex, drugs, and violence into young people's lives. Today's ten- to twelve-year-olds, says one executive of a children's television channel, have about

In recent decades, some people have become concerned that U.S. society is shortening childhood, pushing children to grow up faster and faster. Do films such as *Thirteen*, which show young girls dressing and behaving as if they were much older, encourage a "hurried childhood"? Do you see this as a problem or not?

the same interests and experiences typical of twelve- to fourteen-year-olds a generation ago (K. Hymowitz, 1998). Perhaps this is why today's children, compared to kids fifty years ago, have higher levels of stress and anxiety (Gorman, 2000).

ADOLESCENCE

At the same time that industrialization created childhood as a distinct stage of life, adolescence emerged as a buffer between childhood and adulthood. We generally link *adolescence*, or the teenage years, with emotional and social turmoil as young people struggle to develop their own identities. Again, we are tempted to attribute teenage rebelliousness and confusion to the biological changes of puberty. But it correctly reflects cultural inconsistency. For example, the mass media glorify sex, and schools hand out condoms, even as parents urge restraint. Consider, too, that an eighteen-year-old may face the adult duty of going to war but lacks the adult right to drink a beer. In short,

December 26, 2004

Adultescent

By JOHN TIERNEY

Adultescent came of age in 2004, but only as a word. The adult it describes is too busy playing Halo 2 on his Xbox or watching SpongeBob at his parents' house to think about growing up. The editors of the *Webster's New World College Dictionary* chose *adultescent* as word of the year; they said there were enough examples to constitute a "Peter Pandemic."

Since 1970, the median age for Americans to marry has risen four years, to 25 for women and 27 for men. Meanwhile, the proportion of people in their early 30s who have never married has tripled.

There are four million Americans between 25 and 34 still living with their parents, not always happily, as the apartments.com Web site discovered last year when it offered $10,000 for the best essay from an adultescent desperate for money to get his or her own place. The winner was a 25-year-old woman who told of sharing a room with her 17-year-old brother.

But being unencumbered by rent—or mortgages or children—can leave lots of disposable income, which is why marketers have happily focused on adultescents since at least 1996. That was the year an article in the magazine *Precision Marketing* referred to the "adultescent marketplace," the earliest citation discovered by Paul McFedries, the author of the wordspy.com Web site.

Other variations would later appear—*adultolescents, adulescents, kidults* and *rejuveniles*—but nothing else quite captured the person with teenage tastes and an adult credit card. Someone free to do nothing, like the characters on *Seinfeld*, or party all night, like the ones in *Sex in the City*. Someone with a connoisseur's passion for plasma televisions, Kelly bags, Harry Potter movies and low-riding Gap jeans. Someone with a ritual call at birthday parties: "30 is the new 20," "40 is the new 30," etc.

One common explanation for the rise in adultescence is the cost of housing and education, which has made it harder for young people (especially in places like New York [City]) to afford homes and children. Another explanation is that young adults now enjoy some pleasures of marriage without the consequences.

But if you ask adultescents why they haven't grown up, they may give you a simple answer: Because they don't have to.

---

adolescence is a time of social contradictions, when people are no longer children but not yet adults.

As is true of all stages of life, adolescence varies according to social background. Most young people from working-class families move directly from high school into the adult world of work and parenting. Wealthier teens, however, have the resources to attend college and perhaps graduate school, stretching adolescence into the late twenties and even the thirties.

 YOUR TURN

Many of our soldiers in Iraq are still teenagers. Why should we not be surprised to learn that most of these young men and women performing adult jobs are from small-town, working-class families?

ADULTHOOD

If stages of the life course were based on biological stages, it would be easy to define *adulthood*. However, as "In the *Times*" explains, deciding when someone is an adult turns out to be more complicated than it may seem.

Regardless of exactly when it begins, adulthood is the time when most of life's accomplishments take place, including pursuing a career and raising a family. Personalities are largely formed by then, although marked changes in a person's environment—such as unemployment, divorce, or serious illness—may cause significant changes to the self.

Early Adulthood

During early adulthood—until about age forty—young adults learn to manage day-to-day affairs for themselves, often juggling conflicting priorities: parents, partner, children, schooling, and work. Women are especially likely to

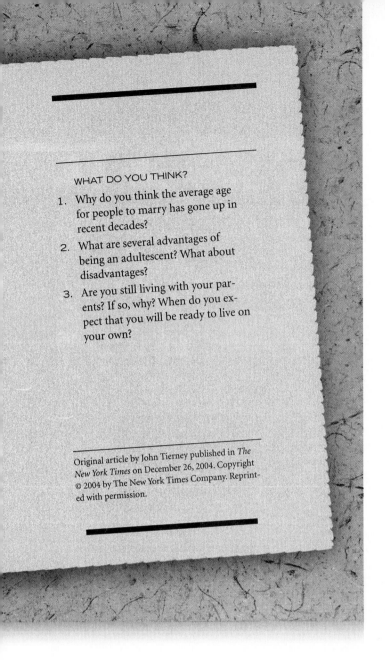

WHAT DO YOU THINK?

1. Why do you think the average age for people to marry has gone up in recent decades?

2. What are several advantages of being an adultescent? What about disadvantages?

3. Are you still living with your parents? If so, why? When do you expect that you will be ready to live on your own?

Original article by John Tierney published in *The New York Times* on December 26, 2004. Copyright © 2004 by The New York Times Company. Reprinted with permission.

try to "do it all," because our culture gives them the major responsibility for child rearing and housework even if they have demanding jobs outside the home.

Middle Adulthood

In middle adulthood—roughly ages forty to sixty—people sense that their life circumstances are pretty well set. They also become more aware of the fragility of health, which the young typically take for granted. Women who have spent many years raising a family find middle adulthood emotionally trying. Children grow up and require less attention, and husbands become absorbed in their careers, leaving some women with spaces in their lives that are difficult to fill. Many women who divorce also face serious financial problems (Weitzman, 1985, 1996). For all these reasons, an increasing number of women in middle adulthood return to school and seek new careers.

For everyone, growing older means facing physical decline, a prospect our culture makes especially painful for women. Because good looks are considered more important for women, wrinkles and graying hair can be traumatic. Men have their own particular difficulties as they get older. Some must admit that they are never going to reach earlier career goals. Others realize that the price of career success has been neglect of family or personal health.

OLD AGE

Old age—the later years of adulthood and the final stage of life itself—begins about the mid-sixties. Again, societies attach different meanings to this stage of life. As explained in Chapter 15 ("Aging and the Elderly"), it is older members of traditional societies who typically control most of the land and other wealth. Also, since traditional societies change slowly, older people possess useful wisdom gained over their lifetime, which earns them much respect.

In industrial societies, however, most younger people work and live apart from their parents, becoming independent of their elders. Rapid change also gives our society a "youth orientation" that defines what is old as unimportant or even obsolete. To younger people, the elderly may seem out of touch with new trends and fashions, and their knowledge and experience may seem of little value.

Perhaps this anti-elderly bias will decline as the share of older people in the United States steadily increases. The percentage of the U.S. population over age sixty-five has more than tripled in the past hundred years, and there are already more seniors than there are teenagers. Life expectancy is still increasing, so most men and women in their mid-sixties (the "young elderly") can look forward to living decades longer. By 2030, the number of seniors will more than double again to 80 million, and the "average" person in the United States will be forty years old (U.S. Census Bureau, 2004).

Old age differs in an important way from earlier stages in the life course. Growing up typically means entering new roles and taking on new responsibilities, but growing old is the opposite experience—leaving roles that provided both satisfaction and social identity. For some people, retirement is a period of restful activity, but for others, it can mean losing valued routines and even outright boredom. Like any life transition, retirement demands learning new patterns while at the same time letting go of habits from the past.

DEATH AND DYING

Through most of human history, low living standards and limited medical technology meant that death from accident or disease could come at any stage of life. Today, however,

The Development of Self among High School Students

Adolescence is a time when people ask questions like "Who am I?" and "What do I want to become?" In the end, we all have to answer these questions for ourselves. But race and ethnicity are likely to have an effect on what our answers turn out to be.

Grace Kao (2000) studied the identity and goals of students enrolled in Johnstown High School, a large (3,000-student) school in a Chicago suburb. Johnstown High is considered a good school, with above-average test scores. It is also racially and ethnically diverse: 47 percent of the students are white, 43 percent are African American, 7 percent are Hispanic, and 3 percent are of Asian descent.

Kao interviewed sixty-three Johnstown students—female and male—both individually and in small groups with others of the same race and ethnicity. Talking with them, she learned how important racial and ethnic stereotypes are in young people's developing sense of self.

What are these stereotypes? White students are seen as hardworking in school and concerned about getting

high grades. African American students are thought to study less, either because they are not as smart or because they just don't try as hard. In any case, students see African Americans at high risk of failure in school. Because the stereotype says that Hispanics are headed for manual occupations—as gardeners or laborers—they are seen as not caring very much about doing well. Finally, Asian American students are seen as hardworking high achievers, either because they are smart or because they spend their time on academics rather than, say, sports.

From her interviews, Kao learned that most students think these stereotypes are true and take them personally. They expect people, including themselves, to perform in school more or less the way the stereotype predicts. In addition, young people—whether white, black, Hispanic, or Asian—mostly hang out with others like themselves, which gives them little chance to find out that their beliefs are wrong.

Students of all racial and ethnic categories say they *want* to do well in school. But not getting to know those who differ from themselves means that

they measure success *only in relation to their own category.* To African American students, in other words, "success" means doing as well as other black students and not flunking out. To Hispanics, "success" means avoiding manual labor and ending up with any job in an office. Whites and Asians, by contrast, define "success" as earning high grades and living up to the high-achievement stereotype. For all these young people, then, "self" develops through the lens of how race and ethnicity are defined by our society.

WHAT DO YOU THINK?

1. Were there racial and ethnic stereotypes, similar to those described here, in your high school? What about your college?
2. Do you think that gender stereotypes affect the performance of women and men in school as much as racial and ethnic stereotypes? Explain.
3. What can be done to reduce the damaging effects of racial and ethnic stereotypes?

85 percent of people in the United States die after age fifty-five (Hoyert, Kung, & Smith, 2005).

After observing many dying people, the psychologist Elisabeth Kübler-Ross (1969) described death as an orderly transition involving five distinct stages. Typically, a person first faces death with *denial,* perhaps out of fear and perhaps because our culture tends to ignore the reality of death. The second phase is *anger,* when a person facing death sees it as a gross injustice. Third, anger gives way to *negotiation* as the person imagines avoiding death by striking a bargain with

God. The fourth response, *resignation,* is often accompanied by psychological depression. Finally, a complete adjustment to death requires *acceptance.* At this point, no longer paralyzed by fear and anxiety, the person whose life is ending now finds peace and makes the most of whatever time remains.

As the share of women and men in old age increases, we can expect our culture to become more comfortable with the idea of death. In recent years, people in the United States have started talking about death more openly, and the trend is to view dying as natural and better than painful or prolonged suffering. More married couples now prepare for death with legal and financial planning. This openness may ease somewhat the pain of the surviving spouse, a consideration for women, who, more often than not, outlive their husbands.

THE LIFE COURSE: PATTERNS AND VARIATIONS

This brief look at the life course points to two major conclusions. First, although each stage of life is linked to the biological process of aging, the life course is largely a social construction. For this reason, people in other societies may experience a stage of life quite differently or, for that matter, not at all. Second, in any society, the stages of the life course present certain problems and transitions that involve learning something new and, in many cases, unlearning familiar routines.

Societies organize the life course according to age, but other forces, such as class, race, ethnicity, and gender, also shape people's lives. This means that the general patterns described in this chapter apply somewhat differently to various categories of people within any society. The Thinking About Diversity box provides an example of how race and ethnicity can shape the academic performance of high school students.

People's life experiences also vary depending on when, in the history of the society, they are born. A **cohort** is *a category of people with something in common, usually their age.* Because age cohorts are generally influenced by the same economic and cultural trends, they tend to have similar attitudes and values. Women and men born in the 1940s and 1950s, for example, grew up during a time of economic expansion that gave them a sense of optimism. Today's college students, who have grown up in an age of economic uncertainty, are less confident of the future.

YOUR TURN

Do you think the war on terror has special importance to today's young people? Why or why not?

Resocialization: Total Institutions

A final type of socialization, experienced by more than 2 million people in the United States, involves being confined—usually against their will—in prisons or mental hospitals. This is the world of the **total institution,** *a setting*

Prisons are one example of a total institution in which inmates dress alike and carry out daily routines under the direct supervision and control of the institutional staff. What do we expect prison to do to young people convicted of crimes? How well do you think prisons do what people expect them to?

in which people are isolated from the rest of society and manipulated by an administrative staff.

According to Erving Goffman (1961), total institutions have three important characteristics. First, staff members supervise all aspects of daily life, including where residents (often called "inmates") eat, sleep, and work. Second, life in a total institution is controlled and standardized, with the same food, uniforms, and activities for everyone. Third, formal rules dictate when, where, and how inmates perform their daily routines.

The purpose of such rigid routines is **resocialization,** *efforts to radically change an inmate's personality by carefully controlling the environment.* Prisons and mental hospitals physically isolate inmates behind fences, barred windows,

THINKING IT THROUGH

Are We Free within Society?

This chapter stresses one key theme: Society shapes how we think, feel, and act. If this is so, then in what sense are we free? To answer this important question, consider the Muppets, puppet stars of television and film. Watching the antics of Kermit the Frog, Miss Piggy, and the rest of the troupe, we almost believe they are real rather than objects controlled from backstage. As the sociological perspective points out, human beings are like puppets in that we, too, respond to backstage forces. Society, after all, gives us a culture and shapes our lives according to class, race, and gender. If this is so, can we really claim to be free?

Sociologists answer this question with many voices. The politically liberal response is that individuals are *not* free of society—in fact, as social creatures, we never could be. But if we have to live in a society with power

over us, it is important to do what we can to make our home as just as possible, by working to lessen class differences and other barriers to opportunity for minorities, including women. Conservatives answer that we *are* free because society can never dictate our dreams. Our history as a nation, right from the revolutionary act that led to its founding, is one story after another of people pursuing personal goals despite great odds.

Both attitudes are found in George Herbert Mead's analysis of socialization. Mead knew that society makes demands on us, sometimes limiting our options. But he also saw that human beings are spontaneous and creative, capable of continually acting on society and bringing about change. Mead noted the power of society while still affirming the human capacity to evaluate, criticize, and ultimately choose and change.

In the end, then, we may seem like puppets, but only on the surface. A crucial difference is that we can stop, look up at the "strings" that make us move, and even yank on them defiantly (Berger, 1963:176). If our pull is strong enough, we can do more than we might think. As Margaret Mead once remarked, "Never doubt that a small group of thoughtful, committed citizens can change the world. Indeed, it is the only thing that ever has."

WHAT DO YOU THINK?

1. Do you think our society gives more freedom to males than to females? Why or why not?
2. Are people in modern, high-income countries more free than those in traditional, low-income nations? Explain your answer.
3. Has learning about socialization increased or decreased your feeling of freedom? Why?

and locked doors and limit their access to the telephone, mail, and visitors. The institution becomes their entire world, making it easier for the staff to bring about personality change—or at least obedience—in the inmate.

Resocialization is a two-part process. First, the staff breaks down the new inmate's existing identity. For example, an inmate must give up personal possessions, including clothing and grooming articles used to maintain a distinctive appearance. Instead, the staff provides standard-issue clothes so that everyone looks alike. The staff subjects new inmates to "mortifications of self," which can include searches, head shaving, medical examinations, fingerprinting, and assignment of a serial number. Once inside the walls, individuals also give up their privacy as guards routinely inspect their living quarters.

In the second part of the resocialization process, the staff tries to build a new self in the inmate through a

system of rewards and punishments. Having a book to read, watching television, or making a telephone call may seem like minor pleasures to the outsider, but in the rigid environment of the total institution, gaining such simple privileges as these can be a powerful motivation to conform. The length of confinement typically depends on how well the inmate cooperates with the staff.

Total institutions affect people in different ways. Some inmates may end up "rehabilitated" or "recovered," but others may change little, and still others may become hostile and bitter. Over a long period of time, living in a rigidly controlled environment can leave some *institutionalized,* without the capacity for independent living.

But what about the rest of us? Does socialization crush our individuality or empower us to reach our creative potential? The Thinking It Through box takes a closer look at this important question.

The following learning tools will help you see what you know, identify what you still need to learn, and expand your understanding beyond the text. You can also visit this text's Companion Website™ at http://www.prenhall.com/macionis to find additional practice tests.

KEY POINTS

Social Experience: The Key to Our Humanity

Socialization is the lifelong process by which we develop our humanity and our particular personalities. A century ago, people thought that most human behavior was guided by biological instinct. Today, we know that human behavior is mostly a result of nurture rather than nature. The importance of social experience to human development is seen in the fact that social isolation can lead to permanent damage.

Understanding Socialization

Sigmund Freud's model of the human personality has three parts. The id represents innate human drives (the life and death instincts), the superego is internalized cultural values and norms, and the ego is our ability to resolve competition between the demands of the id and the restraints of the superego.

Jean Piaget believed that human development involves both biological maturation and gaining social experience. He identified four stages of cognitive development: sensorimotor, preoperational, concrete operational, and formal operational.

Lawrence Kohlberg applied Piaget's approach to moral development. We first judge rightness in preconventional terms, according to our individual needs. Next, conventional moral reasoning takes account of parental attitudes and cultural norms. Finally, postconventional reasoning allows us to criticize society itself.

Carol Gilligan studied the effect of gender on moral development and found that males rely on abstract standards of rightness and females look at the effect of decisions on relationships.

To George Herbert Mead, the self comes from social experience and is partly self-directed (the I) and partly guided by society (the me). Infants yet to form the self can only imitate others; later, the self develops through play and games and eventually includes the generalized other. Charles Horton Cooley used the term *looking-glass self* to explain that we see ourselves as we imagine others see us.

Erik H. Erikson identified challenges that individuals face at each stage of life from infancy to old age.

Agents of Socialization

Usually the first setting of socialization, the family has the greatest influence on a child's attitudes and behavior. Schools expose children to greater social diversity and introduce them to impersonal bureaucracy. Peer groups free children from adult supervision and take on great significance during adolescence. The mass media, especially television, have great impact on the socialization process; the average U.S. child spends as much time watching television as attending school or interacting with parents.

Socialization and the Life Course

Each stage of the life course—childhood, adolescence, adulthood, and old age—is socially constructed in ways that vary from society to society. People in high-income countries typically fend off death until old age. Accepting death is part of socialization for the elderly.

Resocialization: Total Institutions

Total institutions, such as prisons and mental hospitals, try to resocialize inmates, that is, to radically change their personalities.

KEY CONCEPTS

socialization (p. 118) the lifelong social experience by which people develop their human potential and learn culture

personality (p. 118) a person's fairly consistent patterns of acting, thinking, and feeling

id (p. 121) Freud's term for the human being's basic drives

ego (p. 121) Freud's term for a person's conscious efforts to balance innate pleasure-seeking drives with the demands of society

superego (p. 121) Freud's term for the cultural values and norms internalized by an individual

sensorimotor stage (p. 122) Piaget's term for the level of human development at which individuals experience the world only through their senses

preoperational stage (p. 122) Piaget's term for the level of human development at which individuals first use language and other symbols

concrete operational stage (p. 122) Piaget's term for the level of human development at which individuals first see causal connections in their surroundings

formal operational stage (p. 122) Piaget's term for the level of human development at which individuals think abstractly and critically

self (p. 124) George Herbert Mead's term for the part of an individual's personality composed of self-awareness and self-image

looking-glass self (p. 125) Cooley's term for a self-image based on how we think others see us

significant others (p. 125) people, such as parents, who have special importance for socialization

generalized other (p. 125) George Herbert Mead's term for widespread cultural norms

and values we use as a reference in evaluating ourselves

peer group (p. 129) a social group whose members have interests, social position, and age in common

anticipatory socialization (p. 130) learning that helps a person achieve a desired position

mass media (p. 130) the means for delivering impersonal communications to a vast audience

cohort (p. 137) a category of people with something in common, usually their age

total institution (p. 137) a setting in which people are isolated from the rest of society and manipulated by an administrative staff

resocialization (p. 137) efforts to radically change an inmate's personality by carefully controlling the environment

SAMPLE TEST QUESTIONS

These questions are similar to those found in the test bank that accompanies this textbook.

Multiple-Choice Questions

1. Kingsley Davis's study of Anna, the girl isolated for five years, shows that
   a. humans have all the same instincts found in other animal species.
   b. without social experience, a child never develops personality.
   c. personality is present in all humans at birth.
   d. many human instincts disappear in the first few years of life.

2. Most sociologists take the position that
   a. humans have instincts that direct behavior.
   b. biological instincts develop in humans at puberty.
   c. it is human nature to nurture.
   d. all of the above.

3. Lawrence Kohlberg explored socialization by studying
   a. cognition.
   b. the importance of gender in socialization.

   c. the development of biological instincts.
   d. moral reasoning.

4. Carol Gilligan added to Kohlberg's findings by showing that
   a. girls and boys typically use different standards in deciding what is right and wrong.
   b. girls are more interested in right and wrong than boys are.
   c. boys are more interested in right and wrong than girls are.
   d. today's children are far less interested in right and wrong than their parents are.

5. The "self," said George Herbert Mead, is
   a. the part of the human personality made up of self-awareness and self-image.
   b. the presence of culture within the individual.
   c. basic drives that are self-centered.
   d. present in infants from birth.

6. Why is the family so important to the socialization process?
   a. Family members provide vital caregiving to infants and children.
   b. Families give children social identity in terms of class, ethnicity, and religion.
   c. Parents greatly affect a child's self-concept.
   d. All of the above are correct.

7. Social class position affects socialization: Lower-class parents tend to stress _____, and well-to-do parents stress _____.
   a. independence; protecting children
   b. independence; dependence
   c. obedience; creativity
   d. creativity; obedience

8. In global perspective, which statement about childhood is correct?
   a. In every society, the first ten years of life are a time of play and learning.
   b. Rich societies extend childhood much longer than poor societies do.
   c. Poor societies extend childhood much longer than rich societies do.
   d. Childhood is defined by being biologically immature.

9. Modern, high-income societies typically define people in old age as
   a. the wisest of all.
   b. the most up-to-date on current fashion and trends.

c. less socially important than younger adults.
d. all of the above.

10. According to Erving Goffman, the purpose of a total institution is
    a. to reward someone for achievement in the outside world.
    b. to give a person more choices about how to live.
    c. to encourage lifelong learning in a supervised context.
    d. to radically change a person's personality or behavior.

ANSWERS: 1(b); 2(c); 3(d); 4(a); 5(a); 6(d); 7(c); 8(b); 9(c); 10(d).

Essay Questions

1. State the two sides of the "nature-nurture" debate. In what important way are nature and nurture not opposed to each other?

2. What are common themes in the ideas of Freud, Piaget, Kohlberg, Gilligan, Mead, and Erikson? In what ways do their theories differ?

APPLICATIONS & EXERCISES

1. Working with several members of your sociology class, gather data by asking classmates and friends to name traits they consider part of "human nature." Compare notes, and discuss the extent to which these traits come from nature or nurture.

2. Find a copy of the book or film *Lord of the Flies*, a tale based on a Freudian model of personality. Jack and his hunters represent the power of the id; Piggy opposes them as the superego; Ralph stands between the two as the ego, the voice of reason. William Golding wrote the

book after taking part in the bloody D-Day landing in France during World War II. Do you agree with his belief that violence is part of human nature?

3. Watch several hours of primetime programming on network or cable television. Keep track of every time any element of violence is shown. For fun, assign each program a "YIP rating," for the number of years in prison a person would serve for committing all the violent acts you witness (Fobes, 1996). On the basis of observing this small (and unrepresentative) sample of programs, what are your conclusions?

INVESTIGATE *with* Research Navigator

Follow the instructions found on page 27 of this text to access the features of **Research Navigator**™. Once at the Web site, enter your Login Name and Password. Then, to use the **ContentSelect**™ database, enter keywords such as "Sigmund Freud," "mass media," and "childhood," and the search engine will supply relevant and recent scholarly and popular press publications. Use the *New York Times* **Search-by-Subject Archive** to find recent news articles related to sociology and the **Link Library** feature to find relevant Web links organized by the key terms associated with this chapter.

CHAPTER SIX

Social Interaction in Everyday Life

How do we create reality in our
face-to-face interactions?

Why do employers try to control their workers'
feelings as well as their on-the-job behavior?

What makes something funny?

HAROLD AND SYBIL are on their way to another couple's home in an unfamiliar area near Wilkes Barre, Pennsylvania. They have been driving in circles looking for Joseph Camp Road, and now they are late. Harold, gripping the wheel ever more tightly, is doing a slow burn. Sybil, sitting next to him, looks straight ahead, afraid to utter a word.

Harold and Sybil are lost in more ways than one: They are unable to understand why they are growing angry at their situation and at each other. Like most men, Harold can't stand getting lost, and the longer he drives around, the more incompetent he feels. Sybil cannot understand why Harold does not pull into a gas station and ask someone where Joseph Camp Road is. If she were driving, she thinks to herself, they would have arrived already and would now be settled comfortably with their friends.

Why don't men like to ask for directions? Because men value their independence, they don't like to ask for help (and they are also reluctant to accept it). To ask someone for assistance is the same as saying, "You know something I don't." If it takes Harold a few more minutes to find the street on his own—and keep his self-respect in the process—he thinks that's the way to go.

Women are more in tune with others and strive for connectedness. From Sybil's point of view, asking for help is right because sharing information builds social bonds and gets the job done. Asking for directions seems as natural to her as searching on his own is to Harold. Obviously, getting lost is sure to result in conflict as long as neither one understands the other's point of view. ■

Such everyday experiences are the focus of this chapter. The central concept is **social interaction,** *the process by which people act and react in relation to others.* We begin by presenting several important sociological concepts that describe the building blocks of common experience and then explore the almost magical way that face-to-face interaction creates the reality in which we live.

Social Structure: A Guide to Everyday Living

October 21, Ho Chi Minh City, Vietnam. This morning we leave the ship and make our way along the docks toward the center of Ho Chi Minh City, known to an earlier generation as Saigon. The government security officers wave us through the heavy metal gates. Pressed against the fence are dozens of men who operate cyclos (bicycles with small carriages attached to the front), the Vietnamese version of taxicabs. We wave them off and spend the next twenty minutes shaking our heads at several drivers who pedal alongside, pleading for our business. The pressure is uncomfortable. We decide to cross the street but realize suddenly that there are no stop signs or signal lights—and the street is an unbroken stream of bicycles, cyclos, motorbikes, and small trucks. The locals don't bat an eye; they just walk at a steady pace across the street, parting waves of vehicles that immediately close in again behind them. Walk right into traffic? With our small children on our backs? Yup, we did it; that's the way it works in Vietnam.

Members of every society rely on social structure to make sense out of everyday situations. As our family's introduction to the streets of Vietnam suggests, the world can be confusing—even frightening—when society's rules are unclear. We now take a closer look at the ways societies set the rules of everyday life.

For a short video ("Sociology and Cultural Relativity") on the difficulty of traveling to unfamiliar places, go to http://www.TheSociologyPage.com

Status

In every society, people build their everyday lives using the idea of **status,** *a social position that a person holds.* In everyday use, the word *status* generally means "prestige," as when we say that a college president has more "status" than a newly hired assistant professor. But sociologically speaking, both "president" and "professor" are statuses within the collegiate organization.

Status is part of our social identity and helps define our relationship to others. As Georg Simmel (1950, orig. 1902), one of the founders of sociology, once pointed out, before we can deal with anyone, we need to know *who* the person is.

STATUS SET

Each of us holds many statuses at once. The term **status set** refers to *all the statuses a person holds at a given time.* A teenage girl is a daughter to her parents, a sister to her brother, a student at her school, and a goalie on her soccer team.

Status sets change over the life course. A child grows up to become a parent, a student graduates to become a lawyer, and a single person marries to become a husband or wife, sometimes becoming single again as a result of death or divorce. Joining an organization or finding a job enlarges our status set; withdrawing from activities makes it smaller. Over a lifetime, people gain and lose dozens of statuses.

ASCRIBED AND ACHIEVED STATUS

Sociologists classify statuses in terms of how people attain them. An **ascribed status** is *a social position a person receives at birth or takes on involuntarily later in life.* Examples of ascribed statuses include being a daughter, a Cuban, a teenager, or a widower. Ascribed statuses are matters about which we have little or no choice.

By contrast, an **achieved status** refers to *a social position a person takes on voluntarily that reflects personal ability and effort.* Achieved statuses in the United States include honors student, Olympic athlete, nurse, software writer, and thief.

In any rigidly ranked setting, no interaction can proceed until people assess each other's social standing. Thus, military personnel wear insignia, clear symbols of their level of authority. Don't we size up one another in much the same way in routine interactions, noting a person's rough age, quality of clothing, and manner for clues about social position?

In the real world, of course, most statuses involve a combination of ascription and achievement. That is, people's ascribed statuses influence the statuses they achieve. People who achieve the status of lawyer, for example, are likely to share the ascribed benefit of being born into relatively well-off families. By the same token, many less desirable statuses, such as criminal, drug addict, or unemployed worker, are more easily achieved by people born into poverty.

YOUR TURN

Make a list of ten important statuses in your own life. Indicate whether each one is ascribed or achieved. Is this difficult to do? Explain your answer.

MASTER STATUS

Some statuses matter more than others. A **master status** is *a status that has special importance for social identity, often shaping a person's entire life.* For most people, a job is a master status because it reveals a great deal about social

THINKING ABOUT DIVERSITY: RACE, CLASS, & GENDER

Physical Disability as a Master Status

Physical disability works in much the same ways as class, gender, or race in defining people in the eyes of others. In the following interviews, two women explain how a physical disability can become a master status—a trait that overshadows everything else about them. The first voice is that of twenty-nine-year-old Donna Finch, who lives with her husband and son in Muskogee, Oklahoma, and holds a master's degree in social work. She is also blind.

Most people don't expect handicapped people to grow up; they are always supposed to be children. . . . You aren't supposed to date, you aren't supposed to have a job, somehow you're just supposed to disappear. I'm not saying this is true of anyone else, but in my own case I think I was more intellectually mature than most children, and more emotionally immature. I'd say that not until the last four or five years have I felt really whole.

Rose Helman is an elderly woman who has retired and lives near New York City. She suffers from spinal meningitis and is also blind.

You ask me if people are really different today than in the '20s and '30s. Not too much. They are still fearful of the handicapped. I don't know if *fearful* is the right word, but uncomfortable at least. But I can understand it somewhat; it happened to me. I once asked a

man to tell me which staircase to use to get from the subway out to the street. He started giving me directions that were confusing, and I said, "Do you mind taking me?" He said, "Not at all." He grabbed me on the side with my dog on it, so I asked him to take my other arm. And he said, "I'm sorry, I have no other arm." And I said, "That's all right, I'll hold onto the jacket." It felt funny hanging onto the sleeve without the arm in it.

WHAT DO YOU THINK?

1. Have you ever had a disease or disability that became a master status? If so, how did others react?
2. How might such a master status affect someone's personality?
3. Can being very fat or very thin serve as a master status? Why or why not?

Modern technology means that most soldiers who lose limbs in war now survive. How do you think loss of an arm or leg affects a person's social identity and sense of self?

Source: Orlansky & Heward (1981).

---

background, education, and income. In a few cases, name is a master status; being in the "Bush" or "Kennedy" family attracts attention and creates opportunities.

A master status can be negative as well as positive. Take, for example, serious illness. Sometimes people, even long-time friends, avoid cancer patients or people with acquired immune deficiency syndrome (AIDS) because of their illnesses. As another example, the fact that all societies limit the opportunities of women makes gender a master status.

Sometimes a physical disability serves as a master status to the point where we dehumanize people by seeing them

only in terms of their disability. The Thinking About Diversity box shows how.

Role

A second important social structure is **role**, *behavior expected of someone who holds a particular status*. A person *holds* a status and *performs* a role (Linton, 1937b). For example, holding the status of student leads you to perform the role of attending classes and completing assignments.

Both statuses and roles vary by culture. In the United States, the status of "uncle" refers to the brother of either your mother or your father. In Vietnam, however, the word for "uncle" is different on the mother's and father's sides of the family, and the two men have different responsibilities. In every society, actual role performance varies according to an individual's unique personality, although some societies permit more individual expression of a role than others.

ROLE SET

Because we hold many statuses at once—a status set— everyday life is a mix of multiple roles. Robert Merton (1968) introduced the term **role set** to identify *a number of roles attached to a single status.*

Figure 6–1 shows four statuses of one person, each status linked to a different role set. First, as a professor, this woman interacts with students (the teacher role) and with other academics (the colleague role). Second, in her work as a researcher, she gathers and analyzes data (the fieldwork role) that she uses in her publications (the author role). Third, the woman occupies the status of "wife," with a marital role (such as confidante and sexual partner) toward her husband, with whom she shares household duties (domestic role). Fourth, she holds the status of "mother," with routine responsibilities for her children (the maternal role), as well as toward their school and other organizations in her community (the civic role).

A global perspective shows that the roles people use to define their lives differ from society to society. In low-income countries, people spend fewer years as students, and family roles are often very important to social identity. In high-income nations, people spend more years as students, and family roles typically are less important to social identity. Another dimension of difference involves housework. As Global Map 6–1 on page 148 shows, especially in poor countries, housework falls heavily on women.

ROLE CONFLICT AND ROLE STRAIN

People in modern, high-income nations juggle many responsibilities demanded by their various statuses and roles. As most mothers (and more and more fathers) can testify, the combination of parenting and working outside the home is physically and emotionally draining. Sociologists thus recognize **role conflict** as *conflict among the roles connected to two or more statuses.*

We experience role conflict when we find ourselves pulled in various directions as we try to respond to the many statuses we hold. One response to role conflict is deciding that "something has to go." More than one politician, for example, has decided not to run for office because of the

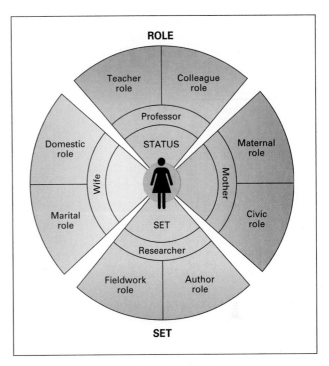

FIGURE 6–1   Status Set and Role Set

A status set includes the statuses a person holds at a given time. Because each status usually involves more than one role, a role set is even larger.

conflicting demands of a hectic campaign schedule and family life. In other cases, people put off having children in order to stay on the "fast track" for career success.

Even roles linked to a single status may make competing demands on us. **Role strain** refers to *tension among the roles connected to a single status.* A college professor may enjoy being friendly with students. At the same time, however, the professor must maintain the personal distance needed in order to evaluate students fairly. In short, performing the various roles attached to even one status can be something of a balancing act.

One strategy for minimizing role conflict is separating parts of our lives so that we perform roles for one status at one time and place and carry out roles connected to another status in a completely different setting. A familiar example of this idea is deciding to "leave the job at work" before heading home to the family.

ROLE EXIT

After she left the life of a Catholic nun to become a university sociologist, Helen Rose Fuchs Ebaugh (1988) began to

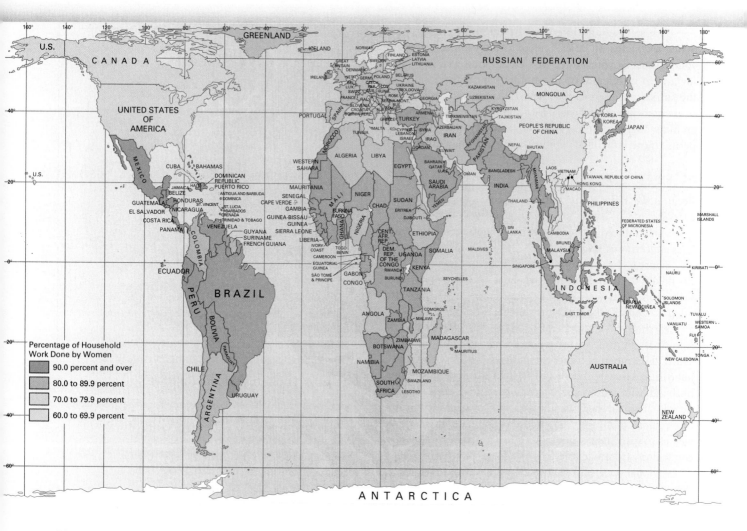

WINDOW ON THE WORLD

GLOBAL MAP 6-1 Housework in Global Perspective

Throughout the world, housework is a major part of women's routines and identities. This is especially true in poor societies of Latin America, Africa, and Asia, where women are not generally in the paid labor force. But our society also defines housework and child care as "feminine" activities, even though a majority of U.S. women work outside the home.

Source: *Peters Atlas of the World* (1990); updated by the author.

Map legend:

Percentage of Household Work Done by Women
- 90.0 percent and over
- 80.0 to 89.9 percent
- 70.0 to 79.9 percent
- 60.0 to 69.9 percent

study her own experience of *role exit,* the process by which people disengage from important social roles. Studying a range of "exes," including ex-nuns, ex-doctors, ex-husbands, and ex-alcoholics, Ebaugh identified elements common to the process of becoming an "ex."

According to Ebaugh, the process begins as people come to doubt their ability to continue in a certain role. As they imagine alternative roles, they ultimately reach a tipping point when they decide to pursue a new life. Even as they are moving on, however, a past role can continue to influence their lives. "Exes" carry with them a self-image shaped by an earlier role, which can interfere with building a new sense of self. For example, an ex-nun may hesitate to wear stylish clothing and makeup.

"Exes" must also rebuild relationships with people who knew them in their earlier life. Learning new social skills is another challenge. For example, Ebaugh reports, ex-nuns who enter the dating scene after decades in the church are often surprised to learn that sexual norms are very different from those they knew when they were teenagers.

The Social Construction of Reality

In 1917, the Italian playwright Luigi Pirandello wrote a play called *The Pleasure of Honesty* about a character named Angelo Baldovino—a brilliant man with a checkered past. Baldovino enters the fashionable home of the Renni family and introduces himself in a peculiar way:

> Inevitably we construct ourselves. Let me explain. I enter this house and immediately I become what I have to become, what I can become: I construct myself. That is, I present myself to you in a form suitable to the relationship I wish to achieve with you. And, of course, you do the same with me. (1962:157–58)

Baldovino's introduction suggests that although behavior is guided by status and role, we have the ability to shape who we are and to guide what happens from moment to moment. In other words, "reality" is not as fixed as we may think.

The phrase **social construction of reality** describes *the process by which people creatively shape reality through social interaction.* This idea is the familiar foundation of the symbolic-interaction approach, described in Chapter 1 ("The Sociological Perspective"). As Baldovino's remark suggests, quite a bit of "reality" remains unclear in everyone's mind, especially in unfamiliar situations. So we present ourselves in terms that suit the setting and our purposes, we try to guide what happens next, and as others do the same, reality emerges.

Social interaction is a complex negotiation that builds reality. Most everyday situations involve at least some agreement about what's going on. But how people see events depends on their different backgrounds, interests, and intentions.

"STREET SMARTS"

What people commonly call "street smarts" is actually a form of constructing reality. In his biography *Down These Mean Streets*, Piri Thomas recalls moving to an apartment in Spanish Harlem. Returning home one evening, young Piri found himself cut off by Waneko, the leader of the local street gang, who was flanked by a dozen others.

Flirting is an everyday experience in reality construction. Each person offers information to the other and hints at romantic interest. Yet the interaction proceeds with a tentative and often humorous air so that either individual can withdraw at any time without further obligation.

"Whatta ya say, Mr. Johnny Gringo," drawled Waneko.

Think man, I told myself, *think your way out of a stomping. Make it good.* "I hear you 104th Street coolies are supposed to have heart," I said. "I don't know this for sure. You know there's a lot of streets where a whole 'click' is made out of punks who can't fight one guy unless they all jump him for the stomp." I hoped this would push Waneko into giving me a fair one. His expression didn't change.

"Maybe we don't look at it that way."

Crazy, man, I cheer inwardly, *the* cabron *is falling into my setup.* . . . "I wasn't talking to you," I said. "Where I come from, the pres is president 'cause he got heart when it comes to dealing."

Waneko was starting to look uneasy. He had bit on my worm and felt like a sucker fish. His boys were now light on me. They were no longer so much interested in stomping me as seeing the outcome between Waneko and me. "Yeah," was his reply. . . .

I knew I'd won. Sure, I'd have to fight; but one guy, not ten or fifteen. If I lost, I might still get stomped, and

People build reality from their surrounding culture. Yet, because cultural systems are marked by diversity and even outright conflict, reality construction always involves tensions and choices. Turkey is a nation with a mostly Muslim population, but it is also a country that has embraced Western culture. Here, women confront starkly different definitions of what is "feminine."

Staton R. Winter, *The New York Times.*

if I won I might get stomped. I took care of this with my next sentence. "I don't know you or your boys," I said, "but they look cool to me. They don't feature as punks."

I had left him out purposely when I said "they." Now his boys were in a separate class. I had cut him off. He would have to fight me on his own, to prove his heart to himself, to his boys, and most important, to his turf. He got away from the stoop and asked, "Fair one, Gringo?" (1967:56–57)

This situation reveals the drama—sometimes subtle, sometimes savage—by which human beings creatively build reality. But of course, not everyone enters a situation with equal standing. If a police officer had driven by when Piri and Waneko were fighting, both young men might have ended up in jail.

THE THOMAS THEOREM

By displaying his wits and fighting with Waneko until they both tired, Piri Thomas won acceptance by the gang. What took place that evening in Spanish Harlem is an example of the **Thomas theorem,** named after W. I. Thomas (1966:301, orig. 1931): *Situations that are defined as real are real in their consequences.*

Applied to social interaction, the Thomas theorem means that although reality is initially "soft" as it is being shaped, it can become "hard" in its effects. In the case we have described, local gang members saw Piri Thomas act in a worthy way, so in their eyes he *became* worthy.

ETHNOMETHODOLOGY

Most of the time, we take social reality for granted. To become more aware of the world we help create, Harold Garfinkel (1967) devised **ethnomethodology,** *the study of the way people make sense of their everyday surroundings.* This approach begins by pointing out that everyday behavior rests on a number of assumptions. When you ask someone the simple question "How are you?" you usually want to know how the person is doing in general, but you might really be wondering how the person is dealing with a specific physical, mental, spiritual, or financial challenge. However, the person being asked probably assumes that you are not really interested in details about any of these things, that you are just "being polite."

One good way to discover the assumptions we make about reality is to purposely break the rules. For example, the next time someone greets you by saying, "How're you doing?" offer details from your last physical examination, or explain all the good and bad things that have happened since you woke up that morning, and see how the person reacts. To test assumptions about how close people should stand to each other while talking, slowly move closer to the other person during the conversation.

The results are predictable, because we all have some idea of what the "rules" of everyday interaction are. The person will most likely become confused or irritated by your unexpected behavior—a reaction that helps us see not only what the rules are but also how important they are to everyday reality.

REALITY BUILDING: CLASS AND CULTURE

People do not build everyday experience out of thin air. In part, how we act or what we see in our surroundings depends on our interests. Gazing at the sky on a starry night, for example, lovers discover romance, and scientists see hydrogen atoms fusing into helium. Social background also affects what we see, which is why residents of Spanish Harlem experience a different world than people living on Manhattan's pricey Upper East Side.

In global perspective, reality construction varies even more. Consider these everyday situations: People waiting for a bus in London typically "queue up" in a straight line; people in New York rarely are so orderly. The law forbids women in Saudi Arabia to drive cars, a ban unheard of in the United States. In the United States, people assume that "a short walk" means a few blocks or a few minutes; in the Andes Mountains of Peru, this same phrase means a few miles.

The point is that people build reality from the surrounding culture. Chapter 3 ("Culture") explains how people the world over find different meanings in specific gestures, so inexperienced travelers can find themselves building an unexpected and unwelcome reality. Similarly, in a study of popular culture, JoEllen Shively (1992) screened western films to men of European descent and to Native American men. The men in both categories claimed to enjoy the films, but for very different reasons. White men interpreted the films as praising rugged people striking out for the West and conquering the forces of nature. Native American men saw in the same films a celebration of land and nature. Given their different cultures, it is as if people in the two groups saw two different films.

Films also have an effect on the reality we all experience. The recent film *Ray*, about the life of the musician Ray Charles, who overcame the challenge of blindness, is only the latest in a series of films that have changed the public's awareness of disabilities. "In the *Times*" on pages 152–53 takes a closer look.

Dramaturgical Analysis: "The Presentation of Self"

Erving Goffman (1922–1982) was another sociologist who studied social interaction, explaining how people live their lives much like actors performing on a stage. If we imagine ourselves as directors observing what goes on in the theater of everyday life, we are doing what Goffman called **dramaturgical analysis**, *the study of social interaction in terms of theatrical performance.*

Dramaturgical analysis offers a fresh look at the concepts of status and role. A status is like a part in a play, and a

role serves as a script, supplying dialogue and action for the characters. Goffman described each individual's "performance" as the **presentation of self,** *a person's efforts to create specific impressions in the minds of others.* This process, sometimes called *impression management,* begins with the idea of personal performance (Goffman, 1959, 1967).

PERFORMANCES

As we present ourselves in everyday situations, we reveal information—consciously and unconsciously—to others. Our performance includes the way we dress (costume), the objects we carry (props), and our tone of voice and gestures (manner). In addition, we vary our performances according to where we are (the set). We may joke loudly in a restaurant, for example, but lower our voices when entering a church. People also design settings, such as homes or offices, to bring about desired reactions in others.

An Application: The Doctor's Office

Consider how a physician uses an office to convey particular information to the audience of patients. The fact that medical doctors enjoy high prestige and power in the United States is clear upon entering a doctor's office. First, the doctor is nowhere to be seen. Instead, in what Goffman describes as the "front region" of the setting, the patient

January 28, 2005

For Disabled, It's Hooray for Hollywood

By CLYDE HABERMAN

To no one's surprise, Jamie Foxx received a best-actor Oscar nomination this week [and later won] for his mesmerizing portrayal of the blind Ray Charles in *Ray*. To the surprise of some, perhaps, this was good news for New Yorkers with disabilities and for the people who help them. When Hollywood turns its [bright] lights on an illness, a disorder, a dysfunction, a handicap—the acceptable word is up to you—the public has a way of paying attention. On good days, that makes life easier for those who treat the problem. On really good days, it can pry money loose from donors.

"It's clear to me that people refer to movies all the time," said Dr. Harold Koplewicz, director of the New York University Child Study Center, which deals with psychiatric illnesses in children. At Lighthouse International, which helps blind and visually impaired people, officials are not counting on the Foxx nomination to bring in cash. But there are other possible rewards, said Barbara Silverstone, the president and chief executive. "Disabilities are being treated in films with much more accuracy, and not just blindness," she said. "A lot can be done to help the cause, so to speak, of raising public awareness."

By now, awareness may have been raised high enough to reach the rafters.

Hollywood has long cast a teary eye on diseases and disorders. "We're still reaping the benefits of *The Miracle Worker*," said Matt Campo, director of development at the Helen Keller National Center for Deaf-Blind Youths and Adults in Sands Point, on Long Island. That film, about the young Helen Keller's struggles, came out in 1962.

But over the last 15 years or so, disabilities have come to be cherished. For a while, from the late 1980s on, it was all but impossible to win a best-actor Oscar without playing a severely troubled character.

There was the autistic Dustin Hoffman in *Rain Man*, the cerebral-palsied Daniel Day-Lewis in *My Left Foot*, the criminally insane Anthony Hopkins in *The Silence of the Lambs*, the blind Al Pacino in *Scent of a Woman*, the AIDS-afflicted Tom Hanks in *Philadelphia*, the retarded Tom Hanks in *Forrest Gump*, the alcoholic Nicolas Cage in *Leaving Las Vegas*, the mentally shattered Geoffrey Rush in *Shine* and the obsessive-compulsive Jack Nicholson in *As Good as It Gets*.

Now we have the cinematically blind Mr. Foxx. For good measure, his competition includes Leonardo DiCaprio, who

---

encounters a receptionist, or gatekeeper, who decides whether and when the patient can meet the doctor. A simple glance around the doctor's waiting room, with patients (often impatiently) waiting to be invited into the inner sanctum, leaves little doubt that the doctor and the staff are in charge.

The "back region" is composed of the examination room plus the doctor's private office. Once inside the office, the patient can see a wide range of props, such as medical books and framed degrees, that give the impression that the doctor has the specialized knowledge necessary to call the shots. The doctor is usually seated behind a desk—the larger the desk, the greater the statement of power—and the patient is given only a chair.

The doctor's appearance and manner offer still more information. The white lab coat (costume) may have the practical function of keeping clothes from becoming dirty, but its social function is to let others know at a glance the physician's status. A stethoscope around the neck and a medical chart in hand (more props) have the same purpose. A doctor uses highly technical language that is often mystifying to the patient, again emphasizing that the doctor is in charge. Finally, patients use the title "doctor," but they, in turn, often are called by their first names, which further shows the doctor's dominant position. The overall message of a doctor's performance is clear: "I will help you, but you must allow me to take charge."

Try doing a similar analysis of the offices of several faculty members on your campus. What differences do you notice? How do you explain the patterns?

played the disturbed Howard Hughes in *The Aviator.*

It's almost enough to make you wonder if it is wise to go to the movies without a medical dictionary. But for those who work with disorders, the benefits from these films and Oscars are unmistakable.

With *Philadelphia,* Mr. Hanks made AIDS sufferers more acceptable to people unfamiliar with the disease, said Ana Oliveira, the executive director of Gay Men's Health Crisis. "They could not only see what AIDS looked like," she said, "they could see what that life looked like." Mr. Hanks then took on AIDS as a cause, said Robert Hagerty, who is in charge of HIV research at the New York University Center for AIDS Research. "If nothing else," he said, "it makes the actor personally identify, and then use his clout to go raise money."

For Dr. Koplewicz, *As Good as It Gets* was a breakthrough. "Jack Nicholson gave OCD a face," he said, referring to obsessive-compulsive disorder. "That translates into two things: destigmatizing it, and eventually permitting people to give money for it." . . .

Realism helps. Ms. Silverstone liked *Scent of a Woman.* Lighthouse International had trained Mr. Pacino for his role. "Why shouldn't a blind person be able to tango?" she said. Indeed. At one point, though, the Pacino character zooms along New York streets behind the wheel of a Ferrari. "We cringed a little at that," Ms. Silverstone said. The concern was that some people would take that scene literally and say, "Look at the crazy things blind people do." There is no such problem with *Ray.* A blind man at a piano? Big deal. Besides, a little perspective can't hurt. "The reason Ray

Charles was so great was not because he was blind," Ms. Silverstone said, "it was because he was talented."

WHAT DO YOU THINK?

1. Can you point to several specific lessons about disabilities that people can learn from films?

2. Why do you think such a large number of recent films have main characters challenged with some kind of disability?

3. Have you seen any of the films mentioned in this article? What were your reactions?

Adapted from the original article by Clyde Haberman published in *The New York Times* on January 28, 2005. Copyright © 2005 by The New York Times Company. Reprinted with permission.

NONVERBAL COMMUNICATION

The novelist William Sansom describes a fictional Mr. Preedy, an English vacationer on a beach in Spain:

> He took care to avoid catching anyone's eye. First, he had to make it clear to those potential companions of his holiday that they were of no concern to him whatsoever. He stared through them, round them, over them—eyes lost in space. The beach might have been empty. If by chance a ball was thrown his way, he looked surprised; then let a smile of amusement light his face (Kindly Preedy), looked around dazed to see that there were people on the beach, tossed it back with a smile to himself and not a smile *at* the people. . . .
>
> [He] then gathered together his beach-wrap and bag into a neat sand-resistant pile (Methodical and Sensible Preedy), rose slowly to stretch his huge frame (Big-Cat Preedy), and tossed aside his sandals (Carefree Preedy, after all). (1956:230–31)

Without saying a single word, Mr. Preedy offers a great deal of information about himself to anyone watching him. This is the process of **nonverbal communication,** *communication using body movements, gestures, and facial expressions rather than speech.*

People use many parts of the body to convey information to others through *body language.* Facial expressions are the most important type of body language. Smiling, for instance, shows pleasure, although we distinguish among the deliberate smile of Kindly Preedy on the beach, a spontaneous smile of joy at seeing a friend, a pained smile of embarrassment after spilling a cup of coffee, and the full, unrestrained smile of self-satisfaction we often associate with winning some important contest.

Eye contact is another key element of nonverbal communication. Generally, we use eye contact to invite social interaction. Someone across the room "catches our eye," sparking a conversation. Avoiding another's eyes, by

Spotting Lies: What Are the Clues?

Deception is common in today's world. There may be no way to rid the world of dishonesty, but researchers have learned a great deal about how to tell when someone is lying. According to Paul Ekman, a specialist in analyzing social interaction, clues to deception are found in four elements of a performance: words, voice, body language, and facial expressions.

1. **Words.** People who are good liars mentally rehearse their lines, but they cannot always avoid inconsistencies that suggest deception. In addition, a simple slip of the tongue—something the person did not mean to say in quite that way—can occur in even a carefully prepared performance. Any such "leak" might indicate that a person is hiding information.

2. **Voice.** Tone and patterns of speech contain clues to deception because they are hard to control. Especially when trying to hide a powerful emotion, a person cannot easily prevent the voice from trembling or breaking. Speed provides another clue: An individual may speak more quickly, suggesting anger, or slowly, indicating sadness.

3. **Body language.** A "leak" conveyed through body language, which is also difficult to control, may tip off an observer to deception. Body movements, sudden swallowing, or rapid breathing may show that a person is nervous. Powerful emotions that flash through a performance and change body language—what Ekman calls "hot spots"—are good clues to deception.

4. **Facial expressions.** Because there are forty-three muscles in the face that humans use to create expressions, facial expressions are even more difficult to control than other body language. Look at the two faces in the photos. Can you tell which is the lying face? It's the one on the left. A real smile is usually accompanied by a relaxed expression and lots of "laugh lines" around the eyes; a phony smile seems forced and unnatural, with fewer wrinkles around the mouth and eyes.

We all try to fake emotions—some of us more successfully than others.

 For more on detecting deception, visit http://www. sciencenews.org/articles/ 20040731/bob8.asp

But the more powerful the emotion, the more difficult it is to deceive others.

WHAT DO YOU THINK?

1. Why can parents usually tell if their children are not being truthful?
2. How might this type of research be useful in the war against terror?
3. Are there "good liars" and "bad liars"? Explain.

Sources: Based on Ekman (1985), F. Golden (1999), and R. Kaufman (2002).

---

contrast, discourages communication. Hands, too, speak for us. Common hand gestures in our society convey, among other things, an insult, a request for a ride, an invitation for someone to join us, or a demand that others stop in their tracks. Gestures also supplement spoken words. For example, pointing at someone in a threatening way gives greater emphasis to a word of warning, just as shrugging the shoulders adds an air of indifference to the phrase "I don't know"

and rapidly waving the arms adds urgency to the single word "Hurry!"

Body Language and Deception

As any actor knows, it is very difficult to pull off a perfect performance. In everyday performances, unintended body language can contradict our planned meaning: A teenage boy offers an explanation for getting home late, for example,

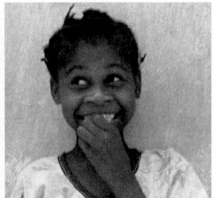

Hand gestures vary widely from one culture to another. Yet people everywhere chuckle, grin, or smirk to indicate that they don't take another person's performance seriously. Therefore, the world over, people who cannot restrain their mirth tactfully cover their faces.

but his mother doubts his words because he avoids looking her in the eye. The movie star on a television talk show claims that her recent flop at the box office is "no big deal," but the nervous swing of her leg suggests otherwise. Because nonverbal communication is hard to control, it offers clues to deception, in much the same way that changes in breathing, pulse rate, perspiration, and blood pressure recorded on a lie detector indicate that a person is lying.

Look at the two faces in the Applying Sociology box. Can you tell which is an honest smile and which is phony? Detecting phony performances is difficult, because no bodily gesture tells us that someone is lying. But because any performance involves so much body language, few people can lie without some slip-up, raising the suspicions of a careful observer. The key to detecting lies is to view the whole performance with an eye for inconsistencies.

GENDER AND PERFORMANCES

Because women are socialized to respond to others, they tend to be more sensitive than men to nonverbal communication. In fact, gender is a central element in personal performances.

Demeanor

Demeanor—the way we act and carry ourselves—is a clue to social power. Simply put, powerful people enjoy more freedom in how they act. Off-color remarks, swearing, or putting your feet on the desk may be acceptable for the boss but rarely for employees. Similarly, powerful people can interrupt others; less powerful people are expected to show respect through silence (Smith-Lovin & Brody, 1989; Henley, Hamilton, & Thorne, 1992; C. Johnson, 1994).

Because women generally occupy positions of lesser power, demeanor is a gender issue as well. As Chapter 13 ("Gender Stratification") explains, 43 percent of all working women in the United States hold clerical or service jobs under the control of supervisors who are usually men. Women, then, learn to craft their personal performances more carefully than men and to defer to men more often in everyday interaction.

Use of Space

How much space does a personal performance require? Power plays a key role here; the more power you have, the more space you use. Men typically command more space than women, whether pacing back and forth before an audience or casually sitting on a bench. Why? Our culture traditionally has measured femininity by how *little* space women occupy—the standard of "daintiness"—and masculinity by how *much* territory a man controls—the standard of "turf" (Henley, Hamilton, & Thorne, 1992).

For both sexes, the concept of **personal space** refers to *the surrounding area over which a person makes some claim to privacy*. In the United States, people typically position themselves several feet apart when speaking; throughout the Middle East, by contrast, people stand much closer. Just about everywhere, men (with their greater social power) often intrude into women's personal space. If a woman moves into a man's personal space, however, he is likely to take it as a sign of sexual interest.

Staring, Smiling, and Touching

Eye contact encourages interaction. In conversations, women hold eye contact more than men. But men have their own brand of eye contact: staring. When men stare at women, they are claiming social dominance and defining women as sexual objects.

Although it often shows pleasure, smiling can also be a sign of trying to please someone or submission. In a male-dominated world, it is not surprising that women smile more than men (Henley, Hamilton, & Thorne, 1992).

Finally, mutual touching suggests intimacy and caring. Apart from close relationships, touching is generally something men do to women (but rarely, in our culture, to other men). A male physician touches the shoulder of his female nurse as they examine a report, a young man touches the back of his woman friend as he guides her across the street, or a male skiing instructor touches young women as he teaches them to ski. In such examples, the intent of touching may be harmless and may bring little response, but it amounts to a subtle ritual by which men claim dominance over women.

YOUR TURN

Watch male-female couples holding hands. In each case, which person has the hand to the front and which has the hand to the rear? Can you see a pattern and offer an explanation?

IDEALIZATION

People behave the way they do for many, often complex, reasons. Even so, Goffman suggests, we construct performances to *idealize* our intentions. That is, we try to convince others (and perhaps ourselves) that what we do reflects ideal cultural standards rather than selfish motives.

Idealization is easily illustrated by returning to the world of doctors and patients. In a hospital, doctors engage in a performance commonly described as "making rounds." Entering the room of a patient, the doctor often stops at the foot of the bed and silently reads the patient's chart. Afterward, doctor and patient talk briefly. In ideal terms, this routine involves a doctor making a personal visit to check on a patient's condition.

In reality, the picture is not so perfect. A doctor may see several dozen patients a day and remember little about many of them. Reading the chart is a chance to recall the patient's name and medical problems, but revealing the impersonality of medical care would undermine the cultural ideal of the doctor as deeply concerned about the welfare of others.

Doctors, college professors, and other professionals typically idealize their motives for entering their chosen careers. They describe their work as "making a contribution to science," "helping others," "serving the community," and even "answering a calling from God." Rarely do they admit the more common, less honorable, motives: the income, power, prestige, and leisure time that these occupations provide.

We all use idealization to some degree. When was the last time you smiled and spoke politely to someone you do not like? Such little lies help us get through everyday life. Even when we suspect others are putting on an act, we are unlikely to challenge their performances, for reasons we shall examine next.

EMBARRASSMENT AND TACT

The famous speaker keeps mispronouncing the dean's name; the visiting ambassador rises from the table to speak, unaware of the napkin still hanging from her neck; the president becomes ill at a state dinner. As carefully as individuals may craft their performances, slip-ups of all kinds occur. The result is *embarrassment,* discomfort following a spoiled performance. Goffman describes embarrassment as "losing face."

Embarrassment is an ever-present danger because idealized performances usually contain some deception. In addition, most performances involve juggling so many elements that one thoughtless moment can shatter the intended impression.

A curious fact is that an audience often overlooks flaws in a performance, allowing an actor to avoid embarrassment. If we do point out a misstep ("Excuse me, but did you know your fly is open?"), we do it quietly and only to help someone avoid even greater loss of face. In Hans Christian Andersen's classic fable "The Emperor's New Clothes," the child who blurts out the truth, that the emperor is parading about naked, is scolded for being rude.

Often members of an audience actually help the performer recover a flawed performance. *Tact,* then, amounts to helping someone "save face." After hearing a supposed expert make an embarrassingly inaccurate remark, for example, people may tactfully ignore the comment, as if it had never been spoken, or with mild laughter treat what was said as a joke. Or they may simply respond, "I'm sure you didn't mean that," hearing the statement but not allowing it to destroy the actor's performance. With this in mind, we can understand Abraham Lincoln's comment, "Tact is the ability to describe others the way they see themselves."

Why is tact so common? Because embarrassment creates discomfort not simply for the actor but for every-one else as well. Just as a theater audience feels uneasy when an actor forgets a line, people who observe awkward behavior

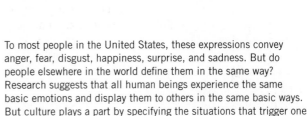

To most people in the United States, these expressions convey anger, fear, disgust, happiness, surprise, and sadness. But do people elsewhere in the world define them in the same way? Research suggests that all human beings experience the same basic emotions and display them to others in the same basic ways. But culture plays a part by specifying the situations that trigger one emotion or another.

are reminded of how fragile their own performances often are. Socially constructed reality thus functions like a dam holding back a sea of chaos. When one person's performance springs a leak, others tactfully help make repairs. Everyone, after all, lends a hand in building reality, and no one wants it suddenly swept away.

In sum, Goffman's research shows that although behavior is spontaneous in some respects, it is more patterned than we often think. Four centuries ago, Shakespeare captured this idea in memorable lines that still ring true:

All the world's a stage,
And all the men and women merely players:
They have their exits and their entrances;
And one man in his time plays many parts.
(*As You Like It*, act 2, scene 7)

Interaction in Everyday Life: Three Applications

The final sections of this chapter illustrate the major elements

Is it possible to build a machine capable of human interaction? Check out http://www.ai.mit.edu/projects/humanoid-robotics-group/

of social interaction by focusing on three dimensions of everyday life: emotions, language, and humor.

EMOTIONS: THE SOCIAL CONSTRUCTION OF FEELING

Emotions, more commonly called *feelings,* are an important element of human social life. In truth, what we *do* often matters less than how we *feel* about it. Emotions seem very personal because they are "inside." Even so, just as society guides our behavior, it guides our emotional life.

The Biological Side of Emotions

Studying people all over the world, Paul Ekman (1980a, 1980b) reports that people everywhere express six basic emotions: happiness, sadness, anger, fear, disgust, and surprise. In addition, Ekman found that people everywhere use much the same facial expressions to show these emotions. Ekman believes that some emotional responses are "wired" into human beings, that is, they are biologically programmed in our facial features, muscles, and central nervous system.

Why? Over the evolution of the human species, emotions may have had a biological root, but they serve a social purpose: supporting group life. Emotions are powerful forces that allow us to overcome our self-centeredness and build connections with others. Thus the capacity for emotion arose in our ancestors along with the capacity for culture (Turner, 2000).

Many of us think emotions are simply part of our biological makeup. While there is a biological foundation to human emotion, sociologists have demonstrated that what triggers an emotion—as well as when, where, and to whom the emotion is displayed—is shaped by culture. For example, many jobs not only regulate a worker's behavior, but also expect workers to display a particular emotion, as in the case of the always-smiling airline flight attendant. Can you think of other jobs that regulate emotions in this way?

The Cultural Side of Emotions

However, culture does play an important role in guiding human emotions. First, Ekman explains, culture defines *what triggers* an emotion. Whether people define the departure of an old friend as joyous (causing happiness), insulting (arousing anger), a loss (producing sadness), or mystical (provoking surprise and awe) has a lot to do with culture. Second, culture provides rules for the *display* of emotions. For example, most people in the United States express emotions more freely with family members than with workplace colleagues. Similarly, we expect children to express emotions to parents, but parents tend to hide their emotions from their children. Third, culture guides how we *value* emotions. Some societies encourage the expression of emotion; others expect members to control their feelings and maintain a "stiff upper lip." Gender also plays a part; traditionally at least, many cultures expect women to show emotions, but they discourage emotional expression by men as a sign of weakness. In some cultures, of course, this pattern is less pronounced or even reversed.

Emotions on the Job

In the United States, most people are freer to express their feelings at home than on the job. The reason, as Arlie Russell Hochschild (1979, 1983) explains, is that the typical company tries to regulate not only the behavior of its employees but also their emotions.  Take the case of an airline flight attendant who offers passengers a drink and a smile. Although this smile may convey real pleasure at serving the customer, Hochschild's study points to a different conclusion: The smile is an emotional script demanded by the airline as the right way to do the job. Therefore, we see that the "presentation of self" described by Erving Goffman can involve not just surface acting but also the "deep acting" of emotions.

With these patterns in mind, it is easy to see that we socially construct our emotions as part of our everyday reality, a process sociologists call *emotion management.* The Thinking Critically box relates the very different emotions displayed by women who decide to have an abortion, depending on their personal view of terminating a pregnancy.

LANGUAGE: THE SOCIAL CONSTRUCTION OF GENDER

As Chapter 3 ("Culture") explains, language is the thread that weaves members of a society into the symbolic web we call culture. Language communicates not only a surface reality but also deeper levels of meaning. One such level involves gender. Language defines men and women differently in terms of both power and value (Henley, Hamilton, & Thorne, 1992; Thorne, Kramarae, & Henley, 1983).

Language and Power

A young man proudly rides his new motorcycle up his friend's driveway and boasts, "Isn't she a beauty?" On the surface, the question has little to do with gender. Yet why does he use the pronoun *she* to refer to his prized possession?

The answer is that men often use language to establish control over their surroundings. A man attaches a female pronoun to a motorcycle (or car, boat, or other object) because it reflects the power of *ownership.* Perhaps this is also why, in the United States and elsewhere, a woman who marries traditionally takes the last name of her husband. Because many of today's married women value their independence, an increasing share (about 15 percent) now keep their own name or combine the two family names.

Language and Value

Typically, the English language treats as masculine whatever has greater value, force, or significance. For instance, the word

THINKING CRITICALLY

Managing Feelings: Women's Abortion Experiences

Few issues today generate as much emotion as abortion. In a study of women's abortion experiences, the sociologist Jennifer Keys (2002) discovered emotional scripts or "feeling rules" that guided how women feel about ending a pregnancy.

Keys explains that emotional scripts arise from the political controversy surrounding abortion. The antiabortion movement defines abortion as a personal tragedy, the "killing of an unborn child." Given this definition, women who terminate a pregnancy through abortion are doing something very wrong and can expect to feel grief, guilt, and regret. So intense are these feelings, according to supporters of this position, that such women often suffer from "postabortion syndrome."

Those who take the pro-choice position have an opposing view of abortion. From this point of view, the woman's problem is the unwanted pregnancy; abortion is an acceptable medical solution. Therefore, the emotion common to women who terminate a pregnancy should be not guilt but relief.

In her research, Keys conducted in-depth interviews with forty women who had recently had abortions and found that all of them used such scripts to "frame" their situation in an antiabortion or pro-choice manner. In part, this construction of reality reflected the women's own attitude about abortion. In addition, however, the women's

partners and friends typically encouraged specific feelings about the event. Ivy, one young woman in the study, had a close friend who was also pregnant. "Congratulations!" she exclaimed when she learned of Ivy's condition. "We're going to be having babies together!" Such a statement established one "feeling rule"—having a baby is *good*—which sent the message to Ivy that her planned abortion should trigger guilt. Working in the other direction, Jo's partner was horrified by the news that she was pregnant. Doubting his own ability to be a father, he blurted out, "I would rather put a gun to my head than have this baby!" His panic not only defined having the child as a mistake but alarmed Jo as well. Clearly, her partner's reaction made the decision to end the pregnancy a matter of relief from a terrible problem.

Medical personnel also play a part in this process of reality construction by using specific terms. Nurses and doctors who talk about "the baby" encourage the antiabortion framing of abortion and provoke grief and guilt. On the contrary, those who use language such as "pregnancy tissue," "fetus," or "the contents of the uterus" encourage the pro-choice framing of abortion as a simple medical procedure leading to relief. Olivia began using the phrase "products of conception," which she picked up from her doctor. Denise spoke of her procedure as

"taking the extra cells out of my body. Yeah, I did feel some guilt when I thought that this was the beginning of life, but my body is full of life—you have lots of cells in you."

After the procedure, most women reported actively trying to manage their feelings. Explained Ivy, "I never used the word 'baby.' I kept saying to myself that it was not formed yet. There was nothing there yet. I kept that in my mind." On the other hand, Keys found that all of the women in her study who leaned toward the antiabortion position did use the term "baby." Gina explained, "I do think of it as a baby. The truth is that I ended my baby's life. . . . Thinking that makes me feel guilty. But—considering what I did—maybe I *should* feel guilty." Believing that what she had done was wrong, in other words, Gina actively called out the feeling of guilt—in part, Keys concluded, to punish herself.

WHAT DO YOU THINK?

1. In your own words, what are "emotional scripts" or "feeling rules"?
2. Can you apply the idea of "feeling rules" to the experience of getting married?
3. In light of this discussion, how correct is it to say that our feelings are not as personal as we may have thought?

Sources: McCaffrey & Keys (2000) and Keys (2002).

virtuous, meaning "morally worthy" or "excellent," comes from the Latin word *vir,* meaning "man." On the other hand, the adjective *hysterical,* meaning "emotionally out of control," is taken from the Greek word *hystera,* meaning "uterus."

In many familiar ways, language also confers different value on the two sexes. Traditional masculine terms such as *king* and *lord* have a positive meaning, and comparable

terms, such as *queen, madam,* and *dame,* can have negative meanings. Similarly, use of the suffixes *-ette* and *-ess* to denote femininity usually devalues the words to which they are added. For example, a *major* has higher standing than a *majorette,* as does a *host* in relation to a *hostess,* or a *master* in relation to a *mistress.* Language both mirrors social attitudes and helps perpetuate them.

THINKING ABOUT DIVERSITY: RACE, CLASS, & GENDER

Gender and Language: "You Just Don't Understand!"

In the story that opened this chapter, Harold and Sybil faced a situation that rings all too true to many people: When they are lost, men grumble to themselves and perhaps blame their partners but avoid asking for directions. For their part, women can't understand why men refuse help when they need it.

Deborah Tannen (1990) explains that men typically define most everyday encounters as competitive. Therefore, getting lost is bad enough without asking for help, which lets someone else get "one up." By contrast, because women traditionally have had a subordinate position, they find it easy to ask for help. Sometimes, Tannen points out, women ask for assistance even when they don't need it.

A similar gender-linked problem common to couples involves what women consider "trying to be helpful" and men call "nagging." Consider the following exchange (adapted from Adler, 1990:74):

SYBIL: What's wrong, honey?

HAROLD: Nothing . . .

SYBIL: Something is bothering you; I can tell.

HAROLD: I told you nothing is bothering me. Leave me alone.

SYBIL: But I can see that there is a problem . . .

HAROLD: OK. Just why do you think there is a problem?

SYBIL: Well, for one thing, you're bleeding all over your shirt.

HAROLD [now irritated]: Yeah, well, it doesn't bother me.

SYBIL [losing her temper]: WELL, IT SURE IS BOTHERING ME!

HAROLD: Fine. I'll go change my shirt.

The problem here is that what one partner *intends* by a comment is not always what the other *hears* in the words. To Sybil, her opening question is an effort at cooperative problem solving. She can see that something is wrong with Harold (who has cut himself while doing yard work), and she wants to help him. But Harold interprets her pointing out his problem as belittling

him and he tries to close off the discussion. Sybil, believing that Harold would be more positive if he understood that she just wants to be helpful, repeats herself. This reaction sets in motion a vicious circle in which Harold, who feels his wife is thinking that he cannot take care of himself, responds by digging in his heels. This response, in turn, makes Sybil all the more sure that she needs to do something. And round it goes until somebody gets really angry.

In the end, Harold agrees to change his shirt but still refuses to discuss the original problem. Defining his wife's concern as "nagging," Harold just wants Sybil to leave him alone. For her part, Sybil fails to understand her husband's view of the situation and walks away convinced that he is a stubborn grouch.

WHAT DO YOU THINK?

1. Do you agree with Tannen that men and women communicate in different ways? Explain your view.
2. In your opinion, what is the reason for any gender difference in how people use language?
3. Do you think that an understanding of Tannen's work can help female-male couples communicate better? Why or why not?

YOUR TURN

In terms of this discussion, do you think that people should follow the traditional practice of using masculine pronouns (*he* and *him*) when not only males are involved ("He who hesitates is lost")? Why or why not?

Given the importance of gender in everyday life, perhaps we should not be surprised that women and men sometimes have trouble communicating with each other. In the Thinking About Diversity box, Harold and Sybil, whose misadventures in trying to find their friends' home opened this chapter, return to illustrate how the two sexes often seem to be speaking different languages.

REALITY PLAY: THE SOCIAL CONSTRUCTION OF HUMOR

Humor plays an important part in everyday life. Everyone laughs at a joke, but few people think about what makes something funny. We can apply many of the ideas developed in this chapter to explain how, by using humor, we "play with reality" (Macionis, 1987).

The Foundation of Humor

Humor is produced by the social construction of reality; it arises as people create and contrast two different realities. Generally, one reality is *conventional,* that is, what people in a specific situation expect. The other reality is *unconventional,* an unexpected violation of cultural patterns. Humor therefore arises from contradiction, ambiguity, and double meanings found in differing definitions of the same situation.

There are countless ways to mix realities and generate humor. Contrasting realities are found in statements that contradict themselves, such as "Nostalgia is not what it used to be"; statements that repeat themselves, such as Yogi Berra's line "It's *déjà vu* all over again"; or statements that mix up words, such as Oscar Wilde's line "Work is the curse of the drinking class." Even switching around syllables does the trick, as in the case of the country song "I'd Rather Have a Bottle in Front of Me than a Frontal Lobotomy."

Of course, a joke can be built the other way around, so that the audience is led to expect an unconventional answer and then receives a very ordinary one. When a reporter asked the famous criminal Willy Sutton why he robbed banks, for example, he replied dryly, "Because that's where the money is." However a joke is constructed, the greater the opposition or difference between the two definitions of reality, the greater the humor.

When telling jokes, the comedian uses various strategies to strengthen this opposition and make the joke funnier. One common technique is to present the first, or conventional, remark in conversation with another actor and then to turn toward the audience (or the camera) to deliver the second, unexpected line. In a Marx Brothers film, Groucho remarks, "Outside of a dog, a book is a man's best friend." Then, raising his voice and turning to the camera, he adds, "And *inside* of a dog, it's too dark to read!" Such "changing channels" emphasizes the difference between the two realities. Following the same logic, stand-up comedians may "reset" the audience to conventional expectations by interjecting the phrase, "But seriously, folks, . . ." between jokes.

Comedians pay careful attention to their performances—the precise words they use and the timing of their delivery. A joke is well told if the comedian creates the sharpest possible opposition between the realities; in a careless performance, the joke falls flat. Because the key to humor lies in the collision of realities, we can see why the climax of a joke is termed the "*punch* line."

The Dynamics of Humor: "Getting It"

After someone tells you a joke, have you ever had to say, "I don't get it"? To "get" humor, you must understand both the conventional and the unconventional realities well enough to appreciate their difference. A comedian may make getting a joke harder by leaving out some important information. In such cases, listeners must pay attention to the stated elements of the joke and then fill in the missing pieces on their own. A simple example is the comment of the movie producer Hal Roach on his one hundredth birthday: "If I had known I would live to be one hundred, I would have taken better care of myself!" Here, getting the joke depends on realizing that Roach must have taken pretty good care of himself in order to make it to one hundred. Or take one of W. C. Fields's lines: "Some weasel took the cork out of my lunch." "What a lunch!" we think to ourselves to "finish" the joke.

Here is an even more complex joke: What do you get if you cross an insomniac, a dyslexic, and an agnostic? Answer: A person who stays up all night wondering if there is a dog. To get this one, you must know that insomnia is an inability to sleep, that dyslexia causes a person to reverse the letters in words, and that an agnostic doubts the existence of God.

Why would a comedian want the audience to make this sort of effort to understand a joke? Our enjoyment of a joke is increased by the pleasure of figuring out all the pieces needed to "get it." In addition, getting the joke makes you an "insider" compared to those who don't "get it." We have all experienced the frustration of *not* getting a joke: fear of being judged stupid, along with a sense of being excluded from a pleasure shared by others. Sometimes someone may tactfully explain the joke so that the other person doesn't feel left out. But as the old saying goes, if a joke has to be explained, it isn't very funny.

The Topics of Humor

All over the world, people smile and laugh, making humor a universal element of human culture. But, because the world's people live in different cultures, humor rarely travels well.

October 1, Kobe, Japan. Can you share a joke with people who live halfway around the world? At dinner, I ask two Japanese college women to tell me a joke. "You know 'crayon'?" Asako asks. I nod. "How do you ask for a crayon in Japanese?" I respond that I have no idea. She laughs

Because humor involves challenging established conventions, most U.S. comedians—including Dave Chappelle—have been social "outsiders," members of racial and ethnic minorities.

out loud as she says what sounds like "crayon crayon." Her companion Mayumi laughs too. My wife and I sit awkwardly, straight-faced. Asako relieves some of our embarrassment by explaining that the Japanese word for "give me" is kureyo, which sounds like "crayon." I force a smile.

What is humorous to the Japanese may be lost on the Chinese, Iraqis, or people in the United States. Even the social diversity of this country means that different types of people will find humor in different situations. New Englanders, southerners, and westerners have their own brands of humor, as do Latinos and Anglos, fifteen- and forty-year-olds, Wall Street bankers and rodeo riders.

But for everyone, topics that lend themselves to double meanings or controversy generate humor. In the United States, the first jokes many of us learned as children concerned bodily functions kids are not supposed to talk about. The mere mention of "unmentionable acts" or even certain parts of the body can dissolve young faces in laughter.

Are there jokes that do break through the culture barrier? Yes, but they must touch on universal human experiences such as, say, turning on a friend:

I think of a number of jokes, but none seems likely to work. Understanding jokes about the United States is difficult for people who know little of our culture. Is there something more universal? Inspiration: "Two fellows are walking in the woods and come upon a huge bear. One guy leans over and tightens up the laces on his running shoes. 'Jake,' says the other, 'what are you doing? You can't outrun this bear!' 'I don't have to outrun the bear,' responds Jake. 'I just have to outrun you!'" Smiles all around.

The controversy found in humor often walks a fine line between what is funny and what is "sick." During the Middle Ages, people used the word *humors* (derived from the Latin *humidus,* meaning "moist") to mean a balance of bodily fluids that regulated a person's health. Researchers today document the power of humor to reduce stress and improve health, confirming the old saying "Laughter is the best medicine" (Haig, 1988; Bakalar, 2005). At the extreme, however, people who always take conventional reality lightly risk being defined as deviant or even mentally ill (a common stereotype shows insane people laughing uncontrollably, and for a long time mental hospitals were known as "funny farms").

Then too, every social group considers certain topics too sensitive for humorous treatment. Of course, you can still joke about them, but doing so risks criticism for telling a "sick" joke (or being labeled "sick" yourself). People's religious beliefs, tragic accidents, or appalling crimes are the stuff of sick jokes or no jokes at all. Even five years later, there have been no jokes about the victims of the September 11, 2001, terrorist attacks.

The Functions of Humor

Humor is found everywhere because it works as a safety valve for potentially disruptive sentiments. Put another way, humor provides an acceptable way to discuss a sensitive topic without appearing to be serious. Having said something controversial, people can use humor to defuse the situation by simply stating, "I didn't mean anything by what I said—it was just a joke!"

People also use humor to relieve tension in uncomfortable situations. One study of medical examinations found that most patients try to joke with doctors to ease their own nervousness (Baker et al., 1997).

Humor and Conflict

Humor may be a source of pleasure, but it can also be used to put down others. Men who tell jokes about women, for example, typically are expressing some measure of hostility toward them (Powell & Paton, 1988; Benokraitis & Feagin, 1995). Similarly, jokes about gay people reveal tensions about sexual orientation. Real conflict can be masked by humor in situations where one or both parties choose not to bring the conflict out into the open (Primeggia & Varacalli, 1990).

"Put-down" jokes make one category of people feel good at the expense of another. After collecting and analyzing jokes from many societies, Christie Davies (1990) confirmed that ethnic conflict is one driving force behind humor in most of the world. The typical ethnic joke makes fun of some disadvantaged category of people, at the same time making the joke teller feel superior. Given the Anglo-Saxon traditions of U.S. society, Poles and other ethnic and racial minorities have long been the butt of jokes in the United States, as have Newfoundlanders in eastern Canada, the Irish in Scotland, Sikhs in India, Turks in Germany, Hausas in Nigeria, Tasmanians in Australia, and Kurds in Iraq.

YOUR TURN

Humor is most common among people with roughly the same social standing. Why is it risky to joke with people who have more power than you do? What about joking with people who have less power?

Disadvantaged people also make fun of the powerful, although usually with some care. Women in the United States joke about men, just as African Americans find humor in white people's ways, and poor people poke fun at the rich. Throughout the world, people target their leaders with humor, and officials in some countries take such jokes seriously enough to arrest those who do not show proper respect (Speier, 1998).

In sum, humor is much more important than we may think. It is a means of mental escape from a conventional world that is never entirely to our liking (Flaherty, 1984, 1990; Yoels & Clair, 1995). This fact helps explain why so many of our nation's comedians are from the ranks of historically marginalized peoples, including Jews and African Americans. As long as we maintain a sense of humor, we assert our freedom and are not prisoners of reality. By putting a smile on our faces, we can change ourselves and the world just a little, hopefully for the better.

MAKING THE GRADE

The following learning tools will help you see what you know, identify what you still need to learn, and expand your understanding beyond the text. You can also visit this text's Companion Website™ at http://www.prenhall.com/macionis to find additional practice tests.

KEY POINTS

Social Structure: A Guide to Everyday Living

Social structure provides guidelines for behavior, making everyday life understandable and predictable.

Status

A major component of social structure is status. Within an entire status set, a master status has special importance for a person's identity. Ascribed statuses are involuntary; achieved statuses are earned. Many statuses we hold are both ascribed and achieved.

Role

Role is the active expression of a status. Tension among the roles linked to two or more statuses causes role conflict; tension among the roles linked to a single status causes role strain.

The Social Construction of Reality

The social construction of reality is the idea that we build the social world through our interactions with others. The Thomas theorem states that situations defined as real are real in their consequences. Ethnomethodology is a strategy to reveal the assumptions and understandings people have of their social world. The social realities people build reflect both their culture and their social standing.

Dramaturgical Analysis: "The Presentation of Self"

Dramaturgical analysis views everyday life as theatrical performance, noting that people try to create particular impressions in the minds of others. Social power affects performances, which is one reason that men's behavior typically differs from women's. Everyday behavior carries the ever-present danger of embarrassment, or "loss of face." People use tact to prevent others' performances from breaking down.

Interaction in Everyday Life: Three Applications

The first application involves emotions. Although the same basic emotions seem to be biologically programmed into all human beings, culture guides what triggers emotions, how we display emotions, and what value we attach to emotion. In everyday life, presentations of self involve managing emotions as well as behavior.

The second application involves gender and language. In various ways, language defines women and men differently, generally to the advantage of men.

The third application involves humor, which stems from creating a difference between conventional and unconventional definitions of a situation. Because humor is an element of culture, people throughout the world find different situations funny.

KEY CONCEPTS

social interaction (p. 144) the process by which people act and react in relation to others

status (p. 145) a social position that a person holds

status set (p. 145) all the statuses a person holds at a given time

ascribed status (p. 145) a social position a person receives at birth or takes on involuntarily later in life

achieved status (p. 145) a social position a person takes on voluntarily that reflects personal ability and effort

master status (p. 145) a status that has special importance for social identity, often shaping a person's entire life

role (p. 146) behavior expected of someone who holds a particular status

role set (p. 147) a number of roles attached to a single status

role conflict (p. 147) conflict among the roles connected to two or more statuses

role strain (p. 147) tension among the roles connected to a single status

social construction of reality (p. 149) the process by which people creatively shape reality through social interaction

Thomas theorem (p. 150) W. I. Thomas's statement that situations that are defined as real are real in their consequences

ethnomethodology (p. 150) Harold Garfinkel's term for the study of the way people make sense of their everyday surroundings

dramaturgical analysis (p. 151) Erving Goffman's term for the study of social interaction in terms of theatrical performance

presentation of self (p. 151) Erving Goffman's term for a person's efforts to create specific impressions in the minds of others

nonverbal communication (p. 153) communication using body movements, gestures, and facial expressions rather than speech

personal space (p. 155) the surrounding area over which a person makes some claim to privacy

SAMPLE TEST QUESTIONS

These questions are similar to those found in the test bank that accompanies this textbook.

Multiple-Choice Questions

1. **Which term defines who and what we are in relation to others?**
   a. role
   b. status
   c. role set
   d. master status

2. **In U.S. society, which of the following might be a master status?**
   a. occupation
   b. physical or mental disability
   c. race or color
   d. all of the above

3. **Role set refers to**
   a. a number of roles found in any one society.
   b. a number of roles attached to a single status.
   c. a number of roles that are more or less the same.
   d. a number of roles within any one organization.

4. **Frank excels at football at his college, but he doesn't have enough time to study as much as he wants to. This problem is an example of**
   a. role set.
   b. role strain.
   c. role conflict.
   d. role exit.

5. The Thomas theorem states that
   a. our statuses and roles are the keys to our personality.
   b. most people rise to their level of incompetence.
   c. people know the world only through their language.
   d. situations defined as real are real in their consequences.

6. Which of the following is the correct meaning of "presentation of self"?
   a. efforts to create impressions in the minds of others
   b. acting out a master status
   c. thinking back over the process of role exit
   d. trying to take attention away from others

7. Paul Ekman points to what as an important clue to deception by another person?
   a. smiling
   b. using tact
   c. inconsistencies in a presentation
   d. all of the above

8. In terms of dramaturgical analysis, tact is understood as
   a. helping someone take on a new role.
   b. helping another person "save face."
   c. making it hard for someone to perform a role.
   d. negotiating a situation to get your own way.

9. In her study of human emotion, Arlie Hochschild explains that companies typically
   a. try to regulate the emotions of workers.
   b. want workers to be unemotional.
   c. encourage people to express their true emotions.
   d. profit from making customers more emotional.

10. People are likely to "get" a joke when they
    a. know something about more than one culture.
    b. have a different social background than the joke teller.
    c. understand the two different realities being presented.
    d. know why someone wants to tell the joke.

Answers: 1(b); 2(d); 3(b); 4(c); 5(d); 6(a); 7(c); 8(b); 9(a); 10(c).

Essay Questions

1. Explain Erving Goffman's idea that we engage in a "presentation of self." What are the elements of this presentation? Apply this approach to an analysis of a professor teaching a class.

2. In what ways are human emotions rooted in our biology? In what ways are emotions guided by culture?

APPLICATIONS & EXERCISES

1. Sketch out your own status set and the role set that goes with it. Identify any master statuses and also any sources of role conflict or role strain.

2. During the next twenty-four hours, every time somebody asks, "How are you?" stop and actually give a complete, truthful answer. What happens when you respond to a polite question in an honest way? Listen to how people respond, and also watch their body language. What can you conclude?

3. Stroll around downtown or at a local mall. Pay attention to how many women and men you find at each location. From your observations, would you conclude that such places are "gendered" so that there are "female spaces" and "male spaces"?

INVESTIGATE with Research Navigator

Follow the instructions on page 27 of this text to access the features of **Research Navigator™**. Once at the Web site, enter your Login Name and Password. Then, to use the **ContentSelect™** database, enter keywords such as "social interaction," "emotions," and "humor," and the search engine will supply relevant and recent scholarly and popular press publications. Use the *New York Times* **Search-by-Subject Archive** to find recent news articles related to sociology and the **Link Library** feature to find relevant Web links organized by the key terms associated with this chapter.

7

Groups and Organizations

How do groups affect the behavior of members?

Why can "who you know" be as important as "what you know"?

In what ways have large business organizations changed in recent decades?

Back in 1948, people in Pasadena, California, paid little attention to the opening of a new restaurant by brothers Maurice and Richard McDonald. Yet this one small business would not only transform the restaurant industry but also introduce a new organizational model copied by countless businesses of all kinds.

The McDonald brothers' basic concept, which was soon called "fast food," was to serve meals quickly and cheaply to large numbers of people. The brothers trained employees to do highly specialized jobs: One person grilled hamburgers while others "dressed" them, made French fries, whipped up milkshakes, and presented the food to the customers in assembly-line fashion.

As the years went by, the McDonald brothers prospered, and they opened several more restaurants, including one in San Bernardino. It was there, in 1954, that Ray Kroc, a traveling blender and mixer salesman, paid them a visit.

Kroc was fascinated by the efficiency of the brothers' system and saw the potential for a whole chain of fast-food restaurants. The three launched the plan as partners. In 1961, in the face

 For a history of McDonald's, go to http://www.wemweb.com/ chr66a/sbr66_museum/sbr66_ museum.html

of rapidly increasing sales, Kroc bought out the McDonalds (who went back to running their original restaurant) and went on to become one of the great success stories of all time. By 1962, the company had sold 1 billion hamburgers, and they stopped counting. Today, more than 30,000 McDonald's restaurants serve 50 million people daily throughout the United States and in 118 other nations around the world. ■

The success of McDonald's is evidence of more than just the popularity of hamburgers and French fries. The organizational principles that guide this company are coming to dominate social life in the United States and elsewhere.

We begin this chapter with an examination of *social groups*, the clusters of people with whom we interact in our daily lives. As you will learn, the scope of group life in the United States expanded greatly during the twentieth century. From a world of families, local neighborhoods, and small businesses, our society now turns on the operation of huge corporations and other bureaucracies that sociologists describe as *formal organizations*. Understanding this expanding scale of social life and appreciating what it means for us as individuals are the main objectives of this chapter.

Social Groups

Almost everyone wants a sense of belonging, which is the essence of group life. A **social group** is *two or more people who identify and interact with one another*. Human beings come together in couples, families, circles of friends, churches, clubs, businesses, neighborhoods, and large organizations. Whatever its form, a group is made up of people with shared experiences, loyalties, and interests. In short, while keeping their individuality, members of social groups also think of themselves as a special "we."

Not every collection of individuals forms a group. People all over the country with a status in common, such as women, homeowners, soldiers, millionaires, college graduates, and Roman Catholics, are not a group but a *category*.

Though they know that others hold the same status, most are strangers to one another. Similarly, students sitting in a large lecture hall interact to a very limited extent. Such a loosely formed collection of people in one place is a *crowd* rather than a group.

However, the right circumstances can quickly turn a crowd into a group. Unexpected events, from power failures to terrorist attacks, can make people bond quickly with strangers.

PRIMARY AND SECONDARY GROUPS

Friends often greet one another with a smile and the simple phrase, "Hi! How are you?" The response usually is, "Fine, thanks. How about you?" This answer is often more scripted than truthful. Explaining how you are *really* doing would make most people feel so awkward that they would beat a hasty retreat.

Social groups fall into one of two types, depending on their members' degree of personal concern for one another. According to Charles Horton Cooley (1864–1929), a **primary group** is *a small social group whose members share personal and lasting relationships.* Joined by *primary relationships,* people spend a great deal of time together, engage

 To learn more about Cooley, visit the Gallery of Sociologists at http://www.TheSociology Page.com

in a wide range of activities, and feel that they know one another pretty well. In short, they show real concern for one another. The family is every society's most important primary group.

Cooley called personal and tightly integrated groups "primary" because they are among the first groups we experience in life. In addition, the family and early play groups have primary importance in the socialization process, shaping attitudes, behavior, and social identity.

Members of primary groups help one another in many ways, but they generally think of the group as an end in itself rather than as a means to some goal. In other words, we prefer to think that family and friendship link people who "belong together." Members of a primary group also tend to view each other as unique and irreplaceable. Especially in the family, we are bound to others by emotion and loyalty. Brothers and sisters may not always get along, but they always remain siblings.

In contrast to the primary group, the **secondary group** is *a large and impersonal social group whose members pursue a specific goal or activity.* In most respects, secondary groups have characteristics opposite to those of primary groups. *Secondary relationships* involve weak emotional ties and little personal knowledge of one another. Most secondary groups are short-term, beginning and ending without particular significance. Students in a college course, who

As human beings, we live our lives as members of groups. Such groups may be large or small, temporary or long-lasting, and can be based on kinship, cultural heritage, or some shared interest.

interact but may not see one another after the semester ends, are one example of a secondary group.

Secondary groups include many more people than primary groups. For example, dozens or even hundreds of people may work together in the same company, yet most of them pay only passing attention to one another. In some cases, time may transform a group from secondary to primary, as with co-workers who share an office for many years and develop closer relationships. But generally, members of a secondary group do not think of themselves as "we." Secondary ties need not be hostile or cold, of course. Interactions among students, co-workers, and business associates are often quite pleasant, even if they are impersonal.

Unlike members of primary groups, who display a *personal orientation,* people in secondary groups have a *goal orientation.* Primary group members define each other according to *who* they are in terms of family ties or personal qualities, but people in secondary groups look to one another for *what* they are, that is, what they can do for each other. In secondary groups, we tend to "keep score," aware of what we give others and what we receive in return. This goal orientation means that secondary-group members usually remain formal and polite. In a secondary relationship, therefore, we ask the question "How are you?" without expecting a truthful answer.

SUMMING UP

Primary Groups and Secondary Groups

	Primary Group ⟵⟶	Secondary Group
Quality of relationships	Personal orientation	Goal orientation
Duration of relationships	Usually long-term	Variable; often short-term
Breadth of relationships	Broad; usually involving many activities	Narrow; usually involving few activities
Perception of relationships	As ends in themselves	As means to an end
Examples	Families, circles of friends	Co-workers, political organizations

The Summing Up table reviews the characteristics of primary and secondary groups. Keep in mind that these traits define two types of groups in ideal terms; most real groups contain elements of both. For example, a women's group on a university campus may be quite large (and therefore secondary), but its members may identify strongly with one another and provide lots of mutual support (making it seem primary).

 Become a member of a virtual group at http://groups.yahoo.com

Many people think that small towns and rural areas have mostly primary relationships and that large cities are characterized by more secondary ties. This generalization is partly true, but some urban neighborhoods—especially those populated by people of a single ethnic or religious category—are very tightly knit.

YOUR TURN

List five social groups that are important in your life. In each case, is the group more primary or more secondary?

GROUP LEADERSHIP

How do groups operate? One important element of group dynamics is leadership. Though a small circle of friends may have no leader at all, most large secondary groups place leaders in a formal chain of command.

Two Leadership Roles

Groups typically benefit from two kinds of leadership. **Instrumental leadership** refers to *group leadership that focuses on the completion of tasks.* Members look to instrumental leaders to make plans, give orders, and get things done. **Expressive leadership,** by contrast, is *group leadership that focuses on the group's well-being.* Expressive leaders take less interest in achieving goals than in raising group morale and minimizing tension and conflict among members.

Because they concentrate on performance, instrumental leaders usually have formal secondary relationships with other members. These leaders give orders and reward or punish members according to how much the members contribute to the group's efforts. Expressive leaders build more personal primary ties. They offer sympathy to a member going through tough times, keep the group united, and lighten serious moments with humor. Typically, successful instrumental leaders enjoy more *respect* from members and expressive leaders generally receive more personal *affection.*

In the traditional U.S. family, the two types of leadership are linked to gender. Historically, cultural norms have given instrumental leadership to men, who, as fathers and husbands, assumed primary responsibility for earning income and making major family decisions. Traditionally, expressive leadership belonged to women: Mothers and wives encouraged supportive and peaceful relationships between family members. One result of this division of labor was that many children had greater respect for their fathers but closer personal ties with their mothers (Parsons & Bales, 1955; Macionis, 1978).

Greater equality between men and women has blurred this gender-based distinction. In family life, as in other settings, women and men now take on both leadership roles.

Three Leadership Styles

Sociologists also describe leadership in terms of decision-making style. *Authoritarian leadership* focuses on instrumental concerns, takes personal charge of decision making, and demands that group members obey orders. Although this leadership style may win little affection from the group, a fast-acting authoritarian leader is appreciated in a crisis.

Democratic leadership is more expressive and makes a point of including everyone in the decision-making process. Although less successful in a crisis situation, democratic leaders generally draw on the ideas of all members to develop creative solutions to problems.

Laissez-faire leadership allows the group to function more or less on its own (*laissez-faire* in French means "leave it alone"). This style typically is the least effective in promoting group goals (White & Lippitt, 1953; Ridgeway, 1983).

GROUP CONFORMITY

Groups influence the behavior of their members by promoting conformity. "Fitting in" provides a secure feeling of belonging, but at the extreme, group pressure can be unpleasant and even dangerous. As experiments by Solomon Asch and Stanley Milgram showed, even strangers can encourage conformity.

Asch's Research

Solomon Asch (1952) recruited students, supposedly to study visual perception. Before the experiment began, he explained to all but one member in a small group that their real purpose was to put pressure on the remaining person. Arranging six to eight students around a table, Asch showed them a "standard" line, as drawn on Card 1 in Figure 7–1, and asked them to match it to one of three lines on Card 2.

Anyone with normal vision could easily see that the line marked "A" on Card 2 is the correct choice. At the beginning of the experiment, everyone made the matches correctly. But then Asch's secret accomplices began answering incorrectly, leaving the naive subject (seated at the table so as to answer next to last) bewildered and uncomfortable.

What happened? Asch found that one-third of all subjects chose to conform by answering incorrectly. Apparently, many of us are willing to compromise our own judgment to avoid the discomfort of being different, even from people we do not know.

Milgram's Research

Stanley Milgram, a former student of Solomon Asch's, conducted conformity experiments of his own. In Milgram's controversial study (1963, 1965; A. G. Miller, 1986), a researcher explained to male recruits that they would be taking part in a study of how punishment affects learning. One by one, he assigned the subjects to the role of teacher and placed another person—actually an accomplice of Milgram's—in a connecting room to pose as a learner.

 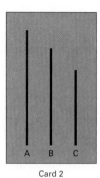

Card 1   Card 2

FIGURE 7–1   Cards Used in Asch's Experiment in Group Conformity

In Asch's experiment, subjects were asked to match the line on Card 1 to one of the lines on Card 2. Most subjects agreed with the wrong answers given by others in their group.

Source: Asch (1952).

The teacher watched as the learner was seated in what looked like an electric chair. The researcher applied electrode paste to one of the learner's wrists, explaining that this would "prevent blisters and burns." The researcher then attached an electrode to the wrist and secured the leather straps, explaining that these would "prevent excessive movement while the learner was being shocked." The researcher assured the teacher that although the shocks would be painful, they would cause "no permanent tissue damage."

The researcher then led the teacher back to the next room, explaining that the "electric chair" was connected to a "shock generator," actually a phony but realistic-looking piece of equipment with a label that read "Shock Generator, Type ZLB, Dyson Instrument Company, Waltham, Mass." On the front was a dial that appeared to regulate electric current from 15 volts (labeled "Slight Shock") to 300 volts (marked "Intense Shock") to 450 volts (marked "Danger: Severe Shock").

Seated in front of the "shock generator," the teacher was told to read aloud pairs of words. Then the teacher was to repeat the first word of each pair and wait for the learner to recall the second word. Whenever the learner failed to answer correctly, the teacher was told to apply an electric shock.

The researcher directed the teacher to begin at the lowest level (15 volts) and to increase the shock by another 15 volts every time the learner made a mistake. And so the teacher did. At 75, 90, and 105 volts, the teacher heard moans from the learner; at 120 volts, shouts of pain; at 270 volts, screams; at 315 volts, pounding on the wall; after that, deadly silence. None of forty subjects assigned to the role of teacher during the initial research even questioned the procedure before reaching 300 volts, and twenty-six of the subjects—almost two-thirds—went all the way to 450 volts. Even Milgram was surprised at how readily people obeyed authority figures.

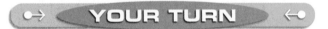

Was Milgram's research ethical, according to the guidelines you read about in Chapter 2, "Sociological Investigation" (see pages 40–41)? Explain your answer.

Milgram (1964) then modified his research to see if groups of ordinary people—not authority figures—could pressure people to administer electrical shocks, as Asch's groups had pressured individuals to match lines incorrectly.

This time, Milgram formed a group of three teachers, two of whom were his accomplices. Each of the three teachers was to suggest a shock level when the learner made an error; the rule was that the group would then administer the *lowest* of the three suggested levels. This arrangement gave the naive subject the power to deliver a lesser shock regardless of what the others said.

The accomplices suggested increasing the shock level with each error, putting pressure on the third member to do the same. The subjects in these groups applied voltages three to four times higher than the levels applied by subjects acting alone. Thus Milgram's research suggests that people are likely to follow the lead of not only legitimate authority figures but also groups of ordinary individuals, even when it means harming another person.

Janis's "Groupthink"

Experts also cave in to group pressure, says Irving L. Janis (1972, 1989). Janis argues that a number of U.S. foreign policy errors, including the failure to foresee Japan's attack on Pearl Harbor during World War II and our ill-fated involvement in the Vietnam War, resulted from group conformity among our highest-ranking political leaders.

Common sense tells us that group discussion improves decision making. Janis counters that group members often seek agreement that closes off other points of view. Janis called this process **groupthink**, *the tendency of group members to conform, resulting in a narrow view of some issue.*

A classic example of groupthink led to the failed invasion of Cuba at the Bay of Pigs in 1961. Looking back, Arthur Schlesinger Jr., an adviser to President John F. Kennedy, confessed to feeling guilty for "having kept so quiet during those crucial discussions in the Cabinet Room," adding that the group discouraged anyone from challenging what, in hindsight, Schlesinger considered "nonsense" (quoted in Janis, 1972:30, 40). Groupthink may also have been a factor in 2003 when U.S. leaders went to war on the assumption that Iraq had stockpiles of weapons of mass destruction.

REFERENCE GROUPS

How do we assess our own attitudes and behavior? Frequently, we use a **reference group,** *a social group that serves as a point of reference in making evaluations and decisions.*

A young man who imagines his family's response to a woman he is dating is using his family as a reference group. A supervisor who tries to predict her employees' reaction to a new vacation policy is using them in the same way. As these examples suggest, reference groups can be primary or secondary. In either case, our need to conform shows how others' attitudes affect us.

We also use groups that we do *not* belong to for reference. Being well prepared for a job interview means showing up dressed the way people in that company dress for work. Conforming to groups we do not belong to is a strategy to win acceptance and illustrates the process of *anticipatory socialization,* described in Chapter 5 ("Socialization").

Stouffer's Research

Samuel A. Stouffer and his colleagues (1949) conducted a classic study of reference group dynamics during World War II. Researchers asked soldiers to rate their own or any competent soldier's chances of promotion in their army unit. You might guess that soldiers serving in outfits with a high promotion rate would be optimistic about advancement. Yet Stouffer's research pointed to the opposite conclusion: Soldiers in army units with low promotion rates were actually more positive about their chances to move ahead.

The key to understanding Stouffer's results lies in the groups against which soldiers measured themselves. Those assigned to units with lower promotion rates looked around them and saw people making no more headway than they were. That is, although they had not been promoted, neither had many others, so they did not feel deprived. However, soldiers in units with a higher promotion rate could easily think of people who had been promoted sooner or more often than they. With such people in mind, even soldiers who had been promoted were likely to feel shortchanged.

The point is that we do not make judgments about ourselves in isolation, nor do we compare ourselves with just anyone. Regardless of our situation in *absolute* terms, we form a subjective sense of our well-being by looking at ourselves in relation to specific reference groups.

IN-GROUPS AND OUT-GROUPS

Each of us favors some groups over others, whether because of political outlook, social prestige, or just manner of dress. On the college campus, for example, left-leaning student activists may look down on fraternity members, whom they consider too conservative; fraternity members, in turn, may snub the computer "nerds" who work too hard. People in just about every social setting make positive and negative evaluations of members of other groups.

Such judgments illustrate another important element of group dynamics: the opposition of in-groups and out-groups. An **in-group** is *a social group toward which a member feels respect and loyalty.* An in-group exists in relation to an **out-group,** *a social group toward which a person feels a sense of competition or opposition.* In-groups and out-groups are based on the idea that "we" have valued traits that "they" lack.

Tensions between groups sharpen the groups' boundaries and give people a clearer social identity. However, members of in-groups generally hold overly positive views of themselves and unfairly negative views of various out-groups.

Power also plays a part in intergroup relations. A powerful in-group can define others as a lower-status out-group. Historically, in countless U.S. towns and cities, many white people viewed people of color as an out-group and subordinated them socially, politically, and economically. Internalizing these negative attitudes, minorities often struggle to overcome negative self-images. In this way, in-groups and out-groups foster loyalty but also generate conflict (Tajfel, 1982; Bobo & Hutchings, 1996).

YOUR TURN

Identify five in-groups and five out-groups at your college. Explain why you define each group as "in" or "out." Would others agree with your choices?

GROUP SIZE

The next time you go to a party, try to arrive first. If you do, you will be able to watch some fascinating group dynamics. Until about six people enter the room, every person who arrives shares a single conversation. As more people arrive, the group divides into two clusters, and it divides again and again as the party grows. Size plays an important role in how group members interact.

To understand why, note the mathematical number of relationships among two to seven people. As shown in

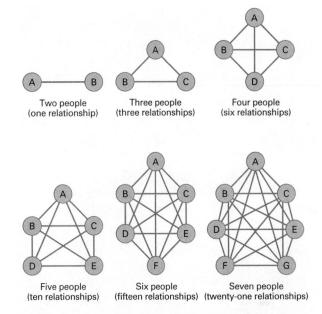

FIGURE 7–2   Group Size and Relationships

As the number of people in a group increases, the number of relationships that link them increases much faster. By the time six or seven people share a conversation, the group usually divides into two.

Source: Created by the author.

Figure 7–2, two people form a single relationship; adding a third person results in three relationships; adding a fourth person yields six. Increasing the number of people one at a time, then, expands the number of relationships much more rapidly since every new individual can interact with everyone already there. Thus by the time seven people join one conversation, twenty-one "channels" connect them. With so many open channels, some people begin to feel left out, and the group usually divides.

The Dyad

The German sociologist Georg Simmel (1858–1918) studied social dynamics in the smallest groups. Simmel (1950, orig. 1902) used the term **dyad** to designate *a social group with two members.*

Simmel explained that social interaction in a dyad is typically more intense than in larger groups because neither member shares the other's attention with anyone else. In the United States, love affairs, marriages, and the closest friendships are dyadic.

But like a stool with only two legs, dyads are unstable. Both members of a dyad must work to keep the relationship going; if either withdraws, the group collapses. Because the

The triad, illustrated by Jonathan Green's painting *Friends,* includes three people. A triad is more stable than a dyad because conflict between any two persons can be mediated by the third member. Even so, should the relationship between any two become more intense in a positive sense, those two are likely to exclude the third.

Jonathan Green, *Friends,* 1992. Oil on masonite, 14 in. × 11 in. © Jonathan Green, Naples, Florida. Collection of Patric McCoy.

stability of marriages is important to society, the marital dyad is supported by legal, economic, and often religious ties.

The Triad

Simmel also studied the **triad,** *a social group with three members,* which contains three relationships, each uniting two of the three people. A triad is more stable than a dyad because one member can act as a mediator should the relationship between the other two become strained. Such group dynamics help explain why members of a dyad (say, a married couple) often seek out a third person (such as a counselor) to discuss tensions between them.

On the other hand, two of the three can pair up to press their views on the third, or two may intensify their relationship, leaving the other feeling left out. For example, when two of the three develop a romantic interest in each other,

they will come to understand the old saying, "Two's company, three's a crowd."

As groups grow beyond three people, they become more stable and capable of withstanding the loss of one or more members. At the same time, increases in group size reduce the intense personal interaction possible only in the smallest groups. This is why larger groups are based less on personal attachment and more on formal rules and regulations.

SOCIAL DIVERSITY: RACE, CLASS, AND GENDER

Race, ethnicity, class, and gender each play a part in group dynamics. Peter Blau (1977; Blau, Blum, & Schwartz, 1982; South & Messner, 1986) points out three ways in which social diversity influences intergroup contact:

1. **Large groups turn inward.** Blau explains that the larger a group is, the more likely its members are to have relationships just among themselves. To enhance social diversity, a college increases the number of international students. These students may add a dimension of difference, but as their numbers rise, they become more likely to form their own social group. Thus efforts to promote social diversity may have the unintended effect of promoting separatism.

2. **Heterogeneous groups turn outward.** The more internally diverse a group is, the more likely its members are to interact with outsiders. Members of campus groups that recruit people of both sexes and various social backgrounds typically have more intergroup contact than those with members of one social category.

3. **Physical boundaries create social boundaries.** To the extent that a social group is physically segregated from others (by having its own dorm or dining area, for example), its members are less likely to interact with other people.

NETWORKS

A **network** is *a web of weak social ties.* Think of a network as a "fuzzy" group containing people who come into occasional contact but who lack a sense of boundaries and belonging. If a group is a "circle of friends," then a network might be described as a "social web" expanding outward, often reaching great distances and including large numbers of people.

Some networks come close to being groups, as is the case with college classmates who stay in touch after graduation through class newsletters and reunions. More commonly, however, a network includes people we *know of*—or who *know of us*—but with whom we interact rarely, if at all.

As one woman with a widespread reputation as a community organizer explains, "I get calls at home, someone says, 'Are you Roseann Navarro? Somebody told me to call you. I have this problem . . .'" (quoted in Kaminer, 1984:94).

Network ties often give us the sense that we live in a "small world." In a classic experiment, Stanley Milgram (1967; Watts, 1999) gave letters to subjects in Kansas and Nebraska intended for a few specific people in Boston who were unknown to the original subjects. No addresses were supplied, and the subjects in the study were told to send the letters to others they knew personally who might know the target people. Milgram found that the target people received the letters with, on average, six subjects passing them on. This result led Milgram to conclude that just about everyone is connected to everyone else by "six degrees of separation." Later research, however, has cast doubt on Milgram's conclusions. Examining Milgram's original data, Judith Kleinfeld (Wildavsky, 2002) points out that most of Milgram's letters (240 out of 300) never arrived at all. Those that did were typically given to subjects who were wealthy, a fact that led Kleinfeld to conclude that rich people are far better connected across the country than ordinary women and men.

Network ties may be weak, but they can be a powerful resource. For immigrants trying to become established in a new community, businesspeople seeking to expand their operations, or anyone looking for a job, *whom you know* is often as important as *what you know* (Hagan, 1998; Petersen, Saporta, & Seidel, 2000).

Networks are based on people's colleges, clubs, neighborhoods, political parties, and personal interests. Obviously, some networks contain people with considerably more wealth, power, and prestige than others; that explains the importance of being "well connected." The networks of more privileged categories of people—such as the members of an expensive country club—are a valuable form of "social capital," which is more likely to lead people to higher-paying jobs (Green, Tigges, & Diaz, 1999; Lin, Cook, & Burt, 2001).

To learn more about new Internet-based social networks, visit http://www.friendster.com

Some people also have denser networks than others; that is, they are connected to more people. Typically, the largest social networks include people who are young, well educated, and living in large cities (Fernandez & Weinberg, 1997; Podolny & Baron, 1997).

Gender also shapes networks. Although the networks of men and women are typically the same size, women include more relatives (and more women) in their networks, and men include more co-workers (and more men). Research suggests that women's ties do not carry quite the same clout as typical "old boy" networks. Even so,

Today's college campuses value social diversity. One of the challenges of this movement is ensuring that all categories of students are fully integrated into campus life. This is not always easy. Following Blau's theory of group dynamics, as the number of minority students increases, these men and women are able to form a group unto themselves, perhaps interacting less with others.

research suggests that as gender equality increases in the United States, the networks of women and men are becoming more alike (Reskin & McBrier, 2000; Torres & Huffman, 2002).

Finally, new information technology has generated a global network of unprecedented size in the form of the Internet. But the Internet has not yet linked the entire world. Global Map 7–1 on page 176 shows that Internet use is high in rich countries and far less common in poor nations.

Formal Organizations

A century ago, most people lived in small groups of family, friends, and neighbors. Today, our lives revolve more and more around **formal organizations,** *large secondary groups organized to achieve their goals efficiently.* Formal organizations, such as business corporations and government agencies, differ from families and neighborhoods in their impersonal and formally planned atmosphere.

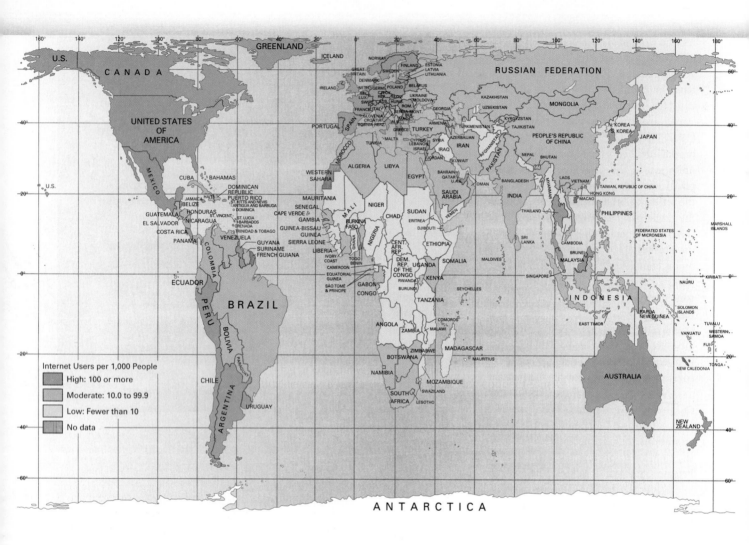

WINDOW ON THE WORLD

GLOBAL MAP 7-1 Internet Users in Global Perspective

This map shows how the Information Revolution has affected countries around the world. In most high-income nations, at least one-third of the population uses the Internet. By contrast, only a small share of people in low-income nations does so. What effect does this have on people's access to information? What does this mean for the future in terms of global inequality?

Sources: International Telecommunication Union (2005) and United Nations Development Programme (2005).

YOUR TURN

Today's world has so many large organizations that we identify them just by initials: IRS, IBM, CIA, PLO, NATO, CNN, WB, WWE, and so on. How many more can you think of?

When you think about it, organizing roughly 300 million people in this country into a single society is truly remarkable, whether it involves paving roads, collecting taxes, schooling children, or delivering the mail. To carry out most of these tasks, we rely on different types of large formal organizations.

TYPES OF FORMAL ORGANIZATIONS

Amitai Etzioni (1975) identified three types of formal organizations, distinguished by the reasons people participate in them: utilitarian organizations, normative organizations, and coercive organizations.

Utilitarian Organizations

Just about everyone who works for income belongs to a *utilitarian organization,* one that pays people for their efforts. Large businesses, for example, generate profits for their owners and income for their employees. Joining a utilitarian organization is usually a matter of individual choice, although most people must join one or another such organization to make a living.

Normative Organizations

People join *normative organizations* not for income but to pursue some goal they think is morally worthwhile. Sometimes called *voluntary associations,* these include community service groups (such as the PTA, the Lions Club, the League of Women Voters, and the Red Cross), as well as political parties and religious organizations. In global perspective, people living in the United States and other high-income nations with relatively democratic political systems are likely to join voluntary associations. A recent study found that 82 percent of first-year college students in the United States claimed to have participated in some volunteer activity within the past year (Curtis, Baer & Grabb, 2001; Schofer & Fourcade-Gourinchas, 2001; Sax et al., 2004).

Coercive Organizations

Coercive organizations have involuntary memberships. People are forced to join these organizations as a form of punishment (prisons) or treatment (some psychiatric hospitals). Coercive organizations have special physical features, such as locked doors and barred windows, and are supervised by security personnel. They isolate people, whom they label "inmates" or "patients," for a period of time in order to radically change their attitudes and behavior. Recall from Chapter 5 ("Socialization") the power of a total institution to change a person's overall sense of self.

It is possible for a single organization to fall into *all* of these categories. For example, a mental hospital serves as a coercive organization for a patient, a utilitarian organization for a psychiatrist, and a normative organization for a hospital volunteer.

ORIGINS OF FORMAL ORGANIZATIONS

Formal organizations date back thousands of years. Elites who controlled early empires relied on government officials to collect taxes, undertake military campaigns, and build monumental structures, from the Great Wall of China to the pyramids of Egypt.

However, early organizations had two limitations. First, they lacked the technology to let people travel over large distances, to communicate quickly, and to collect and store information. Second, these preindustrial societies had traditional cultures, so for the most part ruling organizations tried to preserve cultural systems, not to change them. But during the last few centuries, what Max Weber called a "rational worldview" emerged in parts of the world, a process described in Chapter 4 ("Society"). In Europe and North America, the Industrial Revolution ushered in a new structure for formal organizations concerned with efficiency that Weber called "bureaucracy."

CHARACTERISTICS OF BUREAUCRACY

Bureaucracy is *an organizational model rationally designed to perform tasks efficiently.* Bureaucratic officials regularly create and revise policy to increase efficiency. To appreciate the power and scope of bureaucratic organization, consider that any one of more than 300 million telephones in the United States can connect you within seconds to any other phone in a home, business, automobile, or even a hiker's backpack on a remote mountain trail in the Rocky Mountains. Such instant communication was beyond the imagination of people who lived in the ancient world.

Our telephone system depends on technology such as electricity, fiber optics, and computers. But the system could not exist without the bureaucracy that keeps track of every telephone call—noting which phone calls which other phone, when, and for how long—and then presents this information to more than 100 million telephone users in the form of a monthly bill.

What specific traits promote organizational efficiency? Max Weber (1978, orig. 1921) identified six key elements of the ideal bureaucratic organization:

1. **Specialization.** Our ancestors spent most of their time looking for food and shelter. Bureaucracy, by contrast, assigns individuals highly specialized jobs.

2. **Hierarchy of offices.** Bureaucracies arrange personnel in a vertical ranking of offices. Each person is supervised by "higher-ups" in the organization while in turn supervising others in lower positions. Usually, with few people at the top and many at the bottom, bureaucratic organizations take the form of a pyramid.

3. **Rules and regulations.** Cultural tradition counts for little in a bureaucracy. Instead, rationally enacted rules and regulations guide a bureaucracy's operation.

SUMMING UP

Small Groups and Formal Organizations

	Small Groups	Formal Organizations
Activities	Much the same for all members	Distinct and highly specialized
Hierarchy	Often informal or nonexistent	Clearly defined, corresponding to offices
Norms	General norms, informally applied	Clearly defined rules and regulations
Membership criteria	Variable; often based on personal affection or kinship	Technical competence to carry out assigned tasks
Relationships	Variable and typically primary	Typically secondary, with selective primary ties
Communications	Typically casual and face to face	Typically formal and in writing
Focus	Person-oriented	Task-oriented

Ideally, a bureaucracy operates in a completely predictable way.

4. **Technical competence.** Bureaucratic officials and staff have the technical competence to carry out their duties. Bureaucracies typically hire new members according to set standards and regularly monitor their performance. Such impersonal evaluation contrasts with the ancient custom of favoring relatives, whatever their talents, over strangers.

5. **Impersonality.** Bureaucracy puts rules ahead of personal whim so that both clients and workers are treated in the same way. From this impersonal approach comes the idea of the "faceless bureaucrat."

6. **Formal, written communications.** Someone once said that the heart of bureaucracy is not people but paperwork. Rather than casual, face-to-face talk, bureaucracy relies on formal, written memos and reports, which accumulate in vast files.

Bureaucratic organization promotes efficiency by carefully hiring workers and limiting the unpredictable effects of personal taste and opinion. The Summing Up table reviews the differences between small social groups and large bureaucratic organizations.

ORGANIZATIONAL ENVIRONMENT

No organization operates in a vacuum. The performance of any organization depends not only on its own goals and policies but also on the **organizational environment,** *factors outside an organization that affect its operation.* These factors include technology, economic and political trends, current events, the available workforce, and other organizations.

Modern organizations are shaped by the *technology* of computers, telephone systems, and personal digital assistants (PDAs). Computers give employees access to more information and people than ever before. At the same time, computer technology allows managers to monitor closely the activities of workers (Markoff, 1991).

Economic and political trends affect organizations. All organizations are helped or hurt by periodic economic growth or recession. Most industries also face competition from abroad as well as changes in laws—such as new environmental standards—at home.

Current events can have significant effects on organizations that are far removed from the location of the events themselves. The terrorist attacks of September 11, 2001, for example, were followed by an economic slowdown and an increase in security measures throughout the United States.

Population patterns, such as the size and composition of the surrounding population, also affect organizations. The average age, typical education, and social diversity of a local community determine the available workforce and sometimes the market for an organization's products or services.

Other organizations also contribute to the organizational environment. To be competitive, a hospital must be responsive to the insurance industry and to organizations representing doctors, nurses, and other health care workers. It must also be aware of the equipment and procedures available at nearby facilities, as well as their prices.

THE INFORMAL SIDE OF BUREAUCRACY

Weber's ideal bureaucracy deliberately regulates every activity. In actual organizations, however, human beings are creative (and stubborn) enough to resist bureaucratic

George Tooker's painting *Government Bureau* is a powerful statement about the human costs of bureaucracy. The artist paints members of the public in a drab sameness—reduced from human beings to mere "cases" to be disposed of as quickly as possible. Set apart from others by their positions, officials are "faceless bureaucrats" concerned more with numbers than with providing genuine assistance (notice that the artist places the fingers of the officials on calculators).

George Tooker, *Government Bureau*, 1956. Egg tempera on gesso panel, 19⅝ × 29⅝ inches. The Metropolitan Museum of Art, George A. Hearn Fund, 1956 (56.78). Photograph © 1984 The Metropolitan Museum of Art.

regulation. Informality may amount to simply cutting corners on your job, but it can also provide the flexibility needed to adapt and prosper.

In part, informality comes from the personalities of organizational leaders. Studies of U.S. corporations document that the qualities and quirks of individuals—including personal charisma, interpersonal skills, and the willingness to recognize problems—can have a great effect on organizational outcomes (Halberstam, 1986; Baron, Hannan, & Burton, 1999).

Authoritarian, democratic, and laissez-faire types of leadership (described earlier in this chapter) reflect individual personality as much as any organizational plan. In the "real world" of organizations, leaders sometimes seek to benefit personally by abusing organizational power. Recent high-profile examples include corporate scandals such as the collapse of Enron and other companies. More commonly, leaders take credit for the efforts of the people who work for them. For example, the authority and responsibilities of many secretaries are far greater than their official job titles and salaries suggest.

Communication offers another example of organizational informality. Memos and other written communications are the formal way to spread information throughout an organization. Typically, however, individuals also create informal networks, or "grapevines," that spread information quickly, if not always accurately. Grapevines, using both word of mouth and e-mail, are particularly important to rank-and-file workers because higher-ups often try to keep important information from them.

The spread of e-mail has "flattened" organizations somewhat, allowing even the lowest-ranking employee to bypass immediate superiors and communicate directly with the organization's leader or with all fellow employees at once. Some organizations object to "open-channel" communication and limit the use of e-mail. Microsoft Corporation (whose founder, Bill Gates, has an unlisted e-mail address that helps him limit his mail to hundreds of messages each day) has developed "screens" that filter out messages from everyone except certain approved people (Gwynne & Dickerson, 1997).

Using new information technology as well as age-old human ingenuity, members of organizations often try to break free of rigid rules in order to personalize procedures and surroundings. Such efforts suggest that we should now take a closer look at some of the problems of bureaucracy.

PROBLEMS OF BUREAUCRACY

We rely on bureaucracy to manage everyday life efficiently, but many people are uneasy about large organizations. Bureaucracy can dehumanize and manipulate us, and some say it poses a threat to political democracy.

Bureaucratic Alienation

Max Weber held up bureaucracy as a model of productivity. However, Weber was keenly aware of bureaucracy's ability to *dehumanize* the people it is supposed to serve. The same impersonality that fosters efficiency also keeps officials and

July 25, 2004

The New Magic Bullet: Bureaucratic Imagination

By DOUGLAS JEHL

WASHINGTON—Terrorism has never been a fair fight. . . . It may pit the weak against the strong, the few against the many, but it also pits surprise against habit, indiscriminate attack against rules, the instruments of war against unarmed civilians. It may be asymmetric warfare, in the jargon of the Pentagon, but it is a battle in which the terrorists in many ways have the upper hand.

To the list of holes in the armor of the strong, the Sept. 11 commission has now added another. The failure to foresee the attacks of Sept. 11, 2001, it wrote in its final report, was in large part a failure of imagination—a failure to conceive that "an organization like Al Qaeda headquartered on the other side of the world, in a region so poor that electricity or telephones were scarce, could nonetheless scheme to wield weapons of unprecedented destructive power on the largest cities of the United States."

How now to ignite such imagination? In many ways, the commission's prescription—shaking up the bureaucracy—is as unsatisfying as its diagnosis is accurate. Matched against terrorism, can a bureaucracy ever gain the upper hand?

The recent record does not inspire hope. Remember, for a moment, Richard Reid, whose far-fetched scheme still inspires smiles of disbelief, but who three months after Sept. 11 very nearly blew a plane out of the sky by putting a match to a bomb in his shoe. . . .

After hundreds of pages pulsing with accounts of terrorist daring and bureaucratic inertia, under chapter headings like "We Have Some Planes" and "The System Was Blinking Red," the commission titled its concluding recommendations this way: "How to Do It: A Different Way of Organizing the Government." . . .

"Good people can overcome bad structures," it says. "They should not have to."

Could a better bureaucracy make a difference? That is the case the commission makes in arguing for the creation of a new director of national intelligence, with authority to perceive new problems and break down old barriers. . . .

Of course, bureaucracies respond better to past events than to future responsibilities. (Don't even try to bring that box-cutter on your next cross-country flight.) But with few exceptions, government bureaucracies do not have a reputation for attracting visionary leaders who can imagine, and forestall, the next big surprise.

Bureaucracies are very good at spending money; the government has spent billions of new dollars on counterterrorism since Sept. 11. But given the infinite possibilities for a future attack, there is not enough money in the world to protect against possible strikes.

What bureaucracies do not do well is to move swiftly. The Sept. 11 commission's

---

clients from responding to one another's unique personal needs. Far from it: Officials at large government and corporate agencies must treat each client impersonally as a standard "case."

Formal organizations cause *alienation,* according to Weber, by reducing the human being to "a small cog in a ceaselessly moving mechanism" (1978:988, orig. 1921). Although formal organizations are intended to benefit humanity, Weber feared that humanity might well end up serving formal organizations.

Bureaucratic Inefficiency and Ritualism

Inefficiency, the failure of an organization to carry out the work that it exists to perform, is a familiar problem. According to one report, the General Services Administration, the government agency that buys equipment for federal workers, takes up to three years to process a request for a new computer. This delay ensures that by the time the computer arrives, it is already obsolete (Gwynne & Dickerson, 1997).

The problem of inefficiency is captured in the concept of *red tape,* a term that refers to the red tape used by eighteenth-century English administrators to wrap official parcels and records (Shipley, 1985). To Robert Merton (1968), red tape amounts to a new twist on the already familiar concept of group conformity. He coined the term **bureaucratic ritualism** to describe *a focus on rules and regulations to the point of undermining an organization's goals.* After the terrorist attacks of September 11, 2001, for example, the U.S. Postal Service continued to help deliver mail addressed to Osama bin Laden to a post office in Afghanistan, despite the objections of the FBI. It took an act of Congress to change the policy (Bedard, 2002). "In the *Times*" asks whether large-scale government bureaucracy is up to the task of combating fast-changing global terrorism.

recommendations come 34 months after the attack; its inquiry was delayed by months because of opposition from the White House. Against internal rivalries, bureaucracies find equilibrium in compromise. Despite the urgency with which the commission expressed its findings, the White House and Congress have responded, for the most part, by promising to study the issue carefully.

"It is unrealistic to think they would all be received, considered and passed into law this year," Representative Nancy Pelosi of California, the Democratic House leader, said of the recommendations. "But I would hope that the committees of jurisdiction would quickly review the findings and consider the recommendations." . . .

There are indeed many wise people, including Brent Scowcroft, the former national security adviser, who have long argued privately that a bureaucratic overhaul could make some difference. The current structure, they say, demands too much of the director of central intelligence, whose day-to-day responsibility for running the CIA makes him a less than neutral overseer of the broader range of 15 intelligence agencies.

But by definition, imagination requires new ways of thinking. Here too, the commission had some suggestions, less noticed than the structural changes it recommended, but perhaps ultimately more important.

How best to win the war on terrorism? A starting point, the commission said, is to remember that wars are not best fought by direct means alone, but require diplomacy and other means to address the threat. As an example of imagination, it admiringly quoted from a memorandum written last fall by [Secretary of Defense Donald] Rumsfeld:

"Does the U.S. need to fashion a broad, integrated plan to stop the next generation of terrorists? The U.S. is putting relatively little effort into a long-range plan, but we are putting a great deal of effort into trying to stop terrorists. The cost-benefit ratio is against us!"

WHAT DO YOU THINK?

1. Do you think bureaucracies deal effectively with the unexpected? Why or why not?

2. Why is it hard for bureaucracies to "move swiftly"?

3. What specific suggestions would you make to government anti-terrorism organizations to help them do their job better?

Adapted from the original article by Douglas Jehl published in *The New York Times* on July 25, 2004. Copyright © 2004 by The New York Times Company. Reprinted with permission.

Bureaucratic Inertia

If bureaucrats sometimes have little reason to work especially hard, they have every reason to protect their jobs. Officials typically work to keep an organization going even after its original goal has been realized. As Weber put it, "Once fully established, bureaucracy is among the social structures which are hardest to destroy" (1978:987, orig. 1921).

Bureaucratic inertia refers to *the tendency of bureaucratic organizations to perpetuate themselves.* Formal organizations tend to take on a life of their own beyond their formal objectives. For example, the U.S. Department of Agriculture has offices in nearly every county in all fifty states, even though only one county in seven has any working farms. Usually, an organization stays in business by redefining its goals. For example, the Agriculture Department now performs a broad range of work not directly related to farming, including nutritional and environmental research.

OLIGARCHY

Early in the twentieth century, Robert Michels (1876–1936) pointed out the link between bureaucracy and political **oligarchy,** *the rule of the many by the few* (1949, orig. 1911). According to what Michels called "the iron law of oligarchy," the pyramid shape of bureaucracy places a few leaders in charge of the resources of the entire organization.

Max Weber credited a strict hierarchy of responsibility with high organizational efficiency. But Michels countered that this hierarchical structure also concentrates power and thus threatens democracy because officials can and often do use their access to information, resources, and the media to promote their personal interests.

Furthermore, bureaucracy helps distance officials from the public, as in the case of the corporate president or public official who is "unavailable for comment" to the local press or the U.S. president who withholds documents from

The ideas of scientific management were most successfully applied by Henry Ford, who pioneered the automobile assembly line. As shown in this 1928 photograph of the Dearborn, Michigan, plant, Ford divided up the job of building cars into hundreds of different tasks, each performed by a worker as the cars moved along an assembly line. The result was that new cars could be produced so cheaply that most of these autoworkers could afford to buy one.

Congress claiming "executive privilege." Oligarchy, then, thrives in the hierarchical structure of bureaucracy and reduces the accountability of leaders to the people (Tolson, 1995).

Political competition, term limits, and a system of checks and balances prevent the U.S. government from becoming an out-and-out oligarchy. Even so, incumbents enjoy a significant advantage in U.S. politics. In 2004, as in other recent elections, only 10 percent of congressional officeholders running for reelection were defeated by their challengers.

The Evolution of Formal Organizations

The problems of bureaucracy—especially the alienation it produces and its tendency toward oligarchy—stem from two organizational traits: hierarchy and rigidity. To Weber, bureaucracy was a top-down system: Rules and regulations made at the top guide every facet of people's lives down the chain of command. A century ago in the United States,

Weber's ideas took hold in an organizational model called *scientific management*. We begin with a look at this model and then examine three challenges over the course of the twentieth century that gradually led to a new model, the *flexible organization*.

SCIENTIFIC MANAGEMENT

Frederick Winslow Taylor (1911) had a simple message: Most businesses in the United States were sadly inefficient. Managers had little idea of how to increase their business's output, and workers relied on the same tired skills of earlier generations. To increase efficiency, Taylor explained, business should apply the principles of science. **Scientific management,** then, is *the application of scientific principles to the operation of a business or other large organization.*

Scientific management involves three steps. First, managers carefully observe the task performed by each worker, identifying all the operations involved and measuring the time needed for each. Second, managers analyze their data, trying to discover ways for workers to perform each job more efficiently. For example, managers might decide to give the worker different tools or to reposition various work operations within the factory. Third, management provides guidance and incentives for workers to do their jobs more quickly. If a factory worker moves 20 tons of pig iron in one day, for example, management shows the worker how to do the job more efficiently and then provides higher wages as the worker's productivity rises. Taylor concluded that if scientific principles were applied in this way, companies would become more profitable, workers would earn higher wages, and consumers would pay lower prices.

A century ago, the auto pioneer Henry Ford put it this way: "Save ten steps a day for each of 12,000 employees, and you will have saved fifty miles of wasted motion and misspent energy" (Allen & Hyman, 1999:209). In the early 1900s, the Ford Motor Company and many other businesses followed Taylor's lead and made improvements in efficiency.

The principles of scientific management suggested that workplace power should reside with owners and executives, who paid little attention to the ideas of their workers. As the decades passed, formal organizations faced important challenges, involving race and gender, rising competition from abroad, and the changing nature of work. We now take a brief look at each of these challenges.

THE FIRST CHALLENGE: RACE AND GENDER

In the 1960s, critics pointed out that big businesses and other organizations engaged in unfair hiring practices. Rather than hiring on the basis of competence as Weber had proposed, they had excluded women and other minorities, especially from positions of power. Hiring on the basis of competence is partly a matter of fairness; it is also a matter of increasing the source of talent to promote efficiency.

Patterns of Privilege and Exclusion

Even in the early twenty-first century, as shown in Figure 7–3, non-Hispanic white men in the United States—34 percent of the working-age population—still held 56 percent of management jobs. Non-Hispanic white women made up 34 percent of the population but held just 29 percent of managerial positions (U.S. Equal Employment Opportunity Commission, 2005). The members of other minorities lagged further behind.

Rosabeth Moss Kanter (1977; Kanter & Stein, 1979) points out that excluding women and minorities from the workplace ignores the talents of more than half the population. Furthermore, underrepresented people in an organization often feel like socially isolated out-groups—uncomfortably visible, taken less seriously, and given fewer chances for promotion.

Opening up an organization so that change and advancement happen more often, Kanter claims, improves everyone's on-the-job performance by motivating employees to become "fast-trackers" who work harder and are more committed to the company. By contrast, an organization with many dead-end jobs turns workers into less productive "zombies" who are never asked for their opinion on anything. An open organization encourages leaders to seek out the input of all employees, which usually improves decision making.

The "Female Advantage"

Some organizational researchers argue that women bring special management skills that strengthen an organization. According to Deborah Tannen (1994), women have a greater "information focus" and more readily ask questions in order to understand an issue. Men, on the other hand, have an "image focus" that makes them wonder how asking questions in a particular situation will affect their reputation.

In another study of women executives, Sally Helgesen (1990) found three other gender-linked patterns. First, women place greater value on communication skills than men and share information more than men do. Second, women are more flexible leaders who typically give their employees greater freedom. Third, compared to men, women tend to emphasize the interconnectedness of all organizational operations. Thus women bring a *female advantage* to companies striving to be more flexible and democratic.

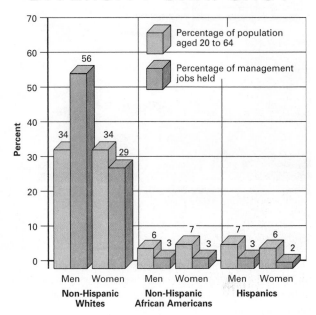

DIVERSITY SNAPSHOT

Percentage of population aged 20 to 64

Percentage of management jobs held

FIGURE 7-3 U.S. Managers in Private Industry by Race, Sex, and Ethnicity, 2003

White men are more likely than their population size suggests to be managers in private industry. The opposite is true for white women and other minorities.

Sources: U.S. Census Bureau (2005) and U.S. Equal Employment Opportunity Commission (2005).

In sum, one challenge to conventional bureaucracy is to become more open and flexible in order to take advantage of the experience, ideas, and creativity of everyone, regardless of race or gender. The result goes right to the bottom line: greater profits.

THE SECOND CHALLENGE: THE JAPANESE WORK ORGANIZATION

In 1980, the U.S. corporate world was shaken to discover that the most popular automobile model sold in this country was not a Chevrolet, Ford, or Plymouth but the Honda Accord, made in Japan. As late as the 1950s, the label "Made in Japan" generally was found on products that were cheap and poorly made. But times had changed. The success of the Japanese auto industry (and shortly afterward, companies making cameras and other products) soon had analysts buzzing about the "Japanese organization." How else could so small a country challenge the world's economic powerhouse?

The best of today's information age jobs—including working at the popular search-engine Web site Google—allow people lots of personal freedom as long as they produce good ideas. At the same time, many other jobs—such as working the counter at McDonald's—involve the same routines and strict supervision found in factories a century ago.

Japanese organizations reflect that country's strong collective spirit. In contrast to the U.S. emphasis on rugged individualism, the Japanese value cooperation. In effect, formal organizations in Japan are more like large primary groups. A generation ago, William Ouchi (1981) highlighted five differences between formal organizations in Japan and those in the United States. First, Japanese companies hired new workers in groups, giving everyone the same salary and responsibilities. Second, many Japanese companies hired workers for life, fostering a strong sense of loyalty. Third, with the idea that employees would spend their entire careers there, many Japanese companies trained workers in all phases of their operations. Fourth, although Japanese corporate leaders took final responsibility for their organization's performance, they involved workers in "quality circles" to discuss decisions that affected them. Fifth, Japanese companies played a large role in the lives of workers, providing home mortgages, sponsoring recreational activities, and scheduling social events. Together, such policies encourage much more loyalty among members of Japanese organizations than is typically the case in their U. S. counterparts.

For decades, people around the world marveled at the economic "miracle" of Japanese organizations. But the praise was premature. Around 1990, the Japanese economy entered a downward trend that is only now showing signs of ending. As a result of this downturn, most Japanese companies no longer offer workers jobs for life or many of the other benefits noted by Ouchi.

THE THIRD CHALLENGE: THE CHANGING NATURE OF WORK

Beyond rising global competition and the need to provide equal opportunity for all, pressure to modify conventional organizations is coming from changes in the nature of work itself. Chapter 4 ("Society") described the shift from industrial to postindustrial production. Rather than working in factories using heavy machinery to make *things,* more and more people are using computers and other electronic technology to create or process *information.* The postindustrial society, then, is characterized by information-based organizations.

Frederick Taylor developed his concept of scientific management at a time when jobs involved tasks that, though often backbreaking, were routine. Workers shoveled coal, poured liquid iron into molds, welded body panels to automobiles on an assembly line, or shot hot rivets into steel girders to build skyscrapers. In addition, many of the industrial workers in Taylor's day were immigrants, most of whom had little schooling and many of whom knew little English. The routine nature of industrial jobs, coupled with the limited skills of the labor force, led Taylor to treat work as a series of fixed tasks, set down by management and followed by employees.

Many of today's information age jobs are very different: The work of designers, artists, writers, composers, programmers, business owners, and others now demands

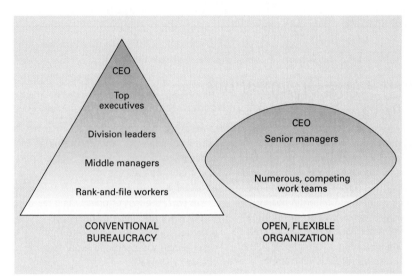

FIGURE 7-4 Two Organizational Models

The conventional model of bureaucratic organizations has a pyramid shape, with a clear chain of command. Orders flow from the top down, and reports of performance flow from the bottom up. Such organizations have extensive rules and regulations, and their workers have highly specialized jobs. More open and flexible organizations have a flatter shape, more like a football. With fewer levels in the hierarchy, responsibility for generating ideas and making decisions is shared throughout the organization. Many workers do their jobs in teams and have a broad knowledge of the entire organization's operation.

Source: Created by the author.

individual creativity and imagination. Here are several ways in which today's organizations differ from those of a century ago:

1. **Creative autonomy.** As one Hewlett-Packard executive put it, "From their first day of work here, people are given important responsibilities and are encouraged to grow" (cited in Brooks, 2000:128). Today's organizations now treat employees with information age skills as a vital resource. Executives can set production goals but cannot dictate how a worker is to accomplish tasks that require imagination and discovery. This gives highly skilled workers *creative freedom,* which means less day-to-day supervision as long as they generate good ideas in the long run.

2. **Competitive work teams.** Organizations typically give several groups of employees the freedom to work on a problem, offering the greatest rewards to those who come up with the best solution. Competitive work teams, a strategy first used by Japanese organizations, draw out the creative contributions of everyone and at the same time reduce the alienation often found in conventional organizations (Maddox, 1994; Yeatts, 1994).

3. **A flatter organization.** By spreading responsibility for creative problem solving throughout the workforce,

 Find out about the Saturn car company's flatter organizational structure at http://www.saturn.com

organizations take on a flatter shape. That is, the pyramid shape of conventional bureaucracy is replaced by an organizational

form with fewer levels in the chain of command, as shown in Figure 7–4.

4. **Greater flexibility.** The typical industrial age organization was a rigid structure guided from the top. Such organizations may accomplish a large amount of work, but they are not especially creative or able to respond quickly to changes in the larger environment. The ideal model in the information age is a more open, *flexible* organization that both generates new ideas and, in a rapidly changing global marketplace, adapts quickly.

What does all this mean for formal organizations? As David Brooks puts it, "The machine is no longer held up as the standard that healthy organizations should emulate. Now it's the ecosystem" (2000:128). Today's "smart" companies seek out intelligent, creative people (America Online's main building is called "Creative Center One") and nurture the growth of their talents.

Keep in mind, however, that many of today's jobs do not involve creative work at all. More correctly, the postindustrial economy has created two very different types of work: high-skill creative work and low-skill service work. Work in the fast-food industry, for example, is routine and

 highly supervised and thus has much more in common with the factory work of a century ago than with the creative teamwork

typical of today's information organizations. Therefore, at the same time that some organizations have taken on a flexible, flatter form, others continue to use the rigid chain of command.

APPLYING SOCIOLOGY

Computer Technology, Large Organizations, and the Assault on Privacy

Late for a meeting with a new client, Sarah drives her car through a yellow light as it turns red at a main intersection. A computer linked to a pair of cameras notes the violation and takes one picture of her license plate and another of her sitting in the driver's seat. In seven days, she receives a summons to appear in traffic court.

Joe calls a toll-free number to check the pollen count. As he listens to a recorded message, caller ID identifies Joe, records the call, and pulls up his profile from a public records database. The computer adds to the profile the fact that Joe suffers from allergies. Several weeks later, tens of thousands of profiles are sold to a drug company, which sends Joe and others a free sample of its new allergy medication.

Julio looks through his mail and finds a letter from a Washington, D.C., data services company telling him that he is one of about 145,000 people whose name, address, Social Security number, and credit file have recently been sold to criminals in California posing as businesspeople. With this information, other people can obtain credit cards or take out loans in his name. (A. Hamilton, 2001; O'Harrow, 2005)

These are all cases showing that today's organizations—which know more about us than ever before and more than most of us realize—pose a growing threat to personal privacy. Large organizations are necessary for today's society to operate. In some cases, organizations using information about us may actually be helpful. But cases of identity theft are on the rise, and personal privacy is on the decline.

In the past, small-town life gave people little privacy. But at least if people knew something about you, you were just as likely to know something about them. Today, unknown people "out there" can access information about each of us all the time.

In part, the loss of privacy is a result of more and more complex computer technology. Are you aware that every e-mail you send and every Web site you visit leaves a record in one or more computers? Most of these records can be retrieved by people you don't know, as well as by employers and other public officials.

Another part of today's loss of privacy reflects the number and size of formal organizations. As explained in this chapter, large organizations tend to treat people impersonally, and they have a huge appetite for information. Mix large organizations with ever more complex computer technology, and it is no wonder that most people in the United States are concerned about who knows what about them and what people are doing with this information.

YOUR TURN

Have you ever had a "dead-end" job? A job that demanded creativity? Which would you prefer and why?

THE "MCDONALDIZATION" OF SOCIETY[1]

As noted in the opening to this chapter, McDonald's has enjoyed enormous success, now operating more than 30,000 restaurants in the United States and around the world. Japan has more than 2,400 Golden Arches, and the world's largest McDonald's is located in China's capital city of Beijing.

McDonald's is far more than a restaurant chain; it is a symbol of U.S. culture. Not only do people around the world associate McDonald's with the United States, but here at home, one poll found that 98 percent of schoolchildren could identify Ronald McDonald, making him as well known as Santa Claus.

Even more important, the organizational principles that underlie McDonald's are coming to dominate our entire society. Our culture is becoming "McDonaldized," an awkward way of saying that we model many aspects of life on this restaurant chain: Parents buy toys at worldwide

---

[1]The term "McDonaldization" was coined by Jim Hightower (1975); much of this discussion is based on Ritzer (1993, 1998, 2000) and Schlosser (2002).

For decades, the level of personal privacy in the United States has been declining. Early in the twentieth century, when state agencies began issuing driver's licenses, for example, they generated files for every licensed driver. Today, officials can send this information at the touch of a button not only to the police but to other organizations as well. The Internal Revenue Service and the Social Security Administration, as well as government agencies that benefit veterans, students, the unemployed, and the poor, all collect mountains of personal information.

Business organizations now do much the same thing, and many of the choices we make end up in a company's database. Most of us use credit—the U.S. population now has more than 1 billion credit cards, an average of five per adult—but the companies that do "credit checks" collect and distribute information about us to almost anyone who asks, including criminals planning to steal our identity.

Then there are the small cameras found not only at traffic intersections but also in stores, public buildings, parking garages, and across college campuses. The number of surveillance cameras that monitor our movements is rapidly increasing with each passing

See who's walking on Fifth Avenue in New York City right now at this Web site: http://www.riotmanhattan.com/riotmanhattan/webcam.html

year. So-called security cameras may increase public safety in some ways—say, by discouraging a mugger or even a terrorist—at the cost of the little privacy we have left.

After the September 11, 2001, terrorist attacks, the federal government took steps (including the USA PATRIOT Act) to strengthen national security. Today, government officials more closely monitor not just who enters the country but the activities of all of us. Increased national security and privacy do not mix.

Some legal protections remain. Each of the fifty states has laws that give citizens the right to examine some records about themselves kept by employers, banks, and credit bureaus. The federal Privacy Act of 1974 also limits the exchange of personal information among government agencies and permits citizens to examine and correct most government files. In response to rising levels of identity theft, Congress is likely to pass more laws to regulate the sale of credit information. But so many organizations, private as well as public, now have information about us—experts estimate that 90 percent of U.S. households are profiled in databases somewhere—that current laws simply cannot effectively address the privacy problem.

WHAT DO YOU THINK?

1. Do you believe that our concern about national security is destroying privacy? How can the loss of privacy threaten our security?

2. Internet search engines such as Yahoo! (http://www.yahoo.com) have "people search" programs that help you locate almost anyone. Do you think such programs pose a threat to personal privacy?

3. Have you checked your credit history recently? Do you know how to reduce the chances of someone stealing your identity? (If not, one place to start is http://www.stopidentitytheft.org).

Sources: Robert Wright (1998), "Online Privacy" (2000), A. Hamilton (2001), Heymann (2002), and O'Harrow (2005).

---

chain stores like Toys 'R' Us; we drive to Jiffy Lube for a ten-minute oil change; face-to-face communication is being replaced more and more by e-mail, voice mail, and instant messaging; more vacations take the form of resorts and tour packages; television presents news in the form of ten-second sound bites; college admissions officers size up students they have never met by their GPA and SAT scores; and professors assign ghost-written textbooks[2] and evaluate students with tests mass-produced for them by publishing companies. The list goes on and on.

[2]A number of popular sociology books were not written by the person whose name appears on the cover. This book is not one of them, and the test bank was also written by the author.

McDonaldization: Three Principles

What do all these developments have in common? According to George Ritzer (1993), the McDonaldization of society rests on three organizational principles:

1. **Efficiency.** Ray Kroc, the marketing genius behind the expansion of McDonald's, set out to serve a hamburger, French fries, and a milkshake to a customer in fifty seconds. Today, one of the company's most popular items is the Egg McMuffin, an entire breakfast in a single sandwich. In the restaurant, customers dispose of their trash and stack their own trays as they walk out the door or, better still, drive away from the pickup window taking whatever mess they make with them. Such efficiency is now central to our way of life. We

tend to think that anything done quickly is, for that reason alone, good.

2. **Uniformity.** The first McDonald's operating manual set the weight of a regular raw hamburger at 1.6 ounces, its size at 3.875 inches across, and its fat content at 19 percent. A slice of cheese weighs exactly half an ounce. Fries are cut precisely 9/32 of an inch thick.

   Think about how many objects around your home, the workplace, and the campus are designed and mass-produced according to a standard plan. Not just our environment but our life experiences—from traveling the nation's interstates to sitting at home viewing television—are more standardized than ever before.

   Almost anywhere in the world, a person can walk into a McDonald's restaurant and receive the same sandwiches, drinks, and desserts prepared in precisely the same way.[3] Uniformity results from a highly rational system that specifies every action and leaves nothing to chance.

3. **Control.** The most unreliable element in the McDonald's system is human beings. After all, people have good and bad days, sometimes let their minds wander, or simply decide to try something a different way. To minimize the unpredictable human element, McDonald's has automated its equipment to cook food at a fixed temperature for a set length of time. Even the cash register at McDonald's is keyed to pictures of the items so that ringing up a customer's order is as simple as possible.

Similarly, automatic teller machines are replacing banks, highly automated bakeries now produce bread while people stand back and watch, and chickens and eggs (or is it eggs and chickens?) emerge from automated hatcheries. In supermarkets, laser scanners at self-checkouts are phasing out human checkers. We do most of our shopping in malls, where everything from temperature and humidity to the kinds of stores and products is carefully controlled and supervised (Ide & Cordell, 1994).

---

[3]As McDonald's has "gone global," a few products have been added or changed according to local tastes. For example, in Uruguay, customers enjoy the McHuevo (hamburger with poached egg on top); Norwegians can buy McLaks (grilled salmon sandwiches); the Dutch favor the Groenteburger (vegetable burger); in Thailand, McDonald's serves Samurai pork burgers (pork burgers with teriyaki sauce); the Japanese can purchase a Chicken Tatsuta Sandwich (chicken seasoned with soy and ginger); Filipinos eat McSpaghetti (spaghetti with tomato sauce and bits of hot dogs); and in India, where Hindus eat no beef, McDonald's sells a vegetarian Maharaja Mac (Sullivan, 1995).

Can Rationality Be Irrational?

There is no doubt about the popularity or efficiency of McDonald's. But there is another side to the story.

Max Weber was alarmed at the increasing rationalization of the world, fearing that formal organizations would cage our imaginations and crush the human spirit. As Weber saw it, rational systems were efficient but dehumanizing. McDonaldization bears him out. Each of the three principles just discussed limits human creativity, choice, and freedom. Echoing Weber, Ritzer states that "the ultimate irrationality of McDonaldization is that people could lose control over the system and it would come to control us" (1993:145). Perhaps even McDonald's understands this—the company has now expanded into more upscale, less McDonaldized restaurants such as Chipotle's and Pret-à-Manger that offer food that is more sophisticated, fresh, and healthful (Philadelphia, 2002).

The Future of Organizations: Opposing Trends

Early in the twentieth century, ever-larger organizations arose in the United States, most taking on the bureaucratic form described by Max Weber. In many respects, these organizations resembled armies led by powerful generals who issued orders to their captains and lieutenants. Foot soldiers, working in the factories, did what they were told.

With the emergence of a postindustrial economy around 1950, as well as rising competition from abroad, many organizations evolved toward a flatter, more flexible model that prizes communication and creativity. Such "intelligent organizations" (Pinchot & Pinchot, 1993; Brooks, 2000) have become more productive than ever. Just as important, for highly skilled people who now enjoy creative freedom, these organizations cause less of the alienation that so worried Max Weber.

But this is only half the story. Though the postindustrial economy has created many highly skilled jobs, it has created even more routine service jobs, such as those offered by McDonald's. Fast-food companies now represent the largest pool of low-wage labor, aside from migrant workers, in the United States (Schlosser, 2002). Work of this kind, which Ritzer terms "McJobs," offers few of the benefits that today's highly skilled workers enjoy. On the contrary, the automated routines that define work in the fast-food industry, telemarketing, and similar fields are very much the same as those that Frederick Taylor described a century ago.

Today, the organizational "flexibility" that gives better-off workers more freedom carries, for rank-and-file employees, the ever-present threat of "downsizing" (Sennett, 1998). Organizations facing global competition are eager to have creative employees, but they are just as eager to cut costs by eliminating as many routine jobs as possible. The net result is that some people are better off than ever, while others worry about holding their jobs and struggle to make ends meet—a trend that Chapter 11 ("Social Class in the United States") explores in detail.

U.S. organizations are the envy of the world for productive efficiency. For example, there are few places on Earth where the mail arrives as quickly and dependably as it does in this country. But we should remember that the future is far brighter for some workers than for others. In addition, as the Applying Sociology box on pages 186–87 explains, organizations pose an increasing threat to our privacy—something to keep in mind as we envision our organizational future.

7 MAKING THE GRADE

The following learning tools will help you see what you know, identify what you still need to learn, and expand your understanding beyond the text. You can also visit this text's Companion Website™ at http://www.prenhall.com/macionis to find additional practice tests.

KEY POINTS

Social Groups

Social groups are building blocks of society that join members as well as perform various tasks. Primary groups tend to be small and person-oriented; secondary groups are typically large and goal-oriented.

Leadership is one key dimension of group dynamics. Instrumental leadership is concerned with realizing a group's goals; expressive leadership focuses on members' morale and well-being.

The Asch, Milgram, and Janis studies all show that group members often seek agreement and may pressure one another toward conformity. Individuals use reference groups—both ingroups and out-groups—to form attitudes and make evaluations.

Georg Simmel described the dyad as intense but unstable; a triad, he added, can easily turn into a dyad by excluding one member. Peter Blau explored how group size, social diversity, and the physical segregation of groups affect members' behavior.

Social networks are relational webs that link people with little common identity and limited interaction. The Internet is a vast electronic network linking millions of people worldwide.

Formal Organizations

Formal organizations are large secondary groups that try to carry out complex tasks efficiently. They are classified as utilitarian, normative, or coercive, depending on their members' reasons for joining. Bureaucracy, which expands in modern societies, is based on specialization, hierarchy, rules and regulations, technical competence, impersonal interaction, and formal written communication. All formal organizations operate in an environment influenced by technology, political and economic trends, population patterns, and other organizations.

Ideally, bureaucracy promotes efficiency. But Max Weber claimed that bureaucracy can also lead to alienation. Robert Michels linked bureaucracy to the problem of oligarchy.

The Evolution of Formal Organizations

Frederick Taylor's concept of scientific management shaped U.S. organizations a century ago. Since then, organizations have evolved toward a more open and flexible form as they have included a larger share of women and other minorities, responded to global competition, and shifted their focus from industrial production to postindustrial information processing.

The "McDonaldization" of society refers not just to the spread of fast food but also to the expansion of the principles of efficiency, uniformity, and control.

The Future of Organizations: Opposing Trends

The future of organizations is likely to involve opposing trends: toward more creative freedom for highly skilled information workers, and toward increased supervision and discipline for less skilled service workers.

KEY CONCEPTS

social group (p. 168) two or more people who identify and interact with one another

primary group (p. 169) a small social group whose members share personal and lasting relationships

secondary group (p. 169) a large and impersonal social group whose members pursue a specific goal or activity

instrumental leadership (p. 170) group leadership that focuses on the completion of tasks

expressive leadership (p. 170) group leadership that focuses on the group's well-being

groupthink (p. 172) the tendency of group members to conform, resulting in a narrow view of some issue

reference group (p. 172) a social group that serves as a point of reference in making evaluations and decisions

in-group (p. 173) a social group toward which a member feels respect and loyalty

out-group (p. 173) a social group toward which a person feels a sense of competition or opposition

dyad (p. 173) a social group with two members

triad (p. 174) a social group with three members

network (p. 174) a web of weak social ties

formal organization (p. 175) a large secondary group organized to achieve its goals efficiently

bureaucracy (p. 177) an organizational model rationally designed to perform tasks efficiently

organizational environment (p. 178) factors outside an organization that affect its operation

bureaucratic ritualism (p. 180) a focus on rules and regulations to the point of undermining an organization's goals

bureaucratic inertia (p. 181) the tendency of bureaucratic organizations to perpetuate themselves

oligarchy (p. 181) the rule of the many by the few

scientific management (p. 182) Frederick Taylor's term for the application of scientific principles to the operation of a business or other large organization

SAMPLE TEST QUESTIONS

These questions are similar to those found in the test bank that accompanies this textbook.

Multiple-Choice Questions

1. **What term did Charles Cooley give to a small social group whose members share personal and lasting relationships?**
   a. expressive group
   b. in-group
   c. primary group
   d. secondary group

2. **Which type of group leadership is concerned with getting the job done?**
   a. laissez-faire leadership
   b. secondary group leadership
   c. expressive leadership
   d. instrumental leadership

3. **The research done by Solomon Asch, in which subjects were asked to pick lines of the same length, showed that**
   a. groups encourage their members to conform.
   b. most people are stubborn and refuse to change their minds.
   c. groups often generate conflict.
   d. group members rarely agree on everything.

4. **What term refers to a social group that someone uses as a point of reference in making an evaluation or decision?**
   a. out-group
   b. reference group
   c. in-group
   d. primary group

5. **A network is correctly thought of as**
   a. the most close-knit social group.
   b. a category of people with something in common.
   c. a social group in which most people know one another.
   d. a web of weak social ties.

6. From the point of view of a nurse, a hospital is a
   a. normative organization.
   b. coercive organization.
   c. utilitarian organization.
   d. all of the above.

7. Bureaucracy is a type of social organization characterized by
   a. specialized jobs.
   b. offices arranged in a hierarchy.
   c. lots of rules and regulations.
   d. all of the above.

8. According to Robert Michels, bureaucracy always means
   a. inefficiency.
   b. oligarchy.
   c. alienation.
   d. specialization.

9. Rosabeth Moss Kanter claims that large business organizations
   a. need to "open up" opportunity to encourage workers to perform well.
   b. must have clear and stable rules to survive in a changing world.

   c. do well or badly depending on how talented the leader is.
   d. suffer if they do not adopt the latest technology.

10. The term "McDonaldization of society" means that
   a. organizations can provide food for people more efficiently than families can.
   b. impersonal organizations concerned with efficiency, uniformity, and control are becoming more and more common.
   c. it is possible for organizations to both do their job and meet human needs.
   d. society today is one vast social network.

Answers: 1(c); 2(d); 3(a); 4(b); 5(d); 6(c); 7(d); 8(b); 9(a); 10(b).

Essay Questions

1. How do primary groups differ from secondary groups? Give examples of each in your own life.

2. According to Max Weber, what are the six traits that define bureaucracy? What is the advantage of this organizational form? What are several problems that often go along with it?

APPLICATIONS & EXERCISES

1. The next time you are eating at a fast-food restaurant, watch to see how not just employees but also customers are expected to behave in certain ways. For example, many such restaurants expect customers to line up to order, get their own drinks, find their own table, and clean up their own mess. What other norms are at work?

2. Visit any large public building with an elevator. Observe groups of people as they approach the elevator, and enter the elevator with them. Watch their behavior: What happens to conversations as the elevator doors close? Where do people fix their eyes? Can you explain these patterns?

3. Using campus publications or your school's Web page (and some assistance from an instructor), try to draw an organizational pyramid for your college or university. Show the key offices and how they supervise and report to one another.

INVESTIGATE *with* Research Navigator

Follow the instructions on page 27 of this text to access the features of **Research Navigator**™. Once at the Web site, enter your Login Name and Password. Then, to use the **ContentSelect**™ database, enter keywords such as "social network," "bureaucracy," and "Max Weber," and the search engine will supply relevant and recent scholarly and popular press publications. Use the *New York Times* **Search-by-Subject Archive** to find recent news articles related to sociology and the **Link Library** feature to find relevant Web links organized by the key terms associated with this chapter.

8

CHAPTER EIGHT

Sexuality and Society

How did the sexual revolution
change U.S. society?

Why do societies control people's sexual behavior?

What part does sexuality play in social inequality?

D ust swirls from the street as the crowded bus pulls to the curb in downtown Baghdad, and twenty-five-year-old Ali is the first one out the door. He hurries for several blocks past vendors and open stores and then turns down a narrow alley. Halfway along the dark passageway, he walks through a small, open door. This is Abu Abdullah's, a popular brothel in Iraq's capital city. Ali has come to buy sex.

Ali lives in a small village 40 miles west of the city. He is not married. "I don't have enough money to get married," he explains, "so I come here." Abdullah's charges him $1.50 for fifteen minutes alone with a woman.

Under the rule of Saddam Hussein, prostitution was outlawed and severely punished. Women convicted of selling sex were subject to death by beheading. But all that changed after the invasion by the U.S.-led coalition in 2003. Prostitution laws were rarely enforced, and businesses such as Abdullah's soon opened across the city.

Asked about the changes in the past year, Ali shrugs his shoulders, smiles, and says, "Now we have freedom." But not everyone agrees that such freedom is a good thing. Many Iraqis believe that the spread of prostitution, as well as the opening of "adult cinemas" and the easy availability of pornography over the Internet, is weakening their society. Some blame the United States for causing what they see as moral decline (Caryl, 2003). ■

The debate about the proper place for sex in Iraqi society will go on for years to come. Much the same discussion is also taking place in the United States, where people disagree about a number of issues, including the pros and cons of prostitution and pornography and how much sex in movies and on television is too much.

This chapter examines the importance of sex to society and presents what researchers have learned about patterns of sexual behavior. As you will see, sexual attitudes are quite diverse around the world, and here in the United States, beliefs about sex have changed dramatically over the past century. Today, we continue to debate a number of social issues involving sexuality, including gay rights, teen pregnancy, prostitution, and date rape.

Understanding Sexuality

How much of your day does *not* involve thoughts about sexuality? If you are like most people, the answer is "not very much," because sexuality is not just about having sex.

Sexuality is a theme found almost everywhere—on campus, in the workplace, and especially in the mass media. The sex industry, including pornography and prostitution, is a multibillion-dollar business in its own right. Sexuality is an important part of how we think about ourselves as well as how others think about us. In truth, there are few areas of life in which sexuality does not play some part.

Nevertheless, U.S. culture has long treated sex as taboo; even today, many people avoid talking about it. As a result, although sex can produce much pleasure, it also causes confusion, anxiety, and sometimes outright fear. Even scientists long considered sex off limits as a topic of research. It was not until the middle of the twentieth century that researchers turned their attention to this vital dimension of social life. Since then, as this chapter explains, we have discovered a great deal about human sexuality.

SEX: A BIOLOGICAL ISSUE

Sex refers to *the biological distinction between females and males.* From a biological point of view, sex is the way

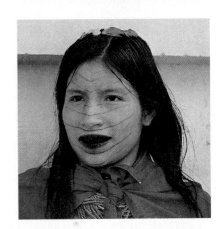

We claim that beauty is in the eye of the beholder, which suggests the importance of culture in setting standards of attractiveness. All of the people pictured here—from Morocco, South Africa, Nigeria, Myanmar, Japan, and Ecuador—are beautiful to members of their own society. At the same time, sociobiologists point out that, in every society on Earth, people are attracted to youthfulness. The reason is that, as sociobiologists see it, attractiveness underlies our choices about reproduction, which is most readily accomplished in early adulthood.

humans reproduce. A female ovum and a male sperm, each containing twenty-three chromosomes (biological codes that guide physical development), combine to form a fertilized embryo. To one of these pairs of chromosomes, which determines the child's sex, the mother contributes an X chromosome and the father contributes either an X or a Y. A second X from the father produces a female (XX) embryo; a Y from the father produces a male (XY) embryo. In this way, a child's sex is determined biologically at the moment of conception.

Within weeks, the sex of an embryo starts to guide its development. If the embryo is male, testicular tissue starts to produce large amounts of testosterone, a hormone that triggers the development of male genitals (sex organs). If little testosterone is present, the embryo develops female genitals. In the United States, about 105 boys are born for every 100 girls, but a higher death rate among males makes females a slight majority by the time people reach their mid-thirties (Mathews & Hamilton, 2005).

SEX AND THE BODY

Some differences in the body set males and females apart. Right from birth, the two sexes have different **primary sex characteristics,** namely, *the genitals, organs used for reproduction.* At puberty, as people reach sexual maturity, additional sex differentiation takes place. At this point, people develop **secondary sex characteristics,** *bodily development, apart from the genitals, that distinguishes biologically mature females and males.* Mature females have wider hips for giving birth, milk-producing breasts for nurturing infants, and deposits of soft, fatty tissue that provides a reserve supply of nutrition during pregnancy and breast-feeding. Mature males typically develop more muscle in the upper body, more extensive body hair, and deeper voices. Of course, these are general differences; some males are smaller and have less body hair and higher voices than some females.

Keep in mind that sex is not the same thing as gender. *Gender* is an element of culture that refers to the personal traits and patterns of behavior (including responsibilities, opportunities, and privileges) that a culture attaches to being female or male. Chapter 13 ("Gender Stratification") describes the importance of gender in social life.

Intersexual People

Sex is not always as clear-cut as we have just described. The term **intersexual people** refers to *people whose bodies (including genitals) have both female and male characteristics.* Another term for intersexual people is *hermaphrodites* (derived from Hermaphroditus, the child of the mythological Greek gods Hermes and Aphrodite, who embodied both sexes). A true hermaphrodite has both a female ovary and a male testis.

However, our culture demands sex to be clear-cut, a fact evident in the requirement that parents record the sex of their new child at birth as either female or male. In the United States, some people respond to hermaphrodites with confusion or even disgust. But attitudes in other cultures are quite different: The Pokot of eastern Africa, for example, pay little attention to what they consider a simple biological error, and the Navajo look on intersexual people with awe, seeing in them the full potential of both the female and the male (Geertz, 1975).

Transsexuals

Transsexuals are *people who feel they are one sex even though biologically they are the other.* Tens of thousands of people in the United States have experienced the feeling of being trapped in a body of the wrong sex and a desire to be the other sex. Most become *transgendered,* meaning that they begin to disregard conventional ideas about how females and males should look and behave. Many go one step further and undergo *gender reassignment,* surgical alteration of their genitals, usually with hormone treatments. This medical procedure is complex and takes months or even years, but it helps many people gain a joyful sense of finally becoming on the outside who they feel they are on the inside (Tewksbury & Gagné, 1996; Gagné, Tewksbury, & McGaughey, 1997).

→ YOUR TURN ←

In 2001, San Francisco became the first city with a health plan for city employees that includes paying the cost of gender reassignment surgery (which can cost $50,000 or more). Would you support enacting similar policies in other places? Why or why not?

SEX: A CULTURAL ISSUE

Sexuality has a biological foundation. But like all elements of human behavior, sexuality is also very much a cultural issue. Biology may explain some animals' mating rituals, but humans have no similar biological program. Although there is a biological "sex drive" in the sense that people find sex pleasurable and may want to engage in sexual activity, our biology does not dictate any specific ways of being sexual any more than our desire to eat dictates any particular foods or table manners.

→ YOUR TURN ←

Looking at the six photos on page 195, do you think that what people in any society consider "beauty" reflects biology or culture? Explain your answer.

Cultural Variation

Almost every sexual practice shows considerable variation from one society to another. In his pioneering study of sexuality in the United States, Alfred Kinsey (1948) found that most heterosexual couples reported having intercourse in a single position—face to face, with the woman on the bottom and the man on top. Halfway around the world, in the South Seas, most couples *never* have sex in this way. In fact, when the people of the South Seas learned of this practice from Western missionaries, they poked fun at it as the strange "missionary position."

Even the simple practice of showing affection varies from society to society. Most people in the United States kiss in public, but the Chinese kiss only in private. The French kiss publicly, often twice (once on each cheek), and the Belgians kiss three times (starting on either cheek). The Maoris of New Zealand rub noses, and most people in Nigeria don't kiss at all.

There is no single view on first-cousin marriages in the United States: Twenty-four states forbid such unions, nineteen allow them, and seven allow them with restrictions.* In general, states that permit first-cousin marriages are found in New England, the Southeast, and the Southwest.

First-Cousin Marriages
☐ Allowed
☐ Allowed with Restrictions
■ Not Allowed

*Of the seven states that allow first-cousin marriages with restrictions, six states permit them only when couples are past childbearing age.

Source: "Cousin Couples" (2005).

Modesty, too, is culturally variable. If a woman stepping into a bath is disturbed, what body parts do you think she would cover? Helen Colton (1983) reports that an Islamic woman covers her face, a Laotian woman covers her breasts, a Samoan woman covers her navel, a Sumatran woman covers her knees, and a European woman covers her breasts with one hand and her genital area with the other.

Around the world, some societies restrict sexuality, and others are more permissive. In China, for example, norms closely regulate sexuality so that few people have sexual intercourse before they marry. In the United States—at least in recent decades—intercourse prior to marriage has become the norm, and some people choose to have sex even without strong commitment.

THE INCEST TABOO

When it comes to sex, do all societies agree on anything? The answer is yes. One cultural universal—an element found in every society the world over—is the **incest taboo,** *a norm forbidding sexual relations or marriage between certain relatives.* In the United States, both law and cultural mores prohibit close relatives (including brothers and sisters, parents and children) from having sex or marrying. But in another example of cultural variation, exactly which family members are included in a society's incest taboo varies from state to state. National Map 8–1 shows that twenty-four U.S. states outlaw marriage between first cousins; twenty-six states do not.

Some societies (such as the North American Navajo) apply incest taboos only to the mother and others on her side of the family. There are also societies on record (including ancient Peru and Egypt) that have approved brother-sister marriages among the nobility to keep power within a single family (Murdock, 1965, orig. 1949).

Why does some form of incest taboo exist everywhere? Part of the reason is biology: Reproduction between close relatives of any species raises the odds of producing offspring with mental or physical problems. But why, of all living species, do only humans observe an incest taboo? This fact suggests that controlling sexuality among close relatives is a necessary element of *social* organization. For one thing, the incest taboo limits sexual competition in families by restricting sex to spouses (ruling out, for example, sex between parent and child). Second, because family ties define people's rights and obligations toward one another, reproduction between close relatives would hopelessly confuse kinship; if a mother and son had a daughter, would the child consider the male a father or a brother? Third, by requiring people to marry outside their immediate families, the incest taboo integrates the larger society as people look beyond their close kin when seeking to form new families.

The incest taboo has long been a sexual norm in the United States and throughout the world. But in this country, many other sexual norms have changed over time. In the twentieth century, as the next section explains, our society experienced both a sexual revolution and a sexual counterrevolution.

September 2, 2003

The Skin Wars Start Earlier and Earlier

By GUY TREBAY

The front lines are drawn in the cool nonspace of every suburban mall. Here, at the Abercrombie & Fitch store in Westchester . . . pictures of half-nude models hang coyly above registers, and shoppers skirmish amiably over cropped miniskirts and skimpy tank tops against an aural backdrop of the White Stripes.

The combatants, if they can be called that, are parents and their daughters, and the fraught territory they are contesting is adolescent sexuality. When *The Washington Post* reported last summer that fashions for girls in the "tween" years were "long on skin, short on modesty," it was noting a reality that many parents of teenagers know only too well. . . .

"The 'whore wars' are a big issue," said Donna Cristen, who was shopping for back-to-school clothing on Thursday with her daughter, Tess, 13. Ms. Cristen's reference was to a term that arose on the Internet, where commentators like Betsy Hart of CNN complained that stores as mainstream as J. C. Penney, Target, and The Limited Too were increasingly carrying clothing that could seem designed to suit the needs of women who work the Lincoln Tunnel on-ramp. . . .

"Everything in stores now is so provocative, you have to keep a close watch," Ms. Cristen said, referring to the plethora of spaghetti strap blouses, midriff-baring tank tops, platform shoes, thongs, T-shirts emblazoned with double entendre slogans and camisoles with built-in bras, all pitched by retailers at girls who have barely crossed the threshold of puberty. . . .

Randi Cardia, who lives in Manhattan and has two teenage daughters, described a majority of the clothes offered for them as "hooker wear." "There are a lot of us out there that are just appalled that someone hasn't taken a stand," Ms. Cardia said. . . .

"It's normal now to see these 12-year-old or younger girls trying to be Britney and Christina, with their pierced belly buttons, their tiny little tube tops, their strappy shoes and their shorts showing the tops of their buttocks," said Ms. Cardia, who, discouraged by the current run of back-to-school offerings, shops with her daughters at stores that cater to boys. . . .

Many schools have been forced to modify dress codes to address concerns that are as much practical as moral. "If you can't sit on the floor in a discussion group about a piece of literature without calling attention to yourself," said John Fierro, the principal of Dorchester Elementary School in Woodcliff Lake, N.J.,

Sexual Attitudes in the United States

What do people in the United States think about sex? Our cultural orientation toward sexuality has always been something of a contradiction. Most European immigrants arrived with rigid ideas about "correct" sexuality, typically limiting sex to reproduction within marriage. The early Puritan settlers of New England demanded strict conformity in attitudes and behavior, and they imposed severe penalties for any sexual "misconduct," even if it took place in the privacy of the home. Some regulation of sexuality has continued ever since. As late as the 1960s, several states legally banned the sale of condoms in stores. Until 2003, when the Supreme Court struck them down, thirteen states had laws forbidding sexual acts between partners of the same sex; "fornication" laws, which are still on the books in eleven states, can be used to punish heterosexual intercourse among unmarried couples.

But this is just one side of the story. As Chapter 3 ("Culture") explains, because U.S. culture is individualistic, many of us believe that people should be free to do pretty much as they wish as long as they cause no direct harm to others. The idea that what people do in the privacy of their own home is *their* business makes sex a matter of individual freedom and personal choice.

When it comes to sexuality, is the United States restrictive or permissive? The answer is both. On one hand, many people in the United States still view sexual conduct as an important sign of personal morality. On the other, as "In the *Times*" explains, sex is strongly promoted by the mass media—even to children as young as ten or twelve—as if to say that "anything goes." Within this complex framework, we turn to changes in sexual attitudes and behavior that have taken place in the United States over the past century.

referring to the micro-miniskirts now popular among middle-school girls, "you're not appropriately dressed." . . .

"In marketing circles, they talk about K.G.O.Y.," an abbreviation for Kids Getting Older Younger, said Alissa Quart, the author of *Branded: The Buying and Selling of Teenagers* (Perseus Books, 2003). "You want to get them younger, so they're full of aspiration not only to look older but to spend older."

That this strategy works seemed clear at Delia's, an apparel store in the Westchester mall, which was packed on Thursday with young shoppers pawing through racks of $22 T-shirts imprinted with phrases like "Parental Guidance Suggested." It is by no means obvious how well such guidance is heard. . . . "You'll never hear a mother say, 'You can't wear that to school,'" she said. . . .

"You don't want to sound censorious or reactionary," Ms. Quart said. "But kids watch HBO. They see late-night TV. They see the 200 channels teeming with quasi-pornographic imagery." . . .

"Parents have to think about a life of commerce these kids are caught up in and teach them some media literacy," Ms. Quart suggested. Kimora Lee Simmons, designer of the hugely popular Baby Phat line, said they also "have to sit their kids down and take some major responsibility when they start wearing clothes that make them look like hootchie mamas, stuff that was never designed with children in mind."

WHAT DO YOU THINK?

1. Why are today's clothing manufacturers encouraging adult patterns of sexuality among young girls?

2. Stars such as Britney Spears and Christina Aguilera have millions of teen fans. How important is sexuality to their performances?

3. Does the pattern described in this article apply only to girls, or does it also apply to boys? Explain your answer.

Adapted from the original article by Guy Trebay published in *The New York Times* on September 2, 2003. Copyright © 2003 by The New York Times Company. Reprinted with permission.

THE SEXUAL REVOLUTION

Over the course of the twentieth century, people witnessed profound changes in sexual attitudes and practices. The first indications of this change came in the 1920s as millions of women and men migrated from farms and small towns to rapidly growing cities. There, living apart from their families and meeting new people in the workplace, young people enjoyed considerable sexual freedom, one reason the decade became known as the "Roaring Twenties."

In the 1930s and 1940s, the Great Depression and World War II slowed the rate of change. But in the postwar period, after 1945, Alfred Kinsey set the stage for what later came to be known as the *sexual revolution.* Kinsey and his colleagues published their first study of sexuality in the United States in 1948, and it raised eyebrows everywhere. Although Kinsey did present some startling results, the national uproar resulted not so much from what he said as from the fact that scientists were actually studying sex, a topic many people were uneasy talking about even in the privacy of their homes.

Kinsey's two books (1948, 1953) became best-sellers partly because they revealed that people in the United States, on average, were far less conventional in sexual matters than most had thought. These books encouraged a new openness toward sexuality, which helped set the sexual revolution in motion.

In the late 1960s, the revolution truly came of age. Youth culture dominated public life, and expressions like "if it feels good, do it" and "sex, drugs, and rock 'n' roll" summed up a new, freer attitude toward sex. The baby boom generation, born between 1946 and 1964, became the first cohort in U.S. history to grow up with the idea that sex was part of people's lives, whether they were married or not.

Over the course of the last century, social attitudes in the United States have become more accepting of human sexuality. What do you see as some of the benefits of this greater openness? What are some of the negative consequences?

Technology also played a part in the sexual revolution. The birth control pill, introduced in 1960, not only prevented pregnancy but also made sex more convenient. Unlike a condom or a diaphragm, which must be applied at the time of intercourse, the pill could be taken anytime during the day. Now women and men could engage in sex spontaneously without any special preparation.

Because women were historically subject to greater sexual regulation than men, the sexual revolution had special significance for them. Society's "double standard" allows (and even encourages) men to be sexually active but expects women to be virgins until marriage and faithful to their husbands afterward. The survey data in Figure 8–1 show the narrowing of the double standard. Among people born between 1933 and 1942 (that is, people who are in their sixties and seventies today), 56 percent of men but just 16 percent of women report having had two or more sexual partners by the time they reached age twenty. Compare this wide gap to the pattern among the baby boomers born between 1953 and 1962 (people now in their forties and fifties), who came of age after the sexual revolution. In this category, 62 percent of men and 48 percent of women say they had two or more sexual partners by age twenty (Laumann et al., 1994:198). The sexual revolution increased sexual activity overall, but it changed women's behavior much more than men's.

Greater openness about sexuality develops as societies become richer and the opportunities for women increase. With these facts in mind, look for a pattern in the global use of birth control shown in Global Map 8–1 on page 202.

THE SEXUAL COUNTERREVOLUTION

The sexual revolution made sex a topic of everyday discussion and sexual activity more a matter of individual choice. However, by 1980, the climate of sexual freedom that had marked the late 1960s and 1970s was criticized by some as evidence of our country's moral decline, and the *sexual counterrevolution* began.

Politically speaking, the sexual counterrevolution was a conservative call for a return to "family values" and a change from sexual freedom back toward what critics saw as the sexual responsibility valued by earlier generations. Critics of the sexual revolution objected not just to the idea of "free love" but to trends such as cohabitation (living together) and unmarried couples having children.

Looking back, the sexual counterrevolution did not greatly change the idea that people should decide for themselves when and with whom to have a sexual relationship. But whether for moral reasons or concerns about sexually transmitted diseases (STDs), more people began choosing to limit their number of sexual partners or not to have sex at all.

PREMARITAL SEX

In light of the sexual revolution and the sexual counterrevolution, how much has sexual behavior in the United States really changed? One interesting trend involves premarital sex—sexual intercourse before marriage—among young people.

Consider, first, what U.S. adults *say* about premarital intercourse. Table 8–1 shows that about 35 percent characterize sexual relations before marriage as "always wrong" or "almost always wrong." Another 20 percent consider premarital sex "wrong only sometimes," and more than 40 percent say premarital sex is "not wrong at all." Public opinion is much more accepting of premarital sex today than a generation ago, but even so, our society remains divided on this issue.

Now let's look at what young people *do.* For women, there has been a marked change over time. The Kinsey studies (1948, 1953; see also Laumann et al., 1994) reported that among people born in the early 1900s, about 50 percent of men but just 6 percent of women had had premarital sexual intercourse before age nineteen. Studies of baby boomers, born after World War II, show a slight increase in premarital intercourse among men and a large increase—to about one-third—among women. The most recent studies, targeting men and women born in the 1970s, show that 76 percent of men and 66 percent of women had had premarital sexual intercourse by their senior year in high school (Laumann et al., 1994:323–24). Although general public attitudes remain divided, premarital sex is largely accepted among young people today.

SEX BETWEEN ADULTS

Judging from the mass media, people in the United States are very active sexually. But do popular images reflect reality? The Laumann study (1994), the largest study of sexuality since Kinsey's groundbreaking research, found that frequency of sexual activity varies widely in the U.S. population. One-third of adults report having sex with a partner a few times a year or not at all, another one-third have sex once or several times a month, and the remaining one-third have sex with a partner two or more times a week. In short, no single stereotype accurately describes sexual activity in the United States.

Despite the widespread image of "swinging singles" seen on television shows such as *Sex and the City,* it is married people who have sex most frequently. Married people also report the highest level of satisfaction—both emotional and physical—with their partners (Laumann et al., 1994).

SEX OVER THE LIFE COURSE

Patterns of sexual activity change with age. In the United States, most young men become sexually active by the time they reach sixteen and women by the age of seventeen. By the time they reach their mid-twenties, more than 90 percent of both women and men reported being sexually active with a partner at least once during the past year. The picture begins to change by about age fifty, after which advancing age is

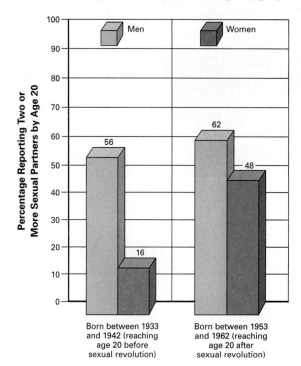

DIVERSITY SNAPSHOT

Percentage Reporting Two or More Sexual Partners by Age 20

Men   Women

Born between 1933 and 1942 (reaching age 20 before sexual revolution): Men 56, Women 16

Born between 1953 and 1962 (reaching age 20 after sexual revolution): Men 62, Women 48

FIGURE 8–1 The Sexual Revolution: Closing the Double Standard

A larger share of men than women report having had two or more sexual partners by age twenty. But the sexual revolution greatly reduced this gender difference.

Source: Laumann et al. (1994:198).

TABLE 8–1

How We View Premarital and Extramarital Sex

Survey Question: "There's been a lot of discussion about the way morals and attitudes about sex are changing in this country. If a man and a woman have sexual relations before marriage, do you think it is always wrong, almost always wrong, wrong only sometimes, or not wrong at all? What about a married person having sexual relations with someone other than the marriage partner?"

	Premarital Sex	Extramarital Sex
"Always wrong"	26.7%	78.5%
"Almost always wrong"	8.0	13.4
"Wrong only sometimes"	19.4	4.2
"Not wrong at all"	43.4	2.1
"Don't know"/No answer	2.5	1.8

Source: *General Social Surveys, 1972–2002: Cumulative Codebook* (Chicago; National Opinion Research Center, 2003), pp. 233–34.

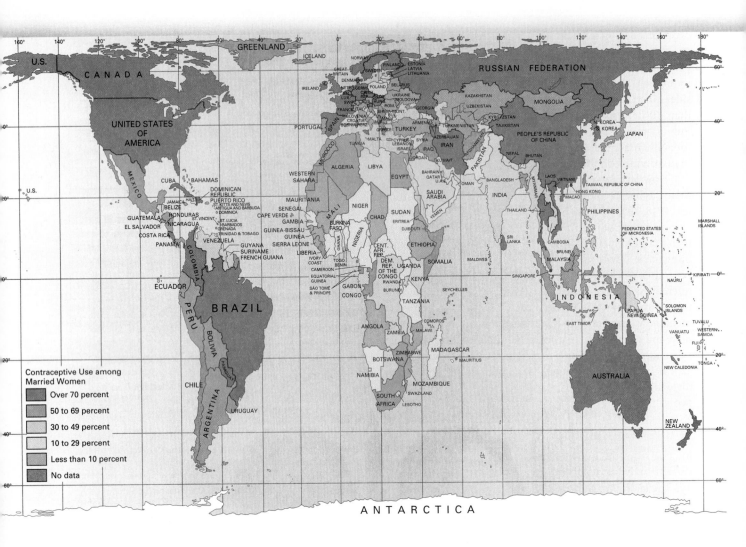

WINDOW ON THE WORLD

GLOBAL MAP 8–1   Contraceptive Use in Global Perspective

The map shows the percentage of married women using modern contraception methods (such as barrier methods, contraceptive pill, implants, injectables, intrauterine contraceptive devices [IUDs], or sterilization). In general, how do high-income nations differ from low-income nations? Can you explain this difference?

Source: Data from United Nations Development Programme (2005).

---

linked to a decline in the share of people who are sexually active. By age sixty, about 15 percent of men and 40 percent of women say they have not been sexually active in the past year. By age seventy, half of women claim not to be sexually active; by age eighty, half of men say the same (Laumann et al., 1994). Contrary to popular stereotypes, these data show that sexual activity is a normal part of life for most older adults.

EXTRAMARITAL SEX

What about sex outside of marriage? This practice, commonly called "adultery" (sociologists prefer the more neutral term "extramarital sex"), is widely condemned. Table 8–1 shows that more than 90 percent of U.S. adults consider a married person having sex with someone other than the marital partner "always wrong" or "almost always wrong." The norm of sexual fidelity within marriage has been and remains a strong element of U.S. culture.

But actual behavior falls short of the cultural ideal. The Laumann study reports that about 25 percent of married men and 10 percent of married women have had at least one extramarital sexual experience. Or stating this the other way around, 75 percent of men and 90 percent of women remain sexually faithful to their partners throughout their married lives (Laumann et al., 1994:214; NORC, 2003:1227).

 YOUR TURN

Why do you think U.S. society has become more accepting of premarital sex but not of extramarital sex?

Sexual Orientation

In recent decades, public opinion about sexual orientation has shown a remarkable change. **Sexual orientation** is *a person's romantic and emotional attraction to another person.* The norm in all human societies is **heterosexuality** (*hetero* is a Greek word meaning "the other of two"), meaning *sexual attraction to someone of the other sex.* Yet in every society, a significant share of people experience **homosexuality** (*homo* is the Greek word for "the same"), *sexual attraction to someone of the same sex.* Keep in mind that people do not necessarily fall into just one of these categories; they may have varying degrees of attraction to both sexes.

The idea that sexual orientation is not clear-cut is confirmed by the existence of a third category: **bisexuality,** *sexual attraction to people of both sexes.* Some bisexual people are equally attracted to males and females; many others are more attracted to one sex than the other. Finally, **asexuality** refers to *a lack of sexual attraction to people of either sex.* Figure 8–2 describes each of these sexual orientations in relation to the others.

It is important to remember that sexual *attraction* is not the same thing as sexual *behavior.* Many people, perhaps even most people, have experienced attraction to someone of the same sex, but far fewer ever engage in same-sex behavior. This is in large part because our culture discourages such actions.

In the United States and around the world, heterosexuality is the norm because, biologically speaking, heterosexual relations permit human reproduction. Even so, most societies tolerate homosexuality. Among the ancient Greeks,

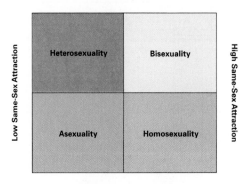

FIGURE 8-2 Four Sexual Orientations

A person's level of same-sex attraction and opposite-sex attraction are two distinct dimensions that combine in various ways to produce four major sexual orientations.

Source: Adapted from Storms (1980).

upper-class men considered homosexuality the highest form of relationship, partly because they looked down on women as intellectually inferior. As men saw it, heterosexuality was necessary only so they could have children, and "real" men preferred homosexual relations (Kluckhohn, 1948; Ford & Beach, 1951; Greenberg, 1988).

WHAT GIVES US A SEXUAL ORIENTATION?

The question of *how* people get a sexual orientation in the first place is a matter that is strongly debated. The arguments cluster into two general positions: sexual orientation as a product of society and sexual orientation as a product of biology.

For a summary of recent research on sexual orientation, go to http://www.davidmyers.org/Brix?pageID=62

Sexual Orientation: A Product of Society

This approach argues that people in any society attach meanings to sexual activity, and these meanings differ from place to place and over time. As Michel Foucault (1990, orig. 1978) points out, for example, there was no distinct category of people called "homosexuals" until a century ago, when scientists and eventually the public as a whole began defining people that way. Throughout history, many people no doubt had what we would call "homosexual

FIGURE 8-3 Sexual Orientation in the United States: Survey Data

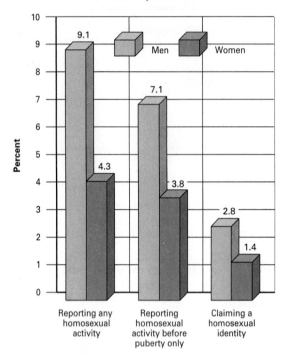

(a) How Many Gay People?

The percentage of people who are classified as having a homosexual orientation depends on how this concept is operationalized. Research suggests that 2.8 percent of adult men and 1.4 percent of adult women claim a homosexual identity.

Source: Adapted from Laumann et al. (1994).

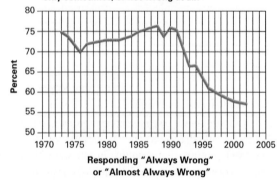

(b) Attitudes toward Homosexual Relations, 1973–2002

Since 1990, the percentage of U.S. adults who disapprove of homosexual relations has been going down and now stands at about 57 percent.

Source: NORC (2003).

experiences." But neither they nor others saw in this behavior the basis for any special identity.

Anthropological studies show that patterns of homosexuality differ from one society to another. In Siberia, for example, the Chukchee Eskimo have a practice in which one man dresses like a female and does a woman's work. The Sambia, who dwell in the Eastern Highlands of New Guinea, have a ritual in which young boys perform oral sex on older men in the belief that eating semen will enhance their masculinity. The existence of such diverse patterns in societies around the world seems to indicate that human sexual expression is socially constructed (Murray & Roscoe, 1998; Blackwood & Wieringa, 1999).

Sexual Orientation: A Product of Biology

A growing body of evidence suggests that sexual orientation is innate, or rooted in human biology in much the same way that people are born right-handed or left-handed. Arguing this position, Simon LeVay (1993) links sexual orientation to the structure of a person's brain. LeVay studied the brains of both homosexual and heterosexual men and found a small but important difference in the size of the hypothalamus, a part of the brain that regulates hormones. Such an anatomical difference, some claim, plays a part in shaping sexual orientation.

> The American Psychological Association posts answers to commonly asked questions about sexual orientation at http://www.apa.org/pubinfo/answers.html

Genetics may also influence sexual orientation. One study of forty-four pairs of brothers—all homosexual—found that thirty-three pairs had a distinctive genetic pattern involving the X chromosome. The gay brothers also had an unusually high number of gay male relatives—but only on their mother's side. Such evidence leads some researchers to think there may be a "gay gene" located on the X chromosome (Hamer & Copeland, 1994).

Critical review Mounting evidence supports the conclusion that sexual orientation is rooted in biology, although the best guess at present is that both nature and nurture play a part. Remember that sexual orientation is not a matter of neat categories. Most people who think of themselves as homosexual have had some heterosexual experiences, just as many people who think of themselves as heterosexual have had some homosexual experiences. Explaining sexual orientation, then, is a complicated job.

There is also a political issue here with great importance for gay men and lesbians. To the extent that sexual orientation is based in biology, homosexuals have no more choice about their sexual orientation than they do about their skin color. If this is so, shouldn't gay men and lesbians expect the same legal protection from discrimination as African Americans? (Herek, 1991)

HOW MANY GAY PEOPLE ARE THERE?

What share of our population is gay? This is a difficult question to answer because, as we have explained, sexual orientation is not a matter of neat categories. In addition, not all people are willing to reveal their sexuality to strangers or even to family members. The pioneering sex researcher Alfred Kinsey (1948, 1953) estimated that about 4 percent of males and 2 percent of females have an exclusively same-sex orientation, although he pointed out that most people experience same-sex attraction at some point in their lives.

Some social scientists put the gay share of the population at 10 percent. But the Laumann (1994) research shows that how homosexuality is defined makes a big difference in the results. As part (a) of Figure 8–3 shows, about 9 percent of U.S. men and about 4 percent of U.S. women between ages eighteen and fifty-nine reported homosexual activity *at some time in their lives.* The second set of numbers in the bar graph shows that fewer men (and even fewer women) had a homosexual experience in childhood but not after puberty. Finally, only 2.8 percent of men and 1.4 percent of women defined themselves as "partly" or "entirely" homosexual.

Kinsey treated sexual orientation as an either-or trait: To be more homosexual was, by definition, to be less heterosexual. But same-sex and other-sex attractions can operate independently. Bisexual people feel a strong attraction to people of both sexes; by contrast, asexual people experience little sexual attraction to people of either sex.

In the Laumann survey, less than 1 percent of adults described themselves as bisexual. But bisexual experiences appear to be fairly common (at least for a time) among younger people, especially on college and university campuses (Laumann et al., 1994; Leland, 1995). Many bisexuals do not think of themselves as either gay or straight, and their behavior reflects elements of both gay and straight living.

THE GAY RIGHTS MOVEMENT

The public's attitude toward homosexuality has been moving toward greater acceptance. Back in 1973, as shown in part (b) of Figure 8–3, about three-fourths of U.S. adults

It was only about thirty years ago (1977) that the first gay character appeared in a television program in the United States. Gay people now have a larger place in our society's popular culture, as suggested by the success of shows including *Queer Eye for the Straight Guy.*

claimed homosexual relations were "always wrong" or "almost always wrong." Although that percentage changed little during the 1970s and 1980s, by 2002 it had dropped below 60 percent (NORC, 2003:234). Among college students, who are generally more tolerant of homosexuality than the general population, we see a similar trend. In 1980, about half of college students supported laws prohibiting homosexual relationships; by 2004, as Figure 8–4 on page 206 shows, only one-third felt this way (Astin et al., 2002; Sax et al., 2004).

In large measure, this change was brought about by the gay rights movement, which began in the middle of the twentieth century. Up to that time, most people in this country did not discuss homosexuality, and it was common for companies (including the federal government and the armed forces) to fire anyone who was accused of being gay. Mental health professionals, too, took a hard line, describing homosexuals as "sick," sometimes placing them in mental hospitals where, it was hoped, they might be "cured." It is no surprise that most lesbians and gay men remained "in the closet," closely guarding the secret of their sexual orientation. But the gay rights movement gained strength during the 1960s. One early milestone occurred in

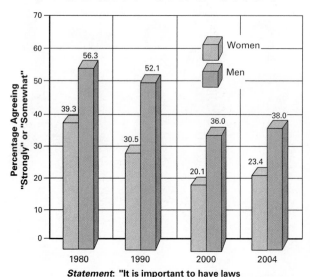

STUDENT SNAPSHOT

Women

Men

Percentage Agreeing
"Strongly" or "Somewhat"

39.3
56.3
30.5
52.1
20.1
36.0
23.4
38.0

1980   1990   2000   2004

Statement: "It is important to have laws
prohibiting homosexual relationships."

FIGURE 8–4   Opposition to Homosexual
Relationships: Attitudes of First-Year
College Students, 1980–2004

Despite a recent increase in opposition to homosexual relationships, the historical trend among college students is toward
greater tolerance, a view held by a large majority.

Sources: Astin et al. (2002) and Sax et al. (2004).

1973, when the American Psychiatric Association declared
that homosexuality was not an illness but simply "a form of
sexual behavior."

The gay rights movement also began using the term
homophobia to describe *discomfort over close personal interaction with people thought to be gay, lesbian, or bisexual*
(Weinberg, 1973). The concept of homophobia, "fear of
sameness," turns the tables on society: Instead of asking,
"What's wrong with gay people?" the question becomes
"What's wrong with people who can't accept a different sexual orientation?"

In 2004, a number of cities and towns began to allow
gay couples to marry, although these unions were later declared illegal. But gay marriage is now legal in the state of
Massachusetts and gay civil unions (marriage without the
name) are legal in Vermont and Connecticut. At the same
time, seventeen states have enacted laws that forbid gay
marriage and prohibit recognizing such marriages performed elsewhere.

↔ YOUR TURN ↔

What changes in laws regarding gay marriage do you expect over the next ten years? Why?

Sexual Issues and Controversies

Sexuality lies at the heart of a number of controversies in
the United States today. Here we take a look at four key issues: teen pregnancy, pornography, prostitution, and sexual
violence.

TEEN PREGNANCY

Because it carries the risk of pregnancy, being sexually
active—especially having intercourse—demands a high
level of responsibility. Teenagers may be biologically mature
enough to conceive, but
many are not emotionally
secure enough to appre-
ciate the consequences
of their actions. Surveys show that there are almost 1 million teen pregnancies in the United States each year, most of
them unplanned. This country's rate of births to teens is
higher than that of all other high-income countries and is
twice the rate in Canada (Darroch et al., 2001).

For young women of all racial and ethnic categories,
weak families and low income sharply raise the risk of
becoming sexually active and having an unplanned child. To
make matters worse, having unplanned children raises the
risk that young women (as well as young fathers-to-be) will
not finish school and will end up poor (Alan Guttmacher
Institute, 2002).

Did the sexual revolution raise the level of teenage
pregnancy? Perhaps surprisingly, the answer is no. The rate
of pregnancy among U.S. teens in 1950 was higher than it is
today, partly because people back then married at a younger
age. Because abortion was against the law, many pregnancies led to quick marriages. As a result, there were many
pregnant teenagers, but almost 90 percent were married.
Today, the number of pregnant teens is lower, but in about
80 percent of cases, the women are unmarried. In a slight
majority (57 percent) of such cases, these women keep their
babies; in the remainder, they have abortions (29 percent)
or miscarriages (14 percent) (Alan Guttmacher Institute,
2004). National Map 8–2 shows the pregnancy rates for
women between the ages of fifteen and nineteen throughout the United States.

Visit the Web site of the National Campaign to Prevent Teen
Pregnancy at http://www.
teenpregnancy.org

Teenage Pregnancy Rates
across the United States

The map shows pregnancy rates for 2000 for women aged fifteen to nineteen. In what regions of the country are rates high? Where are they low? What explanation can you offer for these patterns?

Source: Alan Guttmacher Institute (2004).

Pregnancies per
1,000 Women
Aged 15 to 19

■ Above average
■ Average
□ Below average

YOUR TURN

In light of the fact that 80 percent of today's pregnant teens are unmarried, what should the fathers of these children provide for their children?

PORNOGRAPHY

Pornography is *sexually explicit material intended to cause sexual arousal*. But what is or is not pornographic has long been a matter of debate. Recognizing that different people view portrayals of sexuality differently, the U.S. Supreme Court gives local communities the power to decide for themselves what violates "community standards" of decency and lacks "redeeming social value."

Definitions aside, pornography is very popular in the United States: X-rated videos, telephone "sex lines," a host of sexually explicit movies and magazines, and thousands of Internet Web sites make up a thriving industry that takes in more than $10 billion each year. The vast majority of consumers of pornography are men.

Traditionally, people have criticized pornography on *moral* grounds. As national surveys confirm, 60 percent of U.S. adults are concerned that "sexual materials lead to a breakdown of morals" (NORC, 2003:235). Today, however, pornography is also seen as a *power* issue because most of it degrades women, portraying them as the sexual playthings of men.

Some critics also claim that pornography is a cause of violence against women. Although it is difficult to prove a scientific cause-and-effect relationship between what people view and how they act, the public shares a concern about pornography and violence, with almost half of adults holding the opinion that pornography encourages people to commit rape (NORC, 2003:235).

Although people everywhere object to sexual material they find offensive, many also value the principle of free speech and the protection of artistic expression. Nevertheless, pressure to restrict pornography is building from an unlikely coalition of conservatives (who oppose pornography on moral grounds) and liberals (who condemn it for political reasons).

PROSTITUTION

Prostitution is *the selling of sexual services*. Often called "the world's oldest profession," prostitution has been widespread throughout recorded history. In the United States today, about one in five adult men reports having paid for sex at some time (NORC, 2003:1226). Because most people think of sex as an expression of intimacy between two people, they find the idea of sex for money disturbing. As a result, prostitution is against the law everywhere in the United States except for parts of rural Nevada.

Around the world, prostitution is most common in poor countries, where patriarchy is strong and traditional cultural norms limit women's ability to earn a living. Global Map 8–2 on page 208 shows where in the world prostitution is most widespread.

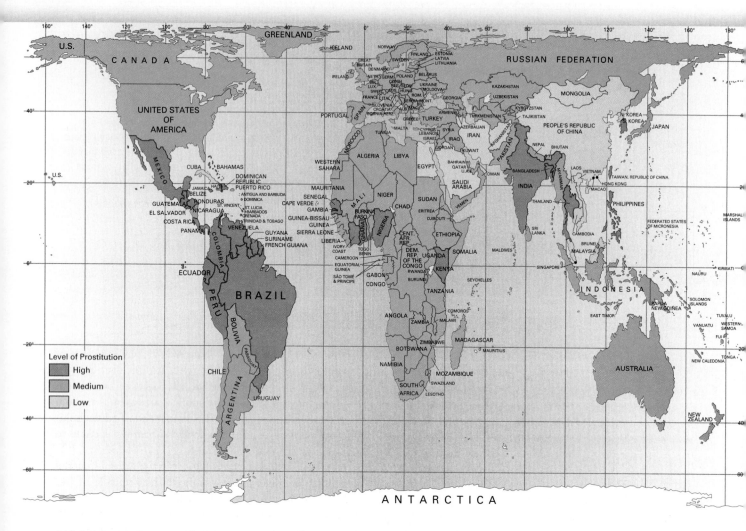

WINDOW ON THE WORLD

GLOBAL MAP 8–2 Prostitution in Global Perspective

Generally speaking, prostitution is widespread in societies where women have low standing. Officially, at least, the People's Republic of China boasts of gender equality, including the elimination of "vice" such as prostitution, which oppresses women. By contrast, in much of Latin America, where patriarchy is strong, prostitution is common. In many Islamic societies, patriarchy is also strong, but religion is a counterbalance, so prostitution is limited. Western, high-income nations have a moderate amount of prostitution.

Sources: *Peters Atlas of the World* (1990) and Mackay (2000).

Types of Prostitution

Most prostitutes (many prefer the morally neutral term "sex workers") are women, and they fall into different categories. *Call girls* are elite prostitutes, typically young, attractive, and well-educated women who arrange their own "dates" with clients by telephone. The classified pages of any large city newspaper contain numerous ads for "escort services," by which women (and sometimes men) offer both companionship and sex for a fee.

Brothels like this one are found in rural counties of Nevada. Some people claim that legalizing prostitution permits the government to protect the health and safety of "sex workers," who have the opportunity to earn a good income. Others claim that selling sex is degrading to women as well as men, and that women's economic opportunity should not depend on selling themselves in this way. Where do you stand on the issue of legalized prostitution? Why?

In the middle category are prostitutes employed in "massage parlors" or brothels under the control of managers. These sex workers have less choice about their clients, receive less money for their services, and get to keep no more than half of what they make.

At the bottom of the sex-worker hierarchy are *streetwalkers,* women and men who "work the streets" of large cities. Some female streetwalkers are under the control of male pimps who take most of their earnings. Many others are addicts who sell sex in order to buy the drugs they need. Both types of people are at high risk of becoming the victims of violence (Davidson, 1998; Estes, 2001).

Most prostitutes offer heterosexual services. However, gay prostitutes also trade sex for money. Researchers report that many gay prostitutes end up selling sex after having suffered rejection by family and friends because of their sexual orientation (Weisberg, 1985; Boyer, 1989; Kruks, 1991).

A Victimless Crime?

Prostitution is against the law almost everywhere in the United States, but many people consider it a victimless crime (defined in Chapter 9, "Deviance," as a crime in which there are no obvious victims). As a result, instead of enforcing prostitution laws all the time, police stage only occasional crackdowns. This policy reflects a desire to control prostitution while recognizing that it is impossible to totally eliminate it.

Many people take a "live and let live" attitude about prostitution and say that adults ought to be able to do as they please so long as no one is forced to do anything. But is prostitution really victimless? The sex trade subjects many

women to abuse and outright violence and also plays a part in spreading sexually transmitted diseases, including AIDS. In addition, many poor women—especially in low-income nations—become trapped in a life of selling sex. Thailand, in Southeast Asia, has 2 million prostitutes, representing about 10 percent of all women in the labor force. Many of these women begin working before they are teenagers, suffer physical abuse, and become infected with HIV (Wonders & Michalowski, 2001).

In the past, the focus of attention has been on the women who earn money as sex workers. But prostitution would not exist at all if it were not for demand on the part of men. For this reason, law enforcement is now more likely to target "Johns" when they attempt to buy sex.

SEXUAL VIOLENCE: RAPE AND DATE RAPE

Ideally, sexual activity occurs within a loving relationship between consenting adults. In reality, however, sex can be twisted by hate and violence. Here we consider two types of sexual violence: rape and date rape.

Rape

Although some people think rape is motivated only by a desire for sex, it is actually an expression of power—a violent act that uses sex to hurt, humiliate, or control another person. According to the Federal Bureau of Investigation, about 93,000 women are raped each year. This number reflects only the reported cases, and the actual number of rapes is almost certainly several times higher (Federal Bureau of Investigation, 2004).

Experts agree that one factor that contributes to the problem of sexual violence on the college campus is the widespread use of alcoholic beverages. What policies are in force on your campus to discourage the kind of drinking that leads to one person imposing sex on another?

The official government definition of rape is "the carnal knowledge of a female forcibly and against her will." Thus official rape statistics include only victims who are women. But men, too, are raped—in perhaps 10 percent of all cases. Most men who rape men are not homosexual; they are heterosexuals who are motivated by a desire not for sex but to dominate another person.

Date Rape

A common myth is that rape involves strangers. In reality, however, only about 33 percent of rapes fit this pattern. About 67 percent of rapes involve people who know one another—more often than not, pretty well—and these crimes usually take place in familiar surroundings, especially the home and the campus. For this reason, the term "date rape" or "acquaintance rape" is used to refer to forcible sexual violence against women by men they know (Laumann et al., 1994; U.S. Bureau of Justice Statistics, 2005).

A second myth, often linked to date rape, is that the victim of rape must have done something to encourage the man and make him think she wanted to have sex. Perhaps the victim agreed to go out with the offender. Maybe she even invited him into her room. But of course, acting in this way no more justifies rape than it would any other kind of physical assault.

Although rape is a physical attack, it often leaves emotional and psychological scars. Beyond the brutality of being physically violated, rape by an acquaintance also undermines a victim's sense of trust. Psychological scars are especially serious among the half of rape victims who are under eighteen; one-third of these young victims are attacked by their own fathers or stepfathers (Greenfield, 1996).

How common is date rape? One study found that about 20 percent of a sample of high school girls in the United States reported being the victim of sexual or physical violence inflicted by boys they were dating (Dickinson, 2001).

Nowhere has the issue of date rape been more widely discussed than on college campuses, where the danger of date rape is high. The collegiate environment promotes easy friendships and encourages trust among young people who still have much to learn about relationships and about themselves. Yet as the Applying Sociology box on page 211 explains, the same college environment that encourages communication provides few social norms to help guide young people's sexual experiences. To counter the problem, many schools now actively address myths about rape. In addition, greater attention is now focused on the abuse of alcohol, which increases the likelihood of sexual violence.

A government report on the sexual victimization of college women is available at http://www.ojp.usdoj.gov/bjs/abstract/svcw.htm

Theoretical Analysis of Sexuality

Applying sociology's various theoretical approaches gives us a better understanding of human sexuality. The following sections discuss the three major approaches, and the Applying Theory table on page 212 highlights the key insights of each approach.

APPLYING SOCIOLOGY

When Sex Is Only Sex: The Campus Culture of "Hooking Up"

Have you ever been in a sexual situation and not been sure of the right thing to do? Most colleges and universities highlight two important rules. First, sexual activity must take place only when both participants have given clear statements of consent. The consent principle is what makes "having sex" different from date rape. Second, no one should knowingly expose another person to a sexually transmitted disease, especially when the partner is unaware of the danger.

These rules are very important; yet they say little about the larger issue of what sex *means*. For example, when is it "right" to have a sexual relationship? Do you have to really know the other person? If you do have sex, are you obligated to see the person again?

Two generations ago, there were informal rules for campus sex. Dating was considered part of the courtship process. That is, "going out" was the way in which women and men evaluated each other as possible marriage partners while they sharpened their own sense of what they wanted in a mate. Because, on average, marriage took place in the early twenties, many college students became engaged and married while they were still in school. In this cultural climate, sex became part of a relationship along with a commitment—a serious interest in the other person as a possible marriage partner.

Of course, not all sexual activity fell under the umbrella of courtship. A fair share of men (and some women, too) have always looked for sex where they could find it. But in an era that linked sex and courtship, it was easy to understand how casual sex could leave one partner feeling "used."

Today, the sexual culture of the campus is very different. Partly because people now marry much later, the culture of courtship is all but gone. About three-fourths of women in a recent national survey point to a new campus pattern, the culture of "hooking up." What exactly is "hooking up"? Most describe it in words like these: "When a girl and a guy get together for a physical encounter—anything from kissing to having sex—and don't necessarily expect anything further."

Student responses to the survey suggest that "hookups" have three characteristics. First, most couples who hook up know little about each other. Second, a typical hookup involves people who have been drinking alcohol, usually at a campus party. Third, most women are critical of the culture of hooking up and express little satisfaction with these encounters. Certainly, some women (and men) who hook up simply walk away, happy to have enjoyed a sexual experience free of further obligation. But given the powerful emotions that sex can unleash, hooking up often leaves someone wondering

what to expect next: "Will you call me tomorrow?" "Will I see you again?"

The survey asked women who had experienced a recent hookup to report how they felt about the experience a day later. A majority of respondents said they felt "awkward," about half felt "disappointed" and "confused," and one in four felt "exploited." Clearly, for many people, sex is more than a physical encounter. In addition, because today's campus climate is very sensitive to charges of sexual exploitation, there is a need for clearer standards of fair play.

WHAT DO YOU THINK?

1. How extensive is the pattern of hooking up on your campus? Are you aware of differences in these types of encounters between heterosexuals and homosexuals?

2. What do you see as the advantages of sex without commitment? What are the disadvantages of this kind of relationship? Are men and women likely to answer this question differently? Explain.

3. Do you think college students need more guidance about sexual issues? If so, who should provide this guidance?

Source: Based in part on Marquardt & Glenn (2001).

STRUCTURAL-FUNCTIONAL ANALYSIS

The structural-functional approach highlights the contribution of any social pattern to the overall operation of society. Because sexuality can have such important consequences, society regulates this type of behavior.

The Need to Regulate Sexuality

From a biological point of view, sex allows our species to reproduce. But culture and social institutions regulate *with whom* and *when* people reproduce. For example, most societies condemn a married person for having sex with someone

APPLYING THEORY
SEXUALITY

	Structural-Functional Approach	Symbolic-Interaction Approach	Social-Conflict Approach
What is the level of analysis?	Macro-level	Micro-level	Macro-level
What is the importance of sexuality for society?	Society depends on sexuality for reproduction. Society uses the incest taboo and other norms to control sexuality in order to maintain social order.	Sexual practices vary among the many cultures of the world. Some societies allow individuals more freedom than others in matters of sexual behavior.	Sexuality is linked to social inequality. U.S. society regulates women's sexuality more than men's, which is part of the larger pattern of men dominating women.
Has sexuality changed over time? How?	Yes. As advances in birth control technology separate sex from reproduction, societies relax some controls on sexuality.	Yes. The meanings people attach to virginity and other sexual matters are all socially constructed and subject to change.	Yes and no. Some sexual standards have relaxed, but society still defines women in sexual terms, just as homosexual people are harmed by society's heterosexual bias.

other than a spouse. To allow sexual passion to go unchecked would threaten family life, especially the raising of children.

The fact that the incest taboo exists everywhere shows that no society permits completely free choice in sexual partners. Reproduction by family members other than married partners would break down the system of kinship and hopelessly confuse human relationships.

Historically, the social control of sexuality was strong, mostly because sex often led to childbirth. We see these controls at work in the traditional distinction between "legitimate" reproduction (within marriage) and "illegitimate" reproduction (outside marriage). But once a society develops the technology to control births, its sexual norms become more permissive. This occurred in the United States, where over the course of the twentieth century, sex moved beyond its basic reproductive function and became accepted as a form of intimacy and even recreation (Giddens, 1992).

Latent Functions: The Case of Prostitution

It is easy to see that prostitution is harmful because it spreads disease and exploits women. But are there latent functions that help explain why prostitution is so widespread? According to Kingsley Davis (1971), prostitution performs several useful functions. It is one way to meet the sexual needs of a large number of people who may not have ready access to sex, including soldiers, travelers, people who are not physically attractive, or people too poor to attract a marriage partner (such as Ali in the opening to this chapter). Some people favor prostitution because they want sex without the "trouble" of a relationship. As one analyst

put it, "Men don't pay for sex, they pay so they can leave" (Miracle, Miracle, & Baumeister, 2003:421).

Critical review The structural-functional approach helps us see the important part sexuality plays in the organization of society. The incest taboo and other cultural norms also suggest that society has always paid attention to who has sex with whom and, especially, who reproduces with whom.

Functionalist analysis sometimes ignores gender; when Kingsley Davis wrote of the benefits of prostitution for society, he was really talking about the benefits to some *men*. In addition, the fact that sexual patterns change over time, just as they differ in remarkable ways around the world, gets little attention using the functionalist approach. To appreciate the varied and changeable character of sexuality, we now turn to the symbolic-interaction approach.

SYMBOLIC-INTERACTION ANALYSIS

The symbolic-interaction approach highlights how, as people interact, they construct everyday reality. As Chapter 6 ("Social Interaction in Everyday Life") explains, people sometimes construct very different realities, so the views of one group or society may well differ from those of another. In the same way, our understanding of sexuality can and does change over time.

The Social Construction of Sexuality

Almost all social patterns involving sexuality saw considerable change over the course of the twentieth century. One good illustration is the changing importance of virginity. A century ago, our society's norm—for women, at least—was virginity before marriage. This norm was strong because there was no effective means of birth control, and virginity was the only guarantee a man had that his bride-to-be was not carrying another man's child.

Today, because birth control has separated sex from reproduction, the virginity norm has weakened considerably. In the United States, among people born between 1963 and 1974, just 16.3 percent of men and 20.1 percent of women reported being virgins at first marriage (Laumann et al., 1994:503).

Another example of our society's construction of sexuality involves young people. A century ago, childhood was a time of innocence in sexual matters. In recent decades, however, thinking has changed. Although few people encourage sexual activity between children, most people believe that children should be educated about sex by the time they are teenagers so that they can make intelligent choices about their behavior as they grow older.

Global Comparisons

Around the world, different societies attach different meanings to sexuality. For example, the anthropologist Ruth Benedict (1938), who spent years learning the ways of life of the Melanesian people of southeastern New Guinea, reported that adults paid little attention when young children engaged in sexual experimentation with one another. Parents in Melanesia shrugged off such activity because, before puberty, sex cannot lead to reproduction. Is it likely that most parents in the United States would respond the same way?

Sexual practices also vary from culture to culture. Male circumcision of infant boys (the practice of removing all or part of the foreskin of the penis) is common in the United States but rare in most other parts of the world. A practice sometimes referred to incorrectly as female circumcision (the removal of the clitoris) is rare in the United States and much of the world but common in parts of Africa and the Middle East (Crossette, 1995; Huffman, 2000). (For more about this practice, more accurately called "female genital mutilation," see the box on page 349.)

Critical review The strength of the symbolic-interaction approach lies in revealing the constructed character of familiar social patterns. Understanding that people "construct" sexuality, we can better appreciate the variety of sexual practices found over the course of history and around the world.

One limitation of this approach, however, is that not all sexual practices are so variable. Throughout our own

The control of women's sexuality is a common theme in human history. During the Middle Ages, Europeans devised the "chastity belt"—a metal device locked about a woman's groin that prevented sexual intercourse (and probably interfered with other bodily functions as well). While such devices are all but unknown today, the social control of sexuality continues. Can you point to examples?

history—and around the world—men are more likely to see women in sexual terms than the other way around. Some broader social structure must be at work in a pattern that is this widespread, as we shall see in the next section, on the social-conflict approach.

SOCIAL-CONFLICT ANALYSIS

As you have seen in earlier chapters, the social-conflict approach (particularly the gender-conflict or feminist approach) highlights dimensions of inequality. This approach shows how sexuality both reflects patterns of social inequality and helps perpetuate them.

Sexuality: Reflecting Social Inequality

Recall our discussion of prostitution, a practice outlawed almost everywhere in the United States. Enforcement of prostitution laws is uneven at best, especially when it comes to who is and is not likely to be arrested. Although two people are involved, the record shows that police are far more

From a social-conflict point of view, sexuality is not so much a "natural" part of our humanity as it is a socially constructed pattern of behavior. Sexuality plays an important part in social inequality: By defining women in sexual terms, men devalue them as objects. Would you consider the behavior shown here to be "natural" or socially directed? Why?

likely to arrest (less powerful) female prostitutes than (more powerful) male clients. Similarly, of all women engaged in prostitution, it is streetwalkers—women with the least income and those most likely to be minorities—who face the highest risk of arrest (COYOTE, 2004). We might also wonder whether so many women would be involved in prostitution in the first place if they had the same economic opportunities as men.

More generally, which categories of people in U.S. society are most likely to be defined in terms of sexuality? The answer, once again, is those with less power: women compared to men, and people of color compared to whites. In this way, sexuality—which is a natural part of human life—is used by society to define some categories of people as less worthy.

↔ **YOUR TURN** ←

Do you think women more than men are defined in terms of their sexuality? What effect does being defined in sexual terms have on women's opportunities?

Sexuality: Creating Social Inequality

Social-conflict theorists, especially feminists, point to sexuality as the root of inequality between women and men. Defining women in sexual terms amounts to devaluing them from full human beings into objects of men's interest and attention. Is it any wonder that the word *pornography* comes from the Greek word *porne,* meaning "a man's sexual slave"?

If men define women in sexual terms, it is easy to see pornography—almost all of which is consumed by males—as a power issue. Because pornography typically shows women focused on pleasing men, it supports the idea that men have power over women.

Some radical critics doubt that this element of power can ever be removed from heterosexual relations (A. Dworkin, 1987). Most social-conflict theorists do not reject heterosexuality, but they do agree that sexuality can and does degrade women. Our culture often describes sexuality in terms of sport (men "scoring" with women) and violence ("slamming," "banging," and "hitting on," for example, are verbs used for both fighting and sex).

Queer Theory

Finally, social-conflict theory has taken aim not only at the domination of women by men but also at heterosexuals dominating homosexuals. In recent years, as many lesbians and gay men have sought public acceptance, a gay voice

 The Queer Resources Directory looks at a wide range of issues from a queer theory perspective: http://www.qrd.org/qrd/

has arisen in sociology. The term **queer theory** refers to *a growing body of research findings that challenges the heterosexual bias in U.S. society.*

Queer theory begins with the claim that our society is characterized by **heterosexism,** *a view that labels anyone who is not heterosexual as "queer."* Our heterosexual culture victimizes a wide range of people, including gay men, lesbians, bisexuals, intersexuals, transsexuals, and even asexual people. Although most people agree that bias against women (sexism) and people of color (racism) is wrong, heterosexism is widely tolerated and sometimes well within the law. For example, U.S. military forces cannot legally discharge a female soldier simply for "acting like a woman" because this would be a clear case of gender discrimination. But the military forces can discharge her for homosexuality if she is a sexually active lesbian.

Heterosexism is also part of everyday culture. When we describe something as "sexy," for example, don't we really mean attractive to *heterosexuals*?

YOUR TURN

Can you think of three attitudes or social patterns (like the one in the preceding sentence) that are examples of heterosexism?

Critical review The social-conflict approach shows that sexuality is both a cause and an effect of inequality. In particular, it helps us understand men's power over women and heterosexual people's domination of homosexual people.

At the same time, this approach overlooks the fact that many people do not see sexuality as a power issue. On the contrary, many couples enjoy a vital sexual relationship that deepens their commitment to one another. In addition, the social-conflict approach pays little attention to steps U.S. society has taken toward reducing inequality. Today's men are less likely to describe women as sex objects than they were a few decades ago. One of the most important issues in

the workplace today is insuring that all employees remain free from sexual harassment. Rising public concern (see Chapter 13, "Gender Stratification") has reduced the abuse of sexuality in the workplace. Likewise, there is ample evidence that the gay rights movement has secured greater opportunities and social acceptance for gay people.

This chapter closes with a look at what is perhaps the most divisive issue involving sexuality: **abortion,** *the deliberate termination of a pregnancy.* There seems to be no middle ground in this controversial issue. The Thinking It Through box on pages 216–17 helps explain why.

MAKING THE GRADE

The following learning tools will help you see what you know, identify what you still need to learn, and expand your understanding beyond the text. You can also visit this text's Companion Website™ at http://www.prenhall.com/macionis to find additional practice tests.

KEY POINTS

Understanding Sexuality

U.S. culture long defined sex as a taboo topic. The Kinsey research was among the first to study human sexuality.

Sex refers to the biological distinction between females and males, which is determined at conception as a male sperm joins a female ovum. Gender is a cultural concept referring to the personal traits and social positions that members of a society attach to being female or male. Males and females are distinguished not only by their genitals (primary sex characteristics) but also by bodily development as they mature

(secondary sex characteristics). Intersexual people (also called "hermaphrodites") have some combination of both male and female genitalia. Transsexuals are people who feel they are one sex even though biologically they are the other.

For most species, sex is rigidly directed by biology; for human beings, sex is a matter of cultural definition as well as personal choice. Patterns of kissing, modesty, and standards of beauty all vary around the world, revealing the cultural foundation of sexual practices.

Sexual Attitudes in the United States

Over the course of history, social attitudes toward sexuality have become more permissive. The sexual revolution, which came of age in the 1960s and 1970s, brought discussion of sexuality out into the open. Research shows that changes in sexuality were greater for women than for men. By 1980, a sexual counterrevolution was taking form, condemning permissiveness and urging a return to more conservative "family values."

The share of people in the United States who have premarital sexual intercourse increased during the twentieth century. Today, research shows that about three-fourths of young

THINKING IT THROUGH
The Abortion Controversy

A black van pulls up in front of the storefront in a busy section of the city. Two women get out of the front seat and cautiously look up and down the street. After a moment, one nods to the other and they open the rear door to let a third woman out of the van. Standing to the right and left of the woman, the two quickly escort her inside the building.

This scene might describe two federal marshals taking a convict to a police station, but it is actually an account of two clinic workers helping a woman who has decided to have an abortion. Why are they so cautious? Anyone who has read the papers in recent years knows about the angry confrontations at abortion clinics across North America. Some opponents have even targeted and killed several doctors who carried out abortions. This procedure—some 850,000 of which are performed each year—is one of the most hotly debated issues today.

Abortion has not always been so controversial. In colonial times,

midwives and other healers performed abortions with little community opposition and with full approval of the law. But controversy arose about 1850, when early medical doctors wanted to eliminate the competition they faced from midwives and other traditional health providers, whose income came largely from ending pregnancies. By 1900, medical doctors had succeeded in getting every state to pass a law banning abortion.

Such laws greatly reduced the number of abortions. Those that remained were done "underground," as secretly as possible. Many women who wanted abortions—especially those who were poor—had little choice but to seek help from unlicensed "back alley" abortionists, sometimes with tragic results.

By the 1960s, opposition to anti-abortion laws was rising. In 1973, the U.S. Supreme Court made a landmark decision (in the cases of *Roe* v. *Wade* and *Doe* v. *Bolton*), striking down all state laws banning abortion. In effect,

this action established a woman's legal access to abortion nationwide.

Today, the abortion controversy continues. On one side of the issue are people who describe themselves as "pro-choice," supporting a woman's right to choose abortion and defending the Supreme Court's 1973 decision. On the other side are those who call themselves "pro-life," opposing abortion as morally wrong; these people would like to see the Supreme Court reverse its 1973 decision.

How strong is the support for each side of the abortion controversy? A recent national survey asked a sample of adults the question "Should it be possible for a pregnant woman to obtain a legal abortion if the woman wants it for any reason?" In response, 41.9 percent said yes (placing them in the pro-choice camp) and 55.5 percent said no (the pro-life position); the remaining 2.6 percent offered no opinion (NORC, 2003:227).

A closer look shows that circumstances make a big difference in how

---

men and two-thirds of young women have intercourse by their senior year in high school.

Among U.S. adults, the level of sexual activity varies: One-third report having sex with a partner a few times a year or not at all; another one-third have sex once or several times a month; the remaining one-third have sex two or more times a week. Although extramarital sex is widely condemned, about 25 percent of married men and 10 percent of married women report being sexually unfaithful to their spouses at some time.

Sexual Orientation

Sexual orientation refers to a person's romantic and emotional attraction to another person. Four major orientations are heterosexuality, homosexuality, bisexuality, and asexuality. Sexual orientation reflects both biological and cultural factors.

The share of the population that is homosexual depends on how researchers define "homosexuality." About 9 percent of adult men and 4 percent of adult women report engaging in some homosexual activity; 2.8 percent of men and 1.4 percent of women consider themselves homosexual.

The gay rights movement has gained greater acceptance for gay people in recent decades. Largely because of this movement, the share of the U.S. population condemning homosexuality as morally wrong has decreased steadily to less than 60 percent.

Sexual Issues and Controversies

Nearly 1 million teenagers become pregnant each year in the United States. The rate of teenage pregnancy has dropped since 1950, when many teens married and had children. Today, most

people see this issue. The figure shows that large majorities of U.S. adults favor legal abortion if a pregnancy seriously threatens a woman's health, if the pregnancy is a result of rape, or if a fetus is likely to have a serious defect. The bottom line is that about 42 percent support access to abortion under *any* circumstances, but nearly 90 percent support access to abortion under *some* circumstances.

Many of those who take the pro-life position feel strongly that abortion amounts to killing unborn children—some 40 million since *Roe* v. *Wade* was passed in 1973. To them, people never have the right to end innocent life in this way. But pro-choice advocates are no less committed to the position that women must have control over their own bodies. If pregnancy decides the course of women's lives, women will never be able to compete with men on equal terms, whether it is on campus or in the workplace. Therefore, access to legal, safe abortion is a necessary condition to women's full participation in society.

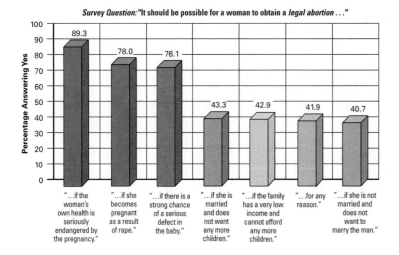

Survey Question: "It should be possible for a woman to obtain a *legal abortion* . . ."

Percentage Answering Yes

- 89.3 — "...if the woman's own health is seriously endangered by the pregnancy."
- 78.0 — "...if she becomes pregnant as a result of rape."
- 76.1 — "...if there is a strong chance of a serious defect in the baby."
- 43.3 — "...if she is married and does not want any more children."
- 42.9 — "...if the family has a very low income and cannot afford any more children."
- 41.9 — "...for any reason."
- 40.7 — "...if she is not married and does not want to marry the man."

When Should the Law Allow a Woman to Choose Abortion?

The extent of public support for legal abortion depends on exactly how the issue is presented.

Source: NORC (2003).

WHAT DO YOU THINK?

1. The more conservative, pro-life position sees abortion as a moral issue, and the more liberal, pro-choice position views abortion as a power issue. Compare these positions to how conservatives and liberals view the issue of pornography.

2. Surveys show that men and women have almost the same opinions about abortion. Does this surprise you? Why or why not?

3. Why do you think the abortion controversy is often so bitter? Do you think our nation can find a middle ground on this issue?

pregnant teens are not married and are at high risk of dropping out of school and being poor.

With no universal definition of pornography, the law allows local communities to set standards of decency. Conservatives condemn pornography as immoral; liberals condemn it as demeaning to women.

Prostitution, the selling of sexual services, is against the law almost everywhere in the United States. Although many people think of prostitution as a victimless crime, others point out that it victimizes women and spreads sexually transmitted diseases.

Some 93,000 rapes are reported each year in the United States, but the actual number is likely several times greater. Rapes are violent crimes in which victims and offenders typically know one another.

Theoretical Analysis of Sexuality

The structural-functional approach highlights society's need to regulate sexual activity. One universal norm is the incest taboo, which keeps family relations clear.

The symbolic-interaction approach emphasizes the various meanings people attach to sexuality. Societies differ from one another in terms of sexual attitudes and practices, and sexual patterns can change in a society over time.

According to the social-conflict approach, one way men dominate women is by devaluing them to the level of sexual objects. Queer theory points to the norm of heterosexism that defines anything different as "queer."

sex (p. 194) the biological distinction between females and males

primary sex characteristics (p. 195) the genitals, organs used for reproduction

secondary sex characteristics (p. 195) bodily development, apart from the genitals, that distinguishes biologically mature females and males

intersexual people (p. 196) people whose bodies (including genitals) have both female and male characteristics

transsexuals (p. 196) people who feel they are one sex even though biologically they are the other

incest taboo (p. 197) a norm forbidding sexual relations or marriage between certain relatives

sexual orientation (p. 203) a person's romantic and emotional attraction to another person

heterosexuality (p. 203) sexual attraction to someone of the other sex

homosexuality (p. 203) sexual attraction to someone of the same sex

bisexuality (p. 203) sexual attraction to people of both sexes

asexuality (p. 203) a lack of sexual attraction to people of either sex

homophobia (p. 206) discomfort over close personal interaction with people thought to be gay, lesbian, or bisexual

pornography (p. 207) sexually explicit material intended to cause sexual arousal

prostitution (p. 207) the selling of sexual services

queer theory (p. 214) a growing body of research findings that challenges the heterosexual bias in U.S. society

heterosexism (p. 214) a view that labels anyone who is not heterosexual as "queer"

abortion (p. 215) the deliberate termination of a pregnancy

SAMPLE TEST QUESTIONS

These questions are similar to those found in the test bank that accompanies this textbook.

Multiple-Choice Questions

1. What is the term for humans who have some combination of female and male genitalia?
   a. asexual people
   b. bisexual people
   c. transsexual people
   d. intersexual people

2. A global perspective on human sexuality shows us that
   a. although sex involves our biology, it is also a cultural trait that varies from place to place.
   b. people everywhere in the world have the same sexual practices.
   c. people in all societies are uncomfortable talking about sex.
   d. all of the above.

3. Why is the incest taboo found in every society?
   a. It limits sexual competition between members of families.
   b. It helps define people's rights and obligations toward one another.
   c. It integrates members of a family within the larger society.
   d. All of the above are correct.

4. The sexual revolution came of age during the
   a. 1890s.
   b. 1920s.
   c. 1960s.
   d. 1980s.

5. Survey data show that the largest share of U.S. adults reject which of the following?
   a. extramarital sex
   b. homosexuality
   c. premarital sex
   d. sex simply for pleasure

6. According to the Laumann study of sexuality in the United States,
   a. only one-third of the adult population is sexually active.
   b. there is great diversity in levels of sexual activity so that no one stereotype is correct.
   c. single people have more sex than married people.
   d. most married men admit to cheating on their wives at some point in their marriage.

7. What is the term meaning "sexual attraction to people of both sexes"?
   a. heterosexuality
   b. homosexuality
   c. bisexuality
   d. asexuality

8. Compared to 1950, the U.S. rate of teenage pregnancy today is
   a. higher.
   b. the same, but more teens become pregnant by choice.

c. the same, but more pregnant teens are married.

d. lower.

9. **By what point in their lives do most young people in the United States today become sexually active?**

   a. when they marry

   b. by the middle of college

   c. by the end of high school

   d. by age thirteen

10. **If we look back in history, we see that once a society develops birth control technology,**

    a. social control of sexuality becomes more strict.

    b. the birth rate actually goes up.

    c. attitudes about sexuality become more permissive.

    d. people no longer care about incest.

Answers: 1(d); 2(a); 3(d); 4(c); 5(a); 6(b); 7(c); 8(d); 9(c); 10(c).

Essay Questions

1. What was the "sexual revolution"? What changed? Can you point to reasons for the change?

2. Of the issues discussed in this chapter (prostitution, teen pregnancy, pornography, sexual violence, and abortion), which do you think is the most important for U.S. society today? Why?

APPLICATIONS & EXERCISES

1. The most complete study of sexual patterns in the United States to date is *The Social Organization of Sexuality: Sexual Practices in the United States* by Edward Laumann and others. Get a copy from your campus or community library, and read a chapter or two. Did what you read surprise you? Why or why not?

2. Contact your school's student services office, and ask for information about the extent of sexual violence on your campus. Do people typically report such crimes? What policies and procedures does your school have to respond to sexual violence?

3. Use the campus library and Internet sources to learn more about the experiences of women and men involved in prostitution. As you learn more, decide whether you think prostitution should be considered a "victimless crime."

INVESTIGATE *with* Research Navigator

Follow the instructions on page 27 of this text to access the features of **Research Navigator™**. Once at the Web site, enter your Login Name and Password. Then, to use the **ContentSelect™** database, enter keywords such as "sexuality," "prostitution," "transgender," and "abortion," and the search engine will supply relevant and recent scholarly and popular press publications. Use the *New York Times* **Search-by-Subject Archive** to find recent news articles related to sociology and the **Link Library** feature to find relevant Web links organized by the key terms associated with this chapter.

9

Deviance

Why is deviance found in all societies?

How does *who* and *what* are defined as deviant reflect social inequality?

What effect has punishment had in reducing crime in the United States?

The black SUV rolled through the gates of the federal women's prison in Alderson, West Virginia, threading its way among the sea of news reporters, many of whom leaned toward the vehicle to catch a glimpse of the famous woman sitting in back. Martha Stewart had just been released from jail. Stewart was sent to prison in 2004 after being convicted of lying about an improper stock deal. After five months behind bars, she was eager to get home. Soon after leaving the prison, the woman who made a fortune explaining how to live well boarded a private jet that whisked her to her 153-acre ranch in Katonah, New York. Within three days, she reported to her probation officer who placed an electronic monitor on her ankle and explained that she would have to spend the next five months at home under house arrest.

The day after her release, Wes Smith, who is a postal carrier in Katonah, smiled at reporters as he delivered mail to Stewart's home. "She's served her time. She's probably a changed person. Maybe she learned her lesson" (Fitzgerald, 2005). ■

This chapter explores crime, criminals, and punishment. One important lesson is that individuals convicted of wrongdoing do not always fit the common stereotype of the "street" criminal. The chapter also tackles the larger question of why societies develop standards of right and wrong in the first place. As we shall see, law is simply one part of a complex system of social control: Society teaches us all to conform, at least most of the time, to countless rules. We begin our investigation by defining several basic concepts.

What Is Deviance?

Deviance is *the recognized violation of cultural norms.* Norms guide almost all human activities, so the concept of deviance is quite broad. One category of deviance is **crime,** *the violation of a society's formally enacted criminal law.* Even criminal deviance spans a wide range of behavior, from minor traffic violations to sexual assault to murder.

Most familiar examples of nonconformity are negative instances of rule breaking, such as stealing from a campus bookstore, assaulting a fellow student, or driving while intoxicated. But we also define especially righteous people—students who speak up too much in class or people who are overly enthusiastic about new computer technology—as deviant, even if we give them a measure of respect. What deviant actions or attitudes—whether negative or positive—

have in common is some element of *difference* that causes us to think of another person as an "outsider" (H. Becker, 1966).

Not all deviance involves action or even choice. The very *existence* of some categories of people can be troublesome to others. To the young, elderly people may seem hopelessly "out of it," and to some heterosexuals, the mere presence of gay people may cause discomfort. Able-bodied people often view people with disabilities as an out-group, just as rich people may shun the poor for falling short of their standards.

SOCIAL CONTROL

All of us are subject to **social control,** *attempts by society to regulate people's thoughts and behavior.* Often this process is informal, as when parents praise or scold their children or when friends make fun of a classmate's choice of music. Cases of serious deviance, however, may involve the **criminal justice system,** *a formal response by police, courts, and prison officials to alleged violations of the law.*

How a society defines deviance, *who* is branded as deviant, and *what* people decide to do about deviance all have to do with the way society is organized. Only gradually, however, have people recognized that deviance

 Learn more about juvenile delinquency at http://www. ojjdp.ncjrs.org/

is much more than a matter of individual choice, as this chapter now explains.

THE BIOLOGICAL CONTEXT

Chapter 5 ("Socialization") explained that a century ago, most people understood—or more correctly, misunderstood—human behavior to be the result of biological instincts. Early interest in criminality thus focused on biological causes. In 1876, Cesare Lombroso (1835–1909), an Italian physician who worked in prisons, theorized that criminals stand out physically, with low foreheads, prominent jaws and cheekbones, hairiness, and unusually long arms. All in all, Lombroso claimed that criminals look like our apelike ancestors.

Had Lombroso looked more carefully, he would have found the physical features he linked to criminality throughout the entire population. We now know that no physical traits distinguish criminals from noncriminals.

In the middle of the twentieth century, William Sheldon took a different approach, suggesting that body structure might predict criminality (Sheldon, Hartl, & McDermott, 1949). He cross-checked hundreds of young men for body type and criminal history and concluded that criminality was most likely among boys with muscular, athletic builds. Sheldon Glueck and Eleanor Glueck (1950) confirmed Sheldon's conclusion but cautioned that a powerful build does not necessarily *cause* criminality. Parents, they suggested, tend to be somewhat distant from powerfully built sons, who in turn grow up to show less sensitivity toward others. Moreover, in a self-fulfilling prophecy, people who expect muscular boys to be bullies may act in ways that bring about the aggressive behavior they expect.

Today, genetics research seeks possible links between biology and crime. In 2003, scientists at the University of Wisconsin reported results of a twenty-five year study of crime among 400 boys. The researchers collected DNA samples from each boy and noted any trouble they had with the law. The researchers concluded that genetic factors (especially defective genes that, say, make too much of an enzyme) together with environmental factors (especially abuse early in life) were strong predictors of adult crime and violence. They noted, too, that these factors together were a better predictor of crime than either one alone (Lemonick, 2003; Pinker, 2003).

Critical review Biological theories offer a limited explanation of crime. The best guess at present is that biological traits in combination with environmental factors explain some serious crime. But most of the actions we define as deviant are carried out by people who are physically quite normal.

Deviance is always a matter of difference. Deviance emerges in everyday life as we encounter people whose appearance or behavior differs from what we consider to be "right." Who is the "deviant" in this photograph? From whose point of view?

In addition, because a biological approach looks at the individual, it offers no insight into how some kinds of behaviors come to be defined as deviant in the first place. Therefore, although there is much to be learned about how human biology may affect behavior, research currently puts far greater emphasis on social influences.

PERSONALITY FACTORS

Like biological theories, psychological explanations of deviance focus on abnormality in the individual personality. Some personality traits are inherited, but most psychologists think that personality is shaped primarily by social experience. Deviance, then, is viewed as the result of "unsuccessful" socialization.

Classic research by Walter Reckless and Simon Dinitz (1967) illustrates the psychological approach. Reckless and Dinitz began by asking a number of teachers to categorize twelve-year-old male students as either likely or unlikely to get into trouble with the law. They then interviewed both the boys and their mothers to assess each boy's self-concept and how he related to others. Analyzing their results, Reckless and Dinitz found that the "good boys" displayed a strong conscience (what Freud called superego), could handle frustration, and identified with cultural norms and values. The "bad boys," by contrast, had a weaker conscience, displayed little tolerance of frustration, and felt out of step with conventional culture.

As we might expect, the "good boys" went on to have fewer run-ins with the police than the "bad boys." Because all the boys lived in an area where delinquency was widespread, the investigators attributed staying out of trouble to a personality that controlled deviant impulses. Based on this conclusion, Reckless and Dinitz called their analysis *containment theory.*

Critical review Psychologists have shown that personality patterns have some connection to deviance. Some serious criminals are psychopaths who do not feel guilt or shame, have no fear of punishment, and have little sympathy for the people they harm (Herpertz & Sass, 2000). However, as we noted in the case of biological factors, most serious crimes are committed by people whose psychological profiles are normal.

Both the biological and psychological approaches view deviance as a trait of individuals. The reason that these approaches have had limited value in explaining deviance is that wrongdoing has more to do with the organization of society. We now turn to a sociological approach, which explores where ideas of right and wrong come from, why people define some rule breakers but not others as deviant, and what role power plays in this process.

THE SOCIAL FOUNDATIONS OF DEVIANCE

Although we tend to view deviance as the free choice or personal failings of individuals, all behavior—deviance as well as conformity—is shaped by society. Three social foundations of deviance identified here will be detailed later in this chapter:

1. **Deviance varies according to cultural norms.** No thought or action is inherently deviant; it becomes deviant only in relation to particular norms. Because norms vary from place to place, deviance also varies. State law permits prostitution in rural areas of Nevada, although the practice is outlawed in the rest of the United States. Eleven states have gambling casinos; twenty-eight have casinos on Indian reservations. In all other states, casino gambling is illegal.

Further, most cities and towns have at least one unique statute. For example, Mobile, Alabama, outlaws the wearing of stiletto-heeled shoes; in Juneau, Alaska, it is illegal to bring a flamingo into a barbershop; South Padre Island, Texas, bans the wearing of neckties; Mount Prospect, Illinois, has a law against keeping pigeons or bees; Topeka, Kansas, bans snowball fights; Hoover, South Dakota, does not allow fishing with a kerosene lantern; and Beverly Hills regulates the number of tennis balls allowed on the court at one time (Sanders & Horn, 1998; R. Steele, 2000).

Around the world, deviance is even more diverse. Albania outlaws any public display of religious faith, such as "crossing" oneself; Cuba and Vietnam can prosecute citizens for meeting with foreigners; Malaysia does not allow women to wear tight-fitting jeans; police in Iran can arrest a woman simply for wearing makeup; and Saudi Arabia bans the sale of red flowers on Valentine's Day.

2. **People become deviant as others define them that way.** Everyone violates cultural norms at one time or another. Have you ever walked around talking to yourself or "borrowed" a pen from your workplace? Whether such behavior defines us as criminal or mentally ill depends on how others perceive, define, and respond to it.

3. **Both norms and the way people define rule-breaking involve social power.** The law, declared Karl Marx, is the means by which powerful people protect their interests. A homeless person who stands on a street corner speaking out against the government risks arrest for disturbing the peace; a mayoral candidate during an election campaign does exactly the same thing and gets police protection. In short, norms and how we apply them reflect social inequality.

The Functions of Deviance: Structural-Functional Analysis

The key insight of the structural-functional approach is that deviance is a necessary part of social organization. This point was made a century ago by Emile Durkheim.

DURKHEIM'S BASIC INSIGHT

In his pioneering study of deviance, Emile Durkheim (1964a, orig. 1893; 1964b, orig. 1895) made the surprising statement that there is nothing abnormal about deviance. In fact, it performs four essential functions:

1. **Deviance affirms cultural values and norms.** As moral creatures, people must prefer some attitudes and behaviors to others. But any definition of virtue rests on an opposing idea of vice: There can be no good without evil and no justice without crime. Deviance is needed to define and support morality.

2. **Responding to deviance clarifies moral boundaries.** By defining some individuals as deviant, people draw a boundary between right and wrong. For example, a college marks the line between academic honesty and cheating by punishing students who cheat on exams.

3. **Responding to deviance brings people together.** People typically react to serious deviance with shared outrage. In doing so, Durkheim explained, they reaffirm the moral ties that bind them. For example, after the September 11, 2001, terrorist attacks, people across the United States were joined by a common desire to protect the country and bring those responsible to justice.

4. **Deviance encourages social change.** Deviant people push a society's moral boundaries, suggesting alternatives to the status quo and encouraging change. Today's deviance, declared Durkheim, can become tomorrow's morality (1964b:71). For example, rock 'n' roll, condemned as immoral in the 1950s, became a multibillion-dollar industry just a few years later; in recent years, hip-hop music has followed the same path.

Deviance is difference that makes a difference. Deviance emerges in everyday life as we encounter people whose appearance or behavior differs from what we consider "normal" or "right." Playing his music on the streets of New York City, the Naked Cowboy is "different" in a way that provides pleasure to many people passing by.

YOUR TURN

Keeping in mind Durkheim's claim that society creates deviance to mark moral boundaries, why do we often define people only in terms of their deviance, as when we call someone "an addict" or "a thief"?

An Illustration: The Puritans of Massachusetts Bay

Kai Erikson's (2005b, orig. 1966) classic study of the Puritans of Massachusetts Bay brings Durkheim's theory to life. Erikson shows that even the Puritans, a disciplined and highly religious group, created deviance to clarify their moral boundaries. In fact, Durkheim might well have had the Puritans in mind when he wrote:

> Imagine a society of saints, a perfect cloister of exemplary individuals. Crimes, properly so called, will there be unknown; but faults which appear [insignificant] to the layman will create there the same scandal that the ordinary offense does in ordinary consciousness. . . . For the same reason, the perfect and upright man judges his smallest failings with a severity that the majority reserve for acts more truly in the nature of an offense. (1964b:68–69)

Deviance is not a matter of a few "bad apples" but a necessary condition of "good" social living.

Deviance may be found in every society, but the *kind* of deviance people generate depends on the moral issues they seek to clarify. The Puritans, for example, experienced a number of "crime waves," including the well-known outbreak of witchcraft in 1692. With each response, the Puritans answered questions about the range of proper beliefs by celebrating some of their members and condemning others as deviant.

Erikson discovered that even though the offenses changed, the proportion of people the Puritans defined as

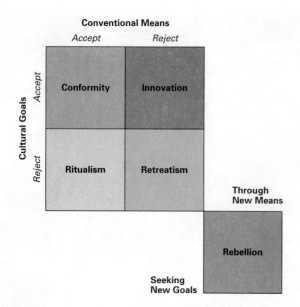

FIGURE 9-1   Merton's Strain Theory of Deviance

Combining a person's view of cultural goals and the conventional means to obtain them allowed Robert Merton to identify various types of deviants.

Source: Merton (1968).

deviant remained steady over time. This stability, he concluded, confirms Durkheim's claim that society creates deviants to mark its changing moral boundaries. In other words, by constantly defining a small number of people as deviant, the Puritans maintained the moral shape of their society.

MERTON'S STRAIN THEORY

Some deviance may be necessary for a society to function, but Robert Merton (1938, 1968) argued that too much deviance results from particular social arrangements. Specifically, the extent and kind of deviance depend on whether a society provides the *means* (such as schooling and job opportunities) to achieve cultural *goals* (such as financial success).

Conformity lies in pursuing cultural goals through approved means. Thus the U.S. "success story" is someone who gains wealth and prestige through talent, schooling, and hard work. But not everyone who wants conventional success has the opportunity to attain it. For example, people raised in poverty may have little hope of becoming successful if they play by the rules. According to Merton, the strain between our culture's emphasis on wealth and the lack of opportunities to get rich may encourage some people,

especially the poor, to engage in stealing, drug dealing, or other forms of street crime. Merton called this type of deviance *innovation*—using unconventional means (street crime) to achieve a culturally approved goal (wealth). Figure 9–1 shows that innovation involves accepting a cultural goal (financial success) but rejecting the conventional means (hard work at a "straight" job) in favor of unconventional means (street crime).

The inability to reach a cultural goal may also prompt another type of deviance that Merton calls *ritualism* (see Figure 9–1). For example, many people believe that they cannot achieve the cultural goal of becoming rich; therefore, they rigidly stick to the rules (the conventional means) in order to at least feel respectable.

A third response to the inability to succeed is *retreatism*—the rejection of both cultural goals and means, so that a person in effect "drops out." Some alcoholics, drug addicts, and street people are retreatists. The deviance of retreatists lies in their unconventional lifestyle and also in what seems to be their willingness to live this way.

The fourth response to failure is *rebellion*. Like retreatists, rebels such as radical "survivalists" reject both the cultural definition of success and the conventional means of achieving it, but they go one step further by forming a counterculture supporting alternatives to the existing social order.

DEVIANT SUBCULTURES

Richard Cloward and Lloyd Ohlin (1966) extended Merton's theory, proposing that crime results not simply from limited legitimate (legal) opportunity but also from readily accessible illegitimate (illegal) opportunity. In short, deviance or conformity arises from the *relative opportunity structure* that frames a person's life.

The life of Al Capone, a notorious gangster, illustrates Cloward and Ohlin's theory. As the son of poor immigrants, Capone faced barriers of poverty and ethnic prejudice, which lowered his odds of achieving success in conventional terms. Yet as a young man during Prohibition (when alcoholic beverages were banned in the United States between 1920 and 1933), Capone found in his neighborhood people who could teach him how to sell alcohol illegally—a source of illegitimate opportunity. Where the structure of opportunity favors criminal activity, Cloward and Ohlin predict the development of *criminal subcultures*, such as street gangs.

But what happens when people cannot identify *any* kind of opportunity, legal or illegal? Then deviance may take the form of *conflict subcultures* (armed street gangs), where violence is ignited by frustration and a desire for

Young people cut off from legitimate opportunity often form subcultures that many people view as deviant. Gang subcultures, including tattoos on the fingers, are one way young people gain the sense of belonging and respect denied to them by the larger culture.

respect, or *retreatist subcultures,* in which deviants drop out and may abuse alcohol or other drugs.

Albert Cohen (1971, orig. 1955) suggests that delinquency is most common among lower-class youths because they have the least opportunity to achieve conventional success. Neglected by society, they seek self-respect by creating a delinquent subculture that defines as worthy the traits these youths do have. Being feared on the street may not win many points with society as a whole, but it may satisfy a young person's desire to "be somebody" in the local neighborhood.

Walter Miller (1970, orig. 1958) adds that delinquent subcultures are characterized by (1) *trouble,* arising from frequent conflict with teachers and police; (2) *toughness,* the value placed on physical size and strength, especially among males; (3) *smartness,* the ability to succeed on the streets, to outsmart or "con" others, and to avoid being similarly taken advantage of; (4) *a need for excitement,* the search for thrills, risk, or danger; (5) *a belief in fate,* a sense that people lack control over their own lives; and (6) *a desire for freedom,* often expressed as anger toward authority figures.

Finally, Elijah Anderson (1994, 2002) explains that in poor urban neighborhoods, most people manage to conform to conventional ("decent") values. Yet faced with neighborhood crime and violence, indifference or even hostility from police, and sometimes even neglect by their own parents, some young men decide to live by the "street code." To show that they can survive on the street, a young man displays "nerve," a willingness to stand up to any threat. Following this street code, the young man believes that a violent death is better than being "dissed" (disrespected) by others. Some manage to escape the dangers,

but the risk of ending up in jail—or worse—is very high for these young men, who have been pushed to the margins of our society.

Critical review Durkheim made an important contribution by pointing out the functions of deviance. However, there is evidence that a community does not always come together in reaction to crime; sometimes fear of crime causes people to withdraw from public life (Liska & Warner, 1991; Warr & Ellison, 2000).

Merton's strain theory has been criticized for explaining some kinds of deviance (stealing, for example) better than others (such as crimes of passion or mental illness). In addition, not everyone seeks success in the conventional terms of wealth, as strain theory suggests.

The general argument of Cloward and Ohlin, Cohen, Miller, and Anderson—that deviance reflects the opportunity structure of society—has been confirmed by subsequent research (Allan & Steffensmeier, 1989; Uggen, 1999). However, these theories fall short by assuming that everyone shares the same cultural standards for judging right and wrong. If we define crime as not just burglary and auto theft but the type of illegal stock deals that sent Martha Stewart to prison, then more high-income people will be counted among criminals. There is evidence that people of all social backgrounds are becoming more casual about breaking the rules, as the Thinking Critically box on page 228 explains.

Finally, all structural-functional theories suggest that everyone who breaks important rules will be labeled deviant. However, becoming deviant is actually a highly complex process, as the next section explains.

THINKING CRITICALLY

Deviant (Sub)Culture: Has It Become OK to Break the Rules?

It's been a bad couple of years for the idea of playing by the rules. First, we learn that the executives of not just one but many U.S. corporations are guilty of fraud and outright stealing on a scale most of us cannot even imagine. Then Martha Stewart, the country's lifestyle guru, is sent to jail for trading stocks illegally and lying about it. Perhaps worst of all, the Catholic church, which we hold up as a model of moral behavior, has been stunned by charges that thousands of priests have sexually abused parishioners (most of them children) while church officials busied themselves covering up the crimes. By 2005, more than 300 priests in the United States had been removed from their duties pending investigations of abuse.

There are plenty of ideas about what is causing this widespread wrongdoing. Some people suggest that the pressure to win—by whatever means necessary—in today's highly competitive corporate world can be overwhelming. As one analyst put it, "You can get away with your embezzlements and your lies—but you can never get away with

failing." Still others point to a simple motive: greed.

Such thinking helps explain the wrongdoing among many CEOs, but it offers little insight into the problem of abusive priests. In some ways at least, wrongdoing seems to have become a way of life for just about everybody. For example, the Internal Revenue Service reports that many U.S. taxpayers cheat on their taxes, failing to pay an estimated $200 billion each year (an average of about $1,600 per taxpayer). The music industry claims that it has lost a

Do you consider cheating in school to be wrong? Would you turn in someone you saw cheat? Why or why not?

vast amount of money because of illegal piracy of recordings, a practice especially common among young people. Perhaps most disturbing of all, surveys of high school and college students show that at least half say they cheated on a test at least once during the past year.

Emile Durkheim considered society to be a moral system built on a set of rules about what people should and should not do. Years earlier, another French thinker named Blaise Pascal made the contrasting claim that "cheating is the foundation of society." Today, which of the two statements is closer to the truth?

WHAT DO YOU THINK?

1. In your opinion, how widespread is wrongdoing in U.S. society today?
2. Do you think people who break the rules usually consider what they are doing as wrong? Why or why not?
3. What do you think are the reasons for the apparent increase in dishonesty?

Sources: Based on "Our Cheating Hearts" (2002) and "John Jay Study Reveals Extent of Abuse Problem" (2005).

Labeling Deviance: Symbolic-Interaction Analysis

The symbolic-interaction approach explains how people define deviance in everyday situations. From this point of view, definitions of deviance and conformity are surprisingly flexible.

LABELING THEORY

The main contribution of symbolic-interaction analysis is **labeling theory,** *the idea that deviance and conformity result*

not so much from what people do as from how others respond to those actions. Labeling theory stresses the relativity of deviance, the idea that people may define the same behavior in any number of ways.

Consider these situations: A college student takes an article of clothing from a roommate's drawer; a married woman at a convention in a distant city has sex with an old boyfriend; a mayor gives a big city contract to a major campaign contributor. We might define the first situation as carelessness, borrowing, or theft. The consequences of the second case depend largely on whether the woman's behavior becomes known back home. In the third situation, is the official choosing the best contractor or paying off a political debt? The social construction of reality is a highly variable process of detection, definition, and response.

Explain in your own words Howard Becker's (1966) statement that deviance is nothing more than behavior that people define as deviant.

Primary and Secondary Deviance

Edwin Lemert (1951, 1972) observed that some norm violations—say, skipping school or underage drinking—provoke slight reaction from others and have little effect on a person's self-concept. Lemert calls such passing episodes *primary deviance.*

But what happens if other people notice someone's deviance and make something of it? For example, if people begin to describe a young man as an "alcohol abuser" and exclude him from their friendship group, he may become bitter, drink even more, and seek the company of others who approve of his behavior. The response to primary deviance sets in motion *secondary deviance,* by which a person repeatedly violates a norm and begins to take on a deviant identity. The development of secondary deviance is one application of the Thomas theorem (discussed in Chapter 6, "Social Interaction in Everyday Life"), which states that situations defined as real become real in their consequences.

Stigma

Secondary deviance marks the start of what Erving Goffman (1963) calls a *deviant career.* As people develop a stronger commitment to deviant behavior, they typically acquire a **stigma,** *a powerfully negative label that greatly changes a person's self-concept and social identity.*

A stigma operates as a master status (see Chapter 6), overpowering other aspects of social identity so that a person is discredited in the minds of others and becomes socially isolated. Sometimes an entire community formally stigmatizes an individual through what Harold Garfinkel (1956) calls a *degradation ceremony.* A criminal trial is one example, operating much the way a high school graduation does but in reverse: A person stands before the community to be labeled in a negative rather than a positive way.

Retrospective and Projective Labeling

Once people stigmatize an individual, they may engage in *retrospective labeling,* interpreting someone's past in light of some present deviance (Scheff, 1984). For example, after discovering that a priest has sexually molested a child, others rethink his past, perhaps musing, "He always did want to be around young children." Retrospective labeling, which distorts a person's biography by being highly selective, typically deepens a deviant identity.

Similarly, people may engage in *projective labeling* of a stigmatized person. That is, they use a deviant identity to predict future action. Regarding the priest, people might say, "He's going to keep at it until he gets caught." The more people in someone's social world think such things, the greater is the chance that they will come true.

Labeling Difference as Deviance

Is a homeless man who refuses to allow police to take him to a city shelter on a cold night simply trying to live independently, or is he "crazy"? People have a tendency to treat behavior that irritates or threatens them not simply as "different" but as deviance or even mental illness.

The psychiatrist Thomas Szasz (1961, 1970, 2003, 2004) charges that people are too quick to apply the label of mental illness to conditions that simply amount to a difference we don't like. The only way to avoid this troubling practice, Szasz continues, is to abandon the idea of mental illness entirely. The world is full of people whose "differences" in thought or action may irritate us, but such differences are no grounds for defining someone as mentally ill. Such labeling, Szasz claims, simply enforces conformity to the standards of people powerful enough to impose their will on others.

Most mental health care professionals reject the idea that mental illness does not exist. But they agree that it is important to think critically about how we define "difference." First, people who are mentally ill are no more to blame for their condition than people who suffer from cancer or some other physical problem. Therefore, having a mental or physical illness is no grounds for being labeled "deviant." Second, ordinary people without the medical knowledge to diagnose mental illness should avoid using such labels in an effort to make people conform to certain standards of behavior.

THE MEDICALIZATION OF DEVIANCE

Labeling theory, particularly the ideas of Szasz and Goffman, helps explain an important shift in the way our society understands deviance. Over the past fifty years, the growing influence of psychiatry and medicine in the United States has led to the **medicalization of deviance,** *the transformation of moral and legal deviance into a medical condition.*

Medicalization amounts to swapping one set of labels for another. In moral terms, we evaluate people or

Every once in a while, people commit a crime that is so shocking that we wonder if they are "crazy." Here is an actual security camera photo of Eric Harris and Dylan Klebold as they stalked and killed twelve students and one teacher in Colorado's Columbine High School in 1999. How do you understand such acts? Were these boys "evil," "sick," or simply very misguided?

their behavior as "bad" or "good." However, the scientific objectivity of medicine passes no moral judgment, instead using clinical diagnoses such as "sick" or "well."

To illustrate, until the mid-twentieth century, people generally viewed alcoholics as morally weak people easily tempted by the pleasure of drink. Gradually, however, medical specialists redefined alcoholism so that most people now consider it a disease, rendering people "sick" rather than "bad." In the same way, obesity, drug addiction, child abuse, sexual promiscuity, and other behaviors that used to be strictly moral matters are widely defined today as illnesses for which people need help rather than punishment.

The Difference Labels Make

Whether we define deviance as a moral or a medical issue has three consequences. First, it affects *who responds* to deviance. An offense against common morality usually brings about a reaction from members of the community or the police. A medical label, however, places the situation under the control of clinical specialists, including counselors, psychiatrists, and doctors.

A second difference is *how people respond* to deviance. A moral approach defines deviants as offenders subject to punishment. Medically, however, they are patients who need treatment. Punishment is designed to fit the crime, but treatment programs are tailored to fit the patient and may involve virtually any therapy that a specialist thinks will prevent future illness.

Third, and most important, the two labels differ on *the personal competence of the deviant person*. From a moral

standpoint, whether we are right or wrong, at least we take responsibility for our own behavior. Once defined as sick, however, we are seen as unable to control (or, if "mentally ill," even understand) our actions. People who are labeled incompetent are in turn subjected to treatment, often against their will. For this reason alone, attempts to define deviance in medical terms should be made with extreme caution.

YOUR TURN

An old saying goes, "Sticks and stones can break my bones, but names can never hurt me." What might labeling theory have to say about this idea?

SUTHERLAND'S DIFFERENTIAL ASSOCIATION THEORY

Learning any behavioral pattern, whether conventional or deviant, is a process that takes place in groups. According to Edwin Sutherland (1940), a person's tendency toward conformity or deviance depends on the amount of contact with others who encourage—or reject—conventional behavior. This is Sutherland's theory of *differential association*.

A number of studies confirm the idea that young people are more likely to engage in delinquency if they believe members of their peer groups encourage such activity (Akers et al., 1979; Miller & Mathews, 2001). One recent investigation focused on sexual activity among eighth-grade students. Two strong predictors of such behavior for young girls was having a boyfriend who encouraged sexual relations and having girlfriends they believed would approve of such activity. Similarly, boys were encouraged to become sexually active by friends who rewarded them with high status in the peer group (Little & Rankin, 2001).

HIRSCHI'S CONTROL THEORY

The sociologist Travis Hirschi (1969; Gottfredson & Hirschi, 1995) developed *control theory,* which states that social control depends on people anticipating the consequences of their behavior. Hirschi assumes that everyone finds at least some deviance tempting. But the thought of a ruined career keeps most people from breaking the rules; for some, just imagining the reactions of family and friends is enough. On the other hand, individuals who feel they have little to lose by deviance are likely to become rule-breakers.

All social groups teach their members skills and attitudes that encourage certain behavior. In recent years, discussion on college campuses has focused on the dangers of binge drinking that results in about 300 deaths each year in the United States. How much of a problem is binge drinking on your campus?

Specifically, Hirschi links conformity to four different types of social control:

1. **Attachment.** Strong social attachments encourage conformity. Weak family, peer, and school relationships leave people freer to engage in deviance.

2. **Opportunity.** The greater a person's access to legitimate opportunity, the greater the advantages of conformity. By contrast, someone with little confidence in future success is more likely to drift toward deviance.

3. **Involvement.** Extensive involvement in legitimate activities—such as holding a job, going to school, or playing sports—inhibits deviance (Langbein & Bess, 2002). By contrast, people who simply "hang out" waiting for something to happen have time and energy to engage in deviant activity.

4. **Belief.** Strong belief in conventional morality and respect for authority figures restrain tendencies toward deviance. People who have a weak conscience (and who are left unsupervised) are more open to temptation (Stack, Wasserman, & Kern, 2004).

Hirschi's analysis combines a number of earlier ideas about the causes of deviant behavior. Note that a person's relative social privilege as well as family and community environment are likely to affect the risk of deviant behavior (Hope, Grasmick, & Pointon, 2003).

Critical review The various symbolic-interaction theories all see deviance as process. Labeling theory links deviance not to action but to the *reaction* of others. Thus some

people are defined as deviant and others who think or behave in the same way are not. The concepts of secondary deviance, deviant career, and stigma show how being labeled deviant can become a lasting self-concept.

Yet labeling theory has several limitations. First, because it takes a highly relative view of deviance, labeling theory ignores the fact that some kinds of behavior—such as murder—are condemned just about everywhere. Therefore, labeling theory is most usefully applied to less serious issues, such as sexual promiscuity or mental illness. Second, research on the consequences of deviant labeling does not clearly show whether deviant labeling produces further deviance or discourages it (Smith & Gartin, 1989; Sherman & Smith, 1992). Third, not everyone resists being labeled deviant; some people actively seek it out (Vold & Bernard, 1986). For example, people take part in civil disobedience and willingly subject themselves to arrest in order to call attention to social injustice.

Sociologists consider Sutherland's differential association theory and Hirschi's control theory to be important contributions to our understanding of deviance. But why do society's norms and laws define certain kinds of activities as deviant in the first place? This question is addressed by social-conflict analysis, the focus of the next section.

Deviance and Inequality: Social-Conflict Analysis

The social-conflict approach links deviance to social inequality. That is, *who* or *what* is labeled "deviant" depends on which categories of people hold power in a society.

DEVIANCE AND POWER

Alexander Liazos (1972) points out that the people we tend to define as deviants—those we dismiss as "nuts" and "sluts"—are typically those who share the trait of powerlessness. Bag ladies (not corporate polluters) and unemployed men on street corners (not international arms dealers) carry the stigma of deviance.

Social-conflict theory explains this pattern in three ways. First, all norms and especially the laws of any society generally reflect the interests of the rich and powerful. People who threaten the wealthy, either by taking their property or by advocating a more egalitarian society, are defined as "common thieves" or "political radicals." As noted in Chapter 4 ("Society"), Karl Marx argued that the law and all other social institutions support the interests of the rich. Or as Richard Quinney puts it, "Capitalist justice is by the capitalist class, for the capitalist class, and against the working class" (1977:3).

Second, even if their behavior is called into question, the powerful have the resources to resist deviant labels. The majority of the executives involved in recent corporate scandals have yet to be arrested; very few have gone to jail.

Third, the widespread belief that norms and laws are natural and good masks their political character. For this reason, although we may condemn the *unequal application* of the law, we give little thought to whether the *laws themselves* are really fair or not.

DEVIANCE AND CAPITALISM

In the Marxist tradition, Steven Spitzer (1980) argues that deviant labels are applied to people who interfere with the operation of capitalism. First, because capitalism is based on private control of wealth, people who threaten the property of others—especially the poor who steal from the rich—are prime candidates for being labeled deviant. Conversely, the rich who take advantage of the poor are less likely to be labeled deviant. For example, landlords who charge poor tenants high rents and evict anyone who cannot pay are not considered criminals; they are simply "doing business."

Second, because capitalism depends on productive labor, people who cannot or will not work risk being labeled deviant. Many members of our society think people who are out of work, even through no fault of their own, are somehow deviant.

Third, capitalism depends on respect for authority figures, causing people who resist authority to be labeled as deviant. Examples are children who skip school or talk back to parents and teachers and adults who do not cooperate with employers or police.

Fourth, anyone who directly challenges the capitalist status quo is likely to be defined as deviant. Such has been the case with labor organizers, radical environmentalists, and antiwar activists.

On the other side of the coin, society positively labels whatever supports the operation of capitalism. For example, winning athletes enjoy celebrity status because they express the values of individual achievement and competition, both vital to capitalism. Also, Spitzer notes, we condemn using drugs of escape (marijuana, psychedelics, heroin, and crack) as deviant but encourage drugs (such as alcohol and caffeine) that promote adjustment to the status quo.

The capitalist system also tries to control people who don't fit into the system. The elderly, people with mental or physical disabilities, and Robert Merton's retreatists (people addicted to alcohol or other drugs) are a "costly yet relatively harmless burden" on society. Such people, claims Spitzer, are subject to control by social welfare agencies. But people who openly challenge the capitalist system, including the inner-city underclass and revolutionaries—Merton's innovators and rebels—are controlled by the criminal justice system and, in times of crisis, military forces such as the National Guard.

Note that both the social welfare and criminal justice systems blame individuals, not the system, for social problems. Welfare recipients are considered unworthy freeloaders, poor people who express rage at their plight are labeled rioters, anyone who challenges the government is branded a radical or a communist, and those who try to gain illegally what they will never get legally are rounded up as common criminals.

WHITE-COLLAR CRIME

In a sign of things to come, a Wall Street stockbroker named Michael Milken made headlines back in 1987 when he was jailed for business fraud. Milken attracted attention because not since the days of Al Capone had anyone made so much money in one year: $550 million—about $1.5 million a day (Swartz, 1989).

Milken committed a **white-collar crime,** defined by Edwin Sutherland (1940) as *crime committed by people of high social position in the course of their occupations.*

White-collar crimes do not involve violence and rarely attract police to the scene with guns drawn. Rather, white-collar criminals use their powerful offices to enrich themselves and others, often causing significant public harm in the process. For this reason, sociologists sometimes call white-collar offenses that occur in government offices and corporate board rooms *crime in the suites* as opposed to *crime in the streets.*

The most common white-collar crimes are bank embezzlement, business fraud, bribery, and antitrust violations. Sutherland (1940) explains that such white-collar offenses typically end up in a civil hearing rather than a criminal courtroom. *Civil law* regulates business dealings between private parties, and *criminal law* defines the individual's moral responsibilities to society. In practice, then, someone who loses a civil case pays for damage or injury but is not labeled a criminal. Corporate officials are also protected by the fact that most charges of white-collar crime target the organization rather than individuals.

When white-collar criminals are charged and convicted, they usually escape punishment. A government study found that those convicted of fraud and punished with a fine ended up paying less than 10 percent of what they owed; most managed to hide or transfer their assets to avoid paying up. Among white-collar criminals convicted of the more serious crime of embezzlement, only about half ever served a day in jail. One accounting found that just 59 percent of the embezzlers convicted in the U.S. federal courts served prison sentences; the rest were put on probation or issued a fine (U.S. Bureau of Justice Statistics, 2005; Willing, 2005).

CORPORATE CRIME

Sometimes whole companies, not just individuals, break the law. **Corporate crime** is *the illegal actions of a corporation or people acting on its behalf.*

Corporate crime ranges from knowingly selling faulty or dangerous products to deliberately polluting the environment (Derber, 2004). The collapse of the Enron Corporation in 2001 following extensive violations of business and accounting laws was a very serious case of corporate crime. Estimates of the losses to stockholders and others as a result of all corporate crime exceed $50 billion, which is four times the annual loss in the United States due to common theft (Lavelle, 2002).

As with white-collar crime, most cases of corporate crime go unpunished, and many are never even known to the public. In addition, the cost of corporate crime goes beyond dollars. The collapse of Enron, Global Crossing, and other corporations in recent years has cost tens of

Following the recent collapse of many large corporations due to fraud and other illegal activities, some corporate executives are facing criminal charges. In 2005, Bernard Ebbers, former chief executive officer of WorldCom, was convicted of numerous charges and will serve up to twenty-five years in prison.

thousands of people their jobs and their pensions. Even more seriously, for decades coal-mining companies have knowingly put miners at risk from inhaling coal dust, and hundreds of people die annually of "black lung" disease. The death toll from all job-related hazards that are known to companies probably exceeds 100,000 annually (J. Carroll, 1999; J. Jones, 1999).

ORGANIZED CRIME

Organized crime is *a business supplying illegal goods or services.* Sometimes criminal organizations force people to do business with them, as when a gang extorts money from shopkeepers for "protection." In most cases, however, organized crime involves the sale of illegal goods and services—including sex, drugs, and gambling—to willing buyers.

Organized crime has flourished in the United States for more than a century. The scope of its operations expanded among immigrants, who found that this society was not willing to share its opportunities with them. Some

APPLYING THEORY
DEVIANCE

	Structural-Functional Approach	Symbolic-Interaction Approach	Social-Conflict Approach
What is the level of analysis?	Macro-level	Micro-level	Macro-level
What is deviance? What part does it play in society?	Deviance is a basic part of social organization. By defining deviance, society sets its moral boundaries.	Deviance is part of socially constructed reality that emerges in interaction. Deviance comes into being as individuals label something deviant.	Deviance results from social inequality. Norms, including laws, reflect the interests of powerful members of society.
What is important about deviance?	Deviance is universal: All societies contain deviance.	Deviance is variable: Any act or person may or may not be labeled as deviant.	Deviance is political: People with little power are at high risk for becoming deviant.

ambitious individuals (such as Al Capone, described earlier) made their own success, especially during Prohibition (1920–1933), when the U.S. government banned the production and sale of alcohol.

The Italian Mafia is a well-known example of organized crime. But other criminal organizations involve African Americans, Chinese, Colombians, Cubans, Haitians, Nigerians, and Russians, as well as others of almost every racial and ethnic category. Today, organized crime involves a wide range of activities, from selling illegal drugs to prostitution to credit-card fraud to selling false identification papers to illegal immigrants (Valdez, 1997).

Critical review According to social-conflict theory, a capitalist society's inequality in wealth and power shapes its laws and how they are applied. The criminal justice and social welfare systems thus act as political agents, controlling categories of people who are a threat to the capitalist system.

Like other approaches to deviance, social-conflict theory has its critics. First, this approach implies that laws and other cultural norms are created directly by the rich and powerful. At the very least, this is an oversimplification, as laws also protect workers, consumers, and the environment, sometimes opposing the interests of corporations and the rich.

Second, social-conflict analysis argues that criminality springs up only to the extent that a society treats its members unequally. However, as Durkheim noted, deviance exists in all societies, whatever the economic system.

The sociological explanations for crime and other types of deviance that we have discussed are summarized in the Applying Theory table.

YOUR TURN

Why do you think the public seems less concerned with white-collar crime and corporate crime than with street crime? In light of recent corporate scandals, do you think this pattern is changing?

Deviance, Race, and Gender

What people consider deviant reflects the relative power and privilege of different categories of people. The following sections offer two examples: how racial and ethnic hostility motivates hate crimes and how gender is linked to deviance.

HATE CRIMES

A **hate crime** is *a criminal act against a person or a person's property by an offender motivated by racial or other bias.* A hate crime may express hostility toward someone's race, religion, ancestry, sexual orientation, or physical disability. The federal government recorded about 7,500 hate crimes in 2003.

Most people were stunned by the brutal killing in 1998 of Matthew Shepard, a gay student at the University of Wyoming, by two men motivated by hatred of homosexuals. The National Gay and Lesbian Task Force reports that one in five lesbians and gay men is physically assaulted and more than 90 percent are verbally abused because of sexual orientation (cited in Berrill, 1992:19–20). People who contend with multiple stigmas, such as gay men of color, are

Hate Crime Laws: Do They Punish Actions or Attitudes?

On a cool October evening, nineteen-year-old Todd Mitchell, an African American, was standing with some friends in front of their apartment complex in Kenosha, Wisconsin. They had just seen the film *Mississippi Burning* and were fuming over a scene that showed a white man beating a young black boy while he knelt in prayer.

"Do you feel hyped up to move on some white people?" asked Mitchell. Minutes later, they saw a young white boy walking toward them on the other side of the street. Mitchell commanded, "There goes a white boy; go get him!" The group swarmed around the youngster, beating him bloody and leaving him on the ground in a coma. The attackers took the boy's tennis shoes as a trophy.

Police soon arrested the teenagers and charged them with the beating. Todd Mitchell went to trial as the ringleader, and the jury found him guilty of aggravated battery *motivated by racial hatred*. Instead of the usual two-year sentence, Mitchell went to jail for four years.

As this case illustrates, hate crime laws punish a crime more severely if the offender is motivated by bias against some category of people. Supporters make three arguments in favor of hate crime legislation. First, the offender's intentions are always important in weighing criminal responsibility, so considering hatred an intention is nothing new. Second, a crime motivated by racial or other bias inflames the public mood more than a crime carried out, say, for money. Third, victims of hate crimes typically suffer greater injury than victims of crimes with other motives.

Critics counter that while some hate crime cases involve hard-core racism, most are impulsive acts by young people. Even more important, critics maintain, hate crime laws are a

Read one critic's ideas about hate crime laws at http://www.andrewsullivan.com/politics.php

threat to First Amendment guarantees of free speech. Hate crime laws allow courts to sentence offenders not just for their actions but for their attitudes.

As Harvard law professor Alan Dershowitz cautions, "As much as I hate bigotry, I fear much more the Court attempting to control the minds of its citizens." In short, according to critics, hate crime statutes open the door to punishing beliefs rather than behavior.

In 1993, the U.S. Supreme Court upheld the sentence handed down to Todd Mitchell. In a unanimous decision, the justices stated that the government should not punish an individual's beliefs. But, they reasoned, a belief is no longer protected when it becomes the motive for a crime.

WHAT DO YOU THINK?

1. Do you think crimes motivated by hate are more harmful than those motivated by greed? Why or why not?

2. Do you think minorities such as African Americans should be subject to the same hate crime laws as white people? Why or why not?

3. Do you favor or oppose hate crime laws? Explain your position.

Sources: Terry (1993) and A. Sullivan (2002).

---

especially likely to be victims. Yet it can happen to anyone: A recent study found that about 25 percent of the hate crimes based on race targeted white people (Jenness & Grattet, 2001).

By 2005, forty-six states and the federal government had enacted legislation that increased penalties for crimes motivated by hatred. Supporters are gratified, but opponents charge that such laws, which increase penalties based on the attitudes of the offender, punish "politically incorrect" thoughts. The Thinking About Diversity box takes a closer look at the issue of hate crime laws.

DEVIANCE AND GENDER

Virtually every society in the world applies stricter normative controls to women than to men. Historically, our own society has centered the lives of women on the home. Even today, in the United States, women's opportunities in the workplace, in politics, in athletics, and in the military are more limited than those of men. Elsewhere in the world, the constraints on women are greater still. In Saudi Arabia, women cannot vote or legally operate motor vehicles; in Iran, women who dare to expose their hair in public can be

Our society's definition of crime leads us to consider both the criminal act and the intention of the person committing the act. People cannot be prosecuted simply because others think they look suspicious or believe they are likely to commit crimes at some later point in time. In the recent film *Minority Report*, Tom Cruise plays a character named Anderson who is fleeing from the Precrime police because they are trying to arrest him for a crime they believe he will commit in the future.

whipped; in 2002, a Nigerian court convicted a divorced woman of bearing a child out of wedlock and sentenced her to death by stoning; her life was later spared out of concern for her child (Eboh, 2002).

Gender also figures in the theories of deviance you read about earlier in the chapter. Robert Merton's strain theory, for example, defines cultural goals in terms of financial success. Traditionally, at least, this goal has had more to do with the lives of men because women have been taught to define success in terms of relationships, particularly marriage and motherhood (Leonard, 1982). A more woman-focused theory might recognize the strain that results from the cultural ideal of equality clashing with the reality of gender-based inequality.

According to labeling theory, gender influences how we define deviance because people commonly use different standards to judge the behavior of females and males. Further, because society puts men in positions of power over women, men often escape direct responsibility for actions that victimize women. In the past, at least, men who sexually harassed or assaulted women were labeled only mildly deviant and sometimes escaped punishment entirely.

By contrast, women who are victimized may have to convince others—even members of a jury—that they were not to blame for their own sexual harassment. Research confirms an important truth: Whether people define a situation as deviance—and, if so, who the deviant is—depends on the sex of both the audience and the actors (King & Clayson, 1988).

Finally, despite its focus on social inequality, much social-conflict analysis does not address the issue of gender. If economic disadvantage is a primary cause of crime, as conflict theory suggests, why do women (whose economic position is much worse than men's) commit far *fewer* crimes than men?

Crime

Crime is the violation of criminal laws enacted by a locality, a state, or the federal government. All crimes are composed of two elements: the *act* itself (or in some cases, the failure to do what the law requires) and *criminal intent* (in legal terminology, *mens rea,* or "guilty mind"). Intent is a matter of degree, ranging from willful conduct to negligence. Someone who is negligent does not deliberately set out to hurt anyone but acts (or fails to act) in a way that results in harm. Prosecutors weigh the degree of intent in deciding whether, for example, to charge someone with first-degree murder, second-degree murder, or negligent manslaughter. Alternatively, they may consider a killing justifiable, as in self-defense.

TYPES OF CRIME

In the United States, the Federal Bureau of Investigation gathers information on criminal offenses and regularly reports the results in a publication called *Crime in the United States.* Two major types of crime make up the FBI "crime index."

The Risk of Violent Crime across the United States

This map shows the risk of becoming a victim of violent crime. In general, the risk is highest in low-income, rural counties that have a large population of men between the ages of fifteen and twenty-four. After reading through this section of the text, see whether you can explain this pattern.

Source: *American Demographics* magazine, December 2000 issue. Copyright © 2004 by Crain Communications, Inc.

Risk of Violent Crime
- Above average
- Average
- Below average

Crimes against the person, also called *violent crimes,* are *crimes that direct violence or the threat of violence against others.* Violent crimes include murder and manslaughter (legally defined as "the willful killing of one human being by another"), aggravated assault ("an unlawful attack by one person upon another for the purpose of inflicting severe or aggravated bodily injury"), forcible rape ("the carnal knowledge of a female forcibly and against her will"), and robbery ("taking or attempting to take anything of value from the care, custody, or control of a person or persons by force or threat of force or violence and/or putting the victim in fear"). National Map 9–1 shows the risk of violent crime in counties all across the United States.

Find a report on the violent victimization of college students at http://www.ojp.usdoj.gov/bjs/pub/pdf/vvcs02.pdf

Crimes against property, also called *property crimes,* are *crimes that involve theft of property belonging to others.* Property crimes include burglary ("the unlawful entry of a structure to commit a [serious crime] or a theft"), larceny-theft ("the unlawful taking, carrying, leading, or riding away of property from the possession of another"), auto theft ("the theft or attempted theft of a motor vehicle"), and arson ("any willful or malicious burning or attempt to burn the personal property of another").

A third category of offenses, not included in major crime indexes, is **victimless crimes,** *violations of law in which there are no obvious victims.* Also called *crimes without complaint,* they include illegal drug use, prostitution, and gambling. The term *victimless crime* is misleading, however. How victimless is a crime when young people have to steal to support a drug habit? What about a young pregnant woman who, by smoking crack, permanently harms her baby? Perhaps it is more correct to say that people who commit such crimes are both offenders and victims.

Because public views of victimless crimes vary greatly, laws differ from place to place. In the United States, although gambling and prostitution are legal in very limited areas, both activities are common across the country.

CRIMINAL STATISTICS

Statistics gathered by the Federal Bureau of Investigation show crime rates rising from 1960 to 1990 then declining through 2003. Even so, police count nearly 12 million serious crimes each year. Figure 9–2 on page 238 shows the trends for various serious crimes.

Always read crime statistics with caution, because they include only crimes known to the police. Almost all homicides are reported, but assaults—especially among people who know one another—often are not. Police records include an even smaller share of property crimes, especially when the losses are small.

Researchers check official crime statistics using *victimization surveys,* in which they ask a representative sample of people if they have had any experience with crime. According to such surveys, the crime rate is about three times higher than official reports indicate (Russell, 1995b).

THE STREET CRIMINAL: A PROFILE

Using government crime reports, we can present a general description of the categories of people most likely to be arrested for violent and property crimes.

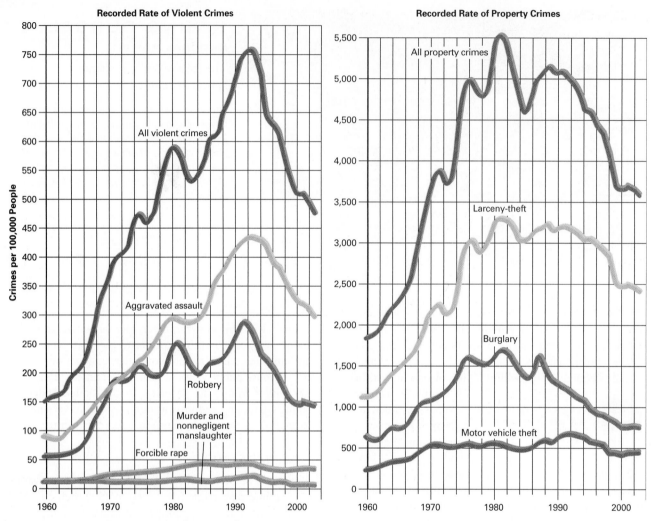

FIGURE 9-2   Crime Rates in the United States, 1960–2003

The graphs represent crime rates for various violent crimes and property crimes during recent decades.
Since about 1990, the trend has been toward lower crime rates.

Source: Federal Bureau of Investigation (2004).

Age

Official crime rates rise sharply during adolescence, peak in the late teens, and then fall as people get older. People between the ages of fifteen and twenty-four represent just 14 percent of the U.S. population, but in 2003 they accounted for 39.3 percent of all arrests for violent crimes and 46.8 percent of arrests for property crimes.

Gender

Although each sex makes up roughly half the population, police collared males in 69.2 percent of all property crime

arrests in 2003; the other 30.8 percent of arrests involved women. In other words, men are arrested more than twice as often as women for property crimes. In the case of violent crimes, the difference is even greater, with 82.2 percent of arrests involving males and just 17.8 percent females (almost a five-to-one ratio).

It may be that law enforcement officials are reluctant to define women as criminals. In global perspective, in fact, the greatest gender difference in crime rates occurs in societies that most severely limit the opportunities of women. In the United States, however, the difference in arrest rates for women and men is narrowing, which probably indicates increasing sexual equality in our society. Between 1994 and 2003, there was a 12.3 percent *increase* in arrests of women and a 6.7 percent *drop* in arrests of men (Federal Bureau of Investigation, 2004).

Social Class

The FBI does not assess the social class of arrested persons, so no statistical data of the kind given for age and gender are available. But research has long indicated that street crime is more widespread among people of lower social position (Thornberry & Farnsworth, 1982; Wolfgang, Thornberry, & Figlio, 1987).

Yet the link between class and crime is more complicated than it appears on the surface. For one thing, many people look on the poor as less worthy than the rich, whose wealth and power confer "respectability" (Tittle, Villemez, & Smith, 1978; Elias, 1986). Although crime—especially violent crime—is a serious problem in the poorest inner-city communities, most of these crimes are committed by a few hardcore offenders. The majority of the people who live in poor communities have no criminal record at all (Wolfgang, Figlio, & Sellin, 1972; Elliott & Ageton, 1980; Harries, 1990).

The connection between social standing and criminality also depends on the type of crime. If we expand our definition of crime beyond street offenses to include white-collar crime and corporate crime, the "common criminal" suddenly looks much more affluent and may live in a $100-million home.

Race and Ethnicity

Both race and ethnicity are strongly linked to crime rates, although the reasons are many and complex. Official statistics show that 70.6 percent of arrests for index crimes in 2003 involved white people. However, the African American arrest rate was higher than the rate for whites in proportion to their representation in the general population. African Americans represent 12.3 percent of the population but 29.1 percent of arrests for property crimes (versus 68.2 percent of arrests for whites) and 37.2 percent of arrests for violent crimes (versus 60.5 percent of arrests for whites) (Federal Bureau of Investigation, 2004).

There are several reasons for the disproportionate number of arrests among African Americans. First, race in the United States closely relates to social standing, which, as we have already explained, affects the likelihood of engaging in street crimes. Many poor people living in the midst of wealth come to perceive society as unjust and therefore are more likely to turn to crime to get their share (Blau & Blau, 1982; E. Anderson, 1994; Martinez, 1996).

Second, black and white family patterns differ: Two-thirds of non-Hispanic black children (compared to one-fourth of

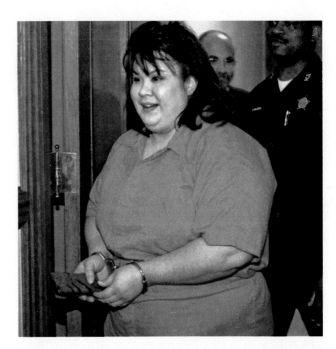

Violent crime is much more likely to involve offenders who are males than females. Of more than 800 people executed for serious crimes since 1977, only ten have been women. Here, Christina Riggs, the only woman on death row in Arkansas, leaves a courtroom in Pulaski County. Why, in your opinion, are men much more likely to be involved in serious, violent crime?

non-Hispanic white children) are born to single mothers. Single parenting carries two risks: Children receive less supervision and experience a greater risk of poverty. With one-third of African American children growing up in poor families (compared to one in seven white children), no one should be surprised at the proportionately higher crime rates for African Americans (Courtwright, 1996; Jacobs & Helms, 1996; U.S. Census Bureau, 2005).

Third, prejudice prompts white police to arrest black people more readily and leads citizens to report African Americans more willingly, so people of color are overly criminalized (Chiricos, McEntire, & Gertz, 2001; Quillian & Pager, 2001; Demuth & Steffensmeier, 2004).

Fourth, remember that the official crime index does not include arrests for offenses ranging from drunk driving to white-collar violations. This omission contributes to the view of the typical criminal as a person of color. If we broaden our definition of crime to include drunk driving, business fraud, embezzlement, stock swindles, and cheating on income tax returns, the proportion of white criminals rises dramatically.

Keep in mind, too, that categories of people with high arrest rates are also at higher risk for being victims of crime.

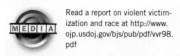

In the United States, for example, African Americans are almost six times as likely to die as a result of homicide as white people (Murphy, 2000; Rogers et al., 2001).

Finally, some categories of the population have unusually low rates of arrest. People of Asian descent, who account for about 4 percent of the population, figure in only 1.2 percent of all arrests. As Chapter 14 ("Race and Ethnicity") explains, Asian Americans enjoy higher-than-average educational achievement and income. Also, Asian American culture emphasizes family solidarity and discipline, both of which keep criminality down.

CRIME IN GLOBAL PERSPECTIVE

By world standards, the crime rate in the United States is high. Although recent crime trends are downward, there were 16,503 murders in the United States in 2003, which amounts to one every half hour around the clock. In large U.S. cities such as New York, rarely does a day pass without someone being killed.

The rate of violent crime (but not property crime) in the United States is several times higher than in Europe. The contrast is even greater between our country and the nations of Asia, including India and Japan, where rates of violent and property crime are among the lowest in the world.

Elliott Currie (1985) suggests that crime stems from our culture's emphasis on individual economic success, frequently at the expense of strong families and neighborhoods. The United States also has extraordinary cultural diversity, a result of centuries of immigration. In addition, economic inequality is higher in this country than in most other high-income nations. Thus our society's relatively weak social fabric, combined with considerable frustration among the poor, generates widespread criminal behavior.

Another factor contributing to violence in the United States is extensive private ownership of guns. About two-thirds of murder victims in the United States die from shootings. Since the early 1990s, the number of shooting deaths in Texas and several other southern states has exceeded the number of automobile-related fatalities. The U.S. rate of handgun deaths is about seven times higher than the rate in Canada, a country that strictly limits handgun ownership.

Surveys suggest that almost half of U.S. households own at least one gun. In fact, there are more guns than adults in this country, and one-third of these weapons are handguns of the type commonly used in violent crime. In large part, gun ownership reflects people's fear of crime, yet the easy availability of guns in this country also makes crime more deadly (J. Wright, 1995; NORC, 2003).

But as critics of gun control point out, waiting periods and background checks at retail gun stores do not keep guns out of the hands of criminals, who almost always obtain guns illegally (J. Wright, 1995). And gun control is not a magic bullet in the war on crime. Elliott Currie (1985) notes, for example, that the number of Californians killed each year by knives exceeds the number of Canadians killed by weapons of all kinds. However, most experts do think that stricter gun control would lower the level of deadly violence.

December 24–25, traveling through Peru. In Lima, Peru's capital city, the concern with crime is obvious. Almost every house is fortified with gates, barbed wire, or broken glass embedded in cement at the top of a wall. Private security forces are everywhere in the rich areas along the coast, where we find the embassies, expensive hotels, and the international airport.

The picture is very different as we pass through small villages high in the Andes to the east. The same families have lived in these communities for generations, and people know one another. No gates and fences here. And we've seen only one police car all afternoon.

Crime rates are high in some of the largest cities of the world, including Manila in the Philippines and São Paulo, Brazil, which have rapid population growth and millions of desperately poor people. Outside of big cities, however, the traditional character of low-income societies and their strong families allow local communities to control crime informally.

Some types of crime have always been multinational, such as terrorism, espionage, and arms dealing (Martin & Romano, 1992). But today, the globalization we are experiencing on many fronts also extends to crime. A recent case in point is the illegal drug trade. In part, the problem of illegal drugs in the United States is a *demand* issue. That is, the demand for cocaine and other drugs in this country is high, and many young people risk arrest or even a violent death for a chance to get rich in the drug trade. But the *supply* side of the issue is just as important. At least 20 percent of the citizens of the South American nation of Colombia depend on cocaine production for their livelihood. Not only is cocaine Colombia's most profitable export, but it outsells all other exports—including coffee—combined. Clearly, drug dealing and many other crimes are closely related to social and economic conditions both in the United States and elsewhere.

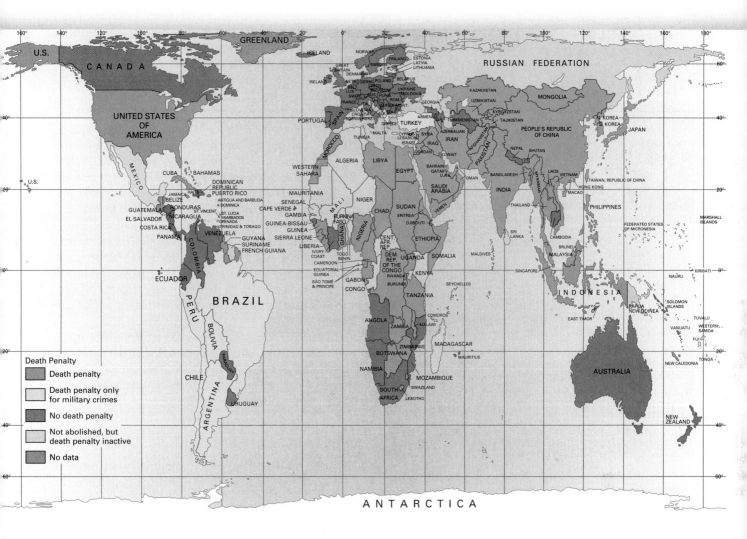

WINDOW ON THE WORLD

GLOBAL MAP 9–1 Capital Punishment in Global Perspective

The map identifies seventy-six countries and territories in which the law allows the death penalty for ordinary crimes; in eleven more, the death penalty is reserved for exceptional crimes under military law or during times of war. The death penalty does not exist in eighty-five countries and territories; in twenty-four more, although the death penalty remains in law, no execution has taken place in more than ten years. Compare rich and poor nations: What general pattern do you see? In what way are the United States and Japan exceptions to this pattern?

Source: Amnesty International (2005a).

Different countries have different strategies for dealing with crime. The use of the death penalty provides a case in point. According to Amnesty International (2005b), four nations (China, Iran, Vietnam, and the United States) account for 97 percent of the world's executions carried out by governments. Global Map 9–1 shows which countries currently use capital punishment. The global trend is toward abolishing the death penalty: Amnesty International (2005b) reports that since 1985, more than fifty nations have ended this practice.

Police must be allowed discretion if they are to handle effectively the many different situations they face every day. At the same time, it is important that the police treat people fairly. Here we see a police officer deciding whether or not to charge a young woman for driving while intoxicated. What factors do you think enter into this decision?

The U.S. Criminal Justice System

The criminal justice system is a society's formal system of social control. We shall briefly introduce the key elements of

the U.S. criminal justice system: police, the courts, and the system of punishment and corrections. First, however, we must understand an important principle that underlies the entire system, the idea of due process.

DUE PROCESS

Due process is a simple but very important idea: The criminal justice system must operate within the bounds of law. This principle is grounded in the first ten amendments

to the U.S. Constitution—known as the Bill of Rights—adopted by Congress in 1791. The Constitution offers various protections to any person charged with a crime, including the right to counsel, the right to refuse to testify against yourself, the right to confront all accusers, freedom from being tried twice for the same crime, and freedom from being "deprived of life, liberty, or property without due process of law." Furthermore, the Constitution gives all people the right to a speedy and public trial, with a jury if desired, and freedom from excessive bail as well as "cruel and unusual" punishments.

 To read the Bill of Rights, go to http://www.archives.gov/national_archives_experience/charters/bill_of_rights.html

In general terms, the concept of due process means that anyone charged with a crime must receive (1) fair notice of the proceedings, (2) a hearing on the charges conducted according to law and with the ability to present a defense, and (3) a judge or jury that weighs evidence impartially (Inciardi, 2000).

Due process limits the power of government, with an eye toward this nation's cultural support of individual rights and freedoms. Of course, deciding exactly how far government can go is an ongoing process that makes up much of the work of the judicial system, especially the U.S. Supreme Court.

POLICE

The police serve as the primary point of contact between the criminal justice system and a society's population. In principle, the police maintain public order by enforcing the law. Of course, there is only so much that the 663,796 full-time police officers in the United States can do to monitor the activities of 300 million people. As a result, the police exercise considerable discretion about which situations warrant their attention and how to handle them.

How do police carry out their duties? In a study of police behavior in five cities, Douglas Smith and Christy Visher (1981; Smith, 1987) concluded that because they must act swiftly, police officers quickly size up situations in terms of six factors. First, the more serious they think the situation is, the more likely they are to make an arrest. Second, officers take account of the victim's wishes in deciding whether or not to make an arrest. Third, the odds of arrest go up the more uncooperative a suspect is. Fourth, officers are more likely to take into custody someone they have arrested before, presumably because this suggests guilt. Fifth, the presence of observers increases the chances of arrest. According to Smith and Visher, the presence of observers prompts police to take stronger control of a situation, if only to move the encounter from the street (the suspect's turf) to the police department (where law officers have the

To increase the power of punishment to deter crime, capital punishment was long carried out in public. Here is a photograph from the last public execution in the United States, with twenty-two-year-old Rainey Bethea standing on the scaffold moments from death in Owensboro, Kentucky, on August 16, 1937. Children as well as adults were in the crowd. Now that the mass media report the story of executions across the country, states carry out capital punishment behind closed doors.

edge). Sixth, all else being equal, police officers are more likely to arrest people of color than whites, perceiving suspects of African or Latino descent as either more dangerous or more likely to be guilty.

COURTS

After arrest, a court determines a suspect's guilt or innocence. In principle, U.S. courts rely on an adversarial process involving attorneys—one representing the defendant and another the state—in the presence of a judge, who monitors legal procedures.

In practice, however, about 90 percent of criminal cases are resolved prior to court appearance through **plea bargaining,** *a legal negotiation in which a prosecutor reduces a charge in exchange for a defendant's guilty plea.* For example, the state may offer a defendant charged with burglary a lesser charge, perhaps possession of burglary tools, in exchange for a guilty plea.

Plea bargaining is widespread because it spares the system the time and expense of trials. A trial is usually unnecessary if there is little disagreement over the facts of the case. In addition, because the number of cases entering the system annually has doubled over the past decade, prosecutors could not bring every case to trial even if they wanted to. By quickly resolving most of their work, the courts channel their resources into the most important cases.

But plea bargaining pressures defendants (who are presumed innocent) to plead guilty. A person can exercise the right to a trial, but only at the risk of receiving a more severe sentence if found guilty. Furthermore, low-income defendants enter the process with the guidance of a public defender—typically an overworked and underpaid attorney who may devote little time to even the most serious cases (Novak, 1999). Plea bargaining may be efficient, but it undercuts both the adversarial process and the rights of defendants.

PUNISHMENT

When a young man is shot dead on the street after leaving a restaurant, some people may wonder why it happened, but almost everyone believes that someone should have to "pay" for the crime. Sometimes the desire to punish is so great that in the end, justice may not be done.

Why should a society punish wrongdoers? Scholars answer with four basic reasons: retribution, deterrence, rehabilitation, and societal protection.

Retribution

The oldest justification for punishment is to satisfy people's need for **retribution,** *an act of moral vengeance by which society makes the offender suffer as much as the suffering caused by the crime.* Retribution rests on a view of society as a moral balance. When criminality upsets this balance,

November 8, 2004

Despite Drop in Crime, an Increase in Inmates

By FOX BUTTERFIELD

The number of inmates in state and federal prisons rose 2.1 percent last year, even as violent crime and property crime fell, according to a study by the Justice Department released yesterday.

The continuing increase in the prison population, despite a drop or leveling off in the crime rate in the past few years, is a result of laws passed in the 1990s that led to more prison sentences and longer terms, said Allen J. Beck, chief of corrections statistics for the department's Bureau of Justice Statistics and an author of the report.

At the end of 2003, there were 1,470,045 men and women in state and federal prisons in the United States, the report found. In addition, counting those inmates in city and county jails and incarcerated juvenile offenders, the total number of Americans behind bars was 2,212,475 on Dec. 31 last year, the report said.

The report estimated that 44 percent of state and federal prisoners in 2003 were black, compared with 35 percent who were white, 19 percent who were Hispanic and 2 percent who were of other races. The numbers have changed little in the last decade.

Statistically, the number of women in prison is growing fast, rising 3.6 percent in 2003. But at a total of 101,179, they are just 6.9 percent of the prison population.

Alfred Blumstein, a criminologist at Carnegie Mellon University, said one of the most striking findings in the report was that almost 10 percent of all American black men ages 25 to 29 were in prison.

Such a high proportion of young black men behind bars not only has a strong impact on black families, Professor Blumstein said, but "in many ways is self-defeating." The criminal justice system is built on deterrence, with being sent to prison supposedly a stigma, he said. "But it's tough to convey a sense of stigma when so many of your friends and neighbors are similarly stigmatized."

In seeking to explain the paradox of a falling crime rate but a rising prison population, Mr. Beck pointed out that FBI statistics showed that from 1994 to 2003 there was a 16 percent drop in arrests for violent crime, including a 36 percent decrease in arrests for murder and a 25 percent decrease in arrests for robbery.

But the tough new sentencing laws led to a growth in inmates being sent to prison, from 522,000 in 1995 to 615,400 in 2002, the report said.

---

punishment in equal measure restores the moral order, as suggested in the ancient saying, "an eye for an eye, a tooth for a tooth."

In the Middle Ages, most people viewed crime as sin—an offense against God as well as society—that required a harsh response. Today, although critics point out that retribution does little to reform the offender, many people consider vengeance reason enough for punishment.

Deterrence

A second justification for punishment is **deterrence,** *the attempt to discourage criminality through the use of punishment.* Deterrence is based on the eighteenth-century Enlightenment idea that humans, as calculating and rational creatures, will not break the law if they think that the pain of punishment will outweigh the pleasure of the crime.

Deterrence emerged as a reform measure in response to the harsh punishments based on retribution. Why put someone to death for stealing if theft can be discouraged with a prison sentence? As the concept of deterrence gained acceptance in industrial societies, the execution and physical mutilation of criminals in most high-income societies were replaced by milder forms of punishment such as imprisonment.

Punishment can deter crime in two ways. *Specific deterrence* is used to convince an individual offender that crime does not pay. Through *general deterrence,* the punishment of one person serves as an example to others.

Rehabilitation

The third justification for punishment is **rehabilitation,** *a program for reforming the offender to prevent later offenses.* Rehabilitation arose along with the social sciences

Similarly, the report found that the average time served by prison inmates rose from 23 months in 1995 to 30 months in 2001.

Among the new measures were mandatory minimum sentencing laws, which required inmates to serve a specified proportion of their time behind bars; truth-in-sentencing laws, which required an inmate to actually serve the time he was sentenced to; and a variety of three-strikes laws increasing the penalties for repeat offenders.

In the three states with the biggest prison systems, California, Texas and Florida, the number of newly admitted inmates grew last year, but the number of those released either fell or remained stable, Mr. Beck said.

Several states with small prison systems had particularly large increases in new inmates, led by North Dakota, up 11.4 percent, and Minnesota, up 10.3 percent.

New York had a 2.8 percent decrease in new inmates, reflecting the continued sharp fall in crime in New York City, Mr. Beck said.

Overall, Mr. Beck said, the prison population is aging. Traditionally the great majority of inmates are men in their 20s and early 30s, but middle-aged inmates, those 40 to 54, account for about half of the increase in the prison population since 1995, he said.

This is a result both of the aging of the general American population and of the longer sentences, Mr. Beck said.

But the number of elderly inmates is still small, despite longer sentences and more life sentences. Those inmates 65 and older were still only 1 percent of the prison population in 2003.

WHAT DO YOU THINK?

1. Why do you think about 10 percent of young African American men are in prison?

2. Do you favor longer sentences as a way to discourage crime? Why or why not?

3. Why do you think the share of prisoners who are women is increasing?

Adapted from the original article by Fox Butterfield published in *The New York Times* on November 8, 2004. Copyright © 2004 by The New York Times Company. Reprinted with permission.

in the nineteenth century. Since then, sociologists have claimed that crime and other deviance spring from a social environment marked by poverty or a lack of parental supervision. Logically, then, if offenders learn to be deviant, they can also learn to obey the rules; the key is controlling their environment. *Reformatories* or *houses of correction* provided controlled settings where people could learn proper behavior (recall the description of total institutions in Chapter 5, "Socialization").

Like deterrence, rehabilitation motivates the offender to conform. In contrast to deterrence and retribution, which simply make the offender suffer, rehabilitation encourages constructive improvement. Unlike retribution, which demands that the punishment fit the crime, rehabilitation tailors treatment to each offender. Thus identical crimes would prompt similar acts of retribution but different rehabilitation programs.

Societal Protection

A final justification for punishment is **societal protection,** *rendering an offender incapable of further offenses temporarily through imprisonment or permanently by execution.* Like deterrence, societal protection is a rational approach to punishment intended to protect society from crime.

Currently, about 2.2 million people are jailed in the United States. As "In the *Times*" explains, the crime rate has gone down in recent years, but the number of offenders locked up across the country has gone up, tripling since 1980. This rise in the prison population reflects both tougher public attitudes toward crime and punishing offenders and an increasing number of drug-related arrests. As a result, the United States now incarcerates a larger share of its population than any other country in the world (U.S. Bureau of Justice Statistics, 2004; Sentencing Project, 2005).

SUMMING UP

Four Justifications for Punishment

Retribution	The oldest justification for punishment.
	Punishment is society's revenge for a moral wrong.
	In principle, punishment should be equal in severity to the deviance itself.
Deterrence	An early modern approach.
	Deviance is considered social disruption which society acts to control.
	People are viewed as rational and self-interested; deterrence works because the pain of punishment outweighs the pleasure of deviance.
Rehabilitation	A modern strategy linked to the development of social sciences.
	Deviance is viewed as the result of social problems (such as poverty) or personal problems (such as mental illness).
	Social conditions are improved; treatment is tailored to the offender's condition.
Societal protection	A modern approach easier to carry out than rehabilitation.
	If society is unable or unwilling to rehabilitate offenders or reform social conditions, people are protected by the imprisonment or execution of the offender.

YOUR TURN

Which of the four reasons for punishment do you think is most important in U.S. society? Why?

Critical review   The Summing Up table reviews the four justifications for punishment. However, an accurate assessment of the consequences of punishment is no simple task.

The value of retribution lies in Durkheim's claim that punishing the deviant person increases society's moral awareness. For this reason, punishment was traditionally a public event. Although the last public execution in the United States took place in Kentucky nearly seventy years ago, today's mass media ensure public awareness of executions carried out inside prison walls (Kittrie, 1971).

Does punishment deter crime? Despite our extensive use of punishment, our society has a high rate of **criminal recidivism,** *later offenses committed by people previously convicted of crimes.* About three-fourths of prisoners in state penitentiaries have been jailed before, and about half will be back in prison within a few years after release (Petersilia, 1997; DeFina & Arvanites, 2002). So does punishment really deter crime? Only about one-third of all crimes are known to police, and of these, only about one in five results in an arrest. The old saying "Crime doesn't pay" rings hollow when we realize that most offenses go unpunished.

General deterrence is even more difficult to investigate scientifically, since we have no way of knowing how people might act if they were unaware of the punishments handed down to others. Opponents of capital punishment point to research suggesting that the death penalty has limited value as a general deterrent and note that the United States is the only Western high-income nation that routinely executes serious offenders. Half of the 3,374 prisoners currently on death row are in just five states: California, Texas, Florida, Pennsylvania, and Ohio.

It is also true that some death sentences have been pronounced against innocent people. Between 1973 and 2003, almost 100 people were released from death row after new evidence established their innocence. How many did not get that chance? Before leaving office in January 2003, Illinois Governor George Ryan claimed that his state's judicial system was seriously flawed and commuted the sentences for all 167 of the state's death row inmates to life in prison (S. Levine, 2003). In 2005, the U.S. Supreme Court struck a blow against capital punishment, ruling that offenders who were younger than eighteen when they committed their crimes cannot be put to death.

Despite growing controversy over the death penalty, a majority of U.S. adults (63 percent) say they support capital punishment for people convicted of murder (NORC, 2003:121). Among first-year college students, support for the death penalty rose between 1970 and 1990 but has declined since then (Astin et al., 2002; Sax et al., 2004).

Prisons provide short-term societal protection by keeping offenders off the streets, but they do little to reshape attitudes or behavior in the long term (Carlson, 1976; R. A. Wright, 1994). Perhaps we should not expect prisons to rehabilitate inmates because, according to Sutherland's theory of differential association, locking up criminals together for years probably strengthens criminal attitudes and skills. Incarceration also stigmatizes prisoners, making jobs hard to find later on (Pager, 2003). In addition, prison breaks the social ties inmates may have in the outside world, which, following Hirschi's control theory, leaves these individuals more likely to commit new crimes upon release.

COMMUNITY-BASED CORRECTIONS

Prisons keep convicted criminals off the streets. But the evidence suggests that they do little to rehabilitate most offenders. Furthermore, prisons are expensive, costing approximately $25,000 per year to support each inmate, in addition to the initial costs of building the facilities.

One alternative to the traditional prison that has been adopted by cities and states across the country is **community-based corrections,** *correctional programs operating within society at large rather than behind prison walls.* Community-based corrections have three main advantages: They reduce costs, reduce overcrowding in prisons, and allow for supervision of convicts while eliminating the hardships of prison life and the stigma that accompanies being imprisoned.

In general, the idea of community-based corrections is not so much to punish as to reform; such programs, therefore, are usually offered to those who have committed less serious offenses and appear to be good prospects for avoiding future criminal violations (Inciardi, 2000).

Probation

One form of community-based corrections is *probation,* a policy permitting a convicted offender to remain in the community under conditions imposed by a court, including regular supervision. Courts may require that a probationer receive counseling, attend a drug treatment program, hold a job, avoid associating with "known criminals," or anything else deemed appropriate. Typically, a probationer must check in with an officer of the court (the *probation officer*) on a regular schedule to make sure the guidelines are being followed. Should the probationer fail to live up to the conditions set by the court or commit a new offense, the court may revoke probation in favor of imprisonment.

Shock Probation

A related strategy is *shock probation,* a policy by which a judge orders a convicted offender to prison for a short time

but then suspends the remainder of the sentence in favor of probation. Shock probation is thus a mix of prison and probation, used to impress on the offender the seriousness of the situation without resorting to full-scale imprisonment. In some cases, shock probation takes place in a special "boot camp" facility where offenders might spend one to three months in a military-style setting intended to teach discipline and respect for authority (Cole & Smith, 2002).

Parole

Parole is a policy of releasing inmates from prison to serve the remainder of their sentences in the local community under the supervision of a parole officer. Although some sentences specifically deny the possibility of parole, most inmates become eligible for parole after serving a certain portion of their sentences. At that time, a parole board evaluates the risks and benefits of the inmate's early release from prison. If parole is granted, the parole board monitors the offender's conduct until the sentence is completed. Should the offender not comply with the conditions of parole or be arrested for another crime, the board can revoke parole and return the offender to prison to complete the sentence.

Critical review Evaluations of probation and parole are mixed. There is little question that these programs are much less expensive than conventional imprisonment; they also free up room in prisons for individuals who commit more serious crimes. Yet research suggests that although probation and shock probation do seem to work for some people, they do not significantly reduce recidivism. Parole is also useful to prison officials as a means to encourage good behavior among inmates. But levels of crime among those released on parole are so high that a number of states have ended their parole programs entirely (Inciardi, 2000).

Such evaluations point to a sobering truth: The criminal justice system cannot eliminate crime. As the Applying Sociology box on page 248 explains, although police, courts, and prisons do affect crime rates, crime and other forms of deviance are not just the acts of "bad people" but reflect the operation of society itself.

↔ **YOUR TURN** ←

Would Emile Durkheim be surprised that the criminal justice system cannot eliminate crime? What about Karl Marx? Explain your answers.

Violent Crime Is Down—but Why?

During the 1980s, crime rates shot upward. Just about everyone lived in fear of violent crime, and in many larger cities, the numbers killed and wounded made whole neighborhoods seem like war zones. There seemed to be no solution to the problem.

In the 1990s, something good and unexpected happened: Serious crime rates began to fall until, by 2000, they were at levels not seen in more than a generation. Why? Researchers point to several reasons:

1. **A reduction in the youth population.** We have already noted that young people (particularly males) are responsible for much violent crime. Between 1990 and 2000, the population aged fifteen to twenty-four dropped by 5 percent (in part because of the legalization of abortion in 1973).

2. **Changes in policing.** Much of the drop in crime (as well as the earlier rise in crime) has taken place in large cities. New York City, where the number of murders fell from 2,245 in 1990 to just 597 in 2003, has adopted a policy of *community policing,* which means that police are concerned not just about making arrests but about preventing crime before it happens. Officers get to know the areas they patrol and stop young men for jaywalking or other minor infractions so they can check them for concealed weapons (the word has gotten around that you can be arrested for carrying a gun). There are also *more* police at work in large cities. Los Angeles added more than 2,000

police officers in the 1990s, which contributed to its drop in violent crime during that period.

3. **More prisoners.** From 1985 to 2005, the number of inmates in U.S. jails and prisons soared from 750,000 to more than 2 million. The main reason for this increase is tough laws that demand prison time for many crimes, especially drug offenses. As one analyst put it, "When you lock up an extra million people, it's got to have some effect on the crime rate" (Franklin Zimring, in Witkin, 1998:31).

4. **A better economy.** The U.S. economy boomed during the 1990s. With unemployment down, more people were working, reducing the likelihood that some would turn to crime out of economic desperation. The logic here is simple: More jobs equals fewer crimes. By the same token, the economic downturn of the early 2000s slowed the downward crime trend.

5. **The declining drug trade.** Many analysts agree that the most important

factor in reducing rates of violent crime was the decline of crack cocaine. Crack came on the scene about 1985, and violence spread as young people—especially in the inner cities and increasingly armed with guns—became part of a booming drug trade. Facing few legitimate job opportunities but with increasing opportunity to make money illegally, a generation of young people became part of a wave of violence. By the early 1990s, however, the popularity of crack began to fall as people saw the damage it was causing to entire communities. This realization, coupled with steady economic improvement and stiffer sentences for drug offenses, helped bring about the turnaround in violent crime.

The current picture looks better relative to what it was a decade ago. But one researcher cautions, "It looks better . . . only because the early 1990s were so bad. So let's not fool ourselves into thinking everything is resolved. It's not."

One reason that crime has gone down is that there are more than 2 million people incarcerated in this country. This has caused severe overcrowding of facilities such as this Maricopa County, Arizona, prison.

WHAT DO YOU THINK?

1. Do you support the policy of community policing? Why or why not?
2. What do you see as the pros and cons of building more prisons?
3. Of all the factors mentioned here, which do you think is the most important in crime control? Which is least important? Why?

Sources: Fagan, Zimring, & Kim (1998), Witkin (1998), Winship & Berrien (1999), Donahue & Leavitt (2000), and R. Rosenfeld (2002).

The following learning tools will help you see what you know, identify what you still need to learn, and expand your understanding beyond the text. You can also visit this text's Companion Website™ at http://www.prenhall.com/macionis to find additional practice tests.

KEY POINTS

What Is Deviance?

Deviance refers to norm violations ranging from bad manners to serious violence. Research suggests that biological factors, in combination with environmental factors, provide a limited explanation of crime. Psychological studies link deviance to abnormal personality resulting from either biological or environmental causes. Psychological theories help explain some types of deviance.

The root of deviance lies in society rather than individuals, because deviance varies according to cultural norms, is socially defined, and reflects patterns of social power.

The Functions of Deviance: Structural-Functional Analysis

Taking the structural-functional approach, Durkheim explained that deviance affirms norms and values, clarifies moral boundaries, brings people together, and encourages social change. Merton's strain theory explains deviance in terms of a society's cultural goals and the means available to achieve them.

Labeling Deviance: Symbolic-Interaction Analysis

The symbolic-interaction approach is the basis of labeling theory, which holds that deviance lies in people's reaction to someone's behavior, not in the behavior itself. Acquiring a stigma of deviance can lead to secondary deviance and a deviant career.

The medicalization of deviance is the transformation of moral and legal deviance into a medical condition. In practice, this means a change from thinking about deviance as "good" or "bad" to thinking in terms of people being "sick" or "well."

Sutherland's differential association theory links deviance to how much others encourage or discourage such behavior. Hirschi's control theory states that people who are well integrated into society are less likely to engage in deviant behavior.

Deviance and Inequality: Social-Conflict Analysis

Based on Karl Marx's ideas, social-conflict theory holds that laws and other norms reflect the interests of powerful members of society. Although white-collar and corporate crimes cause extensive social harm, offenders are rarely branded as criminals.

White-collar offenses are crimes committed by people of high social position as part of their job. Such offenders often end up in civil rather than criminal court. Corporate crime refers to illegal action by a company or people acting on its behalf. Organized crime has a long history in the United States, especially among people with fewer legitimate opportunities.

Deviance, Race, and Gender

Hate crimes, which are motivated by racial or other bias, are most likely to victimize people with multiple disadvantages, such as gay men of color. In the United States and elsewhere, societies control the behavior of women more closely than that of men.

Crime

Official statistics show that arrest rates peak in late adolescence and then drop steadily with advancing age. About 70 percent of the people arrested for property crimes and 82 percent of those arrested for violent crimes are male. Poorer people commit more street crime than people with greater wealth. When white-collar and corporate crimes are included among criminal offenses, however, the socioeconomic difference in criminal activity becomes smaller. More whites than African Americans are arrested for street crimes. However, African Americans are arrested more often than whites in proportion to their respective numbers in the population. Asian Americans have lower-than-average rates of arrest.

The U.S. Criminal Justice System

The idea of due process, which is based in the U.S. Constitution's Bill of Rights, guides the operation of the criminal justice system. Police use a great deal of personal judgment in their work. Arrest is more likely if the offense is serious, bystanders are present, or the accused is African American or Hispanic.

Although it is set up as an adversarial system, U.S. courts resolve most cases through plea bargaining. Though efficient, this method puts less powerful people at a disadvantage.

Justifications of punishment include retribution, deterrence, rehabilitation, and societal protection. Because its consequences are difficult to evaluate scientifically, punishment—like deviance itself—sparks controversy.

Community-based corrections include probation and parole. Such policies lower the cost of supervising people convicted of crimes and reduce prison overcrowding but have not been shown to reduce recidivism.

KEY CONCEPTS

deviance (p. 222) the recognized violation of cultural norms

crime (p. 222) the violation of a society's formally enacted criminal law

social control (p. 222) attempts by society to regulate people's thoughts and behavior

criminal justice system (p. 222) a formal response by police, courts, and prison officials to alleged violations of the law

labeling theory (p. 228) the idea that deviance and conformity result not so much from what people do as from how others respond to those actions

stigma (p. 229) a powerfully negative label that greatly changes a person's self-concept and social identity

medicalization of deviance (p. 229) the transformation of moral and legal deviance into a medical condition

white-collar crime (p. 232) crime committed by people of high social position in the course of their occupations

corporate crime (p. 233) the illegal actions of a corporation or people acting on its behalf

organized crime (p. 233) a business supplying illegal goods or services

hate crime (p. 234) a criminal act against a person or a person's property by an offender motivated by racial or other bias

crimes against the person (violent crimes) (p. 237) crimes that direct violence or the threat of violence against others

crimes against property (property crimes) (p. 237) crimes that involve theft of property belonging to others

victimless crimes (p. 237) violations of law in which there are no obvious victims

plea bargaining (p. 243) a legal negotiation in which a prosecutor reduces a charge in exchange for a defendant's guilty plea

retribution (p. 243) an act of moral vengeance by which society makes the offender suffer as much as the suffering caused by the crime

deterrence (p. 244) the attempt to discourage criminality through the use of punishment

rehabilitation (p. 244) a program for reforming the offender to prevent later offenses

societal protection (p. 245) rendering an offender incapable of further offenses temporarily through imprisonment or permanently by execution

criminal recidivism (p. 246) later offenses committed by people previously convicted of crimes

community-based corrections (p. 247) correctional programs operating within society at large rather than behind prison walls

SAMPLE TEST QUESTIONS

These questions are similar to those found in the test bank that accompanies this textbook.

Multiple-Choice Questions

1. Crime is a special type of deviance that
   a. refers to violations of law.
   b. involves punishment.
   c. refers to any violation of a society's norms.
   d. always involves a particular person as the offender.

2. Emile Durkheim explains that deviance is
   a. defined by the rich and used against the poor.
   b. harmful not just to victims but to society as a whole.
   c. often at odds with public morality.
   d. found in every society.

3. Applying Robert Merton's strain theory, a person selling illegal drugs for a living would be an example of which of the following categories?
   a. conformist
   b. innovator
   c. retreatist
   d. ritualist

4. Labeling theory states that deviance
   a. is a normal part of social life.
   b. always changes people's social identity.
   c. arises not from what people do as much as how others respond.
   d. all of the above.

5. When Jake's friends began calling him a "dope-head," he left the group and spent more time smoking marijuana. He also began hanging out with others who used drugs, and by the end of the term, he had dropped out of college. Edwin Lemert would call this situation an example of
   a. primary deviance.
   b. the development of secondary deviance.
   c. the formation of a deviant subculture.
   d. the beginning of retreatism.

6. A social-conflict approach claims that who a society calls deviant depends on
   a. who has and does not have power.
   b. a society's moral values.
   c. how often the behavior occurs.
   d. how harmful the behavior is.

7. Stealing a laptop computer from the study lounge in a college dorm is an example of which criminal offense?
   a. burglary
   b. auto theft

c. robbery

d. larceny-theft

8. The FBI's criminal statistics used in this chapter to create a profile of the street criminal reflect

a. all crimes that occur.

b. offenses known to the police.

c. offenses that involve violence.

d. offenses resulting in a criminal conviction.

9. Most people arrested for a violent crime in the United States are

a. white.

b. African American.

c. Hispanic.

d. Asian.

10. Which of the following is the oldest justification for punishing an offender?

a. deterrence

b. retribution

c. societal protection

d. rehabilitation

Answers: 1(a); 2(d); 3(b); 4(c); 5(b); 6(a); 7(d); 8(b); 9(a); 10(b).

Essay Questions

1. How does a sociological view of deviance differ from the commonsense idea that bad people do bad things?

2. A recent study (Mauer, 1999) found that one in three black men between the ages of twenty and twenty-nine is in jail, on probation, or on parole. What factors, noted in this chapter, help explain this pattern?

APPLICATIONS & EXERCISES

1. Identity theft is a new type of crime that victimizes as many as 10 million people each year in the United States. Research this phenomenon, and explain how this offense differs from property crime that takes place "on the street." (Consider differences in the crime, the offenders, and the victims.)

2. Rent a wheelchair for a day or two (check with a local pharmacy or medical supply store), and use it as much as possible. Not only will you gain a firsthand understanding of the physical barriers to getting around, but you will also discover that people respond to you in many new ways.

3. Watch an episode of the real-action police show *Cops.* Based on what you see, how would you profile the people who commit crimes?

INVESTIGATE *with* Research Navigator

Follow the instructions on page 27 of this text to access the features of **Research Navigator**™. Once at the Web site, enter your Login Name and Password. Then, to use the **ContentSelect**™ database, enter keywords such as "deviance," "crime," and "prison," and the search engine will supply relevant and recent scholarly and popular press publications. Use the *New York Times* **Search-by-Subject Archive** to find recent news articles related to sociology and the **Link Library** feature to find relevant Web links organized by the key terms associated with this chapter.

10

Social Stratification

What is social stratification?

Why does social inequality exist?

How does social stratification differ
in societies around the world?

ON APRIL 10, 1912, the ocean liner *Titanic* slipped away from the docks of Southampton, England, on its maiden voyage across the North Atlantic to New York. A proud symbol of the new industrial age, the towering ship carried 2,300 men, women, and children, some enjoying more luxury than most travelers today could imagine. Poor passengers crowded the lower decks, journeying to what they hoped would be a better life in the United States.

Two days out, the crew received radio warnings of icebergs in the area but paid little notice. Then, near midnight, as the ship steamed swiftly westward, a lookout was stunned to see a massive shape rising out of the dark ocean directly ahead. Moments later, the *Titanic* collided with a huge iceberg, as tall as the ship itself, which split open its side as if the grand vessel were a giant tin can.

Seawater flooded into the ship's lower levels. Within twenty-five minutes of impact, people were rushing for the lifeboats. By 2:00 A.M., the bow was completely submerged, and the stern rose high above the water. Minutes later, all lights went out. Clinging to the deck, quietly observed by those in lifeboats, hundreds of helpless passengers and crew solemnly passed their final minutes before the ship disappeared into the frigid Atlantic (Lord, 1976). ■

The tragic loss of more than 1,600 lives when the *Titanic* sank made news around the world. Looking back at this terrible accident with a sociological eye, we note that some categories of passengers had much better odds of survival than others. Reflecting that era's traditional ideas about gender, women and children were allowed to board the lifeboats first, with the result that 80 percent of the people who died were men. Class, too, was at work. More than 60 percent of people holding first-class tickets were saved because they were on the upper decks, where warnings were sounded first and lifeboats were accessible. Only 36 percent of the second-class passengers survived, and of the third-class passengers on the lower decks, only 24 percent escaped drowning. On board the *Titanic*, class turned out to mean much more than the quality of accommodations—it was a matter of life or death.

The fate of those aboard the *Titanic* dramatically illustrates how social inequality affects the way people live and sometimes whether they live at all. This chapter explores the important concept of social stratification. Chapter 11 continues the story by examining social inequality in the United States, and Chapter 12 takes a broader look at how our country fits into a global system of wealth and poverty.

What Is Social Stratification?

For tens of thousands of years, humans the world over lived in small hunting and gathering societies. Although members of these bands might single out one person as swifter, stronger, or more skillful in collecting food, everyone had roughly the same social standing. As societies became more complex—a process detailed in Chapter 4 ("Society")—a major change came about. Societies began to elevate specific categories of people above others, giving some parts of the population more wealth, power, and prestige than others.

Social stratification, *a system by which a society ranks categories of people in a hierarchy,* is based on four basic principles:

1. **Social stratification is a trait of society, not simply a reflection of individual differences.** Many of us think of social standing in terms of personal talent and effort, and as a result, we often exaggerate the extent to which we control our own fate. Did a higher percentage of the first-class passengers on the *Titanic* survive because they were better swimmers than

The personal experience of poverty is clear in this photograph of a homeless couple spending the night in a low-cost rooming house. The main sociological insight is that, although we feel the effects of social stratification personally, our social standing is largely the result of the way society (or a world of societies) structures opportunity and reward. To the core of our being, we are all products of social stratification.

second- and third-class passengers? Hardly. They did better because of their privileged position on the ship, which gave them first access to the lifeboats. Similarly, children born into wealthy families are more likely than children born into poverty to enjoy good health, do well in school, succeed in a career, and live a long life. Neither the rich nor the poor created social stratification, yet this system shapes the lives of us all.

2. **Social stratification carries over from generation to generation.** We have only to look at how parents pass their social position on to their children to see that stratification is a trait of societies rather than individuals.

    Some individuals, especially in high-income societies, do experience **social mobility,** *a change in position within the social hierarchy.* Social mobility may be upward or downward. We celebrate the achievements of rare individuals such as Britney Spears and Michael Jordan, both of whom rose from modest beginnings to fame and fortune. Some people move downward because of business failures, unemployment, or illness. More often, people move *horizontally;* they switch from one job to another at about the same social level.

The social standing of most people remains much the same over their lifetimes.

3. **Social stratification is universal but variable.** Social stratification is found everywhere. Yet *what* is unequal and *how* unequal it is varies from one society to another. In some societies, inequality is mostly a matter of prestige; in others, wealth or power is the key element of difference. In addition, some societies contain more inequality than others.

4. **Social stratification involves not just inequality but beliefs as well.** Any system of inequality not only gives some people more than others but also defines these arrangements as fair. Like the *what* of inequality, the explanation of *why* people should be unequal differs from society to society.

Caste and Class Systems

Sociologists distinguish between *closed systems,* which allow for little change in social position, and *open systems,* which permit much more social mobility (Tumin, 1985). The caste system is closed, and the class system is more open.

In India, the traditional caste system still guides people's choice of work, especially in rural areas. Below the four basic castes are the Harijans, people defined as "outcasts" or "untouchables." These people perform jobs, such as cleaning the streets, defined as unclean for others of higher social position.

THE CASTE SYSTEM

A **caste system** is *social stratification based on ascription, or birth*. A pure caste system is closed because birth alone determines a person's entire future, allowing little or no social mobility based on individual effort. People live out their lives in the rigid categories assigned to them, without the possibility of change for the better or worse.

An Illustration: India

Many of the world's societies, most of them agrarian, are caste systems. In India, for example, much of the population still lives in traditional villages where the caste system persists. The Indian system identifies four major castes (or *varna*, a Sanskrit word that means "color"): Brahman, Kshatriya, Vaishya, and Shudra. On the local level, each of these is composed of hundreds of subcaste groups (or *jati*).

From birth, a caste system determines the direction of a person's life. First, with the exception of farming, which is open to everyone, families in each caste perform one type of work, as priests, soldiers, barbers, leather workers, sweepers, and so on.

Second, a caste system demands that people marry others of the same ranking. If people were to have "mixed" marriages with members of other castes, what rank would their children hold? Sociologists call this pattern of marrying within a social category *endogamous* marriage (*endo* stems from the Greek, meaning "within"). According to tradition—this practice is now rare and found only in remote rural areas—Indian parents select their children's marriage partners, often before the children reach their teens.

Third, caste guides everyday life by keeping people in the company of "their own kind." Norms reinforce this practice by teaching, for example, that a "purer" person of a higher caste is "polluted" by contact with someone of lower standing.

Fourth, caste systems rest on powerful cultural beliefs. Indian culture is built on the Hindu tradition that doing the caste's life work and accepting an arranged marriage are moral duties.

Caste and Agrarian Life

Caste systems are typical of agrarian societies because agriculture demands a lifelong routine of hard work. By teaching a sense of moral duty, a caste system ensures that people are disciplined for a lifetime of work and are willing to perform the same jobs as their parents. Thus the caste system has hung on in rural areas of India more than sixty years after being formally outlawed. People living in the industrial cities of India have many more choices about work and marriage partners than people in rural areas.

YOUR TURN

Are there elements of caste in U.S. society? To what extent do parents pass on their social position to children? What about the idea that there are "women's jobs" and "men's jobs"?

Another country dominated by caste is South Africa, although the system of *apartheid*, or separation of the races, is no longer legal and is now in decline. The Thinking Globally box takes a closer look.

Race as Caste: A Report from South Africa

At the southern tip of the African continent lies South Africa, a country about the size of Alaska with a population of about 47 million. For 300 years the native Africans who lived there were ruled by white people, first by the Dutch traders and farmers who settled there in the mid-seventeenth century and then by the British, who colonized the area early in the nineteenth century. By the early 1900s, the British had taken over the entire country, naming it the Union of South Africa.

In 1961, the nation declared its independence from Britain, calling itself the Republic of South Africa, but freedom for the black majority was still decades away. To ensure their political control over the black population, whites created a policy of *apartheid*, or racial separation. Apartheid, written into law in 1948, denied blacks national citizenship, ownership of land, and any voice in the government. As a lower caste, blacks received little schooling and performed menial, low-paying jobs. White people with even average wealth had at least one black household servant.

The white minority claimed that apartheid protected their cultural traditions from the influence of people believed to be inferior beings. When blacks resisted apartheid, whites used brutal military repression to maintain their power.

Even so, steady resistance—especially from younger blacks, who demanded a political voice and economic opportunity—gradually forced change. Criticism from other industrial nations added to the pressure. By the mid-1980s, the tide began to turn as the South African government granted limited political rights to people of mixed race and Asian ancestry. Next came the right of all people to form labor unions, to enter occupations once limited to whites, and to own property. Officials also repealed laws that separated the races in public places.

The pace of change increased in 1990 with the release from prison of Nelson Mandela, who led the fight against apartheid. In 1994, the first national election open to all races made Mandela president—an event that finally ended centuries of white minority rule.

Despite this dramatic political change, social stratification in South Africa is still based on race. Even with the right to own property, one-third of black South Africans have no work, and the majority remain dirt poor. The worst off are some 7 million *ukuhleleleka*, which means "marginal people" in the Xhosa language. Soweto-by-the-Sea may sound like a summer getaway, but it is home to thousands of people who live crammed into shacks made of packing cases, corrugated metal, cardboard, and other discarded materials. There is no electricity for lights or refrigeration. Without plumbing, people use buckets to haul sewerage; women line up to take a turn at a single water tap that serves more than 1,000 people. Jobs are hard to come by, and those who do find work are lucky to earn $250 a month.

South Africa's current president, Thabo Mbeki, who was elected in 1999, leads a nation still crippled by its history of racial caste. Tourism is up and holds the promise of an economic boom in years to come, but the country can break from the past only by providing real opportunity to all its people.

WHAT DO YOU THINK?

1. How has race been a form of caste in South Africa?
2. Although apartheid is no longer law, why does racial inequality continue to shape South African society?
3. Does race operate as an element of caste in the United States? Explain your answer.

Sources: Fredrickson (1981), Wren (1991), Hawthorne (1999), and Mabry & Masland (1999).

THE CLASS SYSTEM

Because a modern economy must attract people to work in many occupations other than farming, it depends on developing people's talents in many diverse fields. This gives rise to a **class system,** *social stratification based on both birth and individual achievement.*

Class systems are more open than caste systems, so people who gain schooling and skills may experience social mobility. As a result, class distinctions become blurred, and even blood relatives may have different social standings. Categorizing people according to their color, sex, or social background comes to be seen as wrong in modern societies as all people gain political rights and, in principle, equal standing before the law. In addition, work is no longer fixed at birth but involves some personal choice. Greater individuality also translates into more freedom in selecting a marriage partner.

Meritocracy

The concept of **meritocracy** refers to *social stratification based on personal merit.* Because industrial societies need to develop a broad range of abilities (beyond farming), stratification is based not just on the accident of birth but also on *merit* (from a Latin word meaning "worthy of praise"), which includes a person's knowledge, abilities, and effort. A rough measure of merit is a person's job and how well it is done. To increase meritocracy, industrial societies expand equality of opportunity and teach people to expect inequality of rewards based on individual performance.

In a pure meritocracy, social position would depend entirely on a person's ability and effort. Such a system would have ongoing social mobility, blurring social categories as individuals continuously move up or down in the system, depending on their latest performance.

Caste societies define "merit" in terms of loyalty to the system—that is, dutifully performing whatever job comes with a person's birth. Caste systems waste human potential, but they are very orderly. A need for order is the reason industrial societies keep some elements of caste—such as letting wealth pass from generation to generation—rather than becoming complete meritocracies. A pure meritocracy would weaken families and other social groupings. After all, economic performance is not everything: Would we want to evaluate our family members solely on how successful they are in their jobs outside the home? Probably not. Class systems in industrial societies move toward meritocracy to promote productivity and efficiency but keep caste elements, such as family, to maintain order and social unity.

YOUR TURN

How much of your social position is due to merit (personal ability and effort), and how much is due to caste (passed on from your parents)?

Status Consistency

Status consistency is *the degree of consistency in a person's social standing across various dimensions of social inequality.* A caste system has limited social mobility and high status consistency, so the typical person has the same relative ranking with regard to wealth, power, and prestige. The greater mobility of class systems produces less status consistency. In the United States, for example, most college professors with advanced academic degrees enjoy high social prestige but earn only average salaries. Low status consistency means that *classes* are much harder to define than *castes.*

ASCRIPTION AND ACHIEVEMENT: THE UNITED KINGDOM

The mix of caste and meritocracy in class systems is well illustrated by the United Kingdom (Great Britain—composed of England, Wales, and Scotland—and Northern Ireland), an industrial nation with a long agrarian history.

The Estate System

In the Middle Ages, England had a castelike system of three *estates.* The *first estate* was the clergy, who were thought to speak with the authority of God. Some clergy were local priests, who lived simple lives. But the highest church officials lived in palaces and presided over an organization that owned much land (which was the major source of wealth); they also had a great deal of power to shape the political events of the day.

The *second estate* was a hereditary nobility that made up barely 5 percent of the population. The royal family—the king and queen at the top of the power structure—as well as lesser nobles (including those titled as dukes, earls, and barons) together owned most of the nation's land. Most of these men and women were wealthy and had no occupation; they thought that engaging in a trade or any other work for income was beneath them. Well tended by servants, nobles used their leisure time to develop skills in horseback riding and warfare and to cultivate refined tastes in art, music, and literature.

In U.S. society, everyone's social position results from a mix of birth and individual achievement. The Wayans brothers, stars of both television and films, were born to a family with ten children in New York and rose to become among the highest-paid people in the country. Such a story is fairly common in the entertainment business, which is relatively open to new talent. How likely would such a story be among athletes? College professors? Lawyers? Bankers?

To prevent vast landholdings from being divided by heirs when the nobles died, the law of *primogeniture* (from the Latin meaning "firstborn") demanded that all landholdings pass to the oldest son or other male relation. Younger sons had to find other means of support. Some became leaders in the church, where they would live as well as they were used to. Others became military officers or judges or took up other professions considered honorable for gentlemen. In an age when no woman could inherit her father's property and few women had the opportunity to earn a living on their own, a noble daughter depended for her security on marrying well.

Below the nobility and the clergy, the vast majority of men and women formed the *third estate,* or commoners. Most commoners were serfs working land owned by nobles or the church. Unlike members of the first or second estates, most had little schooling and were illiterate.

As the Industrial Revolution expanded England's economy, some commoners living in cities made enough money to challenge the nobility. More emphasis on meritocracy, the growing importance of money, and the expansion of schooling and legal rights eventually blurred social rankings and gave rise to a class system.

Perhaps it is a sign of the times that these days, traditional titles are put up for sale by nobles who need money. In 1996, for example, Earl Spencer—the brother of Princess Diana—sold one of his titles, Lord of Wimbledon, to raise the $300,000 he needed to redo the plumbing in one of his large homes (McKee, 1996).

The United Kingdom Today

The United Kingdom has a class system, but caste elements from England's past are still evident today. A small number of British families still holds considerable inherited wealth and enjoys the highest prestige, schooling at excellent universities, and political influence. A traditional monarch,

 London's *Sunday Times* publishes a list of the richest people in Great Britain and other countries. Find the "Rich List" at http://www.sunday-times.co.uk/richlist/

Queen Elizabeth II, is the United Kingdom's head of state, and Parliament's House of Lords is composed of "peers," about half of whom are of noble birth. However, control of government now rests in the House of Commons, where the prime minister and other leaders reach their position by achievement—winning an election—rather than by birth.

Further down in the class hierarchy, roughly one-fourth of the British people form the middle class. Many earn comfortable incomes from professions and business and are likely to have investments in the form of stocks and bonds. Below the middle class, perhaps half of all Britons think of themselves as "working-class," earning modest incomes through manual labor. The remaining one-fourth of the British people make up the lower class, the poor who lack steady work or who work full time but are paid too little to live comfortably. Most lower-class Britons live in the nation's northern and western regions, which have been plagued by the closings of mines and factories.

Today's British class system has a mix of caste elements and meritocracy, producing a highly stratified society with

Can you spot Great Britain's Prince William in this photo? He's just to the right of the center in this "wave" at a recent rugby match. Although he is part of a royal family that traces its ancestry back for a thousand years, today's more egalitarian times encourage "royals" to try to act more "common" in public.

some opportunity to move upward or downward. One result of the historical estate system is that social mobility occurs less often in the United Kingdom than it does in the United States (Kerckhoff, Campbell, & Winfield-Laird, 1985). This more rigid system of inequality in the United Kingdom is reflected in the importance attached to accent. Distinctive patterns of speech develop in any society when people are set off from one another over many generations. People in the United States treat accent as a clue to where a person lives or grew up (we can easily identify a midwestern "twang" or a southern "drawl"). In the United Kingdom, however, accent is a mark of social class, with upper-class people speaking "the King's English" but most people speaking "like commoners." So different are these two accents that the British seem to be, as the saying goes, "a single people divided by a common language."

YOUR TURN

What do the distinctive accents of poor people in rural areas or the inner cities of the United States say about their social history?

ANOTHER EXAMPLE: JAPAN

Social stratification in Japan also mixes caste and meritocracy. Japan is both the world's oldest continuously operating monarchy and a modern society where wealth follows individual achievement.

Feudal Japan

By the fifth century C.E., Japan was an agrarian society with a rigid caste system in which an imperial family ruled over nobles and commoners. The emperor ruled by divine right (meaning that he claimed that God intended him to rule), and his military leader (or *shogun*) enforced the emperor's rule with the help of regional nobles or warlords.

Below the nobility were the *samurai,* a warrior caste whose name means "to serve." This second rank of Japanese society was made up of soldiers who learned martial arts and who lived by a code of honor based on absolute loyalty to their leaders.

As in Great Britain, most people in Japan at this time in history were commoners who worked very hard to live from day to day. Unlike their European counterparts, however, Japanese commoners were not lowest in rank. At the bottom were the *burakumin,* or "outcasts," looked down on by both lord and commoner. Like the lowest caste groups in India, these outcasts lived apart from others, performed the most distasteful work, and could not change their social standing.

Modern Japan

By the 1860s (the time of the Civil War in the United States), the nobles realized that Japan's traditional caste system would prevent the country from entering the modern industrial era. Besides, as in Britain, some nobles were happy to

After the collapse of the Soviet Union in 1991, that nation began a transition toward a market economy. Since then, some people have become quite rich, but others have lost their jobs as old, inefficient factories closed. As a result, the problem of poverty has become widespread, affecting perhaps one-third of the Russian people. Scenes like this one are all too common.

have their children marry wealthy commoners who had more money than they did. As Japan opened up to the larger world, the traditional caste system weakened. In 1871, the Japanese legally banned the social category of "outcast," although today some people still look down on those whose ancestors held this rank. After Japan's defeat in World War II, the nobility lost their privileges, so only the emperor remains as a symbol of Japan's traditions, but he has little real power.

Social stratification in Japan is much different from the rigid caste system of centuries ago. Today, Japanese society consists of "upper," "upper-middle," "lower-middle," and "lower" classes. The exact lines between these classes are unclear to most Japanese, and many people do move between classes over time. But because Japanese culture tends to respect tradition, family background is never far from the surface when sizing up someone's social standing. Officially, everyone is equal before the law, but in reality, many people still look at one another through the centuries-old lens of caste.

Finally, traditional ideas about gender continue to shape Japanese society. Legally, the two sexes are equal, but men dominate women in many ways. Because Japanese parents are more likely to send sons than daughters to college, there is a significant gender gap in education. With the recent economic downturn in Japan, many more women have entered the labor force. But most working women fill lower-level support positions in the corporate world, only rarely assuming leadership roles. In short, individual achievement in Japan's modern class system operates in the shadow of centuries of traditional male privilege (Norbeck, 1983; M. Brinton, 1988; H. French, 2002).

CLASSLESS SOCIETIES? THE FORMER SOVIET UNION

Nowhere in the world do we find a society without some degree of social inequality. Yet some nations have claimed to be classless.

The Russian Revolution

The former Union of Soviet Socialist Republics (USSR), which rivaled the United States as a military superpower in the mid- to late twentieth century, was born out of a revolution in Russia in 1917. The Russian Revolution ended the feudal estate system ruled by nobles and transferred farms, factories, and other productive property from private ownership to state control.

The Russian Revolution was guided by the ideas of Karl Marx, who wrote that private ownership of productive property is the basis of social classes (see Chapter 4, "Society"). When the state took control of the economy, Soviet officials boasted that they had created the first modern, classless society.

Critics, however, pointed out that based on their jobs, the Soviet people actually were stratified into four unequal categories. At the top were high government officials, or *apparatchiks*. Next came the Soviet intelligentsia, including lower government officials, college professors, scientists, physicians, and engineers. Below them were manual workers and, at the lowest level, the rural peasantry.

In reality, the Soviet Union was not really classless at all. But putting factories, farms, colleges, and hospitals under state control did create more economic equality (although

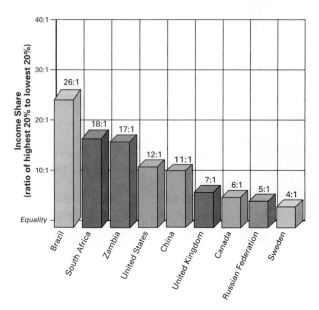

Income Share
(ratio of highest 20% to lowest 20%)

40:1

30:1

26:1

20:1

18:1 17:1

12:1 11:1

10:1

7:1 6:1 5:1 4:1

Equality

Brazil South Africa Zambia United States China United Kingdom Canada Russian Federation Sweden

FIGURE 10-1   Economic Inequality in Selected
Countries

Many low- and middle-income countries have greater economic
inequality than the United States. But this country has more
economic inequality than most high-income nations.

These data are the most recent available, representing income share for various years
between 1998 and 2003.

Sources: U.S. Census Bureau (2005) and World Bank (2005).

with sharp differences in power) than in capitalist societies
such as the United States.

The Modern Russian Federation

In 1985, Mikhail Gorbachev came to power in the Soviet
Union with a new economic program known as *perestroika*,
meaning "restructuring." Gorbachev saw that although the
Soviet system had reduced economic inequality, living standards were far behind those of other industrial nations.
Gorbachev tried to generate economic growth by reducing
the inefficient centralized control of the economy.

Gorbachev's economic reforms turned into one of the
most dramatic social movements in history. People in the
Soviet Union and in other socialist countries of Eastern Europe blamed their poverty and their lack of basic freedoms on
the repressive ruling class of Communist party officials. Beginning in 1989, people throughout Eastern Europe toppled

their socialist governments, and in 1991, the Soviet Union itself collapsed, remaking itself as the Russian Federation.

The Soviet Union's story shows that social inequality
involves more than economic resources. Soviet society did
not have the extremes of wealth and poverty found in the
United Kingdom, Japan, and the United States. But an elite
class existed all the same, one based on political power
rather than wealth.

What about social mobility in so-called classless societies? During the twentieth century, there was as much upward social mobility in the Soviet Union as in the United
States. Rapidly expanding industry and government drew
many poor rural peasants into factories and offices. This
trend illustrates what sociologists call **structural social mobility**, *a shift in the social position of large numbers of people
due more to changes in society itself than to individual efforts.*

*November 24, Odessa, Ukraine. The first
snow of our voyage flies over the decks as
our ship docks at Odessa, the former Sovi-
et Union's southernmost port on the Black Sea. A short
distance away, we gaze up the Potemkin Steps—the
steep stairway leading to the city, where the first
shots of the Russian Revolution rang out. It has
been several years since our last visit, and much has
changed; in fact, the Soviet Union itself has collapsed.
Has life improved? For some people, certainly: There
are now chic boutiques where well-dressed shoppers
buy fine wines, designer clothes, and imported per-
fumes. But for most, life seems much worse. Flea
markets line the curbs as families sell their home furnishings. When meat costs $4 a pound and the average
person earns about $30 a month, people become des-
perate. Even the city has to save money by turning off
street lights at eight o'clock. The spirits of most people
seem as dim as Odessa's streets.*

During the 1990s, the forces of structural social mobility in the new Russian Federation turned downward. One
indicator is that the average life span for Russian men
dropped by eight years and for women by two years. Many
factors are involved in this decline, including Russia's poor
health care system, but the Russian people clearly have suffered in the turbulent period of economic change that
began in 1991 (Bohlen, 1998; Gerber & Hout, 1998).

In the long run, closing inefficient state industries may
improve the nation's economic performance. But in the
short run, most citizens face hard times as living standards

fall. As businesses return to private ownership, the gap between rich and poor has grown. Today, some Russians praise the recent changes while others hang on, patiently hoping for better times.

CHINA: EMERGING SOCIAL CLASSES

Sweeping political and economic change has affected not just the Russian Federation but also the People's Republic of China. After the Communist revolution in 1949, the state took control of all farms, factories, and other productive property. Communist party leader Mao Zedong declared all types of work to be equally important, so officially, social classes no longer existed.

The new program greatly reduced economic inequality. But as in the Soviet Union, social differences remained. The country was ruled by a political elite with enormous power and considerable privilege; below them were managers of large factories as well as skilled professionals; next came industrial workers; at the bottom were rural peasants, who were not even allowed to leave their villages and migrate to cities.

Further economic change came in 1978 when Mao died and Deng Xiaoping became China's leader. The state gradually loosened its hold on the economy, allowing a new class of business owners to emerge. Communist party leaders remain in control of the country, and some have prospered as they have joined the ranks of the small but wealthy elite who control new privately run industries. Much of this new economic growth has been concentrated in coastal areas, where living standards have soared far above those in China's rural interior.

Today, a new class system is emerging with a mix of the old political hierarchy and a new business hierarchy. Economic inequality in China has increased, and, as Figure 10–1 shows, it is now about as great as in the United States. At this early stage, scholars point to the new system's complexity and debate its likely future. But one lesson of China is clear: With new patterns of inequality emerging over time, social stratification is highly dynamic (Bian, 2002).

IDEOLOGY: THE POWER BEHIND STRATIFICATION

How do societies persist without sharing resources more equally? The highly stratified British estate system and the caste system in Japan each survived for centuries, and for 2,000 years people in India accepted the idea that they should be privileged or poor based on the accident of birth.

A major reason that social hierarchies endure is **ideology,** *cultural beliefs that justify particular social arrangements, including patterns of inequality.* A belief—for

In recent decades, the government of China has permitted a market economy to operate in limited areas of the country. The result has been increased production and the emergence of a new business class with a lifestyle similar to that of wealthy people in the United States.

example, the idea that rich people are smart and poor people are lazy—is ideological to the extent that it defines the rich as worthy and suggests that those who are less well off deserve their poverty.

Plato and Marx on Ideology

According to the ancient Greek philosopher Plato (427–347 B.C.E.), every culture considers some type of inequality fair. Although Karl Marx understood this, he was far more critical of inequality than Plato. Marx criticized capitalist societies for defending wealth and power in the hands of a few as "a law of the marketplace." Capitalist law, he continued, defines the right to own property and ensures that money stays within the same families from one generation to the next. In short, Marx concluded, culture and institutions combine to support a society's elite, which is why established hierarchies last a long time.

THINKING CRITICALLY

Is Getting Rich "the Survival of the Fittest"?

"The survival of the fittest"—we have all heard these words used to describe society as a competitive jungle. The phrase was coined by one of sociology's pioneers, Herbert Spencer (1820–1903), whose ideas about social inequality are still widespread today.

Spencer, who lived in England, eagerly followed the work of the natural scientist Charles Darwin (1809–1882). Darwin's theory of biological evolution holds that a species changes physically over thousands of generations as it adapts to the natural environment. Spencer distorted Darwin's theory, applying it to the operation of society: Society became the "jungle" with the "fittest" people rising to wealth and the "failures" sinking into miserable poverty.

It is no surprise that Spencer's views were popular among the rising U.S. industrialists of the day. John D. Rockefeller (1839–1937), who made a fortune building the oil industry, recited Spencer's "social gospel" to young children in Sunday school. As Rockefeller saw it, the growth of giant corporations—and the astounding wealth of their owners—was merely a result of "the survival of the fittest," a basic fact of nature. Neither Spencer nor Rockefeller had much sympathy for the poor, seeing poverty as evidence of not measuring up in a competitive world. Spencer opposed social welfare programs, saying that they penalized society's "best" members (through taxes) and rewarded society's "worst" members (through welfare benefits).

Today's sociologists are quick to point out that society is far from a meritocracy, as Spencer claimed. And it is not the case that companies or individuals who generate lots of money necessarily benefit society. Yet Spencer's view that people get what they deserve in life remains part of our individualistic culture.

WHAT DO YOU THINK?

1. What did Herbert Spencer mean when he said society encourages "the survival of the fittest"?
2. Why do you think that Spencer's ideas are still popular in the United States today?
3. Do you think that how much you earn represents your importance to society? Why or why not?

Historical Patterns of Ideology

Ideology changes along with a society's economy and technology. Because agrarian societies depend on most people devoting themselves to lifelong labor, they develop caste systems that view performing the duties of a person's social position a moral responsibility. With the rise of industrial capitalism, an ideology of meritocracy arises, defining wealth and power as prizes to be won by those who perform the best. This change means that the poor—often the targets of charity under feudalism—are looked down on as personally undeserving. This harsh view is found in the ideas of the early sociologist Herbert Spencer, as explained in the Thinking Critically box.

History shows how difficult it is to change social stratification. However, challenges to the status quo always arise. The traditional idea that a "woman's place is in the home," for example, has given way to increased economic opportunities for women in many societies today. The continuing progress toward racial equality in South Africa demonstrates widespread rejection of the ideology of apartheid.

The Functions of Social Stratification

Why does social stratification exist at all? One answer, consistent with the structural-functional approach, is that social inequality plays a vital part in the operation of society. This argument was set forth more than sixty years ago by Kingsley Davis and Wilbert Moore (1945).

THE DAVIS-MOORE THESIS

The **Davis-Moore thesis** states that *social stratification has beneficial consequences for the operation of a society.* How else, ask Davis and Moore, can we explain the fact that some form of social stratification has been found in every society?

Davis and Moore note that modern societies have hundreds of occupational positions of varying importance. Certain jobs—say, washing windows, cutting grass, or answering a telephone—are fairly easy and can be performed by almost anyone. Other jobs—such as designing new generations of

computers or transplanting human organs—are difficult and demand the scarce talents of people with extensive (and expensive) training.

Therefore, Davis and Moore explain, the greater the functional importance of a position, the more rewards a society attaches to it. This strategy promotes productivity and efficiency because rewarding important work with income, prestige, power, and leisure encourages people to do these jobs and to work better, longer, and harder. In short, unequal rewards (which is what social stratification is) benefit society as a whole.

Davis and Moore claim that any society could be egalitarian, but only to the extent that people are willing to let *anyone* perform *any* job. Equality would also demand that someone who carries out a job poorly be rewarded the same as someone who performs it well. Such a system clearly would offer little incentive for people to try their best, reducing a society's productive efficiency.

The Davis-Moore thesis suggests the reason for stratification; it does not state precisely what rewards a society should give to any occupational position or just how unequal rewards should be. It merely points out that positions a society considers more important must carry enough reward to draw talented people away from less important work.

YOUR TURN

Use the Davis and Moore logic to explain why professors give grades from A to F. What would happen if they gave everyone the same grade? Explain.

Critical review Although the Davis-Moore thesis is an important contribution to understanding social stratification, it has provoked criticism. Melvin Tumin (1953) wondered, first, how we assess the importance of a particular occupation. Perhaps the high rewards our society gives to physicians results partly from deliberate efforts by the medical profession to limit the supply of physicians and thereby increase the demand for their services.

Furthermore, do rewards actually reflect the contribution someone makes to society? With income exceeding $200 million per year, Oprah Winfrey earns more in one day than the U.S. president earns all year. Would anyone argue that hosting a talk show is more important than leading a country? And what about members of the U.S. military in Iraq? Facing the risks of combat, they earn only about $12,000 a year. Then there are many cases like that of Larry Ellison, the chief executive officer of Oracle who, even as the

value of his company slid downward, still earned $700 million, an amount that would take a typical U.S. soldier almost 60,000 years to earn (M. Benjamin, 2002; Broder, 2002; Dunn, 2003). Do corporate executives deserve such megasalaries for their "contributions to society"?

Second, Tumin claimed that Davis and Moore ignore how caste elements of social stratification can *prevent* the development of individual talent. Born to privilege, rich children have opportunities to develop their abilities, which is something many gifted poor children never have.

Third, living in a society that places so much emphasis on money, we tend to overestimate the importance of high-paying work; how do stockbrokers or people who trade international currencies really contribute to society? For the same reason, it is difficult for us to see the value of work that is not oriented toward making money, such as parenting, creative writing, playing music in a symphony, or just being a good friend to someone in need (Packard, 2002).

Do corporate CEOs deserve their high salaries? The AFL-CIO offers a critical view at its Web site, where it tracks CEO salaries: http://www.aflcio.org/corporateamerica/paywatch/

Societies differ in the importance they attach to both money and inequality. "In the *Times*" on pages 266–67 explains that in Europe, people's ideas about how to live differ from those common in the United States.

Finally, by suggesting that social stratification benefits all of society, the Davis-Moore thesis ignores how social inequality promotes conflict and even outright revolution. This criticism leads us to the social-conflict approach, which provides a very different explanation for social inequality.

Stratification and Conflict

Social-conflict analysis argues that rather than benefiting society as a whole, social stratification benefits some people and disadvantages others. This analysis draws heavily on the ideas of Karl Marx, with contributions from Max Weber.

KARL MARX: CLASS CONFLICT

Karl Marx, whose ideas are discussed fully in Chapter 4 ("Society"), explained that most people have one of two basic relationships to the means of production: They either own productive property or labor for others. Different productive roles arise from different social classes. In medieval Europe, the nobility and church officials owned the land on which peasants labored as farmers. In industrial class systems, the capitalists (or the bourgeoisie) own the factories, which use the labor of workers (the proletarians).

July 29, 2004

Love of Leisure, and Europe's Reasons

By **KATRIN BENNHOLD**

COPENHAGEN—Between mountains of suitcases and children racing each other with luggage trolleys at the airport of this Scandinavian capital, Maibritt Ditlev, husband Anders and daughter Lotte in tow, remarked that her whole country seemed to be going on vacation. "In Europe we like our summer holidays," she said. . . . In fact, she works part time because she treasures time off. "We have a nice house and can afford to go on two family holidays a year—what would we need more money for?"

This image of a casual Western European work ethic tends to be viewed with just short of scorn by the world's other wealthy economies. As Europeans like the Ditlevs happily continue to trade income for a slice of leisure time that would be unthinkable in the United States or Asia, the gloomy headlines about Europe's economic future multiply.

Europe, the standard criticism goes, has not matched the American expansion for most of the last decade and has even fallen behind Japan in recent quarters. Its citizens are on average almost 30 percent poorer than their counterparts on the other side of the Atlantic, according to the Organization for Economic Cooperation and Development, a group of 30 countries committed to democracy and the market economy. . . .

Is Europe, with the shortest workweeks and longest holidays in the world, doomed to lag behind, a victim of its penchant for more leisure and a too generous welfare state?

One response: If the answer is yes, then so what? . . .

Over the last half century, Western Europeans have gradually opted to work less and take longer vacations. They have put in place varying national versions of public universal health care, education and retirement benefits. They have set up a complex web of minimum income legislation, including unemployment subsidies and disability benefits, and basic social welfare, in an effort to limit the risk of destitution. . . .

As Joaquín Almunia, European commissioner for economic and monetary affairs, put it, for Europeans, economic growth is a tool, not an end in itself.

"We are not in a race with the U.S.," he said. "Our goal is not to grow as fast as the U.S. or anybody else, but to do what we need to protect our economic and social model. . . ."

The European Union faces challenges, including a stagnant, aging population, chronic underemployment and competitive pressures from the eight new Eastern

---

Marx lived during the nineteenth century, a time in history when a few industrialists in the United States were amassing great fortunes. Andrew Carnegie, J. P. Morgan, John D. Rockefeller, and John Jacob Astor (one of the few very rich passengers to die on the *Titanic*) lived in fabulous mansions staffed by dozens of servants. Even by today's standards, their incomes were staggering. For example, Andrew Carnegie earned about $20 million a year in 1900 (more than $100 million in today's dollars), when the average worker earned roughly $500 a year (Baltzell, 1964; Pessen, 1990).

Marx explained that capitalist society *reproduces the class structure in each new generation*. This happens as families gain wealth and pass it down from generation to generation. But, he predicted, oppression and misery would eventually drive the working majority to come together to overthrow capitalism.

Critical review Marx has had enormous influence on sociological thinking. But his revolutionary ideas—calling for the overthrow of capitalist society—also make his work highly controversial.

One of the strongest criticisms of Marxism is that it denies a central idea of the Davis-Moore thesis: that a system of unequal rewards is necessary to place talented people in the right jobs and to motivate them to work hard. Marx separated reward from performance; his egalitarian ideal was based on the principle "from each according to his ability; to each according to his needs" (Marx & Engels, 1972:388, orig. 1848). However, failure to reward individual performance may be precisely what caused the low productivity of the former Soviet Union and other socialist economies around the world. Defenders of Marxism respond to such criticism by asking why we assume that humanity is inherently selfish rather than

European members and Asian growth markets like China and India. . . .

But for all the bad publicity the European economy receives, it is not performing that poorly. The combined gross domestic product of the 15 members of the European Union before the expansion on May 1 lagged behind that of the United States by about one percentage point a year in the last decade, largely because the region's population expanded at less than half the pace of United States'. . . .

Polls show that Europeans are by and large happy to pay high taxes in return for social services, and anecdotal evidence suggests that the concept of well-being in Europe is less linked to material wealth than it is in the United States.

"Americans move from the 20,000-square-foot house to the 30,000-square-foot house to the 40,000-square-foot house. It's a different mentality," said Ken-neth S. Rogoff, an economist at Harvard University and former chief economist of the International Monetary Fund. . . .

Still, some economists say Europe's social model is costing it dearly. In a society that prides itself on egalitarian values, too many people are unemployed or outside the labor market, doubly raiding public coffers by not paying taxes and often receiving benefits at the same time. The jobless rate in the European Union's 15 old members rose to 7.8 percent last year, compared with 6.1 percent in the United States. . . .

A generous welfare state does not only have costs. Europe has less child poverty, a lower incidence of illiteracy and a smaller prison population than the United States. . . . Europeans have a slightly higher life expectancy and can hope to spend more of their old age in good health than Americans. . . .

"The main difference with the U.S. is that we spend more time enjoying life," said Jorgen Ronnest, director for international affairs at the Danish Employers' Confederation. . . . "And if you look around, maybe we don't need more refrigerators and more cars. . . ."

WHAT DO YOU THINK?

1. Based on this article, what are the major differences between the European and U.S. societies?

2. Do you agree with the European approach to life? Why or why not?

3. How do you think European and U.S. views of inequality differ?

Adapted from the original article by Katrin Bennhold published in *The New York Times* on July 29, 2004. Copyright © 2004 by The New York Times Company. Reprinted with permission.

Elisabetta Povoledo of the *International Herald Tribune* contributed to this article.

social; individual rewards are not the only way to motivate people to perform their social roles (M. S. Clark, 1991; Fiske, 1991).

A second problem is that the revolutionary change Marx predicted has failed to happen, at least in advanced capitalist societies. The next section suggests why.

WHY NO MARXIST REVOLUTION?

Despite Marx's prediction, capitalism is still thriving. Why have industrial workers not overthrown capitalism? Ralf Dahrendorf (1959) suggested four reasons:

1. **The fragmentation of the capitalist class.** Today, millions of stockholders, rather than single families, own most large companies. Day-to-day corporate operations are in the hands of a large class of managers, who may or may not be major stockholders. With stock widely held—about 50 percent of U.S. adults own stocks—more and more people have a direct stake in the capitalist system.

2. **A higher standard of living.** As Chapter 16 ("The Economy and Work") explains, a century ago, most workers were in factories or on farms employed in **blue-collar occupations,** *lower-prestige jobs that involve mostly manual labor.* Today, most workers are engaged in **white-collar occupations,** *higher-prestige jobs that involve mostly mental activity.* These jobs are in sales, management, and other service fields. Most of today's white-collar workers do not think of themselves as an "industrial proletariat." Just as important, the average income in the United States rose almost tenfold over the course of the twentieth century, even

allowing for inflation, and the number of hours in the workweek decreased. In short, most workers today are far better off than workers were a century ago, an example of structural mobility. One result of this rising standard of living is that people are more willing to accept the status quo.

3. **More worker organizations.** Workers today have the right to form labor unions that make demands of management and to back up their demands with threats of work slowdowns and strikes. As a result, labor disputes are settled without threatening the capitalist system.

4. **Greater legal protections.** Over the past century, the government passed laws to make workplaces safer. In addition, unemployment insurance, disability protection, and Social Security now provide workers with greater financial security.

Most workers in the United States today have service jobs; instead of farming or working in a factory, they work with other people. Some analysts say that the spread of service work has made many people feel that they are "getting ahead" and reduced class conflict in U.S. society; others claim that many service jobs actually provide lower pay, fewer benefits, and less job security than many factory jobs of the past. Which argument do you think is more correct? Why?

A Counterpoint

These developments suggest that U.S. society has smoothed many of capitalism's rough edges. Yet many observers claim that Marx's analysis of capitalism is still largely valid (Domhoff, 1983; Stephens, 1986; Boswell & Dixon, 1993; Hout, Brooks & Manza, 1993). First, wealth remains highly concentrated, with 40 percent of all privately owned property in the hands of just 1 percent of the U.S. population (Keister, 2000). Second, many of today's white-collar jobs offer no more income, security, or satisfaction than factory work did a century ago. Third, many benefits enjoyed by today's workers came about through the class conflict Marx described, and workers still struggle to hold on to what they have. Fourth, although workers have gained some legal protections, ordinary people still face disadvantages that the law cannot overcome. Therefore, social-conflict theorists conclude, the absence of a socialist revolution in the United States does not disprove Marx's analysis of capitalism.

YOUR TURN

Applied to inequality in the United States, do you think Marx's analysis is accurate? Why or why not?

MAX WEBER: CLASS, STATUS, AND POWER

Max Weber, whose approach to social analysis is described in Chapter 4 ("Society"), agreed with Karl Marx that social stratification causes social conflict, but he viewed Marx's economics-based model as simplistic. Instead, he claimed that social stratification involves three distinct dimensions of inequality.

The first dimension is economic inequality—the issue so important to Marx—which Weber termed *class* position. Weber did not think of classes as well-defined categories but as a continuum ranging from high to low. Weber's second dimension is *status*, or social prestige, and the third is *power*.

The Socioeconomic Status Hierarchy

Marx viewed social prestige and power as simple reflections of economic position and did not treat them as distinct dimensions of inequality. But Weber noted that status consistency in modern societies is often quite low: A local official might exercise great power yet have little wealth or social prestige.

Weber, then, portrays social stratification in industrial societies as a multidimensional ranking rather than a hierarchy of clearly defined classes. In line with Weber's thinking, sociologists use the term **socioeconomic status (SES)** to refer to *a composite ranking based on various dimensions of social inequality.*

Inequality in History

Weber claimed that each of his three dimensions of social inequality stands out at different points in the evolution of human societies. Status, or social prestige, is the main difference in agrarian societies, taking the form of honor. Members of these societies (whether nobles or servants) gain status by conforming to cultural norms that correspond to their rank.

Industrialization and the development of capitalism eliminate traditional rankings based on birth but create striking financial inequality. Thus, in an industrial society, the crucial difference between people is the economic dimension of class.

Over time, industrial societies witness the growth of a bureaucratic state. Bigger government and the spread of all types of other organizations make power more important in the stratification system. Especially in socialist societies, where government regulates many aspects of life, high-ranking officials become the new ruling elite.

This historical analysis points to a final difference between Weber and Marx. Marx thought societies could eliminate social stratification by abolishing the private ownership of productive property that is the basis of capitalism. Weber doubted that overthrowing capitalism would significantly lessen social stratification. It might reduce economic differences, he reasoned, but socialism would increase inequality by expanding government and concentrating power in the hands of a political elite. Popular uprisings against socialist bureaucracies in Eastern Europe and the former Soviet Union support Weber's position.

Critical review Weber's multidimensional view of social stratification has influenced sociologists greatly. But critics (particularly those who favor Marx's ideas) argue that although social class boundaries may have blurred, industrial and postindustrial societies still show striking patterns of social inequality.

As we shall see in Chapter 11 ("Social Class in the United States"), income inequality has increased recently in the United States. Although some people still favor Weber's multidimensional hierarchy, in light of this trend others think that Marx's view of the rich versus the poor is closer to the truth.

The extent of social inequality in agrarian systems is greater than that found in industrial societies. One indication of the unchallenged power of rulers is the monumental structures built over years with the unpaid labor of common people. Although the Taj Mahal in India is among the world's most beautiful buildings, it is merely a tomb for a single individual.

Stratification and Interaction

Because social stratification has to do with the way an entire society is organized, sociologists (Marx and Weber included) typically treat it as a macro-level issue. But a micro-level analysis of social stratification is also important because people's social standing affects their everyday interactions.

In most communities, people socialize primarily with others of more or less the same social standing. To

When Class Gets Personal: Picking (with) Your Friends

The sound of banjo music drifted across the field late one summer afternoon. I lay down my brush, climbed over the fence I had been painting, and walked toward the sound of the music to see what was going on. That's how I met my neighbor Max, a retired factory worker who lived just up the road. Max was a pretty good "picker," and within an hour, I was back on his porch with my guitar. I called Howard, a friend who teaches at the college, and he showed up a little while later, six string in hand. The three of us jammed for a couple of hours, smiling all the while.

The next morning, I was mowing the grass in front of the house when Max came walking down the road. I turned off the mower as he got closer. "Hi, Max," I said. "Thanks for having us over last night. I really had fun."

"Don't mention it," Max responded with a wave. Then he stopped and shook his head a little and added, "Ya know, I was thinkin' after you guys left. I mean, it was really somethin' how you guys looked like you were having a great time. With somebody like *me!*"

"Well, yeah," I replied, not sure of what he meant. "You sure played better than we did."

Max looked down at the ground, embarrassed by the compliment. Then he added, "What I mean is that you guys were having a good time with somebody like *me*. You're both professors, right? *Doctors,* even . . ."

WHAT DO YOU THINK?

1. Why did Max assume that two college teachers would not enjoy spending time with him?
2. How does his reaction suggest that people take social position personally?
3. Can you think of a similar experience you have had with someone of a different social position?

some extent, this is because we tend to live near others like ourselves. In any public setting, such as a downtown shopping area, if you watch people for even a few minutes, you will see that couples or groups tend to contain individuals whose appearance and shopping habits are similar. People with very different social standing commonly keep their distance from one another. Well-dressed people walking down the street on their way to an expensive restaurant, for example, might move across the sidewalk or even cross the street to avoid getting close to others they think are homeless people. The Applying Sociology box gives another example of how differences in social class position can affect interaction.

Finally, just about everyone realizes that the way we dress, the car we drive (or the bus we ride), and even the food and drink we order at the campus snack bar say something about our budget and personal tastes. Sociologists use the term **conspicuous consumption** to refer to *buying and using products because of the "statement" they make about social position.* Ignoring the water fountain in favor of paying for bottled water tells people you have extra money to spend. And no one needs a $100,000 automobile to get around, of course, but being seen in such a vehicle says "I have arrived" in more ways than one.

The Applying Theory table summarizes the contributions of the three theoretical approaches to social stratification.

APPLYING THEORY

SOCIAL STRATIFICATION

	Structural-Functional Approach	Social-Conflict Approach	Symbolic-Interaction Approach
What is the level of analysis?	Macro-level	Macro-level	Micro-level
What is social stratification?	Stratification is a system of unequal rewards that benefits society as a whole.	Stratification is a division of a society's resources that benefits some and harms others.	Stratification is a factor that guides people's interaction in everyday life.
What is the reason for our social position?	Social position reflects personal talents and abilities in a competitive economy.	Social position reflects the way society divides resources.	The products we consume all make a "statement" about social position.
Are unequal rewards fair?	Yes. Unequal rewards boost economic production by encouraging people to work harder and try new ideas. Linking greater rewards to more important work is widely accepted.	No. Unequal rewards only serve to divide society, creating "haves" and "have-nots." There is widespread opposition to social inequality.	Maybe. People may or may not define inequality as fair. People may view their social position as a measure of self-worth, justifying inequality in terms of personal differences.

Stratification and Technology: A Global Perspective

We can weave together a number of observations made in this chapter to show that a society's technology affects its type of social stratification. This analysis draws on Gerhard Lenski's model of sociocultural evolution, detailed in Chapter 4 ("Society").

HUNTING AND GATHERING SOCIETIES

With simple technology, hunters and gatherers produce only what is necessary for day-to-day living. Some people may produce more than others, but the group's survival depends on all sharing what they have. Thus no categories of people are better off than others.

HORTICULTURAL, PASTORAL, AND AGRARIAN SOCIETIES

As technological advances create a surplus, social inequality increases. In horticultural and pastoral societies, a small elite controls most of the surplus. Large-scale agriculture is more productive still, and striking inequality—as great as at any time in history—places the nobility in an almost god-like position over the masses.

INDUSTRIAL SOCIETIES

Industrialization turns the tide, pushing inequality downward. Prompted by the need to develop individual talents, meritocracy takes hold and weakens the power of the traditional elites. Industrial productivity also raises the standard of living of the historically poor majority. Specialized work demands schooling for all, sharply reducing illiteracy. A literate population, in turn, presses for a greater voice in political decision making, reducing inequality and lessening men's domination of women.

Over time, even wealth becomes somewhat less concentrated (contradicting Marx's prediction). In the 1920s, the richest 1 percent of the U.S. population owned about 40 percent of all wealth, a figure that fell to 30 percent by the 1980s (Williamson & Lindert, 1980; Beeghley, 1989; U.S House of Representatives, 1992). Such trends help explain why Marxist revolutions occurred in *agrarian* societies—such as Russia (1917), Cuba (1959), and Nicaragua (1979)—where social inequality is most pronounced, rather than in industrial societies as Marx had predicted. However, wealth inequality increased after 1990 and is once again about the same as it was in the 1920s (Keister, 2000).

THE KUZNETS CURVE

In human history, then, technological advances first increase but then moderate the extent of social stratification. Greater inequality is functional for agrarian societies, but industrial societies benefit from a less unequal system. This historical trend, recognized by the Nobel Prize–winning economist Simon Kuznets (1955, 1966), is illustrated by the Kuznets curve, shown in Figure 10–2 on page 272.

Social inequality around the world generally supports the Kuznets curve. Global Map 10–1 on page 273 shows that high-income nations that have passed through the

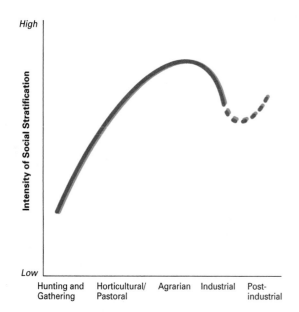

High

Intensity of Social Stratification

Low

Hunting and   Horticultural/   Agrarian   Industrial   Post-
Gathering   Pastoral   industrial

FIGURE 10-2   Social Stratification and
Technological Development:
The Kuznets Curve

The Kuznets curve shows that greater technological sophistication
generally is accompanied by more pronounced social stratification.
The trend reverses itself as industrial societies relax rigid, castelike
distinctions in favor of greater opportunity and equality under the
law. Political rights are more widely extended, and there is even
some leveling of economic differences. However, the emergence of
postindustrial society has brought an upturn in economic
inequality, as indicated by the broken line added by the author.

Source: Created by the author, based on Kuznets (1955) and Lenski (1966).

industrial era (including the United States, Canada, and the
nations of Western Europe) have somewhat less income inequality than nations in which a larger share of the labor

 The Web site of the Center on
Budget and Policy Priorities has
data and analysis of issues involving U.S. social inequality:
http://www.cbpp.org

force remains in farming
(as is common in Latin
America and Africa). In-
come inequality reflects
not just technological development but also political and
economic priorities. Of all high-income nations, the United
States has the greatest income inequality.

And what of the future? Figure 10–2 shows that extending the trend described by Kuznets to the postindustrial era
(the broken line) reveals increasing social inequality. As the
Information Revolution moves ahead, U.S. society is experiencing greater economic inequality (see Chapter 11), suggesting that the long-term trend may differ from what
Kuznets observed fifty years ago (Nielsen & Alderson, 1997).

Social Stratification:
Facts and Values

The year was 2081 and everybody was finally equal. They
weren't only equal before God and the law. They were
equal every which way. Nobody was smarter than anybody else. Nobody was better looking than anybody else.
Nobody was stronger or quicker than anybody else. All
this equality was due to the 211th, 212th, and 213th
Amendments to the Constitution and the unceasing
vigilance of agents of the Handicapper General.

With these words, the novelist Kurt Vonnegut Jr.
(1968:7) begins the story of "Harrison Bergeron," an imaginary account of a future United States in which all social inequality has been abolished. Vonnegut warns that although
attractive in principle, equality can be a dangerous concept
in practice. His story describes a nightmare of social engineering in which every individual talent that makes one
person different from another is systematically neutralized
by the government.

To eliminate differences that make one person "better"
than another, Vonnegut's state requires that physically
attractive people wear masks that make them average looking, that intelligent people wear earphones that generate dis-
tracting noise, and that the best athletes and dancers be fitted
with weights to make them as clumsy as everyone else. In
short, although we may imagine that social equality would
liberate people to make the most of their talents, Vonnegut
concludes that an egalitarian society could exist only if
everyone is reduced to the lowest common denominator.

Like Vonnegut's story, all of this chapter's explanations
of social stratification involve value judgments. The Davis-
Moore thesis states not only that social stratification is universal but also that it is necessary to make society highly
productive. Class differences in U.S. society, from this point
of view, reflect both variation in human abilities and the relative importance of different jobs. This makes complete
equality undesirable because it could be achieved only in an
inefficient society that cared little for developing individual
talent and rewarding excellence.

Social-conflict analysis, advocated by Karl Marx, takes a
much more positive view of equality. Marx thought that inequality is harmful because it causes both human suffering
and conflict between haves and have-nots. As he saw it, social stratification springs from injustice and greed. As a result, Marx wanted people to share resources equally.

The Thinking It Through box on page 274 addresses the
connection between intelligence and social class. This issue is
among the most troublesome in social science, partly because
of the difficulty in defining and measuring "intelligence" but

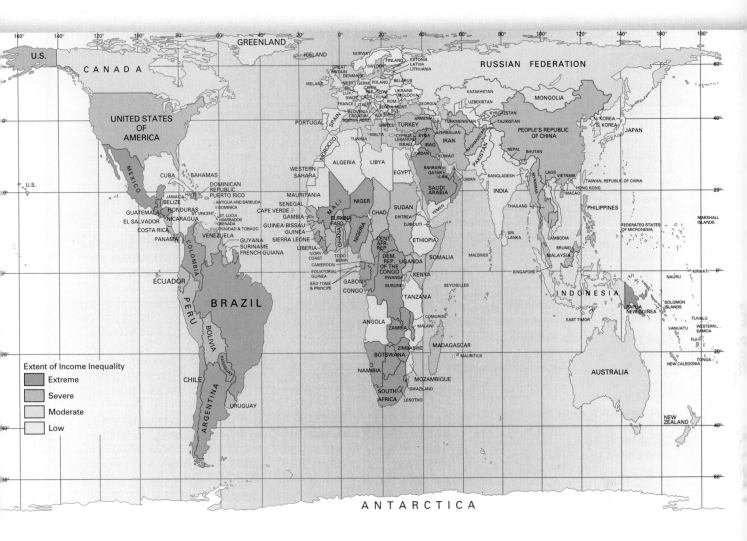

WINDOW ON THE WORLD

GLOBAL MAP 10-1   Income Inequality in Global Perspective

Societies throughout the world differ in the rigidity and extent of their social stratification and their overall standard of living. This map highlights income inequality. Generally speaking, the United States stands out among high-income nations, such as Great Britain, Sweden, Japan, and Australia, as having greater income inequality. The less economically developed countries of Latin America and Africa, including Colombia, Brazil, and the Central African Republic, as well as much of the Arab world, exhibit the most pronounced inequality of income. Is this pattern consistent with the Kuznets curve?

Source: Based on Gini coefficients obtained from World Bank (2005).

also because the idea that elites are somehow "better" than others challenges our democratic culture.

The next chapter ("Social Class in the United States") examines inequality in our own nation, highlighting recent economic polarization. Then, in Chapter 12 ("Global Stratification"), we survey social inequality throughout the world, explaining why some nations have so much more wealth than others. As you will learn, at all levels the study of social stratification involves a mix of facts and values about the shape of a just society.

The Bell Curve Debate: Are Rich People Really Smarter?

It is rare when a social science book captures the attention of people across the country. But *The Bell Curve: Intelligence and Class Structure in American Life* (1994) by Richard J. Herrnstein and Charles Murray did this and more. The book ignited a firestorm of controversy over why social stratification divides our society and, just as important, what should be done about it.

The Bell Curve is a long book that addresses many complex issues, but it makes eight major claims:

1. Something we can describe as "general intelligence" exists; people with more of it tend to be more successful in their careers than those with less.

2. At least half the variation in human intelligence is transmitted genetically from parents to children; the remaining variability is due to environmental factors that affect socialization.

3. During the past century—and especially since the Information Revolution began several decades ago—intelligence has become more necessary to perform our society's most important jobs.

4. At the same time, the most selective U.S. colleges and universities have shifted their admissions policies away from favoring children of inherited wealth to admitting young people with high grades and the highest scores on standardized tests such as the Scholastic Assessment Test (SAT), American College Testing Program (ACT), and Graduate Record Examination (GRE).

5. As a result of these changes in the workplace and on campus, our society is now dominated by a "cognitive elite," people who are not only better educated but actually more intelligent.

6. As very intelligent people interact with others like themselves—both on the campus and in the workplace—the odds are high that they will pair up, marry, and have intelligent children, extending the "cognitive elite" into another generation.

7. A similar process is at work at the other end of the social ladder: Poor people who, on average, have lower intelligence have become socially segregated and tend to marry others like themselves, thus passing along their more modest abilities to their children.

8. Herrnstein and Murray therefore conclude that because membership in the affluent elite or the impoverished underclass is at least partly rooted in genetically inherited intelligence, we should not be surprised that the poor are more likely to have higher rates of crime and drug abuse. Further, we should expect that programs such as Head Start and affirmative action will do little to help the poor.

Evaluating the claims made in *The Bell Curve* must begin with a hard look at the concept of intelligence. Critics of the book argue that most of what we call "intelligence" is the result not of genetic inheritance but of socialization. Intelligence tests, in other words, do not measure cognitive *ability* as much as they measure cognitive *performance*. Average IQ scores have been rising as the U.S. population becomes more educated. If schooling is so important to intelligence, then educational advantages alone would explain why rich children perform better on such tests.

Most researchers who study intelligence agree that genetics plays a part in children's intelligence, but most conclude that only 25 to 40 percent of intelligence is inherited—less than Herrnstein and Murray claim. Therefore, *The Bell Curve* misleads readers when it states that social stratification is a natural product of differences in inherited intelligence. Critics claim this book echoes the social Darwinism popular a century ago, which justified the great wealth of industrial tycoons as "the survival of the fittest."

Could it be that the more today's competitive society seems like a jungle, the more people think of stratification as a matter of nature rather than nurture? But even if it is flawed, *The Bell Curve* raises important issues. If some people are smarter than others, shouldn't we expect them to end up in higher social positions? Shouldn't we expect the people who rise to the top in most fields to be at least a little smarter than the rest of us? If this is true, is it fair? Finally, what can our society do to ensure that all people will have the opportunity to develop their abilities as fully as possible?

WHAT DO YOU THINK?

1. Do you think there is such a thing as "general intelligence"? Why or why not?

2. Do you think that well-off people, on average, are more intelligent than people of low social position? If so, how do you know which factor is the cause and which the effect?

3. Do you think social scientists should study issues such as differences in human intelligence if their results could justify social inequality? Why or why not?

Sources: Herrnstein & Murray (1994), Jacoby & Glauberman (1995), Kohn (1996), and Arrow, Bowles, & Durlauf (2000).

The following learning tools will help you see what you know, identify what you still need to learn, and expand your understanding beyond the text. You can also visit this text's Companion Website™ at http://www.prenhall.com/macionis to find additional practice tests.

KEY POINTS

What Is Social Stratification?

Social stratification, the ranking of categories of people in a hierarchy, (1) is a trait of society, not just a result of individual differences; (2) carries over from generation to generation; (3) is universal but variable; and (4) is supported by cultural beliefs.

Caste and Class Systems

Caste systems, which are typical of agrarian societies, are based on ascription (birth), permit little social mobility, and shape a person's entire life, including occupation and marriage. Class systems, which are typical of industrial societies, mix caste with meritocracy and allow some social mobility based on individual achievement. Both types of social stratification are supported by ideology—cultural values and beliefs—that defines certain kinds of inequality as just.

The Functions of Social Stratification

The Davis-Moore thesis states that social stratification is found in all societies because it promotes economic productivity. Unequal rewards attract the most able people to the most important jobs and encourage good performance. Critics of the Davis-Moore thesis note that (1) it is difficult to assess the functional importance of any job fairly, (2) stratification prevents many people from developing their abilities, and (3) stratification benefits some at the expense of others, causing social conflict.

Stratification and Conflict

Karl Marx claimed that social stratification generates conflict. In industrial-capitalist societies, the capitalists or bourgeoisie own the means of production, seek profits, and dominate the proletarians, who provide labor in exchange for wages. The socialist revolution that Marx predicted has not occurred, at least in industrial societies such as the United States. Some sociologists consider this to be evidence that Marx was wrong, but others point out that U.S. society still has striking social inequality and class conflict.

Max Weber identified three dimensions of social inequality: economic class, social status or prestige, and power. Because people's standing on the three dimensions may differ, stratification is not a matter of clear classes but takes the form of a multidimensional hierarchy.

Stratification and Interaction

In everyday life, people typically socialize with others of similar social standing. People may decide to dress in certain ways or buy certain products in order to increase their social standing in the eyes of others. Conspicuous consumption refers to buying and using products because of the "statement" they make about social position.

Stratification and Technology: A Global Perspective

Through most of history, advancing technology has increased social stratification. Some reversal of this trend occurs in industrial societies, as shown by the Kuznets curve. Even so, postindustrial U.S. society shows some increase in economic inequality.

Social Stratification: Facts and Values

People's beliefs about social inequality reflect not just facts but also politics and values concerning how a society should be organized.

KEY CONCEPTS

social stratification (p. 254) a system by which a society ranks categories of people in a hierarchy

social mobility (p. 255) a change in position within the social hierarchy

caste system (p. 256) social stratification based on ascription, or birth

class system (p. 258) social stratification based on both birth and individual achievement

meritocracy (p. 258) social stratification based on personal merit

status consistency (p. 258) the degree of consistency in a person's social standing across various dimensions of social inequality

structural social mobility (p. 262) a shift in the social position of large numbers of people due more to changes in society itself than to individual efforts

ideology (p. 263) cultural beliefs that justify particular social arrangements, including patterns of inequality

Davis-Moore thesis (p. 264) the assertion that social stratification is a universal pattern because it has beneficial consequences for the operation of a society

blue-collar occupations (p. 267) lower-prestige jobs that involve mostly manual labor

white-collar occupations (p. 267) higher-prestige jobs that involve mostly mental activity

socioeconomic status (SES) (p. 269) a composite ranking based on various dimensions of social inequality

conspicuous consumption (p. 270) buying and using products because of the "statement" they make about social position

SAMPLE TEST QUESTIONS

These questions are similar to those found in the test bank that accompanies this textbook.

Multiple-Choice Questions

1. *Social stratification* refers to
   a. job specialization.
   b. ranking categories of people in a hierarchy.
   c. the fact that some people work harder than others.
   d. inequality of personal talent and individual effort.

2. **Looking back in history and around the world today, we see that social stratification may involve differences in**
   a. how unequal people are.
   b. what resources are unequally distributed.
   c. why a society claims people should be unequal.
   d. all of the above.

3. **A caste system is social stratification**
   a. based on individual achievement.
   b. based on meritocracy.
   c. based on birth.
   d. in which people are likely to change their social position over time.

4. **Sally has two advanced degrees, earns an average salary, and is working at a low-prestige job. Which concept best describes her situation?**
   a. low status consistency
   b. horizontal social mobility
   c. upward social mobility
   d. high status consistency

5. **According to the Davis-Moore thesis,**
   a. equality is functional for society.
   b. the more inequality a society has, the more productive it is.
   c. more important jobs must offer enough rewards to draw talent from less important work.
   d. societies with more meritocracy are less productive than those with caste systems.

6. **Karl Marx claimed that society "reproduces the class structure." By this, he meant that**
   a. society benefits from inequality.
   b. class differences are passed on from one generation to the next.
   c. class differences are the same everywhere.
   d. a society without classes is impossible.

7. **Max Weber claimed that social stratification is based on**
   a. economic class.
   b. social status or prestige.
   c. power.
   d. all of the above.

8. **A society with which type of productive technology has the least amount of social stratification?**
   a. hunting and gathering
   b. horticultural/pastoral
   c. industrial
   d. postindustrial

9. **Keeping in mind the Kuznets curve, which type of society has the most social stratification?**
   a. hunting and gathering
   b. horticultural/pastoral
   c. agrarian
   d. industrial

10. The "bell curve" thesis suggests that which of the following is more important than ever to social position in the United States?
   a. family background
   b. intelligence
   c. hard work
   d. who you know

Answers: 1(b); 2(d); 3(c); 4(a); 5(c); 6(b); 7(d); 8(a); 9(c); 10(b).

Essay Questions

1. Explain why social stratification is a creation of society, not just a reflection of individual differences.

2. How do caste and class systems differ? How are they the same? Why does industrialization introduce a measure of meritocracy into social stratification?

 APPLICATIONS & EXERCISES

1. Write down three examples of social stratification on your college campus, and indicate in what ways the students represented are unequal. Does family background or individual talent seem to be more important in creating these social differences?

2. Sit down with parents, grandparents, or other relatives, and talk about how your family's social position has changed over the last three generations. Has social mobility taken place? If so, describe the change. Was it caused by the effort of individuals or changes in society itself?

3. The "seven deadly sins," the human failings recognized by the Catholic church during the Middle Ages, were pride, greed, envy, anger, lust, gluttony, and sloth. Why are these traits dangerous to an agrarian caste system? Are they a threat to a modern, capitalist class system? Why or why not?

 INVESTIGATE *with* Research Navigator

Research Navigator.com
RESOURCES FOR COLLEGE RESEARCH ASSIGNMENTS

Follow the instructions on page 27 of this text to access the features of **Research Navigator™**. Once at the Web site, enter your Login Name and Password. Then, to use the **ContentSelect™** database, enter keywords such as "social class," "social mobility," and "Karl Marx," and the search engine will supply relevant and recent scholarly and popular press publications. Use the *New York Times* **Search-by-Subject Archive** to find recent news articles related to sociology and the **Link Library** feature to find relevant Web links organized by the key terms associated with this chapter.

11

Social Class in the United States

How is income and wealth divided within the U.S. population?

What factors place people in different social classes?

Why is the poverty rate higher among some categories of people in the United States than others?

ROSA URIAS LEANS FORWARD, pushing and pulling the vacuum cleaner across the hardwood floors, a motion she has repeated hundreds of times to the point that her right wrist and elbow are sore. It is now almost five o'clock in the afternoon, and this forty-five-year-old single mother of two is on her third cleaning job of the day. She works with her cousin Melitsa Sermiento, thirty-six, cleaning nine apartments and five houses each week. The two women, who both came to the United States from El Salvador, divide the money they earn, giving each one an annual income of about $28,000, barely enough to pay the bills in New York City.

But there is no shortage of work cleaning homes. Hundreds of thousands of New Yorkers make more than enough money to hire people like Rosa and Melitsa to dust their tables, mop their floors, and scrub their sinks and toilets while they are out doing their high-paying jobs, working out at the health club, or having lunch with friends.

Rosa reaches up over the bathroom sink to turn on a light so she can see better. She pulls the silver chain, but it breaks and she stands there with part of the chain hanging from her hand. She looks over at Melitsa and both do their best to laugh it off. Then Rosa turns serious and says softly, in Spanish, "My daughter tells me I need some new dreams" (Eisenstadt, 2004). ∎

New York may be a single large city, but the social world in which Rosa and Melitsa live is not the same as the social world of the people who hire these women. How different are the lives of the richest people in the United States and the lives of those who work hard all day just to get by? What about the lives of those who do not even have the security of work? This chapter answers all these questions, explaining some of the different "worlds" found in U.S. society, how different we are, and why the differences are getting bigger.

Dimensions of Social Inequality

The United States differs from most European nations and Japan in never having had a titled nobility. With the significant exception of our racial history, we have never known a caste system that rigidly ranks categories of people.

Even so, U.S. society is highly stratified. Not only do the rich have most of the money, but they also receive the most schooling, enjoy the best health, and consume the most

goods and services. Such privilege contrasts sharply with the poverty of millions of women and men who worry about paying next month's rent or a doctor's bill when a child becomes ill. Many people think of the United States as a middle-class society, but is this really the case?

YOUR TURN

Why do you think so many people view the United States as a "middle-class society" in which most people have more or less equal social standing?

INCOME

One important dimension of inequality is **income,** *earnings from work or investments.* The Census Bureau reports that the median U.S. family income in 2004 was $55,327. The first part of Figure 11–1 illustrates the distribution of

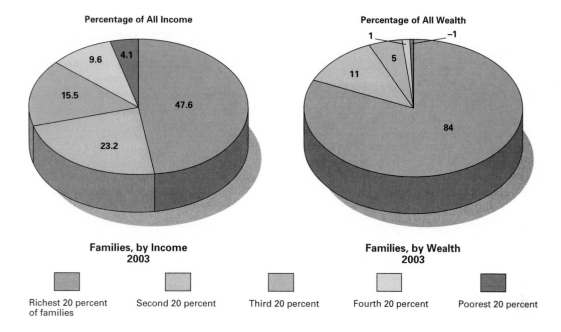

Percentage of All Income

9.6 4.1

15.5

47.6

23.2

Percentage of All Wealth

1   −1

5

11

84

**Families, by Income
2003**

**Families, by Wealth
2003**

Richest 20 percent of families

Second 20 percent

Third 20 percent

Fourth 20 percent

Poorest 20 percent

FIGURE 11–1   Distribution of Income and Wealth in the United States

Income, and especially wealth, is divided unequally in U.S. society.

Sources: Income data from U.S. Census Bureau (2005); wealth data are author estimates based on Keister (2000) and Russell & Mogelonsky (2000).

income among all U.S. families.[1] The richest 20 percent of families (earning at least $98,000 annually, with a mean of about $165,000) received 47.6 percent of all income, while the bottom 20 percent (earning less than $24,000, with a mean of about $14,000) received only 4.1 percent.

Table 11–1 on page 282 provides a closer look at income distribution. In 2003, the highest-paid 5 percent of U.S. families earned at least $170,000 (averaging almost $300,000), or 20.5 percent of all income, more than the total earnings of the lowest-paid 40 percent. At the very top of the income pyramid, the richest half of 1 percent earned at least $1.5 million. In short, while a small number of people earn very high incomes, the majority make do with far less.

---

[1]The Census Bureau reports both mean and median incomes for families ("two or more persons related by blood, marriage, or adoption") and households ("two or more persons sharing a living unit"). In 2003, mean family income was $68,563, higher than the median ($52,680) because high-income families pull up the mean but not the median. For households, these figures are somewhat lower—a mean of $59,067 and a median of $43,318—largely because families average 3.1 people and households average 2.6.

WEALTH

Income is only a part of a person's or family's **wealth,** *the total value of money and other assets, minus outstanding debts.* Wealth—including stocks, bonds, and real estate—is distributed more unequally than income. Recent reductions in taxes on income earned by individuals and wealth passed from one generation to the next are likely to make this inequality greater (Wahl, 2003).

The second part of Figure 11–1 shows the distribution of wealth. The richest 20 percent of U.S. families own roughly 84 percent of the country's wealth. High up in this privileged category are the wealthiest 5 percent of families—the "very rich," who own 60 percent of all private property. Richer still, with wealth in the tens of millions of dollars, are the 1 percent of families that qualify as "super-rich" and possess about 40 percent of this nation's privately held resources (Keister, 2000; Keister & Moller, 2000). At the top of the wealth pyramid, the ten richest U.S. families have a combined net worth of more than $226 billion (Miller & Newcomb, 2005). This amount

Read a government report on U.S. wealth inequality at http://www.census.gov/prod/2003pubs/p70-88.pdf

TABLE 11–1

U.S. Family Income, 2003

Highest-paid . . .	Annually earns at least . . .
0.5%	$1,500,000
1	347,000
5	170,000
10	116,000
20	98,000
30	76,500
40	65,000
50	54,500
60	42,000
70	31,500
80	24,000
90	10,000

Source: U.S. Census Bureau (2005) and author calculations.

equals the total property of 3.1 million average families, including enough people to fill the cities of Chicago, Illinois; Chattanooga, Tennessee; and Clearwater, Florida.

The wealth of the average U.S. household, currently about $71,600, rose through the 1990s and fell somewhat with the economic downturn beginning in 2000. Household wealth reflects the value of homes, cars, investments, insurance policies, retirement pensions, furniture, clothing, and all other personal property, minus a home mortgage and other debts. The wealth of average people is not only less than that of the rich, however, but also different in kind. Most people's wealth centers on a home and a car—that is, property that generates no income—but the wealth of the rich is mostly in the form of stocks and other income-producing investments.

When financial assets are balanced against debts, the lowest-ranking 40 percent of U.S. families have virtually no wealth at all. The negative percentage shown in Figure 11–1 for the poorest 20 percent of the population means that these families actually live in debt.

POWER

In the United States, wealth is an important source of power. The small proportion of families that controls most of the nation's wealth also shapes the agenda of the entire society. As explained in Chapter 17 ("Politics and Government"), some sociologists argue that such concentrated wealth weakens democracy because the political system serves the interests of the super-rich.

YOUR TURN

Everyone, regardless of social class, has the same right to vote. But can you think of ways in which the rich have more power to shape U.S. society than the rest of us?

OCCUPATIONAL PRESTIGE

In addition to generating income, work is also an important source of social prestige. We commonly evaluate each other according to the kind of work we do, giving greater respect to those who do what we consider important work and less respect to others with more modest jobs.

Sociologists measure the relative prestige of various occupations (NORC, 2003). Table 11–2 shows that people give high prestige to occupations such as physician, lawyer, and engineer that require extensive training and generate high income. By contrast, less prestigious work—as a waitress or janitor, for example—pays less and requires less schooling. Occupational prestige rankings are much the same in all high-income nations (Lin & Xie, 1988).

In any society, high-prestige occupations go to privileged categories of people. In Table 11–2, for example, the highest-ranking occupations are dominated by men. We have to go thirteen jobs down the list to find "registered nurse," a career chosen mostly by women.

YOUR TURN

Identify the jobs in Table 11–2 that have traditionally been performed by people of color. What pattern do you discover?

SCHOOLING

Industrial societies have expanded opportunities for schooling, but some people still receive much more education than others. Table 11–3 on page 284 shows the levels of schooling achieved by U.S. women and men aged twenty-five and older. In 2004, although 85 percent completed high school, only about 28 percent were college graduates.

Schooling affects both occupation and income, since most (but not all) of the better-paying white-collar jobs shown in Table 11–2 require a college degree or other advanced study. Most blue-collar jobs, which bring lower income and social prestige, require less schooling.

TABLE 11–2

The Relative Social Prestige of Selected Occupations in the United States

White-Collar Occupations	Prestige Score	Blue-Collar Occupations	White-Collar Occupations	Prestige Score	Blue-Collar Occupations
Physician	86		Funeral director	49	
Lawyer	75		Real estate agent	49	
College/university professor	74		Bookkeeper	47	
Architect	73			47	Machinist
Chemist	73			47	Mail carrier
Physicist/astronomer	73		Musician/composer	47	
Aerospace engineer	72			46	Secretary
Dentist	72		Photographer	45	
Member of the clergy	69		Bank teller	43	
Psychologist	69			42	Tailor
Pharmacist	68			42	Welder
Optometrist	67			40	Farmer
Registered nurse	66			40	Telephone operator
Secondary school teacher	66			39	Carpenter
Accountant	65			36	Bricklayer/stonemason
Athlete	65			36	Child care worker
Electrical engineer	64		File clerk	36	
Elementary school teacher	64			36	Hairdresser
Economist	63			35	Baker
Veterinarian	62			34	Bulldozer operator
Airplane pilot	61			31	Auto body repairer
Computer programmer	61		Retail apparel salesperson	30	
Sociologist	61			30	Truck driver
Editor/reporter	60		Cashier	29	
	60	Police officer		28	Elevator operator
Actor	58			28	Garbage collector
Radio/TV announcer	55			28	Taxi driver
Librarian	54			28	Waiter/waitress
	53	Aircraft mechanic		27	Bellhop
	53	Firefighter		25	Bartender
Dental hygienist	52			23	Farm laborer
Painter/sculptor	52			23	Household laborer
Social worker	52			22	Door-to-door salesperson
	51	Electrician		22	Janitor
Computer operator	50			09	Shoe shiner

Source: Adapted from *General Social Surveys, 1972–2002: Cumulative Codebook* (Chicago: National Opinion Research Center, 2003), pp. 1488–1506.

U.S. Stratification: Merit and Caste

As we discussed in Chapter 10 ("Social Stratification"), the U.S. class system is partly a meritocracy in that social position reflects individual talent and effort. But it also has caste elements, because birth plays a part in what we become later in life.

ANCESTRY

Nothing affects social standing in the United States as much as being born into a particular family, which has a strong bearing on schooling, occupation, and income. Research suggests that more than one-third of our country's richest individuals—those with hundreds of millions of dollars in wealth—acquired some of their fortunes from inheritance (Miller & Newcomb, 2005). Inherited poverty shapes the future of tens of millions of others.

RACE AND ETHNICITY

Race is closely linked to social position in the United States. White people receive more schooling than African Americans

TABLE 11–3

Schooling of U.S. Adults, 2004 (aged 25 and over)

	Women	Men
Not a high school graduate	**14.6%**	**15.2%**
8 years or less	6.1	6.5
9–11 years	8.5	8.7
High school graduate	**85.4**	**84.8**
High school only	32.8	31.1
1–3 years of college	26.5	24.3
College graduate or more	26.1	29.4

Source: U.S. Census Bureau (2005).

and have higher overall occupational standing. The median African American family's income was $35,158 in 2004, just 58 percent of the $60,969 earned by non-Hispanic white families. This inequality in income makes a real difference in people's lives. For example, non-Hispanic white families are more likely to own their homes (76 percent do) than black families (49 percent) (U.S. Census Bureau, 2005).

Some of the racial difference in income results from the larger share of single-parent families among African Americans. Comparing only families headed by married couples, African Americans earned 80 percent as much as non-Hispanic white families.

Over time, the income difference builds into a huge wealth gap (Altonji, Doraszelski, & Segal, 2000). A recent survey of U.S. households by the government's Federal Reserve found that median wealth for minority families (about $17,100) is just 14 percent of the median ($120,900) for non-Hispanic whites (Aizcorbe, Kennickell, & Moore, 2003). Even among families who *do* have a lot of money, race makes a difference, as the Thinking About Diversity box explains.

Social ranking involves ethnicity as well. People of English ancestry have always enjoyed the most wealth and the greatest power in U.S. society. The Latino population—now the largest U.S. racial or ethnic minority—has long been disadvantaged. In 2004, the median income among Hispanic families was $35,401, which is 58 percent of the comparable figure for all non-Hispanic white families. A detailed examination of how race and ethnicity affect social standing is presented in Chapter 14 ("Race and Ethnicity").

GENDER

Of course, both men and women are found in families at every class level. Yet on average, women have less income,

wealth, and occupational prestige than men. Among single-parent families, those headed by a woman are about six times more likely to be poor than those headed by a man. Chapter 13 ("Gender Stratification") examines the link between gender and social stratification.

Social Classes in the United States

As Chapter 10 ("Social Stratification") explained, rankings in a caste system are rigid and obvious to all. Defining social categories in a more fluid class system such as ours, however, is not so easy.

There is an old joke about a couple who orders a pizza, asking that it be cut into six slices because they aren't hungry enough to eat eight. Sociologists do the same thing with social class; some recognize more classes than others. At one extreme, people find as many as six or even seven social classes; at the other, some follow Karl Marx and see two major classes: capitalists and proletarians. Still others side with Max Weber, claiming that people form not classes but a multidimensional status hierarchy.

Defining classes in U.S. society is difficult because of our relatively low level of status consistency. Especially toward the middle of the hierarchy, people's standing in one dimension may not be the same as their standing in another. For example, a government official may have the power to administer a multimillion-dollar budget yet may earn only a modest personal income. Similarly, many members of the clergy enjoy great prestige but moderate power and low pay. Or consider a lucky day trader on the stock market who wins no special respect but makes a lot of money.

Finally, the social mobility typical of class systems—again, most pronounced around the middle—means that social position may change during a person's lifetime, further blurring class boundaries. With these issues in mind, we will describe four general rankings: the upper class, the middle class, the working class, and the lower class.

THE UPPER CLASS

Families in the upper class—5 percent of the U.S. population—earn at least $170,000 a year, and some earn ten times that much or more. As a general rule, the more a family's income comes from inherited wealth in the form of stocks and bonds, real estate, and other investments, the stronger a family's claim to being upper-class.

In 2005, *Forbes* magazine profiled the richest 374 people in the United States who were worth at least $1 billion (and as much as $51 billion) (Miller & Newcomb, 2005). These people form the core of the upper class, or Karl Marx's "capitalists"—the owners of the means of production or most of

The Color of Money: Being Rich in Black and White

African American families earn 58 cents for every dollar a non-Hispanic white family earns, which helps explain why black families are three times as likely to be poor. But there is another side to black America—an affluent side—that has grown dramatically in recent decades.

The number of affluent families—those with incomes over $75,000 a year—is increasing faster among African Americans than among whites. According to Census Bureau statistics for 2003, 1.5 million African American families (17 percent) were financially well-off, nearly ten times the number in 1970 (taking inflation into account). About 16 percent of Latino families were well-off, along with 38 percent of non-Hispanic white families.

The color of money is the same for everyone, but black and white affluence differs in several ways. First, well-off people of African descent are *not as rich* as their white counterparts. Sixty percent of affluent non-Hispanic white families (23 percent of all such families) earn more than $100,000 a year, compared to 50 percent of affluent African American families (9 percent of all black families).

Second, African Americans are more likely than white people to achieve affluence through multiple incomes. Among non-Hispanic white people, 12.8 percent of men and 4.1 percent of women earn more than $75,000; among African Americans, the same is true of just 5.5 percent of men and 2.3 percent of women. Rich black families are more likely to contain two or more working people.

Third, affluent African Americans are more likely to get their income from salaries rather than investments. More

Will Smith and Jada Pinkett Smith are among the most well-known and affluent African Americans in the world. But race still has a lot to do with which families are wealthy.

than 80 percent of wealthy white families have investment income, compared to two-thirds of affluent African American families.

Beyond differences in income, affluent people of color must deal with social barriers that do not limit whites. Even African Americans with the money to purchase a home, for example, may find they are unwelcome as neighbors. This is one reason that a smaller share of well-off African American families (54 percent) live in the suburbs (the richest areas of the country) than affluent white families (68 percent).

Affluent Americans come in all colors. But having money does not completely overcome the racial barriers in the United States.

WHAT DO YOU THINK?

1. What do you think are some of the reasons for the rising number of well-off African American families?

2. In what ways are affluent African Americans still disadvantaged by their race?

3. Do you think affluent African Americans feel less secure about their social position than affluent whites? Why or why not?

the nation's private wealth. Many upper-class people are business owners, top executives in large corporations, or senior government officials. In the past, the upper class has been composed mostly of white Anglo-Saxon Protestants, but this is less true today (Pyle & Koch, 2001).

Upper-Uppers

The *upper-upper class,* sometimes called "blue bloods" or simply "society," includes less than 1 percent of the U.S. population (Coleman & Neugarten, 1971; Baltzell, 1995).

People often distinguish between the "new rich" and those with "old money." Men and women who suddenly begin to earn high incomes tend to spend their money on status symbols because they enjoy the new thrill of high-roller living and they want others to know of their success. Those who grow up surrounded by wealth, on the other hand, are used to a privileged way of life and are more quiet about it. Thus, the conspicuous consumption of the lower-upper class (left) can differ dramatically from the more private pursuits and understatement of the upper-upper class (right).

Membership is almost always the result of birth, as suggested by the joke that the easiest way to become an upper-upper is to be born one. Most of these families possess enormous wealth, which is primarily inherited. For this reason, members of the upper-upper class are said to have "old money."

Set apart by their wealth, upper-uppers live in old, exclusive neighborhoods, such as Beacon Hill in Boston, Rittenhouse Square in Philadelphia, the Gold Coast of Chicago, and Nob Hill in San Francisco. Their children typically attend private schools with others of similar background and complete their schooling at high-prestige colleges and universities. In the tradition of European aristocrats, they study liberal arts rather than vocational skills.

Women of the upper-upper class do volunteer work for charitable organizations. Such activities serve a dual purpose: They help the larger community, and they build networks that broaden this elite's power (Ostrander, 1980, 1984).

Lower-Uppers

Most upper-class people actually fall into the *lower-upper class*. The queen of England is in the upper-upper class based not on her fortune of $500 million but on her family tree. J. K. Rowling, author of the Harry Potter books, is worth even more—almost $1 billion—but this woman (who was once on welfare) is a member of the lower-upper

class. The major difference, in other words, is that lower-uppers are the "working rich" who get their money mostly by earning it rather than inheritance. These well-to-do families—who make up 3 or 4 percent of the U.S. population—generally live in large homes in expensive neighborhoods, own vacation homes near the water or in the mountains, and send their children to private schools and good colleges. Yet most of the "new rich" do not gain entry into the clubs and association of "old money" families.

In the United States, what we often call the "American Dream" has been to earn enough to join the ranks of the lower-upper class. The athlete who signs a million-dollar contract, the actress who lands a starring role in a Hollywood film, the computer whiz who starts a successful Internet company, and even the person who hits it big by winning the lottery are the talented achievers and lucky people who reach the lower-upper class.

THE MIDDLE CLASS

Made up of 40 to 45 percent of the U.S. population, the large middle class has a tremendous influence on our culture. Television programs and movies usually show middle-class people, and most commercial advertising is directed at these average consumers. The middle class contains far more racial and ethnic diversity than the upper class.

Upper-Middles

People in the top half of this category are called the *upper-middle class,* based on above-average income in the range of $80,000 to $170,000 a year. Such income allows upper-middle-class families to live in a comfortable house in a fairly expensive area, own several automobiles, and build investments. Two-thirds of upper-middle-class children graduate from college, and postgraduate degrees are common. Many go on to high-prestige careers as physicians, engineers, lawyers, accountants, and business executives. Lacking the power of the richest people to influence national or international events, upper-middles often play an important role in local political affairs.

Average-Middles

The rest of the middle class falls close to the center of the U.S. class structure. *Average-middles* typically work at less prestigious white-collar jobs as bank branch managers, high school teachers, and government office workers, or in highly skilled blue-collar jobs such as electrical work and carpentry. Family income is between $40,000 and $80,000 a year, which is roughly the national average.[2] Middle-class people typically build up a small amount of wealth over the course of their working lives, mostly in the form of a house and a retirement account. Middle-class men and women are likely to be high school graduates, but the odds are just fifty-fifty that they will complete a college degree, usually at a less expensive, state-supported school.

THE WORKING CLASS

About one-third of the population falls within the working class (sometimes called the *lower-middle class*). In Marxist terms, the working class forms the core of the industrial proletariat. Their blue-collar jobs usually yield a family income of between $25,000 and $40,000 a year, somewhat below the national average. Working-class families have little or no wealth and are vulnerable to financial problems caused by unemployment or illness.

Many working-class jobs provide little personal satisfaction—requiring discipline but rarely imagination—and subject workers to continual supervision. These jobs also offer fewer benefits, such as medical insurance and pension plans. About half of working-class families own their own homes, usually in lower-cost neighborhoods. College

For decades, farm families who worked hard could expect to fall within the U.S. middle class. But the trend toward large-scale agribusiness has put the future of the small family farm in doubt. Although many young people in rural areas are turning away from farming toward other careers, some carry on, incorporating high technology into their farm management in their determined efforts to succeed.

becomes a reality for only about one-third of working-class children.

THE LOWER CLASS

The remaining 20 percent of our population make up the lower class. Low income makes their lives insecure and difficult. In 2004, the federal government classified 40 million people (12.7 percent of the population) as poor. Millions more—called the "working poor"—are slightly better off, holding low-prestige jobs that provide little satisfaction and minimal income. Barely half manage to complete high school, and only one in four ever reaches college.

Society segregates the lower class, especially when the poor are racial or ethnic minorities. About 40 percent of lower-class families own their own homes, typically in the least desirable neighborhoods. Although poor neighborhoods are usually found in our inner cities, lower-class families also live in rural communities, especially across the South.

Most communities contain people of various class levels. In the country as a whole, however, some areas are wealthier than others. National Map 11–1 on page 288 shows one measure of social class—per capita income—for all the counties in the United States.

---

[2]In some parts of the United States where the cost of living is very high (say, San Francisco), a family might need $150,000 or more in annual income to reach the middle class.

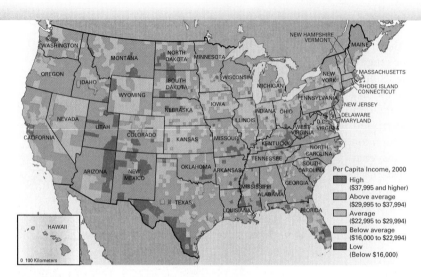

SEEING OURSELVES

NATIONAL MAP 11–1

Per Capita Income across the United States, 2000

This map shows the median per-person income (that is, how much money, on average, a person has to spend) in the more than 3,000 counties that make up the United States, for the year 2000. The richest counties, shown in dark green, are not spread randomly across the country. Nor are the poorest U.S. counties, which are shown in dark red. Looking at the map, what patterns do you see in the distribution of wealth and poverty across the United States? What can you say about wealth and poverty in urban and rural areas?

YOUR TURN

If you were trying to assess someone's social class position and could ask only one question, what would it be? Explain the reason for your choice.

The Difference Class Makes

Social stratification affects nearly every dimension of our lives. We will briefly examine some of the ways social standing is linked to our health, values, politics, and family life.

HEALTH

Health is closely related to social standing. Children born into poor families are three times more likely to die from disease, neglect, accidents, or violence during their first years of life than children born into privileged families. Among adults, people with above-average incomes are almost twice as likely as low-income people to describe their health as excellent. In addition, richer people live, on average, seven years longer because they eat more nutritious food, live in safer and less stressful environments, and receive better medical care (Lethbridge-Cejku & Vickerie, 2005).

VALUES AND ATTITUDES

Some cultural values vary from class to class. The "old rich" have an unusually strong sense of family history because their social position is based on wealth passed down from generation to generation. Secure in their birthright privileges, upper-uppers also favor understated manners and tastes; many "new rich" engage in conspicuous consumption, using homes, cars, and even airplanes as status symbols to make a statement about their social position.

Affluent people with greater education and financial security are also more tolerant of controversial behavior such as homosexuality. Working-class people, who grow up in an atmosphere of greater supervision and discipline and are less likely to attend college, tend to be less tolerant (Baltzell, 1979a, orig. 1958; Lareau, 2002; NORC, 2003).

POLITICS

Do political attitudes follow class lines? The answer is yes, but the pattern is complex. A desire to protect their wealth prompts well-off people to be more conservative on *economic* issues, favoring, for example, lower taxes. But on *social* issues—such as abortion and gay rights—highly educated, more affluent people are more liberal. People of lower social standing, by contrast, tend to be economic liberals, favoring government social programs that support the poor, but typically have more conservative values on social issues (NORC, 2003).

A clearer pattern emerges when it comes to political involvement. Higher-income people, who are better served by the system, are more likely to vote and to join political organizations than people with low incomes. In presidential elections, three-fourths of adults with family incomes of $75,000 vote, compared to about half of those with family incomes of $50,000 (Samuelson, 2003).

FAMILY AND GENDER

Social class also shapes family life. Generally, lower-class families are somewhat larger than middle-class families because of earlier marriage and less use of birth control. Another family pattern is that working-class parents encourage children to conform to conventional norms and to respect authority figures. Parents of higher social standing pass on different "cultural capital" to their children, teaching them to express their individuality and imagination more freely. In both cases, parents are looking to the future: The odds are that less privileged children will have jobs that require them to follow rules and that more privileged children will have careers that require more creativity (Kohn, 1977; McLeod, 1995; Lareau, 2002).

The more money a family has, the more parents can develop their children's talents and abilities. One study found that an affluent family earning $105,000 a year will spend $269,520 raising a child born in 2004 to the age of eighteen. Middle-class people, with an annual income of $55,500, will spend $184,320, and a lower-income family, earning less than $41,700, will spend $133,370 (Lino, 2005). Privilege leads to privilege as family life reproduces the class structure in each generation.

Class also shapes our world of relationships. In a classic study of married life, Elizabeth Bott (1971, orig. 1957) found that most working-class couples divide their responsibilities according to gender roles; middle-class couples, by contrast, are more egalitarian, sharing more activities and expressing greater intimacy. More recently, Karen Walker (1995) discovered that working-class friendships typically serve as sources of material assistance; middle-class friendships are likely to involve shared interests and leisure pursuits.

Social Mobility

Ours is a dynamic society marked by significant social movement. Earning a college degree, landing a higher-paying job, or marrying someone who earns a good income contributes to *upward social mobility;* dropping out of school, losing a job, or becoming divorced (especially for women) may result in *downward social mobility.*

Compared to high-income people, low-income people are half as likely to report good health and, on average, live about seven fewer years. The toll of low income—played out in inadequate nutrition, little medical care, and high stress—is easy to see on the faces of the poor, who look old before their time.

Over the long term, social mobility is not so much a matter of changes in individuals as changes in society itself. In the first half of the twentieth century, for example, industrialization expanded the U.S. economy, pushing up living standards. Even people who were not good swimmers rode the rising tide of prosperity. More recently, *structural social mobility* in a downward direction has dealt many people economic setbacks.

Sociologists distinguish between shorter- and longer-term changes in social position. **Intragenerational social mobility** is *a change in social position occurring during a person's lifetime.* **Intergenerational social mobility,** *upward or downward social mobility of children in relation to their parents,* is important because it usually reveals long-term changes in society, such as industrialization, that affect everyone.

The mass media are full of suggestions that upward social mobility is within reach of everyone. Recent television shows, including *The Bachelor*, *The Bachelorette*, and *How to Marry a Millionaire* (shown above), spread the message that getting rich is as easy as saying "I do." How realistic is this claim?

MYTH VERSUS REALITY

In few societies do people think about "getting ahead" as much as in the United States. Moving up, after all, is the American Dream. But is there as much social mobility as we like to think?

Studies of intergenerational mobility (almost all of which, unfortunately, have focused only on men) show that almost 40 percent of the sons of blue-collar workers take white-collar jobs and about 30 percent of sons born into white-collar families end up doing blue-collar work. *Horizontal mobility*—a change of occupation at the same class level—is even more common; overall, about 80 percent of sons show at least some type of social mobility in relation to their fathers (Blau & Duncan, 1967; Featherman & Hauser, 1978; Hout, 1998).

Research points to four general conclusions about social mobility in the United States:

1. **Social mobility over the course of the past century has been fairly high.** The widespread belief that the United States allows considerable social mobility is true. Mobility is what we would expect in an industrial class system.

2. **The long-term trend in social mobility has been upward.** Industrialization, which greatly expanded the U.S. economy, and the growth of white-collar work over the course of the twentieth century have raised living standards.

3. **Within a single generation, social mobility is usually small.** Most young families increase their income over time as they gain education and skills. For example, a typical family headed by a thirty-year-old earned about $52,000 in 2004; a typical family headed by a fifty-year-old earned $73,000 (U.S. Census Bureau, 2005). Yet only a few people move "from rags to riches" (the way J. K. Rowling did) or lose a lot of money (a number of hip-hop stars who made it big had little money a few years later). Most social mobility involves limited movement *within* one class level rather than striking moves *between* classes.

4. **Social mobility since the 1970s has been uneven.** Real income (adjusted for inflation) rose steadily during the twentieth century until the 1970s. Between 1975 and 1985, gains were far smaller. During the 1980s, real income changed little for many people, rising slowly during the 1990s and falling again after 2000. But general trends do not show the experiences of different categories of people, as the next section explains.

MOBILITY BY INCOME LEVEL

Figure 11–2 shows how U.S. families at different income levels made out between 1980 and 2003. Well-to-do families (the highest 20 percent, but not all the same families over the entire period) saw their incomes jump 57 percent, from an average $104,132 in 1980 to $163,322 in 2003. People in the middle of the population also had gains, but more modest ones. The lowest-income 20 percent saw only a 2.3 percent increase in earnings.

For families at the top of the income scale (the highest 5 percent), recent decades have brought a windfall. These families, with an average income of almost $150,000 in 1980, were making $281,467 in 2003—almost twice as much (U.S. Census Bureau, 2005).

MOBILITY: RACE, ETHNICITY, AND GENDER

White people in the United States have always been in a more privileged position than people of African or Hispanic descent. Through the economic expansion of the 1980s and 1990s, many more African Americans entered the ranks of the wealthy. But overall, the real income of African Americans has changed little in three decades. African American family income as a percentage of white family income was only slightly higher (62 percent) in 2004 than it was in 1970 (60 percent). Compared with white families, Latino families in the United States lost ground between 1975 (when their average income was 67 percent as much as that of white families) and 2004 (when it had slipped to 58 percent) (Featherman & Hauser, 1978; Pomer, 1986; U.S. Census Bureau, 2005).

Historically, women in U.S. society have had less opportunity for upward mobility than men, because most working women hold clerical jobs (such as secretary) and service positions (such as food server) that offer few opportunities for advancement and higher pay. When marriages end in divorce (as almost half do), women commonly experience downward social mobility because they not only lose income but also no longer have many benefits, including health care and insurance coverage (Weitzman, 1996).

Over time, the earnings gap between women and men has been narrowing. Women working full time in 1980 earned 60 percent as much as men working full time; by 2004, women were earning 77 percent as much (U.S. Census Bureau, 2005).

THE AMERICAN DREAM: STILL A REALITY?

The expectation of upward social mobility is deeply rooted in U.S. culture. Through most of our history, the economy has grown steadily, raising living standards. Even today, for some people at least, the American Dream is alive and well. In 2004, 20 percent of U.S. families earned $100,000 or more, compared with just 3 percent back in 1967 (in dollars controlled for inflation). There are now at least 5 million millionaires in the United States, four times the number a decade ago (D'Souza, 1999; Rank & Hirschl, 2001; U.S. Census Bureau, 2005).

Yet not all indicators are positive. Note these disturbing trends:

1. **For many workers, earnings have stalled.** The annual income of a fifty-year-old man working full time climbed 49 percent between 1958 and 1974 (from $25,671 to $38,190 in constant 2001 dollars). Between 1974 and 2001, however, this worker's income rose only slightly, even as the number of hours worked increased and the cost of necessities like housing, education, and medical care went way up (Russell, 1995a; U.S. Census Bureau, 2002).

2. **Multiple job-holding is up.** According to the Bureau of Labor Statistics, 4.7 percent of the U.S. labor force

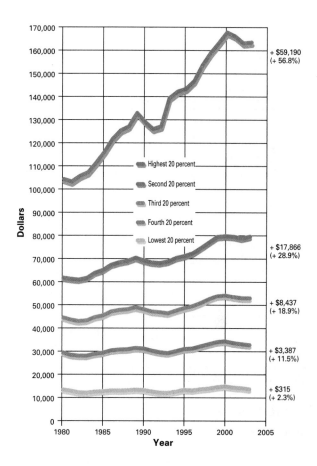

FIGURE 11–2 Mean Annual Income, U.S. Families, 1980–2003 (in 2003 dollars, adjusted for inflation)

Today, there is a greater gap between high-income families and low-income families than there was in 1980.

Source: U.S. Census Bureau (2005).

worked at two or more jobs in 1975; by 2004, the share had risen to 5.4 percent.

3. **More jobs offer little income.** In 1979, the Census Bureau classified 12 percent of full-time workers as "low-income earners" because they made less than $6,905 a year. By 1998, this segment had increased to 15.4 percent, earning less than $15,208 (the same level of income adjusted for inflation).

4. **Young people are remaining at home.** For the first time in history, half of young people aged eighteen to twenty-four are living with their parents. Since 1975, the average age at marriage has moved upward four years (to 25.3 years for women and 27.1 years for men).

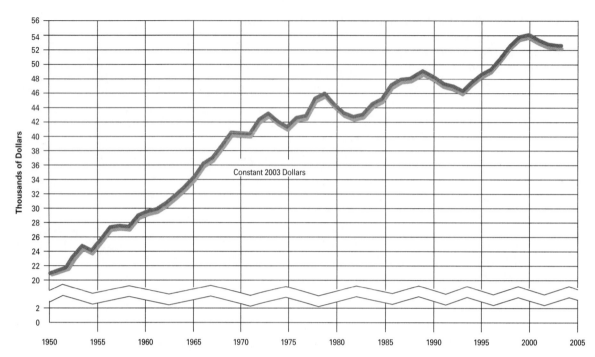

FIGURE 11-3   Median Annual Income, U.S. Families, 1950–2003

Average family income in the United States grew rapidly between 1950 and 1970. Since then, however, the increase has been smaller.

Source: U.S. Census Bureau (2005).

Over the last generation, more people have become rich, and the rich have become richer. At the very top of the pile, as the Applying Sociology box explains, the highest-paid corporate executives have enjoyed a runaway rise in their earnings. Yet the increasing share of low-paying jobs has also brought downward mobility for millions of families, feeding the fear that the chance to enjoy a middle-class lifestyle is slipping away. As Figure 11–3 shows, although median income doubled between 1950 and 1973, it has grown by only 25 percent since then (U.S. Census Bureau, 2005).

THE GLOBAL ECONOMY AND THE U.S. CLASS STRUCTURE

Underlying the shifts in U.S. class structure is global economic change. Much of the industrial production that gave U.S. workers high-paying jobs a generation ago has moved overseas. With less industry at home, the United States now serves as a vast market for industrial goods such as cars and popular items like stereos, cameras, and computers made in China, Japan, Korea, and elsewhere.

High-paying jobs in manufacturing, held by 26 percent of the U.S. labor force in 1960, support only 12 percent of workers today. In their place, the economy now offers service work, which often pays far less. A traditionally high-paying corporation like USX (formerly United States Steel) now employs fewer people than the expanding McDonald's chain, and fast-food clerks make only a fraction of what steelworkers earn.

The global reorganization of work has not been bad news for everyone. On the contrary, the global economy is driving upward social mobility for educated people who specialize in law, finance, marketing, and computer technology. Global economic expansion has also helped push up the stock market (even with the recent declines) almost tenfold between 1980 and 2005, reaping profits for families with money to invest.

But the same trend has hurt many average workers, who have lost their factory jobs and now perform low-wage service work. In addition, many companies have downsized—cutting the ranks of their workforce—to stay competitive in world markets. As a result, even though 60 percent of all families contain two or more workers—more than twice the

APPLYING SOCIOLOGY
As CEOs Get Richer: The Great Mansions Return

I grew up in Elkins Park, Pennsylvania, an older suburban community just north of Philadelphia. Elkins Park was at that time and still is a mostly middle-class community, although, like most of suburbia, some neighborhoods boast bigger houses than others.

What was special about the Elkins Park of my childhood was that scattered over the area were a handful of great mansions, built a century ago by early Philadelphia industrialists. At that time, just about all there was to the town was these great "estates," along with fields and meadows. By about 1940, however, most of the land was split off into lots for the homes of newer middle-class suburbanites. The great mansions suddenly seemed out of place, with heirs trying to figure out how to pay the rising property taxes. As a result, many of the great mansions were sold, the buildings were taken down, and the land was subdivided.

In the 1960s, when I was a teenager, a short ride on my bicycle could take me past what was left of the Breyer estate (built by the founder of the ice-cream company and now the township police building), the Curtis estate (built by a magazine publisher, now transformed into a community park), and the Wanamaker estate (built by the founder of a large Philadelphia department store, now gone entirely). Probably the grandest of them all was the Wiedner estate, modeled after a French château, complete with doorknobs and window pulls covered in gold; it now stands empty.

In their day, these structures were not just homes to families with many servants; they also served as monuments to a time when the rich

were, well, *really* rich. By contrast, the community that emerged on the grounds once owned by these wealthy families is middle-class, with homes built on smaller lots.

But did the so-called Gilded Age of great wealth disappear forever? Hardly. By the 1980s, a new wave of great mansions was being built in the United States. Take architect Thierry Despont, who mostly designs huge houses for super-rich people. One of Despont's "smaller" homes might be 20,000 square feet (about ten times the size of the average U.S. house), and the larger ones go all the way up to 60,000 square feet (as big as any of the Elkins Park mansions built a century ago and almost the size of the White House). These megahomes have kitchens as large as college classrooms, exercise rooms, indoor swimming pools, and even indoor tennis courts.

Megahouses are being built by newly rich chief executive officers (CEOs) of large corporations. CEOs have always made more money than most people, but recent years have witnessed executive pay soaring out of sight. Between 1970 and 2005, the average U.S. family saw only a modest increase in income (about 20 percent after inflation is taken into account). Yet according to *Fortune* magazine, during that period the average annual compensation for the 100 highest-paid

CEOs skyrocketed from $1.3 million (about 40 times the earnings of an average worker of that time) to $37.5 million (roughly a 2,800 percent increase and equal to 1,000 times as much as the earnings of today's average worker). Some CEOs, of course, earn far more: In the year before Enron collapsed, for example, Kenneth Lay earned about $150 million. Assuming that Lay worked forty-eight hours per week and fifty weeks that year, that sum amounts to more than $60,000 *per hour.*

Some analysts argue that in today's competitive global economy, many CEOs are true "superstars" who build company profits and deserve every penny they earn. Some take a less generous view, suggesting that CEOs have stacked their corporate boards of directors with friends, who then paid them back by approving enormous paychecks and bonuses. In any case, executive pay has become a national scandal. In light of this situation (not to mention the many cases of outright fraud and theft that are bringing executives like Kenneth Lay to trial), it appears that we have been living in an era of unbridled greed.

WHAT DO YOU THINK?

1. Do you consider increasing economic inequality a problem? Why or why not?
2. How many times more than an average worker should a CEO earn? Explain your answer.
3. Do you think that very high CEO pay hurts stockholders? What about the general public? Why or why not?

Sources: Based on Krugman (2002) and with material from Myers (2000).

FIGURE 11-4 The Poverty Rate in the United States, 1960–2004

The share of our population in poverty fell dramatically between 1960 and 1970. Since then, the poverty rate has remained between 10 and 15 percent of the population.

Source: U.S. Census Bureau (2005).

share in 1950—many families are working harder simply to hold on to what they have (A.L. Nelson, 1998; J.M. Schlesinger, 1998; Sennett, 1998).

Do you feel that you are likely to end up with a higher social position than your parents? The same? Lower? Why? How much of the mobility you expect is due to changes in U.S. society?

Poverty in the United States

Social stratification creates both "haves" and "have-nots." All systems of social inequality create poverty, or at least **relative poverty,** *the deprivation of some people in relation to those who have more.* A more serious but preventable problem is **absolute poverty,** *a deprivation of resources that is life-threatening.*

As Chapter 12 ("Global Stratification") explains, about 1 billion human beings—one person in six—are at risk of absolute poverty. Even in the affluent United States, families go hungry, live in inadequate housing, and suffer poor health because of serious poverty.

THE EXTENT OF U.S. POVERTY

In 2004, the government classified 40 million men, women, and children—12.7 percent of the population—as poor. This count of relative poverty refers to families with incomes below an official poverty line, which for a family of four in that year was set at $19,307. The poverty line is about three times what the government estimates people must spend for food. But the income of the average poor family was just 60 percent of this amount. This means that the typical poor family had to get by on less than $12,000 in 2004 (U.S. Census Bureau, 2005). Figure 11–4 shows that the official poverty rate fell during the 1960s and has stayed about the same since then.

WHO ARE THE POOR?

Although no single description fits all poor people, poverty is pronounced among certain categories of our population. Where these categories overlap, the problem is especially serious.

Age

A generation ago, the elderly were at greatest risk for poverty. But thanks to better retirement programs offered today by private employers and the government, the poverty rate for people over age sixty-five fell from 30 percent in 1967 to 9.8 percent—well below the national average—in 2004. Looking at it from another angle, 9 percent (3.5 million) of the poor are elderly people.

Today the burden of poverty falls most heavily on children. In 2004, 17.8 percent of people under age eighteen (13 million children) were poor. Put another way, 35 percent of the U.S. poor are children.

Race and Ethnicity

Two-thirds of all poor people are white; 24 percent are African Americans. But in relation to their overall numbers, African Americans are about three times as likely as non-Hispanic whites to be poor. In 2004, 24.3 percent of African Americans (9 million people) lived in poverty, compared to 21.9 percent of Hispanics (9.1 million), 9.8 percent of Asians and Pacific Islanders (1.2 million), and 8.6 percent of non-Hispanic whites (16.9 million). The poverty gap between whites and minorities has changed little since 1975.

African American artist Henry Ossawa Tanner captured the humility and humanity of impoverished people in his painting *The Thankful Poor*. This insight is important in a society that tends to define poor people as morally unworthy and deserving of their bitter plight.

Henry Ossawa Tanner (1859-1937), *The Thankful Poor*. Private collection. Art Resource, N.Y.

People of color have especially high rates of child poverty. Among African American children, 32.8 percent are poor; the comparable figures are 28.6 percent among Hispanic children and 10.5 percent among non-Hispanic white children (U.S. Census Bureau, 2005).

Gender and Family Patterns

Of all poor people age eighteen or older, 60 percent are women and 40 percent are men. This difference reflects the fact that women who head households are at high risk of poverty. Of all poor families, 51 percent are headed by women with no husband present; just 8 percent of poor families are headed by single men.

The United States has experienced the **feminization of poverty,** *the trend of women making up an increasing proportion of the poor.* In 1960, 25 percent of all poor households were headed by women; the majority of poor families had both wives and husbands in the home. By 2004, however, the share of poor households headed by a single woman had more than doubled to 51 percent.

The feminization of poverty is one result of a larger change: the rapidly increasing number of households at all class levels headed by single women. This trend, coupled with the fact that households headed by women are at high risk of poverty, helps explain why women and their children make up an increasing share of the poor in the United States.

Urban and Rural Poverty

The greatest concentration of poverty is found in central cities, where the 2003 poverty rate stood at 17.5 percent. The poverty rate in suburbs is 9.1 percent. Thus the poverty rate for urban areas as a whole is 12.1 percent—lower than the 14.2 percent found in rural areas. National Map 11–2 on page 296 shows that most of the counties with the highest poverty rate in the United States are rural.

EXPLAINING POVERTY

For the richest nation on Earth to contain tens of millions of poor people raises serious questions. It is true, as some analysts remind us, that most poor people in the United States are far better off than the poor in other countries: 41 percent of U.S. poor families own a home, 70 percent own a car, and only a few percent report often going without food (Rector, 1998; Gallagher, 1999). But there is little doubt that poverty harms the well-being of millions of people in this country.

Why is there poverty in the first place? We will present two opposing explanations for poverty that lead to a lively and important political debate.

One View: Blame the Poor

One approach holds that *the poor are mostly responsible for their own poverty.* Throughout our history, people in the

NATIONAL MAP 11-2

Poverty across the United States

This map shows that the poorest counties in the United States—where the poverty rate is more than twice the national average—are in Appalachia, spread across the Deep South, along the border with Mexico, near the Four Corners region of the Southwest, and in the Dakotas. Can you suggest some reasons for this pattern?

Source: U.S. Census Bureau (2001).

Percentage of Population below the Poverty Level

- 45.4% to 68.0%
- 26.2% to 45.3%
- 17.2% to 26.1%
- 11.0% to 17.1%
- 0.0% to 10.9%

United States have placed a high value on self-reliance, convinced that social standing is mostly a matter of individual talent and effort. According to this view, society offers plenty of opportunities to anyone able and willing to take advantage of them. Therefore, the poor are those who cannot or will not work, women and men with few skills, little schooling, and limited motivation.

In his study of poverty in Latin American cities, the anthropologist Oscar Lewis (1961) noted that many poor become trapped in a *culture of poverty*, a lower-class subculture that can destroy people's ambition to improve their lives. Raised in poor families, children become resigned to their situation, producing a self-perpetuating cycle of poverty.

In 1996, hoping to break the cycle of poverty in the United States, Congress changed the welfare system, which had provided federal funds to assist poor people since 1935.

 A report on food scarcity in the United States is found at http://www.ers.usda.gov/Publications/fanrr42/

The federal government continues to send money to the states to distribute to needy people, but benefits carry strict time limits—in most cases, no more than two years at a stretch and a total of five years as an individual moves in and out of the welfare system. The stated purpose of this reform was to force people to be self-supporting and move them away from dependency on government.

Counterpoint: Blame Society

A different position, argued by William Julius Wilson (1996a, 1996b; Mouw, 2000), holds that *society is primarily responsible for poverty*. Wilson points to the loss of jobs in the inner cities as the primary cause of poverty, claiming that there is simply not enough work to support families. Wilson sees any apparent lack of trying on the part of poor

people as a *result* of little opportunity rather than a *cause* of poverty. From Wilson's point of view, Lewis's analysis amounts to "blaming the victims" for their own suffering. The Thinking Critically box provides a closer look at Wilson's argument and how it would shape public policy.

Critical review The U.S. public is evenly divided over whether the government or people themselves should take responsibility for reducing poverty (NORC, 2003). Government statistics show that 52 percent of the heads of poor households did not work at all during 2004, and an additional 29 percent worked only part time (U.S. Census Bureau, 2005). Such facts seem to support the "blame the poor" side of the argument, because one major cause of poverty is *not holding a job*.

But the *reasons* that people do not work seem more in step with the "blame society" position. Middle-class women may be able to combine working and child rearing, but this is much harder for poor women who cannot afford child care, and few employers provide child care programs. As William Julius Wilson explains, many people are idle not because they are avoiding work but because there are not enough jobs to go around. In short, the most effective way to reduce poverty is to ensure a greater supply of jobs as well as child care for parents who work (Wilson, 1996a; Pease & Martin, 1997; Duncan, 1999; Bainbridge, Meyers, & Waldfogel, 2003).

THE WORKING POOR

Not all poor people are jobless. The *working poor* command the sympathy and support of people on both sides of the poverty debate. In 2004, 19 percent of heads of poor families (1.5 million women and men) worked at least fifty

When Work Disappears: The Result Is Poverty

The U.S. economy has created tens of millions of new jobs in recent decades. Yet African Americans who live in inner cities have faced a catastrophic loss of work. William Julius Wilson points out that, although people continue to talk about welfare reform, neither major political party (Democrats or Republicans) has said anything about the lack of work in central cities.

With the loss of inner-city jobs, Wilson continues, for the first time in U.S. history a large majority of the adults in our inner cities are not working. Studying the Washington Park area of Chicago, Wilson found a troubling trend. Back in 1950, most adults in this African American community had jobs, but by the mid-1990s, two-thirds did not. As one elderly woman who moved to the neighborhood in 1953 explained:

> When I moved in, the neighborhood was intact. It was intact with homes, beautiful homes, mini-mansions, with stores, laundromats, with Chinese cleaners. We had drugstores. We had hotels. We had doctors over on 39th Street. We had doctors' offices in the neighborhood. We had the middle class and the upper-middle class. It has gone from affluent to where it is today. (Wilson, 1996b:28)

Why has this neighborhood declined? Wilson's eight years of research point to one answer: There are barely any jobs. It is the loss of work that has pushed people into desperate poverty, weakened families, and made people

turn to welfare. In nearby Woodlawn, Wilson identified more than 800 businesses that had operated in 1950; today, just 100 remain. In addition, a number of major employers in the past—including Western Electric and International Harvester—closed their plant doors in the late 1960s. The inner cities have fallen victim to economic change, including downsizing and the loss of industrial jobs that have moved overseas.

Wilson paints a grim picture. But he also believes the answer lies in creating new jobs. Wilson proposes attacking the problem in stages. First, the government could hire people to do all kinds of work, from clearing slums to putting up new housing. Such a program, modeled on the Works Progress Administration (WPA) enacted in 1935 during the Great Depression, would move people from welfare to work and in the process create much-needed hope. In addition, federal and state governments must improve schools by enacting performance standards and providing more funding. Of special

importance is teaching children language skills and computer skills to prepare them for the jobs being created by the Information Revolution. Improved regional public transportation would connect cities (where people need work) and suburbs (where most jobs now are). In addition, more affordable child care would help single mothers and fathers balance the responsibilities of employment and parenting.

Wilson claims that his proposals are well grounded in research. But he knows that politics revolves around other considerations as well. For one thing, because the public *thinks* there are plenty of jobs, it is hard to change the perception that the poor are simply avoiding work. He also concedes that his proposals, at least in the short term, are more expensive than continuing to funnel welfare assistance to jobless communities.

But what are the long-term costs of allowing our cities to decay while suburbs prosper? On the other hand, what would be the benefits of giving everyone the hope and satisfaction that are supposed to define our way of life?

William Julius Wilson spent years studying neighborhoods like this one in Chicago. He now teaches at Harvard University in Boston.

WHAT DO YOU THINK?

1. If Wilson were running for public office, do you think he would be elected? Why or why not?
2. In your opinion, why are people so reluctant to see inner-city poverty as a problem?
3. Do you agree with Wilson's analysis of poverty? Why or why not?

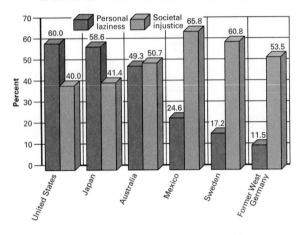

GLOBAL SNAPSHOT

Survey Question: "Why are there people in this country who live in need?"

FIGURE 11-5 Assessing the Causes of Poverty

In the United States (and also in Japan), more people explain poverty in terms of personal laziness than societal injustice. In most high-income nations (including European countries) and in lower-income nations (such as Mexico), more people point to societal injustice rather than personal laziness as the cause of poverty.

Note: Percentages for each country may not add up to 100 because less frequently identified causes of poverty were omitted from this figure.

Source: Inglehart et al. (2000).

weeks of the year and yet could not escape poverty. Another 29 percent of these heads of families (2.3 million people) remained poor despite part-time employment. Put differently, about 4 percent of full-time workers earn so little that they remain poor (U.S. Census Bureau, 2005). A key cause of working poverty is the fact that a full-time worker earning $6 per hour—above the 2005 minimum wage of $5.15 per hour—cannot lift an urban family of four above the poverty line.

 For a profile of the working poor, visit http://www.bls.gov/cps/cpswp2003.pdf

Another category we might call the "working near-poor" includes another 5.6 million families that are only slightly better off, earning more than those officially counted as poor but less than 150 percent of the poverty line. Among these families, 52 percent include at least one full-time worker. With only low-wage jobs available, people who work hard can boost incomes above the poverty line, but not by much (O'Hare, 2002).

In sum, individual ability and personal initiative do play a part in shaping social position. However, the weight of sociological evidence points to society—not individual

character traits—as the primary cause of poverty, because a rising share of available jobs offers only low wages. In addition, the poor are *categories* of people—female heads of families, people of color, people isolated from the larger society in inner-city areas—who face special barriers and limited opportunities.

The Thinking It Through box takes a closer look at the current welfare debate. Understanding this important social issue can help us decide how our society should respond to the problem of poverty, as well as the problem of homelessness discussed next.

HOMELESSNESS

We have no exact count of homeless people. Fanning out across the cities of the United States on the night of March 27, 2000, Census Bureau officials counted 170,706 people at emergency and homeless shelters. But experts estimate that a full count is probably at least 500,000 on any given night, with as many as seven times that number—3.5 million people—homeless at some time during the course of a year. In addition, the evidence suggests that the number of homeless people in the United States is going up (U.S. Census Bureau, 2000; Wickham, 2000; Marks, 2001; L. Kaufman, 2004). "In the *Times*" on pages 300–301 provides a closer look at the problem of homelessness.

The familiar stereotypes of homeless people—men sleeping in doorways and women carrying everything they own in a shopping bag—have been replaced by the

 A report by the U.S. Conference of Mayors on homelessness is found at http://usmayors.org/uscm/hungersurvey/2004/onlinereport/HungerAndHomelessnessReport2004.pdf

"new homeless": people thrown out of work because of plant closings, women who take their children and leave home to escape domestic violence, women and men forced out of apartments by rent increases, and others unable to meet mortgage or rent payments because of low wages or no work at all. Today, no stereotype paints a complete picture of the homeless.

The majority of homeless people report that they do not work, but 44 percent say they work at least part time (U.S. Department of Housing and Urban Development, 1999). Working or not, all homeless people have one thing in common: *poverty*. For that reason, the explanations of poverty just presented also apply to homelessness. Some people blame the *personal traits* of the homeless themselves. One-third of homeless people are substance abusers, and one-fourth are mentally ill. More broadly, a fraction of 1 percent of our population, for one reason or another, seems unable to cope with our complex and highly competitive society (Bassuk, 1984; Whitman, 1989).

THINKING IT THROUGH

The Welfare Dilemma

In 1996, Congress ended federal public assistance, which guaranteed some income to all poor people. New, state-run programs were enacted, which require people who receive aid to get job training or find work—or have their benefits cut off.

What, exactly, is welfare? The term "welfare" refers to many policies and programs designed to improve the well-being of some of the U.S. population. Until the welfare reform of 1996, most people used the term to refer to just one part of the overall system: Aid for Dependent Children (AFDC), a program of monthly financial support for parents (mostly single women) to care for themselves and their children. In 1996, some 5 million households received AFDC for some part of the year.

Conservatives opposed AFDC, claiming that, rather than reducing child poverty, AFDC made the problem worse, in two ways. First, they argue that AFDC weakened families, because for years after the program began, it paid benefits to poor mothers only if no husband lived in the home. As a result, AFDC operated as an economic incentive to women to have children outside marriage, which conservatives link to the rapid rise of out-of-wedlock births among poor people. To conservatives, marriage is one key to reducing poverty: Fewer than one in ten married-couple families are poor; more than nine in ten AFDC families were headed by an unmarried woman.

Second, conservatives believe that welfare encouraged poor people to become dependent on government handouts, the main reason that eight of ten poor heads of households did not have full-time jobs. Furthermore, only 5 percent of single mothers receiving AFDC worked full time, compared to more than half of non-poor single mothers. Conservatives say that welfare strayed

from its original purpose of short-term help to nonworking women with children (say, after divorce or death of a husband) and became a way of life. Once trapped in dependency, poor women would raise children who were also likely to be poor as adults.

Liberals have a different view. Why, they ask, do people object to government money going to poor mothers and children when most "welfare" actually goes to richer people? The AFDC budget was $25 billion annually—no small sum, to be sure—but just half of the $50 billion in home mortgage deductions that homeowners pocket each year. And it pales in comparison to the $300 billion in annual Social Security benefits provided to senior citizens, most of whom are not poor. And what about "corporate welfare" to big companies? Their tax write-offs and other benefits run into hundreds of billions of dollars per year.

Liberals add that the stereotype of do-nothing "welfare queens" masks the fact that most poor families who turn to public assistance are truly needy. The typical AFDC household received barely $400 per month, hardly enough to attract people to a life of welfare dependency. In constant dollars, AFDC payments actually declined over the years. Liberals fault public assistance as a "Band-Aid approach" to the serious social problems of too few jobs and too much income inequality in the United States.

As for the charge that public assistance weakens families, liberals agree that the proportion of single-parent families has risen, but they do not see AFDC as the reason. Rather, they see single parenting as a broad cultural trend found at all class levels in many countries.

Figure 11–5 shows that people in the United States, more than people in

other industrial nations, tend to see poverty as a mark of laziness and personal failure. It should not be surprising, then, that Congress replaced the federal AFDC program with state-run programs called Temporary Assistance for Needy Families (TANF). The federal government provides funding, and states set their own qualifications and benefits, but they must limit assistance to two consecutive years (with a lifetime limit of five years).

By 2004, TANF had moved more than half of single parents on welfare into jobs or job training. In addition, the rate of out-of-wedlock births has fallen. Supporters of welfare reform see the new program as a success. But critics point out that many of the people who are now working earn so little that they are hardly better off than before, and half of these workers have no health insurance. In other words, the reform has greatly reduced the number of people receiving welfare, but it has done little to reduce poverty. In addition, say the critics, many of these working women now spend less time with their children. For these reasons, the welfare debate goes on.

WHAT DO YOU THINK?

1. How does our cultural emphasis on self-reliance help explain the controversy surrounding public assistance? Why do people not criticize benefits (like home mortgage deductions) for more well-off people?
2. Do you approve of the benefit time limits built into the new TANF program? Why or why not?
3. Why do you think the welfare reforms have done little to reduce poverty?

Sources: Corcoran et al. (2000), U.S. Department of Health and Human Services (2000), Rogers-Dillon (2001), Hofferth (2002), Lichter & Crowley (2002), and Lichter & Jayakody (2002).

☞ Times

The New York Times

June 29, 2004

Surge in Homeless Families Sets Off Debate on Cause

By LESLIE KAUFMAN

ST. CLOUD, Minn.—In small cities like this one and big ones like Kansas City, Mo., and New York, families are knocking on the doors of homeless shelters in growing numbers. Inside a faded yellow-brick Victorian on a block near downtown here, dozens of families know of the increase firsthand.

Behind the front door, the 11 rooms of the Landon House Shelter are packed with homeless parents and their children, often exceeding the 48-bed capacity and requiring the staff to roll out cots. . . .

"We are always full," said Darlene Johnson, executive director of the shelter. "Pretty much bursting out of the seams." . . .

This wind-swept Plains city of 60,000 about 60 miles northwest of Minneapolis has seen the number of families requesting shelter climb by 45 percent in the last decade, to an average of 124 fam-

ilies a night. The number of homeless families in Minnesota tripled to 1,341 a night in 2003 from 434 in 1991, when the state first started conducting surveys every three years, and most of the last increase came in rural areas like this one.

And Minnesota is not alone. . . . The Urban Institute, a research group in Washington that surveyed homeless assistance providers in 1996, . . . found that at least 1.4 million children and 2 million adults were homeless, but that number has surely grown as cities like Columbus, Ohio; Philadelphia; St. Louis; and New York have all reported surges at their homeless shelters for the last two or three years. . . .

Family homelessness first emerged as a national problem in the mid-1980s. After a public outcry over the wretched conditions endured by many such families living in crumbling converted hotels, President Ronald Reagan in 1987 signed the McKinney Act, which gave states money to build emergency shelters and

help such families. In the years since, billions in federal dollars have financed an explosion in the number of such shelters. In 2003 alone, the federal government spent $1.3 billion on more than 3,700 local programs that run shelters. . . .

Some liberals have expressed concern that these shelters have done little more than hide a shameful epidemic from public view, while conservatives have argued that they have become an expensive magnet for poor families who are unhappy with their living situations and are seeking government help. Yet almost everyone agrees that the number of families knocking on their doors continues to swell. . . .

Many academics and advocates for the homeless cite a widening gulf between income and rents. Real pay for the bottom 10 percent of wage earners rose less than 1 percent in adjusted dollars from 1979 to 2003. . . . Welfare payments buy less than half of what they did

Other people see homelessness as resulting from *societal factors,* including low wages and a lack of low-income housing (Kozol, 1988; Bohannan, 1991; L. Kaufman, 2004). Supporters of this position note that one-third of the homeless consists of entire families, and they point to children as the fastest-growing category of the homeless.

  YOUR TURN

Our society has been more generous with the "worthy" poor (such as elderly people) than with the "unworthy" poor (such as able-bodied people who, we assume, should take care of themselves). Why do you think we have not done more to reduce poverty among children, who surely fall into the "worthy" category?

No one disputes that a large proportion of homeless people is personally impaired to some degree, but cause and effect are difficult to untangle. Structural changes in the U.S. economy, coupled with reduced aid to low-income people and a real estate market that puts housing out of the reach of the poorest members of U.S. society, all contribute to homelessness.

Finally, social stratification extends far beyond the borders of the United States. In fact, the most striking social inequality is found not within any one nation but in the different living standards from nation to nation around the world. In Chapter 12 ("Global Stratification"), we broaden our investigation of stratification by looking at global inequality.

in 1970, and millions of families no longer receive them at all.

By contrast, housing costs have nearly tripled since 1979, . . . and . . . city governments have been steadily eliminating public housing. . . .

If tight rental markets tell part of the story, they are clearly not the whole story. Since the 1980s, a significant body of research has developed to show that the heads of homeless families, like their single, street-sleeping male counterparts, are often drug addicts or mentally impaired or both.

The families are also disproportionately African American and usually headed by unwed mothers or women fleeing domestic violence. . . .

Critics of the shelter system argue that it may be abetting personal dysfunction. The shelter system constructed with federal dollars after the McKinney Act was a vast improvement over the shoddy hotels of the 1980s. Many programs, particularly in New York, place families in the shelter at the top of the list for government subsidized rental apartments, an incentive that New York is considering dropping.

Such a system actually encourages families to enter the shelter system, argues Howard Husock, who teaches at the John F. Kennedy School of Government at Harvard University, particularly those who are doubled up with relatives or living in otherwise uncomfortable situations because of personal choices, including unwed motherhood. . . .

[Philip F.] Mangano, the Bush administration's homelessness chief, said . . . the emergency shelter system that Washington had built might have been a misuse of money.

"If we had an opportunity to go back, we might have created a different response on homeless[ness], one that focused more on investing in housing," he said. "We spent billions of dollars and have had 20 years of shuffling homeless people from one side of town to the other, from one homeless program to another. It is a disgrace."

WHAT DO YOU THINK?

1. Why do you think homelessness is not discussed much by our political leaders in Congress?

2. What are some of the reasons for homelessness given in the article? Which do you think is most important? Why?

3. What changes in our national policy toward homelessness would you support? Why?

Adapted from the original article by Leslie Kaufman published in *The New York Times* on June 29, 2004. Copyright © 2004 by The New York Times Company. Reprinted with permission.

MAKING THE GRADE

The following learning tools will help you see what you know, identify what you still need to learn, and expand your understanding beyond the text. You can also visit this text's Companion Website™ at http://www.prenhall.com/macionis to find additional practice tests.

KEY POINTS

Dimensions of Social Inequality

Social stratification in the United States involves inequality of income, wealth, power, and prestige. White-collar jobs generally offer greater income and prestige than blue-collar work. Many of the jobs typically held by women offer low social prestige or income. Schooling is also a resource that is distributed unequally. Eighty-five percent of people over age twenty-five complete high school, but only 28 percent are college graduates.

U.S. Stratification: Merit and Caste

Although U.S. society is partly a meritocracy, at birth children receive the social position of their parents. Family ancestry, race and ethnicity, and gender all affect people's social standing.

Social Classes in the United States

The upper class (5 percent of the population) includes the richest and most powerful families. Most members of the upper-upper class, or the "old rich," inherit their wealth; the lower-upper class, or the "new rich," work at high-paying jobs. The middle class (40 to 45 percent) enjoys financial security, but only upper-middle-class people have substantial wealth. With below-average incomes, most members of the working class or lower-middle class (33 percent) have blue-collar jobs, and only one-third of their children reach college. About 20 percent of the U.S. population belongs to the lower class; more than half of these people live below the government's poverty line.

The Difference Class Makes

People with above-average incomes have better health than those whose income is below average. Social class standing also shapes some values and political attitudes. Children born into families with higher social standing receive a great advantage in the form of "cultural capital."

Social Mobility

Some social mobility is common in the United States, as it is in other high-income countries. Typically, however, only small changes occur from one generation to the next. Due to the growing global economy, the wealthiest families in the United States now earn more than ever. There have been only slight increases in average income among families near the bottom of the class system.

Poverty in the United States

The government classifies 40 million people as poor. About 35 percent of the poor are children under age eighteen. Two-thirds of the poor are white, but African Americans and Hispanics are disproportionately represented among people with low income. The *feminization of poverty* means that more poor families are headed by women.

The *culture of poverty* thesis suggests that poverty is caused by shortcomings in the poor themselves. Others believe that poverty is caused by society's unequal distribution of jobs and wealth. The U.S. cultural emphasis on individual responsibility helps explain why public assistance for the poor has long been controversial.

 **KEY CONCEPTS**

income (p. 280) earnings from work or investments

wealth (p. 281) the total value of money and other assets, minus outstanding debts

intragenerational social mobility (p. 289) a change in social position occurring during a person's lifetime

intergenerational social mobility (p. 289) upward or downward social mobility of children in relation to their parents

relative poverty (p. 294) the deprivation of some people in relation to those who have more

absolute poverty (p. 294) a deprivation of resources that is life-threatening

feminization of poverty (p. 295) the trend of women making up an increasing proportion of the poor

---

SAMPLE TEST QUESTIONS

These questions are similar to those found in the test bank that accompanies this textbook.

Multiple-Choice Questions

1. **Which term refers to earnings from work or investments?**
   a. income
   b. assets
   c. wealth
   d. power

2. **The wealthiest 20 percent of people in the United States own about how much of the country's privately owned wealth?**
   a. 34 percent
   b. 54 percent
   c. 84 percent
   d. 94 percent

3. **About what share of U.S. adults over the age of twenty-five are college graduates?**
   a. 10 percent
   b. 28 percent
   c. 40 percent
   d. 68 percent

4. **In the United States, average income for African American families is what share of average income for non-Hispanic white families?**
   a. 98 percent
   b. 85 percent
   c. 75 percent
   d. 58 percent

5. **Which of the following is another term for the "working class"?**
   a. upper-middle class
   b. average-middle class
   c. lower-middle class
   d. lower class

6. In terms of health, people living in high-income families
   a. live in safer and less stressful environments.
   b. are more likely to describe their own health as "excellent."
   c. live longer lives.
   d. all of the above.

7. Which quintile (20 percent) of the U.S. population has seen the greatest change in income over the last generation?
   a. the top quintile
   b. the middle quintile
   c. the lowest quintile
   d. All quintiles have seen the same change.

8. Change in social position during a person's own lifetime is called
   a. intergenerational social mobility.
   b. intragenerational social mobility.
   c. structural social mobility.
   d. horizontal social mobility.

9. In 2004, about what share of the U.S. population was officially counted as poor?
   a. 42.7 percent   b. 22.5 percent
   c. 12.7 percent   d. 2.5 percent

10. Which age category of the U.S. population has the highest percentage of people in poverty?
   a. seniors over age sixty-five
   b. middle-aged people
   c. young people in their twenties
   d. children

Answers: 1(a); 2(c); 3(b); 4(d); 5(c); 6(d); 7(a); 8(b); 9(c); 10(d).

Essay Questions

1. We often hear people say that the United States is a "middle-class society." Where does this idea come from? Based on what you have read in this chapter, how true do you think this claim is? Why?

2. What is the extent of poverty in the United States? Who are the poor in terms of age, race and ethnicity, and gender?

APPLICATIONS & EXERCISES

1. Develop several questions that, taken together, will let you measure social class position. The trick is to decide what you think social class really means. Then try your questions on several adults, refining the questions as you proceed.

2. During an evening of television viewing, assess the social class level of the characters you see on various shows. In each case, explain why you assign someone a particular social position. What patterns do you find?

3. Governor Arnold Schwarzenegger of California recently said, "In this country, it doesn't make any difference where you were born. It doesn't make any difference who your parents were. It doesn't make any difference if, like me, you couldn't even speak English until you were in your twenties. America gave me opportunities, and my immigrant dreams came true. I want other people to get the same chances I did, the same opportunities. And I believe they can." Ask a number of people who came to the United States from another country the extent to which they agree or disagree with this statement.

INVESTIGATE with Research Navigator

Follow the instructions on page 27 of this text to access the features of **Research Navigator**™. Once at the Web site, enter your Login Name and Password. Then, to use the **ContentSelect**™ database, enter keywords such as "homelessness," "welfare reform," and "poverty," and the search engine will supply relevant and recent scholarly and popular press publications. Use the *New York Times* **Search-by-Search Archive** to find recent news articles related to sociology and the **Link Library** feature to find relevant Web links organized by the key terms associated with this chapter.

Global Stratification

What share of the world's people live
in absolute poverty?

Why are some of the world's countries
so rich and others so poor?

Are rich nations making global poverty
better or worse? How?

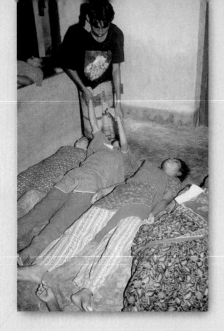

MORE THAN 1,000 workers were busily sewing together polo shirts on the fourth floor of the garment factory in Narsingdi, a small town about thirty miles northeast of Bangladesh's capital city of Dhaka. The thumping of hundreds of sewing machines combined to produce a steady roar that never stopped throughout the long working day.

But in an instant everything changed—an electric gun a worker used to shoot spot remover gave off a spark, which ignited the flammable liquid. Suddenly, a work table burst into flames. Nearby workers rushed to smother the fire with shirts, but there was no stopping the blaze: In a room filled with combustible materials, the flames spread quickly.

The workers scrambled toward the narrow staircase that led to the street. At the bottom, however, the human wave pouring down the steep steps collided with a folding metal gate across the doorway that was kept locked to prevent workers from leaving during work hours. Panicked, the people turned, only to be pushed back by the hundreds behind them. In a single terrifying minute of screaming voices, thrusting legs, and pounding hearts, dozens were crushed and trampled. By the time the gates were opened and the fire put out, fifty-two garment workers lay dead.

Garment factories like this one are big business in Bangladesh, where clothing makes up 75 percent of the country's total economic exports. Half of the garments shipped from Bangladesh end up in clothing stores in the United States. The reason so much of the clothing we buy is made in poor countries like Bangladesh is simple economics—Bangladeshi garment workers labor for close to twelve hours a day, typically seven days a week, and yet earn only between $400 and $500 a year, which is just a few percent of what a garment worker makes in the United States.

Tanveer Chowdhury manages the garment factory owned by his family. Speaking to reporters, he complained bitterly about the tragedy. "This fire has cost me $586,373, and that does not include $70,000 for machinery and $20,000 for furniture. I made commitments to meet deadlines, and I still have the deadlines. I am now paying for air freight at $10 a dozen when I should be shipping by sea at 87 cents a dozen."

There was one other cost Mr. Chowdhury did not mention. To compensate families for the loss of their loved ones in the fire, he eventually agreed to pay $1,952 per person. In Bangladesh, life—like labor—is cheap (based on Bearak, 2001). ■

These garment workers in Bangladesh are part of the roughly 1 billion of the world's people who work hard every day and yet remain poor. As this chapter explains, although poverty is a reality in the United States and other nations, the greatest social inequality is not *within* nations but *between* them (Goesling, 2001). We can understand the full dimensions of poverty only by exploring **global stratification,** *patterns of social inequality in the world as a whole.*

Global Stratification: An Overview

Chapter 11 ("Social Class in the United States") described social inequality in the United States. In global perspective, however, social stratification is far greater. Figure 12–1 divides the world's total income by fifths of the population. Recall from Chapter 11 that the richest 20 percent of the U.S. population earn about 48 percent of the national income (see Figure 11–1 on page 281). The richest 20 percent of global population, however, receive about 80 percent of world income. At the other extreme, the poorest 20 percent of the U.S. population earn 4 percent of our national income; the poorest fifth of the world's people struggles to survive on just 1 percent of global income.

Because some countries are so much richer than others, even people in the United States with income below the government's poverty line live far better than the majority of the Earth's people. The average person living in a rich nation such as the United States is extremely well-off by world standards. At the very top of the pyramid, the wealth of the world's richest person (Bill Gates in the United States, who was worth about $51 billion in 2005) equals the total economic output of the world's forty-five poorest *countries* (Miller & Newcomb, 2005; United Nations Development Programme, 2005).

A WORD ABOUT TERMINOLOGY

Classifying the world's 192 nations into categories ignores many striking differences. These nations have rich and varied histories, speak different languages, and take pride in distinctive cultures. However, various models have been developed that help distinguish countries on the basis of global stratification.

One such model, developed after World War II, labeled the rich, industrial countries the "First World," less industrialized, socialist countries the "Second World," and nonindustrialized, poor countries the "Third World." But the "three worlds" model is now less useful. For one thing, it was a product of Cold War politics by which the capitalist West (the First World) faced off against the socialist East (the Second World), while other nations (the Third World) remained more or less on the sidelines. But the sweeping changes in Eastern Europe and the collapse of the former Soviet Union mean that a distinctive Second World no longer exists.

A second problem is that the "three worlds" model lumped together more than 100 countries as the Third World. In reality, some relatively better-off nations of the Third World (such as Chile in South America) have industrialized enough that they have fifteen times the

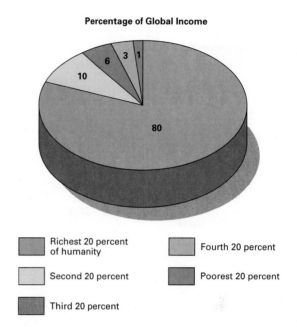

Percentage of Global Income

- Richest 20 percent of humanity
- Second 20 percent
- Third 20 percent
- Fourth 20 percent
- Poorest 20 percent

FIGURE 12-1   Distribution of World Income

Global income is very unequal, with the richest 20 percent of the world's people earning eighty times as much as the poorest 20 percent.

Sources: Calculated by the author based on United Nations Development Programme (2000) and World Bank (2001).

per-person productivity of the poorest countries of the world (including Ethiopia in East Africa).

These facts call for a modestly revised system of classification. Here we define the fifty *high-income countries* as the richest nations with the highest overall standards of living. The world's eighty *middle-income countries* are not as rich; they are nations with a standard of living about average for the world as a whole. The remaining sixty *low-income countries* are nations with a low standard of living in which most people are poor.

This model has two advantages over the older "three worlds" system. First, it focuses on economic development rather than whether societies are capitalist or socialist. Second, it gives a better picture of the relative economic development of various countries because it does not lump together all lower-income nations into a single "Third World."

When ranking countries, keep in mind that there is social stratification within every nation. In Bangladesh, for example, members of the Chowdhury family, who own the garment factory noted in the chapter-opening story, earn as

Japan represents the world's high-income countries, in which industrial technology and economic expansion have produced material prosperity. The presence of market forces is evident in this view of downtown Tokyo (above, left). The Russian Federation represents the middle-income countries of the world. Industrial development and economic performance were sluggish under socialism; as a result, Moscow residents had to wait in long lines for their daily needs (above, right). The hope is that the introduction of a market system will raise living standards, although in the short run, Russian citizens must adjust to increasing economic inequality. Bangladesh (left) represents the world's low-income countries. As the photograph suggests, these nations have limited economic development and rapidly increasing populations. The result is widespread poverty.

much as $1 million per year, which is several thousand times more than their workers earn. Of course, the full extent of global inequality is even greater, because the wealthiest people in rich countries such as the United States live worlds apart from the poorest people in low-income nations such as Bangladesh, Haiti, or Sudan.

HIGH-INCOME COUNTRIES

In nations where the Industrial Revolution first took place more than two centuries ago, productivity increased more than 100-fold. To understand the power of industrial and computer technology, consider that the Netherlands, one small European nation, is more productive than the whole continent of Africa south of the Sahara Desert; likewise, tiny South Korea outproduces all of India.

Global Map 12–1 shows that the high-income nations of the world include the United States and Canada, Argentina and Chile, the nations of Western Europe, Israel, Saudi Arabia, South Africa, Singapore, Hong Kong (now part of the People's Republic of China), Japan, South Korea, Australia, and New Zealand.

These countries cover roughly 25 percent of the Earth's land area, including parts of five continents, and they lie mostly in the Northern Hemisphere. In 2005, the total population of these nations was about 1.1 billion, or about 18 percent of the Earth's people. About three-fourths of the people in high-income countries live in or near cities.

Significant cultural differences exist among high-income countries; for example, the nations of Europe recognize more than thirty official languages. But these societies have something in common: They all produce enough economic goods and services to enable their people to lead a comfortable life. Per capita income (that is, average income per person per year) ranges from about $10,000 annually (in Chile and South Africa) to more than $37,000 annually (in the United States and Norway). In fact,

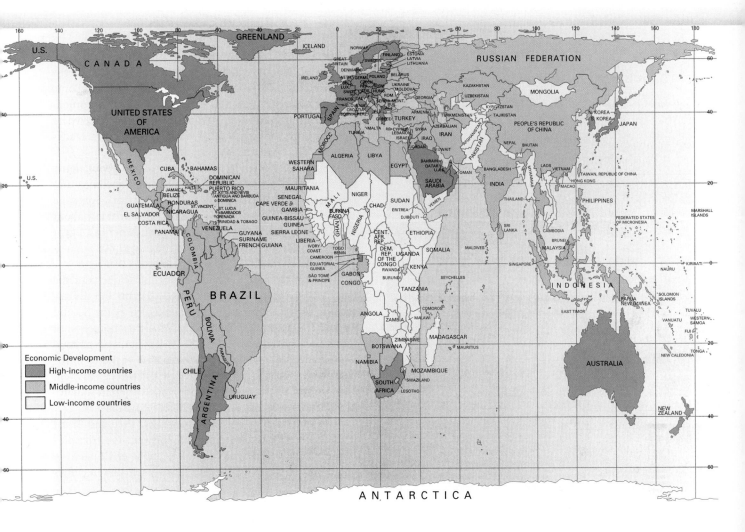

WINDOW ON THE WORLD

GLOBAL MAP 12-1   Economic Development in Global Perspective

In high-income countries—including the United States, Canada, Chile, Argentina, the nations of Western Europe, South Africa, Israel, Saudi Arabia, Australia, and Japan—a highly productive economy provides people, on average, with material plenty. Middle-income countries—including most of Latin America and Asia—are less economically productive, with a standard of living about average for the world as a whole but far below that of the United States. These nations also have a significant share of poor people who are barely able to feed and house themselves. In the low-income countries of the world, poverty is severe and widespread. Although small numbers of elites live very well in the poorest nations, most people struggle to survive on a small fraction of the income common in the United States.

Note: Data for this map are provided by the United Nations. Each country's economic productivity is measured in terms of its gross domestic product (GDP), which is the total value of all the goods and services produced by a country's economy within its borders in a given year. Dividing each country's GDP by the country's population gives us the per capita (per-person) GDP and allows us to compare the economic performance of countries of different population sizes. High-income countries have a per capita GDP of more than $10,000. Many are far richer than this, however; the figure for the United States exceeds $37,000. Middle-income countries have a per capita GDP ranging from $2,500 to $10,000. Low-income countries have a per capita GDP of less than $2,500. Figures used here reflect the United Nations "purchasing power parities" system, which is an estimate of what people can buy using their income in the local economy.

Source: Based on data from United Nations Development Programme (2005). Map projection from *Peters Atlas of the World* (1990).

When Hurricane Katrina flooded the city of New Orleans, most of the population evacuated, leaving behind those who were too old, too sick, or too poor to make their way to safety. This disaster revealed that, although the United States is a high-income nation, our society contains more serious poverty than most people realize.

MIDDLE-INCOME COUNTRIES

Middle-income countries have a per capita income of between $2,500 and $10,000, roughly the median for the world's nations. Two-thirds of the people in middle-income countries live in cities, and industrial jobs are common. The remaining one-third of people live in rural areas, where most are poor and lack access to schools, medical care, adequate housing, and even safe drinking water.

Looking at Global Map 12–1, we see that about eighty of the world's nations fall into the middle-income category. At the high end are Mexico (Latin America), Botswana (Africa), and Malaysia (Asia), where annual income is about $9,000. At the low end are Ecuador (Latin America), Egypt (Africa), and Indonesia (Asia), with roughly $3,000 annually in per capita income.

One cluster of middle-income countries includes the countries that once made up the Soviet Union and the nations of Eastern Europe (in the past known as the Second World). These countries had mostly socialist economies until popular revolts between 1989 and 1991 swept their governments aside. Since then, these nations have begun to introduce market systems, but so far the results have been uneven. Some (including Poland) have improving economies, but living standards in others (including Russia) have fallen.

Other middle-income nations include Peru and Brazil in South America and Namibia and Botswana in Africa. Recently, both India and the People's Republic of China have entered the middle-income category, which now includes most of Asia.

Taken together, middle-income countries span roughly 55 percent of the Earth's land area and include about 4.5 billion people, or about 70 percent of humanity. Some countries (such as Russia) are far less crowded than others (such as El Salvador), but compared to high-income countries, these societies are densely populated.

people in high-income countries enjoy 79 percent of the world's total income.

Keep in mind that high-income countries have many low-income people. The Thinking About Diversity box profiles the striking poverty that exists along the southern border of the United States.

Production in rich nations is capital-intensive; it is based on factories, big machinery, and advanced technology. Most of the largest corporations that design and market computers, as well as most computer users, are located in high-income countries. High-income countries control the world's financial markets, so daily events in the financial exchanges of New York, London, and Tokyo affect people throughout the world.

YOUR TURN

Why do you think most people from high-income countries who travel to middle- or low-income nations do so as tourists, but most who travel from middle- or low-income nations to high-income countries do so as immigrants?

LOW-INCOME COUNTRIES

Low-income countries, where most people are very poor, are mostly agrarian societies with some industry. Many of

THINKING ABOUT DIVERSITY:
RACE, CLASS, & GENDER

Las Colonias: "America's Third World"

"We wanted to have something for ourselves," explains Olga Ruiz, who has lived in the border community of College Park, Texas, for eleven years. There is no college in College Park, nor does this dusty stretch of rural land have sewer lines or even running water. Yet this town is one of some 1,800 settlements that have sprouted up in southern Texas along the 1,200-mile border from El Paso down to Brownsville. Together, they are home to perhaps 700,000 people, a number expected to pass 1 million by 2010.

Many people speak of *las colonias* (Spanish for "the colonies") as "America's Third World" because these desperately poor communities look much like their counterparts in Mexico or many other middle- or low-income nations. But this is the United States, and almost all of the people living in the *colonias* are Hispanic Americans, 85 percent of them legal residents and more than half U.S. citizens.

Anastacia Ledsema, now seventy-two years old, moved to a *colonia* called Sparks more than forty years ago. Born in Mexico, Ledsema married a Texas man, and together they paid $200 for a quarter-acre lot in a new border community. For months, they

camped out on their land. Step by step, they invested their labor and their money to build a modest house. Not until 1995 did their small community get running water—a service that had been promised by developers years before. When the water line finally did arrive, however, things changed more than they expected. "When we got water," recalls Ledsema, "that's when so many people came in." The population of Sparks quickly doubled to about 3,000, overwhelming the water supply so that sometimes the faucet does not run at all.

The residents of all the *colonias* know that they are poor. Indeed, the Census Bureau recently declared the county surrounding one border

community to be the poorest in the entire United States. Concerned over the lack of basic services in so many of these communities, Texas officials have banned any new settlements. But most of the people who move here—even those who start off sleeping in their cars or trucks—see these communities as the first step on the path to the American Dream. Oscar Solis, a neighborhood leader in Panorama Village, a community with a population of about 150, is proud to show visitors around the small but growing town. "All of this work we have done ourselves," he says with a smile, "to make our dreams come true."

WHAT DO YOU THINK?

1. Are you surprised that such poverty exists in the United States? Why or why not?
2. Why do you think such communities get little attention from the U.S. mass media?
3. To what extent do you think people living in these communities will have their "dreams come true"? Explain.

Source: Based on Schaffer (2002).

these sixty nations, identified in Global Map 12–1 on page 309, are found in Central and East Africa and Asia. Low-income countries cover 20 percent of the planet's land area and are home to 12 percent of its people. Population density is generally high, although greater in Asian countries (such as Bangladesh and Pakistan) than in Central African nations (like Chad and the Democratic Republic of the Congo).

In poor countries, one-third of the people live in cities; most inhabit villages and farms as their ancestors have done for centuries. About half the world's people are farmers, most of whom follow cultural traditions. With limited

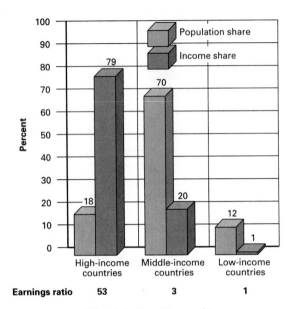

FIGURE 12-2 The Relative Share of Income and Population by Level of Economic Development

For every dollar earned by people in low-income countries, people in high-income countries earn $53.

Sources: Calculated by the author based on United Nations Development Programme (2000) and World Bank (2001).

industrial technology, they cannot be very productive, one reason that many suffer severe poverty. Hunger, disease, and unsafe housing shape the lives of the world's poorest people.

People living in affluent nations such as the United States find it hard to understand the scope of human need in much of the world. From time to time, televised pictures of famine in very poor countries such as Ethiopia and Bangladesh give us shocking glimpses of the poverty that makes every day a life-and-death struggle for many in low-income nations. Behind these images lie cultural, historical, and economic forces that we shall explore in the remainder of this chapter.

Global Wealth and Poverty

> October 14, Manila, Philippines. What caught my eye was how clean she was—a girl no more than seven or eight years old. She was wearing a freshly laundered dress, and her

hair was carefully combed. She stopped to watch us, following us with her eyes: Camera-toting Americans stand out in this, one of the poorest neighborhoods in the entire world.

Fed by methane from decomposing garbage, the fires never go out on Smokey Mountain, the vast garbage dump on the north side of Manila. Smoke covers the hills of refuse like a thick fog. But Smokey Mountain is more than a dump; it is a neighborhood that is home to thousands of people. It is hard to imagine a setting more hostile to human life. Amid the smoke and the squalor, men and women do what they can to survive. They pick plastic bags from the garbage and wash them in the river, and they collect cardboard boxes or anything else they can sell. What chance do their children have, coming from families that earn only a few hundred dollars a year, with hardly any opportunity for schooling, year after year breathing this foul air? Against this backdrop of human tragedy, one lovely little girl has put on a fresh dress and gone out to play.

Now our taxi driver threads his way through heavy traffic as we head for the other side of Manila. The change is amazing: The smoke and smell of the dump give way to neighborhoods that could be in Miami or Los Angeles. A cluster of yachts floats on the bay in the distance. No more rutted streets; now we glide quietly along wide boulevards lined with trees and filled with expensive Japanese cars. We pass shopping plazas, upscale hotels, and high-rise office buildings. Every block or so we see the gated entrance to another exclusive residential community with security guards standing watch. Here, in large, air-conditioned homes, the rich of Manila live—and many of the poor work.

Low-income nations are home to some rich and many poor people. The fact that most people live with incomes of just a few hundred dollars a year means that the burden of poverty is far greater than among the poor of the United States. This is not to suggest that U.S. poverty is a minor problem. In so rich a country, too little food, substandard housing, and no medical care for tens of millions of people—almost half of them children—amount to a national tragedy.

THE SEVERITY OF POVERTY

Poverty in poor countries is more severe than it is in rich countries. A key reason that the quality of life differs so much around the world is that economic productivity is lowest in precisely the regions where population growth is highest. Figure 12–2 shows the proportion of world population and global income for countries at each level of economic development. High-income countries are by far the most advantaged, with 79 percent of global income supporting just 18 percent of humanity. In middle-income nations, 70 percent of the world's people earn 20 percent of global income. This leaves 12 percent of the planet's population with just 1 percent of global income. In short, for every dollar received by individuals in a low-income country, someone in a high-income country takes home $53.

Table 12–1 shows the extent of wealth and well-being in specific countries around the world. The first column of figures gives gross domestic product (GDP) for a number of high-, middle-, and low-income countries.[1] The United States, a large and highly productive nation, had a 2003 GDP of more than $10 trillion; Japan's GDP was more than $4 trillion. A comparison of GDP figures shows that the world's richest nations are thousands of times more productive than the poorest countries.

The second column of figures in Table 12–1 divides GDP by the entire population size to give an estimate of what people can buy using their income in the local economy. The per capita GDP for rich countries like the United States, Sweden, and Canada is very high, exceeding $26,000. For middle-income countries, such as Mexico and the Russian Federation, the figures are in the $7,000 range. In the world's low-income countries, per capita GDP is just a few hundred dollars. In the Central African Republic or in Ethiopia, for example, a typical person labors all year to make what the average worker in the United States earns in a week.

The last column of Table 12–1 measures quality of life in the various nations. This index, calculated by the United Nations, is based on income, education (extent of adult literacy and average years of schooling), and longevity (how long people typically live). Index values are decimals that fall between extremes of one (highest) and zero (lowest). By this calculation, Norwegians enjoy the highest quality of life (.963), with residents of the United States close behind (.944). At the other extreme, people in the African nation of Niger have the lowest quality of life (.281).

---

[1]Gross domestic product (GDP) is the value of all the goods and services produced by a country's economy within its borders in a given year.

TABLE 12–1

Wealth and Well-Being in Global Perspective, 2003

Country	Gross Domestic Product (US$ billions)	GDP per Capita (PPP US$)*	Quality of Life Index
High-Income			
Norway	221	37,670	.963
Australia	522	29,632	.955
Sweden	302	26,750	.949
Canada	857	30,677	.949
United States	10,949	37,562	.944
Japan	4,301	27,967	.943
United Kingdom	1,795	27,147	.939
France	1,758	27,677	.938
South Korea	605	17,971	.901
Middle-Income			
Eastern Europe			
Russian Federation	433	9,230	.795
Romania	57	7,277	.792
Belarus	18	6,052	.786
Ukraine	50	5,491	.766
Latin America			
Mexico	626	9,168	.814
Brazil	492	7,790	.792
Venezuela	85	4,919	.772
Asia			
Malaysia	104	9,512	.796
Thailand	143	7,595	.778
People's Republic of China	1,417	5,003	.755
Middle East			
Iran	137	6,995	.736
Syria	22	3,576	.721
Africa			
Algeria	67	6,107	.722
Botswana	8	8,714	.565
Low-Income			
Latin America			
Haiti	3	1,742	.475
Asia			
Cambodia	4	2,078	.571
Pakistan	82	2,097	.527
Bangladesh	52	1,770	.520
Africa			
Guinea	4	2,097	.466
Ethiopia	7	711	.367
Central African Republic	1	1,089	.355
Niger	3	835	.281

*These data are the United Nations' purchasing power parity (PPP) calculations, which avoid currency rate distortion by showing the local purchasing power of each domestic currency.

Source: United Nations Development Programme, *Human Development Report 2005* (New York: United Nations Development Programme, 2005).

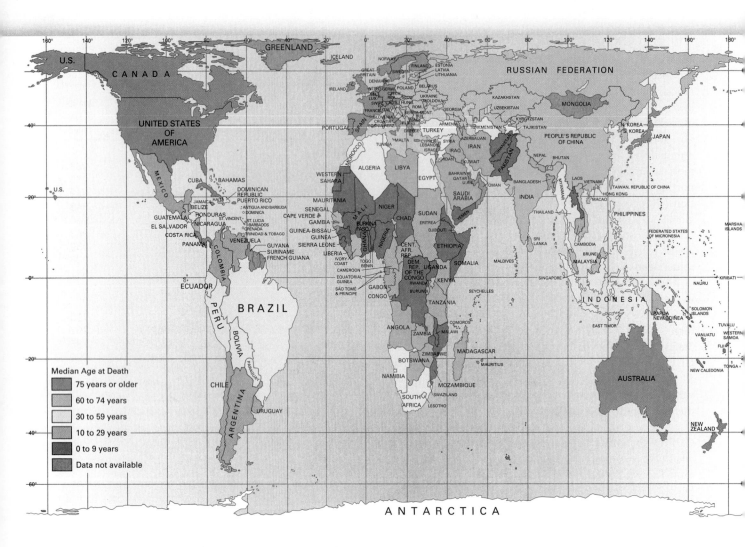

WINDOW ON THE WORLD

GLOBAL MAP 12-2 Median Age at Death in Global Perspective

This map identifies the age below which half of all deaths occur in any year. In the high-income countries of the world, including the United States, it is mostly the elderly who face death, that is, people aged seventy-five or older. In middle-income countries, including most of Latin America, most people die years or even decades earlier. In low-income countries, especially in Africa and parts of Asia, it is children who die, half of them never reaching their tenth birthday.

Sources: World Bank (1993), with updates by the author; map projection from *Peters Atlas of the World* (1990).

Relative versus Absolute Poverty

The distinction between relative and absolute poverty, made in Chapter 11 ("Social Class in the United States"), has an important application to global inequality. People living in rich countries generally focus on *relative poverty*, meaning that some people lack resources that are taken for granted by others. By definition, relative poverty exists in every society, rich or poor.

More important in global perspective, however, is *absolute poverty*, a lack of resources that is life-threatening.

Find a report by the World Bank on strategies to reduce global poverty at http://www1.worldbank.org/publications/pdfs/14978frontmat.pdf

Human beings in absolute poverty lack the nutrition necessary for health and long-term survival. To be sure, some absolute poverty exists in the United States. But such immediately life-threatening poverty strikes only a very small proportion of the U.S. population; in low-income countries, by contrast, one-third or more of the people are in desperate need.

Because absolute poverty is deadly, one global indicator of this problem is median age at death. Global Map 12–2 identifies the age by which half of all people born in a nation die. In rich societies, most people die after the age of seventy-five; in poor countries, half of all deaths occur among children under the age of ten.

THE EXTENT OF POVERTY

Poverty in poor countries is more widespread than it is in rich nations such as the United States. Chapter 11 ("Social Class in the United States") noted that the U.S. government officially classifies almost 13 percent of the population as poor. In low-income countries, however, most people live no better than the poor in the United States, and many are far worse off. As Global Map 12–2 shows, the high death rates among children in Africa indicate that absolute poverty is greatest there, where half the population is malnourished. In the world as a whole, at any given time, 15 percent of the people—about 1 billion—suffer from chronic hunger, which leaves them less able to work and puts them at high risk of disease (Kates, 1996; United Nations Development Programme, 2001). "In the *Times*" on pages 316–17 explains the difficulty that the United Nations is having measuring the extent of serious poverty in the world.

The typical adult in a rich nation such as the United States consumes about 3,500 calories a day, an excess that contributes to widespread obesity and related health problems. The typical adult in a low-income country not only does more physical labor but consumes just 2,000 calories a day. The result is undernourishment: too little food or not enough of the right kinds of food.

In the ten minutes it takes to read this section of the chapter, about 300 people in the world who are sick and weakened from hunger will die. This number amounts to about 40,000 people a day, or 15 million people each year. Clearly, easing world hunger is one of the most serious responsibilities facing humanity today.

POVERTY AND CHILDREN

Death comes early in poor societies, where families lack adequate food, safe water, secure housing, and access to

Tens of millions of children fend for themselves every day on the streets of Latin America, where many fall victim to disease, drug abuse, and outright violence. What do you think must be done to put an end to scenes like this one in San Salvador, the capital city of El Salvador?

medical care. Organizations fighting child poverty estimate that at least 100 million children living in cities in poor countries beg, steal, sell sex, or work for drug gangs to provide income for their families. Such a life almost always means dropping out of school and puts children at high risk of disease and violence. Many girls, with little or no access to medical assistance, become pregnant, a case of children who cannot support themselves having children of their own.

Analysts estimate that another 100 million of the world's children leave their families altogether, sleeping and living on the streets as best they can or perhaps trying to migrate to the United States. Roughly 50 million of these street children are found in Latin American cities such as

 Read more about the lives of street children at http://www.hrw.org/children/street.htm

Mexico City and Rio de Janeiro, where half of all children grow up in poverty. Many people in the United States know these cities as exotic travel destinations, but they are also home to thousands of street children living in makeshift huts, under bridges, or in alleyways (J. Ross, 1996; United Nations Development Programme, 2000; Collymore, 2002).

February 3, 2005

U.N. Aims to Cut Poverty in Half as Experts Wonder How to Measure It

By ALAN B. KRUEGER

One of the United Nations' top goals is to cut in half the proportion of people living in extreme poverty by 2015. . . . Accurately monitoring poverty is essential for knowing whether the goal is achieved and whether antipoverty strategies are working.

But measuring poverty is difficult for a particular country, let alone the world. . . . Angelina Jolie challenged celebrities at the World Economic Forum in Davos, Switzerland, . . . to know "absolutely what they're talking about" when it comes to poverty, yet even experts would have trouble meeting her standard. . . .

First, establishing a poverty line . . . involves an element of arbitrariness. For many poor families, not having enough money amounts to not having enough food. But there is no particular threshold level of income or expenditures above which people automatically become fully functioning, nourished members of society.

"Poverty lines are as much political as scientific constructions," said Angus Deaton, a Princeton economist and expert on economic development. In such places as different as the United States and India, the poverty line was initially set with reference to minimum standards of food consumption. Yet over time, . . . the poverty lines in both countries were adjusted to keep pace with overall price inflation, not the price of food or the share of food in the average family's budget. . . .

The U.N. has set the line for extreme poverty at living on less than $1 a day. This threshold has obvious rhetorical appeal and surely qualifies as extreme poverty by any standard in developed countries; it is also not far off the poverty line used by many of the poorest countries themselves. . . .

To convert the $1 poverty line into foreign currencies, the World Bank uses indexes of "purchasing power parity." Simply put, these indexes reflect the cost of buying a standard bundle of goods in each country.

Although it is desirable to use purchasing indexes, they are not available for all countries and are skewed toward . . . the wealthiest households, not the poorest, when they are available. Another problem is that the bundle of goods that poor families actually buy varies from country to country because of differences in tastes and availability. . . .

Once the poverty line is set in local currency, the consumption of a representative sample of households must be compared with the line to determine the

---

 YOUR TURN

How do you think the experience of "childhood" as a stage of the life course differs in high- and low-income countries?

POVERTY AND WOMEN

In rich societies, much of the work women do is undervalued, underpaid, or overlooked entirely. In poor societies, women face even greater disadvantages. Most of the people who work in sweatshops like the one described in the opening to this chapter are women.

To make matters worse, tradition keeps women out of many jobs in low-income nations; in Bangladesh, for example, women work in garment factories because that society's conservative Muslim religious norms bar them from most other paid work and limit their opportunity for advanced schooling (Bearak, 2001). At the same time, traditional norms in poor societies give women primary responsibility for child rearing and maintaining the household. The United Nations estimates that in poor countries, men own 90 percent of the land, a far greater gender disparity in wealth than is found in high-income nations. It is no surprise, then, that about 70 percent of the world's 1 billion people living near absolute poverty are women (C. Hymowitz, 1995).

Finally, most women in poor countries receive little or no reproductive health care. Limited access to birth control keeps women at home with their children, keeps the birth rate high, and limits the economic production of the country.

percent of people getting by on less than $1 a day. (Each household's consumption is spread equally among its members, another leap of faith.)

Again, this is harder than it sounds. The World Bank typically relies on whatever government surveys that countries routinely produce.

But there is no uniform standard in the way countries collect and process their data. . . .

Consider India, home to 33 percent of the world's poor—or 20 percent, depending on how the data are collected. . . .

Perhaps the best one can hope for is consistency of measurement within countries to detect changes in poverty over time. . . .

The herculean measurement problems aside, careful research by Shaohua Chen and Martin Ravallion of the World Bank indicates that much progress has been made toward the goal of halving poverty in China and India. But, they found, little progress has occurred in Latin America and Africa, and the former Soviet states are slipping into deeper poverty. Because China and India accounted for 60 percent of the world's poor in 1990, the goal of halving poverty may be achieved a decade from now, even while many regions see no progress. . . .

An essential prerequisite is to improve poverty statistics and ensure their integrity.

Although the process of setting a poverty line is necessarily political, the task of measuring poverty should be insulated from political influences. The World Bank, however, is an inherently political institution.

Yet no other international body currently has the expertise or resources to monitor worldwide poverty. . . .

This may not be a cause that celebrities are ready to line up for, but improving poverty data will put the world in a better position to monitor progress and evaluate poverty reduction strategies by the time the poverty line is moved up to $2 a day.

WHAT DO YOU THINK?

1. Why are poverty lines as much political as scientific?

2. Why is measuring poverty an important part of the effort to reduce poverty?

3. Do you think global poverty will be reduced by half within the next decade? Why or why not?

Adapted from the original article by Alan B. Krueger published in *The New York Times* on February 3, 2005. Copyright © 2005 by The New York Times Company. Reprinted with permission.

Alan B. Krueger is the Bendheim professor of economics and public affairs at Princeton University.

SLAVERY

Poor societies have many problems in addition to hunger, including illiteracy, warfare, and even slavery. The British Empire banned slavery in 1833, followed by the United States in 1865. But according to Anti-Slavery International (ASI), as many as 200 million men, women, and children (about 3 percent of humanity) still live in conditions that amount to slavery.

ASI distinguishes four types of slavery. The first is *chattel slavery,* in which one person owns another. The number of chattel slaves is difficult to estimate because this practice is against the law almost everywhere. But the buying and selling of slaves still takes place in many countries in Asia, the Middle East, and especially Africa. The Thinking Globally box on page 318 describes the reality of one slave's life in the African nation of Mauritania.

A second, more common form of bondage is *child slavery,* in which desperately poor families send their children out into the streets to beg or steal or do whatever they can to survive. Perhaps 100 million children—many in the poorest countries of Latin America and Africa—fall into this category.

Third, *debt bondage* is the practice by which employers pay workers wages, but not enough to cover the food and housing provided by the employer. Unable to settle their debts, workers cannot leave and are therefore slaves. Many workers in sweatshops in poor countries fall into this category.

Fourth, *servile forms of marriage* may also amount to slavery. In India, Thailand, and some African nations, families marry off women against their will. Many end up as slaves working for their husband's family; some are forced into prostitution.

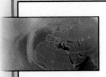
"God Made Me to Be a Slave"

Fatma Mint Mamadou is a young woman living in North Africa's Islamic Republic of Mauritania. Asked her age, she pauses, smiles, and shakes her head. She has no idea when she was born. Nor can she read or write. What she knows is tending camels, herding sheep, hauling bags of water, sweeping, and serving tea to her owners. This young woman is one of perhaps 90,000 slaves in Mauritania.

In the central region of this nation, having dark brown skin almost always means being a slave to an Arab owner. Fatma accepts her situation; she has known nothing else. She explains in a matter-of-fact voice that she is a slave like her mother before her and her grandmother before that. "Just as God created a camel to be a camel," she shrugs, "he created me to be a slave."

Fatma, her mother, and her brothers and sisters live in a squatter settlement on the edge of Nouakchott, Mauritania's capital city. Their home is a nine-by-twelve-foot hut that they built from wood scraps and other materials found at construction sites. The roof is nothing more than a piece of cloth; there is no plumbing or furniture. The nearest water comes from a well a mile down the road.

In this region, slavery began 500 years ago, about the time Columbus sailed west toward the Americas. As Arab and Berber tribes raided local villages, they made slaves of the people,

and so it has been for dozens of generations ever since. In 1905, the French colonial rulers of Mauritania banned slavery. After the nation gained independence in 1961, the new government reaffirmed the ban. But such proclamations have done little to change strong traditions. Indeed, people like Fatma have no idea what "freedom to choose" means.

The next question is more personal: "Are you and other girls ever raped?"

Again, Fatma hesitates. With no hint of emotion, she responds, "Of course, in the night the men come to breed us. Is that what you mean by rape?"

WHAT DO YOU THINK?

1. How does tradition play a part in keeping people in slavery?
2. Why do you think the world still tolerates slavery?
3. Explain the connection between slavery and poverty.

Human slavery continues to exist in the twenty-first century.

Source: Based on Burkett (1997).

Finally, one additional form of slavery is *human trafficking,* the moving of men, women, and children from one place to another for the purpose of performing forced labor. Women or men are brought to a new country with the promise of a job and then forced to become prostitutes or farm laborers, or people adopt children from another country and then force them to work in sweatshops. Such activity is big business: Next to trading in guns and drugs, trading in people brings the greatest profit to organized crime around the world (Orhant, 2002).

In 1948, the United Nations issued its Universal Declaration of Human Rights, which states, "No one shall be held in slavery or servitude; slavery and the slave trade shall be

Read the UN's Universal Declaration of Human Rights at http://www.un.org/rights/50/decla.htm

prohibited in all their forms." Unfortunately, nearly six decades later, this social evil persists.

EXPLANATIONS OF GLOBAL POVERTY

What accounts for the severe and extensive poverty throughout much of the world? The rest of this chapter weaves together explanations from the following facts about poor societies:

1. **Technology.** About one-quarter of people in low-income countries farm the land using human muscle

or animal power. With limited energy sources, economic production is modest.

2. **Population growth.** As Chapter 22 ("Population, Urbanization, and Environment") explains, the poorest countries have the world's highest birth rates. Despite the death toll from poverty, the populations of many poor countries in Africa, for example, double every twenty-five years. In these countries, half the people are teenagers or younger. With so many people entering their childbearing years, a wave of population growth will roll into the future. In recent years, for example, the population of Chad has been swelling by 3.3 percent annually, so even with economic development, living standards have fallen.

3. **Cultural patterns.** Poor societies are usually traditional. Holding on to long-established ways of life means resisting change—even changes that promise a richer material life. The Applying Sociology box on page 320 explains how traditional people in India respond to their poverty differently than poor people in the United States.

4. **Social stratification.** Low-income societies distribute their wealth very unequally. Chapter 10 ("Social Stratification") explained that social inequality is greater in agrarian societies than in industrial societies. In Brazil, for example, half of all farmland is owned by just 1 percent of the people (Bergamo & Camarotti, 1996).

5. **Gender inequality.** Gender inequality in poor societies keeps women from holding jobs, which typically means they have many children. An expanding population, in turn, slows economic development. Many analysts conclude that raising living standards in much of the world depends on improving the social standing of women.

6. **Global power relationships.** A final cause of global poverty lies in the relationships between the nations of the world. Historically, wealth flowed from poor societies to rich nations through **colonialism,** *the process by which some nations enrich themselves through political and economic control of other nations.* The countries of Western Europe colonized much of Latin America beginning roughly 500 years ago. Such global exploitation allowed some nations to develop economically at the expense of other nations.

Although 130 former colonies gained their independence during the twentieth century, exploitation continues through **neocolonialism** (*neo* is the Greek for "new"), *a new form of global power relationships that involves not direct political control but economic exploitation by multinational corporations.* A **multinational corporation** is a *large business that operates in many countries.* Corporate leaders often impose their will on countries where they do business to create favorable economic conditions, just as colonizers did in the past (Bonanno, Constance, & Lorenz, 2000).

Global Stratification: Theoretical Analysis

There are two major explanations for the unequal distribution of the world's wealth and power: *modernization theory* and *dependency theory.* Each theory suggests a different solution to the suffering of hungry people in much of the world.

MODERNIZATION THEORY

Modernization theory is *a model of economic and social development that explains global inequality in terms of technological and cultural differences between nations.* Modernization theory emerged in the 1950s, a time when U.S. society was fascinated by new developments in technology. To showcase the power of productive technology and also to counter the growing influence of the Soviet Union, U.S. policymakers drafted a market-based foreign policy that has been with us ever since.[2]

Historical Perspective

Until a few centuries ago, the entire world was poor. Because poverty is the norm throughout human history, modernization theory claims that it is *affluence* that demands an explanation.

Affluence came within reach of a growing share of people in Western Europe during the late Middle Ages as world exploration and trade expanded. Soon the Industrial Revolution was under way, transforming first Western Europe and then North America. Industrial technology coupled with the spirit of capitalism created new wealth as never before. At first, this new wealth benefited only a few. But industrial technology was so productive that gradually the living standard of even the poorest people began to improve. Absolute poverty, which had plagued humanity throughout history, was finally in decline.

---

[2]This discussion of modernization theory draws on Rostow (1960, 1978), Bauer (1981), Berger (1986), Firebaugh (1996), and Firebaugh & Sandu (1998).

"Happy Poverty" in India: Making Sense of a Strange Idea

Although India has become a middle-income nation, its per capita GDP is just $2,892, less than one-tenth that in the United States. For this reason, India is home to one-fourth of the world's hungry people.

But most North Americans do not readily understand the reality of poverty in India. Many of the country's 1.1 billion people live in conditions far worse than those our society labels "poor." A traveler's first experience of Indian life can be shocking. Chennai (formerly known as Madras), for example, one of India's largest cities with 7 million inhabitants, seems chaotic to an outsider—streets choked with motorbikes, trucks, carts pulled by oxen, and waves of people. Along the roadway, vendors sit on burlap cloths selling fruits, vegetables, and cooked food while people nearby talk, bathe, and sleep.

Although some people live well, Chennai is dotted with more than a thousand shanty settlements, home to half a million people from rural villages who have come in search of a better life. Shantytowns are clusters of huts built with branches, leaves, and pieces of discarded cardboard and tin. These dwellings offer little privacy and lack refrigeration,

running water, and bathrooms. A visitor from the United States may feel uneasy in such an area, knowing that the poorest sections of our own inner cities seethe with frustration and sometimes explode with violence.

But India's people understand poverty differently than we do. No restless young men hang out at the corner, no drug dealers work the streets, and there is little danger of violence. In the United States, poverty often means anger and isolation; in India, even shantytowns are organized around strong families—children, parents, and often grandparents—who offer a smile of welcome to a stranger.

For traditional people in India, life is shaped by *dharma,* the Hindu concept of duty and destiny that teaches

people to accept their fate, whatever it may be. Mother Teresa, who worked among the poorest of India's people, went to the heart of the cultural differences: "Americans have angry poverty," she explained. "In India, there is worse poverty, but it is a happy poverty."

Perhaps we should not describe anyone who clings to the edge of survival as happy. But poverty in India is eased by the strength and support of families and communities, a sense that life has a purpose, and a worldview that encourages each person to accept whatever life offers. As a result, a visitor may well come away from a first encounter with Indian poverty in confusion: "How can people be so poor, and yet apparently content, active, and *joyful?*"

WHAT DO YOU THINK?

1. What did Mother Teresa mean when she said that in parts of India there is "happy poverty"?
2. How might an experience like this in a very poor community change the way you think of being "rich"?
3. Do you know of any poor people in the United States who have attitudes toward poverty similar to these people in India? What would make people seem to accept being poor?

During the twentieth century, the standard of living in high-income countries, where the Industrial Revolution began, jumped at least fourfold. Many middle-income nations in Asia and Latin America have industrialized, and they, too, have become richer. But with limited industrial technology, low-income countries have changed much less.

The Importance of Culture

Why didn't the Industrial Revolution sweep away poverty the world over? Modernization theory points out that not every society wants to adopt new technology. Doing so takes a cultural environment that emphasizes the benefits of material wealth and new ideas.

In rich nations such as the United States, most parents expect their children to enjoy years of childhood, largely free from the responsibilities of adult life. This is not the case in poor nations across Latin America, Africa, and Asia. Poor families depend on whatever income their children can earn, and many children as young as six or seven work full days weaving or performing other kinds of manual labor. Child labor lies behind the low prices of many products imported for sale in this country.

Modernization theory identifies *tradition* as the greatest barrier to economic development. In some societies, strong family systems and a reverence for the past discourage people from adopting new technologies that would raise their living standards. Even today, many people—from the North American Amish to Islamic people in rural regions of the Middle East and Asia to the Semai of Malaysia—oppose technological advances as a threat to their family relationships, customs, and religious beliefs.

Max Weber (1958, orig. 1904–05) found that at the end of the Middle Ages, Western Europe's cultural environment favored change. As discussed in Chapter 4 ("Society"), the Protestant Reformation reshaped traditional Catholic beliefs to generate a progress-oriented way of life. Wealth—looked on with suspicion by the Catholic church—became a sign of personal virtue, and the growing importance of individualism steadily replaced the traditional emphasis on family and community. Taken together, these new cultural patterns nurtured the Industrial Revolution.

Rostow's Stages of Modernization

Modernization theory holds that the door to affluence is open to all. As technological advances spread around the world, all societies should gradually industrialize. According to Walt W. Rostow (1960, 1978), modernization occurs in four stages:

1. **Traditional stage.** Socialized to honor the past, people in traditional societies cannot easily imagine how life can be very different. Therefore, they build their lives around families and local communities, following well-worn paths that allow for little individual freedom or change. Life is often spiritually rich but lacking in material goods.

   A century ago, much of the world was in this initial stage of economic development. Nations such as Bangladesh, Niger, and Somalia are still at the traditional stage and remain poor.

2. **Take-off stage.** As a society shakes off the grip of tradition, people start to use their talents and imagination, sparking economic growth. A market emerges as people produce goods not just for their own use but to trade with others for profit. Greater individualism, a willingness to take risks, and a desire for material goods also take hold, often at the expense of family ties and time-honored norms and values.

   Great Britain reached take-off by about 1800, the United States by 1820. Thailand, a middle-income country in eastern Asia, is now in this stage. Such development typically is speeded by help from rich nations, including foreign aid, the availability of advanced technology and investment capital, and opportunities for schooling abroad.

3. **Drive to technological maturity.** During this stage, "growth" is a widely accepted idea that fuels a society's pursuit of higher living standards. A diversified economy drives a population eager to enjoy the

Modernization theory claims that corporations that build factories in low-income nations help people by providing them with jobs and higher wages than they had before; dependency theory views these factories as "sweatshops" that exploit workers. Following the dependency theory approach, these students are staging a protest at Gap and Nike stores in Boston.

benefits of industrial technology. At the same time, however, people begin to realize (and sometimes regret) that industrialization is eroding traditional family and local community life. Great Britain reached this point by about 1840, the United States by 1860. Today, Mexico, the U.S. territory of Puerto Rico, and South Korea are among the nations driving to technological maturity.

Absolute poverty is greatly reduced in nations in this stage of development. Cities swell with people who leave rural villages in search of economic opportunity. Specialization creates the wide range of jobs that we find in our economy today. An increasing

focus on work makes relationships less personal. Growing individualism generates social movements demanding greater political rights. Societies approaching technological maturity also provide basic schooling for all their people and advanced training for some. The newly educated consider tradition "backward" and

push for further change. The social position of women steadily approaches that of men.

4. **High mass consumption.** Economic development steadily raises living standards as mass production stimulates mass consumption. Simply put, people soon learn to "need" the expanding array of goods that their society produces.

The United States, Japan, and other rich nations moved into this stage by 1900. Now entering this level of economic development are two former British colonies that are prosperous small societies of eastern Asia: Hong Kong (part of the People's Republic of China) and Singapore (independent since 1965).

The Role of Rich Nations

Modernization theory claims that high-income countries play four important roles in global economic development:

1. **Controlling population.** Since population growth is greatest in the poorest societies, rising population can overtake economic advances. Rich nations can help limit population growth by exporting birth control technology and promoting its use. Once economic development is under way, birth rates should decline, as they have in industrialized nations, because children are no longer an economic asset.

2. **Increasing food production.** Rich nations can export high-tech farming methods to poor nations to increase agricultural yields. Such techniques, collectively referred to as the Green Revolution, include new hybrid seeds, modern irrigation methods, chemical fertilizers, and pesticides for insect control.

3. **Introducing industrial technology.** Rich nations can encourage economic growth in poor societies by introducing machinery and information technology, which raise productivity. Industrialization also shifts the labor force from farming to skilled industrial and service jobs.

4. **Providing foreign aid.** Investment capital from rich nations can boost the prospects of poor societies trying to reach Rostow's take-off stage. Foreign aid can raise farm output by helping poor countries buy more fertilizer and build irrigation projects. In the same way, financial and technical assistance can help build power plants and factories to improve industrial output. Each year, the United States provides about $12 billion in foreign aid to developing countries.

Critical review Modernization theory has many influential supporters among social scientists (Parsons, 1966; W. E. Moore, 1977, 1979; Bauer, 1981; Berger, 1986; Firebaugh & Beck, 1994; Firebaugh, 1996, 1999; Firebaugh & Sandu, 1998). For decades, it has shaped the foreign policy of the United States and other rich nations. Supporters point to rapid economic development in Asia—including South Korea, Taiwan, Singapore, and Hong Kong—as proof that the affluence that accompanied industrialization in Western Europe and North America is within reach of other countries.

YOUR TURN

Is the level of material consumption the only way, or the best way, to measure quality of life? Explain your answer.

But modernization theory comes under fire from socialist countries (and left-leaning analysts in the West) as little more than a defense of capitalism. Its most serious flaw, according to critics, is that modernization simply has not occurred in many poor countries. The United Nations reported that living standards in a number of nations, including Haiti and Nicaragua in Latin America and Sudan, Ghana, and Rwanda in Africa, are actually lower today than in 1960 (United Nations Development Programme, 1996).

A second criticism of modernization theory is that it fails to recognize how rich nations, which benefit from the status quo, often block paths to development for poor countries. Centuries ago, critics charge, rich countries industrialized from a position of global strength. Can we expect poor countries today to do so from a position of global weakness?

Third, modernization theory treats rich and poor societies as separate worlds, ignoring the ways in which international relations have affected all nations. Many countries in Latin America and Asia are still struggling to overcome the harm caused by colonialism, which boosted the fortunes of Europe.

Fourth, modernization theory holds up the world's most developed countries as the standard for judging the rest of humanity, revealing an ethnocentric bias. We should remember that our Western idea of "progress" has caused us to rush headlong into a competitive, materialistic way of life, which uses up the world's scarce resources and pollutes the natural environment.

Fifth, and finally, modernization theory suggests that the causes of global poverty lie almost entirely in the poor societies themselves. Critics see this analysis as little more than blaming the victims for their own problems. Instead, these critics argue, an analysis of global inequality should focus just as much on the behavior of rich nations as it does on the behavior of poor ones.

Concerns such as these reflect a second major approach to understanding global inequality: dependency theory.

DEPENDENCY THEORY

Dependency theory is *a model of economic and social development that explains global inequality in terms of the historical exploitation of poor nations by rich ones.* This analysis puts the primary responsibility for global poverty on rich nations, which for centuries have systematically impoverished low-income countries and made them *dependent* on the rich ones. This destructive process continues today.

Historical Perspective

Everyone agrees that before the Industrial Revolution, there was little affluence in the world. Dependency theory asserts, however, that people living in poor countries were actually better off economically in the past than their descendants are now. André Gunder Frank (1975), a noted supporter of this theory, argues that the colonial process that helped develop rich nations also *underdeveloped* poor societies.

Dependency theory is based on the idea that the economic positions of rich and poor nations of the world are linked and cannot be understood apart from each other. Poor nations are not simply lagging behind rich ones on the "path of progress"; rather, the prosperity of the most developed countries came largely at the expense of less developed ones. In short, some nations became rich only because others became poor. Both are products of the global commerce beginning five centuries ago.

The Importance of Colonialism

Late in the fifteenth century, Europeans began exploring the Americas to the west, Africa to the south, and Asia to the east to establish colonies. They were so successful that a century ago, Great Britain controlled about one-fourth of the world's land, boasting that "the sun never sets on the British Empire." The United States, itself originally a collection of small British colonies on the eastern seaboard of North America, soon pushed across the continent, purchased Alaska, and gained control of Haiti, Puerto Rico, Guam, the Philippines, the Hawaiian Islands, part of Panama, and Guantanamo Bay in Cuba.

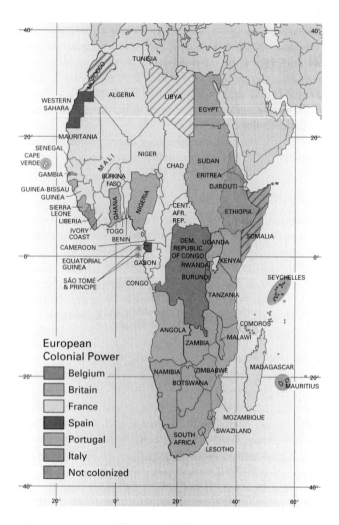

FIGURE 12-3 Africa's Colonial History

For more than a century, most of Africa was colonized by European nations, with France dominating in the northwest region of the continent and Great Britain dominating in the east and south.

Meanwhile, Europeans and Africans engaged in a brutal form of human exploitation—the slave trade—from about 1500 until 1850. Even as the world was rejecting slavery, Europeans took control of most of the African continent, as Figure 12–3 shows. European powers dominated most of the continent until the early 1960s.

Formal colonialism has almost disappeared from the world. However, according to dependency theory, political liberation has not translated into economic independence. Far from it—the economic relationship between poor and rich nations continues the colonial pattern of domination. This neocolonialism is the heart of the capitalist world economy.

Wallerstein's Capitalist World Economy

Immanuel Wallerstein (1974, 1979, 1983, 1984) explains global stratification using a model of the "capitalist world economy." Wallerstein's term *world economy* suggests that the prosperity of some nations and the poverty and dependency of other countries result from a global economic system. He traces the roots of the global economy to the beginning of colonization 500 years ago, when Europeans began gathering wealth from the rest of the world. Because the world economy is based in the high-income countries, it is capitalist in character.[3]

Wallerstein calls the rich nations the *core* of the world economy. Colonialism enriched this core by funneling raw materials from around the world to Western Europe, where they fueled the Industrial Revolution. Today, multinational corporations operate profitably worldwide, channeling wealth to North America, Western Europe, Australia, and Japan.

Low-income countries, on the other hand, represent the *periphery* of the world economy. Drawn into the world economy by colonial exploitation, poor nations continue to support rich ones by providing inexpensive labor and a vast market for industrial products. The remaining countries are considered the *semiperiphery* of the world economy. They include middle-income countries like Mexico and Brazil that have closer ties to the global economic core.

According to Wallerstein, the world economy benefits rich societies (by generating profits) and harms the rest of the world (by causing poverty). The world economy thus makes poor nations dependent on rich ones. This dependency involves three factors:

1. **Narrow, export-oriented economies.** Poor nations produce only a few crops for export to rich countries. Examples include coffee and fruit from Latin American nations, oil from Nigeria, hardwoods from the Philippines, and palm oil from Malaysia.

    Today's multinational corporations purchase raw materials cheaply in poor societies and transport them to core nations where factories process them for profitable sale. Thus poor nations develop few industries of their own.

2. **Lack of industrial capacity.** Without an industrial base, poor societies face a double bind: They count on

---

[3]Based on Wallerstein's ideas, this section also draws on Frank (1980, 1981), Delacroix & Ragin (1981), Bergesen (1983), Dixon & Boswell (1996), and Kentor (1998).

Although the world continues to grow richer, billions of people are being left behind. The shantytown of Cité Soleil ("City of the Sun") near Port-au-Prince, the capital of Haiti, is built around an open sewer. What would you estimate life expectancy to be in such a place?

rich nations to buy their inexpensive raw materials and try to buy from them whatever expensive manufactured goods they can afford. In a classic example of this dependency, British colonialists encouraged the people of India to raise cotton but prevented them from weaving their own cloth. Instead, the British shipped Indian cotton to their own textile mills in Birmingham and Manchester, manufactured the cloth, and shipped finished goods back to India, where the very people who harvested the cotton bought the garments.

Dependency theorists claim that the Green Revolution—widely praised by modernization theorists—works the same way. Poor countries sell cheap raw materials to rich nations and then try to buy expensive fertilizers, pesticides, and machinery in return. Rich countries profit from this exchange more than poor nations.

3. **Foreign debt.** Unequal trade patterns have plunged poor countries into debt to the core nations. Collectively, the poor nations of the world owe rich countries some $2.6 trillion; hundreds of billions of dollars are owed to the United States. Such staggering debt paralyzes a country, causing high unemployment and rampant inflation (World Bank, 2005).

The Role of Rich Nations

Modernization theory and dependency theory assign very different roles to rich nations. Modernization theory holds that rich countries *produce wealth* through capital investment and new technology. Dependency theory views global inequality in terms of how countries *distribute wealth,* arguing that rich nations have *overdeveloped* themselves as they have *underdeveloped* the rest of the world.

Dependency theorists dismiss the idea that programs developed by rich countries to control population and boost agricultural and industrial output raise living standards in poor countries. Instead, they claim, such programs actually benefit rich nations and the ruling elites, not the poor majority, in low-income countries (Kentor, 2001).

Hunger activists Frances Moore Lappé and Joseph Collins (1986; Lappé, Collins, & Rosset, 2001) maintain that the capitalist culture of the United States encourages people to think of poverty as somehow inevitable. In this line of reasoning, poverty results from "natural" processes, including having too many children, and natural disasters such as droughts. But global poverty is far from inevitable; in their view, it results from deliberate policies. Lappé and Collins point out that the world already produces enough food to allow every person on the planet to become quite fat. Moreover, India and most of Africa actually *export* food, even though many of their own people go hungry.

According to Lappé and Collins, the contradiction of poverty amid plenty stems from the rich-nation policy of producing food for profits, not people. That is, corporations in rich nations cooperate with elites in poor countries to grow and export profitable crops such as coffee, which means using land that could otherwise produce basics such

APPLYING THEORY
GLOBAL POVERTY

	Modernization Theory	Dependency Theory
Which theoretical approach is applied?	Structural-functional approach	Social-conflict approach
How did global poverty come about?	The whole world was poor until some countries developed industrial technology, which allowed mass production and created affluence.	Colonialism moved wealth from some countries to others, making some nations poor as it made other nations rich.
What are the main causes of global poverty today?	Traditional culture and a lack of productive technology.	Neocolonialism—the operation of multinational corporations in the global, capitalist economy.
Are rich countries part of the problem or part of the solution?	Rich countries are part of the solution, contributing new technology, advanced schooling, and foreign aid.	Rich countries are part of the problem, making poor countries economically dependent and in debt.

as beans and corn for local families. Governments of poor countries support the practice of growing for export because they need food profits to repay foreign debt. According to Lappé and Collins, the capitalist corporate structure of the global economy is at the core of this vicious cycle.

Critical review The main idea of dependency theory is that no nation becomes rich or poor in isolation because a single global economy shapes the destiny of all nations. Pointing to continuing poverty in Latin America, Africa, and Asia, dependency theorists claim that development simply cannot proceed under the constraints now imposed by rich countries. Rather, they call for radical reform of the entire world economy so that it operates in the interests of the majority of people.

Critics charge that dependency theory wrongly treats wealth as if no one gets richer without someone else getting poorer. Corporations, small business owners, and farmers can and do create new wealth through hard work and imaginative use of new technology. After all, they point out, the entire world's wealth has increased sixfold since 1950.

Second, dependency theory is wrong in blaming rich nations for global poverty because many of the world's poorest countries (like Ethiopia) have had little contact with rich nations. On the contrary, a long history of trade with rich countries has dramatically improved the economies of many nations, including Sri Lanka, Singapore, and Hong Kong (all former British colonies), as well as South Korea and Japan. In short, say the critics, most evidence shows that foreign investment by rich nations encourages economic

growth, as modernization theory claims, not economic decline, as dependency theorists claim (E.F. Vogel, 1991; Firebaugh, 1992).

Third, critics call dependency theory simplistic for pointing the finger at a single factor—capitalism—as the cause of global inequality (Worsley, 1990). Dependency theory views poor societies as passive victims and ignores factors inside these countries that contribute to their economic problems. Sociologists have long recognized the vital role of culture in shaping people's willingness to embrace or resist change. Under the rule of the ultratraditional Muslim Taliban, for example, Afghanistan became economically isolated, and its living standards sank to among the lowest in the world. Is it reasonable to blame capitalist nations for that country's stagnation?

Nor can rich societies be held responsible for the reckless behavior of foreign leaders whose corruption and militaristic campaigns impoverish their countries. Examples include the regimes of Ferdinand Marcos in the Philippines, François Duvalier in Haiti, Manuel Noriega in Panama, Mobutu Sese Seko in Zaire (today's Democratic Republic of the Congo), and Saddam Hussein in Iraq. Some leaders even use food supplies as weapons in internal political struggles, leaving the masses starving, as in the African nations of Ethiopia, Sudan, and Somalia. Likewise, many countries throughout the world have done little to improve the status of women or control population growth.

Fourth, critics say that dependency theory is wrong to claim that global trade always makes rich nations richer and poor nations poorer. For example, in 2004 the United States had a trade deficit of $666 billion, meaning that this nation imports two-thirds of a trillion dollars more than it sells abroad. The single greatest debt was to China, whose profitable trade has now pushed that country into the ranks of middle-income countries (Crutsinger, 2005).

Fifth, critics fault dependency theory for offering only vague solutions to global poverty. Most dependency theorists urge poor nations to end all contact with rich countries, and some call for nationalizing foreign-owned industries. In other words, dependency theory is really an argument for some sort of world socialism. In light of the difficulties that socialist societies (even rich socialist countries such as the former Soviet Union) have had in meeting the needs of their own people, critics ask, should we really expect such a system to rescue the entire world from poverty?

The Applying Theory table summarizes the main arguments of modernization theory and dependency theory.

Which approach—modernization theory or dependency theory—do you find more convincing? Why?

Global Stratification: Looking Ahead

Among the most important trends in recent decades is the development of a global economy. In the United States, rising production and sales abroad bring profits to many corporations and their stockholders, especially those who already have substantial wealth. At the same time, the global economy has moved manufacturing jobs abroad, closing factories in this country and hurting many average workers. The net result: economic polarization in the United States.

People who support the global economy claim that the expansion of trade results in benefits for all countries involved. For this reason, they endorse policies like the North American Free Trade Agreement (NAFTA). Critics of expanding globalization make other claims: Manufacturing jobs are being lost in the United States, and more manufacturing now takes place abroad where workers are underpaid and few laws ensure their safety in the workplace. In addition, other critics of expanding globalization point to the ever greater stress that our economy places on the natural environment.

But perhaps the greatest concern is the vast economic inequality that exists between the world's countries. The concentration of wealth in high-income countries, coupled with the grinding poverty in low-income nations, may well be the biggest problem facing humanity in the twenty-first century.

Both modernization theory and dependency theory offer some understanding of this urgent problem. In evaluating these theories, we must consider empirical evidence. Over the course of the twentieth century, living standards rose in most of the world. Even the economic output of the poorest 25 percent of the world's people almost tripled over the course of the twentieth century. However, the economic output of the other 75 percent of the world's people increased about sixfold. By this measure, although all people are better off in *absolute* terms, there was almost twice as much *relative* economic inequality in the world in 2000 as there was in 1900. As Figure 12–4 on page 328 suggests, the poorest of the world's people are being left behind.

Most of this economic polarization took place between 1900 and 1970. Since 1970, the degree of economic inequality worldwide has declined. In addition, the world's poorest people—those living on less than $1 per day—now number about half of what they were in 1970 (Schultz, 1998; Firebaugh, 1999, 2000; Sala-i-Martin, 2002).

The greatest reduction in poverty has taken place in Asia, a region generally seen as an economic success story. Back in 1970, 75 percent of global $1-per-day poverty was found in Asia; by 2000, that figure had fallen to 15 percent. Since then, both India and China have joined the ranks of the middle-income nations (Sala-i-Martin, 2002; United Nations Development Programme, 2004).

Latin America represents a mixed case. During the 1970s, this region enjoyed significant economic growth; during the 1980s and 1990s, however, there was little overall improvement. The share of the global $1-per-day poverty was the same in 2000 (3 percent) as it was in 1970 (Sala-i-Martin, 2002).

Would you pay more for a cup of coffee to ensure that it was made using beans for which a farmer in a low-income country was paid a higher price? Why or why not?

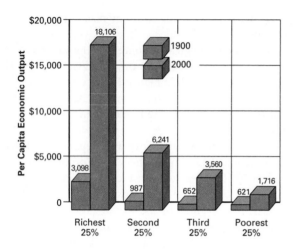

FIGURE 12-4 The World's Increasing Economic Inequality

The gap between the richest and poorest people in the world is twice as big as it was a century ago.

Source: International Monetary Fund (2000).

Africa, especially the countries south of the Sahara Desert, represents a region of economic decline. There the extent of extreme poverty has become worse. In 1970, sub-Saharan Africa accounted for 11 percent of $1-per-day poverty; by 2000, this share had risen to 66 percent (Sala-i-Martin, 2002).

These trends in economic performance have caused both modernization and dependency theorists to revise their views. Governments have played a large role in the economic growth that has occurred in Asia and elsewhere; this fact challenges modernization theory and its free-market approach to development. On the other hand, since the upheavals in the former Soviet Union and Eastern Europe, a global reevaluation of socialism has been taking place. Because socialist nations have a record of decades of poor economic performance and political repression, many low-income nations are unwilling to follow the advice of dependency theory and place economic development entirely under government control.

Although the world's future is uncertain, we have learned a great deal about global stratification. One insight offered by modernization theory is that poverty is partly a *problem of technology.* A higher standard of living for a surging world population depends on the ability of poor nations to raise their agricultural and industrial productivity. A second insight, derived from dependency theory, is that global inequality is also a *political issue.* Even with higher productivity, the human community must address crucial questions concerning how resources are distributed, both within societies and around the globe.

Although economic development raises living standards, it also places greater strains on the natural environment. As nations such as India and China—with a combined population of 2.4 billion—become more affluent, their people will consume more energy and other resources (China has recently passed Japan to become the second largest consumer of oil, behind the United States) and create more pollution.

Finally, the vast gulf that separates the world's richest and poorest people puts everyone at greater risk of war and terrorism as the poorest people challenge the social arrangements that threaten their existence (Lindauer & Weerapana, 2002). In the long run, we can achieve peace on this planet only by ensuring that all people enjoy a significant measure of dignity and security.

YOUR TURN

Based on what you have read here and elsewhere, do you think that global hunger fifty years from now will be more or less serious? Explain your answer.

The following learning tools will help you see what you know, identify what you still need to learn, and expand your understanding beyond the text. You can also visit this text's Companion Website™ at http://www.prenhall.com/macionis to find additional practice tests.

Global Stratification: An Overview

Around the world, social stratification is more pronounced than in the United States. About 18 percent of the world's people live in industrialized, high-income countries such as the United States and receive 79 percent of all income. Another 70 percent of humanity live in middle-income countries with significant industrialization, receiving about 20 percent of all income. Twelve percent of the world's people live in low-income countries with limited industrialization and earn only 1 percent of global income.

Global Wealth and Poverty

Although relative poverty is found everywhere, low-income societies struggle with widespread, absolute poverty. Worldwide, the lives of some 1 billion people are at risk because of poor nutrition. About 15 million people, most of them children, die annually from diseases caused by inadequate nutrition. Nearly everywhere in the world, women are more likely than men to live in poverty. Gender bias against women is greatest in poor, agrarian societies.

The poverty found in much of the world is a complex problem reflecting limited industrial technology, rapid population growth, traditional cultural patterns, internal social stratification, male domination, and global power relationships.

Global Stratification: Theoretical Analysis

Modernization theory maintains that successful development requires giving up cultural traditions that discourage the use of new technology. The modernization theorist Walt Rostow identifies four stages of development: the traditional stage, take-off, the drive to technological maturity, and high mass consumption. Arguing that rich societies hold the keys to creating wealth, modernization theory claims rich nations can help poor nations by providing population control programs, agricultural technology such as hybrid seeds and fertilizers that increase food production, industrial technology that includes machinery and information technology, and foreign aid to help pay for power plants and factories.

Critics of modernization theory say that rich nations do not spread economic development around the world. Further, they claim, because rich nations including the United States now control the global economy, today's poor nations cannot follow the same path to development taken by rich nations centuries ago.

Dependency theory claims that global wealth and poverty are the historical products of the capitalist world economy. The capitalist world economy emerged about 500 years ago with the spread of colonialism and continues today with the operation of multinational corporations. Immanuel Wallerstein views the high-income countries as the advantaged "core" of the capitalist world economy; middle-income nations are the "semiperiphery," and poor societies form the global "periphery." Three key factors—export-oriented economies, a lack of industrial capacity, and foreign debt—make poor countries dependent on rich nations.

Critics of dependency theory argue that this approach overlooks the sixfold increase in the world's wealth since 1950 and note that the world's poorest societies have had weak, not strong, ties to rich countries.

Global Stratification: Looking Ahead

Both modernization theory and dependency theory offer useful insights into global inequality. The theories agree that there is an urgent need to address the various problems caused by worldwide poverty.

KEY CONCEPTS

global stratification (p. 306) patterns of social inequality in the world as a whole

colonialism (p. 319) the process by which some nations enrich themselves through political and economic control of other nations

neocolonialism (p. 319) a new form of global power relationships that involves not direct political control but economic exploitation by multinational corporations

multinational corporation (p. 319) a large business that operates in many countries

modernization theory (p. 319) a model of economic and social development that explains global inequality in terms of technological and cultural differences between nations

dependency theory (p. 323) a model of economic and social development that explains global inequality in terms of the historical exploitation of poor nations by rich ones

SAMPLE TEST QUESTIONS

These questions are similar to those found in the test bank that accompanies this textbook.

Multiple-Choice Questions

1. **In global perspective, the richest 20 percent of all people earn about what share of the entire world's income?**
   a. 20 percent
   b. 40 percent
   c. 60 percent
   d. 80 percent

2. **The United States, Canada, and Japan are all considered**
   a. high-income countries.
   b. middle-income countries.
   c. low-income countries.
   d. Each of these three countries falls into a different category.

3. **Low-income nations**
   a. are evenly spread in all world regions.
   b. lie mostly in Africa and Asia.
   c. are all in Latin America.
   d. contain a majority of the world's people.

4. **China and India are now**
   a. the world's poorest countries.
   b. among the world's low-income nations.
   c. among the world's middle-income nations.
   d. among the world's high-income nations.

5. **Which of the following is the range of annual personal income for people living in middle-income nations?**

   a. $250 to $1,000
   b. $1,000 to $2,500
   c. $2,500 to $10,000
   d. $10,000 to $25,000

6. **How does poverty in poor nations compare to poverty in the United States?**
   a. In poor nations, poverty is more likely to involve men.
   b. In most poor nations, the problem of poverty has been all but solved.
   c. In poor nations, most people do not consider poverty a problem.
   d. In poor nations, there is far more absolute poverty.

7. *Neocolonialism* **refers to the process by which**
   a. rich countries gain new colonies to replace older ones.
   b. multinational corporations dominate the economy of a poor country.
   c. rich countries grant independence to their former colonies.
   d. large corporations do business in many countries at once.

8. **Which of the following statements is the basis of modernization theory?**
   a. The main cause of poverty in the world is low productivity due to simple technology and traditional culture.
   b. Poor nations can never become rich if they remain part of the global capitalist economy.
   c. The main cause of poverty in the world is the operation of multinational corporations.
   d. Most poor nations were richer in the past than they are today.

9. **According to Walt Rostow, which is the final stage of economic development?**

a. drive to technological maturity
b. traditional
c. high mass consumption
d. take-off

10. **Dependency theory differs from modernization theory by saying that**
   a. poor nations are responsible for their own poverty.
   b. capitalism is the best way to produce economic development.
   c. economic development is not a good idea for poor countries.
   d. global stratification results from the exploitation of poor countries by rich countries.

Essay Questions

1. What are the differences between relative and absolute poverty? Describe global social stratification using both concepts.

2. Why do many analysts claim that economic development in low-income countries depends on raising the social standing of women?

APPLICATIONS & EXERCISES

1. Page through several issues of any current newsmagazine or travel magazine, and notice any stories or advertising mentioning low-income countries (selling, say, coffee from Colombia or exotic vacations to India). What picture of life in low-income countries does the advertising present? In light of what you have learned in this chapter, how accurate does this image seem to you?

2. Millions of students from abroad study on U.S. campuses. See if you can identify a woman and a man on your campus who were raised in poor countries. After explaining that you have been studying global stratification, ask if they are willing to share information about what life is like back home. If they are, ask about stratification as well as their social position in their home countries.

3. Pick five of the global maps in this text (the full list is found in the preface on page xx), and identify social traits of high-income countries and those of low-income countries. Try to use both modernization theory and dependency theory to explain the patterns you find.

INVESTIGATE *with* Research Navigator

Follow the instructions on page 27 of this text to access the features of **Research Navigator™**. Once at the Web site, enter your Login Name and Password. Then, to use the **ContentSelect™** database, enter keywords such as "colonialism," "global poverty," and "slavery," and the search engine will supply relevant and recent scholarly and popular press publications. Use the *New York Times* **Search-by-Search Archive** to find recent news articles related to sociology and the **Link Library** feature to find relevant Web links organized by the key terms associated with this chapter.

13

Gender Stratification

How is gender a creation of society?

What difference does gender make
in people's lives?

Why is gender an important dimension
of social stratification?

At first we traveled quite alone . . . but before we had gone many miles, we came on other wagon-loads of women, bound in the same direction. As we reached different cross-roads, we saw wagons coming from every part of the country and, long before we reached Seneca Falls, we were a procession.

So wrote Charlotte Woodward in her journal as she made her way along the rutted dirt roads leading to Seneca Falls, a small town in upstate New York. The year was 1848, a time when slavery was legal in much of the United States and the social standing of all women, regardless of color, was far below that of men. Back then, in much of the country, women could not own property, keep their wages if they were married, draft a will, file lawsuits in a court (including lawsuits seeking custody of their children), or attend college, and husbands were widely viewed as having unquestioned authority over their wives and children.

Some 300 women gathered at Wesleyan Chapel in Seneca Falls to challenge this second-class citizenship. They listened as their leader, Elizabeth Cady Stanton, called for expanding women's rights and opportunities, including the right to vote. At that time, most people considered such a proposal absurd and outrageous. Even many attending the conference were shocked by the idea: Stanton's husband, Henry, rode out of town in protest (Gurnett, 1998). ∎

Much has changed since the Seneca Falls convention, and many of Stanton's proposals are now widely accepted as matters of basic fairness. But as this chapter explains, women and men still lead different lives, in the United States and elsewhere in the world; in most respects, men are still in charge. This chapter explores the importance of gender and explains how, like class position, gender is a major dimension of social stratification.

Gender and Inequality

Chapter 8 ("Sexuality") explained the biological differences that divide the human population into categories of female and male. **Gender** refers to *the personal traits and social positions that members of a society attach to being female or male.* Gender operates as a dimension of social organization, shaping how we interact with others and how we think about ourselves. More important, gender also involves *hierarchy,* ranking men and women differently in terms of power, wealth, and other resources. This is why sociologists speak of **gender stratification,** *the unequal distribution of*

wealth, power, and privilege between men and women. Gender, in short, affects the opportunities and constraints we face throughout our lives.

MALE-FEMALE DIFFERENCES

Many people think there is something "natural" about gender distinctions because biology does make one sex different from the other. But we must be careful not to think of social differences in biological terms. In 1848, for example, women were denied the vote because many people assumed that women did not have enough intelligence or interest in politics. Such attitudes had nothing to do with biology; they reflected the *cultural* patterns of that time and place.

Another example is athletic performance. In 1925, most people—both women and men—believed that the best women runners could never compete with men in a marathon. Today, as Figure 13–1 shows, the gender gap has greatly narrowed, and the fastest women routinely post better times than the fastest men of decades past. Here again, most of the differences between men and women turn out to be socially created.

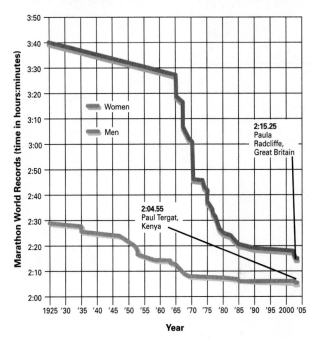

YOUR TURN

Do you think female and male athletes should compete on the same teams? Why or why not? Do you think whether you are a woman or a man affects your answer?

There are some differences in physical ability between the sexes. On average, males are 10 percent taller, 20 percent heavier, and 30 percent stronger, especially in their upper bodies (Ehrenreich, 1999). On the other hand, women outperform men in the ultimate game of life itself: Life expectancy for men in the United States is 74.8 years, and women can expect to live 80.1 years (Hoyert, Kung, & Smith, 2005).

In adolescence, males do a bit better in mathematics, and females show stronger verbal skills, a difference that reflects both biology and socialization (Maccoby & Jacklin, 1974; Baker et al., 1980; Lengermann & Wallace, 1985; Tavris & Wade, 2001). However, research does not point to any difference in overall intelligence between males and females.

Biologically, then, men and women differ in limited ways; neither one is naturally superior. But culture can define the two sexes very differently, as the global study of gender described in the next section shows.

GENDER IN GLOBAL PERSPECTIVE

The best way to see the cultural foundation of gender is by comparing one society to another. Three important studies highlight just how different "masculine" and "feminine" can be.

The Israeli Kibbutz

In Israel, collective settlements are called *kibbutzim*. The *kibbutz* (the singular form of the word) is an important setting for research because gender equality is one of its stated goals; men and women share in both work and decision making.

In kibbutzim, both sexes share most everyday jobs. Both men and women take care of children, cook and clean, repair buildings, and make day-to-day decisions concerning life in the kibbutz. Girls and boys are raised in the same way, and from the first weeks of life, children live together in dormitories. Women and men in kibbutzim have achieved remarkable (although not complete) social equality, evidence that cultures define what is feminine and what is masculine.

Margaret Mead's Research

The anthropologist Margaret Mead carried out ground-breaking research on gender. If gender is based on the

DIVERSITY SNAPSHOT

FIGURE 13-1 Men's and Women's Athletic Performance

Do men naturally outperform women in athletic competition? The answer is not obvious. Early in the twentieth century, men outpaced women by more than an hour in marathon races. But as opportunities for women in athletics have increased, women have been closing the performance gap. Only ten minutes separate the current world marathon records for women and for men (both set in 2003).

Sources: *Christian Science Monitor*, © 1995 Christian Science Monitor and Marathonguide.com (2005). Adapted with permission of the *Christian Science Monitor*.

biological differences between men and women, she reasoned, people everywhere should define "feminine" and "masculine" in the same way; if gender is cultural, these conceptions should vary.

Mead studied three societies in New Guinea (1963, orig. 1935). In the mountainous home of the Arapesh, Mead observed men and women with remarkably similar attitudes and behavior. Both sexes, she reported, were cooperative and sensitive to others—in short, what our culture would label "feminine."

Moving south, Mead then studied the Mundugumor, whose headhunting and cannibalism stood in striking contrast to the gentle ways of the Arapesh. In this culture, both

Sex is a biological distinction that develops prior to birth. Gender is the meaning that a society attaches to being female or male. Gender differences are a matter of power, because what is defined as masculine typically has more importance than what is feminine. Infants begin to learn the importance of gender by the way parents treat them. Do you think this child is a girl or a boy? Why?

sexes were typically selfish and aggressive, traits we define as more "masculine."

Finally, traveling west to the Tchambuli, Mead discovered a culture that, like our own, defined females and males differently. But, Mead reported, the Tchambuli *reversed* many of our notions of gender: Females were dominant and rational, and males were submissive, emotional, and nurturing toward children. Based on her observations, Mead concluded that culture is the key to gender differences, because what one society defines as masculine another may see as feminine.

Some critics view Mead's findings as "too neat," as if she saw in these three societies just the patterns she was looking for. Deborah Gewertz (1981) challenged what she called Mead's "reversal hypothesis," pointing out that Tchambuli males are really the more aggressive sex. Gewertz explains that Mead visited the Tchambuli (who actually call themselves the Chambri) during the 1930s, after they had lost much of their property in tribal wars, and observed men rebuilding their homes, a temporary role for Chambri men.

George Murdock's Research

In a broader study of more than 200 preindustrial societies, George Murdock (1937) found some global agreement about which tasks are feminine and which masculine. Hunting and warfare, Murdock concluded, generally fall to men, and home-centered tasks such as cooking and child care tend to be women's work. With their simple technology, preindustrial societies apparently assign roles reflecting men's and women's physical characteristics. With greater size and strength, men hunt game and protect the group; because women bear children, they do most of the work in the home.

But beyond this general pattern, Murdock found much variety. Consider agriculture: Women did the farming in about the same number of societies as men; in most, the two sexes shared this work. When it came to many other tasks—from building shelters to tattooing the body—Murdock found that societies of the world were as likely to turn to one sex as the other.

→ ← **YOUR TURN** ← →

Did you grow up in a home in which females and males had different jobs and responsibilities? How did this affect your view of gender?

In Sum: Gender and Culture

Global comparisons show that overall, societies do not consistently define tasks as either feminine or masculine. With industrialization, the importance of muscle power declines, further reducing gender differences (Nolan & Lenski, 2004). In sum, gender is too variable across cultures to be a simple expression of biology; what it means to be female and male is mostly a creation of society.

PATRIARCHY AND SEXISM

Although conceptions of gender vary, everywhere in the world we find some degree of **patriarchy** (literally, "the rule of fathers"), *a form of social organization in which males dominate females.* Despite mythical tales of societies run by

In every society, people assume certain jobs, patterns of behavior, and ways of dressing are "naturally" feminine while others are just as obviously masculine. But in global perspective, we see remarkable variety in such social definitions. These men, Wodaabe pastoral nomads who live in the African nation of Niger, are proud to engage in a display of beauty most people in our society would consider feminine.

female "Amazons," **matriarchy,** *a form of social organization in which females dominate males,* has never been documented in human history.

Although some degree of patriarchy may be universal, women's power can rival that of men. During the 1700s and 1800s among the Seneca of North America, for example, women did the farming and controlled the food supply. Seneca men had to obtain women's support for their objectives (such as a military campaign), or women could simply withhold the necessary food (Freedman, 2002).

Around the world, as Global Map 13–1 on page 338 shows, there is significant variation in the relative power and privilege of females and males. According to the United Nations' gender development index, Norway, Australia, and Iceland give women the highest social standing; by contrast, women in the African nations of Niger, Burkina Faso, Mali, Sierra Leone, and Chad have the lowest social standing compared to men. Of the world's nations, the United States was ranked eighth in terms of gender equality (United Nations Development Programme, 2005).

The justification for patriarchy is **sexism,** *the belief that one sex is innately superior to the other.* Sexism is not just a matter of individual attitudes; it is built into the institutions of society. *Institutional sexism* is found throughout the economy, with women concentrated in low-paying jobs. Similarly, the legal system has long excused violence against women, especially on the part of boyfriends, husbands, and fathers.

The Costs of Sexism

Sexism limits the talents and ambitions of the half of the human population who are women. Although men benefit

in some respects from sexism, their privilege comes at a high price. Masculinity in our culture encourages men to engage in many high-risk behaviors: using tobacco and alcohol, playing dangerous sports, and driving recklessly. As Marilyn French (1985) argues, patriarchy leads men to seek control, not only of women but also of themselves and their world. This is why masculinity is closely linked not only to accidents but also to suicide, violence, and stress-related diseases. The *Type A personality*—marked by chronic impatience, driving ambition, competitiveness, and free-floating hostility—is a recipe for heart disease and almost perfectly matches the behavior that our culture considers masculine (Ehrenreich, 1983).

Finally, as men seek control over others, they lose opportunities for intimacy and trust. As one analyst put it, competition is supposed to "separate the men from the boys." In practice, however, it separates men from men and everyone else (Raphael, 1988).

Is Patriarchy Inevitable?

In preindustrial societies, women have little control over pregnancy and childbirth, which limits the scope of their lives. In those same societies, men's greater height and physical strength are highly valued resources. But industrialization, including birth control technology, gives people choices about how to live. In societies like our own, biological differences offer little justification for patriarchy.

But males are dominant in the United States and elsewhere. Does this mean that patriarchy is inevitable? Some researchers claim that biological factors such as differences in hormones and slight differences in brain structure "wire"

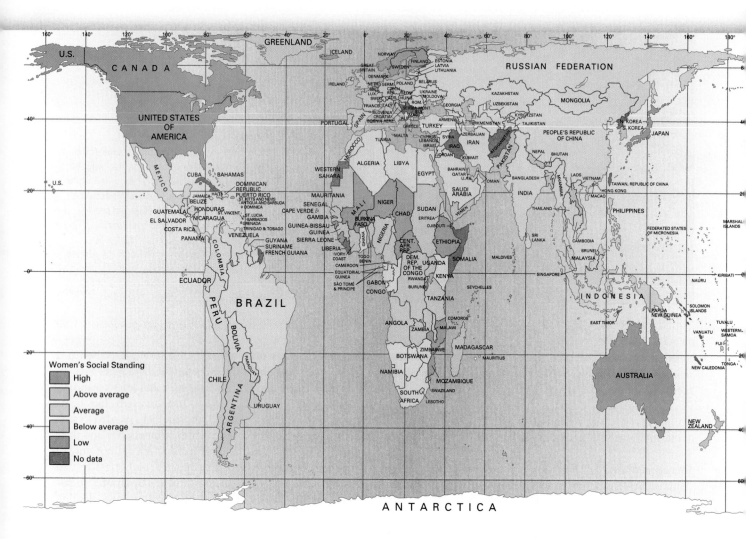

GLOBAL MAP 13–1 Women's Power in Global Perspective

Women's social standing in relation to men's varies around the world. In general, women live better in rich countries than in poor countries. Even so, some nations stand out: In the nations of Norway, Australia, and Iceland, women come closest to social equality with men.

Source: Data from Seager (2003).

the two sexes with different motivations and behaviors—especially aggressiveness in males—making patriarchy difficult, perhaps even impossible, to eliminate (S. Goldberg, 1974; Rossi, 1985; Popenoe, 1993b; Udry, 2000). However, most sociologists believe that gender is socially constructed and *can* be changed. Just because no society has yet eliminated patriarchy does not mean that we must remain prisoners of the past.

To understand why patriarchy continues today, we next examine how gender is rooted and reproduced in society, a process that begins in childhood and continues throughout our lives.

Gender and Socialization

From birth until death, gender shapes human feelings, thoughts, and actions. Children quickly learn that their society considers females and males different kinds of people; by about age three, they begin to think of themselves in these terms.

In the past, many people in the United States traditionally described women using terms such as "emotional," "passive," and "cooperative." By contrast, men were described in opposing terms, as "rational," "active," and "competitive." It is curious that we were taught for so long to think of gender in terms of one sex being opposite to the other, especially because women and men have so much in common and also because research suggests that most young people develop personalities that are some mix of these feminine and masculine traits (Bem, 1993).

Just as gender affects how we think of ourselves, so it teaches us how to behave. **Gender roles** (or **sex roles**) are *attitudes and activities that a society links to each sex*. A culture that defines males as ambitious and competitive encourages males to seek out positions of leadership and play team sports. To the extent that females are defined as deferential and emotional, they are expected to be supportive helpers and quick to show their feelings.

GENDER AND THE FAMILY

The first question people usually ask about a newborn—"Is it a boy or a girl?"—has great importance because the answer involves not just sex but the likely direction of the child's life. In fact, gender is at work even before the birth of a child because, especially in lower-income nations, parents hope their firstborn will be a boy rather than a girl.

Soon after birth, family members welcome infants into the "pink world" of girls or the "blue world" of boys (Bernard, 1981). Parents even send gender messages in the way they handle infants. One researcher at an English university presented an infant dressed as either a boy or a girl to a number of women; her subjects handled the "female" child tenderly, with frequent hugs and caresses, and treated the "male" child more roughly, often lifting him up high in the air or bouncing him on the knee (Bonner, 1984; Tavris & Wade, 2001). The lesson to children is clear: The female world revolves around cooperation and emotion, and the male world puts a premium on independence and action.

GENDER AND THE PEER GROUP

About the time they enter school, children begin to move outside the family and make friends with others of the same age. Considerable research shows that young children tend to form single-sex play groups (Martin & Fabes, 2001).

Peer groups teach additional lessons about gender. After spending a year observing children at play, Janet Lever (1978) concluded that boys favor team sports that have complex rules and clear objectives such as scoring runs or making touchdowns. Such games nearly always have winners and losers, reinforcing masculine traits of aggression and control.

Girls, too, play team sports. But, Lever explains, girls also play hopscotch, jump rope, or simply talk, sing, or dance. These activities have few rules, and rarely is "victory" the ultimate goal. Instead of teaching girls to be competitive, Lever explains, female peer groups promote the interpersonal skills of communication and cooperation, presumably the basis for girls' future roles as wives and mothers.

The games we play offer important lessons for our later lives. Lever's observations recall Carol Gilligan's gender-based theory of moral reasoning, discussed in Chapter 5 ("Socialization"). Boys, Gilligan (1982) claims, reason according to abstract principles. For them, "rightness" amounts to "playing by the rules." Girls, on the other hand, consider morality a matter of responsibility to others.

GENDER AND SCHOOLING

Gender shapes our interests and beliefs about our own abilities, guiding areas of study and, eventually, career choices (Correll, 2001). In high school, more girls than boys learn secretarial skills and take vocational classes such as cosmetology and food services. Classes in woodworking and auto mechanics attract mostly young men.

In college, the pattern continues, with men overly represented in mathematics and the sciences, including physics, chemistry, and biology. Women cluster in the humanities (such as English), the fine arts (painting, music, dance, and drama), and the social sciences (including anthropology and sociology). New areas of study are also likely to be gender-typed: More men than women take computer science, and more women than men enroll in courses in gender studies.

YOUR TURN

What is your declared or likely major? What share of students in this major are female and what share are male? Does the pattern agree with those described here?

Television crime shows such as *CSI* have male lead characters with women in supporting roles largely to provide romantic interest. Can you think of other television shows that display this pattern?

GENDER AND THE MASS MEDIA

Since television first captured the public imagination in the 1950s, white males have held center stage; racial and ethnic minorities were all but absent from television until the early 1970s. Even when both sexes appeared on camera, men generally played the brilliant detectives, fearless explorers, and skilled surgeons. Women played the less capable characters and were often important only for the sexual interest they added to the story.

Historically, advertisements have shown women in the home, cheerfully using cleaning products, serving food, and modeling clothes. Men predominate in ads for cars, travel, banking services, and alcoholic beverages. The authoritative

"voiceover"—the faceless voice that describes a product on television and radio—is almost always male (D.M. Davis, 1993).

A careful study of gender in advertising reveals that men usually appear taller than women, implying male superiority. Women, by contrast, are more frequently presented lying down (on sofas and beds) or, like children, seated on the floor. Men's facial expressions and behavior give off an air of competence and imply dominance; women often appear childlike, submissive, and sexual. Men focus on the products being advertised, and women often focus on the men (Goffman, 1979; Cortese, 1999).

Advertising also actively perpetuates what Naomi Wolf calls the "beauty myth." The Applying Sociology box takes a closer look.

Gender and Social Stratification

Gender affects more than how people think and act. It is also about social hierarchy. The reality of gender stratification can be seen, first, in the world of work.

WORKING WOMEN AND MEN

Back in 1900, just 20 percent of U.S. women were in the labor force. Today, the figure has tripled, to 60 percent, and  74 percent of these working women work full time. The traditional view that earning an income is a man's role no longer holds true.

Factors that have changed the U.S. labor force include the decline of farming, the growth of cities, shrinking family size, and a rising divorce rate. The United States, along with most other nations of the world, considers women working for income the rule rather than the exception. Women now represent almost half the U.S. paid labor force, and half of U.S. married couples depend on two incomes.

A report on women in the labor force can be found at http://www.bls.gov/cps/wlf-databook-2005.pdf

In the past, many women in the U.S. labor force were childless. But today, 59 percent of married women with children under age six are in the labor force, as are 76 percent of married women with children between six and seventeen years of age. For never-married, widowed, divorced, or separated women with children, the comparable figures are 71 percent of women with younger children and 82 percent of women with older children (U.S. Department of Labor, 2005).

APPLYING SOCIOLOGY
The Beauty Myth

The Duchess of Windsor once remarked, "A woman cannot be too rich or too thin." The first half of her observation might apply to men as well, but certainly not the second. The answer lies in the fact that the vast majority of ads placed by the $20-billion-a-year cosmetics industry and the $40-billion diet industry target women.

According to Naomi Wolf (1990), certain cultural patterns create a "beauty myth" that is damaging to women. The beauty myth arises, first, because society teaches women to measure their worth in terms of physical appearance. Yet the standards of beauty embodied in the *Playboy* centerfold or the 100-pound New York fashion model are out of reach of most women.

The way society teaches women to prize relationships with men, whom they presumably attract with their beauty,

also contributes to the beauty myth. Striving for beauty drives women to be extremely disciplined but also forces them to be highly attuned and responsive to men. In short, beauty-minded women try to please men and avoid challenging male power.

The beauty myth affects males as well: Men should want to possess

beautiful women. Thus our ideas about beauty reduce women to objects and motivate men to possess women as if they were dolls rather than human beings.

In sum, there can be little doubt that the idea of beauty is important in everyday life. The question, according to Wolf, is whether beauty is about how we look or how we act.

WHAT DO YOU THINK?

1. How does the beauty myth apply differently to men and women?

2. Do you agree that the great importance attached to women's beauty is a problem? Why or why not?

3. Among people with physical disabilities, do you think women or men face more serious issues of "looking different"?

Gender and Occupations

Although women are closing the gap with men as far as working for income is concerned, the work done by the two sexes remains very different. The U.S. Department of Labor (2005) reports a high concentration of women in two job types. Administrative support work draws 23 percent of working women, most of whom are secretaries or other office workers. These are often called "pink-collar jobs" because 76 percent are filled by women. Another 20 percent of employed women do service work. Most of these jobs are in food service industries, child care, and health care.

Table 13–1 on page 342 shows the ten occupations with the highest concentrations of women. These jobs tend to be at the low end of the pay scale, with limited opportunities

for advancement and with men as supervisors (U.S. Department of Labor, 2005).

Men dominate most other job categories, including the building trades, where 99 percent of bricklayers, stonemasons, and heavy equipment mechanics are men. Likewise, men make up 87 percent of police officers, 86 percent of engineers, 71 percent of lawyers and physicians, and 63 percent of corporate managers. According to a recent survey, the top earners in *Fortune* 500 corporations were 2,141 men (95 percent of the total) and 118 women (5 percent). Just 17 of the 1,000 largest U.S. corporations have a woman chief executive officer (Catalyst, 2004, 2005; U.S. Department of Labor, 2005).

 Find reports on all aspects of women in business at http://www.catalystwomen.org/bookstore/freematerials.shtml#lea

TABLE 13–1

Jobs with the Highest Concentrations of Women, 2004

Occupation	Number of Women Employed	Percentage in Occupation Who Are Women
1. Dental hygienist	130,000	98.8%
2. Preschool or kindergarten teacher	656,000	98.1
3. Secretary or administrative assistant	3,522,000	96.9
4. Dental assistant	242,000	96.5
5. Speech-language pathologist	93,000	95.1
6. Child care worker	1,332,000	94.5
7. Licensed practical or licensed vocational nurse	517,000	94.3
8. Word processor or typist	319,000	93.5
9. Occupational therapist	84,000	92.7
10. Receptionist or information clerk	1,373,000	92.4

Source: U.S. Department of Labor (2005).

Gender stratification in the workplace is easy to see: Female nurses assist male physicians, female secretaries serve male executives, and female flight attendants are under the command of male airplane pilots. In any field, the greater the income and prestige associated with a job, the more likely it is to be held by a man. For example, women represent 98 percent of kindergarten teachers, 82 percent of elementary school teachers, 55 percent of secondary school educators, 39 percent of college and university professors, and 21 percent of college and university presidents (*Chronicle of Higher Education,* 2005; U.S. Department of Labor, 2005).

How are women kept out of certain jobs? By defining some kinds of work as "masculine," companies define women as unsuitable workers. In a study of coal mining in southern West Virginia, Suzanne Tallichet (2000) found that most men considered it "unnatural" for women to join them working in the mines. Women who did, therefore, risked being defined as "unnatural" and subject to labeling as "sexually loose" or as lesbians. Such labeling made these women outcasts, presented a challenge to holding the job, and made advancement all but impossible.

In the corporate world, as already noted, the higher in the company we look, the fewer women we find. You hardly ever hear anyone say that women don't belong at the top levels of a company. But many people seem to feel this way, which can prevent women from being promoted. Sociologists describe this barrier as a *glass ceiling* that is not easy to see but blocks women's careers all the same (Benokraitis & Feagin, 1995).

One challenge to male domination in the workplace comes from women who are entrepreneurs. Women now own more than 9 million small businesses in the United States, twice the number of a decade ago and more than one-third of the total. Although a large majority of these businesses are one-person operations, women-owned businesses employ one-fourth of the entire labor force. Through starting their own businesses, women have shown that they can make opportunities for themselves outside larger, male-dominated companies (U.S. Small Business Administration, 2001b).

HOUSEWORK: WOMEN'S "SECOND SHIFT"

In the United States, we have always been of two minds about housework: We claim that it is essential to family life, but people get little reward for doing it (Bernard, 1981). Here, as around the world, taking care of the home and children has always been considered "women's work." With women's entry into the labor force, the amount of housework women do has gone down, but the *share* done by women has stayed the same. Figure 13–2 shows that, overall, women average 16.5 hours a week of housework, compared to 9.2 hours for men. As the figure shows, women in all categories do significantly more housework than men (Stapinski, 1998).

Men do support the idea of women entering the paid labor force, and most count on the money women earn. But many men resist taking on a more equal share of household duties (Heath & Bourne, 1995; Harpster & Monk-Turner, 1998; Stratton, 2001).

GENDER, INCOME, AND WEALTH

In 2004, the median earnings of women working full time were $31,223; for men, the figure was $40,798. This means that for every dollar earned by men, women earned about 77 cents. This difference is greater among older workers because older working women typically have less education and seniority than older working men. Earning differences are smaller among younger workers because younger men and women tend to have similar schooling and work experience.

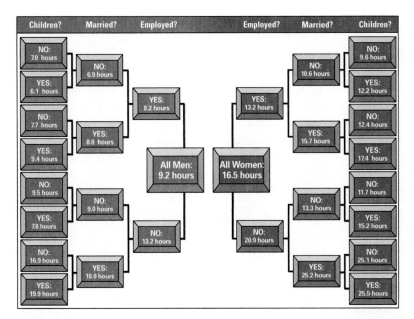

| Children? | Married? | Employed? | | Employed? | Married? | Children? |

NO: 7.0 hours
YES: 6.1 hours
→ **NO:** 6.9 hours
NO: 7.7 hours
YES: 9.4 hours
→ **YES:** 8.8 hours
→ **YES:** 8.2 hours
→ **All Men: 9.2 hours**

NO: 9.5 hours
YES: 7.8 hours
→ **NO:** 9.0 hours
NO: 16.9 hours
YES: 19.9 hours
→ **YES:** 18.0 hours
→ **NO:** 13.2 hours

All Women: 16.5 hours
→ **YES:** 13.2 hours
→ **NO:** 10.6 hours
NO: 9.6 hours
YES: 12.2 hours
→ **YES:** 15.7 hours
NO: 12.4 hours
YES: 17.4 hours

→ **NO:** 13.3 hours
NO: 11.7 hours
YES: 15.2 hours
→ **NO:** 20.9 hours
→ **YES:** 25.2 hours
NO: 25.1 hours
YES: 25.5 hours

FIGURE 13-2 Housework: Who Does How Much?

Overall, women average 16.5 hours of housework per week, compared with 9.2 hours for men. This pattern holds whether people are employed or not, married or not, and parenting or not.

Source: Adapted from Stapinski (1998).

Among all full-time workers of all ages, 34 percent of women earned less than $25,000 in 2004, compared with 23 percent of men. At the upper end of the income scale, men were two-and-one-half times more likely than women (18.5 percent versus 7.2 percent) to earn more than $75,000 (U.S. Census Bureau, 2005).

The *Monthly Labor Review* reports on the gender earnings gap at http://www.bls.gov/opub/mlr/2003/03/art2full.pdf

The main reason women earn less is the *kind* of work they do: largely clerical and service jobs. In effect, jobs and gender interact. People still perceive jobs with less clout as "women's work," just as people devalue certain work simply because it is performed by women (England, Hermsen, & Cotter, 2000; Cohen & Huffman, 2003).

In recent decades, supporters of gender equality have proposed a policy of "comparable worth," paying people not according to the historical double standard but according to the level of skill and responsibility involved in the work. Several nations, including Great Britain and Australia, have adopted comparable worth policies, but these policies have found limited acceptance in the United States. As a result, critics claim, women in this country lose as much as $1 billion in income annually.

A second cause of gender-based income disparity has to do with the family. Both men and women have children, of course, but our culture gives more responsibility for parenting to women. Pregnancy and raising small children keep many young women out of the labor force at a time when their male peers are making significant career advancements. When women workers return to the labor force, they have less job seniority than their male counterparts (Stier, 1996; Waldfogel, 1997).

In addition, women who choose to have children may be unable or unwilling to take on demanding jobs that tie up their evenings and weekends. To avoid role strain, they may take jobs that offer shorter commuting distances, more flexible hours, and employer-provided child care services.

Women pursuing both a career and a family are often torn between their dual responsibilities in ways that men are not. Consider this: At age forty, 90 percent of men but only 35 percent of women in executive positions have at least one child (F.N. Schwartz, 1989). This pattern is also found on campus, where one recent study concluded that young female professors with at least one child were at least 20 percent less likely to have tenure than male professors in the same field (Shea, 2002).

YOUR TURN

Consider the statements "He fathered the child" and "She mothered the child." How do you think gender shapes the meaning of parenting?

Although only about 12 percent of the richest people in the United States are women, a number of women have reached the very top of the economic pyramid. Oprah Winfrey, who became both very wealthy and hugely influential as a result of her television show, is one example. Her business empire includes *O, The Oprah Magazine*.

The two factors noted so far—type of work and family responsibilities—account for about two-thirds of the earnings difference between women and men. A third factor—discrimination against women—accounts for most of the remainder (Fuller & Schoenberger, 1991). Because discrimination is illegal, it is practiced in subtle ways. Women on their way up the corporate ladder often run into the glass ceiling described earlier; company officials may deny its existence, but it effectively prevents many women from rising above middle management.

For all these reasons, women earn less than men in all major occupational categories. Even so, many people think that women own most of this country's wealth, perhaps because women typically outlive men. Government statistics tell a different story: Sixty-one percent of individuals with $1 million or more in assets are men, although widows are highly represented in this elite club (Internal Revenue Service, 2003). Just 12 percent of the individuals identified

in 2005 by *Forbes* magazine as the richest people in the United States were women (Miller & Newcomb, 2005).

GENDER AND EDUCATION

In the past, our society considered schooling more necessary for men, who worked outside the home, than for women, who worked in the home. But times have changed. By 1980, women earned a majority of all associate's and bachelor's degrees; in 2002, their proportion stood at 58 percent (National Center for Education Statistics, 2004).

College doors have opened to women, and the differences in men's and women's majors are becoming smaller. In 1970, for example, women earned just 17 percent of bachelor's degrees in the natural sciences, computer science, and engineering; by 2002, their proportion had doubled to 35 percent.

In 1992, for the first time, women also earned a majority of postgraduate degrees, which often serve as a springboard to high-prestige jobs. In all areas of study in 2002,

 A report on trends in equal education for girls and women can be found at http://nces.ed.gov/pubs2005/equity/

women earned 59 percent of master's degrees and 46 percent of doctorates (including 61 percent of all Ph.D.s in sociology). Women have also broken into many graduate fields that used to be almost all male. For example, in 1970, only a few hundred women earned a master's of business administration (M.B.A.) degree, compared to more than 49,000 in 2002—41 percent of all such degrees (National Center for Education Statistics, 2004).

Despite this progress, men continue to dominate some professional fields. In 2002, men received 52 percent of law degrees (LL.B. and J.D.), 56 percent of medical degrees (M.D.), and 62 percent of dental degrees (D.D.S. and D.M.D.) (National Center for Education Statistics, 2004). Our society still defines high-paying professions (and the drive and competitiveness needed to succeed in them) as masculine. But the share of women in all these professions is rising steadily. For example, the American Bar Association (2005) reports that the law school class of 2007 across the United States is evenly split between women and men.

GENDER AND POLITICS

A century ago, men held virtually every elected office in the United States. By law, women could not even vote in national elections until the passage of the Nineteenth Amendment to the Constitution in 1920. However, a few women were candidates for political office even before they could vote. The Equal Rights party supported Victoria Woodhull for the U.S. presidency in 1872; perhaps it was a sign of the times that she spent election day in a New York City jail.

Table 13–2 identifies later milestones in women's gradual movement into political life.

Today, thousands of women serve as mayors of cities and towns across the United States, and tens of thousands hold responsible administrative posts in the federal government. At the state level, 23 percent of legislators in 2005 were women (up from just 6 percent in 1970). National Map 13–1 on page 346 shows where in the United States women have made the greatest political gains.

 For the latest on women in national politics, visit http://www.cawp.rutgers.edu

Less change has occurred at the highest levels of politics, although a majority of U.S. adults claim they would support a qualified woman for any office, including the presidency. As of 2005, eight of the fifty state governors were women (16 percent), and in Congress, women held 66 of 435 seats in the House of Representatives (15 percent) and 14 of 100 seats (14 percent) in the Senate.

Globally, although women make up half the Earth's population, they hold just 16 percent of seats in the world's 185 parliaments. Although this percentage represents a rise from 3 percent fifty years ago, only in a dozen countries, including Sweden and Norway, do women represent more than one-third of the members of parliament (Inter-Parliamentary Union, 2005).

YOUR TURN

Sweden, Norway, Finland, and Denmark have laws that require at least 25 percent of candidates for elected office to be women. Do you think the United States should adopt such a law? Why or why not?

GENDER AND THE MILITARY

Women have served in the armed forces since colonial times. Yet in 1940, at the outset of World War II, just 2 percent of armed forces personnel were women. By the time of the 2003 war in Iraq, women represented about 7 percent of all deployed U.S. troops and 15 percent of all people in the armed forces.

Clearly, women make up a growing share of the U.S. military, and almost all military assignments are now open to both women and men. But some people object to opening doors in this way, claiming that women lack the physical strength of men. Others reply that military women are better educated and score higher on intelligence tests than military men. But the heart of the issue is our society's deeply

---

TABLE 13–2

Significant "Firsts" for Women in U.S. Politics

1869	Law allows women to vote in Wyoming territory.
1872	First woman to run for the presidency (Victoria Woodhull) represents the Equal Rights party.
1917	First woman elected to the House of Representatives (Jeannette Rankin of Montana).
1924	First women elected state governors (Nellie Taylor Ross of Wyoming and Miriam "Ma" Ferguson of Texas); both followed their husbands into office. First woman to have her name placed in nomination for the vice-presidency at the convention of a major political party (Lena Jones Springs, a Democrat).
1931	First woman to serve in the Senate (Hattie Caraway of Arkansas); completed the term of her husband upon his death and won reelection in 1932.
1932	First woman appointed to the presidential cabinet (Frances Perkins, secretary of labor in the cabinet of President Franklin D. Roosevelt).
1964	First woman to have her name placed in nomination for the presidency at the convention of a major political party (Margaret Chase Smith, a Republican).
1972	First African American woman to have her name placed in nomination for the presidency at the convention of a major political party (Shirley Chisholm, a Democrat).
1981	First woman appointed to the U.S. Supreme Court (Sandra Day O'Connor).
1984	First woman to be successfully nominated for the vice-presidency (Geraldine Ferraro, a Democrat).
1988	First woman chief executive to be elected to a consecutive third term (Madeleine Kunin, governor of Vermont).
1992	Political "Year of the Woman" yields record number of women in the Senate (six) and the House (forty-eight), as well as (1) first African American woman to win election to U.S. Senate (Carol Moseley-Braun of Illinois), (2) first state (California) to be served by two women senators (Barbara Boxer and Dianne Feinstein), and (3) first woman of Puerto Rican descent elected to the House (Nydia Velazquez of New York).
1996	First woman appointed secretary of state (Madeleine Albright).
2000	First First Lady to win elected political office (Hillary Rodham Clinton, senator from New York).
2001	First woman to serve as national security adviser (Condoleezza Rice); first Asian American woman to serve in a presidential cabinet (Elaine Chao).
2002	Record number of women in the Senate (fourteen).
2005	First African American woman appointed secretary of state (Condoleezza Rice); record number of women in the House (sixty-six).

Source: Compiled by the author.

NATIONAL MAP 13-1

Women in State Government across the United States

Although women make up half of U.S. adults, just 23 percent of the seats in state legislatures are held by women. Look at the state-by-state variation in the map. In which regions of the country have women gained the greatest political power? What do you think accounts for this pattern?

Source: Center for American Women and Politics (2005).

Share of State Legislative Seats Held by Women

- High: 30.0% and over
- Above average: 25.0% to 29.9%
- Average: 20.0% to 24.9%
- Below average: 15.0% to 19.9%
- Low: 14.9% and under

U.S. average: 22.5%

---

held view of women as *nurturers*—people who give life and help others—which clashes with the image of women trained to kill.

One reason that women are more integrated into today's military is that technology blurs the distinction between combat and noncombat personnel. A combat pilot can fire missiles by radar at a target miles away; by contrast, nonfighting medical evacuation teams must travel directly into the line of fire (Segal & Hansen, 1992; Wilcox, 1992; Kaminer, 1997).

ARE WOMEN A MINORITY?

A **minority** is *any category of people distinguished by physical or cultural difference that a society sets apart and subordinates.* Given the economic disadvantage of being a woman in our society, it seems reasonable to say that U.S. women are a minority even though they outnumber men.[1]

Even so, most white women do not think of themselves in this way (Lengermann & Wallace, 1985). The reason is partly because, unlike racial minorities (including African Americans) and ethnic minorities (say, Hispanics), white women are well represented at all levels of the class structure, including the very top.

Bear in mind, however, that at every class level, women typically have less income, wealth, education, and power

[1]We use the term "minority" instead of "minority group" because, as explained in Chapter 7 ("Groups and Organizations"), women make up a *category,* not a group. People in a category share a status or identity but generally do not know one another or interact.

than men. Patriarchy makes women dependent on men—first their fathers and later their husbands—for their social standing (Bernard, 1981).

MINORITY WOMEN: INTERSECTION THEORY

If women are defined as a minority, what about minority women? Are they doubly handicapped? This question lies at the heart of **intersection theory,** *the interplay of race, class, and gender, often resulting in multiple dimensions of disadvantage.* Research shows that disadvantages linked to gender and race often combine to produce especially low social standing (Ovadia, 2001).

Income data illustrate the validity of this theory. Looking first at race and ethnicity, the median income in 2004 for African American women working full time was $27,730, which is 85 percent as much as the $32,486 earned by non-Hispanic white women; Hispanic women earned $23,444—just 72 percent as much as their white counterparts. Looking at gender, African American women earned 89 percent as much as African American men, and Hispanic women earned 88 percent as much as Hispanic men.

Combining these disadvantages, African American women earned 61 percent as much as non-Hispanic white men, and Hispanic women earned 51 percent as much (U.S. Census Bureau, 2005). These differences reflect minority women's lower positions in the occupational and educational hierarchies. These data confirm that although gender has a powerful effect on our lives, it never operates alone. Class position, race and ethnicity, and gender form a complex system of disadvantage for some and privilege for others (St. Jean & Feagin, 1998).

VIOLENCE AGAINST WOMEN

As noted in the opening to this chapter, 150 years ago men claimed the right to rule their households, even to the point of using physical discipline against their wives. Even today, a

 Here is a United Nations report on violence against women and girls around the world: http://www.unicef-icdc.org/publications/pdf/digest6e.pdf

great deal of "manly" violence is directed at women. A government report estimates 347,000 aggravated assaults against women annually. To this number can be added 204,000 rapes or sexual assaults and perhaps 1.5 million simple assaults (Goetting, 1999; U.S. Bureau of Justice Statistics, 2005).

Gender violence is also an issue on college and university campuses. A report from the U.S. Department of Justice (2000) states that 1.7 percent of female college students have been victims of rape and another 1.1 percent have been victims of attempted rape. In 90 percent of all cases, the victim knew the offender, and most of the assaults took place in the woman's living quarters.

Off campus, most gender-linked violence also occurs where men and women interact most: in the home. Richard Gelles (cited in Roesch, 1984) argues that with the exception of the police and the military, the family is the most violent organization in the United States, and women suffer most of the injuries (Gelles & Cornell, 1990; Smolowe, 1994).

Violence against women also occurs in casual relationships. As noted in Chapter 9 ("Deviance"), most rapes involve men known, and often trusted, by the victims. Dianne Herman (2001) claims that abuse of women is built into our way of life. All forms of violence against women—from the catcalls that intimidate women on city streets to a pinch in a crowded subway to physical assaults that occur at home—express what she calls a "rape culture" of men trying to dominate women. Sexual violence is fundamentally about *power,* not sex, and therefore should be understood as a dimension of gender stratification.

In global perspective, violence against women is built into different cultures in different ways. One case in point is the practice of female genital mutilation, a painful and often

 For information on female genital mutilation, see http://www.amnesty.org/ailib/intcam/femgen/fgm1.htm

dangerous surgical procedure performed in more than forty countries and known to occur in the

United States, as shown in Global Map 13–2 on page 348. The Thinking About Diversity box on page 349 highlights a case of genital mutilation that took place in California.

VIOLENCE AGAINST MEN

If our way of life encourages violence against women, it may encourage even more violence against men. As noted in

The basic insight of intersection theory is that various dimensions of social stratification—including race and gender—can add up to great disadvantages for some categories of people. Just as African Americans earn less than whites, women earn less than men. Thus, African American women confront a "double disadvantage," earning just 61 cents for every dollar earned by non-Hispanic white men. How would you explain the fact that some categories of people are much more likely to end up in low-paying jobs like this one?

Chapter 9 ("Deviance"), in more than 80 percent of cases in which police make an arrest for a violent crime, including murder, robbery, and assault, the offender is a male. In addition, 57 percent of all victims of violent crime are also men (Federal Bureau of Investigation, 2004; U.S. Bureau of Justice Statistics, 2005).

Our culture tends to define masculinity in terms of aggression and violence. "Real men" work and play hard, speed on the highways, and let nothing stand in their way. A higher crime rate is one result. But even when no laws are broken, men's lives involve more stress and isolation than women's lives, which is one reason that the suicide rate for men is four times higher than for women. In addition, as noted earlier, men live, on average, about five fewer years than women.

Violence is not simply a matter of choices made by individuals. It is built into our way of life, with resulting harm to both men and women. In short, the way any culture constructs gender plays an important part in how violent or peaceful a society will be.

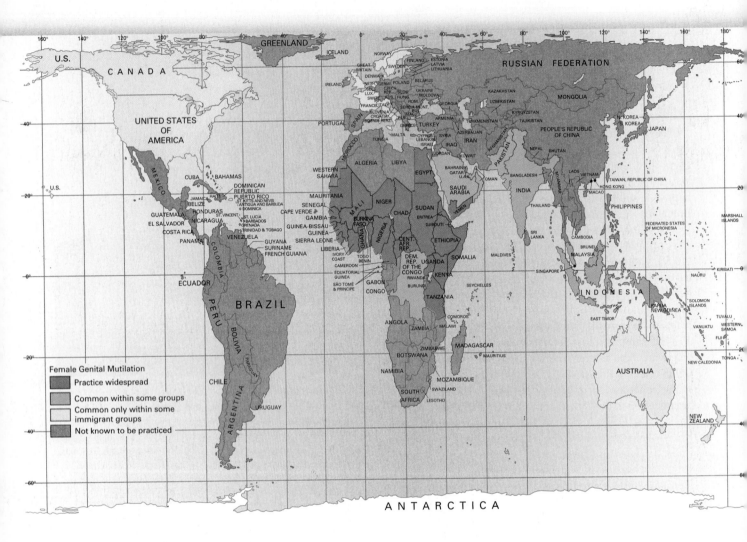

WINDOW ON THE WORLD

GLOBAL MAP 13-2 Female Genital Mutilation in Global Perspective

Female genital mutilation is known to be performed in more than forty countries around the world. Across Africa, the practice is common and affects a majority of girls in the eastern African nations of Sudan, Ethiopia, and Somalia. In several Asian nations, including India, the practice is limited to a few ethnic minorities. In the United States, Canada, several European nations, and Australia, there are reports of the practice among some immigrants.

Source: Data from Seager (2003).

SEXUAL HARASSMENT

Sexual harassment refers to *comments, gestures, or physical contact of a sexual nature that are deliberate, repeated, and unwelcome.* During the 1990s, sexual harassment became an issue of national importance that rewrote the rules for workplace interaction between women and men.

Most (but not all) victims of sexual harassment are women. The reason is that, first, our culture encourages men to be sexually assertive and to see women in sexual terms. As a result, social interaction in the workplace, on campus, and elsewhere can easily take on sexual overtones. Second, most people in positions of power—including

Female Genital Mutilation: Violence in the Name of Morality

Meserak Ramsey, a woman born in Ethiopia and now working as a nurse in California, paid a visit to an old friend's home. Soon after arriving, she noticed her friend's eighteen-month-old daughter huddled in the corner of a room in obvious distress. "What's wrong?" she asked.

Ramsey was shocked when the woman said her daughter had recently had a clitoridectomy, the surgical removal of the clitoris. This type of female genital mutilation—performed by a midwife, a tribal practitioner, or a doctor, and typically without anesthesia—is common in Nigeria, Togo, Somalia, and Egypt and is known to exist in certain cultural groups in other nations around the world. It is illegal in the United States.

Among members of highly patriarchal societies, husbands demand that their wives be virgins at marriage and remain sexually faithful thereafter. The point of female genital mutilation is to eliminate sexual feeling, which, people assume, makes the girl less likely to violate sexual norms and thus be more desirable to men. In about one-fifth of all cases, an even more severe procedure, called infibulation, is performed, in which the entire external genital area is removed and the surfaces are stitched together, leaving only a small hole for urination. Before marriage, a husband retains the right to open the wound and ensure himself of his bride's virginity.

How many women have undergone genital mutilation? Worldwide, estimates place the number at 135 million. In the United States, hundreds or even thousands of such procedures are performed every year. In most cases, immigrant mothers and grandmothers who have themselves been mutilated insist that young girls in their family follow their example. Indeed, many immigrant women demand the procedure *because* their daughters now live in the United States, where sexual mores are more lax. "I don't have to worry about her now," the girl's mother explained to Meserak Ramsey. "She'll be a good girl."

Medically, the consequences of genital mutilation include more than the loss of sexual pleasure. Pain is intense and can persist for years. There is also danger of infection, infertility, and even death. Ramsey knows this all too well: She herself underwent genital mutilation as a young girl. She is one of the lucky ones who has had few medical problems since. But the extent of her suffering is suggested by this story: She invited a young U.S. couple to stay at her home. Late at night, she heard the woman cry out and burst into their room to investigate, only to learn that the couple was making love and the woman had just had an orgasm. "I didn't understand," Ramsey recalls. "I thought that there must be something wrong with American girls. But now I know that there is something wrong with me." Or with a system that inflicts such injury in the name of traditional morality.

WHAT DO YOU THINK?

1. Is female genital mutilation a medical procedure or a means of social control? Explain your answer.
2. Can you think of other examples of physical mutilation imposed on women?
3. What do you think should be done about female genital mutilation in places where it is widespread? Do you think respect for human rights should override respect for cultural differences in this case? Explain your answer.

These young women have just undergone female genital mutilation. What do you think should be done about this practice?

Sources: Based on Crossette (1995) and Boyle, Songora, & Foss (2001).

APPLYING THEORY

GENDER

	Structural-Functional Approach	Social-Conflict Approach
What is the level of analysis?	Macro-level	Macro-level
What does gender mean?	Parsons described gender in terms of two complementary patterns of behavior: masculine and feminine.	Engels described gender in terms of the power of one sex over the other.
Is gender helpful or harmful?	Helpful. Gender gives men and women distinctive roles and responsibilities that help society operate smoothly. Gender builds social unity as men and women come together to form families.	Harmful. Gender limits people's personal development. Gender divides society by giving power to men to control the lives of women. Capitalism makes patriarchy stronger.

business executives, doctors, bureau chiefs, assembly-line supervisors, professors, and military officers—are men who oversee the work of women. Surveys carried out in widely different work settings show that half of the women respondents receive unwanted sexual attention (NORC, 2003).

Sexual harassment is sometimes obvious and direct: A supervisor may ask for sexual favors from an employee and make threats if the advances are refused. Courts have declared such *quid pro quo* sexual harassment (the Latin phrase means "one thing in return for another") to be a violation of civil rights.

More often, however, sexual harassment is a matter of subtle behavior—sexual teasing, off-color jokes, the display of pinups—that may not even be *intended* to harass anyone. But by the *effect* standard favored by many feminists, such actions add up to creating a *hostile environment*. Incidents of this kind are far more complex because they involve different perceptions of the same behavior. For example, a man may think that by repeatedly complimenting a co-worker on her appearance he is simply being friendly. The co-worker may believe that the man is thinking of her in sexual terms and is not taking her work seriously, an attitude that could harm her job performance and prospects for advancement.

Pornography

Chapter 8 ("Sexuality") defined *pornography* as sexually explicit material that causes sexual arousal. Keep in mind, however, that people take different views of what is and what is not pornographic. The law gives local communities the power to define what sexually explicit materials violate "community standards of decency" and "lack any redeeming social value."

People may disagree about what is or is not pornographic, but there is little doubt that in the United States,

pornography is big business. Altogether, sexually explicit videos, movies, magazines, telephone chat, and Internet sites take in more than $10 billion in sales each year.

Traditionally, people have raised concerns about pornography as a *moral* issue. But pornography also plays a part in gender stratification. From this point of view, pornography is really a *power* issue because most pornography dehumanizes women, depicting them as the playthings of men. Worth noting in this context is that the term *pornography* comes from the Greek word *porne,* meaning a woman who acts as a man's sexual slave.

In addition, there is widespread concern that pornography promotes violence against women by portraying them as weak and undeserving of respect. Men may show contempt for women defined this way by striking out against them. Surveys show that about half of U.S. adults think that pornography encourages men to commit rape (NORC, 2003:235).

Like sexual harassment, pornography raises complex and conflicting issues. Despite the fact that some material may offend just about everybody, many support the rights of free speech and artistic expression. Pressure to restrict pornography has increased in recent decades, reflecting both the longstanding concern that pornography weakens morality and more recent concerns that it is demeaning and threatening to women.

YOUR TURN

The Internet has made pornography more accessible; do you think it has become more acceptable as well? Why or why not?

In the 1950s, Talcott Parsons proposed that sociologists interpret gender as a matter of *differences*. As he saw it, masculine men and feminine women formed strong families and made for an orderly society. In recent decades, however, social-conflict theory has reinterpreted gender as a matter of *inequality*. From this point of view, U.S. society places men in a position of dominance over women.

Theoretical Analysis of Gender

Why does gender exist in the first place? Each of sociology's two macro-level approaches, summarized in the Applying Theory table, offers insights about the importance of gender in social organization.

STRUCTURAL-FUNCTIONAL ANALYSIS

The structural-functional approach views society as a complex system of many separate but integrated parts. From this point of view, gender serves as a means to organize social life.

As Chapter 4 ("Society") explained, members of hunting and gathering societies had little power over the forces of biology. Lacking effective birth control, women were frequently pregnant, and the responsibilities of child care kept them close to home. At the same time, men's greater strength made them more suited for warfare and hunting game. Over the centuries, this sexual division of labor became institutionalized and largely taken for granted (Lengermann & Wallace, 1985; Freedman, 2002).

Industrial technology opens up a much greater range of cultural possibilities. With human muscles no longer the main energy source, the physical strength of men becomes less important. In addition, the ability to control reproduction gives women greater choices about how to live. Modern societies relax traditional gender roles as they become more meritocratic because such rigid roles waste an enormous

amount of human talent. Yet change comes slowly because gender is deeply rooted in culture.

Talcott Parsons: Gender and Complementarity

Talcott Parsons (1942, 1951, 1954) argued that keeping some gender differences helps integrate society, at least in its traditional form. Gender forms a *complementary* set of roles that links men and women into family units and gives each sex responsibility for important tasks. Women take the lead in managing the household and raising children. Men connect the family to the larger world as they participate in the labor force.

Therefore, gender plays an important part in socialization. Society teaches boys—presumably destined for the labor force—to be rational, self-assured, and competitive. Parsons called this complex of traits *instrumental* qualities. To prepare girls for child rearing, their socialization stresses *expressive* qualities, such as emotional responsiveness and sensitivity to others.

Society encourages gender conformity by instilling in men and women a fear that straying too far from accepted standards of masculinity or femininity will cause rejection by the other sex. In simple terms, women learn to reject nonmasculine men as sexually unattractive, and men learn to reject unfeminine women. In sum, gender integrates society both structurally (in terms of what people do) and morally (in terms of what they believe).

Critical review Influential a half century ago, this approach has lost much of its standing today. First, functionalism

In the film *Iron Jawed Angels*, Hilary Swank portrays early women's rights activist Alice Paul, who worked tirelessly for passage of the Nineteenth Amendment to the Constitution giving women the right to vote. The United States was fighting World War I at the time, and there was little sympathy for what seemed to be radical ideas about gender. Alice Paul and others were taken to jail, where they began a hunger strike and refused to be force fed (which explains the name of the movie). With the ratification of the Nineteenth Amendment, women gained the right to vote in 1920.

assumes a singular vision of society that is not shared by everyone. Historically, many women have worked outside the home because of economic need, a fact not reflected in Parsons's conventional, middle-class view of family life. Second, Parsons's analysis ignores the personal strains and social costs of rigid, traditional gender roles. Third, in the eyes of those seeking sexual equality, what Parsons describes as gender "complementarity" amounts to little more than women submitting to male domination.

SOCIAL-CONFLICT ANALYSIS

From a social-conflict point of view, gender involves differences not just in behavior but in power as well. Consider the striking similarity between the way ideas about gender benefit men and the way oppression of racial and ethnic minorities benefits white people. Conventional ideas about gender do not make society operate smoothly; they create division and tension, with men seeking to protect their privileges as women challenge the status quo.

As earlier chapters explain, the social-conflict approach draws heavily on the ideas of Karl Marx. Yet as far as gender is concerned, Marx was a product of his time, and his writings focused almost entirely on men. However, his friend and collaborator Friedrich Engels did develop a theory of gender stratification.

Friedrich Engels: Gender and Class

Looking back through history, Engels saw that in hunting and gathering societies, the activities of women and men, although different, had the same importance. A successful hunt brought men great prestige, but the vegetation gathered by women provided most of a group's food supply. As technological advances led to a productive surplus, however, social equality and communal sharing gave way to private property and, ultimately, a class hierarchy. With the rise of agriculture, men gained significant power over women. With surplus wealth to pass on to heirs, upper-class men wanted to be sure who their sons were, which led them to control the sexuality of women. The desire to control property brought about monogamous marriage and the family. Women were taught to remain virgins until marriage, to remain faithful to their husbands thereafter, and to build their lives around bearing and raising one man's children.

According to Engels (1902, orig. 1884), capitalism makes male domination even stronger. First, capitalism creates more wealth, which gives greater power to men as income earners and owners of property. Second, an expanding capitalist economy depends on turning people, especially women, into consumers who seek personal fulfillment through buying and using products. Third, society assigns women the task of maintaining the home to free men to work in factories. The double exploitation of capitalism, as Engels saw it, lies in paying men low wages for their labor and paying women no wages at all.

Critical review Social-conflict analysis is critical of conventional ideas about gender, claiming that society would be better off if we minimized or even did away with this dimension of social structure. One problem with this approach is that it sees conventional families—supported by traditionalists as morally positive—as a social evil. Second, social-conflict analysis minimizes the extent to which women and men live together cooperatively, and often happily, in families. A third problem lies in the assertion that capitalism is the basis of gender stratification. In fact, agrarian societies are typically more patriarchal than industrial-capitalist societies. Although socialist nations—including the People's Republic of China and the former Soviet Union—did move women into the workforce, by and large they provided women with very low pay in sex-segregated jobs (Rosendahl, 1997; Haney, 2002).

Feminism

Feminism is *the advocacy of social equality for women and men, in opposition to patriarchy and sexism.* The first wave of feminism in the United States began in the 1840s as women opposed to slavery, including Elizabeth Cady Stanton and Lucretia Mott, drew parallels between the oppression of African Americans and the oppression of women. Their main objective was obtaining the right to vote, which was finally achieved in 1920. But other disadvantages persisted, causing the rise of a second wave of feminism in the 1960s that continues today.

BASIC FEMINIST IDEAS

Feminism views the personal experiences of women and men through the lens of gender. How we think of ourselves (gender identity), how we act (gender roles), and our sex's social standing (gender stratification) are all rooted in the operation of society.

Although feminists disagree about many things, most support five general principles:

1. **Working to increase equality.** Feminist thinking is strongly political; it links ideas to action. Feminism is critical of the status quo, pushing for change toward social equality for women and men.

2. **Expanding human choice.** Feminists argue that cultural conceptions of gender divide the full range of human qualities into two opposing and limiting spheres: the female world of emotions and cooperation and the male world of rationality and competition. As an alternative, feminists propose a "reintegration of humanity" by which all individuals can develop all human traits (French, 1985).

3. **Eliminating gender stratification.** Feminism opposes laws and cultural norms that limit the education, income, and job opportunities of women. For this reason, feminists have long supported passage of the Equal Rights Amendment (ERA) to the U.S. Constitution, which states, in its entirety, "Equality of rights under the

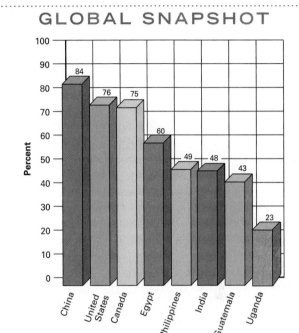

FIGURE 13-3 Use of Contraception by Married Women of Childbearing Age

In the United States, most women of childbearing age use contraception. In many low-income countries, however, most women do not have the opportunity to make this choice.

Source: United Nations Development Programme (2005).

law shall not be denied or abridged by the United States or any State on account of sex." The ERA was first proposed in Congress in 1923. Although surveys show widespread public support, it has yet to become law.

4. **Ending sexual violence.** Today's women's movement seeks to eliminate sexual violence. Feminists argue that patriarchy distorts the relationships between women and men, encouraging violence against women in the form of rape, domestic abuse, sexual harassment, and pornography (A. Dworkin, 1987; Freedman, 2002).

5. **Promoting sexual freedom.** Finally, feminism supports women's control over their sexuality and reproduction. Feminists support the free availability of birth control information. As Figure 13–3 shows, about three-fourths of U.S. women of childbearing age use contraception; the use of contraceptives is far less common in many low-income nations. Most feminists also support a woman's right to choose whether to bear children or end a pregnancy, rather than allowing

men—husbands, physicians, and legislators—to control their reproduction. Many feminists also support gay people's efforts to end prejudice and discrimination in a mostly heterosexual culture (Ferree & Hess, 1995; Armstrong, 2002).

On your campus, do men's organizations (such as fraternities and athletic teams) enjoy special privileges? What about women's organizations?

TYPES OF FEMINISM

Feminists agree on the importance of gender equality, but they disagree on how to achieve it: through liberal feminism, socialist feminism, or radical feminism (Stacey, 1983; L. Vogel, 1983; Ferree & Hess, 1995; Armstrong, 2002; Freedman, 2002).

Liberal Feminism

Liberal feminism is rooted in the classic liberal thinking that individuals should be free to develop their own talents and pursue their own interests. Liberal feminism accepts the basic organization of our society but seeks to expand the rights and opportunities of women, in part by passage of the Equal Rights Amendment. Liberal feminists also support reproductive freedom for all women. They respect the family as a social institution but seek changes, including more widely available maternity and paternity leave and child care for parents who work.

Given their belief in the rights of individuals, liberal feminists think that women should advance according to their own efforts, rather than working collectively for change. Both women and men, through their individual achievement, are capable of improving their lives—as long as society removes legal and cultural barriers.

Socialist Feminism

Socialist feminism evolved from the ideas of Karl Marx and Friedrich Engels. From this point of view, capitalism strengthens patriarchy by concentrating wealth and power in the hands of a small number of men. Socialist feminists do not think the reforms supported by liberal feminism go far enough. The family form created by capitalism must change if we are to replace "domestic slavery" with some collective means of carrying out housework and community-run child care. Replacing the traditional family can come about only through a socialist revolution that creates a state-centered economy to meet the needs of all. Such a basic transformation of society requires that women and men pursue their personal liberation not individually, as liberal feminists propose, but collectively.

Radical Feminism

Like socialist feminism, radical feminism finds liberal feminism inadequate. Radical feminists believe that patriarchy is so deeply rooted in society that even a socialist revolution would not end it. Instead, reaching the goal of gender equality means that society must eliminate gender itself.

One possible way to achieve this goal is to use new reproductive technology (see Chapter 18, "Families") to separate women's bodies from the process of childbearing. With an end to motherhood, radical feminists reason, society could leave behind the entire family system, liberating women, men, and children from the oppression of family, gender, and sex itself (A. Dworkin, 1987). Thus radical feminism envisions an egalitarian and gender-free society, a revolution more sweeping than the one sought by Marx.

OPPOSITION TO FEMINISM

Today, just 20 percent of U.S. adults express attitudes in opposition to feminism, a share that has declined over time (NORC, 2003). Figure 13–4 shows a similar downward trend in opposition to feminism among college students after 1970. Note, however, that there has been little change in attitudes in recent years and that more men than women express antifeminist attitudes.

Feminism provokes criticism and resistance from both men and women who hold conventional ideas about gender. Some men oppose sexual equality for the same reason that many white people have historically opposed social equality for people of color: They do not want to give up their privileges. Other men and women, including those who are neither rich nor powerful, distrust a social movement (especially its radical expressions) that attacks the traditional family and rejects patterns that have guided male-female relations for centuries.

Men who have been socialized to value strength and dominance feel uneasy about feminist ideas of men as gentle and warm (Doyle, 1983). Similarly, some women whose lives center on their husbands and children may think feminism does not value the social roles that give meaning to their lives. In general, resistance to feminism is strongest among women who have the least education and those who do not work outside the home (Marshall, 1985; Ferree & Hess, 1995).

Race and ethnicity play some part in shaping people's attitudes toward feminism. In general, African Americans (especially African American women) express the greatest support of feminist goals, followed by whites, with Hispanic Americans holding somewhat more traditional attitudes when it comes to gender (Kane, 2000).

Resistance to feminism is also found within academic circles. Some sociologists charge that feminism ignores a growing body of evidence that men and women do think and act in somewhat different ways, which may make complete gender equality impossible. Furthermore, say critics, with its drive to increase women's presence in the workplace, feminism undervalues the crucial and unique contribution women make to the development of children, especially in the first years of life (Baydar & Brooks-Gunn, 1991; Popenoe, 1993b; Gibbs, 2001).

Finally, there is the question of *how* women should go about improving their social standing. A large majority of U.S. adults believe that women should have equal rights, but 70 percent also say that women should advance individually, according to their abilities; only 10 percent favor women's rights groups or collective action (NORC, 2003:345).

For these reasons, most opposition to feminism is directed toward its socialist and radical forms, while support for liberal feminism is widespread. In addition, there is an unmistakable trend toward greater gender equality. In 1977, 65 percent of all adults endorsed the statement "It is much better for everyone involved if the man is the achiever outside the home and the woman takes care of the home and family." By 2002, the share supporting this statement had dropped sharply, to 38 percent (NORC, 2003:253).

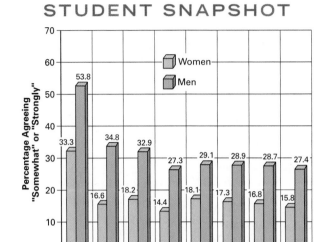

STUDENT SNAPSHOT

Statement: "The activities of married women are best confined to the home and family."

FIGURE 13-4   Opposition to Feminism among First-Year College Students, 1970–2004

The share of college students expressing antifeminist views declined after 1970. Men are still more likely than women to hold such attitudes.

Sources: Astin et al. (2002) and Sax et al. (2004).

Gender: Looking Ahead

Predictions about the future are always a matter of informed guesswork. Just as economists disagree about what the inflation rate will be a year from now, sociologists can offer only general observations about the likely future of gender and society.

Change so far has been remarkable. A century ago, women were second-class citizens, without access to many jobs, barred from political office, and with no right to vote. Although women remain socially disadvantaged, the movement toward equality has surged ahead. Two-thirds of people entering the workforce during the 1990s were women, and in 2000, for the first time, both the husband and wife in a majority of U.S. families were in the paid labor force. Today's economy depends a great deal on the earnings of women.

Many factors have contributed to this change. Perhaps most important, industrialization and recent advances in computer technology have shifted the nature of work from physically demanding tasks that favor male strength to jobs that require thought and imagination. This change puts women and men on an even footing. Also, because birth control technology has given us greater control over reproduction, women's lives are less constrained by unwanted pregnancies.

Many women and men have also deliberately pursued social equality. For example, sexual harassment complaints in the workplace are now taken much more seriously than they were a generation ago. As more women assume positions of power in the corporate and political worlds, social changes in the twenty-first century may be as great as those that have already taken place.

Despite the real change, gender continues to be a matter of inequality and controversy. "In the *Times*" on pages 356–57 explains that a lot of recent television advertising has shown men in unfairly negative terms. But it seems likely that we are seeing movement toward a society in which women and men enjoy equal rights and opportunities.

January 28, 2005

Men Are Becoming the Ad Target of the Gender Sneer

By COURTNEY KANE

Are today's men incompetent, bumbling idiots? Judging by portrayals in some advertising, the answer seems to be yes—much to the dismay of some men.

The portrayals began as a clever reversal of traditional gender roles in campaigns, prompted by the ire of women and feminist organizations over decades of ads using stereotyped imagery of an incompetent, bumbling housewife who needed to be told which coffee or cleanser to buy.

As those images disappeared, the pendulum swung, producing campaigns portraying men in general, and husbands and fathers in particular, as objects of ridicule, pity or even scorn. Among them are ads for Bud Light, Domino's, Hummer, T-Mobile and Verizon.

The "man as a dope" imagery has gathered momentum over the last decade, and critics say that it has spiraled out of control. It is nearly impossible, they say, to watch commercials or read ads without seeing helpless, hapless men.

In the campaigns, which the critics consider misandry (the opposite of misogyny), men act like buffoons, ogling cars and women; are likened to dogs, especially in beer and pizza ads; and bungle every possible household task. It is common for the men in such ads to be set straight by wiser female counterparts, and even for women to smack, swat, punch or kick them in the groin, all in the name of humor.

Most marketers presenting incompetent, silly male characters say their campaigns provide a harmless comedic insight into the male mentality while also appealing to women. But men who describe themselves as rights activists are increasingly speaking out against the ads as a form of male-bashing, especially when the ads disparage the roles that fathers play in their children's lives. . . .

"Men are kind of the last target that's acceptable to make fun of, so they do it," said Glenn Sacks, a commentator who is the host of a national syndicated radio show that focuses on men's and fathers' rights.

Paul Nathanson, who wrote *Spreading Misandry: The Teaching of Contempt for Men in Popular Culture* with Katherine K. Young, said the issue was larger. . . .

"Negative imagery in advertising is part of negative imagery in popular culture in general," Dr. Nathanson said. . . .

Then there are the longer-term effects, Dr. Nathanson said, asking, "How do boys form a healthy identity?" if they

13 MAKING THE GRADE

The following learning tools will help you see what you know, identify what you still need to learn, and expand your understanding beyond the text. You can also visit this text's Companion Website™ at http://www.prenhall.com/macionis to find additional practice tests.

KEY POINTS

Gender and Inequality

Gender refers to the meaning a culture attaches to being female or male. Because society gives men more power and other resources than it gives women, gender is an important dimension of social stratification. Although some degree of gender stratification exists everywhere in the world, the degree of patriarchy varies from one society to another. Gender inequality also varies in any society over the course of history.

Gender and Socialization

Through the socialization process, gender becomes part of our personalities (gender identity) and our actions (gender roles). The major agents of socialization—family, peer groups, schools, and the mass media—reinforce cultural definitions of what is feminine and masculine.

are constantly exposed to anti-male stereotypes. . . .

Martyn Straw, chief strategy officer at BBDO Worldwide in New York, part of the Omnicom Group, offered an explanation.

"In advertising and in general communications," Mr. Straw said, "there is the notion that things that are 'negative' are always much funnier than 'positive,' which can get very schmaltzy."

"In order to not cross over the line into denigration," Mr. Straw said, the situation portrayed in an ad needs to be truthful and funny. If those elements are in place, he added, "it's not really bashing, it's just having a funny look at the way men work sometimes and the way they approach things."

Critics have compiled lists of ads they deem offensive. One Web site, Standyourground.com, in cooperation with the Men's Activism News Network, lists 30 brands it asks men to avoid buying because of what they regard as male-bashing advertising; the list includes Budweiser, Hummer, J. C. Penney and Post-it notes.

One of the companies most cited is Verizon Communications, for a commercial for its Verizon DSL service created by McGarry Bowen in New York. The spot shows a computer-clueless father trying to help his Internet-savvy daughter with her homework online. Mom orders Dad to go wash the dog and leave their daughter alone; the girl flashes an exasperated look of contempt at him.

A Verizon spokesman in New York, John Bonomo, said, "It was not our intention certainly to portray fathers as inessential to families." The commercial has run its scheduled course, he added, and is no longer appearing.

In many ways, said Ann Simonton, coordinator of Media Watch in Santa Cruz, California, an organization that challenges what it considers to be racism, sexism and violence in the media, such commercials play on stereotypes of both sexes. For instance, speaking of the Verizon spot, Ms. Simonton said, "One might be able to interpret the women as being very nagging."

WHAT DO YOU THINK?

1. Do you see any connection between the rise of feminism and negative images of men in advertising? Explain your views.

2. Do you think the "man as dope" image appeals to women? Why or why not?

3. What effect does such advertising have on boys and young men?

Adapted from the original article by Courtney Kane published in *The New York Times* on January 28, 2005. Copyright © 2005 by The New York Times Company. Reprinted with permission.

Gender and Social Stratification

Gender stratification shapes the workplace. Although a majority of women are now in the paid labor force, 43 percent hold clerical or service jobs. Unpaid housework remains a task performed mostly by women, whether or not they hold jobs outside the home. In comparisons of all female and male workers, women earn 77 percent as much as men. This disparity stems from differences in jobs and family responsibilities, as well as from discrimination. Women now earn a slight majority of all bachelor's and master's degrees. Men still receive a slight majority of all doctorates and professional degrees. The number of women in politics has increased sharply in recent decades. Still, the vast majority of elected officials, especially at the national level, are men, and women make up only 15 percent of U.S. military personnel.

Intersection theory investigates the intersection of race, class, and gender, which often causes multiple disadvantages. Because women have a distinctive social identity and are disadvantaged, they are a minority, although most white women do not think of themselves that way. Minority women encounter greater social disadvantages than white women and earn much less than white men.

Violence against women and men is a widespread problem, linked to how society defines gender. Our society is also grappling with the issues of sexual harassment and pornography.

Theoretical Analysis of Gender

Structural-functional analysis suggests that in preindustrial societies, distinctive roles for males and females reflect biological differences between the sexes. In industrial societies, marked gender inequality becomes dysfunctional and gradually decreases. Talcott Parsons claimed that complementary gender roles promote the social integration of families and society as a whole.

Social-conflict analysis views gender as a dimension of social inequality and conflict. Friedrich Engels tied gender stratification to the development of private property.

Feminism

Feminism endorses the social equality of the sexes and opposes patriarchy and sexism. Feminism also seeks to eliminate violence against women and to give women control over their reproduction. There are three variants of feminist thinking: Liberal feminism seeks equal opportunity for both sexes within the existing society; socialist feminism supports abolishing private property as the means to social equality; radical feminism seeks to create a gender-free society. Although two-thirds of adults in the United States support the Equal Rights Amendment, this legislation, first proposed in Congress in 1923, has yet to become part of the U.S. Constitution.

Gender: Looking Ahead

Industrialization and the development of computer technology have made the lives of women and men more alike over the past century. Because gender is deeply rooted in our way of life, change will be gradual, but efforts to increase gender equality continue.

KEY CONCEPTS

gender (p. 334) the personal traits and social positions that members of a society attach to being female or male

gender stratification (p. 334) the unequal distribution of wealth, power, and privilege between men and women

patriarchy (p. 336) a form of social organization in which males dominate females

matriarchy (p. 337) a form of social organization in which females dominate males

sexism (p. 337) the belief that one sex is innately superior to the other

gender roles (**sex roles**) (p. 339) attitudes and activities that a society links to each sex

minority (p. 346) any category of people distinguished by physical or cultural difference that a society sets apart and subordinates

intersection theory (p. 346) the interplay of race, class, and gender, often resulting in multiple dimensions of disadvantage

sexual harassment (p. 348) comments, gestures, or physical contact of a sexual nature that are deliberate, repeated, and unwelcome

feminism (p. 353) the advocacy of social equality for women and men, in opposition to patriarchy and sexism

---

SAMPLE TEST QUESTIONS

These questions are similar to those found in the test bank that accompanies this textbook.

Multiple-Choice Questions

1. Gender is not just a matter of difference but also a matter of
   a. power.
   b. wealth.
   c. prestige.
   d. all of the above.

2. The anthropologist Margaret Mead studied gender in three societies in New Guinea and found that
   a. all societies define femininity in much the same way.
   b. all societies define masculinity in much the same way.
   c. what is feminine in one society may be masculine in another.
   d. the meaning of gender is changing everywhere toward greater equality.

3. For all of us raised in U.S. society, gender shapes our
   a. feelings.
   b. thoughts.
   c. actions.
   d. all of the above.

4. There is a "beauty myth" in U.S. society that encourages
   a. women to believe that their personal importance depends on their looks.
   b. beautiful women to think that they do not need men.
   c. men to improve their physical appearance to get the attention of women.
   d. women to think they are as physically attractive as today's men are.

5. In the United States, what share of women work for income?
   a. 80 percent
   b. 60 percent

c. 40 percent

d. 20 percent

6. **In the U.S. labor force,**

 a. men and women have the same kinds of jobs.

 b. men and women have the same pay.

 c. women are still concentrated in several types of jobs.

 d. a majority of working women hold "pink-collar jobs."

7. **For which of the following categories of people in the United States is it true that women do more housework than men?**

 a. people who work for income

 b. people who are married

 c. people who have children

 d. all of the above

8. **In the United States, women in the labor force working full time earn how much for every dollar earned by men working full time?**

 a. 77 cents

 b. 86 cents

 c. 97 cents

 d. 99 cents

9. **After the 2004 elections, women held about _____ of seats in Congress.**

 a. 5 percent

 b. 15 percent

 c. 35 percent

 d. 55 percent

10. **Which type of feminism accepts U.S. society as it is but wants to give women the same rights and opportunities as men?**

 a. socialist feminism   b. liberal feminism

 c. radical feminism   d. all of the above

Answers: 1(d); 2(c); 3(d); 4(a); 5(b); 6(c); 7(d); 8(a); 9(b); 10(b).

Essay Questions

1. In what ways are sex and gender related? In what ways do they differ?

2. Why is gender considered a dimension of social stratification? How does gender intersect other dimensions of inequality such as class, race, and ethnicity?

APPLICATIONS & EXERCISES

1. Take a walk through a business area of your local community. Which businesses are frequented almost entirely by women? By men? By both men and women? Try to explain the patterns you find.

2. Watch several hours of children's television programming on a Saturday morning. Notice the advertising, which mostly sells toys and breakfast cereal. Keep track of what share of toys are "gendered," that is, aimed at one sex or the other. What traits do you associate with toys intended for boys and those intended for girls?

3. Do some research on the history of women's issues in your state. When was the first woman sent to Congress? What laws once existed that restricted the work women could do? Do any such laws exist today? Did your state support the passage of the Equal Rights Amendment or not? What share of political officials today are women?

INVESTIGATE *with* Research Navigator

Research Navigator.com
RESOURCES FOR COLLEGE RESEARCH ASSIGNMENTS

Follow the instructions on page 27 of this text to access the features of **Research Navigator™**. Once at the Web site, enter your Login Name and Password. Then, to use the **ContentSelect™** database, enter keywords such as "gender," "feminism," and "sexual harassment," and the search engine will sup-

ply relevant and recent scholarly and popular press publications. Use the *New York Times* **Search-by-Search Archive** to find recent news articles related to sociology and the **Link Library** feature to find relevant Web links organized by the key terms associated with this chapter.

Race and Ethnicity

What are race and ethnicity,
and how are they created by society?

Why is the United States known as
a nation of immigrants?

How are race and ethnicity important dimensions
of social inequality today?

In a sociology class at Bronx Community College in New York, the instructor is leading a small-group discussion of race and ethnicity. He explains that there has been a lot of change in how people think about these concepts. He suggests that the students find some examples in books published over the last few decades. Then he asks them "How do you describe yourself?"

Eva Rodriguez is quick to respond. "This is hard for me to answer. Most people think of race as black and white. But it's not. I have both black and white ancestry in me, but you know what? I don't think of myself in that way. I don't think of myself in terms of race at all. You can call me Puerto Rican or call me Hispanic. I prefer the term 'Latina.' Calling myself Latina says I have a mixed racial heritage, and that's what I am. I wish more people understood that race is not clear-cut. I mean, why should I have to choose?"

This chapter examines the meaning of race and ethnicity. We shall see that there are now millions of people in the United States who, like Eva Rodriguez, do not think of themselves in terms of a single category but as a mix of ancestry.

The Social Meaning of Race and Ethnicity

As the opening to this chapter suggests, people frequently confuse "race" and "ethnicity." For this reason, we begin with some definitions.

RACE

A **race** is *a socially constructed category of people who share biologically transmitted traits that members of a society consider important*. People may classify one another racially based on physical characteristics such as skin color, facial features, hair texture, and body shape.

Physical diversity appeared among our human ancestors as the result of living in different geographic regions of the world. In regions of intense heat, for example, humans developed darker skin (from the natural pigment melanin) as protection from the sun; in regions with moderate climates, people have lighter skin. Such differences are literally only skin deep because human beings the world over are members of a single biological species.

The striking variety of physical traits found today is also the product of migration; physical characteristics once common to a single place (such a light skin or curly hair) are now found in many lands. Mixture is especially pronounced in the Middle East (that is, western Asia), historically a crossroads of human migration. Greater physical uniformity characterizes more isolated people, such as the island-dwelling Japanese. But every population has some genetic mixture, and increasing contact among the world's people ensures even more blending of physical characteristics in the future.

Although we think of race in terms of biological elements, race is a socially constructed concept. At one level, different categories of people "see" physical traits differently. For example, research shows that white people rate black subjects as darker in skin tone than black people do (Hill, 2002). Also, a number of people—especially biracial and multiracial people—define themselves and are defined by others differently, depending on the setting (Harris & Sim, 2002). More broadly, entire societies define physical traits differently. Typically, people in the United States "see" fewer racial categories (commonly, black, white, and Asian) than people in Brazil, who distinguish between *branca* (white), *parda* (brown), *morena* (brunette), *mulata* (mulatto), *preta* (black), and *amarela* (yellow) (Inciardi, Surratt, & Telles, 2000). In countries such as the United States, people consider racial differences more important; the people of other countries, such as Brazil, consider them less important.

The range of biological variation in human beings is far greater than any system of racial classification allows. This fact is made obvious by trying to place all of the people pictured here into simple racial categories.

In any society, definitions and meanings concerning race change over time. For example, in 1900, many white people in the United States viewed people of Irish and Italian ancestry as racially different, a practice that was rare by 1950 (Loveman, 1999). Today, the Census Bureau allows people to describe themselves using one or more of sixty-three racial options, so that our society now recognizes a wide range of multiracial people (Porter, 2001).

Racial Types

Scientists invented the concept of "race" in the nineteenth century as they tried to organize the world's physical diversity, identifying three racial types. They called people with relatively light skin and fine hair *Caucasoid,* people with darker skin and coarse hair *Negroid,* and people with yellow or brown skin and distinctive folds on the eyelids *Mongoloid.*

Sociologists consider such terms misleading at best and harmful at worst. For one thing, no society contains biologically "pure" people. The skin color of people we might call "Caucasoid" (or "Indo-European," "Caucasian," or, more

commonly, "white") ranges from very light (typical in Scandinavia) to very dark (in southern India). The same variation exists among so-called "Negroids" ("Africans" or, more commonly, "black" people) and "Mongoloids" (that is, "Asians"). In fact, many "white" people (say, in southern India) actually have darker skin than many "black" people (the Negroid Aborigines of Australia). Overall, the three racial categories differ in only 6 percent of their genes, less than the genetic variation *within* each category (Harris & Sim, 2002; American Sociological Association, 2003).

Why, then, do people make so much of race? With such categories, society ranks people in a hierarchy, which allows some people to feel that they are inherently "better" than others. Because racial ranking shapes access to wealth and prestige, societies may construct racial categories in extreme ways. Throughout much of the twentieth century, for example, many southern states labeled as "colored" anyone with as little as one thirty-second African ancestry (that is, one African American great-great-great-grandparent). Today, the law leaves it up to parents to decide the race of a child. Even so, most members of U.S. society are still very sensitive to racial background.

More people in the United States consider themselves multiracial than ever before. A well-known example is actress Halle Berry, whose mother is white and whose father is African American.

YOUR TURN

How much dating is there between people of different racial categories on your campus? How racially diverse are your school's student organizations and sports teams?

A Trend toward Mixture

Over many generations and throughout the Americas, the genetic traits from around the world have become mixed. Many "black" people have a significant Caucasoid ancestry, just as many "white" people have some Negroid genes. Whatever people may think, race is no black-and-white issue.

Today, people are more willing to define themselves as multiracial. When completing their 2000 census forms, almost 7 million people described themselves by checking two or more racial categories. In addition, the official number of interracial births tripled over the past twenty years to 172,000 annually, about 5 percent of all births.

ETHNICITY

Ethnicity is *a shared cultural heritage*. People define themselves—or others—as members of an *ethnic category* based on common ancestry, language, or religion that gives them a distinctive social identity. The United States is a multiethnic society; although we favor the English language, more than 47 million people (18 percent of the U.S. population) speak Spanish, Italian, German, French, Chinese dialects, or some other language in their homes. In California, more than one-third of the population does so. With regard to religion, the United States is a predominantly Protestant nation, but most people of Spanish, Italian, and Polish descent are Roman Catholic, and many of Greek, Ukrainian, and Russian descent belong to the Eastern Orthodox church. More than 6 million Jewish Americans have ancestral ties to various nations around the world. With a population estimated at between 2 and 8 million, Muslim men and women now outnumber Episcopalians in the United States.

Like the reality of race, the meaning of ethnicity is socially constructed, becoming important only because society defines it that way. For example, U.S. society defines people of Spanish descent as "Latin," even though Italy probably has a more "Latin" culture than Spain. People of Italian descent are not viewed as Latin but as "European" and therefore less different (Camara, 2000; Brodkin, 2001). Like racial differences, the importance of ethnic differences can change over time. A century ago, Catholics and Jews were considered "different" in the mostly Protestant United States. This is much less true today.

Keep in mind that *race* is constructed from *biological* traits and *ethnicity* is constructed from *cultural* traits. However, the two often go hand in hand. For example, Japanese Americans have distinctive physical traits and, for those who hold to a traditional way of life, a distinctive culture as well. Table 14–1 presents the broad sweep of racial and ethnic diversity in the United States, as recorded by the 2000 census.

On an individual level, people play up or play down cultural traits, depending on whether they want to fit in or stand apart from the surrounding society. Immigrants may drop their cultural traditions or, like many people of Native American descent in recent years, try to revive their heritage. For most people, ethnicity is more complex than race because they identify with several ethnic backgrounds. The golf star Tiger Woods describes himself as one-eighth American Indian, one-fourth Thai, and one-fourth Chinese, as well as one-eighth white and one-fourth black (J.E. White, 1997).

MINORITIES

March 3, Dallas, Texas. Sitting in the lobby of just about any hotel in a major U.S. city presents a lesson in contrasts: The majority of the guests checking in and out are white; the majority of hotel employees who carry luggage, serve the food, and clean the rooms are people of color.

As defined in Chapter 13 ("Gender Stratification"), a **minority** is *any category of people distinguished by physical or cultural difference that a society sets apart and subordinates.* Minority standing can be based on race, ethnicity, or both. As shown in Table 14–1, non-Hispanic white people (71 percent of the total) are still a majority of the U.S. population. But the share of minorities is increasing. Today, minorities are a majority in three states (California, New Mexico, and Hawaii) and in half the country's 100 largest cities. By about 2050, minorities are likely to form a majority of the entire U.S. population. National Map 14–1 on page 366 shows where a minority-majority already exists.

Minorities have two important characteristics. First, they share a *distinctive identity,* which may be based on physical or cultural traits. Second, minorities experience *subordination.* As the rest of this chapter shows, U.S. minorities typically have lower income, lower occupational prestige, and limited schooling. These facts mean that class, race, and ethnicity, as well as gender, are overlapping and reinforcing dimensions of social stratification. The Thinking About Diversity box on page 367 profiles the struggles of recent Latin American immigrants.

Of course, not all members of any minority category are disadvantaged. Some Latinos are quite wealthy, certain Chinese Americans are celebrated business leaders, and African Americans are among our nation's leading scholars. But even job success rarely allows individuals to escape their minority standing. As described in Chapter 6 ("Social Interaction in Everyday Life"), race or ethnicity often serves as a *master status* that overshadows personal accomplishments.

Minorities usually make up a small proportion of a society's population, but this is not always the case. Black South Africans are disadvantaged even though they are a numerical majority in their country. In the United States, women represent slightly more than half the population but still lack many of the opportunities and privileges enjoyed by men.

⟶ YOUR TURN ⟵

Do you think all U.S. people of color, rich and poor alike, should be considered minorities? Why or why not?

TABLE 14–1
Racial and Ethnic Categories in the United States, 2000

Racial or Ethnic Classification*	Approximate U.S. Population	Percentage of Total Population
Hispanic descent	**35,305,818**	**12.5%**
Mexican	20,640,711	7.3
Puerto Rican	3,406,178	1.2
Cuban	1,241,685	0.4
Other Hispanic	10,017,244	3.6
African descent	**34,658,190**	**12.3**
Nigerian	165,481	0.1
Ethiopian	86,918	<
Cape Verdean	77,103	<
Ghanaian	49,944	<
South African	45,569	<
Native American descent	**2,475,956**	**0.9**
American Indian	1,815,653	0.6
Eskimo	45,919	<
Other Native American	614,384	0.2
Asian or Pacific Island descent	**10,641,833**	**3.8**
Chinese	2,432,585	0.9
Filipino	1,850,314	0.7
Asian Indian	1,678,765	0.6
Vietnamese	1,122,528	0.4
Korean	1,076,872	0.4
Japanese	796,700	0.3
Cambodian	171,937	<
Hmong	169,428	<
Laotian	168,707	<
Other Asian or Pacific Islander	1,173,997	0.4
West Indian descent	**1,869,504**	**0.7**
Arab descent	**1,202,871**	**0.4**
Non-Hispanic European descent	**194,552,774**	**70.9**
German	42,885,162	15.2
Irish	30,528,492	10.8
English	24,515,138	8.7
Italian	15,723,555	5.6
Polish	8,977,444	3.2
French	8,309,908	3.0
Scottish	4,890,581	1.7
Dutch	4,542,494	1.6
Norwegian	4,477,725	1.6
Two or more races	**6,826,228**	**2.4**

*People of Hispanic descent may be of any race. Many people also identify with more than one ethnic category. Therefore, figures total more than 100 percent.

< indicates less than 1/10 of 1 percent.

Sources: U.S. Census Bureau (2001, 2002, 2004).

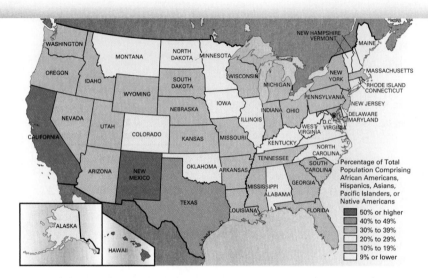

Percentage of Total Population Comprising African Americans, Hispanics, Asians, Pacific Islanders, or Native Americans

- 50% or higher
- 40% to 49%
- 30% to 39%
- 20% to 29%
- 10% to 19%
- 9% or lower

Prejudice

November 19, Jerusalem, Israel. We are driving along the outskirts of this historic city—a holy place to Jews, Christians, and Muslims—when Razi, our taxi driver, spots a small group of Falasha—Ethiopian Jews—on a street corner. "Those people over there," he points as he speaks, "they are different. They don't drive cars. They don't want to improve themselves. Even when our country offers them schooling, they don't take it." He shakes his head at the Ethiopians and drives on.

Prejudice is *a rigid and unfair generalization about an entire category of people*. Prejudice is unfair because all people in some category are rigidly described as the same based on little or no direct evidence. Prejudice may target people of a particular social class, sex, sexual orientation, age, political affiliation, physical disability, race, or ethnicity.

Prejudices are *prejudgments* that can be either positive or negative. Our positive prejudices tend to exaggerate the virtues of people like ourselves, and our negative prejudices condemn those who differ from us. Negative prejudice can

 Take a test for prejudice at http://www.tolerance.org/hidden_bias/index.html

be expressed as anything from mild avoidance to outright hostility. Because such attitudes are rooted in culture, everyone has at least some measure of prejudice.

STEREOTYPES

Prejudice often takes the form of a **stereotype** (*stereo* is derived from a Greek word meaning "solid"), *an exaggerated description applied to every person in some category*. Many white people hold stereotypical views of minorities. Stereotyping is especially harmful to minorities in the workplace. If company officials see workers only in terms of a stereotype, they will make assumptions about their abilities, steering them toward certain jobs and limiting their access to better opportunities (R. L. Kaufman, 2002).

Minorities, too, stereotype whites and other minorities (T. W. Smith, 1996; Cummings & Lambert, 1997). Surveys show, for example, that more African Americans than whites express the belief that Asians engage in unfair business practices and that more Asians than whites criticize Hispanics for having too many children (Perlmutter, 2002).

YOUR TURN

Do you see negative stereotypes in common phrases such as "French kiss," "Dutch treat," "Indian giver," or being "gypped" (a reference to Gypsies)?

Hard Work: The Immigrant Life in the United States

Early in the morning, it is already hot in Houston as a line of pick-up trucks snakes slowly into a dusty yard, where 200 laborers have been gathering since dawn, hoping for a day's work. The driver of the first truck  opens his window and tells the foreman that he is looking for a crew to spread boiling tar on a roof. Abdonel Cespedes, the foreman, turns to the crowd, and after a few minutes, three workers step forward and climb into the back of the truck. The next driver is looking for two experienced housepainters. The scene is repeated over and over as men and a few women leave to dig ditches, spread cement, hang drywall, open clogged septic tanks, or crawl under houses to poison rats.

As each driver pulls into the yard, the foreman asks, "How much?" Most offer $5 an hour. Cespedes automatically responds, "$6.50; the going rate is $6.50 for an hour's hard work." Sometimes he convinces them to pay that much, but usually not. The workers, who come from Mexico, El Salvador, and Guatemala, know that dozens of them will end up with no work at all on this day. Most accept $5 an hour because they know, when the long day is over, $50 is better than nothing.

Labor markets like this one are common in large cities, especially across the southwestern United States. The surge in immigration in recent years has brought millions of people to this country in search of work, and most have little schooling and speak little English.

Manuel Barrera has taken a day's work moving the entire contents of a store to a storage site. He arrives at the boarded-up store and gazes at the mountains of heavy furniture that he must carry out to a moving van, drive across town, and then carry again. He sighs when he realizes how hot it is outside and that it is even hotter inside the building. He will have no break for lunch. No one says anything about toilets. Barrera shakes his head: "I will do this kind of work because it puts food on the table. But I did not foresee it would turn out like this."

The hard truth is that immigrants to the United States do the jobs that no one else wants. At the bottom level of the national economy, they perform low-skill jobs in restaurants and hotels and on construction crews, and they work in private homes cooking, cleaning, and caring for children. Across the United States, about half of all housekeepers, household cooks, tailors, and restaurant waiters are men or women born abroad. Few immigrants make much more than the official minimum wage ($5.15 per hour), and it is rare that immigrant workers receive any health or pension benefits. Many well-off families take the labor of immigrants as much for granted as their sport utility vehicles and cell phones.

WHAT DO YOU THINK?

1. In what ways do you or members of your family depend on the low-paid labor of immigrants?
2. Do you think there is anything wrong with paying someone the current minimum wage for hard work if the person hired agrees? Why or why not?
3. Why has there always been opposition to large numbers of immigrants entering the United States?

Source: Based on Booth (1998).

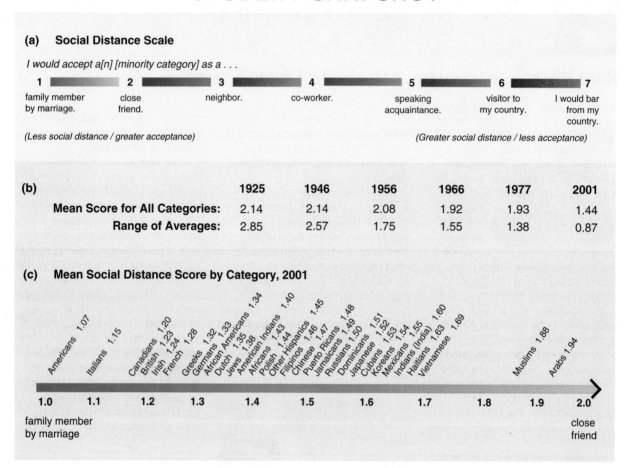

(a)   Social Distance Scale

I would accept a[n] [minority category] as a . . .

1	2	3	4	5	6	7
family member by marriage.	close friend.	neighbor.	co-worker.	speaking acquaintance.	visitor to my country.	I would bar from my country.

(Less social distance / greater acceptance)   *(Greater social distance / less acceptance)*

(b)

	1925	1946	1956	1966	1977	2001
Mean Score for All Categories:	2.14	2.14	2.08	1.92	1.93	1.44
Range of Averages:	2.85	2.57	1.75	1.55	1.38	0.87

(c)   Mean Social Distance Score by Category, 2001

Americans 1.07, Italians 1.15, Canadians 1.20, British 1.23, Irish 1.24, French 1.28, Greeks 1.32, Germans 1.33, African Americans 1.34, Dutch 1.35, Jews 1.38, American Indians 1.40, Africans 1.43, Polish 1.44, Other Hispanics 1.45, Filipinos 1.46, Chinese 1.47, Puerto Ricans 1.48, Jamaicans 1.49, Russians 1.50, Dominicans 1.51, Japanese 1.52, Cubans 1.53, Koreans 1.54, Mexicans 1.55, Indians (India) 1.60, Haitians 1.63, Vietnamese 1.69, Muslims 1.88, Arabs 1.94

1.0   1.1   1.2   1.3   1.4   1.5   1.6   1.7   1.8   1.9   2.0

family member by marriage   close friend

FIGURE 14-1   Bogardus Social Distance Research

The social distance scale is a good way to measure prejudice. Over time, U.S. college students have become less prejudiced toward all racial and ethnic minorities. However, they are still more accepting of some categories of people than others.

Source: Parrillo (2003b).

MEASURING PREJUDICE: THE SOCIAL DISTANCE SCALE

One measure of prejudice is *social distance*, that is, how closely people are willing to interact with members of some category. Eighty years ago, Emory Bogardus (1925) developed the *social distance scale* shown in Figure 14–1. Bogardus asked students at U.S. colleges and universities to look at this scale and indicate how closely they were willing to interact with people in thirty racial and ethnic categories. At one extreme, students could express the greatest social distance (most negative prejudice) by declaring that a particular category of people should be barred from the country entirely (point 7); at the other extreme, students could express the least social distance (most social acceptance) by saying they would accept members of a particular category into their family through marriage (point 1).

Bogardus (1925, 1967; Owen, Elsner, & McFaul, 1977) found that people felt much more social distance from some categories than from others. In general, students in his surveys expressed the most social distance from Hispanics,

African Americans, Asians, and Turks, by indicating that they would be willing to tolerate such people as co-workers but not as neighbors, friends, or family members. Students expressed the least social distance from those from northern and western Europe, including English and Scottish people, and also Canadians, indicating that they were willing to include them in their families by marriage.

What patterns of social distance do we find among college students today? A recent study using the same social distance scale reported three major findings (Parrillo, 2003b):[1]

1. **Student opinion shows a trend toward greater social acceptance.** Today's students express less social distance from all minorities than students did decades ago. Figure 14–1 shows that the average (mean) score on the social distance scale declined from 2.14 in 1925 to 1.93 in 1977 to 1.44 in 2001. Respondents (81 percent of whom were white) showed notably greater acceptance of African Americans, a category that moved up from near the bottom in 1925 to the top one-third in 2001.

2. **People see less difference between various minorities.** The earliest studies found the range (spread of averages) of social distance for different minorities equal to almost three points on the scale. As the figure shows, the most recent research produced averages with a range of less than one point.

3. **The terrorist attacks of September 11, 2001, may have reduced social acceptance of Arabs and Muslims.** The recent study was conducted several weeks after September 11, 2001. Perhaps the fact that the nineteen men who attacked the World Trade Center and the Pentagon were Arabs and Muslims is part of the reason that students ranked these categories last on the social distance scale. However, not a single student gave Arabs or Muslims a 7, indicating that they should be barred from the country. On the contrary, the 2001 scores (1.94 for Arabs and 1.88 for Muslims) show higher social acceptance than students in 1977 expressed toward eighteen of the thirty categories of people studied.

---

[1]Parrillo dropped seven of the categories used by Bogardus (Armenians, Czechs, Finns, Norwegians, Scots, Swedes, and Turks), claiming they were no longer visible minorities. He added nine new categories (Africans, Arabs, Cubans, Dominicans, Haitians, Jamaicans, Muslims, Puerto Ricans, and Vietnamese), claiming these are visible minorities today. This change probably encouraged higher social distance scores, making the trend toward decreasing social distance all the more significant.

Recent research measuring student attitudes shows declining prejudice towards all racial and ethnic categories of the U.S. population. Even so, attitudes towards Muslims and Arab Americans are the most negative, probably a result of publicity surrounding global terrorism. Here, Arab Americans speak out against what they feel is the negative depiction of Arabs in the film *True Lies*.

YOUR TURN

What factors might account for the trend toward less prejudice shown in this research? Consider factors in the country as a whole and also on campus.

RACISM

A powerful and harmful form of prejudice, **racism** is *the belief that one racial category is innately superior or inferior to another.* Racism has existed throughout world history. Despite their many achievements, the ancient Greeks, the peoples of India, and the Chinese all considered people unlike themselves inferior.

Does Race Affect Intelligence?

Are Asian Americans smarter than white people? Is the typical white person more intelligent than the average African American? Throughout the history of the United States, many people have painted one category of people as intellectually more gifted than another and used this thinking to justify privileges for the allegedly superior category and even to bar supposedly inferior people from entering this country.

Scientists know that the distribution of human intelligence forms a "bell curve," as shown in the figure. They define average intelligence as an *intelligence quotient* (IQ) score of 100 (technically, an IQ score is mental age, as measured by a test, divided by age in years, with the result multiplied by 100; thus an eight-year-old who performs like a ten-year-old has an IQ of $10 \div 8 = 1.25 \times 100 = 125$).

In a controversial study of intelligence and social inequality, Richard Herrnstein and Charles Murray (1994) claim that race is related to measures of intelligence. They say that the average IQ for people with European ancestry is 100, for people with East Asian ancestry is 103, and for people with African ancestry is 90.

Such assertions go against our democratic and egalitarian beliefs that no racial type is naturally better than another. Some critics charge that intelligence tests are not valid and even that the concept of intelligence has little real meaning.

Most social scientists believe that IQ tests do measure something important that we think of as intelligence, and they agree that *individuals* vary in intellectual aptitude. But they reject the

idea that any *category* of people, on average, is naturally smarter than any other. So how do we explain the overall differences in IQ scores by race?

Thomas Sowell (1994, 1995) explains that most of this difference results not from biology but from environment. In some skillful sociological detective work, Sowell traced IQ scores for various racial and ethnic categories throughout the twentieth century. He found that on average, early twentieth century immigrants from European nations such as Poland, Lithuania, Italy, and Greece, as well as from Asian countries including China and Japan, scored 10 to 15 points below the U.S. average. But by the end of the twentieth century, people in these same categories had IQ scores that were average or above average. Among Italian Americans, for example, average IQ jumped almost 10 points; among Polish and Chinese Americans, the increase was almost 20 points.

Because genetic changes occur over thousands of years and most people in these categories marry others like themselves, biological factors cannot explain such a rapid rise in IQ scores. The only reasonable explanation is changing cultural patterns. The descendants of early immigrants

improved their intellectual performance as their standard of living rose and their opportunity for schooling increased.

Sowell found that much the same was true of African Americans. Historically, the average IQ score of African Americans living in the North has been about 10 points higher than the average score of those living in the South. Among the descendants of African Americans who migrated from the South to the North after 1940, IQ scores went up just as they did with descendants of European and Asian immigrants. Thus environmental factors appear to be critical in explaining differences in IQ among various categories of people.

According to Sowell, these test score differences tell us that *cultural patterns matter*. Asians who score high on tests are no smarter than other people, but they have been raised to value learning and pursue excellence. African Americans are no less intelligent than anyone else, but they carry a legacy of disadvantage that can undermine self-confidence and discourage achievement.

WHAT DO YOU THINK?

1. If IQ scores reflect people's environment, are they valid measures of intelligence? Could they be harmful?
2. According to Thomas Sowell, why do some racial and ethnic categories show dramatic short-term gains in average IQ scores? Do you agree?
3. Do you think parents and schools influence a child's IQ score? If so, how?

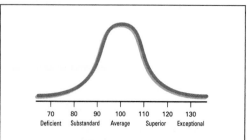

IQ: The Distribution of Intelligence

Racism has also been widespread throughout the history of the United States, where ideas about racial inferiority supported slavery. Today, overt racism in this country

Racism can give rise to hate crimes. For more information, go to http://www.civilrights.org/issues/hate/

has decreased because more people believe in evaluating people, in Martin Luther King Jr.'s words, "not by the color of their skin but the content of their character."

Even so, racism remains a serious social problem, as some people think that certain racial and ethnic categories are smarter than others. As the Applying Sociology box explains, however, racial differences in mental abilities result from environment rather than biology.

THEORIES OF PREJUDICE

Where does prejudice come from? Social scientists provide several answers to this question, focusing on frustration, personality, culture, and social conflict.

Scapegoat Theory

Scapegoat theory holds that prejudice springs from frustration among people who are themselves disadvantaged (Dollard et al., 1939). Take the case of a white woman frustrated by her low-paying job in a textile factory. Directing hostility at the powerful factory owners carries the obvious risk of being fired; therefore, she may blame her low pay on the presence of minority co-workers. Her prejudice does not improve her situation, but it is a relatively safe way to express anger, and it may give her the comforting feeling that at least she is superior to someone.

A **scapegoat,** then, is *a person or category of people, typically with little power, whom people unfairly blame for their own troubles.* Because they are usually "safe targets," minorities are often used as scapegoats.

Authoritarian Personality Theory

T. W. Adorno and colleagues (1950) considered extreme prejudice a personality trait of certain individuals. This conclusion is supported by research showing that people who express strong prejudice toward one minority typically do so toward all minorities. These *authoritarian personalities* rigidly conform to conventional cultural values and see moral issues as clear-cut matters of right and wrong. People with authoritarian personalities also view society as naturally competitive and hierarchical, with "better" people (like themselves) inevitably dominating those who are weaker (including all minorities).

Adorno also found that people tolerant toward one minority are likely to be accepting of all. They tend to be more

flexible in their moral judgments and treat all people as equals.

Adorno thought that people with little schooling and those raised by cold and demanding parents tend to develop authoritarian personalities. Filled with anger and anxiety as children, they grow into hostile, aggressive adults who seek out scapegoats.

Culture Theory

A third theory claims that although extreme prejudice may be found in some people, some prejudice is found in everyone. Why? Because prejudice is embedded in culture, as the Bogardus social distance studies illustrate. Bogardus found that students across the country had similar attitudes toward specific racial and ethnic categories, feeling closer to some and more distant from others.

Another reason to think that prejudice is cultural is that minorities express the same attitudes as white people toward categories other than their own. Such patterns suggest that individuals hold prejudices because they live in a "culture of prejudice," which teaches us to view certain categories of people as "better" or "worse" than others.

Conflict Theory

A fourth explanation proposes that prejudice is used as a tool by powerful people to oppress others. Anglos who look down on Latino immigrants in the Southwest, for example, can get away with paying the immigrants low wages for hard work. Similarly, all elites benefit when prejudice divides workers along racial and ethnic lines and discourages them from working together to advance their common interests (Geschwender, 1978; Olzak, 1989).

According to another conflict-based argument, made by Shelby Steele (1990), minorities themselves encourage *race consciousness* to win greater power and privileges. Because of their historic disadvantage, minorities claim that they are victims entitled to special consideration based on their race. Although this strategy may bring short-term gains, Steele cautions that such thinking often sparks a backlash from whites or others who oppose "special treatment" on the basis of race or ethnicity.

→ YOUR TURN ←

Which of these four theories of prejudice (scapegoat, authoritarian personality, culture, conflict) do you find most convincing? Why?

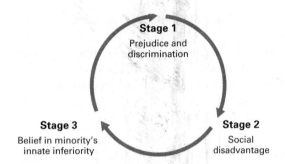

Stage 1
Prejudice and discrimination

Stage 3
Belief in minority's innate inferiority

Stage 2
Social disadvantage

Stage 1: Prejudice and discrimination begin, often as an expression of ethnocentrism or an attempt to justify economic exploitation.

Stage 2: As a result of prejudice and discrimination, a minority is socially disadvantaged, occupying a low position in the system of social stratification.

Stage 3: This social disadvantage is then interpreted not as the result of earlier prejudice and discrimination but as evidence that the minority is innately inferior, unleashing renewed prejudice and discrimination by which the cycle repeats itself.

FIGURE 14–2 Prejudice and Discrimination: The Vicious Circle

Prejudice and discrimination can form a vicious circle, perpetuating themselves.

Discrimination

Closely related to prejudice is **discrimination,** *unequal treatment of various categories of people. Prejudice refers to attitudes,* but *discrimination is a matter of action.* Like prejudice, discrimination can be either positive (providing special advantages) or negative (creating obstacles) and ranges from subtle to blatant.

INSTITUTIONAL PREJUDICE AND DISCRIMINATION

We typically think of prejudice and discrimination as the hateful ideas or actions of specific people. But Stokely Carmichael and Charles Hamilton (1967) pointed out that far greater harm results from **institutional prejudice and discrimination,** *bias built into the operation of society's institutions,* including schools, hospitals, the police, and the

 Do banks unfairly refuse loans to African American applicants? Go to http://www.hud.gov/library/bookshelf18/pressrel/subprime.html

workplace. For example, researchers have found that banks reject home mortgage applications from minorities at a higher rate than those from white people, even when income and quality of neighborhood are held constant (Gotham, 1998).

According to Carmichael and Hamilton, people are slow to condemn or even recognize institutional prejudice and discrimination because it often involves respected public officials and long-established practices. A case in point is *Brown v. Board of Education of Topeka,* the 1954 Supreme Court decision that ended the legal segregation of schools. The principle of "separate but equal" schooling had been the law of the land, supporting racial inequality by allowing school segregation. Despite this change in the law, half a century later, most U.S. students still attend schools that are overwhelmingly of one race (Barnes, 2004). In 1991, the courts declared that neighborhood schools will never provide equal education as long as our population is segregated, with most African Americans living in central cities and most white people and Asian Americans living in suburbs.

PREJUDICE AND DISCRIMINATION: THE VICIOUS CIRCLE

Prejudice and discrimination reinforce each other. The Thomas theorem, discussed in Chapter 6 ("Social Interaction in Everyday Life"), offers a simple explanation of this fact: *Situations that are defined as real become real in their consequences* (W. I. Thomas, 1966:301, orig. 1931).

As Thomas recognized, stereotypes become real to people who believe them and sometimes even to those who are victimized by them. Prejudice on the part of white people toward people of color does not produce *innate* inferiority, but it can produce *social* inferiority, pushing minorities into low-paying jobs, inferior schools, and racially segregated housing. Then, as white people see social disadvantage as evidence that minorities do not measure up, they begin a new round of prejudice and discrimination, giving rise to a vicious circle in which each perpetuates the other, as shown in Figure 14–2.

Majority and Minority: Patterns of Interaction

Sociologists describe patterns of interaction among racial and ethnic categories in a society in terms of four models: pluralism, assimilation, segregation, and genocide.

PLURALISM

Pluralism is *a state in which people of all races and ethnicities are distinct but have equal social standing.* In other words, people who differ in appearance or social heritage all share resources roughly equally.

The United States is pluralistic to the extent that all people have equal standing under the law. In addition, large cities contain countless "ethnic villages," where people proudly display the traditions of their immigrant ancestors. These include New York's Spanish Harlem, Little Italy, and Chinatown; Philadelphia's Italian "South Philly"; Chicago's Little Saigon; and Latino East Los Angeles. New York City alone has 189 different ethnic newspapers (P. Paul, 2001; Logan, Alba, & Zhang, 2002).

But the United States is not truly pluralistic for three reasons. First, although most people value their cultural heritage, few want to live just with others exactly like themselves (NORC, 2003). Second, our tolerance of social diversity goes only so far. One reaction to the rising number of U.S. minorities is a social movement to make English the nation's official language. Third, as we shall see later in this chapter, people of various colors and cultures do *not* have equal social standing.

ASSIMILATION

Many people think of the United States as a "melting pot" in which different nationalities blend together. But rather than everyone "melting" into some new cultural pattern, most minorities have adopted the dominant culture established by our earliest settlers. Why? Because doing so is both the path to upward social mobility and a way to escape the prejudice and discrimination directed at more visible foreigners. Sociologists use the term **assimilation** to describe *the process by which minorities gradually adopt patterns of the dominant culture.* Assimilation can involve changing modes of dress, values, religion, language, and friends.

The amount of assimilation varies by category. For example, Canadians have "melted" more than Cubans, the Dutch more than Dominicans, Germans more than the Japanese. Multiculturalists oppose making assimilation a goal because it suggests that minorities are "the problem" and defines them (rather than majority people) as the ones who need to do all the changing.

Note that assimilation involves changes in ethnicity but not in race. For example, many descendants of Japanese immigrants discard their ethnic traditions but retain their racial identity. In order for racial traits to diminish over generations, **miscegenation,** or *biological reproduction by partners of different racial categories,* must occur. Although interracial marriage is becoming more common, it still amounts to only 3 percent of all U.S. marriages (U.S. Census Bureau, 2004).

SEGREGATION

Segregation is *the physical and social separation of categories of people.* Some minorities, especially religious orders like the Amish, voluntarily segregate themselves. However,

In an effort to force assimilation, the U.S. Bureau of Indian Affairs took American Indian children from their families and placed them in boarding schools like this one—Oklahoma's Riverside Indian School. There, they were taught the English language by non-Indian teachers with the goal of making them into "Americans." As this photo from about 1890 suggests, discipline in these schools was strict.

majorities usually segregate minorities by excluding them. Residential neighborhoods, schools, occupations, hospitals, and even cemeteries may be segregated. Pluralism encourages distinctiveness without disadvantage, but segregation enforces separation that harms a minority.

Racial segregation has a long history in the United States, beginning with slavery and evolving into racially separated housing, schools, buses, and trains. Court decisions such as the 1954 *Brown* case have reduced *de jure* (Latin, meaning "by law") discrimination in this country. However, *de facto* ("in actual fact") segregation continues to this day in the form of countless neighborhoods that are home to people of a single race.

Despite some recent decline, segregation persists in the United States. For example, Livonia, Michigan, is 96 percent white, and neighboring Detroit is 83 percent African American. Kurt Metzger (2001) explains, "Livonia was pretty much created by white flight [from Detroit]." Further, research shows that across the country, whites (especially those with young children) avoid neighborhoods where African Americans live (Emerson, Yancey, &

SEEING OURSELVES

NATIONAL MAP 14-2
Land Controlled by Native Americans, 1790 to Today

In 1790, Native Americans controlled three-fourths of the land that eventually became today's United States. Today, Native Americans control 314 reservations, scattered across the United States, that account for just 2 percent of the country's land area. How would you characterize these locations?

Chai, 2001; Krysan, 2002). At the extreme, Douglas Massey and Nancy Denton (1989) document the *hypersegregation* of poor African Americans in some inner cities. Hypersegregation means having little contact of any kind with people outside the local community. Hypersegregation is the daily experience of about 20 percent of poor African Americans.

YOUR TURN

In your city or town, can you identify minority neighborhoods? Which categories of people live there? To what degree is your community racially or ethnically segregated?

GENOCIDE

Genocide is *the systematic killing of one category of people by another.* This deadly form of racism and ethnocentrism violates nearly every recognized moral standard, yet it has occurred time and time again in human history.

Genocide was common in the history of contact between Europeans and the original inhabitants of the Americas. From the sixteenth century on, the Spanish, Portuguese, English, French, and Dutch forcibly colonized vast empires. Although most native people died from diseases brought by Europeans, against which they had no natural defenses,

many who opposed the colonizers were killed deliberately (Matthiessen, 1984; Sale, 1990).

Genocide also occurred during the twentieth century. Unimaginable horror befell European Jews during Adolf Hitler's reign of terror, known as the Holocaust. From about 1935 to 1945, the Nazis murdered more than 6 million Jewish men, women, and children, along with gay people, Gypsies, and people with handicaps. The Soviet dictator Josef Stalin murdered on an even greater scale, killing perhaps 30 million real and imagined enemies during decades of violent rule. Between 1975 and 1980, Pol Pot's communist regime in Cambodia butchered all "capitalists," a category that included anyone able to speak a Western language. In all, some 2 million people (one-fourth of the population) perished in the Cambodian "killing fields" (Shawcross, 1979).

Tragically, genocide continues today. Recent examples include Hutus killing Tutsis in the African nation of Rwanda and Serbs killing Bosnians in the Balkans of Eastern Europe.

These four patterns of minority-majority interaction have all been played out in the United States. Although many people proudly point to patterns of pluralism and assimilation, it is also important to recognize the degree to which U.S. society has been built on segregation (of African Americans) and genocide (of Native Americans). The remainder of this chapter examines how these four patterns have shaped the history and present social standing of major racial and ethnic categories in the United States.

Race and Ethnicity in the United States

> Give me your tired, your poor,
> Your huddled masses yearning to breathe free,
> The wretched refuse of your teeming shore,
> Send these, the homeless, tempest-tossed to me:
> I lift my lamp beside the golden door.

These words by Emma Lazarus, inscribed on the Statue of Liberty, express cultural ideals of human dignity, personal freedom, and economic opportunity. The United States has provided more of the "good life" to more immigrants than any other nation. About 1 million immigrants come to this country every year, and their many ways of life create a social mosaic that is especially evident in large cities. "In the *Times*" on pages 376–77 provides a look at ethnic diversity in New York City.

However, as a survey of this country's racial and ethnic minorities will show, our country's golden door has opened more widely for some than for others. We turn next to the history and current social standing of the major categories of the U.S. population.

NATIVE AMERICANS

The term "Native Americans" refers to many different societies—including the Aztec, Inca, Aleut, Eskimo, Cherokee, Zuni, Sioux, and Mohawk—that first settled the Western Hemisphere. Some 30,000 years before Christopher Columbus (1446–1506) landed in the Americas, migrating peoples crossed a land bridge from Asia to North America where the Bering Strait (off the coast of Alaska) lies today. Gradually, they made their way throughout North and South America.

When the first Europeans arrived late in the fifteenth century, Native Americans numbered in the millions. But by 1900, after centuries of conflict and even acts of genocide, the "vanishing Americans" numbered just 250,000 (Dobyns, 1966; Tyler, 1973). The land they controlled also shrank dramatically, as shown in National Map 14–2.

Columbus first referred to Native Americans that he encountered (on the Bahama Islands) as "Indians" because he mistakenly thought he had reached his destination of India. Columbus found the native people passive and peaceful, in stark contrast to the materialistic and competitive Europeans. Yet Europeans justified the seizure of Native American land by calling their victims thieves and murderers (Josephy, 1982; Matthiessen, 1984; Sale, 1990).

After the Revolutionary War, the new U.S. government took a pluralistic approach to Native American societies, seeking to gain more land through treaties. Payment for the land was far from fair, however, and when Native Americans

---

TABLE 14–2

The Social Standing of Native Americans, 2000

	Native Americans	Entire U.S. Population
Median family income	$33,144*	$50,891
Percentage in poverty	25.7%*	11.3%
Completion of four or more years of college (age 25 and over)	11.5%	25.6%

*Data are for 1999.

Sources: U.S. Census Bureau (2004).

---

resisted the surrender of their homelands, the U.S. government simply used its superior military power to evict them. By the early 1800s, few Native Americans remained east of the Mississippi River.

In 1871, the United States declared Native Americans wards of the government and adopted a strategy of forced assimilation. Relocated to specific territories designated as "reservations," Native Americans continued to lose their land and were well on their way to losing their culture as well. Reservation life encouraged dependency, replacing ancestral languages with English and traditional religion with Christianity. Officials of the Bureau of Indian Affairs took children from their parents and put them in boarding schools, where they were resocialized as "Americans." Authorities gave local control of reservation life to the few Native Americans who supported government policies, and they distributed reservation land, traditionally held collectively, as private property to individual families (Tyler, 1973).

Not until 1924 were Native Americans entitled to U.S. citizenship. After that, many migrated from reservations, adopting mainstream cultural patterns and marrying non–Native Americans. Today, four out of ten Native Americans consider themselves biracial or multiracial (Raymond, 2001; Wellner, 2001), and many large cities now contain sizable Native American populations. However, as Table 14–2 shows, Native American income is far below the U.S. average, and relatively few Native Americans earn a college degree.[2]

---

[2]In making comparisons of education and, especially, income, keep in mind that various categories of the U.S. population have different median ages. In 2000, the median age for all U.S. people was 35.3 years. Non-Hispanic white people have a median age of 38.6 years; for Native Americans, the figure is 28.0 years. Because people's schooling and income increase over time, this age difference accounts for some of the disparities shown in Table 14–2.

January 30, 2005

Around the World in Five Boroughs

By JOSEPH BERGER

In a growing number of New York City neighborhoods, it is English that is the foreign language. "The Newest New Yorkers 2000," a 265-page report released last week on how immigration has transformed the city's landscape and life, counted 17 neighborhoods where a majority of the residents were born outside the United States.

In one, Elmhurst in Queens, seven out of 10 residents were born abroad. A stranger stepping out of the neighborhood's subway exit at 75th Street and Broadway would quickly see a large sign proclaiming "Learn English" at the entrance to the American Language Communication Center. There, 1,200 people a week take English classes, some to achieve something as modest as advancing to waiter from busboy.

On that block and the next, a beauty parlor is Indian, a money transmission shop is Ecuadorean, a bakery and Seventh-Day Adventist Church are Chinese, and a video store and dry cleaner are Korean. The owner of Bollywood Beauty Salon Karim Budhwani, an Indian Muslim from Bombay, has learned a smattering of Spanish so he can intelligently give a *corte de pelo* (a haircut) to a Latino customer. He is also proud that for three years he has employed a Jew from the former Soviet Union, Alex Arkadiy, as a hair stylist....

Elmhurst's polyglot character has become commonplace for much of the city, even in neighborhoods not previously known for their diversity. Several communities have been refashioned by the immigrant tide that gave New York City 2.9 million foreign-born residents in 2000 compared with 2.1 million in 1990.

Bensonhurst and Bay Ridge, once so inherently third- and fourth-generation Italian-American that the character of Tony Manero and his family were based there in the 1977 film classic *Saturday Night Fever*, now have a population that is 40 percent foreign born. One-fifth of that foreign-born population of 78,585 residents are from China, while Russians and Ukrainians also abound, and immigrants from Italy make up only 11 percent. Woodside and Sunnyside in Queens were once Irish bastions, but now, 6 out of 10 residents were born abroad in countries like Bangladesh, China, Colombia and Ecuador....

The ethnic history of New York has been characterized by a checkerboard, with Italians tending to live in Italian neighborhoods, Jews in Jewish neighborhoods, and so on. But the report found neighborhoods where a stew would be a more apt metaphor.

Of the 74,639 foreign-born residents of Elmhurst, 19 percent came from China, 12 percent from Colombia, 11.7 percent from Ecuador, 8.4 percent from Mexico, 7.1 percent from Korea,

---

From in-depth interviews with Native Americans in a western city, Joan Albon (1971) linked low Native American social standing to a range of cultural factors, including a noncompetitive view of life and a reluctance to pursue higher education. In addition, she noted, many Native Americans have dark skin, which makes them targets of prejudice and discrimination.

Members of many Native American nations have recently reclaimed pride in their cultural heritage. Traditional cultural organizations report a surge in new membership applications, and many children can speak native languages better than their parents. The legal right of Native Americans to govern their reservations has enabled some tribes to build profitable gaming casinos. But the wealth produced from gambling has enriched relatively few Native peoples, and most profits go to non-Indian investors (Bartlett & Steele, 2002). While some prosper, most Native Americans remain severely disadvantaged and share a profound sense of the injustice they have suffered at the hands of white people.

For more information on Native Americans, visit http://www.nativeweb.org

WHITE ANGLO-SAXON PROTESTANTS

White Anglo-Saxon Protestants (WASPs) were not the first people to inhabit the United States, but they soon dominated this nation after European settlement began. Most WASPs are of English ancestry, but the category also includes people from Scotland and Wales. With some 28 million people of English ancestry, 10 percent of our society claims some WASP background, and WASPs are found at all class levels.

5.6 percent from India and 5.2 percent from the Philippines. The exotic flavor would have been portrayed as even richer if the census had included children born here to immigrant parents among its count. . . .

Other neighborhoods are also becoming more cosmopolitan. Bedford-Stuyvesant, long identified as black American, had 16,200 residents who were born abroad, about 28 percent. Most were Caribbean blacks from Jamaica, Trinidad and Tobago, and Guyana. While Borough Park has long been depicted as Hasidic, the report found that it has 35,900 immigrants, one-fifth of whom are Chinese. Park Slope may be identified with brownstone-dwelling children of privilege, but it has 18,700 immigrants, 11 percent of whom are Mexicans. . . .

Despite the amalgamated example of Elmhurst, the report found that many newer immigrants still choose to live among compatriots, at least at first.

Guyanese immigrants are settling in Richmond Hill, Queens, once a heavily German and Irish enclave that saw its immigrant population double during the 1990s. People from the Caribbean countries of Guyana (17,555) and Trinidad and Tobago (4,975) now predominate, and almost all are descendants of contract laborers who left India for the Caribbean in the 19th and early 20th centuries. . . .

The immigrant wave touched every corner of the city. The Bronx has not only had surges of Dominicans moving from apartments in Washington Heights to those in Highbridge, but Jamaicans now make up almost a quarter of the residents of Wakefield, a northeastern neighborhood of one- and two-family homes. Even Staten Island, the whitest of the city's boroughs, has changed. Neighborhoods like New Springville have large numbers of Koreans, Indians and Chinese, and New Brighton–Grymes Hill is home to 8,000 Mexicans.

None of these trends surprise Mr. Budhwani, the Elmhurst hair salon owner.

"Every stranger can stay in New York City and feel more comfortable here than in any other state," he said.

WHAT DO YOU THINK?

1. In what specific ways does an increasing number of immigrants change city life?

2. Do you think the immigrant character of many New York neighborhoods is anything new? Why or why not?

3. Why do you think more of today's neighborhoods are ethnically mixed, in contrast to the one-ethnicity pattern of neighborhoods in the past?

Adapted from the original article by Joseph Berger published in *The New York Times* on January 30, 2005. Copyright © 2005 by The New York Times Company. Reprinted with permission.

Many people associate WASPs with elite communities along the East and West Coasts. But the highest concentrations of WASPs are in Utah (because of migrations of Mormons with English ancestry), Appalachia, and northern New England (because of historic immigration).

Historically, WASP immigrants were highly skilled and motivated to achieve by what we now call the Protestant work ethic. Because of their high social standing, WASPs were not subject to the prejudice and discrimination experienced by other categories of immigrants. In fact, the historical dominance of WASPs has led others to want to become more like them (K. W. Jones, 2001).

WASPs were never one single group; especially in colonial times, considerable hostility separated English Anglicans and Scottish Presbyterians (Parrillo, 1994). But in the nineteenth century, most WASPs joined together to oppose the arrival of "undesirables" such as Germans in the 1840s and Italians in the 1880s. Those who could afford it sheltered themselves in exclusive suburbs and restrictive clubs. Thus the 1880s—the decade that the Statue of Liberty first welcomed immigrants to the United States—also saw the founding of the first country club with exclusively WASP members (Baltzell, 1964).

By about 1950, however, WASP wealth and power had peaked, as indicated by the 1960 election of John Fitzgerald Kennedy as the first Irish Catholic president. Yet the WASP cultural legacy remains. English is this country's dominant language, and Protestantism the majority religion. Our legal system also reflects our English origins. But the historical dominance of WASPs is most evident in the widespread use of the terms *race* and *ethnicity* to refer to everyone but them.

The efforts of these four women greatly advanced the social standing of African Americans in the United States. Pictured above, from left to right: Sojourner Truth (1797–1883), born a slave, became an influential preacher and outspoken abolitionist who was honored by President Lincoln at the White House. Harriet Tubman (1820–1913), after escaping from slavery herself, masterminded the flight from bondage of hundreds of African American men and women via the "Underground Railroad." Ida Wells-Barnett (1862–1931), born to slave parents, became a partner in a Memphis newspaper and served as a tireless crusader against the terror of lynching. Marian Anderson (1902–1993), an exceptional singer whose early career was restrained by racial prejudice, broke symbolic "color lines" by singing in the White House (1936) and on the steps of the Lincoln Memorial to a crowd of almost 100,000 people (1939).

AFRICAN AMERICANS

Although Africans accompanied European explorers to the New World in the fifteenth century, most accounts mark the beginning of black history in the United States as 1619, when a Dutch trading ship brought twenty Africans to Jamestown, Virginia. Whether these people arrived as slaves or indentured servants who paid their passage by agreeing to work for a period of time, being of African descent on these shores soon became virtually the same as being a slave. In 1661, Virginia enacted the first law recognizing slavery (Sowell, 1981).

Slavery was the foundation of the southern colonies' plantation system. White people ran plantations using slave labor, and until 1808, some were also slave traders. Traders—including Europeans, Africans, and North Americans—forcibly transported some 10 million Africans to various countries in the Americas, including 400,000 to the United States. On small sailing ships, hundreds of slaves were chained together for the several weeks it took to cross the Atlantic Ocean. Filth and disease killed many and drove others to suicide. Overall, perhaps half died en route (Franklin, 1967; Sowell, 1981).

Surviving the miserable crossing was a mixed blessing, as the journey's end brought with it a life of servitude. Although some slaves worked in cities at various trades, most labored in the fields, often from daybreak until sunset and even longer during the harvest. The law allowed owners

to use whatever disciplinary measures they deemed necessary to ensure that slaves were obedient and hardworking. Even killing a slave rarely prompted legal action. Owners also divided slave families at public auc-

Read personal accounts of slavery at http://lcweb2.loc.gov/ammem/snhtml

tions, where human beings were bought and sold as property. Unschooled and dependent on their owners for all their basic needs, slaves had little control over their lives (Franklin, 1967; Sowell, 1981).

Some free persons of color lived in both the North and the South, laboring as small-scale farmers, skilled workers, and small-business owners. But the lives of most African Americans stood in glaring contradiction to the principles of equality and freedom on which the United States was founded. The Declaration of Independence states,

> We hold these Truths to be self-evident, that all Men are created equal, that they are endowed by their Creator with certain unalienable Rights, that among these are Life, Liberty, and the Pursuit of Happiness.

However, most white people did not apply these ideals to black people. In the *Dred Scott* case of 1857, the U.S. Supreme Court addressed the question "Are blacks citizens?" by writing, "We think they are not, and that they are not included, and were not intended to be included, under the word 'citizens' in the Constitution, and can therefore claim none of the rights and privileges which that instrument provides for and secures for citizens of the United States" (quoted in Blaustein & Zangrando, 1968:160). Thus arose what Swedish sociologist Gunnar Myrdal (1944) termed the "American dilemma": a democratic society's denial of basic rights and freedoms to an entire category of people. People would speak of equality, in other words, but do little to make all categories of people equal. On the contrary, many white people resolved this dilemma by defining black people as innately inferior and undeserving of equality (Leach, 2002).

In 1865, the Thirteenth Amendment to the Constitution outlawed slavery. Three years later, the Fourteenth Amendment reversed the *Dred Scott* ruling, giving citizenship to all people born in the United States. The Fifteenth Amendment, ratified in 1870, stated that neither race nor previous condition of servitude could deprive anyone of the right to vote. However, so-called *Jim Crow laws*—classic cases of institutional discrimination—segregated U.S. society into two racial castes. Especially in the South, white people beat and lynched black people (and some white people) who challenged the racial hierarchy.

The twentieth century brought dramatic changes for African Americans. After World War I, tens of thousands of men, women, and children fled the South as part of the "Great Migration," seeking jobs in northern factories. Although most did find more economic opportunity, few escaped racial prejudice and discrimination, which placed them lower in the social hierarchy than white immigrants arriving from Europe.

In the 1950s and 1960s, a national civil rights movement led to landmark judicial decisions outlawing segregated schools and overt discrimination in employment and public accommodations. The Black Power movement gave African Americans a renewed sense of pride and purpose.

Despite these gains, people of African descent continue to occupy a lower social position in the United States, as shown in Table 14–3. The median income of African American families in 2004 ($35,158) was only 58 percent of non-Hispanic white family income ($60,969), a ratio that has changed little in thirty years.[3] Black families remain three times as likely as white families to be poor.

---

[3]Here again, a median age difference (non-Hispanic white people, 38.6; black people, 30.2) accounts for some of the income and educational disparities. More important is a higher proportion of one-parent families among blacks than whites. If we compare only married-couple families, African Americans (median income $54,095 in 2004) earned 80 percent as much as non-Hispanic whites ($68,003).

TABLE 14–3

The Social Standing of African Americans, 2004

	African Americans*	Entire U.S. Population
Median family income	$35,158	$55,327
Percentage in poverty	24.7%	12.7%
Completion of four or more years of college (age 25 and over)	17.6%	27.7%

*For purposes of comparison with other tables in this chapter, 2000 data are as follows: median family income, $34,204; percentage in poverty, 22.1%; completion of four or more years of college, 16.6%.

Sources: U.S. Census Bureau (2000, 2001, 2005).

The number of African Americans securely in the middle class rose by more than half between 1980 and 2004; 35 percent earn $50,000 or more. But most African Americans are still working-class or poor, and in recent years, many have seen earnings slip as urban factory jobs, vital to residents of central cities, have been lost to other countries where labor costs are lower. This is one reason that black unemployment is more than twice as high as white unemployment; among African American teenagers in many cities, the figure exceeds 40 percent (R. A. Smith, 2002; U.S. Department of Labor, 2005).

Since 1980, African Americans have made remarkable educational progress. The share of adults completing high school rose from half to more than three-fourths, nearly closing the gap between whites and blacks. Between 1980 and 2004, the share of African American adults with at least a college degree rose from 8 to more than 17 percent. But as Table 14–3 shows, African Americans are still at just over half the national standard when it comes to completing four years of college.

The political clout of African Americans has also increased. As a result of black migration to the cities and white flight to the suburbs, half of this country's ten largest cities have elected African American mayors. Yet in 2005, African Americans accounted for just 41 members of the House of Representatives (9.4 percent of 435), one member (out of 100) in the Senate, and no state governors.

In sum, for nearly 400 years, African Americans have struggled for social equality. As a nation, the United States has come far in this pursuit. Overt discrimination is now illegal, and research documents a long-term decline in prejudice against African Americans (Firebaugh & Davis, 1988; J. Q. Wilson, 1992; NORC, 2003).

Although sometimes portrayed as a successful "model minority," Asian Americans are highly diverse and, like other categories of people, include both rich and poor. These young people contend with many of the same patterns of prejudice and discrimination familiar to members of other minorities.

In 1913, nearly fifty years after the abolition of slavery, W. E. B. Du Bois pointed to the extent of black achievement but cautioned that racial caste remained strong in the United States. Almost a century later, this racial hierarchy persists.

YOUR TURN

In your opinion, how much change has there been in racial prejudice and discrimination against African Americans in the past twenty-five years? Explain your position.

ASIAN AMERICANS

Although Asian Americans share some physical traits, enormous cultural diversity characterizes this category of people with ancestors from dozens of nations. In 2000, the total number of Asian Americans exceeded 10 million, approaching 4 percent of the U.S. population. The largest category of Asian Americans is people of Chinese ancestry (2.4 million), followed by those of Filipino (1.8 million), Asian Indian (1.7 million), Vietnamese (1.1 million), Korean (1 million), and Japanese (800,000) descent. More than one-third of Asian Americans live in California.

Young Asian Americans command attention and respect as high achievers and are disproportionately represented at our country's best colleges and universities. Many of their elders, too, have made economic and social gains; most Asian Americans now live in middle-class suburbs. Yet despite (and sometimes because of) this achievement, Asian Americans often find that others are aloof or outright hostile toward them (O'Hare, Frey, & Fost, 1994; Chua-Eoan, 2000).

At the same time, the "model minority" image of Asian Americans hides the fact that many Asian Americans remain poor. We now focus on the history and current standing of Chinese Americans and Japanese Americans—the longest-established Asian American minorities—and conclude with a brief look at the most recent arrivals.

Chinese Americans

Chinese immigration to the United States began in 1849 with the economic boom of California's Gold Rush. New towns and businesses sprang up overnight, and the demand for cheap labor attracted some 100,000 Chinese immigrants. Most Chinese workers were young men willing to take tough, low-status jobs that whites did not want. But the economy soured in the 1870s, and desperate whites began to compete with the Chinese for whatever work could be found. Suddenly, the hardworking Chinese were seen as a threat. In short, economic hard times led to prejudice and discrimination (Ling, 1971; Boswell, 1986). Soon laws were passed barring Chinese people from many occupations, and public opinion turned strongly against "the Yellow Peril."

In 1882, the U.S. government passed the first of several laws limiting Chinese immigration. This action caused domestic hardship because in the United States, Chinese men outnumbered Chinese women by twenty to one. This sex imbalance drove the Chinese population down to only 60,000 by 1920. Because Chinese women already in the United States were in high demand, they soon lost much of their traditional submissiveness to men (Hsu, 1971; Lai, 1980; Sowell, 1981).

Responding to racial hostility, some Chinese moved east; many more sought the relative safety of urban Chinatowns. There Chinese traditions flourished, and kinship networks, called *clans*, provided financial assistance to individuals and represented the interests of all. At the same time, however, living in an all-Chinese community discouraged residents from learning English, which limited their job opportunities (Wong, 1971).

A renewed need for labor during World War II prompted President Franklin Roosevelt to end the ban on Chinese immigration in 1943 and to extend the rights of citizenship

TABLE 14–4

The Social Standing of Asian Americans, 2004

	All Asian Americans**	Chinese Americans*	Japanese Americans*	Korean Americans*	Filipino Americans*	Entire U.S. Population
Median family income	$65,482	$64,000	$79,000	$53,000	$72,000	$55,327
Percentage in poverty	9.8%	9.8%	4.9%	9.6%	4.4%	12.7%
Completion of four or more years of college (age 25 and over)	49.4%	53.4%	45.4%	45.4%	51.4%	27.7%

*Author estimates based on latest available data.

**For purposes of comparison with other tables in this chapter, 2000 data for all Asians are as follows: median family income, $62,617; percentage in poverty, 10.8%; completion of four or more years of college, 43.9%.

Sources: U.S. Census Bureau (2000, 2001, 2005).

to Chinese Americans born abroad. Many responded by moving out of Chinatowns and pursuing cultural assimilation. In Honolulu in 1900, for example, 70 percent of Chinese people lived in Chinatown; today, the figure is below 20 percent.

By 1950, many Chinese Americans had experienced upward social mobility. Today, people of Chinese ancestry are no longer limited to self-employment in laundries and restaurants; many hold high-prestige positions, especially in fields related to science and information technology.

As shown in Table 14–4, the median family income of Chinese Americans in 2004 ($64,000) stood above the national average ($55,327). The higher income of all Asian Americans reflects a larger number of family members in the labor force.[4] Chinese Americans also have a record of educational achievement, with twice the national average of college graduates.

Despite their successes, many Chinese Americans still grapple with subtle (and sometimes blatant) prejudice and discrimination. Such hostility is one reason that poverty remains a problem for many Chinese Americans. The problem of poverty is most common among

Visit the Organization of Chinese Americans at http://www.ocanatl.org/

people who remain in the socially isolated Chinatowns working in restaurants or otherlow-paying jobs, raising the question of whether racial and ethnic enclaves help their residents or exploit them (Portes & Jensen, 1989; Kinkead, 1992; Gilbertson & Gurak, 1993).

Japanese Americans

Japanese immigration to the United States began slowly in the 1860s, reaching only 3,000 by 1890. Most were men who came to the Hawaiian Islands (annexed by the United States in 1898 and made a state in 1959) as a source of cheap labor. After 1900, however, as the number of Japanese immigrants to California rose (reaching 140,000 by 1915), white hostility increased (Takaki, 1998). In 1907, the United States signed an agreement with Japan curbing the entry of men— the chief economic threat—while allowing women to enter this country to ease the Japanese sex ratio imbalance. In the 1920s, state laws in California and elsewhere segregated the Japanese and banned interracial marriage, just about ending further Japanese immigration. Not until 1952 did the United States extend citizenship to foreign-born Japanese.

Immigrants from Japan and China differed in three important ways. First, there were fewer Japanese immigrants, so they escaped some of the hostility directed toward the more numerous Chinese. Second, the Japanese knew more about the United States than the Chinese did, which helped them assimilate (Sowell, 1981). Third, Japanese immigrants preferred rural farming to clustering in cities, which made them less visible. But many white people objected to Japanese ownership of farmland, so in 1913, California barred

---

[4]Median age for all Asian Americans in 2000 was 32.7 years, somewhat below the national median of 35.3 and the non-Hispanic white median of 38.6. But specific categories vary widely in median age: Japanese, 36.1; Chinese, 32.1; Filipino, 31.1; Korean, 29.1; Asian Indian, 28.9; Cambodian, 19.4; Hmong, 12.5 (U.S. Census Bureau, 2000, 2001).

Of all categories of Asian Americans, immigrants from India have the greatest economic achievement due, in part, to overrepresentation in many high-paying professions. Parminda Nagra, who plays an Indian doctor, is featured on the popular television show *ER*.

further purchases. Many foreign-born Japanese (called *Issei*) responded by placing farmland in the names of their U.S.-born children (*Nisei*), who were constitutionally entitled to citizenship.

Japanese Americans faced their greatest crisis after Japan bombed the U.S. naval fleet at Hawaii's Pearl Harbor on December 7, 1941. Rage was directed at the Japanese living in the United States. Some people feared that Japanese Americans would spy for Japan or commit acts of sabotage. Within a year, President Franklin Roosevelt signed Executive Order 9066, an unprecedented action designed to ensure national security by detaining people of Japanese ancestry in military camps. Authorities soon relocated 110,000 people of Japanese descent (90 percent of the total in this country) to remote inland reservations (Sun, 1998).

Concern about national security always rises in times of war, but Japanese internment was sharply criticized. First, it targeted an entire category of people, not a single one of whom was known to have committed any disloyal act. Second, most of those imprisoned were *Nisei*, U.S. citizens by birth. Third, the United States was also at war

with Germany and Italy, but no comparable action was taken against people of German or Italian ancestry.

Relocation meant selling homes, furnishings, and businesses on short notice for pennies on the dollar. As a result, almost the entire Japanese American population was economically devastated. In military prisons—surrounded by barbed wire and guarded by armed soldiers—families crowded into single rooms, often in buildings that had previously sheltered livestock. The internment ended in 1944 when the Supreme Court declared it unconstitutional. In 1988, Congress awarded $20,000 to each victim as token compensation for the hardships they suffered.

After World War II, Japanese Americans staged a dramatic recovery. Having lost their traditional businesses, many entered new occupations; driven by cultural values stressing the importance of education and hard work, Japanese Americans have enjoyed remarkable success. In 2004, the median income of Japanese American households was almost 50 percent higher than the national average. The rate of poverty among Japanese Americans was less than half the national figure.

Upward social mobility has encouraged cultural assimilation and intermarriage. Younger generations of Japanese Americans rarely live in residential enclaves, as many Chinese Americans do, and most marry non-Japanese partners. In the process, some have abandoned their traditions, including the Japanese language. A high proportion of Japanese Americans, however, belong to associations as a way of maintaining their ethnic identity (Fugita & O'Brien, 1985). Still, some appear to be caught between two worlds: no longer culturally Japanese yet, because of racial differences, not completely accepted in the larger society.

To learn about Japanese culture and society, go to http://www.jinjapan.org

Recent Asian Immigrants

More recent immigrants from Asia include Filipinos, Indians, Koreans, Vietnamese, Guamanians, and Samoans. The Asian American population increased by 48 percent between 1990 and 2000 and currently accounts for one-third of all immigration to the United States (U.S. Department of Homeland Security, 2005). A brief look at Koreans and Filipinos—both from countries that have had special ties to the United States—shows the social diversity of people arriving from Asia.

Koreans Korean immigration to the United States followed the U.S. involvement in the Korean War (1950–53). U.S. troops in South Korea experienced Korean culture firsthand, and some soldiers found Korean spouses. For

The strength of family bonds and neighborhood ties is evident in Carmen Lomas Garza's painting *Barbacoa para Cumpleaños* (Birthday Party Barbecue).

Carmen Lomas Garza, *Barbacoa para Cumpleaños* (Birthday Party Barbecue). Alkyds on canvas, 38 × 48 inches. © 1993 Carmen Lomas Garza (reg. 1994). Photo credit: M. Lee Fatherree. Collection of Federal Reserve Bank of Dallas.

South Koreans, contact with the troops raised interest in the United States.

The entrepreneurial spirit is strong among all Asian immigrants. Asians are slightly more likely than Latinos, three times more likely than African Americans, and eight times more likely than Native Americans to own and operate small businesses (U.S. Small Business Administration, 2001a). Among all Asian Americans, Koreans are the most likely to own small businesses. For example, residents of New York City know that most small grocery stores there are Korean-owned; in Los Angeles, Koreans operate a large share of liquor stores.

Although many Koreans work long hours in businesses such as these, Korean American families earn slightly below average incomes, as shown in Table 14–4. In addition, Korean Americans face limited social acceptance, even among other categories of Asian Americans.

Filipinos The large number of immigrants from the Philippines is explained partly by the fact that the United States controlled the Philippine Islands between 1898, when Spain ceded it to this country as partial settlement of the Spanish-American War, and 1946, when the Philippines became an independent republic.

The data in Table 14–4 show that Filipinos generally have fared well. But a closer look reveals a mixed pattern, with some Filipinos highly successful in the professions (especially in medicine) and others struggling to get by in low-skill jobs (Parrillo, 1994).

For many Filipino families, the key to high income is working women. Almost three-fourths of Filipino American women are in the labor force, compared to just half of Korean American women. Many of these women are professionals, reflecting the fact that 42 percent of Filipino American women have a four-year college degree, compared with 26 percent of Korean American women.

In sum, a survey of Asian Americans presents a complex picture. The Japanese come closest to gaining social acceptance, but surveys reveal greater prejudice against Asian Americans than against African Americans (Parrillo, 2003a). Median income data suggest that many Asian Americans have prospered. But these numbers reflect the fact that many Asian Americans live in Hawaii, California, and New York, where incomes are high but so are living costs (Takaki, 1998). Then too, many Asian Americans remain poor. One thing is clear—their high immigration rate means that people of Asian ancestry are sure to play a central role in U.S. society in the decades to come.

HISPANIC AMERICANS/LATINOS

In 2000, the number of people of Hispanic descent in the United States topped 35 million (12.5 percent of the

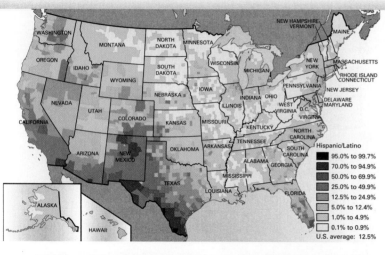

NATIONAL MAP 14–3

The Concentration of Hispanics or Latinos, African Americans, and Asian Americans, by County, 2000

In 2000, people of Hispanic or Latino descent represented 12.5 percent of the U.S. population, compared with 12.3 percent African Americans and 3.6 percent Asian Americans. These three maps show the geographic distribution of these categories of people in 2000. Comparing them, we see that the southern half of the United States is home to far more minorities than the northern half. But do the three concentrate in the same areas? What patterns do the maps reveal?

Source: U.S. Census Bureau (2001).

Hispanic/Latino
- 95.0% to 99.7%
- 70.0% to 94.9%
- 50.0% to 69.9%
- 25.0% to 49.9%
- 12.5% to 24.9%
- 5.0% to 12.4%
- 1.0% to 4.9%
- 0.1% to 0.9%
- U.S. average: 12.5%

African American
- 70.0% to 86.5%
- 50.0% to 69.9%
- 25.0% to 49.9%
- 12.3% to 24.9%
- 5.0% to 12.2%
- 1.0% to 4.9%
- 0.0% to 0.9%
- U.S. average: 12.3%

Asian American
- 25.0% to 46.0%
- 12.5% to 24.9%
- 3.6% to 12.4%
- 1.0% to 3.5%
- 0.0% to 0.9%
- U.S. average: 3.6%

TABLE 14–5

The Social Standing of Hispanic Americans, 2004

	All Hispanics**	Mexican Americans*	Puerto Ricans*	Cuban Americans*	Entire U.S. Population
Median family income	$35,401	$33,533	$30,095	$35,217	$55,327
Percentage in poverty	21.9%	22.8%	26.1%	16.5%	12.7%
Completion of four or more years of college (age 25 and over)	12.1%	7.5%	14.0%	18.6%	27.7%

*Data are for 2003.

**For purposes of comparison with other tables in this chapter, 2000 data for all Hispanics are as follows: median family income, $35,050; percentage in poverty, 21.2%; completion of four or more years of college, 10.6%.

Sources: U.S. Census Bureau (2000, 2001, 2003, 2005).

population), surpassing the number of African Americans (12.3 percent) and making Hispanics the largest racial or ethnic minority. However, keep in mind that few people who fall into this category describe themselves as "Hispanic" or "Latino." Like Asian Americans, Hispanics are really a cluster of distinct populations, each of which identifies with a particular ancestral nation (Marín & Marín, 1991). About two out of three Hispanics (some 20 million) are Mexican Americans, or "Chicanos." Puerto Ricans are next in population size (3.4 million), followed by Cuban Americans (1.2 million). Many other nations of Latin America are represented by smaller numbers.

Although the Hispanic population is increasing all over the country, most Hispanic Americans still live in the Southwest. One out of four Californians is a Latino (in

 For information about Hispanic/Latino culture, go to http://www1.lanic.utexas.edu/la/region/hispanic

greater Los Angeles, almost half the people are Latino). National Map 14–3 shows the U.S. counties in which Hispanic, African American, Asian American, and Native American populations are the largest minority.

Median family income for all Hispanics—$35,401 in 2004—is well below the national average.[5] As the following sections explain, however, some categories of Hispanics fare better than others.

[5]The 2000 median age of the U.S. Hispanic population was 25.8 years, well below the national median of 35.3 years. This differential accounts for some of the disparity in income and education.

Mexican Americans

Some Mexican Americans are descendants of people who lived in a part of Mexico annexed by the United States after the Mexican American War (1846–48). Most, however, are more recent immigrants. Indeed, more immigrants now come to the United States from Mexico than from any other country.

Like many other immigrants, many Mexican Americans have worked as low-wage laborers, on farms and in factories. Table 14–5 shows that the 2003 median family income for Mexican Americans was $33,533, about two-thirds the national average. Almost one-fourth of Chicano families are poor, nearly twice the national average. Despite gains since 1980, Mexican Americans still have a high dropout rate and receive much less schooling than the U.S. population as a whole.

Puerto Ricans

Puerto Rico (like the Philippines) became a possession of the United States when the Spanish-American War ended in 1898. In 1917, Puerto Ricans (but not Filipinos) became U.S. citizens.

New York City is home to 800,000 Puerto Ricans. However, about one-third of this community is severely disadvantaged. Adjusting to cultural patterns on the mainland—including, for many, learning English—is one major challenge; also, Puerto Ricans with dark skin encounter prejudice and discrimination. As a result, more people return to Puerto Rico each year than arrive. During the 1990s, the Puerto Rican population of New York actually fell by 100,000 (Navarro, 2000).

Affirmative Action: Solution or Problem?

Barbara Gruttner, who is white, claimed that she was the victim of racial discrimination. She maintained that the University of Michigan Law School had unfairly denied her application for admission while admitting many less qualified African American applicants. The basis of her claim was the fact that Michigan, a state university, admitted just 9 percent of white students with her grade point average and law school aptitude test scores while admitting 100 percent of African American applicants with comparable scores.

In 2003, the U.S. Supreme Court heard Gruttner's complaint in a review of the admissions policies of both the law school and the undergraduate program at the University of Michigan. In a 6–3 decision, the Court ruled against Gruttner, claiming that the University of Michigan Law School could use a policy of affirmative action that takes account of the race of applicants in the interest of creating a socially diverse student body. At the same time, however, the Court struck down the university's undergraduate admissions policy, which awarded points not only for grades and college board scores but also for being a member of an under-represented minority. A point system of this kind, the Court ruled, is too close

to the rigid quota systems rejected by the Court in the past.

With this ruling, the Supreme Court continued to oppose any quota-like systems while at the same time reaffirming the importance of racial diversity on the campus. Thus colleges and universities can take account of race in order to increase the number of traditionally underrepresented students as

long as race is treated as one variable in a process that evaluates each applicant as an individual (Stout, 2003).

How did the controversial policy of affirmative action begin? The answer takes us back to the end of World War II, when the U.S. government funded higher education for veterans of all races. The G.I. Bill held special promise for African Americans, most of whom needed financial assistance to enroll in college. The program was so successful that by 1960, some 350,000 black men and women were on college campuses with government funding.

There was just one problem: These individuals were not finding the kinds of jobs for which they were qualified. In short, educational opportunity was not producing economic opportunity.

As a result, in the early 1960s, the Kennedy administration devised a program of "affirmative action" to provide broader opportunities to qualified minorities. Employers were instructed to monitor hiring, promotion, and admissions policies to eliminate discrimination—even if unintended—against minorities.

Defenders of affirmative action see it, first, as a sensible response to our nation's racial and ethnic history, especially for African Americans, who

---

This "revolving door" pattern limits assimilation. Three-fourths of Puerto Rican families in the United States speak Spanish at home, compared to about half of Mexican American families (Sowell, 1981; Stevens & Swicegood, 1987). Speaking Spanish keeps ethnic identity strong but limits economic opportunity. Puerto Ricans also have a higher incidence of woman-headed households than other

Hispanics, a pattern that puts families at greater risk of poverty.

Table 14–5 on page 385 shows that the 2003 median family income for Puerto Ricans was $30,095, a little more than half the national average. Although long-term mainland residents have made economic gains, more recent immigrants from Puerto Rico continue to struggle to find

suffered through two centuries of slavery and a century of segregation under Jim Crow laws. Throughout our history, they claim, being white gave people a big advantage. They see minority preference today as a step toward fair compensation for unfair majority preference in the past.

Second, given our racial history, many analysts doubt that the United States will ever become a color-blind society. They claim that because prejudice and discrimination are rooted deep in the fabric of U.S. society, simply claiming that we are color-blind does not mean everyone will compete fairly.

Third, supporters maintain that affirmative action has worked. Where would minorities be if the government had not enacted this policy four decades ago? Major employers, such as fire and police departments in large cities, began hiring minorities and women for the first time only because of affirmative action. This program has played an important part in expanding the African American middle class. Affirmative action has also increased racial diversity on campus, which benefits everyone, and has advanced the careers of an entire generation of black students.

About 80 percent of African Americans claim that affirmative action is needed to secure equal opportunity. But affirmative action draws criticism from others. A 2003 poll shows that 73 percent of white people and 56 percent of Hispanics oppose preferences for African Americans. As opposition to this affirmative action policy was building during the 1990s, courts began to trim back such policies. Critics argue, first, that affirmative action started out as a temporary remedy to ensure fair competition but became a system of "group preferences" and quotas. In other words, the policy did not remain true to the goal of promoting color blindness as set out in the 1964 Civil Rights Act. By the 1970s, it had become "reverse discrimination," favoring people not because of performance but because of race, ethnicity, or sex.

Second, critics argue that affirmative action divides society. If racial preferences were wrong in the past, they are wrong now. Why should whites today, many of whom are far from privileged, be penalized for past discrimination that was in no way their fault? Our society has undone most of the institutional prejudice and discrimination of earlier times, opponents continue, so that minorities can and do enjoy success according to personal merit. Giving entire categories of people special treatment compromises standards of excellence, calls into question the real accomplishments of minorities, and offends public opinion.

A third argument against affirmative action is that it benefits those who need it least. Favoring minority-owned corporations or holding places in law school helps already privileged people. Affirmative action has done little for the African American underclass that needs the most help.

In sum, there are good arguments for and against affirmative action, and people who want our society to have more racial or ethnic equality fall on both sides of the debate. The disagreement is not whether people of all colors should have equal opportunity but whether the current policy of affirmative action is part of the solution or part of the problem.

WHAT DO YOU THINK?

1. In view of the fact that society historically has favored males over females and whites over people of color, would you agree that white males have received more "affirmative action" than anyone? Why or why not?

2. Should affirmative action include only disadvantaged categories of minorities (say, African Americans and Native Americans) and exclude more affluent categories (such as Japanese Americans)? Why or why not?

3. Should state universities admit applicants with an eye toward advancing minorities in order to lessen racial inequality? Do you think that goal is more or less important than the goal of admitting the most qualified individuals? Explain your answer.

Sources: Bowen & Bok (1999), Kantrowitz & Wingert (2003), and NORC (2003).

work. Overall, Puerto Ricans remain the most socially disadvantaged Hispanic minority.

Cuban Americans

Within a decade after the 1959 Marxist revolution led by Fidel Castro, 400,000 Cubans had fled to the United States. Most settled in Miami. Those who came were, for the most part, highly educated business and professional people who wasted little time becoming as successful in the United States as they had been in their homeland.

Table 14–5 shows that the 2003 median household income for Cuban Americans was $35,217, above that of other Hispanics yet still well below the national average.

The 1.2 million Cuban Americans living in the United States today have managed a delicate balancing act, achieving in the larger society while holding on to much of their traditional culture. Of all Hispanics, Cubans are the most likely to speak Spanish in their homes: eight out of ten families do. However, cultural distinctiveness and highly visible communities, such as Miami's Little Havana, provoke hostility from some people.

WHITE ETHNIC AMERICANS

The term "white ethnics" recognizes the ethnic heritage and social disadvantages of many white people. White ethnics are non-WASPs whose ancestors lived in Ireland, Poland, Germany, Italy, or other European countries. More than half the U.S. population falls into one or more white ethnic categories.

High rates of emigration from Europe during the nineteenth century first brought Germans and Irish and then Italians and Jews to our shores. Despite cultural differences, all shared the hope that the United States would offer greater political freedom and economic opportunity than their homelands. Most did live better in this country, but the belief that "the streets of America were paved with gold" turned out to be a far cry from reality. Many immigrants found only hard labor for low wages.

White ethnics also endured their share of prejudice and discrimination. Many employers shut their doors to immigrants, posting signs that warned "None need apply but Americans" (Handlin, 1941:67). By 1921, the federal government had passed a quota system greatly limiting immigration, especially by southern and eastern Europeans, who were likely to have darker skin and different cultural backgrounds than the dominant WASPs. This system continued until 1968.

In response to this hostility, many white ethnics formed supportive residential enclaves. Some also established footholds in certain businesses and trades: Italian Americans entered the construction industry; the Irish worked in construction and in civil service jobs; Jews predominated in the garment industry; many Greeks (like the Chinese) worked in the retail food business (W. M. Newman, 1973).

Many working-class people still live in traditional neighborhoods, although those who prospered have gradually assimilated. Most descendants of immigrants who labored in sweatshops and lived in crowded tenements now lead more comfortable lives. As a result, their ethnic heritage has become a source of pride.

Race and Ethnicity: Looking Ahead

The United States has been and will remain a land of immigrants. Immigration has brought striking cultural diversity and tales of hope, struggle, and success told in hundreds of languages.

Most immigrants arrived in a great wave that peaked about 1910. The next two generations saw gradual economic gains and at least some assimilation. The government also extended citizenship to Native Americans (1924), foreign-born Filipinos (1942), Chinese Americans (1943), and Japanese Americans (1952).

Another wave of immigration began after World War II and swelled as the government relaxed immigration laws in the 1960s. Today, about 1.5 million people come to the United States each year (about 1 million who enter legally and perhaps 500,000 people who enter illegally). This is twice the number that arrived during the "Great Immigration" a century ago (although newcomers now enter a country that has five times as many people). Today's immigrants come not from Europe but from Latin America and Asia, with Mexicans, Asian Indians, and Filipinos arriving in the largest numbers.

Many new arrivals face the same kind of prejudice and discrimination experienced by those who came before them. Indeed, recent years have witnessed rising hostility toward foreigners (sometimes termed *xenophobia*, with Greek roots meaning "fear of what is strange"). In 1994, California voters passed Proposition 187, which cut off social services (including schooling) to illegal immigrants. More recently, voters there mandated that all children learn English in school. Since 2000, some landowners along the southwest border of the United States have taken up arms to discourage the large number of illegal immigrants crossing the border from Mexico, and some political candidates have called for drastic action to cut off further immigration. More broadly, as the Thinking It Through box on pages 386–87 explains, the debate over affirmative action rages as hotly as ever.

Like those who came before, today's immigrants try to blend into U.S. society without completely giving up their traditional culture. Some still build racial and ethnic enclaves so that in many cities across the country, the Little Havanas and Koreatowns of today stand alongside the Little Italys and Chinatowns of the past. In addition, new arrivals still carry the traditional hope that their racial and ethnic identities can be a source of pride and strength rather than a badge of inferiority.

The following learning tools will help you see what you know, identify what you still need to learn, and expand your understanding beyond the text. You can also visit this text's Companion Website™ at http://www.prenhall.com/macionis to find additional practice tests.

The Social Meaning of Race and Ethnicity

Races are socially constructed categories by which societies set apart people with various physical traits. Although scientists identified three broad categories—Caucasoids, Mongoloids, and Negroids—there are no pure races.

Ethnicity is based not on biology but on a shared cultural heritage. Just as people may or may not choose to emphasize their cultural distinctiveness, societies may or may not set categories of people apart because of their cultural heritage.

Minorities, including people of various races and ethnicities, are categories of people society sets apart, making them both distinct and disadvantaged.

Prejudice

Prejudice is a rigid and unfair generalization about a category of people. The social distance scale is one measure of prejudice. Racism, a destructive type of prejudice, asserts that one race is innately superior or inferior to another.

Discrimination

Discrimination is a pattern of action by which a person treats various categories of people unequally.

Majority and Minority: Patterns of Interaction

Pluralism means that racial and ethnic categories, although distinct, have equal social standing. Assimilation is a process by which minorities gradually adopt the patterns of the dominant culture. Segregation is the physical and social separation of categories of people. Genocide is the extermination of a category of people.

Race and Ethnicity in the United States

Native Americans, the earliest human inhabitants of the Americas, have endured genocide, segregation, and forced assimilation. Today, the social standing of Native Americans is well below the national average.

WASPs predominated among the original European settlers of the United States, and many continue to enjoy high social position today.

African Americans experienced two centuries of slavery. Emancipation in 1865 gave way to segregation by law. Today, despite legal equality, African Americans are still disadvantaged.

Chinese and Japanese Americans have suffered both racial and ethnic hostility. Although some prejudice and discrimination continue, both categories now have above-average income and schooling. Asian immigrants, especially Koreans and Filipinos, now account for one-third of all immigration to the United States.

Hispanics, the largest U.S. minority, include many ethnicities sharing a Spanish heritage. Mexican Americans, the largest Hispanic minority, are concentrated in the Southwest. Cubans, concentrated in Miami, are the most affluent Hispanic category; Puerto Ricans, one-third of whom live in New York, are the poorest.

White ethnics are non-WASPs of European ancestry. Although they made gains during the twentieth century, many white ethnics still struggle for economic security.

Race and Ethnicity: Looking Ahead

Immigration has increased in recent years. No longer primarily from Europe, most immigrants now arrive from Latin America and Asia.

KEY CONCEPTS

race (p. 362) a socially constructed category of people who share biologically transmitted traits that members of a society consider important

ethnicity (p. 364) a shared cultural heritage

minority (p. 365) any category of people distinguished by physical or cultural difference that a society sets apart and subordinates

prejudice (p. 366) a rigid and unfair generalization about an entire category of people

stereotype (p. 366) an exaggerated description applied to every person in some category

racism (p. 369) the belief that one racial category is innately superior or inferior to another

scapegoat (p. 371) a person or category of people, typically with little power, whom people unfairly blame for their own troubles

discrimination (p. 372) unequal treatment of various categories of people

institutional prejudice and discrimination (p. 372) bias built into the operation of society's institutions

pluralism (p. 372) a state in which people of all races and ethnicities are distinct but have equal social standing

assimilation (p. 373) the process by which minorities gradually adopt patterns of the dominant culture

miscegenation (p. 373) biological reproduction by partners of different racial categories

segregation (p. 373) the physical and social separation of categories of people

genocide (p. 374) the systematic killing of one category of people by another

---

SAMPLE TEST QUESTIONS

These questions are similar to those found in the test bank that accompanies this textbook.

Multiple-Choice Questions

1. Race refers to _____ considered important by a society, and ethnicity refers to _____.
   a. biological traits; cultural traits
   b. cultural traits; biological traits
   c. differences; what we have in common
   d. what we have in common; differences

2. What share of the U.S. population consists of people of Hispanic ancestry?
   a. 42.5 percent
   b. 32.5 percent
   c. 22.5 percent
   d. 12.5 percent

3. A minority is defined as a category of people who
   a. have physical traits that make them different.
   b. are less than half the society's population.
   c. are defined as both different and disadvantaged.
   d. are below average in terms of income.

4. In this country, three states now have a "minority majority." Which of the following is NOT one of them?
   a. California
   b. Florida
   c. Hawaii
   d. New Mexico

5. Research using the Bogardus social distance scale shows that U.S. college students
   a. are less prejudiced than students fifty years ago.
   b. believe Arabs and Muslims should be kept out of the country.
   c. have the strongest prejudice against African Americans.
   d. all of the above.

6. Prejudice is a matter of _____, and discrimination is a matter of _____.
   a. biology; culture
   b. attitudes; behavior
   c. choice; social structure
   d. what rich people think; what rich people do

7. The United States is not truly pluralistic because
   a. part of our population lives in "ethnic enclaves."
   b. this country has a history of slavery.
   c. different racial and ethnic categories are unequal in social standing.
   d. all of the above.

8. Which term is illustrated by immigrants from Ecuador learning to speak the English language?
   a. genocide
   b. segregation
   c. assimilation
   d. pluralism

9. During the late 1400s, the first Europeans came to the Americas; Native Americans
   a. followed shortly thereafter.
   b. had just migrated from Asia.

c. came with them from Europe.

d. had inhabited this land for 30,000 years.

10. **Which of the following is the largest category of Asian Americans in the United States?**

   a. Chinese American

   b. Japanese American

   c. Korean American

   d. Vietnamese American

ANSWERS: 1(a); 2(d); 3(c); 4(b); 5(a); 6(b); 7(c); 8(c); 9(d); 10(a).

Essay Questions

1. What is the difference between race and ethnicity? What does it mean to say that race and ethnicity are socially constructed?

2. What is a minority? Support the claim that African Americans and Asian Americans are both minorities in the United States using specific facts from the chapter.

APPLICATIONS & EXERCISES

1. Does your college or university take account of race and ethnicity in its admissions policies? Ask to speak with an admissions officer to see what you can learn about your school's policies and the reasons for them. Ask whether there is a "legacy" policy that favors applicants with a parent who attended the school.

2. Surveys show that the average white person in the United States thinks this country is 33 percent African American (the real figure is 12.3 percent). Quiz several friends or family members about what share of the U.S. population is white, Hispanic, African American, and Asian American, and compare the results to Table 14–1 on page 365. Why do you think white people exaggerate the African American population? (C.A. Gallagher, 2003)

3. Interview immigrants on your campus or in your local community about their homeland and their experiences since arriving in the United States. How do their experiences compare to what you have read in this chapter?

INVESTIGATE *with* Research Navigator

Follow the instructions on page 27 of this text to access the features of **Research Navigator™**. Once at the Web site, enter your Login Name and Password. Then, to use the **ContentSelect™** database, enter keywords such as "race," "ethnicity," and "segregation," and the search engine will supply relevant and recent scholarly and popular press publications. Use the *New York Times* **Search-by-Subject Archive** to find recent news articles related to sociology and the **Link Library** feature to find relevant Web links organized by the key terms associated with this chapter.

15

Aging and the Elderly

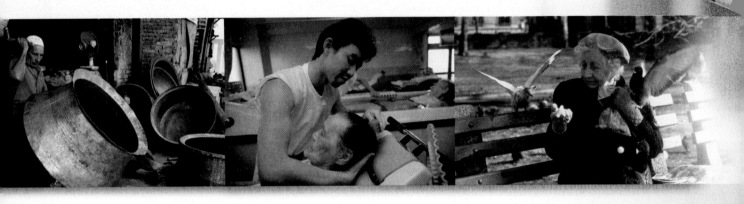

What is the "graying of the United States"?

How is age a dimension of social inequality?

Why are the elderly devalued in modern societies?

For Lynn Stock, the week had not gone well. On Monday, she was notified by her employer, the electronics retailer Best Buy, that she was being laid off. Stock had until the end of the week to clean out her office and be out the door. It was now Friday, and on her final day at work she was to attend what the company called an "outpatient session," an hour's coaching for the people being let go on how to improve their chances of finding another job.

When Stock walked into the room, she was stunned. There were about thirty people in the session, and three-fourths of them were older workers. Stock, who is fifty-one, began talking with others who had been fired. They soon learned that the average age of employees at the company was twenty-nine and that 82 of the 126 people who had been laid off that week were at least forty years old. As a result, she and several dozen other workers decided to sue Best Buy for age discrimination. Officials at Best Buy denied the charge and said that the company will defend itself when the case comes to court (Alster, 2005). ■

This case illustrates an important truth in U.S. society: Social stratification is not just about class, gender, and race; it is also about age. This chapter explains that older people face a number of disadvantages, including lower income, prejudice, and discrimination in the workplace. These facts are becoming more important all the time because the number of older people in the U.S. population is greater than ever and rising rapidly.

The Graying of the United States

A quiet but powerful revolution is reshaping the United States. As shown in Figure 15–1, in 1900, the United States was a young nation, with half the population under age twenty-three; just 4 percent had reached sixty-five. But the number of elderly people—women and men aged sixty-five or older—increased tenfold during the last century. By 2004, the number of seniors exceeded 36 million. Seniors outnumbered teenagers, and they accounted for 12.4 percent of the entire population. By 2030, the number of seniors will double again to 71 million, and the average age of the country's people will be almost forty (Himes, 2001; U.S. Census Bureau, 2004).

In high-income nations, the share of elderly people is increasing rapidly. There are two reasons for this increase: low birth rates (people are having fewer children) and increasing longevity (people are living longer).

In the United States, the ranks of the elderly will swell even more rapidly as the first of the baby boomers—some 75 million strong—reach age sixty-five in 2011. As recent political debate shows, there are serious questions about the ability of the current Social Security system to meet the needs of so many older people.

 Find information on aging and older people at the National Institute on Aging Web site: http://www.nia.nih.gov/

THE BIRTH RATE: GOING DOWN

The birth rate in the United States has been falling for more than a century. This is the usual trend as societies industrialize. Because children are more likely to survive into adulthood, couples bear fewer children. In addition, although children are an economic asset to farming families, they are an economic liability to families in industrial societies. In other words, children no longer add to their family's financial well-being but instead are a major expense.

Finally, as more and more women work outside the home, they choose to have fewer children. This choice is made possible by advances in birth control technology during the past century.

LIFE EXPECTANCY: GOING UP

Life expectancy in the United States is going up. In 1900, a typical female born in the United States could ex-

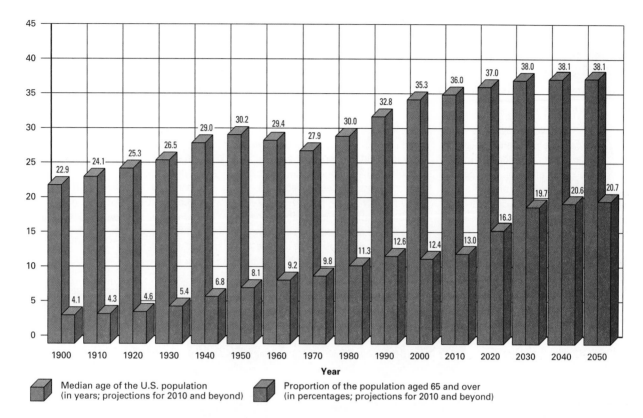

| | 1900 | 1910 | 1920 | 1930 | 1940 | 1950 | 1960 | 1970 | 1980 | 1990 | 2000 | 2010 | 2020 | 2030 | 2040 | 2050 |

Median age: 22.9, 24.1, 25.3, 26.5, 29.0, 30.2, 29.4, 27.9, 30.0, 32.8, 35.3, 36.0, 37.0, 38.0, 38.1, 38.1

Proportion aged 65 and over: 4.1, 4.3, 4.6, 5.4, 6.8, 8.1, 9.2, 9.8, 11.3, 12.6, 12.4, 13.0, 16.3, 19.7, 20.6, 20.7

Year

■ Median age of the U.S. population
(in years; projections for 2010 and beyond)

■ Proportion of the population aged 65 and over
(in percentages; projections for 2010 and beyond)

FIGURE 15-1 The Graying of U.S. Society

The proportion of the U.S. population over the age of sixty-five tripled during the last century. The median age of the U.S. population has now passed thirty-five years and will continue to rise.

Source: U.S. Census Bureau (2004).

pect to live just forty-eight years, and a male, forty-six years. By contrast, females born in 2003 can look forward to living 80.1 years, and males can expect to live 74.8 years (Hoyert, Kung, & Smith, 2005).

This longer life span is one result of the Industrial Revolution. Greater material wealth and advances in medicine have raised living standards so that people benefit from better housing and nutrition. In addition, medical advances have almost eliminated infectious diseases—such as smallpox, diphtheria, and measles—that killed many infants and children a century ago. Other medical advances help us fend off cancer and heart disease, which claim most of the U.S. population, but now later in life.

As life becomes longer, the oldest segment of the U.S. population—people over eighty-five—is increasing rapidly and is already forty times greater than in 1900. These men and women now number 4.9 million (about 1.7 percent of the total population). Their numbers will grow to

almost 21 million (about 5 percent of the total) by the year 2050 (U.S. Census Bureau, 2004).

This major increase in the elderly population will change our society in many ways. As the number of older people retiring from the labor force goes up, the proportion of nonworking adults— already about ten times greater than in 1900— will demand ever more health care and other resources. The ratio of working-age adults to nonworking elderly people, called the *old-age dependency ratio,* will fall from the current level of five to one to about three to one by the year 2050. With fewer and fewer workers to support tomorrow's swelling elderly population, what security can today's young people expect in their old age? The Thinking Globally box on page 396 takes a closer look at a country where the graying of the population is taking place even faster than in the United States: Japan.

A U.S. Department of Agriculture report on the effects of aging in rural communities is found at http://www.ers.usda. gov/publications/rdrr90/ rdrr90.pdf

Can Too Many Be Too Old? A Report from Japan

With an average age of forty-one, the population of Japan is among the oldest in the world. One cause of the aging Japanese population is a declining birth rate, which has fallen to just 1.3 children born for every woman. A second cause of Japan's aging population is increasing life expectancy. Girls born in Japan in 2004 can expect to live, on average, 85 years, and boys can expect to live 78 years.

Looking ahead, Japan's future population patterns alarm many people. First, the low birth rate means that Japan's population is now decreasing and will fall from 127 million today to about 110 million by 2050. Second, by 2050, half the Japanese population will be older than fifty-three. This means that the country's labor force will shrink by millions of people, which could reduce the country's economic output

and dramatically lower living standards. Third, the Japanese worry about how they will support their growing population of seniors. Today, there are three workers for every person over sixty-five. By 2050, the old-age dependency ratio will fall to about one to one. At this point, elderly people would not receive nearly as much income as they currently enjoy.

The importance of the Japanese case is that it is not unique. Other

nations, including Italy and Spain, have populations almost as old as Japan's, and by 2050, they will face the same problems. The United States is among the "youngest" of the high-income countries. But what happens elsewhere will happen here, too. It is just a matter of time.

WHAT DO YOU THINK?

1. Living longer is generally thought to be a good thing. What are some of the problems that come with an aging population?
2. When a nation's average age passes fifty, what changes to popular culture might you expect?
3. How might immigration be a strategy to raise the old-age dependency ratio?

Source: Based on E. Porter (2004).

AN AGING SOCIETY: CULTURAL CHANGE

As the average age of the population rises and the share over age sixty-five climbs ever higher, cultural patterns are likely to change. Through much of the twentieth century, the young rarely mixed with the old, so that most people learned little about old age. But as this country's elderly population steadily increases, age segregation will decline. Younger people will see more seniors on the highways, at shopping malls, in movie theaters, and at sporting events. In addition, the design of buildings—including homes, stores, stadiums, and college classrooms—is likely to change to ease access for older shoppers, sports fans, and students.

Of course, the extent of contact with older people depends a great deal on where in the country you live. This is because the elderly represent a far greater share of the population in some regions, especially in the midsection, from

North Dakota and Minnesota down to Texas. National Map 15–1 looks at the residential patterns of people aged sixty-five and older.

When thinking about how an aging population will change our ways of life, keep in mind that seniors are socially diverse. Being "elderly" is a category open to everyone, if we are lucky enough to live that long. Elders in the United States are women and men of all classes, races, and ethnic backgrounds.

YOUR TURN

In what specific ways would colleges and universities change if more older people were to take part in campus life?

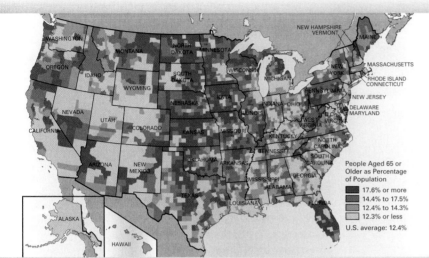

SEEING OURSELVES

NATIONAL MAP 15–1

The Elderly Population
across the United States

Common sense suggests that elderly people live in
the Sunbelt, enjoying the warmer climate of the
South and Southwest. Although it is true that
Florida has a disproportionate share of people over
age sixty-five, it turns out that most counties with
high percentages of older people are in the Midwest. What do you think accounts for this pattern?
Hint: Which regions of the United States do
younger people leave in search of jobs?

Source: U.S. Census Bureau (2001).

THE "YOUNG OLD" AND THE "OLD OLD"

Analysts sometimes distinguish two cohorts of the elderly, roughly equal in size (Himes, 2001). The younger elderly are between sixty-five and seventy-five and typically live independently with good health and financial security; they are likely to be living as couples. The older elderly are past age seventy-five and are more likely to have health and money problems and to be dependent on others. Because of their greater longevity, women outnumber men in the elderly population, an imbalance that grows greater with advancing age. Among the "oldest old," those over age eighty-five, 69 percent are women.

Growing Old: Biology and Culture

Studying the graying of a society's population is the focus of **gerontology** (derived from the Greek word *geron,* meaning "an old person"), *the study of aging and the elderly.* Gerontologists—who work in many disciplines, including medicine, psychology, and sociology—investigate not only how people change as they grow old but also the different ways in which societies around the world define old age.

BIOLOGICAL CHANGES

Aging consists of gradual, ongoing changes in the body. But how we experience life's transitions—whether we welcome our maturity or complain about physical decline—depends largely on how our cultural system defines the various stages of life. In general, U.S. culture takes a positive view of biological changes that occur early in life. Through childhood and

adolescence, people look forward to expanding opportunities and responsibilities.

But today's youth-oriented culture takes a dimmer view of the biological changes that happen later on. Few people receive congratulations for getting old, at least not until they reach eighty-five or ninety. Rather, we offer sympathy to friends as they turn forty, fifty, and sixty and make jokes to avoid facing up to the fact that advancing age will put us all on a slippery slope of physical and mental decline. In short, we assume that by age fifty or sixty, people stop growing *up* and begin growing *down.*

Growing old brings on predictable changes: gray hair, wrinkles, height and weight loss, and declining strength and vitality. After age fifty, bones become more brittle, so injuries take longer to heal, and the odds of developing chronic illnesses (such as arthritis and diabetes) and life-threatening conditions (like heart disease and cancer) rise. The senses—taste, sight, touch, smell, and especially hearing—become less sharp with age (Treas, 1995; Metz & Miner, 1998).

Though health becomes more fragile with advancing age, most older people are not disabled by their physical condition. Only about one in ten seniors reports trouble walking, and fewer than one in five needs intensive care in a hospital or nursing home. No more than 1 percent of the elderly are bedridden. Overall, only 26 percent of people over age sixty-five characterize their health as "fair" or "poor"; 74 percent consider their overall condition "good" or "excellent." In fact, the share of seniors reporting good or excellent health is going up (Lethbridge-Cejku & Vickerie, 2005).

Of course, some elders have better health than others. Health problems are more common among people over age seventy-five. In addition, because women typically live

The reality of growing old is as much a matter of culture as it is of biology. In the United States, being elderly often means being inactive; yet in many other countries of the world, elders often continue many familiar and productive routines.

longer than men, they suffer more from chronic disabilities like arthritis. Well-to-do people also fare better because they live and work in safer and more healthful environments and can afford better medical care. Almost 80 percent of elderly people with incomes over $35,000 assess their own health as "excellent" or "good," but that figure drops below half for people with incomes under $20,000. Lower income and stress linked to prejudice and discrimination also explain why 60 percent of older African Americans assess their health in positive terms, compared to 75 percent of elderly white people (Feagin, 1997; U.S. Federal Agency on Aging-Related Statistics, 2005).

PSYCHOLOGICAL CHANGES

Just as we tend to overstate the physical problems of old age, we sometimes exaggerate the psychological changes that accompany growing old. The common view about intelligence over the life course can be summed up as "What goes up must come down."

If we measure skills like sensorimotor coordination—the ability to arrange objects to match a drawing—we do find a steady decline after midlife. The ability to learn new material and to think quickly also decline, although not until around age seventy. But the ability to apply familiar ideas holds steady with advancing age, and the capacity for thoughtful reflection and spiritual growth actually increases (Baltes & Schaie, 1974; Metz & Miner, 1998).

We all wonder if we will think or feel differently as we get older. Gerontologists report that for better or worse, the answer is usually no. The most common personality changes with advancing age are becoming less materialistic, more mellow in attitudes, and more thoughtful. Generally, two elderly people who were childhood friends would recognize in each other the same personality traits that brought them together as youngsters (Neugarten, 1977; Wolfe, 1994).

AGING AND CULTURE

November 1, Kandy, Sri Lanka. Our little van struggles up the steep mountain incline. Breaks in the lush vegetation offer spectacular views that interrupt our conversation about growing old. "Then there are no old-age homes in your country?" I ask. "In Colombo and other cities, I am sure," our driver responds, "but not many. We are not like you Americans." "And how is that?" I counter, stiffening a bit. His eyes remain fixed on the road: "We would not leave our fathers and mothers to live alone."

When do people grow old? How do younger people regard society's oldest members? How do elderly people view themselves? The answers people give to these questions vary from society to society, showing that although aging is a biological process, it is also a matter of culture.

How long and how well people live depend, first, on a society's technology and standard of living. Through most of human history, as the English philosopher Thomas Hobbes (1588–1679) put it, people's lives were "nasty, brutish, and short" (although Hobbes himself made it to the ripe old age of ninety-one). In his day, most people married and had children as teenagers, became middle-aged in their twenties, and died from various illnesses in their thirties and forties. Many great men and women never reached what we would call old age at all: The English poet Keats died at age twenty-six; Mozart, the Austrian composer, at thirty-five. Among famous writers, none of the three Brontë sisters lived to the end of her thirties; Edgar Allan Poe died at forty, Henry David Thoreau at forty-five, Oscar Wilde at forty-six, and Shakespeare at fifty-two.

By about 1900, however, rising living standards and advancing medical technology in the United States and West-

For a report on aging in global perspective, go to http://www.census.gov/prod/2001pubs/p95-01-1.pdf

ern Europe had extended longevity to about age fifty. As Global Map 15–1 on page 400 shows, this is still the figure in many low-income countries today. In high-income nations, however, increasing affluence has added almost thirty more years to the average life span.

Just as important as longevity is the value societies attach to their senior members. As Chapter 10 ("Social Stratification") explains, all societies distribute basic resources unequally. We now turn to the importance of age in this process.

AGE STRATIFICATION: A GLOBAL SURVEY

Like race, ethnicity, and gender, age is a basis for social ranking. **Age stratification** is *the unequal distribution of wealth, power, and privilege among people at different stages of the life course.* Age stratification varies according to a society's level of technological development.

Hunting and Gathering Societies

As Chapter 4 ("Society") explains, without the technology to produce a surplus of food, hunters and gatherers must be nomadic. This means that survival depends on physical strength and stamina. As members of these societies grow old (in this case, about age thirty), they become less active and may even be considered an economic burden and, when food is in short supply, abandoned (Sheehan, 1976).

Pastoral, Horticultural, and Agrarian Societies

Once societies develop the technology to raise their own crops and animals, they produce a surplus. In such societies, some individuals build up considerable wealth over a lifetime. Of all age categories, the most privileged are typically the elderly, a pattern called **gerontocracy,** *a form of social organization in which the elderly have the most wealth, power, and prestige.* Old people, particularly men, are honored and sometimes feared by their families, and they remain active leaders of society until they die. This respect for the elderly also explains the widespread practice of ancestor worship in agrarian societies.

Industrial and Postindustrial Societies

Industrialization pushes living standards upward and advances medical technology, both of which increase human life expectancy. But although industrialization adds to the *quantity* of life, it can harm the *quality* of life for older people. Contrary to the practice in traditional societies, industrial societies give little power and prestige to the elderly. The reason is that with industrialization, the prime source of wealth shifts from land (typically controlled by the oldest members of society) to businesses and other goods (usually owned and managed by younger people). For all low-income nations, 76 percent of men and 44 percent of women over the age of sixty-five remain in the labor force. In high-income countries, these percentages are far smaller: 23 percent of men and 16 percent of women. The fact that older people move out of the paid labor force is one reason that the peak earning years among U.S. workers is about age fifty, after which earnings decline (United Nations Population Division, 1999; U.S. Census Bureau, 2005).

In high-income countries, younger people move away from their parents to pursue their careers, depending less on their parents and more on their own earning power. In addition, because industrial, urban societies change rapidly, the skills, traditions, and life experiences that served the old may seem unimportant to the young. Finally, the tremendous productivity of industrial nations means that not all members of a society need to work, so most of the very old and the very young play nonproductive roles.

The long-term effect of all these factors transforms *elders* (a word with positive connotations) into *the elderly* (a term that carries far less prestige). In postindustrial societies such as the United States and Canada, economic and political leaders are usually people between the ages of forty and sixty who combine experience with up-to-date skills. Even as the U.S. population, on average, is getting older, the country's corporate executives are getting younger—declining from an average age of fifty-nine in 1980 to fifty-five today (Herring, 2005).

In rapidly changing sectors of the economy, especially the high-tech fields, many key executives are younger still, sometimes barely out of college. Industrial societies often give older people only marginal participation in the economy because they lack the knowledge and training demanded in a fast-changing marketplace.

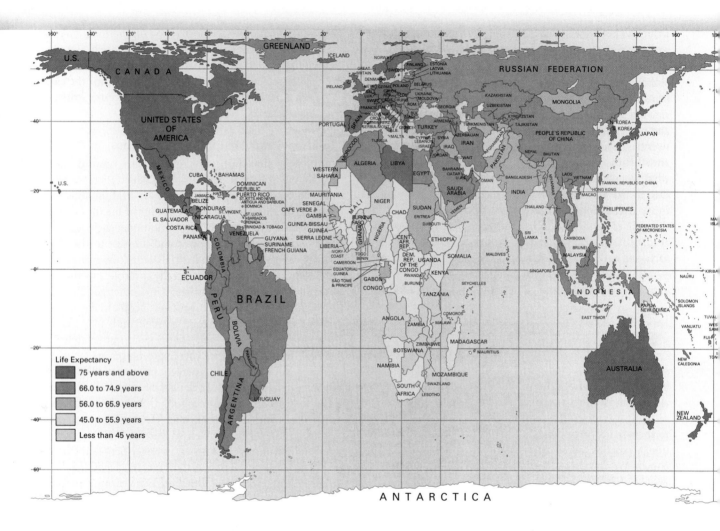

WINDOW ON THE WORLD

GLOBAL MAP 15–1   Life Expectancy in Global Perspective

Life expectancy shot upward over the course of the twentieth century in high-income countries, including Canada, the United States, Western Europe, Japan, and Australia. A newborn in the United States can now expect to live about seventy-seven years, and our life expectancy would be greater still were it not for the high risk of death among infants born into poverty. Because poverty is the rule in much of the world, lives are correspondingly shorter, especially in parts of Africa, where life expectancy may be less than forty years.

Source: Population Reference Bureau (2005).

Some occupations are dominated by older people. The average farmer is fifty-three; the average age of the entire U.S. labor force is only thirty-nine. More than one-third of today's farmers are over the age of sixty-five. Older people also predominate in other traditional occupations, working as barbers, tailors, and shop clerks, and in jobs that involve minimal physical activity, such as night security guards (Yudelman & Kealy, 2000).

Our society is sometimes described as a "youth culture." Do you agree? Explain your answer.

Japan: An Exceptional Case

Throughout the last century, Japan stood out as an exception to the rule that industrialization lowers the social standing of older people. Not only is the share of seniors in Japan increasing as fast as anywhere in the world, but Japan's more traditional culture gives older people great importance. Most elders in Japan live with an adult daughter or son, and they play a significant role in family life. Elderly men in Japan are also more likely than their U.S. counterparts to stay in the labor force, and in many Japanese corporations, the oldest employees enjoy the greatest respect. But Japan is becoming more like other industrial nations, where growing old means giving up some measure of social importance. In addition, a long economic downturn has left Japanese families less able to care for their older members, which may further weaken the traditional importance of elders (Yates, 1986; Ogawa & Retherford, 1997).

Transitions and Challenges of Aging

We confront change at each stage of life. Old age has its rewards, but of all stages of the life course, it presents the greatest challenges.

Physical decline in old age is less serious than most younger people think. But even so, older people endure pain, limit their activities, increase their dependency on others, lose dear friends and relatives, and face up to their own mortality. Because our culture places such a high value on youthfulness, aging in the United States often means added fear and self-doubt. As one retired psychologist commented about old age, "Don't let the current hype about the joys of retirement fool you. They are not the best of times. It's just that the alternative is even worse" (Rubenstein, 1991).

 Find data on the well-being of the U.S. elderly population at http://www.agingstats.gov

FINDING MEANING

Chapter 5 ("Socialization") presented Erik Erikson's (1963, orig. 1950; 1980) theory that elderly people must resolve a tension of "integrity versus despair." No matter how much they still may be learning and achieving, older people recognize that their lives are nearing an end. Thus elderly people spend more time reflecting on their past, remembering disappointments as well as accomplishments. Integrity, to Erikson, means assessing your life realistically. Without such honesty, this stage of life may turn into a time of despair—a dead end with little positive meaning.

In a classic study of people in their seventies, Bernice Neugarten (1971) found that some people cope with growing

TABLE 15–1

Living Arrangements of the Elderly, 2003

	Men	Women
Living alone	18.8%	39.7%
Living with spouse	71.2	41.1
Living with other relatives or nonrelatives	10.0	19.2

In 2000, 4.5 percent of elderly people lived in nursing homes. This number includes people from all of the above categories.

Sources: U.S. Census Bureau (2001, 2004).

older better than others. Worst off are those who fail to come to terms with aging; they develop *disintegrated and disorganized personalities* marked by despair. Many of these people end up as passive residents of hospitals or nursing homes.

Slightly better off are people with *passive-dependent personalities.* They have little confidence in their abilities to cope with daily events, sometimes seeking help even if they do not really need it. Always in danger of social withdrawal, their level of life satisfaction is relatively low.

A third category develop *defended personalities,* living independently but fearful of aging. They try to shield themselves from the reality of old age by fighting to stay youthful and physically fit. Although it is good to be concerned about health, setting unrealistic standards breeds stress and disappointment.

Most of Neugarten's subjects, however, displayed what she termed *integrated personalities,* coping well with the challenges of growing old. As Neugarten sees it, the key to successful aging lies in keeping personal dignity and self-confidence while accepting growing old.

SOCIAL ISOLATION

Being alone can cause anxiety at any age, but isolation is most common among elderly people. Retirement closes off one source of social interaction, physical problems may limit mobility, and negative stereotypes of the elderly as "over the hill" may discourage younger people from close social contact with them.

But the greatest cause of social isolation is the death of significant others, especially the death of a spouse. One study found that almost three-fourths of widows and widowers cited loneliness as their most serious problem (Lund, 1989).

The problem of social isolation falls more heavily on women because they typically outlive their husbands. Table 15–1 shows that 70 percent of men aged sixty-five and

January 30, 2005

Under One Roof, Aging Together Yet Alone

By JANE GROSS

STRATFORD, Conn., Jan. 28—Everyone complains about the food. Nobody wants to sit with the misfits. There are leaders and followers, social butterflies and loners, goody-goodies and trouble-makers. Friendships are intense and so are rivalries. Everybody knows everybody else's business.

Except for the traffic jam of wheel-chairs and walkers, the dining room at the Atria assisted living community here might as well be a high school cafeteria.

Mary Mercandante, 88, has an expla-nation for the restive, gossipy environ-ment when old people are forced to live under one roof, even in a top-notch place like this. "Nobody wants to be here," said Mrs. Mercandante....

When introduced in the mid-1980s in the United States, assisted living was hailed as a dignified alternative to nurs-ing homes.... The monthly costs, which

average $2,524 nationwide and thou-sands of dollars more here in Connecti-cut's wealthiest county, include a common dining room, transportation, housekeeping, activities meant to relieve isolation, and à la carte services for changing personal care and medical needs. In the last decade the number of elderly Americans in assisted living has tripled, to nearly one million, and indus-try experts say the residents, overwhelm-ingly widowed women with an average age of 85, have steadily grown older and frailer. A study by the National Center for Assisted Living, an industry group, shows that half the residents have some degree of cognitive impairment, three-quarters need help bathing, 8 in 10 can-not administer their own medication and more than 90 percent can no longer cook or do housework....

Only a few sociologists and public health researchers have studied the social organization and daily preoccupations

of these communities. Dr. Catherine Hawes, a professor of health policy at Texas A&M University, is one. She de-scribes them as "high school all over again, without the expectations." ...

This stage in life, experts agree, is bleaker than most Americans admit. Humbled by the loss of control and fearful of the future, many older peo-ple complain incessantly, most often about the food. Also, in a cruel sorting process, they ostracize others more im-paired than themselves. The hierarchy by disability "is really fear," said David Vail, executive director of Atria Strat-ford and president of the Connecticut Assisted Living Association, an industry group. "They don't want to look at what they might become." Both the cranki-ness and the cliques are on view in the dining room of the Atria Stratford, home to 120 residents, many of whom good-humoredly call themselves "in-mates." But also on view are acts of

over live with spouses, but only 40 percent of elderly women do. In addition, 40 percent of older women (especially the "older elderly") live alone, compared to 19 percent of older men (U.S. Census Bureau, 2004).

For most older people, family members are the major source of social support. The majority of U.S. seniors have at least one adult child living no more than 10 miles away. About half of these nearby children visit their parents at least once a week, although much research confirms that daughters are more likely than sons to visit regularly (Lin & Rogerson, 1994; Rimer, 1998).

Social isolation is not always a matter of physically being by yourself. "In the *Times*" describes the experiences of aging women and men in an assisted living facility who, although living in the company of others, often feel very alone.

RETIREMENT

Work provides us not only with earnings but also with an important part of our personal identity. Therefore, retire-ment means not only a reduction in income but also less so-cial prestige and perhaps some loss of purpose in life.

Some organizations help ease this transition. Colleges and universities, for example, confer the title "professor emeritus" (*emeritus* is from the Latin, meaning "fully earned") on retired fac-ulty members, many of whom are permitted to keep library privileges, a parking space, and an e-mail account. These highly experi-enced faculty can be a valuable resource not only to stu-dents but to younger professors as well (Parini, 2001).

 Visit the Administration on Aging Web site to learn about programs and services related to aging: http://www.aoa.gov

exceptional kindness, budding friendships and sparks of romance between flirtatious women who dress for dinner and chivalrous men who hold their chairs. . . .

Leaving an assisted living community, on average after two and a half years, is rarely voluntary. Three residents died at Atria Stratford in December. Others, when their assets are gone, will go to nursing homes, which charge 40 percent more on average but accept government reimbursement. . . .

Most states in the last few years have begun small, experimental programs that permit Medicaid to pay a portion of the cost of assisted living: the personal care and medical services that are tacked on to the monthly charge, but not the rent itself. . . .

Statewide, Mr. Vail said, there are 9,800 assisted living units and only 75 Medicaid waiver slots. So he advises families to calculate when their money will

run out and move before that point, since nursing homes, if they have a high enough percentage of Medicaid patients, can push those with assets to the top of the waiting list.

Pat Jordan, 94, whose wife died here last year . . . , is a charmer. His arrival in the country kitchen or the arts and crafts room brings a blush to the faces of at least two women. . . .

"But I have no love interest in anyone. I don't think my Florence would like it." But Colleen Douglas, the activity director, has not given up hope. . . .

Mr. Jordan is her best shot at every activity director's dream: a wedding. "Nobody wants a romance in this building more than I do," Ms. Douglas said. "So if I'm moving in a woman who still has her mind and walks, I go to Mr. Jordan. So far he's still mourning his wife. But I'll keep trying."

Adapted from the original article by Jane Gross published in *The New York Times* on January 30, 2005. Copyright © 2005 by The New York Times Company. Reprinted with permission.

WHAT DO YOU THINK?

1. The facility described in this article is among the best in the country. Why are some people there not very happy?

2. Given that the average cost of an assisted living facility is $30,000 per year, what share of the U.S. population is likely to even consider living in such a place?

3. Given the problems described in this assisted living facility, what do you imagine is the experience of older people living in less desirable nursing homes?

Because seniors are socially diverse, there is no single formula for successful retirement. Part-time work occupies many people entering old age and provides some extra cash as well. Grandparenting is an enormous source of pleasure for many older people. Volunteer work is another path to rewarding activity, especially for those who have saved enough so that they do not have to work—one reason that volunteerism is increasing more among seniors than in any other age category (Gardyn, 2000; Savishinsky, 2000; Shapiro, 2001).

Although retirement is a familiar idea, the concept developed only within the past century or so in high-income countries. High-income societies are so productive that not everyone needs to work; in addition, advanced technology places a premium on up-to-date skills. Therefore, retirement emerged as a strategy to permit younger workers—

presumably, those with the most current knowledge and training—to have the largest presence in the labor force. Fifty years ago, most companies in the United States even had a mandatory retirement age, typically between sixty-five and seventy, although Congress enacted laws phasing out such policies in the 1970s so that few exist today (one exception is airline pilots, who must stop flying before they turn sixty). In high-income countries, private and public pension programs make it financially possible for older people to retire, an opportunity that does not exist for most people living in poor nations.

At the same time, retirement patterns reflect the health of the national economy. Generally speaking, when economic times are good, people save more and think about retiring early. Such has been the case in the United States: As the economy expanded during the 1980s and 1990s, more

APPLYING SOCIOLOGY

Back to Work! Will We Ever Get to Retire?

Old age was looking like the "golden years" for sixty-year-old Martha Perry. She had worked hard for decades, and it had paid off. The sale of her small business, added to years of regular savings, netted her a total of about $1 million. With additional income from Social Security, Perry figured she was set for the rest of her life. She looked forward to playing golf, enjoying an active social life, and traveling around the world.

That was before the stock market tumble that began in 2000. Two years later, her accountant gave her some bad news: Her nest egg had lost almost half its value. With barely half the income she expected—only about $16,000 a year—Perry's travel plans have been put on hold. "I'm going to have to look for part-time work," she says, shaking her head. "But something tells me it's going to end up being full-time work."

The recent recession has hit everyone hard, but older people who rely on investment income have suffered more than most. Many have seen their retirement vanish as quickly as the money in their 401(k) investment portfolios. Like millions of others, Martha Perry is reading the want ads.

This trend helps explain why the share of older people in the labor force has changed direction and is now going up. Certainly, some seniors are happy to continue their careers, and others enjoy working part time. But in the past, many did so by choice, enjoying their jobs but knowing they could retire whenever they wanted to. Now people fear they no longer have a choice. Worse, they wonder whether they will ever be able to step out of the labor force. For those who do not like the

SOCIOLOGY WORK

jobs they have, of course, the future will be far less happy.

All economic downturns come to an end. But analysts caution that investment gains are unlikely to return to the double-digit levels of the 1990s anytime soon. The bottom line: less talk about "early retirement" and more older people in the workforce.

WHAT DO YOU THINK?

1. What is the relationship between how well the economy is doing and people's retirement plans?
2. Why does "phased retirement" for many older people really mean "delayed retirement"?
3. Do you know anyone who has had a pension reduced or cancelled by a corporation? How has that affected the person's financial security?

Source: Kadlec (2002).

people retired earlier, causing the median retirement age to fall from sixty-eight in 1950 to sixty-three by 2000. The economic downturn that began in 2000 has had the opposite effect: Today we hear talk about "staged retirement," in which people continue working well past the age of sixty-five, reducing their hours as they build greater financial security. Even the mandatory retirement age of airline pilots may be pushed back (Kadlec, 2002; McCartney, 2005).

Some retired people, faced with declining value of their investments, are realizing that to make ends meet, they may have to go back to work. The Applying Sociology box takes a closer look.

AGING AND POVERTY

By the time they reach sixty-five, most people have paid off their home mortgages and their children's college expenses. But the costs of medical care, household help, and home

utilities (like heat) typically go up. At the same time, retirement often means a significant decline in income. Even so, today's seniors have more wealth than ever before, with a median net worth of about $160,000 in 2000. Most of this amount is in the value of their home, however, and many do not have enough savings or pension benefits to be self-supporting (Himes, 2001). For most people over age sixty-five, the major source of income is Social Security. Not surprisingly, then, the risk of poverty rises after midlife, as shown in Figure 15–2.

The poverty rate among the elderly fell sharply from about 35 percent in 1960 to 9.8 percent in 2004—below the 12.7 percent rate for the entire population. Since about 1980, seniors have posted a 35 percent increase in average income (in constant dollars), double the increase in income of people under thirty-five (U.S. Census Bureau, 2005).

Several factors have boosted the financial strength of seniors. Better health now allows people who want to work to stay in the labor force, and more of today's couples earn two incomes. Government policy, too, has played a part; programs benefiting the elderly (including Social Security) amount to almost half of all government spending, even as spending on children has remained flat. Even so, some people have lost some of the pension income they were counting on, and more workers are not receiving pension benefits at all.

Disadvantages linked to race and ethnicity persist in old age. In 2004, the poverty rate among elderly Hispanics (18.7 percent) and African Americans (23.9 percent) was two to three times higher than the rate for elderly, non-Hispanic whites (8.3 percent) (U.S. Census Bureau, 2005).

Gender also shapes the lives of people as they age. Among full-time workers, women over sixty-five had median earnings of $26,640 in 2004, compared to $37,378 for men over sixty-five. A quick calculation shows that these older full-time working women earned just 71 percent as much as comparable men. Thus the income gap linked to gender is greater among older people than among younger people (recall from Chapter 13 that *all* working women earn 77 percent as much as *all* working men). This is because older women typically have much less schooling than men their age, so they hold lower-paying jobs.

But because most elderly people have retired from the labor force, a more realistic financial picture must take account of all seniors. When we include both those who are working and those who are not, median individual income is far lower: $11,789 for women, which is 57 percent of the $20,527 earned by men (U.S. Census Bureau, 2005). In light of these low averages, it is easy to see why seniors are concerned about the costs of health care and prescription drugs, which are rising fast and may double by 2010 (Fetto, 2003a).

In the United States, although the elderly are doing better than in the past, growing old (especially for women and other minorities) still increases the risk of poverty. One study found that poor elderly households typically spend three-fourths of their income on basic necessities, which means that these people are just getting by (Koelln, Rubin, & Picard, 1995).

Finally, poverty among the elderly is often hidden from view. Because of personal pride and a desire to remain independent, many elderly people hide financial problems, even from their own families. People who have supported their children for years find it difficult to admit that they can no longer provide for themselves.

CAREGIVING

In an aging society, the need for caregiving is bound to increase. **Caregiving** refers to *informal and unpaid care provided to a dependent person by family members, other relatives, or friends.* Although parents provide caregiving to children, the term is more often applied to the needs of

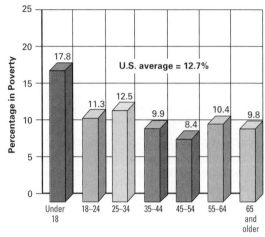

DIVERSITY SNAPSHOT

FIGURE 15-2 U.S. Poverty Rates, by Age, 2004

The highest poverty rate is for young people. But among older people, the rate rises once again.

Source: U.S. Census Bureau (2005).

elderly men and women. Indeed, today's middle-aged adults are called the "sandwich generation" because many will spend as much time caring for their aging parents as for their own children.[1]

Who Are the Caregivers?

Surveys show that 80 percent of caregiving to elders is provided by family members, in most cases by one person. Most caregivers live close to the older person. In addition, 75 percent of all caregiving is provided by women, most often daughters and, next, wives. The gender norm is so strong that daughters-in-law are more likely than sons to care for an aging parent (Himes, 2001).

About two-thirds of caregivers are married, and one-third are also responsible for young children. When we add the fact that half of all caregivers also have a part- or full-time job, it is clear that caregiving is a responsibility over and above what most people already consider a full day's work. Half of all primary caregivers spend more than twenty hours per week providing elder care.

_____

[1]This discussion of caregiving is based on Lund (1993) and additional information provided by Dale Lund.

Elder Abuse

Abuse of older people takes many forms, from passive neglect to active torment; it includes verbal, emotional, financial, and physical harm. About 1 to 2 million elderly people (3 percent) suffer serious maltreatment each year, and three times as many (about 10 percent) suffer abuse at some point. Like other forms of family violence, abuse of the elderly often goes unreported because the victims are reluctant to talk about their plight (Holmstrom, 1994; M. Thompson, 1997, 1998; National Center on Elder Abuse, 2005).

Many caregivers deal with fatigue, emotional distress, and guilt over not being able to do more. Abuse is most likely to occur if the caregiver not only finds the work difficult but also (1) works full time, (2) cares for young children, (3) is poor, (4) feels little affection for the older person, (5) finds the elderly person very difficult, and (6) gets no support or help from others.

But the relatively small share of cases involving abuse should not overshadow the positive side of caregiving. Helping another person is a selfless act of human kindness that affirms the best in us and provides a source of personal enrichment and satisfaction (Lund, 1993).

AGEISM

In earlier chapters, we explained how ideology—including racism and sexism—serves to justify the social disadvantages of minorities. In the same way, sociologists use the term **ageism** for *prejudice and discrimination against older people.* Elderly people are the primary targets of ageism, although middle-aged people can suffer as well. Examples of ageism include passing over qualified older job applicants in favor of younger workers or, as described in the opening to this chapter, firing older workers first.

Like racism and sexism, ageism can be blatant (as when a college decides not to hire a sixty-year-old professor because of her age) or subtle (as when a nurse speaks to elderly patients in a condescending tone, as if they were children). Also like racism and sexism, ageism builds physical traits into stereotypes. In the case of the elderly, some people consider gray hair, wrinkled skin, and stooped posture signs of personal incompetence. Negative stereotypes portray the aged as helpless, confused, unable to deal with change, and generally unhappy. Even "positive" images of sweet little old ladies and eccentric old gentlemen are stereotypes that gloss over individuality and ignore years of experience and accomplishment (Butler, 1975; E. Cohen, 2001).

Sometimes ageism contains a bit of truth. Statistically speaking, older people are more likely than younger people to be mentally and physically impaired. But we slip into ageism when we make unfair generalizations about an entire category of people.

Betty Friedan (1993), a pioneer of today's feminist movement, believes ageism is deeply rooted in our culture. Friedan points out that few elderly people appear in the mass media; only a small percentage of television shows, for example, feature main characters over sixty. More generally, when most of us think about older people, it is often in negative terms: This older man *lacks* a job, that older woman has *lost* her vitality, and seniors *look back* to their youth. In short, says Friedan, we often treat being old as if it were a disease, marked by decline and deterioration, for which there is no cure.

Even so, Friedan believes that older women and men in the United States are discovering that they have more to contribute than others give them credit for. Advising small business owners, designing housing for the poor, teaching children to read—there are countless ways in which older people can help others and at the same time enhance their own lives.

YOUR TURN

On your campus, are the most popular faculty members younger instructors or older instructors? Does age play into a professor's student evaluations?

THE ELDERLY: A MINORITY?

Elderly people in the United States face social disadvantages. Does that mean that the elderly are a minority in the same way as, say, African Americans or women?

The elderly appear to meet the definition of a minority because they have a clear social identity based on their age, and they are subject to prejudice and discrimination. But Gordon Streib (1968) counters that we should not think of elderly people as a minority. First, minority status is usually both permanent and exclusive. That is, a person is an African American or a woman *for life* and cannot become part of the dominant category of whites or men. But being elderly is an *open* status because people are elderly for only part of their lives, and everyone who has the good fortune to live long enough grows old.

Second, the seniors at highest risk of being poor or otherwise disadvantaged fall into categories of people—women, African Americans, Hispanics—who are at highest risk of being poor throughout the life course. As Streib sees it, it is not so much that the old grow poor as that the poor grow old.

If so, old people are not a minority in the same sense as other categories. It might be better to say that the elderly are a part of our population that faces special challenges based on age.

→ YOUR TURN ←

Do you think elderly people should be considered a minority? Explain your position.

Theoretical Analysis of Aging

We now apply sociology's theoretical approaches to gain insight into how society shapes the lives of the elderly. We consider structural-functional, symbolic-interaction, and social-conflict approaches in turn.

STRUCTURAL-FUNCTIONAL ANALYSIS: AGING AND DISENGAGEMENT

Drawing on the ideas of Talcott Parsons—an architect of the structural-functional approach—Elaine Cumming and William Henry (1961) explain that the physical decline and death that accompany aging can disrupt society. In response, society *disengages* the elderly, gradually transferring statuses and roles from the old to the young so that tasks are performed with minimal interruption. **Disengagement theory** is *the idea that society functions in an orderly way by disengaging people from positions of responsibility as they reach old age.*

Disengagement ensures the orderly operation of society by removing aging people from productive roles before they are no longer able to perform them. Another benefit of disengagement in a rapidly changing society is that it makes room for young workers, who typically have the most up-to-date skills and training. Disengagement provides benefits to aging people as well. Although most sixty-year-olds in the United States wish to keep working, most begin to think about retirement and perhaps cut back a bit on their workload. Exactly when people begin to disengage from their careers, of course, depends on their health, enjoyment of the job, and financial situation.

Retiring does not mean being inactive. Some people start a new career or a different job, while others pursue hobbies or engage in volunteer work. In general, people in their sixties start to think less about what they *have been doing* and begin to think more about what they *want to do*

In the United States, it is common for businesses to offer a "senior discount" to people over sixty-five (or sometimes even fifty-five). What is the reason for this practice? Would you prefer a policy of offering discounts to single parents with children, a category of people at much higher risk of poverty?

with the rest of their lives (Palmore, 1979; Schultz & Heckhausen, 1996; Voltz, 2000).

Critical review   Disengagement theory explains why rapidly changing high-income societies tend to define their oldest members as socially marginal. But there are several limitations to this approach.

First, especially in recent years, many workers have found they cannot disengage from paid work because they need the income. Second, some elderly people—whether they are rich or poor—simply do not want to disengage from work they enjoy. Disengagement may also mean losing friends and social prestige. Third, it is not clear that the societal benefits of disengagement outweigh its social costs, which include the loss of human resources and the need to take care of people who might otherwise be able to support themselves. As the numbers of elderly people swell, finding ways to help seniors remain independent is a high priority. Fourth, any rigid system of disengagement does not take account of the widely differing abilities of the elderly. This concern leads us to the symbolic-interaction approach.

SYMBOLIC-INTERACTION ANALYSIS: AGING AND ACTIVITY

Drawing on the symbolic-interaction approach, **activity theory** is *the idea that a high level of activity increases personal satisfaction in old age.* Because everyone bases social identity on many roles, disengagement is bound to reduce satisfaction and meaning in the lives of older people. What seniors need is not to be pushed out of roles but to have many productive or recreational options. The importance of having choices is especially great for today's sixty-five-year-old, who can look forward to about twenty more years of life (T. Smart, 2001; M. W. Walsh, 2001).

Activity theory does not reject the idea of job disengagement; it simply says that people need to find new roles to replace those they leave behind. Research confirms that elderly people who maintain a high activity level find the most satisfaction in their lives.

Activity theory also recognizes that the elderly are diverse, with highly variable interests, needs, and physical abilities. For this reason, the activities that people choose and the pace at which they pursue them are always an individual matter (Neugarten, 1977; Moen, Dempster-McClain, & Williams, 1992).

Critical review Activity theory shifts the focus of analysis from the needs of society (as stated in disengagement theory) to the needs of the elderly themselves. It emphasizes the social diversity of elderly people and highlights the importance of choice in any government policy.

A limitation of this approach is that it assumes that elders are both healthy and competent, which may or may not be the case. Another problem with this approach is that it ignores the fact that many of the problems older people face—such as poverty—have more to do with society than with themselves. We turn now to that point of view: social-conflict theory.

SOCIAL-CONFLICT ANALYSIS: AGING AND INEQUALITY

A social-conflict analysis is based on the idea that access to opportunities and social resources differs for people in different age categories. For this reason, age is a dimension of social stratification. In the United States, middle-aged people enjoy the greatest power and the most opportunities and privileges, and the elderly and children have a higher risk of poverty. Employers who replace senior workers with younger men and women in order to keep wages low may not intend to discriminate against older people. However, according to recent court rulings, if such policies have the effect of causing special harm to older people, they amount to discrimination.

The social-conflict approach claims that our industrial-capitalist economy creates an age-based hierarchy. In line with Marxist thought, Steven Spitzer (1980) points out that a profit-oriented society devalues any category of people that is less productive. To the extent that older people do not work, our society labels them as mildly deviant.

Social-conflict analysis also draws attention to various dimensions of social inequality within the elderly population. Differences of class, race, ethnicity, and gender divide older people as they do everyone else. For this reason, some seniors have far greater economic security, access to better medical care, and more options for personal satisfaction in old age than others. Likewise, elderly white people typically enjoy advantages denied to older minorities. And women—an increasing majority as people age—suffer the social and economic disadvantages of both sexism and ageism.

Critical review The social-conflict approach adds to our understanding of the aging process by highlighting age-based inequality and explaining how capitalism devalues elderly people who are less productive. But critics claim that the real culprit is *industrialization*. As evidence they point to the fact that the elderly are not better off under a socialist system, as a Marxist analysis implies. Furthermore, the idea that either industrialization or capitalism necessarily causes the elderly to suffer is challenged by the long-term rise in income and well-being experienced by seniors in the United States.

Death and Dying

To every thing there is a season,
And a time for every matter under heaven:
A time to be born and a time to die . . .

These well-known lines from the biblical book of Ecclesiastes state two basic truths about human existence: the fact of birth and the inevitability of death. Just as life varies throughout history and around the world, death has many faces. We conclude this chapter with a brief look at the changing character of death, the final stage in the process of growing old.

HISTORICAL PATTERNS OF DEATH

In the past, death was a familiar part of life. Many children died soon after birth, a fact that led many parents to delay naming children until they were one or two years old. For those fortunate enough to survive infancy, illness, accidents, and natural catastrophes made life uncertain at best.

Sometimes food shortages forced societies to protect the majority by sacrificing the least productive members.

Infanticide is the killing of newborn infants, and *geronticide* is the killing of the elderly.

Because death was commonplace, it was readily accepted. Medieval Christianity assured believers that death fit into the divine plan for human existence. Here is how the historian Philippe Ariès describes Sir Lancelot, one of King Arthur's knights of the Round Table, preparing for death when he thinks he is mortally wounded:

> His gestures were fixed by old customs, ritual gestures which must be carried out when one is about to die. He removed his weapons and lay quietly upon the ground. . . . He spread his arms out, his body forming a cross . . . in such a way that his head faced east toward Jerusalem. (1974:7–8)

As societies gradually learned more about health and medicine, death became less of an everyday experience. Fewer children died at birth, and accidents and disease took a smaller toll among adults. As a result, most people living in high-income societies today view dying as extraordinary, something that happens to the very old or to younger people in rare and tragic cases. Back in 1900, about one-third of all deaths in the United States occurred before the age of five and fully two-thirds before the age of fifty-five. Today, by contrast, 85 percent of our population die *after* the age of fifty-five. Death and old age are closely linked in our culture.

In many traditional societies, people express great respect not only for elders but also for their ancestors. Dani villagers in New Guinea mummified the body of this elder in a sitting position so that they could continue to honor him and feel his presence in their daily lives.

THE MODERN SEPARATION OF LIFE AND DEATH

Now removed from everyday experience, death somehow seems unnatural. Social conditions prepared our ancestors to accept death, but modern society's youth culture and aggressive medical technology foster a desire for eternal youth and immortality. Death has become separated from life.

Death is also *physically* removed from everyday activities. The clearest evidence of this is that many of us have never seen a person die. Our ancestors typically died at home in the presence of family and friends, but most deaths today occur in impersonal settings such as hospitals and nursing homes. Even in hospitals, dying patients occupy a special part of the building, and hospital morgues are located well out of sight of patients and visitors alike (Ariès, 1974; Lee, 2002).

YOUR TURN

Ask members of your class if they have ever seen a person die. Does the response support the idea that modern society separates death from life?

ETHICAL ISSUES: CONFRONTING DEATH

In a society in which technology gives us the power to prolong life, moral questions about when and how people should die are more pressing than ever. For example, the national debate in 2005 surrounding the death of Terri Schiavo, kept alive by mechanical means for fifteen years, was not just about the fate of one woman; many people feel we need a better understanding of what the "right to die" rules should be.

When Does Death Occur?

Perhaps the most basic question is the most difficult: Exactly how do we define death? Common sense suggests that life ceases when breathing and heartbeat stop. But the ability of medical personnel to resuscitate someone after a heart attack and artificially sustain breathing makes such definitions of death obsolete. Medical and legal experts in the United States continue to debate the meaning of death, but many now consider death an *irreversible* state involving no response to stimulation, no movement or breathing, no reflexes, and no indication of brain activity (Wall, 1980; D. G. Jones, 1998).

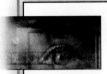

THINKING CRITICALLY

Death on Demand: Euthanasia in the Netherlands

Marcus Erich picked up the telephone and called his brother Arjen. In a quiet voice, thirty-two-year-old Marcus announced, "It's Friday at five o'clock." When the time came, Arjen was there, having driven to his brother's farmhouse an hour south of Amsterdam. They said their final good-byes. Soon afterward, Marcus's physician arrived. Marcus and the doctor spoke for a few moments, and then the doctor prepared a "cocktail" of barbiturates and other drugs. As Marcus drank the mixture, he made a face, joking, "Can't you make this sweeter?"

As the minutes passed, Marcus lay back and his eyes closed. But after half an hour, he was still breathing. At that point, according to their earlier agreement, the physician administered a lethal injection. Minutes later, Marcus's life came to an end.

Events like this take us to the heart of the belief that people have a "right

to die." Marcus Erich was dying from the virus that causes AIDS. For five years, his body had been wasting away, and he was suffering greatly with no hope of recovery. He wanted his doctor to end his life.

The Netherlands, a small nation in northwestern Europe, has gone further than any other in the world in allowing mercy killing, or euthanasia. A 1981 Dutch law allows a physician to assist in a suicide if the following five conditions are met:

1. The patient must make a voluntary, well-considered, and repeated request to a doctor for help in dying.

2. The patient's suffering must be unbearable and without prospect of improvement.

3. The doctor and the patient must discuss alternatives.

4. The doctor must consult with at least one colleague who has access

to the patient and the patient's medical records.

5. The assisted suicide must be performed in accordance with sound medical practice.

Official records indicate that doctors end 3,000 to 4,000 lives per year in the Netherlands. But because many cases are never reported, the actual number may be as much as double that.

WHAT DO YOU THINK?

1. What advantages and benefits do you see in the Dutch law permitting physician-assisted suicide?

2. What are the disadvantages or dangers of such a law?

3. Overall, do you support or oppose such a law? Explain your position.

Sources: Based on della Cava (1997) and Mauro (1997).

The Right-to-Die Debate

Terri Schiavo remained alive without evidence of being conscious or responsive to her surroundings for fifteen years following a heart attack that cut off blood to her brain. Debate surrounding this case, which ended when her feeding tube was removed, shows that many people are less afraid of death than of the prospect of being kept alive at all costs. In other words, medical technology that can sustain life also threatens personal freedom by letting doctors or others rather than the dying person decide when life is to end. In response, people who support a right-to-die movement now seek control over their deaths just as they seek control over their lives (Ogden, 2001).

After thoughtful discussion, patients, families, and physicians may decide not to take "heroic measures" to keep a person alive. Physicians and family members may decide to issue a "do not resuscitate" order, which will allow a

patient to die. *Living wills*—documents stating which medical procedures an individual wants and does not want under specific conditions—are now widely used.

A more difficult issue involves mercy killing, or **euthanasia**—*assisting in the death of a person suffering from an incurable disease.* Euthanasia (from the Greek, meaning "a good death") poses an ethical dilemma because it involves not just refusing treatment but actively taking steps to end life. Some people see euthanasia as an act of kindness, while others consider it a form of murder.

Is there a right to die? People with incurable diseases can choose not to have treatment that might prolong their lives. But whether a doctor should be allowed to help bring about death is a matter of debate. In only one state—Oregon—have voters passed a right-to-die initiative (the Death with Dignity Act, 1997). Although this law has been challenged repeatedly ever since, Oregon physicians can legally

Unlike a hospital, which tries to save and extend life, a hospice tries to give dying people greater comfort. The setting is, as much as possible, personal, and the dying person can have the companionship and support of family members.

assist in ending the lives of patients; in 2002, Oregon physicians legally assisted in thirty-eight suicides (McCall, 2003). In 1997, the U.S. Supreme Court, in *Vacco* v. *Quill*, declared that the U.S. Constitution recognizes no right to die.

Supporters of the right-to-die movement hold up as a model the Netherlands, which has the most permissive euthanasia law in the world. How does the Dutch system operate? The Thinking Critically box takes a closer look.

Should the United States hold the line on euthanasia or follow the lead of the Dutch? Right-to-die advocates maintain that a person facing extreme suffering should be able to choose to live or die. And if death is the choice, medical assistance can help people toward a "good death." Surveys show that a majority of U.S. adults support giving people the option of dying with a doctor's help (D. E. Rosenbaum, 1997; NORC, 2003).

On the other side of the debate, opponents fear that laws allowing physician-assisted suicide invite abuse. Pointing to the Netherlands, critics cite surveys indicating that in most cases, the five conditions for physician-assisted suicide are not met. In particular, most physicians do not consult with another doctor or even report the euthanasia to authorities. Of greater concern is the fact that in about one-fifth of all physician-assisted suicides, the patient never explicitly asks to die. This is so even though half of these patients are conscious and capable of making decisions for themselves (Gillon, 1999). Such facts lead opponents to argue that legalizing physician-assisted suicide puts a nation on a slippery slope toward more and more euthanasia. How can we be sure, they ask, that ill people won't be pushed into accepting death by doctors who consider suicide the right choice for the terminally ill or by family members who are weary of caring for them or want to avoid the expenses of medical treatment?

However the right-to-die debate turns out, our society has now entered a new era when it comes to dying. More often, individuals, family members, and medical personnel must face death not as a medical fact but as a negotiated outcome.

BEREAVEMENT

Elisabeth Kübler-Ross (1969) found that most people usually confront their own death in stages (see Chapter 5, "Socialization"). Initially, individuals react with *denial*, followed by *anger;* then they try *negotiation*, hoping for divine intervention. Gradually, they fall into *resignation* and finally reach *acceptance.*

According to some researchers, bereavement follows the same pattern of stages. Those close to a dying person, for instance, may initially deny the reality of impending death and then, with time, gradually reach a point of acceptance. Other investigators, however, question any linear "stage theory," arguing that bereavement is a personal and unpredictable process (Lund, Caserta, & Dimond, 1986; Lund, 1989; Cutcliffe, 1998). What experts do agree on, however, is the fact that how family and friends view an impending death has an effect on the person who is dying. By accepting an approaching death, others help the dying person do the same; denying death isolates the dying person, who is unable to share feelings and experiences with others.

Many dying people find support in the *hospice movement.* Unlike a hospital, which is designed to cure disease, a hospice helps people have a good death. These care centers

As they become a larger share of the U.S. population in years to come, older people will probably play a larger part in popular culture. Clint Eastwood, shown here with Hilary Swank on the set of the 2005 Oscar nominated–film *Million Dollar Baby*, remains a mega-star at the age of seventy-five. Do you think this pattern is more typical of older men than of older women? Why?

Visit the Web site of the National Hospice and Palliative Care Organization: http://www.nhpco.org

for dying people try to minimize pain and suffering—either at the center or at home—and encourage family members to stay close by. Most hospices also provide social support for family members experiencing bereavement (Foliart & Clausen, 2001).

Under the best of circumstances, bereavement often involves profound grief. Research documents that bereavement is less intense for someone who accepts the death of a loved one and has brought satisfactory closure to the relationship. Such closure also allows family and friends to better comfort one another after death occurs.

Reaching closure is not possible when a death is unexpected. Especially in such cases, social disorientation may be profound and may last for years. One study of middle-aged women who had recently experienced the death of their husbands found that many felt they had lost not only a spouse but also their reason for living. Therefore, dealing successfully with bereavement requires the time and social support necessary to form a new sense of self and recognize new life options (Atchley, 1983; Danforth & Glass, 2001). With the number of older people in the United States increasing so fast, understanding death and dying is taking on greater importance.

Aging: Looking Ahead

This chapter has explored the graying of the United States and other high-income nations. By 2050, the elderly population of this country will exceed the population of the entire nation in 1900. In addition, one in four of tomorrow's seniors will be over eighty-five. In decades to come, then, society's oldest members will gain a far greater voice in everyday life. Younger people will find careers relating to gerontology—the study of the elderly—are sure to gain in importance.

With more elderly people living longer and longer, will our society have the support services to sustain them? Remember that as the needs of the elderly increase, a smaller share of younger people will be there to respond and pay the bills with their taxes. What about the spiraling medical costs of an aging society?

As the baby boomers enter old age, some analysts paint a doomsday picture of the United States, with desperate and dying elderly people everywhere (Longino, 1994).

But there is also good news. For one thing, the health of tomorrow's elderly people (that is, today's middle-aged adults) is better than ever: Smoking is way down, and more people are becoming aware of the national problem of obesity and are eating more healthfully. Such trends suggest that the elderly may well become more vigorous and independent. Tomorrow's seniors also will enjoy the benefits of steadily advancing medical technology, although, as the Thinking It Through box explains, how much of the country's medical resources older people can claim is already being hotly debated.

Another positive sign is the growing financial strength of the elderly. Although recent years have been stressful, it is likely that tomorrow's elderly will be more affluent than ever before. The baby boomers will be the first generation of U.S. seniors with women who have been in the labor force most of their lives, a fact reflected in their substantial savings and pensions.

At the same time, younger adults will face a mounting responsibility to care for aging parents. A falling birth rate coupled with a growing elderly population will demand that middle-aged people perform an increasing share of caregiving for the very old.

Most of us need to learn more about caring for aging parents, which includes far more than meeting physical needs. More important lessons involve communicating, expressing love, and facing up to eventual death. In caring for our parents, we will also teach important lessons to our children, including the skills they will need, one day, to care for us.

THINKING IT THROUGH

Setting Limits: Must We "Pull the Plug" on Old Age?

As the U.S. elderly population soars, as new technology gives us more power to prolong life, and as medical care gets increasingly expensive, many now wonder just how much old age we can afford. Currently, about half the average person's lifetime spending for medical care occurs during the final years of life, and the share is rising. Against the spiraling costs of prolonging life, we well may ask if what is medically possible is morally desirable. In the decades to come, warns gerontologist Daniel Callahan (1987), an elderly population ready and eager to extend their lives will eventually force us either to "pull the plug" on old age or shortchange everyone else.

To even raise this issue, Callahan admits, seems cold and heartless. But consider that the bill for the elderly's health topped $200 billion in 2002—more than twice what it cost in 1980. This dramatic increase reflects the current policy of directing more and more medical resources to studying and treating the diseases and disabilities of old age.

So Callahan makes the case for limits. First, the more we spend on behalf of the elderly, the less we have to provide for others. With poverty a growing problem among children, can we afford to spend more and more on the oldest members of our society?

Second, a *longer* life does not necessarily mean a *better* life. Cost aside, does heart surgery that prolongs the life of an eighty-four-year-old woman a year or two necessarily improve the quality of her life? Cost considered, would those resources yield more "quality of life" if used, say, to give a ten-year-old child a kidney transplant? Or to provide basic care and comfort to hundreds of low-income seniors?

Third, we need to reconsider our view of death as an enemy to be conquered at all costs. Rather, he suggests, a more realistic position for an aging society is to treat death as a natural end to the life course. If we cannot make peace with death for our own well-being, then in a society with limited resources, we must do it for the benefit of others.

But not everyone agrees. Shouldn't people who have worked all their lives and made our society what it is enjoy our generosity in their final years?

Would it be right to deny medical care to aging people able and willing to pay for it?

In the twenty-first century, we face questions that few would have imagined even fifty years ago: Is peak longevity good for everyone? Is it even *possible* for everyone?

WHAT DO YOU THINK?

1. Should doctors and hospitals use a double standard, offering more complete care to the youngest people and more limited care to society's oldest members? Why or why not?
2. Do you think that a goal of the medical establishment should be to extend life at all costs? Explain your position.
3. How should society balance the needs of high-income seniors with the needs of those with little or no money to pay for medical care as they age?

Sources: Callahan (1987), Kapp (2001), and U.S. Census Bureau (2004).

15 MAKING THE GRADE

The following learning tools will help you see what you know, identify what you still need to learn, and expand your understanding beyond the text. You can also visit this text's Companion Website™ at http://www.prenhall.com/macionis to find additional practice tests.

KEY POINTS

The Graying of the United States

The proportion of elderly people in the U.S. population has risen from 4 percent in 1900 to 12 percent today; by 2030, 20 percent of our people will be elderly.

Growing Old: Biology and Culture

Gerontology, the study of aging and the elderly, focuses on how people change in old age and on how various cultures define aging. Most younger people exaggerate the extent of disability among the elderly. Growing old is accompanied by a rising rate of disease and disability, but most seniors are healthy. Psychological research confirms that growing old does not result in overall loss of intelligence or radical changes in personality.

The age at which people are defined as old varies: Until several centuries ago, old age began as early as thirty. In poor societies today, where life expectancy is low, people become old at fifty or even forty. Worldwide, industrialization fosters a decline in the social standing of the elderly relative to younger people.

Transitions and Challenges of Aging

As people age, they face a number of problems, including social isolation brought on by retirement, physical disability, and the death of friends or a spouse. To deal with these issues, most elderly people enjoy the support of family members.

Since 1960, poverty among the elderly has dropped. The aged poor include categories of people—such as single women and people of color—who are at high risk of poverty at any age.

Most caregiving for the elderly population is performed by family members, typically women.

Ageism—prejudice and discrimination against old people—is used to justify age stratification. Although income falls among seniors, the fact that this category includes men and women of all races, ethnicities, and social classes suggests that older people are not a minority.

Theoretical Analysis of Aging

Disengagement theory, based on the structural-functional approach, suggests that society helps the elderly disengage from positions of social responsibility before the onset of disability or death. This process provides for the orderly transfer of statuses and roles from the older to the younger generation.

Activity theory, based on the symbolic-interaction approach, claims that a high level of activity increases people's personal satisfaction in old age.

Age stratification is a focus of the social-conflict approach. A capitalist society's emphasis on economic efficiency leads to the devaluation of those who are less productive, including the elderly.

Death and Dying

Modern society has set death apart from everyday life. This avoidance of death also reflects the fact that most people in high-income societies die in old age. Recent trends suggest that people are confronting death more directly and seeking control over the process of dying.

Aging: Looking Ahead

As the number of older people in U.S. society increases, we face important questions about how to meet their needs. Medical costs are rising rapidly, but tomorrow's elderly are likely to be more affluent than ever before.

KEY CONCEPTS

gerontology (p. 397) the study of aging and the elderly

age stratification (p. 399) the unequal distribution of wealth, power, and privilege among people at different stages of the life course

gerontocracy (p. 399) a form of social organization in which the elderly have the most wealth, power, and prestige

caregiving (p. 405) informal and unpaid care provided to a dependent person by family members, other relatives, or friends

ageism (p. 406) prejudice and discrimination against older people

disengagement theory (p. 407) the idea that society functions in an orderly way by

disengaging people from positions of responsibility as they reach old age

activity theory (p. 408) the idea that a high level of activity increases personal satisfaction in old age

euthanasia (p. 410) assisting in the death of a person suffering from an incurable disease; also known as *mercy killing*

SAMPLE TEST QUESTIONS

These questions are similar to those found in the test bank that accompanies this textbook.

Multiple-Choice Questions

1. **Where in the world is the share of the elderly population increasing most quickly?**
   a. low-income nations
   b. all the world's nations
   c. high-income nations
   d. the United States

2. **What is the average (median) age of the U.S. population?**
   a. 65 years
   b. 55 years
   c. 45 years
   d. 35 years

3. As we look at older and older people in the United States, we find a larger share of
   a. men.
   b. women.
   c. well-off people.
   d. married people.

4. What effect does industrialization have on the social standing of the oldest members of a society?
   a. Social standing goes down.
   b. There is little or no effect.
   c. Social standing goes up.
   d. Social standing goes up for men and down for women.

5. The term "gerontocracy" means a society where
   a. there is a lot of social inequality.
   b. men dominate women.
   c. religious leaders are in charge.
   d. the oldest people have the most wealth, power, and prestige.

6. The idea of retirement first appears in which type of society?
   a. hunting and gathering societies
   b. pastoral societies
   c. industrial societies
   d. postindustrial societies

7. In the United States, the poverty rate for people over the age of sixty-five is
   a. higher than the national average.
   b. the same as the national average.
   c. lower than the national average.
   d. higher than among any other age category.

8. Which category of people in the United States provides most of the caregiving to elderly people?
   a. professionals working in the home
   b. nurses
   c. other elderly people
   d. women

9. The structural-functional approach to aging involves
   a. disengagement theory.
   b. activity theory.
   c. social inequality.
   d. all of the above.

10. A document in which a person states which, if any, medical procedures he or she wishes to be used under specific conditions is known as a
    a. death wish.
    b. living will.
    c. legal trust.
    d. power of attorney.

Answers: 1(c); 2(d); 3(b); 4(a); 5(d); 6(c); 7(c); 8(d); 9(a); 10(b).

Essay Questions

1. What is the "graying of the United States"? What two factors are causing this trend? What are some of the likely consequences of this trend for our way of life?

2. How is ageism like sexism and racism? How is it different? If older people are disadvantaged, should they be considered a minority? Why or why not?

APPLICATIONS & EXERCISES

1. Ask several faculty nearing retirement and several who have already retired about the practices and policies of your college or university for helping older faculty when they retire. Based on what you learn, decide whether retiring from an academic career is harder or easier than retiring from other kinds of work, and explain why.

2. Look through an issue of a popular magazine—say, *Time, Newsweek,* or *People*—and note pictures of men and women in news stories and advertising. What share of the pictures show elderly people? In what types of advertising are they featured?

3. Obtain a copy of a living will (do an online search), and try to respond to all the questions it asks. How does filling out this form affect your thinking about death?

INVESTIGATE *with* Research Navigator

Research Navigator.com
RESOURCES FOR COLLEGE RESEARCH ASSIGNMENTS

Follow the instructions on page 27 of this text to access the features of **Research Navigator**™. Once at the Web site, enter your Login Name and Password. Then, to use the **ContentSelect**™ database, enter keywords such as "caregiving," "ageism," and "death," and the search engine will supply relevant and recent scholarly and popular press publications. Use the *New York Times* **Search-by-Subject Archive** to find recent news articles related to sociology and the **Link Library** feature to find relevant Web links organized by the key terms associated with this chapter.

16

CHAPTER SIXTEEN

The Economy and Work

How does change in the economy reshape society?

What makes capitalist and socialist economies different?

Why have the types of jobs available in the United States changed over the last fifty years?

Here's a quick quiz about the U.S. economy (Hint: All five questions have the same right answer):

- Which business do 100 million people in the United States visit each week?

- Which U.S. company, on average, opens a new store every day?

- Which U.S. company is the largest employer in the country after the federal government?

- Which U.S. company will create nearly 800,000 new jobs over the next five years?

- Which single company accounted for 25 percent of all the growth in U.S. economic output during the second half of the 1990s?

You have probably guessed that the correct answer is Wal-Mart, the global discount store chain founded by Sam Walton, who opened his first store in Arkansas in 1962. By 2005, Wal-Mart had $285 billion in sales from 3,600 stores in the United States and 1,500 stores in other countries, from Brazil to China.

Wal-Mart has made a lot of shoppers happy, but not everyone is pleased about the company's rapid expansion across the United States. Opponents have formed a social movement to keep Wal-Mart out of their local communities, fearing the loss of local businesses and, in some cases, local culture. Critics also claim that the merchandising giant pays low wages, keeps out unions, and sells many products made in sweatshops abroad (Rousseau, 2002; Saporito, 2003). ■

This chapter examines the economy, widely considered the most influential of all social institutions. (The other major social institutions are examined in the chapters that follow.) As the story of Wal-Mart's expansion suggests, the economy of the United States and the entire world is dominated by a number of giant corporations. Who benefits from these megabusinesses? Who loses? What is it like to work for one of these corporations? To answer these questions, sociologists study how the economy operates as well as the nature of work and what it means to each of us.

The Economy: Historical Overview

The **economy** is *the social institution that organizes a society's production, distribution, and consumption of goods and services.* As an institution, the economy operates in a generally predictable manner. *Goods* are commodities ranging from necessities (food, clothing, shelter) to luxury items (cars, swimming pools, yachts). *Services* are activities that benefit others (for example, the work of priests, physicians, teachers, and software specialists).

We value goods and services because they ensure survival or because they make life easier or more interesting. Also, what people produce as workers and what they buy as consumers are important parts of social identity, as when we say, "He's a steelworker," or "She drives a Mercedes." How goods and services are distributed, too, shapes the lives of everyone by giving more resources to some and fewer to others.

The economies of modern high-income nations are the result of centuries of social change. We turn now to three technological revolutions that reorganized production and, in the process, transformed social life.

THE AGRICULTURAL REVOLUTION

Members of the earliest human societies were hunters and gatherers living off the land. In these technologically simple

As societies industrialize, a smaller share of the labor force works in agriculture. In the United States, much of the agricultural work that remains is performed by immigrants from lower-income nations. These farm workers, who came to this country from Mexico, travel throughout North Carolina during the tobacco harvest.

societies, there was no distinct economy. Rather, producing and consuming were all part of family life.

As Chapter 4 ("Society") explained, when people harnessed animals to plows, beginning some 5,000 years ago, a new agricultural economy was created that was fifty times more productive than hunting and gathering. The resulting surplus meant that not everyone had to produce food, so many took on specialized work: making tools, raising animals, or building dwellings. Soon towns sprang up, linked by networks of traders dealing in food, animals, and other goods. These four factors—agricultural technology, job specialization, permanent settlements, and trade—made the economy a distinct social institution.

THE INDUSTRIAL REVOLUTION

By the mid-eighteenth century, a second technological revolution was under way, first in England and then in North America. The development of industry was even more powerful than the rise of agriculture in bringing change to the economy. Industrialization changed the economy in five fundamental ways:

1. **New sources of energy.** Throughout history, "energy" had meant the muscle power of people or animals. But in 1765, the English inventor James Watt introduced the steam engine. One hundred times stronger than muscle power, early steam engines soon drove heavy machinery.

2. **Centralization of work in factories.** Steam-powered machines soon moved work from homes to factories, the centralized and impersonal workplaces housing the machines.

3. **Manufacturing and mass production.** Before the Industrial Revolution, most people grew or gathered raw materials (such as grain, wood, or wool). In an industrial economy, the focus shifts so that most people work to turn raw materials into a wide range of finished products (such as furniture and clothing).

4. **Specialization.** Centuries ago, people worked at home as artisans making products from start to finish. In the factory, a worker repeats a single task over and over, making only a small contribution to the finished product. Such specialization has raised productivity but lowered the skill level of the average worker.

5. **Wage labor.** Instead of working for themselves, factory workers became wage laborers working for strangers, who often cared less for them than for the machines they operated.

↔ YOUR TURN ↔

Look back to page 306 and read the story at the beginning of Chapter 12 about the fire in the Bangladeshi sweatshop. What was the owner's biggest concern?

The Industrial Revolution gradually raised the standard of living as countless new products and services fueled

Women in the Mills of Lowell, Massachusetts

Few people paid much attention as Francis Cabot Lowell, ancestor of two prominent Boston families, the Cabots and the Lowells, stepped off a ship returning from England in 1810. But Lowell carried with him documents that would change the course of the U.S. economy: plans, based on machinery operating in England, for this country's first power loom textile factory (Eisler, 1977; Wertheimer, 1982).

Lowell built his factory beside a waterfall on the Merrimack River in Massachusetts so that he could use waterpower to turn large looms to weave cloth. Soon the productive factory had transformed a small farming village into a thriving industrial town that at his death was renamed in his honor.

From the outset, 90 percent of the mill workers were women. Factory owners preferred women because they could be paid $2 to $3 a week, half the wages men received. Many immigrant men were willing to work for such low wages, but often prejudice disqualified "foreigners" from any job at all.

Recruiters, driving wagons through the small towns of New England,

urged parents to send their daughters to the mills, where, they promised, the young women would be properly supervised as they learned skills and discipline. The offer appealed to many parents, who could barely provide for their children, and the prospect of getting out on their own surely excited many young women. Back then, there were few occupations open to women, and those that were—including teaching and household service—paid even less than factory work.

At the Lowell factory, young women lived in dormitories, paying one-third of their wages for room and board. They were subject to a curfew and, as a

condition of employment, regularly attended church. Any morally questionable conduct (such as bringing men to their rooms) resulted in firm disciplinary action.

Besides fulfilling their promise to parents, factory owners had another motive for their strict rules: They knew that closely supervised women were not able to organize. Working twelve or thirteen hours a day, six days a week, the Lowell employees had good reason to seek improvements in their working conditions. Yet any public criticism of the factory, or even possession of "radical" literature, could cost a worker her job.

WHAT DO YOU THINK?

1. How did race, ethnicity, and gender shape the workforce in the early textile mills?

2. What do you think about how closely supervised the women workers were? Can you think of similar controls in the workplace today?

3. Compare the textile mills in Lowell to the Bangladeshi sweatshop described in the opening of Chapter 12. How are they similar? How do they differ?

an expanding marketplace. Yet the benefits of industrial technology were shared very unequally, especially at the beginning. Some factory owners made vast fortunes, while the majority of industrial workers lived close to poverty.

Children, too, worked in factories or in coal mines for pennies a day. Women working in factories were among the lowest paid, and they endured special problems, as the Thinking About Diversity box explains.

THE INFORMATION REVOLUTION AND POSTINDUSTRIAL SOCIETY

By about 1950, the nature of production was changing once again. The United States was creating a **postindustrial economy,** *a productive system based on service work and high technology.* Automated machinery (and more recently, robotics) has reduced the role of human labor in factory production and expanded the ranks of clerical workers and managers. The postindustrial era is marked by a shift from industrial work to service work.

Driving this change is a third technological breakthrough: the computer. Just as the Industrial Revolution did two-and-a-half centuries ago, the Information Revolution has introduced new kinds of products and new forms of communication and has altered the character of work. In general, there have been three significant changes:

1. **From tangible products to ideas.** The industrial era was defined by the production of goods; in the postindustrial era, people work with symbols. Computer programmers, writers, financial analysts, advertising executives, architects, editors, and all sorts of consultants make up the labor force of the information age.

2. **From mechanical skills to literacy skills.** The Industrial Revolution required mechanical skills, but the Information Revolution requires literacy skills: speaking and writing well and, of course, knowing how to use a computer. People able to communicate effectively enjoy new opportunities; people without these skills face fewer opportunities.

3. **From factories to almost anywhere.** Industrial technology drew workers into factories located near power sources, but computer technology allows people to work almost anywhere. Laptop and wireless computers and cell phones now turn the home, a car, or even an airplane into a "virtual office." In short, new information technology blurs the line between work and home life.

YOUR TURN

What are two advantages and two disadvantages of being able to work almost anywhere? Do you think the benefits of the "anywhere office" outweigh the downsides?

SECTORS OF THE ECONOMY

The three revolutions just described reflect a shifting balance among the three sectors of a society's economy. The

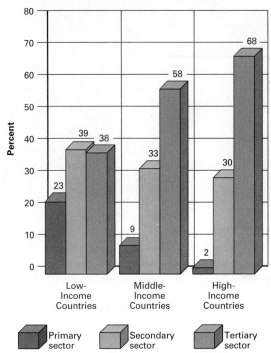

GLOBAL SNAPSHOT

FIGURE 16–1 The Size of Economic Sectors by Income Level of Country

As countries become richer, the primary sector of the economy becomes smaller and the tertiary or service sector becomes larger.

Sources: Estimates based on United Nations Development Programme (2000) and World Bank (2000).

primary sector is *the part of the economy that draws raw materials from the natural environment.* The primary sector—agriculture, raising animals, fishing, forestry, and mining—is largest in low-income nations. Figure 16–1 shows that 23 percent of the economic output of low-income countries is from the primary sector, compared to 9 percent of economic activity in middle-income nations and just 2 percent in high-income countries such as the United States.

The **secondary sector** is *the part of the economy that transforms raw materials into manufactured goods.* This sector grows quickly as societies industrialize. It includes operations such as refining petroleum into gasoline and turning metals into tools and automobiles. The globalization of industry means that just about all the world's countries have a significant share of their workers in the secondary sector.

The rise of a global economy means that more and more products originally produced in one country are now made and consumed around the world. What do you see as some of the good consequences of globalization? What about harmful consequences?

Figure 16–1 shows that the secondary sector accounts for a greater share of economic output in low-income countries than it does in high-income nations.

The **tertiary sector** is *the part of the economy that involves services rather than goods.* Accounting for 38 percent of the labor force in low-income countries, the tertiary sector grows with industrialization and dominates the economies of middle-income countries (58 percent of economic output) and high-income, postindustrial nations (68 percent). About 77 percent of the U.S. labor force is in service work, including secretarial and clerical work and positions in food service, sales, law, health care, law enforcement, advertising, and teaching.

THE GLOBAL ECONOMY

New information technology is drawing people around the world closer together and creating a **global economy,** *expanding economic activity that crosses national borders.* The development of a global economy has five major consequences.

First, we see a global division of labor: Different regions of the world specialize in one sector of economic activity. As Global Map 16–1 shows, agriculture represents about half the total economic output of the world's poorest countries. Global Map 16–2 indicates that most of the economic

output of high-income countries, including the United States, is in the service sector. The poorest nations, then, specialize in producing raw materials, and the richest nations, including the United States, specialize in the production of various services.

Second, an increasing number of products pass through more than one nation. Look no further than your morning coffee: The beans may have been grown in Colombia and transported to New Orleans on a freighter registered in Liberia, made in Japan using steel from Korea and fueled by oil from Venezuela.

Third, national governments no longer control the economic activity that takes place within their borders. In fact, governments cannot even regulate the value of their national currencies because dollars, euros, pounds sterling, and yen are traded around the clock in the financial markets of New York, London, and Tokyo. Global markets are a network using satellite communications to link the world's cities.

A fourth consequence of the global economy is that a small number of businesses, operating internationally, now controls a vast share of the world's economic activity. A rough estimate is that the 600 largest multinational companies account for half the entire world's economic output (Kidron & Segal, 1991; Gergen, 2002).

Fifth and finally, the globalization of the economy raises concerns about the rights and opportunities of workers. Critics of this trend claim that the United States is losing jobs—especially factory jobs—to low-income nations. Workers here face lower wages and higher unemployment, and most workers in low-income nations are paid extremely low wages. As a result, say critics, the global expansion of capitalism threatens the well-being of workers throughout the world.

The world is still divided into 192 politically distinct nations. But increasing international economic activity makes "nationhood" less significant than it was even a decade ago.

Economic Systems: Paths to Justice

October 20, Saigon, Vietnam. Sailing up the narrow Saigon River is an unsettling experience for anyone who came of age during the 1960s. We need to remember that Vietnam is a country, not a war, and that thirty years have passed since the last U.S. helicopter lifted off the rooftop of the U.S. embassy, ending our country's presence there.

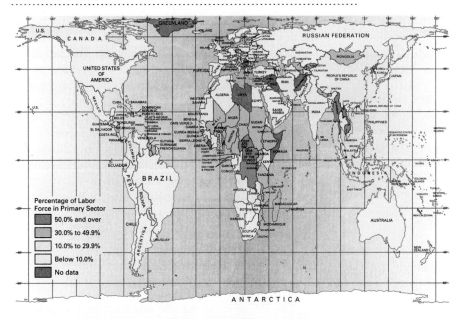

Agricultural Employment in Global Perspective

The primary sector of the economy is largest in the nations that are least developed. Thus in the poor countries of Africa and Asia, up to half of all workers are farmers. This picture is altogether different in the world's most economically developed countries—including the United States, Canada, Great Britain, and Australia—which have 2 percent of their labor force in agriculture.

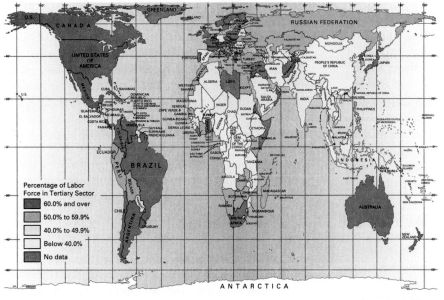

Service-Sector Employment in Global Perspective

The tertiary sector of the economy becomes ever larger as a nation's income level rises. In the United States, Canada, the countries of Western Europe, Australia, and Japan, about two-thirds of the labor force performs service work.

Sources: Data from United Nations Development Programme (2000) and World Bank (2000, 2001); map projection from *Peters Atlas of the World* (1990).

Saigon is on the brink of becoming a boomtown. Neon signs bathe the city's waterfront in color; hotels, bankrolled by Western corporations, push skyward from a dozen construction sites; taxi meters record fares in U.S. dollars, not Vietnamese dong; Visa and American Express stickers decorate the doors of fashionable shops that cater to tourists from Japan, France, and the United States.

There is a heavy irony here: After decades of fighting, the loss of millions of human lives, and the victory of communist forces, the Vietnamese are doing an about-face and turning toward capitalism. What we see today is what might well have happened had the U.S. forces won the war.

Every society's economic system makes a statement about *justice* by determining who is entitled to what. Two general economic models are capitalism and socialism. No nation anywhere in the world has an economy that is completely one or the other; capitalism and socialism represent two ends of a continuum along which all real-world economies can be located. We will look, in turn, at each of these two models.

CAPITALISM

Capitalism is *an economic system in which natural resources and the means of producing goods and services are privately owned*. An ideal capitalist economy has three distinctive features:

1. **Private ownership of property.** In a capitalist economy, individuals can own almost anything. The more capitalist an economy is, the more private ownership there is of wealth-producing property, such as factories, real estate, and natural resources.

2. **Pursuit of personal profit.** A capitalist society encourages the accumulation of private property and considers the profit motive natural, simply a matter of doing business. The Scottish philosopher Adam Smith (1723–1790) claimed that from individuals pursuing their self-interest, an entire society prospers (1937, orig. 1776).

3. **Competition and consumer choice.** A purely capitalist economy is a free-market system with no government interference (sometimes called a *laissez-faire economy*, from the French words meaning "leave it alone"). Adam Smith stated that a freely competitive economy regulates itself by the "invisible hand" of the law of supply and demand.

   Consumers regulate a free-market economy, Smith explained, by selecting the goods and services offering the greatest value. As producers compete for the customer's business, they provide the highest-quality goods at the lowest possible prices. In Smith's time-honored phrase, from narrow self-interest comes the "greatest good for the greatest number of people." Government control of an economy, on the other hand, distorts market forces by reducing the quantity

and quality of goods; in the process, it shortchanges consumers.

"Justice" in a capitalist system amounts to freedom of the marketplace, where a person can produce, invest, and buy according to individual self-interest. The increasing popularity of Wal-Mart, described in the opening to this chapter, reflects the fact that customers think they get a lot for their money.

The United States is considered a capitalist nation because most businesses are privately owned. However, it is not purely capitalist because government plays a large role in the economy. The government owns and operates a number of businesses, including almost all of this country's schools, roads, parks and museums, the U.S. Postal Service, the Amtrak railroad system, and the entire U.S. military. The U.S. government also had a major hand in building the Internet. In addition, governments use taxation and other forms of regulation to influence what companies produce, control the quality and cost of merchandise, and motivate consumers to conserve natural resources.

The U.S. government also sets minimum wage levels, enforces workplace safety standards, regulates corporate mergers, provides farm price supports, and supplements the income of a majority of its people in the form of Social Security, public assistance, student loans, and veterans' benefits. Local, state, and federal governments combined are the country's biggest employer, with 17 percent of the nonfarm labor force on their payrolls (U.S. Census Bureau, 2004).

SOCIALISM

Socialism is *an economic system in which natural resources and the means of producing goods and services are collectively owned*. In its ideal form, a socialist economy rejects each of the three characteristics of capitalism just described in favor of three opposite features:

1. **Collective ownership of property.** A socialist economy limits rights to private property, especially property used to generate income. Government controls such property and makes housing and other goods available to all, not just to the people with the most money.

2. **Pursuit of collective goals.** The individualistic pursuit of profit goes against the collective orientation of socialism. What capitalism celebrates as the "entrepreneurial spirit," socialism condemns as greed; individuals are urged to work for the common good of all.

3. **Government control of the economy.** Socialism rejects capitalism's laissez-faire approach in favor of a *centrally controlled* or *command economy* operated by

Capitalism still thrives in Hong Kong (left), evident in streets choked with advertising and shoppers. Socialism is more the rule in China's capital of Beijing (right), a city dominated by government buildings rather than a downtown business district.

the government. Commercial advertising thus plays little role in socialist economies.

"Justice" in a socialist context means not competing to gain wealth but meeting everyone's basic needs in a roughly equal manner. From a socialist point of view, the common capitalist practice of giving workers as little in pay and benefits as possible to boost company earnings is putting profits before people and is unjust.

The People's Republic of China and some two dozen other nations in Asia, Africa, and Latin America model their economies on socialism, placing almost all wealth-generating property under state control (McColm et al., 1991; Freedom House, 2005). The extent of world socialism has declined in recent years as the countries in Eastern Europe and the former Soviet Union have geared their economies toward a market system.

Socialism and Communism

Many people think of *socialism* and *communism* as the same thing, but they are not. **Communism** is *a hypothetical economic and political system in which all members of a society are socially equal.* Karl Marx viewed socialism as one important step on the path toward the ideal of a communist society that abolishes all class divisions. In many socialist societies today, the dominant political party describes itself

as communist, but the communist goal has not been achieved in any society.

Why? For one thing, social stratification involves differences in power as well as wealth. Socialist societies have reduced economic differences by regulating people's range of choices. In the process, government did not "wither away," as Marx imagined it would. Rather, government has grown, giving socialist political elites enormous power and privilege.

Marx might have agreed that a communist society is a *utopia* (from Greek words meaning "no place"). Yet Marx considered communism a worthy goal and might well have objected to so-called Marxist societies such as North Korea, the People's Republic of China, and Cuba for falling short of the promise of communism.

WELFARE CAPITALISM AND STATE CAPITALISM

Some nations of Western Europe, including Sweden and Italy, have market-based economies but also offer broad social welfare programs. Analysts call this third type of economic system **welfare capitalism,** *an economic and political system that combines a mostly market-based economy with extensive social welfare programs.*

Under welfare capitalism, the government owns some of the largest industries and services, such as transportation, the mass media, and health care. In Sweden and Italy,

Societies with mostly capitalist economies are very productive, providing a high overall standard of living. At the same time, however, these societies distribute income and wealth very unequally. In what social classes do you think people express the most, and the least, support for the mostly capitalist economy of the United States?

about 12 percent of economic production is "nationalized," or state-controlled. Most industry is left in private hands, although it is subject to extensive government regulation. High taxation (aimed especially at the rich) funds a wide range of social welfare programs, including universal health care and child care (Olsen, 1996).

Yet another blend of capitalism and socialism is **state capitalism,** *an economic and political system in which companies are privately owned but cooperate closely with the government.* State capitalism is the rule among the nations along the Pacific Rim. Japan, South Korea, and Singapore are all capitalist countries, but their governments work in partnership with large companies, supplying financial assistance and controlling foreign imports to help their businesses compete in world markets (Gerlach, 1992).

RELATIVE ADVANTAGES OF CAPITALISM AND SOCIALISM

Which economic system works best? Comparing economic models is difficult because all countries mix capitalism and socialism to varying degrees. In addition, nations differ in cultural attitudes toward work, access to natural resources, levels of technological development, and patterns of trade. Despite such complicating factors, some crude comparisons are revealing.

Economic Productivity

One key dimension of economic performance is productivity. A commonly used measure of economic output is gross domestic product (GDP), the total value of all goods and services produced annually. Per capita (per person) GDP allows us to compare the economic performance of nations of different population sizes.

The output of mostly capitalist countries at the end of the 1980s varied somewhat, but averaging the figures for the United States, Canada, and the nations of Western Europe yielded a per capita GDP of about $13,500. The comparable figure for the mostly socialist former Soviet Union and nations of Eastern Europe was about $5,000. This means that the capitalist countries outproduced the socialist nations by a ratio of 2.7 to 1 (United Nations Development Programme, 1990). A recent comparison of socialist North Korea (per capita GDP of $1,000) and capitalist South Korea ($18,000) provides an even sharper contrast (Omestad, 2003).

Economic Equality

The distribution of resources within a population is another important measure of how well an economic system works. A comparative study of Europe in the mid-1970s, when that region was split between mostly capitalist and mostly socialist countries, compared the earnings of the richest 5 percent of the population and the poorest 5 percent (Wiles, 1977). Societies with mostly capitalist economies had a ratio of 10 to 1; the ratio for socialist countries was about 5 to 1. In other words, capitalist economies support a higher overall standard of living, but with greater income inequality. Said another way, socialist economies create more economic equality but with a lower overall living standard.

Personal Freedom

One additional consideration in evaluating capitalism and socialism is the personal freedom each gives its people.

Global comparisons indicate that socialist economies generate greater economic equality, although living standards remain relatively low. Capitalist economies, by contrast, generate more economic inequality but have relatively high living standards. As the Russian Federation has moved from socialism toward capitalism, there is widespread evidence of increasing economic inequality, including the building of large mansions by those who have become rich. This complex is being built by a business tycoon in the suburbs of the Russian capital, an area coming to be known as "the Beverly Hills of Moscow."

Capitalism emphasizes *freedom to* pursue personal self-interest. Capitalism, after all, depends on the freedom of producers and consumers to interact, with little interference by the state. Socialism, by contrast, emphasizes *freedom from* basic want. The goal of equality requires the state to regulate the economy, which in turn limits the personal choices and opportunities for citizens.

No system has yet been able to offer both political freedom and economic equality. In the capitalist United States, the political system guarantees many personal freedoms, but these freedoms are not worth as much to a poor person as to a rich one. By contrast, China or Cuba has more economic equality, but people cannot speak out or travel freely within or outside of the country.

CHANGES IN SOCIALIST COUNTRIES

In 1989 and 1990, the nations of Eastern Europe, which had been seized by the Soviet Union at the end of World War II, overthrew their socialist regimes. These nations—including the German Democratic Republic, Czechoslovakia, Hungary, Romania, and Bulgaria—are moving toward capitalist market systems after decades of state-controlled economies. In 1991, the Soviet Union itself formally dissolved, and the new Russian Federation has introduced some free-market principles. Within a decade, three-fourths of former Soviet government enterprises were partly or entirely in private hands (Montaigne, 2001).

There were many reasons for these sweeping changes. First, the capitalist economies far outproduced their socialist counterparts. The socialist economies were successful in achieving economic equality, but living standards were low compared to those of Western Europe. Second, Soviet

socialism was heavy-handed, rigidly controlling the media and restricting individual freedoms. In short, socialism did away with *economic* elites, as Karl Marx predicted, but as Max Weber foresaw, socialism increased the power of *political* elites.

So far, the market reforms in Eastern Europe are proceeding unevenly. Some nations (the Czech Republic, Slovakia, Poland, and the Baltic states of Latvia, Estonia, and Lithuania) are doing relatively well, but others (Romania, Bulgaria, and the Russian Federation) have been buffeted by price increases and falling living standards. Officials hope that expanding production will eventually bring a turn-around. However, the introduction of a market economy has brought with it an increase in economic inequality (Buraway, 1997; World Bank, 2005).

Work in the Postindustrial Economy

Economic change is taking place not just in the socialist world but also in the United States. In 2004, a total of 139 million people in the United States—representing almost two-thirds of those aged sixteen and over—were working for income. A larger share of men (68.2 percent) than women (56.0 percent) had jobs, although the gap is closing.

 The Bureau of Labor Statistics Web site offers a wide range of data and reports at http://www.bls.gov

Among men, 59.3 percent of African Americans were employed, compared with 70.4 percent of whites, 71.6 percent of Asians, and 75.1 percent of Hispanics. Among women, 55.5 percent of African Americans were employed, compared to 56.1 percent of whites, 55.1 percent of Asians, and 51.8 percent of Hispanics.

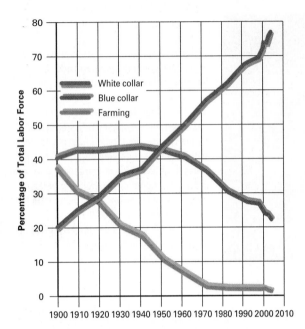

FIGURE 16-2 The Changing Pattern of Work in the United States, 1900–2004

Compared to a century ago, work in the United States now involves mostly white-collar service jobs.

Source: Estimates based on U.S. Department of Labor (2005).

THE DECLINE OF AGRICULTURAL WORK

In 1900, about 40 percent of U.S. workers were farmers. In 2004, just 1.6 percent were employed in agriculture. The family farm of yesterday has been replaced by *corporate agribusinesses.* Land is now more productive, but this change has caused painful adjustments across the country as a way of life is lost (Dudley, 2000). Figure 16–2 shows the shrinking role of the primary sector in the U.S. economy.

FROM FACTORY WORK TO SERVICE WORK

A century ago, industrialization swelled the ranks of blue-collar workers. By 1950, however, a white-collar revolution had moved a majority of workers into service occupations. By 2004, 77 percent of the labor force worked in the service sector, and 92 percent of new jobs were being created in this sector (U.S. Department of Labor, 2005).

As Chapter 11 ("Social Class in the United States") explained, the expansion of service work is one reason many people call the United States a middle-class society. But much service work—including sales and clerical positions

and jobs in hospitals and restaurants—pays much less than older factory jobs. This means that many of the jobs in today's postindustrial society provide only a modest standard of living.

THE DUAL LABOR MARKET

Sociologists see the jobs in today's economy falling into two categories. The **primary labor market** offers *jobs that provide extensive benefits to workers.* This segment of the labor market includes the traditional white-collar professions such as medicine and law, as well as upper-management positions. These are jobs that people think of as *careers,* interesting work that provides high income, job security, and opportunity for advancement.

Few of these advantages apply to work in the **secondary labor market,** *jobs that provide minimal benefits to workers.* This segment of the labor force is employed in low-skilled, blue-collar assembly-line operations and low-level service-sector jobs, including clerical positions. Workers in the secondary labor market receive lower income, have less job security and fewer benefits, and find less satisfaction in their work. Women and other minorities are overly represented in the secondary labor market workforce (J. I. Nelson, 1994; Kalleberg, Reskin, & Hudson, 2000).

YOUR TURN

Do you think the jobs provided by colleges to students on financial aid typically provide a fair level of pay and benefits? Explain your position.

LABOR UNIONS

The changing U.S. economy has seen a decline in **labor unions,** *organizations of workers that seek to improve wages and working conditions through various strategies, including negotiations and strikes.* During the Great Depression of the 1930s, union membership increased rapidly until it reached more than one-third of nonfarm workers by 1950. By 1970, union rolls had peaked at almost 25 million. Since then, membership has declined to about 13 percent of nonfarm workers, or 15.8 million men and women. Looking more closely, 37 percent of government workers are members of unions, compared to just 8 percent of private sector (nongovernmental) workers (Clawson & Clawson, 1999; Goldfield, 2000).

The pattern of union decline holds in other high-income countries, yet unions claim a far smaller share of workers in the United States than elsewhere. From a low of about 19 percent in Japan, union membership climbs to about 31 percent in Canada, between 30 and 40 percent in much of Europe, and a high of 77 percent in Sweden (International Labour Organisation, 2002).

The widespread decline in union memberships reflects the shrinking industrial sector of the economy. Newer service jobs—such as sales jobs at retailers like Wal-Mart, described in the chapter opening—are less likely to be unionized. Citing low wages and numerous worker complaints, unions are trying to organize Wal-Mart employees, so far without success. The weak economy of the past few years has given unions a short-term boost. But long-term gains probably depend on the ability of unions to adapt to the new global economy. Union members in the United States, used to seeing foreign workers as "the enemy," will have to build new international alliances (Greenhouse, 2000; Rousseau, 2002).

PROFESSIONS

All kinds of jobs today are called *professional*—we hear of professional tennis players, professional house cleaners, and even professional exterminators. As distinct from *amateur* (from the Latin for "lover," meaning someone who acts out of love for the activity itself), a professional does some task for a living. But what exactly is a *profession*?

A **profession** is *a prestigious white-collar occupation that requires extensive formal education.* People performing this kind of work make a profession, or public declaration, of their willingness to work according to certain principles. Professions include the ministry, medicine, law, academia, architecture, accountancy, and social work. An occupation is considered a profession to the extent that it demonstrates the following four characteristics (W.J. Goode, 1960; Ritzer & Walczak, 1990):

1. **Theoretical knowledge.** Professionals have a theoretical understanding of their field rather than mere technical training. Anyone can master first-aid skills, for example, but physicians have a theoretical understanding of human health. This means that tennis players, house cleaners, and exterminators do not really qualify as "professionals."

2. **Self-regulating practice.** The typical professional is self-employed, "in private practice" rather than working for a company. Professionals oversee their own work and observe a code of ethics.

3. **Authority over clients.** Because of their expertise, professionals are sought out by clients, who value their advice and follow their directions.

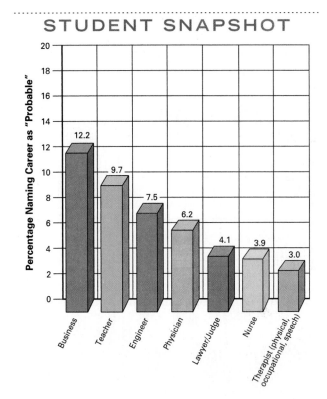

STUDENT SNAPSHOT

FIGURE 16-3 The Careers Most Commonly Named as Probable by First-Year College Students, 2004

Today's college students expect to enter careers that pay well and carry high prestige.

Source: Sax et al. (2004).

4. **Community orientation rather than self-interest.** The traditional professing of duty states an intention to serve others rather than merely to seek income.

In almost all cases, professional work requires not just a college degree but also a graduate degree. Not surprisingly, therefore, professions are well represented among the occupations beginning college students say they hope to get after graduation, as shown in Figure 16–3.

Many occupations that do not qualify as true professions nonetheless seek to *professionalize* their services. Claiming professional standing often begins by renaming the work to suggest special, theoretical knowledge, moving the field away from its original, lesser reputation. Stockroom workers become "inventory supply managers," and exterminators are reborn as "insect control specialists."

DIVERSITY SNAPSHOT

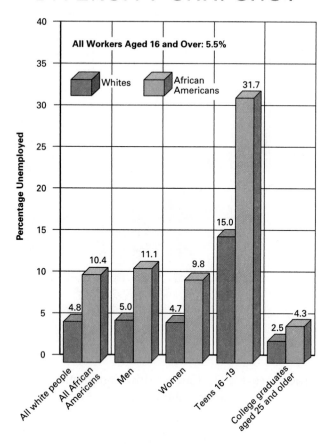

All Workers Aged 16 and Over: 5.5%

Whites | African Americans

Category	Whites	African Americans
All white people	4.8	—
All African Americans	—	10.4
Men	5.0	11.1
Women	4.7	9.8
Teens 16–19	15.0	31.7
College graduates aged 25 and older	2.5	4.3

FIGURE 16-4   Official U.S. Unemployment Rates for Various Categories of Adults, 2004

Although college graduates have low risk of unemployment, race is related to unemployment for all categories of people.

Source: U.S. Department of Labor (2005).

Interested parties may also form a professional association that certifies their skills. This organization then licenses its members, writes a code of ethics, and emphasizes the work's importance in the community through various public relations efforts. To win public acceptance, a professional association may also establish schools or other training facilities and perhaps start a professional journal (Abbott, 1988). Not all occupations try to claim professional status. Some *paraprofessionals,* including paralegals and medical technicians, possess specialized skills but lack the extensive theoretical education required of full professionals.

SELF-EMPLOYMENT

Self-employment—earning a living without working for an organization—was once common in the United States. About 80 percent of the labor force was self-employed in 1800, compared to just 7.5 percent of workers today (8.8 percent of men and 6.0 percent of women) (U.S. Department of Labor, 2005).

Lawyers, physicians, and other professionals are well represented among the ranks of the self-employed. But most self-employed workers are small business owners, plumbers, carpenters, freelance writers, editors, artists, and long-distance truck drivers. In all, the self-employed are more likely to have blue-collar than white-collar jobs.

Visit the Web site of the Small Business Administration at http://www.sba.gov

Women now own nearly 40 percent of this country's small businesses, and the share is rising. The 9.1 million firms owned by U.S. women now employ almost 30 million people and generate close to $4 trillion in annual sales (U.S. Small Business Administration, 2001b).

UNEMPLOYMENT AND UNDEREMPLOYMENT

Every society has some unemployment. Few young people entering the labor force find a job right away; workers may leave their jobs to seek new work or stay at home raising children; some may be on strike; others suffer from long-term illnesses; and still others are illiterate or without the skills to perform useful work.

But unemployment is not just an individual problem; it is also caused by the economy itself. Jobs disappear as occupations become obsolete, businesses change the way they do business, companies downsize to become more competitive, or firms close in the face of foreign competition or economic recession. Since 1980, the 500 largest U.S. businesses have eliminated some 5 million jobs—one-fourth of the total. The economic slowdown that began in 2000 led to millions of people losing their jobs, especially people with white-collar jobs who had typically weathered downturns in the past (Cullen, 2002).

For an article on minority unemployment, go to http://www.brookings.edu/es/urban/publications/offnerexsum.htm

In 2004, 8.1 million people over the age of sixteen were unemployed, about 5.5 percent of the civilian labor force. Some regions of the country, especially rural areas, have unemployment rates double the national average. Today, research shows that rural residents are at especially high risk of unemployment (Stofferahn, 2000).

Figure 16–4 shows that unemployment among African Americans (10.4 percent) is more than twice the rate among white people (4.8 percent). For both races, men have slightly higher levels of unemployment than women.

Underemployment is also a problem for millions of workers. The government reports that more than 32 million people work part time, that is, less than thirty-five hours a week. Although 80 percent are satisfied with this arrangement, 20 percent (6 million workers) say they want more work but cannot find it (U.S. Department of Labor, 2005).

The economic downturn in recent years has created a new kind of underemployment. The bankruptcy of large corporations, including Enron and WorldCom, has left at least 1 million workers—the ones lucky enough to have kept their jobs—with lower salaries, fewer benefits such as health care, and smaller pensions or no pensions at all. In an era of greater global competition and weaker worker organizations, many people have been able to keep their jobs only by agreeing to cutbacks in pay or to the loss of other benefits (Eisenberg, 2001; K. Clark, 2002).

THE UNDERGROUND ECONOMY

The U.S. government requires individuals and businesses to report their economic activity, especially earnings. Unreported income makes a transaction part of the **underground economy,** *economic activity involving income not reported to the government as required by law.*

Most of us participate in the underground economy in small ways from time to time: A family makes extra money by holding a garage sale, or teenagers baby-sit for neighbors without reporting the income. Much more of the underground economy is due to criminal activity, such as prostitution, bribery, theft, illegal gambling, loan-sharking, and the sale of illegal drugs.

But the largest segment of contributors to the underground economy is people who fail to report some or all of their legally earned income when it comes time to file income tax returns. Self-employed persons such as carpenters, physicians, and small business owners may understate their income on tax forms; food servers and other service workers may not report their earnings from tips. Individually, the amounts people fail to report may be small, but taken together, U.S. taxpayers fail to pay as much as $300 billion annually in federal taxes (Kuttner, 2004).

YOUR TURN

In what ways have you been part of the underground economy? Do you think not paying taxes on any earned income is always wrong? Why or why not?

Unemployment means not having a job and the income it provides. But it also means not having the respect that comes from being self-reliant in a society that expects people to take care of themselves. How does the sociological perspective help us to understand being out of work as more than a personal problem?

WORKPLACE DIVERSITY: RACE AND GENDER

In the past, white men have been the mainstay of the U.S. labor force. However, the nation's proportion of minorities is rising rapidly. The African American population is increasing faster than the population of non-Hispanic white people. The rate of increase in the Asian American population is even greater. And the rate of increase in the Hispanic population is greatest of all.

Such dramatic changes are likely to affect U.S. society in countless ways. Not only will more and more workers be women and other minorities, but the workplace will have to develop programs and policies that meet the needs of a socially diverse workforce and also encourage everyone to work together effectively and respectfully. The Thinking About Diversity box on page 432 takes a closer look at some of the issues involved in our changing workplace.

THINKING ABOUT DIVERSITY:
RACE, CLASS, & GENDER

Twenty-First-Century Diversity: Changes in the Workplace

An upward trend in the U.S. minority population is changing the workplace. As the figure shows, the number of non-Hispanic white men in the U.S. labor force will rise by a modest 3 percent between 2002 and 2012, the number of African American men will increase by 20 percent, the number of Hispanic men will increase by 29 percent, and the number of Asian American men will increase by a much greater 54 percent.

Among non-Hispanic white women, the projected rise is 3 percent; among African American women, 19 percent; and among Hispanic women, 38 percent. Asian women will show the greatest gains, estimated at 47 percent.

Within a decade, non-Hispanic white men will represent just 35 percent of all workers, a figure that will continue to drop (Toossi, 2004). Therefore, companies that welcome social diversity will tap the largest talent pool and enjoy a competitive advantage.

Welcoming social diversity means, first, recruiting talented workers of both sexes as well as all racial and cultural backgrounds.

But developing the potential of all employees requires meeting the needs of women and other minorities, which may not be the same as those of white men. For example, child care at the workplace is a big issue for working mothers with small children.

Second, businesses must develop effective ways to deal with tension that arises from social differences. They will have to work harder to ensure that workers are treated equally and

respectfully, which means having zero tolerance for racial or sexual harassment.

Third, companies will have to rethink current promotion practices. At present, only 8 percent of Fortune 500 top executives are women, and just 4 percent are other minorities (Catalyst, 2005). In a survey of U.S. companies, the U.S. Equal Employment Opportunity Commission (2005) confirmed that non-Hispanic white men, who make up 34 percent of adults aged twenty to sixty-four, hold 56 percent of management jobs; the comparable figures are 34 and 29 percent, respectively, for non-Hispanic white women, 13 and 6 percent for non-Hispanic African Americans, and 13 and 5 percent for Hispanics.

WHAT DO YOU THINK?

1. What underlying factors are increasing the diversity of the U.S. workplace?

2. In what specific ways do you think businesses should support minority workers?

3. In what other settings (such as schools) is social diversity becoming more important?

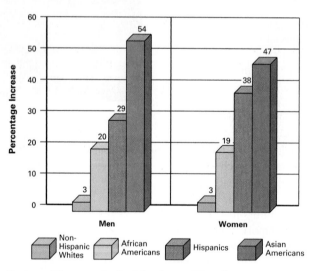

Projected Increase in the Numbers of People in the U.S. Labor Force, 2002–2012

Looking ahead, the share of minorities in the U.S. labor force will increase much faster than the share of white men and women.

Source: Toossi (2004).

NEW INFORMATION TECHNOLOGY AND WORK

July 2, Ticonderoga, New York. The manager of the local hardware store scans the bar codes of a bagful of items. "The computer doesn't just total the costs," she explains. "It also keeps track of inventory, placing orders from the warehouse and deciding which products to continue to sell and which to drop." "Sounds like what you used to do, Maureen," I respond with a smile. "Yep," she nods, with no smile at all.

Another workplace issue is the increasing role of computers and other new information technology. The Information Revolution is changing what people do in a number of ways (Rule & Brantley, 1992; Vallas & Beck, 1996):

1. **Computers are deskilling labor.** Just as industrial machinery replaced the master craftsworkers of an earlier era, computers now threaten the skills of managers. More business  operations are based not on executive decisions but on computer modeling. In other words, a machine decides whether to place an order, stock a dress in a certain size and color, or approve a loan application.

2. **Computers are making work more abstract.** Most industrial workers have a hands-on relationship with their product. Postindustrial workers use symbols to perform abstract tasks, such as making a company more profitable or making software more user-friendly.

3. **Computers limit workplace interaction.** As workers spend more time at computer terminals, they become increasingly isolated from other workers.

4. **Computers increase employers' control of workers.** Computers allow supervisors to monitor employees' output continuously, whether they work at computer terminals or on assembly lines.

5. **Computers allow companies to relocate work.** Because computer technology allows information to flow almost anywhere instantly, the symbolic work in today's economy may not take place where we might think. We have all had the experience of calling a business (say, a hotel or a toy store) located in our own town only to find that we are talking to a person at a computer workstation thousands of miles away. "In the *Times*" on pages 434–35 explains how McDonald's is using new information technology to outsource the job of taking orders at the local drive-through to call centers hundreds or thousands of miles away.

Such changes remind us that technology is not socially neutral. Rather, it changes the relationships between people in the workplace, shapes the way we work, and often alters the balance of power between employers and employees. Understandably, then, people welcome some aspects of the Information Revolution and oppose others.

Corporations

At the core of today's capitalist economy lies the **corporation,** *an organization with a legal existence, including rights*

In today's corporate world, computers are changing the nature of work just as factories did more than a century ago. In what ways is computer-based work different from factory work? In what ways is it the same?

and liabilities, separate from that of its members. Incorporating makes an organization a legal entity, able to enter into contracts and own property. Of the more than 25 million businesses in the United States, 5 million are incorporated (U.S. Census Bureau, 2004). Incorporating shields the wealth of owners from lawsuits that result from business debts or harm to consumers; it can also mean a lower tax rate on the company's profits.

ECONOMIC CONCENTRATION

Most U.S. corporations are small, with assets of less than $500,000, so a small number of very large corporations dominates our country's economy. In 2001, about 2,000 corporations had assets exceeding $2.5 billion, representing three-fourths of all corporate assets (Internal Revenue Service, 2004).

The largest U.S. corporation in terms of sales is Wal-Mart, with more than $100 billion in total assets. Wal-Mart employs more people than the state governments of California, Texas, Colorado, New York, and Florida combined. Its sales ($285 billion in 2005) equal the tax revenues of nearly half the states.

July 18, 2004

A Drive-Through Lane to the Next Time Zone

By MICHAEL FITZGERALD

Pull off Interstate 55 near Cape Girardeau, Mo., and into the drive-through lane of a McDonald's next to the highway and you'll get fast, friendly service, even though the person taking your order is not in the restaurant—or even in Missouri.

The order taker is in a call center in Colorado Springs, more than 900 miles away, connected to the customer and to the workers preparing the food by high-speed data lines. Even some restaurant jobs, it seems, are not immune to outsourcing.

The man who owns the Cape Girardeau restaurant, Shannon Y. Davis, has linked it and 3 other of his 12 McDonald's franchises to the Colorado call center, which is run by another McDonald's franchisee, Steven T. Bigari. And he did it for the same reasons that other business owners have embraced call

centers: lower costs, greater speed and fewer mistakes.

Cheap, quick and reliable telecommunications lines let the order takers in Colorado Springs converse with customers in Missouri, take an electronic snapshot of them, display their order on a screen to make sure it is right, then forward the order and the photo to the restaurant kitchen. The photo is destroyed as soon as the order is completed. . . . People picking up their burgers never know that their order traverses two states and bounces back before they can even start driving to the pickup window. . . . Mr. Davis said . . . he had dreamed of doing something like this for more than a decade. "We could not wait to go with it." . . .

Mr. Bigari, who owns 12 McDonald's franchises and created the call center for his own restaurants, was happy to oblige—for a small fee per transaction. . . .

Central to the system's success . . . is the way it pairs customers' photos with their orders; by increasing accuracy, the system cuts down on the number of complaints and therefore makes the service faster.

In the fast-food business, time is truly money: shaving even five seconds off the processing time of an order is significant. Mr. Bigari . . . cut order time . . . by slightly more than 30 seconds, to about 1 minute, 5 seconds, on average. That's less than half the average . . . for all McDonald's, and among the fastest of any franchise in the country. . . . His drive-throughs now handle 260 cars an hour, . . . 30 more than they did before he started the call center. While Mr. Bigari has been eager to embrace technology—he and his robotic French fry maker warranted mention in the book *Fast Food Nation*—he said he didn't care much for it. "I don't know tech," he said. "I know about people who like to eat hamburgers." And

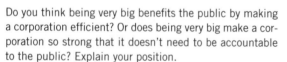

YOUR TURN

Do you think being very big benefits the public by making a corporation efficient? Or does being very big make a corporation so strong that it doesn't need to be accountable to the public? Explain your position.

CONGLOMERATES AND CORPORATE LINKAGES

Economic concentration has created the **conglomerate,** *a giant corporation composed of many smaller corporations.* Conglomerates form as corporations enter new markets, spin off new companies, or merge with other companies.

For example, Pepsico is a conglomerate that includes Pepsi-Cola, Frito-Lay, Gatorade, Tropicana, and Quaker. Many conglomerates are linked because they own each other's stock, the result being worldwide corporate alliances of staggering size. General Motors, for example, owns Opel (Germany), Vauxhall (Great Britain), and half of Saab (Sweden) and has partnerships with Suzuki, Isuzu, and Toyota (Japan). Similarly, Ford owns Jaguar and Aston Martin (Great Britain) and a share of Mazda (Japan), Kia (Korea), and Volvo (Sweden).

Corporations are also linked through *interlocking directorates,* networks of people who serve as directors of many corporations (Weidenbaum, 1995; Kono et al., 1998). These boardroom connections give corporations access to valuable information about other companies' products and marketing strategies. Although perfectly

he knows that people who like to eat hamburgers don't like the wait or the mistakes that often occur at drive-throughs. . . .

Mr. Bigari spent six years looking for a technology company that could meet his needs. . . . He had almost given up when he met with a start-up company called Exit41 Inc., named for its highway exit in Andover, Mass. . . .

Working together, Mr. Bigari and software engineers from Exit41 put a small call center in the back of one of his restaurants in May 2003. Within a couple of weeks, the store was filling orders 30 percent faster and making fewer mistakes. Mr. Bigari . . . now employs 53 people in the call center, which operates 24 hours a day.

Though his operators earn, on average, 40 cents an hour more than his line employees, he has cut his overall labor costs by a percentage point, even as drive-through sales have increased. He said the call center saved enough in six months to cover the cost of setting it up, in part because he no longer had to employ as many people on the overnight shift.

"This transforms my business," Mr. Bigari said. "It's bigger than drive-through." . . .

Mr. Bigari is so enthusiastic about the call-center idea that he has expanded it beyond the drive-through window at his seven restaurants that use the system. While he still offers counter service at those restaurants, most customers now order through the call center, using phones with credit card readers on tables in the seating area. Play areas at the restaurants have them, too, so a parent can place an order over the phone, pay with a credit card and have the food delivered.

The next step, Mr. Bigari said, is to use his call centers to take cellphone orders, something the futurist Paul Saffo said would become commonplace in the next two years. Mr. Bigari plans to test cellphone ordering this summer.

WHAT DO YOU THINK?

1. As a customer, does it make any difference to you whether the person taking your food order at a drive-through is right there at the window or thousands of miles away? Why or why not?

2. How do you think "outsourcing" jobs in this way affects the way people in the restaurant do their jobs?

3. In general, do you think computer technology is changing the workplace for the better or for the worse? Explain your answer.

Adapted from the original article by Michael Fitzgerald published in *The New York Times* on July 18, 2004. Copyright © 2004 by The New York Times Company. Reprinted with permission.

legal, such linkages may encourage illegal activity, such as price fixing, as the companies share information about their pricing policies.

CORPORATIONS: ARE THEY COMPETITIVE?

According to the capitalist model, businesses operate independently in a competitive market. But in light of the extensive linkages that exist between them, it is obvious that large corporations do not operate independently. Also, a few large corporations dominate many markets, so they are not truly competitive.

Federal law forbids any company from establishing a **monopoly,** *the domination of a market by a single producer*, because with no competition, such a company could simply charge whatever it wanted for its products. But **oligopoly,** *the domination of a market by a few producers*, is both legal and common. Oligopoly arises because the huge investment needed to enter a major market, such as the auto industry, is beyond the reach of all but the biggest companies. In addition, competition means risk, which big business tries to avoid.

The federal government seeks to regulate corporations in order to protect the public interest. Yet as recent corporate scandals have shown, regulation is often too little too late, resulting in companies harming millions of people. The U.S. government is the corporate world's single biggest customer, and in some cases it steps in to support struggling corporations, sometimes with billion-dollar bailout programs. As the Applying Sociology box on page 436 explains, state governments' aid to corporations has drawn fire from critics as "corporate welfare."

Them That's Got, Gets: The Case of Corporate Welfare

Would you like the government to slash your income taxes and cancel sales tax on your purchases? What about offering you money to buy a new house at a below-market interest rate? Would you like the government to hook up all your utilities free of charge and pay your water and electric bills?

For an ordinary person, such deals sound too good to be true. But our tax money is doing exactly that—not for families but for big corporations. All a large company has to do is declare a willingness to relocate and then wait for the offers from state and local governments to come pouring in.

Supporters call government aid to corporations "public-private partnerships." They point to the jobs corporations create, sometimes in areas hard hit by earlier business closings. For a city or county with a high unemployment rate, the promise of a new factory is simply too good to pass up. If incentives in the form of tax relief or free utilities are needed to seal the deal, the money is considered well spent.

Critics call such arrangements "corporate welfare." They agree that companies create new jobs, but they point out that the corporations get much more than they give. In 1991, for example, the state of Indiana offered $451 million in incentives to lure United Airlines to build an aircraft maintenance facility there. United built the facility and hired 6,300 people. But some simple math shows that the cost to Indiana came out to be a whopping $72,000 per job. Much the same happened in 1993, when Alabama offered $253 million in incentives to Mercedes-Benz to build an automobile assembly plant in Tuscaloosa. The plant opened and 1,500 people were hired—at an average cost to Alabama of $169,000 for each worker. In 1997, Pennsylvania gave $307 million in incentives to a Norwegian company to reopen part of Philadelphia's naval shipyard. Once the deal was signed, 950 people were hired, at a cost of $323,000 per job. In 2002, Georgia spent $67,000 per job to bring in a new Daimler-Benz auto plant. Across the country, the pattern is much the same. Government support to corporations exceeds $15 billion each year, more than the welfare given to people who are poor.

Although new plants do create some jobs, most jobs are simply moved from one place to another. In addition, not all jobs pay well. Nor is there any guarantee that once settled, a corporation will stay, since businesses are free to make a better deal and move again to another location.

WHAT DO YOU THINK?

1. Why are local government officials so eager to attract business?
2. Do you think ordinary people benefit from corporate tax relief policies? Explain your answer.
3. Overall, do you support tax breaks for corporations? Why or why not?

Sources: Adapted from Bartlett & Steele (1998) and various news reports.

CORPORATIONS AND THE GLOBAL ECONOMY

Corporations have grown so large that they now account for most of the world's economic output. The biggest corporations are based in the United States, Japan, and Western Europe, but their marketplace is the entire world. In fact, many large U.S. companies such as McDonald's and chipmaker Intel earn most of their money outside the United States.

Global corporations recognize that poor countries contain most of the world's people and resources. In addition, labor costs are attractively low: A manufacturing worker in Mexico, whose average hourly wage is $2.21, labors for almost two weeks to earn what a worker in the United States (at an average $17.12 per hour) or Japan ($16.68 per hour) earns in a single day.

As Chapter 12 ("Global Stratification") explained, the impact of multinationals on poor countries is controversial. Modernization theorists claim that multinationals, by unleashing the great productive power of capitalism, raise living standards in poor nations, offering them tax revenues, new jobs, and advanced technology that together accelerate economic growth (Berger, 1986; Firebaugh & Beck, 1994; Firebaugh & Sandu, 1998).

Dependency theorists counter that multinationals make global inequality worse, blocking the development of local industries and pushing poor countries to make goods for export rather than food and other products for local people. From this standpoint, multinationals make poor nations poorer and increasingly dependent on rich nations

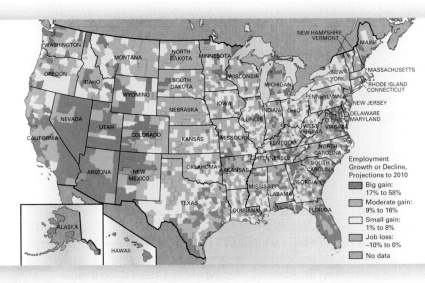

The economic prospects of counties across the United States are not the same. Much of the mid-section of the country is projected to lose jobs. By contrast, the coastal regions and most of the West are rapidly gaining jobs. What factors might account for this pattern?

Source: Used with permission of Woods & Poole Economics, Washington, D.C.

Employment
Growth or Decline,
Projections to 2010

Big gain:
17% to 58%

Moderate gain:
9% to 16%

Small gain:
1% to 8%

Job loss:
–10% to 0%

No data

(Wallerstein, 1979; Walton & Ragin, 1990; Dixon & Boswell, 1996; Kentor, 1998).

Modernization theory hails the market as the key to progress and affluence for all the world's people, and dependency theory calls for replacing market systems with government-based economic policies. The Thinking It Through box on page 438 takes a closer look at the issue of market versus government economies.

The Economy: Looking Ahead

Social institutions are a society's way of meeting people's needs. But as we have seen, the U.S. economy only partly succeeds in this mission. Although highly productive, our economy provides for some people much better than for others.

The Information Revolution has caused tremendous changes in the economy. First, the share of the U.S. labor force in manufacturing is half what it was in 1960; service work, especially computer-related jobs, makes up the difference. For industrial workers, the postindustrial economy has brought rising unemployment and declining wages. Our society must face up to the challenge of providing millions of men and women with the language and computer skills they need to succeed in the new economy. Yet as the economic collapse of many dot-coms in 2001 shows, even this new type of work is not immune to a downturn. In addition, there are regional differences in the economic outlook: National Map 16–1 shows which regions are projected to gain jobs and which are expected to lose them by the end of the decade.

A second transformation that marks the new century is the expansion of the global economy. Two centuries ago, the ups and downs of a local economy reflected events and trends in a single town. One century ago, communities were economically linked so that one town's prosperity depended on producing goods demanded by people elsewhere in the country. Today, it makes little sense to speak of a national economy, because what we pay at the pump for gasoline here in the United States has much to do with increasing demand for oil in China and India. As both producers and consumers, we are now responding to factors and forces that are both distant and unseen.

Finally, analysts around the world are rethinking conventional economic models. The global economy shows that socialism is less productive than capitalism, one important reason behind the collapse of the socialist regimes in Eastern Europe and the Soviet Union. But capitalism has its own problems, including corporate scandal and high levels of inequality, and now operates with significant government regulation.

What will be the long-term effects of these changes? Two conclusions seem certain. First, the economic future of the United States and other nations will be played out in a global arena. The new postindustrial economy in the United States has emerged as more industrial production has moved to other nations. Second, it is imperative that we address the related issues of global inequality and population increase. We are at a fork in the road: Whether the global economy ultimately reduces or deepens the gap between rich and poor societies may well steer our planet toward peace or war.

The Market: Does the "Invisible Hand" Look Out for Us or Pick Our Pockets?

"The market" or "government planning"? Governments rely on one or the other to determine what products and services companies will produce and what people will consume. So important is this question that the answer has much to do with how nations define themselves, choose their allies, and identify their enemies.

Historically, U.S. society has relied on the "invisible hand" of the market to make economic decisions. Market dynamics move prices up or down according to the supply of products and buyer demand. The market thus links the efforts of countless people, each of whom—to restate Adam Smith's insight—is motivated only by self-interest. Defenders of the market system—most notably economists Milton Friedman and Rose Friedman (1980)—claim that a more or less freely operating market system is the key to this country's high standard of living.

But others point to the contributions government makes to the U.S. economy. First, government must step in to carry out tasks that no private company could do as well, such as defending the country against enemies abroad or terrorists at home. Government (in partnership with private companies) also plays a key role in building and maintaining public projects such as roads, utilities, schools, libraries, and museums.

But the Friedmans counter that whatever the task, government usually ends up being very inefficient. They claim that for most people, the least satisfying goods and services available today—public schools, the postal service, and passenger railroad service—

are government-operated. The products we most enjoy—household appliances, computers and other new electronics, fashionable clothes—are products of the market. Some government presence in the economy is necessary, but the Friedmans and other supporters of free markets believe that minimal state regulation best serves the public interest.

But supporters of government intervention in the economy make other arguments. First, they claim that the market has incentives to produce only what is profitable. Few private companies set out to meet the needs of poor people because, by definition, poor people have little money to spend.

Second, the market has certain self-destructive tendencies that only the government can curb. In 1890, for example, the government passed the Sherman Antitrust Act to break up the monopolies that controlled the nation's oil and steel production. In the decades since then—and especially after President Franklin Roosevelt's New Deal of the 1930s—government has taken a strong regulatory role to control inflation (by setting interest rates), enhance the well-being of workers (by imposing workplace safety standards), and benefit consumers (by setting standards for product quality). Despite such interventions, advocates of a stronger government role point out that corporations continue to engage in wrongdoing, and they are so powerful that the government cannot effectively challenge them.

Third, because the market magnifies social inequality, the government must step in on the side of social justice. Since capitalist economies

concentrate income and wealth in the hands of a few, it is necessary for government to tax the rich at a higher rate to ensure that wealth reaches more of the population.

Does the market's "invisible hand" look out for us or pick our pockets? Although most people in the United States favor a free market, they also support government intervention that benefits the public. In recent years, public confidence in corporations has fallen, and confidence in the federal government has gone up (NORC, 2003). Government's job is not only to ensure national security but also to maintain economic stability. Therefore, government helps businesses by providing investment capital, maintaining roads and other public services, and protecting companies from foreign competition. It is no surprise, then, that people in the United States and around the world continue to debate the best balance of market forces and government decision making.

WHAT DO YOU THINK?

1. Do you agree or disagree with the statement that "a government is best that governs least"? Why?
2. Based on what you have read in this chapter, in what specific ways might people's everyday lives reflect whether a society's economy is more a market system or more government-centered?
3. What is your impression of the successes and failures of socialist economic systems? What about "welfare capitalism" as found in Sweden?

16 MAKING THE GRADE

The following learning tools will help you see what you know, identify what you still need to learn, and expand your understanding beyond the text. You can also visit the text's Companion Website™ at http://www.prenhall.com/macionis to find additional practice tests.

KEY POINTS

The Economy: Historical Overview

The economy is the major social institution through which a society produces, distributes, and consumes goods and services. In technologically simple societies, the economy is simply part of family life. Agrarian societies show some productive specialization. Industrialization rapidly expands the economy through greater specialization and new energy sources that power machines in large factories. The postindustrial economy is characterized by a shift from producing goods to providing services. Just as the Industrial Revolution propelled the industrial economy of the past, the Information Revolution is now advancing the postindustrial economy.

The primary sector of the economy, which generates raw materials, is the largest sector in low-income countries. In all nations, the secondary, manufacturing sector represents about one-third of the economy. The tertiary, service sector dominates the economy in high-income countries.

The expanding global economy now produces and consumes products and services across national boundaries. Today, the 600 largest corporations, operating internationally, account for most of the world's economic output.

Economic Systems: Paths to Justice

Capitalism is based on the private ownership of productive property and the pursuit of profit in a competitive marketplace. Socialism is grounded in the collective ownership of productive property through government control of the economy. Although the U.S. economy is predominantly capitalist, government is broadly involved in economic life. Government plays a greater role in the "welfare capitalist" economies of some Western European nations, such as

Sweden, and the "state capitalism" of many Asian nations, including Japan.

Capitalism is very productive, providing a high average standard of living. A capitalist system allows the freedom to act according to self-interest. Socialism is less productive but generates greater economic equality and offers everyone freedom from basic want.

Work in the Postindustrial Economy

In the United States, agricultural work has declined to just 1.6 percent of the labor force. Blue-collar jobs account for just 22 percent of the labor force. The share of white-collar service occupations has increased to 77 percent of the labor force.

Although work in the primary labor market provides greater rewards, many new jobs in the United States are service positions in the secondary labor market. A profession is a special category of white-collar work based on theoretical knowledge, self-regulating practice, authority over clients, and a claim to serving the community. Today, 7.5 percent of U.S. workers are self-employed. Although many professionals fall into this category, most self-employed workers have blue-collar occupations.

Unemployment has many causes, including the operation of the economy itself; in 2004, 5.5 percent of the U.S. labor force was without work. The underground economy, which includes criminal as well as legal activity, generates income unreported to the government.

Corporations

Corporations form the core of the U.S. economy. The largest corporations, which are conglomerates, account for most corporate assets and profits. Many large corporations operate as multinationals, producing and distributing products in nations around the world.

The Economy: Looking Ahead

In the future, our society must prepare more people to perform the type of work being created by the Information Revolution. In addition, the expanding global economy means we produce and consume in response to distant factors and forces in other parts of the world.

KEY CONCEPTS

economy (p. 418) the social institution that organizes a society's production, distribution, and consumption of goods and services

postindustrial economy (p. 421) a productive system based on service work and high technology

primary sector (p. 421) the part of the economy that draws raw materials from the natural environment

secondary sector (p. 421) the part of the economy that transforms raw materials into manufactured goods

tertiary sector (p. 422) the part of the economy that involves services rather than goods

global economy (p. 422) expanding economic activity that crosses national borders

capitalism (p. 424) an economic system in which natural resources and the means of producing goods and services are privately owned

socialism (p. 424) an economic system in which natural resources and the means of producing goods and services are collectively owned

communism (p. 425) a hypothetical economic and political system in which all members of a society are socially equal

welfare capitalism (p. 425) an economic and political system that combines a mostly market-based economy with extensive social welfare programs

state capitalism (p. 426) an economic and political system in which companies are privately owned but cooperate closely with the government

primary labor market (p. 428) jobs that provide extensive benefits to workers

secondary labor market (p. 428) jobs that provide minimal benefits to workers

labor unions (p. 428) organizations of workers that seek to improve wages and working conditions through various strategies, including negotiations and strikes

profession (p. 429) a prestigious white-collar occupation that requires extensive formal education

underground economy (p. 431) economic activity involving income not reported to the government as required by law

corporation (p. 433) an organization with a legal existence, including rights and liabilities, separate from that of its members

conglomerate (p. 434) a giant corporation composed of many smaller corporations

monopoly (p. 435) the domination of a market by a single producer

oligopoly (p. 435) the domination of a market by a few producers

SAMPLE TEST QUESTIONS

These questions are similar to those found in the test bank that accompanies this textbook.

Multiple-Choice Questions

1. **The economy is the social institution that guides**
   a. the production of goods and services.
   b. the distribution of goods and services.
   c. the consumption of goods and services.
   d. all of the above.

2. **The early textile factories in New England, where the Industrial Revolution began in the United States, employed**
   a. mostly women who were paid half the wages earned by men.
   b. mostly immigrants who had just arrived from Asia and Latin America.
   c. people who had been in the United States the longest.
   d. all of the above.

3. **Building houses and making cars are examples of production in which economic sector?**
   a. the primary sector
   b. the secondary sector
   c. the tertiary sector
   d. the service sector

4. **Which of the following marks the rise of a postindustrial economy?**
   a. the spread of factories
   b. declining rates of consumption
   c. the development of computer technology
   d. larger machinery

5. **Today, about what share of the U.S. labor force has industrial (secondary sector) jobs?**
   a. one-fourth
   b. one-half
   c. two-thirds
   d. nine-tenths

6. **The globalization of the economy is causing which of the following?**
   a. Certain areas of the world are specializing in one sector of economic activity.
   b. Industrial jobs in the United States are being lost.
   c. More and more products pass through several nations.
   d. All of the above are correct.

7. **A capitalist society's approach to economic "justice" amounts to**
   a. doing what is best for society's poorest members.
   b. freedom of the marketplace.
   c. making everyone more or less socially equal.
   d. all of the above.

8. **Socialist economies differ from capitalist economies by**
   a. being more productive.
   b. creating less economic equality.
   c. creating more economic equality.
   d. making greater use of commercial advertising.

9. **In the United States, what percentage of nonfarm workers are members of a labor union?**
   a. 13 percent
   b. 33 percent

   c. 53 percent
   d. 73 percent

10. **The largest 2,000 corporations, each with assets exceeding $2.5 billion, represent about what share of all corporate assets in the United States?**
    a. 10 percent
    b. 25 percent
    c. 50 percent
    d. 75 percent

Answers: 1(d); 2(a); 3(b); 4(c); 5(a); 6(d); 7(b); 8(c); 9(a); 10(d).

Essay Questions

1. In what specific ways did the Industrial Revolution change the U.S. economy? How is the Information Revolution changing the economy once again?

2. What key characteristics distinguish capitalism from socialism? Compare these two systems in terms of productivity, economic inequality, and extent of personal freedoms.

APPLICATIONS & EXERCISES

1. Do some research to learn about the economy of your state, including the type of work people do, the unemployment rate, and what trends are under way. A good place to start is the Web site for the U.S. Bureau of Labor Statistics at http://www.bls/org.

2. Visit a discount store such as Wal-Mart or Kmart and do a little "fieldwork" in an area of the store that interests

you. Pick ten products and see where each is made. Do the results support the existence of a global economy?

3. Find out what share of the faculty on your campus have temporary teaching contracts. Talk to two tenured professors and two visiting professors. What differences can you find in their working conditions and their attitudes toward their jobs?

INVESTIGATE *with* Research Navigator

Follow the instructions on page 27 of this text to access the features of **Research Navigator**™. Once at the Web site, enter your Login Name and Password. Then, to use the **ContentSelect**™ database, enter keywords such as "unemployment," "corporations," and "capitalism," and the search engine will supply relevant and recent scholarly and popular press publications. Use the *New York Times* **Search-by-Search Archive** to find recent news articles related to sociology and the **Link Library** feature to find relevant Web links organized by the key terms associated with this chapter.

17

Politics and Government

How do political systems vary around the world?

Why do critics say that U.S. society is not truly democratic?

What are some of the causes of war?

At the end of January 2005, people poured into the streets all across Iraq to select the people who now serve as their leaders. The idea of electing leaders was new and exciting for many of the voters; for decades the country had been ruled by a dictator who tolerated no political opposition. But not everybody was lining up to vote. An organized movement opposed both the elections and the presence of U.S. forces in the country. To keep citizens from the polls, they threatened that the streets would run with the blood of anyone who dared to vote. In a country in which suicide bombings and other attacks happen every day, people have good reason to take such warnings seriously. Others, including many Sunni Muslims, did not wish to take part in an election that seemed likely to elect mostly Shiite Muslims, which would limit the Sunnis' power (Wines, 2005).

Despite all these concerns, about 60 percent of eligible Iraqi voters went to the polls. In fact, the turnout in Iraq exceeded the turnout in the 2004 U.S. presidential election. Perhaps Iraq can boast that it is well on the road to becoming a democracy. Or maybe the United States is not as democratic as we like to think. ■

Questions about who has the power to make decisions in any society lead us to the issue of politics. Formally, **politics**—or "the polity"—is *the social institution that distributes power, sets a society's goals, and makes decisions.* The fact that millions of people in the United States do not take part in elections (even without the threats found in nations such as Iraq) and the fact that this country is divided over the military campaign to change the political system in Iraq suggest that politics is often a matter of controversy.

Power and Authority

The sociologist Max Weber (1978, orig. 1921) claimed that every society is based on **power,** which he defined as *the ability to achieve desired ends despite resistance from others.* The use of power is the business of **government,** *a formal organization that directs the political life of a society.* Governments demand compliance on the part of a population; yet Weber noted that most governments do not openly threaten their people. Most of the time, people respect (or at least accept) their society's political system.

No government, Weber continued, is likely to keep its power for very long if compliance came *only* from the threat of brute force, because there could never be enough police to watch everyone—and who would watch the police? Every

government, therefore, tries to make itself seem legitimate in the eyes of the people. This brings us to Weber's concept of **authority,** *power that people perceive as legitimate rather than coercive.* How do governments transform raw power into more stable authority? Weber pointed to three ways: traditional authority, rational-legal authority, and charismatic authority.

TRADITIONAL AUTHORITY

Preindustrial societies, said Weber, rely on **traditional authority,** *power legitimized by respect for long-established cultural patterns.* Woven into a population's collective memory, traditional authority means that people accept a system, usually one of hereditary leadership, simply because it has always been that way. In centuries past, Chinese emperors were legitimized by tradition, as were nobles in medieval Europe. The power of tradition can be so strong that, for better or worse, people typically come to view traditional rulers as almost godlike.

Traditional authority declines as societies industrialize. Hannah Arendt (1963) pointed out that traditional authority remains strong only as long as everyone shares the same beliefs and way of life. Modern scientific thinking, the specialization demanded by industrial production, and the social change and cultural diversity brought on by immigration all combine to weaken tradition. Therefore, a

U.S. president would never claim to rule by the grace of God, as many rulers in the ancient world did. Even so, some upper-class families with names like Bush, Kennedy, Roosevelt, and Rockefeller are so well established in our country's political life that their members may enter the political arena with some measure of traditional authority (Baltzell, 1964).

Traditional authority is also a source of strength for *patriarchy*, the domination of women by men. This traditional form of power is still widespread, although it is increasingly challenged. Less controversial is the traditional authority parents have over their children. As children, most of us can remember challenging a parent's demand by asking "Why?" only to hear the response "Because I said so!" Answering this way, the parent makes clear that the demand is not open for debate; to respond otherwise would ignore the parent's traditional authority over the child and put the two on an equal footing.

RATIONAL-LEGAL AUTHORITY

Weber defined **rational-legal authority** (sometimes called *bureaucratic authority*) as *power legitimized by legally enacted rules and regulations*. Rational-legal authority is power legitimized in the operation of lawful government.

As Chapter 7 ("Groups and Organizations") explains, Weber viewed bureaucracy as the type of organization that dominates in rational-thinking, modern societies. The same rational worldview that promotes bureaucracy also erodes traditional customs and practices. Instead of looking to the past, members of today's high-income societies seek justice through formally enacted rules of law.

Rationally enacted rules also guide the use of power in everyday life. The authority of deans and classroom teachers, for example, rests on the offices they hold in bureaucratic colleges and universities. The police, too, depend on rational-legal authority. In contrast to traditional authority, rational-legal authority comes not from family background but from a position in government organization. A traditional monarch rules for life, but a modern president accepts and gives up power according to law, which shows that presidential authority lies in the office, not in the person.

YOUR TURN

Why do we call police and many other people who exercise rational authority "officers"?

CHARISMATIC AUTHORITY

Finally, Weber claimed that power can turn into authority through charisma. **Charismatic authority** is *power legitimized by extraordinary personal abilities that inspire devotion and obedience*. Unlike traditional and rational-legal authority, charismatic authority depends less on a person's ancestry or office and more on individual personality.

Charismatic leaders have surfaced throughout history, using their personal skills to turn an audience into followers. Often they make their own rules and challenge the status quo. Examples of charismatic leaders can be as different as Jesus of Nazareth and Adolf Hitler. The fact that they and others, such as India's liberator, Mahatma Gandhi, and the

 For more about the life of Dr. King, go to http://www.lib.lsu.edu/hum/mlk

U.S. civil rights leader Martin Luther King Jr., succeeded in transforming the society around them explains why charismatics are almost always highly controversial, and it probably explains why few of them die of old age.

Because charismatic authority flows from a single individual, the leader's death creates a crisis for the movement the leader has created. For the movement to survive, Max Weber explained, what must happen is the **routinization of charisma**, *the transformation of charismatic authority into some combination of traditional and bureaucratic authority*. After the death of Jesus, followers institutionalized his teachings, creating a church built on tradition and bureaucracy. Routinized in this way, the Roman Catholic Church has lasted for 2,000 years and in 2005 elected its 266th leader, Pope Benedict XVI.

Politics in Global Perspective

Political systems have changed over the course of history. Technologically simple hunting and gathering societies, once found all over the planet, operated like large families without formal governments. Leadership generally fell to a man with unusual strength, hunting skill, or personal charisma. But with few resources, such leaders might control their own people but could never rule a large area (Nolan & Lenski, 2004).

Agrarian societies are larger, with specialized jobs and a material surplus. In these societies, a small elite gains control of most of the wealth and power, moving politics from the family to become a social institution in its own right. This is the point in history when leaders start to claim a divine right to rule, gaining some measure of Weber's traditional authority. Leaders may also benefit from rational-legal authority to the extent that their rule is supported by law.

In 2005, just 28 of the world's 192 nations were political monarchies where single families pass power from generation to generation. Here, the African nation of Swaziland celebrates the coronation of a young king.

As societies grow even bigger, politics takes the form of a national government, or *political state*. But the effectiveness of a political state depends on the available technology. Centuries ago, armies moved slowly on foot, and communication over even short distances was uncertain. For this reason, the early political empires—such as Mesopotamia in the Middle East about 5,000 years ago—took the form of many small *city-states*.

More complex technology brings about the larger-scale system of *nation-states*. Currently, the world has 192 independent nation-states, each with a somewhat distinctive political system. Generally, however, they fall into four categories: monarchy, democracy, authoritarianism, and totalitarianism.

MONARCHY

Monarchy (with Latin and Greek roots meaning "one ruler") is *a political system in which a single family rules from generation to generation*. Monarchy is commonly found in the ancient agrarian societies; the Bible, for example, tells of great kings such as David and Solomon. In the world today, twenty-eight nations have royal families;[1] some trace their ancestry back for centuries. In Weber's terms, then, monarchy is legitimized by tradition.

During the Middle Ages, *absolute monarchs* in much of the world claimed a monopoly of power based on divine

---

[1]In Europe, Sweden, Norway, Denmark, Great Britain, the Netherlands, Liechtenstein, Luxembourg, Belgium, Spain, and Monaco; in the Middle East, Jordan, Saudi Arabia, Oman, Qatar, Bahrain, and Kuwait; in Africa, Lesotho, Swaziland, and Morocco; in Asia, Brunei, Samoa, Tonga, Thailand, Malaysia, Cambodia, Nepal, Bhutan, and Japan.

right. Today, claims of divine right are rare, although monarchs in a number of nations—including Kuwait, Saudi Arabia, and Bahrain—still exercise almost absolute control over their people.

With industrialization, monarchs gradually pass from the scene in favor of elected officials. All the European nations with royal families today are *constitutional monarchies*, meaning that their monarchs are little more than symbolic heads of state; actual governing is the responsibility of elected officials, led by a prime minister and guided by a constitution. In these nations, nobility formally reigns, but elected officials actually rule.

DEMOCRACY

The historical trend in the modern world is toward **democracy**, *a political system that gives power to the people as a whole*. More correctly, a system of *representative democracy* puts authority in the hands of leaders chosen by the people who, from time to time, compete for office in elections.

Most high-income countries of the world claim to be democratic (including those that still have royal families). Industrialization and democratic government go together because both require a literate populace. Also, the traditional legitimization of power in an agrarian monarchy gives way, with industrialization, to rational-legal authority. Thus democracy and rational-legal authority are linked just like monarchy and traditional authority.

But high-income countries such as the United States are not truly democratic for two reasons. First, there is the problem of bureaucracy. The U.S. federal government has 2.7 million regular employees, 1.4 million uniformed military

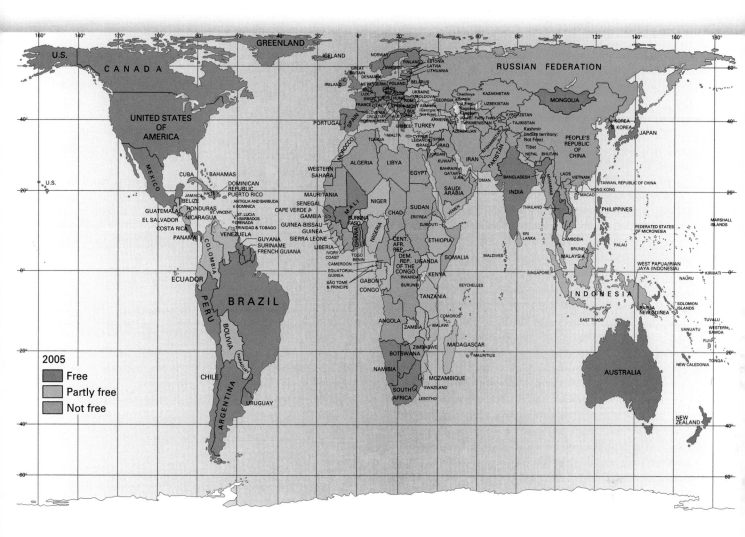

WINDOW ON THE WORLD

GLOBAL MAP 17-1   Political Freedom in Global Perspective

In 2005, a total of 89 of the world's 192 nations, containing 44 percent of all people, were politically "free"; that is, they offered their citizens extensive political rights and civil liberties. Another 54 countries, which included 19 percent of the world's people, were "partly free," with more limited rights and liberties. The remaining 49 nations, home to 37 percent of humanity, fall into the category of "not free." In these countries, government sharply restricts individual initiative. Between 1980 and 2005, democracy made significant gains, largely in Latin America and Eastern Europe. In Asia, India (containing 1 billion people) returned to the "free" category in 1999. In 2000, Mexico joined the ranks of nations considered "free" for the first time.

Source: Freedom House (2005).

personnel, and 8 million employees paid by various grants and special funding—about 12 million workers in all. In addition, another 18 million people work in almost 88,000 local governments across the country. Most people who run the government are never elected by anyone and do not have to answer directly to the people.

The second problem involves economic inequality, since rich people have far more political power than poor people. Both George W. Bush and John Kerry, who ran for the presidency in 2004, are very wealthy men, and in the game of politics, "money talks." Given the even greater resources of billion-dollar corporations, how well does our "democratic" system hear the voices of "average people"?

Still, democratic nations do provide many rights and freedoms. Global Map 17–1 on page 447 shows one assessment of the extent of political freedom around the world. According to Freedom House, an organization that tracks political trends, 89 of the world's 192 nations (with 44 percent of the global population) were "free," respecting many civil liberties, in 2005. This represents a gain for freedom: Just 76 nations were free a decade earlier (Freedom House, 2005).

Democracy and Freedom: Capitalist and Socialist Approaches

Despite the problems we have just described, rich capitalist nations such as the United States claim to operate as democracies. Of course, socialist countries like Cuba and the People's Republic of China make the same claim. This curious fact suggests that we need to look more closely at *political economy*, the interplay of politics and economics.

The political life of the United States, Canada, and the nations of Europe is largely shaped by the economic principles of capitalism, described in Chapter 16 ("The Economy and Work"). The pursuit of profit within a market system requires that "freedom" be defined in terms of people's right to act in their own self-interest. Thus the capitalist approach to political freedom translates into personal liberty, the freedom to act in whatever ways maximize personal profit or other advantage. From this point of view, "democracy" means that individuals have the right to select their leaders from among those running for office.

However, capitalist societies are marked by a striking inequality of income and wealth. If everyone acts according to self-interest, the inevitable result is that some people have much more power to get their way than others. It is this elite that dominates the economic and political life of the society.

By contrast, socialist systems claim they are democratic because their economies meet everyone's basic needs for housing, schooling, work, and medical care. Despite being a much poorer country than the United States, for example, Cuba provides basic medical care to all its people regardless of their ability to pay.

But critics of socialism counter that the extensive government regulation of social life in these countries is oppressive. The socialist governments of China and Cuba, for example, do not allow their people to move freely within or across their borders and tolerate no organized political opposition.

These contrasting approaches to democracy and freedom raise an important question: Can economic equality and political liberty go together? To foster economic equality, socialism limits the choices of individuals. Capitalism, on the other hand, provides broad political liberties, which in practice mean little to the poor.

YOUR TURN

In your opinion, what is the most important way in which people can be "free"? Are civil liberties or economic security more important? Explain your answer.

AUTHORITARIANISM

Some nations prevent their people from having a voice in politics. **Authoritarianism** is *a political system that denies the people participation in government.* An authoritarian government is indifferent to people's needs, offers them no voice in selecting leaders, and uses force in response to dissent or opposition. The absolute monarchies in Saudi Arabia and Bahrain are authoritarian, as is the military junta in Ethiopia. Usually, people resist heavy-handed government. But not always. The Thinking Globally box looks at the "soft authoritarianism" that thrives in the small Asian nation of Singapore.

TOTALITARIANISM

October 22, near Saigon, Vietnam. Six U.S. students in our study-abroad program have been arrested, allegedly for talking to Vietnamese students and taking pictures at the university. The Vietnamese minister of education has canceled the reception tonight, claiming that meetings between our students and their students threaten Vietnam's security.

"Soft Authoritarianism" or Planned Prosperity?
A Report from Singapore

Singapore is on the tip of the Malay peninsula and has a population of 4.3 million. To many of its people, the tiny nation seems an Asian paradise. Surrounded by poor societies grappling with rapidly growing populations, rising crime rates, and dirty, sprawling cities, Singapore stands apart with its affluence, cleanliness, and safety. Visitors from the United States sometimes say it seems more of a theme park than a country.

Since gaining its independence from Malaysia in 1965, Singapore has startled the world with its economic development and its high per capita income. In contrast to the United States, Singapore has scarcely any social problems such as crime, slums, unemployment, or children living in poverty. There are hardly any traffic jams, and you won't find graffiti on subway cars or litter in the streets.

The key to Singapore's orderly environment is the ever-present government, which actively promotes traditional morality and regulates just about everything. The state owns and manages most of the country's housing and has a hand in many businesses. It provides tax breaks for family planning and for the completion of additional years of schooling. To limit traffic, the government slaps hefty surcharges on cars, pushing the price of a basic sedan up to around $40,000.

Singapore has tough anticrime laws that mandate death by hanging for drug dealing and permit police to hold a person suspected of a crime without charge or trial. The government has outlawed some religious groups (including Jehovah's Witnesses) and bans pornography outright. To keep the city clean, the state forbids smoking in public, bans eating on its subways, imposes stiff fines for littering, and even regulates the use of chewing gum.

In economic terms, Singapore does not fit the familiar categories. Government control of many businesses, including television stations, telephone service, airlines, and taxis, seems socialist. Yet unlike most socialist enterprises, these businesses operate efficiently and very profitably. Singapore's capitalist culture applauds economic growth (although the government cautions people against being too

materialistic), and hundreds of multinational corporations are based here.

Singapore's political climate is as unusual as its economy. Freedom House (2005) characterizes Singapore as "partly free." The law provides for elections of political leaders, but one party—the People's Action party—has dominated the political process since independence and controls almost all the seats in the country's parliament.

Singapore is not a democratic country in the conventional sense. But most people in this prospering nation are quite happy with their way of life. Singapore's political system offers a simple bargain: Government demands loyalty from its people; in return, it gives them security and prosperity. Critics charge that this system amounts to a "soft authoritarianism" that controls people's lives and stifles political dissent. But most of the people of Singapore know the struggles of living elsewhere and, for now at least, consider the trade-off a good one.

WHAT DO YOU THINK?

1. What aspects of political life in Singapore do you like? Why?
2. What aspects of political life in Singapore do you not like? Why?
3. Would you say that Singapore offers a better life than the United States? Why or why not?

The most intensely controlled political form is **totalitarianism,** *a highly centralized political system that extensively regulates people's lives.* Totalitarianism emerged in the twentieth century as technological advances gave governments the ability to rigidly control their populations. The

Vietnamese government closely monitors the activities of not just visitors but all its citizens. Similarly, the government of North Korea uses surveillance equipment and powerful computers to control its people by collecting and storing information about them.

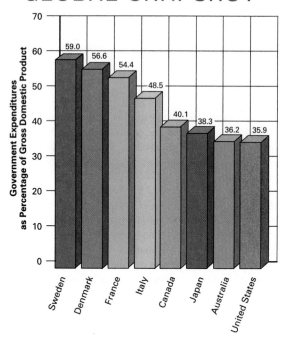

GLOBAL SNAPSHOT

FIGURE 17-1 The Size of Government, 2003

Government activity accounts for a smaller share of economic output in the United States compared to other high-income countries.

Source: U.S. Census Bureau (2004).

Although some totalitarian governments claim to represent the will of the people, most seek to bend people to the will of the government. As the term itself implies, such governments have a *total* concentration of power, allowing no organized opposition. Denying the people the right to assemble and controlling access to information, these governments create an atmosphere of isolation and fear. In the Soviet Union, for example, ordinary citizens had no access to telephone directories, copying equipment, fax machines, or even accurate city maps.

Socialization in totalitarian societies is intensely political, with the goal of obedience and commitment to the system. In North Korea, one of the world's most totalitarian states, pictures of leaders and political messages are everywhere, reminding citizens that they owe total allegiance to the state. Government-controlled schools and mass media present only official versions of events.

Totalitarian governments span the political spectrum from fascist (including Nazi Germany) to communist (including North Korea). In all cases, however, one party claims total control of the society and permits no opposition.

A GLOBAL POLITICAL SYSTEM?

Chapter 16 ("The Economy and Work") described the emergence of a global economy, in which large corporations operate with little regard to national boundaries. Is globalization changing politics in the same way? On one level, the answer is no. Although most of the world's economic activity is international, the planet remains divided into nation-states, just as it has been for centuries. The United Nations (founded in 1945) was a small step toward global government, but to date its political role in the world has been limited.

On another level, however, politics has become a global process. For some analysts, multinational corporations have created a new political order because of their enormous power to shape events throughout the world. In other words, politics is dissolving into business as corporations grow larger than governments.

Also, the Information Revolution has moved national politics onto the world stage. E-mail, text messaging, and cellular phones mean that few countries can conduct their political affairs in complete privacy.

Finally, several thousand *nongovernmental organizations* (NGOs) seek to advance global issues, such as human rights (Amnesty International) or an ecologically sustainable world (Greenpeace). NGOs will continue to play a key part in expanding the global political culture.

In sum, just as individual nations are losing control of their own economies, governments cannot fully manage the political events occurring within their borders.

Politics in the United States

After fighting a war against Britain to gain political independence, the United States replaced the British monarchy with a representative democracy. Our nation's political development reflects a cultural history as well as its capitalist economy.

U.S. CULTURE AND THE RISE OF THE WELFARE STATE

The political culture of the United States can be summed up in a word: individualism. This emphasis is found in the Bill of Rights, which guarantees freedom from undue government interference. It was this individualism that the nineteenth-century poet and essayist Ralph Waldo Emerson had in mind when he said, "The government that governs best is the government that governs least."

Lower-income people have more pressing financial needs and so they tend to focus on economic issues, such as the level of the minimum wage. Higher-income people, by contrast, provide support for many social issues, such as animal rights.

But most people stop short of Emerson's position, believing that government is necessary to defend the country, operate highway systems and schools, maintain law and order, and help people in need. To accomplish these things, the U.S. government has grown into a vast and complex **welfare state,** *government agencies and programs that provide benefits to the population.* Government benefits begin even before birth (through prenatal nutrition programs) and continue into old age (through Social Security and Medicare). Some programs are especially important to the poor, who are not well served by our capitalist economic system; but students, farmers, homeowners, small business operators, veterans, performing artists, and even executives of giant corporations also get various subsidies and supports. In fact, a majority of U.S. adults look to government for at least part of their income.

Today's welfare state is the result of a gradual increase in the size and scope of government. In 1789, the presence of the federal government amounted to little more than a flag in most communities, and the entire federal budget was a mere $4.5 million ($1.50 for each person in the nation). Since then, it has risen steadily, reaching $2.3 trillion in 2004 ($7,900 per person).

When our nation was founded, one government employee served every 1,800 citizens. Today, about one in six workers in the United States is a government employee, which is more people than are engaged in manufacturing (U.S. Census Bureau, 2004).

Despite this growth, the U.S. welfare state is still smaller than those of many other high-income nations. Figure 17–1 shows that government is larger in most of Europe, especially in Scandinavian countries such as Denmark and Sweden.

THE POLITICAL SPECTRUM

Who supports a bigger welfare state? Who wants to cut it back? Answers to these questions reveal attitudes that form the *political spectrum,* which ranges from extremely liberal on the left to extremely conservative on the right. About one-fourth of U.S. adults say they fall on the liberal, or "left," side, and one-third describe themselves as conservative, placing themselves on the political "right." The remaining 40 percent claim to be moderates, in the political "middle" (NORC, 2003:98).

The political spectrum helps us understand two types of issues. *Economic issues* focus on economic inequality. *Social issues* involve moral questions about how people ought to live.

Economic Issues

Economic liberals support both extensive government regulation of the economy and a larger welfare state in order to

STUDENT SNAPSHOT

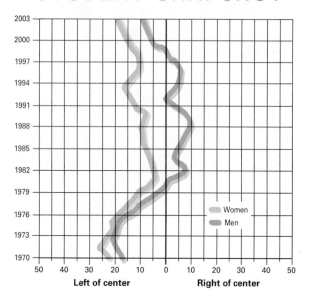

FIGURE 17–2 Left-Right Political Identification of College Students, 1970–2003

Student attitudes moved to the right after 1970 and shifted left in the mid-1990s. College women tend to be a bit more liberal than college men.

Sources: Astin et al. (2002) and Sax et al. (2003).

reduce income inequality. The government can reduce inequality by taxing the rich more heavily and providing more benefits to the poor. Economic conservatives want to limit the hand of government in the economy and allow market forces more freedom, claiming that this produces more jobs and makes the economy more productive.

Social Issues

Social issues are moral questions, ranging from abortion to the death penalty to gay rights to the treatment of minorities. Social liberals support equal rights and opportunities for all categories of people, view abortion as a matter of individual choice, and oppose the death penalty because it has been unfairly applied to minorities.

The "family values" agenda of social conservatives supports traditional gender roles and opposes gay marriage, affirmative action, and other "special programs" for minorities. Social conservatives condemn abortion as morally wrong and support the death penalty.

Of the two major U.S. political parties, the Republican party is more conservative on both economic and social

issues, and the Democratic party is more liberal. Yet each party has conservative and liberal wings, so there may be little difference between a liberal Republican and a conservative Democrat. In addition, Republicans as well as Democrats favor big government when it advances their particular aims. Conservative Republicans (like Presidents Ronald Reagan and George W. Bush) used government power to strengthen the military, for example, just as more liberal Democrats (like President Bill Clinton) increased taxes (especially on the rich) to fund a larger "social safety net."

 To review legislation currently before Congress, visit http:// thomas.loc.gov

YOUR TURN

On social issues, are you more liberal or more conservative? What about on economic issues?

Class, Race, and Gender

Well-to-do people tend to be conservative on economic issues (because they have wealth to protect) but liberal on social issues (largely due to higher levels of education). Low-income people display the opposite pattern, being economically liberal yet socially conservative (Erikson, Luttbeg, & Tedin, 1980; McBroom & Reed, 1990).

African Americans, both rich and poor, tend to be more liberal than whites (especially on economic issues) and for half a century have voted Democratic (almost 90 percent supported Democrat John Kerry in 2004). Historically, Latinos, Asian Americans, and Jews have also supported the Democratic party.

Women tend to be more liberal than men. Among U.S. adults, more women lean toward the Democrats, and more men vote for Republican candidates. Figure 17–2 shows how this pattern has changed over time among college students. Although there have been changes in student attitudes— to the right in the 1970s and to the left beginning in the mid-1990s—college women have remained more liberal than college men (Astin et al., 2002; NORC, 2003; Sax et al., 2003).

Party Identification

Because many people hold mixed political attitudes, with liberal views on some issues and conservative stands on others, party identification in this country is weak. Surveys show that about 43 percent favor the Democratic party and

APPLYING SOCIOLOGY
The Rural-Urban Divide: Election 2004

An important dimension of political difference in the United States involves where people live. Political attitudes and voting patterns in rural and urban places are quite different. Sociologists have long debated why these differences exist.

Take a look at National Map 17–1 on page 454, which shows the county-by-county results for the 2004 presidential election. The first thing that stands out is that Republican George W. Bush won 80 percent of U.S. counties—about 2,500 out of almost 3,200 ("Bush" counties appear in red on the map). Democrat John Kerry won in about 700 counties ("Kerry" counties appear in blue).

Why did Bush win so many more counties but only 51 percent of the popular vote? Republican counties tend to be rural, with relatively small populations. Democrats, by contrast, do better in the counties containing large

cities. In Oregon, for example, Kerry won enough votes in Portland to carry the entire state, even though almost all the remaining counties went for Bush.

The national pattern has led many political analysts to distinguish urban "blue states" that vote Democratic and rural "red states" that vote Republican. Looking more closely, at the county level, there appears to be a political divide between "liberal, urban America" and "conservative, rural America."

What accounts for this difference? Rural counties typically are home to people who have lived in one place for a long time, who are more traditional and family-oriented in their values, and who are more likely to be religious. Such people tend to vote Republican. In the polls taken among voters in the 2004 presidential election, 80 percent of people who supported George Bush said that what mattered most to them was "moral values."

Urban areas are home to more minorities, young and single people, and lower-income people, all of whom are more likely to vote Democratic. Polls indicated that 80 percent of voters who supported John Kerry said that what mattered most to them was "the economy and jobs."

WHAT DO YOU THINK?

1. Can you find your county on the map? Which way did most people vote? Can you explain why?
2. Can you explain the Republican concern about "moral values"? What about the Democratic concern about "the economy and jobs"?
3. If Republicans are to do better in urban areas, how must they change their message? What changes would help Democrats do better in rural areas?

---

35 percent favor the Republican party; however, just 15 percent claim to be "strong Democrats," and just 12 percent claimed to be "strong Republicans." Almost 20 percent say they are "independent" (NORC, 2003). This lack of strong party identification is one reason each of the two major parties gains or loses power from election to election. Democrats held the White House in 1996 and gained ground in Congress in 1996, 1998, and 2000. In 2002 and 2004, the tide turned as Republicans made gains in Congress and kept control of the White House.

There is also an urban-rural divide in U.S. politics: People in urban areas typically vote Democratic and those in rural areas Republican. The Applying Sociology box takes a closer look at the national political scene, and National Map 17–1 on page 454 shows the county-by-county results for the 2004 election.

 To learn more about how researchers conduct political polls, go to http://faculty.vassar.edu/lowry/polls.html

SPECIAL-INTEREST GROUPS

For years, people throughout the United States have debated the private ownership of firearms. Organizations such as the Brady Campaign to Prevent Gun Violence support stricter gun laws; other organizations, including the National Rifle Association, strongly oppose such measures. Each of these organizations is an example of a **special-interest group,** *people organized to address some economic or social issue.* Special-interest groups, which include associations of older adults, fireworks producers, and environmentalists, among others, are strong in nations where political parties tend to be weak. Special-interest groups employ *lobbyists* to work on their behalf, trying to get members of Congress to support their goals. Washington, D.C., is home to more than 34,000 lobbyists.

A **political action committee (PAC)** is *an organization formed by a special-interest group, independent of political*

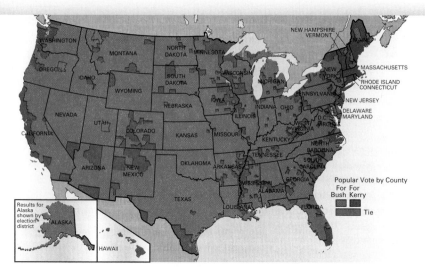

parties, to raise and spend money in support of political goals. Political action committees channel most of their funds directly to candidates likely to support their interests. Since they were created in the 1970s, the number of PACs has grown rapidly to more than 4,000 (Federal Election Commission, 2005).

Because of the rising costs of political campaigns, most candidates eagerly accept support from political action committees. In the 2004 congressional elections, 34 percent of all campaign funding came from PACs, and senators seeking reelection received, on average, at least $1 million each in PAC contributions. Supporters of this practice claim that PACs represent the interests of a vast assortment of businesses, unions, and church groups, thereby increasing political participation. Critics counter that organizations supplying cash to politicians expect to be treated favorably in return, so that in effect, PACs try to buy political influence (Cook, 1993; Center for Responsive Politics, 2005).

In 2004, the candidates for the U.S. presidency spent a total of about $4 billion on their campaigns, and another $4 billion was spent by those running for all other political offices. Does having the most money matter? The answer is yes: 90 percent of the candidates with the most money ended up winning the election. Concerns about the power of money have led to demands for campaign finance reforms. In 2002, Congress passed a modest reform, limiting the amount of unregulated money that candidates are allowed to collect. Despite this change, the 2004 presidential and congressional races still set new records for campaign spending.

VOTER APATHY

As the story that opened this chapter suggested, many people in the United States do not vote. In fact, U.S. citizens are less likely to vote today than they were a century ago. In the 2000 presidential election, which turned on a few hundred votes, only half of all registered voters went to the polls. In 2004, participation rose to 60 percent, still lower than in almost all other high-income countries.

Who is and is not likely to vote? Research shows that women are slightly more likely than men to cast a ballot. People over sixty-five are much more likely to vote than college-age adults (half of whom have not even registered). Non-Hispanic white people are more likely to vote (66 percent voted in 2004) than African Americans (56 percent), and Hispanics (28 percent) are the least likely of all to vote. Generally speaking, people with a bigger stake in U.S. society—homeowners, parents with young children, people with more schooling and good jobs—are more likely to vote. Income matters, too: People earning more than $75,000 are more likely to vote (76 percent voted in 2004) than people earning less than $10,000 (60 percent voted) (U.S. Census Bureau, 2005).

 Learn more about voting, public opinion, and political participation at this Web site: http://www.umich.edu/~nes/

YOUR TURN

Why do you think most of today's young people do not vote? Have you registered to vote?

Of course, we should expect some nonvoting because at any given time, millions of people are sick or away from home or have recently moved to a new neighborhood and have forgotten to reregister. In addition, registering and voting depend on the ability to read and write, which discourages tens of millions of U.S. adults with limited literacy skills. Finally, people with physical disabilities that limit mobility have a lower turnout than the general population (Schur & Kruse, 2000; Brians & Grofman, 2001).

Conservatives suggest that apathy is really *indifference* to politics among people who are, by and large, content with their lives. Liberals and especially radicals on the far left of the political spectrum counter that apathy reflects *alienation* from politics among people who are so deeply dissatisfied with society that they doubt that elections make any real difference. Because the disadvantaged and powerless people are least likely to vote, the liberal explanation for apathy is probably closer to the truth.

SHOULD CONVICTED CRIMINALS VOTE?

Although the right to vote is at the very foundation of our country's claim to being democratic, forty-eight of the fifty states (all except Vermont and Maine) have laws that bar felons—people in jail, on probation, or on parole after being convicted of serious crimes—from voting. Four states go further and bar many or all ex-felons from ever voting again. For this reason, about 5 million people (including 1.4 million African American men) in the United States have lost their right to vote.

Should government take away political rights as a type of punishment? The legislatures of most of our fifty states have said yes. But critics point out that this practice may be politically motivated, because preventing convicted criminals from voting makes a difference in the way U.S. elections turn out. Convicted felons show better than a two-to-one preference for Democratic over Republican candidates. Even allowing for expected voter apathy, one recent study concluded that if these laws were not in force, Democrats would have won more congressional races and in 2000 Al Gore would have defeated George W. Bush for the presidency (Uggen & Manza, 2002).

Theoretical Analysis of Power in Society

Sociologists have long debated how power is spread throughout the U.S. population. Power is a very difficult topic to study because decision making is complex and often takes place behind closed doors. Despite this difficulty, researchers have developed three competing models of power in the United States.

THE PLURALIST MODEL: THE PEOPLE RULE

The **pluralist model,** closely linked to structural-functional theory, is *an analysis of politics that sees power as spread among many competing interest groups.* Pluralists claim, first, that politics is an arena of negotiation. With limited resources, no organization can expect to realize all its goals. Organizations therefore operate as *veto groups,* realizing some success but mostly keeping opponents from achieving all their ends. The political process relies heavily on creating alliances and compromises among numerous interest groups so that policies gain wide support. In short, pluralists see power as spread widely throughout society, with all people having at least some voice in the political system (Dahl, 1961, 1982; Rothman & Black, 1998).

THE POWER-ELITE MODEL: A FEW PEOPLE RULE

The **power-elite model,** based on social-conflict theory, is *an analysis of politics that sees power as concentrated among the rich.* The term *power elite* was coined by C. Wright Mills (1956), who argued that a small upper class holds most of society's wealth, prestige, and power.

Mills claimed that members of the power elite head up the three major sectors of U.S. society: the economy, the government, and the military. The power elite is made up of the "super-rich" (corporate executives and major stockholders); top officials in Washington, D.C., and state capitals around the country; and the highest-ranking officers in the U.S. military.

Further, Mills explained, these elites move from one sector to another, building power as they go. Vice President Dick Cheney, for example, has moved back and forth between powerful positions in the corporate world and the federal government. Colin Powell moved from a top position in the U.S. military to become secretary of state. More broadly, when President George W. Bush took office, he assembled a cabinet in which all but one member were already millionaires.

Power-elite theorists say that the United States is not a democracy because the concentration of wealth and power is simply too great for the average person's voice to be heard. They reject the pluralist idea that various centers of power serve as checks and balances on one another. From this point of view, those at the top are powerful enough that they face no real opposition (Bartlett & Steele, 2000; Moore et al., 2002).

APPLYING THEORY
POLITICS

	Pluralist Model	Power-Elite Model	Political-Economy Model
Which theoretical approach is applied?	Structural-functional approach	Social-conflict approach	Social-conflict approach
How is power spread throughout society?	Power is spread widely so that all groups have some voice.	Power is concentrated in the hands of top business, political, and military leaders.	Power is directed by the operation of the capitalist economy.
Is the United States a democracy?	Yes. Power is spread widely enough to make the country a democracy.	No. Power is too concentrated for the country to be a democracy.	No. The capitalist economy sets political decision making, so the country is not a democracy.

THE MARXIST MODEL: THE SYSTEM IS BIASED

A third approach to understanding U.S. politics is the **Marxist political-economy model,** *an analysis that explains politics in terms of the operation of a society's economic system.* Like the power-elite model, the Marxist model rejects the idea that the United States operates as a political democracy. But the power-elite model focuses on just the enormous wealth and power of certain individuals; the Marxist model goes further and sees bias rooted in this nation's institutions, especially its economy. As noted in Chapter 4 ("Society"), Karl Marx claimed that a society's economic system (capitalist or socialist) shapes its political system. Therefore, the power elites do not simply appear out of nowhere; they are creations of capitalism itself.

From this point of view, reforming the political system—say, by limiting the amount of money that rich people can contribute to political candidates—is unlikely to bring about true democracy. The problem does not lie in the *people* who exercise great power or the *people* who don't vote; the problem is rooted in the *system* itself, what Marxists call the "political economy of capitalism." In other words, as long as the United States has a mostly capitalist economy, the majority of people will be shut out of politics, just as they are exploited in the workplace.

Critical review The Applying Theory table summarizes the three models of the U.S. political system. Which of these three models is correct? Over the years, research has shown support for each one. In the end, how you think our political system ought to work is as much a matter of political values as of scientific fact.

Classic research by Nelson Polsby (1959) supports the pluralist model. Polsby studied the political scene in New Haven, Connecticut, and concluded that key decisions on various issues—including education, urban renewal, and the electoral nominating process—were made by different groups. Polsby concluded that in New Haven, no one group—not even the upper class—ruled all the others.

Robert Lynd and Helen Lynd (1937) studied Muncie, Indiana (which they called "Middletown," to suggest that it was a typical city), and documented the fortune amassed by a single family, the Balls, from their business manufacturing glass canning jars. Their findings support the power-elite position. The Lynds showed how the Ball family dominated the city's life, pointing to that family's name on a local bank, a university, a hospital, and a department store. In Muncie, according to the Lynds, the power elite boiled down more or less to a single family.

From the Marxist perspective, the point is not to look at which individuals make decisions. Rather, as Alexander Liazos (1982:13) explains in his analysis of the United States, "The basic tenets of capitalist society shape everyone's life: the inequalities of social classes and the importance of profits over people." As long as the basic institutions of society are organized to meet the needs of the few rather than the many, Liazos concludes, a democratic society is impossible.

Clearly, the U.S. political system gives almost everyone the right to participate in the political process through elections. But the power-elite and Marxist models point out that at the very least, the U.S. political system is far less democratic than most people think. Most citizens may have the right to vote, but the major political parties and their candidates typically support only positions that are acceptable to the most powerful segments of society and consistent with the operation of our capitalist economy.

Whatever the reasons, many people in the United States appear to be losing confidence in their leaders. More than 80 percent of U.S. adults report having, at best, only "some confidence" that members of Congress and other government officials will do what is best for the country (NORC, 2003:977, 1132).

Power beyond the Rules

In politics, there is always disagreement over a society's goals and the means to achieve them. A political system tries to resolve these controversies within a system of rules. But political activity sometimes breaks the rules or tries to do away with the entire system.

REVOLUTION

Political revolution is *the overthrow of one political system in order to establish another.* Reform involves change *within* a system, through modification of the law or, in the extreme case, a *coup d'état* (in French, literally, "stroke of the state"), in which one leader topples another. Revolution involves change in the type of system itself.

No political system is immune to revolution, nor does revolution produce any one kind of government. Our country's Revolutionary War (1775–81) replaced colonial rule by the British monarchy with a representative democracy. French revolutionaries in 1789 also overthrew a monarch, only to set the stage for the return of monarchy in the person of Napoleon. In 1917, the Russian Revolution replaced monarchy with a socialist government built on the ideas of Karl Marx. In 1991, a second Russian revolution dismantled the socialist Soviet Union, and the nation was reborn as the Russian Federation, which has been moving toward a market system although it has yet to provide a greater political voice for its people.

Despite their striking variety, revolutions share a number of traits (Tocqueville, 1955, orig. 1856; Skocpol, 1979; Tilly, 1986):

1. **Rising expectations.** Common sense suggests that revolution would be more likely when people are severely deprived, but history shows that most revolutions occur when people's lives are improving. Rising expectations, rather than bitterness and despair, make revolutions more likely.

2. **Unresponsive government.** Revolutions become more likely when a government is unwilling to reform itself, especially when demands for reform by powerful segments of society are ignored.

3. **Radical leadership by intellectuals.** The English philosopher Thomas Hobbes (1588–1679) claimed that intellectuals provide the justification for revolution, and universities are often the center of political change. Students played a critical role in China's prodemocracy movement and the uprisings in Eastern Europe.

4. **Establishing a new legitimacy.** Overthrowing a political system is not easy, but ensuring a revolution's

Increasing security in a time of danger generally means reducing freedom. As part of the ongoing war on terrorism, security teams are far more evident in public places. In what ways does increased police surveillance threaten our freedoms?

long-term success is harder still. Some revolutionary movements are held together mostly by hatred of the past regime and fall apart once new leaders are installed. Revolutionaries must also guard against counterrevolutionary drives led by overthrown leaders. This explains the speed and ruthlessness with which victorious revolutionaries typically dispose of former leaders.

Scientific analysis cannot declare that a revolution is good or bad. The full consequences of such an upheaval depend on personal values and typically become evident only after many years. Fifteen years after its revolution, the future of the former Soviet Union remains uncertain.

TERRORISM

On September 11, 2001, terrorists hijacked four commercial airliners; one crashed in a wooded area, and the other three were flown into public buildings full of people. The attack killed more than 3,000 innocent people (representing sixty-eight nations), injured many thousands more, completely destroyed the twin towers of the World Trade Center in New York City, and seriously damaged the Pentagon in Washington, D.C. Not since the attack on Pearl Harbor at the outbreak of World War II had the United States suffered such a blow. Indeed, this event was the most serious terrorist act ever recorded.

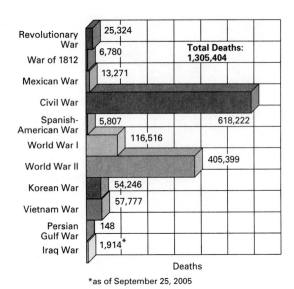

Revolutionary War	25,324
War of 1812	6,780
Mexican War	13,271
Civil War	
Spanish-American War	5,807
World War I	116,516
World War II	
Korean War	54,246
Vietnam War	57,777
Persian Gulf War	148
Iraq War	1,914*

Total Deaths: 1,305,404

618,222

405,399

Deaths

*as of September 25, 2005

FIGURE 17–3 Deaths of Americans in Eleven U.S. Wars

Almost half of all U.S. deaths in war occurred during the Civil War (1861–1865).

Sources: Compiled from various sources by Maris A. Vinovskis (1989) and the author.

Terrorism refers to *acts of violence or the threat of violence used as a political strategy by an individual or a group.* Like revolution, terrorism is a political act beyond the rules of established political systems. According to Paul Johnson (1981), terrorism has four distinguishing characteristics.

First, terrorists try to paint violence as a legitimate political tactic, even though such acts are condemned by virtually every nation. Terrorists also bypass (or are excluded from) established channels of political negotiation. Therefore, terrorism is a weaker organization's strategy against a stronger enemy. In recent decades, terrorism has become

 Read the U.S. State Department's annual report on global terrorism at http://www.state.gov/s/ct/rls/pgtrpt/

commonplace in international politics. In 2004, there were 651 acts of terrorism worldwide, which claimed 1,907 lives and injured 6,704 people. Most of those killed were in the Middle East, linked to either the conflict between Israel and the Palestinians or the conflict in Iraq. But many nations were involved, including both Spain and Russia, where the bloodiest attacks of the year occurred (U.S. Department of State, 2005).

Second, terrorism is used not just by groups but also by governments against their own people. *State terrorism* is the

use of violence, generally without support of law, by government officials as a way to control the population. State terrorism is lawful in some authoritarian and totalitarian states, which survive by creating widespread fear and intimidation. Saddam Hussein, for example, relied on secret police and state terror to protect his power in Iraq.

Third, democratic societies reject terrorism in principle, but they are especially vulnerable to terrorists because they give extensive civil liberties to their people and have less extensive police networks. In contrast, totalitarian regimes make widespread use of state terrorism, but their extensive police power gives individuals few opportunities for acts of terror against the government.

Fourth and finally, terrorism is always a matter of definition. Governments claim the right to maintain order, even by force, and may label opposition groups that use violence as "terrorists." Political differences may explain why one person's "terrorist" is another's "freedom fighter" (Jenkins, 2003).

Although hostage taking and outright killing provoke popular anger, taking action against terrorists is difficult. Because most terrorist groups are shadowy organizations with no formal connection to any established state, identifying the parties responsible may be difficult. In addition, any military response risks confrontation with other governments. Yet as the terrorism expert Brian Jenkins warns, the failure to respond "encourages other terrorist groups, who begin to realize that this can be a pretty cheap way to wage war" (quoted in Whitaker, 1985:29).

Do you think you will live to see a world free from terrorism? Why or why not?

War and Peace

Perhaps the most critical political issue is **war,** *organized, armed conflict among the people of two or more nations, directed by their governments.* War is as old as humanity, but understanding it is crucial today because humanity now has weapons that can destroy the entire planet.

At almost any moment during the twentieth century, nations somewhere in the world were engaged in violent conflict. In its short history, the United States has participated in eleven large-scale wars. From the Revolutionary War to the Iraq War, more than 1.3 million U.S. men and women have been killed in armed conflicts, as shown in Figure 17–3, and many times that number have been injured. Thousands more died in "undeclared wars" and limited military actions in the Dominican Republic, Nicaragua, Lebanon, Grenada, Panama, Haiti, Bosnia, and elsewhere.

Read a firsthand account by a survivor of the dropping of an atomic bomb on Hiroshima at http://www.coara.or.jp/~ryoji/abomb/e-index.html

THE CAUSES OF WAR

Wars occur so often that we might think that there is something natural about armed confrontation. But there is no evidence that human beings must wage war under any particular circumstances. On the contrary, governments around the world usually have to force their people to go to war.

Like all forms of social behavior, warfare is a product of *society* that is more common in some places than others. The Semai of Malaysia, among the most peace-loving of the world's peoples, rarely resort to violence. In contrast, the Yąnomamö (see the box on page 63) are quick to wage war.

If society holds the key to war or peace, under what circumstances do humans go to battle? Quincy Wright (1987) cites five factors that promote war:

1. **Perceived threats.** Societies mobilize in response to a perceived threat to their people, territory, or culture. Leaders justified the recent U.S.-led military campaign to disarm Iraq, for example, by stressing the threat that Saddam Hussein posed to the United States.

2. **Social problems.** When internal problems generate widespread frustration at home, a society's leaders may divert public attention by attacking an external "enemy" as a form of scapegoating. Although U.S. leaders claimed that the war in Iraq was a matter of national security, there is little doubt that the onset of the war diverted attention from the struggling national economy and boosted the popularity of President Bush.

3. **Political objectives.** Poor nations, such as Vietnam, have used wars to end foreign domination. On the other hand, powerful countries, such as the United States, may benefit from a periodic show of force (recall the deployments of troops in Somalia, Haiti, Bosnia, Afghanistan, and Iraq) to increase global political standing.

4. **Moral objectives.** Nations rarely claim that they are going to war to gain wealth and power. Instead, their leaders infuse military campaigns with moral urgency. By calling the 2003 invasion of Iraq "Operation Iraqi

There is an old saying that all is fair in love and war, but wars (like relationships) are actually carried out according to rules. The recent war on terrorism has raised questions about the rights of captured enemy combatants, most of whom are not soldiers in any nation's army. Should the prisoners held at the U.S. base in Guantanamo Bay, Cuba, be treated according to the rules of war as spelled out in the United Nations Geneva Convention? Should they have access to the U.S. courts as U.S. citizens do?

Freedom," U.S. leaders portrayed the mission as a morally justified war of liberation from an evil tyrant.

5. **The absence of alternatives.** A fifth factor promoting war is the absence of alternatives. Although the goal of the United Nations is to maintain international peace by finding alternatives to war, the UN has had limited success in preventing conflict between nations.

SOCIAL CLASS AND THE MILITARY

In World War II, three-fourths of the men in the United States in their late teens and twenties served in the military.

Those who did not were considered ineligible due to some physical or mental problem. Today, by contrast, there is no draft and fighting is done by a volunteer military. But not every member of our society is equally likely to volunteer.

One recent study concluded that the military has few young people who are rich and also few who are very poor. Rather, it is primarily working-class people who look to the

In recent years, the world has become aware of the death and mutilation caused by millions of land mines placed in the ground during wartime and left there afterward. Civilians—many of them children—maimed by land mines receive treatment in this Kabul, Afghanistan, clinic.

military for a job, to get some money to go to college, or simply to get out of the small town they grew up in. In addition, the largest number of young enlistees comes from the South, where local culture is more supportive of the military and where most military bases are located. As two analysts put it, "America's military seems to resemble the makeup of a two-year commuter or trade school outside Birmingham or Biloxi far more than that of a ghetto or barrio or four-year university in Boston" (Halbfinger & Holmes, 2003:1).

Given this profile of military recruits, it is easy to understand why the armed forces are trying to boost their numbers by offering financial incentives. "In the *Times*" on pages 462–63 describes some of the strategies being used by the Marine Corps to attract larger numbers of recruits.

YOUR TURN

Does it seem fair or unfair that the defense of this country falls heavily on working-class people? Explain your position.

IS TERRORISM A NEW KIND OF WAR?

After the terrorist attacks on September 11, 2001, U.S. government officials spoke of terrorism as a new kind of war.

War has historically followed certain patterns: It is played out according to some basic rules, the warring parties are known to each other, and the objectives of the warring parties—which generally involve control of territory—are clearly stated.

Terrorism breaks from these patterns. The identity of terrorist individuals and organizations may not be known, those involved may deny their responsibility, and their goals may be unclear. The 2001 terrorist attacks against the United States were not attempts to defeat the nation militarily or to secure territory. They were carried out by people representing not a country but a cause, one not well understood in the United States. In short, they were expressions of anger and hate, an effort to destabilize the country and create widespread fear.

Conventional warfare is symmetrical, with two nations sending their armies into battle. By contrast, terrorism is an unconventional form of warfare, an asymmetrical conflict in which a small number of attackers uses terror and their own willingness to die to level the playing field against a much more powerful enemy. Although the terrorists may be ruthless, the nation under attack must exercise restraint in its response to terrorism because little may be known about the identity and location of those responsible. It is for this reason that the United States has had limited success in ending the insurgency in Iraq.

THE COSTS AND CAUSES OF MILITARISM

The cost of armed conflict extends far beyond battlefield casualties. Together, the world's nations spend almost $1 trillion annually ($159 for every person on the planet) for military purposes. Spending this much diverts resources from the desperate struggle for survival by hundreds of millions of poor people.

Defense is the U.S. government's second largest expenditure (after Social Security), accounting for 20 percent of all federal spending, which amounted to $414 billion in 2004. The war on terrorism and the Iraq War have only pushed this number higher. In recent years, the United States has emerged as the world's only superpower, with more military might than the next nine countries combined (Gergen, 2002).

For decades, military spending went up as a result of the *arms race* between the United States and the Soviet Union, which dropped out of the race after its collapse in

1991. But some analysts (those who support power-elite theory) link high military spending to the domination of U.S. society by a **military-industrial complex,** *the close association of the federal government, the military, and defense industries.* The roots of militarism, then, lie not just in external threats to our security but also in the institutional structures here at home (Marullo, 1987; Barnes, 2002b).

A final reason for continuing militarism is regional conflict. During the 1990s, for example, localized wars broke out in Bosnia, Chechnya, and Zambia, and tensions today run high between Israel and the Palestinians, as well as between India and Pakistan. Even limited wars have the potential to grow and draw in other countries, including the United States. India and Pakistan—both nuclear powers—moved to the brink of war in 2002. In 2003, the announcement by North Korea that it, too, had nuclear weapons raised tensions in Asia. In 2005, Iran continues to develop nuclear technology, raising fears that this nation may soon have an atomic bomb.

NUCLEAR WEAPONS

Despite the easing of superpower tensions, the world still contains 20,000 nuclear warheads, representing a destructive power of five tons of TNT for every person on the planet. If even a small fraction of this stockpile is used in war, life as we know it could end on much of the Earth. Albert Einstein, whose genius contributed to the development of nuclear weapons, reflected, "The unleashed power of the atom has changed everything *save our modes of thinking,* and we thus drift toward unparalleled catastrophe." In short, nuclear weapons make unrestrained war unthinkable in a world not yet capable of peace.

The United States, the Russian Federation, Great Britain, France, the People's Republic of China, Israel, India, Pakistan, and North Korea all have nuclear weapons. The danger of catastrophic war increases with **nuclear proliferation,** *the acquisition of nuclear weapons technology by more and more nations.* Although a few nations stopped the development of nuclear weapons—Argentina and Brazil halted work in 1990, and South Africa dismantled its arsenal in 1991—by 2025 as many as fifty nations could have the ability to fight a nuclear war. Such a trend makes even the smallest regional conflict very dangerous to the entire planet.

MASS MEDIA AND WAR

The Iraq War was the first war in which television crews traveled with U.S. troops, reporting as the campaign unfolded. The mass media provided ongoing and detailed reports of events; cable television made available live coverage of the war twenty-four hours a day, seven days a week.

Media outlets critical of the war—especially the Arab news channel Al-Jazeera—tended to report the slow pace of the conflict, the casualties to the U.S. and allied forces, and the deaths and injuries suffered by Iraqi civilians, information that would increase pressure to end the war. Media outlets supportive of the war—including most news organizations in the United States—tended to report the rapid pace of the war and the casualties to Saddam Hussein's forces and to downplay harm to Iraqi civilians as minimal and unintended. In sum, the power of the mass media to provide selective information to a worldwide audience means that television and other media are almost as important to the outcome of a conflict as the military that are doing the actual fighting.

PURSUING PEACE

How can the world reduce the dangers of war? Here are the most recent approaches to peace:

1. **Deterrence.** The logic of the arms race linked security to a "balance of terror" between the superpowers. The principle of *mutual assured destruction (MAD)* means that the side launching a first-strike nuclear attack against the other will face greater retaliation. This deterrence policy kept the peace during more than fifty years of the Cold War between the United States and the Soviet Union. But this strategy fueled an enormously expensive arms race and had little effect on nuclear proliferation, which represents a growing threat to peace. Deterrence also does little to stop terrorism or to prevent war started by a powerful nation (such as the United States) against a weaker foe (such as the Taliban regime in Afghanistan or Saddam Hussein's Iraq).

2. **High-technology defense.** If technology created the weapons, perhaps it can also protect us from them. Such is the claim of the *strategic defense initiative (SDI).* Under SDI, satellites and ground installations would destroy enemy missiles soon after they were launched. Partly in response to the recent terrorist attacks, two-thirds of U.S. adults now support SDI (Thompson & Waller, 2001; "Female Opinion," 2002). However, critics claim that the system, which they refer to as "Star Wars," would be, at best, a leaky umbrella. Others worry that building such a system will spark another massive arms race.

3. **Diplomacy and disarmament.** Some analysts believe that the best path to peace is diplomacy rather than

February 25, 2005

For the Few and the Proud, Concern over the "Few" Part

By ERIC SCHMITT

WASHINGTON, Feb. 24—The Iraq war's dampening effect on recruiting has led to a plan by the Marine Corps to put hundreds of additional recruiters on the streets over the next several months and offer new re-enlistment bonuses of up to $35,000....

Recruiters and other military officials say the "Falluja effect"—a steady drumbeat of military casualties from Iraq, punctuated by graphic televised images of urban combat—is searing an image into the public eye that Marine officers say is difficult to overcome.

The Marines make up about 21 percent of the 150,000 military personnel in Iraq now but have suffered 31 percent of the military deaths there, according to Pentagon statistics.

The Army and other services have often increased the number of recruiters and dangled incentives to bolster their enlistment efforts in lean years. But for the Marines, steps of this magnitude, including the largest one-time increase in recruiters in recent memory, are unheard of in a service whose macho image has historically been a magnet for young people seeking adventure and danger in a military career.

General Michael W. Hagee, the Marine Corps commandant, predicted on Thursday that the Marines would achieve their overall recruiting goal for this fiscal year, even after the service missed its monthly quota in January, the first such lapse in nearly a decade. But General Hagee indicated that recruiters were facing some of toughest conditions they have ever faced....

"What the recruiters are telling us is that they have to spend more time with the parents," General Hagee said. "Parents have influence, and rightly so, on the decision these young men and young women are going to make. They're saying, 'It's not maybe a bad idea to join the Marine Corps, but why don't you consider it a year from now, or two years from now; let's think about this.'"

At issue is the Marines' decision to rebuild its recruiting ranks, which had fallen recently to 2,410 full-time recruiters from 2,650 before the Iraq war, as commanders siphoned off Marines who had been scheduled for recruiting duty to perform combat duty in Iraq and Afghanistan....

In a reflection of the difficult market for Marine recruiters, the service offers bonuses of up to $35,000 to retain combat veterans of Iraq and Afghanistan.

What is unusual about these incentives is that the Marines Corps for the first time is offering re-enlistment bonuses, averaging $20,000, to its most junior infantrymen, rather than relying mainly on inexperienced troops fresh from boot camp to replenish the infantry. About 75 percent of enlisted

---

technology (Dedrick & Yinger, 1990). Teams of diplomats working together can increase security by reducing, rather than building, weapons stockpiles.

But disarmament has limitations. No nation wants to be weakened by letting down its defenses. Successful diplomacy depends on everyone involved making efforts to resolve a common problem (Fisher & Ury, 1988). Although the United States and the Soviet Union succeeded in negotiating arms reduction agreements, the world now faces increasing threats from other nations such as North Korea.

4. **Resolving underlying conflict.** In the end, reducing the dangers of war may depend on resolving underlying conflicts by promoting a more just world. Poverty, hunger, and illiteracy are all root causes of war. Perhaps the world needs to reconsider the wisdom of spending thousands of times as much money on militarism as we do on efforts to find peaceful solutions (Sivard, 1988; Kaplan & Schaffer, 2001).

Politics: Looking Ahead

Change in political systems is ongoing. Several problems and trends are likely to be important as the twenty-first century unfolds.

One troublesome problem in the United States is the inconsistency between our democratic ideals and our low turnout at the polls. Perhaps, as conservative pluralist theorists say, many people do not bother to vote because they are

Marines leave the service after their first tour, requiring a steady stream of recruits moving through training centers in San Diego and Parris Island, S.C.

"We need infantrymen," General Hagee said, explaining the shift in bonus priorities. "That's what we're using over there on the ground."

General Hagee said the initial wave of bonuses had increased re-enlistment rates among infantry units, but Marine officials said they did not have specific figures readily available.

The Marines' decision to strengthen recruiting comes as the Army has added hundreds of new recruiters and is pushing incoming recruits into training as fast as possible.

In a wide-ranging breakfast interview with reporters, General Hagee touched on several issues regarding Iraq that military specialists say contribute to the climate of concern among potential recruits and their parents.

General Hagee said the military had an all-out effort under way to combat the remotely detonated roadside bombs that are the No. 1 killer of American troops in Iraq. The Marines, he said, are using a sophisticated computer program to help identify potential vulnerabilities of supply convoys protected by electronic jamming devices.

When it comes to recruiting, the traditional enticements of military service, like travel, education benefits and the Marine Corps mystique, now must vie with the concerns of recruits and their parents, recruiters say.

WHAT DO YOU THINK?

1. The "volunteer army" attracts mostly young people with fewer career options. Do you think it is fair that the typical recruit is a working-class man or woman?

2. Would you support a military draft that would give all young people, regardless of social background, the same chances of being called into the military? Why or why not?

3. Do you think offering re-enlistment bonuses to increase the share of experienced soldiers is a good idea? Explain your position.

Adapted from the original article by Eric Schmitt published in *The New York Times* on February 25, 2005. Copyright © 2005 by The New York Times Company. Reprinted with permission.

content with their lives. On the other hand, liberal power-elite theorists may be right in their view that people withdraw from a system that concentrates wealth and power in the hands of so few people. Or perhaps, as radical Marxist critics claim, people find that our political system gives little real choice, limiting options and policies to those that support our capitalist economy. In any case, the current high level of apathy indicates that significant political reform is needed.

A second issue is the global rethinking of political models. The Cold War between the United States and the Soviet Union encouraged people to think of politics in terms of the two opposing models, capitalism and socialism. Today, however, people are more likely to consider a broader range of political systems that links government to the economy in various ways. "Welfare capitalism," as found in Sweden, or "state capitalism," as found in Japan and South Korea, are just two possibilities. In all cases, promoting the broadest democratic participation is an important goal. The Thinking It Through box on page 464 takes a look at the debate over the chances for democratic governments emerging in the world's Islamic countries.

Third, we still face the danger of war in many parts of the world. Even as the United States and the Russian Federation dismantle some warheads, vast stockpiles of nuclear weapons remain, and nuclear technology continues to spread around the world. In addition, new superpowers are likely to arise (the People's Republic of China and India are likely candidates), and regional conflicts and terrorism are likely to continue. We can only hope (and vote!) for leaders who will find nonviolent solutions to the age-old problems that provoke war, putting us on the road to world peace.

THINKING IT THROUGH

Islam and Freedom: A "Democracy Gap"?

Freedom is a goal that is celebrated throughout the world. In different cultural settings, of course, "freedom" means different things. And as this chapter has explained, other nations understand "freedom" differently than we do in the United States.

Freedom House, an organization that monitors political freedom around the world, tracks people's right to vote and to express ideas and move about without undue interference from government. It reports that the part of the world with the least political freedom stretches from Africa through the Middle East to Asia (see Global Map 17–1 on page 447).

Many of the nations that this organization characterizes as "not free" have populations that are largely Islamic. Freedom House reports that 47 of the world's 192 nations have an Islamic majority population. As the figure shows, just 11 (23.4 percent) of these 47 countries have democratic governments, and Freedom House rates only one—Mali—as "free." Of the 145 nations without a majority Islamic population, 110 (75.9 percent) have democratic governments, and 84 are rated as "free." In other words, countries without Islamic majorities are three times more likely to have democratic governments as countries with Islamic majorities. Freedom House concludes that countries with an Islamic majority display a "democracy gap" (Karatnycky, 2002).

This relative lack of democracy holds for all world regions that contain Islamic-majority nations—Africa, central Europe, the Middle East, and Asia. The pattern is especially strong among the sixteen Islamic-majority states in the Middle East and North Africa that are ethnically Arabic—none is an electoral democracy.

What explains this "democracy gap"? Freedom House points to four factors. First, countries with Islamic-majority populations typically are less economically developed, with limited schooling and widespread poverty. Second, these countries have cultural traditions that rigidly control the lives of women, providing them with few economic, educational, or political opportunities. Third, although most other countries limit the power of religious elites in government, and some (including the United States) even require a "separation of church and state," Islamic-majority nations support giving Islamic leaders political power. In just two recent cases—Iran and Afghanistan under the Taliban—Islamic leaders have actually taken formal control of the government; more commonly, religious leaders do not hold office but exert considerable influence on political outcomes.

Fourth and finally, the enormous wealth that comes from Middle Eastern oil also plays a part in preventing democratic government. In Iraq, Saudi Arabia, Kuwait, Qatar, and other nations, this resource has provided astounding riches to a small number of families, money that they can use to shore up their political control. In addition, oil wealth permits elites to build airports and other modern facilities without encouraging broader economic development that would raise the living standards of the majority.

For all these reasons, Freedom House concludes that the road to democracy for Islamic-majority nations is likely to be long. But today's patterns may not predict those of tomorrow. In 1950, very few Catholic-majority countries (mostly in Europe and Latin America) had democratic governments. Today, however, most of these nations are democratic. Note, too, that a majority of the world's Muslim people—who live in Nigeria, Turkey, Bangladesh, India, Indonesia, and the United States—already live under democratic governments.

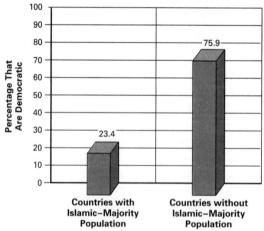

Democracy in Countries with and without Islamic-Majority Populations

Today, democratic government is much less common in countries with Islamic-majority populations. Fifty years ago, the same was true of countries with Catholic-majority populations.

Source: Karatnycky (2002).

WHAT DO YOU THINK?

1. Do you think the United States is right or wrong in the way it is seeking to bring about a democratic political system in Iraq? Why?
2. Do you expect greater democracy in Islamic-majority countries fifty years from now? Why or why not?
3. Can you point to several reasons that Muslim people might object to the kind of political system we call "democracy"? Explain.

The following learning tools will help you see what you know, identify what you still need to learn, and expand your understanding beyond the text. You can also visit this text's Companion Website™ at http://www.prenhall.com/macionis to find additional practice tests.

KEY OINTS

Power and Authority

Politics is the major social institution by which a society distributes power and organizes decision making. Max Weber explained that raw power is transformed into authority by tradition, rationally enacted rules and regulations, or the personal charisma of a leader.

Politics in Global Perspective

Monarchy, based on traditional authority, is common in preindustrial societies. Although constitutional monarchies persist in some industrial nations, industrialization favors democracy based on rational-legal authority and extensive bureaucracy.

Authoritarian political regimes deny people participation in government. Totalitarian political systems go even further, rigidly regulating people's everyday lives.

The world is divided into 192 politically independent nation-states. A political trend, however, is the growing wealth and power of multinational corporations that operate around the world. In an age of computers and other new information technology, governments can no longer control the flow of information across their boundaries.

Politics in the United States

Government has expanded in the United States during the past two centuries and now offers many public benefits and to some extent regulates the economy. The welfare state in the United States is smaller than in most other high-income nations.

The political spectrum—from the liberal left to the conservative right—involves attitudes on economic issues (such as government regulation of the economy) and social issues (including the rights and opportunities of various segments of the population).

Affiliation with political parties is relatively weak in the United States. Special-interest groups advance the political aims of specific segments of the population. These groups employ lobbyists and political action committees (PACs) to influence the political process.

Political apathy runs high in the United States: 60 percent of eligible voters went to the polls in the 2004 presidential election. Millions of people convicted of serious crimes lose their right to vote.

Theoretical Analysis of Power in Society

The pluralist model holds that political power is spread widely in the United States; the power-elite model takes an opposing view, arguing that power is concentrated in a small, wealthy segment of the population. The Marxist political-economy view claims that our political agenda is determined by our capitalist economy, meaning that true democracy is impossible.

Power beyond the Rules

Revolution radically transforms a political system. Terrorism, another unconventional political tactic, employs violence in the pursuit of political goals and is widely used by groups against a much more powerful enemy. Terrorism is emerging as a new form of asymmetrical warfare.

War and Peace

War is armed conflict directed by governments. The development and spread of nuclear weapons have increased the threat of global catastrophe. World peace ultimately depends on resolving the tensions and conflicts that fuel militarism.

Politics: Looking Ahead

U.S. society claims to be democratic but fails to involve almost half the adult population in the political process. Addressing the problem of political apathy is an important challenge for the decades ahead. In addition, the United States and other nations must face up to the dangers of war, especially the spread of nuclear technology used to make weapons that threaten the entire planet.

politics (p. 444) the social institution that distributes power, sets a society's goals, and makes decisions

power (p. 444) the ability to achieve desired ends despite resistance from others

government (p. 444) a formal organization that directs the political life of a society

authority (p. 444) power that people perceive as legitimate rather than coercive

traditional authority (p. 444) power legitimized by respect for long-established cultural patterns

rational-legal authority (p. 445) power legitimized by legally enacted rules and regulations; also known as *bureaucratic authority*

charismatic authority (p. 445) power legitimized by extraordinary personal abilities that inspire devotion and obedience

routinization of charisma (p. 445) the transformation of charismatic authority into some combination of traditional and bureaucratic authority

monarchy (p. 446) a political system in which a single family rules from generation to generation

democracy (p. 446) a political system that gives power to the people as a whole

authoritarianism (p. 448) a political system that denies the people participation in government

totalitarianism (p. 449) a highly centralized political system that extensively regulates people's lives

welfare state (p. 451) government agencies and programs that provide benefits to the population

special-interest group (p. 453) people organized to address some economic or social issue

political action committee (PAC) (p. 453) an organization formed by a special-interest group, independent of political parties, to raise and spend money in support of political goals

pluralist model (p. 455) an analysis of politics that sees power as spread among

many competing interest groups

power-elite model (p. 455) an analysis of politics that sees power as concentrated among the rich

Marxist political-economy model (p. 456) an analysis that explains politics in terms of the operation of a society's economic system

political revolution (p. 457) the overthrow of one political system in order to establish another

terrorism (p. 458) acts of violence or the threat of violence used as a political strategy by an individual or a group

war (p. 458) organized, armed conflict among the people of two or more nations, directed by their governments

military-industrial complex (p. 461) the close association of the federal government, the military, and defense industries

nuclear proliferation (p. 461) the acquisition of nuclear weapons technology by more and more nations

SAMPLE TEST QUESTIONS

These questions are similar to those found in the test bank that accompanies this textbook.

Multiple-Choice Questions

1. According to Max Weber, power is defined as
   a. "the shadow of wealth."
   b. the ability to achieve desired ends, despite resistance from others.
   c. a society's form of government.
   d. the creation of bureaucracy.

2. Max Weber claimed that the main difference between power and authority is that
   a. power is a better way to hold a society together.
   b. authority is based on brute force.

   c. power involves a special claim to justice.
   d. people typically view authority as legitimate rather than coercive.

3. Modern societies, including the United States, rely mostly on which type of authority?
   a. charismatic authority
   b. traditional authority
   c. rational-legal authority
   d. no authority

4. In which type of political system does power reside in the hands of the people as a whole?
   a. democracy   b. aristocracy
   c. totalitarianism   d. monarchy

5. When sociologists use the term "political economy," they are referring to
   a. the fact that people "vote with their pocketbook."
   b. the fact that the political and economic systems are linked.

c. any democratic political system.

d. the most efficient form of government.

6. **The claim that socialist societies are democratic typically is based on the fact that**

   a. their members have considerable personal liberty.

   b. these societies have no elite.

   c. these societies meet the basic economic needs of everyone.

   d. these societies have a high standard of living.

7. **Which type of government concentrates all power in one place and rigidly regulates people's lives?**

   a. an aristocratic government

   b. a democratic government

   c. an authoritarian government

   d. a totalitarian government

8. **In the 2004 U.S. presidential election, about what share of registered voters actually cast a vote?**

   a. close to 100 percent   b. about 80 percent

   c. about 60 percent   d. about 20 percent

9. **The Marxist political-economy model suggests that**

   a. power is concentrated in the hands of a small "power elite."

b. an antidemocratic bias is built into the capitalist system.

c. power is spread widely throughout society.

d. many people do not vote because they are basically satisfied with their lives.

10. **Which war resulted in the highest loss of life to people in the United States?**

    a. the Civil War   b. World War II

    c. the Korean War   d. the Vietnam War

Answers: 1(b); 2(d); 3(c); 4(a); 5(b); 6(c); 7(d); 8(c); 9(b); 10(a).

Essay Questions

1. What is the difference between authority and power? How do preindustrial and industrial societies create authority in different ways?

2. Compare and contrast the pluralist, power-elite, and Marxist political-economy models of societal power. Which of these models do you think makes the most sense? Why?

APPLICATIONS & EXERCISES

1. The following Web site provides data on how people voted in the 2004 presidential election by gender, age, race, income, religion, and other variables: http://www.cnn.com/ELECTION/2004/pages/results/states/US/P/00/epolls.0.html Visit this site, and develop a profile of the typical Democratic voter and the typical Republican voter. Which variables best predict differences in voting preference?

2. With several classmates or friends, make a list of political leaders who have demonstrated personal charisma. Discuss why each person is on the list. Do you think personal charisma today is something more than "being good on television"? If so, precisely what is it?

3. Freedom House, an organization that studies civil rights and political liberty around the world, publishes an annual report, *Freedom in the World.* Find a copy in the library, or examine global trends and the political profile of any country on the Web at http://www.freedomhouse.org

INVESTIGATE *with* Research Navigator

Follow the instructions on page 27 of this text to access the features of **Research Navigator**™. Once at the Web site, enter your Login Name and Password. Then, to use the **ContentSelect**™ database, enter keywords such as "democracy," "war," and "terrorism," and the search engine will supply relevant

and recent scholarly and popular press publications. Use the *New York Times* **Search-by-Subject Archive** to find recent news articles related to sociology and the **Link Library** feature to find relevant Web links organized by the key terms associated with this chapter.

18

Families

What is a family?

How are families in the United States changing?

Why is there a debate over the future of the family?

osa Yniguez is one of seven children who grew up in Jalisco, Mexico, in a world in which families were proud of having many children. Rosa remembers visiting the home of friends of her parents who had a clock in their living room with a picture of each of their twelve children where the numbers on the clock face would be.

Now thirty-five years old, Yniguez is living in the United States and working as a cashier in a San Francisco department store near her home. Recalling her childhood, she says, "In Mexico, many of the families I knew had six, eight, ten children. Sometimes more. But I came to this country to get ahead. That is simply impossible with too many kids." As a result of her desire to keep her job and make a better life for her family, Yniguez has decided to have no more than the three children she has now.

Hispanics have become the largest racial or ethnic minority in the United States because of a traditionally high birth rate and large families. But today more and more Latinas are making the same decision as Rosa Yniguez and opting to have fewer children. Studies show that the birth rate for all immigrant women has dropped by 30 percent during the past decade (Navarro, 2004). ■

Families have been with us for a very long time. But as this story indicates, U.S. families are changing in response to a number of factors, including the desire of women to have more career options and to provide better lives for their children. In fact, the family is changing faster than any other social institution (Bianchi & Spain, 1996). This chapter explores the changes in family life, as well as the diversity of families both around the world and here in the United States.

Families: Basic Concepts

The **family** is *a social institution found in all societies that unites people in cooperative groups to care for one another, including any children.* Family ties are also called **kinship,** *a social bond based on common ancestry, marriage, or adoption.* All societies contain families, but exactly whom people call their kin has varied through history and varies today from one culture to another. From the point of view of any individual, families change as we grow up, leaving the family into which we were born to form a family of our own.

Here as in other countries, families form around **marriage,** *a legal relationship, usually involving economic cooperation, sexual activity, and childbearing.* The traditional belief in the United States is that people should marry before having children; this expectation is found in the word *matrimony,* which in Latin means "the condition of motherhood." Today two-thirds of children are born to married couples, but one-third are born to single women who may or may not live with a partner.

Families, then, have become more diverse. Which relationships are and are not considered a family can have important consequences, because companies typically extend benefits such as health care only to family members.

The U.S. Census Bureau, which collects data used by sociologists, counts as families only people living together who are linked by "blood, marriage, or adoption."[1] All

---

[1]According to the U.S. Census Bureau, there were 111 million U.S. households in 2003. Of these, 75.6 million (68 percent) meet the bureau's definition of "family." The remaining living units contained single people or unrelated individuals living together. In 1960, 85 percent of all households were families.

Families in the United States have many diverse forms, and celebrity couples represent them all. After living together, Ashton Kutcher, age 27, and Demi Moore, age 42, were recently married. They live with her three children from a previous marriage, who refer to Kutcher as "My Other Dad." Rosie O'Donnell and Kelli Carpenter married in San Francisco in 2004, but their marriage was later voided by the California Supreme Court. They live with Rosie's three adopted children.

Census Bureau data in this chapter are based on that definition. However, the trend in the United States is toward a broader definition of families to include both homosexual and heterosexual partners and unmarried as well as married couples who live together. These *families of affinity* are made up of people who think of themselves as a family and wish others to see them that way.

Families: Global Variations

How closely related do people have to be in order to be part of a family? In preindustrial societies, people commonly recognize the **extended family,** *a family consisting of parents and children as well as other kin.* This large group is sometimes called the *consanguine family* because it includes everyone with "shared blood." With industrialization, however, increasing social mobility and geographic migration give rise to the **nuclear family,** *a family composed of one or two parents and their children.* The nuclear family is also called the *conjugal family,* meaning "based on marriage." Although many people in our society think of kinship in terms of extended families, most people carry out daily routines within a nuclear family.

The family is changing most quickly in nations that have a large welfare state (see Chapter 17, "Politics and Government"). In the Thinking Globally box on page 472, the sociologist David Popenoe takes a look at Sweden, which, he claims, is home to the weakest families in the world.

MARRIAGE PATTERNS

Cultural norms, and often laws, identify people as suitable or unsuitable marriage partners. Some marital norms promote **endogamy,** *marriage between people of the same social category.* Endogamy limits potential partners to people of the same age, race, religion, or social class. By contrast, **exogamy** is *marriage between people of different social categories.* In rural areas of India, for example, people are expected to marry someone of the same caste (endogamy) but from a different village (exogamy). The reason for endogamy is that people of similar position pass along their standing to their offspring, maintaining the traditional social hierarchy. Exogamy, on the other hand, links communities and encourages the spread of culture.

In high-income nations, laws permit only **monogamy** (from the Greek, meaning "one union"), *marriage that unites two partners.* Global Map 18–1 on page 474 shows that monogamy is the rule throughout North and South America as well as Europe, although many countries in Africa and southern Asia permit **polygamy** (from the Greek, meaning "many unions"), *marriage that unites a person with two or more spouses.* Polygamy has two forms.

The Weakest Families on Earth? A Report from Sweden

The Swedes have managed to avoid many of the social problems—violent crime, drug abuse, and savage poverty—that blight whole cities in the United States. Instead, this Scandinavian nation seems to fulfill the promise of the modern welfare state, with a large and professional government bureaucracy that sees to virtually all human needs.

But one drawback of an expanding welfare state, according to David Popenoe (1991, 1994), is that Sweden has the weakest families on Earth. Because people look to the government, not spouses, for economic assistance, Swedes are less likely to marry than members of any other high-income society. For the same reason, Sweden also has a high share of adults living alone (36 percent compared to 24 percent in the United States). In addition, a large proportion of couples live together outside marriage (28 percent, versus 7 in the United States), and more than half of all Swedish children (compared to one-third in the United States) are born to unmarried parents. Average household size in Sweden is also the smallest in the world (2.0 persons, versus 2.6 in the United States). Finally, Swedish couples, whether married or not, are more likely to break up than partners in any other high-income nation.

Popenoe claims that a growing culture of individualism and self-fulfillment, along with the declining influence of religion, began

eroding Swedish families in the 1960s. The movement of women into the labor force also played a part. Today Sweden has the lowest proportion of women who are homemakers (10 percent, versus 22 percent in the United States) and the highest percentage of women in the labor force (77 percent, versus 59 percent in the United States).

But most important, according to Popenoe, is the expansion of the welfare state. The Swedish government offers its citizens a lifetime of services. Swedes can count on the government to deliver and school their children, provide comprehensive health care, support them when they are out of work, and pay for their funerals.

Many Swedes supported this welfare state, thinking it would *strengthen* families. But as Popenoe sees it, government is really *replacing* families. Take the case of child care: The Swedish government operates child care centers, staffed by professionals and available regardless of parents' income. However, the government gives

nothing to parents who wish to care for children in their own home. In effect, government benefits encourage people to let the state do what family members used to do for themselves.

But if Sweden's system has solved so many social problems, why should anyone care about the family getting weaker? For two reasons, says Popenoe. First, it is very expensive for government to provide many "family" services; this is the main reason that Sweden has one of the highest rates of taxation in the world. Second, it is unlikely that government employees in large child care centers can provide children with the same love and emotional security given by two parents living as a family. Popenoe believes that small, intimate groups do some things better than large organizations.

WHAT DO YOU THINK?

1. Do you agree with Popenoe that government should not replace families? Explain your answer.
2. In the United States, we have a much smaller welfare state than in Sweden; should our government do more for its people? Why or why not?
3. With regard to children, list two specific things that government can do better than parents and two things that parents do better than government.

By far the more common form is **polygyny** (from the Greek, meaning "many women"), *marriage that unites one man and two or more women.* For example, Islamic nations in the Middle East and Africa permit men up to four wives. Even so, most Islamic families are monogamous because few men can afford to support several wives and even more children.

Polyandry (from the Greek, meaning "many men" or "many husbands") is *marriage that unites one woman and two or more men.* This extremely rare pattern exists in Tibet, a mountainous land where agriculture is difficult. There, polyandry discourages the division of land into parcels too small to support a family and divides the work of farming among many men.

Most of the world's societies have at some time permitted more than one marital pattern. Even so, most marriages have been monogamous (Murdock, 1965, orig. 1949). This historical preference for monogamy reflects two facts of life: Supporting several spouses is very expensive, and the number of men and women in most societies is roughly equal.

YOUR TURN

Given the high level of divorce in the United States, do you think "serial monogamy" would be a better description of our marriage system than "monogamy"? Explain your position.

RESIDENTIAL PATTERNS

Just as societies regulate mate selection, they also designate where a couple lives. In preindustrial societies, most newlyweds live with one set of parents who offer them protection, support, and assistance. Most common is the norm of **patrilocality** (Greek for "place of the father"), *a residential pattern in which a married couple lives with or near the husband's family.* But some societies (such as the North American Iroquois) favor **matrilocality** (meaning "place of the mother"), *a residential pattern in which a married couple lives with or near the wife's family.* Societies that engage in frequent local warfare tend toward patrilocality, so sons are close to home to offer protection. On the other hand, societies that engage only in distant warfare may be either patrilocal or matrilocal, depending on whether its sons or daughters have greater economic value (Ember & Ember, 1971, 1991).

Industrial societies show yet another pattern. Finances permitting, they favor **neolocality** (from the Greek, meaning "new place"), *a residential pattern in which a married couple lives apart from both sets of parents.*

PATTERNS OF DESCENT

Descent refers to *the system by which members of a society trace kinship over generations.* Most preindustrial societies trace kinship through either the father's side or the mother's side of the family. **Patrilineal descent,** the more common pattern, is *a system tracing kinship through men.* In this pattern, children are related to others only through their fathers, so that fathers pass property on to their sons. Patrilineal descent characterizes most pastoral and agrarian societies, in which men produce the most valued resources. Less common is **matrilineal descent,** *a system tracing kinship through women.* Matrilineal descent, in which mothers pass property to their daughters, is found more frequently in horticultural societies, where women are the main food producers.

Industrial societies with greater gender equality recognize **bilateral descent** ("two-sided descent"), *a system tracing kinship through both men and women.* In this pattern, children recognize people on both the father's side and the mother's side as relatives.

YOUR TURN

Based on this discussion, how would you explain the common practice in the United States of a woman taking her husband's name after marriage?

PATTERNS OF AUTHORITY

Worldwide, polygyny, patrilocality, and patrilineal descent are dominant and reflect the global pattern of patriarchy. But in industrial societies like the United States, more egalitarian family patterns are evolving, especially as the share of women in the labor force goes up. However, men are still typically heads of households, and most U.S. parents give children their father's last name.

Theoretical Analysis of Families

As in earlier chapters, the three major theoretical approaches offer a range of insights about the family. We can use all three to gain a deeper understanding of family life.

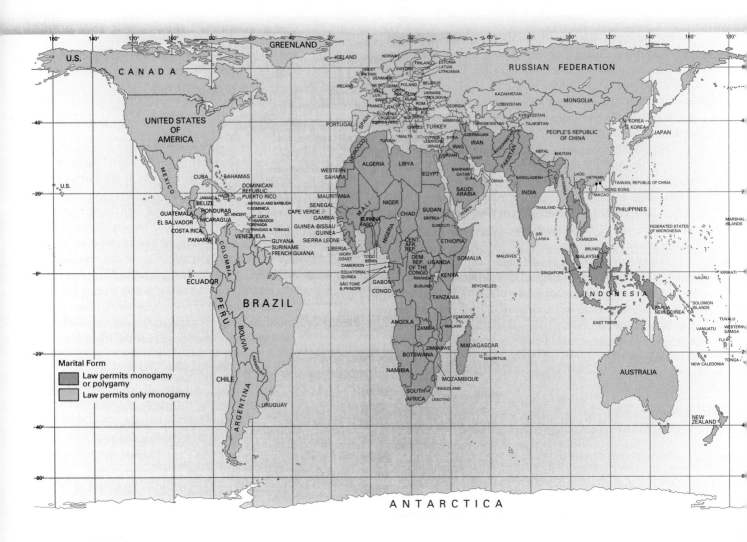

WINDOW ON THE WORLD

GLOBAL MAP 18-1 Marital Form in Global Perspective

Monogamy is the only legal form of marriage throughout the Western Hemisphere and in much of the rest of the world. In most African nations and in southern Asia, however, polygamy is permitted by law. In many cases, this practice reflects the historic influence of Islam, a religion that allows a man to have up to four wives. Even so, most marriages in these countries are monogamous, primarily for financial reasons.

Source: *Peters Atlas of the World* (1990).

FUNCTIONS OF THE FAMILY: STRUCTURAL-FUNCTIONAL ANALYSIS

According to the structural-functional approach, the family performs many vital tasks. In fact, the family operates as the backbone of society.

1. **Socialization.** As explained in Chapter 5 ("Socialization"), the family is the first and most important setting for child rearing. Ideally, parents help children become well-integrated, contributing members of society (Parsons & Bales, 1955). Of course, family socialization continues throughout the life cycle. Adults

The family is a basic building block of society because it performs important functions, such as conferring social position and regulating sexual activity. To most family members, however, the family (at least in ideal terms) is a "haven in a heartless world" in which individuals enjoy the feeling of belonging and find emotional support. Marc Chagall conveyed the promise of marriage in his painting, *To My Wife*. Looking at the painting, how does the artist characterize marriage?

Marc Chagall (1887–1985), painting, *To My Wife*, 1933–44. Georges Pompidou Centre, Paris. The Bridgeman Art Library, London. © 2003 Artists Rights Society (ARS), New York/ADAGP, Paris.

change within marriage, and as any parent knows, mothers and fathers learn as much from their children as their children learn from them.

2. **Regulation of sexual activity.** Every culture regulates sexual activity in the interest of maintaining kinship organization and property rights. The **incest taboo** is *a norm forbidding sexual relations or marriage between certain relatives*. Although the incest taboo exists in every society, exactly which relatives cannot marry varies from one culture to another. The matrilineal Navajo, for example, forbid marrying any relative of one's mother. Our bilateral society applies the incest taboo to both sides of the family but limits it to close relatives, including parents, grandparents, siblings, aunts, and uncles (National Map 8–1 on page 197 shows which states allow or forbid first-cousin marriages). But even brother-sister (but not parent-child) marriages existed among the ancient Egyptian, Incan, and Hawaiian nobility (Murdock, 1965, orig. 1949).

Reproduction between close relatives of any species can result in mental and physical damage to offspring. Yet only human beings observe an incest taboo, a fact suggesting that the key reason for controlling incest is social. Why? First, the incest taboo limits sexual competition in families by restricting sex to spouses. Second, because kinship defines people's rights and obligations toward one another, reproduction among close relatives would hopelessly confuse kinship ties and threaten social order. Third, forcing

people to marry outside their immediate families ties together the larger society.

3. **Social placement.** Families are not needed for people to reproduce, but they help maintain social organization. Parents pass on their own social identity—in terms of race, ethnicity, religion, and social class—to their children at birth.

4. **Material and emotional security.** Many people view the family as a "haven in a heartless world," offering physical protection, emotional support, and financial assistance. Perhaps this is why people living in families tend to be happier, healthier, and wealthier than people living alone (Goldstein & Kenney, 2001; U.S. Census Bureau, 2005).

Critical review Structural-functional analysis explains why society, at least as we know it, is built on families. But this approach glosses over the diversity of U.S. family life and ignores how other social institutions (such as government) could meet some of the same human needs. Finally, structural-functionalism overlooks negative aspects of family life, including patriarchy and family violence.

YOUR TURN

To understand what your family means to you, make a list of all the benefits of family life, and then try to find an alternative source (such as friends, clubs, or government) for each one.

Women have long been taught to see marriage as the key to a happy life. Social-conflict theory, however, points to the fact that marriage often means a lifetime sentence of unpaid domestic labor. Susan Pyzow's painting, *Bridal Bouquet,* makes the point.

© Susan Pyzow, *Bridal Bouquet,* watercolor on paper, 10 × 13.5 in. Studio SPM Inc.

INEQUALITY AND THE FAMILY: SOCIAL-CONFLICT AND FEMINIST ANALYSIS

Like the structural-functional approach, the social-conflict approach, including feminist analysis, considers the family as central to our way of life. But rather than focusing on ways that kinship benefits society, this approach points out how the family perpetuates social inequality.

1. **Property and inheritance.** Friedrich Engels (1902, orig. 1884) traced the origin of the family to men's need (especially in the upper classes) to identify heirs so that they could hand down property to their sons.

Families thus concentrate wealth and reproduce the class structure in each new generation.

2. **Patriarchy.** Feminists link the family to patriarchy. To know their heirs, men must control the sexuality of women. Families therefore transform women into the sexual and economic property of men. A century ago in the United States, most wives' earnings belonged to their husbands. Today women still bear most of the responsibility for child rearing and housework (Benokraitis & Feagin, 1995; Stapinski, 1998; England, 2001).

3. **Racial and ethnic inequality.** Racial and ethnic categories persist over generations because most people marry others like themselves. Endogamous marriage supports racial and ethnic hierarchies.

Critical review Social-conflict and feminist analysis shows another side of family life: its role in social stratification. Engels criticized the family as supporting capitalism. But noncapitalist societies also have families (and family problems). The family may be linked to social inequality, as Engels argued, but the family carries out societal functions not easily accomplished by other means.

CONSTRUCTING FAMILY LIFE: MICRO-LEVEL ANALYSIS

Both structural-functional and social-conflict analyses view the family as a structural system. By contrast, micro-level analysis explores how individuals shape and experience family life.

Symbolic-Interaction Analysis

Ideally, family living offers an opportunity for *intimacy,* a word with Latin roots meaning "sharing fear." As family members share many activities over time, they build emotional bonds. Of course, the fact that parents act as authority figures often limits their closeness with younger children. Only as children approach adulthood do kinship ties open up to include sharing confidences with greater intimacy (Macionis, 1978).

Social-Exchange Analysis

Social-exchange analysis, another micro-level approach, describes courtship and marriage as forms of negotiation (Blau, 1964). Dating allows each person to assess the advantages and disadvantages of a potential spouse. In essence, exchange analysts suggest, people "shop around" for partners to make the best "deal" they can.

In patriarchal societies, gender roles dictate the elements of exchange: Men bring wealth and power to the marriage

APPLYING THEORY

FAMILY

	Structural-Functional Approach	Social-Conflict and Feminist Approach	Symbolic-Interaction Approach
What is the level of analysis?	Macro-level	Macro-level	Micro-level
What is the importance of the family for society?	The family performs vital tasks, including socializing the young and providing emotional and financial support for members.	The family perpetuates social inequality by handing down wealth from one generation to the next.	The reality of family life is constructed by members in their interaction.
	The family helps regulate sexual activity.	The family supports patriarchy as well as racial and ethnic inequality.	Courtship typically brings together people who offer the same level of advantages.

marketplace, and women bring beauty. The importance of beauty explains women's traditional concern with their appearance. But as women have joined the labor force, they are less dependent on men to support them, and so the terms of exchange are converging for men and women.

→ **YOUR TURN** ←

Thinking about the "marriage marketplace," why do you think women have traditionally been less willing than men to reveal their age?

Critical review Micro-level analysis balances structural-functional and social-conflict visions of the family as an institutional system. Both the interaction and exchange viewpoints focus on the individual experience of family life. However, micro-level analysis misses the bigger picture: Family life is similar for people in the same social and economic categories. The Applying Theory table summarizes what we can learn by applying each of the theoretical approaches to family life.

Stages of Family Life

The family is a dynamic institution, with marked changes across the life course. New families begin with courtship and evolve as the new partners settle into the realities of married life. Next, for most couples at least, come the years spent developing careers and raising children, leading to the later years of marriage after the children have left home to form families of their own. We will look briefly at each of these four stages.

COURTSHIP

November 2, Kandy, Sri Lanka. Winding through the rain forest of this beautiful island, our van driver, Harry, recounts how he met his wife. Actually, he explains, it was more of an arrangement: The two families were both Buddhist and of the same caste. "We got along well, right from the start," recalls Harry. "We had the same background. I suppose she or I could have said no. But love marriages happen in the city, not in the village where I grew up."

In rural Sri Lanka, as in rural areas of low- and middle-income countries throughout the world, most people consider courtship too important to be left to the young (Stone, 1977). *Arranged marriages* are alliances between extended families of similar social standing and usually involve an exchange not just of children but also of wealth and favors. Romantic love has little to do with marriage, and parents may make such arrangements when their children are very young. A century ago in Sri Lanka and India, for example, half of all girls married before reaching age fifteen (Mayo, 1927; Mace & Mace, 1960). As the Thinking Globally box on page 478 explains, child marriage is still found in some parts of the world today.

Because traditional societies are more culturally homogeneous, almost all young men and women have been well socialized to be good spouses. Therefore, parents can arrange marriages with little thought about whether or not the two individuals involved are *personally* compatible because they know that the partners will be *culturally* compatible.

Industrialization erodes the importance of extended families and weakens tradition. Young people in industrial

Early to Wed: A Report from Rural India

Sumitra Jogi cries as her wedding is about to begin. Are they tears of joy? Not exactly. This "bride" is an eleven-month-old squirming in the arms of her mother. The groom? A boy of six.

In a remote, rural village in India's western state of Rajasthan, two families gather at midnight to celebrate a traditional wedding ritual. It is May 2, in Hindu tradition an especially good day to marry. Sumitra's father smiles as the ceremony begins; her mother cradles the infant, who has fallen asleep. The groom, dressed in a special costume with a red and gold turban on his head, gently reaches up and grasps the baby's hand. Then, as the ceremony reaches its conclusion, the young boy leads the child and mother around the wedding fire three-and-one-half times, as the audience beams at the couple's first steps together as husband and wife.

Child weddings are illegal in India, but in the rural regions, traditions are strong and marriage laws are hard to enforce. As a result, thousands of children marry

each year. "In rural Rajasthan," explains one social welfare worker, "all the girls are married by age fourteen. These are poor, illiterate families, and they don't want to keep girls past their first menstrual cycle."

For the immediate future, Sumitra Jogi will remain with her parents. But in eight or ten years, a second ceremony will send her to live with her husband's family, and her married life will begin.

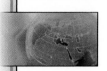

The two-year-old girl on the left is breastfeeding during her wedding ceremony in a small village in the state of Rajasthan, India; her new husband is eight years old. Although outlawed, such arranged marriages involving children are still known to take place in traditional, remote areas of India.

If the responsibilities of marriage lie years in the future, why do families push their children to marry at such an early age? Parents of girls know that the younger the bride, the smaller the dowry offered to the groom's family. Then, too, when girls marry this young, there is no question about their virginity, which raises their value on the marriage market. Arranged marriages are an alliance between families. No one thinks about love or the fact that the children are too young to understand what is taking place (J. W. Anderson, 1995).

WHAT DO YOU THINK?

1. Why are arranged marriages common in very traditional regions?
2. List several advantages and disadvantages of arranged marriages from the point of view of the families involved. Do you think the advantages outweigh the disadvantages? Why or why not?
3. Can you point to ways in which mate selection in the United States is "arranged" by society?

---

societies choose their own mates and delay marriage until they have gained the financial security needed to live apart from their parents and the experience needed to select a suitable partner. During this time, dating sharpens courtship skills and allows sexual experimentation.

Check out how people use the Internet to find partners at http://www.syl.com

Romantic Love

Our culture celebrates *romantic love*—affection and sexual passion for another person—as the basis for marriage. We find it hard to imagine marriage without love, and popular culture—from fairy tales like "Cinderella" to today's television sitcoms and dramas—portrays love as the key to a successful marriage.

Our society's emphasis on romance motivates young people to "leave the nest" to form new families of their own, and physical passion can help a new couple through the difficult adjustments of living together (W. J. Goode, 1959). On the other hand, because feelings change over time, romantic love is a less stable foundation for marriage than social and economic considerations, which is one reason that the divorce rate is much higher in the United States than in nations in which culture is a stronger guide in the choice of a partner.

But even in our country, sociologists point out, society aims Cupid's arrow more than we like to think. Most people fall in love with others of the same race, of comparable age, and of similar social class. Our society "arranges" marriages by encouraging **homogamy** (literally, "like marrying like"), *marriage between people with the same social characteristics.*

→ **YOUR TURN** ←

How similar are your parents (or you and your spouse) in terms of age, social class, race, ethnicity, and education?

SETTLING IN: IDEAL AND REAL MARRIAGE

Our culture gives the young an idealized, "happily ever after" picture of marriage. Such optimism can lead to disappointment, especially for women, who are taught to view marriage as the key to happiness. Also, romantic love involves a good deal of fantasy: We fall in love with others not always as they are but as we want them to be (Berscheid & Hatfield, 1983).

Sexuality, too, can be a source of disappointment. In the romantic haze of falling in love, people may see marriage as an endless sexual honeymoon, only to face the sobering realization that sex becomes a less-than-all-consuming passion. Although the frequency of marital sex does decline over time, about two in three married people report that they are satisfied with the sexual dimension of their relationship. In general, couples with the best sexual relationships experience the most satisfaction in their marriages. Sex may not be the key to marital bliss, but more often than not, good sex and good relationships usually go together (Blumstein & Schwartz, 1983; Laumann et al., 1994).

Infidelity—*sexual activity outside marriage*—is another area where the reality of marriage does not match our cultural ideal. In a recent survey, 92 percent of U.S. adults said sex outside of marriage is "always wrong" or "almost

"Son, you're all grown up now. You owe me two hundred and fourteen thousand dollars."

always wrong." Even so, 21 percent of men and 13 percent of women indicated on a private, written questionnaire that they had been sexually unfaithful to their partners at least once (NORC, 2003:234, 1227).

CHILD REARING

Despite the demands children make on us, adults in this country overwhelmingly identify raising children as one of life's greatest joys. Today about half of U.S. adults say that two children is the ideal number, and few people want more than three (NORC, 2003: 1071, 230). This is a change from two centuries ago, when *eight* children was the U.S. average.

Big families pay off in preindustrial societies because children supply needed labor. This is why members of such societies view having children as a wife's duty, and without effective birth control, childbearing is a regular event. Of course, a high death rate in preindustrial societies prevents many children from reaching adulthood; as late as 1900, one-third of children born in the United States died by age ten.

Economically speaking, industrialization transforms children from an asset to a liability. It now costs more than $200,000 to raise one child, including college tuition (Lino, 2005). No wonder the average size of the U.S. family dropped steadily during the twentieth century to one child per family![2]

The trend toward smaller families is most pronounced in high-income nations. The picture differs in low-income countries in Latin America, Asia, and especially Africa, where many women have few alternatives to bearing children. In such societies, as a glance back to Global Map 1–1 on page 4 shows, between four and six children is still the norm.

Parenting is a very expensive, lifelong commitment. As our society has given people greater choices about family life, more U.S. adults have decided to delay childbirth or to remain childless. In 1960, almost 90 percent of women between twenty-five and twenty-nine who had ever married had at least one child; today, this proportion is just 69 percent (U.S. Census Bureau, 2003).

About two-thirds of parents in the United States say they would like to devote more of their time to child rearing (Snell, 1990; K. Clark 2002). But unless we accept a lower standard of living, economic realities demand that most parents pursue careers outside the home, even if that means devoting less time to their families. For many families, including the Yniguez family described in the opening to this chapter, having fewer children is an important step toward raising their standard of living.

Children of working parents spend most of the day at school. But after school, some 3.3 million children (15 percent of six- to twelve-year-olds) are *latchkey kids* who are left to fend for themselves (Vandivere et al., 2003). Traditionalists in the "family values" debate charge that many mothers work at the expense of their children, who receive less parenting. Progressives counter that such criticism targets women for wanting the same opportunities men have long enjoyed.

Congress took a step toward easing the conflict between family and job responsibilities by passing the Family and Medical Leave Act in 1993.  This law allows up to ninety days of unpaid leave from work because of a new child or a serious family emergency. Still, most adults in this country have

to juggle parental and job responsibilities. When parents work, who cares for the kids? The Applying Sociology box provides the answer.

THE FAMILY IN LATER LIFE

Increasing life expectancy in the United States means that couples who stay married do so for a longer and longer time. By about age sixty, most have finished the task of raising children. At this point, marriage brings a return to living with only a spouse.

Like the birth of children, their departure—creating the "empty nest"—requires adjustments, although a marriage often becomes closer and more satisfying. Years of living together may have lessened a couple's sexual passion, but understanding and commitment often increase.

Personal contact with children usually continues because most older adults live a short distance from at least one of their children. One-third of all U.S. adults (60 million) are grandparents. Most grandparents help with child care and other responsibilities. Among African Americans, who have a high rate of single parenting, grandmothers have an especially important position in family life (Clemetson, 2000; U.S. Census Bureau, 2003).

The other side of the coin is that more adults in midlife now care for aging parents. The "empty nest" may not be filled by a parent coming to live in the home, but many adults find that caring for parents, who now live to eighty and beyond, can be as taxing as raising young children. The oldest of the "baby boomers"—now sixty—are called the "sandwich generation" because many (especially women) will spend as many years caring for their aging parents as they did caring for their children (Lund, 1993).

The final and surely the most difficult transition in married life comes with the death of a spouse. Because of their greater life expectancy and the fact that women usually marry men several years older than themselves, wives typically outlive their husbands. Wives can thus expect to spend some years as widows. The challenge of living alone following the death of a spouse is especially great for men, who usually have fewer friends than widows and may lack housekeeping skills.

U.S. Families:
Class, Race, and Gender

Dimensions of inequality—social class, ethnicity and race, and gender—are powerful forces that shape marriage and family life. This discussion addresses each factor in turn, but bear in mind that they overlap in our lives.

---

[2]According to the U.S. Census Bureau, the median number of children per family was 0.87 in 2003. Among all families, the medians were 0.79 for whites, 1.05 for African Americans, and 1.18 for Hispanics.

APPLYING SOCIOLOGY
Who's Minding the Kids?

Traditionally, the task of providing daily care for young children fell to stay-at-home mothers. But with a majority of mothers and fathers now in the labor force, finding quality, affordable child care is a high priority for parents.

The figure shows the various arrangements reported by working mothers to care for children under the age of five. The majority of these children, 53 percent, receive care at home from a parent (27 percent) or a relative (26 percent). The remaining 47 percent are cared for by a nonrelative: 29 percent attend preschool or a day care program, 13 percent go to the home of a nonrelative, and only 5 percent of children are cared for in their own home by a nanny or babysitter (Urban Institute, 2004).

The use of day care programs has doubled over the past decade because many

 A report on the quality of child care given by relatives can be found at http://www.urban.org/UploadedPDF/311161_snapshots3_No23.pdf

parents cannot find affordable in-home care for their children. Some day care

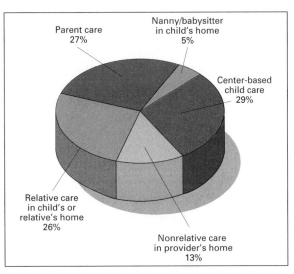

Parent care 27%

Nanny/babysitter in child's home 5%

Center-based child care 29%

Relative care in child's or relative's home 26%

Nonrelative care in provider's home 13%

Working mothers report that a majority of their young children receive care in the home.

centers are so big that they amount to "tot lots" where parents "park" their children for the day. The impersonality of such settings and the rapid turnover in staff prevent the warm and consistent nurturing that young children need in order to develop a sense of trust.

But other child care centers offer a secure and healthful environment. Research suggests that *good* care centers are good for children; *bad* facilities are not.

WHAT DO YOU THINK?

1. Why do so many parents have trouble finding affordable child care? Should employers do more?
2. As parents, would you and your partner be willing to limit your working hours to allow child care at home? Why or why not?
3. How can parents assess the quality of a child care center? What should you look for?

SOCIAL CLASS

Social class determines both a family's financial security and its range of opportunities. Interviewing working-class women, Lillian Rubin (1976) found that wives thought a good husband was one who held a steady job, did not drink too much, and was not violent. Rubin's middle-class respondents, by contrast, never mentioned such things; these women simply *assumed* that a husband would provide a safe and secure home. Their ideal husband was someone they could talk to easily, sharing feelings and experiences.

Clearly, what women (and men) think they can hope for in marriage—and what they end up with—is linked to

their social class. Much the same holds for children; boys and girls lucky enough to be born into more affluent families enjoy better mental and physical health, develop more self-confidence, and go on to greater achievement than children born to poor parents (Fitzpatrick, 1988; McLeod & Shanahan, 1993; Duncan et al., 1998).

ETHNICITY AND RACE

As Chapter 14 ("Race and Ethnicity") discusses, ethnicity and race are powerful social forces that can affect family life. Keep in mind, however, that American Indian, Latino, and African American families (like all families) do not fit any single stereotype (Allen, 1995).

April 5, 2005

Crisis of Indian Children Intensifies as Families Fail

By SARAH KERSHAW

LUMMI INDIAN RESERVATION, Wash., March 29—The very full house on Gumel Place was steeped in the usual loud weekend chaos when 14-year-old Cecilia Morris burst through the door.

"Hey," she said. "Is Mom in jail?"

No, said her uncle, Jasper Cladoosby, but her mother had gone back into drug treatment. Her father is the one in prison.

Mr. Cladoosby, 27, who is raising four of his own children along with Cecilia and two of her sisters, is one of possibly hundreds of uncles, aunts, grandparents and others caring for children whose parents are unable to raise them because of dire poverty, alcoholism and epidemic drug abuse on this reservation on Bellingham Bay in Northwest Washington. . . .

Tribal officials here estimate that fewer than half of the 1,500 children on the reservation are living with a parent full time. A breakdown of the American Indian family, mirrored throughout reservations across the country, has been building for generations but is now growing worse, tribal and outside experts say.

The crisis gained new attention this month after a troubled youth went on a shooting rampage on the Red Lake reservation in northern Minnesota. The broken family of the teenager, Jeff Weise, 16, who the police say killed nine people and then himself, is typical among Indians. With his father dead and his mother disabled by a drunken-driving accident, he was staying with his grandmother on the reservation, after living with his mother, before her accident, in Minneapolis. . . .

Even though tribes have made great strides over the last two decades in keeping children from troubled homes, a cascade of statistics paints a bleak picture of the roughly 850,000 Indian and Alaska Native youths, about half of them living on Indian reservations, according to the Census Bureau. Compared with whites and with other minorities, Indians have extremely high teenage suicide rates, are more likely to get into fights at school and carry weapons to school, and have high rates of substance abuse, several recent reports show. . . .

According to the latest federal statistics, nearly 10,000 Indian and Alaska Native children, or about 1.2 percent, are in foster care, living with relatives or others. (Indians and Alaska Natives make up 1.5 percent of the nation's population.) The federal data, from the Department of Health and Human Services, show that

American Indian Families

American Indians display a wide variety of family types. Some patterns emerge, however, among people who migrate from tribal reservations to cities. Women and men who arrive in cities often seek out others—especially kin and members of the same tribe—for help getting settled. One recent study, for example, tells the story of two women migrants to the San Francisco area who met at a meeting of an Indian organization and realized that they were of the same tribe. The women and their children decided to share an apartment, and soon after, the children began to refer to one another as brothers, sisters, and cousins. As the months passed, the two mothers came to think of themselves as sisters.

Migration also creates many "fluid households" with changing membership. In another case from the same research, a large apartment in San Francisco was rented by a woman, her aunt, and their children. Over the course of the next month, however, they welcomed into their home more than thirty other urban migrants, who stayed for a short time until they found housing of their own. Such patterns of mutual assistance, often involving real and fictional kinship, are common among all low-income people (Lobo, 2002).

American Indians who leave tribal reservations for the cities typically are better off than those who stay behind. Because people on reservations have a hard time finding work, they cannot easily form stable marriages, and problems such as alcoholism and drug abuse shatter the ties between parent and child. "In the *Times*" describes the crisis facing families on the Lummi Indian reservation in Washington, where half the children do not live with even one of their biological parents.

about 1.8 percent of black children and about 0.5 percent of white children are in foster care....

Many experts say the crisis for Indian children stems not so much from living without their parents—the role of the extended family in child rearing is crucial in Indian culture—but from a lack of mental health services and recreation on reservations, some so destitute that there is no swimming pool or basketball court, let alone a counselor.

Money for health and mental health care on reservations, which comes mostly from the federal government but is increasingly supplemented by gambling revenues, falls far short of the demand, many experts say.

Here at Lummi Nation, the Silver Reef Casino opened in 2002 but has only recently begun to yield steady profits. The tribe has invested $2 million in a new home, scheduled to open April 13, that can hold 28 troubled children; a "safe home" for youths; and more counselors. Now, there are seven counselors available for the 1,500 children, well above the national average for Indians.

But tribal officials acknowledge that Lummi families still bear the brunt of caring for neglected children and emotionally supporting them....

Justin Zollner, ... 16, has an anger problem. The ... father has "been out of the picture" for a long time....

Justin has uncles who live nearby, and they attend his football games and take him canoe racing, a passionate pursuit for the tribe....

Still, it is painful when Justin talks, fairly often, about missing his father. "Right now, I kind of wish my dad was still here because I've played football for like seven years now, and he never got to watch me." ...

WHAT DO YOU THINK?

1. How does this article show the effect of societal structures such as poverty on families?

2. How do you think poverty and weak parent-child ties affect the children described in this article?

3. What should be done to address the problems discussed in this article?

Adapted from the original article by Sarah Kershaw published in *The New York Times* on April 5, 2005. Copyright © 2005 by The New York Times Company. Reprinted with permission.

Latino Families

Many Latinos enjoy the loyalty and support of extended families. Traditionally, too, Latino parents exercise considerable control over children's courtship, considering marriage an alliance of families, not just a union based on romantic love. Some Latino families also follow conventional gender roles, encouraging machismo—strength, daring, and sexual conquest—among men and treating women with respect but also close supervision.

However, assimilation into the larger society is changing these traditional patterns. In the opening story to this chapter, we explained that many women who come to California from Mexico favor smaller families. Similarly, many Puerto Ricans who migrate to New York do not maintain the strong extended family ties they knew in Puerto Rico. Traditional male authority over women has also lessened, especially among affluent Latino families, whose number has tripled in the past twenty years (O'Hare, 1990; Lach, 1999; Navarro, 2004).

Some Hispanics have prospered, but the overall social standing of this segment of the U.S. population remains below average. The U.S. Census Bureau (2005) reports that the typical Hispanic family had an income of $35,401 in 2004, or 64 percent of the national average. Many Hispanic families suffer the stress of unemployment and other poverty-related problems.

African American Families

African American families face economic disadvantages: The typical African American family earned $35,158 in 2004, which was 64 percent of the national average. People of African ancestry are three times as likely as whites to be

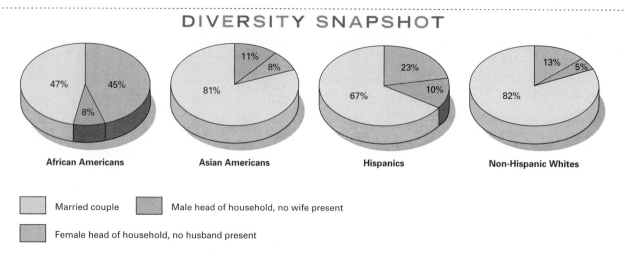

FIGURE 18–1 Family Form in the United States, 2004

All racial and ethnic categories show variations in family form.

Source: U.S. Census Bureau (2005).

poor, and poverty means that both parents and children are likely to experience unemployment and a dangerous physical environment of crime and drug abuse.

A high risk of unemployment and poverty among African Americans makes maintaining a stable marriage difficult. Consider that 27 percent of African American women in their forties have never married, compared to about 9 percent of white women of the same age. This means that African American women—often with children—are more likely to be single heads of households. Figure 18–1 shows that women headed 45 percent of all African American families in 2004, compared to 23 percent of Hispanic families, 13 percent of non-Hispanic white families, and 11 percent of Asian or Pacific Islander families (Harknett & McLanahan, 2004; U.S. Census Bureau, 2005).

Regardless of race, single-mother families are always at high risk of poverty. Nineteen percent of single families headed by non-Hispanic white women are poor. Higher yet, the poverty rate among families headed by African American women (38 percent) and Hispanic women (39 percent) is strong evidence of how the intersection of class, race, and gender can put women at a disadvantage. African American families with both wife and husband in the home, which represent 47 percent of the total, are much stronger economically, earning 80 percent as much as comparable non-Hispanic white families. But 68 percent of African American children are born to single women, and 33 percent of African American boys and girls are growing up

poor, meaning that these families carry much of the burden of child poverty in the United States (Martin et al., 2003; U.S. Census Bureau, 2005).

Ethnically and Racially Mixed Marriages

Most spouses have similar social backgrounds with regard to class and race. But over the course of the twentieth century, ethnicity came to matter less and less. In recent decades, for example, a woman of German and French ancestry might readily marry a man of Irish and English background without inviting disapproval from their families or from society in general.

Race has been a more powerful barrier. Before a 1967 Supreme Court decision (*Loving* v. *Virginia*), interracial marriage was illegal in sixteen states. Today, African, Asian, and Native Americans represent 17 percent of the U.S. population; if people ignored race in choosing spouses, we would expect about the same share of marriages to be mixed. The actual proportion of mixed marriages is 5.4 percent, showing that race still matters in social relations. But the number of racially mixed marriages is rising steadily.

The single most common type of interracial married couple is a white husband and an Asian wife, which accounts for about 14 percent of all interracial married couples. About one-fourth of all interracial married couples contain a husband (13 percent) or a wife (12 percent) who claimed a multiple-race identity in the 2000 census. Interracial married couples are likely to live in the west; more than 10 percent of all married couples are interracial in five states: Hawaii, Alaska, California, Nevada, and Oklahoma (Lee & Edmonston, 2005).

Surveys report that most U.S. teens now claim they have dated someone of another race. Do you think the proportion of mixed-race marriages will rise in the next twenty years? Why or why not?

GENDER

Jessie Bernard (1982) said that every marriage is actually *two* different relationships: a woman's marriage and a man's marriage. The reason is that few marriages are composed of two equal partners. Although patriarchy has weakened, most people still expect men to be older and taller than their wives and to have more important, better-paying jobs.

Why, then, do many people think that marriage benefits women more than men? The positive stereotype of the carefree bachelor contrasts sharply with the negative image of the lonely spinster, suggesting that women are fulfilled only through being wives and mothers.

However, Bernard continued, married women in fact have poorer mental health, less happiness, and more passive attitudes toward life than single women. Married men, on the other hand, generally live longer, mentally are better off, and report being happier overall than single men. These differences suggest why, after divorce, men are more eager than women to find a new partner.

Bernard concluded that there is no better assurance of long life, health, and happiness for a man than a woman well socialized to devote her life to taking care of him and providing the security of a well-ordered home. She was quick to add that marriage *could* be healthful for women if husbands did not dominate wives and expect them to do almost all the housework.

Transitions and Problems in Family Life

The newspaper columnist Ann Landers once remarked that one marriage in twenty is wonderful, five in twenty are good, ten in twenty are tolerable, and the remaining four are "pure hell." Families can be a source of joy, but for some, the reality falls far short of the ideal.

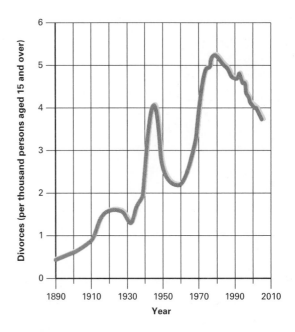

FIGURE 18–2 Divorce Rate for the United States, 1890–2004

Over the long term, the U.S. divorce rate has gone up. Since about 1980, however, the trend has been downward.

Source: Munson & Sutton (2005).

DIVORCE

U.S. society strongly supports marriage, and about nine out of ten people at some point "tie the knot." But many of today's marriages unravel. Figure 18–2 shows the tenfold increase in the U.S. divorce rate over the past century. In 2004, almost four in ten marriages were ending in divorce (for African Americans, the rate was about six in ten). Ours is the highest divorce rate in the world, about one-and-one-half times higher than in Canada and Japan, and nearly six times higher than in Italy (Japanese Ministry of Health, Labour, and Welfare, 2005).

The high U.S. divorce rate has many causes (Furstenberg & Cherlin, 1991; Etzioni, 1993; Popenoe, 1999; Greenspan, 2001):

1. **Individualism is on the rise.** Today's family members spend less time together. We have become more individualistic and more concerned about personal happiness and earning income than about the well-being of families and children.

2. **Romantic love fades.** Because our culture bases marriage on romantic love, relationships may fail as sexual

Divorce may be a solution for a couple in an unhappy marriage, but it can be a problem for children who experience the withdrawal of a parent from their social world. In what ways can divorce be harmful to children? Is there a positive side to divorce? How might separating parents better prepare their children for the transition of parental divorce?

passion fades. Many people end a marriage in favor of a new relationship that promises renewed excitement and romance.

3. **Women are less dependent on men.** Women's increasing participation in the labor force has reduced wives' financial dependence on husbands. Therefore, women find it easier to leave unhappy marriages.

4. **Many of today's marriages are stressful.** With both partners working outside the home in most cases, jobs leave less time and energy for family life. This makes raising children harder than ever. Children do stabilize some marriages, but divorce is most common during the early years of marriage, when many couples have young children.

5. **Divorce is socially acceptable.** Divorce no longer carries the powerful stigma it did several generations ago. Family and friends are now less likely to discourage couples in conflict from divorcing.

6. **Legally, a divorce is easier to get.** In the past, courts required divorcing couples to show that one or both were guilty of behavior such as adultery or physical abuse. Today all states allow divorce if a couple simply thinks the marriage has failed. Concern about easy divorces, shared by more than half of U.S. adults, has led some states to consider rewriting their marriage laws (Nock, Wright, & Sanchez, 1999; Phillips, 2001; NORC, 2003).

Who Divorces?

At greatest risk of divorce are young spouses—especially those who marry after a brief courtship—who lack money and emotional maturity. The chance of divorce also rises if the couple marries after an unexpected pregnancy or if one or both partners have substance abuse problems. People whose parents divorced also have a higher divorce rate themselves. Researchers suggest that a role-modeling effect is at work: Children who see parents go through divorce are more likely to consider divorce themselves (Amato, 2001). Finally, people who are not religious are more likely to divorce than those who have strong religious beliefs.

Divorce is also more common when both partners have successful careers, perhaps because of the strains of a two-career marriage but also because financially secure people do not feel they have to stay in an unhappy home. Finally, men and women who divorce once are more likely to divorce again, probably because high-risk factors follow them from one marriage to another (Glenn & Shelton, 1985).

Divorce and Children

Because mothers usually gain custody of children but fathers typically earn more income, the well-being of children often depends on fathers' making court-ordered child support payments. As Figure 18–3 indicates, courts award child support in 59 percent of all divorces involving children. Yet in any given year, half the children legally entitled to support receive only partial payments (which can be as little as $1) or no payments at all. Some 3.4 million "deadbeat dads" fail to support their youngsters. In response, federal legislation now mandates that employers withhold money from the earnings of fathers or mothers who fail to pay up; it is a serious crime to refuse to make child support payments or to move to another state to avoid making them (U.S. Census Bureau, 2003).

The effects of divorce on children go beyond financial support. Divorce can tear young people from familiar surroundings, entangle them in bitter feuding, and distance them from a parent they love. Most serious of all, many children blame themselves for their parents' breakup. Divorce changes the course of many children's lives, causing emotional and behavioral problems and raising the risk of dropping out of school and getting into trouble with the law. Many experts counter that divorce is better for children than their staying in a family torn by tension and violence. In any case, parents should remember that if they consider divorce, more than their own well-being is at stake (Wallerstein & Blakeslee, 1989; Popenoe, 1996; Amato & Sobolewski, 2001).

REMARRIAGE

Four out of five people who divorce remarry, most within five years. Nationwide, almost half of all marriages are now remarriages for at least one partner. Men, who benefit more from wedlock, are more likely than women to remarry.

Remarriage often creates *blended families,* composed of children and some combination of biological parents and stepparents. With brothers, sisters, half siblings, a stepparent—not to mention a biological parent who might live elsewhere and be married to someone else with other children—young people in blended families face the challenge of defining many new relationships and deciding just who is part of the nuclear family.

 Learn more about remarriage and other family issues at http://www.cdc.gov/nchs/data/series/sr_23/sr23_022.pdf

Parents often have trouble defining responsibility for household work among people unsure of their relations to each other. When the custody of children is an issue, ex-spouses can be an unwelcome presence for people in a new marriage. Although blended families require that members adjust to their new circumstances, they offer both young and old the chance to relax rigid family roles (Furstenberg & Cherlin, 2001; McLanahan, 2002).

YOUR TURN

A girl who has been an only child becomes part of a "blended family" and suddenly has two older brothers. What adjustments might she have to make?

FAMILY VIOLENCE

The ideal family is a source of pleasure and support. However, the disturbing reality of many homes is **family violence,** *emotional, physical, or sexual abuse of one family member by another.* The sociologist Richard J. Gelles calls

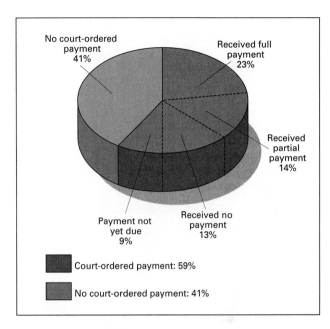

FIGURE 18-3 Payment of Child Support after Divorce

In half of all cases of court-ordered child support, the full payment is never received.

Source: U.S. Census Bureau (2003).

the family "the most violent group in society with the exception of the police and the military" (quoted in Roesch, 1984:75).

Violence against Women

Family brutality often goes unreported to police. Even so, the U.S. Bureau of Justice Statistics (2005) estimates that about 700,000 people are victims of domestic violence each year. Of this total, 73 percent of cases involve violence against women, and the remaining 27 percent involve violence against men. Fully 33 percent of women who are victims of homicide (but just 4 percent of men) are killed by spouses or, more often, ex-spouses. Nationwide, the death toll from family violence is about 1,250 women each year. Overall, women are more likely to be injured by a family member than to be mugged or raped by a stranger or hurt in an automobile accident (Shupe, Stacey, & Hazlewood, 1987; Blankenhorn, 1995; Federal Bureau of Investigation, 2004).

Historically, the law defined wives as the property of their husbands, so no man could be charged with raping his wife. Today, however, all states have enacted *marital*

than nonvictims to form stable relationships later on (Cherlin et al., 2004).

Violence against Children

Family violence also victimizes children. Each year, there are roughly 3 million reports of alleged child abuse or neglect, about 1,500 of them involving a child's death. Child abuse entails more than physical injury; abusive adults misuse power and trust to damage a child's emotional well-being. Child abuse and neglect are most common among the youngest and most vulnerable children (Besharov & Laumann, 1996).

Learn more about child abuse at http://www.nncc.org

Although child abusers conform to no simple stereotype, they are more likely to be women (58 percent) than men (42 percent). But almost all abusers share one trait—having been abused themselves as children. Research shows that violent behavior in close relationships is learned; in families, violence begets violence (Browning & Laumann, 1997; S. Levine, 2001; National Clearinghouse on Child Abuse and Neglect Information, 2005).

Alternative Family Forms

Most families in the United States are composed of a married couple who raise children. But in recent decades, our society has displayed greater diversity in family life.

ONE-PARENT FAMILIES

Twenty-eight percent of U.S. families with children under eighteen have only one parent in the household, a proportion that more than doubled during the last generation. Put another way, 28 percent of U.S. children now live with only one parent, and about half will do so before reaching eighteen. One-parent families—75 percent of which are headed by a single mother—result from divorce, death, or an unmarried woman's decision to have a child.

Single parenthood increases a woman's risk of poverty because it limits her ability to work and to further her education. The opposite is also true: Poverty raises the odds that a young woman will become a single mother (Trent, 1994). But single parenthood goes well beyond the poor: One-third of women in the United States become pregnant as teenagers, and many decide to raise their children whether they marry or not. Looking back to Figure 18–1, note that 53 percent of African American families are headed by a single parent. Single parenting is less common among Hispanics (33 percent), Asian Americans (19 percent), and

In recent years, the proportion of young people who cohabit—that is, live together without being married—has risen sharply. This trend contributes to the debate over what is and is not a family: Do you consider a cohabiting couple a family? Why or why not?

rape laws. The law no longer regards domestic violence as a private family matter; it gives victims more options. Now, even without a formal separation or divorce, a woman can obtain court protection from an abusive spouse, and all states have "stalking laws" that forbid an ex-partner from following or otherwise threatening the other partner. Communities across the United States have established shelters to provide counseling and temporary housing for women and children driven from their homes by domestic violence.

Finally, the harm caused by domestic violence goes beyond the physical injuries. Victims often lose their ability to trust others. One recent study found that women who had been physically or sexually abused were much less likely

non-Hispanic whites (18 percent). In many single-parent families, mothers turn to their own mothers for support. In the United States, then, the rise in single parenting is tied to a declining role for fathers and the growing importance of grandparenting.

Research shows that growing up in a one-parent family usually disadvantages children. Some studies claim that because a father and a mother each make distinctive contributions to a child's social development, one parent has a hard time doing as good a job alone. But the most serious problem for one-parent families, especially if that parent is a woman, is poverty. On average, children growing up in a single-parent family start out poorer, get less schooling, and end up with lower incomes as adults. Such children are also more likely to be single parents themselves (Popenoe, 1993a; Blankenhorn, 1995; Wu, 1996; Duncan et al., 1998; Kantrowitz & Wingert, 2001; McLanahan, 2002).

COHABITATION

Cohabitation is *the sharing of a household by an unmarried couple.* The number of cohabiting couples in the United States increased from about 500,000 in 1970 to about 5.6 million today (5 million heterosexual couples and 600,000 homosexual couples), or about 9 percent of all couples (U.S. Census Bureau, 2003).

In global perspective, cohabitation is a long-term form of family life, with or without children, that is common in Sweden and other Scandinavian nations. But it is rare in more traditional (especially Roman Catholic) nations such as Italy. Cohabitation is gaining in popularity in the United States, with almost half of people between ages twenty-five and forty-four having cohabited at some point.

Cohabiting tends to appeal to more independent-minded individuals as well as those who favor gender equality (Brines & Joyner, 1999). Most couples cohabit for no more than a few years; at that point, about half decide to marry and half split up. Mounting evidence suggests that living together may actually discourage marriage because partners (especially men) become used to low-commitment relationships. For this reason, cohabiting couples who have children—currently representing about one in eight births in the United States—may not always be long-term parents. Figure 18–4 shows that just 5 percent of children born to cohabiting couples will live until age eighteen with both biological parents, if the parents remain unmarried. The share rises to 36 percent among children whose parents marry at some point, but even this is half of the 70 percent figure among children whose parents married before they were born. When cohabiting couples with children separate, the involvement of both parents, including financial support,

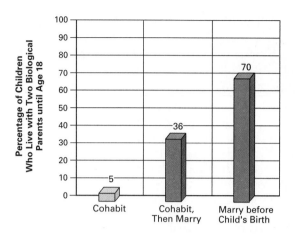

FIGURE 18–4 Parental Involvement in Children's Lives: Cohabiting and Married Parents

Marriage increases the odds that parents will share the same household with their child.

Source: Phillips (2001).

is far from certain (Popenoe & Whitehead, 1999; Booth & Crouter, 2002; Scommegna, 2002).

GAY AND LESBIAN COUPLES

In 1989, Denmark became the first country to permit lawful same-sex marriages. This change extended social legitimacy to gay and lesbian couples and equalized advantages in inheritance, taxation, and joint property ownership. The Netherlands (2001), Belgium (2003), Canada (2003), and Spain (2005) have followed suit. Fifteen other European countries now recognize gay civil partnerships (Knox, 2004).

In the United States, the states of Vermont, Connecticut, and Hawaii, as well as a number of major cities, including San Francisco and New York, have passed laws giving limited marital benefits to gay and lesbian couples. Still, the U.S. Congress passed a law in 1996 defining marriage as joining one man and one woman, and until 2004, gay marriage remained illegal in all fifty states.

Then the pace of change accelerated. In 2004, the supreme court of Massachusetts ruled that gay and lesbian couples had a right to marry, and legal marriages began in May of that year (subject to possible new legislation in the future). The Massachusetts court decision prompted officials in San Francisco and a number of other U.S. cities to

THINKING IT THROUGH
Should We Save the Traditional Family?

What are "traditional families"? Are they vital to our way of life or a barrier to progress? People use the term *traditional family* to mean a married couple who, at some point in their lives, raise children. Statistically speaking, traditional families are less common than they used to be. In 1950, as the figure shows, 90 percent of U.S. households were families—using the Census Bureau's definition of two or more persons related by blood, marriage, or adoption. By 2004, just 68 percent of households were families, due to rising levels of divorce, cohabitation, and singlehood.

"Traditional family" is more than just a term; it is also a moral statement. Belief in the traditional family implies giving high value to becoming and staying married, putting children ahead of careers, and favoring two-parent families over various "alternative lifestyles."

On one side of the debate, David Popenoe (1993) warns that there has been a serious erosion of the traditional family since 1960. At that time, married couples with young children accounted for almost half of all households; today, the figure is 23 percent. Singlehood is up, from 10 percent of households in 1960 to 24 percent today. And the divorce rate has risen by 60 percent since 1960, so that nearly four in ten of today's marriages end in

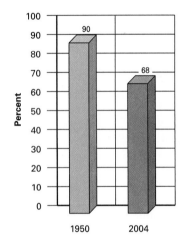

Share of U.S. Households That the Census Bureau Classifies as Families, 1950 and 2004

Families were a smaller share of all U.S. households in 2004 compared to 1950.

permanent separation. Because of divorce and the increasing number of children born to single women, the share of youngsters who will live with just one parent before age eighteen has quadrupled since 1960 to 50 percent. In other words, just one in four of today's children will grow up with two parents and go on to maintain a stable marriage as an adult.

In light of such data, Popenoe concludes, it may not be an exaggeration to say that the family is falling apart. He sees a fundamental shift from a "culture of marriage" to a "culture of divorce." Traditional vows of marital commitment—"till death do us part"—now amount to little more than "as long as I am happy." Daniel Yankelovich (1994:20) summed it up this way:

The quest for greater individual choice clashed directly with the obligations and social norms that held families and communities together in earlier years. People came to feel that questions of how to live and with whom to live were a matter of individual choice not to be governed by restrictive norms. As a nation, we

perform thousands of marriages for gay and lesbian couples, despite state laws banning such unions. Courts later declared those marriages to be illegal. In the November 2004 elections, voters in thirteen states passed ballot measures changing their state constitutions to recognize only marriages between one man and one woman.

The trend in public opinion is toward greater support for homosexual relationships. Currently, about one-third of U.S. adults support gay marriage, and half support civil unions providing the rights enjoyed by married couples (Gallup, 2002).

Most gay couples with children in the United States are raising the offspring of previous heterosexual unions; others have adopted children. But many gay parents are quiet about their sexual orientation, not wishing to draw unwelcome attention to their children or to themselves. In several widely publicized cases, courts have removed children from the custody of homosexual couples, citing the "best interests" of the children.

Gay parenting challenges many traditional ideas. But it also shows that many gay couples value family life as highly as heterosexuals do.

came to experience the bonds of marriage, family, children, job, community, and country as constraints that were no longer necessary. Commitments have loosened.

The negative consequences of the cultural trend toward weaker families, Popenoe continues, are obvious and can be found everywhere: As we pay less and less attention to children, the crime rate among young people goes up, along with a host of other problem behaviors including underage smoking and drinking, premarital sex, and teen suicide.

As Popenoe sees it, we must work hard and act quickly to reverse current trends. Government cannot be the solution and may even be part of the problem: Since 1960, as families have weakened, government spending on social programs has soared fivefold. To save the traditional family, says Popenoe, we need a cultural turnaround similar to what happened with regard to cigarette smoking. In this case, we must replace our "me first" attitudes with commitment to our spouse and children and publicly endorse the two-parent family as best for the well-being of children.

Judith Stacey (1993) provides a feminist viewpoint, saying "good riddance" to the traditional family. In her view, the traditional family is more problem than solution:

> The family is not here to stay. Nor should we wish it were. On the contrary, I believe that all democratic people, whatever their kinship preferences, should work to hasten its demise. (Stacey, 1990:269)

The main reason for rejecting the traditional family, Stacey explains, is that it perpetuates social inequality. Families play a key role in maintaining the class hierarchy, by transferring wealth as well as "cultural capital" from one generation to another. Feminists criticize the traditional family's patriarchal form, which subjects women to their husbands' authority and gives them most of the responsibility for housework and child care. From a gay rights perspective, she adds, a society that values traditional families also denies homosexual men and women equal participation in social life.

Stacey thus applauds the breakdown of the family as social progress. She does not view the family as a necessary social institution but as a political construction that elevates one category of people—affluent white males—above others, including women, homosexuals, and poor people.

Stacey also claims that the concept of "traditional family" is increasingly irrelevant in a diverse society in which both men and women work for income. What our society needs, Stacey concludes, is not a return to some golden age of the family but political and economic change, including income parity for women, universal health care and child care, programs to reduce unemployment, and expanded sex education in the schools. Such measures not only help families but also ensure that people in diverse family forms receive the respect and dignity they deserve.

WHAT DO YOU THINK?

1. To strengthen families, David Popenoe suggests that parents put children ahead of their own careers by limiting their joint workweek to sixty hours. Do you agree? Why or why not?

2. Judith Stacey thinks that marriage is weaker today because women are rejecting patriarchal relationships. What do you think about this argument?

3. Do we need to change family patterns for the well-being of our children? As you see it, what specific changes are called for?

SINGLEHOOD

Because nine out of ten people in the United States marry, we tend to view singlehood as a temporary stage of life. However, increasing numbers of people are choosing to live alone. In 1950, only one household in ten contained a single person. By 2003, this share had risen to one in four, a total of 29 million single adults (U.S. Census Bureau, 2004).

Most striking is the rising number of single young women. In 1960, 28 percent of U.S. women aged twenty to twenty-four were single; by 2003, the proportion had soared to 74 percent. Underlying this trend is women's greater participation in the labor force. Although most of these women will marry later on, women who are economically secure view a husband as a matter of choice rather than a financial necessity (Edwards, 2000).

By midlife, many unmarried women sense a lack of available men. Because we expect a woman to "marry up," the older a woman is, the more education she has, and the better her job, the more difficulty she has finding a suitable husband.

New Reproductive Technology and the Family

Recent medical advances involving *new reproductive technology* are also changing families. In 1978, England's Louise Brown became the world's first "test-tube baby." Since then, tens of thousands of children have been conceived this way. A decade from now, 2 or 3 percent of the children in high-income nations may result from new reproductive technologies.

Test-tube babies are the product of *in vitro fertilization,* in which doctors unite a woman's egg and a man's sperm "in glass" (usually not a test tube but a shallow dish) rather than in a woman's body. Doctors then either implant the resulting embryo in the womb of the woman who is to bear the child or freeze it for use at a later time.

At present, new reproductive technologies help some couples who cannot conceive by conventional means. These techniques may eventually help reduce the incidence of birth defects. Genetic screening of sperm and eggs allows medical specialists to increase the odds of having a healthy baby. But new reproductive technology also raises difficult and troubling questions: When one woman carries an embryo formed from the egg of another, who is the mother? When a couple divorces, which spouse is entitled to decide what is to be done with the frozen embryos? Should parents use genetic screening to select the physical traits of their child? Such questions remind us that technology changes faster than our ability to understand the consequences of its use (A. Cohen, 1998; Nock, Wright, & Sanchez, 1999).

Families: Looking Ahead

Family life in the United States will continue to change in years to come, and with change comes controversy. Advocates of "traditional family values" line up against those who support greater personal choice; the Thinking It Through box on pages 490–91 outlines some of the issues. Sociologists cannot predict the outcome of this debate, but we can suggest five likely future trends.

First, the divorce rate is likely to remain high, even in the face of evidence that marital breakups harm children.

Today's marriages are about as durable as they were a century ago, when many were cut short by death. The difference is that now more couples *choose* to end marriages that fail to live up to their expectations. Thus although the divorce rate has declined since 1980, it is unlikely to return to the low rates that marked the early decades of the twentieth century.

Second, family life in the twenty-first century will be more diverse than ever. Cohabiting couples, one-parent families, gay and lesbian families, and blended families are all on the rise. Most families are still based on marriage, and most married couples still have children. But the diversity of family forms implies a trend toward more personal choice.

Third, men will play a limited role in child rearing. In the 1950s, a decade that many people view as the "golden age" of families, men began to withdraw from active parenting (Snell, 1990; Stacey, 1990). In recent years, a small countertrend—the stay-at-home dad—is evident, with some older, highly educated fathers staying at home with young children, many using computer technology to continue

 Visit a Web site for stay-at-home fathers at http://www.slowlane.com

their work. But the stay-at-home dad represents no more than 10 percent of fathers with young children (Gardner, 1996; U.S. Census Bureau, 2004). The bigger picture is that the high U.S. divorce rate and the increase in single motherhood are weakening children's ties to fathers and increasing children's risk of poverty.

Fourth, families will continue to feel the effects of economic changes. In many homes, both household partners work, reducing marriage and family to the interaction of weary men and women who try to fit a little "quality time" with their children into an already full schedule. The long-term effects of the two-career couple on families as we have known them are likely to be mixed.

Fifth and finally, the importance of new reproductive technology will increase. Ethical concerns about whether what *can* be done *should* be done will surely slow these developments, but new forms of reproduction will continue to alter the traditional experience of parenthood.

Despite the changes and controversies that have shaken the family in the United States, most people still report being happy as partners and parents. Marriage and family life are likely to remain foundations of our society for generations to come.

The following learning tools will help you see what you know, identify what you still need to learn, and expand your understanding beyond the text. You can also visit the text's Companion Website™ at http://www.prenhall.com/macionis to find additional practice tests.

KEY POINTS

Families: Basic Concepts

All societies are built on kinship. Family forms vary across cultures and over time.

Families: Global Variations

In industrialized societies such as the United States, marriage is monogamous. Many preindustrial societies, however, permit polygamy, of which there are two types: polygyny and polyandry. In global perspective, patrilocality is most common, but industrial societies favor neolocality and a few societies have matrilocal residence. Industrial societies use bilateral descent, and preindustrial societies are either patrilineal or matrilineal.

Theoretical Analysis of Families

Structural-functional analysis identifies major family functions: socialization of the young, regulation of sexual activity, social placement, and provision of material and emotional support. Social-conflict theories, including feminist analysis, explore how the family perpetuates social inequality by transmitting divisions based on class, ethnicity, race, and gender. Micro-level analysis highlights the variety of family life as experienced by various family members.

Stages of Family Life

Courtship leads to the formation of new families. Romantic love is central to mate selection in the United States but not in much of the rest of the world. Even in this country, romantic love usually joins people with similar social backgrounds.

The vast majority of married couples have children, although family size has decreased over time. The main reason for this decline is industrialization, which transforms children into economic liabilities, encourages women to gain an education and join the labor force, and reduces infant mortality. Married life changes as children leave home to form families of their own. Many middle-aged couples care for aging parents, and many older couples are active grandparents. The final transition in marriage begins with the death of a spouse, usually the husband.

U.S. Families: Class, Race, and Gender

Families differ according to class position, race, and ethnicity. Latino families, for example, are more likely than others to maintain extended kinship ties. African American families are more likely to be headed by single women. Among all categories of people, well-to-do families enjoy the most options and the greatest financial security.

Gender affects family dynamics since husbands dominate in most marriages. Research suggests that marriage provides more benefits for men than for women.

Transitions and Problems in Family Life

The divorce rate today is ten times what it was a century ago; nearly four in ten current marriages will end in divorce. Most people who divorce—especially men—remarry, often forming blended families that include children from previous marriages. Family violence, which victimizes mostly women and children, is far more common than official records indicate. Most adults who abuse family members were themselves abused as children.

Alternative Family Forms

Our society's family life is becoming more varied. One-parent families, cohabitation, gay and lesbian couples, and singlehood have proliferated in recent years. Although only in Massachusetts does the law recognize same-sex marriages, many gay men and lesbians form long-lasting relationships and, increasingly, are raising children.

New Reproductive Technology and the Family

New reproductive technology is changing conventional ideas of parenthood. This technology makes parenthood possible for couples who cannot conceive children in the usual way, but it also raises ethnical questions about the extent to which parents can "design" their children.

Families: Looking Ahead

In the near future, divorce rates are likely to remain high and families will continue to be diverse. Fathers are likely to continue to play a limited role in the lives of many children.

family (p. 470) a social institution found in all societies that unites people in cooperative groups to care for one another, including any children

kinship (p. 470) a social bond based on common ancestry, marriage, or adoption

marriage (p. 470) a legal relationship, usually involving economic cooperation, sexual activity, and childbearing

extended family (p. 471) a family consisting of parents and children as well as other kin; also known as a *consanguine family*

nuclear family (p. 471) a family composed of one or two parents and their children; also known as a *conjugal family*

endogamy (p. 471) marriage between people of the same social category

exogamy (p. 471) marriage between people of different social categories

monogamy (p. 471) marriage that unites two partners

polygamy (p. 471) marriage that unites a person with two or more spouses

polygyny (p. 473) marriage that unites one man and two or more women

polyandry (p. 473) marriage that unites one woman and two or more men

patrilocality (p. 473) a residential pattern in which a married couple lives with or near the husband's family

matrilocality (p. 473) a residential pattern in which a married couple lives with or near the wife's family

neolocality (p. 473) a residential pattern in which a married couple lives apart from both sets of parents

descent (p. 473) the system by which members of a society trace kinship over generations

patrilineal descent (p. 473) a system tracing kinship through men

matrilineal descent (p. 473) a system tracing kinship through women

bilateral descent (p. 473) a system tracing kinship through both men and women

incest taboo (p. 475) a norm forbidding sexual relations or marriage between certain relatives

homogamy (p. 479) marriage between people with the same social characteristics

infidelity (p. 479) sexual activity outside marriage

family violence (p. 487) emotional, physical, or sexual abuse of one family member by another

cohabitation (p. 489) the sharing of a household by an unmarried couple

---

SAMPLE TEST QUESTIONS

These questions are similar to those found in the test bank that accompanies this textbook.

Multiple-Choice Questions

1. The family is a social institution that is found in
   a. most but not all societies.
   b. low-income nations but typically not in high-income nations.
   c. high-income nations but typically not in low-income nations.
   d. every society.

2. What is the term sociologists use for a family containing parents, children, and other kin?
   a. a nuclear family
   b. an extended family
   c. a family of affinity
   d. a conjugal family

3. A system of marriage that unites one woman with two or more men is called
   a. polygamy.
   b. polygyny.
   c. polyandry.
   d. bilateral marriage.

4. Sociologists claim that marriage in the United States follows the principle of homogamy, which means that partners are
   a. people of the same sex.
   b. people who are socially alike in terms of class, age, and race.
   c. people who marry due to social pressure.
   d. selected based on love rather than by parents.

5. Which of the following are included among the functions of the family?
   a. socialization of children
   b. regulation of sexual activity
   c. social placement of children
   d. all of the above

6. Which theoretical approach states that people select partners who have about the same to offer as they do?
   a. the structural-functional approach
   b. the social-exchange approach
   c. the social-conflict approach
   d. the feminist approach

7. Which of the following transitions in married life is usually the hardest for people?
   a. the birth of the second child
   b. the last child leaving home
   c. the death of a spouse
   d. retiring from the labor force

8. In the United States, many Latino families are characterized by
   a. strong extended kinship.
   b. parents exerting a great deal of control over their children's courtship.
   c. traditional gender roles.
   d. all of the above.

9. For which category of the U.S. population is the highest proportion of children born to single women?
   a. African Americans
   b. Asian Americans
   c. Hispanic Americans
   d. non-Hispanic white Americans

10. Which category of people in the United States is at the highest risk of divorce?
    a. gay and lesbian couples
    b. young people who marry after a short courtship
    c. a couple whose parents never experienced divorce
    d. a couple facing a wanted and expected pregnancy

Answers: 1(d); 2(b); 3(c); 4(b); 5(d); 6(b); 7(c); 8(d); 9(a); 10(b).

Essay Questions

1. Sociologists point to ways in which family life reflects not just individual choices but the structure of society as well. Provide three examples of how society shapes family life.

2. Overall, do you think families in the United States are becoming weaker or simply more diverse? Support your position.

APPLICATIONS & EXERCISES

1. Parents and grandparents can be a wonderful source of information about changes in marriage and the family. Ask them at what ages they married, what their married lives have been like, and what changes in family life today stand out for them. Compare the answers of two or more relatives. Are they very different?

2. Relationships with various family members differ. With which family member—mother, father, brother, sister— do you most readily share confidences? Who in your family would be the last to know? Why? Which family member would you turn to first in a crisis, and why?

3. A recent survey found that just one-third of families eat dinner together often (D. G. Myers, 2000:179). Are family meals part of your routine? What other regular family rituals do you participate in? Do members of your family feel that they spend enough time together?

INVESTIGATE *with* Research Navigator

Follow the instructions on page 27 of this text to access the features of **Research Navigator**™. Once at the Web site, enter your Login Name and Password. Then, to use the **ContentSelect**™ database, enter keywords such as "family," "cohabitation," and "divorce," and the search engine will supply relevant and recent scholarly and popular press publications. Use the *New York Times* **Search-by-Subject Archive** to find recent news articles related to sociology and the **Link Library** feature to find relevant Web links organized by the key terms associated with this chapter.

19

Religion

Why is the United States more religious
than other high-income nations?

What effects does being religious have
on social behavior?

How do religions in the East and the West differ?

With its many churches, synagogues, temples, and mosques (a recent study put the figure at one house of worship for every 865 people), one nation stands out as among the most religious on Earth. For its entire history, its leaders have proclaimed that God is responsible for its prosperity and liberty; today, four out of five of this nation's people say they have "experienced God's presence or a spiritual force." Together, they give more than $55 billion each year to religious organizations—more than the total economic output of most low-income countries. In schools, their children stand before the national flag and pledge their allegiance to "one nation under God" (Sheler, 2002).

You have already guessed that the country described is the United States. But although the United States is a religious nation, it is also a country of immigrants, and as a result, its people imagine God in many different ways. In countless places of worship—from soaring Gothic cathedrals in New York City to small storefront tabernacles in Los Angeles—Christians, Muslims, Jews, Buddhists, Hindus, Sikhs, Jains, Zoroastrians, and followers of dozens of other religions can be found (Yang & Ebaugh, 2001; Sheler, 2002). One scholar of religion recently described the United States as the world's most religiously diverse nation, a country in which Hindu and Jewish children go to school together and Muslims, Buddhists, and Sikhs work in the same factories and offices as Protestants and Catholics (Eck, 2001). As you shall see, many more people in the United States today are spiritual without being part of an organized religion. ■

This chapter begins by explaining what religion is from a sociological point of view. We then explore the changing face of religious belief throughout history and around the world and examine the vital and sometimes controversial place of religion in today's society.

Religion: Basic Concepts

The French sociologist Emile Durkheim stated that religion involves "things that surpass the limits of our knowledge" (1965:62, orig. 1915). We define most objects, events, or experiences as **profane** (from the Latin, meaning "outside the temple"), *an ordinary element of everyday life.* But we also consider some things **sacred,** *set apart as extraordinary, inspiring awe and reverence.* Setting the sacred apart from the profane is the essence of all religious belief. **Religion,** then, is *a social institution involving beliefs and practices based on recognizing the sacred.*

There is great diversity in matters of faith, and nothing is sacred to everyone on Earth. Although people regard most books as profane, Jews believe the Torah (the first five books of the Hebrew Bible or Old Testament) is sacred, in the same way that Christians revere the Old and New Testaments of the Bible and Muslims exalt the Qur'an (Koran).

But no matter how a community of believers draws religious lines, Durkheim (1965, orig. 1915) explained, people understand profane things in terms of their everyday usefulness: We log on to the Internet with our computer or turn a key to start our car. What is sacred we reverently set apart from everyday life, giving it a "forbidden" or "holy" aura. Marking the boundary between the sacred and the profane, for example, Muslims remove their shoes before entering a mosque, to avoid defiling a sacred place with soles that have touched the profane ground outside.

The sacred is embodied in **ritual,** or *formal, ceremonial behavior.* Holy communion is the central ritual of Christianity; to the Christian faithful, the wafer and wine consumed during communion are never treated in a profane way as food but as the sacred symbols of the body and blood of Jesus Christ.

RELIGION AND SOCIOLOGY

Because religion deals with ideas that transcend everyday experience, neither common sense nor sociology can prove or disprove religious doctrine. Religion is a matter of **faith,** *belief based on conviction rather than scientific evidence.* The New Testament of the Bible defines faith as "the conviction of things not seen" (Hebrews 11:1) and urges Christians to "walk by faith, not by sight" (2 Corinthians 5:7).

Some people with strong faith may be disturbed by the thought of sociologists turning a scientific eye on what they hold sacred. However, a sociological study of religion is no threat to anyone's faith. Sociologists study religion just as they study the family, to understand religious experiences around the world and how religion is tied to other social institutions. They make no judgments that a specific religion is right or wrong. Rather, scientific sociology takes a more worldly approach, asking why religions take a particular form in one society or another and how religious activity affects society as a whole.

 Find online resources for the study of religion at http://www.princeton.edu/~csrelig/links/links.html

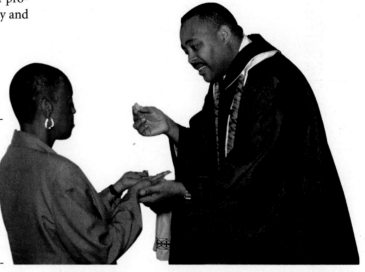

Regularly taking part in religious rituals sharpens the distinction between the sacred and the profane. The wafer used in the Christian ritual of holy communion is never thought of in the everyday sense of food; rather, it is a sacred symbol of the body of Christ.

Theoretical Analysis of Religion

Sociologists apply the major theoretical approaches to the study of religion just as they do to any other topic. Each approach provides distinctive insights into the way religion shapes social life.

FUNCTIONS OF RELIGION: STRUCTURAL-FUNCTIONAL ANALYSIS

According to Durkheim (1965, orig. 1915), society has a life and power of its own beyond the life of any individual. In other words, society itself is godlike, shaping the lives of its members and living on beyond them. Practicing religion, people celebrate the awesome power of their society.

No wonder people around the world transform certain everyday objects into sacred symbols of their collective life. Members of technologically simple societies do this with a **totem,** *an object in the natural world collectively defined as sacred.* The totem—perhaps an animal or an elaborate work of art—becomes the centerpiece of ritual, symbolizing the power of society over the individual. In our society, the flag

is treated with respect and is not used in a profane way (say, as clothing) or allowed to touch the ground.

Similarly, putting the words "In God We Trust" on all currency (a practice started back in the 1860s at the time of the Civil War) or adding the words "under God" to the Pledge of Allegiance (in 1954) symbolizes some widespread beliefs that tie society together. Across the United States, local communities also gain a sense of unity by linking totems to sports teams: from the New England Patriots to the Iowa State University Cyclones to the San Francisco 49ers.

Durkheim identified three major functions of religion that contribute to the operation of society:

1. **Social cohesion.** Religion unites people through shared symbolism, values, and norms. Religious thought and ritual establish rules of fair play, organizing our social life.

2. **Social control.** Every society uses religious ideas to promote conformity. By defining God as a "judge," many religions encourage people to obey cultural norms. Religion can also be used to back up the power of political systems. In the Middle Ages, royalty claimed to rule by "divine right," so that obedience was seen as doing God's will. Few of today's political leaders make this claim, but many publicly ask for

Religion is founded on the concept of the sacred—that which is set apart as extraordinary and which demands our submission. Bowing, kneeling, or prostrating oneself are all ways of symbolically surrendering to a higher power. These Buddhist pilgrims are making their way to a holy place on Mount Kallas in western Tibet.

God's blessing, implying that their efforts are right and just.

3. **Providing meaning and purpose.** Religious belief offers the comforting sense that our brief lives serve some greater purpose. Strengthened by such beliefs, people are less likely to despair in the face of change or even tragedy. For this reason, we mark major life course transitions—including birth, marriage, and death—with religious observances.

Critical review In Durkheim's structural-functional analysis, religion represents the collective life of society. The major weakness of this approach is that it downplays religion's dysfunctions, especially the fact that strongly held beliefs can generate social conflict. Terrorists have

claimed that God supports their actions, and many nations march to war under the banner of their God. A study of conflict in the world would probably show that religious beliefs have provoked more violence than differences of social class.

CONSTRUCTING THE SACRED: SYMBOLIC-INTERACTION ANALYSIS

From a symbolic-interaction point of view, religion (like all of society) is socially constructed (although perhaps with divine inspiration). Through various rituals—from daily prayers to annual religious observances like Easter or Passover—people sharpen the distinction between the sacred and the profane. Peter Berger (1967:35–36) claims that placing our small, brief lives within some "cosmic frame of reference" gives us the appearance of "ultimate security and permanence."

Marriage is a good example. If two people look on marriage as merely a contract, they can walk away whenever they want to. Their bond makes far stronger claims on them when it is defined as holy matrimony, which is surely one reason that the divorce rate is lower among people with strong religious beliefs. More generally, whenever human beings face uncertainty or life-threatening situations—such as illness, natural disaster, terrorist attack, or war—we turn to our sacred symbols.

⟶ **YOUR TURN** ⟵

List several specific events in the recent history of our country or your community when people turned to religious symbols. Explain what happened.

Critical review Using the symbolic-interaction approach, people use religion to give everyday life sacred meaning. Berger adds that the sacred's ability to give special meaning to society depends on ignoring the fact that it is socially constructed. After all, how much strength could we gain from beliefs we saw as mere strategies for coping with tragedy? Also, this micro-level analysis ignores religion's link to social inequality, to which we now turn.

INEQUALITY AND RELIGION: SOCIAL-CONFLICT ANALYSIS

The social-conflict approach highlights religion's support of social inequality. Karl Marx claimed that religion serves

APPLYING THEORY
RELIGION

	Structural-Functional Approach	Symbolic-Interaction Approach	Social-Conflict Approach
What is the level of analysis?	Macro-level	Micro-level	Macro-level
What is the importance of religion for society?	Religion performs vital tasks, including uniting people and controlling behavior.	Religion strengthens marriage by giving it (and family life) sacred meaning.	Religion supports social inequality by claiming that the social order is just.
	Religion gives life meaning and purpose.	People often turn to sacred symbols for comfort when facing danger and uncertainty.	Religion turns attention from problems in this world to a "better world to come."

ruling elites by legitimizing the status quo and diverting people's attention from social inequities.

Today, the British monarch is the formal head of the Church of England, illustrating the close ties between religious and political elites. In such a society, working for political change would mean opposing the church and, by implication, God. Religion also encourages people to endure without complaint social problems of this world while they look hopefully to a "better world to come." In a well-known statement, Marx dismissed religion as "the sigh of the oppressed creature, the sentiment of a heartless world, and the soul of soulless conditions. It is the opium of the people" (1964:27, orig. 1848).

Religion and social inequality are also linked through gender. Virtually all the world's major religions are patriarchal, as the Thinking About Diversity box on pages 502–03 explains.

Critical review Social-conflict analysis reveals the power of religion to support social inequality. Yet religion also promotes change toward equality. For example, nineteenth-century religious groups in the United States played an important part in the movement to abolish slavery. In the 1950s and 1960s, religious organizations and their leaders were the core of the civil rights movement. In the 1960s and 1970s, many clergy opposed the Vietnam War, and today many support progressive causes such as feminism and gay rights.

The Applying Theory table summarizes the three theoretical approaches to understanding religion.

YOUR TURN

Can you think of an example of a nation using the idea of "converting heathens" to justify controlling other societies? Explain.

Religion and Social Change

Religion is not just the conservative force portrayed by Karl Marx. At some points in history, as Max Weber (1958, orig. 1904–05) explained, religion has promoted dramatic social change.

MAX WEBER: PROTESTANTISM AND CAPITALISM

Max Weber argued that particular religious ideas set into motion a wave of change that brought about the Industrial Revolution in Western Europe. The rise of industrial capitalism was encouraged by Calvinism, a movement within the Protestant Reformation.

As Chapter 4 ("Society") explains in detail, John Calvin (1509–1564) was a leader in the Protestant Reformation who preached the doctrine of predestination. According to Calvin, an all-powerful and all-knowing God had selected some people for salvation but condemned most to eternal damnation. Each individual's fate, sealed before birth and known only to God, was either eternal glory or endless hellfire.

Driven by anxiety over their fate, Calvinists understandably looked for signs of God's favor in this world and came to see prosperity as a sign of divine blessing. Religious conviction and a rigid devotion to duty led Calvinists to work all the time, and many amassed great wealth. But money was not for selfish spending or for sharing with the poor, whose plight they saw as a mark of God's rejection. As agents of God's work on Earth, Calvinists believed that they best fulfilled their "calling" by reinvesting profits and achieving ever-greater success in the process.

All the while, Calvinists lived thrifty lives and adopted technological advances, which laid the groundwork for the rise of industrial capitalism. In time, the religious fervor that motivated early Calvinists weakened, leaving a profane "Protestant work ethic." To Max Weber, industrial capitalism

THINKING ABOUT DIVERSITY:
RACE, CLASS, & GENDER

Religion and Patriarchy: Does God Favor Males?

Why do two-thirds of adults in the United States say they think of God as "father" rather than "mother" (NORC, 2003: 146)? It is probably because we link godly traits such as wisdom and power to men. Just about all the world's religions tend to favor males, a fact evident in passages from their sacred writings.

The Qur'an (Koran), the sacred text of Islam, declares that men are to dominate women:

> Men are in charge of women. . . . Hence good women are obedient. . . . As for those whose rebelliousness you fear, admonish them, banish them from your bed, and scourge them. (quoted in W. Kaufman, 1976:163)

Christianity, the major religion of the Western world, also supports patriarchy. Many Christians revere Mary, the mother of Jesus, but the New Testament also includes the following passages:

> A man . . . is the image and glory of God; but woman is the glory of man. For man was not made from woman, but woman from man. Neither was man created for woman, but woman for man. (1 Corinthians 11:7–9)

> As in all the churches of the saints, the women should keep silence in the churches. For they are not permitted to speak, but should be subordinate, as even the law says. If there is anything they desire to know, let them ask their husbands

itself arose as a "disenchanted" religion, further showing the power of religion to alter the shape of society.

LIBERATION THEOLOGY

Historically, Christianity has reached out to oppressed people, urging all to a stronger faith in a better life to come. In recent decades, however, some church leaders and theologians have taken a decidedly political approach and endorsed **liberation theology,** *the combining of Christian principles with political activism, often Marxist in character.*

This social movement started in the 1960s in Latin America's Roman Catholic Church. Today, Christian activists continue to help people in poor nations liberate themselves from abysmal poverty. Their message is simple: Social oppression runs counter to Christian morality, so as a matter of faith and justice, Christians must promote greater social equality.

Pope Benedictine XVI, like Pope John Paul II before him, condemns liberation theology for distorting traditional church doctrine with left-wing politics. Nevertheless, the liberation theology movement has gained strength in the poorest countries of Latin America, where many people's Christian faith drives them to improve conditions for the poor and oppressed (Neuhouser, 1989; J. E. Williams, 2002).

Types of Religious Organizations

Sociologists categorize the hundreds of different religious organizations found in the United States along a continuum, with *churches* at one end and *sects* at the other. We can describe any actual religious organization in relation to these two ideal types by locating it on the church-sect continuum.

at home. For it is shameful for a woman to speak in church. (1 Corinthians 14:33–35)

Wives, be subject to your husbands, as to the Lord. For the husband is the head of the wife as Christ is the head of the church. . . . As the church is subject to Christ, so let wives also be subject in everything to their husbands. (Ephesians 5:22–24)

Let a woman learn in silence with all submissiveness. I permit no woman to teach or to have authority over men; she is to keep silent. For Adam was formed first, then Eve; and Adam was not deceived, but the woman was deceived and became a transgressor. Yet woman will be saved through bearing children, if she continues in faith and love and holiness, with modesty. (1 Timothy 2:11–15)

Judaism also has traditionally supported patriarchy. Male Orthodox Jews say the following words in daily prayer:

Blessed art thou, O Lord our God, King of the Universe, that I was not born a gentile.

Blessed art thou, O Lord our God, King of the Universe, that I was not born a slave.

Blessed art thou, O Lord our God, King of the Universe, that I was not born a woman.

Many patriarchal religions also exclude women from the clergy. Today, Islam and the Roman Catholic Church ban women from the priesthood, as do about half of Protestant denominations. But a growing number of Protestant religious organizations, including the  Church of England, ordain women, who now represent 18 percent of U.S. clergy. Orthodox Judaism upholds the traditional prohibition against women serving as rabbis, but Reform and Conservative Judaism look to both men and women as spiritual leaders. Across the United States, the

proportion of women in seminaries has never been higher (now roughly one-third), which is more evidence of a trend toward greater equality (Chaves, 1997; Nesbitt, 1997).

Feminists argue that unless traditional ideas of gender are removed from our understanding of God, women will never be equal to men in the church. The theologian Mary Daly puts the matter bluntly: "If God is male, then male is God" (quoted in Woodward, 1989:58).

WHAT DO YOU THINK?

1. Are you or other members of your family affiliated with a religious organization? If so, what evidence of patriarchy do you see in this religion?
2. Why do you think many religions encourage people to think of God as male?
3. Can you think of God in terms that do not include gender? Explain your answer.

CHURCH

Drawing on the ideas of his teacher Max Weber, Ernst Troeltsch (1931) defined a **church** as *a type of religious organization that is well integrated into the larger society.* Churchlike organizations usually persist for centuries and include generations of the same families. Churches have well-established rules and regulations and expect leaders to be formally trained and ordained.

Though concerned with the sacred, a church accepts the ways of the profane world. Church members think of God in intellectual terms (say, as a force for good) and favor abstract moral standards ("Do unto others as you would have them do unto you") over specific rules for day-to-day living. By teaching morality in safely abstract terms, church leaders avoid social controversy. For example, many congregations celebrate the unity of all peoples but say little about their own lack of racial diversity. By downplaying this type

of conflict, a church makes peace with the status quo (Troeltsch, 1931).

A church may operate with or apart from the state. As its name implies, a **state church** is *a church formally allied with the state.* State churches have existed throughout human history. For centuries, Roman Catholicism was the official religion of the Roman Empire, and Confucianism was the official religion of China until early in the twentieth century. Today, the Anglican church is the official church of England, and Islam is the official religion of Morocco, Pakistan, and Iran. State churches count everyone in the society as a member, which sharply limits tolerance of religious differences.

A **denomination,** by contrast, is *a church, independent of the state, that recognizes religious pluralism.* Denominations exist in nations, including the United States, that formally separate church and state. This country has dozens of Christian denominations—including Catholics, Baptists,

In global perspective, the range of religious activity is truly astonishing. Members of this Southeast Asian cult show their devotion to God by suspending themselves in the air using ropes and sharp hooks that pierce their skin.

Episcopalians, Presbyterians, and Lutherans—as well as various categories of Judaism, Islam, and other traditions. Although members of any denomination hold to their own doctrine, they recognize the right of others to have other beliefs.

SECT

The second general religious form is the **sect,** *a type of religious organization that stands apart from the larger society.* Sect members have rigid religious convictions and deny the beliefs of others. Churches try to appeal to everyone (the term *catholic* also means "universal"), but a sect instead forms an exclusive group. To members of a sect, religion is not just one aspect of life but a firm plan for how to live. In extreme cases, members of a sect withdraw completely from society in order to practice their religion without interference. The Amish community is one example of a North

American sect that isolates itself. Because our culture generally considers religious tolerance a virtue, members of sects are sometimes accused of being narrow-minded in insisting that they alone follow the true religion (Kraybill, 1994; P.W. Williams, 2002).

In organizational terms, sects are less formal than churches. Sect members may be highly spontaneous and emotional in worship, compared to members of churches, who tend to listen passively to their leaders. Sects also reject the intellectualized religion of churches, stressing instead the personal experience of divine power. Rodney Stark (1985:314) contrasts a church's vision of a distant God ("Our Father, who art in Heaven") with a sect's more immediate God ("Lord, bless this poor sinner kneeling before you now").

Churches and sects also have different patterns of leadership. The more churchlike an organization, the more likely that its leaders are formally trained and ordained. Sectlike organizations, which celebrate the personal presence of God, expect their leaders to exhibit divine inspiration in the form of **charisma** (from the Greek, meaning "divine favor"), *extraordinary personal qualities that can infuse people with emotion and turn them into followers.*

Sects generally form as breakaway groups from established religious organizations (Stark & Bainbridge, 1979). Their psychic intensity and informal structure make them less stable than churches, and many sects blossom only to disappear soon after. The sects that do endure typically become more like churches, with declining emphasis on charismatic leadership as they become more bureaucratic.

To sustain their membership, many sects actively recruit, or *proselytize,* new members. Sects highly value the experience of *conversion,* a personal transformation or religious rebirth. For example, members of Jehovah's Witnesses go door to door to share their faith with others in the hope of attracting new members.

Finally, churches and sects differ in their social composition. Because they are more closely tied to the world, well-established churches tend to include people of high social standing. Sects attract more disadvantaged people. A sect's openness to new members and its promise of salvation and personal fulfillment appeal to people who feel they are social outsiders.

CULT

A **cult** is *a religious organization that is largely outside a society's cultural traditions.* Most sects spin off from conventional religious organizations. However, a cult typically forms around a highly charismatic leader who offers a compelling message about a new and very different way of life.

Animism is widespread among Native Americans, who live respectfully within the natural world on which they depend for their survival. These Aleuts live in Eklutna, a village north of Anchorage, Alaska, which has been inhabited by people with much the same way of life for almost 500 years. Animists see a divine force present not only in themselves but in everything around them.

As many as 5,000 cults exist in the United States (Marquand & Wood, 1997).

Because some cult principles or practices are unconventional, the popular view is that they are deviant or even evil. The suicides of thirty-nine members of California's Heaven's Gate cult in 1997—people who claimed that dying was a doorway to a higher existence, perhaps in the company of aliens from outer space—confirmed the negative image the public holds of most cults. In short, calling any religious community a "cult" amounts to dismissing its members as crazy (Shupe, 1995; Gleick, 1997).

This charge is unfair because there is nothing basically wrong with this kind of religious organization. Many long-standing religions—Christianity, Islam, and Judaism included—began as cults. Of course, few cults exist for very long. One reason is that they are even more at odds with the larger society than sects. Many cults demand that members not only accept their doctrine but also adopt a radically new lifestyle. This is why people sometimes accuse cults of brainwashing their members, although research suggests that most people who join cults experience no psychological harm (Kilbourne, 1983; P. W. Williams, 2002).

YOUR TURN

Over time, can a religious organization change from its beginnings as a cult or a sect to being a church? Explain. Can you give an example of such a transformation?

Religion in History

Like other social institutions, religion shows marked variation according to time and place. Let us look at several ways in which religion has changed over the course of history.

RELIGION IN PREINDUSTRIAL SOCIETIES

Early hunters and gatherers practiced **animism** (from the Latin, meaning "the breath of life"), *the belief that elements of the natural world are conscious life forms that affect humanity.* Animistic people view forests, oceans, mountains, and even the wind as spiritual forces. Many Native American societies are animistic, which explains their reverence for the natural environment.

Belief in a single divine power responsible for creating the world began with pastoral and horticultural societies, which first appeared 10,000 to 12,000 years ago. The conception of God as a "shepherd" arose because Christianity, Judaism, and Islam had their beginnings among pastoral peoples.

Religion gains importance in agrarian societies, which develop a specialized priesthood in charge of religious organizations. The central role of religion is seen in the huge cathedrals that dominated the towns of medieval Europe.

RELIGION IN INDUSTRIAL SOCIETIES

The Industrial Revolution introduced a growing emphasis on science. More and more, people looked to doctors and scientists for the knowledge and comfort they used to get from priests. But religion persists in industrial societies because science is powerless to address issues of ultimate meaning in human life. In other words, learning *how* the world works is a matter for scientists, but *why* we and the rest of the universe exist at all is a question of faith.

World Religions

The diversity of religions in the world is almost as wide-ranging as the diversity of culture itself. Many of the thousands of different religions are found in just one place and have few followers. But

 Learn more about different religions at http://www. adherents.com

there are a number of *world religions,* which are widely known and have millions of adherents. We shall briefly describe six world religions, which together claim 4 billion believers—two-thirds of humanity.

CHRISTIANITY

Christianity is the most widespread religion, with 2 billion followers, almost one-third of the world's people. Most Christians live in Europe or the Americas; more than 85 percent of the people in the United States and Canada identify with Christianity. As shown in Global Map 19–1, people who think of themselves as Christian represent a large share of the population in many world regions, with the notable exceptions of northern Africa and Asia. European colonization spread Christianity throughout much of the world over the past 500 years. Its dominance in the West is shown by the fact that our calendar numbers years from the birth of Jesus Christ.

As noted earlier, Christianity began as a cult, drawing elements from Judaism, a much older religion. Like many cults, Christianity was built on the personal charisma of a leader, Jesus of Nazareth, who preached a message of personal salvation. Jesus did not directly challenge the political power of his day, the Roman Empire, telling his followers to "render therefore to Caesar things that are Caesar's" (Matthew 22:21). But his message was revolutionary all the same, promising that faith and love would triumph over sin and death.

Christianity is one example of **monotheism,** *belief in a single divine power.* This new religion was quite different from the Roman Empire's traditional **polytheism,** *belief in many gods.* Yet Christianity views the Supreme Being as a sacred Trinity: God the Creator; Jesus Christ, Son of God and Redeemer; and the Holy Spirit, a Christian's personal experience of God's presence.

The claim that Jesus was divine rests on accounts of his final days on Earth. Brought to trial as a threat to established political leaders, Jesus was tried in Jerusalem and sentenced to death by crucifixion, a common means of execution at the time. This explains why the cross became a sacred Christian symbol. According to Christian belief, three days after his execution, Jesus arose from the dead, showing that he was the Son of God.

Jesus' followers, especially his twelve closest associates, known as the apostles, spread Christianity throughout the Mediterranean region. At first, the Roman Empire persecuted Christians. But by the fourth century, the empire had adopted Christianity as a state church—the official religion of what became known as the Holy Roman Empire.

Christianity took various forms, including the Roman Catholic Church and the Orthodox church, based in Constantinople (now Istanbul, Turkey). Toward the end of the Middle Ages, the Protestant Reformation in Europe gave rise to hundreds of new denominations. In the United States, dozens of these denominations—the Baptists and Methodists are the two largest—command sizable followings (W. Kaufman, 1976; Jacquet & Jones, 1991).

ISLAM

Islam has about 1.2 billion followers, which is almost one-fifth of humanity. Followers of Islam are called Muslims. A majority of people in the Middle East are Muslims, so we tend to associate Islam with Arabs in that region of the world. But most of the world's Muslims live elsewhere: Global Map 19–2 shows that most people in northern Africa and Indonesia are Muslims. In addition, large concentrations of Muslims are found in western Asia in Pakistan, India, Bangladesh, and the southern republics of the former Soviet Union. Because Muslims have a higher birth rate than followers of any other major religion, it is possible that Islam could become the world's dominant religion by the end of this century.

Estimates of the Muslim population of the United States range from 2 to 8 million, making Islam a significant part of our country's religious life. The Muslim population

 Read a report on Muslims in the United States at http://www. cair-net.org/mosquereport /index.html

is not only large but quite diverse. It includes Arab Americans and others with Middle Eastern ancestry, Asian Americans, and African Americans (Blank, 1998; Eck, 2001; *Society,* 2004).

Islam is the word of God as revealed to Muhammad, who was born in the city of Mecca (now in Saudi Arabia) about the year 570. To Muslims, Muhammad is a prophet, not a divine being as Jesus is to Christians. The text of the Qur'an (Koran), which is sacred to Muslims, is the word of

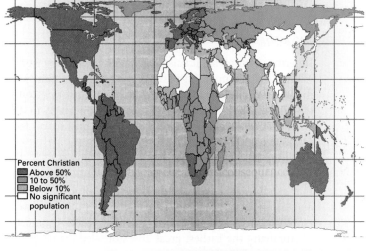

GLOBAL MAP 19–1
Christianity in Global Perspective

Source: *Peters Atlas of the World* (1990).

Percent Christian
Above 50%
10 to 50%
Below 10%
No significant
population

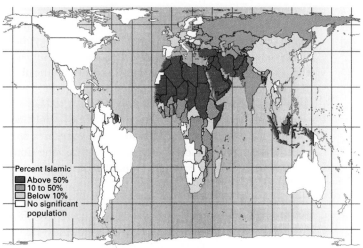

GLOBAL MAP 19–2
Islam in Global Perspective

Source: *Peters Atlas of the World* (1990).

Percent Islamic
Above 50%
10 to 50%
Below 10%
No significant
population

Allah (Arabic for "God") as transmitted through Muhammad, Allah's messenger. In Arabic, the word *islam* means both "submission" and "peace," and the Qur'an urges submission to Allah as the path to inner peace. Muslims express this personal devotion in a ritual of prayers five times each day.

After the death of Muhammad, Islam spread rapidly. Although divisions arose among Muslims, all accept the Five Pillars of Islam: (1) recognizing Allah as the one, true God and Muhammad as God's messenger; (2) ritual prayer; (3) giving alms to the poor; (4) fasting during the month of Ramadan; and (5) making a pilgrimage at least once in a

lifetime to the Sacred House of Allah in Mecca (Weeks, 1988; El-Attar, 1991). Like Christianity, Islam holds people accountable to God for their deeds on Earth. Those who live obediently will be rewarded in heaven, and evildoers will suffer unending punishment.

Muslims are also required to defend their faith, which has led to calls for holy wars against unbelievers (in roughly the same way that medieval Christians fought in the Crusades). Recent decades have witnessed a rise in militancy and anti-Western feeling in much of the Muslim world, where many people see the United States as both militarily threatening and representing a way of life that they view as

Many religions promote literacy because they demand that followers study sacred texts. As part of their upbringing, most Islamic parents teach their children lessons from the Qur'an (Koran); later, the children will do the same for a new generation of believers.

materialistic and immoral. Many Westerners—who typically know little about Islam and often stereotype all Muslims in terms of the terrorist actions of a few—respond with confusion and sometimes hostility (Eck, 2001; Ryan, 2001).

Many people in the United States also view Muslim women as among the most socially oppressed people on Earth. There are differences among Muslim nations in terms of rights given to women: Tunisia allows women far more opportunities than, say, Saudi Arabia, which does not allow women to vote or even drive a car (Ganley, 1998). It is true that many Muslim women lack some of the personal freedoms enjoyed by Muslim men. Yet many—perhaps even most—accept the mandates of their religion and find security in a system that guides the behavior of both women and men (Peterson, 1996). Defenders of Islam also point out that patriarchy was well established in the Middle East long before the birth of Muhammad and that Islam actually improved the social position of women by requiring husbands to deal justly with their wives. For example, Islam permits a

man to have up to four wives, but it requires men to have only one wife if having more would cause him to treat any woman unjustly (Qur'an, "The Women," v. 3).

JUDAISM

In terms of numbers, Judaism's 15 million followers worldwide make it something less than a world religion. Jews make up a majority of the population in only one country—Israel. But Judaism has special importance to the United States because the largest concentration of Jews (6 million people) is found in North America.

Jews look to the past as a source of guidance in the present and for the future. Judaism has deep historical roots that extend 4,000 years before the birth of Christ to the ancient societies of Mesopotamia. At this time, Jews were animistic, but this belief changed after Jacob—grandson of Abraham, the earliest great ancestor—led his people to Egypt.

Jews survived centuries of slavery in Egypt. In the thirteenth century B.C.E., Moses, the adopted son of an Egyptian princess, was called by God to lead the Jews from bondage. This exodus (this word's Latin and Greek roots mean "a marching out") from Egypt is remembered by Jews today in the annual ritual of Passover. Once liberated, the Jews became monotheistic, recognizing a single, all-powerful God.

A distinctive concept of Judaism is the *covenant,* a special relationship with God by which the Jews became God's "chosen people." The covenant implies a duty to observe God's law, especially the Ten Commandments as revealed to Moses on Mount Sinai. Jews regard the Old Testament of the Bible as both a record of their history and a statement of the obligations of Jewish life. Of special importance are the Bible's first five books (Genesis, Exodus, Leviticus, Numbers, and Deuteronomy), called the *Torah* (a word meaning "teaching" and "law"). In contrast to Christianity's central concern with personal salvation, Judaism emphasizes moral behavior in this world.

Judaism has three main denominations. Orthodox Jews (including more than 1 million people in the United States) strictly observe traditional beliefs and practices, wear traditional dress, segregate men and women at religious services, and eat only kosher foods. Such traditional practices set off Orthodox Jews in the United States from the larger society, making them the most sectlike. In the mid-nineteenth century, many Jews wanted to join in with the larger society, which led to the formation of more churchlike Reform Judaism (now including more than 1.3 million people in this country). A third segment, Conservative Judaism (with about 2 million U.S. adherents), has established a middle ground between the other two denominations.

Whatever the denomination, Jews share a cultural history of oppression as a result of prejudice and discrimination. A collective memory of centuries of slavery in Egypt, conquest by Rome, and persecution in Europe has shaped the Jewish identity. It was Jews in Italy who first lived in an urban ghetto (this word comes from the Italian *borghetto,* meaning "settlement outside of the city walls"), and this residential segregation soon spread to other parts of Europe.

Jewish immigration to the United States began in the mid-1600s. The early immigrants who prospered were assimilated into largely Christian communities. But as great numbers entered the country at the end of the nineteenth century, prejudice and discrimination against Jews—commonly termed *anti-Semitism*—increased. During World War II, anti-Semitism reached a vicious peak as the Nazi regime in Germany systematically annihilated 6 million Jews.

Today, the social standing of Jews is well above average. Still, many Jews are concerned about the future of their religion because in the United States, only half the children growing up in Jewish households are learning Jewish culture and ritual, and more than half marry non-Jews (Eisen, 1983; Dershowitz, 1997; Van Biema, 1997; Keister, 2003).

 For information about Jewish life, go to http://www.ujc.org

HINDUISM

Hinduism is the oldest of all the world religions, originating in the Indus River valley about 4,500 years ago. Today, there are about 800 million Hindus, which is 12 percent of the world's people. Global Map 19–3 on page 510 shows that Hinduism remains an Eastern religion, mostly practiced in India and Pakistan, but with a significant presence in southern Africa and Indonesia.

Over the centuries, Hinduism and the culture of India have blended so that now one is not easily described apart from the other (although India also has a sizable Muslim population). This connection also explains why Hinduism, unlike Christianity, Islam, and Judaism, has not diffused widely to other nations. But with 1.5 million followers in the United States, Hinduism is an important part of our country's cultural diversity.

Hinduism differs from most other religions in that it is not linked to the life of any single person. In addition, Hinduism envisions God as a universal moral force rather than a specific entity. For this reason, Hinduism—like other Eastern religions, as we shall see shortly—is sometimes described as an "ethical religion." Hindu beliefs and practices vary widely, but all Hindus believe that they have moral responsibilities, called *dharma.* Dharma, for example, calls people to observe the traditional caste system, described in Chapter 10 ("Social Stratification").

Another Hindu principle, *karma,* involves a belief in the spiritual progress of the human soul. To a Hindu, each action has spiritual consequences, and proper living results in moral development. Karma works through *reincarnation,* a cycle of death and rebirth by which a person is reborn into a spiritual state corresponding to the moral quality of a previous life. Unlike Christianity and Islam, Hinduism recognizes no ultimate judgment at the hands of a supreme god. But in the ongoing cycle of rebirth, it may be said that people get what they deserve. For those who reach *moksha,* the state of spiritual perfection, the soul will no longer be reborn.

The case of Hinduism shows that not all religions can be neatly labeled as monotheistic or polytheistic. Hinduism is monotheistic insofar as it views the universe as a single moral system; yet Hindus see this moral force at work in every element of nature. Hindus connect to this moral force through their private meditation and rituals, which vary from village to village across the vast nation of India. Many also participate in public events, such as the *Kumbh Mela,* which every twelve years brings some 20 million pilgrims to bathe in the purifying waters of the sacred Ganges River.

Hinduism is not well understood by most people in the United States, although elements of Hindu thought have entered the "New Age" movement discussed later in this chapter. But almost 2 million people in this country claim Asian Indian ancestry, and the number of immigrants from India is rising, which is making Hinduism more and more important in the United States (W. Kaufman, 1976; Larson, 2000; Eck, 2001).

BUDDHISM

Twenty-five hundred years ago, the rich culture of India gave rise to Buddhism. Today, some 350 million people, or 5 percent of humanity, are Buddhists, and almost all live in Asia. As shown in Global Map 19–4 on page 510, Buddhists are a majority of the population in Myanmar (Burma), Thailand, Cambodia, and Japan. Buddhism is also widespread in India and the People's Republic of China. Buddhism has much in common with Hinduism: It recognizes no god of judgment, sees each daily action as having spiritual consequences, and believes in reincarnation. But like Christianity, Buddhism has origins in the life of one person.

Siddhartha Gautama was born to a high-caste family in Nepal in 563 B.C.E. Even as a young man, he was deeply spiritual. At the age of twenty-nine, he experienced a personal transformation, which led him to years of travel and

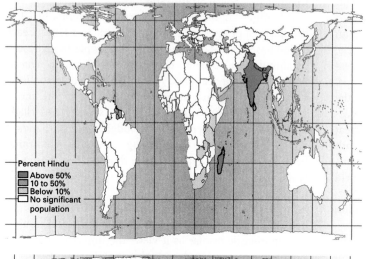

GLOBAL MAP 19-3

Hinduism in Global Perspective

Source: *Peters Atlas of the World* (1990).

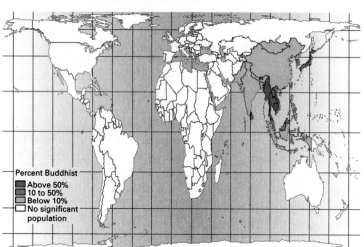

GLOBAL MAP 19-4

Buddhism in Global Perspective

Source: *Peters Atlas of the World* (1990).

meditation. By the end of this journey, he achieved what Buddhists describe as *bodhi*, or enlightenment. By gaining an understanding of the essence of life, Gautama became the Buddha.

Drawn by his personal charisma, followers spread the Buddha's teachings—the *dhamma*—across India. In the third century B.C.E., India's ruler became a Buddhist and sent missionaries throughout Asia, transforming Buddhism into a world religion.

Buddhists believe that much of life involves suffering. This idea is rooted in the Buddha's own travels in a very poor society. But, the Buddha claimed, the solution to suffering is not wealth. On the contrary, a concern with money holds back spiritual development. Instead, the Buddha taught that we must use meditation to move beyond selfish concerns and desires. Only by quieting the mind can people connect with the power of the larger universe—the goal described as *nirvana,* a state of enlightenment and peace (E. J. Thomas, 1975; Van Biema, 1997; Eck, 2001).

CONFUCIANISM

From about 200 B.C.E. until the beginning of the twentieth century, Confucianism was a state church—the official religion of China. After the 1949 revolution, the communist government of the new People's Republic of China repressed all religious expression. But even today, hundreds of millions of Chinese are still influenced by Confucianism. China is still home to Confucian thought, although Chinese immigration has spread this religion to other nations in Southeast Asia. Perhaps 100,000 followers of Confucius live in North America.

Confucius, whose Chinese name was K'ung-Fu-tzu, lived between 551 and 479 B.C.E. Like the Buddha, Confucius was deeply moved by people's suffering. The Buddha's response was sectlike—a spiritual withdrawal from the world. Confucius took a more churchlike approach, instructing his followers to engage the world according to a code of moral conduct. In the same way that Hinduism became part of the Indian way of life, Confucianism became linked to the traditional culture of China.

A central idea of Confucianism is *jen,* meaning "humaneness." In practice, this means that we must always place moral principle above our self-interest, looking to tradition for guidance in how to live. In the family, Confucius taught, each of us must be loyal and considerate. For their part, families must remember their duties toward the larger community. In this model, layers of moral obligation unite society as a whole.

Of all world religions, Confucianism stands out as lacking a clear sense of the sacred. Perhaps Durkheim would have said that Confucianism is the celebration of the sacred character of society itself. Others might call Confucianism less a religion than a model of disciplined living. However you look at it, Confucianism shares with religion a body of beliefs and practices that seek moral goodness and social harmony (Schmidt, 1980; McGuire, 1987; Ellwood, 2000).

RELIGION: EAST AND WEST

You may already have noticed two general differences between the belief systems of Eastern and Western societies. First, religions that arose in the West (Christianity, Islam, Judaism) have a clear focus on God. Eastern religions (Hinduism, Buddhism, Confucianism), however, tend to be ethical codes; they make a less clear-cut distinction between the sacred and the profane.

Second, followers of Western religions join together in congregations, worshiping together in a special place at a regular time. Followers of Eastern religions, by contrast, express their religion in their daily lives. Temples do exist, but they are used by individuals rather than groups according to no special schedule. In a country like Japan, temples are as likely to be filled with tourists as with worshipers.

Great Britain's Prince Charles greets his guest, the Dalai Lama, the religious and political leader of the Tibetan people. The Dalai Lama is the best-known Buddhist teacher in the world. He received the Nobel Peace Prize in 1989 for his efforts to liberate his people from Chinese control through nonviolent means.

These two differences are important, but they do not overshadow a common element of all religions: a call to move beyond selfish, everyday concerns in pursuit of a higher moral purpose. Religions may take different paths to this goal, but they all encourage a spiritual sense that there is more to life than what we see around us.

Religion in the United States

As noted in the opening to this chapter, the United States is one of the most religious of the high-income nations of the world. As Figure 19–1 on page 512 shows, eight in ten members of our society say they gain "comfort and strength from religion," a higher share than in most other countries.

That said, scholars debate exactly how religious we are. Some claim that religion remains central to our way of life, but others conclude that a decline of the traditional family and the growing importance of science are weakening religious faith (Greeley, 1989; Woodward, 1992a; Hadaway, Marler, & Chaves, 1993).

RELIGIOUS AFFILIATION

National surveys show that about 85 percent of U.S. adults identify with a religion (NORC, 2003:131). Table 19–1 on page 513 shows that more than 52 percent of U.S. adults

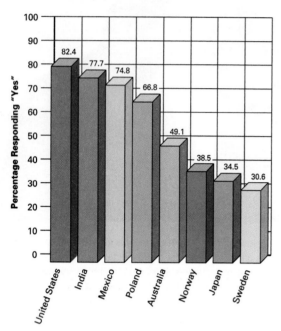

GLOBAL SNAPSHOT

Survey Question: "Do you gain comfort and strength from religion?"

FIGURE 19-1   Religiosity in Global Perspective

Religion is stronger in the United States than in many other nations.

Source: Inglehart et al. (2000).

RELIGIOSITY

Religiosity is *the importance of religion in a person's life.* However, exactly how religious we are depends on precisely how we operationalize this concept. For example, 86 percent of U.S. adults claim to believe in a divine power, although just 60 percent claim that they "know that God exists and have no doubts about it" (NORC, 2003:357). Fifty-six percent of adults say they pray at least once a day, but just 30 percent report attending religious services on a weekly or almost-weekly basis (NORC, 2003:133, 140).

Clearly, the question "How religious are we?" has no easy answer, and it is likely that many people in the United States claim to be more religious than they really are. Although most people in the United States say they are at

least somewhat religious, probably no more than about one-third actually are. Religiosity also varies among denominations. Members of sects are the most religious of all, followed by Catholics and then "mainstream" Protestant denominations such as Episcopalians, Methodists, and Presbyterians. In general, older people are more religious than younger people, and women are more religious than men (Hadaway, Marler, & Chaves, 1993; Sherkat & Ellison, 1999; Miller & Stark, 2002).

What difference does being more religious make? Researchers have linked a number of social patterns to strong religious beliefs, including low rates of delinquency among young people and low rates of divorce among adults. According to one recent study, religiosity helps unite children, parents, and local communities in ways that benefit young people, increasing their educational achievement (Muller & Ellison, 2001).

YOUR TURN

Would our society be better off or worse off if more people were more religious? Explain your answer.

RELIGION: CLASS, ETHNICITY, AND RACE

Religious affiliation is related to a number of other factors, including social class, ethnicity, and race.

Social Class

A study of *Who's Who in America,* which profiles U.S. high achievers, showed that 33 percent of the people who gave a religious affiliation were Episcopalians, Presbyterians, and

consider themselves Protestants, 24 percent are Catholics, and about 2 percent say they are Jewish. Large numbers of people follow dozens of other religions, from animism to Zen Buddhism, making our society the most religiously diverse of any on Earth (Eck, 2001).

About 90 percent of U.S. adults report that they had at least some formal religious instruction when growing up, and 60 percent say they belong to a religious organization today (NORC, 2003:355). National Map 19–1 on page 514 shows the share of people who claim to belong to any church across the United States.

National Map 19–2 on page 514 goes a step further, showing that the religion most people identify with varies by region. New England and the Southwest are mostly Catholic, the South is mostly Baptist, and in the northern Plains states, Lutherans predominate. In and around Utah, most people belong to the Church of Jesus Christ of Latter-Day Saints, whose followers are more commonly known as Mormons.

United Church of Christ members, denominations that together account for less than 10 percent of the population. Jews, too, enjoy high social position, with this 2 percent of the population accounting for 12 percent of the listings in *Who's Who*.

Research shows that other denominations, including Congregationalists, Methodists, and Catholics, have moderate social standing. Lower social standing is typical of Baptists, Lutherans, and members of sects. Of course, there is considerable variation within all denominations (Davidson, Pyle, & Reyes, 1995; Waters, Heath, & Watson, 1995; Keister, 2003).

Ethnicity

Throughout the world, religion is tied to ethnicity, mostly because one religion stands out in a single nation or geographic region. Islam predominates in the Arab societies of the Middle East, Hinduism is fused with the culture of India, and Confucianism runs deep in Chinese society. Christianity and Judaism do not follow this pattern; although these religions are mostly Western, Christians and Jews are found all over the world.

Religion and national identity are joined in the United States as well. For example, we have Anglo-Saxon Protestants, Irish Catholics, Russian Jews, and people of Greek Orthodox heritage. This linking of nation and creed results from the influx of immigrants from nations with a single major religion. Still, nearly every ethnic category displays some religious diversity. For example, people of English ancestry may be Protestants, Roman Catholics, Jews, Hindus, Muslims, or followers of other religions.

Race

Scholars claim that the church is both the oldest and the most important social institution within the African American community. Transported to the Western Hemisphere in slave ships, most Africans became Christians, the dominant religion in the Americas, but they blended Christian belief with elements of African religions. Guided by this religious mix, African American Christians have developed rituals that seem, by European standards, quite spontaneous and emotional (Frazier, 1965; Roberts, 1980; Paris, 2000).

When African Americans migrated from the rural South to the industrial cities of the North around 1940, the church played a major role in addressing the problems of dislocation, poverty, and prejudice (Pattillo-McCoy, 1998). Black churches have also provided an important avenue of achievement for talented men and women. Ralph Abernathy, Martin Luther King Jr., and Jesse Jackson have all achieved world recognition for their work as religious leaders.

TABLE 19–1

Religious Identification in the United States, 2002

Religion	Percentage Indicating Preference
Protestant denominations	**52.8%**
Baptist	17.4
Methodist	7.5
Lutheran	5.4
Presbyterian	2.9
Episcopalian	2.1
All others or no denomination	17.5
Catholic	**24.3**
Jewish	**1.7**
Other or no answer	**7.4**
No religious preference	**13.7**

Source: *General Social Surveys, 1972–2002: Cumulative Codebook* (Chicago: National Opinion Research Center, 2003), pp. 131–32.

Recent years have witnessed an increasing number of non-Christian African Americans, especially in large U.S. cities. Among them, the most common non-Christian religion is Islam, with an estimated 1 million African American followers (Paris, 2000).

Religion in a Changing Society

June 4, Ticonderoga, New York. Our summer church is small—maybe forty people attend on a typical Sunday. These days, Ed Keller says, it's tough for churches to survive with kids' sports teams scheduling practices and games on Sunday morning, Wal-Mart and the other discount stores open for shopping, and many dog-tired people taking advantage of the chance to sleep a little later. Ed thinks that our modern world sometimes seems less than "church-friendly."

All social institutions evolve over time. Just as the economy, politics, and the family have changed over the course of the past century, so has our society's religious life.

SECULARIZATION

Secularization is *the historical decline in the importance of the supernatural and the sacred.* Secularization (from Latin, meaning "the present age") is commonly associated with

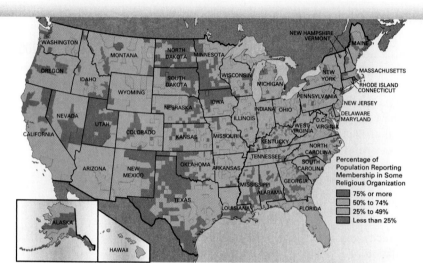

NATIONAL MAP 19–1

Religious Membership across the United States

In general, people in the United States are more religious than people in other high-income nations. Yet membership in a religious organization is more common in some parts of the country than in others. What pattern do you see in the map? Can you explain the pattern?

Source: From Rodger Doyle, *Atlas of Contemporary America.* Copyright © 1994 by Facts on File, Inc. Reprinted with the permission of Facts on File, Inc.

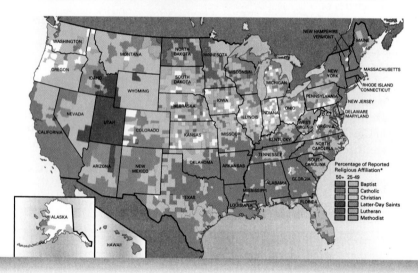

NATIONAL MAP 19–2

Religious Diversity across the United States

In most counties, at least 25 percent of people who report having an affiliation are members of the same religious organization. Thus, although the United States is religiously diverse at the national level, most people live in communities where one denomination predominates. What historical facts might account for this pattern?

*When two or more churches have 25 to 49 percent of the membership in a county, the largest is shown. When no church has 25 percent of the membership, that county is left blank.

Source: Glenmary Research Center (2002).

modern, technologically advanced societies in which science is the major way of understanding.

Today, we are more likely to experience the transitions of birth, illness, and death in the presence of physicians (with scientific knowledge) than of religious leaders (whose knowledge is based on faith). This shift alone suggests that religion's relevance to our everyday lives has declined. Harvey Cox explains:

> The world looks less and less to religious rules and rituals for its morality or its meanings. For some, religion provides a hobby, for others a mark of national or ethnic identification, for still others an aesthetic delight. For fewer and fewer does it provide an inclusive and commanding system of personal and cosmic values and explanations. (1971:3)

If Cox is right, should we expect religion to disappear someday? Most sociologists say no. The vast majority of people in the United States still say they believe in God, and more people claim to pray each day than vote in national elections. In addition, religious affiliation today is actually proportionately higher than it was in 1850. And one of the most watched movies of 2004 was Mel Gibson's *Passion of the Christ,* which portrayed the final days leading up to the crucifixion of Jesus.

Our society does not seem to be on the road to secularization. It is true that some dimensions of religiosity (such as belief in life after death) have declined, but others (such as religious affiliation) have increased. Similarly, some religious organizations have lost members, but others find their membership increasing. Among college students, as Figure 19–2 shows, the share of first-year students saying they have no religious preference has gone up, more than doubling between 1980 and 2004. But this share is still just a minority. Putting all this together, the claim that religion is declining in this country may be off the mark (Gorski, 2000; Stark & Finke, 2000; Hout & Fischer, 2002; Sax et al., 2004).

As we look at religious change, people disagree about what is good or bad. Conservatives tend to see any weakening of religion as a mark of moral decline. Progressives view secularization as liberation from the all-encompassing beliefs of the past, giving people more choice about what to believe. Secularization has also helped bring some practices of many religious organizations, such as ordaining only men, into line with widespread social attitudes that support greater gender equality.

An important event that helped spark the secularization debate took place in 1963, when the U.S. Supreme Court banned prayer in public schools as a violation of the constitutional separation of church and state. In recent years, however, religion has returned to many public schools—the Applying Sociology box on page 516 takes a closer look at this trend.

According to the secularization thesis, religion should weaken in high-income nations as people enjoy higher living standards and greater security. A global perspective shows that this thesis holds for the countries of Western Europe, where most measures of religiosity have declined and are now low. But the United States—the richest country of all—is an exception, because, as we have explained, religion remains quite strong in our country and may even be getting stronger. "In the *Times*" on pages 518–19 takes a closer look at this issue and offers an explanation for this curious pattern.

CIVIL RELIGION

One expression of secularization is the rise of what sociologist Robert Bellah (1975) calls **civil religion**, *a quasi-religious loyalty binding individuals in a basically secular society.* In other words, formal religion may lose power, but citizenship takes on religious qualities. Most people in the United States consider our way of life a force for moral good in the world. Many people also find religious qualities in political movements, whether liberal or conservative (Williams & Demerath, 1991).

Civil religion also involves a range of rituals, from singing the national anthem at sporting events to waving the flag at public parades. At all such events, the U.S. flag serves as a sacred symbol of our national identity, and we expect people to treat it with respect.

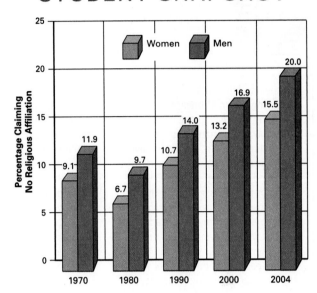

FIGURE 19-2 Religious Nonaffiliation among First-Year College Students, 1970–2004

The share of students claiming no religious affiliation has risen in recent decades.

Sources: Astin et al. (2002) and Sax et al. (2004).

"NEW AGE" SEEKERS: SPIRITUALITY WITHOUT FORMAL RELIGION

December 29, Machu Picchu, Peru. We are ending the first day exploring this magnificent city built by the Inca people high in the Andes Mountains. Lucas, a local shaman, or religious leader, is leading a group of twelve travelers in a ceremony of thanks. He kneels on the dirt floor of the small stone building and places offerings—corn and beans, sugar, plants of all colors, and even bits of gold and silver—in front of him as gifts to Mother Earth as he prays for harmony, joy, and the will to do good for one another. His words and the magic of the setting make the ceremony very moving.

In recent decades, an increasing number of people are seeking spiritual development outside of established religious organizations. This trend has led some analysts to conclude that the United States is becoming a *postdenomination*

APPLYING SOCIOLOGY
Should Students Pray in School?

It is late afternoon on a cloudy spring day in Minneapolis, and two dozen teenagers have come together to pray. They share warm smiles as they enter the room. As soon as everyone is seated, the prayers begin, with one voice following another. One girl prays for her brother; a boy prays for the success of an upcoming food drive; another asks God to comfort a favorite teacher who is having a hard time. Then they join their voices to pray for all the teachers at their school who are not Christians. Following the prayers, the young people sing Christian songs, discuss a Scripture lesson, and bring their meeting to a close with a group hug (Van Biema, 1998, 1999).

What is so unusual about this prayer meeting is that it is taking place in Room 133 of Patrick Henry High School, a *public* institution. In public schools from coast to coast, something of a religious revival is taking place as more and more students hold meetings like this one.

You would have to be at least fifty years old to remember when it was routine for public school students to start the day with Bible reading and prayer. In 1963, the Supreme Court ruled that religion in the schools violated the separation of church and state set by the U.S. Constitution, making any religious activity in a public

school illegal. But from the moment the ruling was announced, critics charged that by supporting a wide range of other activities and clubs while banning any religious activity, schools were really being *antireligious.* In 1990, the Supreme Court handed down a new ruling, stating that religious groups can meet on school property as long as group membership is voluntary, the meetings are held outside regular class hours, and students rather than adults run them.

Today, student religious groups have formed in perhaps one-fourth of all public schools. Evangelical Christian organizations such as First Priority

and National Network of Youth are using the Internet as well as word of mouth in an effort to expand the place of religion in every public school across the country. However, opponents of school prayer worry that religious enthusiasm may lead some students to pressure others to join their groups. Such disagreements ensure that the debate over prayer in school will continue.

WHAT DO YOU THINK?

1. Do you think that religious clubs should have the same freedom to operate on school grounds as other organizations? Why or why not?

2. The writers of our Constitution stated in the First Amendment that Congress should not establish any official religion and should also pass no law that would interfere with the free practice of religion. How do you think this amendment applies to the issue of prayer in school?

3. In 1995, President Bill Clinton said, "Nothing in the First Amendment converts our public schools into religion-free zones." Do you think schools should support spiritual education and development as they would, say, athletic development? Why or why not?

Although some U.S. colleges and universities are operated by religious organizations, most offer a secular education. At secular schools, do you think religious groups should be treated the same in terms of funding as any other groups? Why or why not?

society. In simple terms, more people seem to be spiritual seekers, believing in a vital spiritual dimension to human existence that they pursue more or less separately from membership in any formal denomination.

What exactly is the difference between this "New Age" focus on spirituality and a traditional concern with religion? As one analysis (Cimino & Lattin, 1999:62) puts it:

[Spirituality] is the search for ... a religion of the heart, not the head. It's a religious expression that downplays doctrine and dogma, and revels in direct experience of the divine—whether it's called the "holy spirit" or "divine consciousness" or "true self." It's practical and personal, more about stress reduction than salvation, more therapeutic than theological. It's about feeling good rather than being good. It's as much about the body as the soul.

New Age "seekers" are people in pursuit of spiritual growth, often using the age-old technique of meditation. The goal of this activity is to quiet the mind so that, by moving away from everyday concerns, one can hear an inner, divine voice. Countless people attest to the spiritual value of meditation; it has also been linked to improved physical health.

Millions of people in the United States take part in New Age spirituality. The anthropologist and spiritual teacher Hank Wesselman (2001:39–42) identifies five core values that define this approach:

1. **Seekers believe in a higher power.** There exists a higher power, a vital force that is within all things and all people. Humans, then, are partly divine.

2. **Seekers believe we're all connected.** Everything and everyone is interconnected as part of a universal divine pattern.

3. **Seekers believe in a spirit world.** The physical world is not all there is; a more important spiritual reality (or "spirit world") also exists.

4. **Seekers want to experience the spirit world.** Spiritual development means gaining the ability to experience the spirit world. Many seekers come to understand that helpers and teachers who dwell in the spirit world can and do touch their lives.

5. **Seekers pursue transcendence.** Various techniques (such as yoga, meditation, and prayer) give people an increasing ability to rise above the immediate physical world (the experience of "transcendence"), which is seen as the larger purpose of life.

From a traditional point of view, this New Age concern with spirituality may seem more like psychology than religion (Tucker, 2002). Yet like civil religion, it is a new form of religious interest in the modern world.

YOUR TURN

Can you see elements of both Western and Eastern religions in New Age spirituality? Explain.

RELIGIOUS REVIVAL: "GOOD OL'-TIME RELIGION"

At the same time as New Age spirituality is becoming more popular, a great deal of change has been going on in the world of organized religion. In the United States, membership in liberal mainstream denominations such as Episcopalian and Presbyterian has dropped by almost 50 percent since 1960. During the same period, affiliation with more conservative religious organizations (including the Mormons, the Seventh-Day Adventists, and especially Christian sects) has risen just as fast.

These opposing trends suggest that secularization may be self-limiting: As many churchlike organizations become more worldly, many people leave them in favor of more sectlike communities offering a more intense religious experience (Stark & Bainbridge, 1981; Jacquet & Jones, 1991; Iannaccone, 1994; Hout, Greeley, & Wilde, 2001).

Religious Fundamentalism

Fundamentalism is *a conservative religious doctrine that opposes intellectualism and worldly accommodation in favor of restoring traditional, otherworldly religion.* In the United

November 21, 2004

Give Them Some of That Free-Market Religion

By EDUARDO PORTER

The 2004 election, in which religious conservatives helped deliver the presidency to George W. Bush, brings up an interesting economic question: Why is the United States, the world's most prosperous and educated democracy, so religious?

The United States is rather unusual in this regard, an enclave of intense religious devotion in the mostly secular club of industrial democracies. . . . Over the past 10 years or so a growing group of mostly American sociologists has deployed a novel theory to explain the United States' apparently anomalous behavior: supply-side economics. Americans, they say, are fervently religious because there are so many churches competing for their devotion.

Old-school sociology holds that as nations become more prosperous, healthy and educated, demand for the support that religion provides declines.

People do not suddenly lose faith as they grow rich, these sociologists argue. Rather, they gradually go less to church—reducing their children's exposure to religion. Meanwhile, secular institutions take over functions, like education, formerly controlled by the church. Religious attendance, they argue, wanes from one generation to the next.

In economic terms, demand for religion drops as its perceived benefits diminish compared with the cost of participating. . . .

The industrial democracies in Asia and Europe seem to bear this out. According to the Pew Global Attitudes Project two years ago, only 20 percent of Germans, 12 percent of Japanese and 11 percent of the French say religion plays a very important role in their lives. In a 1991 multinational survey, a quarter of all Dutch said they were atheists. . . .

But this line of analysis cannot account for the most modern and rich country of them all.

According to the Pew survey, 60 percent of Americans said religion had a very important role in their lives; 48 percent believed that the United States has a special protection from God; 54 percent said they had an "unfavorable" view of atheists.

And religious expression in the United States seems to have grown, not diminished, with socioeconomic development. . . . In 1890, 45 percent of Americans were members of a church. By 2000, that figure was 62 percent. . . .

The supply-side view . . . posits that demand for religion has little to do with economic development. Instead, what creates change is the supply of religious services.

That is, Americans are more churchgoing and pious than Germans or Canadians because the United States has the most open religious market, with dozens

States, fundamentalism has made the greatest gains among Protestants. Southern Baptists, for example, are the largest religious community in the country. But fundamentalism has also grown among Catholics and Jews.

In response to what they see as the growing influence of science and the weakening of the conventional family, religious fundamentalists defend what they call "traditional values." As they see it, liberal churches are simply too open to compromise and change. Religious fundamentalism is distinctive in five ways (Hunter, 1983, 1985, 1987):

1. **Fundamentalists take the words of sacred texts literally.** Fundamentalists insist on a literal reading of sacred texts such as the Bible to counter what they see as excessive intellectualism among more liberal religious organizations. For example, fundamentalist Christians believe that God created the world in seven days precisely as described in the biblical book of Genesis.

2. **Fundamentalists reject religious pluralism.** Fundamentalists believe that tolerance and relativism water down personal faith. Therefore, they maintain that their religious beliefs are true and other beliefs are not.

3. **Fundamentalists pursue the personal experience of God's presence.** In contrast to the worldliness and intellectualism of other religious organizations, fundamentalism seeks a return to "good old-time religion" and spiritual revival. To fundamentalist Christians, being "born again" and having a personal relationship with Jesus Christ should be evident in a person's everyday life.

4. **Fundamentalists oppose "secular humanism."** Fundamentalists think accommodation to the changing world weakens religious faith. They reject "secular humanism," our society's tendency to look to scientific experts rather than God for guidance about how to

of religious denominations competing vigorously to offer their flavor of salvation, becoming extremely responsive to the needs of their parishes....

The suppliers of religion then try to stoke demand. "The potential demand for religion has to be activated," said Rodney Stark, a sociologist at Baylor University. "The more members of the clergy that are out there working to expand their congregations, the more people will go to church."

. . . This free-market theory also fits well with the explosion of religion across Latin America, where the weakening of the longstanding Catholic monopoly has led to all sorts of evangelical Christian churches and to an overall increase of religious expression.

The supply-siders say their model even explains secular Europe. Europeans, they argue, are fundamentally just as religious as Americans, with similar metaphysical concerns, but they suffer from an uncompetitive market—lazy, quasi-monopolistic churches that have been protected from competition by the state. "Wherever you've got a state church, you have empty churches," Mr. Stark said.

The free-market argument is not absolutely watertight, however. Islamic states, for instance, have very strong quasi-state churches and high religious participation. And some European sociologists argue that there is much more religious competition in Europe than the supply-siders acknowledge.

And in the United States, the most religious states and counties are those most dominated by a single denomination—Mormon, Baptist or Pentecostal—not those where there is most competition....

Whatever its shortcomings, the free-market theory might also offer solace for those concerned about the creeping influence of religion in American government. That's because the theory posits that for religion to thrive, it must remain clearly separate from the state.

"Our pluralism helps religion expand," said Gary Wills, [a] historian. "The separation of church and state protected religion from anticlericalism."

WHAT DO YOU THINK?

1. Are there regions in the world in which the secularization thesis seems to hold? Which regions?

2. Can you think of other reasons that the people of the United States may be more religious than people in other high-income nations? If so, what are they?

3. Do you agree with the argument made in this article? Why or why not?

Adapted from the original article by Eduardo Porter published in *The New York Times* on November 21, 2004. Copyright © 2004 by The New York Times Company. Reprinted with permission.

live. There is nothing new in this tension between science and religion; it has existed for several centuries, as the Thinking It Through box on page 520 explains.

5. **Many fundamentalists endorse conservative political goals.** Although fundamentalism tends to back away from worldly concerns, some fundamentalist leaders (including Ralph Reed, Pat Robertson, and Gary Bauer) have entered politics to oppose what they call the "liberal agenda," including feminism and gay rights. Fundamentalists oppose abortion and gay marriages; they support the traditional two-parent family, seek a return of prayer in schools, and criticize the mass media for coloring stories with a liberal bias (Manza & Brooks, 1997; Thomma, 1997; Rozell, Wilcox, & Green, 1998).

Opponents regard fundamentalism as rigid and self-righteous. But many find in fundamentalism, with its greater religious certainty and emphasis on the emotional experience of God's presence, an appealing alternative to the more intellectual, tolerant, and worldly "mainstream" denominations (Marquand, 1997).

Which religions are fundamentalist? In recent years, the world has become familiar with an extreme form of fundamentalist Islam that is intolerant of other beliefs and even supports violence against Western culture. In the United States, the term is most correctly applied to conservative Christian organizations in the evangelical tradition, including Pentecostals, Southern Baptists, Seventh-Day Adventists, and Assemblies of God. Several national religious movements, including Promise Keepers (a men's organization) and Chosen Women, have a fundamentalist orientation. In national surveys, 30 percent of U.S. adults describe their religious upbringing as "fundamentalist," 40 percent claim a "moderate" upbringing, and 24 percent, a "liberal" background (NORC, 2003:150).

THINKING IT THROUGH
Does Science Threaten Religion?

About 400 years ago, the Italian physicist and astronomer Galileo (1564–1642) helped start the Scientific Revolution with a series of startling discoveries. Dropping objects from the Leaning Tower of Pisa, he discovered some of the laws of gravity; making his own telescope, he observed the stars and found that Earth orbited the sun, not the other way around.

For his trouble, Galileo was challenged by the Roman Catholic Church, which had preached for centuries that Earth stood motionless at the center of the universe. Galileo only made matters worse by responding that religious leaders had no business talking about matters of science. Before long, he found his work banned and himself under house arrest.

As Galileo's treatment shows, right from the start, science has had an uneasy relationship with religion. In the twentieth century, the two clashed again over the issue of creation. Charles Darwin's masterwork, *On the Origin of Species,* states that humanity evolved from lower forms of life over a billion years. Yet this theory seems to fly in the face of the biblical account of creation found in Genesis, which states that "God created the heavens and the earth," introducing life on the third day and, on the fifth and sixth days, animal life, including human beings fashioned in God's own image.

Galileo would certainly have been an eager observer of the famous "Scopes monkey trial." In 1925, the state of Tennessee put a small-town science teacher named John Thomas Scopes on trial for teaching Darwinian evolution in the local high school. State law forbade teaching "any theory that denies the story of the Divine Creation of man as taught in the Bible" and especially the idea that "man descended from a lower order of animals." Scopes was found guilty and fined $100. His conviction was reversed on appeal, so the case never reached the U.S. Supreme Court, and the Tennessee law stayed on the books until 1967. A year later, the Supreme Court, in *Epperson* v. *Arkansas* struck down all such laws as unconstitutional government support of religion.

Today—almost four centuries after Galileo was silenced—many people still debate the apparently conflicting claims of science and religion. A third of U.S. adults believe that the Bible is the literal word of God, and many of them reject any scientific findings that run counter to it (NORC, 2003:157).

But a middle ground is emerging: Half of U.S. adults (and also many church leaders) say the Bible is a book of truths inspired by God without being correct in a literal, scientific sense. That is, science and religion are two different ways of understanding that answer different questions. Both Galileo and Darwin devoted their lives to investigating *how* the natural world works. Yet only religion can address *why* we and the natural world exist in the first place.

This basic difference between science and religion helps explain why our nation is both the most scientific and the most religious in the world. As one scientist recently noted, the mathematical odds that a cosmic "big bang" 12 billion years ago created the universe and led to the formation of life as we know it is even smaller than the chance of winning a state lottery twenty weeks in a row. Doesn't such a scientific fact suggest an intelligent and purposeful power in our creation? Can't a person be a religious believer and at the same time a scientific investigator?

In 1992, a Vatican commission concluded that the church's silencing of Galileo was wrong. Today, most scientific and religious leaders agree that science and religion represent important but different truths. Many also believe that in today's rush to scientific discovery, our world has never been more in need of the moral guidance provided by religion.

WHAT DO YOU THINK?

1. Why do you think some scientific people reject religious accounts of human creation? Why do some religious people reject scientific accounts?
2. Do you think the sociological study of religion challenges anyone's faith? Why or why not?
3. About half of U.S. adults think science is changing our way of life too fast. Do you agree? Why or why not?

Sources: Based on Gould (1981), Huchingson (1994), and Applebome (1996).

The Electronic Church

In contrast to local congregations of years past, some religious organizations, especially fundamentalist ones, have become electronic churches featuring "prime-time preachers" (Hadden & Swain, 1981). Electronic religion is found only in the United States. It has made Billy Graham, Robert Schuller, and others more famous than all but a few clergy of the past. About 5 percent of the national television audience (some 10 million people) regularly view religious television, and 20 percent (about 40 million) watch or listen to some religious program every week (NORC, 2003).

Religion: Looking Ahead

The popularity of media ministries, the growth of fundamentalism, new forms of spiritualism, and the connection of millions of people to mainstream churches show that religion will remain a major part of modern society for decades to come. High levels of immigration from many religious countries (in Latin America and elsewhere) will intensify as well as diversify the religious character of U.S. society in the twenty-first century (Yang & Ebaugh, 2001).

The world is becoming more complex, and change seems to move more rapidly than our ability to make sense of it all. But rather than weakening religion, this process fires the religious imagination. Science is simply unable to provide answers to the most basic human questions about the purpose of our lives. As new technology gives us the power to change, extend, and even create life, we are faced with increasingly difficult moral questions. Against this backdrop of uncertainty, it is little wonder that many people look to their faith for guidance and hope.

19 MAKING THE GRADE

The following learning tools will help you see what you know, identify what you still need to learn, and expand your understanding beyond the text. You can also visit the text's Companion Website™ at http://www.prenhall.com/macionis to find additional practice tests.

KEY POINTS

Religion: Basic Concepts

Religion is a major social institution based on setting the sacred apart from the profane. Religion is grounded in faith rather than scientific evidence, and people express their religious beliefs through various rituals. Sociologists study how religion is linked to other social patterns but make no claims about the truth of any religious belief.

Theoretical Analysis of Religion

Durkheim explained that through religion, we celebrate the power of our society. His structural-functional analysis suggests that religion promotes social cohesion and conformity and gives meaning and purpose to life.

Using the symbolic-interaction approach, Peter Berger explains that we socially construct religious beliefs in the same way that we build all the reality we experience. We are especially likely to seek religious meaning when faced with life's uncertainties and disruptions.

Social-conflict analyst Karl Marx claimed that religion justifies the status quo. In this way, religion supports inequality and discourages change toward a more just and equal society.

Religion and Social Change

Max Weber argued, in opposition to Marx, that religion can encourage social change. He showed how Calvinism contributed to the rise of industrial capitalism. Liberation theology, a fusion of Christian principles and political activism, tries to encourage social change.

Types of Religious Organizations

Churches are religious organizations well integrated into their society. They fall into two categories: state churches and denominations. Sects are the result of religious division and are marked by charismatic leadership and suspicion of the larger society. Cults are religious organizations based on new and unconventional beliefs and practices.

Religion in History

Technologically simple human societies were generally animistic, with religion existing only as a part of family life. In more complex societies, religion emerges as a distinct social institution.

World Religions

Followers of six world religions—Christianity, Islam, Judaism, Hinduism, Buddhism, and Confucianism—represent three-fourths of all humanity. Western religions (the first three) share a focus on God and have well-defined congregations; Eastern religions (the second three) tend to be ethical codes largely fused with the broader culture.

Religion in the United States

The United States is one of the most religious and religiously diverse nations. How researchers operationalize "religiosity" affects the results. In the United States, 85 percent of adults identify with a religion and 60 percent profess a firm belief in God, but just 30 percent say they attend religious services weekly.

Religion in a Changing Society

Secularization is the historical decline in the importance of the supernatural and the sacred. In the United States, although some indicators of religiosity (like membership in mainstream churches) have declined, others (membership in sects) have increased.

Therefore, it is doubtful that secularization will bring an end to religion. In a more secular society, civil religion takes the form of quasi-religious patriotism that ties people to their society.

Spiritual seekers are part of the growing "New Age" movement that pursues spiritual development outside conventional religious organizations. These seekers believe in a higher power that links everything; they use meditation and prayer to move beyond the physical world to experience the spiritual world.

Also on the rise is fundamentalism, which opposes religious accommodation to the world. Fundamentalists take the words of religious texts literally and reject religious diversity as they pursue the personal experience of God's presence.

Religion: Looking Ahead

Some of the continuing appeal of religion lies in the inability of science to address timeless questions about the ultimate meaning of human existence.

KEY CONCEPTS

profane (p. 498) an ordinary element of everyday life

sacred (p. 498) set apart as extraordinary, inspiring awe and reverence

religion (p. 498) a social institution involving beliefs and practices based on recognizing the sacred

ritual (p. 498) formal, ceremonial behavior

faith (p. 499) belief based on conviction rather than scientific evidence

totem (p. 499) an object in the natural world collectively defined as sacred

liberation theology (p. 502) the combining of Christian principles with political activism, often Marxist in character

church (p. 503) a type of religious organization that is well integrated into the larger society

state church (p. 503) a church formally allied with the state

denomination (p. 503) a church, independent of the state, that recognizes religious pluralism

sect (p. 504) a type of religious organization that stands apart from the larger society

charisma (p. 504) extraordinary personal qualities that can infuse people with emotion and turn them into followers

cult (p. 504) a religious organization that is largely outside a society's cultural traditions

animism (p. 505) the belief that elements of the natural world are conscious life forms that affect humanity

monotheism (p. 506) belief in a single divine power

polytheism (p. 506) belief in many gods

religiosity (p. 512) the importance of religion in a person's life

secularization (p. 513) the historical decline in the importance of the supernatural and the sacred

civil religion (p. 515) a quasi-religious loyalty binding individuals in a basically secular society

fundamentalism (p. 517) a conservative religious doctrine that opposes intellectualism and worldly accommodation in favor of restoring traditional, otherworldly religion

SAMPLE TEST QUESTIONS

These questions are similar to those found in the test bank that accompanies this textbook.

Multiple-Choice Questions

1. **What term did Emile Durkheim use to refer to the everyday elements of our lives?**
   a. religion   b. profane
   c. sacred   d. ritual

2. **Faith, or belief in religious matters, is best described as**
   a. what we learn from science.
   b. what our senses tell us.
   c. our cultural traditions.
   d. conviction in things unseen.

3. **The reason sociologists study religion is to learn**
   a. the meaning of life.
   b. whether a particular religion is true or not.
   c. how patterns of religious activity affect society.
   d. which religious organization they wish to join.

4. Which of the following is *not* one of the important functions of religion, according to Durkheim?
   a. generating social conflict
   b. generating social cohesion
   c. providing social control
   d. providing meaning and purpose

5. Peter Berger claims that we are most likely to turn to religion when we experience
   a. social conflict.
   b. the best of times.
   c. familiar, everyday routines.
   d. important events that are out of our control.

6. Which sociologist explained how religion helps support social inequality?
   a. Emile Durkheim   b. Karl Marx
   c. Max Weber   d. Ernst Troeltsch

7. Which type of religious organization is most integrated into the larger society?
   a. cult   b. church
   c. sect   d. all of the above

8. A sect is a type of religious organization that
   a. has formally trained leaders.
   b. is well integrated into the larger society.

   c. rejects the importance of charisma.
   d. stands apart from the larger society.

9. Which of the following religions is found in the United States?
   a. Islam   b. Judaism
   c. Christianity   d. all of the above

10. The term "secularization" refers to which of the following?
    a. religion becoming more important in people's lives
    b. increasing popularity of fundamentalism
    c. the decline in the importance of religion and the sacred
    d. churches resisting social change

ANSWERS: 1(b); 2(d); 3(c); 4(a); 5(d); 6(b); 7(b); 8(d); 9(d); 10(c).

Essay Questions

1. What is the basic distinction between the sacred and the profane that underlies all religious belief?

2. In what ways do churches, sects, and cults differ?

APPLICATIONS & EXERCISES

1. Some colleges are very religious; others are very secular. Investigate the place of religion on your campus. Is your school affiliated with a religious organization? Was it ever? Is there a chaplain or other religious official? See if you can learn from campus sources what share of students regularly attend any religious service.

2. Develop five questions that might be used on a questionnaire or in an interview to measure how religious people

are. Present them to several people. Use the results to show that how religious people appear to be depends on exactly what questions you ask them.

3. Is religion getting weaker? To evaluate the claim that our society is undergoing secularization, go to the library or local newspaper office and obtain an issue of your local newspaper published fifty years ago and, if possible, one published 100 years ago. Compare the amount of attention to religious issues then and now.

INVESTIGATE *with* Research Navigator

Follow the instructions on page 27 of this text to access the features of **Research Navigator**™. Once at the Web site, enter your Login Name and Password. Then, to use the **ContentSelect**™ database, enter keywords such as "religion," "cults," and "Islam," and the search engine will supply relevant

and recent scholarly and popular press publications. Use the *New York Times* **Search-by-Subject Archive** to find recent news articles related to sociology and the **Link Library** feature to find relevant Web links organized by the key terms associated with this chapter.

Education

How is a nation's schooling affected by its level
of economic development?

What are the serious problems of U.S. schools?

Why is education an important dimension
of social inequality?

When Lisa Addison was growing up in Baltimore, her teachers always said she was smart and should go to college. "I liked hearing that," she recalls. "But I didn't know what to do about it. No one in my family had ever gone to college. I didn't know what courses to take in high school. I had no idea of how to apply to a college. How would I pay for it? What would it be like if I got there?"

Discouraged and uncertain, Addison found herself "kind of goofing off in school." After finishing high school, she spent the next fifteen years working as a waitress in a restaurant and then as a kitchen helper in a catering company. Now, at the age of thirty-eight, Addison has decided to go back to school. "I don't want to do this kind of work for the rest of my life. I *am* smart. I can do better. At this point, I am ready for college."

Addison took a giant step through the door of the Community College of Baltimore County, speaking to counselors and setting her sights on an associate's degree in business. When she finishes the two-year program, she plans to transfer to a four-year university to complete a bachelor's degree. Then she hopes to go back into the food service industry—but this time as a better-paid manager (Toppo & DeBarros, 2005). ■

Higher education is part of the American dream for 80 percent of young people in the United States. But many face the types of challenges that delayed Lisa Addison in her journey toward a college degree. Especially for people growing up in low-income families, often with parents who are not college graduates, the odds of getting to college are very small.

Who goes to college in the United States? What difference does higher education make in the type of job you get or the money you make? This chapter answers these questions by focusing on **education**, *the social institution through which society provides its members with important knowledge, including basic facts, job skills, and cultural norms and values.* In high-income nations such as the United States, education is largely a matter of **schooling**, *formal instruction under the direction of specially trained teachers.*

Education: A Global Survey

Throughout the United States, young people expect to spend much of their first eighteen years in school. This was not the case a century ago, when just a small elite in the United States had the privilege of attending school. Even today, most young people in poor countries receive only a few years of formal schooling.

SCHOOLING AND ECONOMIC DEVELOPMENT

The extent of schooling in any society is tied to its level of economic development. In low- and middle-income countries, which are home to most of the world's people, families and communities teach young people important knowledge and skills. Formal schooling, and especially learning that is not directly connected to survival, is available mainly to wealthy people who do not need to work. After all, the Greek root of the word *school* means "leisure." In ancient Greece, famous teachers such as Socrates, Plato, and Aristotle taught aristocratic, upper-class men. The same was true in ancient China, where the famous philosopher K'ung-Fu-tzu (Confucius) shared his wisdom with a privileged few.

December 30, the Quechua region, Peru. High in the Andes Mountains of Peru, families send their children to the local school. But "local" can mean 3 miles or more, and

In many low-income nations, girls are as likely to work as to attend school. In Afghanistan under the strict rule of the Taliban, girls were all but absent from school. By the beginning of 2002, however, the picture was changing. Here we see girls at the Manu Chera school for girls in central Kabul completing a classroom assignment.

there are no buses, so these children, almost all from poor families, walk an hour or more each way. Schooling is required by law, but in the rural highlands, some parents prefer to keep their children at home where they can help with the farming and livestock.

Today, the limited schooling that takes place in lower-income countries reflects the national culture. In Iran, for example, schooling is closely tied to Islam. Similarly, schooling in Bangladesh (Asia), Zimbabwe (Africa), and Nicaragua (Latin America) has been shaped by the distinctive cultural traditions of these nations.

All lower-income countries have one trait in common when it comes to schooling: There is not very much of it. In the world's poorest nations (including several in Central Africa), only half of all children ever get to school; worldwide, only half of all children ever get to the secondary grades. As a result, about one-third of the world's people cannot read or write. Global Map 20–1 on page 528 shows the extent of illiteracy around the world, and the following national comparisons illustrate the link between the extent of schooling and economic development.

SCHOOLING IN INDIA

India has recently become a middle-income country, but people there still earn only about 8 percent of U.S. average income, and most poor families depend on the earnings of children. Even though India has outlawed child labor, many children continue to work in factories—weaving rugs or making handicrafts—up to sixty hours per week, which greatly limits their chances for schooling.

Today, 81 percent of children in India complete primary school, typically in crowded schoolrooms where one teacher may face as many as sixty children, twice as many as in the average U.S. public school classroom. Less than half of Indian children go on to secondary school, and very few enter college. As a result, 39 percent of India's people are not able to read and write.

Patriarchy also shapes Indian education. Indian parents are joyful at the birth of a boy, because he and his future wife will both contribute income to the family. But there are economic costs to raising a girl: Parents must provide a dowry (a gift of wealth to the groom's family), and after her marriage, a daughter's work benefits her husband's family. Therefore, many Indians see less reason to invest in the schooling of girls, so only 30 percent of girls (compared to 45 percent of boys) reach the secondary grades. So what do the girls do while the boys are in school? Most of the children working in Indian factories are girls—a family's way of benefiting from their daughters while they can (United Nations Development Programme, 1995).

SCHOOLING IN JAPAN

Schooling has not always been part of the Japanese way of life. Before industrialization brought mandatory education in 1872, only a privileged few attended school. Today, Japan's educational system is widely praised for producing some of the world's highest achievers.

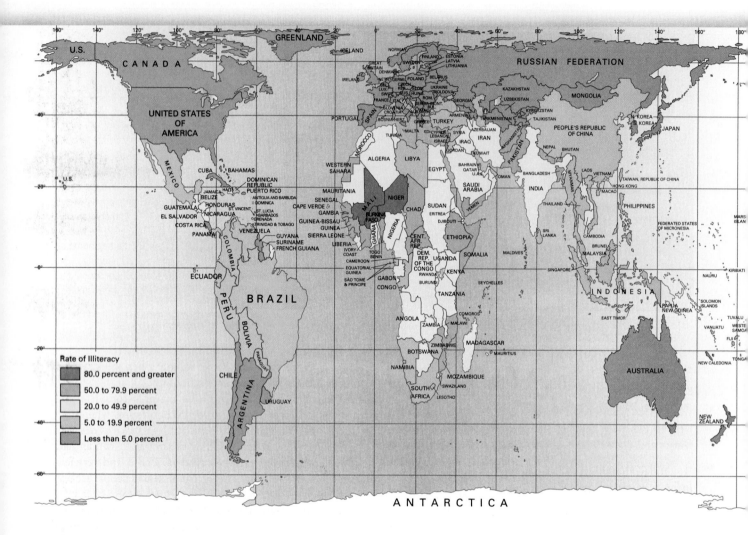

WINDOW ON THE WORLD

GLOBAL MAP 20–1 Illiteracy in Global Perspective

Reading and writing skills are widespread in high-income countries, where illiteracy rates generally are below 5 percent. In much of Latin America, however, illiteracy is more common, one consequence of limited economic development. In twenty-two nations—sixteen of them in Africa—illiteracy is the rule rather than the exception; there, people rely on the oral tradition of face-to-face communication rather than the written word.

Source: United Nations Development Programme (2005); map projection from *Peters Atlas of the World* (1990).

The early grades concentrate on transmitting Japanese traditions, especially a sense of obligation to family. Starting in their early teens, students take a series of difficult and highly competitive examinations. Their scores on these written tests, which are like the Scholastic Assessment Test (SAT) in the United States, decide the future of all Japanese students.

More men and women graduate from high school in Japan (96 percent) than in the United States (85 percent). But these competitive examinations allow just half of high school graduates—compared to 62 percent in the United States—to enter college. Understandably, Japanese students (and their parents) take entrance examinations very seriously, and about half attend "cram schools" to prepare for them.

Japanese schooling produces impressive results. In a number of fields, notably mathematics and science, Japanese students outperform students in every other high-income nation, including the United States.

SCHOOLING IN GREAT BRITAIN

During the Middle Ages, schooling was a privilege of the British nobility, who studied classical subjects, having little concern for the practical skills needed to earn a living. But as the Industrial Revolution created a need for an educated labor force, and as working-class people demanded access to schools, a rising share of the population entered the classroom. British law now requires every child to attend school until age sixteen.

Traditional class differences still affect British schooling. Most wealthy families send their children to what the British call *public schools,* what we would refer to as private boarding schools. These elite schools enroll about 7 percent of British students and teach not only academic subjects but also the special patterns of speech, mannerisms, and social graces of the British upper class. Because these academies are very expensive, most British students attend state-supported day schools (Ambler & Neathery, 1999).

The British have tried to reduce the importance of social background in schooling by expanding their university system and linking admission to competitive entrance examinations. For those who score the highest, the government pays most of the college costs. But many well-to-do children who do not score very well still manage to get in to Oxford or Cambridge, the most prestigious British universities, on a par with our own Yale, Harvard, and Princeton. Many "Oxbridge" graduates go on to positions at the top of the British power elite: More than two-thirds of the highest-ranking members of the British government, for example, have "Oxbridge" degrees (Sampson, 1982; Gamble, Ludlam, & Baker, 1993).

These brief sketches of schooling in India, Japan, and Great Britain show the crucial importance of economic development. In poor countries, many children—especially girls—work rather than go to school. Rich nations enact mandatory education laws to prepare an industrial workforce as well as to satisfy demands for greater equality. But a nation's history and culture still matter, as we see in the intense competition of Japanese schools, the traditional social stratification that shapes schools in Great Britain, and, in the next section, the practical emphasis found in the schools of the United States.

TABLE 20–1

Educational Achievement in the United States, 1910–2004*

Year	High School Graduates	College Graduates	Median Years of Schooling
1910	13.5%	2.7%	8.1
1920	16.4	3.3	8.2
1930	19.1	3.9	8.4
1940	24.1	4.6	8.6
1950	33.4	6.0	9.3
1960	41.1	7.7	10.5
1970	55.2	11.0	12.2
1980	68.7	17.0	12.5
1990	77.6	21.3	12.4
2000	84.1	25.6	12.7
2004	85.2	27.7	n/a

*For people twenty-five years of age and over. Percentage of high school graduates includes those who go on to college. Percentage of high school dropouts can be calculated by subtracting percentage of high school graduates from 100 percent.

Source: U.S. Census Bureau (2005).

SCHOOLING IN THE UNITED STATES

The United States was among the first countries to set a goal of mass education. By 1850, about half the young people between the ages of five and nineteen were enrolled in school. By 1918, all states had passed a *mandatory education law* requiring children to attend school until the age of sixteen or the completion of the eighth grade. Table 20–1 shows that a milestone was reached in the mid-1960s when for the first time a majority of U.S. adults had high school diplomas. Today, more than four out of five have high school educations, and more than one in four have a four-year college degree.

The U.S. educational system is shaped by both our high standard of living (which means that young people typically do not have to work) and our democratic principles (the idea that schooling should be provided to everyone). Thomas Jefferson thought the new nation could become democratic only if people "read and understand what is going on in the world" (quoted in Honeywell, 1931:13). Today, the United States has an outstanding record of higher education for its people: No other country has as large a share of adults with university degrees (U.S. Census Bureau, 2004).

Schooling in the United States also tries to promote *equal opportunity.* National surveys show that most people think schooling is crucial to personal success, and a majority also believe that everyone has the chance to get an education consistent with personal ability and talent (NORC, 2003). However, this opinion expresses our cultural ideals rather than reality. A century ago, for example, few women had the chance to go to college, and even today, most men and women who attend college come from families with above-average incomes.

 For the report, "Trends in Educational Equity of Girls and Women," go to http://nces. ed.gov/pubs2005/equity/

In the United States, the educational system stresses the value of *practical* learning, knowledge that prepares people for future jobs. This emphasis is in line with what the educational philosopher John Dewey (1859–1952) called *progressive education,* having the schools make learning relevant to people's lives. Similarly, students seek out subjects of study that they feel will give them an advantage when they are ready to compete in the job market. For example, as concerns about international terrorism have risen in recent years, so have the numbers of students choosing to study geography, international conflict, and Middle Eastern history and culture (M. Lord, 2001).

YOUR TURN

What is your career goal? Are the courses you are taking geared to helping you realize this goal?

The Functions of Schooling

Structural-functional analysis looks at ways in which formal education supports the operation and stability of society. We look briefly at five ways that this happens.

SOCIALIZATION

Technologically simple societies look to families to transmit a way of life from one generation to the next. As societies gain complex technology, they turn to trained teachers to develop and pass on the specialized knowledge that adults will need for their jobs.

In primary school, children learn language and basic mathematical skills. Secondary school builds on this foundation, and for many students, college allows further specialization. In addition, all schooling teaches cultural values and norms. For example, civics classes instruct students in our political way of life, and rituals such as saluting the flag foster patriotism. Likewise, activities such as

spelling bees develop competitive individualism and a sense of fair play.

CULTURAL INNOVATION

Faculty at colleges and universities create culture as well as pass it on to students. Research in the sciences, the social sciences, the humanities, and the fine arts leads to discovery and changes in our way of life. For example, medical research at major universities has helped increase life expectancy, just as research by sociologists and psychologists helps us learn how to better enjoy our lives so we can take advantage of our longevity.

SOCIAL INTEGRATION

Schooling molds a diverse population into one society sharing norms and values. This is one reason that states enacted mandatory education laws a century ago at a time when immigration was very high. In light of the ethnic diversity of many urban areas today, schooling continues to serve this same purpose.

SOCIAL PLACEMENT

Schools identify talent and match instruction to ability. Schooling increases meritocracy by rewarding talent and hard work regardless of social background and provides a path to upward social mobility.

LATENT FUNCTIONS OF SCHOOLING

Schooling also serves several less widely recognized functions. It provides child care for the growing number of one-parent and two-career families. In addition, schooling occupies thousands of young people in their teens and twenties who would otherwise be competing for limited opportunities in the job market. High schools, colleges, and universities also bring together people of marriageable age. Finally, schools establish networks that serve as a valuable career resource throughout life.

Critical review   Structural-functional analysis stresses ways in which formal education supports the operation of a modern society. However, this approach overlooks how the classroom behavior of teachers and students can vary from one setting to another, a focus of the symbolic-interaction approach discussed next. In addition, structural-functional analysis says little about many problems of our educational system and how schooling helps reproduce the class structure in each generation, which is the focus of social-conflict analysis found in the final theoretical section of the chapter.

Schooling and Social Interaction

The basic idea of the symbolic-interaction approach is that people create the reality they experience in their day-to-day interaction. We use this approach to explain how stereotypes can shape what goes on in the classroom.

THE SELF-FULFILLING PROPHECY

Chapter 6 ("Social Interaction in Everyday Life") presented the Thomas theorem, which states that situations people define as real become real in their consequences. Put another way, people who expect others to act in certain ways often encourage that very behavior. Doing so, people set up a *self-fulfilling prophecy.*

Jane Elliott, an elementary school teacher in the all-white community of Riceville, Iowa, carried out a simple experiment that showed how a self-fulfilling prophecy can take place in the classroom. Back in 1968, Elliot was teaching a fourth-grade class when Dr. Martin Luther King Jr. was assassinated. Her students were puzzled and asked why a national hero had been brutally shot. Elliott responded by asking her white students what they thought about people of color, and she was stunned to find out that they held many powerful and negative stereotypes.

To show the class the harmful effects of such stereotypes, Elliott performed a classroom experiment. She found that almost all of the children in her class had either blue eyes or brown eyes. She told the class that children with brown eyes were smarter and worked harder than children with blue eyes. To be sure everyone could easily tell which category a child fell into, pieces of brown or blue colored cloth were pinned to every student's collar.

Elliott recalls the effect of this "lesson" on the way students behaved: "It was just horrifying how quickly they became what I told them they were." Within half an hour, Elliot continued, a blue-eyed girl named Carol had changed from a "brilliant, carefree, excited little girl to a frightened, timid, uncertain, almost-person." Not surprisingly, in the hours that followed, the brown-eyed students came to life, speaking up more and performing better than they had done before. The prophecy had been fulfilled: Because the brown-eyed children thought they were superior, they became superior in their classroom performance—as well as "arrogant, ugly and domineering" toward the blue-eyed children. For their part, the blue-eyed children began underperforming, becoming the inferior people they believed themselves to be.

Graduation from college is an important event in the lives of an ever-increasing number of people in the United States. Look over the discussion of the functions of schooling on page 530. How many of these functions do you think people in college are aware of? Can you think of other social consequences of going to college?

By the end of the day, Elliott took time to explain to everyone what they had experienced. She applied the lesson to race, pointing out that if white children thought they were superior to black children, they would expect to do better in school, just as many children of color who live in the shadow of the same stereotypes would underperform in school. The children also realized that the society that teaches these stereotypes, as well as the hate that often goes with them, encourages the kind of violence that ended the life of Dr. King (Kral, 2000).

Critical review The symbolic-interaction approach explains how we all build reality in our everyday interactions with others. When school officials define some students as "gifted," for example, we can expect teachers to treat them differently and the students themselves to behave differently as a result of having been labeled in this way. If students and teachers come to believe that one race is academically superior to another, the behavior that follows may be a self-fulfilling prophecy.

One limitation of this approach is that people do not just make up such beliefs about superiority and inferiority. Rather, these beliefs are built into a society's system of social inequality, which brings us to the social-conflict approach.

Sociological research has documented the fact that young children living in low-income communities typically learn in classrooms like the one on the left, with large class sizes and low budgets that do not provide for high technology and other instructional materials. Children from high-income communities typically enjoy classroom experiences such as the one shown on the right, with small classes and the latest learning technology.

Schooling and Social Inequality

Social-conflict analysis explains how schooling both causes and perpetuates social inequality. In this way, it can explain how stereotypes of "good" and "bad" students described in the symbolic-interaction discussion arise in the first place. In addition, a social-conflict approach challenges the structural-functional idea that schooling develops everybody's talents and abilities by claiming that schooling plays a part in social stratification.

SOCIAL CONTROL

Schooling is a way of controlling people, reinforcing acceptance of the status quo. Samuel Bowles and Herbert Gintis (1976) claim that the rise of public education in the late nineteenth century came at exactly the same time that factory owners needed an obedient and disciplined workforce. Once in school, immigrants learned not only the English language but also the importance of following orders.

STANDARDIZED TESTING

Here is a question of the kind historically used to measure the academic ability of school-age children in the United States:

Painter is to painting as _____ is to sonnet.
(a) driver   (b) poet   (c) priest   (d) carpenter

The correct answer is "(b) poet": A painter creates a painting just as a poet creates a sonnet. This question supposedly measures logical reasoning, but getting the right answer also depends on knowing what each term means. Students who are unfamiliar with the sonnet as a Western European form of written verse are not likely to answer the question correctly.

The organizations that create standardized tests claim that this type of bias has been all but eliminated because they carefully study response patterns and drop any question that favors one racial or ethnic category. But critics insist that some bias based on class, race, or ethnicity will always exist in formal testing. Because questions will always reflect our society's dominant culture, minority students are placed at a disadvantage (Crouse & Trusheim, 1988; Putka, 1990).

SCHOOL TRACKING

Despite controversy over standardized tests, most schools in the United States use them for **tracking,** *assigning students to different types of educational programs*, such as college preparatory classes, general education, and vocational and technical training.

Tracking supposedly helps teachers meet each student's individual needs and abilities. However, one education critic, Jonathan Kozol (1992), considers tracking an example of "savage inequalities" in our school system. Most students from privileged backgrounds do well on standardized tests and get into higher tracks, where they receive the best the school can offer. Students from disadvantaged backgrounds typically do less well on these tests and end up in lower tracks, where teachers stress memorization and put little focus on creativity.

NATIONAL MAP 20–1

Teachers' Salaries
across the United States

In 2004, the average public school teacher in the United States earned $46,752. The map shows the average teacher salary for all the states; they range from a low of $33,236 in South Dakota to a high of $57,337 in Connecticut. Looking at the map, what pattern do you see? What do high-salary (and low-salary) states have in common?

Source: National Education Association, *Rankings and Estimates: Rankings of the States and Estimates of School Statistics 2004.* Washington, D.C.: NEA, 2004, p. 19.

Average Annual Teacher Salaries

$55,000 and above
$50,000 to $54,999
$45,000 to $49,999
$40,000 to $44,999
Below $40,000

U.S. average: $46,752

Based on these concerns, schools across the United States are cautious about making tracking assignments and give students the chance to move from one track to another. Some schools have even dropped tracking entirely. Tracking can help match instruction with students' abilities, but rigid tracking can have a powerful impact on students' learning and self-concept. Young people who spend years in higher tracks tend to see themselves as bright and able; students in lower tracks end up with less ambition and low self-esteem (Bowles & Gintis, 1976; Oakes, 1985; Kilgore, 1991; Kozol, 1992).

INEQUALITY AMONG SCHOOLS

Just as students are treated differently within schools, schools themselves differ in important ways. The biggest difference is between public and private schools.

Public and Private Schools

Across the United States, about 90 percent of the 54 million primary and secondary school children attend state-funded public schools. The rest go to private schools.

Most private school students attend one of the 8,000 *parochial schools* (from the Latin, meaning "of the parish") operated by the Roman Catholic Church. The Catholic school system grew rapidly a century ago as cities swelled with immigrants, helping the new arrivals keep their religious heritage in a new and mostly Protestant society. Today, after decades of flight from the inner city by white people, many parochial schools enroll non-Catholics, including a growing number of African Americans whose families seek an alternative to the neighborhood public school.

Protestants also have private schools, often known as Christian academies. These schools are favored by parents who want religious instruction for their children as well as higher academic and disciplinary standards (James, 1989; Dent, 1996).

There are also about 6,000 nonreligious private schools that enroll mostly young people from well-to-do families. These are typically prestigious and expensive preparatory ("prep") schools, modeled on British boarding schools, that not only provide strong academic programs but also teach the way of life of the upper class. Many "preppies" maintain lifelong school-based networks that provide numerous social advantages.

Are private schools better than public schools? Research shows that, holding social background constant, students in private schools do outperform those in public schools. The advantages of private schools include smaller classes, more demanding coursework, and greater discipline (Coleman, Hoffer, & Kilgore, 1981; Coleman & Hoffer, 1987).

Inequality in Public Schooling

But even public schools are not all the same. Differences in funding result in unequal resources; as a result, children in more affluent areas receive a better education than children living in poor communities. National Map 20–1 shows one key way resources differ: Average teacher salaries vary more than $20,000 in a state-by-state comparison.

Dramatic differences in local funding for education exist across the United States. Winnetka, Illinois, one of the richest suburbs in the United States, spends more than $13,000 each year on each of its students, compared to less than $8,000 in poor areas like Laredo, Texas, and in recent years,

Schooling in the United States: Savage Inequality

"Public School 261? Head down Jerome Avenue and look for the mortician's office." Off for a day studying the New York City schools, Jonathan Kozol parks his car and walks toward PS 261. Finding PS 261 is not easy because the school has no sign. In fact, the building is a former roller rink and doesn't look much like a school at all.

The principal explains that this is in a minority area of the North Bronx, so the population of PS 261 is 90 percent African American and Hispanic. Officially, the school should serve 900 students, but it actually enrolls 1,300. The rules say class size should not exceed thirty-two, but Kozol observes that it sometimes approaches forty. Because the school has just one small cafeteria, the children must eat in three shifts. After lunch, with no place to play, students squirm in their seats until told to return to their classrooms. Only one classroom in the entire school has a window to the world outside.

Toward the end of the day, Kozol remarks to a teacher about the overcrowding and the poor condition of the building. She sums up her thoughts: "I had an awful room last year. In the winter, it was 56 degrees. In the summer, it was up to 90." "Do the children ever comment on the building?" Kozol asks. "They don't say," she responds, "but they know. All these kids see TV. They know what suburban schools are like. Then they look around them at their school. They don't comment on it, but you see it in their eyes. They understand."

Several months later, Kozol visits PS 24, in the affluent Riverdale section of New York City. This school is set back from the road, beyond a lawn planted with magnolia and dogwood trees, which are now in full bloom. On one side of the building is a playground for the youngest children; behind the school are playing fields for the older kids. Many people pay the high price of a house in Riverdale because the local schools have such an excellent reputation. There are 825 children here; most are white and a few are Asian, Hispanic, or African American. The building is in good repair. It has a large library and even a planetarium. All the classrooms have windows with bright curtains.

Entering one of the many classes for gifted students, Kozol asks the children what they are doing today. A young girl answers confidently, "My name is Laurie, and we're doing problem solving." A tall, good-natured boy continues, "I'm David. One thing that we do is logical thinking. Some problems, we find, have more than one good answer." Kozol asks if such reasoning is innate or if it is something a child learns. Susan, whose smile reveals her braces, responds, "You know some things to start with when you enter school. But we learn some things that other children don't. We learn certain things that other children don't know because we're *taught* them."

WHAT DO YOU THINK?

1. Are there differences between schools in your city or town? Explain.
2. Why do you think there is little public concern about schooling inequality?
3. What changes would our society have to make to eliminate schooling inequality?

Source: Adapted from Kozol (1992:85–88, 92–96).

these differences have grown (Edwards, 1998; Winter, 2004). In response, Vermont passed Act 60, a law that distributes tax money equally across that state. The Thinking About Diversity box shows that funding for public schools can vary even from neighborhood to neighborhood in a single city.

Differences in funding also benefit whites (who typically live in richer communities) over minorities. For this reason, some districts enacted a policy of *busing,* transporting students to achieve racial balance and more equal opportunity in schools. Although only 5 percent of U.S. schoolchildren are bused to schools outside their neighborhoods, this policy is controversial. Supporters claim that given the reality of racial segregation, the only way government will adequately fund schools in poor, minority neighborhoods is if white children from richer areas attend. Critics respond that busing is expensive and undermines the concept of neighborhood schools. But almost everyone agrees on one thing: Given the racial imbalance of most urban areas, an effective busing scheme would have to join inner cities and suburbs, a plan that has never been politically possible.

Inequality in schooling is not only about money. A classic report by a research team headed by James Coleman (1966) confirmed that students in mostly minority schools suffer from larger class size, insufficient libraries, and fewer science labs. But the Coleman report cautioned that more money by itself would not magically ensure educational quality. More important are the cooperative efforts and enthusiasm of teachers, parents, and the students themselves. In other words, even if school funding were exactly the same everywhere, students who benefit from more *social capital*—that is, those whose parents value schooling, read to their children, and encourage the development of imagination—would still perform better. In short, we should not expect schools alone to overcome social inequality (Schneider et al., 1998; Israel, Beaulieu, & Hartless, 2001).

Recent research confirms the important influence of home environment on school performance. A research team led by Douglas Downey (Downey, von Hippel, & Broh, 2004) studied the rate at which school-age children gain skills in reading and mathematics. Because U.S. children go to school six to seven hours a day, five days a week, and do not attend school during summer months, the researchers calculate that children spend only about 13 percent of their waking hours in school. During the school year, high-income children learn somewhat more quickly than low-income children, but the learning disparity is far greater during the summer season when children are not in school. The researchers conclude that differences in the home and local neighborhood matter most in children's learning. As shown in Figure 20–1, schools may not be equal for all children, but they do level the playing field somewhat by reducing the great differences in children's home environments.

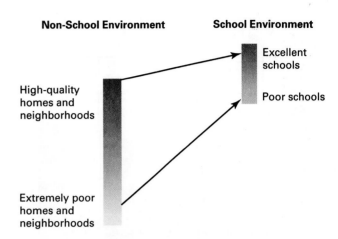

Non-School Environment   **School Environment**

High-quality homes and neighborhoods

Extremely poor homes and neighborhoods

Excellent schools

Poor schools

FIGURE 20–1   Home and School Environments: Effects on Learning

Because children spend only 13 percent of their waking hours in school, the home environment has a greater effect on learning than the school environment. Schools—even poor ones—help to narrow the learning gap between advantaged and disadvantaged children, but they are not able to close the gap completely.

Source: D.B. Downey, P.T. von Hippel, and B.A. Broh, "Are Schools the Great Equalizer?", *American Sociological Review*, vol. 69 no. 5 (October 2004), p. 614, Fig. 1. Reprinted by permission.

YOUR TURN

Are there specific ways parents can improve children's learning? How did your parents affect your learning?

ACCESS TO HIGHER EDUCATION

Schooling is the main path to good jobs. But only 62 percent of U.S. high school graduates enroll in college the fall after graduation. Overall, among young people eighteen to twenty-four years old, about 32 percent are enrolled in college (National Center for Education Statistics, 2004).

A crucial factor affecting access to U.S. higher education is family income. College is expensive: Even at state-supported institutions, annual tuition averages at least $3,000, and admission to the most exclusive private colleges and universities exceeds $40,000 a year. As shown in Figure 20–2 on page 536, two-thirds of children from families with incomes above $75,000 annually (roughly the richest 30 percent, who fall within the upper-middle class and upper class) attend college, but only 27 percent of young people from families earning less than $20,000 go on to higher education (U.S. Census Bureau, 2004).

These economic differences are one reason that the education gap between whites and minorities widens at the college level. As Figure 20–3 on page 537 shows, African Americans are not quite as likely as non-Hispanic whites to graduate from high school and are much less likely to complete four or more years of college. Hispanics, many of whom speak Spanish as their first language, have a lower rate of high school graduation, but again, the gap is much greater when it comes to college degrees. Schooling is an important path to social mobility in our society, but the promise of schooling has not overcome the racial inequality that exists in the United States.

Completing college brings many rewards, including intellectual and personal growth, as well as higher income. In the last forty years, as our economy has shifted to work that requires processing information, the gap in average income between people who complete only high school and those who earn a

SOCIOLOGY WORK

DIVERSITY SNAPSHOT

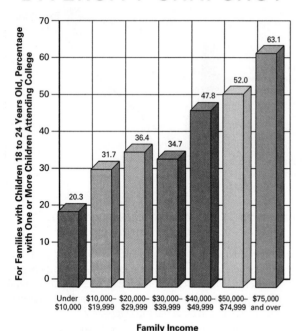

FIGURE 20-2   College Attendance and Family Income, 2002

The higher a family's income, the more likely it is that children will attend college.

Source: U.S. Census Bureau (2004).

four-year college degree has more than doubled. Today, a college degree adds as much as $1 million to a person's lifetime income. Table 20–2 gives details. In 2004, men with an eighth-grade education typically earned $21,659, high school graduates averaged $35,725, and college graduates averaged $57,220. The ratios in parentheses show that a man with a bachelor's degree earns more than two-and-one-half times as much as a man with eight or fewer years of schooling. Across the board, women earn less than men; added years of schooling boosts women's income, but more slowly. Keep in mind that for both men and women, some of the increased earnings have to do with social background, because those with the most schooling are likely to come from relatively well-off families to begin with.

GREATER OPPORTUNITY: EXPANDING HIGHER EDUCATION

With some 15.9 million people enrolled in colleges and universities, the United States is the world leader in providing a college education to its people. This country also enrolls more students from abroad than any other.

One reason for this achievement is that there are more than 4,000 colleges and universities in the United States. This number includes 2,324 four-year institutions (which award bachelor's degrees) as well as 1,844 two-year colleges (which award associate's degrees). Although some two-year colleges are private, most are publicly funded community colleges that serve a local area (usually a county) and charge a low tuition (National Center for Education Statistics, 2004).

For general news and information about higher education, go to http://chronicle.com

Because higher education is a key path to better jobs and higher income, the government makes money available to help certain categories of people pay the costs of college. After World War II, the GI Bill provided college funds to veterans, with the result that tens of thousands of men and women were able to attend college. Some branches of the military continue to offer college money to enlistees; in addition, the government funds a number of grants and scholarships for veterans.

Community Colleges

Since the 1960s, the expansion of state-funded community colleges has further increased access to higher education. According to the National Center for Education Statistics (2004), the 1,844 two-year colleges across the United States now enroll 39 percent of all college undergraduates.

Community colleges provide a number of specific benefits. First, their low tuition cost places college courses and degrees within the reach of millions of families that could not otherwise afford a college education. Today, community colleges enroll many students who are the first in their family to pursue a college degree. The low cost of community colleges is especially important during periods of economic recession. When the economy slumps and people lose their jobs, college enrollments soar, especially at community colleges.

Second, community colleges have special importance for minorities. Currently, half of all African American and Hispanic undergraduates in the United States attend community colleges.

Third, although it is true that community colleges serve local populations, two-year colleges also attract students from around the world. Many community colleges recruit students from abroad, and more than one-third of all foreign students enrolled on a U.S. campus are studying at community colleges (Briggs, 2002; D. Golden, 2002).

Finally, the top priority of faculty who work at large universities is typically research, but the most important job for community college faculty is teaching. Thus, although teaching loads are high (usually four or five classes each semester), community colleges appeal to faculty who find their greatest pleasure in the classroom. Community college students often get more attention from faculty than students at large universities (Jacobson, 2003).

PRIVILEGE AND PERSONAL MERIT

If attending college is a rite of passage for rich men and women, as social-conflict analysis suggests, then *schooling transforms social privilege into personal merit.* But given our cultural emphasis on individualism, we tend to see credentials as badges of ability rather than as symbols of family affluence (Sennett & Cobb, 1973).

When we congratulate the new graduate, we rarely recognize the resources—in terms of both financial and social capital—that made this achievement possible. Yet young people from families with incomes exceeding $100,000 a year average more than 200 points higher on the SAT college entrance examination than young people from families with less than $10,000 in annual income. The richer students are more likely to get into college; once there, they are also more likely to complete their studies and get a degree. In a *credential society*—one that evaluates people on the basis of their schooling—companies hire job applicants with the best education. This process ends up helping people with advantages to begin with and harming those who are already disadvantaged (Collins, 1979).

Critical review Social-conflict analysis links formal education to social inequality to show how schooling transforms privilege into personal worthiness and social disadvantage into personal deficiency. However, the social-conflict approach overlooks the extent to which schooling provides upward social mobility for talented women and men from all backgrounds. In addition, despite the claims that schooling supports the status quo, today's college curricula challenge social inequality on many fronts.

The Applying Theory table on page 538 sums up what the theoretical approaches show us about education.

Problems in the Schools

An intense debate revolves around schooling in the United States. Perhaps because we expect our schools to do so much more than merely teach—equalize opportunity, instill discipline, and fire the imagination—people are divided on whether public schools are doing

 For details on this national poll, go to http://www.pdkintl. org/kappan/k0509pol.htm

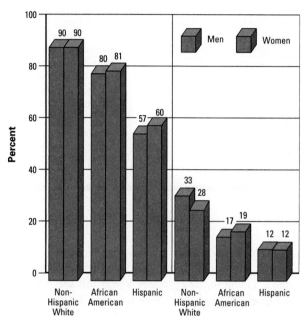

DIVERSITY SNAPSHOT

FIGURE 20-3 Educational Achievement for Various Categories of People, Aged 25 Years and Over, 2004

U.S. society still provides less education to minorities.

Source: U.S. Census Bureau (2005).

TABLE 20–2

Median Income by Sex and Educational Attainment*

Education	Men	Women
Professional degree	$100,000 (4.6)	$75,036 (4.4)
Doctorate	82,401 (3.8)	68,875 (4.0)
Master's	71,530 (3.3)	51,316 (3.0)
Bachelor's	57,220 (2.6)	41,681 (2.4)
1–3 years of college	41,895 (1.9)	30,816 (1.8)
4 years of high school	35,725 (1.6)	26,029 (1.5)
9–11 years of school	26,277 (1.2)	19,162 (1.1)
0–8 years of school	21,659 (1.0)	17,023 (1.0)

*Persons aged twenty-five years and over working full time, 2004. The earnings ratio, in parentheses, indicates how many times the lowest income level a person with additional schooling earns.

Source: U.S. Census Bureau (2005).

APPLYING THEORY

EDUCATION

	Structural-Functional Approach	Symbolic-Interaction Approach	Social-Conflict Approach
What is the level of analysis?	Macro-level	Micro-level	Macro-level
What is the importance of education for society?	Schooling performs many vital tasks for the operation of society, including socializing the young and encouraging discovery and invention to improve our lives. Schooling helps unite a diverse society by teaching shared norms and values.	How teachers and others define students can become real to everyone and affect students' educational performance.	Schooling maintains social inequality through unequal schooling for rich and poor. Within individual schools, tracking provides privileged children with a better education than poor children.

their job. Although almost half of adults give schools in their local community a grade of A or B, just about as many give a grade of C or below (Rose & Gallup, 2005).

DISCIPLINE AND VIOLENCE

When many of today's older teachers think back to their own student days, school "problems" consisted of talking out of turn, chewing gum, breaking the dress code, or cutting class. Today, schools are grappling with serious issues such as drug and alcohol abuse, teenage pregnancy, and outright violence. Although almost everyone agrees that schools should teach personal discipline, many think the job is no longer being done.

Schools do not create violence; in most cases, violence spills into the schools from the surrounding society. In the wake of a number of school shootings in recent years, many school districts have adopted zero-tolerance policies that require suspension or expulsion for serious misbehavior.

STUDENT PASSIVITY

If some schools are plagued by violence, many more are filled with students who are bored. Some of the blame for passivity can be placed on television (which now consumes more of young people's time than school), parents (who are not involved enough with their children), and the students themselves. But schools, too, play a part, since our educational system itself generates student passivity (Coleman, Hoffer, & Kilgore, 1981).

Bureaucracy

The small, personal schools that served countless local communities a century ago have evolved into huge educational

factories. In a study of high schools across the United States, Theodore Sizer (1984:207–9) identified five ways in which large, bureaucratic schools undermine education:

1. **Rigid uniformity.** Bureaucratic schools run by outside specialists (such as state education officials) generally ignore the cultural character of local communities and the personal needs of their children.

2. **Numerical ratings.** School officials define success in terms of numerical attendance records and dropout rates and "teach to the tests," hoping to raise achievement test scores. In the process, they overlook dimensions of schooling that are difficult to quantify, such as creativity and enthusiasm.

3. **Rigid expectations.** Officials expect fifteen-year-olds to be in the tenth grade and eleventh-graders to score at a certain level on a standardized verbal achievement test. Rarely are exceptionally bright and motivated students permitted to graduate early. Similarly, poor performers are pushed on from grade to grade.

4. **Specialization.** Students in middle school and high school learn Spanish from one teacher, receive guidance from another, and are coached in sports by still others. Although specialized teachers may know more about their subjects, students experience this division of labor as a continual shuffling from one fifty-minute period to another throughout the school day. As a result, no school official comes to know the child well.

5. **Little individual responsibility.** Highly bureaucratic schools do not empower students to learn on their own. Similarly, teachers have little say in what they

teach in their classes and how they do it; any change in the pace of learning might disrupt the system.

Of course, with 54 million schoolchildren in the United States, schools must be bureaucratic to get the job done. But Sizer recommends that we "humanize" schools by reducing rigid scheduling, cutting class size, and training teachers more broadly so that they become more involved in the lives of their students. Overall, as James Coleman (1993) suggested, schools need to be less "administratively driven" and more "output-driven." Perhaps this transformation could begin by ensuring that graduation from high school depends on what students have learned rather than simply on the number of years spent in the building.

YOUR TURN

California recently capped the size of classes in the first three grades at twenty students. What benefits would such a policy have for the country as a whole? What would be the costs?

For all categories of people in the United States, dropping out of school greatly reduces the chances to get a good job and earn a secure income. Why is the dropout rate particularly high among Hispanic Americans?

College: The Silent Classroom

Passivity is also common among college and university students. Sociologists rarely study the college classroom—a curious fact, considering how much time they spend there. One exception was a study at a coeducational university where David Karp and William Yoels (1976) found that even in small classes, only a few students spoke up. Thus passivity seems to be a classroom norm, and students may even become irritated if one of their number is especially talkative.

According to Karp and Yoels, most students think classroom passivity is their own fault. Yet as anyone who observes young people *outside* class knows, they are usually active and vocal. Therefore, it is schools that teach students to be passive and to view instructors as experts who serve up "truth." Students find little value in classroom discussion and see their proper role as listening quietly and taking notes. As a result, the researchers estimate, just 10 percent of college class time is used for discussion.

Faculty can bring students to life in their classrooms by making use of four teaching strategies: (1) calling on students by name when they volunteer, (2) positively reinforcing student participation, (3) asking analytical rather than

factual questions and giving students time to answer, and (4) asking for student opinions even when no one volunteers a response (Auster & MacRone, 1994).

YOUR TURN

How many of your classes encourage active student discussion? Is participation more common in some disciplines than in others? Why?

DROPPING OUT

If many students are passive in class, others are not there at all. The problem of *dropping out*—quitting school before earning a high school diploma—leaves young people (many of whom are disadvantaged to begin with) unprepared for the world of work and at high risk of poverty.

The dropout rate has declined slightly in recent decades; currently 10.7 percent of people between the ages of sixteen and twenty-four have dropped out of school, a total of some 3.8 million young women and men. Dropping out is least pronounced among non-Hispanic whites (7.3 percent), higher among non-Hispanic African

May 24, 2005

The College Dropout Boom

By DAVID LEONHARDT

CHILHOWIE, Va.—One of the biggest decisions Andy Blevins has ever made ... never seemed like much of a decision at all. ...

In the summer of 1995, he was moving boxes of soup cans, paper towels and dog food across the floor of a supermarket warehouse. ... The job had sounded impossible when he arrived fresh off his first year of college. ...

But hard work done well was something he understood, even if he was the first college boy in his family. Soon he was making bonuses on top of his $6.75 an hour, more money than either of his parents made. His girlfriend was around, and so were his hometown buddies. ...

It was just about the perfect summer. ...

So he quit college ... and ... joined one of the largest and fastest-growing groups of young adults in America. He became a college dropout, though *nongraduate* may be the more precise term.

Many people like him plan to return to get their degrees, even if few actually do. Almost one in three Americans in their mid-20s now fall into this group, up from one in five in the late 1960s, when the Census Bureau began keeping such data. Most come from poor and working-class families.

The phenomenon has been largely overlooked in the glare of positive news about the country's gains in education. Going to college has become the norm throughout most of the United States. ... At elite universities, classrooms are filled with women, blacks, Jews and Latinos, groups largely excluded two generations ago. The American system of higher learning seems to have become a great equalizer.

In fact, though, colleges have come to reinforce many of the advantages of birth. On campuses that enroll poorer students, graduation rates are often low. ... Only 41 percent of low-income students entering a four-year college managed to graduate within five years, the Department of Education found in a study last year, but 66 percent of high-income students did. That gap had grown over recent years. ...

That loss of ground is all the more significant because a college education matters much more now than it once did. ... College graduates have received steady pay increases over the past two decades, while the pay of everyone else has risen little more than the rate of inflation.

As a result, despite one of the great education explosions in modern history, economic mobility ... has stopped rising, researchers say. Some recent studies suggest that it has declined over the last generation. ... Ten years after trading college for the warehouse, Mr. Blevins ... has worked his way up to produce buyer,

---

Americans (10.9 percent), and highest of all among Hispanics (27.0 percent) (National Center for Education Statistics, 2004).

Some students drop out because of problems with the English language, others because of pregnancy, and some because they must work to help support their family. The dropout rate (10.7 percent) among children growing up in the bottom 20 percent of households by income is more than six times as high as that (1.7 percent) for youngsters whose households fall in the top 20 percent (National Center for Education Statistics, 2004). These data suggest that many dropouts are young people whose parents also have little schooling, revealing a multigenerational cycle of disadvantage. "In the *Times*" shows how class position shapes the decision to leave college in the lives of many young people.

ACADEMIC STANDARDS

Perhaps the most serious educational issue confronting our society is the quality of schooling. *A Nation at Risk,* a comprehensive report on the quality of U.S. schools published in 1983 by the National Commission on Excellence in Education (NCEE), begins with this alarming statement:

> If an unfriendly foreign power had attempted to impose on America the mediocre educational performance that exists today, we might well have viewed it as an act of war. As it stands, we have allowed this to happen to ourselves. (1983:5)

Supporting this conclusion, the report notes that "nearly 40 percent of seventeen-year-olds cannot draw inferences from written material; only one-fifth can write a persuasive essay; and only one-third can solve mathematical

earning $35,000 a year with health benefits and a 401(k) plan. He is on a path typical for someone who attended college without getting a four-year degree. Men in their early 40s in this category made an average of $42,000 in 2000. Those with a four-year degree made $65,000. . . .

Mr. Blevins says he has many reasons to be happy. He lives with his wife, Karla, and their year-old son, Lucas, in a small blue-and-yellow house at the end of a cul-de-sac in the middle of a stunningly picturesque Appalachian valley. . . .

But he does think about what might have been. . . .

College degree or not, Mr. Blevins has the kind of life that many Americans say they aspire to. He fills it with family, friends, church and a five-handicap golf game. . . .

Mr. Blevins also sings in a quartet called the Gospel Gentlemen. . . .

On a still-dark February morning, with the winter's heaviest snowfall on the ground, Andy Blevins scraped off his Jeep and began his daily drive to the supermarket warehouse. As he passed the home of Mike Nash, his neighbor and fellow gospel singer, he noticed that the car was still in the driveway. For Mr. Nash, a school counselor and the only college graduate in the singing group, this was a snow day.

Mr. Blevins later sat down with his calendar and counted to 280: the number of days he had worked last year. Two hundred and eighty days—six days a week most of the time—without ever really knowing what the future would hold. . . .

So the decision was made. On May 31, Andy Blevins says, he will return to Virginia Highlands, taking classes at night. . . .

He thinks he can get his bachelor's degree in three years. If he gets it at all, he will have defied the odds.

Adapted from the original article by David Leonhardt published in *The New York Times* on May 24, 2005. Copyright © 2005 by The New York Times Company. Reprinted with permission.

problems requiring several steps" (NCEE, 1983:9). Furthermore, scores on the SAT show little improvement over time. In 1967, median scores for students were 516 on the mathematical test and 543 on the verbal test; by 2005, the average in mathematics had risen slightly to 520, and the verbal average had slipped to just 508. Nationwide, one-third of high school students—and more than half in urban schools—fail to master even the basics in reading, math, and science on the National Assessment of Educational Progress examination (Marklein, 2000; Barnes, 2002a).

For many, even basic literacy is at issue. **Functional illiteracy,** *a lack of the reading and writing skills needed for everyday living,* is a problem for one in eight children who leave secondary school in the United States. For older people, the problem is even worse: Overall, some 40 million U.S. adults (about 20 percent of the total) read and write at an eighth-grade level or below. The extent of functional illiteracy in the United States is below that of middle-income nations (such as Poland) but higher than in other high-income countries (such as Canada or the countries of Europe).

A Nation at Risk recommended drastic reform. First, it called for schools to require *all* students to complete several years of English, mathematics, social studies, general science, and computer science. Second, schools should not promote students until they meet achievement standards. Third, teacher training must improve, and teachers' salaries must be raised to draw talent into the profession. The report concluded that schools must meet public expectations and that citizens must be prepared to pay for a job well done.

STUDENT SNAPSHOT

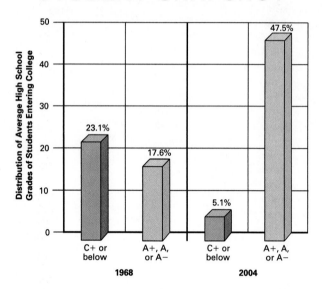

FIGURE 20–4 Grade Inflation in U.S. High Schools

In recent decades, teachers have given higher and higher grades to students.

Source: Sax et al. (2004).

What has happened in the years since this report was issued? In some respects, schools have improved. A report by the Center on Education Policy (2000) noted a decline in the dropout rate, a trend toward schools' offering more challenging courses, and a larger share of high school graduates going to college. Despite several tragic cases of shootings, school violence overall was down during the 1990s. At the same time, the evidence suggests that a majority of elementary school students are falling below standards in reading; in many cases, they can't read at all. In short, although some improvement is evident, much remains to be done.

The United States spends more on schooling its children than almost any other country. Even so, U.S. eighth-graders place seventeenth in the world in science achievement and twenty-eighth in mathematics (Bennett, 1997; Finn & Walberg, 1998). Cultural values play a big part in how well students perform. For example, U.S. students are generally less motivated and do less homework than students in Japan. Japanese young people also spend sixty more days in school each year than U.S. students. Perhaps one approach to improving schools is simply to have students spend more time there.

→   YOUR TURN   ←

Recall that U.S. students spend only about 13 percent of their waking hours in school. Do you think they should spend more time in school? Explain your answer.

GRADE INFLATION

Academic standards depend on using grades that have clear meaning and are awarded for work of appropriate quality. Yet recent decades have seen substantial *grade inflation,* the awarding of higher and higher grades for average work. Though not necessarily found in every school, grade inflation is evident in both high schools and colleges.

One recent study of high school grades shows how dramatic the change has been. In 1968, as Figure 20–4 shows, the high school records of students who had just entered college included more grades of C+ and below than grades of A-, A, and A+. By 2004, however, these A grades outnumbered grades of C+ and below by nine to one (Sax et al., 2004).

A few colleges and universities have enacted policies that limit the share of A's (generally to one-third of all grades). But there is little evidence that grade inflation will slow down anytime soon. As a result, the C grade (which used to mean "average") may all but disappear, making every student "above average."

What accounts for grade inflation? In part, today's teachers are concerned about the morale and self-esteem of their students and are not as "tough" as they used to be. At the same time, however, the ever more competitive process of getting into college and graduate school puts increasing pressure on high schools and colleges to award high grades (Astin et al., 2002).

Recent Issues in U.S. Education

Our society's schools continuously confront new challenges. This section explores several recent and important educational issues.

SCHOOL CHOICE

Some analysts claim that our public schools teach poorly because they have no competition. Giving parents options about schooling their children might force all schools to do a better job. This is the essence of a policy called *school choice.*

Charter schools are public schools that are given the freedom to try out new policies and programs, often with good results. In this Los Angeles charter school, teacher and students benefit from the latest in computer technology.

The goal of school choice is to create a market for schooling so that parents and students can shop for the best value. According to one proposal, the government would give vouchers to families with school-age children and allow them to spend that money at public, private, or parochial schools. In recent years, major cities, including Indianapolis, Minneapolis, Milwaukee, Cleveland, Chicago, and Washington, D.C., as well as the states of Florida and Illinois, have experimented with choice plans aimed at making public schools perform better to win the confidence of families. In addition, the Children's Scholarship Fund, a privately funded charity, has supported 40,000 children who wish to attend nonpublic schools and has more than 1 million children on its waiting list (M. Lord, 2002).

Supporters claim that giving parents a choice about where to enroll their children is the only sure way to improve all schools. But critics charge that school choice amounts to giving up on our nation's commitment to public education and that it will do little to improve schools in central cities, where the need is greatest (A. Cohen, 1999; Morse, 2002b).

In 2002, President George W. Bush signed a new education bill that downplayed vouchers in favor of another approach to greater choice. Starting in the 2005–06 school year, all public schools must test every child in reading, mathematics, and science in grades three through eight. Although the federal government may provide more aid to schools where students do not perform well, if those schools do not show improvements in test scores over a period of time, their students will have the choice of either special tutoring or transportation to another school (Lindlaw, 2002).

A more modest type of school choice involves *magnet schools,* 3,000 of which now exist across the country. Magnet schools offer special facilities and programs that promote educational excellence in a particular field, such as computer science, foreign languages, science and mathematics, or the arts. In school districts with magnet schools, parents can choose the school best suited to their child's particular talents and interests.

Another school choice strategy involves *charter schools,* public schools that are given more freedom to try out new policies and programs. There are about 3,500 such schools in forty states, Washington, D.C., and Puerto Rico; they enroll more than 1 million students, about half of whom are minorities. In many of these schools, students have demonstrated high academic achievement—a requirement for renewal of the charter (U.S. Charter Schools, 2005).

A final development in the school choice movement is *schooling for profit.* Advocates of this plan say that school systems can be operated by private profit-making companies more efficiently than by local governments. Private schooling is nothing new, of course; more than 27,000 schools in the United States are currently run by private organizations and religious groups. What is new is that hundreds of public schools, enrolling hundreds of thousands of students, are now run by private businesses for profit.

and against privately run public schools—run high, and each side claims it speaks for the well-being of those caught in the middle: the schoolchildren (Caruso, 2002; McGurn, 2002; Winters, 2002).

HOME SCHOOLING

Home schooling is gaining popularity across the United States. About 1.1 million children (more than 2 percent of all school-age children) have their formal schooling at home. This means that home schooling involves more school-age children than magnet schools, charter schools, and for-profit schools combined.

Why do parents undertake the enormous challenge of schooling their own children? Some twenty years ago, most of the parents who pioneered home schooling (which is now legal in every state) did so in order to give their children a strongly religious upbringing. Today, however, many are mothers and fathers who simply do not believe that public schools are doing a good job and who think they can do better. To benefit their children, they are willing to alter work schedules and relearn algebra or other necessary subjects. Many belong to groups in which parents pool their efforts, specializing in what each knows best.

Advocates of home schooling point out that given the poor performance of many public schools, no one should be surprised that a growing number of parents are willing to step in to teach their own children. In addition, this system works—on average, students who learn at home outperform those who learn in school. Critics argue that home schooling reduces the amount of funding going to local public schools, which ends up hurting the majority of students. As one critic adds, home schooling "takes some of the most affluent and articulate parents out of the system. These are the parents who know how to get things done with administrators" (Chris Lubienski, quoted in Cloud & Morse, 2001:48).

SCHOOLING PEOPLE WITH DISABILITIES

Many of the 5 million children with disabilities in the United States face special challenges getting to and from school; once there, many with crutches or wheelchairs cannot negotiate stairs and other obstacles inside school buildings. Other children with developmental disabilities such as mental retardation require extensive personal attention from specially trained teachers. Because of these challenges, many children with mental and physical disabilities have received a public education only after persistent efforts by parents and other concerned citizens (Horn & Tynan, 2001).

Educators have long debated the best way to teach children with disabilities. On one hand, such children may benefit from separate facilities staffed by specially trained teachers. On the other hand, children are less likely to be stigmatized as "different" if they are included in regular classrooms. One way to "mainstream" children with special needs is to provide them with teaching assistants who offer the help they need throughout the day.

Research confirms that many public school systems suffer from bureaucratic bloat, spending too much and teaching too little. And our society has long looked to competition to improve quality. Evidence suggests that for-profit schools have greatly reduced administrative costs, but the educational results appear mixed. Although several companies claim to have improved student learning, some cities have cut back on business-run schools. In recent years, school boards in Baltimore, Miami, Hartford, and Boston have canceled the contracts of for-profit schooling corporations. But other cities are deciding to give for-profit schooling a try. For example, after Philadelphia's public school system failed to graduate one-third of its students, the state of Pennsylvania took over that city's schools and has recently turned over most of them to for-profit companies. Emotions—both for

About half of all children with disabilities are schooled in special facilities; the rest attend public schools, many in regular classes. Most schools avoid expensive "special education" in favor of **mainstreaming**, *integrating students with disabilities or special needs into the overall educational program*. Mainstreaming is a form of *inclusive education* that works best for physically impaired students who have no difficulty keeping up academically with the rest of the class. A benefit of putting children with and without disabilities in the same classroom is allowing everyone to learn to interact with people who are different from themselves.

ADULT EDUCATION

In 2000, more than 88 million U.S. adults over age twenty-five were enrolled in some type of schooling. These older students range in age from the mid-twenties to the seventies and beyond. From another angle, they make up 21 percent of students in degree-granting programs. Adults in school are more likely to be women than men, and most have above-average incomes.

Why do adults return to the classroom? The most obvious reasons given are to advance a career or train for a new job (66 percent), but many (43 percent) also point to the simple goal of personal enrichment (U.S. Census Bureau, 2004).

THE TEACHER SHORTAGE

A major challenge for U.S. schools is hiring enough teachers to fill the classrooms. A number of factors—including low salaries, frustration, and retirement, as well as rising enrollment and a reduction in class size—have combined to create more than 200,000 teaching vacancies in the United States each year.

How will these slots be filled? About the same number of people graduate with education degrees annually. Most of them do not have a degree in a specific academic area, such as mathematics, biology, or English, and many have trouble passing state certification tests in the area they wish to teach.

As a result, schools have adopted new recruitment strategies. Some analysts suggest that community colleges could play a larger role in teacher education. Others support using incentives such as higher salaries and signing bonuses to attract people who have already established successful careers. In addition, states could make teaching certification easier to get. Finally, many school districts are going global—actively recruiting in countries such as Spain, India, and the Philippines to bring talented women and men from around the world to U.S. classrooms (M. Lord, 2001; Philadelphia, 2001; Evelyn, 2002).

YOUR TURN

Have you considered a career in teaching? If so, why? If not, what could be done to make the field more appealing to you?

The debates about education in the United States extend beyond the issues noted here. The Applying Sociology box on page 546 highlights the declining share of male students on college campuses.

Schooling: Looking Ahead

Although the United States still leads the world in sending people to college, the public school system continues to struggle with serious problems. In terms of quality of schooling, this country has fallen well behind many other high-income nations, a fact that calls into question the future strength of the United States on the world stage.

Many of the problems of schooling discussed in this chapter have their roots in the larger society. We cannot expect schools *by themselves* to provide high-quality education. Schools will improve only to the extent that students, teachers, parents, and local communities commit themselves to educational excellence. In short, educational dilemmas are *social* problems, and there is no quick fix.

For much of the twentieth century, there were just two models for education in the United States: public schools run by the government and private schools operated by nongovernmental organizations. In the last decade, however, many new ideas about schooling have come on the scene, including schooling for profit and a wide range of "choice" programs. In the decades ahead, we are likely to see some significant changes in mass education, guided in part by social science research pointing out the consequences of different strategies.

Another factor that will continue to reshape schools is new information technology. Today, all but the poorest primary and secondary schools use computers for instruction. Computers prompt students to be more active and allow them to progress at their own pace. For students with disabilities who cannot write using a pencil, computers permit easier self-expression.

Even so, computers will never bring to the educational process the personal insight or imagination of a motivated human teacher. Nor can computers tap what one teacher calls the "springs of human identity and creativity" that we discover by exploring literature and language rather than

APPLYING SOCIOLOGY
The Twenty-First-Century Campus: Where Are the Men?

A century ago, the campuses of colleges and universities across the United States might as well have hung out a sign that read "Men Only." Almost all of the students and faculty were male. There were a small number of women's colleges, but many more schools—including some of the best-known U.S. universities such as Yale, Harvard, and Princeton—barred women outright.

Since then, women have won greater social equality. By 1980, the number of women enrolled at U.S. colleges finally matched the number of men.

In a surprising turn of events, the share of women on campus has continued to increase. As a result, in 2001, men accounted for only 44 percent of all U.S. undergraduates. Meg DeLong noticed the gender imbalance right away when she moved into her dorm at the University of Georgia at Athens; she soon learned that just 39 percent of her first-year class-mates were men. In some classes, there were few men, and women usually dominated discussions. Out of class, DeLong and many other women soon complained that having so few men on campus hurt their social life. Not surprisingly, most of the men felt otherwise (Fonda, 2000).

What accounts for the shifting gender balance on U.S.

campuses? One theory is that young men are drawn away from college by the lure of jobs, especially in computer science and high technology. This pattern is sometimes termed the "Bill Gates syndrome," after the Microsoft founder, who dropped out of college and soon became the world's richest person. In addition, analysts point to an anti-intellectual male culture. Young women are drawn to learning and seek to do well in school, but young men attach less importance to studying and dismiss schoolwork as "something for girls." Rightly or wrongly, more men seem to think they can get a good job without investing years of their lives and a considerable amount of money in getting a college degree.

The gender gap is evident in all racial and ethnic categories and at all class levels. Among African Americans on campus, only 36 percent are men.

The lower the income level, the greater the gender gap in college attendance.

Many college officials are concerned about this trend. In an effort to attract more balanced enrollments, some colleges are adopting what amounts to affirmative action programs that favor males. But courts in several states have already ruled such policies illegal. Many colleges, therefore, are turning to more active recruitment; admissions officers are paying special attention to male applicants and stressing a college's strength in mathematics and science—areas that traditionally have attracted men. In the same way that colleges across the country are striving to increase their share of minority students, the hope is that they can also succeed in attracting a larger share of men.

WHAT DO YOU THINK?

1. Among high school students, are men less concerned than women about academic achievement? Why or why not?
2. Is there a gender imbalance on your campus? Does it create problems? What problems? For whom?
3. What programs or policies do you think might increase the number of men going to college?

simply manipulating mathematical codes. Despite the growing number of computers in the classroom, these machines have yet to change teaching and learning in any fundamental sense or even to replace the traditional writing on the blackboard. Nor will technology ever solve the problems—including violence and rigid bureaucracy—that plague our schools. What we need is a broad plan for social change that renews this country's early ambition to provide high-quality universal schooling, a goal that has so far eluded us.

The following learning tools will help you see what you know, identify what you still need to learn, and expand your understanding beyond the text. You can also visit the text's Companion Website™ at http://www.prenhall.com/macionis to find additional practice tests.

KEY POINTS

Education: A Global Survey

Education is the major social institution for transmitting knowledge and skills, as well as teaching cultural norms and values. In preindustrial societies, education occurs informally within the family; industrial societies develop formal systems of schooling to educate their children. The United States was among the first countries to undertake compulsory mass education, reflecting both democratic political ideals and the needs of the industrial-capitalist economy.

The Functions of Schooling

Structural-functional analysis highlights major functions of schooling, including socialization, cultural innovation, social integration, and the placement of people in the social hierarchy. Latent functions of schooling include providing child care and building social networks.

Schooling and Social Interaction

The symbolic-interaction approach helps us understand that stereotypes can have important consequences for how people act. If students think they are academically superior, they are likely to perform better; students who think they are inferior are likely to perform less well.

Schooling and Social Inequality

Social-conflict analysis links schooling to the hierarchy involving class, race, and gender. Formal education also serves as a means of generating conformity to produce obedient adult workers. The use of standardized achievement tests is controversial. Some people see them as a reasonable measure of academic aptitude and learning, but others say they are culturally biased tools that may lead to labeling less privileged students as personally deficient.

Tracking is another controversial issue. Some people see tracking as a way to provide appropriate instruction for students with different interests and aptitudes; others say that tracking gives privileged youngsters a richer education.

The great majority of young people in the United States attend state-funded public schools. Most private schools offer a religious education. A small proportion of students—usually the most well-to-do—attend elite private preparatory schools.

Problems in the Schools

Most adults in the United States are critical of public schools. Violence permeates many schools, especially those in poor neighborhoods. The bureaucratic character of schools also fosters high dropout rates and student passivity.

Declining academic standards are reflected in today's lower average scores on achievement tests, the functional illiteracy of a significant proportion of high school graduates, and grade inflation.

Recent Issues in U.S. Education

The school choice movement seeks to make schools more responsive to the public. Innovative options include magnet schools, schooling for profit, and charter schools, all of which are topics of continuing policy debate. In addition, an increasing number of parents now choose to school their children at home.

Historically, children with mental or physical disabilities were schooled in special classes. Mainstreaming affords them broader opportunities and exposes all children to a more diverse student population.

Adults represent a growing proportion of college students in the United States. Most older learners are women who are engaged in job-related study.

Schooling: Looking Ahead

Students in the United States lag behind those of other high-income nations in academic performance. But because the problems of our schools have their roots in the larger society, improvement will require a national commitment.

The Information Revolution is changing the way we learn, and schools now make widespread use of computers. Although these machines permit interactive, self-paced learning, they are important tools but not solutions to many educational problems in the United States.

KEY CONCEPTS

education (p. 526) the social institution through which society provides its members with important knowledge, including basic facts, job skills, and cultural norms and values

schooling (p. 526) formal instruction under the direction of specially trained teachers

tracking (p. 532) assigning students to different types of educational programs

functional illiteracy (p. 541) a lack of the reading and writing skills needed for everyday living

mainstreaming (p. 545) integrating students with disabilities or special needs into the overall educational program

SAMPLE TEST QUESTIONS

These questions are similar to those found in the test bank that accompanies this textbook.

Multiple-Choice Questions

1. In the United States and in other countries, laws requiring all children to attend school were enacted following
   a. national independence.
   b. the Industrial Revolution.
   c. World War II.
   d. the computer age.

2. Japan differs from the United States in that getting into college depends more on
   a. athletic ability.
   b. race and ethnicity.
   c. family money.
   d. scores on achievement tests.

3. What share of the U.S. adult population has completed high school?
   a. 45 percent
   b. 65 percent
   c. 85 percent
   d. 99 percent

4. Using a structural-functional approach, schooling carries out the task of
   a. tying together a diverse population.
   b. creating new culture.
   c. socializing young people.
   d. all of the above.

5. A social-conflict approach highlights how education
   a. reflects and reinforces social inequality.
   b. helps prepare students for their future careers.
   c. has both latent and manifest functions.
   d. all of the above.

6. The importance of community colleges to U.S. higher education is reflected in the fact that they
   a. greatly expand the opportunity to attend college.
   b. enroll almost 40 percent of all U.S. college students.
   c. enroll half of all African American and Hispanic college students.
   d. all of the above.

7. What share of people in the United States between age sixteen and twenty-four drop out before completing high school?
   a. 1 percent
   b. 11 percent
   c. 21 percent
   d. 31 percent

8. Support for the school choice movement is based on the claim that U.S. public schools perform poorly because
   a. they have no competition.
   b. many schools lack enough funding.
   c. of a high national poverty rate.
   d. too many parents are not involved in the schools.

9. This chapter provides lots of evidence to support the claim that
   a. U.S. schools are better than those in other high-income nations.
   b. most public schools perform well; most private schools do not.
   c. without involving the entire society, schools cannot improve the quality of education.
   d. all of the above.

10. About what share of all U.S. college students today are men?
   a. 64 percent
   b. 54 percent
   c. 44 percent
   d. 34 percent

ANSWERS: 1(b); 2(d); 3(c); 4(d); 5(d); 6(a); 7(b); 8(a); 9(c); 10(c).

Essay Questions

1. Why does industrialization lead societies to expand their systems of schooling? In what ways has schooling in the United States been shaped by our economic, political, and cultural systems?

2. From a structural-functional perspective, why is schooling important to the operation of society? From a social-conflict point of view, how does schooling reproduce social inequality in each generation?

APPLICATIONS & EXERCISES

1. Make a visit to a secondary school near your college or home. Does it have a tracking policy? If so, find out how it works. How much importance does a student's social background have in making a tracking assignment?

2. Most people agree that teaching our children is important work. Yet teachers earn relatively low salaries. Check the prestige ranking for teachers in Table 11–2 on page 283. See what you can learn about the average salaries of teachers in your community, and compare it to the pay of other workers. Do you think teachers are paid enough?

3. Since the passage of the Americans with Disabilities Act of 1990, schools have tried to "accommodate" students with a broader range of physical and mental disabilities. Talk to officials on your campus about policies at your school and how laws of this kind are changing education.

INVESTIGATE *with* Research Navigator

Follow the instructions on page 27 of this text to access the features of **Research Navigator**™. Once at the Web site, enter your Login Name and Password. Then, to use the **ContentSelect**™ database, enter keywords such as "tracking," "illiteracy," and "school choice," and the search engine will supply relevant and recent scholarly and popular press publications. Use the *New York Times* **Search-by-Subject Archive** to find recent news articles related to sociology and the **Link Library** feature to find relevant Web links organized by the key terms associated with this chapter.

21

CHAPTER TWENTY-ONE

Health and Medicine

How is health a social issue?

What categories of the U.S. population
have the best health?

Why is there an obesity epidemic
in the United States?

Krista Peters says she cannot remember a time in her life when she was not on a diet. The sixteen-year-old, who lives in a small Pennsylvania town, shakes her head. "It's, like, I can't do anything about it. I know I don't look good. My mom says I shouldn't eat so much; the nurse at school says the same thing. But if it's up to me, then why can't I ever lose any weight?"

Peters does have a weight problem. Although she stands just 5 feet 2 inches tall, she weighs 240 pounds. Doctors would call her seriously obese, and the longer she remains so heavy, the greater her odds of serious disease and even death at a young age.

Krista Peters is not alone. In a society where fast food has become something of a national dish and people use the word "supersize" as a verb, people all across the United States are getting fat. Not some people—*most* people. According to the experts, about two-thirds of U.S. adults are overweight.

Being overweight is not just a matter of looks. It is a serious health issue. People like Krista Peters are at high risk for heart disease, stroke, and diabetes. Each year, about 300,000 people in the United States die early from diseases related to being overweight.

It is easy to dismiss being overweight as a personal flaw. The choices we make do matter, but we are up against some powerful cultural forces. Consider the fact that the U.S. population is confronted with unhealthy fast food at every turn. Our national consumption of potato chips and other salty snacks, sugar-rich soft drinks, pizza, and candy bars rises every year. One reason that car companies and airlines have had to make seats bigger is to fit more and more "supersized" people (Bellandi, 2003; Cullen, 2003; Witt, 2004). ■

What Is Health?

The World Health Organization defines **health** as *a state of complete physical, mental, and social well-being* (1946:3).

MEDIA Learn more about the World Health Organization at http://www.who.int/en/

This definition underscores the major theme of this chapter: Health is not just a matter of personal choice, nor it is only a biological issue; patterns of well-being and illness are rooted in the organization of society.

HEALTH AND SOCIETY

Society shapes people's health in four major ways:

1. **Cultural patterns define health.** Standards of health vary from place to place. A century ago, yaws, a contagious skin disease, was so common in sub-Saharan Africa that people there considered it normal (Dubos, 1980). In the United States, a rich diet is so common that most adults and about one-fourth of children are overweight. "Health," therefore, is sometimes a matter of having the same disease as your neighbors (Pinhey, Rubinstein, & Colfax, 1997).

   What people see as healthful also reflects what they think is morally good. Members of our society (especially men) think a competitive way of life is "healthy" because it fits our cultural mores, but stress contributes to heart disease and many other illnesses. People who object to homosexuality on moral grounds call this sexual orientation "sick," even though it is natural from a biological point of view. Thus ideas about health act as a form of social control, encouraging conformity to cultural norms.

2. **Cultural standards of health change over time.** In the early twentieth century, some doctors warned women not to go to college because higher education strained the female brain. Others claimed that masturbation was a threat to health. We know now that both of these ideas are false. Fifty years ago, on the other hand, few doctors understood the dangers of cigarette smoking or too much sun exposure, practices that we now recognize as serious health risks. Even patterns of basic hygiene change over time. Today, 75 percent of U.S. adults report bathing every day; back in 1950, only 30 percent said the same (Gallup, 2000).

3. **A society's technology affects people's health.** As shown in Table 21–1, the three leading causes of death in the United States a century ago were all contagious diseases. Today, improved living standards and advancements in medical technology have sharply reduced the number of deaths from such diseases.

   The poor sanitation and inadequate medical resources in poor societies today is an important reason that infectious diseases are common in these countries. Industrialization does raise living standards and improve health. But industrial technology also creates new health threats. As Chapter 22 ("Population, Urbanization, and Environment") explains, high-income ways of life threaten human health by overtaxing the world's resources and creating pollution.

4. **Social inequality affects people's health.** All societies distribute resources unequally. Overall, the rich have far better physical and mental health than the poor.

Health: A Global Survey

We see the close link between health and social life in the fact that human well-being improved over the long course of history as societies developed more advanced technology. Differences in societal development are also the cause of striking differences in health around the world today.

HEALTH IN HISTORY

With only simple technology, our ancestors could do little to improve health. Hunters and gatherers faced frequent food shortages, which sometimes forced mothers to abandon their children. Those lucky enough to survive infancy were still vulnerable to injury and illness, so half died by the age of twenty and few lived to the age of forty (Scupin, 2000; Nolan & Lenski, 2004).

As societies developed agriculture, food became more plentiful. Yet social inequality also increased, so the elites enjoyed better health than the peasants and slaves, who

TABLE 21–1

Leading Causes of Death in the United States, 1900 and 2003

1900	2003
1. Influenza and pneumonia	1. Heart disease
2. Tuberculosis	2. Cancer
3. Stomach and intestinal disease	3. Stroke
4. Heart disease	4. Lung disease (noncancerous)
5. Cerebral hemorrhage	5. Accidents
6. Kidney disease	6. Diabetes
7. Accidents	7. Influenza and pneumonia
8. Cancer	8. Alzheimer's disease
9. Disease in early infancy	9. Kidney disease
10. Diphtheria	10. Blood disease

Sources: Information for 1900 is from William C. Cockerham, *Medical Sociology*, 2d ed. (Englewood Cliffs, N.J.: Prentice Hall, 1986), p. 24; information for 2003 is from Donna L. Hoyert, Hsiang-Ching Kung, & Betty L. Smith, *National Vital Statistics Reports*, vol. 53, no. 15 (Hyattsville, Md.: National Center for Health Statistics, 2005).

lived in crowded, unsanitary shelters and often went hungry. In the growing cities of medieval Europe, human waste and other refuse piled up in the streets, spreading infectious diseases, and plagues periodically wiped out entire towns (Mumford, 1961).

HEALTH IN LOW-INCOME COUNTRIES

December 25, Yucay, Peru. We're attending the Christmas Day street festival in this small village in the Andes Mountains. There is much excitement and happiness everywhere. Oddly, perhaps, I notice that not one of the hundreds of people who have passed by along the main street is wearing glasses. One Peruvian friend says that in this poor community, there are no optometrists or eye doctors, and no one has any extra money to afford glasses.

In much of the world, severe poverty cuts decades off the life expectancy enjoyed in rich countries. A look back at Global Map 15–1, on page 400, shows that people in most parts of Africa have a life expectancy of barely fifty, and in the poorest countries, most people die before reaching their teens.

The World Health Organization reports that 1 billion people around the world—about one person in six—suffer from serious illness due to poverty. Bad health can result both from eating a single type of food and, more commonly,

Average health varies from place to place throughout the United States. This map shows the results of a survey that asked people across the country about their personal health, including their smoking habits, nutritional diet, and frequency of illness. Looking at the map, what pattern do you see? Can you explain it?

Source: *American Demographics*, October 2000, p. 50. Reprinted with permission from *American Demographics*. © 2004 by Crain Communications, Inc.

Quality of Health
- Very good/Excellent
- Good
- Fair
- Poor

from simply having too little to eat. Malnutrition kills people of all ages, especially children.

In low-income countries, sanitation is also a killer. Safe drinking water is as hard to come by as a balanced diet, and bad water carries a number of infectious diseases, including influenza, pneumonia, and tuberculosis, which are widespread killers in poor societies today. To make matters worse, medical personnel are few and far between; as a result, the world's poorest people—many of whom live in Central Africa—never see a physician.

In poor nations with minimal medical care, it is no wonder that 10 percent of children die within a year of their birth. In some countries, half the children never reach adulthood. For those who do grow up, illness and poverty form a vicious circle: Poverty breeds disease, which in turn undermines the ability to work. When medical technology does control infectious disease, the populations of poor nations rise. Without resources to ensure the well-being of the people they have now, poor societies can ill afford population increases. Therefore, programs that lower death rates in poor countries will succeed only if they are coupled with programs that reduce birth rates.

HEALTH IN HIGH-INCOME COUNTRIES

By 1800, as the Industrial Revolution took hold, factory jobs in the cities attracted people from all over the countryside. Cities quickly became overcrowded, a condition creating serious sanitation problems. Factories fouled the air with smoke, which few recognized as a health threat until well into the twentieth century. Accidents in the workplace were common.

Industrialization gradually improved health in Western Europe and North America by providing better nutrition and safer housing for most people. After 1850, medical advances began to control infectious diseases. In 1854, for example, Dr. John Snow mapped the street addresses of London's cholera victims and found they all had drunk contaminated water from the same well. Not long afterward, scientists linked cholera to a specific bacterium and developed a vaccine against the deadly disease. Armed with scientific knowledge, early environmentalists campaigned against age-old practices such as discharging raw sewage into the same rivers used for drinking water. By the early twentieth century, death rates from infectious diseases had fallen sharply.

A glance back at Table 21–1 shows that the leading killers in 1900—influenza and pneumonia—account for just a small percentage of deaths today in high-income countries such as the United States. It is now chronic illnesses, such as heart disease, cancer, and stroke, that cause most deaths, usually in old age.

Health in the United States

Because the United States is a rich nation, health is generally good by world standards. Still, some categories of people are better off than others.

WHO IS HEALTHY? AGE, GENDER, CLASS, AND RACE

Social epidemiology is *the study of how health and disease are distributed throughout a society's population.* Just as early

Masculinity: A Threat to Health?

Doctors call it "coronary-prone behavior." Psychologists call it the "Type A personality." Almost everyone recognizes it as our culture's concept of masculinity. This combination of attitudes and behavior, common among men in our society, includes (1) chronic impatience ("C'mon! Get outta my way!"), (2) uncontrolled ambition ("I've gotta have it . . . I *need* that!"), and (3) free-floating hostility ("Why are so many people *such idiots?*").

This pattern, although normal from a cultural point of view, is one major reason that men who are driven to succeed are at high risk of heart disease. By acting out the Type A personality, we may get the job done, but we set in motion complex biochemical processes that are very hard on the human heart.

Here are a few questions to help you assess your own degree of risk (or that of someone important to you):

1. **Do you believe you have to be aggressive to succeed?** Do "nice guys finish last"? If your answer to this question is yes, for your heart's sake, try to remove hostility from your life.

One starting point: Eliminate profanity from your speech. Try replacing aggression with compassion, which can be surprisingly effective in dealing with other people. Medically speaking, compassion and humor—rather than irritation and aggravation—will improve your health.

2. **How well do you handle uncertainty and opposition?** Do you have moments when you fume "Why won't the waiter take my order?" or "This customer just doesn't get it!"? We all like to know what's going on, and we like others to agree with us. But the world often doesn't work this way. Accepting uncertainty and

opposition makes us more mature and certainly healthier.

3. **Are you uncomfortable showing positive emotions?** Many men think giving and accepting love—from women, from children, and from other men—is a sign of weakness. But the medical truth is that love supports health and anger damages it.

As human beings, we have a great deal of choice about how to live. Think about the choices you make, and reflect on how our society's idea of masculinity often makes us hard on others (including those we love) and—just as important—hard on ourselves.

WHAT DO YOU THINK?

1. Does masculinity have to be harmful to health? Explain.
2. Why do you think so many people are unaware that our culture's definition of masculinity can be dangerous to our health?
3. How can sociology play a part in changing men's behavior for the better?

Sources: Based on Friedman & Rosenman (1974) and M.P. Levine (1990).

social epidemiologists traced the spread of epidemic diseases, researchers today examine the connection between health and our physical and social environments. National Map 21–1 surveys the health of the population of the United States, where there is a twenty-year difference in average life expectancy between the richest and poorest communities. Patterns of health can be viewed in terms of age, gender, social class, and race.

For information on nutrition and health, go to http://www.nal.usda.gov/fnic/etext/000056.html

Age and Gender

Death is now rare among young people. Still, young people do fall victim to accidents and, more recently, to acquired immune deficiency syndrome (AIDS).

Across the life course, women have better health than men. First, girls are less likely than boys to die before or immediately after birth. Then, as socialization begins, males become more aggressive and individualistic, which contributes to their higher rates of accidents, violence, and suicide. As the Applying Sociology box explains, the combination

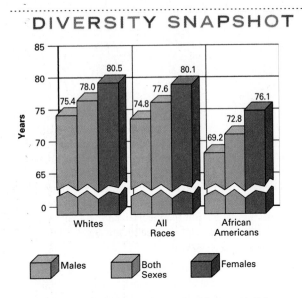

DIVERSITY SNAPSHOT

FIGURE 21–1 Life Expectancy of U.S. Children Born in 2003

Both gender and race have a powerful effect on life expectancy.

Source: Hoyert, Kung, & Smith (2005).

of chronic impatience, uncontrolled ambition, and frequent outbursts of hostility that doctors call "coronary-prone behavior" is a fairly close match with our culture's definition of masculinity.

Social Class and Race

Infant mortality—the death rate among children under one year of age—is twice as high for disadvantaged children as for children born into privileged families. Although the health of the richest children in our nation is the best in the world, our poorest children are as vulnerable to disease as those in low-income nations such as Nigeria and Vietnam.

Researchers tell us that 72 percent of adults in families with incomes over $35,000 think their health is excellent or very good, but only 46 percent of adults in families earning less than $20,000 say the same. Conversely, only about 6 percent of higher-income people describe their health as fair or poor, compared with 25 percent of low-income people. Having a higher income and greater wealth boosts people's health by improving their nutrition, enabling them to receive better health care, and allowing them to live in safer and less stressful surroundings (Krueger et al., 2003; Lethbridge-Cejku & Vickerie, 2005).

Poverty among African Americans—at three times the white rate—helps explain why black people are more likely to die in infancy and, as adults, are more likely to suffer the effects of violence, drug abuse, and poor health (Hayward et al., 2000). Figure 21–1 shows that the life expectancy of white children born in 2003 is five years greater than that of African Americans (78.0 years compared to 72.8). Gender is an even stronger predictor of health than race, since African American women outlive men of either race. From another angle, 80 percent of white men—but just 66 percent of African American men—live to age sixty-five. The comparable figures for women are 88 percent for whites and 79 percent for African Americans.

CIGARETTE SMOKING

Cigarette smoking tops the list of preventable hazards to health. Only after World War I did smoking become popular in this country. Despite growing evidence of its dangers, smoking remained fashionable even a generation ago. Today, however, an increasing number of people consider smoking a mild form of social deviance.

The popularity of cigarettes peaked in 1960, when 45 percent of U.S. adults smoked. By 2003, only 22 percent were still lighting up (Centers for Disease Control and Prevention, 2005). Quitting is difficult because cigarette smoke contains nicotine, a physically addictive drug. Many people smoke to cope with stress: Divorced and separated people are likely to smoke, as are lower-income people, the unemployed, and people serving in the armed forces. A larger share of men (24 percent) than women (19 percent) smoke. But cigarettes, the only form of tobacco popular with women, have taken a toll on women's health. By 1987, lung cancer surpassed breast cancer as a cause of death among U.S. women, who now account for 41 percent of all smoking-related deaths (Center for Disease Control and Prevention, 2005).

Some 440,000 men and women in the United States die prematurely each year as a direct result of cigarette smoking, a figure that exceeds the death toll from alcohol, cocaine, heroin, homicide, suicide, automobile accidents, and AIDS combined (Centers for Disease Control and Prevention, 2005). Smokers also suffer more frequent minor illnesses such as the flu, and pregnant women who smoke increase the likelihood of spontaneous abortion and low-birthweight babies. Even nonsmokers exposed to cigarette smoke have a higher risk of smoking-related diseases.

Tobacco is an $83 billion industry in the United States. In 1997, the tobacco industry admitted that cigarette smoking is harmful to health and agreed to stop marketing cigarettes to young people. Despite the antismoking trend in the United States, the percentage of college students who smoke has been creeping up, to 29 percent in 2001 (Centers for Disease Control and Prevention, 2002). In addition, the use of chewing tobacco—known to cause cancers of the mouth and throat—is increasing among the young.

The tobacco industry has increased its sales abroad, especially in low-income countries where there is less regulation of tobacco products. In many countries, especially in Asia, a large majority of men smoke. Worldwide, more than 1 billion adults (about 30 percent of the total) smoke, consuming some 6 trillion cigarettes annually, and smoking is on the rise. The good news is that about ten years after quitting, an ex-smoker's health is about as good as that of someone who never smoked at all.

YOUR TURN

Researchers report that the less schooling people have, the more likely they are to smoke. Why do you think this is the case?

EATING DISORDERS

An **eating disorder** is *an intense form of dieting or other unhealthy method of weight control driven by the desire to be very thin.* One eating disorder, anorexia nervosa, is characterized by dieting to the point of starvation; another is bulimia, which involves binge eating followed by induced vomiting to avoid weight gain.

Eating disorders have a significant cultural component; 95 percent of people who suffer from anorexia nervosa or bulimia are women, mostly from affluent white families. For women, U.S. culture equates slenderness with being successful and attractive to men. Conversely, we tend to stereotype overweight women (and, to a lesser extent, men) as lazy, sloppy, and even stupid (M. P. Levine, 1987).

Research shows that most college-age women believe that "guys like thin girls," being thin is critical to physical attractiveness, and they are not as thin as men would like. In fact, most college women want to be even thinner than most college men want them to be. Most men express more satisfaction with their body shape (Fallon & Rozin, 1985).

Because few women approach our culture's unrealistic standards of beauty, many women develop a low self-image. Our idealized image of beauty leads many young women to diet to the point of risking their health and even their lives. The Thinking About Diversity box on page 558 explains

Mary-Kate Olsen, shown on the right with her twin sister Ashley Olsen, is among the many young women celebrities who have struggled with an eating disorder. To what extent do you think the mass media are responsible for encouraging young women to be so thin that some even put their lives at risk? Explain your view.

how the introduction of U.S. culture to the island of Fiji soon resulted in a sharp increase in eating disorders among women.

OBESITY

Eating disorders such as anorexia nervosa and bulimia are not the biggest eating-related problem in the United States. There is an increasingly serious problem of obesity in the population as a whole. As noted in the opening to this chapter, the government reports that two-thirds of U.S. adults are

 This government Web site provides health news and statistical data on a wide range of health topics: http://www.cdc.gov

overweight, which is defined as being 10 to 30 pounds over a healthy weight. Half of all overweight people in the United States are clinically obese, which means that they are at least 30 pounds over their healthy weight. National Map 21–2 on page 559 shows the percentage of people who are medically obese in the United States.

Gender and Eating Disorders: A Report from Fiji

In 1995, television came to Fiji, a small group of islands in the South Pacific Ocean. A single cable channel carried programming from the United States, Great Britain, and Australia. Anne Becker (1999), a Harvard researcher specializing in eating disorders, read the news with great interest, wondering what effect the new culture being poured in via television would have on young women there.

Traditionally, Fijian culture emphasizes good nutrition and looking strong and healthy. The idea of dieting to look very thin was almost unknown. So it is not surprising that in 1995, Becker found that just 3 percent of teenage girls reported ever vomiting to control their weight. By 1998, however, a striking change was taking place, with 15 percent of teenage girls—a fivefold increase—reporting this practice. Becker also found that 62 percent of girls claimed they had dieted during the previous month and 74 percent reported feeling "too big" or "fat."

The rapid rise in eating disorders in Fiji, which Becker linked to the introduction of television, shows the power of culture to shape patterns of health. Eating disorders, including anorexia nervosa and bulimia, are even more common in the United States, where about half of college women report engaging in such behavior, even though most of these women, medically speaking, are not overweight. Fijian women are now being taught what many women in the United States already believe: "You are never too thin to feel fat."

WHAT DO YOU THINK?

1. Why are eating disorders a social issue as well as a medical issue?
2. At what age do you think that young girls learn that "you are never too thin to feel fat"? How do they learn this?
3. What social changes might reduce the rate of eating disorders among U.S. women?

Being overweight can limit physical activity and raises the risk of a number of serious diseases, including heart disease, stroke, and diabetes. According to the U.S. government, the cost of treating diseases caused by obesity plus the cost of lost days at work due to such illnesses equals about $117 billion every year. Most seriously, some 300,000 people die each year in the United States from disease related to being overweight (Carmona, 2003; Ferraro & Kelley-Moore, 2003).

A cause for national concern is the fact that about one in four young people in this country is already overweight. This trend suggests that the medical problems of this new generation will be even greater as they reach middle age.

What are the social causes of obesity? One factor is that we live in a society in which more and more people have jobs that keep them sitting in front of computer screens rather than engaging in the type of physical labor that was common a century ago. Even when we are not on the job, most of the work around the house is done by machines (or other people). Children spend more of their time sitting as well—watching television or playing video games.

Then, of course, there is diet. The typical person in the United States is eating more salty and fatty food than ever before. And meals are also getting bigger: The Department of Agriculture recently reported that in 2000, the typical U.S. adult consumed 140 more pounds of food in a year than was true a decade earlier. Comparing old and new editions of cookbooks, recipes that used to say they would feed six now say they will feed four. The odds of being overweight go up among people with lower incomes partly because they may lack the education to make healthy choices and partly because stores in low-income communities offer a greater selection of low-cost, high-fat snack foods and fewer healthful fruits and vegetables (Hellmich, 2002).

↔ YOUR TURN ↔

Calculate your *body mass index* (BMI): [weight in pounds/(height in inches)^2] × 703. A BMI of 18.5–24.9 is normal; 25.0–29.9 is considered overweight, 30.0 and above is obese. Where does your BMI fall? Were you surprised by the results?

According to the government, two-thirds of U.S. adults are overweight, meaning that they are at least ten pounds over a healthy weight. About half of all overweight people are clinically obese, which means they are at least thirty pounds overweight. This map shows the share of the population that is obese for counties across the United States. Looking at the map, what can you say about the regions that have the highest rates of obesity?

Source: *Time* (June 7, 2004). Copyright © 2004 Time, Inc. Reprinted by permission.

SEXUALLY TRANSMITTED DISEASES

Sexual activity, though both pleasurable and vital to the continuation of our species, can transmit more than fifty kinds of *sexually transmitted diseases* (STDs). Because our culture associates sex with sin, some people regard these diseases not only as illnesses but also as marks of immorality.

STDs grabbed national attention during the "sexual revolution" of the 1960s, when infection rates rose as people began sexual activity earlier and with a greater number of partners. The rise in STDs is an exception to the general decline of infectious diseases during the twentieth century. By the late 1980s, the rising dangers of STDs—especially AIDS—generated a sexual counterrevolution as people moved away from casual sex (Kain, 1987; Laumann et al., 1994). The following sections briefly describe several common STDs.

Gonorrhea and Syphilis

Gonorrhea and syphilis, among the oldest known diseases, are caused by microscopic organisms that are almost always transmitted by sexual contact. Untreated, gonorrhea causes sterility; syphilis damages major organs and can result in blindness, mental disorders, and death.

In 2003, some 335,000 cases of gonorrhea and 34,000 cases of syphilis were recorded in the United States, although the actual numbers may be several times higher. Most cases are contracted by non-Hispanic African Americans (70 percent), with lower numbers among non-Hispanic whites (20 percent), Latinos (9 percent), and Asian Americans and Native Americans (under 2 percent) (Centers for Disease Control and Prevention, 2004).

Both gonorrhea and syphilis can easily be cured with antibiotics such as penicillin. Thus neither is a major health problem in the United States.

Genital Herpes

Genital herpes is a virus that infects at least 45 million adolescents and adults in the United States (one in five). Though far less dangerous than gonorrhea and syphilis, herpes is incurable. People with genital herpes may not have any symptoms, or they may experience periodic, painful blisters on the genitals accompanied by fever and headache. Although not fatal to adults, pregnant women with genital herpes can transmit the disease during a vaginal delivery, and it can be deadly to a newborn. Therefore, women with active infections typically give birth by cesarean section (Sobel, 2001).

AIDS

The most serious of all sexually transmitted diseases is acquired immune deficiency syndrome (AIDS). Identified in 1981, it is incurable and almost always fatal, although a few people have lived with the disease for more than twenty years. AIDS is caused by the human immunodeficiency virus (HIV), which attacks white blood cells, weakening the immune system. AIDS thus makes a person vulnerable to a wide range of diseases that eventually cause death.

AIDS deaths in the United States numbered 18,017 in 2003. But officials recorded some 43,000 new cases in the United States that year, raising the total number of cases on record to more than 929,000. Of these, about 524,000 have died (Centers for Disease Control and Prevention, 2004).

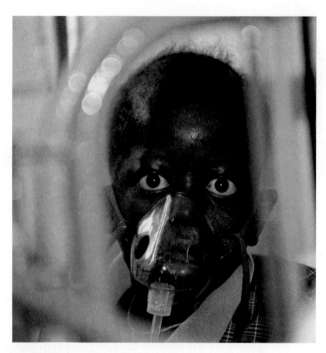

In the African nation of Kenya, there are about 500 deaths from AIDS every day. In parts of sub-Saharan Africa, the epidemic is so great that half of all children will become infected with HIV. This young Nairobi child, who already has AIDS, is fighting for his life.

Globally, HIV infects some 40 million people—half of them under the age of twenty-five—and the number is rising rapidly. The global AIDS death toll now exceeds 20 million, with about 2 percent of these deaths in the United States. Around the world each day, 8,700 people die of AIDS and 14,000 more are infected. As Global Map 21–1 shows, Africa (especially south of the Sahara) has the highest HIV infection rate and accounts for 66 percent of all world cases. A recent United Nations study found that across much of sub-Saharan Africa, fifteen-year-olds face a fifty-fifty chance of becoming infected with HIV. The risk is especially high for girls, not only because HIV is transmitted more easily from men to women but also because many African cultures encourage women to be submissive to men. According to some analysts, the AIDS crisis now threatens the political and economic security of Africa, which affects the entire world (Ashford, 2002; United Nations, 2004).

 For information on United Nations efforts to combat AIDS, go to http://www.unaids.org

Upon infection, people with HIV display no symptoms at all, so most are unaware of their condition. Symptoms of AIDS may not appear for a year or longer, but during this time an infected person may infect others. Within five years, one-third of infected people in the United States develop full-blown AIDS; half develop AIDS within ten years, and almost all become sick within twenty years. In low-income countries, the progression of this illness is much more rapid, with many people dying within a few years.

HIV is infectious but not contagious. That is, HIV is transmitted from person to person through blood, semen, or breast milk but not through casual contact such as shaking hands, hugging, sharing towels or dishes, or swimming together or even by coughing and sneezing. The risk of transmitting the virus through saliva (as in kissing) is extremely low. The chance of transmitting HIV through sexual activity is greatly reduced by the use of latex condoms. However, abstinence or an exclusive relationship with an uninfected person are the only sure ways to avoid infection.

Specific behaviors put people at high risk of HIV infection. The first is *anal sex,* which can cause rectal bleeding, allowing easy transmission of HIV from one person to another. The fact that many homosexual and bisexual men engage in anal sex helps explain why these categories of people account for 48 percent of AIDS cases in the United States.

Sharing needles used to inject drugs is a second high-risk behavior. At present, intravenous drug users account for 27 percent of persons with AIDS. Sex with an intravenous drug user is also very risky. Because intravenous drug use is more common among poor people in the United States, AIDS is now becoming a disease of the socially disadvantaged. Minorities make up the majority of people with AIDS: African Americans (12 percent of the population) account for 40 percent of people with AIDS, and Latinos (13 percent of the population) represent 19 percent of AIDS cases. Almost 80 percent of all women and children with the disease are African American or Latino. By contrast, Asian Americans and Native Americans together account for only about 1 percent of people with AIDS (Centers for Disease Control and Prevention, 2004).

Using any drug, including alcohol, also increases the risk of HIV infection to the extent that it impairs judgment. In other words, even people who understand what places them at risk of infection may act less responsibly if they are under the influence of alcohol, marijuana, or some other drug.

As Figure 21–2 on page 562 shows, only 16 percent of people with AIDS in the United States became infected through heterosexual contact (although heterosexuals, infected in various ways, account for more than 30 percent of AIDS cases). But heterosexual activity does transmit HIV, and the danger rises with the number of sexual partners, especially if they fall into high-risk categories. Worldwide,

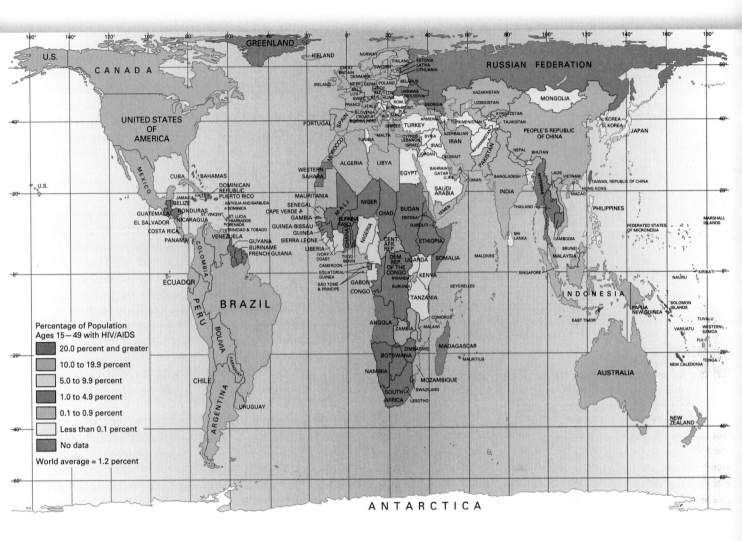

WINDOW ON THE WORLD

GLOBAL MAP 21-1   HIV/AIDS Infection of Adults in Global Perspective

Sixty-four percent of all global HIV infections are in sub-Saharan Africa. In countries such as Botswana and Swaziland, more than one-third of people between the ages of fifteen and forty-nine are infected with HIV/AIDS. This very high infection rate reflects the prevalence of other sexually transmitted diseases and infrequent use of condoms, two factors that promote transmission of HIV. All of Southeast Asia accounts for about 17 percent of global HIV infections. In Cambodia, 2 to 3 percent of people aged fifteen to forty-nine are now infected. All of North and South America taken together account for 8 percent of global HIV infections. In the United States, 0.6 percent of people aged fifteen to forty-nine are infected. The incidence of infection in Muslim nations is extremely low by world standards.

Sources: Population Reference Bureau (2003, 2005); and United Nations (2004); map projection from *Peters Atlas of the World* (1990).

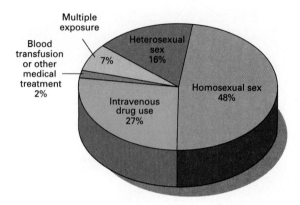

FIGURE 21–2 Types of Transmission for Reported U.S. AIDS Cases as of 2003

There are several ways in which people can be infected with HIV.

Source: Centers for Disease Control and Prevention (2004).

heterosexual relations are the primary means of HIV transmission, accounting for two-thirds of all infections.

In the United States, treating just one person with AIDS costs hundreds of thousands of dollars, and this figure may rise as new therapies appear. Government health programs, private insurance, and personal savings rarely cover more than a fraction of the cost of treatment. In addition, there is the mounting cost of caring for children orphaned by AIDS—at least 75,000 in the United States alone, and worldwide exceeding 15 million. Overall, there is little doubt that AIDS represents both a medical and a social problem of monumental proportions.

The U.S. government responded slowly to the AIDS crisis, largely because the earliest people to be infected, gay men and intravenous drug users, were widely viewed as deviant. But funds allocated for AIDS research and education have increased rapidly (now totaling some $17 billion annually), and researchers have identified some drugs, including protease inhibitors, that suppress the symptoms of the disease. But educational programs remain the most effective weapon against AIDS, since prevention is the only way to stop a disease that so far has no cure.

ETHICAL ISSUES SURROUNDING DEATH

Now that technological advances are giving human beings the power to draw the line separating life and death, we must decide how and when to do so. In other words, questions about the use of medical technology have added an ethical dimension to health and illness.

When Does Death Occur?

Common sense suggests that life ceases when breathing and heartbeat stop. But the ability to replace a heart and artificially sustain respiration makes that definition of death obsolete. Medical and legal experts in the United States now define death as an *irreversible* state involving no response to stimulation, no movement or breathing, no reflexes, and no indication of brain activity (Ladd, 1979; Wall, 1980; D.G. Jones, 1998).

Do People Have a Right to Die?

Today, medical personnel, family members, and patients themselves face the agonizing burden of deciding when a terminally ill person should die. Among the most difficult cases are the roughly 10,000 people in the United States in a permanent vegetative state who cannot express their desires about life and death. Generally speaking, the first duty of physicians and hospitals is to protect a patient's life. Even so, a mentally competent person in the process of dying may refuse medical treatment and even nutrition, either at the time or, in advance, through a "living will," a document stating the extent of medical care a person would or would not want in the event of an illness or injury that leaves the person unable to make decisions.

The case of Terri Schiavo, who died in 2005 after her feeding tube was removed, showed how difficult such decisions can be—for fifteen years, she was unable to speak for herself but had no living will. The Schiavo case was more difficult still because family members disagreed about whether she would have wanted to remain alive or not.

What about Mercy Killing?

Mercy killing is the common term for **euthanasia,** *assisting in the death of a person suffering from an incurable disease.* Euthanasia (from the Greek, meaning "a good death") poses an ethical dilemma, being at once an act of kindness and a form of killing.

Whether there is a "right to die" is one of today's most difficult issues. All people with incurable diseases have a right to refuse treatment that might prolong their lives. But whether a doctor should be allowed to help bring about death is at the heart of the debate. In 1994, three states—Washington, California, and Oregon—asked voters whether doctors should be able to help people who wanted to die. Only Oregon's proposition passed, and the law was quickly challenged and remained tied up in state court until 1997, when Oregon voters again endorsed it. Since then, Oregon doctors have legally assisted in the death of a few dozen terminally ill patients. In 1997, however, the U.S. Supreme Court decided that under the U.S. Constitution, there is no "right to die," a decision that has slowed the spread of such laws.

Supporters of *active* euthanasia—allowing a dying person to enlist the services of a physician to bring on a quick death—argue that there are circumstances (such as when a dying person suffers great pain) that make death preferable to life. Critics counter that permitting active euthanasia invites abuse (see Chapter 15, "Aging and the Elderly"). They fear that patients will feel pressure to end their lives in order to spare family members the burden of caring for them and the high costs of hospitalization. Research in the Netherlands, where physician-assisted suicide is legal, indicates that about one-fifth of all such deaths have occurred without a patient explicitly requesting to die (Gillon, 1999).

In the United States, a majority of adults express support for giving terminally ill people the right to choose to die with a doctor's help (NORC, 2003). Therefore, the right-to-die debate is sure to continue.

The Medical Establishment

Medicine is *the social institution that focuses on fighting disease and improving health.* Through most of human history, health care was the responsibility of individuals and their families. Medicine emerges as a social institution only as societies become more productive and people take on specialized work.

Members of agrarian societies today still turn to various traditional health practitioners, including herbalists and acupuncturists, who play a central part in improving health. In industrial societies, medical care falls to specially trained and licensed professionals, from anesthesiologists to X-ray technicians. Today's medical establishment in the United States has taken form over the last 150 years.

THE RISE OF SCIENTIFIC MEDICINE

In colonial times, doctors, herbalists, druggists, midwives, and ministers practiced the healing arts. But not all were effective: Unsanitary instruments, lack of anesthesia, and simple ignorance made surgery a terrible ordeal, and doctors probably killed as many people as they saved.

Doctors made medicine into a science, studying the human body and how it works, emphasizing surgery and the use of drugs to fight disease. Pointing to their specialized knowledge, doctors gradually established themselves as self-regulating professionals with medical degrees. The American Medical Association (AMA) was founded in 1847 and symbolized the growing acceptance of a scientific model of medicine.

Still, traditional approaches to health care had their supporters. The AMA opposed them by seeking control of

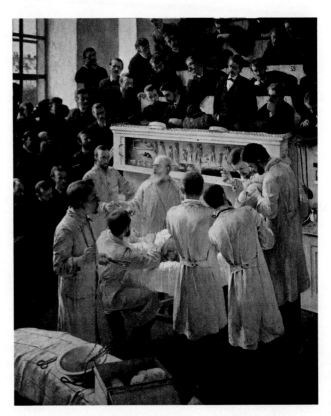

The rise of scientific medicine during the nineteenth century resulted in new skills and technology for treating many common ailments that had afflicted humanity for centuries. At the same time, however, scientific medicine pushed forms of health care involving women to the margins and placed medicine under the control of men living in cities. We see this pattern in the A. F. Seligmann painting *General Hospital*, showing an obviously all-male medical school class in Vienna in 1880.

the certification process. In the early 1900s, state licensing boards agreed to certify only doctors trained in scientific programs approved by the AMA. As a result, schools teaching other healing skills began to close, which soon limited the practice of medicine to individuals holding an M.D. degree. In the process, both the prestige and the income of physicians rose dramatically; today, men and women with M.D. degrees earn, on average, $250,000 annually.

Practitioners who did things differently, such as osteopathic physicians, concluded that they had no choice but to fall in line with AMA standards. Thus osteopaths (with D.O. degrees), originally trained to treat illness by manipulating the skeleton and muscles, today treat illness with drugs in much the same way as medical doctors (with M.D. degrees). Chiropractors, herbal healers, and midwives still practice using traditional methods, but they have lower standing

Between Faith and Medicine, How Clear a Line?

August 18, 2004

By MICHAEL WINES

JOHANNESBURG, Aug. 17—South Africa is having a serious debate over how to license its doctors. Legislators are pondering minimum requirements for medical practice, rules of professional ethics and standards for quality of care. A government research council is conducting double-blind, placebo-controlled tests on potential new prescription drugs. Insurance companies are considering new claims-reimbursement guidelines.

It is the very model of a modern regulatory process, with one exception: These doctors are *sangomas*—diviners, who cure with combinations of herbal potions, readings of scattered bones and second opinions from long-dead ancestors. Disbelievers long pinned them with the offensive label "witch doctors." Today's politically correct term is "traditional healers."

By any name, they pose an exquisitely difficult question: How does this, Africa's most Westernized nation, accredit as legally recognized physicians a group whose members largely confound empirical Western standards?

It is a sterling example of the tightrope South Africans walk every day: melding modern and ancient; Western and African; black and white and mixed-race culture, while still accommodating the distinctive virtues of each. . . .

This nation has about 23,000 Western-style physicians—and perhaps 14 times as many healers of various types. By some reckonings, more than 8 in 10 South Africans turn to traditional healers for help with both medical and personal problems, even if they also see a Western-educated doctor.

But something dogs the sangomas: a legacy of illness and death. . . . So-called traditional surgeons perform a circumcision ritual on thousands of teenage males each year, leaving dozens dead, maimed or infected with HIV through the use of unclean knives. Others die or suffer permanent kidney or liver damage from traditional remedies that include toxic elements like chromium salts. . . .

From the government's standpoint, licensing sangomas as physicians cracks the door open to regulating practices and medicines that now cause untold misery. . . .

The trade-off is that sangomas and related healers would acquire the legal status of any other physician—although in a separate class—and many of the coveted powers and benefits that implies, including medical insurance.

And that raises a host of thorny empirical questions: What distinguishes a real sangoma from a fly-by-night, when many traditional healers claim to be called to their profession by ancestors, not trained at schools? What is a safe and effective traditional prescription? If a diagnosis based on consultation with ancestors or examination of bones proves fatally wrong, is

---

within the medical profession. The tension and conflict between scientific medicine and traditional healing continues today, both in the United States and in many other countries. "In the *Times*" explains the current controversy over the licensing of traditional healers in South Africa.

Scientific medicine, taught in expensive, urban medical schools, also changed the social profile of doctors so that most came from privileged backgrounds and practiced in cities. Women, who had played a large part in many fields of healing, were pushed aside by the AMA. Some early medical schools did focus on the training of women and African Americans, but gradually most of these schools ran out of money and closed. Only in recent decades has the social diversity of medical doctors increased, with women and African Americans representing 29 percent and 6 percent, respectively, of all physicians (U.S. Department of Labor, 2005).

HOLISTIC MEDICINE

Recently in the United States, the scientific model of medicine has been tempered by the more traditional model of **holistic medicine,** *an approach to health care that emphasizes the prevention of illness and takes into account a person's entire physical and social environment.* Holistic practitioners agree on the need for drugs, surgery, artificial organs, and high technology, but they emphasize treatment of the whole person rather than symptoms and focus on health rather than disease. There are three foundations of holistic health care (Gordon, 1980; Patterson, 1998):

1. **Treat patients as people.** Holistic practitioners concern themselves not only with symptoms but also with how environment and lifestyle affect their patients. Holistic practitioners extend the bounds of conventional medicine, taking an active role in fighting

that malpractice? The South Africa branch of Doctors for Life International argues that the government promotes malpractice—and gives traditional healers a free ride—if it equates sangoma methods . . . with those of Western doctors. . . .

Many sangomas spend years in apprenticeships . . . and Western science is starting to acknowledge a scientific basis for many herbal remedies and non-Western medical disciplines like acupuncture. Why, they say, should traditional healing be any different? . . .

South Africa's Medical Research Council, which tests drugs, is already examining traditional remedies aimed at the mass market and those for which specific benefits are claimed. But it will not try to certify nostrums prescribed by sangomas to individual patients, no matter how peculiar, unless a sangoma or patient requests it. . . .

For their part, insurers will be legally bound to cover medical claims from licensed healers, said David Strauss, a senior officer with Discovery Health, South Africa's largest medical insurer. Despite snide remarks from some insurers about payment for prescriptions of elephant dung—a not-uncommon traditional remedy—the law allows insurers to pay only for medicines and procedures certified by the government as safe and effective.

And what will be safe and effective sangoma practice? An interim regulatory body, composed of government appointees and traditional doctors, would act as a sort of self-regulatory body for the industry. But many details of how sangomas would be regulated are left to the discretion of the health minister, a decided advocate of traditional medicine. . . .

The fact of the matter—even in 21st-century, Western-leaning South Africa—is that many people here look first to traditional healers for solace and help when illness strikes, and to Western-trained doctors only second, if at all. What's more, they seem content with that.

WHAT DO YOU THINK?

1. In a nation with tens of thousands of doctors trained in scientific medicine, why do you think so many people use the services of traditional healers?

2. What do people see as the advantages and disadvantages of scientific medicine? What do they see as the advantages and disadvantages of traditional healing practices?

3. Do you think it is fair that scientific standards are being used to evaluate the traditional healers? Why or why not?

Adapted from the original article by Michael Wines published in *The New York Times* on August 18, 2004. Copyright © 2004 by The New York Times Company. Reprinted with permission.

poverty, environmental pollution, and other dangers to public health.

2. **Encourage responsibility, not dependency.** In the scientific model, patients are dependent on physicians. Holistic medicine tries to shift some responsibility for health from physicians to people themselves by encouraging health-promoting behavior. Holistic medicine thus favors an *active* approach to *health,* rather than a *reactive* approach to *illness.*

3. **Provide personal treatment.** Conventional medicine locates medical care in impersonal offices and hospitals, both disease-centered settings. By contrast, holistic practitioners favor, as much as possible, a personal and relaxed environment such as the home.

In sum, holistic care does not oppose scientific medicine but shifts the emphasis from treating disease toward achieving the greatest well-being for everyone. Because the AMA currently recognizes more than fifty medical specialties, it is clear that there is a need for practitioners who are concerned with the whole patient.

How much responsibility should you take for your own health? In what ways can a society improve the health of the population?

PAYING FOR MEDICAL CARE: A GLOBAL SURVEY

As medicine has come to rely on high technology, the costs of providing medical care have skyrocketed. Countries

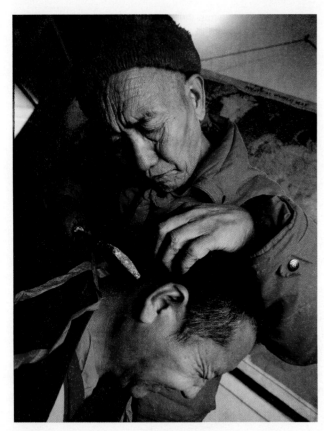

Traditional healers work to improve people's health throughout the world, especially in low-income nations. Here, a Chinese practitioner treats a patient by burning rolled herbs into his scalp.

throughout the world use various strategies to meet these costs.

Medicine in Socialist Nations

In nations with mostly socialist economies, government provides medical care directly to the people. These countries hold that all citizens have the right to basic medical care. This means that doctors and hospitals are paid not by patients but by the government, using public funds. The state owns and operates medical facilities and pays salaries to doctors and other medical care workers, who are government employees.

The People's Republic of China This economically growing but mostly agrarian nation faces the immense task of providing for the health of more than 1 billion people. China has experimented with private medicine, but the government controls most medical care.

China's "barefoot doctors," roughly comparable to U.S. paramedics, bring some modern methods of medical care to millions of peasants in rural villages. Otherwise, traditional healing arts, including acupuncture and the use of medicinal herbs, are still widely practiced in China. The Chinese approach to health is based on a holistic concern for the interplay of mind and body (Kaptchuk, 1985).

The Russian Federation The Russian Federation is transforming a state-dominated economy into more of a market system. For this reason, medical care is in transition. Nonetheless, the idea that everyone has a right to basic medical care remains widespread.

As in China, people do not choose a physician but report to a local government-operated health facility. Physicians have much lower incomes than medical doctors in the United States, earning about the same salary as skilled industrial workers (by contrast, doctors earn roughly five times as much as industrial workers in the United States). Also, about 70 percent of Russian doctors are women, compared to 29 percent in the United States. As in our society, occupations dominated by women in the Russian Federation offer fewer financial rewards.

In recent years, the Russian Federation has suffered setbacks in health care, partly because of a falling standard of living, as the Thinking Globally box explains. A rising demand for medical care has strained a bureaucratic system that at best provides highly standardized and impersonal care. The optimistic view is that as market reforms proceed, both living standards and the quality of medical services will improve. In Russia's uncertain times, what does seem certain is that inequalities in medical care will increase (Specter, 1995; Landsberg, 1998).

Medicine in Capitalist Nations

People living in nations with mostly capitalist economies usually pay for medical care out of their own pockets. However, because high cost puts medical care beyond the reach of many people, government programs underwrite much of the expense.

Sweden In 1891, Sweden began a mandatory, comprehensive system of government medical care. Citizens pay for this program with their taxes, which are among the highest in the world. Typically, physicians are government employees, and most hospitals are government-managed. Because this medical system resembles that found in socialist societies, Sweden's system is called **socialized medicine,** *a medical care system in which the government owns and operates most medical facilities and employs most physicians.*

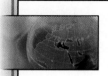

THINKING GLOBALLY
When Health Fails: A Report from Russia

Night is falling in Pitkyaranta, a small town on the western edge of Russia, near the Finnish border. Andrei, a thirty-year-old man with a weathered face and a long ponytail, weaves his way through the deepening shadows along a busy street. He has spent much of the afternoon in a bar with friends watching music videos, smoking cigarettes, and drinking vodka. Andrei is a railroad worker, but several months ago he was laid off. "Now," he explains bitterly, "I have nothing to do but drink and smoke." Andrei shrugs off a question about his health. "The only thing I care about is finding a job. I am a grown man. I don't want to be supported by my mother and father." Andrei still thinks of himself as young, yet according to current health patterns in Russia, his life is half over (Landsberg, 1998).

After the collapse of the Soviet Union in 1991, living conditions worsened steadily. One result, say doctors, is lots of stress—especially on men who earn too little to support their families or are out of work entirely. Few people eat well anymore, but Russian

men now drink and smoke more than ever. The World Health Organization reports that alcohol abuse is Russia's number one killer, with cigarette smoking not far behind.

In towns like Pitkyaranta, signs of poor health are everywhere: Women no longer breast-feed their babies, adults suffer higher rates of accidents and illness, and like Andrei, people look old

before their time. Doctors work to stop the health slide, but with poorly equipped hospitals, they are simply overwhelmed. Life expectancy has dropped several years for women and even more dramatically for men, who now live an average of just fifty-nine years, about the same as fifty years ago. Just 100 miles to the west in Finland, where economic trends are far better, men live to an average of seventy-five years.

Among young Russian men like Andrei, a joke is making the rounds. Their health may be failing, they say, but this cloud has a silver lining: At least they no longer have to worry about retirement.

WHAT DO YOU THINK?

1. Based on this report, in what ways is health in Russia a social issue as well as a medical matter?
2. In general, how does a society's economic health relate to the physical health of its people?
3. Can you think of stories similar to this one that involve the United States?

Great Britain In 1948, Great Britain also established socialized medicine by creating a dual system of medical service. All British citizens are entitled to medical care provided by the National Health Service, but those who can afford to may go to doctors and hospitals that operate privately.

Canada Since 1972, Canada has had a "single-payer" model of medical care that provides care to all Canadians. Like a giant insurance company, the Canadian government pays doctors and hospitals according to a set schedule of fees. Like Great Britain, Canada also has some physicians

working outside the government-funded system and setting their own fees, although costs are regulated by the government.

Canada boasts of providing care for everyone at a lower cost than the (nonuniversal) medical system in the United States. However, the Canadian system uses less state-of-the-art technology and responds more slowly, meaning that people may wait months to receive major surgery. But the Canadian system provides care for all citizens, regardless of income, unlike the United States, where lower-income people are often denied medical care (Rosenthal, 1991; Macionis & Gerber, 2005).

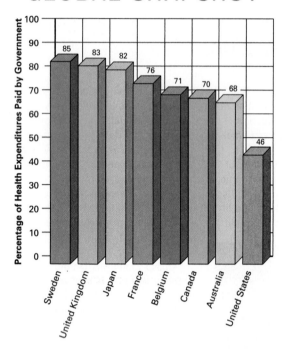

GLOBAL SNAPSHOT

FIGURE 21–3   Extent of Socialized Medicine
in Selected Countries

Of all high-income countries, the United States has the smallest percentage of government-provided medical care.

Sources: U.S. Census Bureau (2004) and World Bank (2005).

July 31, Montreal, Canada. I am visiting the home of an oral surgeon who appears (judging by the large home) to be doing pretty well. Yet he complains that the Canadian government, in an effort to hold down medical costs, caps doctors' salaries at about $125,000 (U.S.). Therefore, he explains, many specialists have left Canada for the United States, where they can earn much more; other doctors and dentists simply limit their practices.

Japan   Physicians in Japan have private practices, but a combination of government programs and private insurance pays their patients' medical costs. As shown in Figure 21–3, the Japanese approach medical care much as the Europeans do, with most medical expenses paid through government.

PAYING FOR MEDICAL CARE: THE UNITED STATES

The United States stands alone among industrialized nations in having no universal, government-sponsored program of medical care. Ours is a **direct-fee system,** *a medical care system in which patients pay directly for the services of physicians and hospitals.* Europeans look to government to fund about 80 percent of their medical costs (paid for through taxation), but the U.S. government pays just 46 percent of this country's medical costs (U.S. Census Bureau, 2004).

Read the government report *Healthy People 2010* at http://www.cdc.gov/nchs/hphome.htm

In the United States, rich people can purchase the best medical care in the world. Yet the poor are worse off than their counterparts in Europe. This difference explains the relatively high death rates among both infants and adults in the United States compared to those in many European countries (United Nations Development Programme, 2005).

Why does the United States have no national medical care program? First, because our culture stresses self-reliance, our society has limited government. Second, political support for a national medical program has not been strong, even among labor unions, which have concentrated on winning medical care benefits from employers. Third, the AMA and the health insurance industry have strongly and consistently opposed national medical care (Starr, 1982).

Expenditures for medical care in the United States increased dramatically from $12 billion in 1950 to more than $1.5 trillion in 2002. This sum amounts to more than $4,000 per person, more than any other nation in the world spends for medical care. Who pays the medical bills?

YOUR TURN

The head of the Ford Motor Company said recently that in building a car, the cost of medical care is now greater than the cost of steel. How do you think the rising cost of medical care affects an average family's budget?

Private Insurance Programs

In 2004, about 174 million people (60 percent) received some medical care benefits from a family member's employer or labor union. Another 27 million people (8 percent) purchased private coverage on their own. Combining these figures, 68 percent of the U.S. population has private insurance, although few such programs pay all medical costs (U.S. Census Bureau, 2005).

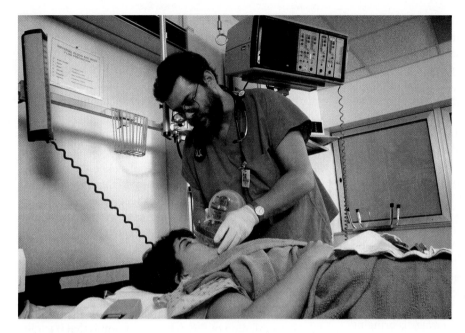

Throughout the United States, there is a serious shortage of nurses. One strategy for filling the need is for nursing programs to recruit more men into this profession; currently, men account for only 8 percent of nurses with R.N. degrees.

Public Insurance Programs

In 1965, Congress created Medicare and Medicaid. Medicare pays a portion of the medical costs of men and women over age sixty-five; in 2004, it covered 39 million women and men, 14 percent of the population. In the same year, Medicaid, a medical insurance program for the poor, provided benefits to 38 million people, about 13 percent of the population. An additional 11 million veterans (4 percent of the population) can obtain free care in government-operated hospitals. In all, 27 percent of this country's people get medical benefits from the government, but most also have private insurance.

Health Maintenance Organizations

About 72 million people (25 percent) in the United States belong to a **health maintenance organization (HMO),** *an organization that provides comprehensive medical care to subscribers for a fixed fee.* HMOs vary in their costs and benefits, and none provides full coverage. Fixed fees make these organizations profitable to the extent that their subscribers stay healthy; therefore, many take a preventive approach to health. At the same time, HMOs have been criticized for refusing to pay for medical procedures that they consider unnecessary. Congress is currently debating the extent to which patients can sue HMOs in order to obtain better care.

In all, 84 percent of the U.S. population has some medical care coverage, either private or public. Yet most plans do not provide full coverage, so a serious illness threatens even middle-class people with financial hardship. Most programs also exclude certain medical services, such as dental care and treatment for mental health and substance abuse problems. Worse, 46 million people (about 16 percent of the population) have no medical insurance at all, even though 73 percent of these people are working. Almost as many lose their medical coverage temporarily each year due to layoffs or job changes. Caught in the medical care bind are mostly low- to moderate-income people who do not qualify for Medicaid yet cannot afford the cost of the preventive medical care they need to stay healthy (Brink, 2002; U.S. Census Bureau, 2005).

Should the United States follow the lead of other high-income countries and enact a government program of medical care for everyone? Why or why not?

THE NURSING SHORTAGE

Another important issue in medical care is the shortage of nurses across the United States. In 2004, there were some 2.5 million nurses (people with the degree of R.N., registered nurse), but about 7 percent of the available jobs (roughly 139,000 positions) were unfilled.

The main cause of the shortage is that fewer people are entering the nursing profession. During the past decade, enrollments in nursing programs have dropped by one-third, even as the need for nurses (driven by the aging of the U.S. population) goes up. Why this decline? One factor is that today's young women have a wide range of occupational choices, and fewer are drawn to the traditionally female occupation of nursing. This fact is evident in the rising median age of working nurses, which is now forty-three. Another is that many of today's nurses are unhappy with their working conditions, citing heavy patient loads, too much required overtime, a stressful working environment, and a lack of recognition and respect from supervisors, physicians, and hospital managers. In fact, one recent survey found that a majority of working nurses say they would not recommend the field to others, and many R.Ns are leaving the field for other jobs.

A hopeful sign is that the nursing shortage is bringing change to this profession. Salaries, which range from about $45,000 for general-duty nurses to $100,000 for certified nurse-anesthetists, are rising, although slowly. Some hospitals and physicians are also offering signing bonuses in efforts to attract new nurses. In addition, nursing programs are trying harder to recruit a more diverse population, seeking more minorities (which are currently underrepresented) and more men (who now make up only 8 percent of R.N.s) (DeFrancis, 2002a, 2002b; R. W. Dworkin, 2002; Yin, 2002).

Theoretical Analysis of Health and Medicine

Each of sociology's major theoretical approaches helps us organize and interpret facts and issues concerning human health.

STRUCTURAL-FUNCTIONAL ANALYSIS: ROLE THEORY

Talcott Parsons (1951) viewed medicine as society's strategy to keep its members healthy. According to this model, illness is dysfunctional because it undermines people's abilities to perform their roles.

The Sick Role

Society responds to sickness not only by providing medical care but also by affording people a **sick role,** *patterns of behavior defined as appropriate for people who are ill.* According to Parsons, the sick role releases people from normal obligations such as going to work or attending classes. To prevent abuse of this privilege, however, people cannot simply claim to be ill; they must "look the part" and in serious cases get the help of a medical expert. After assuming the sick role, the patient must want to get better and must do whatever is needed to regain good health, including cooperating with health professionals.

The Physician's Role

Physicians evaluate people's claims of sickness and help restore the sick to normal routines. To do this, physicians use their specialized knowledge and expect patients to cooperate with them, providing necessary information and following "doctor's orders" to complete the treatment.

Critical review Parsons's analysis links illness and medicine to the broader organization of society. Others have extended the concept of the sick role to some nonillness situations such as pregnancy (Myers & Grasmick, 1989).

One limitation of the sick-role concept is that it applies to acute conditions (like the flu or a broken leg) better than to chronic illnesses (like heart disease), which may not be reversible. In addition, a sick person's ability to assume the sick role (to take time off from work to regain health) depends on the patient's resources; many working poor, for example, cannot afford to assume a sick role. Finally, illness is not entirely dysfunctional; it can have some positive consequences: Many people who experience serious illness find it provides the opportunity to reevaluate their lives and gain a better sense of what is truly important (D. G. Myers, 2000; Ehrenreich, 2001).

Finally, critics point out that Parsons's analysis gives doctors, rather than patients, the primary responsibility for health. A more prevention-oriented approach gives each of us as individuals the responsibility to pursue health.

SYMBOLIC-INTERACTION ANALYSIS: THE MEANING OF HEALTH

According to the symbolic-interaction approach, society is less a grand system than a complex and changing reality. In this model, health and medical care are socially constructed by people in everyday interaction.

The Social Construction of Illness

If both health and illness are socially constructed, people in a poor society may view hunger and malnutrition as normal. Similarly, many members of our own society give little thought to the harmful effects of a rich diet.

Our response to illness also is based on social definitions that may or may not square with medical facts. People with AIDS may be forced to deal with fear and prejudice that has no medical basis. Likewise, students may pay no attention to signs of real illness on the eve of a vacation but head for the infirmary hours before a midterm examination with a case of the sniffles. In short, health is less an objective fact than a negotiated outcome.

How people define a medical situation may actually affect how they feel. Medical experts marvel at *psychosomatic* disorders (a fusion of Greek words for "mind" and "body"), when state of mind guides physical sensations (Hamrick, Anspaugh, & Ezell, 1986). Applying sociologist W. I. Thomas's theorem (presented in Chapter 6, "Social Interaction in Everyday Life"), we can say that once health or illness is defined as real, it can become real in its consequences.

The Social Construction of Treatment

Also in Chapter 6, we used Erving Goffman's dramaturgical approach to explain how physicians tailor their physical surroundings (their office) and their behavior (the "presentation of self") so that others see them as competent and in charge.

The sociologist Joan Emerson (1970) further illustrates this process of reality construction in her analysis of the gynecological examination carried out by a male doctor. This situation is vulnerable to serious misinterpretation, since a man's touching of a woman's genitals is conventionally viewed as a sexual act and possibly an assault.

To ensure that people define the situation as impersonal and professional, the medical staff wear uniforms and furnish the examination room with nothing but medical equipment. The doctor's manner and overall performance are designed to make the patient feel that to him, examining the genital area is no different from treating any other part of the body. A female nurse is usually present during the examination, not only to assist the physician but also to avoid any impression that a man and a woman are "alone together."

Managing situational definitions in this way is only rarely taught in medical schools. The oversight is unfortunate because, as Emerson's analysis shows, understanding how people construct reality in the examination room is as important as mastering the medical skills required for treatment.

YOUR TURN

How might sociological insights help doctors improve their relationships with patients and perhaps even reduce the likelihood of being sued?

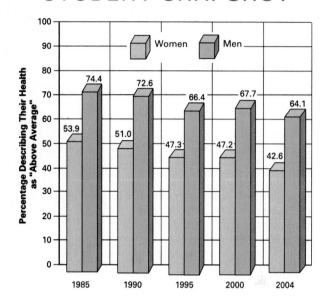

FIGURE 21-4 Self-Assessment of Physical Health by First-Year College Students, 1985–2004

Since 1985, a smaller share of students have described their health as "above average."

Sources: Astin et al. (2002) and Sax et al. (2004).

Critical review The symbolic-interaction approach reveals that what people view as healthful or harmful depends on numerous factors that are not, strictly speaking, medical. This approach also shows that in any medical procedure, both patient and medical staff engage in a subtle process of reality construction.

Critics fault the symbolic-interaction approach for implying that there are no objective standards of well-being. Certain physical conditions do indeed cause definite changes in people, regardless of how we view those conditions. People who lack sufficient nutrition and safe water, for example, suffer from their unhealthy environment, whether they define their surroundings as normal or not.

Figure 21–4 shows that since 1985, the share of first-year college students in the United States who describe their physical health as "above average" has been dropping. Do you think this trend reflects changing perceptions or a real decline in health (due, say, to eating more unhealthy food)?

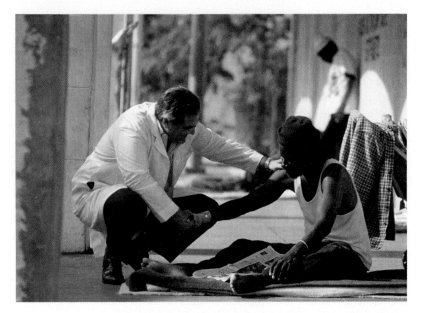

Despite the efforts of exemplary physicians such as Dr. Joe Greer, homeless people throughout the United States have a great need for medical support but receive little health care. In your opinion, what changes are needed to meet the needs of society's most vulnerable members?

SOCIAL-CONFLICT ANALYSIS: HEALTH AND INEQUALITY

Social-conflict analysis points out the connection between health and social inequality and, taking a cue from Karl Marx, ties medicine to the operation of capitalism. Researchers have focused on three main issues: access to medical care, the effects of the profit motive, and the politics of medicine.

Access to Care

Health is important to everyone. Yet by requiring individuals to pay for medical care, capitalist societies allow the richest people to have the best health. The access problem is more serious in the United States than in other high-income nations because we do not have a universal medical care system.

Conflict theorists argue that capitalist medical care provides excellent medical care for the rich but not for the rest of the population. Most of the 46 million people who lack medical care coverage at present have moderate to low incomes.

The Profit Motive

Some conflict analysts go further, arguing that the real problem is not access to medical care but the character of capitalist medicine itself. The profit motive turns physicians, hospitals, and the pharmaceutical industry into multibillion-dollar corporations. The quest for higher profits encourages physicians to recommend unnecessary tests and surgery and to rely too much on drugs rather than focusing on the improvement of people's living conditions.

Of about 25 million surgical operations performed in the United States each year, three-fourths are elective, which means that they are intended to promote long-term health and are not prompted by a medical emergency. Of course, any medical procedure or use of drugs is risky and results in harm to between 5 and 10 percent of patients. Therefore, social-conflict theorists argue, the decision to perform surgery reflects the financial interests of surgeons and hospitals as well as the medical needs of patients (Cowley, 1995; Nuland, 1999).

Finally, say conflict theorists, our society is all too tolerant of physicians having a direct financial interest in the tests and procedures they order for their patients (Pear & Eckholm, 1991). Medical care should be motivated by a concern for people, not profits.

Medicine as Politics

Although science declares itself politically neutral, scientific medicine frequently takes sides on important social issues. For example, the medical establishment has always strongly opposed government medical care programs. The history of medicine itself shows how racial and sexual discrimination have been supported by "scientific" opinions about, say, the inferiority of women (Leavitt, 1984). Consider the diagnosis of "hysteria," a term that has its origins in the Greek word *hyster,* meaning "uterus." In choosing this word to describe a wild, emotional state, the medical profession suggested that being a woman is somehow the same as being irrational.

APPLYING THEORY

HEALTH

	Structural-Functional Approach	Symbolic-Interaction Approach	Social-Conflict Approach
What is the level of analysis?	Macro-level	Micro-level	Macro-level
How is health related to society?	Illness is dysfunctional for society because it prevents people from carrying out their daily roles. The sick role releases people who are ill from responsibilities while they try to get well.	Societies define "health" and "illness" differently according to their living standards. How people define their own health affects how they actually feel (psychosomatic conditions).	Health is linked to social inequality, with rich people having more access to care than poor people. Capitalist medical care places the drive for profits over the needs of people, treating symptoms rather than addressing poverty as a cause of illness.

Even today, according to conflict theory, scientific medicine explains illness exclusively in terms of bacteria and viruses, ignoring the damaging effects of poverty. In effect, scientific medicine hides the bias in our medical system by transforming this social issue into simple biology.

Critical review Social-conflict analysis provides still another view of the relationships among health, medicine, and society. According to this approach, social inequality is the reason some people have better health than others.

The most common objection to the conflict approach is that it minimizes the gains in U.S. health brought about by scientific medicine and higher living standards. Though there is plenty of room for improvement, health indicators for our population as a whole rose steadily over the course of the twentieth century and compare well with those of other industrial nations.

In sum, sociology's three major theoretical approaches explain why health and medicine are social issues. The Applying Theory table sums up what they teach us.

But advancing technology will not solve every health problem. On the contrary, as the Thinking It Through box on page 574 explains, today's advancing technology is raising new questions and concerns.

The renowned French scientist Louis Pasteur (1822–1895), who spent much of his life studying how bacteria cause disease, said just before he died that health depends less on bacteria than on the social environment in which the bacteria are found (Gordon, 1980:7). Explaining Pasteur's insight is sociology's contribution to human health.

Health and Medicine: Looking Ahead

In the early 1900s, deaths from infectious diseases like diphtheria and measles were common. Because scientists had yet to develop penicillin and other antibiotics, even a small wound might become infected, and a simple infection from a minor wound was sometimes life-threatening. Today, a century later, most members of U.S. society—at least most young people—take good health and long life for granted. Although the increasing obesity epidemic is cause for concern, it seems reasonable to expect the improvements in U.S. health to continue during the twenty-first century.

Another encouraging trend is that more people are taking responsibility for their own health. Every one of us can live better and longer if we avoid tobacco, eat healthful meals in moderation, and exercise regularly.

Many health problems will continue to plague U.S. society in the decades to come. The biggest problem, discussed throughout this chapter, is this nation's double standard in health: more well-being for the rich and higher rates of disease for the poor. International comparisons show that the United States lags in some measures of human health because we neglect the people at the margins of our society. An important question, then, is how a rich society can afford to let millions of people live without the security of medical care.

Finally, we find that health problems are far greater in low-income nations than they are in the United States. The good news is that life expectancy for the world as a whole has been on the rise—from forty-eight years in 1950 to sixty-seven years today—and the biggest gains have been made in poor countries (Population Reference Bureau, 2005). But in much of Latin America, Asia, and especially Africa, hundreds of millions of adults and children lack not only medical attention but also adequate food and safe drinking water. Improving the health of the world's poorest people is a critical challenge for the twenty-first century.

The Genetic Crystal Ball: Do We Really Want to Look?

The liquid in the laboratory test tube seems ordinary enough, like a syrupy form of water. But this liquid is one of the greatest medical breakthroughs of all time; it may even hold the key to life itself. The liquid is deoxyribonucleic acid, or DNA, the spiraling molecule found in cells of the human body that contains the blueprint for making each one of us human as well as different from every other person.

The human body is composed of some 100 trillion cells, most of which contain a nucleus of twenty-three pairs of chromosomes (one of each pair comes from each parent). Each chromosome is packed with DNA, in segments called genes. Genes guide the production of protein, the building block of the human body.

If genetics sounds complicated (and it is), the social implications of genetic knowledge are even more complex. Scientists discovered the structure of the DNA molecule in 1952, and in recent years they have made great gains in "mapping" the human genome. Charting the genetic landscape may lead to understanding how each bit of DNA shapes our being. But do we really want to turn the key to unlock the secrets of life itself? What do we do with this knowledge once we have it?

In the Human Genome Project, many scientists see a chance to prevent certain illnesses before they even begin. Research already has identified genetic abnormalities that cause some forms of cancer, sickle-cell anemia, muscular dystrophy, Huntington's disease, cystic fibrosis, and other crippling and deadly afflictions. In the future, genetic screening—a scientific "crystal ball"—could let people know their medical destiny and allow doctors to manipulate segments of DNA to prevent diseases before they appear.

But many people urge caution in such research, warning that genetic information can easily be abused. At its worst, genetic mapping opens the door to Nazi-like efforts to breed a "super-race." In 1994, the People's Republic of China began to regulate marriage and childbirth to prevent "new births of inferior quality."

It seems inevitable that some parents will want to use genetic testing to evaluate the health (or even the eye and hair color) of their future children. This technology may give them the opportunity to abort a fetus because it falls short of their standards or to create "designer children."

Then there is the issue of "genetic privacy." Can a prospective spouse request a genetic evaluation of her fiancé before agreeing to marry? Can a life insurance company demand genetic testing before issuing a policy? Can an employer screen job applicants to weed out those whose future illnesses might drain the company's medical care funds? Clearly, what is scientifically possible is not always morally desirable. Society is already struggling with questions about the proper use of our expanding knowledge of human genetics. Such ethical dilemmas will only multiply as genetic research moves forward in the years to come.

WHAT DO YOU THINK?

1. Traditional wedding vows join couples "in sickness and in health." Do you think individuals have a right to know the future health of their potential partner before tying the knot? Why or why not?

2. Do you think parents should be able to genetically "design" their children? Why or why not?

3. Is it right that private companies doing genetic research are able to patent their discoveries so that they can profit from the results, or should this information be made available to everyone? Explain your answer.

Scientists are learning more and more about the genetic factors that prompt the eventual development of serious diseases. If offered the opportunity, would you want to undergo a genetic screening that would predict the long-term future of your own health?

Sources: D. Thompson (1999) and Golden & Lemonick (2000).

The following learning tools will help you see what you know, identify what you still need to learn, and expand your understanding beyond the text. You can also visit this text's Companion Website™ at http://www.prenhall.com/macionis to find additional practice tests.

KEY POINTS

What Is Health?

Health is a social issue because personal well-being depends on a society's technology and its distribution of resources. A society's culture shapes definitions of health and patterns of medical care.

Health: A Global Survey

Historically, human health was poor by today's standards. Health improved dramatically in Western Europe and North America in the nineteenth century, first because of industrialization and later because of medical advances. A century ago, infectious diseases were leading killers; today, most people in the United States die in old age of chronic illnesses such as heart disease, cancer, or stroke.

Poor nations suffer from inadequate sanitation, hunger, and other problems linked to poverty. Life expectancy is about twenty years less than in the United States; in the poorest nations, half the children do not survive to adulthood.

Health in the United States

More than three-fourths of U.S. children born today will live to at least age sixty-five. Throughout the life course, women have better health than men, and people of high social position enjoy better health than the poor.

Current issues in U.S. health care include cigarette smoking, which is the greatest preventable cause of death, the obesity epidemic, the recent increase in sexually transmitted diseases, and ethical dilemmas associated with advancing medical technology.

The Medical Establishment

Health care was historically a family concern but has become the responsibility of trained specialists. The model of scientific medicine is the foundation of the U.S. medical establishment. The holistic approach seeks to give people greater responsibility for their own health.

Socialist nations define medical care as a right that governments offer equally to everyone. Capitalist nations view medical care as a commodity to be purchased, although most capitalist governments support medical care through socialized medicine or national health insurance.

The United States, with a direct-fee system, is the only high-income nation with no comprehensive medical care program. Most people have private or government health insurance. About 46 million people in the United States do not have medical insurance.

Theoretical Analysis of Health and Medicine

A major part of the structural-functional analysis of health is the sick role, which excuses the ill person from routine social responsibilities. The symbolic-interaction approach investigates how health and medical treatments are largely matters of socially constructed definitions. Social-conflict analysis focuses on the unequal distribution of health and medical care. It criticizes the U.S. medical establishment for its overreliance on drugs and surgery, the dominance of the profit motive, and its overemphasis on the biological rather than the social causes of illness.

Health and Medicine: Looking Ahead

Health has improved in the United States during the past century. Future improvements are also likely, especially to the extent that people take greater responsibility for their own health and this country reduces the current double standard by which the rich have far better medical care than the poor.

KEY CONCEPTS

health (p. 552) a state of complete physical, mental, and social well-being

social epidemiology (p. 554) the study of how health and disease are distributed throughout a society's population

eating disorder (p. 557) an intense form of dieting or other unhealthy method of weight control driven by the desire to be very thin

euthanasia (p. 562) assisting in the death of a person suffering from an incurable disease; also known as *mercy killing*

medicine (p. 563) the social institution that focuses on fighting disease and improving health

holistic medicine (p. 564) an approach to health care that emphasizes the prevention of illness and takes into account a person's entire physical and social environment

socialized medicine (p. 566) a medical care system in which the government owns and operates most medical facilities and employs most physicians

direct-fee system (p. 568) a medical care system in which patients pay directly for the services of physicians and hospitals

health maintenance organization (HMO) (p. 569) an organization that provides comprehensive medical care to subscribers for a fixed fee

sick role (p. 570) patterns of behavior defined as appropriate for people who are ill

---

SAMPLE TEST QUESTIONS

These questions are similar to those found in the test bank that accompanies this textbook.

Multiple-Choice Questions

1. **Health is a social issue because**
   a. cultural patterns define what people view as healthy.
   b. social inequality affects people's health.
   c. a society's technology affects people's health.
   d. all of the above.

2. **In the very poorest nations of the world today, a majority of people die before reaching**
   a. their teens.
   b. the age of fifty.
   c. the age of sixty-five.
   d. the age of seventy-five.

3. **The Industrial Revolution reduced deaths caused by _____, which increased the share of deaths caused by _____.**
   a. disease; war
   b. starvation; accidents
   c. infectious disease such as influenza; chronic conditions such as heart disease
   d. chronic conditions such as heart disease; infectious disease such as influenza

4. **Social epidemiology is the study of**
   a. which bacteria cause a specific disease.
   b. the distribution of health and illness in a population.
   c. what kind of people become doctors.
   d. the distribution of doctors around the world.

5. **What is the largest cause of death among young people in the United States?**
   a. cancer
   b. influenza
   c. accidents
   d. AIDS

6. **In the United States, which category of people has the highest life expectancy?**
   a. African American men
   b. white men
   c. African American women
   d. white women

7. **In the United States, the greatest preventable cause of death is**
   a. sexually transmitted diseases.
   b. automobile accidents.
   c. cigarette smoking.
   d. AIDS.

8. About what share of U.S. adults are overweight?
   a. two-thirds
   b. half
   c. one-third
   d. one-fifth

9. Which sexually transmitted disease is most common among U.S. adults?
   a. AIDS
   b. genital herpes
   c. gonorrhea
   d. syphilis

10. A social-conflict analysis claims that capitalism harms human health because
    a. it does not encourage people to take control of their own health.
    b. it gives physicians little financial incentive to work.

c. it reduces average living standards.
d. it makes quality of care dependent on income.

Answers: 1(d); 2(a); 3(c); 4(b); 5(c); 6(d); 7(c); 8(a); 9(b); 10(d).

Essay Questions

1. Why is health as much a social as a biological issue? How does a social-conflict analysis of health and medicine point to the need to define health as a societal issue?

2. Describe Talcott Parsons's structural-functional analysis of health and illness. What is the sick role? When and how is it used?

APPLICATIONS & EXERCISES

1. Take a trip to the local courthouse or city hall to find public records showing people's cause of death and age at death. Compare such records for 1905 and 2005. What patterns do you find in life expectancy and causes of death?

2. Get a course catalogue from a medical school (or visit a school's Web site) and see how much, if any, of the curriculum deals with the social dimensions of medical care.

3. Interview a midwife (many list their services in the Yellow Pages) about her work helping women deliver babies. How do midwives differ from medical obstetricians in their approach?

INVESTIGATE *with* Research Navigator

Research Navigator.com
RESOURCES FOR COLLEGE RESEARCH ASSIGNMENTS

Follow the instructions on page 27 of this text to access the features of **Research Navigator**™. Once at the Web site, enter your Login Name and Password. Then, to use the **ContentSelect**™ database, enter keywords such as "obesity," "AIDS," "cigarette smoking," and "euthanasia," and the search engine will supply relevant and recent scholarly and popular press publications. Use the *New York Times* **Search-by-Subject Archive** to find recent news articles related to sociology and the **Link Library** feature to find relevant Web links organized by the key terms associated with this chapter.

22

Population,
Urbanization,
and Environment

Why do many people worry about the rapid rate
of global population increase?

What are the typical experiences
of city living?

How is the state of the natural environment
a social issue?

L ooking for a new place to live after you finish college? Crosby, North Dakota, would really like you to call it home. The town's officials will do more than welcome you—they will give you a free piece of land to build a house. As a bonus, they will throw in a free membership in the local country club.

Ellsworth, Kansas, also wants you. The town leaders will match Crosby's offer of free land and go one better, paying you $1,000 cash toward a down payment on your new home.

Perhaps the best deal of all is found in Plainville, Kansas. In addition to free land, you can forget about property taxes for the next ten years!

Why are these towns so eager to attract new residents? The answer is that they are all in the Great Plains, the central region of the United States extending from North Dakota all the way down to Texas, which has lost much of its population in recent decades. People in Crosby (current population 1,100), Elsworth (2,500), and Plainville (2,000) are offering these fantastic deals because they are worried that unless there is a turnaround, their towns may disappear like hundreds of other nearby communities already have (Greene, 2005). ■

All across the Great Plains, many towns are hanging on by a thread. This chapter investigates population patterns, explaining why people move from place to place, why some cities get so large, and why small towns sometimes die. We shall also look at how population change and our way of life affect the physical environment.

Demography: The Study of Population

When humans first began to cultivate plants some 12,000 years ago, Earth's entire *Homo sapiens* population was only about 5 million, about the number living in Minnesota today. Very slow growth pushed the global total in 1 B.C.E. to perhaps 300 million, or about the population of the United States today.

Starting around 1750, world population began to spike upward. We now add 74 million people to the planet each year; in 2005, the total world population was 6.5 billion.

The causes and consequences of this drama are the basis of **demography,** *the study of human population.* Demography (from Greek, meaning "description of people") is a cousin of sociology that analyzes the size and composition of a population and studies how and why people move from place to place. Demographers not only collect statistics but also raise important questions about the effects of population growth and suggest how it might be controlled. The following sections present basic demographic concepts.

FERTILITY

The study of human population begins with how many people are born. **Fertility** is *the incidence of childbearing in a country's population.* During her childbearing years, from the onset of menstruation (typically in the early teens) to menopause (usually in the late forties), a woman is capable of bearing more than twenty children. But *fecundity,* or maximum possible childbearing, is sharply reduced by cultural norms, finances, and personal choice.

Demographers describe fertility using the **crude birth rate,** *the number of live births in a given year for every 1,000 people in a population.* To calculate a crude birth rate, divide the number of live births in a year by the society's total population and multiply the result by 1,000. In the United States in 2004, there were 4.1 million live births in a population of 295 million; if you do the math, you will see that the resulting crude birth rate for that year was 13.9 (Munson & Sutton, 2005).

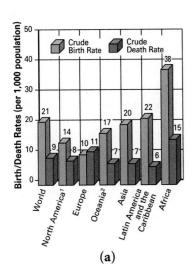

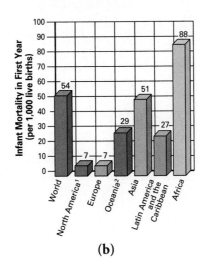

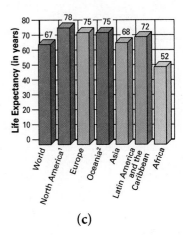

(a)   (b)   (c)

FIGURE 22-1   (a) Crude Birth Rates and Crude Death Rates,
(b) Infant Mortality Rates, and
(c) Life Expectancy around the World, 2004

By world standards, North America has low birth and death rates, very low infant mortality rates, and high life expectancy.

[1] United States and Canada.

[2] Australia, New Zealand, and South Pacific Islands.

Source: Population Reference Bureau (2005).

January 18, Coshocton County, Ohio. Having just finished the mountains of meat and potatoes that make up a typical Amish meal, we have gathered in the living room of Jacob Raber, a member of this rural Amish community. Mrs. Raber, a mother of four, is telling us about Amish life. "Most of the women I know have five or six children," she says with a smile, "but certainly not everybody—some have eleven or twelve!"

A country's birth rate is described as "crude" because it is based on the entire population, not just women in their childbearing years. In addition, this measure ignores differences between various categories of the population: Fertility among the Amish, for example, is quite high, and fertility among Asian Americans is low. But the crude measure is easy to calculate and allows rough comparisons of the fertility of one country or region in relation to others. Part (a) of Figure 22–1 shows that on a global scale, the crude birth rate of North Americans is low.

YOUR TURN

Can you point to specific ways in which your life would be different if you had five or six brothers and sisters, compared to one or two?

MORTALITY

Population size also reflects **mortality**, *the incidence of death in a country's population.*. To measure mortality, demographers use a **crude death rate,** *the number of deaths in a given year for every 1,000 people in a population.* This time, we take the number of deaths in a year, divide by the total population, and multiply the result by 1,000. In 2004, there were 2.4 million deaths in the U.S. population of 295 million, yielding a crude death rate of 8.1 (Munson & Sutton, 2005). Part (a) of Figure 22–1 shows that this rate is about average.

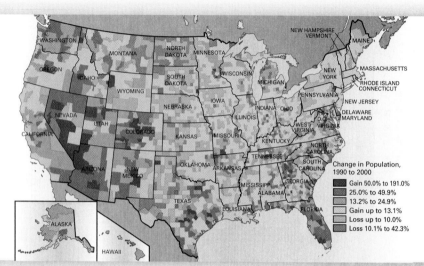

This map, based on results of the 2000 census, shows that population is moving from the heartland of the United States toward the coasts. What do you think is causing this internal migration? What types of people do you think remain in counties that are losing population?

Source: U.S. Census Bureau (2001).

Change in Population, 1990 to 2000

- Gain 50.0% to 191.0%
- 25.0% to 49.9%
- 13.2% to 24.9%
- Gain up to 13.1%
- Loss up to 10.0%
- Loss 10.1% to 42.3%

A third useful demographic measure is the **infant mortality rate,** *the number of deaths among infants under one year of age for each 1,000 live births in a given year.* To compute infant mortality, divide the number of deaths of children under one year of age by the number of live births during the same year and multiply the result by 1,000. In 2004, there were 27,300 infant deaths and 4.1 million live births in the United States. Dividing the first number by the second and multiplying the result by 1,000 yields an infant mortality rate of 6.7. Part (b) of Figure 22–1 indicates that, by world standards, North American infant mortality is low.

But remember the differences among various categories of people. For example, African Americans, with nearly three times the burden of poverty as whites, have an infant mortality rate of 14.4—more than twice the white rate of 5.8.

Low infant mortality greatly raises **life expectancy,** *the average life span of a country's population.* U.S. males born in 2003 can expect to live 74.8 years, and females can look forward to 80.1 years. As part (c) of Figure 22–1 shows, life expectancy in North America is twenty-six years greater than is typical of low-income countries of Africa.

MIGRATION

Population size is also affected by **migration,** *the movement of people into and out of a specified territory.* Movement into a territory, or *immigration,* is measured as an *in-migration rate,* calculated as the number of people entering an area for every 1,000 people in the population. Movement out of a territory, or *emigration,* is measured in terms of an *out-migration rate,* the number leaving for every 1,000 people.

Both types of migration usually occur at once; the difference is the *net migration rate.*

All nations experience internal migration, that is, movement within their borders from one region to another. National Map 22–1 shows where the U.S. population is moving, and the places left behind (as suggested by the chapter opening, notice the heavy losses in the Plains States in the middle of the country). Migration is sometimes voluntary, as when people leave a small town and move to a larger city. In such cases, "push-pull" factors are typically at work; a lack of jobs "pushes" people to move, and more opportunity elsewhere "pulls" them to a larger city. Migration can also be involuntary, such as the forcible transport of 10 million Africans to the Western Hemisphere as slaves.

POPULATION GROWTH

Fertility, mortality, and migration all affect the size of a society's population. In general, rich nations (such as the United States) grow as much from immigration as from natural increase; poor nations (such as Pakistan) grow almost entirely from natural increase.

To calculate a population's natural growth rate, demographers subtract the crude death rate from the crude birth rate. The natural growth rate of the U.S. population in 2004 was 5.8 per 1,000 (the crude birth rate of 13.9 minus the crude death rate of 8.1), or about 0.6 percent annual growth.

Global Map 22–1 on page 584 shows that population growth in the United States and other high-income nations is well below the world average of 1.2 percent. Earth's low-growth continents are Europe (currently posting a slight

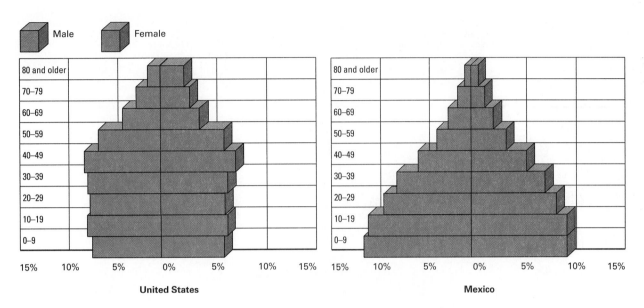

Male   Female

United States

Mexico

FIGURE 22–2   Age-Sex Population Pyramids for the United States and Mexico, 2005

By looking at the shape of a country's population pyramid, you can tell its level of economic development and predict future levels of population increase.

Source: U.S. Census Bureau (2005).

decline, expressed as a *negative* 0.1 percent annual rate), North America (0.6 percent), and Oceania (1.0 percent). Close to the global average are Asia (1.3 percent) and Latin America (1.6 percent). The highest growth region in the world is Africa (2.3 percent).

A handy rule of thumb for estimating population growth is to divide a society's population growth rate into the number 70; this yields the *doubling time* in years. Thus an annual growth rate of 2 percent (found in parts of Latin America) doubles a population in thirty-three years, and a 3 percent growth rate (found in some countries in Africa) drops the doubling time to just twenty-three years. The rapid population growth of the poorest countries is deeply troubling because these countries can barely support the populations they have now.

YOUR TURN

Saudi Arabia's current population growth rate is 2.7 percent. At this rate, how long will it take the Saudi population to double?

POPULATION COMPOSITION

Demographers also study the makeup of a society's population at a given point in time. One variable is the **sex ratio,** *the number of males for every 100 females in a nation's population.* In 2004, the sex ratio in the United States was 96, or 96 males for every 100 females. Sex ratios are usually below 100 because, on average, women outlive men. In India, however, the sex ratio is 106, because many parents value sons more than daughters and may either abort a female fetus or, after birth, give more care to a male infant, raising the odds that a female child will die.

A more complex measure is the **age-sex pyramid,** *a graphic representation of the age and sex of a population.* Figure 22–2 presents the age-sex pyramids for the populations of the United States and Mexico. Higher mortality with advancing age gives these figures a rough pyramid shape. In the U.S. pyramid, the bulge in the middle reflects high birth rates during the *baby boom* from the mid-1940s to the mid-1960s. The contraction for people in their twenties and thirties reflects the subsequent *baby bust.* The birth rate has continued to decline from its high of 25.3 in 1957 to 13.9 in 2004.

Comparing the U.S. and Mexican age-sex pyramids shows different demographic trends. The age-sex pyramid

WINDOW ON THE WORLD

GLOBAL MAP 22-1   Population Growth in Global Perspective

The richest countries of the world—including the United States, Canada, and the nations of Europe—have growth rates below 1 percent. The nations of Latin America and Asia typically have growth rates around 1.5 percent, which double a population in forty-seven years. Africa has an overall growth rate of 2.3 percent (despite only small increases in countries with a high rate of AIDS), which cuts the doubling time to thirty years. In global perspective, we see that a society's standard of living is closely related to its rate of population growth: Population is rising fastest in the world regions that can least afford to support more people.

Source: Population Reference Bureau (2005); map projection from *Peters Atlas of the World* (1990).

Annual Population Growth
- 3.0 percent and higher
- 2.0 to 2.9 percent
- 1.0 to 1.9 percent
- Below 1.0 percent

for Mexico, like that of other lower-income nations, is wide at the bottom (reflecting higher birth rates) and narrows quickly by what we would term middle age (due to higher mortality). In short, Mexico is a much younger society, with a median age of twenty-five, compared to thirty-five in the United States. With a larger share of females still in their childbearing years, Mexico's crude birth rate (23) is nearly twice our own (13.9), and its annual rate of population growth (1.9 percent) is three times the U.S. rate (0.6 percent).

History and Theory of Population Growth

In the past, people wanted large families because human labor was the key to productivity. In addition, until rubber condoms were invented 150 years ago, the prevention of pregnancy was uncertain at best. But high death rates from infectious diseases put a constant brake on population growth.

A major demographic shift began about 1750 as the world's population turned upward, reaching the 1 billion mark by 1800. This milestone (which took all of human history to reach) was repeated barely a century later in 1930, when a second billion people were added to the planet.

 To find out more about U.S. demography, go to http://www.census.gov

In other words, not only was population increasing but also the *rate* of growth was accelerating. Global population reached 3 billion by 1962 (just thirty-two years later) and 4 billion by 1974 (only twelve years after that). The rate of world population increase has stabilized recently, but our planet passed the 5 billion mark in 1987 and the 6 billion mark in 1999. In no previous century did the world's population even double. In the twentieth century, it quadrupled.

Currently, the world is adding about 74 million people each year; 96 percent of this increase is in poor countries. Experts predict that Earth's population will reach between 8 billion and 9 billion by 2050 (O'Neill & Balk, 2001). Given the world's troubles feeding the present population, such an increase is a matter of urgent concern.

MALTHUSIAN THEORY

The sudden population growth 250 years ago sparked the development of demography. Thomas Robert Malthus (1766–1834), an English economist and clergyman, warned that population increase would soon lead to social chaos. Malthus (1926, orig. 1798) calculated that population would increase in what mathematicians call a *geometric progression,* illustrated by the series of numbers 2, 4, 8, 16, 32, and so on. At such a rate, Malthus concluded, world population would soon soar out of control.

Food production would also increase, Malthus explained, but only in *arithmetic progression* (as in the series 2, 3, 4, 5, 6, and so on) because even with new agricultural technology, farmland is limited. Thus Malthus presented a distressing vision of the future: people reproducing beyond what the planet could feed, leading ultimately to widespread starvation and war over what resources were left.

This street scene in Calcutta, India, conveys the vision of the future found in the work of Thomas Robert Malthus, who feared that population increase would overwhelm the world's resources. After reading the next few pages, can you explain why Malthus had such a serious concern about population? How is demographic transition theory a more hopeful analysis?

Malthus recognized that artificial birth control or abstinence might change his prediction. But he found one morally wrong and the other quite impractical. Famine and war therefore stalked humanity in Malthus's mind, and he was justly known as "the dismal parson."

Critical review Fortunately, Malthus's prediction was flawed. First, by 1850, the European birth rate began to drop, partly because children were becoming an economic liability rather than an asset and partly because people began using artificial birth control. Second, Malthus underestimated human ingenuity: Modern irrigation techniques, fertilizers, and pesticides increased farm production far more than he could have imagined.

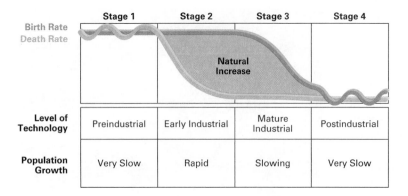

	Stage 1	Stage 2	Stage 3	Stage 4
Birth Rate **Death Rate**			**Natural Increase**	
Level of Technology	Preindustrial	Early Industrial	Mature Industrial	Postindustrial
Population Growth	Very Slow	Rapid	Slowing	Very Slow

FIGURE 22–3 Demographic Transition Theory

Demographic transition theory links population change to a society's level of technological development.

Some criticized Malthus for ignoring the role of social inequality in world abundance and famine. For example, Karl Marx (1967, orig. 1867) objected to viewing suffering as a "law of nature" rather than the curse of capitalism. More recently, "critical demographers" have claimed that saying poverty is caused by high birth rates in low-income countries amounts to blaming the victims. On the contrary, they see global inequality as the real issue (Horton, 1999; Kuumba, 1999).

Still, Malthus offers an important lesson. Habitable land, clean water, and fresh air are limited resources, and greater economic productivity has taken a heavy toll on the natural environment. In addition, medical advances have lowered death rates, pushing up world population. Common sense tells us that no level of population growth can go on forever. People everywhere must become aware of the dangers of population increase.

DEMOGRAPHIC TRANSITION THEORY

A more complex analysis of population change is **demographic transition theory,** *the thesis that population patterns reflect a society's level of technological development.* Figure 22–3 shows the demographic consequences at four levels of technological development. Preindustrial, agrarian societies (Stage 1) have high birth rates because of the economic value of children and the absence of birth control. Death rates are also high because of low living standards and limited medical technology. Outbreaks of disease neutralize births, so population rises and falls with only a modest overall increase. This was the case for thousands of years in Europe before the Industrial Revolution.

Stage 2, the onset of industrialization, brings a demographic transition as death rates fall due to greater food supplies and scientific medicine. But birth rates remain high, resulting in rapid population growth. It was during

Europe's Stage 2 that Malthus formulated his ideas, which accounts for his pessimistic view of the future. The world's poorest countries today are in this high-growth stage.

In Stage 3, a mature industrial economy, the birth rate drops, curbing population growth once again. Fertility falls because most children survive to adulthood and because high living standards make raising children expensive. In short, affluence transforms children from economic assets into economic liabilities. Smaller families, made possible by effective birth control, are also favored by women working outside the home. As birth rates follow death rates downward, population growth slows further.

Stage 4 corresponds to a postindustrial economy in which the demographic transition is complete. The birth rate keeps falling, partly because dual-income couples gradually become the norm and partly because the cost of raising children continues to increase. This trend, linked to steady death rates, means that population grows only very slowly or even decreases. This is the case today in Japan, Europe, and the United States.

Critical review Demographic transition theory suggests that the key to population control lies in technology. Instead of the runaway population increase feared by Malthus, this theory sees technology slowing growth and spreading material plenty.

Demographic transition theory is linked to modernization theory, one approach to global development discussed in Chapter 12 ("Global Stratification"). Modernization theorists are optimistic that poor countries will solve their population problems as they industrialize. But critics, notably dependency theorists, strongly disagree. Unless there is a redistribution of global resources, they maintain, our planet will become increasingly divided into industrialized "haves," enjoying low population growth, and nonindustrialized "have-nots," struggling in vain to feed more and more people.

Fertility in the United States has fallen during the past century and is now quite low. But some categories of the U.S. population have much higher fertility rates. One example is the Amish, a religious society living in rural areas of Ohio, Pennsylvania, and other states. It is common for Amish couples to have five, six, or more children. Why do you think the Amish favor large families?

GLOBAL POPULATION TODAY: A BRIEF SURVEY

What can we say about population in today's world? Drawing on the discussion so far, we can identify important patterns and reach several conclusions.

The Low-Growth North

When the Industrial Revolution began in the Northern Hemisphere, the population increase in Western Europe and North America was a high 3 percent annually. But in

 To find out more about population growth, go to http://www.populationconnection.org

the centuries since, the growth rate has steadily declined, and in 1970, it fell below 1 percent. As our postindustrial society settles into Stage 4, the U.S. birth rate is less than the replacement level of 2.1 children per woman, a point demographers term **zero population growth**—*the level of reproduction that maintains population in a steady state.* More than sixty nations, almost all of them rich, are at or below the point of zero population growth.

Factors holding down population in these postindustrial societies include a high proportion of men and women in the labor force, rising costs of raising children, trends toward later marriage and singlehood, and widespread use of contraceptives and abortion.

In high-income nations, then, population increase is not the pressing problem that it is in poor countries. On the contrary, many governments in high-income countries are concerned about a future problem of ·*underpopulation* because declining population may be difficult to reverse and because the swelling ranks of the elderly can look to fewer and fewer young people for support (P. McDonald, 2001; Kent & Mather, 2002).

YOUR TURN

What effect do you think our country's high level of immigration (which typically brings young people) will have on our ability to support more and more older people?

The High-Growth South

Population is a critical problem in poor nations of the Southern Hemisphere. No nation of the world lacks industrial technology entirely; demographic transition theory's Stage 1 applies today to remote rural areas of low-income nations. But much of Latin America, Africa, and Asia is at Stage 2, with a mix of agrarian and industrial economies. Advanced medical technology, supplied by rich countries, has sharply reduced death rates, but birth rates remain high. This is why poor countries now account for two-thirds of Earth's people and 96 percent of global population increase.

In poor countries throughout the world, birth rates have fallen from an average of about six children per woman in 1950 to about three today. But fertility this high will only in-

 Read about population control in South Asia at http://www.asia-initiative.org/

tensify global poverty. At a 1994 global population conference in Cairo, delegates from 180 nations

agreed that a key element in controlling world population growth was improving the status of women. The Thinking About Diversity box on page 588 takes a closer look.

In much of the world, mortality is falling. To limit population growth, the world—especially poor countries—must control births as successfully as it is fending off deaths.

Empowering Women: The Key to Controlling Population Growth

Sohad Ahmad lives with her husband in a farming village 50 miles south of Cairo, Egypt's capital. Ahmad lives a poor life, like hundreds of millions of other women in the world. Yet her situation differs in an important respect: She has had only two children and will have no more.

Why do Ahmad and her husband reject the conventional wisdom that children are an economic asset? One part of the answer is that Egypt's growing population has already created such a demand for land that Ahmad's family could not afford more even if they had the children to farm it. But the main reason is that she does not want her life defined only by childbearing.

Like Ahmad, more women in Egypt are taking control of their fertility and seeking educational and economic opportunities. For this reason, Egypt has made great progress in reducing its annual population growth from 3.0 percent just ten years ago to 2.0 percent today.

With its focus on raising the standing of women, the 1994 Cairo conference broke new ground. Past population control programs have simply tried to make birth control technology available to women. This effort is vital, since only half the world's married women use effective birth control. But even with birth control available, the population continues to expand in societies that define women's primary responsibility as raising children.

Dr. Nafis Sadik, an Egyptian woman who heads the United Nations efforts at population control, sums up the new approach to lowering birth rates this way: *Give women more life choices, and they will have fewer children.* In other words, women who have access to schooling and jobs, who can decide when and whether to marry, and who bear children as a matter of choice will limit their own fertility. Schooling must be available to older women, too, Sadik adds, because elders exercise great influence in local communities.

Evidence from countries around the world is that controlling population and raising the social standing of women go hand in hand.

A simple truth: Women who have more opportunity for schooling and paid work have fewer children. As more women attend school in traditional societies, the fertility rate in these countries is falling.

WHAT DO YOU THINK?

1. Why do many analysts claim that controlling population depends on expanding women's choices?
2. What specific laws or programs can you suggest that might reduce women's childbearing?
3. Is population control an issue for people in rich countries as well as those in poor countries? Why or why not?

Sources: Ashford (1995), Axinn & Barber (2001), and Population Reference Bureau (2005).

Urbanization: The Growth of Cities

October 8, Hong Kong. The cable train grinds to the top of Victoria Peak, where we behold one of the world's most spectacular vistas: the city of Hong Kong at night! A million bright, colorful lights ring the harbor as ships, ferries, and traditional Chinese junks churn by. Few places match Hong Kong for sheer energy. This small city is as economically productive as the state of Wisconsin or the nation of Finland. We could sit here for hours entranced by the spectacle of Hong Kong.

For most of human history, the sights and sounds of great cities such as Hong Kong, New York, and Los Angeles were simply unimaginable. Our distant ancestors lived in small, nomadic groups, moving as they depleted vegetation or hunted migratory game. The tiny settlements that marked the emergence of civilization in the Middle East some 12,000 years ago held only a small fraction of the Earth's population. Today the largest three or four cities of the world hold as many people as the entire planet did back then.

Urbanization is *the concentration of population into cities.* Urbanization redistributes and concentrates population within a society and transforms many patterns of social life. We will trace these changes in terms of three urban revolutions: the emergence of cities 10,000 years ago, the development of industrial cities after 1750, and the explosive growth of cities in poor countries today.

THE EVOLUTION OF CITIES

Cities are a relatively new development in human history. Only about 12,000 years ago did our ancestors begin founding permanent settlements, which paved the way for the *first urban revolution.*

The First Cities

As explained in Chapter 4 ("Society"), hunting and gathering forced people to move all the time; however, once our ancestors discovered how to domesticate animals and cultivate crops, they were able to stay in one place. Raising their own food also created a material surplus, which freed some people from food production and allowed them to build shelters, make tools, weave cloth, and take part in religious rituals. The emergence of cities led to both specialization and higher living standards.

The first city was Jericho, which lies to the north of the Dead Sea in what is now the West Bank. When first settled some 10,000 years ago, it was home to only 600 people. But as the centuries passed, cities grew to tens of thousands of people and became the centers of vast empires. By 3000 B.C.E., Egyptian cities flourished, as did cities in China about 2000 B.C.E. and in Central and South America about 1500 B.C.E. In North America, however, only a few Native American societies formed settlements; widespread urbanization had to await the arrival of European settlers in the seventeenth century.

Preindustrial European Cities

European cities date back some 5,000 years to the Greeks and later the Romans, both of whom created great empires and founded cities across Europe, including Vienna, Paris, and London. With the fall of the Roman Empire, the so-called Dark Ages began as people withdrew within defensive walled settlements and warlords battled for territory. Only in the eleventh century did Europe become more peaceful; trade flourished once again, allowing cities to grow.

Medieval cities were quite different from those familiar to us today. Beneath towering cathedrals, the narrow and winding streets of London, Brussels, and Florence teemed with merchants, artisans, priests, peddlers, jugglers, nobles, and servants. Occupational groups such as bakers, carpenters, and metalworkers clustered together in distinct sections or "quarters." Ethnicity also defined communities as residents tried to keep out people who differed from themselves. The term "ghetto" (from the Italian *borghetto,* meaning "outside the city walls") was first used to describe the neighborhood in Venice into which Jews were segregated.

Industrial European Cities

As the Middle Ages came to a close, steadily increasing commerce enriched a new urban middle class, or *bourgeoisie* (French, meaning "townspeople"). With more and more money, the bourgeoisie soon rivaled the hereditary nobility.

By about 1750, the Industrial Revolution triggered a *second urban revolution,* first in Europe and then in North America. Factories unleashed tremendous productive power, causing cities to grow bigger than ever before. London, the largest European city, reached 550,000 people by 1700 and exploded to 6.5 million by 1900 (A. F. Weber, 1963, orig. 1899; Chandler & Fox, 1974).

Cities not only grew but changed shape as well. Older winding streets gave way to broad, straight boulevards to handle the increasing flow of commercial traffic. Steam and electric trolleys soon crisscrossed the expanding cities. Because land was now a commodity to be bought and sold, developers divided cities into regular-sized lots (Mumford, 1961). The center of the city was no longer the cathedral but a bustling central business district filled with banks, retail stores, and tall office buildings.

With a new focus on business, cities became more crowded and impersonal. Crime rates rose. Especially at the outset, a few industrialists lived in grand style, but most men, women, and children barely survived by working in factories.

Organized efforts by workers to improve their lives eventually brought changes to the workplace, better housing, and the right to vote. Public services such as water, sewerage, and electricity further improved urban living. Today some urbanites still live in poverty, but a rising standard of living has partly fulfilled the city's historical promise of a better life.

A century ago, as this scene from the film *Gangs of New York* suggests, people living in cities used the streets for most of their daily activities. Today, by contrast, the idea of "living on the streets" is associated with the poor and homeless. Why do you think street life is less valued today than it was in the past?

THE GROWTH OF U.S. CITIES

Most of the Native Americans who inhabited North America for thousands of years before the arrival of Europeans were migratory people who formed few permanent settlements. The spread of villages and towns came after European colonization.

Colonial Settlement, 1565–1800

In 1565, the Spanish built a settlement at Saint Augustine, Florida, and in 1607, the English founded Jamestown, Virginia. The first lasting settlement, however, came in 1624, when the Dutch established New Amsterdam, later renamed New York.

New York and Boston (founded by the English in 1630) started out as tiny villages in a vast wilderness. They resembled medieval towns in Europe, with narrow, winding streets that still curve through lower Manhattan and downtown Boston. When the first census was completed in 1790, as Table 22–1 shows, just 5 percent of the nation's people lived in cities.

Urban Expansion, 1800–1860

Early in the nineteenth century, as cities along the East Coast became bigger, towns sprang up along the transportation routes that opened the American West. By 1860, Buffalo, Cleveland, Detroit, and Chicago were changing the face of the Midwest, and about one-fifth of the entire U.S. population lived in cities.

Urban expansion was greatest in the northern states; New York City, for example, had ten times the population of Charleston, South Carolina. The division of the United States into the industrial-urban North and the agrarian-rural South was one underlying cause of the Civil War (A. Schlesinger, 1969).

The Metropolitan Era, 1860–1950

The Civil War (1861–65) gave an enormous boost to urbanization as factories strained to produce weapons. Waves of people deserted the countryside for cities in hopes of finding better jobs. Joining them were tens of millions of immigrants, mostly from Europe, forming a culturally diverse urban mix.

In 1900, New York's population soared past the 4 million mark, and Chicago, a city of only 100,000 people in 1860, was closing in on 2 million. Such growth marked the era of the **metropolis** (from the Greek, meaning "mother city"), *a large city that socially and economically dominates an urban area.* Metropolises became the economic centers of the United States. By 1920, urban areas were home to a majority of the U.S. population.

Industrial technology pushed the urban skyline ever higher. In the 1880s, steel girders and mechanical elevators permitted buildings to rise more than ten stories high. In 1930, New York's Empire State Building was hailed as an urban wonder, reaching 102 stories into the clouds.

Urban Decentralization, 1950–Present

The industrial metropolis reached its peak about 1950. Since then, something of a turnaround—termed *urban decentralization*—has occurred as people have spread out within the urban area. They have left downtown areas for outlying **suburbs**, *urban areas beyond the political boundaries of a city*. The old industrial cities of the Northeast and Midwest stopped growing, and some lost considerable population in the decades after 1950. At the same time, suburban populations increased rapidly. The urban landscape of densely packed central cities evolved into sprawling suburban regions.

SUBURBS AND URBAN DECLINE

Imitating European nobility, some of the rich had townhouses in the city as well as country homes beyond the city limits. But not until after World War II did ordinary people find a suburban home within their reach. With more and more cars, new four-lane highways, government-backed mortgages, and inexpensive tract homes, the suburbs grew rapidly. By 1999, most of the U.S. population lived in the suburbs and shopped at nearby malls rather than in the older and more distant downtown shopping districts (Pederson, Smith, & Adler, 1999; Macionis & Parrillo, 2004).

As many older cities of the Snowbelt—the Northeast and Midwest—lost higher-income taxpayers to the suburbs, they struggled to pay for expensive social programs for the poor who remained. Many cities fell into financial crisis, and inner-city decay became severe. Especially to white suburbanites, the inner cities became synonymous with slums, crime, drugs, unemployment, the poor, and minorities (Stahura, 1986; Galster, 1991).

The urban critic Paul Goldberger (2002) points out that the decline of central cities also has led to a decline in the importance of public space. Historically, the heart of city life was played out on public streets. The French word for a sophisticated person is *boulevardier,* which literally means "street person." However, this term has a negative meaning in the United States today. The active life that once took place on public streets and in public squares now takes place in shopping malls, cineplex lobbies, and gated communities—all privately owned spaces. Further reducing the vitality of today's urban places is the spread of television, the Internet, and other media that people use without leaving home.

> **YOUR TURN**
>
> Do you think of city streets as a place for socializing or simply as routes to some destination? Do you know of any cases of cities banning traffic from certain streets to create pedestrian areas?

TABLE 22–1

Urban Population of the United States, 1790–2000

Year	Population (in millions)	Percentage Urban
1790	3.9	5.1%
1800	5.3	6.1
1820	9.6	7.3
1840	17.1	10.5
1860	31.4	19.7
1880	50.2	28.1
1900	76.0	39.7
1920	105.7	51.3
1940	131.7	56.5
1960	179.3	69.9
1980	226.5	73.7
2000	281.4	79.0

Source: U.S. Census Bureau (2004).

POSTINDUSTRIAL SUNBELT CITIES

As older Snowbelt cities fell into decline, Sunbelt cities in the South and the West began to grow rapidly. The soaring populations of cities such as Los Angeles and Houston reflect a population shift to the Sunbelt, where 60 percent of U.S. people now live. In addition, most of today's immigrants enter the country in the Sunbelt region. In 1950, nine of the ten biggest U.S. cities were in the Snowbelt; in 2004, seven of the top ten were in the Sunbelt (U.S. Census Bureau, 2005).

Unlike their colder counterparts, Sunbelt cities came of age *after* urban decentralization began. So although cities like Chicago have long been enclosed by a ring of politically independent suburbs, cities like Houston have pushed their boundaries outward to include suburban communities. Chicago covers 227 square miles; Houston is more than twice that size, and the greater Houston urban area covers almost 9,000 square miles—an area the size of New Jersey.

The great sprawl of Sunbelt cities has drawbacks. Many people in cities like Atlanta, Dallas, Phoenix, and Los Angeles complain that growth results in traffic-clogged roads leading to poorly planned housing developments and schools that cannot keep up with the inflow of children. Not surprisingly, in light of this growth, voters in many communities across the United States have passed ballot initiatives seeking to limit urban sprawl (Lacayo, 1999; Romero & Liserio, 2002).

The rural rebound has been most pronounced in towns that offer spectacular natural beauty. There are times when people living in the scenic town of Park City, Utah, cannot even find a parking space.

MEGALOPOLIS: THE REGIONAL CITY

Another result of urban decentralization is urban regions or regional cities. The U.S. Census Bureau (2005) recognizes 362 *metropolitan statistical areas* (MSAs). These areas include at least one city with 50,000 or more people. The bureau also recognizes 560 *micropolitan statistical areas,* urban areas with at least one city of 10,000 to 50,000 people. *Core based statistical areas* (CBSAs) include both metropolitan and micropolitan statistical areas.

The biggest CBSAs contain millions of people and cover large areas that extend into several states. In 2000, the largest MSA was New York and its adjacent urban areas in Long Island, western Connecticut, northern New Jersey, and eastern Pennsylvania, with a total population of more than 21 million. Next in size is the CBSA in southern California that includes Los Angeles, Riverside, and Long Beach, with a population of more than 16 million.

As regional cities grow, they begin to overlap. In the early 1960s, the French geographer Jean Gottmann (1961) coined the term **megalopolis** to designate *a vast urban region containing a number of cities and their surrounding suburbs.* Along the East Coast, a 400-mile megalopolis stretches all the way from New England to Virginia. Other supercities cover the eastern coast of Florida and stretch from Cleveland west to Chicago.

EDGE CITIES

Urban decentralization has also created *edge cities,* business centers some distance from the old downtowns. Edge cities—a mix of corporate office buildings, shopping malls, hotels, and entertainment complexes—differ from suburbs, which contain mostly homes. The population of suburbs peaks at night, but the population of edge cities peaks during the workday.

As part of expanding urban regions, most edge cities have no clear physical boundaries. Some do have names, including Las Colinas (near the Dallas–Fort Worth airport), Tyson's Corner (in Virginia, near Washington, D.C.), and King of Prussia (northwest of Philadelphia). Other edge cities are known only by the major highways that flow through them, including Route 1 in Princeton, New Jersey, and Route 128 near Boston (Garreau, 1991; Macionis & Parrillo, 2004).

THE RURAL REBOUND

Over the course of U.S. history, as shown by the data in Table 22–1, the urban population of the nation has increased steadily. Immigration has played a part in this increase because most newcomers settle in cities. At the same time, there has been considerable migration from rural areas to urban places, typically by people seeking greater economic opportunity.

However, in the 1990s, three-fourths of the rural counties across the United States gained population, a trend analysts have called the "rural rebound." Most of this gain resulted from the migration of people from urban areas. This trend has not affected all rural places: As the opening to this chapter explains, many small towns in rural areas (especially in the Plains States) are struggling simply to stay

Peasant Dance (above, c. 1565), by Pieter Breughel the Elder, conveys the essential unity of rural life forged by generations of kinship and neighborhood. By contrast, Ernest Fiene's *Nocturne* (left) communicates the impersonality common to urban areas. Taken together, these paintings capture Tönnies's distinction between *Gemeinschaft* and *Gesellschaft*.

Pieter Breughel the Elder (c. 1525/30–1569), *Peasant Dance*, c. 1565, Kunsthistorisches Museum, Vienna/Superstock. Ernest Fiene (1894–1965), *Nocturne*. Photograph © Christie's Images.

alive. But even there, losses slowed during the 1990s (K. M. Johnson, 1999; D. Johnson, 2001).

The greatest gains have come to rural communities that offer scenic and recreational attractions, such as lakes, mountains, and ski areas. People are drawn to rural communities not only by their natural beauty but also by their slower pace: less traffic, a lower crime rate, and cleaner air. A number of companies have relocated to rural counties, which has increased economic opportunity for the rural population (K. M. Johnson, 1999; Johnson & Fuguitt, 2000).

Urbanism as a Way of Life

Early sociologists in Europe and the United States focused their attention on the rise of cities and how urban life differed from rural life. We briefly present their accounts of urbanism as a way of life.

FERDINAND TÖNNIES: *GEMEINSCHAFT* AND *GESELLSCHAFT*

In the late nineteenth century, the German sociologist Ferdinand Tönnies (1855–1937) studied how life in the new industrial metropolis differed from life in rural villages. From this contrast, he developed two concepts that have become a lasting part of sociology's terminology.

Tönnies (1963, orig. 1887) used the German word *Gemeinschaft* (meaning roughly "community") to refer to *a type of social organization in which people are closely tied by kinship and tradition.* The *Gemeinschaft* of the rural village joins people in what amounts to a single primary group.

By and large, argued Tönnies, *Gemeinschaft* is absent in the modern city. On the contrary, urbanization creates *Gesellschaft* (a German word meaning roughly "association"), *a type of social organization in which people come together only on the basis of individual self-interest.* In the *Gesellschaft* way of life, individuals are motivated by their own needs rather than by a desire to help improve the well-being of everyone. City dwellers display little sense of community or common identity and look to others mainly when they need something. Tönnies saw in urbanization a weakening of close, long-lasting social relations in favor of the brief and impersonal ties—or secondary relationships—typical of business.

EMILE DURKHEIM: MECHANICAL AND ORGANIC SOLIDARITY

The French sociologist Emile Durkheim (see Chapter 4, "Society") agreed with much of Tönnies's thinking about cities. However, Durkheim countered that urbanites do not lack social bonds; they simply organize social life differently than rural people.

Durkheim described traditional, rural life as *mechanical solidarity*, social bonds based on common sentiments and shared moral values. With its emphasis on tradition, Durkheim's concept of mechanical solidarity bears a striking similarity to Tönnies's *Gemeinschaft*. Urbanization erodes mechanical solidarity, Durkheim explained, but it also generates a new type of bonding, which he called *organic solidarity*, social bonds based on specialization and interdependence. This concept, which parallels Tönnies's *Gesellschaft*, reveals an important difference between the two thinkers. Both thought the growth of industrial cities weakened tradition, but Durkheim optimistically pointed to a new kind of solidarity. Where people had been joined by *likeness*, Durkheim now saw them joined by *difference*.

For Durkheim, urban society offered more individual choice, moral tolerance, and personal privacy than people find in rural villages. In sum, something is lost in the process of urbanization, but much is gained.

GEORG SIMMEL: THE BLASÉ URBANITE

The German sociologist Georg Simmel (1858–1918) offered a microanalysis of cities, studying how urban life shapes individual experience. According to Simmel, individuals perceive the city as a crush of people, objects, and events. To prevent being overwhelmed by all this stimulation, urbanites develop a *blasé attitude*, tuning out much of what goes on around them. Such detachment does not mean that city dwellers lack compassion for others; they simply keep their distance as a survival strategy so they can focus their time and energy on those who really matter to them.

THE CHICAGO SCHOOL:
ROBERT PARK AND LOUIS WIRTH

Sociologists in the United States soon joined the study of rapidly growing cities. Robert Park, a leader of the first U.S. sociology program at the University of Chicago, sought to add a street-level perspective by getting out and studying real cities. As he said of himself, "I suspect that I have actually covered more ground, tramping about in cities in different parts of the world, than any other living man" (1950:viii). Walking the streets, Park found the city to be an organized mosaic of distinctive ethnic communities, commercial centers, and industrial districts. Over time, he observed these "natural areas" develop and change in relation to one another. To Park, the city was a living organism—a human kaleidoscope.

Another major figure in the Chicago School of urban sociology was Louis Wirth (1897–1952). Wirth (1938) is best

known for blending the ideas of Tönnies, Durkheim, Simmel, and Park into a comprehensive theory of urban life.

Wirth began by defining the city as a setting with a large, dense, and socially diverse population. These traits result in an impersonal, superficial, and transitory way of life. Living among millions of others, urbanites come into contact with many more people than residents of rural areas. So

when city people notice others at all, they usually know them not in terms of *who they are* but *what they do*—as, for instance, the bus driver, florist, or grocery store clerk. Specialized urban relationships are pleasant for all concerned, but we should remember that self-interest rather than friendship is usually the main reason for the interaction.

Finally, limited social involvement coupled with great social diversity make city dwellers more tolerant than rural villagers. Rural communities often jealously enforce their narrow traditions, but the heterogeneous population of a city rarely shares any single code of moral conduct (Wilson, 1985, 1995).

Critical review   In both Europe and the United States, early sociologists presented a mixed view of urban living. Rapid urbanization troubled Tönnies, and Wirth saw personal ties and traditional morality lost in the anonymous rush of the city. Durkheim and Park emphasized urbanism's positive face, pointing to more personal freedom and greater personal choice.

One problem with all these views is that they paint urbanism in broad strokes that overlook the effects of class, race, and gender. There are many kinds of urbanites—rich and poor, black and white, Anglo and Latino, women and men—all leading distinctive lives (Gans, 1968). As the Thinking About Diversity box explains, the share of minorities in the largest U.S. cities increased sharply during the 1990s. We see social diversity most clearly in cities, where various categories of people are large enough to form visible communities (Macionis & Parrillo, 2004).

URBAN ECOLOGY

Sociologists (especially members of the Chicago School) developed **urban ecology,** *the study of the link between the physical and social dimensions of cities.* For example, why are cities located where they are? The first cities emerged in fertile regions where the ecology favored raising crops. Preindustrial people, concerned with defense, built their cities on mountains (ancient Athens was perched on an outcropping of rock) or surrounded by water (Paris and Mexico City were founded on islands). With the coming of the Industrial Revolution,

Census 2000: Minorities Now a Majority in the Largest U.S. Cities

According to the results of the 2000 census, minorities—Hispanics, African Americans, and Asians—are now a majority of the population in 48 of the 100 largest U.S. cities, up from 30 in 1990.

What accounts for the change? One reason is that large cities have been losing their non-Hispanic white population. Santa Ana, California, for example, lost 38 percent of its 1990 white population; the drop was 40 percent in Birmingham, Alabama, and a whopping 53 percent in Detroit, Michigan. The white share of the population of all 100 of the largest cities fell from 52.1 percent in 1990 to 43.8 percent in 2000, as the figure shows.

But perhaps the biggest reason for the minority-majority trend is the increase in immigration. Immigration, coupled with higher birth rates among new immigrants, resulted in a 43

percent gain in the Hispanic population (almost 4 million people) of the

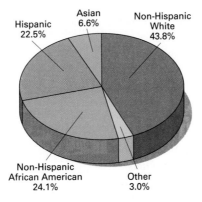

Hispanic 22.5%
Asian 6.6%
Non-Hispanic White 43.8%
Non-Hispanic African American 24.1%
Other 3.0%

Population Profile for the 100 Largest U.S. Cities, 2000

Racial and ethnic minorities make up a majority of the population of this country's largest cities.

Source: U.S. Census Bureau (2001).

largest 100 cities between 1990 and 2000. The Asian population also surged by 40 percent (more than 1.1 million people). The African American population was steady over the course of the 1990s. Political officials and other policy makers have been watching these figures closely, for the future vitality of the largest U.S. cities depends on meeting the needs and welcoming the contributions of the swelling minority populations.

WHAT DO YOU THINK?

1. Why do you think white people are leaving central cities?
2. What positive changes does a minority-majority bring to a city?
3. What are some specific challenges faced by cities with large populations of new immigrants?

Sources: Based on Schmitt (2001) and U.S. Census Bureau (2001).

---

economic considerations situated all the major U.S. cities near rivers and natural harbors that facilitated trade.

Urban ecologists also study the physical design of cities. In 1925, Ernest W. Burgess, a student and colleague of Robert Park's, described land use in Chicago in terms of *concentric zones.* City centers, Burgess observed, are business districts bordered by a ring of factories, followed by residential rings with housing that becomes more expensive the farther it is from the noise and pollution of the city's center.

Homer Hoyt (1939) refined Burgess's observations, noting that distinctive districts sometimes form *wedge-shaped sectors.* For example, one fashionable area may develop next to another, or an industrial district may extend outward from a city's center along a train or trolley line.

Chauncy Harris and Edward Ullman (1945) added yet another insight: As cities decentralize, they lose their

single-center form in favor of a *multicentered model.* As cities grow, residential areas, industrial parks, and shopping districts typically push away from one another. Few people wish to live close to industrial areas, for example, so the city becomes a mosaic of distinct districts.

Social area analysis investigates what people in particular neighborhoods have in common. Three factors seem to explain most of the variation: family patterns, social class, and race and ethnicity (Shevky & Bell, 1955; Johnston, 1976). Families with children look for areas with single-family homes or large apartments and good schools. The rich seek high-prestige neighborhoods, often in the central city near cultural attractions. People with a common race or ethnic heritage cluster in distinctive communities.

Finally, Brian Berry and Philip Rees (1969) tie together many of these insights. They explain that distinct family types tend to settle in the concentric zones described by Burgess. Specifically, households with few children tend to cluster toward the city's center, and those with more children live farther away. Social class differences are primarily responsible for the sector-shaped districts described by Hoyt—for instance, the rich occupy one "side of the tracks," and the poor, the other. And racial and ethnic neighborhoods are found at various points throughout the city, consistent with Harris and Ullman's multicentered model.

URBAN POLITICAL ECONOMY

In the late 1960s, many large U.S. cities were rocked by major riots. In the wake of this unrest, some analysts turned away from the ecological approach to a social-conflict understanding of city life. The *urban political economy* model applies Karl Marx's analysis of conflict in the workplace to conflict in the city (Lindstrom, 1995).

Political economists disagree with the ecological approach, which sees the city as a natural organism with particular districts and neighborhoods developing according to an internal logic. They claim that city life is defined by people with power: corporate leaders and political officials. Capitalism, which transforms the city into real estate traded for profit and concentrates wealth in the hands of a few, is the key to understanding city life. From this point of view, for example, the decline in industrial Snowbelt cities after 1950 was the result of deliberate decisions by the corporate elite to move their production facilities to the Sunbelt (where labor is cheaper and less likely to be unionized) or to move them out of the country entirely to low-income nations (Molotch, 1976; Castells, 1977, 1983; Feagin, 1983; Lefebvre, 1991; Jones & Wilson, 1999).

Critical review   The fact that many U.S. cities are in crisis, with widespread poverty, high crime, and barely functioning schools, seems to favor the political economy model over the urban ecology approach. But one criticism applies to both: They focus on U.S. cities during a limited period of history. Much of what we know about industrial cities does not apply to preindustrial U.S. towns in our own past or to the rapidly growing cities in many poor nations today. It is unlikely that any single model of cities can account for the full range of urban diversity.

Urbanization in Poor Nations

November 16, Cairo, Egypt. People call the vast Muslim cemetery in Old Cairo the "City of the Dead." In truth, it is very

much alive: Tens of thousands of squatters have moved into the mausoleums, making this place an eerie mix of life and death. Children run across the stone floors, clotheslines stretch between the monuments, and an occasional television antenna protrudes from a tomb roof. With Cairo's population increasing at the rate of 1,000 people a day, families live where they can.

As noted earlier, twice in its history, the world has experienced a revolutionary expansion of cities. The first urban revolution began about 12,000 years ago with the first urban settlements and continued until permanent settlements were in place on several continents. About 1750, the second urban revolution took off; it lasted for two centuries as the Industrial Revolution spurred rapid growth of cities in Europe and North America.

A third urban revolution is now under way. Today, approximately 75 percent of people in industrial societies are already city dwellers. But extreme urban growth is occurring in low-income nations. In 1950, about 25 percent of the people in poor countries lived in cities; in 2005, the figure was close to 50 percent. In 1950, only seven cities in the world had populations over 5 million, and only two of these were in low-income countries. By 2005, forty-nine cities had passed this mark, and thirty-two of them were in less developed nations (Brockerhoff, 2000; GeoHive, 2005).

This third urban revolution is taking place because many poor nations have entered the high-growth Stage 2 of demographic transition theory. Falling death rates have fueled population increases in Latin America, Asia, and especially Africa. For urban areas, the rate of increase is *twice* as high because in addition to natural increase, millions of people leave the countryside each year in search of jobs, health care, education, and conveniences such as running water and electricity.

Cities do offer more opportunities than rural areas, but they provide no quick fix for the massive problems of escalating population and grinding poverty. Many cities in less economically developed nations—including Mexico City, Egypt's Cairo, India's Calcutta, and Manila in the Philippines—are simply unable to meet the basic needs of much of their populations. All these cities are surrounded by wretched shantytowns—settlements of makeshift homes built from discarded materials. As noted in Chapter 12 ("Global Stratification"), even city dumps are home to thousands of poor people, who pick through the piles of waste hoping to find enough to make it through another day.

Environment and Society

The human species has prospered, rapidly increasing the population of the planet. An increasing share of the global population now lives in cities, complex settlements that offer the promise of a better life than that found in rural villages.

But these advances have come at a high price. Never before in history have human beings placed such demands on the planet. This disturbing development brings us to the final section of this chapter: the interplay between the natural environment and society. Like demography, **ecology** is another cousin of sociology, formally defined as *the study of the interaction of living organisms and the natural environment*. Ecology rests on the research of natural scientists as well as social scientists. In this text, we focus on the aspects of ecology that involve familiar sociological concepts and issues.

The **natural environment** is *Earth's surface and atmosphere, including living organisms, air, water, soil, and other resources necessary to sustain life*. Like every other species, humans depend on the natural environment to survive. Yet with our capacity for culture, humans stand apart from other species; we alone take deliberate action to remake the world according to our own interests and desires, for better and for worse.

Why is the environment of interest to sociologists? Simply because environmental problems—from pollution to acid rain to global warming—do not arise from the natural world operating on its own. Rather, as we shall explain, such issues result from the organized patterns of collective living, so they are *social* problems (L. Marx, 1994).

THE GLOBAL DIMENSION

The study of the natural environment requires a global perspective. The reason is simple: Regardless of political divisions among nations, the planet is a single **ecosystem,** *a system composed of the interaction of all living organisms and their natural environment.*

The Greek meaning of *eco* is "house," reminding us that this planet is our home and that all living things and their natural environment are interrelated. A change in any part of the natural environment ripples throughout the entire global ecosystem.

Consider, from an ecological point of view, our national love of eating hamburgers. People in North America (and increasingly around the world) have created a huge demand for beef, which has greatly expanded the ranching industry in Brazil, Costa Rica, and other Latin American nations. To produce the lean meat sought by fast-food corporations, cattle in Latin America feed on grass, which requires a great

The most important insight sociology offers about our physical world is that environmental problems do not simply "happen." Rather, the state of the natural environment reflects the ways in which social life is organized—how people live and what they think is important. The greater the technological power of a society, the greater that society's ability to threaten the natural environment.

deal of land. Latin American ranchers get the land for grazing by clearing thousands of square miles of forests each year. These tropical forests are vital to maintaining Earth's atmosphere. Deforestation ends up threatening everyone, including people in the United States enjoying hamburgers (N. Myers, 1984a).

TECHNOLOGY AND THE ENVIRONMENTAL DEFICIT

Sociologists point to a simple formula: $I = PAT$, where environmental impact (I) reflects a society's population (P), its level of affluence (A), and its level of technology (T). Members of societies with simple technology—the hunters and gatherers described in Chapter 4 ("Society")—hardly affect the environment because they are small in number, are poor, and have only simple technology. On the contrary, nature affects their lives as they follow the migration of game, watch the rhythm of the seasons, and suffer from natural catastrophes such as fires, floods, droughts, and storms.

Societies at intermediate stages of technological development have a somewhat greater capacity to affect the environment. Such societies are both larger and richer. But the environmental impact of horticulture (small-scale farming), pastoralism (the herding of animals), and even agriculture (the use of animal-drawn plows) is limited because people still rely on muscle power for producing food and other goods.

Humans' ability to control the natural environment increased dramatically with the Industrial Revolution. Muscle power gave way to engines that burn fossil fuels: coal at first and then oil. Such machinery affects the environment in two ways: We consume more natural resources, and we release more pollutants into the atmosphere. Even more important, armed with industrial technology, we are able to bend nature to our will, tunneling through mountains, damming rivers, irrigating deserts, and drilling for oil in the arctic wilderness and on the ocean floor. This explains why people in rich nations, who represent just 18 percent of humanity, now use 80 percent of the world's energy (G. T. Miller, 1992; York, Rosa, & Deitz, 2002).

The environmental impact of industrial technology goes beyond energy consumption. Just as important is the fact that members of industrial societies produce 100 times more goods than people in agrarian societies do. Higher living standards in turn increase the problem of solid waste (since people ultimately throw away most of what they produce) and pollution (since industrial production generates smoke and other toxic substances).

From the start, people recognized the material benefits of industrial technology. But only a century later did they begin to see the long-term effects on the natural environment. Today, we realize that the technological power to make our lives better can also put the lives of future generations at risk, and there is a national debate about how to address this issue.

Evidence is mounting that we are running up an **environmental deficit,** *profound long-term harm to the natural environment caused by humanity's focus on short-term material affluence* (Bormann, 1990). The concept of environmental deficit is important for three reasons. First, it reminds us that environmental concerns are *sociological,* reflecting societies' priorities about how people should live. Second, it suggests that much environmental damage—to the air, land, and water—is *unintended.* By focusing on the short-term benefits of, say, cutting down forests, strip mining, or using throwaway packaging, we fail to see their long-term environmental effects. Third, in some respects, the environmental deficit is *reversible.* Societies have created environmental problems but can also undo many of them.

CULTURE: GROWTH AND LIMITS

Whether we recognize environmental dangers and decide to do something about them is a cultural matter. Thus along with technology, culture has powerful environmental consequences.

The Logic of Growth

One of the core values that underlies social life in the United States is *material comfort,* the belief that money and the things it buys enrich our lives. We also believe in the idea of *progress,* thinking the future will be better than the present. In addition, we look to *science* to make our lives easier and more rewarding. In simple terms, "having things is good," "life gets better," and "people are clever." Taken together, such cultural values form the *logic of growth.*

Can you point to ways in which the mass media and our popular culture (music, films, and television) encourage people to support the logic of growth?

An optimistic view of the world, the logic of growth holds that more powerful technology has improved our lives and new discoveries will continue to do so in the future. Throughout the history of the United States and other high-income nations, the logic of growth has been the driving force behind settling the wilderness, building towns and roads, and pursuing material affluence.

However, "progress" can lead to unexpected problems, including strain on the environment. The logic of growth responds by arguing that people (especially scientists and other technology experts) will find a way out of any problem that growth places in our path. For example, if the world runs short of oil, we will come up with hydrogen, solar, or nuclear engines or some other as yet unknown technology to meet the world's energy needs.

Environmentalists counter that the logic of growth is flawed because it assumes that natural resources such as oil, clean air, fresh water, and topsoil will always be plentiful. We can and will exhaust these *finite* resources if we continue to pursue growth at any cost. Echoing Malthus, environmentalists warn that if we call on Earth to support increasing numbers of people, we will surely deplete finite resources, destroying the environment—and ourselves—in the process.

The Limits to Growth

If we cannot invent our way out of the problems created by the logic of growth, perhaps we need another way of thinking about the world. Environmentalists therefore counter that growth must have limits. Stated simply, the *limits-to-growth thesis* is that humanity must put in place policies to control the growth of population, production, and use of resources in order to avoid environmental collapse.

In *The Limits to Growth,* a controversial book that was influential in launching the environmental movement, Donella Meadows and her colleagues (1972) used a computer model to calculate the planet's available resources, rates of population growth, amount of land available for cultivation, levels of industrial and food production, and amount of pollutants released into the atmosphere. The authors concede that any long-range predictions are speculative, and some critics think they are plain wrong (Simon, 1981). But right or wrong, the conclusions of the study call for serious consideration. First, the authors claim that we are quickly consuming Earth's finite resources. Supplies of oil, natural gas, and other energy sources are already falling sharply and will continue to drop, a little faster or slower depending on the conservation policies of rich nations and the speed with which other nations industrialize. Within the next 100 years, resources will run out and cripple industrial output, which will also cause a decline in food production.

This limits-to-growth theory shares Malthus's pessimism about the future. People who accept it doubt that current patterns of life are sustainable for even another century. If so, we face a fundamental choice: Either we make deliberate changes in how we live, or widespread hunger and conflict will force change on us.

YOUR TURN

Are you willing to pay higher prices for products (such as hybrid cars or things made with recycled materials) that are better for the environment? Why or why not?

SOLID WASTE: THE DISPOSABLE SOCIETY

Across the United States, people generate a massive amount of solid waste—about 1.4 billion pounds *each and every day.* Figure 22–4 shows the average composition of a typical community's trash.

As a rich nation of people who value convenience, the United States has become a *disposable society.* We consume more products than virtually any other nation, and many of these products have throwaway packaging. For example, fast food is served with cardboard, plastic, and Styrofoam containers that we throw away within minutes. Countless other products—from film to fishhooks—are elaborately packaged to make the products more attractive to the customer and to discourage tampering and theft.

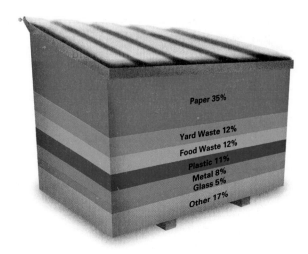

FIGURE 22-4 Composition of Community Trash

We throw away a wide range of material, with paper the single largest part of our trash.

Source: U.S. Environmental Protection Agency (2005).

Manufacturers market soft drinks, beer, and fruit juices in aluminum cans, glass jars, and plastic containers, which not only consume finite resources but also generate mountains of solid waste. Then there are countless items intentionally designed to be disposable: pens, razors, flashlights, batteries, even cameras. Other products, from light bulbs to automobiles, are designed to have a limited useful life and then become unwanted junk. As Paul Connett (1991) points out, even the words we use to describe what we throw away—*waste, litter, trash, refuse, garbage, rubbish*—show how little we value what we cannot immediately use. But this was not always the case, as the Applying Sociology box on page 600 explains.

Living in a rich society, the average person in the United States consumes 50 times more steel, 170 times more newspaper, 250 times more gasoline, and 300 times more plastic each year than the typical person in a low-income country such as Haiti (G. T. Miller, 1992). This high level of consumption means not only that we in the United States use a disproportionate share of the planet's natural resources but also that we generate most of the world's refuse.

We like to say that we "throw things away." But 80 percent of our solid waste never "goes away." Rather, it ends up in landfills, which are, literally, filling up. Material in landfills can pollute groundwater stored under the surface of the Earth. Although in most places, laws now regulate what can be discarded in a landfill, the Environmental Protection

APPLYING SOCIOLOGY
Why Grandmother Had No Trash

Grandma Macionis, we always used to say, never threw anything away. She was born and raised in Lithuania—the "old country"—where life in a poor village shaped her in ways that never changed, even after she emigrated to the United States as a young woman and settled in Philadelphia.

After opening a birthday present, she would carefully save the box, wrapping paper, and ribbon, which meant as much to her as the gift they contained. Buying a present for her was difficult, because Grandma never wore new clothes or wanted anything that she did not already have. Her kitchen knives were worn narrow from decades of sharpening, and all her garbage was recycled as compost for her vegetable garden.

As strange as Grandma sometimes seemed to her grandchildren, she was a product of her culture. A century ago,

in fact, there was little "trash." If a pair of socks wore thin, people mended them, probably more than once. When they were beyond repair, they were used as rags for cleaning or sewn (with other old clothing) into a quilt. Everything had value—if not in one way, then in another.

During the twentieth century, as women joined men in working outside the home, income went up and families began buying more and more "time-saving" products. Before long, few people cared about the home recycling that Grandma practiced. Soon cities sent crews from block to block to pick up truckloads of discarded material. The era of "trash" had begun.

WHAT DO YOU THINK?

1. Just as Grandma Macionis was a product of her culture, so are we. What cultural values make people today demand time-saving products and "convenience" packaging?
2. Do you think that the recycling of household waste in the United States will expand in the decades to come? Why or why not?
3. Would you support laws that limited trash by requiring people to recycle? Why or why not?

Agency has identified 30,000 dump sites across the United States containing hazardous materials that are polluting water both above and below the ground. In addition, what goes into landfills all too often stays there, sometimes for centuries. Tens of millions of tires, diapers, and other items we bury in landfills each year do not decompose but remain as an unwelcome legacy for future generations.

Environmentalists argue that we should address the problem of solid waste by doing what many of our grandparents did: Turn "waste" into a resource. One way to do this is through *recycling,* reusing resources we would otherwise discard. Recycling is an accepted practice in Japan and many other nations, and it is becoming more common in the United States, where we now reuse about 30 percent of waste materials. The share is increasing as laws require reuse of certain materials such as glass bottles and aluminum cans. But recycling is expanding slowly because our nation's market-based economy encourages any activity only to the

extent that it is profitable. "In the *Times*" on pages 602–03 describes a global dimension to recycling.

WATER AND AIR

Oceans, lakes, and streams are the lifeblood of the global ecosystem. Humans depend on water for drinking, bathing, cooking, recreation, and a host of other activities.

According to what scientists call the *hydrologic cycle,* Earth naturally recycles water and refreshes the land. The process begins as heat from the sun causes Earth's water, 97 percent of which is in the oceans, to evaporate and form clouds. Because water evaporates at lower temperatures than most pollutants, the water vapor that rises from the seas is relatively pure, leaving various contaminants behind. Water then falls to Earth as rain, which drains into streams and rivers and finally returns to the sea. Two major concerns about water, then, are supply and pollution.

Water Supply

Only about 1 percent of Earth's water is suitable for drinking. It is not surprising, then, that for thousands of years, water rights have figured prominently in laws around the world. Today, some regions of the world, especially the tropics, enjoy plentiful fresh water, using a small share of the available supply. However, high demand, coupled with modest reserves, makes water supply a matter of concern in much of North America and Asia, where people look to rivers rather than rainfall for their water. In China, deep aquifers are dropping rapidly. In the Middle East, water supply is reaching a critical level. Iran is rationing water in its capital city. In Egypt, the Nile River provides just one-sixth as much water per person as it did in 1900. Across northern Africa and the Middle East, as many as 1 billion people may lack the water they need for irrigation and drinking by 2025 (Postel, 1993; "China Faces Water Shortage," 2001).

Rising population and the development of more complex technology have greatly increased the world's appetite for water. The global consumption of water (now estimated at 4 billion cubic feet per year) has tripled since 1950 and is rising steadily. As a result, even in those parts of the world that receive plenty of rainfall, people are using groundwater faster than it can be replenished naturally. In the Tamil Nadu region of southern India, for example, so much groundwater is being used that the water table has fallen 100 feet over the last several decades. Mexico City—which has sprawled to some 1,400 square miles—has pumped so much water from its underground aquifer that the city has sunk 30 feet during the past century and continues to drop about 2 inches per year. Farther north in the United States, the Ogallala aquifer, which lies below seven states from South Dakota to Texas, is now dropping by about 18 inches a year, raising fears that it will run dry within several decades.

In light of such developments, we must face the reality that water is a valuable, finite resource. Greater conservation of water by individuals (the average person consumes 10 million gallons in a lifetime) is part of the answer. However, households around the world account for just 10 percent of water use. It is even more crucial that we curb water consumption by industry, which uses 20 percent of the global total, and farming, which consumes 70 percent of the total for irrigation.

Perhaps new irrigation technology will reduce the future demand for water. But here again, we see how population

Water is vital to life, and it is also in short supply. The state of Gujarat, in western India, has experienced a decade-long drought. In the village of Natwarghad, people crowd together, lowering pots into the local well, taking what little water is left.

increase, as well as economic growth, strains our ecosystem (Postel, 1993; Population Action International, 2000).

Water Pollution

In large cities from Mexico City to Cairo to Shanghai, many people have no choice but to drink contaminated water. Infectious diseases like typhoid, cholera, and dysentery, all caused by waterborne microorganisms, spread rapidly through these populations. Besides ensuring ample *supplies* of water, then, we must protect the *quality* of water.

Water quality in the United States is generally good by global standards. However, even here the problem of water pollution is steadily growing. According to the Sierra Club, an environmental activist organization, rivers and streams across the United States absorb some 500 million pounds of toxic waste each year. This pollution results not just from intentional dumping but also from the runoff of agricultural fertilizers and lawn chemicals.

A special problem is *acid rain*—rain made acidic by air pollution—which destroys plant and animal life. Acid rain (or snow) begins with power plants burning fossil fuels (oil and coal) to generate electricity; this burning releases sulfuric and nitrous oxides into the air. As the wind sweeps these gases into the atmosphere, they react with the air to form sulfuric and nitric acids, which turns atmospheric moisture acidic.

This is a clear case of one type of pollution causing another: Air pollution (from smokestacks) ends up

November 15, 2004

Glasses, Scalpels, Bikes: Turning Waste into Help

By LIA MILLER

Every year, Americans throw away millions of items that would be welcomed in poorer countries, and a wide range of groups make it their mission to recycle them. Some of these campaigns are decades old and well known, others are more spontaneous, and still others fill special niches. Here are three organizations that illustrate these possibilities.

The Lions Club Ever since Helen Keller challenged members of the Lions Clubs in 1925 to become "knights of the blind in this crusade against darkness," they have donated much of their volunteer resources to vision services.

The best-known part of this effort is the recycling of eyeglasses, which are collected in more than 13,000 collection boxes and sent to seven recycling centers in the United States. There, members clean the glasses, determine the prescription using a machine known as a lensometer and categorize each pair by prescription. Since 1994, Lions Clubs have distributed more than 20 million pairs of glasses in countries like Angola, Brazil, Cambodia, Gambia, Ghana, Mexico, Romania, Rwanda, Sri Lanka and Tajikistan.

Information: lionsclubs.org

Pedals for Progress In the mid-1970s, David Schweidenback was a Peace Corps volunteer in Ecuador. He noticed that his neighbor, a carpenter, was one of the most well-off men in his town. His bicycle allowed him to do more than anyone else: he could carry more tools and get to more places faster. When Mr. Schweidenback returned to the United States, he knew he wanted to send bikes to Ecuador.

In 1991, he decided to try collecting some bicycles. His goal was to get 12 bikes; he got almost 150. He soon realized that he could put his plan into effect on a much larger scale, and Pedals for Progress was born.

Mr. Schweidenback did not simply want to send bikes. He thought that the bikes could be a tool to help change the lives of the people in the community that received them.

Pedals for Progress collects bikes by working with about 150 civic organizations, like the Eagle Scouts, the Girl Scouts and Rotary Clubs, to sponsor collection drives in their communities.

The bikes are checked to make sure they are in fairly good working order before they are shipped.

Pedals for Progress then coordinates with a nonprofit group working in an area of a developing country in need of transportation alternatives. It helps the group receive the bikes and open a rudimentary bicycle shop. This shop then hires local people and trains them to

contaminating water (in lakes and streams that collect acid rain). Acid rain is truly a global phenomenon because the regions that suffer the harmful effects may be thousands of miles from the original pollution. For instance, British power plants have caused acid rain that has devastated forests and fish in Norway and Sweden, up to 1,000 miles to the northeast. In the United States, we see a similar pattern as midwestern smokestacks have harmed the natural environment of upstate New York and New England.

Air Pollution

Because we are surrounded by air, most people in the United States are more aware of air pollution than contaminated water. One of the unexpected consequences of industrial technology, especially the factory and the motor vehicle, has been a decline in air quality. In London in the mid-twentieth century, factory smokestacks, automobiles, and coal fires used to heat homes all added to what was probably the worst urban air quality of the last century. What some British jokingly called "pea soup" was in reality a deadly mix of pollution: Over five days in 1952, an especially thick haze that hung over London killed 4,000 people.

Air quality improved in the final decades of the twentieth century. Rich nations passed laws that banned high-pollution heating, including the coal fires that choked London fifty years ago. In addition, scientists devised ways to make factories as well as automobiles and trucks operate more cleanly.

If high-income countries can breathe a bit more easily than they once did, the problem of air pollution in poor societies is becoming more serious. One reason is that people in low-income countries still rely on wood, coal, peat, and other "dirty" fuels for cooking fires and to heat their

repair the bicycles. The bikes are sold at a very low cost to local residents.

The hope is that in the majority of cases, the proceeds from the nonprofit agency's bike shop will pay for more shipments of donated bikes, spurring a continuing process.

Goodwill Industries in Panama City, for example, has just received its 12th shipment of bicycles since 2000.

Information: p4p.org

MedShare International Every year, billions of dollars' worth of usable medical equipment is thrown out. Because of the United States' stringent regulations for medical equipment, a large portion of what is thrown away is unused.

After learning this statistic six years ago, A. B. Short and Robert Freeman decided to start a nonprofit group that could somehow take that waste and make it useful to people in other countries. The two men had been partners 10 years earlier when they founded Cafe 458, an innovative soup kitchen in Atlanta that is run like a restaurant.

MedShare International works in partnership with 15 local Georgia hospitals, where collection barrels for recyclable items have been set up. The equipment MedShare collects runs the gamut from sutures and sterile gloves to stethoscopes, hospital beds and infant incubators.

MedShare has worked with hospitals in more than 80 countries, shipping to places like Armenia, Cameroon, China, Haiti, Liberia and Peru. The hospitals order items they want from an online catalog. This helps the program stick to one of the most important pieces of advice the founders got when they were doing their initial research: never donate anything overseas that hasn't been asked for.

"So often, things are donated where it's like, 'I've got this, here it is, take it," says Mr. Short. "But it's the fact that the power of choosing is in the hands of the recipient instead of in the hands of the giver that makes it a quality donation."

Information: medshareinternational.org

WHAT DO YOU THINK?

1. Do you agree with the basic idea of recycling things discarded by people living in rich countries by sending them to people living in poor nations? Why or why not?

2. In your opinion, have the programs described in the article been successful? Why or why not?

3. Can you think of other "global solutions" to environmental problems? What are they?

Adapted from the original article by Lia Miller published in *The New York Times* on November 15, 2004. Copyright © 2004 by The New York Times Company. Reprinted with permission.

homes. In addition, nations eager to encourage short-term industrial development may pay little attention to the longer-term dangers of air pollution. As a result, many cities in Latin America, Eastern Europe, and Asia are plagued by air pollution as bad as London's pea soup fifty years ago.

THE RAIN FORESTS

Rain forests are *regions of dense forestation, most of which circle the globe close to the equator.* The largest tropical rain forests are in South America (notably Brazil), west-central Africa, and Southeast Asia. In all, the world's rain forests cover some 2 billion acres, or 7 percent of Earth's total land surface.

Like other global resources, rain forests are falling victim to the needs and appetites of the surging world population. As noted earlier, to meet the demand for beef, ranchers in Latin America burn forested areas to increase their supply of grazing land. We are also losing rain forests to the hardwood trade. People in rich nations pay high prices for mahogany and other woods because, as the environmentalist Norman Myers (1984b:88) puts it, they have "a penchant for parquet floors, fine furniture, fancy paneling, weekend yachts, and high-grade coffins." Under such economic pressure, the world's rain forests are now just half their original size, and they continue to shrink by about 1 percent (65,000 square miles) annually, which amounts to about an acre every second. Unless we stop this loss, the rain forests will vanish before the end of this century, and with them will go protection for Earth's biodiversity and climate.

For more information about rain forests, visit http://www.rainforestweb.org

Members of small, simple societies, such as the Tan't Batu in the Philippines, live in harmony with nature; they do not have the technological means to greatly affect the natural world. Although we in complex societies like to think of ourselves as superior to such people, the truth is that there is much we can—and must—learn from them.

Global Warming

Why are rain forests so important? One reason is that they cleanse the atmosphere of carbon dioxide (CO_2). Since the beginning of the Industrial Revolution, the amount of carbon dioxide produced by humans, mostly from factories and automobiles, has risen sharply. Much of this carbon dioxide is absorbed by the oceans. But plants also take in carbon dioxide and expel oxygen. This is why rain forests are vital to maintaining the chemical balance of the atmosphere.

The problem is that production of carbon dioxide is rising while the amount of plant life on Earth is shrinking. To make matters worse, rain forests are being destroyed mostly by burning, which releases even more carbon dioxide into the atmosphere. Experts estimate that the atmospheric concentration of carbon dioxide is now 20 to 30 percent higher than it was 150 years ago (Revkin, 2002).

High above Earth, carbon dioxide acts like the glass roof of a greenhouse, letting heat from the sun pass through to the surface while preventing much of it from radiating away from the planet. The result of this *greenhouse effect,* say ecologists, is **global warming,** *a rise in Earth's average temperature due to an increasing concentration of carbon dioxide in the atmosphere.* Over the past century, the global temperature has risen about 1 degree Fahrenheit (to an average of 58° F). Scientists warn that it could rise by 5° F to 10° F

during this century, which would melt vast areas of the polar ice caps and raise the sea level to cover low-lying land around the world. Were this to happen, water would cover all of Bangladesh, for example, and much of the coastal United States, including Washington, D.C., right up to the steps of the White House. On the other hand, the U.S. Midwest, currently one of the most productive agricultural regions in the world, probably would become arid.

Not all scientists share this vision of future global warming. Some point out that global temperature changes have been taking place throughout history, apparently with little or nothing to do with rain forests. Higher concentrations of carbon dioxide in the atmosphere might speed up plant growth The Heinz Center publishes analyses of society's effect on the natural environment at http://www.heinzctr.org/publications.htm (since plants thrive on this gas), and this increase would correct the imbalance and push Earth's temperature downward once again. But a consensus is building that global warming is a problem that threatens the future of all of us (K. A. McDonald, 1999; Kerr, 2005).

YOUR TURN

How do you think global warming could affect you personally?

Declining Biodiversity

Clearing rain forests also reduces Earth's *biodiversity* because rain forests are home to almost half the planet's living species.

On Earth, there are as many as 30 million species of animals, plants, and microorganisms. Several dozen unique species of plants and animals cease to exist every day. Given the vast numbers of living species, why should we be concerned by the loss of a few? Environmentalists give four reasons. First, our planet's biodiversity provides a varied source of human food. Using agricultural high technology, scientists can "splice" familiar crops with more exotic plant life, making food more bountiful as well as more resistant to insects and disease. Thus biodiversity helps feed our planet's rapidly increasing population.

Second, Earth's biodiversity is a vital genetic resource used by medical and pharmaceutical researchers to produce hundreds of new compounds each year that cure disease and improve our lives. For example, children in the United States now have a good chance of surviving leukemia, a disease that was almost a sure killer two generations ago, because of a compound derived from a tropical flower called the rosy periwinkle. The oral birth control pill, used by tens of millions of women in this country, is another product of plant research involving the Mexican forest yam.

Third, with the loss of any species of life—whether it is the magnificent California condor, the famed Chinese panda, the spotted owl, or even a single species of ant—the beauty and complexity of our natural environment are diminished. And there are clear warning signs of such loss: Three-fourths of the world's 9,000 species of birds are declining in number.

Finally, unlike pollution, the extinction of any species is irreversible and final. An important ethical question, then, is whether we who live today have the right to impoverish the world for those who live tomorrow (N. Myers, 1991; E. O. Wilson, 1991; Brown et al., 1993).

ENVIRONMENTAL RACISM

Conflict theory has given rise to the concept of **environmental racism,** *the pattern by which environmental hazards are greatest for poor people, especially minorities.* Historically, factories that spew pollution have stood near neighborhoods of the poor and people of color. Why? In part, the poor themselves were drawn to factories in search of work, and their low incomes often meant they could afford housing only in undesirable neighborhoods. Sometimes the only housing that fit their budgets stood in the very shadow of the plants and mills where they worked.

Nobody wants a factory or dump nearby, but the poor have little power to resist. Through the years, the most serious environmental hazards have been located near Newark, New Jersey (not in upscale Bergen County), in southside Chicago (not wealthy Lake Forest), or on Native American reservations in the West (not in affluent suburbs of Denver or Phoenix) (Commission for Racial Justice, 1994; Bohon & Humphrey, 2000).

Looking Ahead: Toward a Sustainable Society and World

The demographic analysis presented in this chapter points to some disturbing trends. We see, first, that Earth's population has reached record levels because birth rates remain high in poor nations and death rates have fallen just about everywhere. Reducing fertility will remain a pressing need throughout this century. Even with some recent decline in the rate of population increase, the nightmare Thomas Malthus described is still a real possibility, as the Thinking It Through box on page 606 explains.

Further, population growth remains greatest in the poorest countries of the world, those without the means to support their present populations, much less their future

ones. Supporting 74 million additional people on our planet each year, 70 million of whom are in low-income countries, will require a global commitment to provide not only food but housing, schools, and employment as well. The well-being of the entire world may ultimately depend on resolving the economic and social problems of poor, overly populated countries and bridging the widening gulf between "have" and "have-not" nations.

Urbanization is continuing, especially in poor countries. Throughout human history, people have sought out cities in the hope of finding a better life. But the sheer numbers of people who live in the emerging global supercities—Mexico City, São Paulo (Brazil), Kinshasa (Democratic Republic of the Congo), Bombay (India), Manila (the Philippines)—have created urban problems on a massive scale.

Around the world, humanity is facing a serious environmental challenge. Part of this problem is population increase, which is greatest in poor countries. But part of the problem is the high levels of consumption in rich nations such as our own. By increasing the planet's environmental deficit, our present way of life is borrowing against the well-being of our children and their children. Globally, members of rich societies, who currently consume so much of Earth's resources, are mortgaging the future security of the poor countries of the world.

The answer, in principle, is to create an **ecologically sustainable culture,** *a way of life that meets the needs of the present generation without threatening the environmental legacy of future generations.* Sustainable living depends on three strategies.

First, the world needs to *bring population growth under control.* The current population of 6.5 billion is already straining the natural environment. Clearly, the higher the world's population climbs, the more difficult environmental problems will become. Even if the recent slowing of population growth continues, the world will have 8 billion people by 2050. Few analysts think that the planet can support this many people; most argue that we must hold the line at about 7 billion, and some argue that we must *decrease* population in the coming decades (Smail, 2007).

 To read more about population increase, the environment, and global inequality, go to http:// www.peopleandplanet.net

A second strategy is to *conserve finite resources.* This means meeting our needs with a responsible eye toward the future by using resources efficiently, seeking alternative sources of energy, and in some cases, learning to live with less.

A third strategy is to *reduce waste.* Whenever possible, simply using less is the best solution. But recycling programs, too, are part of the answer.

In the end, making all these strategies work depends on a more basic change in the way we think about ourselves

THINKING IT THROUGH

Apocalypse: Will People Overwhelm the Planet?

Are you worried about the world's increasing population? Think about this: By the time you finish reading this box, more than 1,000 people will have been added to our planet. By this time tomorrow, global population will have risen by more than 200,000. Currently, as the table shows, there are four births for every two deaths on the planet, pushing the world's population upward by 74 million annually. Put another way, global population growth amounts to adding another Egypt to the world each year.

It is no wonder that many demographers and environmentalists are deeply concerned about the future. Earth has an unprecedented population: The 2 billion people we have added since 1974 alone exceed the planet's total in 1900. Might Thomas Robert Malthus—

who predicted that overpopulation would push the world into war and suffering—be right after all? Lester Brown and other *neo-Malthusians* predict a coming apocalypse if we do not change our ways. Brown (1995) admits that Malthus failed to imagine how much technology (especially fertilizers and altering plant genetics) could boost the planet's agricultural output. But he maintains that Earth's rising population is rapidly outstripping its finite resources. Families in many poor countries can find little firewood; members of rich countries are depleting the oil reserves; everyone is draining our supply of clean water and poisoning the planet with waste. Some analysts argue that we have already passed Earth's "carrying capacity" for population and we need to hold the line or even reduce

global population to ensure our long-term survival.

But other analysts, the *anti-Malthusians,* sharply disagree. Julian Simon (1995) points out that two centuries after Malthus predicted catastrophe, Earth supports almost six times as many people who, on average, live longer, healthier lives than ever before. With more advanced technology, people have devised ways to increase productivity and limit population increase. As Simon sees it, this is cause for celebration. Human ingenuity has consistently proved the doomsayers wrong, and Simon is betting it will continue to do so.

WHAT DO YOU THINK?

1. Where do you place your bet? Do you think Earth can support 8 or 10 billion people? Explain your reasoning.
2. Ninety-six percent of current population growth is in poor countries. What does this mean for the future of rich nations? For the future of poor ones?
3. What should people in rich countries do to ensure the future of children everywhere?

Global Population Increase

	Births	Deaths	Net Increase
Per year	130,013,274	56,130,242	73,883,032
Per month	10,834,440	4,677,520	6,156,919
Per day	356,201	153,781	202,419
Per hour	14,842	6,408	8,434
Per minute	247	107	141
Per second	4.1	1.8	2.3

Sources: Based in part on Brown (1995), Simon (1995), Scanlon (2001), and Smail (2007).

and our world. Our *egocentric* outlook sets our own interests as standards for how to live, but a sustainable environment demands an *ecocentric* outlook that helps us see how the present is tied to the future and why everyone must work together. Most nations in the southern half of the world are *underdeveloped*, unable to meet the basic needs of their people. At the same time, most countries in the northern half of the world are *overdeveloped*, using more resources than the planet can sustain over time. The changes needed to create a sustainable ecosystem will not come easily, and they will be costly. But the price of not responding to the growing environmental deficit will certainly be greater (Kellert &

Bormann, 1991; Brown et al., 1993; Population Action International, 2000).

Finally, consider that the great dinosaurs dominated this planet for some 160 million years and then perished forever. Humanity is far younger, having existed for a mere 250,000 years. Compared to the rather dimwitted dinosaurs, our species has the gift of great intelligence. But how will we use this ability? What are the chances that our species will continue to flourish 160 million years—or even 1,000 years—from now? The answer depends on the choices that will be made by one of the 30 million species living on Earth: human beings.

The following learning tools will help you see what you know, identify what you still need to learn, and expand your understanding beyond the text. You can also visit this text's Companion Website™ at http://www.prenhall.com/macionis to find additional practice tests.

KEY POINTS

Demography: The Study of Population

Fertility and mortality, measured as crude birth rates and crude death rates, are major factors affecting population size. In global terms, U.S. population growth is low. Migration has special importance to the historical growth of the United States. Demographers use age-sex pyramids to show graphically the composition of a population and to project population trends. *Sex ratio* refers to a society's balance of females and males.

History and Theory of Population Growth

Historically, world population grew slowly because high birth rates were largely offset by high death rates. About 1750, a demographic transition began as world population rose sharply, mostly due to falling death rates. Thomas Robert Malthus warned that population growth would outpace food production and the result would be social calamity. Demographic transition theory, however, contends that technological advances gradually slow population increase. World population is expected to reach between 8 billion and 9 billion by 2050. Most of this increase will take place in poor societies.

Urbanization: The Growth of Cities

The first urban revolution began with the appearance of cities about 10,000 years ago. By about 2,000 years ago, cities had emerged in most regions of the world except for North America. Preindustrial cities have low-rise buildings; narrow, winding streets; and personal social ties.

A second urban revolution began about 1750 as the Industrial Revolution spurred rapid urban growth in Europe. The physical form of cities changed as planners created wide, regular streets to allow for easier trade. The emphasis on commerce and the increasing size of cities made urban life more anonymous.

Urbanism came to North America with Europeans, who settled in towns along the Atlantic coastline. By 1850, hundreds of new cities had been founded from coast to coast. By 1920, a majority of the U.S. population lived in urban areas, and the largest metropolises were home to millions of people. About 1950, cities began to decentralize with the growth of suburbs and edge cities. Nationally, Sunbelt cities—but not the older Snowbelt cities—are increasing in size and population.

Urbanism as a Way of Life

Rapid urbanization in Europe during the nineteenth century led early sociologists to contrast rural and urban life. Ferdinand Tönnies built his analysis on the concepts of *Gemeinschaft* and *Gesellschaft*, and Emile Durkheim used similar concepts of mechanical solidarity and organic solidarity. Georg Simmel claimed that the overstimulation of city life produced a blasé attitude in urbanites.

At the University of Chicago in the United States, Robert Park claimed that cities permit greater social freedom. Louis Wirth saw large, dense, heterogeneous populations creating an impersonal and self-interested, though tolerant, way of life. Other researchers have explored urban ecology and urban political economy.

Urbanization in Poor Nations

A third urban revolution is now occurring in poor countries. Today, most of the world's largest cities are found in less developed nations.

Environment and Society

The state of the environment is a social issue because it reflects how human beings organize social life. Societies increase the environmental deficit by focusing on short-term benefits and ignoring the long-term consequences brought on by their way of life. The more complex a society's technology, the greater its capacity to alter the natural environment.

The "logic of growth" thesis supports economic development, claiming that people can solve environmental problems as they arise. The opposing "limits to growth" thesis states that societies must curb development to prevent eventual environmental collapse.

Environmental issues include disposing of solid waste and protecting the quality of air and water. The supply of clean water is already low in some parts of the world. Rain forests help remove carbon dioxide from the atmosphere and are home to a large share of this planet's living species. Under pressure from commercial interests, the world's rain forests are now half their original size and are shrinking by about 1 percent annually. *Environmental racism* refers to the pattern by which the poor, especially minorities, suffer most from environmental hazards.

Looking Ahead: Toward a Sustainable Society and World

To achieve a sustainable environment that does not threaten the well-being of future generations, we must control world population, conserve finite resources, and reduce waste and pollution.

KEY CONCEPTS

Population

demography (p. 580) the study of human population

fertility (p. 580) the incidence of child-bearing in a country's population

crude birth rate (p. 580) the number of live births in a given year for every 1,000 people in a population

mortality (p. 581) the incidence of death in a country's population

crude death rate (p. 581) the number of deaths in a given year for every 1,000 people in a population

infant mortality rate (p. 582) the number of deaths among infants under one year of age for each 1,000 live births in a given year

life expectancy (p. 582) the average life span of a country's population

migration (p. 582) the movement of people into and out of a specified territory

sex ratio (p. 583) the number of males for every 100 females in a nation's population

age-sex pyramid (p. 583) a graphic representation of the age and sex of a population

demographic transition theory (p. 586) the thesis that population patterns reflect a society's level of technological development

zero population growth (p. 587) the level of reproduction that maintains population in a steady state

Urbanization

urbanization (p. 589) the concentration of population into cities

metropolis (p. 590) a large city that socially and economically dominates an urban area

suburbs (p. 591) urban areas beyond the political boundaries of a city

megalopolis (p. 592) a vast urban region containing a number of cities and their surrounding suburbs

Gemeinschaft (p. 593) a type of social organization in which people are closely tied by kinship and tradition

Gesellschaft (p. 593) a type of social organization in which people come together only on the basis of individual self-interest

urban ecology (p. 594) the study of the link between the physical and social dimensions of cities

Environment

ecology (p. 597) the study of the interaction of living organisms and the natural environment

natural environment (p. 597) Earth's surface and atmosphere, including living organisms, air, water, soil, and other resources necessary to sustain life

ecosystem (p. 597) a system composed of the interaction of all living organisms and their natural environment

environmental deficit (p. 598) profound long-term harm to the natural environment caused by humanity's focus on short-term material affluence

rain forests (p. 603) regions of dense forestation, most of which circle the globe close to the equator

global warming (p. 604) a rise in Earth's average temperature due to an increasing concentration of carbon dioxide in the atmosphere

environmental racism (p. 605) the pattern by which environmental hazards are greatest for poor people, especially minorities

ecologically sustainable culture (p. 605) a way of life that meets the needs of the present generation without threatening the environmental legacy of future generations

SAMPLE TEST QUESTIONS

These questions are similar to those found in the test bank that accompanies this textbook.

Multiple-Choice Questions

1. *Demography* is defined as the study of
   a. democratic political systems.
   b. human culture.
   c. human population.
   d. the natural environment.

2. Which region of the world has *both* the lowest birth rate and the lowest infant mortality rate?
   a. Latin America
   b. Europe
   c. Africa
   d. Asia

3. Typically, high-income nations grow mostly from _____, and low-income nations grow from _____.
   a. immigration; natural increase
   b. emigration; natural increase
   c. natural increase; immigration
   d. internal migration; natural increase

4. In general, the higher the average income of a country,
   a. the faster the population increase.
   b. the slower the population increase.
   c. the lower the level of immigration.
   d. the lower the level of urbanization.

5. In the United States, urban decentralization has caused
   a. the expansion of suburbs.
   b. the development of vast urban regions.
   c. the growth of edge cities.
   d. all of the above.

6. **Which term was used by Ferdinand Tönnies to refer to a type of social organization in which people come together on the basis of individual self-interest?**
   a. mechanical solidarity
   b. organic solidarity
   c. *Gesellschaft*
   d. *Gemeinschaft*

7. **The world's third urban revolution is now taking place in**
   a. the United States.
   b. Europe and Japan.
   c. middle-income nations.
   d. low-income nations.

8. **The *environmental deficit* refers to**
   a. long-term harm to the environment caused by a short-sighted focus on material affluence.
   b. the public's lack of interest in the natural environment.
   c. the fact that natural scientists ignore the social dimensions of environmental problems.
   d. the lack of funding for important environmental programs.

9. **Which of the following statements reflects the "limits to growth" thesis?**
   a. People are rapidly consuming Earth's finite resources.
   b. Whatever problems technology creates, technology can solve.

   c. Quality of life on Earth is getting better.
   d. Higher living standards today will benefit future generations.

10. ***Environmental racism* is the idea that**
    a. few minorities are found within the environmental movement.
    b. prejudice is the major cause of pollution and other environmental problems.
    c. environmental dangers are greatest for the poor and minorities.
    d. all of the above.

ANSWERS: 1(c); 2(b); 3(a); 4(b); 5(d); 6(c); 7(d); 8(a); 9(a); 10(c).

Essay Questions

1. According to demographic transition theory, how does economic development affect population patterns?

2. According to Ferdinand Tönnies, Emile Durkheim, Georg Simmel, and Louis Wirth, what characterizes urbanism as a way of life? Note several differences in the ideas of these thinkers.

APPLICATIONS & EXERCISES

1. Here is an illustration of the problem of runaway growth (Milbrath, 1989:10): "A pond has a single water lily growing on it. The lily doubles in size each day. In thirty days, it covers the entire pond. On which day does it cover half the pond?" When you realize the answer, discuss the implications of this example for population increase.

2. Draw a mental map of a city familiar to you with as much detail of specific places, districts, roads, and

transportation facilities as you can. Compare your map to a real one or, better yet, a map drawn by someone else. Try to account for the differences.

3. As an interesting exercise, carry a trash bag around for a single day, and collect everything you throw away. Most people are surprised to find that the average person in the United States discards close to 5 pounds of paper, metal, plastic, and other materials daily (over a lifetime, that's about 50 tons).

INVESTIGATE *with* Research Navigator

Follow the instructions on page 27 of this text to access the features of **Research Navigator™**. Once at the Web site, enter your Login Name and Password. Then, to use the **ContentSelect** database, enter keywords such as "demography," "urbanism," and "global warming," and the search engine will supply relevant and recent scholarly and popular press publications. Use the *New York Times* **Search-by-Subject Archive** to find recent news articles related to sociology and the **Link Library** feature to find relevant Web links organized by the key terms associated with this chapter.

23

Collective Behavior and Social Movements

What are the various types
of collective behavior?

Why do social movements arise?

How do social movements
bring about change?

On December 26, 2004, at one minute before 8 o'clock in the morning, a massive earthquake shook the floor of the Indian Ocean just off the western tip of the island of Sumatra, Indonesia. As the ocean floor shifted violently, it produced a tsunami, a massive wall of water, as high as 100 feet, that raced across the ocean and slammed into shorelines of not only Indonesia but Thailand to the northeast and Sri Lanka, India, and the coast of Africa to the west.

The huge waves rolled over the coastline, destroying everything and everyone in their path. Buildings were washed from their foundations, cars and trains were pushed around as if they were toys, and in a matter of seconds, entire communities were literally washed away. More than 230,000 people were killed, making the tsunami one of the deadliest natural disasters in recorded history. ■

 For images of the tsunami, go to http://www.waveofdestruction.org/photos/

What happens to people when their world is suddenly torn apart by unexpected events? How do communities cope with such devastation? Studying disasters is one example of the work sociologists do when they investigate **collective behavior,** *activity involving a large number of people that is unplanned, often controversial, and sometimes dangerous.*

This chapter investigates various types of collective behavior—including what happens when people are faced with disasters, mobs and riots, panic and mass hysteria, rumor and gossip, and fashions and fads. In addition, we will examine social movements, a type of collective behavior aimed at changing people's lives in some important way.

Studying Collective Behavior

Collective behavior is difficult for sociologists to study for three reasons:

1. **Collective behavior is diverse.** Collective behavior involves a wide range of human action. At first glance, it is difficult to see what disasters have in common with fads, rumors, and mob behavior.

2. **Collective behavior is hard to explain.** Sometimes a rumor, like the claim that there would be a military draft if President Bush won the 2004 presidential election, spreads all across the United States. But other rumors quickly die out. Why does one rumor catch on but others do not?

3. **Much collective behavior is transitory.** Sociologists have long studied social institutions such as the family because they are continuing parts of society. Disasters, rumors, and fads, however, come and go quickly.

Some researchers point out that these problems apply not just to collective behavior but to most forms of human behavior (Aguirre & Quarantelli, 1983). In addition, collective behavior is not always so surprising; anyone can predict that crowds will form at sporting events and music festivals, and sociologists can study these gatherings firsthand or record them on videotape to study later. Researchers can even anticipate some natural disasters such as tornadoes, which are common in some parts of the United States, and be ready to study how people respond to such events (D. L. Miller, 1985).

As a result of their efforts, sociologists now know a great deal about collective behavior. The most basic lesson is that all collective behavior involves the action of some **collectivity,** *a large number of people whose minimal interaction occurs in the absence of well-defined and conventional norms.* Collectivities are of two types. A *localized collectivity* refers to people physically close to one another, as in the case of crowds and riots. A *dispersed collectivity* or *mass behavior* involves people who influence one another despite being spread over a large area. Examples of this type of collective behavior include rumors, public opinion, and fashion.

Be sure to keep in mind how collectivities differ from the already familiar concept of social groups (see Chapter 7, "Groups and Organizations"). Here are three key differences:

1. **People who are part of collectivities have little or no social interaction.** People in groups interact frequently and directly. People in mobs or other localized collectivities interact very little. Most people taking part in dispersed collectivities, such as a fad, do not interact at all.

2. **Collectivities have no clear social boundaries.** Group members share a sense of identity, but people engaged in collective behavior usually do not. People in a local crowd may have the same object of their attention, such as someone on a ledge threatening to jump, but they feel little sense of unity. Individuals involved in dispersed collectivities, such as the students involved in the rumor about the possibility of a military draft, have almost no awareness of shared membership. To give another example, people may share concerns over many issues, but usually it is difficult to say exactly who falls within the ranks of, say, the environmental or feminist movement.

3. **Collectivities generate weak and unconventional norms.** Conventional cultural norms usually regulate the behavior of people in groups. Some collectivities, such as people traveling together on an airplane, do observe conventional norms, but their interaction is usually limited to polite small talk with respect for the privacy of others sitting nearby. Other collectivities—such as excited fans after a game who take to the streets drinking and overturning cars—behave according to no clear guidelines (Weller & Quarantelli, 1973; Turner & Killian, 1993).

Localized Collectivities: Crowds

One major form of collective behavior is the **crowd,** *a temporary gathering of people who share a common focus of attention and who influence one another.* Most of our ancestors never saw a large crowd: In medieval Europe, for example, about the only time large numbers of people gathered in one place was when armies faced off on the battlefield (Laslett, 1984). Today, however, crowds of 25,000 or more are common at rock concerts, sporting events, and even the registration halls of large universities.

YOUR TURN

Do you think people go to athletic games or musical events in part because they enjoy the experience of being in a large crowd? Explain your answer.

Several years ago, college students at the University of Colorado at Boulder engaged in two nights of partying that turned violent, drawing more than 100 police to the campus to restore order. Such occurrences, usually following sports events, have become common in recent years. Reading the description below, what type of crowd behavior is this? What are the reasons for this behavior?

All crowds are not alike. Herbert Blumer (1969) identified four categories of crowds:

A *casual crowd* is a loose collection of people who interact little, if at all. People lying on a beach or people who rush to the scene of an automobile accident have only a passing awareness of one another.

A *conventional crowd* results from deliberate planning, as illustrated by a country auction, a college lecture, or a celebrity's funeral. In each case, the behavior of people involved follows a clear set of norms.

An *expressive crowd* forms around an event with emotional appeal, such as a religious revival, a NASCAR race, or the New Year's Eve celebration in New York City's Times Square. Excitement is the main reason people join expressive crowds, which makes this spontaneous experience exhilarating for those involved.

An *acting crowd* is a collectivity motivated by an intense, single-minded purpose, such as an audience rushing the doors of a concert hall or fleeing from a mall after hearing gunshots. Acting crowds are set in motion by powerful emotions, which can sometimes trigger mob violence.

Any crowd can change from one type to another. In 2001, for example, a conventional crowd of more than 10,000 fans filed into a soccer stadium in Johannesburg, South Africa, to watch a match between two rival teams. After a goal was scored, the crowd erupted and people began to push toward the field. Within seconds, an acting crowd had formed, and a stampede began, which ended up crushing forty-seven people to death (Nessman, 2001).

Deliberate action by a crowd is not simply the product of rising emotions. Participants in *protest crowds*—a fifth category we can add to Blumer's list—may stage marches, boycotts, sit-ins, and strikes for political purposes (McPhail & Wohlstein, 1983). The antiwar demonstrations that have taken place on many campuses and in many large cities since the beginning of the Iraq War are examples of protest crowds. Sometimes protest crowds have the low-level energy characteristic of a conventional crowd; at other times, people become emotional enough to form an acting crowd.

MOBS AND RIOTS

When an acting crowd turns violent, the result may be the birth of a **mob,** *a highly emotional crowd that pursues a violent or destructive goal.* Despite, or perhaps because of, their intense emotions, mobs tend to dissipate quickly. How long a mob continues to exist depends on its precise goals and whether its leadership tries to inflame or calm the crowd.

Lynching is the most notorious example of mob behavior in the United States. The term is derived from Charles Lynch, who lived in Virginia during the colonial period and tried to enforce law and order in his community before there were formal police and courts. The word *lynch* soon came to mean violence and murder carried out beyond the law.

Lynching has always been colored by race. After the Civil War, lynch mobs terrorized newly freed African Americans. Any person of color who challenged white superiority risked being hanged or burned alive by hateful whites.

Lynch mobs—typically composed of poor whites who felt threatened by competition from freed slaves—reached their peak between 1880 and 1930. Police recorded some 5,000 lynchings in that period, though many more undoubtedly occurred. Often lynchings were popular events, attracting hundreds of spectators; sometimes victims were killed quickly, but others were tortured before being put to death. Most of these terrorist killings took place in the Deep South, where the farming economy depended on a cheap and obedient labor force. On the western frontier, lynch mobs targeted people of Mexican and Asian descent. In about 25 percent of reported lynchings, whites killed other whites. Lynching women was rare; only about 100 such cases are known, almost all involving women of color (White, 1969, orig. 1929; Grant, 1975; Lacayo, 2000).

A highly energized crowd with no particular purpose is a **riot,** *a social eruption that is highly emotional, violent, and undirected.* Unlike the action of a mob, a riot usually has no clear goal, except perhaps to express dissatisfaction. The cause of most riots is some longstanding anger or grievance;

violent action is ignited by some minor incident that causes people to start destroying property and harming other persons (Smelser, 1962; M. Rosenfeld, 1997). A mob action usually ends when some specific violent goal is accomplished (such as a lynching); a riot tends to go on until participants run out of steam or police and community leaders gradually bring participants under control.

Throughout our nation's history, riots have been sparked by social injustice. Industrial workers, for example, have rioted to vent rage over unfair working conditions. In 1886, a bitter struggle by Chicago factory workers for an eight-hour workday led to the explosive Haymarket Riot, which left eleven dead and scores injured. Prison inmates sometimes express anger and despair through riots.

In addition, race riots have occurred in this country with striking regularity. Early in the twentieth century, crowds of whites attacked African Americans in Chicago, Detroit, and other cities. In the 1960s, seemingly trivial events sparked rage at continuing prejudice and discrimination, causing violent riots in numerous inner-city ghettos. In Los Angeles in 1992, the acquittal of police officers involved in the beating of motorist Rodney King set off an explosive riot. Violence and fires killed more than fifty people, injured thousands, and destroyed property worth hundreds of millions of dollars.

Not all riots are fired by hate. They can also begin with very positive feelings. In 2000, for example, young men celebrating New York City's National Puerto Rican Day began spraying water on young women in the crowd. During the next few hours, sexual violence erupted as dozens of women were groped, stripped, and assaulted—apparently resulting, as one report put it, from a mixture of "marijuana, alcohol, hot weather, testosterone idiocy, and lapses in police [protection]" (Barstow & Chivers, 2000:1). On a number of state university campuses, a win by the home sports team was all it took to send hundreds of students into the streets, drinking and soon lighting fires and battling with police. As one analyst put it, in an "anything goes" culture, some people think they can do whatever they feel like doing (Pitts, 2000).

CROWDS, MOBS, AND SOCIAL CHANGE

April 13, Cincinnati, Ohio. The city has been under siege all week by African American demonstrators enraged by the police shooting of an unarmed black man. In the mayhem, however, dozens of innocent people, both black and white, have been seriously hurt by flying bricks and swinging baseball bats. Does such violence help bring attention to a just cause, or does it just make things worse?

The 2003 meeting of the World Trade Organization in Seattle, Washington, was the occasion for protests by those opposed to the expanding global marketplace. After reading the theories of crowd behavior on pages 615 and 616, try to apply each theory to an event such as this one. Which approach seems to make the most sense to you? Why?

What does a riot accomplish? Ordinary people can gain power when they act collectively. The Cincinnati demonstrators succeeded in calling national attention to their claim of racial bias on the part of police and causing that police department to carefully review officer conduct. The power of the crowd to challenge the status quo and sometimes to force social change is the reason crowds are controversial. Throughout history, defenders of the status quo have feared "the mob" as a threat. By contrast, those seeking change have supported collective action.

EXPLAINING CROWD BEHAVIOR

What accounts for the behavior of crowds? Social scientists have developed several explanations.

Contagion Theory

An early explanation of collective behavior was offered by the French sociologist Gustave Le Bon (1841–1931). According to Le Bon's *contagion theory* (1960, orig. 1895), crowds exert a hypnotic influence over their members. Shielded by the anonymity found in large numbers, people forget about personal responsibility and give in to the contagious emotions of the crowd. A crowd thus assumes a life of its own, stirring up emotions and driving people toward irrational, even violent, action.

Critical review Le Bon's idea that crowds provide anonymity and can generate strong emotions is surely true. Yet as Clark McPhail (1991) points out, a considerable body

of research shows that "the madding crowd" does not take on a life of its own; its actions result from the policies and decisions made by specific individuals. In the case of the 2003 nightclub fire in Rhode Island that killed ninety-seven people, the high death toll did not result simply from the crowd "going wild" and becoming trapped inside the flaming building. Later investigation showed that the band had used dangerous fireworks onstage, flames ignited flammable soundproofing material on the ceiling, and the room had no sprinkler system. As a result, fire engulfed the entire building in minutes, before many people realized what was happening (Apuzzo, 2003; Forliti, 2003).

Finally, although collective behavior may involve strong emotions, such feelings may not be irrational, as contagion theory suggests. Emotions—as well as action—can reflect real fear (as in the nightclub fire) or result from a sense of injustice (as in the Cincinnati racial protests) (Jasper, 1998).

Convergence Theory

Convergence theory holds that crowd behavior comes not from the crowd itself but from the particular people who join in. From this point of view, a crowd is a convergence of like-minded individuals. Contagion theory states that crowds cause people to act in a certain way; convergence theory says the opposite, claiming that people who wish to act in a certain way come together to form crowds.

In recent years, the crowds that formed at demonstrations opposing the Iraq War, for example, did not cause participants to become antiwar. On the contrary, participants came together because of their political attitudes.

Critical review   By linking crowds to broader social forces, convergence theory rejects Le Bon's claim that crowd behavior is irrational in favor of the view that people in crowds express existing beliefs and values. But in fairness to Le Bon, people sometimes do things in a crowd that they would not have the courage to do alone, because crowds can spread responsibility among many people. In addition, crowds can intensify an emotion simply by creating a critical mass of like-minded people.

Emergent-Norm Theory

Ralph Turner and Lewis Killian (1993) developed the *emergent-norm theory* of crowd dynamics. These researchers admit that social behavior is never entirely predictable, but if similar interests draw people into a crowd, distinctive patterns of behavior may emerge.

According to Turner and Killian, crowds begin as collectivities containing people with mixed interests and motives. Especially in the case of expressive, acting, and protest crowds, norms may be vague and changing. Consider how many Iraqi citizens began looting government buildings after U.S. troops toppled Saddam Hussein; over time, although some continued to steal anything they could carry, others tried to stop the lawlessness. In short, people in crowds make their own rules as they go along.

Critical review   Emergent-norm theory represents a middle-ground approach to crowd dynamics. Turner and Killian (1993) explain that crowd behavior is neither as irrational as contagion theory suggests nor as deliberate as convergence theory implies. Certainly, crowd behavior reflects the desires of participants, but it is also guided by norms that emerge as the situation unfolds.

Decision making does play a role in crowd behavior, although people watching from the sidelines may not realize it. For example, frightened people clogging the exits of a burning nightclub may appear to be victims of irrational panic, but from their point of view, fleeing a rapidly spreading fire makes a lot of sense.

Emergent-norm theory points out that people in a crowd take on different roles. Some step forward as leaders; others become lieutenants, rank-and-file followers, inactive bystanders, and even opponents (Weller & Quarantelli, 1973; Zurcher & Snow, 1981).

Which of the theories presented here—contagion theory, convergence theory, or emergent-norm theory—best explains your own experiences with crowd behavior? Why?

Dispersed Collectivities: Mass Behavior

It is not just people clustered together in crowds who take part in collective behavior. **Mass behavior** refers to *collective behavior among people spread over a wide geographic area.*

RUMOR AND GOSSIP

A common type of mass behavior is **rumor,** *unconfirmed information that people spread informally, often by word of mouth.* People pass along rumors through face-to-face communication, of course, but today's modern technology—including telephones, the mass media, e-mail, and the Internet—spreads rumors faster and farther than ever before.

Rumor has three main characteristics:

1. **Rumor thrives in a climate of uncertainty.** Rumors arise when people lack clear and certain information about an important issue. The fact that no one really knew the government's position on the possibility of a military draft helps explain why rumors were flying in the months before the 2004 presidential election.

2. **Rumor is unstable.** People change a rumor as they pass it along, usually giving it a "spin" that serves their own interests. The Democrats had one version of the draft rumor; Republicans had a different story.

3. **Rumor is difficult to stop.** The number of people aware of a rumor increases very quickly because each person spreads information to many others. Rumors go away eventually, but in general, the only way to control rumors is for a believable source to issue a clear and convincing statement of the facts.

Rumor can trigger the formation of crowds or other collective behavior. For this reason, officials establish rumor-control centers during a crisis in order to manage information. Yet some rumors persist for generations, perhaps just because people enjoy them; the Thinking Critically box gives a classic example.

Visit a site that tracks the truth about Internet rumors: http://www.nonprofit.net/hoax

Gossip is *rumor about people's personal affairs.* Charles Horton Cooley (1962, orig. 1909) explained that rumor involves some issue many people care about, but gossip interests only a small circle of people who know a particular person. This is why rumors spread widely but gossip tends to be localized.

The Rumor Mill: Paul Is Dead!

Probably the best-known rock group of the twentieth century was the Beatles—Paul McCartney, John Lennon, George Harrison, and Ringo Starr—whose music caused a cultural revolution in the 1960s. However, today's young people may not know the rumor that circulated about Paul McCartney at the height of the group's popularity (Rosnow & Fine, 1976; Kapferer, 1992).

On October 12, 1969, a young man telephoned a Detroit disk jockey to say that he had discovered the following "evidence" that Paul McCartney was dead:

1. At the end of the song "Strawberry Fields Forever" on the *Magical Mystery Tour* album, if you filter out the background noise, you will hear a voice saying, "I buried Paul!"
2. The phrase "Number 9, Number 9, Number 9" from the song "Revolution 9" on *The Beatles* (commonly known as the "White Album"), when played backward, seems to say, "Turn me on, dead man!"

Two days later, the University of Michigan student newspaper ran a story titled "McCartney Is Dead: Further Clues Found." It sent millions of Beatles fans racing for their albums to look for the following:

3. A picture inside the *Magical Mystery Tour* album shows John, George, and Ringo wearing red carnations, but Paul is wearing a black flower.
4. The cover of the *Sergeant Pepper's Lonely Hearts Club Band* album

shows a grave with yellow flowers arranged in the shape of Paul's bass guitar.
5. On the inside of that album, McCartney wears an armpatch with the letters "OPD." Is this the initials of some police department or confirmation that Paul had been "officially pronounced dead"?
6. On the back cover of the same album, three Beatles are facing forward but McCartney has his back to the camera.
7. On the album cover of *Abbey Road*, John Lennon is clothed as a clergyman, Ringo Starr wears an undertaker's black tie, and George Harrison is clad in workman's attire as if ready to dig a grave. For his part, McCartney is barefoot, which is how Tibetan ritual says to prepare a corpse for burial.
8. Also on the cover of *Abbey Road*, John Lennon's Volkswagen appears behind Paul with the license plate "28 IF," as if to say that McCartney would be *28 if* he were alive.

The rumor was that McCartney had died of head injuries suffered in an automobile accident in November 1966 and that after the accident, record company executives had secretly replaced Paul with a double.

Of course, McCartney is very much alive and still touring. He still jokes about the "Paul is dead" episode, and few doubt that he dreamed up some of the details of his own "death," with a little help from his friends. But the story has a serious side, showing how quickly rumors can arise and how they spread in a climate of distrust. In the late 1960s, many young people were quite ready to believe that the media and other powerful interests were concealing McCartney's death.

Back in 1969, McCartney himself denied the rumor in a *Life* magazine interview. But thousands of suspicious readers noticed that on the other side of the page with McCartney's picture was an ad for an automobile: Holding this page up to the light, the car lay across McCartney's chest and blocked his head. Another clue!

WHAT DO YOU THINK?

1. What kinds of issues give rise to rumors?
2. What types of rumors have circulated recently on your campus? What made them begin? What made them go away?
3. Overall, do you think rumors are helpful, harmful, or harmless? Why?

Communities use gossip as a means of social control, using praise and blame to encourage people to conform to local norms. Also, people gossip about others to raise their own standing as social "insiders" or to put other people down (Baumgartner, 1998; Nicholson, 2001). Yet no community wants gossip to get out of control so that no one knows what to believe, which is why people who gossip too much are criticized as "busybodies."

PUBLIC OPINION AND PROPAGANDA

Another type of dispersed collective behavior is **public opinion,** *widespread attitudes about controversial issues.* Exactly who is, or is not, included in any "public" depends on the issue involved. Over the years in the United States, "publics" have formed over numerous controversial issues, from global warming and air pollution to handguns and health care. More recently, the public has debated affirmative action, campaign finance reform, and government funding of public radio and television.

Whatever the issue, a small share of people have no opinion at all; this may be due to either ignorance or indifference. Even on some important issues, a surprising share of the population has no clear opinions. One recent study, for example, found that 60 percent of U.S. adults claimed they did not understand the U.S. income tax system well enough to know if they supported it or not (M. Rosenbaum, 2003).

Also, not everyone's opinion carries the same weight. Some categories of people are more likely to be asked for their opinion, and what they say will have more clout because they are better educated, wealthier, and better connected. By forming an organization, various categories of people can increase their voice. Through the American Medical Association, for example, physicians have a lot to say about medical care in the United States, just as members of the National Education Association have a great deal of influence on public education.

Special-interest groups and political leaders all try to shape public tastes and attitudes by using **propaganda,** *information presented with the intention of shaping public opinion.* Although we tend to think of propaganda in negative terms, it is not necessarily false. A thin line separates information from propaganda; the difference depends mostly on the presenter's intention. We offer *information* to enlighten others; we use *propaganda* to sway people toward our own point of view. Political speeches, commercial advertising, and even some college lectures may include propaganda in an effort to steer people toward thinking or acting in some specific way.

YOUR TURN

Have you ever taken a course in which the information presented by the professor, one of the readings, or a film seemed to be propaganda? What made it seem that way? Ask some of your classmates if they agree with you.

FASHIONS AND FADS

Fashions and fads also involve people spread over a large area. A **fashion** is *a social pattern favored by a large number of people.* People's tastes in clothing, music, and automobiles, as well as ideas about politics, change often, going in and out of fashion.

In preindustrial societies, clothing and personal appearance change very little, reflecting traditional *style.* Women and men, the rich and the poor, lawyers and carpenters wear distinctive clothes and hairstyles that reflect their occupations and social standing (Lofland, 1973; Crane, 2000).

In industrial societies, however, established style gives way to changing fashion. For one thing, modern people care less about tradition and are often eager to try out new "lifestyles." Higher rates of social mobility also cause people to use their "looks" to make a statement about themselves. The German sociologist Georg Simmel (1971, orig. 1904) explained that rich people are usually the trendsetters, because they attract lots of attention and they have the money to spend on luxuries. As the U.S. sociologist Thorstein Veblen (1953, orig. 1899) put it, fashion involves *conspicuous consumption* as people buy expensive products (from bottled water to Hummers) not because they need such things but simply to show off their wealth.

Ordinary people who want to look wealthy are eager to buy less expensive copies of what the rich make fashionable. In this way, a fashion moves downward through the class structure. But eventually, the fashion loses its prestige when too many average people now share "the look," so the rich move on to something new. In short, fashions are born along the Fifth Avenues and Rodeo Drives of the rich, gain popularity in Targets and Wal-Marts across the country, and eventually are pushed aside in favor of something new.

Since the 1960s, however, there has been a reversal of this pattern in the United States, and many fashions favored by rich people are drawn from people of lower social position. This pattern began with blue jeans, which have long been worn by people doing manual labor. During the civil rights and antiwar movements of the 1960s, jeans became popular among college students who wanted to identify with "ordinary people." Today, cargo pants and other emblems of the hip-hop culture allow even the most affluent entertainers and celebrities to mimic the styles that began among the inner-city poor. Even rich and famous people often identify with their ordinary roots: In one of her songs, Jennifer Lopez sings, "Don't be fooled by the rocks that I've got, I'm still, I'm still Jenny from the block."

A **fad** is *an unconventional social pattern that people embrace briefly but enthusiastically.* Fads, sometimes called *crazes,* are common in high-income societies, where many people have the money to spend on amusing, if often frivolous, products. During the 1950s, two young Californians produced a brightly colored plastic hoop, a version of a toy popular in Australia, that you can swing around your waist by gyrating the hips. The "hula hoop" became a national craze. In less than a year, hula hoops all but vanished, only to reappear from time to time. Pokémon cards are another example of the rise and fall of a fad (Aguirre, Quarantelli, & Mendoza, 1988).

How do fads differ from fashions? Fads capture the public imagination but quickly burn out. Because fashions reflect basic cultural values like individuality and sexual attractiveness, they tend to stay around for a while. Therefore, a fashion—but rarely a fad—becomes a more lasting part of popular culture. Streaking, for instance, was a fad that came out of nowhere and soon vanished; blue jeans, however, is an example of fashion that originated in the rough mining camps of Gold Rush California in the 1870s and is still popular today.

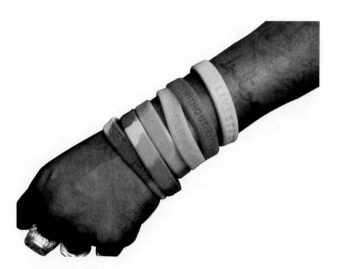

A recent fad among young people in the United States is the wearing of colorful plastic bracelets to express support for various organizations and causes, including efforts to find a cure for AIDS, breast cancer, and other diseases.

PANIC AND MASS HYSTERIA

A **panic** is *a form of collective behavior in which people in one place react to a threat or other stimulus with irrational, frantic, and often self-destructive behavior.* The classic illustration of a panic is people streaming toward the exits of a crowded theater after someone yells, "Fire!" As they flee, they trample one another, blocking the exits so that few actually escape.

Closely related to panic is **mass hysteria** or **moral panic,** *a form of dispersed collective behavior in which people react to a real or imagined event with irrational and even frantic fear.* Whether the cause of the hysteria is real or not, a large number of people take it very seriously.

One example of a moral panic is the controversy set off by flag burning during the Vietnam War; a more recent example is fear of AIDS or of people with AIDS. Sometimes

 To hear the 1938 radio broadcast that started a national panic, go to http://www.waroftheworlds.org

such situations pose little real danger to anyone: There is almost no chance of becoming infected with HIV by simply interacting with someone who has AIDS. At another level, however, a fear of AIDS can become a danger if it were to give rise to a hate crime targeting a person with AIDS.

One factor that makes moral panics common in our society is the influence of the mass media. Diseases, disasters, and deadly crime all get intense coverage by television and other media, which hope to gain an audience. As Erich Goode (2000:549) points out, "The mass media *thrive* on scares; contributing to moral panics is the media's stock in trade."

Mass hysteria is sometimes triggered by an event that, at the extreme, sends people into chaotic flight. Of course, people who see others overcome by fear may become more afraid themselves, and the hysteria feeds on itself. When a small plane flew into restricted air space over Washington, D.C., in 2005, officials ordered the evacuation of the Capitol and other government buildings. The order sent people running into the streets, although at the time there was no real danger at all.

DISASTERS

A **disaster** is *an event, generally unexpected, that causes extensive harm to people and damage to property.* Disasters are of three types[1]. Floods, hurricanes, earthquakes, forest fires, and the 2004 tsunami described in the opening to this chapter are all examples of *natural disasters.* A second type is the *technological disaster,* which is widely regarded as an *accident* but is more accurately a failure to control technology. The 11 million gallons of oil spilled when the *Exxon Valdez* tanker ran aground off the coast of Alaska in 1989 or the nuclear accident at the Chernobyl power plant in Ukraine in 1986 were both technological disasters. A third type of disaster is the *intentional disaster,* in which one or more organized groups deliberately harms others. War, terrorist attacks, and the genocide that took place in Yugoslavia

---

[1]The first two types are based on Erikson (2005a). The third type is added by the author.

Sociologists classify disasters into three types. Hurricane Katrina, which brought massive flooding to New Orleans, is an example of a natural disaster. The 1989 grounding of the tanker ship *Exxon Valdez*, which spilled 11 million gallons of crude oil off the coast of Alaska, was a technological disaster. The slaughter of 1 million people in the African nation of Rwanda in 1994 is an example of intentional disaster.

(1992–1995) and Rwanda (1994) are examples of intentional disasters.

The full scope of the harm caused by disasters may become evident only many years after the event takes place. The Applying Sociology box provides an example of a technological disaster that is still affecting people and their descendants more than fifty years after it occurred.

Kai Erikson (1976, 1994, 2005a) has investigated dozens of disasters of all types. From his investigations of floods, nuclear contamination, oil spills, and genocide, Erikson reached three major conclusions about the social consequences of disasters. First, we all know that disasters harm people and destroy property; but what most people don't realize is that disasters also cause serious damage to human community. When a dam burst and sent a mountain of water down West Virginia's Buffalo Creek in 1972, it killed 125 people, destroyed 1,000 homes, and left 4,000 people homeless. After the waters had gone and help was streaming into the area, the people were paralyzed by the loss of family members and friends but also the loss of their entire way of life. Even more than thirty years later, they have been unable to rebuild the community life that they once knew. We can know when disasters start, Erikson points out, but we cannot know when they will

finally end. In addition, when disasters strike, it is the poor that suffer the most. This lesson was made clear when Hurricane Katrina struck New Orleans in 2005: "In the *Times*" on pages 622–23 provides a look at the lives of two families in the weeks after the event.

Second, Erikson explains that the social damage is more serious when an event involves some toxic substance, as is common with technological disasters. As the case of radiation falling on Utrik Island shows us, people feel "poisoned" when they have been exposed to a dangerous substance that they fear and over which they have no control. People in Ukraine felt much the same way after the 1986 explosion and radiation leak at the Chernobyl nuclear plant.

Third, the social damage is most serious when the disaster is caused by the actions of other people. This can happen through negligence or carelessness (in the case of technological disasters) or through willful action (in the case of intentional disasters). Our belief that "other people will do us no harm" is a basic foundation of social life, Erikson claims. But when others act carelessly (as in the case of the *Exxon Valdez* oil spill in Alaska in 1989) or intentionally in ways that harm us (as in the case of genocide in Yugoslavia from 1992 to 1995), those who survive typically lose their trust in others to a degree that may never go away.

A Never-Ending Atomic Disaster

It was just after dawn on March 1, 1954, and the air was already warm on Utrik Island, a small bit of coral and volcanic rock in the South Pacific that is one of the Marshall Islands. The island was home to 159 people, who lived by fishing much as their ancestors have done for centuries. The population knew only a little about the outside world—a missionary from the United States taught the local children, and two dozen military personnel lived at a small U.S. weather station with an airstrip that received one plane each week.

At 6:45 A.M., the western sky suddenly lit up brighter than anyone had ever seen, and seconds later, a rumble like a massive earthquake rolled across the island. Some of the Utrik people thought the world was coming to an end. Their world, at least as they had known it, had changed forever.

About 160 miles to the west, on Bikini Island, the United States military had just detonated an atomic bomb, a huge device with 1,000 times the power of the bomb used at the end of World War II to destroy the Japanese city of Hiroshima. The enormous blast vaporized the entire island and sent a massive cloud of dust and radiation into the atmosphere. The military expected the winds to take the cloud north into an open area of the ocean, but the cloud blew east instead. By noon, the radiation cloud engulfed a Japanese fishing boat ironically called the *Lucky Dragon*, exposing the twenty-three people on

board to a dose of radiation that would eventually sicken or kill them all. By the end of the afternoon, the deadly cloud reached Utrik Island.

The cloud was made up of coral and rock dust, all that was left of Bikini Island. The dust fell softly on Utrik Island, and the children, who remembered pictures of snow shown to them by their missionary teacher, ran out to play in the white powder that was piling up everywhere. No one realized that it was contaminated with deadly radiation.

Three-and-one-half days later, the U.S. military landed planes on Utrik Island and informed all the people that they would have to leave immediately,

bringing nothing with them. For three months, the island people were held on another military base, and then they were taken home.

Many of the people who were on the island that fateful morning died young, typically from cancer or some other disease associated with radiation exposure. But even today, those who survived consider themselves and their island poisoned by the radiation, and they believe that the poison will never go away. The radiation may or may not still be in their bodies, but it has worked its way deep into their culture. More than fifty years after the bomb exploded, people still talk about the morning that "everything changed." The damage from this disaster turns out to be much more than medical—it is a social transformation that has left the people with a deep belief that they are all sick, that life will never be the same, and that people could have prevented the disaster but did not.

WHAT DO YOU THINK?

1. In what sense is a disaster like this one never really over?
2. In what ways did the atomic bomb test change the culture of the Utrik people?
3. The U.S. government never formally took responsibility for what happened. What do you think the government should do now?

Source: Based on K. T. Erikson (2005a).

Social Movements

A **social movement** is *an organized activity that encourages or discourages social change.* Social movements are among the most important types of collective behavior because they often have lasting effects on the shape of our society.

Social movements are common in the modern world, but this was not always the case. Preindustrial societies are tightly bound by tradition, making social movements extremely rare. However, the many subcultures and countercultures found in industrial and postindustrial societies encourage social movements dealing with a wide range of

September 5, 2005

Hurricane Katrina: A Tale of Two Families

By JODI WILGOREN

BATON ROUGE, La., Sept. 4—It was moving day for the families of Gaynell Porretto and Tracy Jackson, the first page of the next chapter in their Hurricane Katrina horror stories.

Mrs. Porretto's four-car caravan crammed with a lifetime of photo albums, a few changes of clothes and coolers of drinks pulled up to a yellow house with a wide front porch that she had just rented for $600 in the humble hamlet of Arnaudville, La.

It is 125 miles from her storm-sacked home in the New Orleans suburb of Metairie, half the size for twice as many people, but she can see the church steeple from the yard, and her son is signed up for football at the nearby high school. . . .

Outside the New Orleans airport, Ms. Jackson's four sickly and hungry children, ages 1, 3, 5 and 7, were sprawled on a skycap's cart as she slogged through the sweaty, snail-like line, the baby atop a blue plastic bin filled with what they had scrounged from strangers.

It is all they have, their $2,000 cash savings burned up with their belongings—including birth certificates—in a post-flood fire at their apartment in uptown New Orleans. Even as they waited to board a plane, they did not know where they were taking it. . . .

Just as it ripped through levees to send water pouring through New Orleans, the storm cleaved a harsh chasm among the region's refugees, providing a stark portrait of the vast divide between America's haves and have-nots.

The more than 100 members of Mrs. Porretto's extended family have cars that carried them out last Sunday morning, well before the hurricane hit.

Ms. Jackson, who does not know how to drive, escaped on foot only after the floodwaters started filling her apartment on Tuesday, walking first to a bridge, then to the squalid Superdome.

Mrs. Porretto, 51, has an American Express card that covered her $564.26 bill at the Hilton in Lafayette, La. . . . Ms. Jackson, 24, does not have a bank account, and her husband, Jerel Brown, spent their last $25 to buy fish and shrimp from men grilling on the street in the chaos, so now there is nothing in the pockets of his baggy jeans but a crushed pack of Benson & Hedges. . . .

Mrs. Porretto, a court clerk, and her husband, Joel, a retired police officer, are hardly rich. But as they embark on life in exile, they look like royalty compared with Mr. Brown, Ms. Jackson and their children. . . .

Nearly one in four of New Orleans' 445,000 residents live in poverty, many of them in neighborhoods like the one where the Jackson-Brown clan huddled in a $350-a-month two-bedroom apartment across from a dilapidated and

---

public issues. In recent decades, for example, the gay rights movement has won legal changes in numerous cities and several states, forbidding discrimination based on sexual orientation and allowing formal domestic partnership and in some places even legal gay marriage. Like any social movement that seeks change, the gay rights movement has prompted a countermovement made up of traditionalists who want to limit the social acceptance of homosexuality. In today's society, almost every important public issue gives rise to a social movement favoring change and an opposing countermovement resisting it.

TYPES OF SOCIAL MOVEMENTS

Sociologists classify social movements according to several variables (Aberle, 1966; Cameron, 1966; Blumer, 1969). One variable asks, *Who is changed?* Some movements target selected people, and others try to change everyone. A second variable asks, *How much change?* Some movements seek only limited change in our lives, and others pursue radical transformation of society. Combining these variables results in four types of social movements, shown in Figure 23–1 on page 624.

Alterative social movements are least threatening to the status quo because they seek limited change in only a part of the population. Their aim is to help certain people *alter*

Visit the Promise Keepers Web site at http://www. promisekeepers.org

their lives. Promise Keepers, one example of an alterative social movement, encourages men to live more spiritual lives and be more supportive of their families.

Redemptive social movements also target specific people, but they seek radical change. Their aim is to help certain

dangerous housing project; 69 percent of the city is black, and the median household income is $31,369. To the west in Metairie, where Ellen DeGeneres grew up, the median income is $41,265, just below the national average, 87 percent of the 145,000 residents are white, and fewer than 1 in 10 are poor. . . .

On Saturday, as [Mrs. Porretto and her sister] unpacked the storm-survival arsenal they had amassed at the hotel—pounds of ham for sandwiches and a new toaster oven, all manner of snacks and condiments, even a bottle of olives to ease Mrs. Porretto's arthritis—a neighbor stopped by with a box of cleaning supplies. . . .

On moving day, Mrs. Porretto wore a clean T-shirt and fresh lipstick. Two hours' drive away at the airport, Ms. Jackson was braless under her soiled shirt and had a blue bandana covering her unwashed hair.

Ms. Jackson, Mr. Brown, their children, a nephew and a friend they call Auntie left New Orleans last Sunday morning, to stay with a friend. But they went back on Tuesday, and as the water rose to waist level, they fled with no provisions. After two nights shielding the baby's eyes from dead bodies at the feces-infested Superdome, they set out for the convention center, where rumors of rapes and worse left them taking turns sleeping on the floor in fear for their children's safety. . . .

Now, Ms. Jackson is wondering whether she will be able to enroll her children in school without identification—even her own Social Security card is gone. . . . Standing in the sweltering line, Mr. Brown occasionally lashed out, slapping the leg of a child on the move or barking at others in line for pushing. When an older woman passed out on the curb, he pushed through the crowd to pour water down her head and back. "Where's the help?" he called out. "We need help!" . . .

WHAT DO YOU THINK?

1. How did Hurricane Katrina remind people in the United States of social class differences? Do you think most people were aware of the kind of class differences described here?

2. What are several specific factors that make poor people more vulnerable than richer people when a natural disaster strikes?

3. We tend to think of hurricanes and other disasters of this kind as both natural and inevitable. In what ways are the consequences of such disasters also products of the way society is organized?

Adapted from the original article "In [a] Tale of Two Families, a Chasm Between Haves and Have-Nots" by Jodi Wilgoren published in *The New York Times* on September 5, 2005. Copyright © 2005 by The New York Times Company. Reprinted with permission.

---

people *redeem* their lives. For example, Alcoholics Anonymous is an organization that helps people with an alcohol addiction achieve a sober life.

Reformative social movements aim for only limited social change but target everyone. Multiculturalism, described in Chapter 3 ("Culture"), is an educational and political movement that advocates working toward social equality for people of all races and ethnicities. Reformative social movements generally work inside the existing political system. Some are *progressive*, promoting a new social pattern, and others are *reactionary*, trying to preserve the status quo or to revive past social patterns. Thus just as multiculturalists push for greater racial equality, so white supremacist organizations try to maintain the historical dominance of white people.

Revolutionary social movements are the most extreme of all, seeking the basic transformation of an entire society. Sometimes pursuing specific goals, sometimes spinning utopian dreams, these social movements reject existing social institutions as flawed in favor of a radically new alternative. Both the left-wing Communist party (pushing for government control of the entire economy) and the right-wing militia groups (advocating the destruction of "big government") seek to radically change our way of life (van Dyke & Soule, 2002).

YOUR TURN

Have you ever taken part in a social movement or witnessed one in action on your campus? If so, which of the four types best describes the movement?

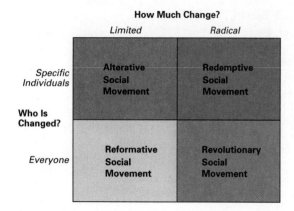

How Much Change?

	Limited	Radical
Specific Individuals	Alterative Social Movement	Redemptive Social Movement
Everyone	Reformative Social Movement	Revolutionary Social Movement

Who Is Changed?

FIGURE 23-1 Four Types of Social Movements

There are four types of social movements based on who is changed and how great the change is.

Source: Based on Aberle (1966).

CLAIMS MAKING

In 1981, the Centers for Disease Control and Prevention began to track a strange disease that was killing people, most of them homosexual men. The disease came to be known as AIDS (acquired immune deficiency syndrome). Although this is a deadly disease, there was little public attention and few stories in the mass media. It was only about five years later that the public became aware of the rising number of deaths and began to think of AIDS as a serious social threat.

The change in public thinking was the result of **claims making**, *the process of trying to convince the public and public officials of the importance of joining a social movement to address a particular issue.* In other words, for a social movement to form, some issue has to be defined as a problem that demands public attention. Usually, claims making begins with a small number of people. In the case of AIDS, the gay community in large cities (notably San Francisco and New York) mobilized to convince people of the dangers posed by this deadly disease. Over time, if the mass media give the issue attention and public officials speak out on behalf of the problem, it is likely that the social movement will gain strength.

Considerable public attention has now been given to AIDS, and there is ongoing research aimed at finding a cure for this deadly disease. The process of claims making goes on all the time for dozens of issues. Today, for example, a movement to ban the use of cellular telephones in automobiles has pointed to the thousands of automobile accidents each year related to the use of phones while driving; some states have now passed laws banning this practice, and debate continues in others (McVeigh, Welch, & Bjarnason, 2003; Macionis, 2005).

EXPLAINING SOCIAL MOVEMENTS

Because social movements are intentional and long-lasting, sociologists find this type of collective behavior easier to explain than brief episodes of mob behavior or mass hysteria described earlier in the chapter. Several theories have gained importance.

Deprivation Theory

Deprivation theory holds that social movements seeking change arise among people who feel deprived. People who feel they lack enough income, safe working conditions, basic political rights, or plain human dignity may organize a social movement to bring about a more just state of affairs (Morrison, 1978; J. D. Rose, 1982).

The rise of the Ku Klux Klan and the passage of Jim Crow laws by whites intent on enforcing segregation in the South after the Civil War illustrate deprivation theory. With the end of slavery, white landowners lost a source of free labor and poorer whites lost the claim that they were socially superior to African Americans. This change produced a sense of deprivation, prompting whites to try to keep all people of color "in their place" (Dollard et al., 1939). African Americans' deprivation was far greater, of course,

 For information on hate groups around the country, visit http://www.splcenter.org/intel /history.jsp

but as minorities in a racist society, they had little opportunity to organize. During the twentieth century, however, African Americans did organize successfully in pursuit of racial equality.

As Chapter 7 ("Groups and Organizations") explained, deprivation is a relative concept. Regardless of anyone's absolute amount of money and power, people feel either good or bad about their situation only by comparing themselves to some other category of people. **Relative deprivation,** then, is *a perceived disadvantage arising from some specific comparison* (Stouffer et al., 1949; Merton, 1968).

Alexis de Tocqueville's study of the French Revolution offers a classic illustration of relative deprivation (1955, orig. 1856). Why did rebellion occur in progressive France where feudalism was breaking down rather than in more traditional Germany, where peasants were much worse off? Tocqueville's answer was that as bad as their condition was, German peasants had known nothing but feudal servitude and thus had no basis for feeling deprived. French peasants, by contrast, had seen improvements in their lives that made them eager for more change. Consequently, the French—but not the Germans—felt relative deprivation. As Tocqueville saw it, increasing freedom and prosperity did not satisfy people as much as it sparked their desire for an even better life.

Closer to home, Tocqueville's insight helps explain patterns of rioting during the 1960s. Protest riots involving

A curious fact is that rioting by African Americans in U.S. cities during the 1960s was more common in the North (here, in Detroit), where good factory jobs were available and living standards were higher, rather than in the South, where a larger share of people lived in rural areas with lower incomes. Relative deprivation theory explains this contradiction by pointing out that it was in the North—where life had improved—that people came to expect equality. Relative to that goal, the reality of second-class citizenship became intolerable.

African Americans took place not in the South, where many black people lived in miserable poverty, but in Detroit, where the auto industry was booming, black unemployment was low, and black home ownership was highest in the country (Thernstrom & Thernstrom, 1998).

Critical review Deprivation theory challenges our commonsense assumption that the worst-off people are the most likely to organize for change. People do not organize simply because they suffer in an absolute sense; rather, social movements arise out of a sense of *relative* deprivation. Both Tocqueville and Marx—as different as they were in many ways—agreed on the importance of relative deprivation in the formation of social movements.

But most people experience some discontent all the time, so deprivation theory leaves us wondering why social movements arise among some categories of people and not others. A second problem is that deprivation theory suffers from circular reasoning: We assume that deprivation causes social movements, but often the only evidence of deprivation is the social movement itself (Jenkins & Perrow, 1977). A third limitation is that this approach focuses on the cause of a social movement and tells us little about what happens after movements take form (McAdam, McCarthy, & Zald, 1988).

Mass-Society Theory

William Kornhauser's *mass-society theory* (1959) argues that socially isolated people seek out social movements as a way to gain a sense of belonging and importance. From this point of view, social movements are most likely to arise in impersonal, *mass* societies. This theory points out the *personal* as well as the *political* consequences of social movements that offer a

sense of community to people otherwise adrift in society (Melucci, 1989).

It follows, says Kornhauser, that categories of people with weak social ties are those most eager to join a social movement. People who are well integrated socially, by contrast, are unlikely to seek membership in a social movement.

Kornhauser concludes that activists tend to be psychologically vulnerable people who eagerly join groups and can be manipulated by group leaders. For this reason, Kornhauser claims, social movements are rarely very democratic.

Critical review To Kornhauser's credit, his theory focuses on both the kind of society that produces social movements and the kinds of people who join them. But one criticism is that there is no clear standard for measuring the extent to which we live in a "mass society," so his thesis is difficult to test.

A second criticism is that explaining social movements in terms of people hungry to belong ignores the social-justice issues that movements address. Put otherwise, mass-society theory suggests that flawed people—rather than a flawed society—are responsible for social movements.

What does research show about mass-society theory? The record is mixed. Research by Frances Piven and Richard Cloward (1977) supports Kornhauser's approach. Piven and Cloward found that a breakdown of routine social patterns has encouraged poor people to form social movements. Also, a study of the New Mexico State Penitentiary found that when prison programs that promoted social ties among inmates were suspended, inmates were more likely to protest their conditions (Useem, 1997).

But other studies cast doubt on this approach. Some researchers conclude that the Nazi movement in Germany did not draw heavily from socially isolated people (Lipset, 1963; Oberschall, 1973). Similarly, many of the people who took part in urban riots during the 1960s had strong ties to their communities (Sears & McConahay, 1973). Evidence also suggests that most young people who join religious movements have fairly normal family ties (Wright & Piper, 1986). Finally, researchers who have examined the biographies of 1960s political activists find evidence of deep and continuing commitment to political goals rather than isolation from society (McAdam, 1988, 1989; Whalen & Flacks, 1989).

Structural-Strain Theory

One of the most influential theories about social movements was developed by Neil Smelser (1962). *Structural-strain theory* identifies six factors that encourage the development of social movements. Smelser's theory also suggests which factors encourage unorganized mobs or riots and which encourage highly organized social movements. The prodemocracy movement that transformed Eastern Europe during the late 1980s illustrates Smelser's theory.

1. **Structural conduciveness.** Social movements begin to emerge when people come to think their society has some serious problems. In Eastern Europe, these problems included low living standards and political repression by national governments.

2. **Structural strain.** People begin to experience relative deprivation when society fails to meet their expectations. Eastern Europeans joined the prodemocracy movement because they compared their living standards to the higher ones in Western Europe; they also knew that their standard of living was lower than what years of socialist propaganda had led them to expect.

3. **Growth and spread of an explanation.** Forming a well-organized social movement requires a clear statement of not just the problem but also its causes and its solutions. If people are confused about why they are suffering, they will probably express their dissatisfaction in an unorganized way through rioting. In the case of Eastern Europe, intellectuals played a key role in the prodemocracy movement by pointing out economic and political flaws in the socialist system and proposing strategies to increase democracy.

4. **Precipitating factors.** Discontent may exist for a long time before some specific event sparks collective action. Such an event occurred in 1985 when Mikhail Gorbachev came to power in the Soviet Union and began his program of *perestroika* (restructuring). As Moscow relaxed its rigid control over Eastern Europe, people there saw a historic opportunity to reorganize political and economic life and claim greater freedom.

5. **Mobilization for action.** Once people share a concern about some public issue, they are ready to take action—to distribute leaflets, stage protest rallies, and build alliances with sympathetic organizations. The initial success of the Solidarity movement in Poland—helped by the Reagan administration in the United States and by Pope John Paul II in the Vatican—mobilized people throughout Eastern Europe to press for change. The rate of change became faster and faster: What had taken a decade in Poland required only months in Hungary and only weeks in other Eastern European nations.

6. **Lack of social control.** The success of any social movement depends, in large part, on the response of political officials, police, and the military. Sometimes the state moves swiftly to crush a social movement, as happened in the case of prodemocracy forces in the People's Republic of China. But Gorbachev adopted a policy of nonintervention in Eastern Europe, opening the door for change. Ironically, the movements that began in Eastern Europe soon spread to the Soviet Union itself, ending the historic domination of the Communist party in 1991 and producing a new political confederation.

Critical review   Smelser's analysis explains how various factors help or hurt the development of social movements. Structural-strain theory also explains why people may respond to their problems either by forming organized social movements or through spontaneous mob action.

Yet Smelser's theory contains some of the same circularity of argument found in Kornhauser's analysis. A social movement is caused by strain, says Smelser, but the only evidence of underlying strain is often the social movement itself. Finally, structural-strain theory is incomplete, overlooking the important role that resources like the mass media or international alliances play in the success or failure of a social movement (Jenkins & Perrow, 1977; McCarthy & Zald, 1977; Olzak & West, 1991).

Resource-Mobilization Theory

Resource-mobilization theory points out that no social movement is likely to succeed—or even get off the ground—without substantial resources, including money, human labor, office and communications equipment, access to the mass media, and a positive public image. In short, any social movement rises or falls on how well it attracts resources, mobilizes people, and forges alliances.

Outsiders can be just as important as insiders in affecting the outcome of a social movement. Because socially disadvantaged people, by definition, lack the money, contacts,

Social movements are often given great energy by powerful visual images, which is one key idea of culture theory. During World War II, this photo of six soldiers raising the U.S. flag on the tiny Pacific island of Iwo Jima increased morale at home and, later, was the inspiration for a memorial sculpture. Some twenty-five years later, the news included the photo on the right, showing children running from a napalm strike by U.S. planes in South Vietnam. The girl in the middle of the picture had ripped the flaming clothes from her body. This photo increased the strength of the social movement against the war in Vietnam.

leadership skills, and organizational know-how that a successful movement requires, sympathetic outsiders fill the resource gap. In U.S. history, well-to-do white people, including college students, performed a vital service to the black civil rights movement in the 1960s, and affluent men have joined women as leaders of the women's movement.

Resources connecting people are also vital. The 1989 prodemocracy movement in China was fueled by students whose location on campuses clustered together in Beijing allowed them to build networks and recruit new members (Zhao, 1998). More recently, the Internet and cell phones have been important resources that help organizations link hundreds of thousands of people across the country or around the world. Prior to the Iraq War, for example, two individuals using their computers were able to get 120,000 people in 190 countries to sign a petition opposing the war.

The availability of organizing ideas online has helped many social movements to grow over time. For example, "Take Back the Night" is an annual occasion for rallies at which people speak out in opposition to violence against women, children, and families. Using resources available online, even a small number of people can plan and carry out an effective political event (Valocchi, 1996; Passy & Giugni, 2001; Packer, 2003).

 For more about Take Back the Night, go to http://www. campusoutreachservices.com/ resources/tbtnhistory.htm

Critical review Resource-mobilization theory recognizes that resources as well as discontent are necessary to the success of a social movement. Research confirms the importance of forging alliances to gaining resources and notes that movements with few resources may, in desperation, turn to violence to call attention to their cause (Grant & Wallace, 1991; Jenkins, Jacobs, & Agone, 2003).

Critics of this theory counter that "outside" people and resources are not always needed to ensure a movement's success. They argue that even relatively powerless segments of a population can promote change if they are able to organize effectively and have strongly committed members (Donnelly & Majka, 1998). Aldon Morris (1981) adds that the success of the civil rights movement of the 1950s and 1960s was due to people of color who drew mostly on their own skills and resources. A second problem with this theory is that it overstates the extent to which powerful people are willing to challenge the status quo. Some rich white people did provide valuable resources to the black civil rights movement, but probably more often, elites were indifferent or opposed to significant change (McAdam, 1982, 1983; Pichardo, 1995).

Culture Theory

In recent years, sociologists have developed *culture theory*, the recognition that social movements depend not only on material resources and the structure of political power but also on cultural symbols. That is, people in any particular situation are likely to mobilize to form a social movement only to the extent that they develop "shared understandings of the world that legitimate and motivate collective action" (McAdam, McCarthy, & Zald, 1996:6; see also J. E. Williams, 2002).

In part, mobilization depends on a sense of injustice, as suggested by deprivation theory. In addition, people must come to believe that they are not able to respond to their situation effectively by acting alone. Finally, social movements gain strength as they develop symbols and a sense of community that both build strong feelings and direct energy into organized action. Media images of the burning World Trade Center towers after the September 11, 2001, terrorist attacks helped mobilize people to support the "war against terrorism." Likewise, photos of gay couples celebrating their weddings have helped fuel both the gay rights movement and the countermovement trying to prevent the expansion of gay marriage.

Critical review A strength of culture theory is reminding us that social movements depend not just on material resources but also on cultural symbols. At the same time, powerful symbols (such as the flag and ideas about patriotism and respecting our leaders) help support the status quo. How and when symbols turn people from supporting the system toward protest against it are questions in need of further research.

Political-Economy Theory

Marxist *political-economy theory* also has something to say about social movements. From this point of view, social movements arise within capitalist societies because the capitalist economic system fails to meet the needs of the majority of people. Despite great economic productivity, U.S. society is in crisis, with millions of people unable to find good jobs, living below the poverty line, and living without health insurance.

Social movements arise as a response to such conditions. Workers organize in order to demand higher wages, citizens rally for a health policy that will protect everyone, and people march in opposition to spending billions to fund wars at the expense of social welfare programs (Buechler, 2000).

Critical review A strength of political-economy theory is its macro-level approach. Other theories explain the rise of social movements in terms of traits of individuals (such as weak social ties or a sense of relative deprivation) or traits of movements (such as their available resources), but this approach focuses on the institutional structures (the economy and political system) of society itself.

This approach explains social movements concerned with economic issues. But it is less helpful in understanding the recent rise of social movements concerned with noneconomic issues such as obesity, animal rights, or the state of the natural environment.

New Social Movements Theory

A final theoretical approach addresses what are often called "new social movements." *New social movements theory* suggests that recent social movements in the postindustrial societies of North America and Western Europe have a new focus (McAdam, McCarthy, & Zald, 1988; Pakulski, 1993; Wallace, 1996).

First, older social movements, such as those led by labor organizations, are concerned mostly with economic issues, but new social movements tend to focus on improving our social and physical surroundings. The environmental movement, for example, is trying to stop global warming and address other environmental dangers.

Second, most of today's social movements are international, focusing on global ecology, the social standing of

 For information on laws involving animal rights, see http://www.animal-law.org

women and gay people, animal rights, and opposition to war. In other words, as the process of globalization links the world's nations, social movements are becoming global.

Third, most social movements of the past drew strong support from working-class people, but new social movements that focus on noneconomic issues usually draw support from the middle and upper-middle classes. As discussed in Chapter 17 ("Politics and Government"), more affluent people tend to be more conservative on economic issues (because they have wealth to protect) but more liberal on social issues (partly as a result of extensive education). In the United States and other rich nations, the number of highly educated professionals—the people who are most likely to support "new social movements"—is increasing, a fact suggesting that these movements will grow (Jenkins & Wallace, 1996; F. Rose, 1997).

Critical review One strength of new social movements theory is recognizing that social movements have become international along with the global economy. This theory also highlights the power of the mass media and new information technology to unite people around the world in pursuit of political goals.

SUMMING UP

Theories of Social Movements

Deprivation Theory	People experiencing relative deprivation begin social movements. The social movement is a means of seeking change that brings participants greater benefits. Social movements are especially likely when rising expectations are frustrated.
Mass-Society Theory	People who lack established social ties are mobilized into social movements. Periods of social breakdown are likely to spawn social movements. The social movement gives members a sense of belonging and social participation.
Structural-Strain Theory	People come together because of their shared concern about the inability of society to operate as they believe it should. The growth of a social movement reflects many factors, including a belief in its legitimacy and some precipitating event that provokes action.
Resource-Mobilization Theory	People may join for all the reasons noted above and also because of social ties to existing members. But the success or failure of a social movement depends largely on the resources available to it. Also important is the extent of opposition within the larger society.
Culture Theory	People are drawn to a social movement by cultural symbols that define some cause as just. The movement itself usually becomes a symbol of power and justice.
Political-Economy Theory	People unite to address the societal ills caused by capitalism, including unemployment, poverty, and lack of health care. Social movements are necessary because a capitalist economy inevitably fails to meet people's basic needs.
New Social Movements Theory	People who join social movements are motivated by quality-of-life issues, not necessarily economic concerns. Mobilization is national or international in scope. New social movements arise in response to the expansion of the mass media and new information technology.

However, critics claim that this approach exaggerates the differences between past and present social movements. The women's movement, for example, focuses on many of the same issues—workplace conditions and pay—that have concerned labor organizations for decades. Similarly, many people protesting the use of U.S. military power consider economic equality around the world their primary goal.

Each of the seven theories presented here offers some explanation of the emergence of social movements. The Summing Up table summarizes them all.

GENDER AND SOCIAL MOVEMENTS

Gender figures prominently in the operation of social movements. In keeping with traditional ideas about gender in the United States, more men than women tend to take part in public life—including spearheading social movements.

Investigating "Freedom Summer," a 1964 voter registration project in Mississippi, Doug McAdam (1992) found that movement members considered the job of registering African American voters in a hostile white community

dangerous and therefore defined it as "men's work." Many of the women in the movement, despite more years of activist experience, ended up working in clerical or teaching assignments behind the scenes. Only the most exceptionally talented and committed women, McAdam found, were able to overcome the movement's gender barriers. In short, women have played leading roles in many social movements (including the abolitionist and feminist movements in the United States), but male dominance has been the norm even in social movements that otherwise oppose the status quo (Herda-Rapp, 1998).

STAGES IN SOCIAL MOVEMENTS

Despite the many differences that set one social movement apart from another, all unfold in roughly the same way, as shown in Figure 23–2 on page 630. Researchers have identified four stages in the life of the typical social movement (Blumer, 1969; Mauss, 1975; Tilly, 1978):

Stage 1: Emergence Social movements are driven by the perception that all is not well. Some, such as the civil rights and women's movements, are born of widespread dissatisfaction.

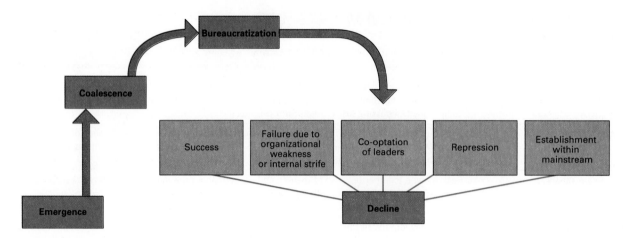

FIGURE 23-2 Stages in the Lives of Social Movements

Social movements typically go through four stages. The last is decline, which may occur for any of five reasons.

Others emerge only as a small vanguard group increases public awareness of some issue. Gay activists, for example, helped raise public concern about the threat posed by AIDS.

Stage 2: Coalescence   After emerging, a social movement must define itself and develop a strategy for "going public." Leaders must determine policies, decide on tactics to be used, build morale, and recruit new members. At this stage, the movement may engage in collective action, such as rallies or demonstrations, to attract the attention of the media and increase public awareness. The movement may also form alliances with other organizations to acquire necessary resources.

Stage 3: Bureaucratization   To become a political force, a social movement must become an established, bureaucratic organization, as described in Chapter 7 ("Groups and Organizations"). As this happens, the movement depends less on the charisma and talents of a few leaders and relies more on a capable staff. When social movements do not become established in this way, they risk dissolving if the leader steps down, as is the case with many organizations of college activists. On the other hand, the National Organization for Women (NOW), despite its changing leadership, is well established and can be counted on to speak for feminists.

But becoming more bureaucratic can also hurt a social movement. Surveying the fate of various social movements in U.S. history, Frances Piven and Richard Cloward (1977) found that leaders sometimes become so engrossed in

building an organization that they neglect the need to keep people "fired up" for change. In such cases, the radical edge of protest is lost.

Stage 4: Decline   Eventually, most social movements begin to decline. Frederick Miller (1983) suggests four reasons this can occur.

First, if members have met their goals, decline may simply signal success. For example, the women's suffrage movement disbanded after it won women in the United States the right to vote. But as is the case with the modern women's movement, winning one victory leads to new goals.

Second, a social movement may fold because of organizational failures, such as poor leadership, loss of interest among members, insufficient funds, or repression by authorities. Some people lose interest when the excitement of early efforts is replaced by day-to-day routine. Fragmentation due to internal conflicts over goals and strategies is another common problem. Students for a Democratic Society (SDS), a student movement opposing the war in Vietnam, splintered into several small factions by the end of the 1960s, as members disagreed over goals and strategies for change.

Third, a social movement can fall apart if leaders are attracted by offers of money, prestige, or power from within the "system." This type of "selling out" is one example of the iron law of oligarchy, discussed in Chapter 7 ("Groups and Organizations"). That is, organizational leaders can use their position to serve their own interests. For example, Vernon Jordan, once head of the activist National Urban League, became a close adviser to President Clinton and a rich and powerful Washington insider. But this process can also work the other way: Some people give up high-paying careers to become activists. Cat Stevens, a rock star of the 1970s, became a Muslim, changed his name to Yusuf Islam, and since then has devoted his life to the spread of his religion.

Fourth and finally, a social movement can be crushed by repression. Officials may destroy a social movement by frightening away participants, discouraging new recruits, and even imprisoning leaders. In general, the more revolutionary the social movement, the more officials try to repress it. Until 1990, the government of South Africa banned the African National Congress (ANC), a political organization seeking to overthrow the state-supported system of apartheid. Even suspected members of the ANC were subject to arrest. Only after 1990, when the government lifted the decades-old ban and released from prison ANC leader Nelson Mandela (who was elected the country's president in 1994) did South Africa begin the journey away from apartheid.

Beyond the reasons noted by Miller, a fifth cause of decline is that a social movement may "go mainstream." Some movements become an accepted part of the system—typically after realizing some of their goals—so they continue to flourish but no longer challenge the status quo. The U.S. labor movement, for example, is now well established; its leaders control vast sums of money and, according to some critics, now have more in common with the business tycoons they opposed in the past than with rank-and-file workers.

SOCIAL MOVEMENTS AND SOCIAL CHANGE

Social movements exist to encourage or to resist social change. Whatever the intention, their success varies from case to case. The civil rights movement has effectively pushed this country toward racial equality, despite opposition from a handful of white supremacist countermovements like the Aryan Nation and what's left of the Ku Klux Klan.

Sometimes we overlook the success of past social movements and take for granted the changes that other people struggled so hard to win. Beginning a century ago, workers' movements in the United States fought to end  child labor in factories, limit working hours, make the workplace safer, and establish workers' right to bargain collectively with employers. Laws protecting the environment are another product of successful social movements. In addition, women today enjoy the greater legal rights and economic opportunities won by earlier generations of women.

As the Thinking It Through box on page 632 explains, some college students become part of movements seeking social and political goals. Keeping in mind the importance of social movements to the future direction of society, what about you? Are you willing to take a stand?

Social Movements: Looking Ahead

Especially since the turbulent 1960s—a decade marked by widespread social protests—U.S. society has been pushed and pulled by many social movements and countermovements calling attention to issues from abortion to financing political campaigns to medical care to war. Of course, different people define the problems in different ways, just as they are likely to settle on different policies as solutions. In short, social movements and the problems they address are always *political* (Macionis, 2005).

For three reasons, the scope of social movements is likely to increase. First, protest should increase as women, African Americans, gay people, and other historically marginalized categories of our population gain a greater political voice. Second, at a global level, the technology of the Information Revolution means that anyone with a television or a personal computer can be well informed about political events, often as soon as they happen. Third, new technology and the emerging global economy mean that social movements are now uniting people throughout the entire world. Because many problems are global in scope, we can expect the formation of international social movements seeking to solve them.

Are You Willing to Take a Stand?

Are you satisfied with our society as it is? Surely, everyone would change some things about our way of life. Indeed, surveys show that if they could, a lot of people would change plenty! There is considerable pessimism about the state of U.S. society: Two-thirds of U.S. adults think that the average person's situation "is getting worse, not better," and three-fourths of respondents stated that most government officials are "not interested" in the average person's problems (NORC, 2003:208).

But in light of such concerns, few people are willing to stand up and try to bring about change. Within the past five years, only 13 percent of U.S. adults have attended a public meeting organized to protest against the government; just 9 percent say they have taken part in a protest march or demonstration (NORC, 2003:974–75).

Many college students probably suspect that age has something to do with such apathy. That is, young people have the interest and idealism to challenge the status quo, but older adults worry only about their families and their jobs. Indeed, one of the popular sayings of the activist 1960s was "You can't trust people over thirty!" But the facts are otherwise: Students entering college in 2004 expressed less interest in political issues than their parents.

Asked to select important goals in life from a list, 34 percent of first-year students included "keeping up with political affairs" and just 21 percent checked off "participating in community action programs." As the figure shows, in the past year, 25

percent of students claimed to discuss politics frequently, and 21 percent say they voted in a student election.

Certainly, people cite some good reasons to avoid political controversy. Any time we challenge the system—whether on campus or in the national political arena—we risk making enemies, losing a job, or perhaps even sustaining physical injury.

But the most important reason that people in the United States avoid joining in social movements may have to do with cultural norms about how change should occur. In our individualistic culture, people favor taking personal responsibility over collective action as a means of addressing social problems. For example, when asked about the best way for women or African Americans to improve their social position, most U.S. adults say that individuals should rely on their own

efforts, and only a few point to women's groups or civil rights activism as the best way to bring about change (NORC, 2003:221, 343, 345). This individualistic orientation explains why adults in this country are half as likely as their European counterparts to join in lawful demonstrations (Inglehart et al., 2000).

Sociology, of course, poses a counterpoint to our cultural individualism. As C. Wright Mills (1959) explained decades ago, many of the problems we encounter as individuals are caused by the structure of society. As a result, said Mills, solutions to many of life's problems depend on collective effort—that is, people willing to take a stand for what they believe.

WHAT DO YOU THINK?

1. Do you think the reluctance of people in the United States to address problems through collective action shows that they are basically satisfied with their lives or that they think individuals acting together can't make a difference? Explain your answer.
2. Have you ever participated in a political demonstration? What were its goals? What did it accomplish?
3. Does it surprise you that nearly 60 percent of eighteen- to twenty-four-year-olds in the United States do not even bother to vote? How would you explain such political apathy?

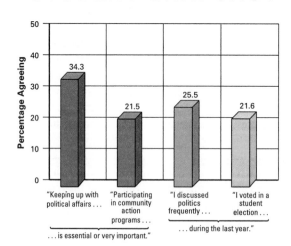

STUDENT SNAPSHOT

Percentage Agreeing

- 34.3 — "Keeping up with political affairs . . . . . . is essential or very important."
- 21.5 — "Participating in community action programs . . .
- 25.5 — "I discussed politics frequently . . .
- 21.6 — "I voted in a student election . . . . . . during the last year."

Political Involvement of Students Entering College in 2004: A Survey

First-year college students are mostly younger people who express limited interest in politics.

Source: Sax et al. (2004).

The following learning tools will help you see what you know, identify what you still need to learn, and expand your understanding beyond the text. You can also visit this text's Companion Website™ at http://www.prenhall.com/macionis to find additional practice tests.

KEY POINTS

Studying Collective Behavior

Collective behavior differs from group behavior in that it involves limited social interaction within vague social boundaries, usually guided by weak and often unconventional norms.

Localized Collectivities: Crowds

Crowds, an important type of collective behavior, take various forms: casual crowds, conventional crowds, expressive crowds, acting crowds, and protest crowds. Crowds that become emotionally intense can create violent mobs and riots. Mobs pursue a specific goal; rioting involves unfocused destruction. Crowd behavior can threaten the status quo, which is why crowds have figured heavily in social change throughout history.

Contagion theory views crowds as anonymous, suggestible, and swayed by rising emotions. Convergence theory states that crowd behavior reflects the desires people bring to them. Emergent-norm theory suggests that crowds develop their own behavioral norms.

Dispersed Collectivities: Mass Behavior

One form of mass behavior is rumor, which thrives in a climate of uncertainty. Rumor involves public issues, and gossip deals with personal issues. Public opinion consists of people's positions on important, controversial issues. Public attitudes change over time, and at any time on any given issue, a small share of people hold no opinion at all.

People living in industrial societies use fashion as a source of social prestige. A fad is more unconventional than a fashion; although people may follow a fad with enthusiasm, it usually goes away in a short time.

A panic (in a local area) or mass hysteria (across an entire society) are types of collective behavior in which people respond to a significant event, real or imagined, with irrational, frantic, and often self-destructive behavior.

Disasters are generally unexpected events that cause great harm to many people. Disasters are of three types: natural disasters (flood or earthquake), technological disasters (oil spill or nuclear plant accident), and intentional disasters (terrorist attack or genocide).

Social Movements

Social movements try to promote or discourage change. Sociologists classify social movements according to the range of people they try to involve and the extent of change they try to accomplish. Social movements engage in claims making to try to convince people that a particular issue should be a matter of public attention.

According to deprivation theory, social movements arise as people feel deprived in relation to some standard of well-being. Mass-society theory holds that people join social movements to gain a sense of belonging and moral direction. Structural-strain theory states that a social movement develops as the result of six factors and that clearly stated grievances encourage the formation of social movements; undirected anger, by contrast, promotes rioting. Resource-mobilization theory ties the success or failure of a social movement to the availability of resources such as money, human labor, and alliances with other organizations. Culture theory notes the importance of symbols as well as material resources to the success of a social movement. The political-economy approach claims that social movements arise within capitalist societies that fail to meet the needs of a majority of people. New social movements theory focuses on quality-of-life issues that are usually international in scope.

A typical social movement proceeds through consecutive stages: emergence (defining the public issue), coalescence (entering the public arena), bureaucratization (becoming formally organized), and decline (due to failure or, sometimes, success).

Social Movements: Looking Ahead

Social movements have had a major effect on U.S. society, especially since the 1960s. With technology linking people as never before, it is likely that social movements, many of them international in scope, will be more common in the future.

KEY CONCEPTS

collective behavior (p. 612) activity involving a large number of people that is unplanned, often controversial, and sometimes dangerous.

collectivity (p. 612) a large number of people whose minimal interaction occurs in the absence of well-defined and conventional norms

crowd (p. 613) a temporary gathering of people who share a common focus of attention and who influence one another

mob (p. 614) a highly emotional crowd that pursues a violent or destructive goal

riot (p. 614) a social eruption that is highly emotional, violent, and undirected

mass behavior (p. 616) collective behavior among people spread over a wide geographic area

rumor (p. 616) unconfirmed information that people spread informally, often by word of mouth

gossip (p. 616) rumor about people's personal affairs

public opinion (p. 618) widespread attitudes about controversial issues

propaganda (p. 618) information presented with the intention of shaping public opinion

fashion (p. 618) a social pattern favored by a large number of people

fad (p. 618) an unconventional social pattern that people embrace briefly but enthusiastically

panic (p. 619) a form of collective behavior in which people in one place react to a

threat or other stimulus with irrational, frantic, and often self-destructive behavior

mass hysteria (moral panic) (p. 619) a form of dispersed collective behavior in which people react to a real or imagined event with irrational and even frantic fear

disaster (p. 619) an event, generally unexpected, that causes extensive harm to people and damage to property

social movement (p. 621) an organized activity that encourages or discourages social change

claims making (p. 624) the process of trying to convince the public and public officials of the importance of joining a social movement to address a particular issue

relative deprivation (p. 624) a perceived disadvantage arising from some specific comparison

SAMPLE TEST QUESTIONS

These questions are similar to those found in the test bank that accompanies this textbook.

Multiple-Choice Questions

1. **Which of the following is true about collective behavior?**
   a. It usually involves a large number of people.
   b. It is often spontaneous.
   c. It is often controversial.
   d. All of the above are correct.

2. **Which of the following is a good example of a collectivity?**
   a. students quietly working out at the college weight room
   b. excited soccer fans throwing bottles as they leave a stadium
   c. students in line at the cafeteria waiting to be served
   d. all of the above

3. **A mob differs from a riot in that the mob**
   a. typically has a clear objective.
   b. is not violent.
   c. does not involve people with intense emotion.
   d. lasts a long time.

4. **Which theory says that "crowds can make people go crazy"?**
   a. emergent-norm theory
   b. convergence theory
   c. contagion theory
   d. subcultural theory

5. **When sociologists speak of "mass behavior," they have in mind**
   a. people taking part in a riot or mob.
   b. many people spread over a large area thinking or acting in a particular way.
   c. irrational behavior on the part of people in a crowd.
   d. people imitating what they see others do.

6. **Which of the following is an example of a technological disaster?**
   a. a forest fire in Yellowstone National Park caused by lightning
   b. the deaths of millions of civilians during World War II
   c. Hurricane Andrew slamming into Florida
   d. the radiation leak from the Chernobyl nuclear power plant

7. **Hula hoops, streaking, and collecting Pokémon cards are all examples of**
   a. style.
   b. fashion.
   c. fads.
   d. popular social movements.

8. Deprivation theory explains that social movements arise among people who
   a. feel adrift in society.
   b. are poor and feel they have little more to lose.
   c. believe that they lack rights, income, or something else that they think they should have.
   d. are moved to action by particular cultural symbols.

9. The claim that social movements cannot arise without things like effort, money, and leadership is made by which theory?
   a. resource-mobilization theory
   b. deprivation theory
   c. mass-society theory
   d. political-economy theory

10. The effect of gender on the operation of social movements in the United States is demonstrated by the fact that
    a. few women are interested in most public issues.
    b. men have usually taken leadership roles.
    c. men tend to avoid participation in social movements.
    d. women typically have taken leadership roles.

Answers: 1(d); 2(b); 3(a); 4(c); 5(b); 6(d); 7(c); 8(c); 9(a); 10(b).

Essay Questions

1. The concept of collective behavior encompasses a broad range of social patterns. List some of these patterns. What traits do they have in common? How do they differ?

2. In what respects do some recent social movements (the environment, animal rights, and gun control) differ from older crusades (the right of workers to form unions or the right of women to vote)?

APPLICATIONS & EXERCISES

1. With ten friends, try this experiment: One person writes down a detailed "rumor" about someone important and then whispers it to the second person, who whispers it to a third, and so on. The last person to hear the rumor writes it down again. Compare the two versions of the rumor. Are you surprised by the results of your experiment? Why or why not?

2. With other members of the class, identify recent fad products. What makes people want them? Why do people lose interest in them so quickly?

3. What social movements are represented by organizations on your campus? Invite several leaders to describe their groups' goals and strategies to your class.

INVESTIGATE *with* Research Navigator

Research Navigator.com
RESOURCES FOR COLLEGE RESEARCH ASSIGNMENTS

Follow the instructions on page 27 of this text to access the features of **Research Navigator™.** Once at the Web site, enter your Login Name and Password. Then, to use the **ContentSelect™** database, enter keywords such as "social movements," "disasters," and "animal rights," and the search engine will supply relevant and recent scholarly and popular press publications. Use the *New York Times* **Search-by-Subject Archive** to find recent news articles related to sociology and the **Link Library** feature to find relevant Web links organized by the key terms associated with this chapter.

24

Social Change:
Traditional, Modern, and
Postmodern Societies

Why do societies change?

How does modern society shape people's lives?

What do sociologists say is good
and bad about today's society?

The five-story, red brick apartment building at 253 East Tenth Street in New York City has been standing for more than a century. In 1900, one of the twenty small apartments in the building was occupied by thirty-nine-year-old Julius Streicher, Christine Streicher, age thirty-three, and their four young children. The Streichers were immigrants, having come in 1885 from their native Germany to New York, where they met and married.

The Streichers probably considered themselves successful. Julius operated a small clothing shop a few blocks from his apartment; Christine stayed at home, raised the children, and did housework. Like most people in the country at that time, neither Julius nor Christine had graduated from high school, and they worked for ten to twelve hours a day, six days a week. Their income—average in the United States for that time—was about $35 a month or about $425 a year. (In today's dollars, that would be slightly more than $8,000, which would put the family well below today's poverty line.) They spent almost half of their income for food; most of the rest went for rent.

Today, Dorothy Sabo resides at 253 East Tenth Street, living alone in the same apartment where the Streichers spent much of their lives. Now eighty-seven, she is retired from a career teaching art at a nearby museum. In many respects, Sabo's life has been far easier than the life the Streichers knew. For one thing, when the Streichers lived there, the building had no electricity (people used kerosene lamps and candles) and no running water (Christine Streicher spent most of every Monday doing laundry, using water she carried from a public fountain at the end of the block). There were no telephones, no television, and of course no computers. Today, Dorothy Sabo takes such conveniences for granted. Although she is hardly rich, her pension and Social Security are several times as much (in constant dollars) as the Streichers earned.

Sabo has her own worries. She is concerned about the environment and often speaks out about global warming. But a century ago, if the Streichers and their neighbors were concerned about "the environment," they probably would have meant the smell coming up from the street. At a time when motor vehicles were just beginning to appear in New York City, carriages, trucks, and trolleys were all pulled by horses—thousands of them. These animals dumped 60,000 gallons of urine and 2.5 million pounds of manure on the streets each and every day (Simon & Cannon, 2001). ■

It is difficult for most people today to imagine how different life was a century ago. Not only was life much harder back then, but it was also much shorter. Statistical records show that 100 years ago, life expectancy was just forty-six years for men and forty-eight years for women, compared to seventy-five and eighty years today.

Learn about the lives of men and women, black and white, living in New York City a century ago at http://www.albany.edu/mumford/1920/groups.html

Over the course of the past century, much has changed for the better. Yet as this chapter explains, social change is not all positive. On the contrary, change has negative consequences, too, creating unexpected new problems. Indeed, as we shall see, early sociologists were mixed in their assessment of *modernity,* changes brought about by the Industrial Revolution. Likewise, today's sociologists point to both good and bad aspects of *postmodernity,* the recent transformations of society caused by the Information Revolution and the postindustrial economy. The one thing that is clear is that—for better and worse—the rate of change has never been faster than it is now.

What Is Social Change?

In earlier chapters, we examined relatively fixed or *static* social patterns, including status and role, social stratification, and social institutions. We also looked at the *dynamic* forces that have shaped our way of life, ranging from innovations in technology to the growth of bureaucracy and the expansion of cities. These are all dimensions of **social change,** *the transformation of culture and social institutions over time.* The process of social change has four major characteristics:

1. **Social change happens all the time.** "Nothing is constant except death and taxes" goes the old saying. Yet even our thoughts about death have changed dramatically as life expectancy in the United States has doubled over the course of a century. Back in 1900, the Streichers and almost all other people in the United States paid little or no taxes on their earnings; taxes increased dramatically over the course of the twentieth century, along with the size and scope of government. In short, just about everything is subject to the twists and turns of change.

    Still, some societies change faster than others. As Chapter 4 ("Society") explained, hunting and gathering societies change quite slowly; members of today's high-income societies, by contrast, experience significant change within a single lifetime.

YOUR TURN

What are the three most important changes that have occurred during your lifetime? Explain your answer.

It is also true that in a given society, some cultural elements change faster than others. William Ogburn's (1964) theory of *cultural lag* (see Chapter 3, "Culture") states that material culture (that is, things) usually changes faster than nonmaterial culture (ideas and attitudes). For example, the genetic technology that allows scientists to alter and perhaps even to create life has developed more rapidly than our ethical standards for deciding when and how to use it.

2. **Social change is sometimes intentional but often unplanned.** Industrial societies actively promote many kinds of change. For example, scientists seek more efficient forms of energy, and advertisers try to convince us that life is incomplete without this or that new gadget. Yet rarely can anyone envision all the consequences of the changes that are set in motion.

    Back in 1900, when the country still relied on horses for transportation, many people looked ahead to motorized vehicles that would carry them in a single day distances that used to take weeks or months. But no one could see how much the mobility provided by automobiles would alter life in the United States, scattering family members, threatening the environment, and reshaping cities and suburbs. Nor could automotive pioneers have predicted the more than 42,000 deaths that occur in car accidents each year in the United States alone.

3. **Social change is controversial.** The history of the automobile shows that social change brings both good and bad consequences. Capitalists welcomed the Industrial Revolution because new technology increased productivity and swelled profits. However, workers feared that machines would make their skills obsolete and resisted the push toward "progress."

    Today, as in the past, changing patterns of social interaction between black people and white people, women and men, and gays and heterosexuals are welcomed by some people and opposed by others.

4. **Some changes matter more than others.** Some changes (such as clothing fads) have only passing significance; others (like the invention of computers) may change the entire world. Will the Information Revolution turn out to be as important as the Industrial Revolution? Like the automobile and television, the computer has both positive and negative effects, providing new kinds of jobs while eliminating old ones, isolating people in offices while linking people in global electronic networks, offering vast amounts of information while threatening personal privacy.

Causes of Social Change

Social change has many causes. In a world linked by sophisticated communication and transportation technology, change in one place often sets off change elsewhere.

These young boys are performing in a hip-hop dance competition in Chengdu, China, in 2005. Hip-hop music, dress style, and dancing have become popular in China, a clear case of cultural diffusion. Cultural patterns move from place to place, but not always with the same understandings of what they mean. How might Chinese youth understand hip-hop differently from the young African Americans in the United States who originated it?

CULTURE AND CHANGE

Chapter 3 ("Culture") identified three important sources of cultural change. First, *invention* produces new objects, ideas, and social patterns. Rocket propulsion research, which began in the 1940s, has produced spacecraft that reach toward the stars. Today we take such technology for granted; during this century, a significant number of people may well travel in space.

Second, *discovery* occurs when people take note of existing elements of the world. Medical advances, for example, offer a growing understanding of the human body. Beyond the direct effects on human health, medical discoveries have stretched life expectancy, setting in motion the "graying" of U.S. society (see Chapter 15, "Aging and the Elderly").

Third, *diffusion* creates change as products, people, and information spread from one society to another. Ralph Linton (1937a) recognized that many familiar elements of our culture came from other lands. For example, the cloth used to make our clothing was developed in Asia, the clocks we see all around us were invented in Europe, and the coins we carry in our pockets were first used in Turkey.

In general, material things diffuse more easily than cultural ideas. That is, new breakthroughs such as the science

of cloning occur faster than our understanding of when—and even whether—they are morally desirable.

CONFLICT AND CHANGE

Tension and conflict in a society also produce change. Karl Marx saw class conflict as the engine that drives societies from one historical era to another (see Chapter 4, "Society," and Chapter 10, "Social Stratification"). In industrial-capitalist societies, he maintained, the struggle between capitalists and workers pushes society toward a socialist system of production.

In the more than 100 years since Marx's death, this model has proved simplistic. Yet Marx correctly foresaw that social conflict arising from inequality (involving not just class but also race and gender) would force changes in every society, including our own, to improve the lives of working people.

IDEAS AND CHANGE

Max Weber also contributed to our understanding of social change. Although Weber agreed that conflict could bring about change, he traced the roots of most social change to ideas. For example, people with charisma (Martin Luther King Jr. was one example) can carry a message that sometimes changes the world.

Weber also highlighted the importance of ideas by showing how the religious beliefs of early Protestants set the stage for the spread of industrial capitalism (see Chapter 4, "Society"). The fact that industrial capitalism developed primarily in areas of Western Europe where the Protestant work ethic was strong proved to Weber (1958, orig. 1904–05) the power of ideas to bring about change.

Ideas also direct social movements. Chapter 23 ("Collective Behavior and Social Movements") explained how change occurs when people join together in the pursuit of a common goal, such as cleaning up the environment or improving the lives of oppressed people.

DEMOGRAPHIC CHANGE

Population patterns also play a part in social change. A century ago, as the chapter opening suggested, the typical household (4.8 people) was almost twice as large as it is today (2.6 people). Women are having fewer children, and more people are living alone. In addition, change is taking place as our population grows older. As Chapter 15 ("Aging and the Elderly") explained, 12 percent of the U.S. population was over age sixty-five in 2000, three times the proportion in 1900. By the year 2030, seniors will account for 20 percent of the total (U.S. Census Bureau, 2004). Medical research and health care services already focus extensively on

NATIONAL MAP 24–1

Who Stays Put? Residential Stability across the United States

Overall, only about 9 percent of U.S. residents have not moved during the last thirty years. Counties with a higher proportion of "long-termers" typically have experienced less change over recent decades: Many neighborhoods have been in place since before World War II, and many of the same families live in them. As you look at the map, what can you say about these stable areas? Why are most of these counties rural and at some distance from the coasts?

Source: U.S. Census Bureau (1996).

---

the elderly, and life will change in countless additional ways as homes and household products are redesigned to meet the needs of older consumers.

Migration within and among societies is another demographic factor that promotes change. Between 1870 and 1930, tens of millions of immigrants entered the industrial cities in the United States. Millions more from rural areas joined the rush. As a result, farm communities declined, cities expanded, and for the first time, the United States became a mostly urban nation. Similarly, changes are taking place today as people move from the Snowbelt to the Sunbelt and mix with new immigrants from Latin America and Asia.

Where in the United States have demographic changes been greatest, and which areas have been least affected? National Map 24–1 provides one answer, showing counties where the largest share of people have lived in their present homes for thirty years or more.

Modernity

A central concept in the study of social change is **modernity,** *social patterns resulting from industrialization*. In everyday usage, *modernity* (its Latin root means "lately") refers to the present in relation to the past. Sociologists include in this catchall concept all of the social patterns set in motion by the Industrial Revolution, which began in Western Europe in the 1750s. **Modernization,** then, is *the process*

of social change begun by industrialization. The timeline inside the front cover of the text highlights important events that mark the emergence of modernity. Table 24–1 on page 642 provides a snapshot of some of the changes that took place during the twentieth century.

FOUR DIMENSIONS OF MODERNIZATION

Peter Berger (1977), in his influential study of social change, identified four major characteristics of modernization:

1. **The decline of small, traditional communities.** Modernity involves "the progressive weakening, if not destruction, of the . . . relatively cohesive communities in which human beings have found solidarity and meaning throughout most of history" (Berger, 1977:72). For thousands of years, in the camps of hunters and gatherers and in the rural villages of Europe and North America, people lived in small communities where social life revolved around family and neighborhood. Such traditional worlds gave each person a well-defined place that, although limiting range of choice, offered a strong sense of identity, belonging, and purpose.

   Small, isolated communities still exist in remote corners of the United States, of course, but they are home to only a small percentage of our nation's people. And their isolation is little more than geographic. Cars, telephones, television, and computers give rural

TABLE 24–1

The United States: A Century of Change

	1900	2000
National population	76 million	281 million
Percentage urban	40%	80%
Life expectancy	46 years (men), 48 years (women)	74 years (men), 79 years (women)
Median age	22.9 years	35.3 years
Average household income	$8,000 (in 2000 dollars)	$40,000 (in 2000 dollars)
Share of income spent on food	43%	15%
Share of homes with flush toilets	10%	98%
Average number of cars	1 car for every 2,000 households	1.3 cars for every household
Divorce rate	about 1 in 20 marriages	about 8 in 20 marriages
Average gallons of petroleum products consumed per person per year	34	1,100

families the pulse of the larger society and connect them to the entire world.

2. **The expansion of personal choice.** Members of traditional, preindustrial societies view their lives as shaped by forces beyond human control—gods, spirits, or simply fate. As the power of tradition weakens, people come to see their lives as an unending series of options, a process Berger calls *individualization.* Many people in the United States, for example, choose a "lifestyle" (sometimes adopting one after another), showing an openness to change. Indeed, a common belief in our modern culture is that people *should* take control of their lives.

3. **Increasing social diversity.** In preindustrial societies, strong family ties and powerful religious beliefs enforce conformity and discourage diversity and change. Modernization promotes a more rational, scientific worldview as tradition loses its hold and people gain more and more individual choice. The growth of cities, the expansion of impersonal bureaucracy, and the social mix of people from various backgrounds combine to foster diverse beliefs and behavior.

4. **Orientation toward the future and a growing awareness of time.** Premodern people focus on the past, but people in modern societies think more about the future. Modern people are not only forward-looking but optimistic that new inventions and discoveries will improve their lives.

   Modern people also organize their daily routines down to the very minute. With the introduction of clocks in the late Middle Ages, Europeans began to think not in terms of sunlight and seasons but in terms of days, hours, and minutes. Preoccupied with personal gain, modern people demand precise measurement of time and are likely to agree that "time is money." Berger points out that one good indicator of a society's degree of modernization is the share of people wearing wristwatches.

Finally, recall that modernization touched off the development of sociology itself. As Chapter 1 ("The Sociological Perspective") explained, the discipline originated in the wake of the Industrial Revolution in Western Europe, where social change was proceeding most rapidly. Early European and U.S. sociologists tried to analyze the rise of modern society and its consequences, both good and bad, for human beings.

FERDINAND TÖNNIES: THE LOSS OF COMMUNITY

The German sociologist Ferdinand Tönnies (1855–1937) produced a lasting account of modernization in his theory of *Gemeinschaft* and *Gesellschaft* (see Chapter 22, "Population, Urbanization, and Environment"). Like Peter Berger, whose work he influenced, Tönnies (1963, orig. 1887)

 For a short biography of Tönnies, visit the Gallery of Sociologists at http://www. TheSociologyPage.com

viewed modernization as the progressive loss of *Gemeinschaft,* or human community. As Tönnies saw it, the Industrial Revolution weakened the social fabric of family and tradition by introducing a businesslike emphasis on facts, efficiency, and money. European and North American societies gradually became rootless and impersonal as people came to associate mostly on the basis of self-interest—the state Tönnies termed *Gesellschaft.*

In response to the accelerating pace of change in the nineteenth century, Paul Gauguin left his native France for the South Seas where he was captivated by a simpler and seemingly timeless way of life. He romanticized this environment in his painting, *Nave Nave Moe (Sacred Spring)*.

Paul Gauguin, French (1848–1903), *Nave Nave Moe (Sacred Spring)*, 1894. Hermitage, St. Petersburg, Russia. Oil on canvas, 73 × 98 cm. © The Bridgeman Art Library International Ltd.

Early in the twentieth century, at least some parts of the United States approximated Tönnies's concept of *Gemeinschaft*. Families that had lived for generations in small villages and towns were bound together in a hardworking, slow-moving way of life. Telephones (invented in 1876) were rare; it wasn't until 1915 that someone placed the first coast-to-coast call (see the timeline inside the front cover of this book). Living without television (introduced in 1933 and not widespread until after 1950), families entertained themselves, often gathering with friends in the evening to share stories, sorrows, or song. Without rapid transportation (Henry Ford's assembly line began in 1908, but cars became commonplace only after World War II), many people's hometown was their entire world.

Inevitable tensions and conflicts divided these communities of the past. But according to Tönnies, because of the traditional spirit of *Gemeinschaft*, people were "essentially united in spite of all separating factors" (1963:65, orig. 1887).

Modernity turns societies inside out so that, as Tönnies put it, people are "essentially separated in spite of uniting factors" (1963:65, orig. 1887). This is the world of *Gesellschaft*, where, especially in large cities, most people live among strangers and ignore the people they pass on the street. Trust is hard to come by in a mobile and anonymous society where people tend to put their personal needs ahead of group loyalty and an increasing majority of adults believe "you can't be too careful" in dealing with people (NORC, 2003:181). No wonder researchers conclude that even as we become more affluent, the social health of modern societies has declined (D. G. Myers, 2000).

Critical review Tönnies's theory of *Gemeinschaft* and *Gesellschaft* is the most widely cited model of modernization. The theory's strength lies in combining various dimensions of change: growing population, the rise of cities, and increasing impersonality in social interaction. But modern life, though often impersonal, still has some degree of *Gemeinschaft*. Even in a world of strangers, modern friendships can be strong and lasting. Some analysts also think that Tönnies favored—perhaps even romanticized—traditional societies while overlooking bonds of family, neighborhood, and friendship that continue to flourish in modern societies.

EMILE DURKHEIM: THE DIVISION OF LABOR

The French sociologist Emile Durkheim, whose work is discussed in Chapter 4 ("Society"), shared Tönnies's interest in the profound social changes that resulted from the Industrial Revolution. For Durkheim (1964a, orig. 1893), modernization is defined by an increasing *division of labor,* or specialized economic activity. Every member of a traditional society performs more or less the same daily round of activities; modern societies function by having people perform highly specific roles.

Durkheim explained that preindustrial societies are held together by *mechanical solidarity,* or shared moral sentiments. In other words, members of preindustrial societies view everyone as basically alike, doing the same kind of work and belonging together. Durkheim's concept of mechanical solidarity is virtually the same as Tönnies's *Gemeinschaft*.

George Tooker's 1950 painting *The Subway* depicts a common problem of modern life: Weakening social ties and eroding traditions create a generic humanity in which everyone is alike yet each person is an anxious stranger in the midst of others.

George Tooker, *The Subway*, 1950, egg tempera on gesso panel, 18⅛ × 36⅛", Whitney Museum of American Art, New York. Purchased with funds from the Juliana Force Purchase Award, 50.23. Photograph © 2000 Whitney Museum of American Art.

With modernization, the division of labor becomes more and more pronounced. To Durkheim, this change means less mechanical solidarity but more of another kind of tie: *organic solidarity,* or mutual dependency between people engaged in specialized work. Put simply, modern societies are held together not by likeness but by difference: All of us must depend on others to meet most of our needs. Organic solidarity corresponds to Tönnies's concept of *Gesellschaft.*

Despite obvious similarities in their thinking, Durkheim and Tönnies viewed modernity somewhat differently. To Tönnies, modern *Gesellschaft* amounts to the loss of social solidarity, because modern people lose the "natural" and "organic" bonds of the rural village, leaving only the "artificial" and "mechanical" ties of the big, industrial city. Durkheim had a different view of modernity, even reversing Tönnies's language to bring home the point. Durkheim labeled modern society "organic," arguing that modern society is no less natural than any other, and he described traditional societies as "mechanical" because they are so regimented. Durkheim viewed modernization not as the *loss* of community but as a change from community based on bonds of likeness (kinship and neighborhood) to community based on economic interdependence (the division of labor). Durkheim's view of modernity is thus both more complex and more positive than Tönnies's view.

Critical review Durkheim's work, which resembles that of Tönnies, is a highly influential analysis of modernity. Of the two, Durkheim was more optimistic; still, he feared that modern societies might become so diverse that they would collapse into *anomie,* a condition in which norms and values are so weak and inconsistent that society provides little moral guidance to individuals. Living with weak moral norms, modern people can become egocentric, placing their own needs above those of others and finding little purpose in life.

The suicide rate—which Durkheim considered a good index of anomie—did in fact increase in the United States over the course of the twentieth century, and the vast majority of U.S. adults report that they see moral questions not in clear terms of right and wrong but in confusing "shades of gray" (NORC, 2003:359). Yet shared norms and values still seem strong enough to give most individuals some sense of meaning and purpose. Whatever the hazards of anomie, most people seem to value the personal freedom modern society gives us.

MAX WEBER: RATIONALIZATION

For Max Weber (also discussed in Chapter 4, "Society"), modernity meant replacing a traditional worldview with a rational way of thinking. In preindustrial societies, tradition acts as a constant brake on change. To traditional people, "truth" is roughly the same as "what has always been" (1978:36, orig. 1921). To modern people, however, "truth" is the result of rational calculation. Because they value efficiency and have little reverence for the past, modern people adopt whatever social patterns allow them to achieve their goals.

Echoing Tönnies and Durkheim, who held that industrialization weakens tradition, Weber declared modern society to be "disenchanted." The unquestioned truths of an earlier time had been challenged by rational thinking. In short, modern society turns away from the gods. Throughout his life, Weber studied various modern "types"—the capitalist, the scientist, the bureaucrat—all of whom share the detached worldview that Weber believed was coming to dominate humanity.

Max Weber maintained that the distinctive character of modern society was its rational worldview. Virtually all of Weber's work on modernity centered on types of people he considered typical of their age: the scientist, the capitalist, and the bureaucrat. Each is rational to the core: The scientist is committed to the orderly discovery of truth, the capitalist to the orderly pursuit of profit, and the bureaucrat to orderly conformity to a system of rules.

Critical review Compared with Tönnies and especially Durkheim, Weber was critical of modern society. He knew that science could produce technological and organizational wonders but worried that science was turning us away from more basic questions about the meaning and purpose of human existence. Weber feared that rationalization, especially in bureaucracies, would erode the human spirit with endless rules and regulations.

Looking at Weber's three "modern types" shown in the drawing, state in your own words what they have in common. What social traits would you expect all of them to lack?

Some of Weber's critics think that the alienation he attributed to bureaucracy actually stemmed from social inequality. That criticism leads us to the ideas of Karl Marx.

KARL MARX: CAPITALISM

For Karl Marx, modern society was synonymous with capitalism; he saw the Industrial Revolution as primarily a *capitalist revolution*. Marx traced the emergence of the bourgeoisie in medieval Europe to the expansion of commerce. The bourgeoisie gradually displaced the feudal aristocracy as the Industrial Revolution gave it a powerful new productive system.

Marx agreed that modernity weakened small communities (as described by Tönnies), sharpened the division of labor (as noted by Durkheim), and fostered a rational worldview (as Weber claimed). But he saw all these simply as conditions necessary for capitalism to flourish. Capitalism, according to Marx, draws population from farms and small towns into an ever-expanding market system centered in cities; specialization is needed for efficient factories; and rationality is exemplified by the capitalists' endless pursuit of profit.

For more on Durkheim, Weber, and Marx, visit the Gallery of Sociologists at http://www.TheSociologyPage.com

Earlier chapters have painted Marx as a spirited critic of capitalist society, but his vision of modernity also includes a good bit of optimism. Unlike Weber, who viewed modern society as an "iron cage" of bureaucracy, Marx believed that social conflict in capitalist societies would sow seeds of revolutionary change, leading to an egalitarian socialism. Such a society, as he saw it, would harness the wonders of industrial technology to enrich people's lives and also rid the world of social classes, the source of social conflict and so much suffering. Although Marx was an outspoken critic of modern society, he nevertheless imagined a future of human freedom, creativity, and community.

Critical review Marx's theory of modernization is a complex theory of capitalism. But he underestimated the dominance of bureaucracy in modern societies. In socialist societies in particular, the stifling effects of bureaucracy turned out to be as bad as, or even worse than, the dehumanizing aspects of capitalism. The upheavals in Eastern Europe and the former Soviet Union in the late 1980s and early 1990s reveal the depth of popular opposition to oppressive state bureaucracies.

YOUR TURN

Of the four theorists just discussed—Tönnies, Durkheim, Weber, and Marx—who was the most optimistic about modern society? Who was the most pessimistic? Explain your responses.

Theoretical Analysis of Modernity

The rise of modernity is a complex process involving many dimensions of change, as described in previous chapters and summarized in the Summing Up table. How can we make sense of so many changes going on all at once? Sociologists have developed two broad explanations of modern society, one guided by the structural-functional approach and one based on social-conflict theory.

STRUCTURAL-FUNCTIONAL THEORY: MODERNITY AS MASS SOCIETY

November 11, on Interstate 275. From the car window, we see BP and Sunoco gas stations, a Kmart and a Wal-Mart, an AmeriSuites hotel, a Bob Evans, a Chi-Chi's Mexican restaurant, and a McDonald's. This road happens to circle Cincinnati. But it could be almost anywhere in the United States.

One broad approach—drawing on the ideas of Ferdinand Tönnies, Emile Durkheim, and Max Weber—understands modernization as the emergence of *mass society* (Kornhauser, 1959; Nisbet, 1966, 1969; Berger, Berger, & Kellner, 1974; Pearson, 1993). A **mass society** is *a society in which prosperity and bureaucracy have weakened traditional social ties.* A mass society is highly productive; on average, people have more income than ever. At the same time, it is marked by weak kinship and impersonal neighborhoods, so individuals often feel socially isolated. Although many people have material plenty, they are spiritually weak and often experience moral uncertainty about how to live.

The Mass Scale of Modern Life

Mass-society theory argues, first, that the scale of modern life has greatly increased. Before the Industrial Revolution, Europe and North America formed a mosaic of countless rural villages and small towns. In these small communities, which inspired Tönnies's concept of *Gemeinschaft,* people lived out their lives surrounded by kin and guided by a shared heritage. Gossip was an informal yet highly effective way to ensure conformity to community standards. These small communities, with their strong moral values and their low tolerance of social diversity, exemplified the state of mechanical solidarity described by Durkheim.

For example, before 1690, English law demanded that everyone participate regularly in the Christian ritual of Holy Communion (Laslett, 1984). On the North American continent, only Rhode Island among the New England colonies tolerated religious dissent. Because social differences were repressed in favor of conformity to established norms, subcultures and countercultures were few, and change proceeded slowly.

Increasing population, the growth of cities, and specialized economic activity driven by the Industrial Revolution gradually altered this pattern. People came to know one another by their jobs (for example, as "the doctor" or "the bank clerk") rather than by their kinship group or hometown. People looked on most others simply as strangers. The face-to-face communication of the village was eventually replaced by the impersonal mass media: newspapers, radio, television, and computer networks. Large organizations steadily assumed more and more responsibility for seeing to the daily tasks that had once been carried out by family, friends, and neighbors; public education drew more and more people to schools; police, lawyers, and courts supervised a formal criminal justice system. Even charity became the work of faceless bureaucrats working for various social welfare agencies.

Geographic mobility and exposure to diverse ways of life all weaken traditional values. People become more tolerant of social diversity, defending individual rights and freedom of choice. Treating people differently because of their race, sex, or religion comes to be defined as backward and unjust. In the process, minorities at the margins of society gain greater power and broader participation in public life.

The mass media give rise to a national culture that washes over traditional differences that set off one region from another. As one analyst put it, "Even in Baton Rouge, La., the local kids don't say 'y'all' anymore; they say 'you guys' just like on TV" (Gibbs, 2000:42). In this way, mass-society theorists fear, transforming people of various backgrounds into a generic mass may end up dehumanizing everyone.

Traditional and Modern Societies: The Big Picture

Elements of Society	Traditional Societies	Modern Societies
Cultural Patterns		
Values	Homogeneous; sacred character; few subcultures and countercultures	Heterogeneous; secular character; many subcultures and countercultures
Norms	Great moral significance; little tolerance of diversity	Variable moral significance; high tolerance of diversity
Time orientation	Present linked to past	Present linked to future
Technology	Preindustrial; human and animal energy	Industrial; advanced energy sources
Social Structure		
Status and role	Few statuses, most ascribed; few specialized roles	Many statuses, some ascribed and some achieved; many specialized roles
Relationships	Typically primary; little anonymity or privacy	Typically secondary; much anonymity and privacy
Communication	Face to face	Face-to-face communication supplemented by mass media
Social control	Informal gossip	Formal police and legal system
Social stratification	Rigid patterns of social inequality; little mobility	Fluid patterns of social inequality; high mobility
Gender patterns	Pronounced patriarchy; women's lives centered on the home	Declining patriarchy; increasing number of women in the paid labor force
Settlement patterns	Small-scale; population typically small and widely dispersed in rural villages and small towns	Large-scale; population typically large and concentrated in cities
Social Institutions		
Economy	Based on agriculture; much manufacturing in the home; little white-collar work	Based on industrial mass production; factories become centers of production; increasing white-collar work
State	Small-scale government; little state intervention in society	Large-scale government; much state intervention in society
Family	Extended family as the primary means of socialization and economic production	Nuclear family retains some socialization functions but is more a unit of consumption than of production
Religion	Religion guides worldview; little religious pluralism	Religion weakens with the rise of science; extensive religious pluralism
Education	Formal schooling limited to elites	Basic schooling becomes universal, with growing proportion receiving advanced education
Health	High birth and death rates; short life expectancy because of low standard of living and simple medical technology	Low birth and death rates; longer life expectancy because of higher standard of living and sophisticated medical technology
Social Change	Slow; change evident over many generations	Rapid; change evident within a single generation

Can you give five examples of "mass culture" that are the same throughout the United States? What elements of culture tend to be distinctive from region to region?

The Ever-Expanding State

In the small-scale preindustrial societies of Europe, government amounted to little more than a local noble. A royal family formally reigned over an entire nation, but without efficient transportation or communication, even absolute monarchs had far less power than today's political leaders.

As technological innovation allowed government to expand, the centralized state grew in size and importance. At the time the United States gained independence from Great Britain, the federal government was a tiny organization with the main purpose of providing national defense. Since then, government has assumed responsibility for more and more areas of social life: schooling the population, regulating wages and working conditions, establishing standards for products of all sorts, and offering financial assistance to the

Social-conflict theory sees modernity not as a mass society but as a class society in which some categories of people are second-class citizens. This six-year-old boy waits for his mother to finish cooking a simple dinner outside their trailer on the Navajo Reservation near Window Rock, Arizona. The family lives without electricity or running water—a situation shared by thousands of other Navajo families.

ill and the unemployed. To pay for such programs, taxes have soared: Today's average worker labors almost four months each year to pay for the broad array of services that government provides.

In a mass society, power resides in large bureaucracies, leaving people in local communities little control over their lives. For example, state officials mandate that local schools must have a standardized educational program, local products must be government-certified, and every citizen must maintain extensive tax records. Although such regulations may protect people and advance social equality, they also force us to deal more and more with nameless officials in distant and often unresponsive bureaucracies, and they undermine the autonomy of families and local communities.

Critical review The growing scale of modern life certainly has positive aspects, but only at the price of losing some of our cultural heritage. Modern societies increase individual rights, tolerate greater social differences, and raise standards of living (Inglehart & Baker, 2000). But they are prone to what Weber feared most—excessive bureaucracy—as well as Tönnies's self-centeredness and Durkheim's anomie. Modern society's size, complexity, and tolerance of diversity all but doom traditional values and family patterns, leaving individuals isolated, powerless, and materialistic. As Chapter 17 ("Politics and Government") noted, voter apathy is a serious problem in the United States. But should we be surprised that individuals in vast, impersonal societies think no one person can make much of a difference?

Critics sometimes say that mass-society theory romanticizes the past. They remind us that many people in small towns were actually eager to set out for a higher standard of living in cities. Moreover, mass-society theory ignores problems of social inequality. Critics say this theory attracts conservatives who defend conventional morality and overlook the historical inequality of women and other minorities.

SOCIAL-CONFLICT THEORY: MODERNITY AS CLASS SOCIETY

The second interpretation of modernity derives largely from the ideas of Karl Marx. From a social-conflict perspective, modernity takes the form of a **class society,** *a capitalist society with pronounced social stratification.* That is, although agreeing that modern societies have expanded to a mass scale, this approach views the heart of modernization as an expanding capitalist economy, marked by inequality (Habermas, 1970; Polenberg, 1980; Blumberg, 1981; Harrington, 1984; Buechler, 2000).

Capitalism

Class-society theory follows Marx in claiming that the increasing scale of social life in modern society results from the growth and greed unleashed by capitalism. Because a capitalist economy pursues ever-greater profits, both production and consumption steadily increase.

According to Marx, capitalism rests on "naked self-interest" (Marx & Engels, 1972:337, orig. 1848). This self-centeredness weakens the social ties that once united small communities. Capitalism also treats people as commodities: a source of labor and a market for capitalist products.

Capitalism supports science, not just as the key to greater productivity but as an ideology that justifies the status quo. That is, modern societies encourage people to view

SUMMING UP

Two Interpretations of Modernity

	Mass Society	Class Society
Process of modernization	Industrialization; growth of bureaucracy	Rise of capitalism
Effects of modernization	Increasing scale of life; rise of the state and other formal organizations	Expansion of the capitalist economy; persistence of social inequality

human well-being as a technical puzzle to be solved by engineers and other experts rather than through the pursuit of social justice. For example, a capitalist culture seeks to improve health through scientific medicine rather than by eliminating poverty, which is a core cause of poor health.

Business also raises the banner of scientific logic, trying to increase profits through greater efficiency. As Chapter 16 ("The Economy and Work") explains, today's capitalist corporations have reached enormous size and control unimaginable wealth as a result of "going global" as multinationals. From the class-society point of view, the expanding scale of life is less a function of *Gesellschaft* than the inevitable and destructive consequence of capitalism.

Persistent Inequality

Modernity has gradually worn away the rigid categories that set nobles apart from commoners in preindustrial societies. But class-society theory maintains that elites persist as capitalist millionaires rather than nobles born to wealth and power. In the United States, we may have no hereditary monarchy, but the richest 5 percent of the population controls about 60 percent of all privately held property.

What of the state? Mass-society theorists argue that the state works to increase equality and combat social problems. Marx disagreed; he doubted that the state could accomplish more than minor reforms because as he saw it, the real power lies in the hands of capitalists, who control the economy. Other class-society theorists add that to the extent that working people and minorities do enjoy greater political rights and a higher standard of living today, these changes were the result of political struggle, not government goodwill. In short, they conclude, despite our pretensions of democracy, most people are powerless in the face of wealthy elites.

Critical review Class-society theory dismisses Durkheim's argument that people in modern societies suffer from anomie, claiming instead that they suffer from alienation and powerlessness. Not surprisingly, then, the class-society interpretation of modernity enjoys widespread support among liberals and radicals who favor greater equality and call for extensive regulation or the abolition of the capitalist marketplace.

A basic criticism of class-society theory is that it overlooks the increasing prosperity of modern societies and the fact that discrimination based on race, ethnicity, and gender is now illegal and is widely viewed as a social problem. In addition, most people in the United States do not want an egalitarian society; they prefer a system of unequal rewards that reflects personal differences in talent and effort.

Based on socialism's failure to generate a high standard of living, few observers think that a centralized economy would cure the ills of modernity. Many other problems in the United States—from unemployment, hunger, and industrial pollution to unresponsive government—are also found in socialist nations.

The Summing Up table contrasts the two interpretations of modernity. Mass-society theory focuses on the increasing scale of life and the growth of government; class-society theory stresses the expansion of capitalism and the persistence of inequality.

MODERNITY AND THE INDIVIDUAL

Both mass- and class-society theories look at the broad societal changes that have taken place since the Industrial Revolution. But from these macro-level approaches we can also draw micro-level insights into how modernity shapes individual lives.

Mass Society: Problems of Identity

Modernity freed individuals from the small, tightly knit communities of the past. Most people in modern societies have the privacy and freedom to express their individuality.

However, mass-society theory suggests that so much social diversity, widespread isolation, and rapid social change make it difficult for many people to establish any coherent identity at all (Wheelis, 1958; Berger, Berger, & Kellner, 1974).

Chapter 5 ("Socialization") explained that people's personalities are largely a product of their social experiences. The small, homogeneous, and slowly changing societies of the past provided a firm, if narrow, foundation for building a personal identity. Even today, the Amish communities that flourish in the United States and Canada teach young men and women "correct" ways to think and behave. Not everyone born into an Amish community can tolerate strict demands for conformity, but most members establish a well-integrated and satisfying personal identity (see Hostetler, 1980; Kraybill & Olshan, 1994).

Mass societies are quite another story. Socially diverse and rapidly changing, they offer only shifting sands on which to build a personal identity. Left to make many life decisions on their own, many people—especially those with greater wealth—face a bewildering array of options. The freedom to choose has little value without standards to help us make good choices, and in a tolerant mass society, people may find little reason to choose one path over another. As a result, many people shuttle from one identity to another, changing their lifestyles, relationships, and even religions in search of an elusive "true self." Given the widespread "relativism" of modern societies, people without a moral compass lack the security and certainty once provided by tradition.

To David Riesman (1970, orig. 1950), modernization brings changes in **social character,** *personality patterns common to members of a particular society.* Preindustrial societies promote what Riesman calls **tradition-directedness,** *rigid conformity to time-honored ways of living.* Members of traditional societies model their lives on those of their ancestors, so that "living a good life" amounts to "doing what our people have always done."

Tradition-directedness corresponds to Tönnies's *Gemeinschaft* and Durkheim's mechanical solidarity. Culturally conservative, tradition-directed people think and act alike. Unlike the conformity sometimes found in modern societies, the uniformity of tradition-directedness is not an effort to imitate a popular celebrity or follow the latest fashions. Instead, people are alike because they all draw on the same solid cultural foundation. Amish women and men exemplify tradition-directedness; in Amish culture, tradition ties everyone to ancestors and descendants in an unbroken chain of righteous living.

Members of diverse and rapidly changing societies consider a tradition-directed personality deviant because it seems so rigid. Modern people, by and large, prize personal flexibility, the capacity to adapt, and sensitivity to others. Riesman calls this type of social character **other-directedness,** *openness to the latest trends and fashions, often expressed by imitating others.* Because their socialization occurs in societies that are continuously in flux, other-directed people develop fluid identities marked by superficiality, inconsistency, and change. They try on different "selves," almost like so many pieces of new clothing, seek out role models, and engage in varied "performances" as they move from setting to setting (Goffman, 1959). In a traditional society, such "shiftiness" makes a person untrustworthy, but in a changing, modern society, the chameleonlike ability to fit in virtually anywhere is very useful.

In societies that value the up-to-date rather than the traditional, people look to others for approval, using members of their own generation rather than elders as role models. Peer pressure can be irresistible to people without strong standards to guide them. Our society urges individuals to be true to themselves. But when social surroundings change so rapidly, how can people develop the self to which they should be true? This problem lies at the root of the identity crisis so widespread in industrial societies today. "Who am I?" is a nagging question that many of us struggle to answer. In truth, this problem is not so much us as the inherently unstable mass society in which we live.

YOUR TURN

Would you call yourself more tradition-directed or more other-directed? Where do you turn for standards in making choices about how to live?

Class Society: Problems of Powerlessness

Class-society theory paints a different picture of modernity's effects on individuals. This approach maintains that persistent social inequality undermines modern society's promise of individual freedom. For some people, modernity serves up great privilege, but for many, everyday life means coping with economic uncertainty and a growing sense of powerlessness (K. S. Newman, 1993; Ehrenreich, 2001).

For racial and ethnic minorities, the problem of relative disadvantage looms even larger. Similarly, although women participate more broadly in modern societies, they continue to run up against traditional barriers of sexism. This approach rejects mass-society theory's claim that people suffer from too much freedom. According to class-society theory,

Mass-society theory relates feelings of anxiety and lack of meaning in the modern world to rapid social change that washes away tradition. This notion of modern emptiness is captured in the photo at the left. Class-society theory, by contrast, ties such feelings to social inequality, by which some categories of people are made into second-class citizens (or not made citizens at all), an idea expressed in the photo at the right.

our society still denies a majority of people full participation in social life.

As Chapter 12 ("Global Stratification") explained, the expanding scope of world capitalism has placed more of Earth's population under the influence of multinational corporations. As a result, about three-fourths of the world's income is concentrated in the high-income nations, where only 18 percent of its people live. Is it any wonder, class-society theorists ask, that people in poor nations seek greater power to shape their own lives?

The problem of widespread powerlessness led Herbert Marcuse (1964) to challenge Max Weber's statement that modern society is rational. Marcuse condemned modern society as irrational for failing to meet the needs of so many people. Although modern capitalist societies produce unparalleled wealth, poverty remains the daily plight of more than 1 billion people. Marcuse adds that technological advances further reduce people's control over their own lives. High technology gives a great deal of power to a small core of specialists—not the majority of people—who now dominate the discussion of issues such as computing, energy production, and medical care. Countering the common view that technology *solves* the world's problems, Marcuse believed that science *causes* them. In sum, class-society theory asserts that people suffer because modern, scientific

societies concentrate both wealth and power in the hands of a privileged few.

MODERNITY AND PROGRESS

In modern societies, most people expect, and applaud, social change. We link modernity to the idea of *progress* (from Latin, meaning "moving forward"), a state of continual improvement. By contrast, we see stability as stagnation.

Given our bias in favor of change, our society tends to regard traditional cultures as backward. But change, particularly toward material affluence, is a mixed blessing. As the Thinking Globally box on pages 652–53 shows, social change is too complex simply to equate with progress.

Even getting rich has both advantages and disadvantages, as the cases of the Kaiapo and the Gullah show. Historically, among people in the United States, a rising standard of living has made lives longer and materially more comfortable. At the same time, many people wonder if today's routines are too stressful, with families often having little time to relax or simply spend time together. Perhaps this is why, in most high-income countries, measures of happiness show a decline over the course of recent decades (D. G. Myers, 2000).

Science, too, has its pluses and minuses. People in the United States are more confident than people in other

Does "Modernity" Mean "Progress"?
Brazil's Kaiapo and Georgia's Gullah Community

The firelight flickers in the gathering darkness. Chief Kanhonk sits, as he has done at the end of the day for many years, ready to begin an evening of animated storytelling (Simons, 2007). This is the hour when the Kaiapo, a small society in Brazil's lush Amazon region, celebrate their heritage. Because the Kaiapo are a traditional people with no written language, the elders rely on evenings by the fire to pass along their culture to their children and grandchildren. In the past, evenings like this have been filled with tales of brave Kaiapo warriors fighting off Portuguese traders who were in pursuit of slaves and gold.

But as the minutes pass, only a few older villagers assemble for the evening ritual. "It is the Big Ghost," one man grumbles, explaining the poor turnout. The "Big Ghost" has indeed descended on them; its bluish glow spills from windows throughout the village.

The Kaiapo children—and many adults as well—are watching sitcoms on television. The installation of a satellite dish in the village several years ago has had consequences far greater than anyone imagined. In the end, what their enemies failed to do with guns, the Kaiapo may well do to themselves with prime-time programming.

The Kaiapo are among the 230,000 native peoples who inhabit Brazil. They stand out because of their striking body paint and ornate ceremonial dress. During the 1980s, they

became rich from gold mining and harvesting mahogany trees. Now they must decide whether their newfound fortune is a blessing or a curse.

To some, affluence means the opportunity to learn about the outside world through travel and television.

To see pictures of Brazil's Kaiapo, go to http://www.ddbstock.com/largeimage/amindns.html

Others, like Chief Kanhonk, are not so sure. Sitting by the fire, he thinks aloud, "I have been saying that people must buy useful things like knives and fishing hooks. Television does not fill the stomach. It only shows our children and grandchildren white people's things." Bebtopup, the oldest priest, nods in agreement: "The night is the time the old people teach the young people. Television has stolen the night" (Simons, 2007).

Far to the north, in the United States, half an hour by ferry from the coast of Georgia,

nations that science improves our lives (Inglehart et al., 2000). But surveys also show that many adults in the United States feel that science "makes our way of life change too fast" (NORC, 2003:346).

New technology has always sparked controversy. A century ago, the introduction of automobiles and telephones allowed more rapid transportation and more efficient communication. But at the same time, such technology weakened traditional attachments to hometowns and even to families. Today, people might well wonder whether computer technology will do the same thing, giving us access to people around the world but shielding us

from the community right outside our doors; providing more information than ever before but in the process threatening personal privacy. In short, we all realize that social change comes faster all the time, but we may disagree about whether a particular change is good or bad for society.

MODERNITY: GLOBAL VARIATION

October 1, Kobe, Japan. Riding the computer-controlled monorail high above the streets of Kobe or the 200-mile-per-hour

lies the swampy island community of Hog Hammock. The seventy African American residents of the island today trace their ancestry back to the first slaves who settled there in 1802.

Walking past the colorful houses nestled among pine trees draped with Spanish moss, visitors feel transported back in time. The local people, known as Gullahs (or, in some places, Geechees) speak a mixture of English and West African languages. They fish, living much as they have for hundreds of years.

But the future of this way of life is now in doubt. Few young people who are raised in Hog Hammock can find work beyond fishing and making traditional crafts. "We have been here nine generations and we are still here," says one local. Then, referring to the island's nineteen children, she adds, "It's not that they don't want to be here, it's that there's nothing here for them—they need to have jobs" (Curry, 2001:41).

Just as important, with people on the mainland looking for waterside homes for vacations or year-round living, the island is now becoming prime real estate. Not long ago, one of the

Learn more about Gullah culture at http://www.knowitall.org/gullahnet

larger houses went up for sale, and the community was shocked to learn that its asking price was more than $1 million. The locals know only too well that higher property values will mean high taxes that few can afford to pay. In short, Hog Hammock is likely to become another Hilton Head, once a Gullah community on the South Carolina coast that is now home to well-to-do people from the mainland.

The odds are that the people of Hog Hammock will be selling their homes and moving inland. But few people are happy at the thought of

selling out, even for a good price. On the contrary, moving away will mean the end of their cultural heritage.

The stories of both the Kaiapo and the people of Hog Hammock show us that change is not a simple path toward "progress." These people may be moving toward modernity, but this process will have both positive and negative consequences. In the end, both groups of people may enjoy a higher standard of living with better shelter, more clothing, and new technology. On the other hand, their new affluence will come at the price of their traditions. The drama of these people is now being played out around the world as more and more traditional cultures are being lured away from their heritage by the affluence and materialism of rich societies.

WHAT DO YOU THINK?

1. Why is social change both a winning and a losing proposition for traditional peoples?
2. Do the changes described here improve the lives of the Kaiapo? What about the Gullah community?
3. Do traditional people have any choice about becoming modern? Explain your answer.

bullet train to Tokyo, we see Japan as the society of the future; its people are in love with high technology. Yet the Japanese remain strikingly traditional in other respects: Few corporate executives and almost no senior politicians are women, young people still show seniors great respect, and public orderliness contrasts with the chaos of many U.S. cities.

Japan is a nation at once traditional and modern. This contradiction reminds us that although it is useful to contrast traditional and modern societies, the old and the new often coexist in unexpected ways. In the People's Republic of China, ancient Confucian principles are mixed with contemporary socialist thinking. In Saudi Arabia and Qatar, the embrace of modern technology is mixed with respect for the ancient principles of Islam. Likewise, in Mexico and much of Latin America, people observe centuries-old Christian rituals even as they struggle to move ahead economically. In short, combinations of traditional and modern are far from unusual; rather, they are found throughout the world. "In the *Times*" on pages 654–55 describes patterns of change coming to a traditional village in Tibet.

November 25, 2004

Modernity Tips Balance in a Remote Corner of Kashmir

By AMY WALDMAN

LEH, Kashmir—The young man wore Western clothes, but he paused as he passed the prayer wheel. Then, without self-consciousness, he mounted the steps and spun, circumambulating the wheel in search of good fortune.

"I feel great because I'm doing something for my God," he said afterward.

The young man, Tsewang Tamchos, 16, is a product of Ladakh, a remote repository of Tibetan Buddhism on a high-altitude Himalayan plateau in the northern areas of Kashmir, a disputed state. But he is a product of a wider world, too: his school in Delhi, the music of Eminem, the ambitions of an upwardly mobile family whose material fortunes improve with each generation.

As in many cultures, the people of Ladakh, a sparsely populated region, live in the fold between tradition and modernity. But few places have provided as concentrated a laboratory for how modernization is tipping that balance.

In less than four decades, Ladakh has gone from being closed to the outside world to reflecting it. With each generation, the ties to the land, to the past, weaken, as options and opportunities widen. The culture and economy have moved from community-oriented to competitive, from living off the land to working for cash and spending it.

For generations, Ladakh, a barren, moonlike landscape punctuated by monasteries, was almost cut off from the outside world. . . . It took 16 days to get to Srinagar, the state's summer capital, across passes that soar above 13,000 feet. Its people developed a way of life attuned to the land, and in tune with one another. Nothing was wasted. . . . Human waste fertilized fields; worn-out clothes patched irrigation channels. . . .

In 1974, Ladakh opened to foreign tourists for the first time, and they quickly became a pillar of the economy. . . .

The influence of outsiders has gradually leached into Ladakh's way of life. Before [as one long-time resident noted], the economy was not based on money. Rich and poor alike needed each other for the harvest. Now rich men can hire laborers from Nepal or poorer Indian states, and many do. "There is a lot of competition now," he said. "Everyone is trying to have a car."

The notion, and the novelty, of competition surfaces in conversations in the car-choked streets of Leh or nearby villages.

At 35, Tashi Palzes is old enough to remember a time with no competition in her village, Phyang Puluhu, which sits on several steep terraces in the valley behind the Phyang monastery.

Today, she, like everyone, is racing against her neighbors, and sees herself as winning. She has not one, but two

Postmodernity

If modernity was the product of the Industrial Revolution, is the Information Revolution creating a postmodern era? A number of scholars think so, and they use the term **postmodernity** to refer to *social patterns characteristic of postindustrial societies.*

Precisely what postmodernism is remains a matter of debate. The term has been used for decades in literary, philosophical, and even architectural circles. It moved into sociology on a wave of social criticism that has been building since the spread of left-leaning politics in the 1960s. Although there are many variants of postmodern thinking, all share the following five themes (Hall & Neitz, 1993; Inglehart, 1997; Rudel & Gerson, 1999):

1. **In important respects, modernity has failed.** The promise of modernity was a life free from want. As postmodernist critics see it, however, the twentieth century was unsuccessful in solving social problems like poverty because many people still lack financial security.

2. **The bright light of "progress" is fading.** Modern people look to the future, expecting that their lives will improve in significant ways. Members (and even leaders) of postmodern societies, however, are less confident about what the future holds. The strong optimism that carried society into the modern era more than a century ago has given way to stark pessimism; most U.S. adults believe that life is getting worse (NORC, 2003:208).

3. **Science no longer holds the answers.** The defining trait of the modern era was a scientific outlook and a confident belief that technology would make life

televisions—the second one in color—and a satellite dish on her roof. She wears not the handspun traditional dress of a Ladakhi woman but a secondhand Gap sweatshirt, bought at the Leh bazaar.

Earlier, she said, villagers did not have much and did not need much. Now they have more needs—better clothes, better education, more televisions—and thus more work. Life is simultaneously more comfortable and more difficult. . . .

In the Leh home of Tsewang Tamchos, too, each generation brings substantial change. His grandparents live in the Nubra Valley, about 75 miles away.

They do not read or write; they farm. They grew up drinking unlimited quantities of butter tea, the salty staple of Ladakhi life.

His father, Tsering Tundup, 44, is a government forester. He says butter tea is bad for his blood pressure, and limits his intake to two cups a day. The house he has built his family in Leh has elements of tradition—the Buddhist prayer room, the wooden ceiling in the kitchen—but in most respects is modern.

His children study out of the state, Tsewang in Delhi and his 19-year-old sister, Tsering, in Chandigarh.

Tsewang's parents want him to be an engineer, and he does as well, but Ladakh has few opportunities for engineers. He would like to live here, but does not know if he will.

He does plan to marry a Ladakhi woman. "I don't want to change my culture," he said. "That's the only thing I have."

WHAT DO YOU THINK?

1. List five examples of cultural diffusion in the article, and explain how they are causing changes to this traditional society.

2. Do you think the only way societies can remain traditional is to remain isolated from the rest of the world? What advantages and disadvantages do you see in doing so?

3. In what specific ways does modern life differ from traditional life in Ladakh?

Adapted from the original article by Amy Waldman published in *The New York Times* on November 25, 2004. Copyright © 2004 by The New York Times Company. Reprinted with permission.

better. But postmodern critics argue that science has not solved many old problems (such as poor health) and has even created new problems (such as pollution and declining natural resources).

Postmodernist thinkers discredit science, claiming that it implies a singular truth. On the contrary, they maintain, there is no one truth. This means that objective reality does not exist; rather, many realities result from social construction.

4. **Cultural debates are intensifying.** Now that more people have all the material things they really need, ideas are taking on more importance. In this sense, postmodernity is also a postmaterialist era, in which more careers involve working with symbols and in which issues such as social justice, the environment, and animal rights command more and more public attention.

5. **Social institutions are changing.** Just as industrialization brought a sweeping transformation to social institutions, the rise of a postindustrial society is remaking society all over again. For example, the postmodern family no longer conforms to any single pattern; on the contrary, individuals are choosing among many new family forms.

Critical review Analysts who claim that the United States and other high-income societies are entering a postmodern era criticize modernity for failing to meet human needs. In defense of modernity, there have been marked increases in longevity and living standards over the course of the past century. Even if we accept postmodernist views that science is bankrupt and progress is a sham, what are the alternatives?

Tracking Change: Is Life in the United States Getting Better or Worse?

We began this chapter with a look at what life was like in a large U.S. city in 1900, more than a century ago. It is easy to see that in many ways, life is far better for us than it was for our grandparents and great-grandparents. In recent decades, however, not all indicators have been good. Here is a look at some trends shaping the United States since 1970

(Miringoff & Miringoff, 1999; D. G. Myers, 2000).

First, the good news: By some measures, shown in the first set of figures, life in this country is clearly improving. Infant mortality has fallen steadily; that is, fewer and fewer children die soon after birth. In addition, an increasing share of people are reaching old age, and after reaching

sixty-five, they are living longer than ever. More good news: The poverty rate among the elderly is well below what it was in 1970. Schooling is another area of improvement: The share of people dropping out of high school is down, and the share completing college is up.

Second, some "no news" results: A number of indicators show that life is about the same as it was in the 1970s.

The good news . . .

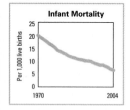

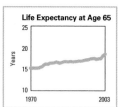

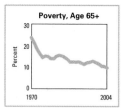

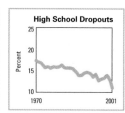

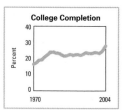

No news . . .

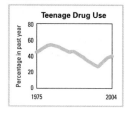

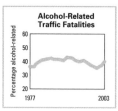

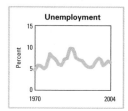

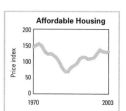

The Applying Sociology box offers evidence suggesting that life in the United States is getting better in some ways but not in others.

Looking Ahead: Modernization and Our Global Future

Back in Chapter 1 (see page 8), we imagined the entire world reduced to a village of 1,000 people. About 180 residents of this "global village" come from high-income countries. Another 180 people are so poor that their lives are at risk.

The tragic plight of the world's poor shows that the world is in desperate need of change. Chapter 12 ("Global Stratification") presented two competing views of why 1 billion people around the world are poor. *Modernization theory* claims that in the past the entire world was poor and that technological change, especially the Industrial Revolution, enhanced human productivity and raised living standards in many nations. From this point of view, the solution to global poverty is to promote technological development around the world.

For reasons suggested earlier, however, global modernization may be difficult. Recall that David Riesman portrayed preindustrial people as *tradition-directed* and likely to resist change. So modernization theorists advocate

The bad news . . .

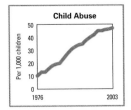

Child Abuse
Per 1,000 children
50
40
30
20
10
0
1976   2003

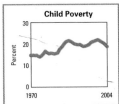

Child Poverty
Percent
30
20
10
0
1970   2004

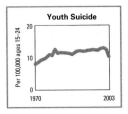

Youth Suicide
Per 100,000 ages 15–24
20
10
0
1970   2003

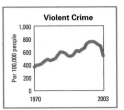

Violent Crime
Per 100,000 people
1,000
800
600
400
200
0
1970   2003

Average Weekly Wages
Dollars
350
300
250
200
1970   1996

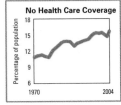

No Health Care Coverage
Percentage of population
18
15
12
9
6
1970   2004

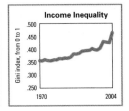

Income Inequality
Gini index, from 0 to 1
.500
.450
.400
.350
.300
.250
1970   2004

For example, teenage drug use was about the same in 2004 as it was a generation ago. Likewise, alcohol-related traffic deaths number about the same. Unemployment has had its ups and downs, but the overall level has stayed about the same. Finally, there was about the same amount of affordable housing in the United States in 2003 as in 1970.

Third, the bad news: By some measures, several having to do with children, the quality of life in the United States has actually fallen. The official rate of child abuse is up, as is the level of child poverty and the rate of suicide among young people. Although the level of violent crime fell through most of the 1990s, it remains above the 1970 level. Average hourly wages, one measure of economic security, show a downward trend, meaning that more families have to rely on two or more earners to maintain family income. The number of people without health insurance is also on the rise. Finally, economic inequality in this country has been increasing.

Overall, the evidence does not support any simple ideas about "progress over time." Social change has been—and probably will continue to be—a complex process that reflects the kinds of priorities we set for this nation as well as our will to achieve them.

WHAT DO YOU THINK?

1. Some analysts claim that U.S. society embodies a paradox: Over decades, we see increasing economic health but declining social health. Based on the data here, do you agree? Why or why not?
2. Which of the trends do you find most important? Why?
3. On balance, do you think the quality of life in the United States is improving? Why or why not?

that the world's rich societies help poor countries grow economically. Industrial nations can speed development by exporting technology to poor regions, welcoming students from these countries, and providing foreign aid to stimulate economic growth.

The review of modernization theory in Chapter 12 points to some success with policies in Latin America and to greater success in the small Asian countries of Taiwan, South Korea, Singapore, and Hong Kong (now part of the People's Republic of China). But jump-starting development in the poorest countries of the world poses greater challenges. And even where dramatic change has occurred, modernization involves a trade-off. Traditional people, such as Brazil's Kaiapo, may gain wealth through economic development, but they lose their cultural identity and values as they are drawn into a global "McCulture," which is based on Western materialism, pop music, trendy clothes, and fast food. One Brazilian anthropologist expressed hope about the future of the Kaiapo: "At least they quickly understood the consequences of watching television. . . . Now [they] can make a choice" (Simons, 2007).

But not everyone thinks that modernization is really an option. According to a second approach to global stratification, *dependency theory*, today's poor societies have little ability to modernize, even if they want to. From this point of view, the major barrier to economic development is not traditionalism but the global domination of rich capitalist societies.

THINKING IT THROUGH

Personal Freedom and Social Responsibility: Can We Have It Both Ways?

Shortly after midnight on a crisp March evening in 1964, a car pulled to a stop in the parking lot of a New York apartment complex. Kitty Genovese had just finished her shift as a manager at a nearby bar. She turned off the headlights, locked the doors of her vehicle, and headed across the blacktop toward the entrance to her building. Seconds later, a man wielding a knife lunged at her, and as she screamed in terror, he stabbed her repeatedly. Windows opened above as curious neighbors looked down to see what was going on. But the attack continued—for more than thirty minutes—until Genovese lay dead in the doorway. The police never identified her killer, and their investigation revealed the stunning fact that *not one of dozens of neighbors who witnessed the attack on Kitty Genovese went to her aid or even called the police.*

Decades after this tragic event, we still confront the question of what we owe others. As members of modern societies, we prize our individual rights and personal privacy, but we sometimes withdraw from public responsibility and turn a cold shoulder to people in need. When a cry for help is met with indifference, have we pushed our modern idea of personal freedom too far? In a cultural climate of expanding individual rights, can we keep a sense of human community?

These questions highlight the tension between traditional and modern social systems, which we can see in the writings of all the sociologists discussed in this chapter. Tönnies, Durkheim, and others concluded that in some respects, traditional community and modern individualism don't mix. That is, society can unite its members in a moral community, but only by limiting their range of personal choices about how to live. In short, although we value both community and autonomy, we can't have it both ways.

The sociologist Amitai Etzioni (1993, 1996, 2003) has tried to strike a middle ground. The *communitarian movement* rests on the simple idea that with rights must come responsibilities. Put another way, our pursuit of self-interest must be balanced by a commitment to the larger community.

Etzioni claims that modern people have become too concerned about individual rights. We expect the system to work for us, but we are reluctant to support the system. For example, we believe that people accused of a crime have the right to their day in court, but fewer and fewer of us are willing to perform jury duty; similarly, we are quick to accept government services but reluctant to support these services with our taxes.

The communitarians advance four proposals to balance individual rights and public responsibilities. First, our society should halt the expanding "culture of rights" by which we put our own interests ahead of social responsibility; the Constitution, which is quoted so often when discussing individual rights,

Dependency theory asserts that rich nations achieved their modernization at the expense of poor ones, plundering poor nations' natural resources and exploiting their human labor. Even today, the world's poorest countries remain locked in a disadvantageous economic relationship with rich nations, dependent on wealthy countries to buy their raw materials and in return provide them with whatever manufactured products they can afford. According to this view, continuing ties with rich societies only perpetuates current patterns of global inequality.

Whichever approach you find more convincing, keep in mind that change in the United States is no longer separate from change in the rest of the world. At the beginning of the twentieth century, most people in today's high-income countries lived in relatively small settlements with limited awareness of the larger world. Today, a century later,

the entire world has become one huge village because the lives of all people are increasingly linked.

The last century witnessed unprecedented human achievement. Yet solutions to many problems of human existence—including finding meaning in life, resolving conflicts between nations, and eliminating poverty—have eluded us. The Thinking It Through box examines one dilemma: balancing individual freedom and personal responsibility. To this list of pressing matters new concerns have been added, such as controlling population growth and establishing an environmentally sustainable society. In the next hundred years, we must be prepared to tackle such problems with imagination, compassion, and determination. Our growing understanding of human society gives us reason to be hopeful that we can get the job done.

does not provide us with the right to do whatever we want. Second, we must remember that all rights involve responsibilities; we cannot simply take from society without giving something back. Third, the well-being of everyone may require limiting our individual rights; for example, pilots and bus drivers who are responsible for public safety may be asked to take a drug test. Fourth, no one can ignore key responsibilities such as upholding the law and responding to a cry for help from someone like Kitty Genovese.

The communitarian movement appeals to many people who believe in both personal freedom and social responsibility. But Etzioni's proposals have drawn criticism from both sides of the political spectrum. To those on the left, serious problems ranging from voter apathy and street crime to disappearing pensions and millions of workers without medical care cannot be solved with some vague notion of "social responsibility." As they see it, what

we need is expanded government programs to protect people and lessen inequality.

Conservatives, on the political right, see different problems in Etzioni's proposals (Pearson, 1995). As they see it, the communitarian movement favors liberal goals, such as confronting prejudice and protecting the environment, but ignores conservative goals such as

In today's world, people can find new ways to express age-old virtues such as concern for their neighbors and extending a hand to those in need. Habitat for Humanity, an organization with chapters in cities and towns across the United States, is made up of people who want to help local families realize their dream of owning a home.

strengthening religious belief and supporting traditional families.

Etzioni responds that the criticism coming from both sides suggests he has found a moderate, sensible answer to a serious problem. But the debate may also indicate that in a society as diverse as the United States, people who are so quick to assert their rights are not so quick to agree on their responsibilities.

WHAT DO YOU THINK?

1. Have you ever failed to come to the aid of someone in need or danger? Why?
2. Nearly half a century ago, President Kennedy stated, "Ask not what your country can do for you—ask what you can do for your country." Do you think people today support this idea? Why or why not?
3. Do you agree with Etzioni's call for balance between individual rights and social responsibilities? Explain your answer.

MAKING THE GRADE

The following learning tools will help you see what you know, identify what you still need to learn, and expand your understanding beyond the text. You can also visit the text's Companion Website™ at http://www.prenhall.com/macionis to find additional practice tests.

KEY POINTS

What Is Social Change?

Every society changes all the time, sometimes faster, sometimes slower. Social change often generates controversy.

Causes of Social Change

Social change takes many forms. Invention produces new objects and ideas; discovery gives us a fresh awareness of things in the world; diffusion spreads objects or ideas from one place to another. Causes of social change include social conflict (Marx) and ideas (Weber), as well as migration and other demographic factors.

Modernity

Modernity refers to the social consequences of industrialization, which include the erosion of traditional communities, expanding personal choice, increasingly diverse beliefs, and a focus on the future.

Ferdinand Tönnies described modernization as the transition from *Gemeinschaft* to *Gesellschaft*, with the decline of traditional community and the rise of individualism.

Emile Durkheim saw modernization as a society's expanding division of labor. Mechanical solidarity, based on shared activities and beliefs, is gradually replaced by organic solidarity, in which specialization makes people interdependent.

Max Weber saw modernity as the decline of tradition and rise of rationality. Weber feared the dehumanizing effects of rational organization.

Karl Marx saw modernity as the triumph of capitalism over feudalism. Capitalism creates social conflict, which Marx claimed would bring about revolutionary change toward an egalitarian socialist society.

Theoretical Analysis of Modernity

According to mass-society theory, modernity increases the scale of life, enlarging the role of government and other formal organizations in carrying out tasks previously performed by families in local communities. Cultural diversity and rapid social change make it difficult for people in modern societies to develop stable identities and to find meaning in their lives.

According to class-society theory, modernity involves the rise of capitalism. By concentrating wealth in the hands of a few, modern capitalist societies generate widespread feelings of powerlessness.

Social change is too complex and controversial simply to be equated with social progress.

Postmodernity

Postmodernity refers to the cultural traits of postindustrial societies. Postmodern criticism of society centers on the failure of modernity, and specifically science, to fulfill its promise of prosperity and well-being.

Looking Ahead:
Modernization and Our Global Future

Modernization theory links global poverty to the power of tradition. Rich nations can help poor countries develop their economies.

Dependency theory explains global poverty as the product of the world economic system. The operation of multinational corporations makes poor nations economically dependent on rich nations.

KEY CONCEPTS

social change (p. 639) the transformation of culture and social institutions over time

modernity (p. 641) social patterns resulting from industrialization

modernization (p. 641) the process of social change begun by industrialization

mass society (p. 646) a society in which prosperity and bureaucracy have weakened traditional social ties

class society (p. 648) a capitalist society with pronounced social stratification

social character (p. 650) personality patterns common to members of a particular society

tradition-directedness (p. 650) rigid conformity to time-honored ways of living

other-directedness (p. 650) openness to the latest trends and fashions, often expressed by imitating others

postmodernity (p. 654) social patterns characteristic of postindustrial societies

SAMPLE TEST QUESTIONS

These questions are similar to those found in the test bank that accompanies this textbook.

Multiple-Choice Questions

1. Sociologists use the term "modernity" to refer to social patterns that emerged
   a. with the first human civilizations.
   b. with the fall of Rome.
   c. after the Industrial Revolution.
   d. along with the Information Revolution.

2. Which of the following are common causes of social change?
   a. invention of new ideas and things
   b. diffusion from one cultural system to another
   c. discovery of existing things
   d. all of the above

3. Karl Marx highlighted the importance of _____ in the process of social change.
   a. immigration and demographic factors
   b. ideas
   c. social conflict
   d. cultural diffusion

4. Max Weber's analysis of how Calvinism helped create the spirit of capitalism highlighted the importance of _____ in the process of social change.

   a. invention
   b. ideas
   c. social conflict
   d. cultural diffusion

5. Which term was used by Ferdinand Tönnies to describe a traditional society?

   a. *Gemeinschaft*
   b. *Gesellschaft*
   c. mechanical solidarity
   d. organic solidarity

6. According to Emile Durkheim, modern societies have

   a. respect for established tradition.
   b. widespread alienation.
   c. common values and beliefs.
   d. an increasing division of labor.

7. For Max Weber, modernity meant the rise of _____; for Karl Marx, modernity meant_____.

   a. capitalism, anomie
   b. rationality, capitalism
   c. tradition, self-interest
   d. specialization, *Gesellschaft*

8. Which of the following statements about modernity as a mass society is *not* correct?

   a. There is more poverty today than in past centuries.
   b. Kinship ties have become weaker.

   c. Bureaucracy, including government, has increased in size.
   d. People experience moral uncertainty about how to live.

9. Sociologists who describe modernity in terms of class society focus on which of the following?

   a. rationality as a way of thinking about the world
   b. mutual interdependency
   c. the rise of capitalism
   d. the high risk of anomie

10. David Riesman described the other-directed social character typical of modern people as

    a. rigid conformity to tradition.
    b. eagerness to follow the latest fashions and fads.
    c. highly individualistic.
    d. all of the above.

Answers: 1(c); 2(d); 3(c); 4(b); 5(a); 6(d); 7(b); 8(a); 9(c); 10(b).

Essay Questions

1. Discuss how Tönnies, Durkheim, Weber, and Marx described modern society. What are similarities and differences in their understandings of modernity?

2. What traits lead some analysts to call the United States a "mass society"? Why do other analysts describe the United States as a "class society"?

APPLICATIONS & EXERCISES

1. Ask an elderly relative or friend to name the most important social changes during his or her lifetime. Do you think your world will change as much during your lifetime?

2. Ask people in your class or friendship group to make five predictions about U.S. society in the year 2050, when

today's twenty-year-olds will be senior citizens. Compare notes. On what issues is there agreement?

3. Do you think the rate of social change has been increasing? Do some research about modes of travel—including walking, riding animals, trains, cars, airplanes, and rockets—throughout history, and see what pattern emerges. How many of these modes of travel were available even 300 years ago?

INVESTIGATE *with* Research Navigator

Follow the instructions on page 27 of this text to access the features of **Research Navigator**™. Once at the Web site, enter your Login Name and Password. Then, to use the **ContentSelect**™ database, enter keywords such as "social change," "modernization," and "postmodernity," and the search engine will supply relevant and recent scholarly and popular press publications. Use the *New York Times* **Search-by-Subject Archive** to find recent news articles related to sociology and the **Link Library** feature to find relevant Web links organized by the key terms associated with this chapter.

PART II:

FROM

INTERSECTIONS:
READINGS IN SOCIOLOGY

EDITED BY

RALPH McNEAL

AND

KATHLEEN TIEMANN

INTERSECTIONS:
READINGS IN SOCIOLOGY

HOW HISTORY AND SOCIOLOGY CAN HELP TODAY'S FAMILIES

STEPHANIE COONTZ

"How History and Sociology Can Help Today's Families," by Stephanie Coontz, reprinted from The Way We Really Are: Coming to Terms with America's Changing Families, *1997, BasicBooks. Copyright © by Stephanie Coontz. pp. 11–32.*

In this article, Stephanie Coontz demonstrates how to apply the sociological imagination through her analysis of contemporary teen-parent conflicts and male-female conflicts. C. Wright Mills had defined sociological imagination as a quality of mind that lets us see how the social, historical, cultural, economic, and political context sways the choices people make in their lives. This article shows how the sociological imagination can help us understand all-too-common conflicts.

When lecture audiences first urged me to talk about how family history and sociology were relevant to contemporary life, I wasn't sure I wanted to abandon the safety of my historical observation post. But my experiences in recent years have convinced me that people are eager to learn whether historians and social scientists can help them improve their grasp of family issues. And I've come to believe that it's our responsibility to try.

I don't want to make false promises about what history and sociology offer. I can't give you five tips to make your relationship last. I don't have a list of ten things you can say to get your kids to do what *you* want and make them think it's what *they* want. Nor can I give kids many useful pointers on how to raise their parents.

But a historical perspective can help us place our personal relationships into a larger social context, so we can distinguish individual idiosyncrasies or problems from broader dilemmas posed by the times in which we live. Understanding the historical background and the current socioeconomic setting of family changes helps turn down the heat on discussion of many family issues. It can alleviate some of the anxieties of modern parents and temper the recriminations that go back

and forth between men and women. Seeing the larger picture won't make family dilemmas go away, but it can reduce the insecurity, personal bitterness, or sense of betrayal that all of us, at one time or another, bring to these issues. Sometimes it helps to know that the tension originates in the situation, not the psyche.

Putting Teen-Parent Conflicts in Perspective

Consider the question of what's happening to American youth. It's extremely difficult for parents today to look at a specific problem that they may have with their teenager, whether this is sneaking out at night or experimenting with alcohol and drugs, without seeing it as a sign of the crisis we are told grips modern youth. Parents tell me they are terrified by headlines about the "epidemic" of teen suicide and by chilling television stories about kids too young to drive a car but old enough to carry an AK-47.

Concerns over adolescent behavior are not entirely new. "Let's Face It," a *Newsweek* cover story of September 6, 1954, declared: "Our Teenagers Are Out of Control." The 1955 film, *Blackboard Jungle,* claimed that teens were "savage" animals because "gang leaders have taken the place of parents." Still, there *are* new structural and historical changes in American life that have recently complicated the transition from early adolescence to young adulthood, making youth-adult relations seem more adversarial.

It doesn't help us understand these changes, however, when people exaggerate the problems of today's teens or turn their normal ups and downs into pathologies. Most teens do not get involved in violence, either as criminals or victims. While teen suicide rates have indeed been increasing, any growth from a low starting point can sound dramatic if presented as a percentage. For example, a 1995 report from the Centers for Disease Control stated that suicides among 10- to 14-year-old youths had "soared" between 1980 and 1992. What this meant in real figures, points out researcher

Mike Males, was that 1 in 60,000 youths in this age group killed themselves in 1992, compared to 1 in 125,000 in 1980. The actual death rate among teens from firearms and poisoning has scarcely changed since the 1950s, but the proportion attributed to suicide has risen dramatically, while the proportion attributed to accident has declined.[1]

Furthermore, many "teen" suicide figures are overstated because they come from a database that includes people aged 15 to 24. Suicide rates for actual teenagers, aged 13 to 19, are among the lowest of any age group. In fact, notes Kirk Astroth, "teens as a whole are *less likely* to commit suicide than any other age group *except* preteens. . . . Occupational surveys consistently show that parents and teachers are *twice* as likely, counselors and psychologists are *four* times as likely, and school administrators are *six* times as likely to commit suicide as are high school students."[2] (When I read this statistic to a teenage acquaintance of mine, he told me dourly, "Yeah, but they'll just say we drove them to it.")

It's not that we have more bad parents or more bad kids today than we used to. It's not that families have lost interest in their kids. And there is no evidence that the majority of today's teenagers are more destructive or irresponsible than in the past. However, relations between adults and teens are especially strained today, not because youths have lost their childhood, as is usually suggested, but because they are not being adequately prepared for the new requirements of adulthood. In some ways, childhood has actually been prolonged, if it is measured by dependence on parents and segregation from adult activities. What many young people have lost are clear paths for gaining experience doing responsible, socially necessary work, either in or out of the home, and for moving away from parental supervision without losing contact with adults.

The most common dilemma facing adolescents, and the one that probably causes the most conflicts with adults, is their "rolelessness" in modern society. A rare piece of hard data in all the speculation about what makes adolescents tick is that young people do better on almost every level when they have meaningful involvement in useful and necessary tasks. This effect exists independently of their relationships with parents and friends. Teens also benefit from taking responsibility for younger or less-fortunate children. As one author observes, teens "need some experience of being older, bigger, stronger, or wiser."[3]

But today's adolescents have very few opportunities to do socially necessary work. The issue of rolelessness has been building for eighty years, ever since the abolition of child labor, the extension of schooling, and the decline in farm work that used to occupy many youths in the summer. The problem has accelerated recently, as many of the paths that once led teenagers toward mastery of productive and social roles have turned into dead ends. Instead of having a variety of routes to adulthood, as was true for most of American history, most youngsters are now expected to stay in high school until age 17 or 18.

High schools were originally designed for the most privileged sector of the populations. Even now they tend to serve well only that half of the high school population that goes on to college. Non-college-bound students often tell me they feel like second-class citizens, not really of interest to the school. And in recent decades a high school degree has lost considerable value as a ticket to a stable job. Even partial college work confers fewer advantages than in the past. Because of these and other trends, researcher Laurence Steinberg claims, adolescence "has become a social and economic holding period."[4]

Parents are expected to do the holding. In 1968, two researchers commented that most teen-parent conflicts stemmed from the fact that "readiness for adulthood comes about two years *later* than the adolescent claims and about two years *before* the parent will admit."[5] There is some evidence that the level of miscalculation has widened for *both* parents and kids.

From the point of view of parents, it is more necessary than ever for kids to stay in school rather than seek full-time work, and to delay marriage or pregnancy. After all, the age at which youths can support themselves, let alone a *family*, has reached a new high in the past two decades. From the kids' point of view, though, this waiting period seems almost unbearable. They not only know a lot more than their folks about modern technology but they feel that they also know more about the facts of life than yesterday's teens. Understandably, they strain at the leash.

The strain is accentuated by the fact that while the age of economic maturation has been rising, the age of physical maturation has been falling. The average age of puberty for girls, for instance, was 16 in 1820, 14 in 1900, and 13 in 1940. Today it is 12, and may still be dropping. For boys, the pace and timing of pubertal development is the most important factor in determining the age at which they first have sex; the influence of parents, friends, income and race is secondary. Although parents and friends continue to exert considerable influence on the age at which girls begin to have sex, there are obvious limits to how long parents can hold their teenagers back.[6]

And even as the job market offers fewer and fewer ways for teens to assert their independence and show that they are more grown up than younger kids, consumer markets and the media offer more and more. Steinberg points out that while teens "have less autonomy to pursue societally-valued *adult* activities" than in the past, they "have more autonomy than did their counterparts previously in matters of leisure, discretionary consumption, and grooming." As a result, adolescents "find it easier to purchase illicit drugs than to obtain legitimate employment."[7]

Another problem for parent-child relations is society's expectation that teens abide by rules and habits that grown-ups have abandoned, and that parents ought to be able to *make* them do so. In preindustrial societies most kids were integrated into almost all adult activities, and right up until the twentieth century there were few separate standards or different laws for teens and adults. For centuries, youth and adults played the same games by the same rules, both literally and figuratively. From "blind man's bluff" to "follow the leader," games we now leave to children were once played by adults as well. There were few special rules or restrictions that applied solely to teens. *All* premarital sex was supposedly out of line with the nineteenth century; teen sex was not singled out as a special problem. In fact, as late as 1886, the "age of consent" for girls was only 10 in more than half the states in the union.[8] However, girls or women who *did* consent to premarital sex were ostracized, regardless of their age.

Today's adults have moved on to new amusements and freedoms, but we want teens to play the old games by the old rules. There may be some good reasons for this, but any segregated group soon develops its own institutions, rules, and value systems, and young people are no exception.

Sports is virtually the only adult-approved and peer-admired realm where teens can demonstrate successive gains in competency, test their limits, and show themselves bigger, stronger, and better than younger children. But for teens who aren't good at sports, or those who reject it as busywork designed to keep them out of trouble, what's left? Music, clothes, drugs, alcohol—the choices differ. Many kids experiment and move on. Others get caught in the quagmire of seeking their identity through consumption. What we often call the youth culture is actually adult marketers seeking to commercially exploit youthful energy and rebellion. But sometimes consumerism seems the only way teens

can show that they are growing up and experimenting with new social identities while adults try to keep them suspended in the children's world of school or summer camp.

Of course, many teens get a lot out of school and summer camp. But the dilemmas of rolelessness often put adolescents and their parents on a collision course. Young people feel that adults are plying them with make-work or asking them to put their lives on hold as they mature. They're pretty sure we didn't put *our* lives on hold at comparable levels of maturity, so they suspect us of hypocrisy. Often, they have a point.

On the other hand, while many parents recognize that risk taking among teenagers hasn't changed much since their own youth, they feel that there are more serious consequences for those behaviors than there used to be, given the presence of AIDS (acquired immune deficiency syndrome), high-tech weapons, and new potent drugs. So adults are not necessarily being hypocritical when they hold kids to higher standards than they met themselves. Many of us fear that the second chances and lucky breaks we get may not be available to the next generation.

Balancing the legitimate fears of adults against the legitimate aspirations of teens is not easy. But it helps for both teens and adults to realize that many of their conflicts are triggered by changes in social and economic arrangements, not just family ones. The best way I've found to personally confirm the sociological studies of rolelessness is to ask older men to talk about their life histories. Some of the most interesting discussions I've had over the past few years have been with men over age 60, whose memories extend beyond the transitional period of the 1960s and 1970s to what teen life was like in the 1930s, 1940s, or early 1950s.

The conversations usually start with comments on irresponsible behavior by today's teenage males. "I'd have had my hide tanned if I'd been caught doing that," someone always says, which generally leads to examples of how they got "whomped" or "taught a lesson." Soon, though, the subject switches to the things these upstanding men *didn't* get caught doing in their youth. And most of the time, it turns out the first lesson they learned by getting whomped was how not to get caught.

When they talk about what *really* set them on the right path, almost every older man I've talked with recalls his first job. "I was supporting myself when I was 17" (16, 18, 19, even 15), or "I was in the army with a job to do," the stories go: "What's the matter with today's kids?" And soon they provide their own answers. The typical job a teenager can get today provides neither the self-pride of economic independence nor the socializing benefits of working alongside adult mentors. Teens work in segregated jobs where the only adult who ever comes around is the boss, almost always in an adversarial role. Few jobs for youth allow them to start at the bottom and move up; the middle rungs of the job ladder have been sawed off. Marking time in dead-end jobs that teach no useful skills for the future, teens remain dependent on their parents for the basic necessities of life, simultaneously resenting that dependence and trying to manipulate it.

The stories older men tell about their first jobs are quite different from those told by today's teens. Even men who later become businessmen or highly educated professionals say that their first jobs were in construction, factory work, or some menial setting where they worked beside older men who were more skilled or highly paid. The senior men teased the youngsters, sending them out for a left-handed hammer or making them the butt of sometimes painful practical jokes, but they also showed kids the ropes and helped protect them from the foreman or boss. And they explained why "putting up with the crap" was worth it. After older men talk for a while about what these work experiences meant to them, they are almost always surprised to find themselves agreeing that the loss of nonparental male mentoring may be a bigger problem for boys today than the rise of single-mother homes.

Even allowing for nostalgia, such work relations seem to have been critical experiences for the socialization of many young men in the past. Such jobs integrated youths into adult society, teaching skills they would continue to use as they aged, instead of segregating them in a separate peer culture. As late as 1940, about 60 percent of employed adolescents aged 16–17 worked in traditional workplaces, such as farms, factories, or construction sites. The jobs they did there, or at least the skills they used, might last well into their adult lives. By 1980, only 14 percent worked in such settings.[9]

Girls, who were excluded from many such jobs, have lost less in this arena of life. Up through the 1960s an adolescent girl typically had more responsibilities at home, from washing dishes to taking care of siblings, than she does today. While such tasks may have prepared girls for adult roles as wives and mothers, they also held girls back from further education or preparation for future work outside the home. The change in work patterns for girls has thus made it *easier* for them to see that they have paths toward adult independence. On the other hand, it raises a different set of tensions between girls and their parents. The decline of the sexual double standard, without an equal decline in economic and social discrimination against women, leads parents to worry that their daughters may have too much opportunity, too early, to engage in sexual risk taking for which girls still pay a far higher price than boys.

Another issue facing teens of both sexes is their increasing exclusion from public space. People talk about how kids today are unsupervised, and they often are; but in one sense teens are under *more* surveillance than in the past. Almost anyone above the age of 40 can remember places where young people could establish real physical, as opposed to psychic, distance from adults. In the suburbs it was undeveloped or abandoned lots and overgrown woods, hidden from adult view, often with old buildings that you could deface without anyone caring. In the cities it was downtown areas where kids could hang out. Many of these places are now gone, and only some kids feel comfortable in the malls that have replaced them.

Much has been written about the gentrification of public space in America, the displacement of the poor or socially marginal from their older niches, followed by fear and indignation from respectable people suddenly forced to actually see the homeless doing what they always used to do. Over the years we have also seen what I think of as an "adultification" of public space. Kids are usually allowed there, as long as they're young enough to be in their parents' charge. But where in your town are teenagers welcome on their own?

Teens today have fewer opportunities than in the past for gradual initiation into productive activities, both at home and in public, and fewer places to demonstrate their autonomy in socially approved ways. At the same time, though, they have more access to certain so-called adult forms of consumption than ever before. This makes it hard for adults to avoid the extremes of overly controlling, lock-'em-up positions on the one hand and frequent breakdowns of supervision on the other. Some parents clearly underprotect their kids. We've all seen parents who are too stressed to monitor their kids effectively or who have had their limits overrun so many times that they have given up. Other parents, however, overprotect their kids, trying to personally compensate for the loss of wider adult contacts and of safe retreats. Both extremes drive kids away. But, in most cases, both are reactions to structural dilemmas facing parents and teens rather than abdications of parental responsibility.

What Social Science Tells Us About Male-Female Conflicts

The same kind of perspective can be useful in sorting through conflicts between modern couples. I vividly remember the first people who forced me to bring my historical and social analysis down to individual cases. Following one of my talks, a couple stood up and described a conflict they were having in their marriage. She complained about how unappreciative he was of the effort she took in making gourmet dinners and keeping the house clean. He said: "Hang on a minute. I never asked her to do any of those things. I can't help it if she has higher standards than I do. I don't *care* what we have for dinner. I don't *care* if the floor gets mopped twice a week." They wanted me to comment on their situation.

This is not fair, I thought, as I tried to wriggle out of doing so. I've just summed up the history of family diversity and changing gender roles since colonial times and they want me to settle a marital argument—over housework, of all things? I'm not a counselor; I don't know anything about mediating these issues. I tried to change the subject, but they wouldn't let up, and the audience was clearly on their side. You think family history is relevant, they seemed to be saying. Prove it.

Trapped, but unwilling to pretend I had therapeutic expertise, I cast about for something in my own research or training that might by any stretch of the imagination be helpful. The only thing that came to mind was a concept I had read about in an academic journal. "So," I said, feeling a bit silly, "perhaps the problem we have here lies in what social scientists would call your 'situated social power.'"[10]

It sounded very academic, even downright pompous, but the more we talked about it, the more I realized this *was* a useful concept for them. In plain English it means that various groups in society have unequal access to economic resources, political power, and social status, and these social differences limit how fair or equal a personal relationship between two individuals from different groups can really be. Such social imbalances affect personal behavior regardless of sincere intentions of both parties to "not let it make a difference."

Teachers, for example, have social power over students. I tell my students that I want them to speak their mind and express their disagreement with me. And I mean it. But often I don't even notice that they continue to defer until someone finally gets angry at me for "dominating the discussion." Even after all these years, my initial reaction is usually indignation.

"I told you to speak up," I want to say; "it's not my fault if you hold back." Then I remind myself that in any situation of unequal power, it's the party with the most power who always assumes that other people can act totally free of outside constraints.

When a person with power pretends not to have it, people with less power feel doubly vulnerable. Although they continue to be unequal, they are now asked to put aside the psychological defenses they have constructed against that inequality, including a certain amount of self-protective guardedness. So they clam up or get sore, which leaves the more powerful person feeling that his or her big-hearted gestures are being rebuffed. This tension arises between people of different races and classes, between employees and supervisors, and between men and women, as well as between my students and me.

With this awareness, I try to remember that my students are never going to feel as free criticizing my work as I'm going to feel criticizing theirs. I have to adjust the structure of my class to facilitate discussion. I need to institute protected spaces for criticism, such as providing anonymous evaluation forms for assessing my performance. But I also have to recognize that our power imbalance will always create tensions between us. I should neither blame my students for that nor feel that I've failed to communicate my "authentic self" to them. None of us exists independently of the social relations in which we operate.

Remembering how helpful this concept is to me in depersonalizing conflicts with students, I reminded the couple that men and women have different options in our society, outside and independent of their personal relationships. Research shows that men are happiest in a relationship when they don't have to do much housework and yet meals get made, clothes get ironed, and the house looks good. This doesn't mean they are chauvinist pigs. Who *wouldn't* be happier under those conditions?

But the wives of such men tend to be depressed. A wife may feel, especially if she jeopardized her earning power by taking time off to raise children, that she can't give up the domestic services she performs, because if her husband *does* get dissatisfied, she has fewer options than he does in the work world, and would be far worse off after a divorce.

Consciously or not, the wife in this particular marriage seemed to be assessing the risk of not keeping a nice house or putting delicious meals on the table, and finding it too high to just relax and let the housework go. But she was also resenting her husband's unwillingness to help out. This very common pattern of seemingly voluntary sacrifice by the woman, followed by resentment for the man's failure to reciprocate, originates outside the individual relationship. The man was probably completely sincere about not caring if the work got done, but he was missing the point. His wife had looked around, seen what happened to wives who failed to please their husbands, and tried extra hard to make her husband happy. He could not understand her compulsion, and resented being asked to participate in what he saw as unnecessary work. Counseling and better communication might help, but would probably not totally remove the little kernel of fear in the wife's heart that stems from her perfectly reasonable assessment of the unequal social and economic options for men and women.

Similarly, two people trying to raise a child while they both work fulltime are going to get stressed or angry. Part of the problem may be that the man isn't doing enough at home (on average, research shows, having a man in the house *adds* hours to a woman's workday). Part of the problem may be that the woman is sabotaging her own stated desire to have the man do more—treating him as an unskilled assistant, refusing to relinquish her control over child-raising decisions, and keeping her domestic standards too high for him to meet. But another part of the problem will remain even if they are the most enlightened individuals in the world.

There's no nonstressful way to divide three full-time jobs between two individuals. Better communication can make the sacrifices more fair, or help clear away the side issues that get entangled with the stress, but the strains are a social problem existing outside the relationship. The solution does not lie in Martians learning to talk Venusian or Venusians being tolerant of the cultural oddities of Martians, as one pop psychologist describes the differences between men and women, but in changing the job structures and social support networks for family life. Until businesses and schools adjust their hours and policies to the realities of two-earner families, even the best-intentioned couples are going to have difficult times.

Improving communication or using the shortcuts offered by self-help books can alleviate some of the conflicts between men and women in this period of rapidly changing roles and expectations. But addressing communication problems alone ignores the differing social options and the patterned experiences of inequality that continually *re-create* such problems between men and women. So people move from one self-help book to another; they try out new encounter groups and memorize new techniques; they slip back and must start all over again. They are medicating the symptoms without solving the problem.

For example, the Venusian-Martian reference comes from best-selling author John Gray, who has found a strikingly effective analogy for getting men and women to realize that they bring different assumptions and experiences to relationships: Men and women, he says, come from different planets. They need to learn each other's culture and language. Gray tells women why men's periodic withdrawals from communication do not mean lack of interest in a relationship. Martians, he says, like to retreat to caves in times of stress, while Venusians tend to crowd around, offering each other support and empathy. He explains to men that women are often just asking for reassurance, not trying to control men's lives, when they pursue subjects past the male comfort zone.[12]

But Gray doesn't urge either sex to make any big changes, merely to take "tiny steps toward understanding the other." He offers women hints on how to ask their partners for help without antagonizing them or making them feel manipulated, but he doesn't demand that men share housework or that women accept the responsibilities that go with egalitarian relationships. For Gray, a healthy relationship exists "when both partners have permission to ask for what they want and need, and they both have permission to say no if they choose." This is certainly better than no one feeling free to ask, but it leaves a rather large set of issues unresolved.[13]

The problem is that many advice books refuse to ask hard questions about the division of household work and decision-making power. In a section called "scoring points with the opposite sex," for example, Gray's advice to women revolves around issues such as not criticizing men for their driving or choice of restaurants. Men, by contrast, are advised: "offer to make dinner," "occasionally offer to wash the dishes," "compliment her on how she looks," "give her four hugs a day," and "don't flick the remote control to different channels when she is watching TV with you."[14]

Now, most women will say that the book would be worth its weight in gold if their husbands would just follow that last tip, but the fact remains that the unequal bargaining power and social support systems for men and women are not addressed, *or even acknowledged*, in this kind of advice. In the long run, failure to address the roots of gender differences perpetuates the problem of communication, or merely replaces one set of misunderstandings with another. As therapist Betty

Carter writes, communicating about feelings rather than addressing issues of power and daily behavior can lead to manipulation that eventually degenerates into mutual blame and psychological name-calling.[15] If we're going to think of men and women as being from different planets, they need more than guidebooks and language translations; we must make sure that the social, economic, and political treaties they operate under are fair to both parties.

It's not only women's dissatisfactions that are addressed by a historical and sociological perspective. Men often complain that feminists ignore male insecurities and burdens, and they have a point. Men *do* feel injured and alienated, despite their economic and political advantages over women of the same social group. But history and sociology can identify the sources of men's pain a lot more accurately than myths about the loss of some heroic age of male bonding when Australian aborigines, Chinese sun kings, and Greek warriors marched to their own drumbeat. Going "back to the woods" makes a nice weekend retreat, but it doesn't help men restructure their long-term relationships or identify the social, economic, and political changes they need to improve their family lives.[16]

Male pain is the other side of male power. Not all men, contrary to the rhetoric of masculinity, can be at the top of the pyramid. The contrast between rhetoric and reality is very painful for men whose race, class, health, or even height does not allow them to wield power, exercise authority, or just cut a figure imposing enough to qualify as a "real man." Even successful men pay a high price for their control and authority. The competitive, hierarchical environments men are encouraged to operate in cut them off from intimacy and penalize them for letting down their guard. The myth that male power is all individually achieved, not socially structured, means masculinity can be lost if it is not constantly proven in daily behavior.[17]

Structural analysis helps us get beyond the question of "who hurts more" to explore the different rewards and penalties that traditional gender roles impose on today's men and women. For girls, societal pressures descend heavily at about age 11 or 12, penalizing them for excelling and creating a sharp drop in their self-esteem. There is overwhelming evidence, for example, that girls are treated in ways that hinder their academic and intellectual development. But sometimes this discrimination takes the form of too easy praise and too little pressure to complete a task, leading boys to feel that "girls get off easy." And almost any parent can testify that boys are subject to a much earlier, more abrupt campaign to extinguish the compassion, empathy, and expression of feelings that young boys initially display as openly as girls. The list of derogatory words for boys who don't act masculine is miles longer than the list of disparaging words for girls who don't act feminine. Boys who don't get the message quickly enough are treated brutally. Those who do get the message find that the very success of their effort to "be a man" earns mistrust and fear as well as admiration. In an article that my male students invariably love, Eugene August points out that people always talk about "innocent women and children" in describing victims of war or terrorism. Is there no such thing as an innocent man?[18]

It's good to get past caricatures of female victims and male villains, but it is too simplistic to say that we just have to accept our differences. A man's fear of failure and discomfort with intimacy, for example, come from his socially structured need to constantly have others affirm his competence, self-reliance, or superiority. This is the downside of what he must do to exercise power and privilege. For women, lack of power often leads to fear of success. The downside of women's comfort with intimacy is discomfort with asserting authority.

As three researchers in the psychology of gender summarize the tradeoffs, boys "get encouraged to be independent and powerful, possibly at the cost of distancing themselves from intimacy." The result is that boys "tend to be overrepresented in the psychopathologies involving aggression." Girls, by contrast, "get rewarded for being compliant and for establishing intimate relations, possibly at the cost of achieving autonomy and control over their choices." This may be why girls are "overrepresented in the psychopathologies involving depression."[19]

The solution suggested by historical and social analysis is not for men and women to feel each other's pain but to equalize their power and access to resources. That is the only way they can relate with fairness and integrity, so that unequal and therefore inherently dishonest relations do not deform their identities. Men must be willing to give up their advantages over women if they hope to build healthy relationships with either sex. Women must be willing to accept tough criticism and give up superficial "privileges" such as being able to cry their way out of a speeding ticket if they hope to develop the inner resources to be high achievers.

· · ·

Endnotes

1. Males, M. (1996). *The scapegoat generation: America's war on adolescents*. Monroe, ME: Common Courage Press, 1996, pp. 229–238; Holinger, P. (1994). *Suicide and homicide among adolescents*. New York: Guilford, p. 37.

2. Astroth, K. (1993, January). Beyond ephebiphobia: Problem adults or problem youths? *Phi Delta Kappan*, p. 413.

3. Maton, K. (1990). Meaningful involvement in instrumental activity and well-being: Studies of older adolescents and at risk urban teen-agers. *American Journal of Community Psychology*, *18*, 297; Hamburg, D. (1992). *Today's children: Creating a future for a generation in crisis*. (New York: Times Books), p. 201.

4. Maddrick, J. (1995). *The end of affluence: The causes of consequences of America's economic dilemma*. New York: Random House, pp. 109–112; Steinberg, L. The logic of adolescence. In P. Edelman & J. Ladner, (Eds.), *Adolescence and poverty: Challenge for the 1990s* (p. 30). Washington, DC: Center for National Policy Press.

5. Stone, L. J., & Church, J. (1968). *Childhood and adolescence: A psychology of the growing person*. New York: Random House, p. 447 (emphasis added).

6. Nightingale, E., & Wolverton, L. (1988, September). Adolescent rolelessness in modern society. Working Paper, Carnegie Council on Adolescent Development, p. 5; (1994). Sex and America's teenagers, Alan Guttmacher Institute, New York, p. 21.

7. Steinberg. The logic of adolescence, p. 30.

8. Luker, K. (1996) *Dubious conceptions: The politics of teenage pregnancy*. Cambridge, MA: Harvard University Press, p. 27.

9. Greenberger, E., & Steinberg, L. (1986). *When teenagers work: The psychological and social costs of adolescent employment*. New York: Basic Books, pp. 58–65.

10. Wartenberg, T. (1988). The situated concept of social power, *Social Theory and Practice*, *14*.

11. Bruce, J., Lloyd, C., & Leonard, A. with Engle, P., & Duffy, N. (1995). *Families in focus: New perspectives on mothers, fathers, and children*. New York: The Population Council, p. 29; Hartmann, H. (1981). The family as the locus of gender, class and political struggle: The example of housework, *Signs*, *6*.

12. Gray, J. (1992). *Men are from Mars, Women are from Venus*. New York: HarperCollins.

13. Peterson, K. (1994, Marsh 28). A global ambassador between the sexes. *USA Today*, pp. 1D and 2D; Gray, J. *Men are from Mars*, p. 265.

14. Gray, J. *Men are from Mars*, pp. 180–184, 199–202. On unequal bargaining power, see Sen, A. (1983). Economics and the family, *Asian Development Review*, *1*.

15. Carter, C. (1996). *Love, honor, and negotiate: Making your marriage work*. New York: Pocket Books. As Andrew Greeley points out in "The Declining Morale of Women" (*Sociology and Social Research*, *173*, 189), women's morale in marriage has declined far more significantly than men's.

Unless their frustrations with the marriage bargain are addressed more directly, not just placated, men and women *could* end up on different planets.

16. The images are taken from Bly, R. (1990). *Iron John: A book about men*. Reading, MA: Addison-Wesley. For a critique, see Connell, R. W. (1992). Drumming up the wrong tree. *Tikkun*, *7*.

17. Brines, J. Economic dependency, gender, and the division of labor at home. *American Journal of Sociology*, *100*, 683; Lehne, G. (1989). Homophobia among men: Supporting and defining the male role. In M. Kimmel & M. Messner (Eds.), *Men's lives* (pp. 416–429). New York: Macmillan.

18. Gilligan, C., Lyons, N., & Hanmer, T. (1990). *Making connections: The relational world of adolescent girls at Emma Willard School*. Cambridge, MA: Harvard University Press; Orenstein, P. (1994). *School girls: Young women, self-esteem, and the confidence gap*. New York: Doubleday; Gilligan, C., & Brown, L. M. (1992). *Meeting at the crossroads: Women's psychology and girls' development*. Cambridge, MA: Harvard University Press; Sadker, M., & Sadker, D. (1994). *Failing at fairness: How American schools cheat girls*. New York: Scribners and Sons; (1992). *How schools shortchange girls: The AAUW report: A study of major findings on girls and education*. Washington, DC: AAUW Educational Foundation; Kann, M. (1986). The costs of being on top. *Journal of the National Association for Women Deans*, *49*; August, E. (1992). Real men don't: Anti-male bias in English. In M. Schaum & C. Flanagan (Eds.), *Gender images: Readings for composition* (pp. 131–141). Boston: Houghton Mifflin.

19. Cowan, P. A., Cowan, C. P., & Kerig, P. K. (1993). Mothers, fathers, sons and daughters: Gender differences in family formation and parenting styles. In P. Cowan et al. (Eds.), *Family, self, and society: Toward a new agenda for family research*. (p. 190). Hillsdale, NJ: Lawrence Erlbaum.

Questions

1. According to Coontz, why is it important for us to view our personal relationships in a larger social context?

2. What is "rolenessness"? Did you (or do you) experience this phenomenon? Explain.

3. What is "situated social power"? Provide an example from your own life to illustrate this concept.

4. What is "adultification"? Describe how you experienced adultification in your teen years.

5. Does Coontz have a sociological imagination? Why or why not?

ETHICS AND POLITICS OF FIELD RESEARCH IN SOUTH AFRICA

IVY N. GODUKA
Central Michigan University

"Ethics and Politics of Field Research in South Africa," by Ivy N. Goduka, reprinted from Social Problems, *Vol. 37, No. 3, August 1990. Copyright © by the Society for the Study of Social Problems. pp. 329–340. www.ucpress.edu*

When sociologists conduct research, they are expected to adhere to a code of ethics that is designed to protect their subjects from harm. One requirement of that code is that, before collecting data, researchers must provide subjects with an "informed consent" form that explains their rights as participants in the project. But what happens when subjects do not seem to understand the informed consent form, or when the code of ethics is relevant in one culture but not in another? This is the very situation that confronted Ivy Goduka when she conducted research on black children in South Africa. As you read this article, think about not only how the code of ethics affected Goduka's research, but also how her personal background and experience helped her successfully complete this project.

I am a black South African. I was born and grew up in Herschel in the homeland of the Transkei. Recently I completed a Ph.D. in the College of Human Ecology at Michigan State University, and for my dissertation I conducted field research (Goduka 1987) on black children in three black residential areas in South Africa: Herschel; the resettlement of Thornhill, in the homeland of the Ciskei; and white-owned farm areas in Queenstown and in Zastron. In the process of conducting that research I became acutely aware of the contradictions inherent in any attempt to apply ethical codes designed in the relatively liberal, economically stable, politically "safe," and literate societies of North America and Europe to research practices in an authoritarian context such as South Africa.

This paper illustrates the disjunctures created when ethical codes designed in one cultural and political context are applied to a quite different one. I draw upon my background as a black South African and my graduate training at Michigan State University. Because I was trained in the United States, and because my research project was funded by the National Science Foundation, I was obligated to abide by the ethical guidelines of the American Sociological Association (1988). I will first describe the political and cultural contexts in South Africa, contrast these with the political and cultural contexts in the United States, and examine the implications of these contexts for research. In an effort to bridge the differences between these two contexts, I will discuss my research topic, its origins, purpose, methods, and data collection procedures. I will then explore the limitations of informed consent and prohibitions against covert research when applied to an authoritarian context such as South Africa.

Research Contexts

South Africa

South Africa is an authoritarian society that gives little or no state protection of individual rights, particularly for blacks. This lack of protection results from the system of apartheid, a policy of rigid racial discrimination that has existed in South Africa since 1948. Many laws and acts have been passed by the South African government that serve to entrench and legalize apartheid. These laws include population registration, land reservation, education, and job reservation acts. These laws and acts deny blacks in South Africa the right to vote and serve to keep them landless, powerless, and lacking in all the basic resources necessary for survival. Because they lack basic resources, blacks are not only illiterate and poverty-stricken but also ignorant, vulnerable, and powerless to make decisions and choices directly affecting their own lives, particularly those regarding family issues.

. . .

Living conditions for blacks in the white-owned farm areas are also very poor. Workers, including children, are housed in large unfurnished sheds with no internal walls or beds. Families live in corrugated iron huts. There is usually no internal water, and there is a general lack of sanitation. Farm life is characterized by what Nasson (1984) calls acute squalor, chronic poverty, and almost total lack of alternative employment opportunities. Farm laborers, and their children who grow up working on the farm, learn to be dependent on white farmers for jobs, food, and housing. Thus, under apartheid, black families not only live under impoverished conditions, they are disenfranchised and prevented from making basic individual decisions about family affairs.

The United States

In contrast to the authoritarian South African context, the laws of the United States are founded on respect for the rights of the individual regardless of race. This respect for individual rights is also emphasized and required in research, particularly in the ethical and legal imperative of informed consent (Lidz et. al. 1984). The state laws regulating informed consent are deeply rooted in the individualistic tradition of the English common law and have been adopted and used in the American legal system. . . .

The guidelines professionally specified for sociologists are outlined by the American Sociological Association (ASA 1988). I followed these ethical guidelines in my research in South Africa. These guidelines are offered as applicable to research on human subjects irrespective of disciplinary area, and illustrate ethical codes current in the various human sciences. They are based on nine major principles (American Sociological Association 1988:4–5). In this paper, only those guidelines that relate to deception and informed consent are cited.

In abridged form, these ASA guidelines are: (1) Sociologists must not knowingly use their professional roles as covers to obtain information for fraudulent or covert purpose. (2) Sociologists must take culturally appropriate steps to secure informed consent and to avoid invasion of privacy. Special actions may be necessary where the individuals studied are illiterate, of very low social status, and/or unfamiliar with social research. (3) Study design and information-gathering techniques should conform to regulations protecting the rights of human subjects, irrespective of source of funding, as outlined by the American Association of University Professors in "Regulations governing research on human subjects" (Academe 1981).

It is clear that the ASA document covers a fair number of specific and somewhat general principles regarding the protection of the research participants. In order to ascertain that researchers in the United States abide by the guidelines on informed consent, universities have attempted to aid researchers and protect the welfare of human subjects in a variety of ways. Consequently, universities have instituted human subjects research review committees that must approve of the ethics of a specific procedure before the research may be conducted.

• • •

The University Committee on Research Involving Human Subjects (UCRIHS) at Michigan State University, where I was studying at the time of this research, did not require a signed consent form prior to starting fieldwork. However, Michigan State's UCRIHS reviewed my proposal to ensure that the rights and welfare of the subjects were not violated. The National Science Foundation which provided funding for this research, also required a copy of the informed consent form prior to approving the application for funding.

The consent form I used as required by UCRIHS at Michigan State University reads as follows:

> Parent/Guardian's Name:
> _____. I freely give consent for my child and I to take part in this study. I understand that my child and I are free to discontinue our participation in the study at any time. My participation and my child's participation in the study does not guarantee any beneficial results to me and to my child. I understand that, at my request, I can receive additional explanation of the study after my participation is completed, and that the results of the study will be treated in strict confidence and we will remain anonymous. Within these restrictions, results of the study will be made available to me at my request (Goduka 1987:260).

At the end of the consent form, the subject is required to attach his/her signature and date it. This document is legally binding on the researcher. It emphasizes individuals over collectivities, and contractual relations between the researcher and the subjects; it assumes the legalistic rights of the subjects, as well as the right to make choices and have control over one's life. As I will illustrate by my discussion of the problems I encountered while attempting to apply the ASA guidelines in my research, the political and cultural conditions that gave rise to the development of such professional codes of research ethics in the United States simply do not exist in South Africa.

Bridging Two Cultures

The Research Project: Methods and Procedures

My research project, which ultimately came to be titled "Behavioral Development of Black South African Children: An Ecological Approach" (Goduka 1987), originated from my own childhood experience in Herschel, in the homeland of the Transkei, and a concern for how black children grow and develop in the rural areas of South Africa under apartheid. Thus, the study's purpose was to examine the physical growth and behavioral development of black elementary school children in South Africa from an ecosystem perspective. A number of selected ecological factors, namely, the area of residence, the type of family structure, parent's socio-economic status, family mobility, and the home environment, were examined as these might modify the nutritional status and the socio-emotional and cognitive development of children.

The sample included 300 children and their parents or guardians from the Xhosa ethnic group. I selected a sub-sample of one hundred children from each of the three areas studied (homeland of the Transkei; resettlement of Thornhill; and white-owned farms). Before children were tested and parents were interviewed, I gave each child who was in the sample a letter explaining the purpose of the research, and a copy of the consent form that the parents were to fill out and give to the child to return to school the following day. Both the letter and a copy of the consent form were first written in English and then translated into Xhosa, a language spoken by the subjects. About one-half (52%) of the parents or guardians filled out the consent forms and returned them to school via their children the next day. My assistants and I made home visits to the other half of the sample to explain the purpose of the study and request that the parent or guardian fill out the informed consent form.

A team of three researchers (two research assistants from the homeland of the Transkei whom I had hired, and myself), assessed children at school for cognitive and social-emotional development. We also took measures of physical growth (height, weight, and head circumference). The assessment and measuring of children took place at school. In most cases testing was done during recess, in other cases it took place after school. The three of us made home visits to observe parent-child interaction and home conditions, and to administer a questionnaire to the parent or guardian of each child in order to obtain demographic data.

· · ·

Ethics and Access

A major problem for me in doing this particular project arose out of my position as a black South African: how to gain access to white-owned farm areas. On the basis of the Group Area's Act, black families may live, work, and move freely only in the homeland and resettlement areas. Similarly, whites, coloreds, and Asians may live only in their designated areas. To live and work in urban areas and on white-owned farms, blacks are required by law to obtain a pass (identification document) and work permit from the white government. The same laws applied to me and my research assistants when conducting research on white-owned farm areas. Unlike the homeland and the resettlement areas, the farm areas are directly under the control of the Pretoria regime, as are the schools in white-owned

areas. Therefore, as black South Africans we had to obtain permission from Pretoria in order to gain entry into the schools in these areas and to interview farm laborers.

While preparing my research proposal, I had to decide whether I would do covert research or be completely open and honest about my project's purpose. The latter, in all probability, would have caused the South African, as well as the Transkeian and Ciskeian governments to refuse me access to the schools and homes. Realizing these difficulties, I decided to use the same strategies that other social scientists have used when dealing with the South African government.

While doing research in South Africa, van den Berghe (1968:185–86) concluded "I decided that I should have no scruples in deceiving the government and that the paramount consideration in my dealings with the state would be to minimize obstacles to my research without compromising my principles." When he applied for a South African visa, he decided that it would be unwise to reveal the real purpose of his study, which was to look at race relations. Instead he stated that the was a social scientist interested in "the spectacular economic development of South Africa" (1988:185–86). He also refused certain customary white privileges, and decided to break some laws that they considered iniquitous or that exposed his non-white friends to embarrassment.

In order to gain access to these research sites, I chose van den Berghe's strategy. For instance, I phrased the title of the study in a way that would not be alarming to the government of South Africa, the school administrators, or the subjects. My research was designed to study black children under apartheid and originally was titled "Behavioral Development of Black South African Children Under Apartheid." After I alerted my guidance committee to problems I would encounter with this title, the committee allowed me to change it. The committee also was afraid that the government of South Africa would view this title as challenging the status quo, and would not allow me access to areas where blacks live. Consequently, I changed the title to "Behavioral Development of Black South African Children: An Ecological Approach" (Goduka 1987). This was a less threatening yet all-inclusive title that would save me from the possibility of refused access or even possibly going to jail. The human ecological framework used in this study also helped in phrasing a title acceptable to the government of South Africa. It was acceptable because it sounded like social science jargon and thus apolitical.

Gaining access to the homeland of the Transkei and the resettlement of Thornhill was easy both because these are "independent" areas assigned to blacks and because we were black and from one of these areas. However, I had to go personally to Pretoria for an interview before the government gave us the approval to enter the white-owned farm areas. Because I am a native of South Africa, I know and understand how the government operates, I knew how to manipulate the system to obtain what I wanted. The first strategy that I devised was to secure the assistance of a white liberal South African who would have credibility for the Pretoria white minority government. I asked my major professor, who was also the director of the study at Michigan State University, to request in writing that the Deputy Director of the National Institute of Personnel Research (NIPR) in Johannesburg supervise my work while I collected data in South Africa. (I had worked for the NIPR before coming to study at Michigan State. The Deputy Director, who is an opponent of apartheid, had been my supervisor at the institute). After he expressed his willingness to supervise the research, his name was given in the letter to the school administrators and parents or guardians. In addition, administrators and parents or guardians were given his telephone number at the institute and were instructed to call him if they had further questions about the project.

An interview with the chief school administrator in Pretoria, which lasted two to three hours, did not give weight to my case primarily because the color of my skin and the fact that I am a woman. What overcame this deficiency, however, was a telephone conversation between the chief school inspector and the Deputy Director of the NIPR. The latter was then asked to write a letter explaining who I was. In the letter he added: "Her university has appointed me as supervisor of her fieldwork in South Africa. I would be grateful if you could give her the assistance that she seeks with a view to completing fieldwork of her Ph.D. research" (Goduka 1987:261e).

Thus, I had to use the NIPR to get into the schools on white-owned farms. I knew the NIPR had more credibilicommittee members, who were thousands of miles ty in the eyes of the government than my away in the United States. Telephone calls to and fro would have been a waste of time and money. However, under normal circumstances, i.e., without the imposition of economic sanctions upon the South African government by the Reagan administration, a call from the United States probably would have carried more weight than the NIPR.

Getting approval from Pretoria made entry to some farm areas easier; however, in other areas we were totally refused entry. The white Boer farmers knew their word was final, and that their treatment of "Kaffirs" or "niggers" (as they referred to us) would not jeopardize their situation. The white farmers have the complete support of the government since they vote for the president, and the economy of South Africa is dependent on what they produce.

Another access problem we had concerned driving around the white-owned farms in the evenings. Because of the political turmoil, marked by extreme tension between blacks and whites, 1986 was a bad year to be in South Africa. Some of the interviews and observations in the farm areas were scheduled in the evening, after the laborers were off work. On several occasions we were stopped on the road because of a road-block and would be late for interviews, or end up missing interview appointments. We were asked to produce passes, or identification cards by white police officers. Failure to do so on the spot led many travellers to be taken away and locked in jail. We were fortunate that we knew the law and were prepared in that respect. Our bags were searched, and the research material would be tossed all over in the trunk. All this was done out of spite: "Die Kaffirs dink hulle is slim"—"these niggers think thay are smart. Who are you to do research?" as one officer commented, laughing sarcastically. We would spend hours being interrogated by young, ignorant, white police officers. Some interviews had to be cancelled because of the state of emergency and declared curfews.

Going back to the homeland after interviews was another problem. Although trust and rapport were established and maintained in some extent with teachers, school children, and parents, we found that villagers, particularly high school students, were suspicious. Not only were we viewed as "outsiders," because the rented car we were using had a Johannesburg registration, but also we were occasionally stopped by villagers for interrogation, and were accused of collaborating with the Pretoria government. The problems we encountered, therefore, came not only from the white establishment but also from some blacks. Having been out of the country for five years. I was viewed as a stranger, especially to young children. However, the presence of the two local teachers who were my research assistants made a great difference. Thus, while conducting research in South Africa was a traumatic experience for me, familiarity with the policy of apartheid and knowing what to expect made the situation somewhat less traumatic. Nonetheless, my conscience has since been bothering me. I do not know to what degree I may have violated ethical codes in the process of meeting the practical need of access, and what penalty I could be made to pay for doing so.

Ethics and Dissemination of Findings

Another major concern I had was how to disseminate the findings to the research participants or to the authorities if they so desired. Although the informed consent the parents had signed stated that "the results of the study will be made available to me at my request," I knew that since I was dealing with an illiterate group, the meaning of the consent form would not be understood. Since no promises were made in writing to the authorities, I decided to send copies of the dissertation to only a few universities in the homelands. For my safety, I did not send a copy to Pretoria. However, suppose the government of Pretoria had forced me to make a written promise to send findings as a condition to obtaining approval to enter white-owned farm areas? If I had signed a contract in order to get what I wanted, then refused to deliver for fear of my safety—would this be regarded as a "criminal act" by the ASA, and would I be made to confess my "sins"? I am not in a position to answer these questions and will leave them up to the Association. However, below I offer a few suggestions that might help alleviate difficulties when scientists transplant ethical codes to authoritarian contexts.

Discussion

. . . To date, very little work has been done either by professional organizations or by individuals to address the special ethical considerations of conducting research in an authoritarian society. Little information has been published about problems involved in undertaking research in repressive societies such as South Africa, the People's Republic of China, the Middle East, the Soviet Union, and various Latin American countries. The lack of such reports may be motivated by the fear (on the part of the researchers and the funding agencies) that the governments of these countries might then make it hard for outsiders to conduct research.

Mosher's (1985) report on his experiences in the People's Republic of China is one rare example. In his thought-provoking and controversial book, *Journey to the Forbidden China*, Mosher relates how he was told by Chinese officials that, despite his stamped travel permit, he had entered a restricted region—and must confess to having willfully violated the People's Republic of China's Travel Regulations for Foreigners. Although he managed to extricate himself from this predicament, this led to his abrupt departure from the PRC and, even worse, to the charge of espionage that the Chinese officials leveled against him.

Certain social scientists have addressed covert research in general rather than research which relates specifically to repressive societies. For example, Bulmer (1982) points out that the researcher may be entitled, and indeed compelled, to adopt covert methods. He maintains that the social scientist is justified in using such measures where necessary in order to achieve the higher objective of scientific truth. Bulmer's argument ties to the context of repressive societies and can be extended to the South African situation. Galliher (1982:159–60) also addresses this issue:

> The question is how much honor is proper for the sociologist in studying the membership and organization of what he considers an essentially dishonorable, morally outrageous, and destructive enterprise? Is not the failure of sociology to uncover corrupt, illegitimate, covert practices of government or industry because of the supposed prohibition of professions tantamount to supporting such practices?

Although Galliher is referring to doing research directly on the powerful (government and industry), one can also conduct research among the oppressed with the intention of exposing those in power.

Appelbaum, Lidz, and Meisel (1987) suggest that discussions of informed consent in medical settings must be supplemented by hands-on training. They propose that students be taught "how to communicate information, facilitate patient participation, and handle questions of impaired competency and voluntariness" (Appelbaum, Lidz, and Meisel 1987:265–66). As my discussion of my own research project has illustrated, securing truly informed consent is just as problematic (if not more so) for researchers doing fieldwork in authoritarian and/or impoverished societies as it is for medical practitioners. Universities should prepare prospective researchers for what lies ahead in the field. The training and guidance that graduate students currently receive about informed consent and what it entails is insufficient. It barely covers the applicability and relevance of informed consent in closed societies.

A major part of graduate training should emphasize that ethical codes designed in one context may not apply across cultures, and/or across time. Ethical codes designed in the relatively liberal, economically stable, politically "safe," and literate societies of North America and Europe are irrelevant to research practices in an authoritarian context such as South Africa. Furthermore, it should be emphasized that some ethical codes that applied in the 1950s may not be applicable in the 1990s. The training should also stress that informed consent is fundamentally limited and limiting. As the guideline regarding informed consent stands at present, it is only suited for use by middle class social scientists for studying middle class populations, or business contractors who fulfill the requirement of knowledgeability, voluntary participation, and competent choice.

Western academic institutions should also study what guidelines work in which places, under what conditions, and for whom, before sending their students to other countries to conduct research. They should consult black South African scholars who are in the United States or abroad to strategize ways for doing research in that country. There is, further, a need for scientists in Africa to Africanize research to meet the needs of Africans, rather than to adopt Anglo- and Euro-centric ethics and methods of research.

Finally, any professional code is useful only as a guideline or as a moral pathfinder sensitizing students, researchers, and supervisors to ethical elements prior, during, and after the project (Punch 1986). When major decisions are to be made, the responsibility should rest with the individual investigator, who presumably is cognizant of the professional codes, the politics, and the culture under which the subjects live. Most important, professional associations must examine the relevance of informed consent in authoritarian societies. I suggest that the research codes include a guideline that reads: "When one conducts research in an authoritarian society, covert research may be necessary in order to expose the powerful." Is this too much of a risk for such associations to take?

References

Academe. (1981, December). Regulations governing research on human subjects: Academic freedom and the institutional review board, 358–370.

American Sociological Association. (1988). Proposed revisions to code of ethics. Washington, DC: American Sociological Association.

Appelbaum, P. S., Lidz, C. W., & Meisel, A. (1987). *Informed consent: Legal theory and clinical practice*. New York: Oxford University Press.

Bulmer, M. (1982). *Social research ethics*. New York: Holmes and Meier.

Galliher, J. F. (1982). The protection of human subjects: a re-examination of the professional code of ethics. In M. Bulmer (Ed.), *Social research ethics*, (pp. 159–160). New York: Holmes and Meier.

Goduka, I. N. (1987). Behavioral development of black South African children: An ecological approach. Ph.D. Dissertation, Michigan State University.

Lidz, C. W., Meisel, A., Zerubavel, E., Carter, M., Sestak, R. M., & Roth, L. H. (1984). *Informed consent: Study of decisionmaking in psychiatry*. New York: The Guilford Press.

Mosher, S. W. (1985). *Journey to the forbidden China*. New York: The Free Press.

Nasson, B. (1984). Bitter harvest: Farm schooling for black South Africans. Second Carnegie Inquiry into Poverty and Development in Southern Africa (Paper no. 97). Rondebosch, Cape Town, School of Economics.

Punch, M. (1986). *The politics and ethics of fieldwork*. London: Sage.

Van den Berghe, P. R.. (1968). Research in South Africa: The story of my experiences with tyranny. In G. Sjoberg (Ed.), *Ethics, politics, and social research*. pp. 185–186). Cambridge: Schenkman.

Questions

1. In what ways does South African culture differ from U.S. culture?

2. How did Goduka's personal background and training make her research project difficult? How did it make it easier? If you were to conduct research in South Africa, how would your background affect the research process?

3. What do you think was the biggest problem that Goduka faced while she was in South Africa?

4. Which of the guidelines listed in the code of ethics of the American Sociological Association (ASA) did Goduka violate? Provide examples to support your argument.

5. What were some dangers that Goduka encountered while doing research in South Africa? Would you have taken these risks? Why or why not?

6. Goduka is one of a growing number of researchers who have had problems doing research in other cultures because the ASA's code of ethics is culture bound. Do you think that the code of ethics should be changed to facilitate cross-cultural research? Why or why not?

7. If a South African researcher were to come to the United States to do research on children, what kinds of problems might he or she encounter? How would these problems compare to those faced by Goduka?

ANYBODY'S SON WILL DO

GWYNNE DYER

"Anybody's Son Will Do," by Gwynne Dyer, reprinted from War, *1985. Copyright © by Crown Publishers.*

How do young men and women become soldiers? How are they taught to kill other human beings? What are the dynamics of the socialization process that allows such a vivid transformation of a person's identity? This selection reveals what is involved in basic training in the U.S. military and how this training helps establish the esprit de corps *that is necessary to make soldiers out of civilians.*

. . . All soldiers are born civilians. The method for turning young men into soldiers—people who kill other people and expose themselves to death—is basic training. It's essentially the same all over the world, and it always has been, because young men everywhere are pretty much alike.

Human beings are fairly malleable, especially when they are young and in every young man there are attitudes for any army to work with: the inherited values and postures, more or less dimly recalled, of the tribal warriors who were once the model for every young boy to emulate. Civilization did not involve a sudden clean break in the way people behave, but merely the progressive distortion and redirection of all the ways in which people in the old tribal societies used to behave, and modern definitions of maleness still contain a great deal of the old warrior ethic. The anarchic machismo of the primitive warrior is not what modern armies really need in their soldiers, but it does provide them with promising raw material for the transformation they must work in their recruits.

Just how this transformation is wrought varies from time to time and from country to country. In totally militarized societies—ancient Sparta, the samurai class of medieval Japan, the areas controlled by organizations like the Eritrean People's Liberation Front today[1]—it begins at puberty or before, when the young boy is immersed in a disciplined society in which only the military values are allowed to penetrate. In more sophisticated modern societies, the process is briefer and more concentrated, and the way it works is much more visible.

. . .

. . . Soldiers are not just robots, they are ordinary human beings with national and personal loyalties, and many of them do feel the need for some patriotic or ideological justification for what they do. But which nation, which ideology, does not matter: men will fight as well and die as bravely for the Khmer Rouge as for "God, King, and Country." Soldiers are the instruments of politicians and priests, ideologues and strategists, who may have high national or moral purposes in mind, but the men down in the trenches fight for more basic motives. The closer you get to the front line, the fewer abstract nouns you hear.

Armies know this. It is their business to get men to fight, and they have had a long time to work out the best way of doing it. All of them pay lip service to the symbols and slogans of their political masters, though the amount of time they must devote to this activity varies from country to country. It is less in the United States than in the Soviet Union, and it is still less in a country like Israel, which actually fights frequent wars. Nor should it be thought that the armies are hypocritical—most of their members really do believe in their particular national symbols and slogans. But their secret is that they know these are not the things that sustain men in combat. . . .

. . . In countries where the army must extract its recruits in their late teens, whether voluntarily or by conscription, from a civilian environment that does not share the military values, basic training involves a brief but intense period of indoctrination whose purpose is not really to teach the recruits basic military skills, but rather to change their values and their loyalties. "I guess you could say we brainwash them a little bit," admitted a U.S. Marine drill instructor, "but you know they're good people." . . .

It's easier if you catch them young. You can train older men to be soldiers; it's done in every major war. But you can never get them to believe that they like it, which is the major reason armies try to get their recruits before they are twenty There are other reasons too, of course, like the physical fitness, lack of dependents, and economic dispensability of teenagers, that make armies prefer them, but the most important qualities teenagers bring to basic training are enthusiasm and naiveté. Many of them actively want the discipline and the closely structured environment that the armed forces will provide, so there is no need for the recruiters to deceive the lads about what will happen to them after they join.

> There is discipline. There is drill. . . . When you are relying on your mates and they are relying on you, there's no room for slackness or sloppiness. If you're not prepared to accept the rules, you're better off where you are.
> —*British army recruiting advertisement, 1976*

People are not born soldiers, they become soldiers. . . . And it should not begin at the moment when a new recruit is enlisted into the ranks, but rather much earlier, at the time of the first signs of maturity, during the time of adolescent dreams.

—Red Star *(Soviet army newspaper), 1973*

Young civilians who have volunteered and have been accepted by the Marine Corps arrive at Parris Island, the Corps East Coast facility for basic training, in a state of considerable excitement and apprehension: most are aware that they are about to undergo an extraordinary and very difficult experience. But they do not make their own way to the base; rather they trickle in to Charleston airport on various flights throughout the day on which their training platoon is due to form, and are held there, in a state of suppressed but mounting nervous tension, until late in the evening. When the buses finally come to carry them the seventy-six miles to Parris Island, it is often after midnight—and this is not an administrative oversight. The shock treatment they are about to receive will work most efficiently if they are worn out and somewhat disoriented when they arrive.

The basic training organization is a machine, processing several thousand young men every month, and every facet and gear of it has been designed with the sole purpose of turning civilians into Marines as efficiently as possible. Provided it can have total control over their bodies and their environment for approximately three months, it can practically guarantee converts. Parris Island provides that controlled environment, and the recruits do not set foot outside it again until they graduate as Marine privates eleven weeks later.

> They're allowed to call home, so long as it doesn't get out of hand—every three weeks or so they can call home and make sure everything's all right, if they haven't gotten a letter or there's a particular set of circumstances. If it's a case of an emergency call coming in, then they're allowed to accept that call; if not, one of my staff will take the message. . . .
>
> In some cases I'll get calls from parents who haven't quite gotten adjusted to the idea that their son had cut the strings—and in a lot of cases that's what they're doing. The military provides them with an opportunity to leave home but they're still in a rather secure environment.
>
> —*Captain Brassington, USMC*

For the young recruits, basic training is the closest thing their society can offer to a formal rite of passage, and the institution probably stands in an unbroken line of descent from the lengthy ordeals by which young males in precivilized groups were initiated into the adult community of warriors. But in civilized societies it is a highly functional institution whose product is not anarchic warriors, but trained soldiers.

Basic training is not really about teaching people skills; it's about changing them so that they can do things they wouldn't have dreamt of otherwise. It works by applying enormous physical and mental pressure to men who have been isolated from their normal civilian environment and placed in one where the only right way to think and behave is the way the Marine Corps wants them to. The key word the men who run the machine use to describe this process is *motivation.*

> I can motivate a recruit and in third phase, if I tell him to jump off the third deck, he'll jump off the third deck. Like I said before, it's a captive audience and I can train that guy; I can get him to do anything I want him to do. . . . They're good kids and they're out to do the right thing. We get some bad lads, but you know, we weed those out. But as far as motivation—here, we can motivate them to do anything you want, in recruit training.
>
> —*USMC drill instructor, Parris Island*

The first three days the raw recruits spend at Parris Island are actually relatively easy, though they are hustled and shouted at continuously. It is during this time that they are documented and inoculated, receive uniforms, and learn the basic orders of drill that will enable young Americans (who are not very accustomed to this aspect of life) to do everything simultaneously in large groups. But the most important thing that happens in "forming" is the surrender of the recruits' own clothes, their hair—all the physical evidence of their individual civilian identities.

During a period of only seventy-two hours, in which they are allowed little sleep, the recruits lay aside their former lives in a series of hasty rituals (like being shaven to the scalp) whose symbolic significance is quite clear to them even though they are quite deliberately given absolutely no time for reflection, or any hint that they might have the option of turning back from their commitment. The men in charge of them know how delicate a tightrope they are walking, though, because at this stage the recruits are still newly caught civilians who have not yet made their ultimate inward submission to the discipline of the Corps.

Forming Day One makes me nervous. You've got a whole new mob of recruits, you know, sixty or seventy depending, and they don't know anything. You don't know what kind of a reaction you're going to get from the stress you're going to lay on them, and it just worries me the first day.

Things could happen, I'm not going to lie to you. Something might happen. A recruit might decide he doesn't want any part of this stuff and maybe take a poke at you or something like that. In a situation like that it's going to be a spur-of-the-moment thing and that worries me.

—*USMC drill instructor*

But it rarely happens. The frantic bustle of forming is designed to give the recruit no time to think about resisting what is happening to him. And so the recruits emerge from their initiation into the system stripped of their civilian clothes, shorn of their hair, and deprived of whatever confidence in their own identity they may previously have had as eighteen-year-olds, like so many blanks ready to have the Marine identity impressed upon them.

The first stage in any conversion process is the destruction of an individual's former beliefs, and confidence, and his reduction to a position of helplessness and need. It isn't really as drastic as all that, of course, for three days cannot cancel out eighteen years; the inner thoughts and the basic character are not erased. But the recruits have already learned that the only acceptable behavior is to repress any unorthodox thoughts and to mimic the character the Marine Corps wants.

• • •

The training, when it starts, seems impossibly demanding physically for most of the recruits—and then it gets harder week by week. There is a constant barrage of abuse and insults aimed at the recruits, with the deliberate purpose of breaking down their pride and so destroying their ability to resist the transformation of values and attitudes that the Corps intends them to undergo. At the same time the demands for constant alertness and for instant obedience are continuously stepped up, and the standards by which the dress and behavior of the recruits are judged become steadily more unforgiving. But it is all carefully calculated by the men who run the machine, who think and talk in terms of the stress they are placing on the recruits: "We take so many c.c.'s of stress and we administer it to each man—they should be a little bit scared and they

should be unsure, but they're adjusting." The aim is to keep the training arduous but just within most of the recruits' capability to withstand. One of the most striking achievements of the drill instructors is to create and maintain the illusion that basic training is an extraordinary challenge, one that will set those who graduate apart from others, when in fact almost everyone can succeed. . . .

Not even physical violence is necessary to effect the transformation, though it has been used by most armies at most times.

It's not what it was fifteen years ago down here. The Marine Corps still occupies the position of a tool which the society uses when it feels like that is a resort that they have to fall to. Our society changes as all societies do, and our society felt that through enlightened training methods we could still produce the same product—and when you examine it, they're right. . . . Our 100 c.c.'s of stress is really all we need, not two gallons of it, which is what it used to be. . . . In some cases with some of the younger drill instructors it was more an initiation than it was an acute test, and so we introduced extra officers and we select our drill instructors to "fine-tune" it.

—*Captain Brassington, USMC*

• • •

Just the sheer physical exercise, administered in massive doses, soon has the recruits feeling stronger and more competent than ever before. Inspections, often several times daily, quickly build up their ability to wear the uniform and carry themselves like real Marines, which is a considerable source of pride. The inspections also help to set up the pattern in the recruits of unquestioning submission to military authority: standing stock-still staring straight ahead, while somebody else examines you closely for faults is about as extreme a ritual act of submission as you can make with your clothes on.

But they are not submitting themselves merely to the abusive sergeant making unpleasant remarks about the hair in their nostrils. All around them are deliberate reminders—the flags and insignia displayed on parade, the military music, the marching formations and drill instructors' cadenced calls—of the idealized organization, the "brotherhood" to which they will be admitted as full members if they submit and conform. Nowhere in the armed forces are the military courtesies so elaborately observed, the staffs' uniforms so immaculate (some DIs change several times a day), and the ritual aspects of military life so highly visible as on a basic training establishment.

Even the seeming inanity of close-order drill has a practical role in the conversion process. It has been over a century since mass formations of men were of any use on the battlefield, but every army in the world still drills its troops, especially during basic training, because marching in formation, with every man moving his body in the same way at the same moment, is a direct physical way of learning two things a soldier must believe: that orders have to be obeyed automatically and instantly, and that you are no longer an individual, but part of a group.

The recruits' total identification with the other members of their unit is the most important lesson of all, and everything possible is done to foster it. They spend almost every waking moment together—a recruit alone is an anomaly to be looked into at once—and during most of that time they are enduring shared hardships. They also undergo collective punishments, often for the misdeed or omission of a single individual (talking in the ranks, a bed not swept under during barracks inspection), which is a highly effective way of suppressing any tendencies toward individualism. And, of course, the DIs place relentless emphasis on competition with other "serials" in training: there may be something infinitely pathetic to outsiders about a marching group of anonymous recruits chanting, "Lift your heads and hold them high, 3313 is a-passin' by," but it doesn't seem like that to the men in the ranks.

Nothing is quite so effective in building up a group's morale and solidarity, though, as a steady diet of small triumphs. Quite early in basic training the recruits begin to do things that seem, at first sight, quite dangerous: descend by ropes from fifty-foot towers, cross yawning gaps hand-over-hand on high wires (known as the Slide for Life, of course), and the like. The common denominator is that these activities are daunting but not really dangerous: the ropes will prevent anyone from falling to his death off the rappelling tower, and there is a pond of just the right depth—deep enough to cushion a falling man, but not deep enough that he is likely to drown—under the Slide for Life. The goal is not to kill recruits, but to build up their confidence as individuals and as a group by allowing them to overcome apparently frightening obstacles.

> You have an enemy here at Parris Island. The enemy that you're going to have at Parris Island is in every one of us. It's in the form of cowardice. The most rewarding experience you're going to have in recruit training is standing on line every evening, and you'll be able to look into each other's eyes, and you'll be able to say to each other with your eyes: "By God, we've made it one more day! We've defeated the coward."
>
> —*Captain Pingree, USMC*

> Number on deck, sir, forty-five . . . highly motivated, truly dedicated, rompin', stompin', bloodthirsty, kill-crazy United States Marine Corps recruits, SIR!
>
> —*Marine chant, Parris Island, 1982*

If somebody does fail a particular test, he tends to be alone, for the hurdles are deliberately set low enough that most recruits can clear them if they try. In any large group of people there is usually a goat: someone whose intelligence or manner or lack of physical stamina marks him for failure and contempt. The competent drill instructor, without deliberately setting up this unfortunate individual for disgrace, will use his failure to strengthen the solidarity and confidence of the rest. When one hapless young man fell off the Slide for Life into the pond, for example, his drill instructor shouted the usual invective—"Well, get out of the water. Don't contaminate it all day"—and then delivered the payoff line: "Go back and change your clothes. You're useless to your unit now."

"Useless to your unit" is the key phrase, and all the recruits know that what it means is "useless in battle." The Marine drill instructors at Parris Island know exactly what they are doing to the recruits, and why. They are not rear-echelon people filling comfortable jobs, but the most dedicated and intelligent NCOs the Marine Corps can find: even now, many of them have combat experience. The Corps has a clear-eyed understanding of precisely what it is training its recruits for—combat—and it ensures that those who do the training keep that objective constantly in sight. . . .

Combat is the ultimate reality that Marines—or any other soldiers, under any flag—have to deal with. Physical fitness, weapons training, battle drills, are all indispensable elements of basic training, and it is absolutely essential that the recruits learn the attitudes of group loyalty and interdependency which will be their sole hope of survival and success in combat. The training inculcates or fosters all of those things, and even by the halfway point in the eleven-week course, the recruits are generally responding with enthusiasm to their tasks.

But there is nothing in all this (except the weapons drill) that would not be found in the training camp of a professional football team. What sets soldiers apart is their willingness to kill. But it is not a willingness that comes easily to most men—even young men who have been provided with uniforms, guns, and official approval to kill those whom their government has designated as enemies. They will, it is true, fall very readily into the stereotypes of the tribal warrior group. Indeed, most of them have had at least a glancing acquaintance in their early teens with gangs (more or less violent, depending on, among other things, the neighborhood), the modern relic of that ancient institution.

And in many ways what basic training produces is the uniformed equivalent of a modern street gang—a bunch of tough, confident lads full of bloodthirsty talk. But gangs don't actually kill each other in large numbers. If they behaved the way armies do, you'd need trucks to clean the bodies off the streets every morning. They're held back by the civilian belief—the normal human belief—that killing another person is an awesome act with huge consequences. . . .

There is such a thing as a "natural soldier": the kind of man who derives his greatest satisfaction from male companionship, from excitement, and from the conquering of physical and psychological obstacles. He doesn't necessarily want to kill people as such, but he will have no objections if it occurs within a moral framework that gives him a justification—like war—and if it is the price of gaining admission to the kind of environment he craves. Whether such men are born or made, I do not know, but most of them end up in armies (and many move on again to become mercenaries, because regular army life in peacetime is too routine and boring).

But armies are not full of such men. They are so rare that they form only a modest fraction even of small professional armies, mostly congregating in the commando-type special forces. In large conscript armies they virtually disappear beneath the weight of numbers of more ordinary men. And it is these ordinary men, who do not like combat at all, that the armies must persuade to kill. Until only a generation ago, they did not even realize how bad a job they were doing.

. . .

Combat of the sort we know today, even at the infantryman's level—let along the fighter pilots—simply could not occur unless military organizations put immense effort into reshaping the behavior of individuals to fit their unusual and exacting requirements. The military institution, for all its imposing presence, is a highly artificial structure that is maintained only by constant endeavor. And if ordinary people's behavior is malleable in the direction the armed forces require, it is equally open to change in other directions. . . .

Endnote

1. Eritrea, an Italian colony from 1885 to 1941, was annexed by Ethiopia in 1962. After a 30-year civil war, Eritrea gained its independence in 1992—Ed.

Questions

1. Why does the military prefer to train young men as opposed to old men? As opposed to women?

2. What does the article title "Anybody's Son Will Do" imply?

3. What procedures does the military use to help strip away a recruit's former identity?

4. A total institution is "a place of residence and work where a large number of like-situated individuals, cut off from the wider society for an appreciable period of time, together lead an enclosed, formally administered round of life" (Goffman, 1961). The three most common total institutions are military training (i.e., bootcamp), mental hospitals, and prisons. How might the process used to resocialize military recruits be applied to one of these other kinds of institutions? How might the process differ?

THE PRESENTATION OF SELF IN EVERYDAY LIFE

ERVING GOFFMAN

"The Presentation of Self in Everyday Life," by Erving Goffman, reprinted from The Presentation of Self in Everyday Life, *1959, Doubleday Anchor Books. Copyright © by Erving Goffman. pp. 1–16. www.randomhouse.com*

Erving Goffman's most lasting contributions to sociology are likely his writings on "impression management." This concept is crucial for understanding what's known as the symbolic interactionist perspective—the belief that interactions are constructed based on the use of mutually understood symbols, objects and language. In the introduction to his classic text, The Presentation of Self in Everyday Life, Goffman presents several key concepts including impression management, the "situation," and sign-vehicles. While reading this selection, think about how these concepts lay the groundwork for the eventual introduction of "front-stage" and "back-stage" and how these concepts are critical for understanding human interaction.

When an individual enters the presence of others, they commonly seek to acquire information about him or to bring into play information about him already possessed. They will be interested in his general socio-economic status, his conception of self, his attitude toward them, his competence, his trustworthiness, etc. Although some of this information seems to be sought almost as an end in itself, there are usually quite practical reasons for acquiring it. Information about the individual helps to define the situation, enabling others to know in advance what he will expect of them and what they may expect of him. Informed in these ways, the others will know how best to act in order to call forth a desired response from him.

For those present, many sources of information become accessible and many carriers (or "sign-vehicles") become available for conveying this information. If unacquainted with the individual, observers can glean clues from his conduct and appearance which allow them to apply their previous experience with individuals roughly similar to the one before them or, more important, to apply untested stereotypes to him. They can also assume from past experience that only individuals of a particular kind are likely to be found in a given social setting. They can rely on what the individual says about himself or on documentary evidence he provides as to who and what he is. If they know, or know of, the individual by virtue of experience prior to the interaction, they can rely on assumptions as to the persistence and generality of psychological traits as a means of predicting his present and future behavior.

However, during the period in which the individual is in the immediate presence of the others, few events may occur which directly provide the others with the conclusive information they will need if they are to direct wisely their own activity. Many crucial facts lie beyond the time and place of interaction or lie concealed within it. For example, the "true" or "real" attitudes, beliefs, and emotions of the individual can be ascertained only indirectly, through his avowals or through what appears to be involuntary expressive behavior. Similarly, if the individual offers the others a product or service, they will often find that during the interaction there will be no time and place immediately available for eating the pudding that the proof can be found in. They will be forced to accept some events as conventional or natural signs of something not directly available to the senses. In Ichheiser's terms,[1] the individual will have to act so that he intentionally or unintentionally *expresses* himself, and the others will in turn have to be *impressed* in some way by him. . . .

Taking communication in both its narrow and broad sense, one finds that when the individual is in the immediate presence of others, his activity will have a promissory character. The others are likely to find that they must accept the individual on faith, offering him a just return while he is present before them in exchange for something whose true value will not be established until after he has left their presence. (Of course, the others also live by inference in their dealings with the physical world, but it is only in the world of social interaction that the objects about which they make inferences will purposely facilitate and hinder this inferential process.) The security that they justifiably feel in making inferences about the individual will vary, of course, depending on such factors as the amount of information they already possess about him, but no amount of such past evidence can entirely obviate the necessity of acting on the basis of inferences. As William I. Thomas suggested:

> It is also highly important for us to realize that we do not as a matter of fact lead our lives, make our decisions, and reach our goals in everyday life either statistically or scientifically. We live by inference. I am, let us say, your guest. You do not know, you cannot determine scientifically, that I will not steal your money or your spoons. But inferentially I will not, and inferentially you have me as a guest.[2]

Let us now turn from the others to the point of view of the individual who presents himself before them. He may wish them to think highly of him, or to think that he thinks highly of them, or to perceive how in fact he feels toward them, or to obtain no clear-cut impression; he may wish to ensure sufficient harmony so that the interaction can be sustained, or to defraud, get rid of, confuse, mislead, antagonize, or insult them. Regardless of the particular objective which the individual has in mind and of his motive for having this objective, it will be in his interests to control the conduct of the others, especially their responsive treatment of him. This control is achieved largely by influencing the definition of the situation which the others come to formulate, and he can influence this definition by expressing himself in such a way as to give them the kind of impression that will lead them to act voluntarily in accordance with his own plan. Thus, when an individual appears in the presence of others, there will usually be some reason for him to mobilize his activity so that it will convey an impression to others which it is in his interests to convey. Since a girl's dormitory mates will glean evidence of her popularity from the calls she receives on the phone, we can suspect that some girls will arrange for calls to be made, and Willard Waller's finding can be anticipated:

> It has been reported by many observers that a girl who is called to the telephone in the dormitories will often allow herself to be called several times, in order to give all the other girls ample opportunity to hear her paged.[3]

Of the two kinds of communication—expressions given and expressions given off—this report will be primarily concerned with the latter, with the more theatrical and contextual kind, the non-verbal, presumably unintentional kind, whether this communication be purposely engineered or not. As an example of what we must try to examine, I would like to cite at length a novelistic incident in which Preedy, a vacationing Englishman, makes his first appearance on the beach of his summer hotel in Spain:

> But in any case he took care to avoid catching anyone's eye. First of all, he had to make it clear to those potential companions of his holiday that they were of no concern to him whatsoever. He stared through them, round them, over them—eyes lost in space. The beach might have been empty. If by chance a ball was thrown his way, he looked surprised; then let a smile of amusement lighten his face (Kindly Preedy), looked round dazed to see that there were people on the beach, tossed it back with a smile to himself and not a smile at the people, and then resumed carelessly his nonchalant survey of space.
>
> But it was time to institute a little parade, the parade of the Ideal Preedy. By devious handlings he gave any who wanted to look a chance to see the title of his book—a Spanish translation of Homer, classic thus, but not daring, cosmopolitan too—and then gathered together his beach-wrap and bag into a neat sand-resistant pile (Methodical and Sensible Preedy), roll slowly to stretch at ease his huge frame (Big-Cat Preedy), and tossed aside his sandals (Carefree Preedy, after all).
>
> The marriage of Preedy and the sea! There were alternative rituals. The first involved the stroll that turns into a run and a dive straight into the water, thereafter smoothing into a strong splashless crawl towards the horizon. But of course not really to the horizon. Quite suddenly he would turn on to his back and thrash great white splashes with his legs, somehow thus showing that he could have swum further had he wanted to,

and then would stand up a quarter out of water for all to see who it was.

> The alternative course was simpler, it avoided the cold-water shock and it avoided the risk of appearing too high-spirited. The point was to appear to be so used to the sea, the Mediterranean, and this particular beach, that one might as well be in the sea as out of it. It involved a slow stroll down and into the edge of the water—not even noticing his toes were wet, land and water all the same to him!—with his eyes up at the sky gravely surveying portents, invisible to others, of the weather (Local Fisherman Preedy).[4]

The novelist means us to see that Preedy is improperly concerned with the extensive impressions he feels his sheer bodily action is giving off to those around him. We can malign Preedy further by assuming that he has acted merely in order to give a particular impression, that this is a false impression, and that the others present receive either no impression at all, or, worse still, the impression that Preedy is affectedly trying to cause them to receive this particular impression. But the important point for us here is that the kind of impression Preedy thinks he is making is in fact the kind of impression that others correctly and incorrectly glean from someone in their midst.

I have said that when an individual appears before others his actions will influence the definition of the situation which they come to have. Sometimes the individual will act in a thoroughly calculating manner, expressing himself in a given way solely in order to give the kind of impression to others that is likely to evoke from them a specific response he is concerned to obtain. Sometimes the individual will be calculating in his activity but be relatively unaware that this is the case. Sometimes he will intentionally and consciously express himself in a particular way, but chiefly because the tradition of his group or social status require this kind of expression and not because of any particular response (other than vague acceptance or approval) that is likely to be evoked from those impressed by the expression. Sometimes the traditions of an individual's role will lead him to give a well-designed impression of a particular kind and yet he may be neither consciously nor unconsciously disposed to create such an impression. The others, in their turn, may be suitably impressed by the individual's efforts to convey something, or may misunderstand the situation and come to conclusions that are warranted neither by the individual's intent nor by the facts. In any case, in so far as the others act *as if* the individual had conveyed a particular impression, we may take a functional or pragmatic view and say that the individual has "effectively" projected a given definition of the situation and "effectively" fostered the understanding that a given state of affairs obtains.

There is one aspect of the others' response that bears special comment here. Knowing that the individual is likely to present himself in a light that is favorable to him, the others may divide what they witness into two parts; a part that is relatively easy for the individual to manipulate at will, being chiefly his verbal assertions, and a part in regard to which he seems to have little concern or control, being chiefly derived from the expressions he gives off. The others may then use what are considered to be the ungovernable aspects of his expressive behavior as a check upon the validity of what is conveyed by the governable aspects. In this a fundamental asymmetry is demonstrated in the communication process, the individual presumably being aware of only one stream of his communication, the witnesses of this stream and one other. For example, in Shetland Isle one crofter's wife, in serving native dishes to a visitor from the mainland of Britain, would listen with a polite smile to his polite claims of liking what he was eating; at the same time she would take note of the rapidity with which the visitor lifted his fork or spoon to his mouth, the eagerness with which he passed food into his mouth, and the gusto expressed in chewing the food, using these signs as a check on the stated feelings of the eater. The same woman, in order to discover what one acquaintance (A) "actually" thought of another acquaintance (B), would wait until B was in the presence of A but engaged in conversation with still another person (C). She would then covertly examine the facial expressions of A as he regarded B in conversation with C. Not being in conversation with B, and not being directly observed by him, A would sometimes relax usual constraints and tactful deceptions, and freely express what he was "actually" feeling about B. This Shetlander, in short, would observe the unobserved observer.

Now given the fact that others are likely to check up on the more controllable aspects of behavior by means of the less controllable, one can expect that sometimes the individual will try to exploit this very possibility, guiding the impression he makes through behavior felt to be reliably informing.[5] For example, in gaining admission to a tight social circle, the participant observer may not only wear an accepting look while listening to an informant, but may also be careful to wear the same look when observing the informant talking to others; observers of the observer will then not as easily discover where he actually stands. A specific illustration may be cited from Shetland Isle. When a neighbor dropped in to have a cup of tea, he would ordinarily wear at least a hint of an expectant warm smile as he passed through the door into the cottage. Since lack of physical obstructions outside the cottage and lack of light within it usually made it possible to observe the visitor unobserved as he approached the house, islanders sometimes took pleasure in watching the visitor drop whatever expression he was manifesting and replace it with a sociable one just before reaching the door. However, some visitors, in appreciating that this examination was occurring, would blindly adopt a social face a long distance from the house, thus ensuring the projection of a constant image.

This kind of control upon the part of the individual reinstates the symmetry of the communication process, and sets the stage for a kind of information game—a potentially infinite cycle of concealment, discovery, false revelation, and rediscovery. It should be added that since the others are likely to be relatively unsuspicious of the presumably unguided aspect of the individual's conduct, he can gain much by controlling it. The others of course may sense that the individual is manipulating the presumably spontaneous aspects of his behavior, and seek in this very act of manipulation some shading of conduct that the individual has not managed to control. This again provides a check upon the individuals behavior, this time his presumably uncalculated behavior, thus re-establishing the asymmetry of the communication process. Here I would like only to add the suggestion that the arts of piercing an individual's effort at calculated unintentionality seem better developed than our capacity to manipulate our own behavior, so that regardless of how many steps have occurred in the information game, the witness is likely to have the advantage over the actor, and the initial asymmetry of the communication process is likely to be retained.

When we allow that the individual projects a definition of the situation when he appears before others, we must also see that the others, however passive their role may seem to be, will themselves effectively project a definition of the situation by virtue of their response to the individual and by virtue of any lines of action they initiate to him. Ordinarily the definitions of the situation projected by the several different participants are sufficiently attuned to one another so that open contradiction will not occur. I do not mean that there

will be the kind of consensus that arises when each individual present candidly expresses what he really feels and honestly agrees with the expressed feelings of the others present. This kind of harmony is an optimistic ideal and in any case not necessary for the smooth working of society. Rather, each participant is expected to suppress his immediate heartfelt feelings, conveying a view of the situation which he feels the others will be able to find at least temporarily acceptable. The maintenance of this surface of agreement, this veneer of consensus, is facilitated by each participant concealing his own wants behind statements which assert values to which everyone present feels obliged to give up service.

. . .

Given the fact that the individual effectively projects a definition of the situation when he enters the presence of others, we can assume that events may occur within the interaction which contradict, discredit, or otherwise throw doubt upon this projection. When these disruptive events occur, the interaction itself may come to a confused and embarrassed halt. Some of the assumptions upon which the responses of the participants had been predicated become untenable, and the participants find themselves lodged in an interaction for which the situation has been wrongly defined and is now no longer defined. At such moments the individual whose presentation has been discredited may feel ashamed while the others present may feel hostile, and all the participants may come to feel ill at ease, nonplussed, out of countenance, embarrassed, experiencing the kind of anomy that is generated when the minute social system of face-to-face interaction breaks down.

In stressing the fact that the initial definition of the situation projected by an individual tends to provide a plan for the co-operative activity that follows—in stressing this action point of view—we must not overlook the crucial fact that any projected definition of the situation also has a distinctive moral character. It is this moral character of projections that will chiefly concern us in this report. Society is organized on the principle that any individual who possesses certain social characteristics has a moral right to expect that others will value and treat him in a correspondingly appropriate way. Connected with this principle is a second, namely that an individual who implicitly or explicitly signifies that he has certain social characteristics ought to have this claim honored by others and ought in fact to be what he claims he is. In consequence, when an individual projects a definition of the situation and thereby makes an implicit or explicit claim to be a person of a particular kind, he automatically exerts a moral demand upon the others, obliging them to value and treat him in the manner that persons of his kind have a right to expect. He also implicitly forgoes all claims to be things he does not appear to be[6] and hence forgoes the treatment that would be appropriate for such individuals. The others find, then, that the individual has informed them as to what is and as to what they ought to see as the "is."

. . .

To summarize, then, I assume that when an individual appears before others he will have many motives for trying to control the impression they receive of the situation. . . . The issues dealt with by stagecraft and stage management are sometimes trivial but they are quite general; they seem to occur everywhere in social life, providing a clear-cut dimension for formal sociological analysis.

Endnotes

1. Ichheiser, G. (1949). Misunderstandings in human relations. Supplement to *The American Journal of Sociology*, 55, 6–7.

2. Quoted in Volkart, E. H. (Ed.) (1951). *Social behavior and personality*. Contributions of W. I. Thomas to Theory and Social Research. New York: Social Science Research Council, 5.

3. Waller, W. The rating and dating complex. *American Sociological Review*. 2, 730.

4. Sansom, W. (1956). *A contest of ladies*. London: Hogarth, 230–232.

5. The widely read and rather sound writings of Stephen Potter are concerned in part with signs that can be engineered to give a shrewd observer the apparently incidental cues he needs to discover concealed virtues the gamesman does not in fact possess.

6. This role of the witness in limiting what it is the individual can be has been stressed by Existentialists, who see it as a basic threat to individual freedom. See Sartre, J.-P. (1956). *Being and nothingness*. (H. E. Barnes, Trans.). New York: Philosophical Library, 365 ff.

Questions

1. Define "sign-vehicles." What is the significance of sign-vehicles?

2. How does the "definition of the situation" affect the presentation of the self?

3. According to Goffman, there are two components of any projected behavior: the governable and the ungovernable. What is the value of the ungovernable aspect of behavior?

4. The concept that Goffman is most known for is "impression management," which includes a front-stage and back-stage component. Explain how the concepts introduced in this selection lead to the development of the front-stage, back-stage distinction.

GROUPTHINK

IRVING L. JANIS

"Groupthink," by Irving L. Janis, reprinted from Groupthink: Psychological Studies of Policy Decisions and Fiascoes, *Second Edition, 1982. Copyright © by Houghton Mifflin. pp. 2–13.*

It seems as if everybody is now familiar with the term "groupthink," the process whereby groups make decisions that run counter to all logic and common sense. However, many people misuse the term, and many others do not have a firm understanding of what contributes to the problem of groupthink. In this selection, Irving Janis defines the phenomenon and explains what group characteristics increase the likelihood that "groupthink" will occur.

Nobody Is Perfect

Year after year newscasts and newspapers inform us of collective miscalculations—companies that have unexpectedly gone bankrupt because of misjudging their market, federal agencies that have mistakenly authorized the use of chemical insecticides that poison our environment, and White House executive committees that have made ill-conceived foreign policy decisions that inadvertently bring the major powers to the brink of war. Most people, when they hear about such fiascoes, simply remind themselves that, after all, "organizations are run by human beings," "to err is human," and "nobody is perfect." But platitudinous thoughts about human nature do not help us to understand how and why avoidable miscalculations are made.

Fiasco watchers who are unwilling to set the problem aside in this easy fashion will find that contemporary psychology has something to say (unfortunately not very much) about distortions of thinking and other sources of human error. The deficiencies about which we know the most pertain to disturbances in the behavior of each individual in a decision-making group—temporary states of elation, fear, or anger that reduce

a person's mental efficiency; chronic blind spots arising from a person's social prejudices; shortcomings in information-processing that prevent a person from comprehending the complex consequences of a seemingly made policy decision. One psychologist has suggested that because the information-processing capabilities of every individual are limited, no responsible leader of a large organization ought to make a policy decision without using a computer that is programmed to spell out all the probable benefits and costs of each alternative under consideration. The usual way of trying to counteract the limitations of individuals' mental functioning, however, is to relegate important decisions to groups.

Imperfections of Group Decisions

Groups, like individuals, have shortcomings. Groups can bring out the worst as well as the best in man. Nietzsche went so far as to say that madness is the exception in individuals but the rule in groups. A considerable amount of social science literature shows that in circumstances of extreme crisis, group contagion occasionally gives rise to collective panic, violent acts of scapegoating, and other forms of what could be called group madness. Much more frequent, however, are instances of mindless conformity and collective misjudgment of serious risks, which are collectively laughed off in a clubby atmosphere of relaxed conviviality. Consider what happened a few days before disaster struck the small mining town of Pitcher, Oklahoma, in 1950. The local mining engineer had warned the inhabitants to leave at once because the town had been accidentally undermined and might cave in at any moment. At a Lion's Club meeting of leading citizens, the day after the warning was issued, the members joked about the warning and laughed uproariously when someone arrived wearing a parachute. What the club members were communicating to each other by their collective laughter was that "sensible people like us know better than to take seriously those disaster warnings; we know it can't happen here, to our fine little town." Within a few days, this collective complacency cost some of the these men and their families their lives. . . .

Effects of Group Cohesiveness

In applying the concepts of group dynamics to recent historic policy decisions, I am extending the work of some pioneering social scientists. The power of a face-to-face group to set norms that influence members were emphasized by leading sociologists early in the twentieth century—Charles Horton Cooley and George Herbert Mead. During the same period, William Graham Sumner postulated that in-group solidarity increases when clashes arise with out-groups.

Kurt Lewin, the social psychologist who began using empirical methods to study group dynamics during the 1940s, called attention to the prerequisites for effective group decisions. He described the typical dilemmas faced by executive committees, including wartime groups of military planners who select bomb targets and peacetime groups of policy-makers who try to improve relations between nations. Lewin emphasized the need for fact-finding and objective appraisal of alternatives to determine whether the chosen means will achieve a group's goals. He warned that the lack of objective standards for evaluating goal achievement allows many opportunities for errors of judgment and faulty decisions. Lewin's analysis of the behavior of small groups also emphasized the importance of group cohesiveness—that is, members' positive valuation of the group and their motivation to continue to belong to it. When group cohesiveness is high, all the members express solidarity, mutual liking, and positive feelings about attending meetings and carrying out the routine tasks of the group. Lewin was most interested in the positive effects of group cohesiveness and did not investigate instances when members of cohesive groups make gross errors and fail to correct their shared misjudgments.

. . .

Conformity to Group Norms

In studies of social clubs and other small groups, conformity pressures have frequently been observed. Whenever a member says something that sounds out of line with the group's norms, the other members at first increase their communication with the deviant. Attempts to influence the nonconformist member to revise or tone down his dissident ideas continue as long as most members of the group feel hopeful about talking him into changing his mind. But if they fail after repeated attempts, the amount of communication they direct toward the deviant decreases markedly. The members begin to exclude him, often quite subtly at first and later more obviously, in order to restore the unity of the group. A social psychological experiment conducted by Stanley Schachter with avocation clubs in an American university—and replicated by Schachter and his collaborators in seven European countries— showed that the more cohesive the group and the more

relevant the issue to the goals of the group, the greater is the inclination of the members to reject a nonconformist. Just as the members insulate themselves from outside critics who threaten to disrupt the unity and esprit de corps of their group, they take steps, often without being aware of it, to counteract the disruptive influence of inside critics who are attacking the group's norms.

The norms to which the members of a cohesive group adhere, as Bion's analysis implies, do not always have a positive effect on the quality of the group's performance. Studies in industrial organizations indicate that while the norms of some work groups foster conscientiousness and high productivity, the norms of other, similar work groups foster slowdowns and socializing activities that reduce productivity. The same type of variation in norms that facilitate or interfere with the group's work objectives may be found among policy-making groups in large organizations. . . .

Conceptions of Political Decision-Making

Group dynamics is still in the early stages of scientific development, and much remains to be learned. At present there are only a few concepts and generalizations in which we can have confidence when we are trying to understand the behavior of policy-making groups. Nevertheless, social scientists concerned with policy-making in the government—most notably, Karl Deutsch, Alexander George, and Joseph de Rivera— have started to use group dynamics concepts that hold the promise of enriching political science. The rapprochement between the two fields, however, is still mainly a perspective for the future rather than a current reality.

. . .

What Is Groupthink?

The group dynamics approach is based on the working assumption that the members of policy-making groups, no matter how mindful they may be of their exalted national status and of their heavy responsibilities, are subjected to the pressures widely observed in groups of ordinary citizens. In my earlier research on group dynamics, I was impressed by repeated manifestations of the effects—both unfavorable and favorable—of the social pressures that typically develop in cohesive groups—in infantry platoons, air crews, therapy groups, seminars, and self-study or encounter groups of executives receiving leadership training. In all these groups, just as in the industrial work groups described by other investigators, members tend to evolve informal norms to preserve friendly intragroup relations and these become part of the hidden agenda at their meetings. When conducting research on groups of heavy smokers at a clinic set up to help people stop smoking, I noticed a seemingly irrational tendency for the members to exert pressure on each other to increase their smoking as the time for the final meeting approached. This appeared to be a collusive effort to display mutual dependence and resistance to the termination of the group sessions.

Sometimes, even long before members become concerned about the final separation, clear-cut signs of pressures toward uniformity subvert the fundamental purpose of group meetings. At the second meeting of one group of smokers, consisting of twelve middle-class American men and women, two of the most dominant members took the position that heavy smoking was an almost incurable addiction. The majority of the others soon agreed that no one could be expected to cut down drastically. One heavy smoker, a middle-aged business executive, took issue with this consensus, arguing that by using will power he had stopped smoking since joining the group and that everyone else could do the same. His declaration was followed by a heated discussion, which continued in the halls of the building after the formal meeting adjourned. Most of the others ganged up against the man who was deviating from the group consensus. Then, at the beginning of the next meeting, the deviant announced that he had made an important decision. "When I joined," he said, "I agreed to follow the two main rules required by the clinic—to make a conscientious effort to stop smoking and to attend every meeting. But I have learned from experience in this group that you can only follow one of the rules, you can't follow both. And so, I have decided that I will continue to attend every meeting but I have gone back to smoking two packs a day and I will not make any effort to stop smoking again until after the last meeting." Whereupon, the other members beamed at him and applauded enthusiastically, welcoming him back to the fold. No one commented on the fact that the whole point of the meetings was to help each individual to cut down on smoking as rapidly as possible. As a psychological consultant to the group, I tried to call this to the members' attention, and so did my collaborator, Dr. Michael Kahn. But during that meeting the members managed to ignore our comments and reiterated their consensus that heavy smoking was

an addiction from which no one would be cured except by cutting down very gradually over a long period of time.

This episode—an extreme form of groupthink—was only one manifestation of a general pattern that the group displayed. At every meeting, the members were amiable, reasserted their warm feelings of solidarity, and sought complete concurrence on every important topic, with no reappearance of the unpleasant bickering that would spoil the cozy atmosphere. The concurrence-seeking tendency could be maintained, however, only at the expense of ignoring realistic challenges (like those posed by the psychological consultants) and distorting members' observations of individual differences that would call into question the shared assumption that everyone in the group had the same type of addiction problem. It seemed that in this smoking group I was observing another instance of the groupthink pattern I had encountered in observations of widely contrasting groups whose members came from diverse sectors of society and were meeting together for social, educational, vocational, or other purposes. Just like the group in the smoking clinic, all these different types of groups had shown signs of high cohesiveness and of an accompanying concurrence-seeking tendency that interfered with critical thinking—the central features of groupthink.

I use the term "groupthink" as a quick and easy way to refer to a mode of thinking that people engage in when they are deeply involved in a cohesive ingroup, when the members' strivings for unanimity override their motivation to realistically appraise alternative courses of action. "Groupthink" is a term of the same order as the words in the newspeak vocabulary George Orwell presents in his dismaying *1984*—a vocabulary with terms such as "doublethink" and "crimethink." By putting groupthink with those Orwellian words, I realize that groupthink takes on an invidious connotation. The invidiousness is intentional: Groupthink refers to a deterioration of mental efficiency, reality testing, and moral judgment that results from in-group pressures.

Seven Characteristics of Groupthink

When I began to investigate the Bay of Pigs invasion, the decision to escalate the Korean War, and other fiascoes, for purposes of studying sources of error in foreign policy decision-making, I was initially surprised to discover the persuasiveness of symptoms of groupthink. Although the symptoms that could be discerned from published accounts of the deliberations did not seem as obtrusive as in the face-to-face groups I had observed directly, nevertheless signs of poor decision-making as a result of concurrence-seeking were unmistakable.

After noting the first few examples of grossly miscalculated policy decisions that seemed at least partly attributable to group processes, I began collecting instances of similar fiascoes from a variety of sources such as Harold Wilensky's *Organizational Intelligence* and Barton Whaley's *Stratagem*. In a short time, with the help of suggestions from colleagues in political science and library research by students in my seminars on group dynamics, I compiled a list of several dozen fiascoes. I cut the list to about two dozen that appeared appropriate for an analysis of group processes. I was looking for instances in which a defective decision was made in a series of meetings by a few policymakers who constituted a cohesive group. By a defective decision, I mean one that results from decision-making practices of extremely poor quality. In other words, the fiascoes that I selected for analysis *deserved* to be fiascoes because of the grossly inadequate way the policymakers carried out their decision-making tasks.

At least seven major defects in decision-making contribute to failures to solve problems adequately. First, the group's discussions are limited to a few alternative courses of action (often only two) without a survey of the full range of alternatives. Second, the group does not survey the objectives to be fulfilled and the values implicated by the choice. Third, the group fails to reexamine the course of action initially preferred by the majority of members from the standpoint of nonobvious risks and drawbacks that had not been considered when it was originally evaluated. Fourth, the members neglect courses of action initially evaluated as unsatisfactory by the majority of the group: They spend little or no time discussing whether they have overlooked nonobvious gains or whether there are ways of reducing the seemingly prohibitive costs that had made the alternatives seem undesirable. Fifth, the members make little or no attempt to obtain information from experts who can supply sound estimates of loses and gains to be expected from alternative courses of actions. Sixth, selective bias is shown in the way the group reacts to factual information and relevant judgments from experts, the mass media, and outside critics. The members show interest in facts and opinions that support their initially preferred policy and take up time in their meetings to discuss them, but they tend to ignore facts and opinions

that do not support their initially preferred policy. Seventh, the members spend little time deliberating about how the chosen policy might be hindered by bureaucratic inertia, sabotaged by political opponents, or temporarily derailed by the common accidents that happen to the best of well-laid plans. Consequently, they fail to work out contingency plans to cope with foreseeable setbacks that could endanger the overall success of the chosen course of action.

I assume that these seven defects and some related features of inadequate decision-making result from groupthink. But, of course, each of the seven can arise from other common causes of human stupidity as well—erroneous intelligence, information overload, fatigue, blinding prejudice, and ignorance. Whether produced by groupthink or by other causes, a decision suffering from most of these defects has relatively little chance of success.

. . .

The Imperfect Link Between Groupthink and Fiascoes

Simply because the outcome of a group decision has turned out to be a fiasco, I do not assume that it must have been the result of groupthink or even that it was the result of defective decision-making. Nor do I expect that every defective decision, whether arising from groupthink or from other causes, will produce a fiasco. . . .

Groupthink is conducive to errors in decision-making, and such errors increase the likelihood of a poor outcome. Often the result is a fiasco, but not always. Suppose that because of lucky accidents fostered by absurd command decisions by the Cuban military leaders, the Kennedy administration's Bay of Pigs invasion had been successful in provoking a civil war in Cuba and led to the overthrow of the Castro regime. Analysis of the decision to invade Cuba would still support the groupthink hypothesis, for the evidence shows that Kennedy's White House group was highly cohesive, clearly displayed symptoms of defective decision-making, and exhibited all the major symptoms of groupthink. Thus, even if the Bay of Pigs decision had produced a triumph rather than a defeat, it would still be an example of the potentially adverse effects of groupthink (even though the invasion would not, in that case, be classified as a fiasco).

Hardhearted Actions by Softheaded Groups

At first I was surprised by the extent to which the groups in the fiascoes I have examined adhered to group norms and pressures toward uniformity. Just as in groups of ordinary citizens, a dominant characteristic appears to be remaining loyal to the group by sticking with the decisions to which the group has committed itself, even when the policy is working badly and has unintended consequences that disturb the conscience of the members. In a sense, members consider loyalty to the group the highest form of morality. That loyalty requires each member to avoid raising controversial issues, questioning weak arguments, or calling a halt to softheaded thinking.

Paradoxically, softheaded groups are likely to be extremely hardhearted toward out-groups and enemies. In dealing with a rival nation, policy-makers comprising an amiable group find it relatively easy to authorize dehumanizing solutions such as large-scale bombings. An affable group of government officials is unlikely to pursue the difficult and controversial issues that arise when alternatives to a harsh military solution come up for discussion. Nor are the members inclined to raise ethical issues that imply that this "fine group of ours, with its humanitarianism and its high-minded principles, might be capable of adopting a course of action that is inhumane and immoral."

Many other sources of human error can prevent government leaders from arriving at well worked out decisions, resulting in failures to achieve their practical objectives and violations of their own standards of ethical conduct. But, unlike groupthink, these other sources of error do not typically entail increases in hardheartedness along with softheadedness. Some errors involve blind spots that stem from the personality of the decision-makers. Special circumstances produce unusual fatigue and emotional stresses that interfere with efficient decision-making. Numerous institutional features of the social structure in which the group is located may also cause inefficiency and prevent adequate communication with experts. In addition, well-known inferences with sound thinking arise when the decision-makers comprise a noncohesive group. For example, when the members have no sense of loyalty to the group and regard themselves merely as representatives of different departments, with clashing interests, the meetings may become bitter power struggles, at the expense of effective decision-making.

The concept of groupthink pinpoints an entirely different source of trouble, residing neither in the individual nor in the organizational setting. Over and beyond all the familiar sources of human error is a powerful source of defective judgment that arises in cohesive groups—the concurrence-seeking tendency, which fosters overoptimism, lack of vigilance, and sloganistic thinking about the weakness and immorality of out-groups. This tendency can take its toll even when the decision-makers are conscientious statesmen trying to make the best possible decisions for their country and for all mankind.

I do not mean to imply that all cohesive groups suffer from groupthink, though all may display its symptoms from time to time. Nor should we infer from the term "groupthink" that group decisions are typically inefficient or harmful. On the contrary, a group whose members have properly defined roles, with traditions and standard operating procedures that facilitate critical inquiry, is probably capable of making better decisions than any individual in the group who works on the problem alone. And yet the advantages of having decisions made by groups are often lost because of psychological pressures that arise when the members work closely together, share the same values, and above all face a crisis situation in which everyone is subjected to stresses that generate a strong need for affiliation. In these circumstances, as conformity pressures begin to dominate, groupthink and the attendant deterioration of decision-making set in.

The central theme of my analysis can be summarized in this generalization, which I offer in the spirit of Parkinson's laws: *The more amiability and esprit de corps among the members of a policy-making in-group, the greater is the danger that independent critical thinking will be replaced by groupthink, which is likely to result in irrational and dehumanizing actions directed against out-groups.*

Sources

Policy decisions and computers: Shepard, 256–263.

Lewin's prerequisites for effective group decisions: Lewin (1947).

Importance of group cohesiveness: Lewin (1952), 145–169.

"Other things . . . self esteem": Cartwright, 105.

Group solidarity and the stresses that beset policy-makers: see George (1974).

Group cohesiveness and members' inclination to reject a nonconformist: Schachter, 1965–181, and Schachter et al. (1954).

Norms of different work groups: Vroom, 223–227, summarizes field research on group productivity by French and Zander, Likert, Seashore, and others. See also Homans.

Stereotypic images that dehumanize outgroups: see Ashmore, 318–339; Sherif et al.; Zimbardo.

Shift toward riskier courses of action: see Brown; Dion, Baron, and Miller; Myers and Lamm; Pruitt Wallach, Kogan, and Bem.

"Presume always . . . rational manner": Morgenthau, 5.

"The best . . . their explanations": Allison, 158–259.

"Most theorists . . . and models": *Ibid.*, 273.

Mutual dependency and resistance to termination of group: Janis (1966).

Major defects in decision-making: Based on Janis and Mann, 10–14.

French and German military errors during World War I: see Tuchman, 45–62, 242–261, 487–488.

References

Allison, G. T. (1971). *Essence of decision: Explaining the Cuban Missile Crisis.* Boston: Little, Brown.

Ashmore, R. (1970). Solving the problem of prejudice. In B. Collins (Ed.), *Social psychology* (pp. 298–339). Reading, MA: Addison-Wesley.

Brown, R. (1965). *Social psychology.* New York: Free Press.

Cartwright, D. (1968). The nature of group cohesiveness. In D. Cartwright & A. Zander (Eds.), *Group dynamics: Research and theory* (3rd ed.). New York: Harper & Row.

Dion, J. L., Baron, R. S., & Miller, N. (1970). Why do groups make riskier decisions than individuals? In L. Berkowitz (Ed.), *Advances in experimental group psychology* (Vol. 5, pp. 306–377). New York: Academic Press.

George, A. (1974). Adaptation to stress in political decision making: The individual, small group, and organizational context. In G. V. Coelho, D. A. Hamburg, & J. E. Adams (Eds.), *Coping and adaptation.* New York: Basic Books.

Homans, G. (1965). Group factors in worker productivity. In H. Proshansky & L. Seidenberg (Eds.), *Basic studies in social psychology* (pp. 592–604). New York: Holt.

Janis, I. L. (1966, August). Field and experimental studies of phases in the development of cohesive face-to-face groups. A paper presented at the 18th International Congress of Psychology of Moscow, U.S.S.R. Mimeo.

Janis, I. L., & Mann, L. (1977). *Decision making: A psychological analysis of conflict, choice, and commitment.* New York: Free Press.

Lewin, K. (1947). Group decision and social change. In T. Newcomb & E. Hartley (Eds.), *Readings in social psychology* (pp. 197–211). New York: Holt, 1947.

Lewin, K. (1952). *Field theory in social science.* London: Tavistock Publications.

Morgenthau, H. (1970). *Politics among nations* (4th ed.). New York: Knopf.

Myers, D. G., & Lamm, H. (1977). The polarizing effect of group discussion. In I. L. Janis (Ed.), *Current trends in psychology: Readings from the American scientist.* Los Altos, CA: Kaufmann.

Pruitt, D. (1971). Choice shifts in group discussion: An introductory review. *Journal of Personality and Social Psychology, 20,* 330–360.

Schachter, S. (1959). *The psychology of affiliation.* Stanford, CA: Stanford University Press.

Schachter, S. et al. (1954). Cross-cultural experiments on threat and rejection. *Human Relations, 7,* 403–439.

Shephard, R. N. (1967). On subjectively optimum selections among multi-attribute alternatives. In W. Edwards & A. Tversky (Eds.), *Decision making.* Baltimore: Penguin Books.

Sherif, M., Harvey, O. J., White, B. J., Hood, W. R., & Sherif, C. W. (1963). *Inter-group conflict and cooperation: The robbers cave experiment.* Norman, OK: University of Oklahoma Press.

Tuchman, B. (1963). *The guns of August.* New York: Dell.

Tuchman, B. (1966). *The proud tower.* New York: Macmillan.

Vroom, V. H. (1969). Industrial social psychology. In G. Lindzey & E. Aronson (Eds.), *The handbook of social psychology* (Vol. 5). Reading, MA: Addison-Wesley.

Wallach, M. A., Kogan, N., & Bem, D. J. (1968). Group influence on risk-taking. In D. Cartwright & A. Zander (Eds.), *Group dynamics: Research and theory* (3rd ed., pp. 430–443). New York: Harper & Row.

Zimbardo, P. (1969). The human choice: Individuation, reason and order versus deindividuation, impulse, and chaos. *Nebraska symposium on motivation 1969* (Vol. 17, pp. 237–307). University of Nebraska Press.

Questions

1. Define "groupthink."

2. What are the two group attributes that Janis contends are most prominent for understanding "groupthink"? Explain.

3. What are the seven elements of "groupthink"? How are the elements interrelated?

4. What role does emotion serve in the "groupthink" process?

5. Think of specific "groupthink" decisions that you have been involved in (since we all have!). To what degree do the seven elements outlined by Janis pertain to your example? Which elements do not seem particularly relevant?

6. Groups are typically composed of people of differing backgrounds, including gender, race, social class, age, and religion. How might these attributes affect "groupthink"? Which of these elements or characteristics might have the greatest effect on "groupthink"? Why?

PATHOLOGY OF IMPRISONMENT

PHILIP G. ZIMBARDO

"Pathology of Imprisonment," by Philip G. Zimbardo, reprinted from Society, *Vol. 9, No. 6, April, 1972. Copyright © by Transaction, Inc. pp. 4–8.*

Philip Zimbardo and his colleagues wanted to study the effects of imprisonment on human behavior, particularly the psychological impacts. They opened a mock prison using carefully screened college students who were "mature, emotionally stable, normal, intelligent college students from middle-class homes throughout the United States and Canada." The results were so shocking that the experiment was aborted after just six days! In this essay, Zimbardo reports on the results. He then comments on why prisons breed pathological behavior and what we might do to prevent this from happening.

I was recently released from solitary confinement after being held therein for 37 months [months!]. A silent system was imposed upon me and to even whisper to the man in the next cell resulted in being beaten by guards, sprayed with chemical mace, blackjacked, stomped and thrown into a strip-cell naked to sleep on a concrete floor without bedding, covering, wash basin or even a toilet. The floor served as toilet and bed, and even there the silent system was enforced. To let a moan escape your lips because of the pain and discomfort . . . resulted in another beating. I spent not days, but months there during my 37 months in solitary. . . . I have filed every writ possible against the administrative acts of brutality. The state courts have all denied the petitions. Because of my refusal to let the things die down and forget all that happened during my 37 months in solitary. . . . I am the most hated prisoner in [this] penitentiary, and called a "hard-core incorrigible."

Maybe I am an incorrigible, but if true, it's because I would rather die than to accept being treated as less than a human being. I have never complained of my prison sentence as being unjustified except through legal means of appeals. I have never put a knife on a guard's throat and demanded my release. I know that thieves must be punished and I don't justify stealing, even though I am a thief myself. But now I don't think I will be a thief when I am released. No, I'm not rehabilitated. It's just that I no longer think of becoming wealthy by stealing. I now only think of killing—killing those who have beaten me and treated me as if I were a dog. I hope and pray for the sake of my own soul and future life of freedom that I am able to overcome the bitterness and hatred which eats daily at my soul, but I know to overcome it will not be easy.

This eloquent plea for prison reform—for humane treatment of human beings, for the basic dignity that is the right of every American—came to me secretly in a letter from a prisoner who cannot be identified because he is still in a state correctional institution. He sent it to me because he read of an experiment I recently conducted at Stanford University. In an attempt to understand just what it means psychologically to be a prisoner or a prison guard, Craig Haney, Curt Banks, Dave Jaffe and I created our own prison. We carefully screened over 70 volunteers who answered an ad in a Palo Alto city newspaper and ended up with about two dozen young men who were selected to be part of this study. They were mature, emotionally stable, normal, intelligent college students from middle-class homes throughout the United States and Canada. They appeared to represent the cream of the crop of this generation. None had any criminal record and all were relatively homogeneous on many dimensions initially.

Half were arbitrarily designated as prisoners by a flip of a coin, the others as guards. These were the roles they were to play in our simulated prison. The guards were made aware of the potential seriousness and danger of the situation and their own vulnerability. They made up their own formal rules for maintaining law, order and respect, and were generally free to improvise new ones during their eight-hour, three-man shifts. The prisoners were unexpectedly picked up at their homes by a city policeman in a squad car, searched, handcuffed, fingerprinted, booked at the Palo Alto station house and taken blindfolded to our jail. There they were stripped, deloused, put into a uniform, given a number and put into a cell with two other prisoners where they expected to live for the next two weeks. The pay was good ($15 a day) and their motivation was to make money.

We observed and recorded on videotape the events that occurred in their prison, and we interviewed and tested the prisoners and guards at various points throughout the study. Some of the videotapes of the actual encounters between the prisoners and guards were seen in the NBC News feature "Chronolog" on November 26, 1971.

At the end of only six days we had to close down our mock prison because what we saw was frightening. It was no longer apparent to most of the subjects (or to us) where reality ended and their roles began. The majority had indeed become prisoners or guards, no longer able to clearly differentiate between role playing and self. There were dramatic changes in virtually every aspect of their behavior, thinking and feeling. In less than a week the experience of imprisonment undid (temporarily) a lifetime of learning; human values were suspended, self-concepts were challenged and the ugliest, most base, pathological side of human nature surfaced. We were horrified because we saw some boys (guards) treat others as if they were despicable animals, taking pleasure in cruelty, while other boys (prisoners) became servile, dehumanized robots who thought only of escape, of their own individual survival and of their mounting hatred for the guards.

We had to release three prisoners in the first four days because they had such acute situational traumatic transactions as hysterical crying, confusion in thinking and severe depression. Others begged to be paroled, and all but three were willing to forfeit all the money they had earned if they could be paroled. By then (the fifth day) they had been so programmed to think of themselves as prisoners that when their request for parole was denied, they returned docilely to their cells. Now, had they been thinking as college students acting in an oppressive experiment, they would have quit once they no longer wanted the $15 a day we used as our only incentive. However, the reality was not quitting an experiment but "being paroled by the parole board from the Stanford County Jail." By the last days, the earlier solidarity among the prisoners (systematically broken by the guards) dissolved into "each man for himself." Finally, when one of their fellows was put in solitary confinement (a small closet) for refusing to eat, the prisoners were given a choice by one of the guards: give up their blankets and the incorrigible prisoner would be let out, or keep their blankets and he would be kept in all night. They voted to keep their blankets and to abandon their brother.

About a third of the guards became tyrannical in their arbitrary use of power, in enjoying their control over other people. They were corrupted by the power of their roles and became quite inventive in their techniques of breaking the spirit of the prisoners and making them feel they were worthless. Some of the guards merely did their jobs as tough but fair correctional officers, and several were good guards from the prisoners' point of view since they did them small favors and were friendly. However, no good guard ever interfered with a command by any of the bad guards; they never intervened on the side of the prisoners, they never told the others to ease off because it was only an experiment,

and they never even came to me as prison superintendent or experimenter in charge to complain. In part, they were good because the others were bad; they needed the others to help establish their own egos in a positive light. In a sense, the good guards perpetuated the prison more than the other guards because their own needs to be liked prevented them from disobeying or violating the implicit guards' code. At the same time, the act of befriending the prisoners created a social reality which made the prisoners less likely to rebel.

By the end of the week the experiment had become a reality, as if it were a Pirandello play directed by Kafka that just keeps going after the audience has left. The consultant for our prison, Carlo Prescott, an ex-convict with 16 years of imprisonment in California's jails, would get so depressed and furious each time he visited our prison, because of its psychological similarity to his experiences that he would have to leave. A Catholic priest who was a former prison chaplain in Washington, D.C. talked to our prisoners after four days and said they were just like the other first-timers he had seen.

But in the end, I called off the experiment not because of the horror I saw out there in the prison yard, but because of the horror of realizing that *I* could have easily traded places with the most brutal guard or become the weakest prisoner full of hatred at being so powerless that I could not eat, sleep or go to the toilet without permission of the authorities. *I* could have become Calley at My Lai, George Jackson at San Quentin, one of the men at Attica or the prisoner quoted at the beginning of this article.

Individual behavior is largely under the control of social forces and environmental contingencies rather than personality traits, character, will power or other empirically unvalidated constructs. Thus we create an illusion of freedom by attributing more internal control to ourselves, to the individual, than actually exists. We thus underestimate the power and persuasiveness of situational controls over behavior because: a) they are often non-obvious and subtle, b) we can often avoid entering situations where we might be so controlled, c) we label as "weak" or "deviant" people in those situations who do behave differently from how we believe we would.

Each of us carries around in our heads a favorable self-image in which we are essentially just, fair, humane and understanding. For example, we could not imagine inflicting pain on others without much provocation or hurting people who had done nothing to us, who in fact were even liked by us. However, there is a growing body of social psychological research which underscores the conclusion derived from this prison study. Many people, perhaps the majority, can be made to do almost anything when put into psychologically compelling situations—regardless of their morals, ethics, values, attitudes, beliefs or personal convictions. My colleague, Stanley Milgram, has shown that more than 60 percent of the population will deliver what they think is a series of painful electric shocks to another person even after the victim cries for mercy, begs them to stop and then apparently passes out. The subjects complained that they did not want to inflict more pain but blindly obeyed the command of the authority figure (the experimenter) who said that they must go on. In my own research on violence, I have seen mild-mannered co-eds repeatedly give shocks (which they thought were causing pain) to another girl, a stranger whom they had rated very favorably, simply by being made to feel anonymous and put in a situation where they were expected to engage in this activity.

Observers of these and similar experimental situations never predict their outcomes and estimate that it is unlikely that they themselves would behave similarly. They can be so confident only when they were outside the situation. However, since the majority of people in these studies do act in non-rational, non-obvious ways, it follows that the majority of observers would also succumb to the social psychological forces in the situation.

With regard to prisons, we can state that the mere act of assigning labels to people and putting them into a situation where those labels acquire validity and meaning is sufficient to elicit pathological behavior. This pathology is not predictable from any available diagnostic indicators we have in the social sciences and is extreme enough to modify in very significant ways fundamental attitudes and behavior. The prison situation, as presently arranged, is guaranteed to generate severe enough pathological reactions in both guards and prisoners as to debase their humanity, lower their feelings of self-worth and make it difficult for them to be part of a society outside of their prison.

For years our national leaders have been pointing to the enemies of freedom, to the fascist or communist threat to the American way of life. In so doing they have overlooked the threat of social anarchy that is building within our own country without any outside agitation. As soon as a person comes to the realization that he is being imprisoned by his society or individuals in it, then, in the best American tradition, he demands

liberty and rebels, accepting death as an alternative. The third alternative, however, is to allow oneself to become a good prisoner—docile, cooperative, uncomplaining, conforming in thought and complying in deed.

Our prison authorities now point to the militant agitators who are still vaguely referred to as part of some communist plot, as the irresponsible, incorrigible troublemakers They imply that there would be no trouble, riots, hostages or deaths if it weren't for this small band of bad prisoners. In other words, then, everything would return to "normal" again in the life of our nation's prisons if they could break these men.

The riots in prisons are coming from within—from within every man and woman who refuses to let the system turn them into an object, a number, a thing or a no-thing. It is not communist inspired, but inspired by the spirit of American freedom. No man wants to be enslaved. To be powerless, to be subject to the arbitrary exercise of power, to not be recognized as a human being is to be a slave.

To be a military prisoner is to become aware that the physical jails are but more blatant extensions of the forms of social and psychological oppression experienced daily in the nation's ghettos. They are trying to awaken the conscience of the nation to the ways in which the American ideals are being perverted, apparently in the name of justice but actually under the banner of apathy, fear and hatred. If we do not listen to the pleas of the prisoners at Attica to be treated like human beings, then we have all become brutalized by our priorities for property rights over human rights. The consequence will not only be more prison riots but a loss of all those ideals on which this country was founded.

The public should be aware that they own the prisons and that their business is failing. The 70 percent recidivism rate and the escalation in severity of crime committed by graduates of our prisons are evidence that current prisons fail to rehabilitate the inmates in any positive way. Rather, they are breeding grounds for hatred of the establishment, a hatred that makes every citizen a target of violent assault. Prisons are a bad investment for us taxpayers. Until now we have not cared, we have turned over to wardens and prison authorities the unpleasant job of keeping people who threaten us out of our sight. Now we are shocked to learn that their management practices have failed to improve the product and instead turn petty thieves into murderers. We must insist upon new management or improved operating procedures

The cloak of secrecy should be removed from the prisons. Prisoners claim they are brutalized by the guards, guards say it is a lie. Where is the impartial test of the truth in such a situation? Prison officials have forgotten that they work for us, that they are only public servants whose salaries are paid by our taxes. They act as if it is their prison, like a child with a toy he won't share. Neither lawyers, judges, the legislature nor the public is allowed into prisons to ascertain the truth unless the visit is sanctioned by authorities and until all is prepared for their visit. I was shocked to learn that my request to join a congressional investigating committee's tour of San Quentin and Soledad was refused, as was that of the news media.

There should be an ombudsman in every prison, not under the pay or control of the prison authority, and responsible only to the courts, state legislature and the public. Such a person could report on violations of constitutional and human rights.

Guards must be given better training than they now receive for the difficult job society imposes upon them. To be a prison guard as now constituted is to be put in a situation of constant threat from within the prison, with no social recognition from the society at large. As was shown graphically at Attica, prison guards are also prisoners of the system who can be sacrificed to the demands of the public to be punitive and the needs of politicians to preserve an image. Social scientists and business administrators should be called upon to design and help carry out this training.

The relationship between the individual (who is sentenced by the courts to a prison term) and his community must be maintained. How can a prisoner return to a dynamically changing society that most of us cannot cope with after being out of it for a number of years? There should be more community involvement in these rehabilitation centers, more ties encouraged and promoted between the trainees and family and friends, more educational opportunities to prepare them for returning to their communities as more valuable members of it than they were before they left.

Finally, the main ingredient necessary to effect any change at all in prison reform, in the rehabilitation of a single prisoner or even in the optimal development of a child is caring. Reform must start with people—especially people with power—caring about the well-being of others. Underneath the toughest, society-hating convict, rebel or anarchist is a human being who wants his existence to be recognized by his fellows and who wants someone else to care about whether he lives or dies and to grieve if he lives imprisoned rather than lives free.

Questions

1. What impact did imprisonment have on group solidarity among the "prisoners" in Zimbardo's study?

2. To what degree did the students internalize their role as "guards"? What effect did this have on their treatment of the student prisoners?

3. How influential is social situation or context in determining behavior? What role does labeling play?

4. What characteristics of prisons contribute to the development of pathological behavior? Explain.

5. Why did the student prisoners take abuse from the guards and suffer through other demeaning behavior if they were there voluntarily?

6. What changes does Zimbardo recommend to make prisons more effective, or at least to make prisons less likely to breed pathological behavior?

OUTSIDERS

HOWARD S. BECKER

"Outsiders," by Howard S. Becker, reprinted from The Outsiders: Studies in the Sociology of Deviance, *1963. pp. 1–18.*

In the selection below, Howard Becker defines the term outsiders as persons who break a rule agreed upon by a group. He also says that rule breakers often perceive a person who enforces a rule as an outsider. In other words, Becker argues that many facets of deviant behavior are 'relative.' This piece provided an early foundation for what has become known as the interactionist theory of deviant behavior.

All social groups make rules and attempt, at some times and under some circumstances, to enforce them. Social rules define situations and the kinds of behavior appropriate to them, specifying some actions as "right" and forbidding others as "wrong." When a rule is enforced, the person who is supposed to have broken it may be seen as a special kind of person, one who cannot be trusted to live by the rules agreed on by the group. He is regarded as an *outsider*.

But the person who is thus labeled an outsider may have a different view of the matter. He may not accept the rule by which he is being judged and may not regard those who judge him as either competent or legitimately entitled to do so. Hence, a second meaning of the term emerges: the rule-breaker may feel his judges are *outsiders*.

In what follows, I will try to clarify the situation and process pointed to by this double-barreled term: the situations of rule-breaking and rule-enforcement and the processes by which some people come to break rules and others to enforce them.

Some preliminary distinctions are in order. Rules may be of a great many kinds. They may be formally enacted into law, and in this case the police power of the state may be used in enforcing them. In other cases, they represent informal agreements, newly arrived at or encrusted with the sanction of age and tradition; rules of this kind are enforced by informal sanctions of various kinds.

Similarly, whether a rule has the force of law or tradition or is simply the result of consensus, it may be the task of some specialized body, such as the police or the committee on ethics of a professional association, to enforce it; enforcement, on the other hand, may be everyone's job or, at least, the job of everyone in the group to which the rule is meant to apply.

Many rules are not enforced and are not, in any except the most formal sense, the kind of rules with which I am concerned. Blue laws, which remain on the statute books though they have not been enforced for a hundred years, are examples. . . . Informal rules may similarly die from lack of enforcement. I shall mainly be concerned with what we can call the actual operating rules of groups, those kept alive through attempts at enforcement.

. . .

Definitions of Deviance

The outsider—the deviant from group rules—has been the subject of much speculation, theorizing, and scientific study. What laymen want to know about deviants is: why do they do it? How can we account for their rule-breaking? What is there about them that leads them to do forbidden things? Scientific research has tried to find answers to these questions. In doing so it has accepted the common-sense premise that there is something inherently deviant (qualitatively distinct) about acts that break (or seem to break) social rules. It has also accepted the common-sense assumption that the deviant act occurs because some characteristic of the person who commits it makes it necessary or inevitable that he should. Scientists do not ordinarily question the label "deviant" when it is applied to particular acts or people but rather take it as given. In so doing, they accept the values of the group making the judgment. . . .

Our first problem, then, is to construct a definition of deviance . . . as the failure to obey group rules. Once we have described the rules of a group enforces on its members, we can say with some precision whether or not a person has violated them and is thus, on this view, deviant.

This view is closest to my own, but it fails to give sufficient weight to the ambiguities that arise in deciding which rules are to be taken as the yardstick against which behavior is measured and judged deviant. A society has many groups, each with its own set of rules, and people belong to many groups simultaneously. A person may break the rules of one group by the very act of abiding by the rules of another group. Is he, then, deviant? Proponents of this definition may object that while ambiguity may arise with respect to the rules peculiar to one or another group in society, there are some rules that are very generally agreed to by everyone, in which case the difficulty does not arise. This, of course, is a question of fact, to be settled by empirical research. I doubt there are many such areas of consensus and think it wiser to use a definition that allows us to deal with both ambiguous and unambiguous situations.

Deviance and the Responses of Others

The sociological view I have just discussed defines deviance as the infraction of some agreed-upon rule. It then goes on to ask who breaks rules, and to search for the factors in their personalities and life situations that might account for the infractions. This assumes that those who have broken a rule constitute a homogeneous category, because they have committed the same deviant act.

Such an assumption seems to me to ignore the central fact about deviance: it is created by society. I do not mean this in the way it is ordinarily understood, in which the causes of deviance are located in the social situation of the deviant or in "social factors" which prompt his action. I mean, rather, that *social groups create deviance by making the rules whose infraction constitutes deviance*, and by applying those rules to particular people and labeling them as outsiders. From this point of view, deviance is *not* a quality of the act the person commits, but rather a consequence of the application by others of rules and sanctions to an "offender." The deviant is one to whom that label has successfully been applied; deviant behavior is behavior that people so label.

Since deviance is, among other things, a consequence of the responses of others to a person's act, students of deviance cannot assume that they are dealing with a homogeneous category when they study people who have been labeled deviant. That is, they cannot assume that these people have actually committed a deviant act or broken some rule, because the process of labeling may not be infallible; some people may be labeled deviant who in fact have not broken a rule. Furthermore, they cannot assume that the category of those labeled deviant will contain all those who actually have broken a rule, for many offenders may escape apprehension and thus fail to be included in the population of "deviants" they study. Insofar as the category lacks homogeneity and fails to include all the cases that belong in it, one cannot reasonably expect to find common factors of personality or life situation that will account for the supposed deviance.

What, then, do people who have been labeled deviant have in common? At the least, they share the label and the experience of being labeled as outsiders. I will begin my analysis with this basic similarity and view deviance as the product of a transaction that takes place between some social group and one who is viewed by that group as a rule-breaker.

. . .

Whether an act is deviant, then, depends on how other people react to it. . . . The response of other people has to be regarded as problematic. Just because one has committed an infraction of a rule does not mean that others will respond as though this had happened. (Conversely, just because one has not violated a rule does not mean that he may not be treated, in some circumstances, as though he had.)

The degree to which other people will respond to a given act as deviant varies greatly. Several kinds of variation seem worth noting. First of all, there is variation over time. A person believed to have committed a given "deviant" act may at one time be responded to much more leniently than he would be at some other time. The occurrence of "drives" against various kinds of deviance illustrates this clearly. At various times, enforcement officials may decide to make an all-out attack on some particular kind of deviance, such as gambling, drug addiction, or homosexuality. It is obviously much more dangerous to engage in one of these activities when a drive is on than at any other time. . . .

The degree to which an act will be treated as deviant depends also on who commits the act and who feels he has been harmed by it. Rules tend to be applied more to some persons than others. Studies of

juvenile delinquency make the point clearly. Boys from middle-class areas do not get as far in the legal process when they are apprehended as do boys from slum areas. The middle-class boy is less likely, when picked up by the police, to be taken to the station; less likely when taken to the station to be booked; and it is extremely unlikely that he will be convicted and sentenced.[1] This variation occurs even though the original infraction of the rule is the same in the two cases. Similarly, the law is differentially applied to Negroes and whites. It is well known that a Negro believed to have attacked a white woman is much more likely to be punished than a white man who commits the same offense; it is only slightly less well known that a Negro who murders another Negro is much less likely to be punished than a white man who commits murder.[2] This, of course, is one of the main points of Sutherland's analysis of white-collar crime: crimes committed by corporations are almost always prosecuted as civil cases, but the same crime committed by an individual is ordinarily treated as a criminal offense.[3]

Some rules are enforced only when they result in certain consequences. The unmarried mother furnishes a clear example. Vincent[4] points out that illicit sexual relations seldom result in severe punishment or social censure for the offenders. If, however, a girl becomes pregnant as a result of such activities the reaction of others is likely to be severe. (The illicit pregnancy is also an interesting example of the differential enforcement of rules on different categories of people. Vincent notes that unmarried fathers escape the severe censure visited on the mother.)

Why repeat these commonplace observations? Because, taken together, they support the proposition that deviance is not a simple quality, present in some kinds of behavior and absent in others. Rather, it is the product of a process which involves responses of other people to the behavior. The same behavior may be an infraction of the rules at one time and not at another; may be an infraction when committed by one person, but not when committed by another; some rules are broken with impunity, others are not. In short, whether a given act is deviant or not depends in part on the nature of the act (that is, whether or not it violates some rule) and in part on what other people do about it.

Some people may object that this is merely a terminological quibble, that one can, after all, define terms by any way he wants to and that if some people want to speak of rule-breaking behavior as deviant without reference to the reactions of others they are free to do so. This, of course, is true. Yet it might be worthwhile to refer to such behavior as *rule-breaking behavior* and reserve the term *deviant* for those labeled as deviant by some segment of society. . . .

If we take as the object of our attention behavior which comes to be labeled as deviant, we must recognize that we cannot know whether a given act will be categorized as deviant until the response of others has occurred. Deviance is not a quality that lies in behavior itself, but in the interaction between the person who commits an act and those who respond to it.

Whose Rules?

I have been using the term "outsiders" to refer to those people who are judged by others to be deviant and thus to stand outside the circle of "normal" members of the group. But the term contains a second meaning, whose analysis leads to another important set of sociological problems: "outsiders," from the point of view of the person who is labeled deviant, may be the people who make the rules he had been found guilty of breaking.

Social rules are the creation of specific social groups. Modern societies are not simple organizations in which everyone agrees on what the rules are and how they are to be applied in specific situations. They are, instead, highly differentiated along social class lines, ethnic lines, occupational lines and cultural lines. These groups need not and, in fact, often do not share the same rules. The problems they face in dealing with their environment, the history and traditions they carry with them, all lead to the evolution of different sets of rules. Insofar as the rules of various groups conflict and contradict one another, there will be disagreement about the kind of behavior that is proper in any given situation.

Italian immigrants who went on making wine for themselves and their friends during Prohibition were acting properly by Italian immigrant standards, but were breaking the law of their new country (as, of course, were many of their Old American neighbors). Medical patients who shop around for a doctor may, from the perspective of their own group, be doing what is necessary to protect their health by making sure they get what seems to them the best possible doctor; but, from the perspective of the physician, what they do is wrong because it breaks down the trust the patient ought to put in his physician. The lower-class delinquent who fights for his "turf" is only doing what he considers necessary and right, but teachers, social workers, and police see it differently.

While it may be argued that many or most rules are generally agreed to by all members of a society, empirical research on a given rule generally reveals variation in people's attitudes. Formal rules, enforced by some specially constituted group, may differ from those actually thought appropriate by most people.[5] Factions in a group may disagree on what I have called actual operating rules. Most important for the study of behavior ordinarily labeled deviant, the perspectives of the people who engage in the behavior are likely to be quite different from those of the people who condemn it. In this latter situation, a person may feel that he is being judged according to rules he has had no hand in making and does not accept, rules forced on him by outsiders.

To what extent and under what circumstances do people attempt to force their rules on others who do not subscribe to them? Let us distinguish two cases. In the first, only those who are actually members of the group have any interest in making and enforcing certain rules. If an orthodox Jew disobeys the laws of kashruth only other orthodox Jews will regard this as a transgression; Christians or nonorthodox Jews will not consider this deviance and would have no interest in interfering. In the second case, members of a group consider it important to their welfare that members of certain other groups obey certain rules. Thus, people consider it extremely important that those who practice the healing arts abide by certain rules; this is the reason the state licenses physicians, nurses, and others, and forbids anyone who is not licensed to engage in healing activities

To the extent that a group tries to impose its rules on other groups in the society, we are presented with a second question: Who can, in fact, force others to accept their rules and what are the causes of their success? This is, of course, a question of political and economic power. . . . Here it is enough to note that people are in fact always *forcing* their rules on others, applying them more or less against the will and without the consent of those others. By and large, for example, rules are made for young people by their elders. Though the youth of this country exert a powerful influence culturally—the mass media of communication are tailored to their interests, for instance—many important kinds of rules are made for our youth by adults. Rules regarding school attendance and sex behavior are not drawn up with regard to the problems of adolescence. Rather, adolescents find themselves surrounded by rules about these matters which have been made by older and more settled people. It is considered legitimate to do this, for youngsters are considered neither wise enough nor responsible enough to make proper rules for themselves.

In the same way, it is true in many respects that men make the rules for women in our society (though in America this is changing rapidly). Negroes find themselves subject to rules made for them by whites. The foreign-born and those otherwise ethnically peculiar often have their rules made for them by the Protestant Anglo-Saxon minority. The middle class makes rules the lower class must obey—in the schools, the courts, and elsewhere.

Differences in the ability to make rules and apply them to other people are essentially power differentials (either legal or extralegal). Those groups whose social position gives them weapons and power are best able to enforce their rules. Distinctions of age, sex, ethnicity, and class are all related to differences in power, which accounts for differences in the degree to which groups so distinguished can make rules for others.

In addition to recognizing that deviance is created by the responses of people to particular kinds of behavior, by the labeling of that behavior as deviant, we must also keep in mind that the rules created and maintained by such labeling are not universally agreed to. Instead, they are the object of conflict and disagreement, part of the political process of society.

Endnotes

1. See Cohen, A. K., & Short, J. F., Jr. Juvenile delinquency. In Merton & Nisbet, (Eds.).

2. Garfinkel, H. (1949). Research notes on inter- and intraracial homicides. *Social Forces, 27*, 369–381.

3. Sutherland, E. H. (1940). White collar criminality. *American Sociological Review, 5*, 1–12.

4. Vincent, C. (1961). *Unmarried mothers.* New York: The Free Press of Glencoe, pp. 3–5.

5. Rose, A. M., & Prell, A. E. (1955). Does the punishment fit the crime?—A study in social valuation. *American Journal of Sociology, 121*, 247–259.

Questions

1. Why does Becker discount the statistical, pathological, and functional views of deviant behavior?

2. What implications are there for labeling theory if Becker is correct in saying that those who label individuals as "deviant" are not infallible?

3. Becker contends that deviant behavior is an interaction between the individual and a group. What does he mean by this statement? Can you think of any examples from your campus that illustrate this point?

4. According to the theoretical framework developed in this article, "Those groups whose social position gives them weapons and power are best able to enforce their rules." Can you think of cases where this is true in American society? What about in other societies? Finally, what are some cases where the "rules" seem *not* to favor the powerful? (That is, what types of behavior are defined as deviant that the powerful would rather have defined as normal?)

RACE AND CLASS IN THE AMERICAN CRIMINAL JUSTICE SYSTEM

DAVID COLE

"Race and Class in the American Criminal Justice System," by David Cole, reprinted from No Equal Justice: Race and Class in the American Criminal Justice System, *1999, The New York Press. Copyright © by David Cole. pp. 1–15.*

In his book No Equal Justice, *David Cole examines inequality in the criminal justice system, paying particular attention to inequities toward race and class. In this selection, he carefully summarizes his major themes and findings. He contends that inequities exist because "our criminal justice system affirmatively depends on inequality." He further argues that inequality in the judicial arena widens the already growing gap between whites and blacks, and between rich and poor, in other areas of society.*

The most telling image from the most widely and closely watched criminal trial of our lifetime is itself an image of people watching television. On one half of the screen black law students at Howard Law School cheer as they watch the live coverage of a Los Angeles jury acquitting O. J. Simpson of the double murder of his ex-wife and her friend. On the other half of the screen, white students at George Washington University Law school sit shocked in silence as they watch the same scene. The split-screen image captures in a moment the division between white and black Americans on the question of O. J. Simpson's guilt. And that division in turn reflects an even deeper divide on the issue of the fairness and legitimacy of American criminal justice.

Before, during, and after the trial, about three quarters of black citizens maintained that Simpson was not guilty, while an equal fraction of white citizens deemed him guilty. More people paid attention to this trial than any other in world history, but neither the DNA evidence nor the dubious reliability of Los Angeles detective Mark Fuhrman altered either group's views on guilt or innocence.

In some respects, the racially divided response to the verdict was understandable. For many black citizens, the acquittal was a sign of hope, or at least payback. For much of our history, the mere allegation that a black man had murdered two white people would have been sufficient grounds for his lynching. Until very recently, the jury rendering judgment on O. J. Simpson would likely have been all white; Simpson's jury, by contrast, consisted of nine blacks, two whites, and an Hispanic. And the prosecution was poisoned by the racism of the central witness, Detective Mark Fuhrman, who had, among other things, called blacks "niggers" on tape and then lied about it on the stand. To many blacks, the jury's "not guilty" verdict demonstrated that the system is not *always* rigged against the black defendant, and that was worth cheering.

The white law students' shock was also understandable. The evidence against Simpson was overwhelming. Simpson's blood had been found at the scene of the murders. The victims' blood had been found in Simpson's white Bronco and on a sock in Simpson's bedroom. And a glove found at Simpson's home had, as prosecutor Marcia Clark put it in her closing argument to the jury, "all of the evidence on it: Ron Goldman, fibers from his shirt; Ron Goldman's hair; Nicole's hair; the defendant's blood; Ron Goldman's blood; Nicole's blood; and the Bronco fiber."[1] The defense's suggestion that the Los Angeles Police Department somehow planted all of this evidence ran directly contrary to their simultaneous (and quite effective) demonstration of the LAPD's "keystone cops" incompetence. To many whites, it appeared that a predominantly black jury had voted for one of their own, and had simply ignored the overwhelming evidence that Simpson was a brutal double murderer.

But there is a deep irony in these reactions. Simpson, of course, was atypical in every way. The very factors that played to his advantage at trial generally work to the disadvantage of the vast majority of black defendants. Simpson had virtually unlimited resources, a jury that identified with him along racial grounds, and celebrity status. Most black defendants, by contrast, cannot afford any attorney, much less a "dream team." Their fate is usually decided by predominantly or exclusively white juries. And most black defendants find that their image is linked in America's mind not with celebrity, but with criminality.

At the same time, the features that worked to Simpson's advantage, and that occasioned such outrage among whites, generally benefit whites.

Whites have a disproportionate share of the wealth in our society, and are more likely to be able to buy a good defense; white defendants generally face juries composed of members of their own race; and a white person's face is not stereotypically associated with crime. Thus, what dismayed whites in Simpson's case is precisely what generally works to their advantage, while what blacks cheered is what most often works to their disadvantage.

Had Simpson been poor and unknown, as most black (and white) criminal defendants are, everything would have been different. The case would have garnered no national attention. Simpson would have been represented by an overworked and underpaid public defender who would not have been able to afford experts to examine and challenge the government's evidence. No one would have conducted polls on the case, and the trial would not have been televised. In all likelihood, Simpson would have been convicted in short order, without serious testing of the evidence against him or the methods by which it was obtained. Whites would have expressed no outrage that a poor black defendant had been convicted, and blacks would have had nothing to cheer about. That, not *California v. O. J. Simpson*, is the reality in American courtrooms across the country today.

In other words, it took an atypical case, one in which minority race and lower socioeconomic class did *not* coincide, in which the defense outperformed the prosecution, and in which the jury was predominantly black, for white people to pay attention to the role that race and class play in criminal justice. Yet the issues of race and class are present in every criminal case, and in the vast majority of cases they play out no more fairly. Of course, they generally work in the opposite direction: the prosecution outspends and outperforms the defense, the jury is predominantly white, and the defendant is poor and a member of a racial minority. In an odd way, then, the Simpson case brought to the foreground issues that lurk beneath the entire system of criminal justice. The system's legitimacy turns on equality before the law, but the system's reality could not be further from that ideal. As Justice Hugo Black wrote over 40 years ago: "There can be no equal justice where the kind of trial a man gets depends on the amount of money he has." He might well have added, "or the color of his skin." Where race and class affect outcomes, we cannot maintain that the criminal law is just.

Equality, however, is a difficult and elusive goal. In our nation, it has been the cause of a civil war, powerful political movements, and countless violent uprisings. Yet the gap between the rich and the poor is larger in the United States today than in any other Western industrialized nation,[2] and has been steadily widening since 1968.[3] In 1989, the wealthiest 1% of U.S. households owned nearly 40% of the nation's wealth. The wealthiest 20% owned more than 80% of the nation's wealth. That leaves precious little for the rest.[4] The income and wealth gap correlates closely with race. Minorities' median net worth is less than 7% that of whites.[5] Nine percent of white families had incomes below the poverty level in 1992, while more than 30% of black families and 26.5% of Hispanic families fell below that level.[6] The consequences of the country's race and class divisions are felt in every aspect of American life, from infant mortality and unemployment, where black rates are double white rates;[7] to public education, where the proportion of black children educated in segregated schools is increasing;[8] to housing, where racial segregation is the norm, integration the rare exception.[9] Racial inequality . . . remains to this day the most formidable of our social problems.

This inequality is in turn reflected in statistics on crime and the criminal justice system. The vast majority of those behind bars are poor; 40% of state prisoners can't even read; and 67% of prison inmates did not have full-time employment when they were arrested. The per capita incarceration rate among blacks is seven times that among whites. African Americans make up about 12% of the general population, but more than half of the prison population. They serve longer sentences, have higher arrest and conviction rates, face higher bail amounts, and are more often the victims of police use of deadly force than white citizens. In 1995, one in three young black men between the ages of 20 and 29 was imprisoned or on parole or probation. If incarceration rates continue their current trends, one in four young black males born today will serve time in prison during his lifetime (meaning that he will be convicted and sentenced to more than one year of incarceration). Nationally, for every one black man who graduates from college, 100 are arrested.[10]

In addition, poor and minority citizens are disproportionately victimized by crime. Poorer and less educated persons are the victims of violent crime at significantly higher rates than wealthy and more educated persons.[11] African Americans are victimized by robbery at a rate 150% higher than whites; they are the victims of rape, aggravated assault, an armed robbery 25% more often than whites.[12] Homicide is the

leading cause of death among young black men.[13] Because we live in segregated communities, most crime is intraracial; the more black crime there is, the more black victims there are. But at the same time, the more law enforcement resources we direct toward protecting the black community from crime, the more often black citizens, especially those living in the inner city, will find their friends, relatives, and neighbors behind bars.

. . . While our criminal justice system is explicitly based on the premise and promise of equality before the law, the administration of criminal law—whether by the officer on the beat, the legislature, or the Supreme Court—is in fact predicated on the exploitation of inequality. My claim is not simply that we have ignored inequality's effects within the criminal justice system, nor that we have tried but failed to achieve equality there. Rather, I contend that *our criminal justice system affirmatively depends on inequality*. Absent race and class disparities, the privileged among us could not enjoy as much constitutional protection of our liberties as we do; and without those disparities, we could not afford the policy of mass incarceration that we have pursued over the past two decades.

White Americans are not likely to want to believe this claim. The principle that all are equal before the law is perhaps the most basic American law; it is that maxim, after all, that stands etched atop the Supreme Court's magnificent edifice. The two most well-known Supreme Court decisions on criminal justice stand for equality before the law, and that is why they are so well known. In *Gideon v. Wainwright*, the Court in 1963 held that states must provide a lawyer at state expense to all defendants charged with a serious crime who cannot afford to hire their own lawyer. . . . Three years later, in *Miranda v. Arizona*, the Court required the police to provide poor suspects with an attorney at state expense and to inform all suspects of their rights before questioning them in custody. In these landmark decisions, the Court sought to ameliorate societal inequalities—both among suspects and between suspects and the state—that undermined the criminal justice system's promise of equality. As the Court stated in *Miranda*, "[w]hile authorities are not required to relieve the accused of his poverty, they have the obligation not to take advantage of indigence in the administration of justice."

The prominence of these decisions, however, is misleading. They were both decided by the Supreme Court under Chief Justice Earl Warren, at a time when the Court was solidly liberal and strongly committed to racial and economic equality. At virtually every juncture since *Gideon* and *Miranda*, the Supreme Court has undercut the principle of equality reflected in those decisions, and has itself "take[n] advantage of indigence in the administration of justice." Today, those decisions stand out as anomalies. *Gideon* is a symbol of equality unrealized in practice; poor defendants are nominally entitled to the assistance of counsel at trial, but the Supreme Court has failed to demand that the assistance be meaningful. Lawyers who have slept through testimony or appeared in court drunk have nonetheless been deemed to have provided their indigent clients "effective assistance of counsel." And today's Court has so diluted *Miranda* that the decision has had little effect on actual police integration practices.

The exploitation of inequality in criminal justice is driven by the need to balance two fundamental and competing interests: the protection of constitutional rights, and the protection of law-abiding citizens from crime. Virtually all constitutional protections in criminal justice have a cost: they make the identification and prosecution of suspected criminals more difficult. Without a constitutional requirement that police have probable cause and a warrant before they conduct searches, for example, police officers would be far more effective in rooting out and stopping crime. Without jury trials, criminal justice administration would be much more efficient. But if police could enter our homes whenever they pleased, we would live in a police state, with no meaningful privacy protection. And absent jury trials, the community would have little check on overzealous prosecutors. Much of the public and academic debate about criminal justice focuses on where we should draw the line between law enforcement interests and constitutional protections. Liberals tend to argue for more rights-protective rules, while conservatives tend to advocate rules that give law enforcement more leeway. But both sides agree, at least in principle, that the line should be drawn in the same place for everyone.

In fact, however, we have repeatedly mediated the tension not by picking one point on the continuum, but in effect by picking two points—one for the more privileged and educated, the other for the poor and less educated. For example, the Supreme Court has ruled that the Fourth Amendment bars police from searching luggage, purses, or wallets without a warrant that is based on probable cause to believe evidence of a crime will be found. But at the same time, the Court permits police officers to approach any citizen—without any basis for suspicion—and request "consent" to search. The officer need not inform the suspect that he has a right to say no. This tactic, not surprisingly, is popular among the police, and is disproportionately targeted at young black men, who are less likely to assert their right to say no. In this way, the privacy of the privileged is guaranteed, but the police still get their evidence, and society does not have to pay the cost in increased crime of extending to everyone the right to privacy that the privileged enjoy. This pattern is repeated throughout the criminal justice system: the Court affirms a constitutional right, but in a manner that effectively protects the right only for the privileged few, while as a practical matter denying the right to those who are less privileged. By exploiting society's "background" inequality, the Court sidesteps the difficult question of how much constitutional protection we could afford if we were willing to ensure that it was enjoyed equally by all people.

Nor is the Supreme Court alone in exploiting inequality in this way. If there is a common theme in criminal justice policy in America, it is that we consistently seek to avoid difficult trade-offs by exploiting inequality. Politicians impose the most serious criminal sanctions on conduct in which they and their constituents are least likely to engage. Thus, a predominantly white Congress has mandated prison sentences for the possession and distribution of crack cocaine one hundred times more severe than the penalties for powder cocaine. African Americans comprise more than 90% of those found guilty of crack cocaine crimes, but only 20% of those found guilty of powder cocaine crimes. By contrast, when white youth began smoking marijuana in large numbers in the 1960s and 1970s, state legislatures responded by reducing penalties and in some states effectively decriminalizing marijuana possession. More broadly, it is unimaginable that our country's heavy reliance on incarceration would be tolerated if the black/white incarceration rates were reversed, and whites were incarcerated at seven times the rate that blacks are. The white majority can "afford" the costs associated with mass incarceration because the incarcerated mass is disproportionately nonwhite.

Similarly, police officers routinely use methods of investigation and interrogation against members of racial minorities and the poor that would be deemed unacceptable if applied to more privileged members of the community. "Consent" searches, pretextual traffic stops, and "quality of life" policing are all disproportionately used against black citizens. Courts assign attorneys to defend the poor in serious criminal trials whom the wealthy would not hire to represent them in traffic court. And jury commissioners and lawyers have long engaged in discriminatory practices that result in disproportionately white juries.

These double standards are not, of course, explicit; on the face of it, the criminal law is color-blind and class blind. But in a sense, this only makes the problem worse. The rhetoric of the criminal justice system sends the message that our society carefully protects everyone's constitutional rights, but in practice the rules assure that law enforcement prerogatives will generally prevail over the rights of minorities and the poor. By affording criminal suspects substantial constitutional protections in theory, the Supreme Court validates the results of the criminal justice system as fair. That formal fairness obscures the systemic concerns that ought to be raised by the fact that the prison population is overwhelmingly poor and disproportionately black.

I am not suggesting that the disproportionate results of the criminal justice system are wholly attributable to racism, nor that the double standards are intentionally designed to harm members of minority groups and the poor. Intent and motive are notoriously difficult to fathom, particularly where there are multiple actors and decisionmakers. . . . In fact, I think it more likely that the double standards have developed because they are convenient mechanisms for avoiding hard questions about competing interests, and it is human nature to avoid hard questions. But whatever the reasons, we have established two systems of criminal justice: one of the privileged, and another for the less privileged. Some of the distinctions are based on race, others on class, but in no true sense can it be said that all are equal before the criminal law. Thus, I take issue with those, like Professor Randall Kennedy, who argue that as long as we can rid the criminal justice system of *explicit* and *intentional* considerations of race, we will have solved the problem of inequality in criminal justice.[14] . . . To suggest that a "color-blind" set of rules is sufficient is to ignore the lion's share of inequality that pervades the criminal justice system today. The disparities I discuss are built into the very structure and doctrine of our criminal justice system, and unless and until we acknowledge and remedy them, we will have "no equal justice."

Equality in criminal justice does not necessarily mean more rights for the criminally accused. Indeed, I think it likely that were we to commit ourselves to equality, the substantive scope of constitutional protections accorded to the accused would be reduced, not expanded. If we had to pay full cost, in law enforcement terms, for the constitutional rights we now claim to protect, the scope of those constitutional rights would probably be cut back for all. But at least we would then strike the balance between law enforcement and constitutional rights honestly. . . .

No one disputes that the criminal justice system's legitimacy depends on equality before the law. . . . There are . . . strong pragmatic reasons for responding to inequality in criminal justice, because a criminal justice system based on double standards both fuels racial enmity and encourages crime.

The racially polarized reactions to the Simpson case illustrate a deep and longstanding racial divide on issues of criminal justice: blacks are consistently more skeptical of the criminal justice system than whites. A long history of racially discriminatory practices in criminal law enforcement has much to do with this skepticism, but it is not just a matter of history: the double standards we rely on today in drawing the lines between rights and law enforcement reinforce black alienation and distrust. Because criminal law governs the most serious sanctions that a society can impose on its members, inequity in its administration has especially corrosive consequences. Perceptions of race and class disparities in the criminal justice system are at the core of the race and class divisions in our society.

The perception and reality of double standards also contribute to the crime problem by eroding the legitimacy of the criminal law and undermining a cohesive sense of community. As any wise ruler knows (and many ineffective despots learn), the most effective way to govern is not through brute force or terror, but by fostering broad social acceptance for one's policies. Where a community accepts the social rules as legitimate, the rule will be largely self-enforcing. Studies have found that most people obey the law not because they fear formal punishment—the risk of actually being apprehended and punished is infinitesimal for all crimes other than murder—but because they and their peers have accepted and internalized the rules, and because they do not want to let their community down. The rules will be accepted, and community pressure to conform will be effective, only to the extent that "the community" believes that the rules are just and that the authority behind them is legitimate. Thus, although the double standards . . . were adopted for the purpose of *reducing* the costs of crime associated with protecting constitutional rights, . . . in the end they undermine the criminal justice system's legitimacy, and thereby *increase* crime and its attendant costs.

When significant sectors of a community view the system as unjust, law enforcement is compromised in at least two ways. First, people feel less willing to co-operate with the system, whether by offering leads to police officers, testifying as witnesses for the prosecution, or entering guilty verdicts as jurors. Second, and more importantly, people are more likely to commit crimes, precisely because the laws forbidding such behavior have lost much of their moral force. When the law loses its moral force, the only deterrents that remain are the strong-arm methods of conviction and imprisonment. We should not be surprised, then, that the United States has the second highest incarceration rate of all developed nations. And it should be no wonder that black America, which has been most victimized by the inequalities built into the criminal justice system, is simultaneously most plagued by crime and most distrustful of criminal law enforcement.

What is to be done? . . . The first step, of course, is to recognize the scope of the problem. Although African-Americans are generally skeptical of the criminal justice system's fairness, their skepticism is not shared by the white majority, nor apparently by the courts. Until now, the courts and legislatures have been extremely reluctant even to allow the issue of inequality in criminal justice to be aired, and have instead impermissibly exploited inequality to make the hard choices of criminal justice seem easier. . . . A realistic response to crime, and in the end our society's survival as a cohesive community, depend on a candid assessment of the uses of inequality in criminal justice.

The second step is to eliminate the double standards. This turns out to be rather straightforward in some instances, but difficult if not impossible in others. We could certainly require, for example, that police officers seeking consent to search informed citizens that they have the right to say no. But wealthy defendants will always be able to outspend poor defendants; not everyone can afford Johnny Cochran. Even an *attempt* to limit such disparities would be a reversal of the current approach, however, which affirmatively exploits them. Such reforms are necessary if the criminal justice system is to regain the legitimacy so critical to effective law enforcement.

But restoring legitimacy through adjusting the rules that govern criminal law enforcement will not be nearly enough. The double standards have also had a devastating impact on black communities, particularly in poor, inner-city enclaves. The racial divide fostered and furthered by inequality in criminal justice has contributed to a spiral of crime and decay in the inner city, corroding the sense of belonging that encourages compliance with the criminal law. Therefore, we cannot limit ourselves to restoring the criminal law's legitimacy, but must also seek to restore the communities that have been doubly ravaged by crime and the criminal justice system. To accomplish this, we must both reinforce and support community-building organizations in the inner cities, and change the way we respond to crime itself.

These remedies go hand in hand. In order to adopt a more effective approach to criminal punishment, we must rebuild communities. In order to rebuilt communities, we must forego our reliance on mass incarceration—a policy that has robbed inner-city neighborhoods of whole generations of young men. We respond to crime today in a self-defeating way, by stigmatizing criminals, cutting them off from their communities, and fostering criminal subcultures that encourage further criminal behavior. In doing so, we undermine one of the most important deterrents to crime: a sense of belonging to a law-abiding community. By the same token, to the extent that we reinforce and reify divisions between individuals and communities, and between the law-enforcing and law-breaking communities, we encourage continuing criminal behavior. If we are to reduce criminal recidivism, we must adopt measures that seek to reintegrate offenders into the community, and that reinforce social ties within and across communities.

This is an ambitious agenda. But unless all Americans begin to see the problem of inequality in criminal justice as their own, and unless we take responsible measures to respond to it, America's crime problem and racial divide will only get worse.

Endnotes

1. Toobin, J. (1995, October 23). A horrible human event. *The New Yorker*, 40.
2. Bradsher, K. (1995, April 17). Gap in wealth in U.S. called widest in West. *N.Y. Times*, p. A1; Bradsher, K. (1995, August 14). Low ranking for poor American children. *N.Y. Times*, p. A9.
3. Holmes, S. A. (1996, June 20). Income disparity between poorest and richest rises. *N.Y. Times*, p. A1.
4. Johnson, E. W. (1997, October 4). Corporate soulcraft in the age of brutal markets. *Business Ethics Quarterly*, 7(4).
5. Bureau of the Census, U.S. Dept of Commerce. *Statistical Abstract of the United States—1993*, 477 (Table 753).
6. Id. at 47 (Table 50), 471 (Table 741), 473 (Table 743).
7. In 1993, the infant mortality rate among whites was 6.8 deaths per 1,000 live births, while the rate among blacks was 16.5 deaths per 1,000 births. U.S. Dept. of Commerce, *Statistical Abstract of the United States—1996*, 93

(Table 127) (Infant Morality Rates, by Race). From 1980 to 1995, the unemployment rate among blacks has always been at least twice that among whites. In 1995, unemployment among blacks was 10.4%, and among whites was 4.9%. Id. at 413 (Table 64) (Unemployed Workers—Summary: 1980 to 1995).

8. Orfield, G., Bachmeier, M. D., James, D. R., & Eitle, T. (1997, April 5). Deepening segregation in American public schools (Harvard Project on School Desegregation.)

9. Massey, D. and Denton, N. (1993). *American apartheid: Segregation and the making of the underclass.* Cambridge, MA: Harvard University Press.

10. Lewen, D. C. (1993). Curing America's addiction to prisons. 20 Fordham Urb. L.J. 641, 646; Tonry, M. (1995). *Malign neglect—Race, crime and punishment in America.* New York: Oxford University Press; Butterfield, F. (1998, August 9). Prison population growing although crime rate drops, 19; Bureau of Justice Statistics. (1996). *Sourcebook of criminal justice statistics—1995*, 474; See also Ayres, I., & Waldfogel, J. (1994). A market test for race discrimination in bail setting. *Stan. L. Rev.*, 46; Maurer, M., & Huling, T. (1995, October 1).*Young black Americans and the criminal justice system: Five years later* (The Sentencing Project); Gates Jr., H. L. (1996, April 29/May 6). The charmer. *The New Yorker*; Mustard, D. B. (1997). Racial, ethnic and gender disparities in sentencing: Evidence from the U.S. federal courts. University of Georgia Economics Working Paper, 97–458.

11. Bachman, R. (1992, June). U.S. Department of Justice, Bureau of Justice Statistics. *Crime victimization in city, suburban, and rural areas: National crime victimization survey report.*

12. Hagan, J. and Peterson, R. (1995). Criminal inequality in America. In J. Hagan & R. Peterson, (Eds.), *Crime and Inequality* (25). Stanford: Stanford University Press.

13. Id. at 16.

14. Kennedy, R. (1997). *Race, crime and the law.* New York: Pantheon.

Questions

1. Summarize the major differences in how blacks and whites perceive the criminal justice system. Are there any similarities? If so, what are they?

2. To what degree do the inequalities in the criminal justice system reflect inequality in other areas of American society (e.g., housing, education, etc.)? Can Cole's belief that inequality is structurally inherent in the criminal justice system be extended to other areas?

3. According to Cole, how do double standards serve to worsen crime? What other effects do double standards have on minorities' communities?

4. Why does Cole claim that key legislative or legal precedents, such as *Gideon vs. Wainwright* (court-provided attorney for the indigent) and *Miranda vs. Arizona* (rights before questioning), are misleading and only give the impression of equity?

5. According to Cole, why is the court's decision to allow certain types of investigations inherently discriminatory? Why are there drastic differences in sentencing for specific types of crime (e.g., crack-cocaine possession versus powder-cocaine possession)? Are there any reasons, other than those provided by Cole, that might explain these apparent inequities?

SOME PRINCIPLES OF STRATIFICATION

KINGSLEY DAVIS AND WILBERT E. MOORE
Princeton University

"Some Principles of Stratification," by Kingsley Davis and Wilbert E. Moore, reprinted from American Sociological Review. *pp. 242–249.*

In this classic essay, Kingsley Davis and Wilbert Moore explore the reasons behind social stratification and inequality. They also provide a framework for understanding variation in stratification between societies. This piece continues to serve as the backbone of the functionalist explanation for inequality.

Starting from the proposition that no society is "classless," or unstratified, an effort is made to explain in functional terms, the universal necessity which calls forth stratification in any social system. Next, an attempt is made to explain the roughly uniform distribution of prestige as between the major types of positions in every society. Since, however, there occur between one society and another part differences in the degree and kind of stratification, some attention is also given to the varieties of social inequality and the variable factors that give rise to them.

Clearly, the present task requires two different lines of analysis—one to understand the universal, the other to understand the variable features of stratification. Naturally each line of inquiry aids the other and is indispensable, and in the treatment that follows the two will be interwoven, although, because of space limitations, the emphasis will be on the universals.

Throughout, it will be necessary to keep in mind one thing—namely, that the discussion relates to the system of positions, not to the individuals occupying those positions. It is one thing to ask why different positions carry different degrees of prestige, and quite another to ask how certain individuals get into those positions. Although, as the argument will try to show, both questions are related, it is essential to keep them separate in our thinking. Most of the literature on stratification has tried to answer the second question (particularly with regard to the ease or difficulty of mobility between strata) without tracking the first. The first question, however, is logically prior and, in the case of any particular individual or group, factually prior.

The Functional Necessity of Stratification

Curiously, however, the main functional necessity explaining the universal presence of stratification is precisely the requirement faced by any society of placing and motivating individuals in the social structure. As a functioning mechanism a society must somehow distribute its members in social positions and induce them to perform the duties of these positions. It must thus concern itself with motivation at two different levels: to instill in the proper individuals the desire to fill certain positions, and, once in these positions, the desire to perform the duties attached to them. Even though the social order may be relatively static in form, there is a continuous process of metabolism as new individuals are born into it, shift with age, and die off. Their absorption into the positional system must somehow be arranged and motivated. This is true whether the system is competitive or non-competitive. A competitive system gives greater importance to the motivation to achieve positions, whereas a non-competitive system gives perhaps greater importance to the motivation to perform the duties of the positions; but in any system both types of motivation are required.

If the duties associated with the various positions were all equally pleasant to the human organism, all equally important to societal survival, and all equally in need of the same ability or talent, it would make no difference who got into which positions, and the problem of social placement would be greatly reduced. But actually it does make a great deal of difference who gets into which positions, not only because some positions are inherently more agreeable than others, but also because some require special talents or training and some are functionally more important than others. Also, it is essential that the duties of the positions be performed with the diligence that their importance requires. Inevitably, then, a society must have, first, some kind of rewards that it can use as inducements, and second, some way of distributing these rewards differentially according to positions. The rewards and their distribution become a part of the social order, and thus give rise to stratification.

One may ask what kind of rewards a society has at its disposal in distributing its personnel and securing essential services. It has, first of all, the things that contribute to sustenance and comfort. It has, second, the things that contribute to humor and diversion. And it has, finally, the things that contribute to self respect and ego expansion. The last, because of the peculiarly social character of the self, is largely a function of the opinion of others, but it nonetheless ranks in importance with the first two. In any social system all three kinds of rewards must be dispensed differentially according to positions.

In a sense the rewards are "built into" the position. They consist in the "rights" associated with the position, plus what may be called its accompaniments or perquisites. Often the rights, and sometimes the accompaniments are functionally related to the duties of the position. (Rights as viewed by the incumbent are usually duties as viewed by other members of the community.) However, there may be a host of subsidiary rights and perquisites that are not essential to the function of the position and have only an indirect and symbolic connection with its duties, but which still may be of considerable importance in inducing people to seek the positions and fulfill the essential duties.

If the rights and perquisites or different positions in a society must be unequal, then the society must be stratified, because that is precisely what stratification means. Social inequality is thus an unconsciously evolved device by which societies ensure that the most important positions are conscientiously filled by the most qualified persons. Hence every society, no matter how simple or complex, must differentiate persons in terms or both prestige and esteem, and must therefore possess a certain amount of institutionalized inequality.

It does not follow that the amount or type of inequality need to be the same in all societies. This is largely a function of factors that will be discussed presently.

The Two Determinants of Positional Rank

Granting the general function that inequality subserves, one can specify the two factors that determine the relative rank of different positions. In general those positions convey the best reward, and hence have the highest rank, which (a) have the greatest importance for the society and (b) require the greatest training or talent. The first factor concerns function and is a matter of relative significance; the second concerns means and is a matter of scarcity.

Differential Functional Importance

Actually a society does not need to reward positions in proportion to their functional importance. It merely needs to give sufficient reward to them to ensure that they will be filled competently. In other words, it must see that less essential positions do not compete successfully with more essential ones. If a position is easily filled, it need not be heavily rewarded, even though important. On the other hand, if it is important but hard to fill, the reward must be high enough to get it filled anyway. Functional importance is therefore a necessary but not a sufficient cause of high rank being assigned to a position.[1]

Differential Scarcity of Personnel

Practically all positions, no matter how acquired, require some form of skill or capacity for performance. This is implicit in the very notion of position, which implies that the incumbent must, by virtue of his incumbency, accomplish certain things.

There are, ultimately, only two ways in which a person's qualifications come about: through inherent capacity or through training. Obviously, in concrete activities both are always necessary, but from a practical standpoint the scarcity may lie primarily in one or the other, as well as in both. Some positions require innate talents of such high degree that the persons who fill them are bound to be rare. In many cases, however, talent is fairly abundant in the population but the training process is so long, costly, and elaborate that relatively few can qualify. Modern medicine, for example, is within the mental capacity of most individuals, but a medical education is so burdensome and expensive that virtually none would undertake it if the position of the M.D. did not carry a reward commensurate with the sacrifice.

If the talents required for a position are abundant and the training easy, the method of acquiring the position may have little to do with its duties. There may be, in fact, a virtually accidental relationship. But if the skills required are scarce by reason of the rarity of talent or the costliness of training, the position, if functionally important, must have an attractive power that will draw the necessary skills in competition with other positions. This means, in effect, that the position must be high in the social scale—must command great prestige, high salary, ample leisure, and the like.

How Variations Are to be Understood

In so far as there is a difference between one system of stratification and another, it is attributable to whatever factors affect the two determinants of differential reward—namely, functional importance and scarcity of personnel. Positions important in one society may not be important in another, because the conditions faced by the societies, or their degree of internal development, may be different. The same conditions, in turn, may affect the question of scarcity; for in some societies the stage or development, or the external situation, may wholly obviate the necessity of certain kinds of skill or talent. Any particular system of stratification, then, can be understood as a product of the special conditions affecting the two aforementioned grounds of differential reward.

Major Societal Functions and Stratification

Religion

The reason why religion is necessary is apparently to be found in the fact that human society achieves its unity primarily through the possession by its members of certain ultimate values and ends in common. Although these values and ends are subjective, they influence behavior, and their integration enables the society to operate as a system. Derived neither from inherited nor from external nature, the have evolved as a part of culture by communication and moral pressure. They must, however, appear to the members of the society to have some reality, and it is the role of religious belief and ritual to supply and reinforce this appearance of reality. Through belief and ritual the common ends and values are connected with an imaginary world symbolized by concrete sacred objects, which would in turn is related in a meaningful way to the facts and trials of the individual's life. Through the worship of the sacred objects and the beings they symbolize, and the acceptance of supernatural prescriptions that are the same time codes of behavior, a powerful control over human conduct is exercised, guiding it along lines sustaining the institutional structure and conforming to the ultimate ends and values. . . .

. . . There is a peculiar relation between the duties of the religious official and the special privileges he enjoys. If the supernatural world governs the destinies of men more ultimately than does the real world, its earthly representative, the person through whom one may communicate with the supernatural, must be a powerful individual. He is a keeper of sacred tradition, a skilled performer of the ritual, and an interpreter of lore and myth. He is in such close contact with the gods that he is viewed as possessing some of their characteristics. He is, in short, a bit sacred, and hence free from some of the more vulgar necessities and controls.

It is no accident, therefore, that religious functionaries have been associated with the very highest positions of power, as in theocratic regimes. Indeed, looking at it from this point of view, one may wonder why it is that they do not get *entire* control over their societies. The functions that prevent this are worthy of note.

In the first place, the amount of technical competence necessary for the performance of religious duties is small. Scientific or artistic capacity is not required. Anyone can set himself up as enjoying an intimate relation with deities, and nobody can successfully dispute him. Therefore, the factor of scarcity of personnel does not operate in the technical sense.

One may assert, on the other hand, that religious ritual is often elaborate and religious lore abstruse, and that priestly ministrations require tact, if not intelligence. This is true, but the technical requirements of the profession are for the most part adventitious, not related to the end in the same way that science is related to air travel. The priest can never be free from competition, since the criteria of whether or not one has genuine contact with the supernatural are never strictly clear. It is this competition that debases the priestly position below what might be expected at first glance. That is why priestly prestige is highest in those societies where membership in the profession is rigidly controlled by the priestly guild itself. That is why, in part at least, elaborate devices are utilized to stress the identification of the person with his office—spectacular costume, abnormal conduct, special diet, segregated residence, celibacy, conspicuous leisure, and the like. In fact, the priest is always in danger of becoming somewhat discredited—as happens in a secularized society—because in a world of stubborn fact, ritual and sacred knowledge alone will not grow crops or build houses. Furthermore, unless he is protected by a professional guild, the priest's identification with the supernatural tends to preclude his acquisition of abundant worldly goods.

* * *

Government

Like religion, government plays a unique and indispensable part in society. But in contrast to religion, which provides integration in terms of sentiments, beliefs, and rituals, it organizes the society in terms of law and authority. Furthermore, it orients the society to the actual rather than the unseen world.

The main functions of government are, internally, the ultimate enforcement of norms, the final arbitration of conflicting interests, and the overall planning and direction of society; and externally, the handling of war and diplomacy. To carry out these functions it acts as the agent of the entire people, enjoys a monopoly of force, and controls all individuals within its territory.

Political action, by definition, implies authority. An official can command because he has authority, and the citizen must obey because he is subject to that authority. For this reason stratification is inherent in the nature of political relationships.

So clear is the power embodied in political position that political inequality is sometimes thought to comprise all inequality. But it can be shown that there are other bases of stratification, that the following controls operate in practice to keep political power from becoming complete: (a) The fact that the actual holders of political office, and especially those determining top policy must necessarily be few in number compared to the total population. (b) The fact that the rulers respect the interest of the group rather than of themselves, and are therefore restricted in their behavior by rules and mores designed to enforce this limitation of interest. (c) The fact that the holder of political office has his authority by virtue of his office and nothing else, and therefore any special knowledge, talent, or capacity he may claim is purely incidental, so that he often has to depend upon others for technical assistance.

In view of these limiting factors, it is not strange that the rulers often have less power and prestige than a literal enumeration of their formal rights would lead one to expect.

Wealth, Property, and Labor

Every position that secures for its incumbent a livelihood is, by definition, economically rewarded. For this reason there is an economic aspect to those positions (e.g., political and religious) the main function of which is not economic. It therefore becomes convenient for the society to use unequal economic returns as a principal means of controlling the entrance of persons into positions and stimulating the performance of their duties. The amount of the economic return therefore becomes one of the main indices of social status.

It should be stressed, however, that a position does not bring power and prestige *because* it draws a high income. Rather, it draws a high income because it is functionally important and the available personnel is for one reason or another scarce. It is therefore superficial and erroneous to regard high income as the cause of a man's power and prestige, just as it is erroneous to think that a man's fever is the cause of his disease.

The economic source of power and prestige is not income primarily, but the ownership of capital goods (including patents, good will, and professional reputation). . . . Even in situations where social values are widely commercialized and earnings are the readiest method of judging social position, income does not confer prestige on a position so much as it induces people to compete for the position. It is true that a man who has a high income as a result of one position may find this money helpful in climbing into another position as well, but this again reflects the effect of his initial, economically advantageous status, which exercises its influence through the medium of money.

· · ·

Technical Knowledge

The function of finding means to single goals, without any concern with the choice between goals, is the exclusively technical sphere. The explanation of why positions requiring great technical skill receive fairly high rewards is easy to see, for it is the simplest case of the rewards being so distributed as to draw talent and motivate training. Why they seldom if ever receive the highest rewards is also clear: the importance of technical knowledge from a societal point of view is never so great as the integration of goals, which takes place on the religious, political, and economic levels. Since the technological level is concerned solely by means, a purely technical position must ultimately be subordinate to other positions that are religious, political, or economic in character.

Nevertheless, the distinction between expert and layman in any social order is fundamental, and cannot be entirely reduced to other terms. Methods of recruitment, as well as of reward, sometimes lead to the erroneous interpretation that technical positions are economically determined. Actually, however, the acquisition of knowledge and skill cannot be accomplished by purchase, although the opportunity to learn may be. The control of the avenues of training may inhere as a sort of property right in certain families or classes, giving them power and prestige in consequence. Such a situation adds an artificial scarcity to the natural scarcity of skills and talents. On the other hand, it is possible

for an opposite situation to arise. The rewards of technical position may be so great that a condition of excess supply is created, leading to at least temporary devaluation of the rewards. Thus "unemployment in the learned professions" may result in a debasement of the prestige of those positions. Such adjustments and readjustments are constantly occurring in changing societies; and it is always well to bear in mind that the efficiency of a stratified structure may be affected by the modes of recruitment for positions. The social order itself, however, sets limits to the inflation or deflation of the prestige of experts: and over-supply tends to debase the rewards and discourage recruitment or produce revolution, whereas an under-supply tends to increase the rewards or weaken the society in competition with other societies.

Particular systems of stratification show a wide range with respect to the exact position of technically competent persons. This range is perhaps most evident in the degree of specialization. Extreme division of labor tends to create many specialists without high prestige since the training is short and the required native capacity relatively small. On the other hand it also ends to accentuate the high position of the true experts—scientists, engineers, and administrators—by increasing their authority relative to other functionally important positions. But the idea of a technocratic social order or a government or priesthood of engineers or social scientists neglects the limitations of knowledge and skills as a basic for performing social functions. To the extent that the social structure is truly specialized the prestige of the technical person must also be circumscribed.

Variation in Stratified Systems

The generalized principles of stratification here suggested form a necessary preliminary to a consideration of types of stratified systems, because it is in terms of these principles that the types must be described. This can be seen by trying to delineate types according to certain modes of variation. For instance, some of the most important modes (together with the polar types in terms of them) seem to be as follows:

(a) The Degree of Specialization.   The degree of specialization affects the fineness and multiplicity of the gradations in power and prestige. It also influences the extent to which particular functions may be emphasized in the invidious system, since a given function cannot receive much emphasis in the hierarchy until it has achieved structural separation from the other functions. Finally, the amount of specialization influences the bases of selection. Polar types: *Specialized, Unspecialized.*

(b) The Nature of the Functional Emphasis. In general when emphasis is put on sacred matters, a rigidity is introduced that tends to limit specialization and hence the development of technology. In addition, a brake is placed on social mobility, and on the development of bureaucracy. When the preoccupation with the sacred is withdrawn, leaving greater scope for purely secular preoccupations, a great development, and rise in status, of economic and technological positions seemingly takes place. Curiously, a concomitant rise in political position is not likely, because it has usually been allied with the religious and stands to gain little by the decline of the latter. It is also possible for a society to emphasize family functions—as in relatively undifferentiated societies where high mortality requires high fertility and kinship forms the main basis of social organization. Main types: *Familistic, Authoritarian (Theocratic* or sacred, and *Totalitarian* or secular), *Capitalistic.*

(c) The Magnitude of Invidious Differences. What may be called the amount of social distance between positions, taking into account the entire scale, is something that should lend itself to quantitative measurement. Considerable differences apparently exist between different societies in this regard, and also between parts of the same society. Polar types: *Equalitarian, Inequalitarian.*

(d) The Degree of Opportunity. The familiar question of the amount of mobility is different from the question of the comparative equality or inequality of rewards posed above, because the two criteria may vary independently up to a point. For instance, the tremendous divergences in monetary income in the United States are far greater than those found in primitive societies, yet the equality of opportunity to move from one rung to the other in the social scale may also be greater in the United States than in a hereditary tribal kingdom. Polar types: *Mobile* (open), *Immobile* (closed).

(e) The Degree of Stratum Solidarity. Again, the degree of "class solidarity" (or the presence of specific organizations to promote class interests) may vary to some extent independently of the other criteria, and hence is an important principle in classifying systems of stratification. Polar types: *Class organized, Class unorganized.*

External Conditions

What state any particular system of stratification is in with reference to each of these modes of variation depends on two things: (1) its state with reference to the other ranges of variation, and (2) the conditions outside the system of stratification which nevertheless influence that system. Among the latter are the following:

(a) The Stage of Cultural Development. As the cultural heritage grows, increased specialization becomes necessary, which in turn contributes to the enhancement of mobility, a decline of stratum solidarity, and a change of functional emphasis.

(b) Situation with Respect to Other Societies. The presence or absence of open conflict with other societies, of free trade relations or cultural diffusion, all influence the class structure to some extent. A chronic state of warfare tends to place emphasis upon the military functions, especially when the opponents are more or less equal. Free trade, on the other hand, strengthens the hand of the trader at the expense of the warrior and priest. Free movement of ideas generally has an effect. Migration and conquest create special circumstances.

(c) Size of the Society. A small society limits the degree to which functional specialization can go, the degree of segregation of different strata, and the magnitude of inequality.

Composite Types

Much of the literature on stratification has attempted to classify concrete systems into a certain number of types. This task is deceptively simple, however, and should come at the end of an analysis of elements and principles, rather than at the beginning. If the preceding discussion has any validity, it indicates that there are a number of modes of variation between different systems, and that any one system is a composite of the society's status with reference to all these modes of variation. The danger of trying to classify whole societies under such rubrics as *caste, feudal,* or *open class* is that one or two criteria are selected and others ignored, the result being an unsatisfactory solution to the problem posed. The present discussion has been offered as a possible approach to the more systematic classification of composite types.

Endnote

1. Unfortunately, functional importance is difficult to establish. To use the position's prestige to establish it, as is often unconsciously done, constitutes circular reasoning from our point of view. There are, however, two independent clues: (a) the degree to which a position is functionally unique, there being no other positions that can perform the same function satisfactorily; (b) the degree to which other positions are dependent on the one in question. Both clues are best exemplified in organized systems of positions built around one major function. Thus, in most complex societies the religious, political, economic, and educational functions are handled by distinct structures not easily interchangeable. In addition, each structure possesses many different positions, some clearly dependent on, if not subordinate to, others. In sum, when an institutional nucleus become differentiated around one main function, and at the same time organizes a large portion of the populations into its relationships, the *key* positions in it are of the highest functional importance. The absence of such specialization does not prove functional unimportance, for the whole society may be relatively unspecialized; but it is safe to assume that the more important functions receive the first and clearest structural differentiation.

Questions

1. Why do Davis and Moore contend that stratification *must* exist in every society?

2. What are the two determinants of positional rank? How do they interplay with one another?

3. According to Davis and Moore, why are religious leaders given relatively high positions in the social hierarchy? What prevents them from having an even higher social position? What about government officials?

4. What role does technical knowledge and training play in determining the status or prestige associated with a particular position?

5. What contributes to variations in stratification across societies?

6. What external conditions affect the type of stratified system that emerges in a society?

7. Think about your own career goal. (If you are still undecided, think of a job that closely matches your interests at this time.) How would Davis and Moore explain that job's relative position in the social hierarchy? Cite the impact of functional importance of the job, the abundance of people available to fill the job, and the length and type of technical training and expertise required, among other factors.

PUBLIC OPINION ON ABORIGINAL RIGHTS

J. RICK PONTING
JERILYNN KIELY

Reprinted by permission from First Nations in Canada: Perspectives on Opportunity, Empowerment, and Self-Determination. *Copyright © 1997 by McGraw-Hill Ryerson.*

Aboriginal rights have long been and still are key issues in Canada's political and social landscape. The long-standing nature of such issues is highlighted by the antiquity of some of Canada's legislation, such as the 1850 Indian Protection Act. In contemporary Canada, the question of Aboriginal rights seems to touch on nearly every aspect of society including housing, employment, land-use and education (to name only a few). If Aboriginal rights are to be granted by the Canadian government (it holds the power with regard to the issue), widespread public support would be necessary because "native" issues are a sensitive topic for politicians seeking election (or re-election). Thus, an important question is: how much public support is there for Aboriginal rights specifically and for Aboriginals in general? In this selection, J. Rick Ponting and Jerilynn Kiely present a broad overview of Canadians' thoughts on Aboriginal rights and compare how the public's opinion changed (or not) over the twenty-year period focused on in this study (1976–1994).

The first national survey on Aboriginal issues was conducted by Ponting and Gibbins in 1976. With few exceptions, such as significant deterioration of support for First Nations in Quebec and British Columbia, the findings from that comprehensive survey still hold true today, as evidenced by the findings from Ponting's detailed, ten-year follow-up national study and an even more detailed 1994 national survey kindly provided to the authors by the Angus Reid Group. We shall discuss the main themes that emerge from those studies. In order to retain focus on the "big picture" and to avoid getting bogged down in detail, we usually report percentages only parenthetically, if at all. Similarly, readers are referred elsewhere (Ponting and Gibbins, 1980: 71–72; Ponting, 1987a: A1–A7) for the methodological details of the surveys. Suffice it to say here that in all three surveys the samples were large (over 1800) and the 1976 and 1986 surveys were conducted using face-to-face interviews in respondents' homes in the official language of the respondent's choice, while the 1994 survey differed by using telephone interviews. All three surveys were conducted by reputable polling firms.[1]

Little Knowledge, Low Priority

Canadians know very little about Aboriginal affairs. In part, that is because we tend to pay little attention to most Aboriginal matters in the mass media and attach a low priority to Aboriginal issues, except when they touch close to home by involving personal inconvenience or threat to our livelihood. The evidence of this widespread ignorance is overwhelming, as measured by such indicators as not knowing the meaning of the term "Aboriginal people," not being aware of the existence of the Indian Act, not being aware of the existence of Aboriginal rights in the Constitution, and over-estimating by a factor of at least two the proportion of Native people in the Canadian population. Around 15 percent of Canadians are almost totally oblivious to Aboriginal matters in this country.

Opposition to Special Status

With the exception of a select few situations, such as First Nations' special relationship with the land, Canadians manifest a pronounced tendency to reject what they view as "special status" for Native people. This is shown in the curve in Figure 1, which plots the distribution of the sample on two indexes, one of which is the Index of Support for Special Status for Natives, in the 1986 survey. A respondent's score on this index is his or her average score on four items dealing with special institutional arrangements for Native people. As with most of the indexes reported in this chapter, this one comprises statements with which respondents are asked to indicate their degree of agreement or disagreement, on a scale ranging from "strongly agree" to "strongly disagree."[2]

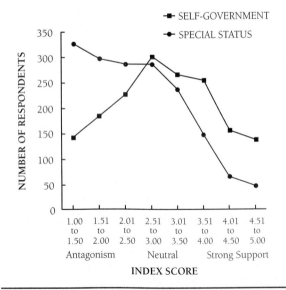

FIGURE 1   Distribution of the Sample on the Index of Support for Special Status and on the Index of Support for Native Self-Government

In Figure 1 we shall observe that most respondents fall at the unsupportive end of the scale measuring support for special status for Native people. In 1986 even stronger opposition to special status was found in most questions that explicitly use the word "special." For instance, in 1986, when respondents were given two statements—one of which described special institutional arrangements for Native people and one of which did not—and were asked to choose the one that came closer to their views, it was repeatedly found that almost two-thirds of respondents opted for the statement that denied special status to Native people. One concrete example of this involved the two statements: "For crimes committed by Indians on Indian reserves, there should be special courts with Indian judges" (only 27 percent chose this); and "Crimes committed by Indians on Indian reserves should be handled in the same way as crimes committed elsewhere" (65 percent chose this). By 1994, there was some softening of this antagonism to special status[3] and the issue had become less clear-cut. Some ambivalence had entered Canadians' minds. On some questions, Canadians were still more antagonistic than supportive.[4] On other questions, though, there was more support than antagonism.[5] Our interpretation of this discrepancy is that it is an indication of Canadians' opinions on Aboriginal issues being rather inchoate. Although opinions on Aboriginal issues are not exactly formless, because Aboriginal issues are so peripheral to most Canadians we should expect a less consistently structured set of opinions on these issues than on some other issues such as the environment or national unity.

Such opposition to "special status" as does exist is probably rooted both in the long-standing opposition of many Canadians outside Quebec to special status in Confederation for Quebec, and in a norm of equality that is widely held among Canadians.

Obviously, Canadians' orientation to "special status" for First Nations could have important implications for the degree of self-determination that is attainable under the federal government's "self-government" legislation. The division of public opinion on this is captured nicely by a 1994 question (L1) pertaining to "self-government for Canada's aboriginal peoples—that is, both status and non-status Indians, the Métis and the Inuit." The remainder of the question, and the equal division of respondents across the three response options, follows:

> Which of the following three broad statements best describes how you feel about aboriginal self-government, or the right of aboriginals to govern themselves?

- Aboriginal peoples in Canada have an historic, existing, inherent right to self-government. (29%)
- The federal and provincial governments should allow aboriginal peoples to govern themselves. (27%)
- Aboriginal people have no more right to self-government than other ethnic groups in Canada. (28%)

We pursue these issues of rights and self-government in more detail below.

Support for Self-Government and Aboriginal Rights

Paradoxically, antagonism toward special status coexists with a support for Native self-government and even for recognition of the inherent right to self-government as an existing Aboriginal or treaty right. For many Canadians, self-government is less a manifestation of special status than a basic democratic right of self-determination. This interpretation is suggested by the fact that in Figure 1 the curve representing the distribution of the sample on an Index of Support for Native Self-Government[6] exhibits a markedly different shape than the curve for the Index of Support for Special Status for Natives. The curve depicting support for Native self-government is akin to the famous bell-shaped curve, and the average score is slightly to the supportive side of the mid-point of the scale. The curve for support for special status is highly skewed.

Surprisingly, even when the notion of the inherent right to self-government was linked with the Charlottetown Accord, defeated in the 1992 nationwide referendum, a small majority of the 1994 sample favoured its recognition as an Aboriginal and treaty right.

The degree of autonomy of First Nations governments from provincial governments is of pivotal importance in defining the fundamental character of First Nations governments. Replacing non-Native bureaucrats with brown-faced bureaucrats who administer essentially the same provincial policies is not self-determination. Yet, that is precisely what a substantial majority (akin to the 1986 survey's two-thirds disapproving of special status) of the 1994 respondents preferred when given the option between two statements, as follows:

Aboriginals could develop and run their own programs in [such areas as health, education and child welfare] without the province having any authority. (19%)

versus

Aboriginals could manage the programs in these areas but they would still be subject to provincial laws and standards. (65%)

Canadians' views of the capability of Aboriginal governments are improving.[7] When Canadians were asked in 1994 "how much confidence you have . . . in terms of the role they might play in working towards some solutions to aboriginal peoples' concerns," the chiefs of large bands garnered majority support, as did national Aboriginal organizations.[8] Also, there is plurality support for the eventual dismantling of the Department of Indian Affairs and Northern Development (DIAND) and strong majority support for the Manitoba approach of transferring DIAND responsibilities to Aboriginal control as "a model for moving towards aboriginal self-government across the country." However, indications are that on the matter of the representativeness of Aboriginal leaders, by 1994 the skeptics had closed the gap on the believers, such that the population had come to be evenly divided.[9]

General Sympathy

To some extent, support for Native self-government and Native rights is a reflection of a more general positive orientation toward, or attitudinal support for, Natives. This might be called "sympathy," if that word can be stripped of connotations of condescension. Overall, the Canadian population in both 1976 and 1986 tended to be more sympathetic than antagonistic toward Native people. This observation is based on respondents' scores on composite indexes of several questions in each survey.[10] In 1986 two separate indexes were used. Only 10–15 percent of Canadians were *consistently* antagonistic (strongly or mildly) toward Native people across both scales. Twice as many were *consistently* supportive. On both indexes, as on the 1976 index, the average score for the sample was well above the mid-point of the scale. Further evidence of a generalized sympathy comes from other questions not included in any of the indexes. For instance, in 1986 a majority (57 percent) disagreed with the statement "Indians are a bunch of complainers" (only 23 percent agreed), and a large majority (71 percent) disagreed with the statement "The more I hear and see about Indians in the news media, the less respect I have for them" (only 13 percent agreed).

However, there has been a deterioration in support for Native people over the almost two decades covered by the surveys. For instance, in 1976 an overwhelming majority (72 percent) agreed with the statement "Indians deserve to be a lot better off economically than they are now." By 1986, only a plurality agreed (48 percent versus 29 percent disagreeing). The question was not asked on the 1994 survey, but it was a smaller plurality that took the pro-Aboriginal stance in response to the following somewhat similar statement: "Most of the problems of aboriginal people are brought on by themselves" (40 percent disagreed; 31 percent agreed). Yet, on another question that might carry moral over-tones to respondents who adhere to the Protestant work ethic, a solid majority of the 1994 sample agreed (57 percent versus 15 percent who disagreed) with the statement "Aboriginal people are hard-working and industrious, and capable of earning their way if given a chance."

The deterioration in support for Native people can be seen in Table 1. There we observe that in Canada as a whole, the victimization stereotype of Indians/Aboriginal people lost about half of its adherents (as a percentage of the total population) between 1976 and 1994, while the alcohol and drug-abuse stereotype almost doubled in prevalence during that period, to the point of reaching parity with the victimization view. Note that in 1976, British Columbia was right at the national average level of sympathy for Native people, but a decade later it was well below the national average. Whereas a majority of Quebeckers, perhaps expressing a shared sense of deprivation as an ethnic minority in Canada, viewed Indians as victims of racism or discrimination in 1976, by 1994 only one-fifth did. The view that alcohol or drugs was the main problem facing Indians was scarcely detectable in Quebec in 1976, but eighteen years later it was not only held by a large minority of Quebeckers, but was notably more prevalent in Quebec than the view of Aboriginal people as victims of racism and discrimination.

Sensitivity to Native People's Special Relationship to the Land

Respondents exhibited a generally supportive opinion for Native people on matters related to land and land-use conflict. Two examples, from among several available in the 1986 survey, are:

- a (slight) majority of Canadians agreed (versus one-third who disagreed) with the statement: "Where Natives' use of land conflicts with natural resource development, Native use should be given priority."

- a near majority disagreed (48 percent versus 37 percent agreeing) that giving Native people special hunting rights "just isn't fair."[11]

On a 1994 question a plurality agreed (44 percent versus 29 percent disagreeing) with the statement: "Aboriginals have a special relationship to the land and can be trusted as better caretakers of the environment."

Opposition to Tactical Assertiveness

Canadians tend not to be accepting of any escalation of First Nations' protest tactics beyond a rather tame level. Protest was a major focus of the 1976 survey (Ponting and Gibbins, 1981), and the 1994 survey also included several questions on the topic. The results are broadly similar over the two decades. In 1976, the use of the courts and of protest marches received majority approval, as did "requesting that a royal commission be formed to study Indians' problems." The majority disapproved of the more assertive tactics of barricading roads or railroads crossing Indian reserves, and threatening violence. Even boycotting private businesses elicited strong disapproval ratings.

In 1994, among five tactics listed, the only one for which approvers outnumbered disapprovers was the blockading of natural resource extraction on land claimed by Aboriginal people.[12] A "peaceful blockade of a major highway to press for speedier action on land claims" met with resounding disapproval as did the strategy of unilaterally asserting sovereignty.[13] Even making a formal complaint to the United Nations was approved by only a little more than a third of the sample (37 percent versus 45 percent disapproving). Similarly, only one-third approved of delaying completion of a resource megaproject.

Regional Variation

To this point, discussion of public opinion has been couched in terms of Canada as a whole. That, however, obscures important variations from one region of the country to another. Those regional variations take on considerable practical significance when one remembers that many of the reforms sought by First Nations require the approval of provincial governments.

In some provinces, notably Saskatchewan and now Quebec, support for Aboriginal people is clearly rather low, while in Ontario support is comparatively high. Table 1 provides examples from the three surveys. Note how Quebeckers stand out as thinking Aboriginal

TABLE 1 Regional Variation in Public Opinion on Aboriginal Issues

Item or Statement	Canada	Atl. Can.	Mtl.	Rest of Que.	Tor.	Rest of ON	MB	SK	AB	Vanc.	Rest of BC
Means Score on Index of:											
Sympathy for Natives, 1976*	3.31	3.10		3.56		3.25	3.15	2.90	3.00		3.30
Sympathy for Natives, 1986*	3.22	3.12	3.17	3.31	3.47	3.30	3.13	2.96	3.13	3.09	2.97
Sympathy for Indians, 1986*	3.29	3.09	3.42	3.45	3.48	3.38	3.39	2.91	3.08	3.04	3.04
Support for Special Status for Native People, 1986*	2.56	2.38	2.15	2.96	2.34	2.45	2.44	2.14	2.07	2.11	2.07
1994 Statement											
It just isn't right for Natives to have special rights that other Canadians don't have.											
% agreeing	41	47	57		24		53	55	47	41	
% disagreeing	34	36	32		30		37	34	36	46	
1994 Question											
Generally speaking, do you think Canada's aboriginal people are being reasonable or unreasonable in terms of their current land claims?											
Reasonable (%)	38	34	30		32		55	53	50	49	
Unreasonable (%)	41	45	66		21		41	43	38	46	
Main (1976)/Most Serious (1994) Problem Facing Indians (1976)/Canada's Aboriginal People (1994) Today?											
% citing racism or discrimination											
1976	39	27	51		36		31		22	44	
1994	21	20	20		18		28		22	24	
% citing alcohol or drugs											
1976	12	7	1		13		28			12	
1994	23	25	30		17		21		29	13	

*Denotes possible range is 1.0 to 5.0, where 5.0 is most sympathetic.

people are being unreasonable in their land claims and how a high proportion of people from that province, along with Manitobans and Albertans, view alcohol or drugs as the most serious problem or issue facing Aboriginal people in Canada. Conversely, alcohol and drugs rank as only the seventh most serious Aboriginal problem in British Columbians' view. All four western provinces also stand apart from the rest of Canada in thinking that Aboriginal people are being reasonable in their land claims.

Table 2 depicts regional variation in answers to the open-ended question asking respondents to name the Aboriginal issue or problem that they think is most serious. In numerous ways, this table reveals that Canadians in different regions have a very different picture of Aboriginal matters. For instance, "Integration into society" is most commonly identified by Quebeckers as the most serious Aboriginal issue or problem, whereas, at the other extreme, it ranks ninth in importance in Saskatchewan. Ontarians and British Columbians rank education as the most serious Aboriginal issue or problem, whereas in Quebec it ranks seventh. Prairie residents stand apart as being more likely to see self-government as a more serious issue than do residents of other provinces. Regional subcultures are reflected in other ways, too. For instance, Alberta, with its frontier ideology's emphasis on self-reliance and "rugged individualism," has a notably higher proportion of respondents citing "lack of initiative or motivation" than do the Atlantic provinces and Quebec, where structural barriers to personal success are more widely recognized and acknowledged.

Regional variation is also pronounced on other measures not shown in Table 1 or 2. For instance, the proportion of the public that is oblivious to Native issues is much larger in Quebec than in the other provinces. In addition, familiarity with Native matters tends to be regionally specific. To the extent that Canadians are familiar with Native matters at all, that familiarity is usually confined to matters in their own region. The 1986 survey found that even on issues that are clearly of national applicability, such as Aboriginal rights in the Constitution or the 1985 amendments to the Indian Act to remove sex discrimination, regional variation emerges in respondents' degree of familiarity.

Causes of Hostility

The 1986 national survey offers some important insights into the causes of hostility toward government policies designed to help Aboriginal people. Using advanced statistical techniques, Langford and Ponting (1992) determined that ethnocentrism is a minor to negligible determinant of hostility. Instead, economic conservativism (the "free enterprise" belief that government should minimize its role in economic relations), prejudice, and perceptions of conflicting group interests[14] between Aboriginals and themselves are key determinants of respondents' policy preferences. Furthermore, there is an important *interaction effect* between prejudice and perceived group conflict. That is, to take a hypothetical example, if a British Columbia logger has a low level of prejudice toward Natives, her perception that Native land claims threaten her livelihood from logging would have little impact on her support for Native self-government or on her support for special status for Natives. However, for another logger in whom the level of prejudice against Native people is high, that same perception that his livelihood is threatened by Native land claims will produce a dramatically lower level of support for both Native self-government and special status for Native people.

It is also possible to analyze these relationships from the opposite side. In doing so, we found that prejudice has very little impact on the dependent variables (support for Native self-government; support for special status for Native people) when the level of perceived group conflict is low. However, when perceived group conflict is high, prejudice again becomes an important determinant of Canadians' policy preferences toward Aboriginal people.

Our findings suggest the utility of distinguishing between two types of prejudice: dormant and activated. Prejudice against a group is dormant when it is unattached to any sense of conflict with that outgroup. Dormant prejudice has minimal effects on policy preferences vis-à-vis that outgroup. On the other hand, prejudice against a group is activated when it is linked to a perception of contemporary conflict with the outgroup. Such activated prejudice has important effects on policy preferences.

Regardless of whether prejudice is dormant, activated, or absent, economic conservatism was found statistically to produce antagonism toward Aboriginals and their preferred policies. Aboriginal people and their supporters might despair at that finding, in light of the contemporary influence of economic conservatism and the fact that substantial state financial participation will be necessary to overcome the effects of past and present racism, as the final report of the Royal Commission on Aboriginal Peoples asserted.

TABLE 2 Most Serious Aboriginal Issue or Problem, by Province, 1994

Problem	Canada		Atlantic Canada		Quebec		Ontario		Manitoba		Saskat.		Alberta		BC	
	Rank	%	Rank	%	Rank	%	Rank	%	Rank	%	Rank	%	Rank	%	Rank	%
Alcohol/drugs	1	23.2	2	24.8	2	29.9	5	17.4	2	28.6	5	20.6	1	28.6	7	13.4
Integration in society	2	22.4	6	14.4	1	38.2	6	16.6	6	14.2	9	8.3	5	18.0	6	15.6
Racism/ discrimination	3	20.8	3	20.4	3	19.6	3	18.4	3	23.3	2	27.7	2.5	21.8	1.5	24.0
Unemployment/ jobs	4	20.2	1	31.2	5	13.7	2	20.4	1	29.4	1	30.5	4	21.3	4	19.8
Education	5	18.9	5	15.1	7	12.6	1	24.6	5	16.3	3	24.1	6	17.7	1.5	24.1
Land claims	6	16.3	10	10.0	4	16.9	4	17.6	8	10.5	8	8.8	7	13.4	3	23.1
Self-government	7	14.8	7	14.1	8.3	10.8	7	14.0	4	20.5	4	21.0	2.5	21.7	5	16.3
Culture/ traditions	8	12.7	4	15.3	6	13.2	8	13.8	10.5	9.8	10	8.0	8	10.6	8	12.0
Poverty	9	10.1	8	11.6	8.3	10.8	9	8.4	10.5	9.9	6	12.6	9	9.3	9.5	11.1
Dependency on gov't/want everything for nothing/too much gov't funding/handouts	10	8.6	9	10.3	8.3	10.8	12	4.7	7	11.4	12	3.7	11	7.8	9.5	11.1
People don't understand them	11	5.5	11	8.9	11	4.9	10	7.5	13	4.2	13	2.8	13	2.6	12	4.3
Lack of initiative or motivation	12.5	4.3	—	0.0	12	2.3	11	5.4	12	7.1	7	11.1	10	8.9	13	2.6
Low self-esteem/ self-worth/self-respect	12.5	4.3	12	3.7	13	1.2	13	3.3	9	10.2	11	7.2	12	7.4	11	8.2
Valid cases	**1493**		**139**		**451**		**395**		**66**		**66**		**160**		**209**	

SOURCE: Angus Reid Group Ltd.

Conclusion

Although public opinion has softened slightly over the years on the issue of "special status" for First Nations, debilitating stereotypes remain alive in a significant minority of the non-Native population. In its broader contours, public opinion is no longer the ally that it was when social scientists first began monitoring it over two decades ago. Canadians have a low tolerance for precisely the kinds of protest strategies and tactics that create leverage for otherwise disempowered peoples. Aboriginal peoples have had to resort to those strategies and tactics and have paid the price in a deteriorating level of support from non-Native people. Furthermore, the very assertiveness that Aboriginal peoples are finding necessary to attain concrete results is likely to bring Aboriginal people into competition with private and commercial interests in the larger society. Non-Native people's perception of such competition as a threat is associated with opposition to government policies favoured by Aboriginal leaders.

Non-Native politicians might seek to discount non-Native public opinion on Aboriginal issues as uninformed, uninterested, and inconsistent. It is all three of those things. However, there are limits to how far politicians in office are willing to go when, as was the case in Canada in the mid-1990s, the courts are waivering, political opponents are seeking to reap political gain from government's policies toward Native people, financial costs increase relentlessly, and the recommended reforms veer off at a 180° angle from the increased level of accountability that the public seeks from the state.

Violence-prone right-wing extremist organizations do exist in Canada, but they have little influence and their main focus has not been on Aboriginal people. Of more concern should be the more influential right-wing ideologues. Their ethnocentric, anti-statist, pro–individual rights, radical egalitarian, fiscal retrenchment philosophy is profoundly antithetical to First Nations' needs. The probability is that they will inject partisan politics into Aboriginal issues such that Aboriginal people, lacking electoral clout, will again be buffeted by political forces that are largely beyond their ability to control. A real danger is that the political atmosphere created by right-wing ideologues will lead the state to offer either mere incremental, tokenistic change, which would exacerbate the problems of distrust of government, or conversely, to offer in desperation some drastic "solution" of radical equality. Neither approach offers true justice in the sense of arrangements that permit the survival and well-being of Indians as Indians (Boldt, 1993: 57).

Notes

1. The 1986 national survey reported here was conducted with the aid of a Sabbatical Leave Fellowship from the Social Sciences and Humanities Research Council of Canada (SSHRCC) and with funding from SSHRCC (Research Grants Division), the Multiculturalism Directorate of the federal Department of the Secretary of State (Canadian Ethnic Studies Research Program), the University of Calgary, and the sale of reports issuing from the study. Data for the 1976 study reported here were collected under a generous grant from the Donner Canadian Foundation. The Angus Reid Group conducted the 1994 study reported here. The authors express their sincere appreciation to these supporters of the projects and to the respondents, research assistants, and other support staff members without whose assistance the projects would not have been possible. Data collection in 1976 and 1986 was done under contract by Complan Research Associates Ltd. and Decima Research Ltd., respectively. Percentages cited in this section do not sum to 100 percent because "Don't Know; No Response" is usually not reported here. In the 1994 survey, the "Don't Know; No Response" category was remarkably constant at about 15 percent of the sample.

2. The statements in the 1986 Index of Support for Special Status for Natives are shown below, and are followed by the percentage of the sample agreeing (strongly or moderately) and then the percentage disagreeing (strongly or moderately) with each one:

    "If Parliament and the elected leaders of the Native people agreed that some Canadian laws would not apply in Native communities, it would be all right with me" (38 percent vs 44 percent);

    "Native schools should not have to follow provincial guidelines on what is taught" (22 percent vs 67 percent);

    "Native governments should have powers equivalent to those of provincial governments" (31 percent vs 51 percent); and

    "Native governments should be responsible to elected Native politicians, rather than to Parliament, for the federal government money they receive" (28 percent vs 44 percent).

3. Given a choice of the RCMP having the "responsibility to enforce the law on aboriginal land reserves regardless of what the band leaders might want" and the RCMP "respect[ing] the wishes of the band leaders and leaving law enforcement up to the members of the reserve," a majority (56 percent of the 1994 sample) chose the former and only 25 percent chose the latter option.

4. For instance, given the statement "It just isn't right for natives to have special rights that other Canadians don't have," 41 percent of the 1994 sample agreed and 34 percent disagreed. Similarly, in that same survey 51 percent agreed with the statement "Aboriginal Canadians who eventually have self-government on their own land base should no longer have any special status or rights," while only half as many (26 percent) disagreed.

5. For instance, almost half (46 percent) of the 1994 sample agreed that "Aboriginals should have certain formally recognized rights such as these [exemption from certain taxes, special hunting and fishing rights]," while only 37 percent disagreed.

6. The Index of Support for Native Self-Government is made up of four items. A respondent's index score is his or her average score across the four items. The items are listed below, and are followed by the percentage of the sample agreeing (strongly or moderately) and then the percentage disagreeing (strongly or moderately):

   "It is important to the future well-being of Canadian society that the aspirations of Native people for self-government be met" (42 percent vs 33 percent);

   "Those provincial premiers who oppose putting the right to Native self-government in the Constitution are harming Native people" (38 percent vs 34 percent);

   "Most Native leaders who call for self-government for Native people are more interested in promoting their own personal career than in helping Native people" (30 percent vs 41 percent); and

   "The Constitution of Canada should specifically recognize the right of Indians to self-government" (41 percent vs 40 percent).

7. In 1986, 30 percent of respondents thought that, if Native governments were adequately funded, they would be more capable than the federal government of meeting Native people's needs, while 18 percent thought the federal government would be more capable, and 37 percent thought that the two would be equally capable. In 1994, a large plurality (46 percent) was of the opinion that "if aboriginal self-government becomes a reality . . . the overall standard of living and living conditions of Canada's aboriginal peoples, let's say 10 years down the road," will improve, whereas 19 percent thought it would stay the same and 18 percent thought it would get worse. Eighteen percent did not express an opinion. The stability of the "anti-Aboriginal" opinion (at 18 percent) over the eight years is noteworthy.

8. The question also asked 1994 respondents how much confidence they have in each of several other players. The full results are as follows, with the numbers in parentheses representing "a lot of confidence," "a fair amount of confidence," "not much confidence," and "no confidence at all," respectively: Chiefs of large Indian bands (9 percent, 45 percent, 19 percent, and 9 percent); your provincial government (6 percent, 43 percent, 24 percent, and 10 percent); the federal government (8 percent, 45 percent, 23 percent, and 8 percent); Canada's justice system (10 percent, 43 percent, 23 percent, and 8 percent); the federal Department of Indian and Northern Affairs (5 percent, 42 percent, 26 percent, and 7 percent); Ovide Mercredi, leader of the Assembly of First Nations (15 percent, 40 percent, 14 percent, and 8 percent); Ron Irwin, the federal Minister of Indian and Northern Affairs (4 percent, 36 percent, 18 percent, and 7 percent); the Royal Commission on Aboriginal Peoples (7 percent, 40 percent, 19 percent, and 7 percent); and national Aboriginal organizations (9 percent, 50 percent, 15 percent, and 5 percent).

9. In 1986, in response to the statement "Most Native leaders who call for self-government for Native people are more interested in promoting their own personal career than in helping Native people," 30 percent agreed (anti-Native) and 41 percent disagreed (pro-Native). The 1994 survey asked: "Now, thinking about Canada's aboriginal leadership as a whole, based on your own impressions, do you think they represent the views and concerns of: all, most, some, or only a few of the aboriginal people in this country?" The responses were: 4 percent for "all"; 38 percent for "most"; 29 percent for "some"; and 13 percent for "only a few."

10. See Ponting and Gibbins (1980: 84–85) and Ponting (1987c: B11–B12) for the items constituting these indexes and for the distribution of the samples on those items.

11. In a 1988 national follow-up study, when the question was reworded to deal with special fishing rights, rather than special hunting rights, the results were virtually identical.

12. The item was phrased as follows: "blocking resource companies from taking natural resources such as timber and minerals from lands claimed by aboriginals." Approval was given by 41.6 percent of the 1994 respondents, while 41.2 percent disapproved.

13. The item read: "Indian bands establishing gaming houses and other gambling facilities on their reserve lands without the approval of other government"; 70 percent disapproved; 15 percent approved.

14. Perceptions of conflicting group interests were measured in terms of such dimensions as the belief that Native people already receive excessive financial assistance from government, and the belief that Native people already exercise considerable power and influence with the federal or provincial government.

References

Boldt, Menno. 1993. *Surviving as Indians. The Challenge of Self-Government.* Toronto: University of Toronto Press.

Decima Research Limited. 1987. *A Study of Canadian Attitudes toward Aboriginal Self-Government.* Toronto: Decima.

Langford, Tom, and J. Rick Ponting. 1992. "Canadians' Responses to Aboriginal Issues: The Role of Prejudice, Perceived Group Conflict, and Economic Conservatism," *Canadian Review of Sociology and Anthropology* 24, 2: 140–66.

Ponting, J. Rick. 1986. *Arduous Journey.* Toronto: McClelland and Stewart.

———. 1987a. *Profiles of Public Opinion on Canadian Natives and Native Issues.* Module 1. *Constitutional Issues.* Calgary: Research Report #87–01, Research Unit for Public Policy Studies, the University of Calgary.

———. 1987b. *Profiles of Public Opinion on Canadian Natives and Native Issues.* Module 2. *Special Status and Self-Government.* Calgary: Research Report #87–02, Research Unit for Public Policy Studies, the University of Calgary.

———. 1987c. *Profiles of Public Opinion on Canadian Natives and Native Issues*. Module 3. *Knowledge, Perceptions, and Sympathy*. Calgary: Research Report #87–03, Research Unit for Public Policy Studies, the University of Calgary.

———. 1988a. *Profiles of Public Opinion on Canadian Natives and Native Issues*. Module 4. *Native People, Finances, and Services*. Calgary: Research Report #88–01, Research Unit for Public Policy Studies, the University of Calgary.

———. 1988b. *Profiles of Public Opinion on Canadian Natives and Native Issues*. Module 5. *Land, Land Claims, and Treaties*. Calgary: Research Report #88–02, Research Unit for Public Policy Studies, the University of Calgary.

Ponting, J. Rick, and Roger Gibbins. 1980. *Out of Irrelevance: A Socio-Political Introduction to Indian Affairs in Canada*. Scarborough, ON: Butterworth.

———. 1981. "The Reactions of English Canadians and French Québécois to Native Indian Protest," *Canadian Review of Sociology and Anthropology* 18, 2: 222–38.

Questions

1. How would you characterize the public's opinion of granting Aboriginals specific rights, such as self-government, from a historical perspective?

2. Summarize the trend between 1976 and 1994 specific to Aboriginal rights.

3. Why is recognizing the regional variation in awareness of Aboriginal needs and support for their rights important?

4. What are two main causes for resistance or lack of support for Aboriginal rights? Explain.

5. It has been more than a decade since the last data point, so the results may not be valid for contemporary Canadian society. Given this, how would you summarize the current public's opinion on Aboriginal rights? Make sure to use some form of evidence to support your view, such as newspaper articles, media reports, etc.

POSITIVE FUNCTIONS OF THE UNDESERVING POOR: USES OF THE UNDERCLASS IN AMERICA

HERBERT J. GANS

"A Positive Function of the Undeserving Poor: Uses of the Underclass in America," by Herbert Gans, reprinted from Politics and Society, *Vol. 22, No. 3, September 1994. Copyright © by Sage Publications. pp. 269–283.*

Below, Herbert Gans examines the role of poverty within society. This is not meant to be a satirical portrayal of why poverty may be good for some people. Rather, Gans examines the functions that poverty serves within a society. He also breaks the functions into several categories, including microsocial, economic, normative, and political. If you've never systematically examined the underlying 'value' of poverty within a society, this article should prove to be eye opening.

Poverty, like any other social phenomenon, can be analyzed in terms of the *causes* which initiate and perpetuate it, but once it exists, it can also be studied in terms of the consequences or *functions* which follow. These functions can be both *positive* and *negative*, adaptive and destructive, depending on their nature and the people and interests affected.

Poverty has many negative functions (or dysfunctions), most for the poor themselves, but also for the nonpoor. Among those of most concern to both populations, perhaps the major one is that a small but visible proportion of poor people is involved in activities which threaten their physical safety, for example street crime, or which deviate from important norms claimed to be "mainstream," such as failing to work, bearing children in adolescence and out of wedlock, and being "dependent" on welfare. In times of high unemployment, illegal and even legal immigrants are added to this list for endangering the job opportunities of native-born Americans.

Furthermore, many better-off Americans believe that the number of poor people who behave in these ways is far larger than it actually is. More important, many think that poor people act as they do because of moral shortcomings that express themselves in lawlessness or in the rejection of mainstream norms. Like many other sociologists, however, I argue that the behavior patterns which concern the more fortunate classes are *poverty-related*, because they are, and have historically been, associated with poverty. After all, mugging is only practiced by the poor. They are in fact caused by poverty, although a variety of other causes must also be at work since most poor people are not involved in any of these activities, including mugging.

Because their criminal or disapproved behavior is ascribed to moral shortcomings, the poor people who resort to it are often classified as unworthy or *undeserving*. For example, even though the failure of poor young men (or women) to work may be the effect of a lack of jobs, they are frequently accused of laziness, and then judged undeserving. Likewise, even though poor young mothers may decide not to marry the fathers of their children, because they, being jobless, cannot support them, the women are still accused of violating conventional familial norms, and also judged undeserving. Moreover, once judged to be undeserving, poor people are then no longer thought to be deserving of public aid that is financially sufficient and secure enough to help them escape poverty.

Judgments of the poor as undeserving are not based on evidence, but derive from a stereotype, even if, like most others, it is a stereotype with a "kernel of truth" (e.g., the monopolization of street crime by the poor). Furthermore, it is a very old stereotype. . . .

It is not difficult to understand why people, poor and more fortunate, are fearful of street crime committed by poor people, and even why the jobless poor and welfare recipients may be perceived as economic threats for not working and drawing on public funds, at least in bad economic times. Also, one can understand why other forms of poverty-related behavior, such as the early sexual activity of poor youngsters and the dramatic number of poor single-parent families are viewed as moral threats, since they violate norms thought to uphold the two-parent nuclear family and related normative bases of the social order. Here, there would seem to be no inherent reason for exaggerating these threats, for example, in the case of welfare recipients who obtain only a tiny proportion of governmental expenditures, or more generally, by stereotyping poor people as undeserving without evidence of what they have and have not done, and why.

One reason, if not the only one, for the exaggeration and the stereotyping, and for the continued attractiveness of the concept of the undeserving poor itself, is that undeservingness has a number of *positive* functions for the better-off population. Some of these functions, or uses, are positive for everyone who is not poor, but most are positive only for some people, interest groups, and institutions, ranging from moderate income to wealthy ones. Needless to say, that undeservingness has uses for some people does not justify it; the existence of functions just helps to explain why it persists.

My notion of function, or empirically observable adaptive consequence, is adapted from the classical conceptual scheme of Robert K. Merton.[1] My analysis will concentrate on those positive functions which Merton conceptualized as *latent*, which are unrecognized and/or unintended, but with the proviso that the functions which are identified as latent will probably not be abolished once they are widely recognized. Positive functions are, after all, also benefits, and people are not necessarily ready to give up benefits, including unintended ones, even if they become aware of them.[2] . . .

Functions of the Undeserving Poor

I will discuss five sets of positive functions: microsocial, economic, normative-cultural, political, and macrosocial, which I divide into 13 specific functions, although

the sets are arbitrarily chosen and interrelated, and I could add many more functions. The functions are not listed in order of importance, for such a listing is not possible without empirical research on the various beneficiaries of undeservingness.

Two Microsocial Functions

1. *Risk reduction.* Perhaps the primary use of the idea of the undeserving poor, primary because it takes place at the microsocial scale of everyday life, is that it distances the labeled from those who label them. By stigmatizing people as undeserving, labelers protect themselves from the responsibility of having to associate with them, or even to treat them like moral equals, which reduces the risk of being hurt or angered by them. Risk reduction is a way of dealing with actual or imagined threats of physical safety, for example from people who might be muggers, or cultural threats attributed to poor youngsters or normative ones imagined to come from welfare recipients. All pejorative labels and stereotypes serve this function, which may help to explain why there are so many such labels.

2. *Scapegoating and displacement.* By being thought undeserving, the stigmatized poor can be blamed for virtually any shortcoming of everyday life which can be credibly ascribed to them—violations of the laws of logic or social causation notwithstanding. Faulting the undeserving poor can also support the desire for revenge and punishment. In a society in which punishment is reserved for legislative, judicial, and penal institutions, *feelings* of revenge and punitiveness toward the undeserving poor supply at least some emotional satisfaction.

Since labeling poor people undeserving opens the door for nearly unlimited scapegoating, the labeled are also available to serve what I call the displacement function. Being too weak to object, the stigmatized poor can be accused of having caused social problems which they did not actually cause and can serve as cathartic objects on which better-off people can unload their own problems, as well as those of the economy, the polity, or of any other institution, for the shortcomings of which the poor can be blamed.

Whether societywide changes in the work ethic are displaced on to "shiftlessness," or economic stagnation on to "welfare dependency," the poor can be declared undeserving for what ails the more affluent. This may also help to explain why . . . the furor about poor "babies having babies" waited for the awareness of rising adolescent sexual activity among the better-off classes in the 1980s—at which point rates of adolescent pregnancy among the poor had already declined. . . .

Three Economic Functions

3. *Economic banishment and the reserve army of labor.* People who have successfully been labeled as undeserving can be banished from the formal labor market. If young people are designated "school dropouts," for example, they can also be thought to lack the needed work habits, such as proper adherence to the work ethic, and may not be offered jobs to begin with. Many ex-convicts are declared unemployable in similar fashion, and some become recidivists because they have no other choice but to go back to their criminal occupations.

Banishing the undeserving also makes room for immigrant workers, who may work for lower wages, are more deferential, and are more easily exploitable by being threatened with deportation. In addition, banishment helps to reduce the official jobless rate, a sometimes useful political function, especially if the banished drop so completely out of the labor force that they are not even available to be counted as "discouraged workers."

The economic banishment function is in many ways a replacement for the old reserve army of labor function, which played itself out when the undeserving poor could be hired as strikebreakers, as defense workers in the case of sudden wartime economic mobilization, as "hypothetical workers," who by their very presence could be used to depress the wages of other workers, or to put pressure on the unions not to make wage and other demands. Today, however, with a plentiful supply of immigrants, as well as of a constantly growing number of banished workers who are becoming surplus labor, a reserve army is less rarely needed—and when needed, can be recruited from sources other than the undeserving poor. . . .

4. *Supplying illegal goods.* The undeserving poor who are banished from other jobs remain eligible for work in the manufacture and sale of illegal goods, including drugs. Although it is estimated that 80 percent of all illegal drugs are sold to Whites who are not poor, the sellers are often people banished from the formal labor market.[3] Other suppliers of illegal goods include the illegal immigrants, considered undeserving in many American communities, who work for garment industry sweatshops manufacturing clothing under illegal conditions.

5. *Job creation.* Perhaps the most important economic function of the undeserving poor today is that their mere presence creates jobs for the better-off population, including professional ones. Since the undeserving poor are thought to be dangerous or improperly socialized, their behavior either has to be

modified so that they act in socially approved ways, or they have to be isolated from the deserving sectors of society. The larger the number of people who are declared undeserving, the larger also the number of people needed to modify and isolate as well as control, guard, and care for them. Among these are the social workers, teachers, trainers, mentors, psychiatrists, doctors and their support staffs in juvenile training centers, "special" schools, drug treatment centers, and penal behavior modification institutions, as well as the police, prosecutors, defense attorneys, judges, court officers, probation personnel and others who constitute the criminal courts, and the guards and others who run the prisons. . . .

More jobs are created in the social sciences and in journalism for conducting research about the undeserving poor and producing popular books, articles, and TV documentaries for the more fortunate who want to learn about them. The "job chain" should also be extended to the teachers and others who train those who serve, control, and study the undeserving poor.

In addition, the undeserving poor make jobs for what I call the salvation industries, religious, civil, or medical, which also try to modify the behavior of those stigmatized as undeserving. Not all such jobs are paid, for the undeserving poor also provide occasional targets for charity and thus offer volunteer jobs of those providing it—and paid jobs for the professional fundraisers who obtain most of the charitable funds these days. . . .

Three Normative Functions

6. *Moral legitimation.* Undeservingness justifies the category of deservingness and thus supplies moral and political legitimacy, almost by definition, to the institutions and social structures that include the deserving and exclude the undeserving. Of these structures, the most important is undoubtedly the class hierarchy, for the existence of an undeserving class or stratum legitimates the deserving classes, if not necessarily all of their class-related behavior. The alleged immorality of the undeserving also gives a moral flavor to, and justification for, the class hierarchy, which may help to explain why upward mobility itself is so praiseworthy.

7. *Norm reinforcement.* By violating, or being imagined as violating, a number of mainstream behavioral patterns and values, the undeserving poor help to reaffirm and reinforce the virtues of these patterns—and to do so visibly, since the violations by the undeserving are highly publicized. As Emile Durkheim pointed out nearly a century ago, norm violations and their punishments also provide an opportunity for preserving and reaffirming the norms. This is not insignificant, for

norms sometimes disparaged as "motherhood" values gain new moral power when they are violated, and their violators are stigmatized.

If the undeserving poor can be imagined to be lazy, they help to reaffirm the Protestant work ethic; if poor single-parent families are publicly condemned, the two-parent family is once more legitimated as ideal. . . .

Enforcing the norms also contributes further to preserving them in another way, for one of the standard punishments of the undeserving poor for misbehaving—as well as a standard obligation in exchange for help—is practicing the mainstream norms, including those that the members of the mainstream may only be preaching, and that might die out if the poor were not required to incorporate them in their behavior. Old work rules that can no longer be enforced in the rest of the economy can be maintained in the regulations for workfare; old-fashioned austerity and thrift are built into the consumption patterns expected of welfare recipients. Economists like to argue that if the poor want to be deserving, they should take any kind of job, regardless of its low pay or demeaning character, reflecting a work ethic which economists themselves have never practiced.

Similarly, welfare recipients may be removed from the rolls if they are found to be living with a man—but the social worker who removes them has every right to cohabit and not lose his or her job. In most states, welfare recipients must observe rules of housecleaning and child care, only the poor are monitored to see if they obey these. Should they use more physical punishment on their children than social workers consider desirable, they can be charged with child neglect or abuse and can lose their children to foster care.[4] . . .

Actually, most of the time most of the poor are as law abiding and observant of mainstream norms as are other Americans. Sometimes they are even more observant; thus the proportion of welfare recipients who cheat is always far below the percentage of taxpayers who do so.[5] Moreover, survey after survey has shown that the poor, including many street criminals and drug sellers, want to hold respectable jobs like everyone else, hope someday to live in the suburbs, and generally aspire to the same American dream as most moderate and middle-income Americans.[6]

8. *Supplying popular culture villains.* The undeserving poor have played a long-term role in supplying American popular culture with villains, allowing the producers of the culture both to reinforce further mainstream norms and to satisfy audience demands for re-

venge, notably by showing that crime and other norm violations do not pay. Street criminals are shown dead or alive in the hands of the police on local television news virtually every day, and more dramatically so in the crime and action movies and television series.

For many years before and after World War II, the criminal characters in Hollywood movies were often poor immigrants, frequently of Sicilian origin. Then they were complemented for some decades by communist spies and other Cold War enemies who were not poor, but even before the end of the Cold War, they were being replaced by Black and Hispanic drug dealers and gang leaders. . . .

Three Political Functions

9. *Institutional scapegoating.* The scapegoating of the undeserving poor mentioned in Function 2 above also extends to institutions which mistreat them. As a result, some of the responsibility for the existence of poverty, slums, unemployment, poor schools, and the like is taken off the shoulders of elected and appointed officials who are supposed to deal with these problems. For example, to the extent that educational experts decide that the children of the poor are learning disabled or that they are culturally or genetically inferior in intelligence, attempts to improve the schools can be put off or watered down.

To put it another way, the availability of institutional scapegoats both personalizes and exonerates social systems. The alleged laziness of the jobless and the anger aimed at beggars take the heat off the failure of the economy, and the imagined derelictions of slum dwellers and the homeless, off the housing industry. In effect, the undeserving poor are blamed both for their poverty and also for the absence of "political will" among the citizenry to do anything about it.

10. *Conservative power shifting.* Once poor people are declared undeserving, they also lose their political legitimacy and whatever little political influence they had before they were stigmatized. Some cannot vote, and many do not choose to vote or mobilize because they know politicians do not listen to their demands. Elected officials might ignore them even if they voted or mobilized, because these officials and the larger polity cannot easily satisfy their demands for economic and other kinds of justice.[7] As a result, the political system is able to pay additional attention to the demands of more affluent constituents. It can therefore shift to the "right."

The same shift to the right also takes place ideologically. Although injustices of poverty help justify the existence of liberals and the more radical left, the undeserving poor themselves provide justification and opportunities for conservatives to attack their ideological enemies on their left. When liberals can be accused of favoring criminals over victims, their accusers can launch and legitimate incursions on the civil liberties and rights of the undeserving poor, and concurrently on the liberties and rights of defenders of the poor. Moreover, the undeservingness of the poor can be used to justify attacks on the welfare state. Charles Murray understood the essence of this ideological function when he argued that welfare and other welfare state legislation for the poor only increased the number of poor people.[8]

11. *Spatial purification.* Stigmatized populations are often used deliberately or not, to stigmatize the areas in which they live, making such areas eligible for various kinds of purification. As a result, "underclass areas" can be torn down and their inhabitants moved to make room for more affluent residents or higher taxpayers.

However, such areas can also be used to isolate stigmatized poor people and facilities by selecting them as locations for homeless shelters, halfway houses for the mentally ill or for ex-convicts, drug treatment facilities, and even garbage dumps, which have been forced out of middle- and working-class areas following NIMBY (not in my backyard) protests. Drug dealers and other sellers of illegal goods also find a haven in areas stigmatized as underclass areas, partly because these supply some customers, but also because police protection in such areas is usually minimal enough to allow illegal activities without significant interference from the law.[9] . . .

Two Macrosocial Functions

12. *Reproduction of stigma and the stigmatized.* For centuries now, undeservingness has given rise to policies and agencies which are manifestly set up to help the poor economically and otherwise to become deserving, but which actually prevent the undeserving poor from being freed of their stigma, and which also manage, unwittingly, to see to it that their children face the same obstacles. In some instances, this process works so speedily that the children of the stigmatized face "anticipatory stigmatization," among them the children of welfare recipients who are frequently predicted to be unable to learn, to work, and to remain on the right side of the law even before they have been weaned.

If this outcome were planned deliberately, one could argue that politically and culturally dominant groups are reluctant to give up an easily accessible and always available scapegoat. In actuality, however, the reproduction function results unwittingly from other intended and seemingly popular practices. For example, the so-called War on Drugs, which has unsuccessfully sought to keep hard drugs out of the United States, but has meanwhile done little to provide drug treatment to addicts who want it, thereby aids the continuation of addiction, street crime, and a guaranteed prison population, not to mention the various disasters that visit the families of addicts and help to keep them poor.

The other major source of reproducing stigma and the stigmatized is the routine activities of the organizations which service welfare recipients, the homeless, and other stigmatized poor, and end up mistreating them. For one thing, such agencies, whether they exist to supply employment to the poor or to help the homeless, are almost certain to be underfunded because of the powerlessness of their clientele. No organization has ever had the funds or power to buy, build, or rehabilitate housing for the homeless in sufficient number. Typically, they have been able to fund or carry out small demonstration projects.

In addition, organizations which serve stigmatized people often attract less well-trained and qualified staff than those with high-status clients, and if the clients are deemed undeserving, competence may become even less important in choosing staff. Then too, helping organizations generally reflect the societal stratification hierarchy, which means that organizations with poor, low-status clients frequently treat them as undeserving. If they also fear some of their clients, they may not only withhold help, but attack the clients on a preemptive strike basis. Last but not least, the agencies that serve the undeserving poor are bureaucracies which operate by rules and regulations that routinize the work, encourage the stability and growth of the organizations, and serve the needs of their staffs before those of their clients.

When these factors are combined, as they often are, and become cumulative, as they often do, it should not be surprising that the organizations cut off escape routes from poverty not only for the clients, but in doing so, also make sure that some of their children remain poor as well.

13. *Extermination of the surplus.* In earlier times, when the living standards of all poor people were at or below subsistence, many died at an earlier age than the better off, thus performing the set of functions for the latter forever associated with Thomas Malthus. Standards of living, even for the very poor, have risen considerably in the last century, but even today, morbidity and mortality rates remain much higher among the poor than among moderate-income people. To

put it another way, various social forces combine to do away with some of the people who have become surplus labor and are no longer needed by the economy.

Several of the killing illnesses and pathologies of the poor change over time; currently, they include AIDS, tuberculosis, hypertension, heart attacks, and cancer, as well as psychosis, substance abuse, street crime, injury and death during participation in the drug trade and other underworld activities, and intraclass homicide resulting from neighborhood conflicts over turf and "respect." Whether the poor people whose only problem is being unfairly stereotyped and stigmatized as undeserving die earlier than other poor people is not known.

Moreover, these rates can be expected to remain high or even to rise as rates of unemployment—and of banishment from labor force—rise, especially for the least skilled. Even the better-off jobless created by the downsizing of the 1990s blame themselves for their unemployment if they cannot eventually find new jobs, become depressed, and in some instances begin the same process of being extruded permanently from the labor market experienced by the least skilled of the jobless.

In effect, contemporary advanced capitalism may well have created the conditions for a new Malthusian hypothesis. In any case, the early departure of poor people from an economy and society which do not need them is useful for those who remain. Since the more fortunate classes have already developed a purposive blindness to the structural causes of unemployment and to the poverty-related causes of pathology and crime that follow, those who benefit from the current job erosion and the possible extermination of the surplus labor may not admit it consciously either. Nonetheless, those left over to compete for scarce jobs and other resources will have a somewhat easier time in the competition, thus assigning undeservingness a final positive function for the more fortunate members of society.[10]

Conclusion

I have described thirteen of the more important functions of the undeserving poor, enough to support my argument that both the idea of the undeserving poor and the stigmas with which some poor people are thus labeled may persist in part because they are useful in a variety of ways to the people who are not poor.

This analysis does not imply that undeservingness will or should persist. Whether it *will* persist is going to be determined by what happens to poverty in America. If it declines, poverty-related crime should also

decline, and then fewer poor people will probably be described as undeserving. If poverty worsens, so will poverty-related crime, as well as the stereotyping and stigmatization of the poor, and any worsening of the country's economy is likely to add to the kinds and numbers of undeserving poor, if only because they make convenient and powerless scapegoats.

The functions that the undeserving poor play cannot, by themselves, perpetuate either poverty or undeservingness, for as I noted earlier, functions are not causes. For example, if huge numbers of additional unskilled workers should be needed, as they were for the World War II war effort, the undeserving poor will be welcomed back into the labor force, at least temporarily. Of course, institutions often try to survive once they have lost both their reasons for existence and their functions. Since the end of the Cold War, parts of the military-industrial establishment both in the United States and Russia have been campaigning for the maintenance of some Cold War forces and weapons to guarantee their own futures, but these establishments also supply jobs to their national economies, and in the United States, for the constituents of elected officials. Likewise, some of the institutions and interest groups that benefit from the existence of undeservingness, or from controlling the undeserving poor, may try to maintain undeservingness and its stigma. . . .

Whether applying the label of undeservingness to the poor *should* persist is a normative question which ought to be answered in the negative. Although people have a right to judge each other, that right does not extend to judging large numbers of people as a single group, with one common moral fault, or to stereotyping them without evidence either about their behavior or their values. Even if a case could be made for judging large cohorts of people as undeserving, these judgments should be distributed up and down the socioeconomic hierarchy, requiring Americans also to consider whether and how people in the working, middle, and upper classes are undeserving.

The same equality should extend to the punishment of crimes. Today, many Americans and courts still treat white-collar and upper-class criminals more leniently than poor ones. The public excuse given is that the street crime of the undeserving poor involves violence and thus injury or death, but as many students of white-collar and corporate crime have pointed out, these also hurt and kill people, and often in larger numbers, even if they do so less directly and perhaps less violently.

Changes also need to be made in the American conception of deviance, which like that of other countries, conflates people whose behavior is *different* with those whose behavior is socially *harmful*. Bearing children without marriage is a long-standing tradition among the poor. Born of necessity rather than preference, it is a poverty-related practice, but it is not, by itself, harmful, or at least not until it can be shown that either the children—or the moral sensibilities of the people who oppose illegitimacy—are significantly hurt. Poor single-parent families are hardly desirable, but as the lack of condemnation of more affluent single-parent parents should suggest, the major problem of such families is not the number of parents, actual or surrogate, in the family, but its poverty.

Finally, because many of the poor are stereotyped unjustly as undeserving, scholars, writers, journalists, and others should launch a systematic and public effort to deconstruct and delegitimate the notion of the undeserving poor. This effort, which is necessary to help make effective antipoverty programs politically acceptable again, should place the following five ideas on the public agenda and encourage discussion as well as dissemination of available research.

The five ideas, all discussed earlier in this article, are that (1) the criminal and deviant behavior among the poor is largely poverty related rather than the product of free choice based on distinctive values; (2) the undeservingness of the poor is an ancient stereotype, and like all stereotypes, it vastly exaggerates the actual dangers that stem from the poor; (3) poverty-related deviance is not necessarily harmful just because it does not accord with mainstream norms; (4) the notion of undeservingness survives in part because of the positive functions it has for the better-off population; and (5) the only certain way to eliminate both this notion and the functions is to eliminate poverty.[11]

Endnotes

1. Merton, R. K. (1949). *Manifest and latent functions*. In R. K. Merton (Ed.), *Social theory and social structure: Toward the codification of social research* (Chapter 1). Glencoe, IL.

2. Actually, some of the functions that follow may in fact have been intended by some interest groups in society, but neither intended nor recognized by others, adding an interesting conceptual variation—and empirical question—to Merton's dichotomy.

3. Harris, R. (1990, April 22). Blacks feel brunt of drug war. *Los Angeles Times*, 1.

4. Poor immigrants who still practice old-country discipline norms are particularly vulnerable to being accused of child abuse.

5. Funiciello, T. (1993). *Tyranny of kindness: Dismantling the welfare system to end poverty in America*. New York: Atlantic Monthly Press, p. 60.

6. See Rank, M. R. (1994). *Living on the edge: The realities of welfare in America*. New York: Columbia University Press, p. 93.

7. In addition, the undeserving poor make a dangerous constituency. Politicians who say kind words about them or who act to represent their interests are likely to be attacked for their words and actions. Jesse Jackson was hardly the first national politician to be criticized for being too favorable to the poor.

8. Murray, C. (1984). *Losing ground: American social policy, 1950–1980*. New York: Basic Books.

9. Since even middle-class drug buyers are willing to travel to underclass areas for drugs, neighborhoods convenient to expressways and bridges that serve the suburbs often become major shopping centers for hard drugs.

10. Killing off the undeserving poor may conflict with the prior function (see Function 12) of reproducing them, but functional analysis describes consequences which do not have to be logically consistent. Moreover, since turning poor people into undeserving ones can be a first step toward eliminating them, Functions 12 and 13 may even be logically consistent.

11. A fuller discussion of policy proposals will appear in my forthcoming book, *Ending the war against the poor*.

Questions

1. List the categories of functions served by poverty that Gans provides. What specific functions are in each category? Which of these functions seem to be the most manifest? Which are more latent?

2. What type of functions does poverty serve from an economic and political perspective? How are these two particular categories of functions intertwined in American society?

3. Of all the functions, which seems to be the most problematic from an applied or policy perspective? In other words, which function would be the most difficult to fill in society if poverty were eliminated?

WHY THE RICH ARE GETTING RICHER AND THE POOR POORER

ROBERT REICH

"Why the Rich Are Getting Richer and the Poor Poorer," by Robert Reich, reprinted from Utne Reader, *January/February 1990. pp. 42–49.*

Robert Reich recognizes that the gap between rich and poor is continuing to grow, despite policies aimed at reducing that inequality. However, he claims that the gap primarily derives from competition in the international economy, not greed or any specific political or social ill within the United States. As you read this article, ask yourself whether Reich makes a convincing argument. Are there more specific issues in the domestic United States that may explain the growing chasm between rich and poor?

Between 1978 and 1987, the poorest fifth of American families became 8% poorer, and the richest fifth became 13% richer. That means the poorest fifth now have less than 5% of the nation's income, while the richest fifth have more than 50%.

This widening gap can't be blamed on the growth in single-family lower-income families, which in fact slowed markedly after the late 1970s. Nor is it due mainly to the stingy social policies of the Reagan years. Granted, food stamp benefits have dropped 13% since 1981 (in real terms), and many states have failed to raise benefits for the poor and unemployed to keep up with inflation. But this doesn't come close to accounting for the growing persistence of economic inequality in the United States. Rather, this disturbing trend is connected to a profound change in the American economy as it merges with the global economy. And because the merging is far from complete, this trend will not stop all by itself anytime soon. It is significant that the growth of inequality can be seen most strikingly among Americans who have jobs. Through most of the postwar era, the wages of Americans at different income levels rose at about the same pace. Although different workers occupied different steps on the escalator, everyone moved up together. In those days poverty was the condition of *jobless* Americans, and the major economic challenge was to create enough jobs for everyone. Once people were safely in the work force, their problems were assumed to be over. Thus "full employment" became a liberal rallying cry.

But in recent years Americans with jobs have been traveling on two escalators—one going up, the other going down. In 1987 the average hourly earnings of non-supervisory workers (adjusted for inflation) were lower than in any year since 1966. Middle-level managers fared much better, although their median real earnings were only slightly above the levels of the 1970s. Executives, however, did spectacularly well. In 1988 alone, CEOs of the 100 largest publicly held industrial corporations received raises averaging almost 12%.

Between 1978 and 1987, as the real earnings of unskilled workers were declining, the real incomes of investment bankers and other securities industry workers rose 21%. It is not unusual for a run-of-the-mill investment banker to bring home comfortably over a million dollars. Meanwhile, the number of impoverished *working* Americans climbed by nearly two million, or 23%, during those same years. Nearly 60% of the 20 million people who now fall below the Census Bureau's poverty line are from families with at least one member in full-time or part-time work.

The American economy now exhibits a wider gap between rich and poor than it has at any other time since World War II. The most basic reason, put simply is that America itself is ceasing to exist as an economic system separate from the rest of the world. One can no more meaningfully speak of an "American economy" than of a "Delaware economy." We are becoming but a region—albeit still a relatively wealthy region—of a global economy. This is a new kind of economy whose technologies, savings, and investments move effortlessly across borders, making it harder for individual nations to control their economic destinies. . . .

New technologies of worldwide communication and transportation have redrawn the economic playing field. American industries no longer compete against Japanese or European industries. Rather, a company with headquarters in the United States, production facilities in Taiwan, and a marketing force spread across many nations competes with another, similarly wide-ranging company. So when General Motors, say, is doing well, that probably is good news for a lot of executives in Detroit, and for GM shareholders across the globe, but it isn't necessarily good news for a lot of assembly-line workers in Detroit, because there may, in fact, be very few GM assembly-line workers in Detroit, or anywhere else in America. The welfare of assembly-line workers in Detroit may depend, instead, on the health of corporations based in Japan or Canada.

More to the point, even if those Canadian and Japanese corporations are doing well, those Detroit workers may be in trouble. For they are increasingly part of an international labor market, encompassing Asia, Africa, Western Europe, and, perhaps before long, Eastern Europe. With relative ease corporations can relocate their production centers to take advantage of low wages. So American workers find themselves settling for low wages in order to hold on to their jobs. More and more, your "competitiveness" as a worker depends not on the fortunes of any American corporation, or of any American industry, but on what function you serve within the global economy.

In order to see in greater detail what is happening to American jobs, it helps to view the work that most Americans do in terms of new categories that reflect how U.S. workers fit into the global economy. Essentially, three road categories are emerging. I call them: 1) symbolic-analytic services; 2) routine production services; and 3) routine personal services.

1. Symbolic-analytic services are based on the manipulation of information: data, words, and oral and visual symbols. Symbolic analysis comprises some (but by no means all) of the work undertaken by people who call themselves lawyers, investment bankers, commercial bankers, management consultants, research scientists, academics, public-relations executives, real estate developers, and even a few creative accountants. Also, many advertising and marketing specialists, art directors, design engineers, architects, writers and editors, musicians, and television and film producers. . . .

Most symbolic analysts work alone or in small teams. If they work with others, they often have partners rather than bosses or supervisors. Their work environments tend to be quiet and tastefully decorated, often within tall steel-and-glass buildings. When they are not analyzing, designing, or strategizing, they are in meetings or on the telephone—giving advice or making deals. Many of them spend an inordinate amount of time in jet planes and hotels. They are generally articulate and well groomed. The vast majority are white males.

Symbolic analysis now accounts for more than 40% of America's gross national product, and almost 20% of our jobs.

The services performed by America's symbolic analysts are in high demand around the world. The Japanese are buying up the insights and inventions of America's scientists and engineers (who are only too happy to sell them at a fat profit). The Europeans, meanwhile, are hiring our management consultants, business strategists, and investment bankers. Developing nations are hiring our civil and design engineers; and almost everyone is buying the output of our pop musicians, television stars, and film producers.

The same thing is happening with the global corporation. The central offices of these sprawling entities, headquartered in America, are filled with symbolic analysts who manipulate information and then export their insights around the world via the corporation's far-flung operations. IBM, for instance, doesn't export machines from the United States; it manufactures its machines in factories all over the globe. IBM world headquarters, in Armonk, New York, exports just strategic planning and related management services.

Thus has the standard of living of America's symbolic analysts risen. They increasingly find themselves part of a global labor market, not a national one. And because the United States has a highly developed economy, and an excellent university system, they find that the services they have to offer are in high demand around the whole world. This ensures that their salaries are quite high.

Those salaries are likely to go even higher in the years ahead, as the world market for symbolic analysis continues to grow. Foreigners are trying to learn these skills and techniques, to be sure, but they still have a long way to go. No other country does a better job of preparing its most fortunate citizens for symbolic analysis than does the United States. None has surpassed America in providing experience and training, often with entire regions specializing in one or another kind of symbolic analysis (New York and Chicago for finance, Los Angeles for music and film, the San Francisco Bay area and greater Boston for science and engineering). In this we can take pride. But for the second major category of American workers—the providers of routine production services—the future doesn't bode well.

2. Routine production services involve tasks that are repeated over and over, as one step in a sequence of steps for producing a finished product. Although we tend to associate these jobs with manufacturing, they are becoming common in banking, insurance, wholesaling, retailing, health care—all industries employing millions of people who spend their days processing data, often putting information into computers or taking it out.

Most people involved in routine production services work with many other people who do similar work, within large, centralized facilities. They are overseen by supervisors, who in turn are monitored by more senior supervisors. They are usually paid an hourly wage. Their jobs are often monotonous. Most of the workers do not have a college education. Those who deal with metal are mostly white males; those who deal with fabrics or information tend to be female and/or minorities.

Decades ago, those kinds of workers were relatively well paid. But in recent years America's providers of routine production services have found themselves in direct competition with millions of foreign workers, most of whom work for a fraction of the pay American workers get. Through the miracle of satellite transmission, even routine data processing can now be undertaken in relatively poor nations, thousands of miles away from the skyscrapers where the data are finally used. This fact has given management ever greater power in bargaining talks. If routine production workers living in America don't agree to reduce their wages, then the work often goes abroad.

And it has. In 1950, routine production services constituted about 30% of our gross national product and well over half of American jobs. Today such ser- vices represent about 20% of the GNP and one fourth of jobs. And the scattering of foreign-owned factories placed here to circumvent American protectionism isn't going to reverse the trend. So the standard of living of America's routine production workers will likely keep declining. The dynamics behind the wage concessions, plant closings, and union-busting that have become commonplace won't be stopped without a major turnaround in labor organizing or political action.

3. Routine personal services also entail simple, repetitive work, but, unlike routine production services, they are provided in person. Included in this employment category are restaurant and hotel workers, barbers and beauticians, retail sales personnel, cab drivers, household cleaners, day-care workers, hospital atten- dants and orderlies, truck drivers, and—among the fastest-growing of all careers—custodians and secu- rity guards.

Like production workers, providers of personal services are usually paid by the hour. They are also carefully supervised and rarely have more than a high school education. But unlike people in the other two categories of work, they are in direct contact with the ultimate beneficiaries of what they do. And the com- panies they work for are often small. In fact, some rou- tine personal-service workers become entrepreneurs. (Most new businesses and new jobs in America come from this sector—which now constitutes about 20% of GNP and 30% of jobs.) Women and minorities make up the bulk of routine personal-service workers.

Apart from the small number who strike out on their own, these workers are paid poorly. They are sheltered from the direct effects of global competition, but not the indirect effects. They often compete with undocu- mented workers willing to work for low wages, or with former or would-be production workers who can't find well-paying production jobs, or with labor-saving ma- chinery (automated tellers, self-service gas pumps) dreamed up by symbolic analysts in America and manu- factured in Asia. And because they tend to be unskilled and dispersed among small businesses, personal-service workers rarely have a union or a powerful lobby group to standup for their interests. When the economy turns sour, they are among the first to feel the effects.

These workers will continue to have jobs in the years ahead and may experience some small increase in real wages. They will have demographics on their side, as the American work force shrinks. But for all

the foregoing reasons, the gap between their earnings and those of the symbolic analysts will continue to grow if present economic trends and labor conditions continue.

These three functional categories—symbolic analysis, routine production services, and routine personal services—cover at least three out of four American jobs. The rest of the nation's work force consists mainly of government employees (includ- ing public school teachers), employees in regulated industries (like utility workers), and government- financed workers (engineers working on defense weapons systems), many of whom are sheltered from global competition. One further clarification: Some traditional job categories overlap several of these categories. People called "secretaries," for example, include those who actually spend their time doing symbolic analysis work closely allied to what their bosses do; those who do routine data entry or re- trieval of a sort that will eventually be automated or done overseas; and those who provide routine personal services.

The important point is that workers in these three functional categories are coming to have different competitive positions in the world economy. Symbolic analysts hold a commanding position in an increasingly global labor market. Routine production workers hold a relatively weak position in an increasingly global labor market. Routine personal service workers still find themselves in a national labor market, but for various reasons they suffer the indirect effects of competition from workers broad.

How should we respond to these trends? One response is to accept them as inevitable consequences of change, but to try to offset their polarizing effects through a truly progressive income tax, coupled with more generous income assistance—including health insurance—for poor working Americans. . . .

A more ambitious response would be to guard against class rigidities by ensuring that any talented American kid can become a symbolic analyst—regard- less of family income or race. But America's gifted but poor children can't aspire to such jobs until the government spends substantially more than it does now to ensure excellent public schools in every city and region and ample financial help when they are ready to attend college.

Of course, it isn't clear that even under those cir- cumstances there would be radical growth in the num- ber of Americans who become research scientists, design engineers, musicians, management consultants, or (even if the world needed them) investment bankers and lawyers. So other responses are also needed. Perhaps the most ambitious would be to increase the numbers of Americans who could apply symbolic analysis to production and to personal services.

There is ample evidence, for example, that access to computerized information can enrich production jobs by enabling workers to alter the flow of materials and components in ways that increase efficiency. Production workers who have broader responsibilities and more control over how production is organized cease to be "routine" workers—becoming, in effect, symbolic analysts at a level very close to the production process. The same transformation can occur in personal-service jobs. Consider, for example, the checkout clerk whose computer enables her to control inventory and decide when to reorder items from the factory.

The number of such technologically empowered jobs, or course, is limited by the ability of workers to learn on the job. That means a far greater number of Americans will need a good grounding in mathematics, basic science, reading, and communication skills. So once again, comfortably integrating the American work force into the new world economy turns out to rest heavily on education. (Better health care, especially prenatal and pediatric care, would also figure in here.)

Education and health care for poor children are apt to be costly. Since poorer working Americans, already under a heavy tax load, can't afford it, the cost would have to be borne by wealthier Americans—who also would have to bear the cost of any income redistribution plans designed to neutralize the polarizing domestic effects of a globalized economy. Thus a central question is the willingness of the more fortunate American citizens—especially symbolic analysts, who constitute much of the most fortunate fifth, with 40% of the nation's income—to bear the burden. But here lies a catch-22. For as our economic fates diverge, the top fifth may be losing its sense of connectedness with the bottom fifth (or even the bottom half) that would elicit such generosity.

The conservative tide that has swept the land during the past decade surely has many causes, but the fundamental changes in our economy should not be discounted as a major factor. It is now possible for the most fortunate fifth to sell their expertise directly in the global market, and thus maintain and enhance their standard of living, even as that of other Americans declines. There is less and less basis for a strong sense of interclass interdependence in America. Meanwhile, the fortunate fifth have also been able to insulate themselves from the less fortunate, by living in suburban enclaves far removed from the effects of poverty. Neither patriotism nor altruism may be sufficient to overcome these realities. Yet without the active support of at least some of the fortunate fifth, it will be more difficult to muster the political will necessary for change. . . .

Questions

1. What has happened to American jobs and wages since World War II?

2. What job categories does Reich say have emerged as part of the global economy?

3. What changes explain the shift in wages, job security, and potential mobility for each of the three categories that Reich describes?

4. What are the likely prospects for wage growth, job security, and mobility for each of the three categories? What traits or attributes explain the differential projections?

5. What, if anything, can be done to help ameliorate the negative picture that Reich presents? How might his recommendations be effectively implemented?

BAITING IMMIGRANTS: HEARTBREAK FOR LATINOS

MERCEDES LYNN DE URIATE
University of Texas–Austin

"Baiting Immigrants: Heartbreak for Latinos," by Mercedes Lynn De Uriate, reprinted from The Progressive, *September 1996. pp. 18–20.*

Immigration has a long, complicated history in the United States. Most recently, the federal government has seemed to focus increasingly on limiting immigration across the U.S.–Mexican border. In the reading below, Mercedes Lynn De Uriate explains how this anti-immigrant attitude has affected "illegals" in the United States. In addition, she explores the impact of this attitude on legal resident-aliens and U.S. citizens who experience anti-immigrant backlash simply because of their surname.

Twenty-one-year-old Gina Cardenas could hardly wait for summer to begin. Long hours of work, study, and persistence had paid off. First she won a prestigious fellowship including a paid internship as a metro reporter at a mid-sized Midwestern newspaper. Then she was accepted to an exchange program at one of Mexico's best-known universities, where, among other things, she would study Spanish.

But next came the notice from the U.S. State Department. Its Houston Passport Agency questioned her right to a passport. Cardenas is the daughter of naturalized immigrant parents. She was born in the United States with the assistance of a midwife at home in Brownsville, a Texas border town.

The agency asked her to supply a "combination of early public documents created at the time of your birth." These included an "attending midwife's report; prenatal and postnatal notes created by the midwife of your mother regarding her pregnancy and delivery; a certified copy of baptismal certificate; your parents' tax, rent, or employment records created at the time of your birth which indicated their U.S. residency; elementary school records showing your name, date, and place of birth and indicating your parents' address or any other document established in your infancy or early childhood that indicates your place of birth."

Cardenas said her first reaction to the notice from the U.S. Passport Agency was one of disbelief. "I mean, this is my own government," she says. "I'm an American!" But her efforts to convince government bureaucrats of this fact dragged on for months. At the last minute her papers came through, allowing her to participate in the program. But not before she had endured significant harassment.

Cardenas was not alone. This year, several other students who were U.S. citizens born to immigrant parents found their government reluctant to certify their citizenship with a passport.

In addition, as a result of Governor Pete Wilson's tirades against illegal aliens and the subsequent passage of Proposition 187, hundreds of California students brought here as babies by parents without government papers—youngsters who have lived here all their lives—found themselves ejected from universities. Most of these students worked full time to pay for their educations in an effort to leave behind economic hardship and gang pressures. Many were forced out just weeks before graduating.

"It is both shortsighted and heartbreaking," says Cristina Bodinger-de Uriarte, a sociology professor at California State University, Los Angeles, an urban campus with one of the most diverse populations in the nation. "Suddenly, within weeks of graduation, students were notified that unless they paid out-of-state tuition,

they must leave school. Students who had worked full-time jobs for four or five years in order to finance their education and escape poverty were penalized. They were already stretched to the financial limit.

"Some of my best students were in tears for days—then they simply disappeared from the student body," she says.

Bodinger-de Uriarte says she does not understand the reasoning behind this push-out policy. "They are mistaken if they believe that these youngsters will return to other countries. Most of them speak no other language, have lived nowhere else, and identify with this country."

The push-out policy is aimed not just at students without documents. It extends to legal immigrants, as well. Regardless of high grades or outstanding accomplishments, regardless of their potential in a country increasingly dependent on global commerce, these students will find it far more difficult to get federally subsidized loans and grants.

According to student advisers who work in foreign-study programs, Spanish-surnamed students are having more and more trouble obtaining government documents. "I cannot remember any other period of time when there was so much trouble with official papers," says Helena Wilkins, who has worked in the University of Texas's study-abroad program for seven years.

Norma Madrid, who captured a prestigious business internship in Spain, also struggled to get proper documents. "She received the same inquiry as Gina did," says Wilkins. "And there was no reason for it. She was an American citizen. Norma badgered the passport people for months trying to get the matter straightened out. Finally, the passport came through."

Another student who almost lost her chance to study abroad was of Indian descent, says Wilkins, "but her name could have been mistaken for a Hispanic name. On the other hand, the government agency had all her paperwork and should have been able to realize that she was not Latina."

What these three students have in common, besides Hispanic-sounding names, are naturalized parents, all of whom had become citizens many years earlier.

Harassment of Latino students is but one component of an increasingly harsh national trend . . . to bar the children of undocumented immigrants from attending school.

• • •

Actually, [this] idea was tried and failed in the 1980s, when the state of Texas attempted to bar undocumented migrant children from classrooms. That effort led to a 1982 U.S. Supreme Court ruling that undocumented youngsters could not be denied a public education.

If a new effort to bar the children of immigrants were to succeed, the results for society at large would be disastrous. The current cost of U.S. illiteracy is already $200 billion annually if one takes into account its role in incarceration, unemployment, health, and welfare. Already, one in five adults—27 million—is functionally illiterate, according to the U.S. Department of Education. Most of those in prison today fall into this category, as do a significant percent of the unemployed.

Republican politicians from Bob Dole to Pete Wilson have built political careers around promises to get tough on immigrants. In a pre-convention television commercial, the Republican National Committee launched a blatant attack on immigrants. As *The New York Times* reported, the ad opens with a shot of the border, and in case there is any misunderstanding, it has a sign saying Mexico. The ad proceeds to show immigrants fleeing up the road under the glare of spotlights. "You spend $5.5 billion to support illegals," the ad screams, adding that "spending for illegals" is "up 12.7% under Clinton." The ad ends up by urging voters to "tell President Clinton: Stop giving illegal benefits to illegals. End wasteful Washington spending."

The blame for immigrant-bashing can't all be placed on Republican politics, however. Bill Clinton has grown increasingly punitive in his policies and opportunistic in his portrayal of undocumented immigrants.

In response to the Republican ad, the Democratic National Committee released its own anti-immigrant ad. Clinton has boosted the number of border-patrol officers, brags the ad, while showing a picture of a brown-skinned man being handcuffed by a border-patrol agent. Another brown-skinned man is shown climbing down a wall with a rope, the *Times* reported, and then the ad shows "two gloved hands clutching a large chisel and trying to pry open a window."

In both the Republican and Democratic ads, Mexicans are portrayed as the only illegal-immigrant group. Thus an entire population is criminalized through visual images meant to incite anger and fear. What's more, the information in the ads is out of context and slippery. . . .

As the Democrats' commercial indicates, Clinton often links immigration to crime.

"As we have worked hard to bring the crime rate down all over America, we've made special efforts in our border communities, because we know we have special responsibilities there," he told San Diegans recently, citing increases in border-patrol agents in Arizona, California, and Texas. He described communities in the Southwest as "under siege" and pointed to the tough line taken by the Administration's Operation Gatekeeper.

In April the President signed anti-terrorism legislation that gives the INS sweeping new powers. One provision of the new law pushes due process aside, and allows for the hasty removal of foreign-born individuals who arrive at ports of entry without proper documentation. The decision is left to the immigration officer on duty, without court hearing or judicial review. The burden of proof of legal entry falls on immigrants. This provision fails to uphold international human-rights laws that were incorporated into the U.S. canon in 1980. Nor does it ensure the legal treatment of refugees protected under the U.N. convention relating to the status of refugees.

. . .

The crackdown on immigrants is based on political propaganda, not reality. Most undocumented individuals arrive on commercial carriers and overstay their visas or cross from Canada, according to the INS. Nevertheless, the United States disproportionately reinforces its southern border. . . .

Most of the individuals who cross the southern border do no take jobs that Americans seek. A 1982 Reagan Administration initiative called Operation Jobs proved this point rather conclusively. For two weeks, beginning on April 26, 1982, dramatic TV visuals showed INS sweeps of workplaces in Fort Worth, Houston, San Francisco, Detroit, Newark. New York, Chicago, and Denver. It was one of the most extensive deportation efforts that the U.S. government had ever undertaken. Within five days, the INS seized 6,000 individuals. Local businesses felt the pinch immediately. In Los Angeles, merchants along Broadway, a main shopping thoroughfare for Latinos, reported a drop in sales of 30 to 80%. Subsequent newspaper reports revealed that the few Americans who took those vacated jobs quit within days because of brutal labor conditions. Two weeks after the raids, the press reported the deportees were once again at work.

Immigrants are not the drain on the social budget they are made out to be. Immigrants pay much more in taxes than they receive in education and social services. Over the course of their working lifetime, immigrants pay an average of $89,437 in state income and sales taxes, far more than the $62,600 it costs to educate a person from kindergarten through 12th grade, according to a study released June 10 by the Tomas Rivera Center in Claremont, California.

The Urban Institute found that legal and illegal immigrants contribute $70.3 billion in tax payments into the system—but draw out only $42.9 billion in total services. Immigrants add billions more to the U.S. economy in consumer spending, the study found.

U.S. businesses have always depended on cheap foreign labor. The United States could not have become the wealthy industrialized leader of the early nineteenth century without both slave labor and European immigrant workers. The railroads were largely built by Chinese immigrants brought in by U.S. development barons for this purpose. Large-scale agricultural production still depends on Mexican workers today.

That's why the borders have remained porous. But in this era of downsizing and falling wages, border rhetoric plays well in Washington, and it's not the businesses that are being blamed, it's their workers.

Cracking down on migrant workers and their children does not address the root causes of immigration to the United States. The main reasons for the migration phenomenon we see around the world are flights for safety, job searches, and travel to reunite families says attorney Schey.

"Yet never have our lawmakers sat down to develop a broad-based plan that would address these motivations," he says. "They have never targeted outflow nations. They have never effectively addressed oppressive regimes—indeed, we often support them, even when their citizens are immigrating in huge numbers. Consider our track record with Iran, Haiti, the Philippines, and El Salvador, to mention just a few."

Anti-immigrant movements throughout our history have ridden the crest of prejudice.

Jeremiah Jenks and W. Jett Lauck, former members of the United States Immigration Commission, observed this pattern in 1912: "Many persons, who have spoken and written in favor of restriction of immigration, have laid great stress upon the evils of society arising from immigration. They have claimed that disease, pauperism, crime, and vice have been greatly increased through the incoming of immigrants. Perhaps no other phase of the questions has aroused so keen feeling, and yet perhaps no other phase of the question has been so little accurate information."

But backlash against immigrant seems to be ingrained in our culture. In 1882, the Chinese Exclusion Act provided the most obvious example. Its forerunner, an 1879 California statewide ballot that passed by a margin of 154,638 to 833, may have set a precedent for the exclusion act, which restricted Chinese immigration for more than 50 years, and for its contemporary counterpart, Proposition 187. The 1952 McCarran-Walter Act was another effort to control ethnic distribution. Among other provisions it established a complicated procedure for admitting Asians, and set up a long list of conditions allowing for deportation. It also granted wide powers of search, seizure, and interrogation to INS agents.

These efforts have portrayed immigrants as criminals, economic parasites, or health risks. In recent years, those targeted most frequently have been Latinos. My own research indicates that over the last century, the U.S. press has exhibited a consistent negative bias against Latinos.

A rise in hate crimes since 1991 shadows the current anti-immigrant rhetoric. In 1994, the Los Angeles County Human Relations Commission reported a 23.5% rise in hate crimes against Latinos. Last November, the Coalition for Humane Immigrant Rights of Los Angeles released an 18-page report. "Hate Unleashed: Los Angeles in the aftermath of 187," which documented 229 cases of "discrimination, denial of services, civil-rights violations, hate speech, and hate crimes" since the passage of Proposition 187.

Gina Cardenas is in many ways a prototypical immigrant success story. Her mother and father met and married in the United States. Both worked hard to give their four children opportunities they never had. Gina, the oldest, is the first in her family to go to college, the first to travel to the nation's capital, the first to receive scholarships. Like many other American children of immigrant parents, Cardenas is a profile of initiative and independence.

Now she is poised to contribute to her nation, pursuing her interest in international relations, and developing her foreign-language skills—valuable assets in the current, global economy. But her government has shown little interest in her contribution, and has treated her with suspicion because of her Mexican name.

Cardenas and thousands of other Latinos are caught in the maelstrom of anti-immigrant sentiment, which has cycled through our history for more than a century. The maelstrom swirls around U.S. economic needs, as the government responds to both urban and agricultural demands.

Today the nation faces major changes as technology retools the workplace, as demographics reconfigure the population and as trade becomes globalized. These changes require discussion of public policies, including immigration.

But instead of looking for solutions, our leaders are carting out the old scapegoats.

Questions

1. To what degree has politics affected the anti-immigrant movement?

2. Is there evidence to support the claim that most immigrants take jobs that Americans would otherwise hold?

3. What socio-cultural and/or structural features of the United States and Mexico contribute to the increased rate of immigration?

4. What effect do you think success stories, such as that of Gina, will have on the anti-immigrant attitudes held by many Americans? Do such stories have the potential to worsen the current situation for Latinos and Latinas in the United States? If so, how?

AFRICAN AMERICAN FAMILIES: A LEGACY OF VULNERABILITY AND RESILIENCE

BEVERLY GREENE

"African American Families: A Legacy of Vulnerability and Resilience," by Beverly Greene, reprinted from National Forum: The Phi Kappa Phi Journal, *Summer 1995, pp. 29–32. Copyright © 1995 by Beverly Greene.*

Many people think of African American families as dysfunctional. Beverly Greene refutes this image. As she sees it, such families are amazingly resilient despite the historical and contemporary racism that they have suffered. As you read this piece, compare the images that you have of African American families with those presented in the article.

• • •

African Americans are one of the oldest and largest groups of persons of color in the United States. The first census in 1790 counted 760,000 African Americans. By 1990, over 30,000,000 were counted. African Americans are descendants of people who belonged to the tribes of the West African coast and were the primary objects of the U.S. slave trade. Many African Americans have Native American and European ancestry as well.

They are perhaps the only ethnic group in the United States whose immigration was wholly involuntary. Entry into the United States was not, as it was for members of white ethnic groups and other groups of persons of color, the result of an effort to better their circumstances or find a more advantageous political climate than their homeland could offer. Instead of bettering their circumstances, their forced departure from the West African coast resulted in pervasive losses. Aside from the loss of life for many, there was a loss of community, the loss of original languages, and the loss of status as human beings for those who survived the Atlantic Passage.

As slaves, literally deprived of all human rights, they were to provide free labor and were bought and sold as any other commodity. Their children were salable commodities as well. In this system, family attachments were routinely ignored as slaves were transported, sold, and regarded as livestock with no regard for their family or important emotional ties. In this context, slave families came to place less emphasis on the role of biological parents because most children were separated from and not raised by them. Rather, children were informally "adopted" and raised by other people in their immediate community in extended rather than nuclear family arrangements. These extended family arrangements are still a prominent feature of contemporary African American families and may be considered a major survival tool.

The struggles of African Americans are often viewed as if they ended with emancipation. This belief ignores over a century more of legal racial discrimination that led to the civil rights struggles which reached a peak in the 1950s and 1960s. Even in the wake of legislation designed to make racial discrimination illegal, discrimination in more subtle, institutionalized forms still operates to this day in ways that continue to challenge the optimal physical, psychological, and economic well-being of African Americans.

Characteristics of African American Families

Characteristics of contemporary African American families represent an interaction of African cultural derivatives, the need to adapt to a racially antagonistic environment, and the influence of American cultural imperatives. They include extended networks of kinship between family members and persons who are not blood-related in complex networks of obligation and support. African Americans as a group are geographically and socioeconomically diverse. However, they share both cultural origins and the need to manage the anxieties and prejudices of a dominant group that is culturally different and that discriminates against African Americans both actively and passively on the basis of race. In some form, all African Americans must make psychological sense out of their disparaged condition, deflect hostility from the dominant group, and negotiate racial barriers under a wide range of circumstances. If the group is to survive, the members must teach their children to do so as well.

In this regard, African American parents have a special task and a unique stressor that are not shared by their white counterparts. These consist of the special things they must do to prepare their children to function in an adaptive fashion without internalizing the dominant culture's negative messages about African American people. In *Children of Color*, Allen and Majidi-Ahi note that teaching African American children how to cope with racism represents a socialization issue that exemplifies all that is distinct about the African American experience in America. A major component of this experience entails the task of communicating to African American children the racial realities and dangers of the world, how to correctly identify and cope with the resulting barriers, and how to seek support for the feelings evoked when confronting these barriers.

Succeeding Against Odds

Despite many historical and contemporary obstacles, African Americans have succeeded against many overwhelming odds in every generation. African American families are an important source of socialization and support for their members and can be an important translator of the dominant culture for African American children. At its best, this system teaches African American children to imitate and function in the dominant culture without believing that its demeaning images of African Americans are true.

Another role of the family is to pass along different kinds of successful coping strategies against racism. One strategy, the heightened sensitivity to the potential for exploitation by white persons, has been referred to by Grier and Cobbs in *Black Rage* as cultural paranoia. While this heightened sensitivity often has been pathologized by the dominant culture, it is a realistic and adaptive way of approaching situations that have frequently been antagonistic. Hopson and Hopson in *Different and Wonderful* suggest that another important coping strategy and a major source of psychological resilience is reflected in the sharing of African cultural derivatives with children while encouraging them to take pride in their ancestry. In *Long Memory*, Mary Berry and John Blassingame note that each generation of African Americans prepares the next for survival in a society that devalues them by passing along "searing vignettes" about what has preceded them. They view this process as a long collective memory that is in and of itself an instrument of survival.

African American families must do all of these things in addition to providing the normal range of basic necessities that all families must provide for their children. In the context of a racist society, however, African American families' ability to do this may be compromised by the institutional barriers that providers in the family invariably confront. In these scenarios there may be a drain on the family's emotional and material resources, making the extended family structure an important resource in this regard. Sharing the burden of child care and child rearing helps to ease this burden in many families and can be seen as an example of resilience.

Multiple Mothering

In *Black Families*, Nancy Boyd-Franklin gives one example of this in what she describes as "multiple mothering." "Multiple mothers" refers to grandmothers, aunts, cousins, close friends, or people considered "kin" to a child's mother. They need not be biologically related. These multiple mothers provide emotional safety valves, sounding boards, and alternative role models to children while often providing their real mothers with important tangible support in the form of child care. These arrangements also emphasize the important role for elder members of the family and the importance of their connection to members of the next generation. It is important to remember this extended family structure when viewing "single-parent families." The fact that African American families may deviate in structure from the White Anglo Saxon Protestant norm does not warrant pathologizing them or presuming that this deviation accounts for family problems.

In what appear to be many single-parent families, extensive networks of other family members, family friends, neighbors, and others are routinely involved in the caretaking of children. Hence, the unmarried status of the mother does not automatically tell us what the rest of the family structure is like. The single-parent family as a large and diverse group among African Americans is not synonymous with teenaged or under-aged mothers. Becoming a parent before one is biologically and emotionally mature, or when it interferes with important developmental tasks of the parent, is certainly not what is recommended. Rather, I suggest that African American family structures be viewed as perhaps having a wider range of flexibility in what is available to its members, reflected in a wider range of persons, in addition to biological parents, involved in parenting roles.

Gender Role Flexibility

Robert Hill, in *The Strengths of Black Families*, identifies major characteristics of African American families: strong kinship bonds, a strong achievement motivation, a strong religious and spiritual orientation, and a strong work orientation. Hill views these characteristics as strengths that have helped African Americans survive and function under difficult circumstances. He further cites gender role flexibility as an important and adaptive characteristic of African American families. This flexibility in gender roles is explained in part as a derivative of the value of interdependence among group members, typical of Western African precolonial cultures, that is unlike the value of rugged individualism of the West. It is also a function of the need to adapt to racism in the United States in many different ways.

One of the features that distinguished African American women from their white counterparts was their role as workers. Aside from being brought into the country as slaves whose primary function was to work, the status of African American women as slaves superseded their status as women. Hence they were not given the courtesies of femininity that were routinely accorded white women. Conventions of femininity considered many forms of labor that were routine for white males inappropriate for white females. Slavery deprived African American women of this protection, and as such their roles as workers did not differ from those of African American males. Hence at the very outset, rigid gender-role stratification among African Americans was not permitted. Later, because African American men faced significant racial barriers

in the workplace and could not fit the idealized image of the Western male provider, women were forced to work to help support the home. Thus, the dominant cultural norm of women remaining in the home while men worked outside the home was never a practical reality for African American families.

This does not mean that there is no sexism within African American families. Tensions are often produced when African American men internalize the dominant culture's value of male domination and female subordination. Working women become the targets of African American male frustration rather than institutional racism. Despite such occurrences, flexibility in gender roles represents another example of an adaptive strategy that has contributed to the survival of African American families.

Summary

African American families have functioned under a legacy of challenges to their survival, beginning with slavery when families were not allowed to exist and when they were continually disrupted by abrupt and permanent separations. Surviving these disruptions, African American families have continued to demonstrate their flexibility and resilience under many adverse circumstances. It is not surprising that many African American families would be in crisis, given the range of routine assaults they face. What is more surprising is that many of these families display a remarkable legacy of adaptive strengths. James Comer, in *Maggie's American Dream*, reminds us that what we learn from survivors will tell us more about the circumvention of problems than will an exclusive focus on victims. African Americans are, if anything, survivors of historical and contemporary circumstances that may increase their vulnerability. However, as survivors, they have much to teach us about resilience.

Questions

1. What are some coping strategies used by African American families?

2. What are multiple mothers? What important functions do they provide?

3. What does Greene mean when she says that African American families have been pathologized? How does pathologizing affect African American families?

4. Watch two prime-time television shows that feature African American families. How are these families depicted? Are these depictions accurate? Do you think that these programs encourage or deter an accurate understanding of African American family life? Explain your answer.

THE LOOKING-GLASS SELF

CHARLES HORTON COOLEY

"The Looking-Glass Self," by Charles Horton Cooley, reprinted from Human Nature and the Social Order, *1902, Scribner's. pp. 179–185.*

Charles Cooley introduced the concept of the looking-glass self nearly a century ago. It is arguably one of the two most basic concepts in social psychology (the other being the distinction between the "I" and the "Me" introduced by George Herbert Mead). In this classic piece, you are invited to study Cooley's original treatment of the concept. As you read the article, ask yourself how often in your everyday interactions you project your sense of "I" in order to gauge others' perceptions of your appearance and behavior.

• • •

That the "I" of common speech has a meaning which includes some sort of reference to other persons is involved in the very fact that the word and the ideas it stands for are phenomena of language and the communicative life. It is doubtful whether it is possible to use language at all without thinking more or less distinctly of some one else, and certainly the things to which we give names and which have a large place in reflective thought are almost always those which are impressed upon us by our contact with other people. Where there is no communication there can be no nomenclature and no developed thought. What we call "me," "mine," or "myself' is, then, not something separate from the general life, but the most interesting part of it, a part whose interest arises from the very fact that it is both general and individual. That is, we care for it just because it is that phase of the mind that is living and striving in the common life, trying to impress itself upon the minds of others. "I" is a militant social tendency, working to hold and enlarge its place in the general current of tendencies. So far as it can it waxes, as all life does. To think of it as apart from society is a palpable absurdity of which no one could be guilty who really saw it as a fact of life.

"Der Mensch erkennt sich nur im Menschen, nur Das Leben lehret jedem was er sei."*

If a thing has no relation to others of which one is conscious he is unlikely to think of it at all, and if he does think of it he cannot, it seems to me, regard it as emphatically his. The appropriative sense is always the shadow, as it were, of the common life, and when we have it we have a sense of the latter in connection with it. Thus, if we think of a secluded part of the woods as "ours," it is because we think, also, that others do not go there. As regards the body I doubt if we have a vivid my-feeling about any part of it which is not thought of, however vaguely, as having some actual or possible reference to someone else. Intense self-consciousness regarding it arises along with instincts or experiences which connect it with the thought of others. Internal organs, like the liver, are not thought of as peculiarly ours unless we are trying to communicate something regarding them, as, for instance, when they are giving us trouble and we are trying to get sympathy.

"I," then, is not all of the mind, but a peculiarly central, vigorous, and well-knit portion of it, not separate from the rest but gradually merging into it, and yet having a certain practical distinctness, so that a man generally shows clearly enough by his language and behavior what his "I" is as distinguished from thoughts he does not appropriate. It may be thought of, as already suggested, under the analogy of a central colored area on a lighted wall. It might also, and perhaps more justly, be compared to the nucleus of a living cell, not altogether separate from the surrounding matter, out of which indeed it is formed, but more active and definitely organized. The reference to other persons involved in the sense of self may be distinct and particular, as when a boy is ashamed to have his mother catch him at something she has forbidden, or it may be vague and general, as when one is ashamed to do something which only his conscience, expressing his sense of social responsibility, detects and disapproves; but it is always there. There is no sense of "I," as in pride or shame, without its correlative sense of you, or he, or they. Even the miser gloating over his hidden gold can feel the "mine" only as he is aware of the world of men over whom he has secret power; and the case is very similar with all kinds of hidden treasure. Many painters, sculptors, and writers have loved to withhold their work from the

---

* *"Only in man does man know himself, life alone teaches each one what he is." Goethe,* Tasso, *act 2, sc. 3.*

world, fondling it in seclusion until they were quite done with it; but the delight in this, as in all secrets, depends upon a sense of the value of what is concealed.

I remarked above that we think of the body as "I" when it comes to have social function or significance, as when we say "I am looking well today," or "I am taller than you are." We bring it into the social world, for the time being, and for that reason put our self-consciousness into it. Now it is curious, though natural, that in precisely the same way we may call any inanimate object "I" with which we are identifying our will and purpose. This is notable in games, like golf or croquet, where the ball is the embodiment of the player's fortunes. You will hear a man say, "I am in the long grass down by the third tee," or "I am in position for the middle arch." So a boy flying a kite will say "I am higher than you," or one shooting at a mark will declare that he is just below the bullseye.

In a very large and interesting class of cases the social reference takes the form of a somewhat definite imagination of how one's self—that is any idea he appropriates—appears in a particular mind, and the kind of self-feeling one has is determined by the attitude toward this attributed to that other mind. A social self of this sort might be called the reflected or looking glass self:

> "Each to each a looking-glass
> Reflects the other that doth pass."

As we see our face, figure, and dress in the glass, and are interested in them because they are ours, and pleased or otherwise with them according as they do or do not answer to what we should like them to be; so in imagination we perceive in another's mind some thought of our appearance, manners, aims, deeds, character, friends, and so on, and are variously affected by it.

A self-idea of this sort seems to have three principal elements: the imagination of our appearance to the other person; the imagination of his judgment of that appearance, and some sort of self-feeling, such as pride or mortification. The comparison with a looking-glass hardly suggests the second element, the imagined judgment, which is quite essential. The thing that moves us to pride or shame is not the mere mechanical reflection of ourselves, but an imputed sentiment, the imagined effect of this reflection upon another's mind. This is evident from the fact that the character and freight of that other, in whose mind we see ourselves, makes all the difference with our feeling. We are ashamed to seem evasive in the presence of a straightforward man, cowardly in the presence of a brave one, gross in the eyes of a refined one, and so on. We always imagine, and in

imagining share, the judgments of the other mind. A man will boast to one person of an action—say some sharp transaction in trade—which he would be ashamed to own to another.

It should be evident that the ideas that are associated with self-feeling and form the intellectual content of the self cannot be covered by any simple description, as by saying that the body has such a part in it, friends such a part, plans so much, etc., but will vary indefinitely with particular temperaments and environments. The tendency of the self, like every aspect of personality, is expressive of far-reaching hereditary and social factors, and is not to be understood or predicted except in connection with the general life. Although special, it is in no way separate—specialty and separateness are not only different but contradictory, since the former implies connection with a whole. The object of self-feeling is affected by the general course of history, by the particular development of nations, classes, and professions, and other conditions of this sort.

Questions

1. What does Cooley mean by saying that a person brings the "I" into the social world?

2. Why does Cooley define the concept of "I" as the "looking glass self"?

3. What are the three principal elements of the looking-glass self?

4. Cite some examples of the looking-glass self in your daily routine.

DECLINING FORTUNES: THE END OF THE SOCIAL CONTRACT

KATHERINE S. NEWMAN

From Declining Fortunes: The Withering of the American Dream *by Katherine S. Newman. Copyright © 1993 by Katherine S. Newman. Reprinted by permission of Basic Books, a member of Perseus Books, L.L.C.*

The average young person today will do worse in the labor market and be of lower socioeconomic standing than their parents. America's traditional "social contract," assuring that hard work and higher education will lead to upward mobility, has been broken. Corporate downsizing, globalization, the boom and subsequent bust of dot.com organizations, and the aging of the baby boom generation are all contributing factors. In this selection, Katherine Newman documents the degree to which the contract has been broken and details the pervasiveness of the consequences.

It is an article of faith among middle-class Americans that every generation will do better than the one that preceded it and that upward mobility is a birthright for those who work hard. By the same token, nothing is due those who slack off and expect a handout. Indeed, the promise of economic success defines our national identity, but it is a cultural premise built upon shifting sands. Our economy has grown increasingly more fragile, buffeted by forces we barely understand and cannot seem to control. With every day that goes by, these unseen hands seem to interfere more and more in our most intimate decisions: when to marry, when to have children, where to live, how easily we can remain close to our extended families, whether we will be able to enjoy our sunset years or will have to fret over every dime. And on all of these counts, the largest living generation of Americans is doing worse, enjoying less of the good life than those who came before, most notably its own parents.

The baby-boom generation feels strangled by this decline. Decisions that were once left to the vagaries of emotion are now calculated down to the last nickel; risks that could once be taken in education or career are now out of the question. If being careful could cure the disease of downward mobility, baby boomers would at least have a strategy for overcoming the obstacles the economy has placed in their way. But in truth, being careful and making all the right choices is no guarantee that the future will work out well. Indeed, for many of the nation's youngest boomers who put aside risks and dreams in favor of the pragmatic course, economic history has been unkind in the extreme. No amount of deferred gratification will buy them the gratification they want: skyrocketing prices, stagnating wages, dissipating promotion prospects, and the relentless pressure of an economy that just does not seem to work any more—these are the forces and trends that are choking them.

At the very least, sympathy would seem to be in order. After fifty years of sustained expansion in the United States, the bandwagon has come to a screeching halt. The brunt of the slowdown has been born by the baby boomers, with more to come as their own children mature into an economy characterized by fits and starts, weak recoveries, and industrial decline. Surely the country must realize that they are deserving of some concern, some recognition of the price they have had to pay for maturing in the wrong place at the wrong time.

Postwar parents, perhaps more than anyone else, know how steep this slide has been: it is after all their flesh and blood that has been exiled from the places where they were born and raised. Long awaited grandchildren are growing up many miles away because the boomers in between cannot afford to live near their hometowns. The Ozzies and Harriets of the 1950s would like to be able to point with pride to the material accomplishments of their adult children as a natural extension of their own talents and drive. Instead, they confront boomerang kids who cannot seem to break free and forty-year-old progeny whose life-styles cannot hold a candle to their own, even if they are managers or professionals. The whole program they so believe in seems to have gone sour and no one really knows why. They take some solace, pointing the finger at elites, often those from other countries but some homegrown as well, who have taken unfair advantage and "jumped the line." Expressions of disgust at the urban "other," the underclass that demands tax dollars and affirmative action, creates a sense of moral superiority and a mandate for rejectionist "throw the bums out" politics. In the end, however, postwar parents believe that the boomers themselves are to blame for wanting it all too soon. They need to "get a new culture," divest themselves of their overblown expectations, and learn to wait their turn.

The problem is, of course, that waiting does not seem to work anymore. Postwar parents who had to wait because their young lives were tangled up in the depression and the war found the pot of gold at the end of the rainbow more by historical chance than anything else. Not that they did not work for it, but their children are working equally hard and are not likely to see the same rewards. They will pay the price for this misfortune for the rest of their lives: delayed entry into the housing market, among other things, will put them at a serious disadvantage from which they are unlikely to recover.

The United States is mired in an economic transformation that may turn out to be as profound as the industrial revolution itself, with consequences that are only vaguely understood by those of us whose lives will be shaped by them. But the decisions we make at this juncture, particularly those that govern the use of federal, state, and local budgets, will shape the very soul of the society we will pass on to the generations yet to come. Will America be a country in which we are our brother's keeper? Or will it be a culture where "every man for himself" summarizes our sense of social responsibility? Will the generations reach across the divides that time and history have placed between them, or will they turn inward and demand their share first, and others be damned? Will our suburban citizens—rapidly becoming the majority—turn their backs on the cities and define the nation's urban problems as someone else's responsibility? There are philosophical questions at issue here that go to the heart of the country's national character. But underlying every moral question lies the simple, irreducible, problem of money: who is going to be allowed to lead the good life to which all middle-class Americans believe they are entitled, and who is going to be shut out.

Jim Florio, the ill-fated governor of New Jersey, knows this changing mood all too well. His state budget has been drowning in a sea of red ink, and his every effort to restore solvency through tax increases has met with resounding rejection. Angry middle-class taxpayers have marched on Trenton in protests that looked like the old days of the antiwar movement, save for the Brooks Brothers suits and the silver hair dotting the crowd. Lowell Weicker, independent governor of Connecticut, discovered the same fury in his constituency when he attempted to introduce a state income tax for the first time in order to preserve the public services the budget could no longer cover. All across the nation, starting with the new-age tax revolt in California (Proposition 13) to its companion measure in Massachusetts (Proposition 21⁄2), voters have thrown local government out of their pocketbooks and issued ultimatums to politicians of all persuasions: find the money somewhere else. Not on my back, Jack.

For a nation that professes a firm belief in education as the proving ground for young people, we have been surprisingly mean in our support of public schools throughout the 1980s and early 1990s. School bond issues that passed without a second thought in the expansive years of the 1950s now fail regularly, leaving local school districts no choice but to fire teachers, cut back on extracurricular activities, skimp on supplies, eliminate enrichment courses, and bear down hard in order to meet prefabricated objectives in standardized test scores, hoping to shield themselves against the criticism that they are wasteful. In 1990, 48 percent of the school budgets in the state of New Jersey were rejected by taxpayers,[1] continuing a trend that had been on the upswing since the mid-1980s.

New Jersey residents were hardly alone: school bond failures have become epidemic throughout the nation.[2] Voters charge that there is altogether too much fat in the public schools, and they have served notice that they are not about to pick up the tab. School officials, however, see their districts as skeletal, their mission threatened, and their very value as educators

under the gun. Since they make little money to begin with, teachers are beginning to ask themselves whether some other way of making a living might be preferable to the beating they are taking at the hands of the public.

If this were merely a matter of squeezing the funds out of the citizens of Pleasanton to educate their own children, this would be bad enough; in fact, it might be regarded as self-destructive. But the political conflict over school expenditures is everywhere crisscrossed by generational and racial turmoil, by the demands of equity and fairness to distribute whatever resources we have to all comers. Retirees whose own children benefited from public education when they moved to towns like Pleasanton, now turn their backs on the needs of today's young families. And while they often do so in the name of elusive standards of efficiency in public education, underlying their rejection of school budgets is the cold fact that they do not want to pay for services they no longer use. The exile of their own progeny from Pleasanton, fueled by ridiculous real estate prices, has exacerbated the tendency to pull out of the social contract at the local level. After all, what's in it for them?[3] If the same logic were ever applied to social security or Medicare, we would surely see the contract that binds the generations fall apart.

The fiercest debates over school funding have come in states like New Jersey and California, where equalization is the issue. Rich districts fight tooth and nail to prevent their coffers from being tapped in favor of communities with far fewer options for funding the public schools. Supreme Court decisions notwithstanding, the well-to-do have made it clear that they are loath to see their money distributed to those less fortunate, particularly when they are of a different skin color or speak a foreign tongue. Jonathan Kozol's searing account of the nation's inner-city school districts, *Savage Inequalities*, stands as a moral indictment of the consequences: poor kids everywhere attend schools without books, without pencils, and with roofs that are caving in and windows that are broken.

We could chalk these inequities up to racism, and many minority advocates as well as their constituents readily draw this conclusion. There can be little doubt that the fortunate residents of Pleasanton are uncomfortable with minorities who live far away, who come to them through media images of crime and unrest. But racism is far too simplistic a diagnosis of the revolts that have blocked the distribution of middle-class tax dollars to the working poor in the cities and suburbs. It is the sharp edge of declining fortunes, the hoarding mentality that derives from the sense that there is not enough to go around, much less extra to fund the demands of the dispossessed.

The business community is also party to the hue and cry over schools and taxes. It is up in arms over the declining quality of public education, worried about the literacy and numeracy problems of a work force it argues is only marginally able to handle entry-level jobs in banks, stores, insurance companies, and fast-food restaurants. Business leaders bemoan the sliding competence of high school graduates and argue that we have yielded our international economic position to the Japanese and the Germans in part because we have abandoned high standards. Hence, the captains of industry promote highly visible schemes to resurrect the educational enterprise, by adopting schools, promoting voucher systems to stimulate competition, and pushing for more resources to be put in the hands of the educational system.

Yet the business community is caught in the same web of contradictory impulses as the average taxpayer: its market position has eroded, income has plummeted. Hence, business is on the lookout for any means of cutting expenses, including business taxes. Communities hungry for economic stability have traded corporate tax breaks for jobs and in the process have left themselves short of the funds they need to operate the public sector. In Florida $32 million went to public education in 1991, a sizable sum. But the amount is trivial compared with the $500 million claimed by Florida businesses as concessions in sales taxes, machinery, and fuel costs.[4] In Cleveland, Ohio, where the public school system was $34 million in the red for the 1991–92 school year, administrators filed a lawsuit arguing that tax breaks for business have seriously eroded the resource base of public schools. Teachers in Washington State walked off the job in protest against corporate tax breaks, singling out the case of the Boeing Company, which, they charge, was exempted from more than $900 million in sales taxes that could have been used to support public education. In Kansas, Texas, and Minnesota, among other places, legislators have pushed to eliminate property-tax concessions for businesses, since this is the revenue source most directly tied to education.

Businesses themselves point to their losing battle with overseas competitors and argue that their performance will only get worse if they are forced to absorb additional tax burdens. Besides, they argue, the schools should be pushed toward greater efficiencies in the name of accountability. As Forrest Coffey, corporate vice president for government affairs at the Boeing Company in Seattle, put the matter: "First they say, 'Give us more money.' Why should I give [the schools] more money? What do I get?" A powerful rhetoric of efficiency has found a great deal of support in a country skeptical of government and of public sector services: school teachers find themselves having to justify their calling in terms more appropriate for the assembly line. How many widgets were turned out per hour; how high are the reading test scores per hour of invested instruction? Educators lament the increased reliance on these stultifying forms of educational processing, though they have little choice but to prove their merit according to this yardstick. Next to the consumer price index, annual statistics on reading scores have become a major benchmark of mayoral efficacy. Meanwhile, the business world and state governments square off against each other in a fight for resources, while municipalities stand by and pray that they will not have to withstand more plant closings, more defections of firms who can always find other states where the economy is bad enough to extract new concessions.

The nation's colleges and universities have been similarly trapped. Federal contributions toward financial aid declined precipitously throughout the 1980s, leaving just enough for the poorest would-be students and relatively little for the struggling middle-income kids. State budgets for higher education have been slashed, a reflection of the weakened political clout of the education industry. University officials have had no choice but to begin stripping the universities first of their support staff and then of their faculty. No one is going to cry themselves to sleep over these problems, except perhaps the students who will be denied access to a college education, a sheepskin that is irreplaceable in this increasingly credential-oriented climate.[5] Because middle-class children know just how important higher education is for job opportunity, the issue of access has become politicized and, on occasion, ugly. The University of California at Berkeley, the nation's premier public university, has been in the spotlight in recent years because of its admissions policies.[6] High-achieving Asian high school students have squared off against African-American students long denied their turn at the elite schools; affirmative action has been embraced and then reversed as the politics of access heats up. Economic constraints on higher education are turning into blocked opportunities, and when this transpires, conflict inevitably intensifies among those critical credentials.

Private universities, including Brown and Columbia, have seen student protests swell over financial-aid policies that threaten to exclude those who cannot afford to pay the astronomical tuition charges of the Ivy League. On both fronts—the public and the private universities—we are seeing a wrenching end to the period of expansion in higher education that began in earnest in the 1960s, democratizing access to the scientific and humanistic knowledge that is the hallmark of a great nation. The country that bestowed the GI Bill on its deserving soldiers and provided generous student-loan programs to the older boomers is about to let higher education become the province of those to the manor born and the poorest of the poor, leaving everyone else standing at the door.

The 1990s are returning us to an earlier era in which birthright determined one's fortunes. Those who can afford the better things in life will have them from the beginning, and those who do not will find it much harder to lay their hands on a middle-class identity. The issue of schools and taxes makes the cleavage between haves and have nots abundantly clear. Other sources of division are less obvious but have the same destructive potential for undermining the social contract. Generational differences are among the least recognized but most important of these "hidden" conflicts.[7] Richard Lamm, the outspoken former governor of Colorado, now a professor of public policy at the University of Denver, recently spoke out about the age-based inequalities in the way we spend our federal budget:

> Congress . . . has just passed a budget that gives approximately 60 percent of our federal social spending to just 12 percent of our citizens: Americans over sixty-five. Yet the elderly have the highest disposable income and the lowest rates of poverty . . . in America. . . . There is little question that the elderly are the most politically powerful group in America. It's highly questionable whether they are the most deserving.[8]

Lamm goes on to explain that Medicare pays for the health costs of thousands of elderly millionaires, while 20 percent of the nation's children go unvaccinated.[9] We allow Medicare to pay for heart transplants, while thirty-one million Americans lack health insurance of any kind. "We have created an excessive sense of entitlement in the elderly," laments the former governor, "and they are vociferous in defending and enlarging their benefits."[10]

Lamm's warning is the first volley in a generational conflict that is not yet full-blown. His voice is not the only one raised against generational privilege. In the early 1990s the *New York Times* began an opin-ion series entitled "Voices from a New Generation," a periodic column in which young Americans at least one generation removed from the boomers have the opportunity to speak up. One particularly angry column was written by Mark Featherman, a young man who works in the library of the Jewish Theological Seminary. Mark complained about the colossal national debt racked up in the 1980s by a nation unwilling to live within its means, noting that his generation would end up having to pay for this binge:

> America had a party in the 1980's and we—the "twentysomething generation"—weren't invited. While high-flying S & L robber barons were making millions with other people's money, while men of bad conscience were constructing investment houses of paper, we were making our way through college and graduate school, taking out loans to finance our educations. Odd, then, that now that the party's over, we should get stuck with the bill.
>
> People are now speaking of the "new austerity." . . . Those doing most of the talking, of course, are those who can afford to be austere; their income is safely tucked away in tax shelters and investments. But for those of us just entering the work force, austerity is not something we have chosen; it was chosen for us. . . . The baby boomers have a long-term lock on the upper levels of the marketplace, and we face increased competition for entry-level jobs. Who will be made to pay for the good times of the last decade? It doesn't take a genius to figure out that it will be us, the youngest and rawest members of the labor force.[11]

Mark is not a happy camper; his age-mates are likely to be just as upset if their prospects continue to decline and they come to identify the source of their problems as older, more privileged generations of Americans.

The disparate fortunes of these generations may well become so blatant that they will catalyze a new kind of political dialogue. As the stresses and strains evident in the boomer generation become clearer, they may well turn around and ask their politicians (not to mention their own parents) why the country seems so uninterested in their problems. They may well want to know why so little attention has been paid to their concerns, particularly in light of how much attention is given to the problems of other groups: the elderly, the poor, the cities. Boomers are likely to open a generational conversation on the subject of equity and it will not be a pleasant one, for their complaints already evoke countercharges that they are a spoiled generation with inflated expectations, a critique they sometimes level at themselves. If the economic prospects of the boomers continue to sag, the country may hear the sound and fury of promises unfulfilled and hard work gone unrewarded. And this will be just the beginning of the generational debate: in time, the "baby-bust" generation will surely ask why they should have to bear the burden of supporting the boomer generation in retirement.[12]

Until that time, we are left with pressing questions of public policy that cannot wait. Who will pay for the national debt? How are we going to compete in the international arena if we refuse to pay for the school bond issues that will fund quality education? The skyrocketing cost of health care threatens to bankrupt workers and employers, and there appears to be no end in sight. The nation's inner cities are suffering from massive neglect, severe unemployment, and persistent poverty. Where will the resources come from to speak to these critical issues?

If the experience of the generations of Pleasanton is any guide, the country is in for a rough ride indeed. Even the generation of the 1960s, with its liberal political history, feels economically vulnerable. Their younger counterparts, the boomers of the Reagan era, are that much less inclined to be sympathetic toward the need to be their brother's keeper. Postwar parents who were lucky enough to be in the right country at the right time are now faced with escalating tax bills that are driving them out of towns like Pleasanton. Their need to marshal their resources in order to support themselves through a long retirement, leaves little to help their boomer progeny. The social concerns that no country can afford to ignore, the problems that festered and then exploded in south central Los Angeles in the spring of 1992, flicker on their TV sets and then dissolve into the great beyond of the increasingly distant cities. Suburban dwellers are too preoccupied and too worried about their own problems and those of their children to leave much room for the demands of the inner city. They want someone else to handle that headache, someone else's resources to pay for it.

This does not augur well for the soul of the country in the twenty-first century. Every great nation draws its strength from a social contract, an unspoken agreement to provide for one another, to reach across the narrow self-interests of generations, ethnic groups, races, classes, and genders toward some vision of the common good. Taxes and budgets—the mundane preoccupations of city hall—express this commitment, or lack of it, in the bluntest fashion. Through these mechanistic devices, we are forced to confront some of the most searching philosophical questions that face any country: what do we owe one another as members of a society? Can we sustain a collective sense of purpose in the face of the declining fortunes that are tearing us apart, leaving those who are able to scramble for advantage and those who are not to suffer out of sight?

There will be little left of the nation if we withdraw into our own little corners and refuse to "pay" for anyone else's needs. if the fortunes of the generations diverge to the point where they cannot see each other's legitimate claims and heartfelt dilemmas, we may well see the development of warring interest groups competing for politically sacred identities: the inviolable elderly, the deserving children, the baby boomers holding IOUs because they have yet to claim their fair share, the burdened baby-bust generation that did not get to "come to the party" in the 1980s. This is a nightmare vision of American politics that we cannot afford to entertain. We cannot allow public policy debates to descend to the level of squabbles over who is spoiled, about which ethnic groups deserve the good life and which should be excluded, about who is really deserving of a decent retirement or adequate medical care. The social contract upon which we all depend requires some recognition of the common rights and legitimate aspirations of all Americans for a share of the good life.

In explaining our fate, American culture tends to subtract large forces from our lives—economic trends, historical moments, and even government policies that privilege one group over another—and looks instead to the individual's character traits or values for answers. Ask members of the postwar generation about their extraordinary experience of upward mobility and you are likely to hear a sermon on the importance of hard work and "your own boot-straps." The GI Bill, low-interest mortgages, and the booming economy of the 1950s and 1960s will barely rate a mention in this tale of upward mobility. But the truth is that the hard work paid off only because economic conditions over which no individual had control made it possible and because government policies provided a helping hand.

In the legacy of the GI Bill, the WPA, and a host of other government initiatives lies the kind of active program for recovery we sorely need today. These programs created confidence that we lack at present that there are measures we can take, investments in the well-being of all Americans that will actually make a difference.[13] The Great Depression was a far worse economic calamity than anything we have seen since, and we found our way out of it. It is true that part of that trajectory of success came about because the United States was arming itself for World War II, a catalyst for government spending that few would want to see repeated. But the lesson we might take from the experience of the nation's recovery from the blight of the 1930s is that we need not assume that nothing can be done to move the economy and the generations that depend upon it out of the current malaise. We can ask and should ask what government can do as well as what private industry can do. And when we have finished that agenda, we must ask as well what we must do for one another if the present generations and those that follow are to claim their own share of the American dream.

Endnotes

1. "Angry Taxpayers Reject 44% of New Jersey School Budgets," *New York Times*, May 2, 1992, p. B1.

2. See Jean Scandlyn, "When the Social Contract Fails: Inter-Generational and Inter-Ethnic, Conflict in an American Suburb," (Ph.D. thesis, Columbia University, 1992).

3. One thing that is "in it for them" is the preservation of the value of their own real estate. The quality of the local public school is essential to property values. On this count, retirees should be concerned to keep quality high. Unfortunately, this interest conflicts with the desire to hold down tax rates, a losing battle in the 1980s.

4. "Educators Complain Business Tax Breaks Are Costing Schools," *New York Times*, May 22, 1991, pp. A1, A23.

5. A college degree is an important hedge against wage losses. The wages of college graduates relative to high school graduates were higher in 1987 than at any other time since 1963. But as Lawrence Mishel and David M. Frankel observe, the average college graduate was still earning less in 1987 than in 1971. The increased wage gap between college and high school graduates reflects "a modest increase in the demand for college-educated workers, not an across-the-board, economy-wide trend toward higher skilled and higher wage jobs." See Mishel and Frankel, *The State of Working America, 1990–91* (Armonk, N.Y.: Economic Policy Institute, M. E. Sharpe, 1991).

6. At the University of California, Berkeley, this was particularly sensitive where the admission of students of Asian origin were concerned. Grade-point averages and test scores would have placed Asian students at the top of the admissions list to such a degree at Berkeley that virtually no room would be left for other ethnic groups, including whites. Responding to this, university officials proposed to rely in part on extracurricular activities, admissions essays, and other unquantifiable characteristics for admissions. Ethnic and racial groups on all sides of this dispute were at each other's throats because access to Berkeley, as well as the rest of the University of California system, is becoming increasingly restricted. See Daniel Seligman, "College in California: The Numbers Game," *Fortune*, February 11, 1991, p. 146; and James S. Gibney, "The Berkeley Squeeze," *New Republic*, April 11, 1988, pp. 15–17.

7. For a look at the favored treatment of the postwar generation by the feds and the comparatively unfavorable plight of the boomers, see Laurence J. Kotlikoff, *Generational Accounting: Knowing Who Pays—and When—for What We Spend* (New York: Free Press, 1992).

8. Richard Lamm, "Again, Age Beats Youth," *New York Times*, Op-Ed, December 2, 1990, p. A32.

9. Lamm is quick to note that Medicare policies were hardly designed for millionaires and that they have been responsible for pulling poverty-stricken seniors out of harm's way far more often than they have been used to coddle the very wealthy. His point, also echoed by H. Ross Perot, is both that a far larger share of our resources go to the elderly than to any other demographic group and that we do not means test the benefits we provide.

10. Perhaps the baby-boom generation should be satisfied with the prospect that they too will one day be the beneficiaries of policies that enhance the lives of the elderly. As we saw in chapter 2, there is reason to question whether the nation will be able to afford such largesse when this colossal generation is ready for retirement. Yet so little attention has been paid to the problems we are likely to see in the social security system (when a small number of workers—today's children—are paying into a system that will have to care for the enormous boomer generation) that the conflicts that will undoubtedly emerge over unbearable tax burdens have barely registered in the public mind. See Kotlikoff, *Generational Accounting*.

11. Mark Featherman, "The 80's Party Is Over, . . ." *New York Times*, Op-Ed, September 24, 1990.

12. This particular complaint may have unpleasant racial dimensions as well. The increasing fertility rates of minorities, particularly Hispanics in the United States may well mean that whites in the boomer generation will be more dependent on racial minorities to pay for their retirement needs than has ever been the case in the past. This is but one more reason for the country to attend to the racial tension growing in the cities and suburbs. For the social security system to work as it was designed, a degree of intergenerational and cross-racial commitment will be needed.

13. Bill Clinton is the only national politician who articulated a program akin to those of the postwar era. He has argued that a national "education bank" should be created that would allow young people to borrow money for college, to be repaid through public service jobs that would rebuild the nation's infrastructure.

Questions

1. How has the breaking of the social contract affected support for public schooling?

2. Explain how generational differences have arisen given the recent downturn in economic prosperity.

3. Katherine Newman's book was published in 1993, prior to the more recent economic downturn and recession. In your opinion, how much worse have political dynamics and intergenerational differences become in the last decade?

4. What are some likely consequences of diminished support for social services, education, and various assistance programs?

5. In your opinion, how might members of "Generation X" respond to the expectation that, as a group, they likely will fare worse than their parents' generation?

JIHAD VS. MCWORLD

BENJAMIN R. BARBER

Benjamin R. Barber is Kekst Professor of Civil Society at the University of Maryland, Director, New York office, The Democracy Collaborative and the author of many books including "Strong Democracy" (1984), "Jihad vs. McWorld" (Times Books, 1995), "The Truth Of Power: Intellectual Affairs in the Clinton White House" (W.W. Norton & Company)

Jihad and McWorld are terms that have recently come into popular usage. McWorld (i.e., globalism) describes globalization from an economic perspective (e.g., McDonalds restaurants built with increasing frequency around the globe). Jihad (i.e., tribalism) describes the political conflict between Muslims and non-Muslims, referring especially to Middle-East conflicts and recent terrorism against the United States, and more generally to conflicts arising between ethnic or religious groups within national borders.

In this selection, Barber details the strengths and weaknesses of each perspective, explains how the two organizing principles work in opposite directions and often undermine democracy, and proposes an alternative that he calls the "confederal option."

The two axial principles of our age—tribalism and globalism—clash at every point except one: they may both be threatening to democracy.

Just beyond the horizon of current events lie two possible political futures—both bleak, neither democratic. The first is a retribalization of large swaths of humankind by war and bloodshed: a threatened Lebanonization of national states in which culture is pitted against culture, people against people, tribe against tribe—a Jihad in the name of a hundred narrowly conceived faiths against every kind of interdependence, every kind of artificial social cooperation and civic mutuality. The second is being borne in on us by the onrush of economic and ecological forces that demand integration and uniformity and that mesmerize the world with fast music, fast computers, and fast food—with MTV, Macintosh, and McDonald's, pressing nations into one commercially homogenous global network: one McWorld tied together by technology, ecology, communications, and commerce. The planet is falling precipitately apart *AND* coming reluctantly together at the very same moment.

These two tendencies are sometimes visible in the same countries at the same instant: thus Yugoslavia, clamoring just recently to join the New Europe, is exploding into fragments; India is trying to live up to its reputation as the world's largest integral democracy while powerful new fundamentalist parties like the Hindu nationalist Bharatiya Janata Party, along with nationalist assassins, are imperiling its hard-won unity. States are breaking up or joining up: the Soviet Union has disappeared almost overnight, its parts forming new unions with one another or with like-minded nationalities in neighboring states. The old interwar national state based on territory and political sovereignty looks to be a mere transitional development.

The tendencies of what I am here calling the forces of Jihad and the forces of McWorld operate with equal strength in opposite directions, the one driven by parochial hatreds, the other by universalizing markets, the one re-creating ancient subnational and ethnic borders from within, the other making national borders porous from without. They have one thing in common: neither offers much hope to citizens looking for practical ways to govern themselves democratically. If the global future is to pit Jihad's centrifugal whirlwind against McWorld's centripetal black hole, the outcome is unlikely to be democratic—or so I will argue.

McWorld, or the Globalization of Politics

Four imperatives make up the dynamic of McWorld: a market imperative, a resource imperative, an information-technology imperative, and an ecological imperative. By shrinking the world and diminishing the salience of national borders, these imperatives have in combination achieved a considerable victory over factiousness and particularism, and not least of all over their most virulent traditional form—nationalism. It is the realists who are now Europeans, the utopians who dream nostalgically of a resurgent England or Germany, perhaps even a resurgent Wales or Saxony. Yesterday's wishful cry for one world has yielded to the reality of McWorld.

The Market Imperative

Marxist and Leninist theories of imperialism assumed that the quest for ever-expanding markets would in time compel nation-based capitalist economies to push against national boundaries in search of an international economic imperium. Whatever else has happened to the scientistic predictions of Marxism, in this domain they have proved farsighted. All national economies are now vulnerable to the inroads of larger, transnational markets within which trade is free, currencies are convertible, access to banking is open, and contracts are enforceable under law. In Europe, Asia, Africa, the South Pacific, and the Americas such markets are eroding national sovereignty and giving rise to entities—international banks, trade associations, transnational lobbies like OPEC and Greenpeace, world news services like CNN and the BBC, and multinational corporations that increasingly lack a meaningful national identity—that neither reflect nor respect nationhood as an organizing or regulative principle.

The market imperative has also reinforced the quest for international peace and stability, requisites of an efficient international economy. Markets are enemies of parochialism, isolation, fractiousness, war. Market psychology attenuates the psychology of ideological and religious cleavages and assumes a concord among producers and consumers—categories that ill fit narrowly conceived national or religious cultures. Shopping has little tolerance for blue laws, whether dictated by pub-closing British paternalism, Sabbath-observing Jewish Orthodox fundamentalism, or no-Sunday-liquor-sales Massachusetts puritanism. In the context of common markets, international law ceases to be a vision of justice and becomes a workaday framework for getting things done—enforcing contracts, ensuring that governments abide by deals, regulating trade and currency relations, and so forth.

Common markets demand a common language, as well as a common currency, and they produce common behaviors of the kind bred by cosmopolitan city life everywhere. Commercial pilots, computer programmers, international bankers, media specialists, oil riggers, entertainment celebrities, ecology experts, demographers, accountants, professors, athletes—these compose a new breed of men and women for whom religion, culture, and nationality can seem only marginal elements in a working identity. Although sociologists of everyday life will no doubt continue to distinguish a Japanese from an American mode, shopping has a common signature throughout the world. Cynics might even say that some of the recent revolutions in Eastern Europe have had as their true goal not liberty and the right to vote but well-paying jobs and the right to shop (although the vote is proving easier to acquire than consumer goods). The market imperative is, then, plenty powerful; but, notwithstanding some of the claims made for "democratic capitalism," it is not identical with the democratic imperative.

The Resource Imperative

Democrats once dreamed of societies whose political autonomy rested firmly on economic independence. The Athenians idealized what they called autarky, and tried for a while to create a way of life simple and austere enough to make the polis genuinely self-sufficient. To be free meant to be independent of any other community or polis. Not even the Athenians were able to achieve autarky, however: human nature, it turns out, is dependency. By the time of Pericles, Athenian politics was inextricably bound up with a flowering empire held together by naval power and commerce—an empire that, even as it appeared to enhance Athenian might, ate away at Athenian independence and autarky. Master and slave, it turned out, were bound together by mutual insufficiency.

The dream of autarky briefly engrossed nineteenth-century America as well, for the underpopulated, endlessly bountiful land, the cornucopia of natural resources, and the natural barriers of a continent walled in by two great seas led many to believe that America could be a world unto itself. Given this past, it has been harder for Americans than for most to accept the inevitability of interdependence. But the rapid depletion of resources even in a country like ours, where they once seemed inexhaustible, and the maldistribution of arable soil and mineral resources on the planet, leave even the wealthiest societies ever more resource-dependent and many other nations in permanently desperate straits.

Every nation, it turns out, needs something another nation has; some nations have almost nothing they need.

The Information-Technology Imperative

Enlightenment science and the technologies derived from it are inherently universalizing. They entail a quest for descriptive principles of general application, a search for universal solutions to particular problems, and an unswerving embrace of objectivity and impartiality.

Scientific progress embodies and depends on open communication, a common discourse rooted in rationality, collaboration, and an easy and regular flow and exchange of information. Such ideals can be hypocritical covers for power-mongering by elites, and they may be shown to be wanting in many other ways, but they are entailed by the very idea of science and they make science and globalization practical allies.

Business, banking, and commerce all depend on information flow and are facilitated by new communication technologies. The hardware of these technologies tends to be systemic and integrated—computer, television, cable, satellite, laser, fiber-optic, and microchip technologies combining to create a vast interactive communications and information network that can potentially give every person on earth access to every other person, and make every datum, every byte, available to every set of eyes. If the automobile was, as George Ball once said (when he gave his blessing to a Fiat factory in the Soviet Union during the Cold War), "an ideology on four wheels," then electronic telecommunication and information systems are an ideology at 186,000 miles per second—which makes for a very small planet in a very big hurry. Individual cultures speak particular languages; commerce and science increasingly speak English; the whole world speaks logarithms and binary mathematics.

Moreover, the pursuit of science and technology asks for, even compels, open societies. Satellite footprints do not respect national borders; telephone wires penetrate the most closed societies. With photocopying and then fax machines having infiltrated Soviet universities and *samizdat* literary circles in the eighties, and computer modems having multiplied like rabbits in communism's bureaucratic warrens thereafter, *glasnost* could not be far behind. In their social requisites, secrecy and science are enemies.

The new technology's software is perhaps even more globalizing than its hardware. The information arm of international commerce's sprawling body reaches out and touches distinct nations and parochial cultures, and gives them a common face chiseled in Hollywood, on Madison Avenue, and in Silicon Valley. Throughout the 1980s one of the most-watched television programs in South Africa was *The Cosby Show*. The demise of apartheid was already in production. Exhibitors at the 1991 Cannes film festival expressed growing anxiety over the "homogenization" and "Americanization" of the global film industry when, for the third year running, American films dominated the awards ceremonies. America has dominated the world's popular culture for much longer, and much more decisively. In November of 1991 Switzerland's once insular culture boasted best-seller lists featuring *Terminator 2* as the No. 1 movie, *Scarlett* as the No. 1 book, and Prince's *Diamonds and Pearls* as the No. 1 record album. No wonder the Japanese are buying Hollywood film studios even faster than Americans are buying Japanese television sets. This kind of software supremacy may in the long term be far more important than hardware superiority, because culture has become more potent than armaments. What is the power of the Pentagon compared with Disneyland? Can the Sixth Fleet keep up with CNN? McDonald's in Moscow and Coke in China will do more to create a global culture than military colonization ever could. It is less the goods than the brand names that do the work, for they convey life-style images that alter perception and challenge behavior. They make up the seductive software of McWorld's common (at times much too common) soul.

Yet in all this high-tech commercial world there is nothing that looks particularly democratic. It lends itself to surveillance as well as liberty, to new forms of manipulation and covert control as well as new kinds of participation, to skewed, unjust market outcomes as well as greater productivity. The consumer society and the open society are not quite synonymous. Capitalism and democracy have a relationship, but it is something less than a marriage. An efficient free market after all requires that consumers be free to vote their dollars on competing goods, not that citizens be free to vote their values and beliefs on competing political candidates and programs. The free market flourished in junta-run Chile, in military-governed Taiwan and Korea, and, earlier, in a variety of autocratic European empires as well as their colonial possessions.

The Ecological Imperative

The impact of globalization on ecology is a cliche even to world leaders who ignore it. We know well enough that the German forests can be destroyed by Swiss and Italians driving gas-guzzlers fueled by leaded gas. We also know that the planet can be asphyxiated by greenhouse gases because Brazilian farmers want to be part of the twentieth century and are burning down tropical rain forests to clear a little land to plough, and because Indonesians make a living out of converting their lush jungle into toothpicks for fastidious

Japanese diners, upsetting the delicate oxygen balance and in effect puncturing our global lungs. Yet this ecological consciousness has meant not only greater awareness but also greater inequality, as modernized nations try to slam the door behind them, saying to developing nations, "The world cannot afford your modernization; ours has wrung it dry!"

Each of the four imperatives just cited is transnational, transideological, and transcultural. Each applies impartially to Catholics, Jews, Muslims, Hindus, and Buddhists; to democrats and totalitarians; to capitalists and socialists. The Enlightenment dream of a universal rational society has to a remarkable degree been realized—but in a form that is commercialized, homogenized, depoliticized, bureaucratized, and, of course, radically incomplete, for the movement toward McWorld is in competition with forces of global breakdown, national dissolution, and centrifugal corruption. These forces, working in the opposite direction, are the essence of what I call Jihad.

Jihad, or the Lebanonization of the World

OPEC, the World Bank, the United Nations, the International Red Cross, the multinational corporation . . . there are scores of institutions that reflect globalization. But they often appear as ineffective reactors to the world's real actors: national states and, to an ever greater degree, subnational factions in permanent rebellion against uniformity and integration—even the kind represented by universal law and justice. The headlines feature these players regularly: they are cultures, not countries; parts, not wholes; sects, not religions; rebellious factions and dissenting minorities at war not just with globalism but with the traditional nation-state. Kurds, Basques, Puerto Ricans, Ossetians, East Timoreans, Quebecois, the Catholics of Northern Ireland, Abkhasians, Kurile Islander Japanese, the Zulus of Inkatha, Catalonians, Tamils, and, of course, Palestinians—people without countries, inhabiting nations not their own, seeking smaller worlds within borders that will seal them off from modernity.

A powerful irony is at work here. Nationalism was once a force of integration and unification, a movement aimed at bringing together disparate clans, tribes, and cultural fragments under new, assimilationist flags. But as Ortega y Gasset noted more than sixty years ago, having won its victories, nationalism changed its strategy. In the 1920s, and again today, it is more often a reactionary and divisive force, pulverizing the very nations it once helped cement together. The force

that creates nations is "inclusive," Ortega wrote in *The Revolt of the Masses*. "In periods of consolidation, nationalism has a positive value, and is a lofty standard. But in Europe everything is more than consolidated, and nationalism is nothing but a mania . . ."

This mania has left the post–Cold War world smoldering with hot wars; the international scene is little more unified than it was at the end of the Great War, in Ortega's own time. There were more than thirty wars in progress last year, most of them ethnic, racial, tribal, or religious in character, and the list of unsafe regions doesn't seem to be getting any shorter. Some new world order!

The aim of many of these small-scale wars is to redraw boundaries, to implode states and resecure parochial identities: to escape McWorld's dully insistent imperatives. The mood is that of Jihad: war not as an instrument of policy but as an emblem of identity, an expression of community, an end in itself. Even where there is no shooting war, there is fractiousness, secession, and the quest for ever smaller communities. Add to the list of dangerous countries those at risk: In Switzerland and Spain, Jurassian and Basque separatists still argue the virtues of ancient identities, sometimes in the language of bombs. Hyperdisintegration in the former Soviet Union may well continue unabated—not just a Ukraine independent from the Soviet Union but a Bessarabian Ukraine independent from the Ukrainian republic; not just Russia severed from the defunct union but Tatarstan severed from Russia. Yugoslavia makes even the disunited, ex-Soviet, nonsocialist republics that were once the Soviet Union look integrated, its sectarian fatherlands springing up within factional motherlands like weeds within weeds within weeds. Kurdish independence would threaten the territorial integrity of four Middle Eastern nations. Well before the current cataclysm Soviet Georgia made a claim for autonomy from the Soviet Union, only to be faced with its Ossetians (164,000 in a republic of 5.5 million) demanding their own self-determination within Georgia. The Abkhasian minority in Georgia has followed suit. Even the good will established by Canada's once promising Meech Lake protocols is in danger, with Francophone Quebec again threatening the dissolution of the federation. In South Africa the emergence from apartheid was hardly achieved when friction between Inkatha's Zulus and the African National Congress's tribally identified members threatened to replace Europeans' racism with an indigenous tribal war. After thirty years of attempted integration using the colonial language (English) as a unifier, Nigeria is now playing with the idea of linguistic multiculturalism—which could mean the cultural breakup of the nation into hundreds of tribal fragments. Even Saddam Hussein has benefited from the threat of internal Jihad, having used renewed tribal and religious warfare to turn last season's mortal enemies into reluctant allies of an Iraqi nationhood that he nearly destroyed.

The passing of communism has torn away the thin veneer of internationalism (workers of the world unite!) to reveal ethnic prejudices that are not only ugly and deep-seated but increasingly murderous. Europe's old scourge, anti-Semitism, is back with a vengeance, but it is only one of many antagonisms. It appears all too easy to throw the historical gears into reverse and pass from a Communist dictatorship back into a tribal state.

Among the tribes, religion is also a battlefield. ("Jihad" is a rich word whose generic meaning is "struggle"—usually the struggle of the soul to avert evil. Strictly applied to religious war, it is used only in reference to battles where the faith is under assault, or battles against a government that denies the practice of Islam. My use here is rhetorical, but does follow both journalistic practice and history.) Remember the Thirty Years War? Whatever forms of Enlightenment universalism might once have come to grace such historically related forms of monotheism as Judaism, Christianity, and Islam, in many of their modern incarnations they are parochial rather than cosmopolitan, angry rather than loving, proselytizing rather than ecumenical, zealous rather than rationalist, sectarian rather than deistic, ethnocentric rather than universalizing. As a result, like the new forms of hypernationalism, the new expressions of religious fundamentalism are fractious and pulverizing, never integrating. This is religion as the Crusaders knew it: a battle to the death for souls that if not saved will be forever lost.

The atmospherics of Jihad have resulted in a breakdown of civility in the name of identity, of comity in the name of community. International relations have sometimes taken on the aspect of gang war—cultural turf battles featuring tribal factions that were supposed to be sublimated as integral parts of large national, economic, postcolonial, and constitutional entities.

The Darkening Future of Democracy

These rather melodramatic tableaux vivants do not tell the whole story, however. For all their defects, Jihad and McWorld have their attractions. Yet, to repeat and insist, the attractions are unrelated to democracy.

Neither McWorld nor Jihad is remotely democratic in impulse. Neither needs democracy; neither promotes democracy.

McWorld does manage to look pretty seductive in a world obsessed with Jihad. It delivers peace, prosperity, and relative unity—if at the cost of independence, community, and identity (which is generally based on difference). The primary political values required by the global market are order and tranquillity, and freedom—as in the phrases "free trade," "free press," and "free love." Human rights are needed to a degree, but not citizenship or participation—and no more social justice and equality than are necessary to promote efficient economic production and consumption. Multinational corporations sometimes seem to prefer doing business with local oligarchs, inasmuch as they can take confidence from dealing with the boss on all crucial matters. Despots who slaughter their own populations are no problem, so long as they leave markets in place and refrain from making war on their neighbors (Saddam Hussein's fatal mistake). In trading partners, predictability is of more value than justice.

The Eastern European revolutions that seemed to arise out of concern for global democratic values quickly deteriorated into a stampede in the general direction of free markets and their ubiquitous, television-promoted shopping malls. East Germany's Neues Forum, that courageous gathering of intellectuals, students, and workers which overturned the Stalinist regime in Berlin in 1989, lasted only six months in Germany's mini-version of McWorld. Then it gave way to money and markets and monopolies from the West. By the time of the first all-German elections, it could scarcely manage to secure three percent of the vote. Elsewhere there is growing evidence that glasnost will go and perestroika—defined as privatization and an opening of markets to Western bidders—will stay. So understandably anxious are the new rulers of Eastern Europe and whatever entities are forged from the residues of the Soviet Union to gain access to credit and markets and technology—McWorld's flourishing new currencies—that they have shown themselves willing to trade away democratic prospects in pursuit of them: not just old totalitarian ideologies and command-economy production models but some possible indigenous experiments with a third way between capitalism and socialism, such as economic cooperatives and employee stock-ownership plans, both of which have their ardent supporters in the East.

Jihad delivers a different set of virtues: a vibrant local identity, a sense of community, solidarity among kinsmen, neighbors, and countrymen, narrowly conceived. But it also guarantees parochialism and is grounded in exclusion. Solidarity is secured through war against outsiders. And solidarity often means obedience to a hierarchy in governance, fanaticism in beliefs, and the obliteration of individual selves in the name of the group. Deference to leaders and intolerance toward outsiders (and toward "enemies within") are hallmarks of tribalism—hardly the attitudes required for the cultivation of new democratic women and men capable of governing themselves. Where new democratic experiments have been conducted in retribalizing societies, in both Europe and the Third World, the result has often been anarchy, repression, persecution, and the coming of new, noncommunist forms of very old kinds of despotism. During the past year, Havel's velvet revolution in Czechoslovakia was imperiled by partisans of "Czechland" and of Slovakia as independent entities. India seemed little less rent by Sikh, Hindu, Muslim, and Tamil infighting than it was immediately after the British pulled out, more than forty years ago.

To the extent that either McWorld or Jihad has a *NATURAL* politics, it has turned out to be more of an antipolitics. For McWorld, it is the antipolitics of globalism: bureaucratic, technocratic, and meritocratic, focused (as Marx predicted it would be) on the administration of things—with people, however, among the chief things to be administered. In its politico-economic imperatives McWorld has been guided by laissez-faire market principles that privilege efficiency, productivity, and beneficence at the expense of civic liberty and self-government.

For Jihad, the antipolitics of tribalization has been explicitly antidemocratic: one-party dictatorship, government by military junta, theocratic fundamentalism—often associated with a version of the *Fuhrerprinzip* that empowers an individual to rule on behalf of a people. Even the government of India, struggling for decades to model democracy for a people who will soon number a billion, longs for great leaders; and for every Mahatma Gandhi, Indira Gandhi, or Rajiv Gandhi taken from them by zealous assassins, the Indians appear to seek a replacement who will deliver them from the lengthy travail of their freedom.

The Confederal Option

How can democracy be secured and spread in a world whose primary tendencies are at best indifferent to it (McWorld) and at worst deeply antithetical to it (Jihad)?

My guess is that globalization will eventually vanquish retribalization. The ethos of material "civilization" has not yet encountered an obstacle it has been unable to thrust aside. Ortega may have grasped in the 1920s a clue to our own future in the coming millennium.

"Everyone sees the need of a new principle of life. But as always happens in similar crises—some people attempt to save the situation by an artificial intensification of the very principle which has led to decay. This is the meaning of the 'nationalist' outburst of recent years . . . things have always gone that way. The last flare, the longest; the last sigh, the deepest. On the very eve of their disappearance there is an intensification of frontiers—military and economic."

Jihad may be a last deep sigh before the eternal yawn of McWorld. On the other hand, Ortega was not exactly prescient; his prophecy of peace and internationalism came just before blitzkrieg, world war, and the Holocaust tore the old order to bits. Yet democracy is how we remonstrate with reality, the rebuke our aspirations offer to history. And if retribalization is inhospitable to democracy, there is nonetheless a form of democratic government that can accommodate parochialism and communitarianism, one that can even save them from their defects and make them more tolerant and participatory: decentralized participatory democracy. And if McWorld is indifferent to democracy, there is nonetheless a form of democratic government that suits global markets passably well—representative government in its federal or, better still, confederal variation.

With its concern for accountability, the protection of minorities, and the universal rule of law, a confederalized representative system would serve the political needs of McWorld as well as oligarchic bureaucratism or meritocratic elitism is currently doing. As we are already beginning to see, many nations may survive in the long term only as confederations that afford local regions smaller than "nations" extensive jurisdiction. Recommended reading for democrats of the twenty-first century is not the U.S. Constitution or the French Declaration of Rights of Man and Citizen but the Articles of Confederation, that suddenly pertinent document that stitched together the thirteen American colonies into what then seemed a too loose confederation of independent states but now appears a new form of political realism, as veterans of Yeltsin's new Russia and the new Europe created at Maastricht will attest.

By the same token, the participatory and direct form of democracy that engages citizens in civic activity and civic judgment and goes well beyond just voting and accountability—the system I have called "strong democracy"—suits the political needs of decentralized communities as well as theocratic and nationalist party dictatorships have done. Local neighborhoods need not be democratic, but they can be. Real democracy has flourished in diminutive settings: the spirit of liberty, Tocqueville said, is local. Participatory democracy, if not naturally apposite to tribalism, has an undeniable attractiveness under conditions of parochialism.

Democracy in any of these variations will, however, continue to be obstructed by the undemocratic and antidemocratic trends toward uniformitarian globalism and intolerant retribalization which I have portrayed here. For democracy to persist in our brave new McWorld, we will have to commit acts of conscious political will—a possibility, but hardly a probability, under these conditions. Political will requires much more than the quick fix of the transfer of institutions. Like technology transfer, institution transfer rests on foolish assumptions about a uniform world of the kind that once fired the imagination of colonial administrators. Spread English justice to the colonies by exporting wigs. Let an East Indian trading company act as the vanguard to Britain's free parliamentary institutions. Today's well-intentioned quick-fixers in the National Endowment for Democracy and the Kennedy School of Government, in the unions and foundations and universities zealously nurturing contacts in Eastern Europe and the Third World, are hoping to democratize by long distance. Post Bulgaria a parliament by first-class mail. Fed Ex the Bill of Rights to Sri Lanka. Cable Cambodia some common law.

Yet Eastern Europe has already demonstrated that importing free political parties, parliaments, and presses cannot establish a democratic civil society; imposing a free market may even have the opposite effect. Democracy grows from the bottom up and cannot be imposed from the top down. Civil society has to be built from the inside out. The institutional superstructure comes last. Poland may become democratic, but then again it may heed the Pope, and prefer to found its politics on its Catholicism, with uncertain consequences for democracy. Bulgaria may become democratic, but it may prefer tribal war. The former Soviet Union may become a democratic confederation, or it may just grow into an anarchic and weak conglomeration of markets for other nations' goods and services.

Democrats need to seek out indigenous democratic impulses. There is always a desire for self-government, always some expression of participation, accountability, consent, and representation, even in traditional hierarchical societies. These need to be identified, tapped, modified, and incorporated into new democratic practices with an indigenous flavor. The tortoises among the democratizers may ultimately outlive or outpace the hares, for they will have the time and patience to explore conditions along the way, and to adapt their gait to changing circumstances. Tragically, democracy in a hurry often looks something like France in 1794 or China in 1989.

It certainly seems possible that the most attractive democratic ideal in the face of the brutal realities of Jihad and the dull realities of McWorld will be a confederal union of semi-autonomous communities smaller than nation-states, tied together into regional economic associations and markets larger than nation-states—participatory and self-determining in local matters at the bottom, representative and accountable at the top. The nation-state would play a diminished role, and sovereignty would lose some of its political potency. The Green movement adage "Think globally, act locally" would actually come to describe the conduct of politics.

This vision reflects only an ideal, however—one that is not terribly likely to be realized. Freedom, Jean-Jacques Rousseau once wrote, is a food easy to eat but hard to digest. Still, democracy has always played itself out against the odds. And democracy remains both a form of coherence as binding as McWorld and a secular faith potentially as inspiriting as Jihad.

Questions

1. Briefly define/explain the terms *tribalism* and *globalism*.

2. What are the McWorld principle's four imperatives? Which are most effective at reducing political boundaries? Which are most effective at generating solidarity and creating cross-national ties?

3. What do Jihad and McWorld promise that can be construed as a positive contribution(s) or outcome(s)?

4. What pitfalls face Jihad and McWorld as organizing principles?

5. To what extent can Jihad potentially fractionalize populations within particular national boundaries?

6. Why does Barber contend that neither Jihad nor McWorld operate under or foster democratic principles?

WHY AMERICANS FEAR THE WRONG THINGS

BARRY GLASSNER

Reprinted from The Culture of Fear: Why Americans Are Afraid of the Wrong Things, *by permission of Basic Books. Copyright © 1999 by Barry Glassner.*

Americans fear many things, and often fear the wrong things. One of the more recent moral panics in American society was the fear of school violence, particularly school shootings. The media continually told us that we were in the middle of an epidemic of growing proportion, legislators told school districts that they had to develop emergency response protocols, and parents mobilized to more effectively reach at-risk youth. Underlying this moral panic was little knowledge of the facts: at its peak, slightly more than 50 children were killed in school shootings in a given year while more than 50 million children were enrolled in school. The truth was that a child has better odds of being struck by lightning or killed at the hands of a family member in his own home than being the victim of school violence. So why do we fear school violence more than lightning or domestic violence? In this selection, Barry Glassner explores why Americans fear the wrong things.

Why are so many fears in the air, and so many of them unfounded? Why, as crime rates plunged throughout the 1990s, did two-thirds of Americans believe they were soaring? How did it come about that by mid-decade 62 percent of us described ourselves as "truly desperate" about crime—almost twice as many as in the late 1980s, when crime rates were higher? Why, on a survey in 1997, when the crime rate had already fallen for a half dozen consecutive years, did more than half of us disagree with the statement "This country is finally beginning to make some progress in solving the crime problem"?[1]

In the late 1990s the number of drug users had decreased by half compared to a decade earlier; almost two-thirds of high school seniors had never used any illegal drugs, even marijuana. So why did a majority of adults rank drug abuse as the greatest danger to America's youth? Why did nine out of ten believe the drug problem is out of control, and only one in six believe the country was making progress?[2]

Give us a happy ending and we write a new disaster story. In the late 1990s the unemployment rate was below 5 percent for the first time in a quarter century. People who had been pounding the pavement for years could finally get work. Yet pundits warned of imminent economic disaster. They predicted inflation would take off, just as they had a few years earlier—also erroneously—when the unemployment rate dipped below 6 percent.[3]

We compound our worries beyond all reason. Life expectancy in the United States has doubled during the twentieth century. We are better able to cure and control diseases than any other civilization in history. Yet we hear that phenomenal numbers of us are dreadfully ill. In 1996 Bob Garfield, a magazine writer, reviewed articles about serious diseases published over the course of a year in the *Washington Post*, the *New York Times*, and *USA Today*. He learned that, in addition to 59 million Americans with heart disease, 53 million with migraines, 25 million with osteoporosis, 16 million with obesity, and 3 million with cancer, many Americans suffer from more obscure ailments such as temporomandibular joint disorders (10 million) and brain injuries (2 million). Adding up the estimates, Garfield determined that 543 million Americans are seriously sick—a shocking number in a nation of 266 million inhabitants. "Either as a society we are doomed, or someone is seriously double-dipping," he suggested.[4]

Garfield appears to have underestimated one category of patients: for psychiatric ailments his figure was 53 million. Yet when Jim Windolf, an editor of the *New York Observer*, collated estimates for maladies ranging from borderline personality disorder (10 million) and sex addiction (11 million) to less well-known conditions such as restless leg syndrome (12 million) he came up with a figure of 152 million. "But give the experts a little time," he advised. "With another new quantifiable disorder or two, everybody in the country will be officially nuts."[5]

Indeed, Windolf omitted from his estimates new-fashioned afflictions that have yet to make it into the *Diagnostic and Statistical Manual of Mental Disorders* of the American Psychiatric Association: ailments such as road rage, which afflicts more than half of Americans, according to a psychologist's testimony before a congressional hearing in 1997.[6]

The scope of our health fears seems limitless. Besides worrying disproportionately about legitimate ailments and prematurely about would-be diseases, we continue to fret over already refuted dangers. Some still worry, for instance, about "flesh-eating bacteria," a bug first rammed into our consciousness in 1994 when the U.S. news media picked up on a screamer headline in a British tabloid, "Killer Bug Ate My Face." The bacteria, depicted as more brutal than anything seen in modern times, was said to be spreading faster than the pack of photographers outside the home of its latest victim. In point of fact, however, we were not "terribly vulnerable" to these "superbugs," nor were they "medicine's worst nightmares," as voices in the media warned.

Group A strep, a cyclical strain that has been around for ages, had been dormant for half a century or more before making a comeback. The British pseudoepidemic had resulted in a total of about a dozen deaths in the previous year. Medical experts roundly rebutted the scares by noting that of 20 to 30 million strep infections each year in the United States fewer than 1 in 1,000 involve serious strep A complications, and only 500 to 1,500 people suffer the flesh-eating syndrome, whose proper name is necrotizing fasciitis. Still the fear persisted. Years after the initial scare, horrifying news stories continued to appear, complete with grotesque pictures of victims. A United Press International story in 1998 typical of the genre told of a child in Texas who died of the "deadly strain" of bacteria that the reporter warned "can spread at a rate of up to one inch per hour."[7]

Roosevelt Was Wrong

We had better learn to doubt our inflated fears before they destroy us. Valid fears have their place; they cue us to danger. False and overdrawn fears only cause hardship....

We all pay one of the costs of panics: huge sums of money go to waste. Hysteria over the ritual abuse of children cost billions of dollars in police investigations, trials, and imprisonments. Men and women went to jail for years "on the basis of some of the most fantastic claims ever presented to an American jury," as Dorothy Rabinowitz of the *Wall Street Journal* demonstrated in a series of investigative articles for which she became a Pulitzer Prize finalist in 1996. Across the nation expensive surveillance programs were implemented to protect children from fiends who reside primarily in the imaginations of adults.[8]

The price tag for our panic about overall crime has grown so monumental that even law-and-order zealots find it hard to defend. The criminal justice system costs Americans close to $100 billion a year, most of which goes to police and prisons. In California we spend more on jails than on higher education. Yet increases in the number of police and prison cells do not correlate consistently with reductions in the number of serious crimes committed. Criminologists who study reductions in homicide rates, for instance, find little difference between cities that substantially expand their police forces and prison capacity and others that do not.[9]

The turnabout in domestic public spending over the past quarter century, from child welfare and antipoverty programs to incarceration, did not even produce reductions in *fear* of crime. Increasing the number of cops

and jails arguably has the opposite effect: it suggests that the crime problem is all the more out of control.[10]

Panic-driven public spending generates over the long term a pathology akin to one found in drug addicts. The more money and attention we fritter away on our compulsions, the less we have available for our real needs, which consequently grow larger. While fortunes are being spent to protect children from dangers that few ever encounter, approximately 11 million children lack health insurance, 12 million are malnourished, and rates of illiteracy are increasing.[11]

I do not contend, as did President Roosevelt in 1933, that "the only thing we have to fear is fear itself." My point is that we often fear the wrong things. In the 1990s middle-income and poorer Americans should have worried about unemployment insurance, which covered a smaller share of workers than twenty years earlier. Many of us have had friends or family out of work during economic downturns or as a result of corporate restructuring. Living in a nation with one of the largest income gaps of any industrialized country, where the bottom 40 percent of the population is worse off financially than their counterparts two decades earlier, we might also have worried about income inequality. Or poverty. During the mid- and late 1990s 5 million elderly Americans had no food in their homes, more than 20 million people used emergency food programs each year, and one in five children lived in poverty—more than a quarter million of them homeless. All told, a larger proportion of Americans were poor than three decades earlier.[12]

One of the paradoxes of a culture of fear is that serious problems remain widely ignored even though they give rise to precisely the dangers that the populace most abhors. Poverty, for example, correlates strongly with child abuse, crime, and drug abuse. Income inequality is also associated with adverse outcomes for society as a whole. The larger the gap between rich and poor in a society, the higher its overall death rates from heart disease, cancer, and murder.

Two Easy Explanations

In the following discussion I will try to answer two questions: Why are Americans so fearful lately, and why are our fears so often misplaced? To both questions the same two-word answer is commonly given by scholars and journalists: premillennial tensions. The final years of a millennium and the early years of a new millennium provoke mass anxiety and ill reasoning, the argument goes. So momentous does the calendric change seem, the populace cannot keep its wits about it.

Premillennial tensions probably do help explain some of our collective irrationality. Living in a scientific era, most of us grant the arbitrariness of reckoning time in base-ten rather than, say, base-twelve, and from the birth of Christ rather than from the day Muhammad moved from Mecca. Yet even the least superstitious among us cannot quite manage to think of the year 2000 as ordinary. Social psychologists have long recognized a human urge to convert vague uneasiness into definable concerns, real or imagined. In a classic study thirty years ago Alan Kerckhoff and Kurt Back pointed out that "the belief in a tangible threat makes it possible to explain and justify one's sense of discomfort."[13]

Some historical evidence also supports the hypothesis that people panic at the brink of centuries and millennia. Witness the "panic terror" in Europe around the year 1000 and the witch hunts in Salem in the 1690s. As a complete or dependable explanation, though, the millennium hypothesis fails. Historians emphasize that panics of equal or greater intensity occur in odd years, as demonstrated by anti-Indian hysteria in the mid 1700s and McCarthyism in the 1950s. Scholars point out too that calendars cannot account for why certain fears occupy people at certain times (witches then, killer kids now).[14]

Another popular explanation blames the news media. We have so many fears, many of them off-base, the argument goes, because the media bombard us with sensationalistic stories designed to increase ratings. This explanation, sometimes called the media-effects theory, is less simplistic than the millennium hypothesis and contains sizable kernels of truth. When researchers from Emory University computed the levels of coverage of various health dangers in popular magazines and newspapers they discovered an inverse relationship: much less space was devoted to several of the major causes of death than to some uncommon causes. The leading cause of death, heart disease, received approximately the same amount of coverage as the eleventh-ranked cause of death, homicide. They found a similar inverse relationship in coverage of risk factors associated with serious illness and death. The lowest-ranking risk factor, drug use, received nearly as much attention as the second-ranked risk factor, diet and exercise.[15]

Disproportionate coverage in the news media plainly has effects on readers and viewers. When Esther Madriz, a professor at Hunter College, interviewed women in New York City about their fears of crime they frequently responded with the phrase "I saw it in the news." The interviewees identified the news media as both the source of their fears and the reason they believed those fears were valid. Asked in a national poll why they believe the country has a serious crime problem, 76 percent of people cited stories they had seen in the media. Only 22 percent cited personal experience.[16]

When professors Robert Blendon and John Young of Harvard analyzed forty-seven surveys about drug abuse conducted between 1978 and 1997, they too discovered that the news media, rather than personal experience, provide Americans with their predominant fears. Eight out of ten adults say that drug abuse has never caused problems in their family, and the vast majority report relatively little direct experience with problems related to drug abuse. Widespread concern about drug problems emanates, Blendon and Young determined, from scares in the news media, television in particular.[17]

Television news programs survive on scares. On local newscasts, where producers live by the dictum "if it bleeds, it leads," drug, crime, and disaster stories make up most of the news portion of the broadcasts. Evening newscasts on the major networks are somewhat less bloody, but between 1990 and 1998, when the nation's murder rate declined by 20 percent, the number of murder stories on network newscasts increased 600 percent (*not* counting stories about O.J. Simpson).[18]

After the dinnertime newscasts the networks broadcast newsmagazines, whose guiding principle seems to be that no danger is too small to magnify into a national nightmare. Some of the risks reported by such programs would be merely laughable were they not hyped with so much fanfare: "Don't miss *Dateline* tonight or YOU could be the next victim!" Competing for ratings with drama programs and movies during prime-time evening hours, newsmagazines feature story lines that would make a writer for "Homicide" or "ER" wince.[19]

"It can happen in a flash. Fire breaks out on the operating table. The patient is surrounded by flames," Barbara Walters exclaimed on ABC's "20/20" in 1998. The problem—oxygen from a face mask ignited by a surgical instrument—occurs "more often than you might think," she cautioned in her introduction, even though reporter Arnold Diaz would note later, during the actual report, that out of 27 million surgeries each year the situation arises only about a hundred times. No matter, Diaz effectively nullified the reassuring numbers as soon as they left his mouth. To those who "may say it's too small a risk to worry about" he presented distraught victims: a woman with permanent scars on her face and a man whose son had died.[20]

The gambit is common. Producers of TV news-magazines routinely let emotional accounts trump objective information. In 1994 medical authorities attempted to cut short the brouhaha over flesh-eating bacteria by publicizing the fact that an American is fifty-five times more likely to be struck by lightning than die of the suddenly celebrated microbe. Yet TV journalists brushed this fact aside with remarks like, "whatever the statistics, it's devastating to the victims" (Catherine Crier on "20/20"), accompanied by stomach-turning videos of disfigured patients.[21]

Sheryl Stolberg, then a medical writer for the *Los Angeles Times*, put her finger on what makes the TV newsmagazines so cavalier: "Killer germs are perfect for prime time," she wrote. "They are invisible, uncontrollable, and, in the case of Group A strep, can invade the body in an unnervingly simple manner, through a cut or scrape." Whereas print journalists only described in words the actions of "billions of bacteria" spreading "like underground fires" throughout a person's body, TV newsmagazines made use of special effects to depict graphically how these "merciless killers" do their damage.[22]

Morality and Marketing

To blame the media is to oversimplify the complex role that journalists play as both proponents and doubters of popular fears. It is also to beg the same key issue that the millennium hypothesis evades: why particular anxieties take hold when they do. Why do news organizations and their audiences find themselves drawn to one hazard rather than another?

The short answer to why Americans harbor so many misbegotten fears is that immense power and money await those who tap into our moral insecurities and supply us with symbolic substitutes.

Endnotes

1. Crime data here and throughout are from reports of the Bureau of Justice Statistics unless otherwise noted. Fear of crime: Esther Madriz, *Nothing Bad Happens to Good Girls* (Berkeley: University of California Press, 1997), ch. 1; Richard Morin, "As Crime Rate Falls, Fears Persist," *Washington Post* National Edition, 16 June 1997, p. 35; David Whitman, "Believing the Good News," *U.S. News & World Report*, 5 January 1998, pp. 45–46.

2. Eva Bertram, Morris Blachman et al., *Drug War Politics* (Berkeley: University of California Press, 1996), p. 10; Mike Males, *Scapegoat Generation* (Monroe, ME: Common Courage Press, 1996), ch. 6; Karen Peterson, "Survey: Teen Drug Use Declines," *USA Today*, 19 June 1998, p. A6; Robert Blendon and John Young, "The Public and the War on Illicit Drugs," *Journal of the American Medical Association* 279 (18 March 1998): 827–32. In presenting these statistics and others I am aware of a seeming paradox: I criticize the abuse of statistics by fearmongering politicians, journalists, and others but hand down precise-sounding numbers myself. Yet to eschew all estimates because some are used inappropriately or do not withstand scrutiny would be as foolhardy as ignoring all medical advice because some doctors are quacks. Readers can be assured I have interrogated the statistics presented here as factual. As notes throughout the book make clear, I have tried to rely on research that appears in peer-reviewed scholarly journals. Where this was not possible or sufficient, I traced numbers back to their sources, investigated the research methodology utilized to produce them, or conducted searches of the popular and scientific literature for critical commentaries and conflicting findings.

3. Bob Herbert, "Bogeyman Economics," *New York Times*, 4 April 1997, p. A15; Doug Henwood, "Alarming Drop in Unemployment," *Extra*, September 1994, pp. 16–17; Christopher Shea, "Low Inflation and Low Unemployment Spur Economists to Debate 'Natural Rate' Theory," *Chronicle of Higher Education*, 24 October 1997, p. A13.

4. Bob Garfield, "Maladies by the Millions," *USA Today*, 16 December 1996, p. A15.

5. Jim Windolf, "A Nation of Nuts," *Wall Street Journal*, 22 October 1997, p. A22.

6. Andrew Ferguson, "Road Rage," *Time*, 12 January 1998, pp. 64–68; Joe Sharkey, "You're Not Bad, You're Sick. It's in the Book," *New York Times*, 28 September 1997, pp. N1, 5.

7. Malcolm Dean, "Flesh-eating Bugs Scare," *Lancet* 343 (June 1994): 1418; "Flesh-eating Bacteria," *Science* 264 (17 June 1994): 1665; David Brown, "The Flesh-eating Bug," *Washington Post* National Edition, 19 December 1994, p. 34; Sarah Richardson, "Tabloid Strep," *Discover* (January 1995): 71; Liz Hunt, "What's Bugging Us," *The Independent*, 28 May 1994, p. 25; Lisa Seachrist, "The Once and Future Scourge," *Science News* 148 (7 October 1995): 234–35. Quotes are from Bernard Dixon, "A Rampant Non-epidemic," *British Medical Journal* 308 (11 June 1994): 1576–77; and Michael Lemonick and Leon Jaroff, "The Killers All Around," *Time*, 12 September 1994, pp. 62–69. More recent coverage: "Strep A Involved in Baby's Death," UPI, 27 February 1998; see also, e.g., Steve Carney, "Miracle Mom," *Los Angeles Times*, 4 March 1998, p. A6; KTLA, "News at Ten," 28 March 1998.

8. Dorothy Rabinowitz, "A Darkness in Massachusetts," *Wall Street Journal*, 30 January 1995, p. A20 (contains quote); "Back in Wenatchee" (unsigned editorial), *Wall Street Journal*, 20 June 1996, p. A18; Dorothy Rabinowitz, "Justice in Massachusetts," *Wall Street Journal*, 13 May 1997, p. A19. See also Nathan and Snedeker, *Satan's Silence*; James Beaver, "The Myth of Repressed Memory," *Journal of Criminal Law and Criminology* 86 (1996): 596–607; Kathryn Lyon, *Witch Hunt* (New York: Avon, 1998); Pam Belluck, "'Memory' Therapy Leads to a Lawsuit

and Big Settlement," *New York Times*, 6 November 1997, pp. A1, 10.

9. Elliott Currie, *Crime and Punishment in America* (New York: Metropolitan, 1998); Tony Pate et al., *Reducing Fear of Crime in Houston and Newark* (Washington, DC: Police Foundation, 1986); Steven Donziger, *The Real War on Crime* (New York: HarperCollins, 1996); Christina Johns, *Power, Ideology and the War on Drugs* (New York: Praeger, 1992); John Irwin et al., "Fanning the Flames of Fear," *Crime and Delinquency* 44 (1998): 32–48.

10. Steven Donziger, "Fear, Crime and Punishment in the U.S.," *Tikkun* 12 (1996): 24–27, 77.

11. Peter Budetti, "Health Insurance for Children," *New England Journal of Medicine* 338 (1998): 541–42; Eileen Smith, "Drugs Top Adult Fears for Kids' Well-being," *USA Today*, 9 December 1997, p. D1. Literacy statistic: Adult Literacy Service.

12. "The State of America's Children," report by the Children's Defense Fund, Washington, DC, March 1998; "Blocks to Their Future," report by the National Law Center on Homelessness and Poverty, Washington, DC, September 1997; reports released in 1998 from the National Center for Children in Poverty, Columbia University, New York; Douglas Massey, "The Age of Extremes," *Demography* 33 (1996): 395–412; Trudy Lieberman, "Hunger in America," *Nation*, 30 March 1998, pp. 11–16; David Lynch, "Rich Poor World," *USA Today*, 20 September 1996, p. B1; Richard Wolf, "Good Economy Hasn't Helped the Poor," *USA Today*, 10 March 1998, p. A3; Robert Reich, "Broken Faith," *Nation*, 16 February 1998, pp. 11–17.

13. Alan Kerckhoff and Kurt Back, *The June Bug* (New York: Appleton-Century-Crofts, 1968), see esp. pp. 160–61.

14. Stephen Jay Gould, *Questioning the Millennium* (New York: Crown, 1997); Todd Gitlin, "Millennial Mumbo Jumbo," *Los Angeles Times Book Review*, 27 April 1997, p. 8.

15. Karen Frost, Erica Frank et al., "Relative Risk in the News Media," *American Journal of Public Health* 87 (1997): 842–45. Media-effects theory: Nancy Signorielli and Michael Morgan, eds., *Cultivation Analysis* (Newbury Park, CA: Sage, 1990); Jennings Bryant and Dolf Zillman, eds., *Media Effects* (Hillsdale, NJ: Erlbaum, 1994); Ronald Jacobs, "Producing the News, Producing the Crisis," *Media, Culture and Society* 18 (1996): 373–97.

16. Madriz, *Nothing Bad Happens to Good Girls*, see esp. pp. 111–14; David Whitman and Margaret Loftus, "Things Are Getting Better? Who Knew," *U.S. News & World Report*, 16 December 1996, pp. 30–32.

17. Blendon and Young, "War on Illicit Drugs." See also Ted Chiricos et al., "Crime, News and Fear of Crime," *Social Problems* 44 (1997): 342–57.

18. Steven Stark, "Local News: The Biggest Scandal on TV," *Washington Monthly* (June 1997): 38–41; Barbara Bliss Osborn, "If It Bleeds, It Leads," *Extra*, September–October 1994, p. 15; Jenkins, *Pedophiles and Priests*, pp. 68–71; "It's Murder," *USA Today*, 20 April 1998, p. D2; Lawrence Grossman, "Does Local TV News Need a National Nanny?" *Columbia Journalism Review* (May 1998): 33.

19. Regarding fearmongering by newsmagazines, see also Elizabeth Jensen et al., "Consumer Alert," *Brill's Content* (October 1998): 130–47.

20. ABC "20/20," 16 March 1998.

21. Thomas Maugh, "Killer Bacteria a Rarity," *Los Angeles Times*, 3 December 1994, p. A29; Ed Siegel, "Roll Over, Ed Murrow," *Boston Globe*, 21 August 1994, p. 14. Crier quote from ABC's "20/20," 24 June 1994.

22. Sheryl Stolberg, "'Killer Bug' Perfect for Prime Time," *Los Angeles Times*, 15 June 1994, pp. A1, 30–31. Quotes from Brown, "Flesh-eating Bug"; and Michael Lemonick and Leon Jaroff, "The Killers All Around," *Time*, 12 September 1994, pp. 62–69.

Questions

1. What are some examples of supporting evidence that Americans fear the wrong things?

2. What are some costs of having misplaced fears?

3. Why does Glassner contend Americans fear the wrong things?

4. Now that the "new millennium" has passed, does the construction of fear seem to have subsided or changed in any way? Explain.

5. Provide two examples of things we are supposed to fear right now in American society. How well do these examples fit the explanation(s) provided by Glassner?

THE USES OF GLOBAL POVERTY: HOW ECONOMIC INEQUALITY BENEFITS THE WEST

DAINA STUKULIS EGLITIS

Copyright © 2004 by Daina Stukulis Eglitis. Reprinted by permission.

In his 1971 article, Herbert Gans used a variant of functionalist theory to argue that poverty serves particular functions or purposes in American society. The logical conclusion from Gans's research is that poverty cannot be eliminated without society's needing to find other ways to serve those functions or purposes. The article was heavily criticized. Many contended that it served no purpose other than to rationalize the existence of poverty, and that such a thesis would jeopardize poverty-relief programs. Over thirty years later, poverty is still an issue in America. Economic, political, and social relations, however, have become more heavily globalized and interconnected, and in this selection, Daina Stukulis Eglitis examines global poverty using Gans's theoretical perspective and presents eleven functions of global poverty.

In the global village, there stand a wide variety of homes, from the stately mansion on the hill, to the modest abode blessed with electricity and running water, to the adequate but unheated (or uncooled) hut, to the flood-prone, tattered shanty cobbled together from gathered scrap. Those who live on the hill are aware of their neighbors, as their neighbors are aware of them. Most inhabitants of the global village recognize that wealth and the accompanying opportunities for education, health care, and consumption are not evenly divided and that a substantial gap exists between the more and less materially blessed populations. Not everyone agrees on why that is the case.

Consider the following comparisons of life in the global village: In 1999, the gross national income in purchasing power parity (GNI PPP)[1] in the United States was $31,910. In Germany the figure was $23,510, and in Australia, $23,850. By contrast, the GNI PPP of China was $3,550, in Indonesia it was $2,660, and in Pakistan, $1,860. On the bottom tier of states, we find countries like Nigeria with a GNI of $770 and Sierra Leone with just $440. If we use the GNI PPP as a yardstick of economic power and the well-being of populations, we may begin to construct a picture of a global system characterized by the massive maldistribution of wealth, economic security, and purchasing power. Our village is one characterized by deep and fundamental stratification.

What have been the responses of well-off states to this global class system with its extremes of wealth and poverty? Not surprisingly, perhaps, political rhetoric has consistently elevated the goal of spreading the prosperity enjoyed by the advanced industrial states of the West around the globe. In remarks made at the United States Coast Guard Academy commencement ceremony in 1989, President George Bush phrased it this way: "What is it that we want to see? It is a growing community of democracies anchoring international peace and stability, and a dynamic free-market system generating prosperity and progress on a global scale.... If we succeed, the next decade and the century beyond will be an era of unparalleled growth, an era which sees the flourishing of freedom, peace, and prosperity around the world."

If shared global prosperity was the goal, it seems safe to say that while there was some modest progress made in areas like Latin America, Eastern Europe, and parts of Asia, "we" did not really succeed, because the global wealth gap is still massive and growing. The rich countries remain rich, and the poor countries, for the most part, remain trapped in desperate, dire poverty. This has not changed.

Another thing that has not changed is the rhetorical commitment to spreading the wealth. In a speech in Coventry, England, in December 2000, President Bill Clinton laid out a "prescription for how the United States might help close the gap between rich and poor nations." And in his farewell address to the nation in January 2001, the President declared that "the global gap requires more than compassion. It requires action."

As of 2002, President George W. Bush has not addressed the question of non-Western development specifically, though it seems relatively safe to say that he too will join the political chorus of support for global prosperity, although his administration seems destined to be defined by a focus on war rather than development.

Western rhetoric, assistance programs, and advice seem to support the goal of global prosperity and its extension to the 1.3 billion who live on less than $1 per day and those millions or even billions more who eke out a sparse existence just above the threshold of absolute poverty. But the reality of prosperity has touched only a relative few countries, while the struggle to meet basic needs touches many more. Social indicators like the GNI PPP highlight the differences we find in our village. But what explains them? Why does global poverty exist and persist? Why does a global class system with a thin layer of rich states and a broad strata of poor countries exist and persist? What explains why some villagers inhabit houses on the mount while others squat in mud huts below? Possible answers are many. This article explores one way of understanding the yawning gap between the planet's wealthiest and poorest states.

In 1971, sociologist Herbert Gans published an article entitled "The Uses of Poverty: The Poor Pay All."[2] In the article, Gans utilized a conservative theoretical perspective in sociology, functionalism, to inquire about the persistence of poverty in America. The functionalist perspective takes as its starting point the position that essentially all institutions and social phenomena that exist in society contribute in some manner to that society—that is, they are functional for society. If they did not contribute to the social order, the functionalists maintain, they would disappear. Using this perspective, functionalists may inquire about, for instance, the functions, both obvious and hidden (or manifest and latent, to use sociologist Robert Merton's terms), of institutions like the education system or the family or social phenomena like punishment for deviance. These social theorists assume that institutions or phenomena exist because they are functional, and hence their guiding question is, What function do they serve?

Gans posed a similar question about poverty, asking, What are the uses of poverty? Clearly, the notion that poverty is functional for society as a whole is ludicrous: Who would suggest that it is functional for those who endure economic deprivation? So Gans offered a modified functionalist analysis: ". . . instead of identifying functions for an entire social system, I shall identify them for the interest groups, socioeconomic classes, and other population aggregates with shared values that 'inhabit' a social system. I suspect that in a modern heterogeneous society, few phenomena are functional or dysfunctional for the society as a whole, and that most result in benefits to some groups and costs to others."

Gans sought to explain the existence and persistence of poverty in modern, wealthy America by highlighting the way that the existence of poverty has benefits for the nonpoor—not just "evil" individuals like the loan shark or the slum lord, but for "normal" members of nonpoor classes. He identified thirteen "uses" of poverty, including the notions that the existence of a poor class "ensures that society's 'dirty work' will be done," that "the poor buy goods others do not want and thus prolong the economic usefulness of such goods," and "the poor can be identified and punished as alleged or real deviants in order to uphold the legitimacy of conventional norms." He was not arguing that poverty is good. He was suggesting that understanding poverty's existence and persistence means recognizing that the poor have positive social and economic functions for the nonpoor. Thus, one would conclude that the elimination of poverty, while elevated as a societal goal, would be, in practice, costly to the nonpoor.

While Gans's theoretically based inquiry into poverty was focused on America's poor, the same question might be asked about the existence of global poverty: What are the "uses" of global poverty for the better-off countries of the world economic system? The purpose of such an inquiry would be, as it was in Gans's inquiry, not to use a functionalist analysis to legitimate poverty or the highly skewed distribution of wealth in the global system, but to contribute to a deeper understanding of why it continues to exist by explaining how its persistence confers benefits on well-off states and their inhabitants.

The argument is not that advanced states are consciously conspiring to keep the poor states destitute: Well-off countries have historically sought to offer help to less developed countries. In reality, however, there are limited incentives for the better-off states to support the full industrial and technological (and even democratic) development of all the states in the global system. To the degree that the existence of a class of poor states is positively functional for wealthy states, we can begin to imagine why development and assistance programs that help ensure survival, but not prosperity, for poor populations are quite characteristic of Western policy.

This article notes eleven "uses" of global poverty. Global poverty is not, from this perspective, functional for the global community as a whole. The notion that the poverty of billions who live in economically marginal states is globally "useful" would be absurd. But it is not absurd to ask how the existence of a class of poor states serves wealthy states. In fact, asking such a question might contribute to a better understanding of the dual phenomena of global poverty and the global "class" system.

Point 1: The existence of global poverty helps ensure the wealth of affordable goods for Western consumers.

The cornucopia of decently priced goods of reasonable quality enjoyed by Western consumers is underpinned by the low-wage work done in low-income countries. The labels on the clothing you are wearing right now likely contain the familiar words "Made in China" or perhaps "Made in Pakistan." Your clothing is probably of reasonable quality, and you likely paid a reasonable (but not necessarily cheap) price for it.

The Western consumer of textiles such as off-the-rack clothing is a beneficiary of a globalized manufacturing process that has seen the movement of manufacturing to low-wage areas located in poor states that provide ready pools of workers needy enough to labor for a pittance. In China, the average hourly wage of apparel workers is about 23 cents. This benefits the consumer of that apparel. The worker herself (workers in this industry are usually female) derives less benefit: The average hourly wage needed to meet basic needs in China, according to Women's Edge, an advocacy group, is 87 cents.[3]

Another way that the impoverished workers of the third world help reduce the cost of goods coming to Western consumers is through their agricultural labor. For instance, the comparably (and sometimes illegally) low wages paid to many poor migrant farm workers from Mexico and Central America in states like

California contribute to America's ample and reasonably priced food supply.

Stories about low-wage workers in developing countries have, in recent years, emerged in the Western press and provoked some expressions of outrage and the formation of groups like United Students Against Sweatshops. These expressions have been small and limited. Imagine, however, the outrage if popular sports shoes, already pricey, climbed another $50 in cost as a result of manufacturers opting for well-paid, unionized labor. Or imagine if the price of a head of iceberg lettuce, America's favorite vegetable, suddenly doubled in price to $3.00. Which outrage would be more potent?

Point 2: The existence of global poverty benefits Western companies and shareholders in the form of increased profit margins.

Labor costs typically constitute a high percentage of a company's expenditures. By reducing labor costs, companies can both keep prices reasonable (which benefits, as noted, the consumer) and raise profit margins. Not surprisingly, then, companies are not likely to locate in—and are more likely to leave—locations where wages are relatively high. The use of poor female workers in the third world is, in this respect, especially "beneficial" to companies. Women comprise about 80 percent of workers in Export Processing Zones and are often paid 20 percent to 50 percent less than male counterparts. The less costly the workforce, the greater the opportunity for profit. Not coincidentally, countries with an ample supply of poor workers willing to work for miserable wages are also countries with lax safety and environmental regulations, which also keeps down the costs to the Western employer and pushes up the profits. Hence, companies benefit directly from the existence of economically deprived would-be workers willing (or not in a position to be unwilling) to work for paltry wages in potentially hazardous, or at least very unpleasant, conditions.

Point 3: The existence of global poverty fosters access to resources in poor states that are needed in or desired by the West.

Poor states may sell raw goods at low prices to Western states, which can transform the resource into a more valuable finished product. The position of the poor states in the world economy makes it less likely that they can derive the full benefit of the resources they possess for the government and people. The case of oil in resource-rich but desperately poor Nigeria is an example. Seven major foreign oil companies operate in Nigeria, all representing interests in wealthy states. The vast majority of benefits from Nigeria's oil has accrued not to the country's people, but to the companies (and consumers) of the wealthy states. There is no attempt to hide this: John Connor, head of Texaco's worldwide exploration and production, talking about a massive oil strike in January 2000, stated that the successful conclusion of the well test "sets the stage for development of a world-class project that will add substantially to the company's resource base."[4] Clearly the failure of Nigeria's people to benefit from the country's resources is also linked to a succession of corrupt governments, but the poverty of the masses and the powerful position of oil companies help to ensure that resistance to exploitation of resources for the benefit of non-Nigerian interests will be marginal.

Point 4: The existence of global poverty helps support Western medical advances.

The poor provide a pool of guinea pigs for the testing of medicines developed for use primarily in the West. The beneficiaries are not the poor themselves consumers of advanced medicine (60 percent of profits are made in the United States, which leads the world in drug consumption) and the pharmaceutical companies, which stand astride a $350 billion (and growing) industry. A series of reports in the *Washington Post* in December 2000 documents the disturbing practice of conducting drug trials on ill inhabitants of poor states. For instance, an unapproved antibiotic was tested by a major pharmaceutical company on sick children during a meningitis epidemic in Nigeria. The country's lax regulatory oversight, the sense among some doctors that they could not object to experiment conditions for political or economic reasons, the dearth of alternative health care options, combined with the desire of the company to rapidly prepare for the market a potential "blockbuster" drug underpinned a situation in which disease victims were treated as test subjects rather than patients. This case highlights the way that non-poor states actually benefit from the existence of poor states with struggling, sick populations. A reporter for the series noted that "companies use the tests to produce new product and revenue streams, but they are also responding to pressure from regulators, Congress, and lobbyists for disease victims to develop new medicines quickly. By providing huge pools of human subjects, foreign trials help speed new drugs to the marketplace—where they will be sold mainly to patients in wealthy countries."[5]

Point 5: The existence of global poverty contributes to the advancement of Western economies and societies with the human capital of poor states.

Poorer states like India have become intellectual feeders of well-educated and bright individuals whose skills cannot be fully rewarded in less developed states. The magnetic draw of a better life in economies that amply reward their human capital pulls the brightest minds from their countries of origin, a process referred to as "brain drain." Advanced economies such as the United States and England are beneficiaries of brain drain. The United States has moved to take advantage of the pool of highly educated workers from the developing world: Congress has passed legislation increasing the number of H-1B visas, or "high-tech visas," to bring up to 600,000 workers to the United States over the next several years. The United States and England offer attractive opportunities to highly educated workers from poorer states. Notably, high-tech companies often pay the foreign workers less than their domestic equivalents would demand.

Point 6: The existence of global poverty may contribute to the pacification of the Western proletariat, or "Workers of the World, A Blue Light Special!"

To some degree, the broad availability of good, inexpensive merchandise may help obscure class divisions in the West, at least in the arena of consumption. It is clear that those with greater wealth can consume more high-quality goods, but low-end "designer" merchandise is accessible to the less well-off in cathedrals of consumption such as Wal-Mart. At K-Mart, for instance, Martha Stewart peddles her wares, intended to transform "homemaking chores...into what we like to call 'domestic art.'" Thanks in part to the low-wage workers in places like China, these goods are available to the unwashed masses (now washed by Martha's smart and cozy towels) as well as to better-situated homemakers. Consumption appears to be one of the great equalizers of modern society. (It is worth noting, though, that many members of the Western working class are also "victims" of global

poverty, since many jobs have gone abroad to low-wage areas, leaving behind, for less educated workers, positions in the less remunerative and less secure service industry or leaving former industrial workers jobless.)

Point 7: Global poverty benefits the West because poor countries make optimal dumping grounds for goods that are dangerous, expired, or illegal.

Wealthy countries and their inhabitants may utilize poorer states as repositories for dangerous or unwanted material such as nuclear waste. The desperation of cash-strapped states benefits better-off countries, which might otherwise have difficulty ridding themselves of the dangerous by-products of their industrial and consumer economies. For instance, in December 2000, the Russian Parliament, in an initial vote on the issue, overwhelmingly supported the amendment of an environmental law to permit the importation of foreign nuclear waste. The alteration of the law was supported by the Atomic Ministry of the Russian Federation, which suggested that over the next decade, Russia might earn up to $21 billion from the importation of spent nuclear fuel from states like Japan, Germany, and South Korea. Likely repositories of the radioactive refuse are Mayak and Krasnoyarsk, already among the most contaminated sites on the planet.

India has also emerged as a dumping ground for hazardous junk from the world's industrial giants. The western Indian city of Alang, for instance, is host to the world's largest shipbreaking yard, where Western-owned ships are sent for dismantling and, ostensibly, recycling. The process of "breaking" the old vessels, however, endangers workers and the environment because it releases asbestos. PCBs, and other toxic wastes.[6]

Point 8: The existence of global poverty provides jobs for specialists employed to assist, advise, and study the world's poor and to protect the "better-off" from them.

Within this group of specialists we find people in a variety of professions. There are those who are professional development workers, operating through organizations like the United States Agency for International Development (USAID) to further "America's foreign policy interests in expanding democracy and free markets while improving the lives of the citizens of the developing world."[7] The Peace Corps is also built around the goal of bringing Western "know-how" to the poor with volunteer programs that promote entrepreneurship and agricultural development.

Academics in fields as diverse as economics, sociology, international affairs, political science, and anthropology study, write about, and "decipher" the lives of the poor and the condition of poor states. Texts on development, articles debating why poverty persists, and books from university presses are only some of the products of this research. Journalists and novelists can build careers around bringing colorful, compelling representations of the poor to the warm living rooms of literate, well-off consumers. Still others are charged with the task of protecting wealthy states from "invasions" of the poor: U.S. border patrols, for instance, employ thousands to keep those seeking better fortunes out of U.S. territory.

Point 9: Global poverty benefits inhabitants of wealthy countries, who can feel good about helping the global poor through charitable work and charitable giving.

From the celebrity-studded musical production "We are the World" to trick-or-treating for UNICEF, those who inhabit the wealthy corners of the world feel good about themselves for sharing their good fortune. The Web site of World Vision, a faith-based charity that offers the opportunity to sponsor poor children, features a speak-out area for contributors. On that site, a young Canadian sponsor wrote, "A few days ago I woke up early and turned the TV on . . . looking at those children made me realize I could help them. I thought if I had enough money to pay for the Internet, cell phone, and a couple of other things I didn't need, I said to myself, [then] why not give that money to people who need it instead of spending it all in (*sic*) luxury and things that are not really important. . . . I immediately picked up the phone and called to sponsor a child! I am happy. I can help someone who needs it!"[8]

Apparently, we need not feel guilt about consuming many times what the unfortunate inhabitants of the world's poor states do if only we are willing to give up a few of our luxuries to help them. Indeed, not only do the poor not inspire guilt, they may inspire positive feelings: As the World Vision writer notes, she feels "happy" because she can "help someone who needs it." No less a figure than the world's

richest man, Bill Gates, is also "dedicated to improving people's lives by sharing advances in health and learning with the global community" through the Gates Foundation.[9]

A related point is that the poor we see on television or hear about in news or music give those of us in wealthy countries the opportunity to feel good about ourselves, regardless of our position in the socioeconomic structure of our own states. Consider the memorable lines from the 1985 Band-Aid song, "Do They Know It's Christmas?" which was produced by British pop artist Bob Geldof as a charitable act to raise money for Ethiopia's famine victims: "And the Christmas bells that ring there are the clanging chimes of doom. Well, tonight, thank God, it's them instead of you." Indeed, even the underpaid blue- or pink-collar worker in the West can relate to that sentiment.

Point 10: The poverty of less developed states makes possible the massive flow of resources westward.

Imagine if large and largely poor countries like China, Nigeria, and India consumed at U.S. rates. At present, Americans consume a tremendously disproportionate share of the world's resources. With their profligate use of all manner of resources, most notably fossil fuels, Americans are the greediest consumers of natural resources on the planet. On both an absolute and per capita basis, most world resources flow westward. Notably, on October 4, 2000, article in the *Seattle Times* reported that bicycles, long a characteristic and popular means of transport for Chinese commuters, are losing popularity: "Increasingly, young Chinese are not even bothering to learn to ride bikes, because growing wealth has unlashed a plethora of transportation choices, public and private."[10] The new transportation of choice is still largely public buses or private taxis; the Chinese have not yet graduated to mass private cars. But it is interesting to ponder whether there would be enough (affordable) oil for everyone if the Chinese, with their growing population and prosperity, became a country of two-vehicle families or developed a taste and market for gas-guzzling sports utility vehicles. In this case, the West likely benefits from the fact that few can afford (at least at present) to consume at the rate its people do.

Point 11: The poorer countries, which reproduce at rates higher than Western states, are useful scapegoats for real and potential global environmental threats.

What is the bigger environmental threat to our planet? Is it the rapid growth of the populations of developing states or the rapid consumption of resources by the much smaller populations of developed states? The overdevelopment of the West may well be the bigger threat, though the growth of populations in third-world countries, which is often linked to conditions of underdevelopment, such as a lack of birth control and the need to have "extra" children as a hedge against high child mortality rates, makes an attractive alternative explanation for those who would not wish to fault the SUV-driving, disposable-diaper using, BBQ-loving American consumer for threats to the global environment. While some Western policymakers express concern about the environmental threats emerging from rapid population growth or the use of "dirty" technology in developing states, there is comparably little serious attention given to the global threat presented by the profligate consumption by Western states. The poor divert attention from the environmental problems caused by Western overconsumption.

I have talked about eleven ways that the continued existence of global poverty benefits those who reside in wealthy states. The argument I have offered to explain the persistence of a strata of poor states and the yawning global gap highlights the idea that while global poverty (and the status quo) is beneficial to the wealthy West, serious steps to alleviate it will not be taken.

It is surely the case that poverty does not have to exist. But while we in the West derive the benefits and bonuses of these economic inequalities, it seems likely that our efforts to support, advise, and assist the less developed states will remain at levels that are financially and politically convenient and feasible, and will target survival rather than true prosperity for those outside our gated, privileged, greedy Western neighborhood. In Gans's words, "Phenomena like poverty can be eliminated only when they become dysfunctional for the affluent or powerful, or when powerless can obtain enough power to change society.

Endnotes

1. The figures in this paragraph come from the Population Reference Bureau Web site (*http://www.prb.org*), which provides excellent demographic data. According to the PRB, the "GNI PPP per capita is gross national income in purchasing power parity divided by mid-year population. . . . GNI PPP refers to gross national income converted to 'international' dollars using a purchasing power parity conversion factor. International dollars indicate the amount of goods or services one could buy in the United States with a given amount of money. GNI PPP provides an indicator of the welfare of people that is comparable across countries free of price and exchange rate distortions that occur when GNI is converted using market exchange rates."

2. *Social Policy*, July/August 1971.

3. Information on issues of trade and Chinese women is available at *http://www.womensedge.org*. The information cited is from the April 2000 Web issue of *Notes from the Edge*.

4. "Texaco in massive oil strike in Nigeria" in *The Namibian*, available online at *http://www.namibian.com.ma/Netstories/2000/January/Marketplace/texaco.html*.

5. Stephens, Joe, "As Drug Testing Spreads, Profits and Lives Hang in Balance," *The Washington Post* 17, (December 2000): A1.

6. Information on both issues is available at the Web site of the environmental group Greenpeace at *http://www.greenpeace.org*.

7. The Web site address is *http://www.usaid.gov*.

8. The charity's Web site address is *http://www.worldvision.org*.

9. The foundation is at *http://www.gatesfoundation.org*.

10. The article is cited at the Web site of the Competitive Enterprise Institute: *http://www.cei.org/CHNReader.asp?ID=1227*.

Questions

1. What are the key premises of functionalist theory?

2. In what way does Eglitis's research rely on a "modified" functionalist perspective?

3. Which of the author's eleven "uses" of global poverty do you find most convincing? Why?

4. Can you categorize or classify Eglitis's points in a way that might generalize the uses of global poverty (e.g., economic, political)?

5. Find and read Herbert Gans's 1971 article, "The Uses of Poverty: The Poor Pay All," *Social Policy* July/August. How are the functions portrayed by Gans in 1971 similar to or different from those discussed by Eglitis in 2004? Explain.

GLOSSARY

abortion   the deliberate termination of a pregnancy

absolute poverty   a deprivation of resources that is life-threatening

achieved status   a social position a person takes on voluntarily that reflects personal ability and effort

activity theory   the idea that a high level of activity increases personal satisfaction in old age

Afrocentrism   emphasizing and promoting African cultural patterns

ageism   prejudice and discrimination against older people

age-sex pyramid   a graphic representation of the age and sex of a population

age stratification   the unequal distribution of wealth, power, and privilege among people at different stages of the life course

agriculture   large-scale cultivation using plows harnessed to animals or more powerful energy sources

alienation   the experience of isolation and misery resulting from powerlessness

animism   the belief that elements of the natural world are conscious life forms that affect humanity

anomie   Durkheim's term for a condition in which society provides too little moral guidance to individuals

anticipatory socialization   learning that helps a person achieve a desired position

ascribed status   a social position a person receives at birth or takes on involuntarily later in life

asexuality   a lack of sexual attraction to people of either sex

assimilation   the process by which minorities gradually adopt patterns of the dominant culture

authoritarianism   a political system that denies the people participation in government

authority   power that people perceive as legitimate rather than coercive

beliefs   specific statements that people hold to be true

bilateral descent   a system tracing kinship through both men and women

bisexuality   sexual attraction to people of both sexes

blue-collar occupations   lower-prestige jobs that involve mostly manual labor

bureaucracy   an organizational model rationally designed to perform tasks efficiently

bureaucratic inertia   the tendency of bureaucratic organizations to perpetuate themselves

bureaucratic ritualism   a focus on rules and regulations to the point of undermining an organization's goals

capitalism   an economic system in which natural resources and the means of producing goods and services are privately owned

capitalists   people who own and operate factories and other businesses in pursuit of profits

caregiving   informal and unpaid care provided to a dependent person by family members, other relatives, or friends

caste system   social stratification based on ascription, or birth

cause and effect   a relationship in which change in one variable (the independent variable) causes change in another (the dependent variable)

charisma   extraordinary personal qualities that can infuse people with emotion and turn them into followers

charismatic authority   power legitimized by extraordinary personal abilities that inspire devotion and obedience

church   a type of religious organization that is well integrated into the larger society

civil religion   a quasi-religious loyalty binding individuals in a basically secular society

claims making   the process of trying to convince the public and public officials of the importance of joining a social movement to address a particular issue

class conflict   conflict between entire classes over the distribution of a society's wealth and power

class consciousness   Marx's term for workers' recognition of themselves as a class unified in opposition to capitalists and ultimately to capitalism itself

class society   a capitalist society with pronounced social stratification

class system   social stratification based on both birth and individual achievement

cohabitation   the sharing of a household by an unmarried couple

cohort   a category of people with something in common, usually their age

collective behavior   activity involving a large number of people that is unplanned, often controversial, and sometimes dangerous

collectivity   a large number of people whose minimal interaction occurs in the absence of well-defined and conventional norms

colonialism   the process by which some nations enrich themselves through political and economic control of other nations

communism   a hypothetical economic and political system in which all members of a society are socially equal

community-based corrections   correctional programs operating within society at large rather than behind prison walls

concept   a mental construct that represents some part of the world in a simplified form

concrete operational stage   Piaget's term for the level of human development at which individuals first see causal connections in their surroundings

conglomerate   a giant corporation composed of many smaller corporations

conspicuous consumption   buying and using products because of the "statement" they make about social position

control   holding constant all variables except one in order to see clearly the effect of that variable

corporate crime   the illegal actions of a corporation or people acting on its behalf

corporation   an organization with a legal existence, including rights and liabilities, separate from that of its members

correlation   a relationship in which two (or more) variables change together

counterculture   cultural patterns that strongly oppose those widely accepted within a society

crime   the violation of a society's formally enacted criminal law

crimes against the person   crimes that direct violence or the threat of violence against others; also known as *violent crimes*

crimes against property   crimes that involve theft of property belonging to others; also known as *property crimes*

criminal justice system   a formal response by police, courts, and prison officials to alleged violations of the law

criminal recidivism   later offenses committed by people previously convicted of crimes

critical sociology   the study of society that focuses on the need for social change

crowd   a temporary gathering of people who share a common focus of attention and who influence one another

crude birth rate   the number of live births in a given year for every 1,000 people in a population

crude death rate   the number of deaths in a given year for every 1,000 people in a population

cult   a religious organization that is largely outside a society's cultural traditions

cultural integration   the close relationships among various elements of a cultural system

cultural lag   the fact that some cultural elements change more quickly than others, disrupting a cultural system

cultural relativism   the practice of judging a culture by its own standards

cultural transmission   the process by which one generation passes culture to the next

cultural universals   traits that are part of every known culture

culture   the values, beliefs, behavior, and material objects that together form a people's way of life

culture shock   personal disorientation when experiencing an unfamiliar way of life

Davis-Moore thesis   the assertion that social stratification is a universal pattern because it has beneficial consequences for the operation of a society

deductive logical thought   reasoning that transforms general theory into specific hypotheses suitable for testing

democracy   a political system that gives power to the people as a whole

demographic transition theory   the thesis that population patterns reflect a society's level of technological development

demography   the study of human population

denomination   a church, independent of the state, that recognizes religious pluralism

dependency theory   a model of economic and social development that explains global inequality in terms of the historical exploitation of poor nations by rich ones

dependent variable   a variable that is changed by another (independent) variable

descent   the system by which members of a society trace kinship over generations

deterrence   the attempt to discourage criminality through the use of punishment

deviance   the recognized violation of cultural norms

direct-fee system   a medical care system in which patients pay directly for the services of physicians and hospitals

disaster   an event, generally unexpected, that causes extensive harm to people and damage to property

discrimination   unequal treatment of various categories of people

disengagement theory   the idea that society functions in an orderly way by disengaging people from positions of responsibility as they reach old age

division of labor   specialized economic activity

dramaturgical analysis   Erving Goffman's term for the study of social interaction in terms of theatrical performance

dyad   a social group with two members

eating disorder   an intense form of dieting or other unhealthy method of weight control driven by the desire to be very thin

ecologically sustainable culture   a way of life that meets the needs of the present generation without threatening the environmental legacy of future generations

ecology   the study of the interaction of living organisms and the natural environment

economy   the social institution that organizes a society's production, distribution, and consumption of goods and services

ecosystem   a system composed of the interaction of all living organisms and their natural environment

education   the social institution through which society provides its members with important knowledge, including basic facts, job skills, and cultural norms and values

ego   Freud's term for a person's conscious efforts to balance innate pleasure-seeking drives with the demands of society

empirical evidence   information we can verify with our senses

endogamy   marriage between people of the same social category

environmental deficit   profound long-term harm to the natural environment caused by humanity's focus on short-term material affluence

environmental racism   the pattern by which environmental hazards are greatest for poor people, especially minorities

ethnicity   a shared cultural heritage

ethnocentrism   the practice of judging another culture by the standards of one's own culture

ethnomethodology   Harold Garfinkel's term for the study of the way people make sense of their everyday surroundings

Eurocentrism   the dominance of European (especially English) cultural patterns

euthanasia   assisting in the death of a person suffering from an incurable disease; also known as *mercy killing*

exogamy   marriage between people of different social categories

experiment   a research method for investigating cause and effect under highly controlled conditions

expressive leadership   group leadership that focuses on the group's well-being

extended family   a family consisting of parents and children as well as other kin; also known as a *consanguine family*

fad   an unconventional social pattern that people embrace briefly but enthusiastically

faith   belief based on conviction rather than scientific evidence

false consciousness   Marx's term for explanations of social problems as the shortcomings of individuals rather than as the flaws of society

family   a social institution found in all societies that unites people in cooperative groups to care for one another, including any children

family violence   emotional, physical, or sexual abuse of one family member by another

fashion   a social pattern favored by a large number of people

feminism   the advocacy of social equality for women and men, in opposition to patriarchy and sexism

feminization of poverty   the trend of women making up an increasing proportion of the poor

fertility   the incidence of childbearing in a country's population

folkways   norms for routine or casual interaction

formal operational stage   Piaget's term for the level of human development at which individuals think abstractly and critically

formal organization   a large secondary group organized to achieve its goals efficiently

functional illiteracy a lack of the reading and writing skills needed for everyday living

fundamentalism a conservative religious doctrine that opposes intellectualism and worldly accommodation in favor of restoring traditional, otherworldly religion

Gemeinschaft a type of social organization in which people are closely tied by kinship and tradition

gender the personal traits and social positions that members of a society attach to being female or male

gender-conflict approach a point of view that focuses on inequality and conflict between women and men

gender roles (sex roles) attitudes and activities that a society links to each sex

gender stratification the unequal distribution of wealth, power, and privilege between men and women

generalized other George Herbert Mead's term for widespread cultural norms and values we use as a reference in evaluating ourselves

genocide the systematic killing of one category of people by another

gerontocracy a form of social organization in which the elderly have the most wealth, power, and prestige

gerontology the study of aging and the elderly

Gesellschaft a type of social organization in which people come together only on the basis of individual self-interest

global economy expanding economic activity that crosses national borders

global perspective the study of the larger world and our society's place in it

global stratification patterns of social inequality in the world as a whole

global warming a rise in Earth's average temperature due to an increasing concentration of carbon dioxide in the atmosphere

gossip rumor about people's personal affairs

government a formal organization that directs the political life of a society

groupthink the tendency of group members to conform, resulting in a narrow view of some issue

hate crime a criminal act against a person or a person's property by an offender motivated by racial or other bias

Hawthorne effect a change in a subject's behavior caused simply by the awareness of being studied

health a state of complete physical, mental, and social well-being

health maintenance organization (HMO) an organization that provides comprehensive medical care to subscribers for a fixed fee

heterosexism a view that labels anyone who is not heterosexual as "queer"

heterosexuality sexual attraction to someone of the other sex

high culture cultural patterns that distinguish a society's elite

high-income countries nations with the highest overall standards of living

holistic medicine an approach to health care that emphasizes the prevention of illness and takes into account a person's entire physical and social environment

homogamy marriage between people with the same social characteristics

homophobia discomfort over close personal interaction with people thought to be gay, lesbian, or bisexual

homosexuality sexual attraction to someone of the same sex

horticulture the use of hand tools to raise crops

hunting and gathering the use of simple tools to hunt animals and gather vegetation for food

hypothesis a statement of a possible relationship between two (or more) variables

id Freud's term for the human being's basic drives

ideal type an abstract statement of the essential characteristics of any social phenomenon

ideology cultural beliefs that justify particular social arrangements, including patterns of inequality

incest taboo a norm forbidding sexual relations or marriage between certain relatives

income earnings from work or investments

independent variable a variable that causes change in another (dependent) variable

inductive logical thought reasoning that transforms specific observations into general theory

industrialism the production of goods using advanced sources of energy to drive large machinery

infant mortality rate the number of deaths among infants under one year of age for each 1,000 live births in a given year

infidelity sexual activity outside marriage

in-group a social group toward which a member feels respect and loyalty

institutional prejudice and discrimination bias built into the operation of society's institutions

instrumental leadership group leadership that focuses on the completion of tasks

intergenerational social mobility upward or downward social mobility of children in relation to their parents

interpretive sociology the study of society that focuses on the meanings people attach to their social world

intersection theory the interplay of race, class, and gender, often resulting in multiple dimensions of disadvantage

intersexual people people whose bodies (including genitals) have both female and male characteristics

interview a series of questions a researcher asks respondents in person

intragenerational social mobility a change in social position occurring during a person's lifetime

kinship a social bond based on common ancestry, marriage, or adoption

labeling theory the idea that deviance and conformity result not so much from what people do as from how others respond to those actions

labor unions organizations of workers that seek to improve wages and working conditions through various strategies, including negotiations and strikes

language a system of symbols that allows people to communicate with one another

latent functions the unrecognized and unintended consequences of any social pattern

liberation theology the combination of Christian principles with political activism, often Marxist in character

life expectancy the average life span of a country's population

looking-glass self Cooley's term for a self-image based on how we think others see us

low-income countries nations with a low standard of living in which most people are poor

macro-level orientation a broad focus on social structures that shape society as a whole

mainstreaming integrating students with disabilities or special needs into the overall educational program

manifest functions the recognized and intended consequences of any social pattern

marriage a legal relationship, usually involving economic cooperation, sexual activity, and childbearing

Marxist political-economy model an analysis that explains politics in terms of the operation of a society's economic system

mass behavior collective behavior among people spread over a wide geographic area

mass hysteria (moral panic) a form of dispersed collective behavior in which people react to a real or imagined event with irrational and even frantic fear

mass media the means for delivering impersonal communications to a vast audience

mass society a society in which prosperity and bureaucracy have weakened traditional social ties

master status a status that has special importance for social identity, often shaping a person's entire life

material culture the physical things created by members of a society

matriarchy a form of social organization in which females dominate males

matrilineal descent a system tracing kinship through women

matrilocality a residential pattern in which a married couple lives with or near the wife's family

measurement a procedure for determining the value of a variable in a specific case

mechanical solidarity Durkheim's term for social bonds, based on common sentiments and shared moral values, that are strong among members of preindustrial societies

medicalization of deviance the transformation of moral and legal deviance into a medical condition

medicine the social institution that focuses on fighting disease and improving health

megalopolis a vast urban region containing a number of cities and their surrounding suburbs

meritocracy social stratification based on personal merit

metropolis a large city that socially and economically dominates an urban area

micro-level orientation a close-up focus on social interaction in specific situations

middle-income countries nations with a standard of living about average for the world as a whole

migration the movement of people into and out of a specified territory

military-industrial complex the close association of the federal government, the military, and defense industries

minority any category of people distinguished by physical or cultural difference that a society sets apart and subordinates

miscegenation biological reproduction by partners of different racial categories

mob a highly emotional crowd that pursues a violent or destructive goal

modernity social patterns resulting from industrialization

modernization the process of social change begun by industrialization

modernization theory a model of economic and social development that explains global inequality in terms of technological and cultural differences between nations

monarchy a political system in which a single family rules from generation to generation

monogamy marriage that unites two partners

monopoly the domination of a market by a single producer

monotheism belief in a single divine power

mores norms that are widely observed and have great moral significance

mortality the incidence of death in a country's population

multiculturalism an educational program recognizing the cultural diversity of the United States and promoting the equality of all cultural traditions

multinational corporation a large business that operates in many countries

natural environment Earth's surface and atmosphere, including living organisms, air, water, soil, and other resources necessary to sustain life

neocolonialism a new form of global power relationships that involves not direct political control but economic exploitation by multinational corporations

neolocality a residential pattern in which a married couple lives apart from both sets of parents

network a web of weak social ties

nonmaterial culture the ideas created by members of a society

nonverbal communication communication using body movements, gestures, and facial expressions rather than speech

norms rules and expectations by which a society guides the behavior of its members

nuclear family a family composed of one or two parents and their children; also known as a *conjugal family*

nuclear proliferation the acquisition of nuclear weapons technology by more and more nations

objectivity personal neutrality in conducting research

oligarchy the rule of the many by the few

oligopoly the domination of a market by a few producers

operationalize a variable specifying exactly what is to be measured before assigning a value to a variable

organic solidarity Durkheim's term for social bonds, based on specialization and interdependence, that are strong among members of industrial societies

organizational environment factors outside an organization that affect its operation

organized crime a business supplying illegal goods or services

other-directedness openness to the latest trends and fashions, often expressed by imitating others

out-group a social group toward which a person feels a sense of competition or opposition

panic a form of localized collective behavior in which people in one place react to a threat or other stimulus with irrational, frantic, and often self-destructive behavior

participant observation a research method in which investigators systematically observe people while joining them in their routine activities

pastoralism the domestication of animals

patriarchy a form of social organization in which males dominate females

patrilineal descent a system tracing kinship through men

patrilocality a residential pattern in which a married couple lives with or near the husband's family

peer group a social group whose members have interests, social position, and age in common

personality a person's fairly consistent patterns of acting, thinking, and feeling

personal space the surrounding area over which a person makes some claim to privacy

plea bargaining a legal negotiation in which a prosecutor reduces a charge in exchange for a defendant's guilty plea

pluralism a state in which people of all races and ethnicities are distinct but have equal social standing

pluralist model an analysis of politics that sees power as spread among many competing interest groups

political action committee (PAC) an organization formed by a special-interest group, independent of political parties, to raise and spend money in support of political goals

political revolution the overthrow of one political system in order to establish another

politics the social institution that distributes power, sets a society's goals, and makes decisions

polyandry marriage that unites one woman and two or more men

polygamy marriage that unites a person with two or more spouses

polygyny marriage that unites one man and two or more women

polytheism belief in many gods

popular culture cultural patterns that are widespread among a society's population

population the people who are the focus of research

pornography sexually explicit material intended to cause sexual arousal

positivism a way of understanding based on science

postindustrial economy a productive system based on service work and high technology

postindustrialism technology that supports an information-based economy

postmodernity social patterns characteristic of postindustrial societies

power the ability to achieve desired ends despite resistance from others

power-elite model an analysis of politics that sees power as concentrated among the rich

prejudice a rigid and unfair generalization about an entire category of people

preoperational stage Piaget's term for the level of human development at which individuals first use language and other symbols

presentation of self Erving Goffman's term for a person's efforts to create specific impressions in the minds of others

primary group a small social group whose members share personal and lasting relationships

primary labor market jobs that provide extensive benefits to workers

primary sector the part of the economy that draws raw materials from the natural environment

primary sex characteristics the genitals, organs used for reproduction

profane an ordinary element of everyday life

profession a prestigious white-collar occupation that requires extensive formal education

proletarians people who sell their labor for wages

propaganda information presented with the intention of shaping public opinion

prostitution the selling of sexual services

public opinion widespread attitudes about controversial issues

queer theory a growing body of research findings that challenges the heterosexual bias in U.S. society

questionnaire a series of written questions a researcher presents to subjects

race a socially constructed category of people who share biologically transmitted traits that members of a society consider important

race-conflict approach a point of view that focuses on inequality and conflict between people of different racial and ethnic categories

racism the belief that one racial category is innately superior or inferior to another

rain forests regions of dense forestation, most of which circle the globe close to the equator

rationality a way of thinking that emphasizes deliberate, matter-of-fact calculation of the most efficient way to accomplish a particular task

rationalization of society Weber's term for the historical change from tradition to rationality as the main mode of human thought

rational-legal authority power legitimized by legally enacted rules and regulations; also known as *bureaucratic authority*

reference group a social group that serves as a point of reference in making evaluations and decisions

rehabilitation a program for reforming the offender to prevent later offenses

relative deprivation a perceived disadvantage arising from some specific comparison

relative poverty the deprivation of some people in relation to those who have more

reliability consistency in measurement

religion a social institution involving beliefs and practices based on recognizing the sacred

religiosity the importance of religion in a person's life

replication repetition of research by other investigators

research method a systematic plan for doing research

resocialization efforts to radically change an inmate's personality by carefully controlling the environment

retribution an act of moral vengeance by which society makes the offender suffer as much as the suffering caused by the crime

riot a social eruption that is highly emotional, violent, and undirected

ritual formal, ceremonial behavior

role behavior expected of someone who holds a particular status

role conflict conflict among the roles connected to two or more statuses

role set a number of roles attached to a single status

role strain tension among the roles connected to a single status

routinization of charisma the transformation of charismatic authority into some combination of traditional and bureaucratic authority

rumor unconfirmed information that people spread informally, often by word of mouth

sacred set apart as extraordinary, inspiring awe and reverence

sample a part of a population that represents the whole

Sapir-Whorf thesis the idea that people see and understand the world through the cultural lens of language

scapegoat a person or category of people, typically with little power, whom people unfairly blame for their own troubles

schooling formal instruction under the direction of specially trained teachers

science a logical system that bases knowledge on direct, systematic observation

scientific management Frederick Taylor's term for the application of scientific principles to the operation of a business or other large organization

scientific sociology the study of society based on systematic observation of social behavior

secondary group a large and impersonal social group whose members pursue a specific goal or activity

secondary labor market jobs that provide minimal benefits to workers

secondary sector the part of the economy that transforms raw materials into manufactured goods

secondary sex characteristics bodily development, apart from the genitals, that distinguishes biologically mature females and males

sect a type of religious organization that stands apart from the larger society

secularization the historical decline in the importance of the supernatural and the sacred

segregation the physical and social separation of categories of people

self George Herbert Mead's term for the part of an individual's personality composed of self-awareness and self-image

sensorimotor stage Piaget's term for the level of human development at which individuals experience the world only through their senses

sex the biological distinction between females and males

sexism the belief that one sex is innately superior to the other

sex ratio the number of males for every 100 females in a nation's population

sexual harassment comments, gestures, or physical contact of a sexual nature that are deliberate, repeated, and unwelcome

sexual orientation a person's romantic and emotional attraction to another person

sick role patterns of behavior defined as appropriate for people who are ill

significant others people, such as parents, who have special importance for socialization

social change the transformation of culture and social institutions over time

social character personality patterns common to members of a particular society

social conflict the struggle between segments of society over valued resources

social-conflict approach a framework for building theory that sees society as an arena of inequality that generates conflict and change

social construction of reality the process by which people creatively shape reality through social interaction

social control attempts by society to regulate people's thoughts and behavior

social dysfunction any social pattern that may disrupt the operation of society

social epidemiology the study of how health and disease are distributed throughout a society's population

social functions the consequences of any social pattern for the operation of society as a whole

social group two or more people who identify and interact with one another

social institutions the major spheres of social life, or societal subsystems, organized to meet human needs

social interaction the process by which people act and react in relation to others

socialism an economic system in which natural resources and the means of producing goods and services are collectively owned

socialization the lifelong social experience by which people develop their human potential and learn culture

socialized medicine a medical care system in which the government owns and operates most medical facilities and employs most physicians

social mobility a change in position within the social hierarchy

social movement an organized activity that encourages or discourages social change

social stratification a system by which a society ranks categories of people in a hierarchy

social structure any relatively stable pattern of social behavior

societal protection rendering an offender incapable of further offenses temporarily through imprisonment or permanently by execution

society people who interact in a defined territory and share a culture

sociobiology a theoretical approach that explores ways in which human biology affects how we create culture

sociocultural evolution Lenski's term for the changes that occur as a society gains new technology

socioeconomic status (SES) a composite ranking based on various dimensions of social inequality

sociological perspective the special point of view of sociology that sees general patterns of society in the lives of particular people

sociology the systematic study of human society

special-interest group people organized to address some economic or social issue

spurious correlation an apparent but false relationship between two (or more) variables that is caused by some other variable

state capitalism an economic and political system in which companies are privately owned but cooperate closely with the government

state church a church formally allied with the state

status a social position that a person holds

status consistency the degree of consistency in a person's social standing across various dimensions of social inequality

status set all the statuses a person holds at a given time

stereotype an exaggerated description applied to every person in some category

stigma a powerfully negative label that greatly changes a person's self-concept and social identity

structural-functional approach a framework for building theory that sees society as a complex system whose parts work together to promote solidarity and stability**

structural social mobility   a shift in the social position of large numbers of people due more to changes in society itself than to individual efforts

subculture   cultural patterns that set apart some segment of a society's population

suburbs   urban areas beyond the political boundaries of a city

superego   Freud's term for the cultural values and norms internalized by an individual

survey   a research method in which subjects respond to a series of statements or questions in a questionnaire or an interview

symbol   anything that carries a particular meaning recognized by people who share a culture

symbolic-interaction approach   a framework for building theory that sees society as the product of the everyday interactions of individuals

technology   knowledge that people use to make a way of life in their surroundings

terrorism   acts of violence or the threat of violence used as a political strategy by an individual or a group

tertiary sector   the part of the economy that involves services rather than goods

theoretical approach   a basic image of society that guides thinking and research

theory   a statement of how and why specific facts are related

Thomas theorem   W. I. Thomas's statement that situations that are defined as real are real in their consequences

total institution   a setting in which people are isolated from the rest of society and manipulated by an administrative staff

totalitarianism   a highly centralized political system that extensively regulates people's lives

totem   an object in the natural world collectively defined as sacred

tracking   assigning students to different types of educational programs

tradition   values and beliefs passed from generation to generation

traditional authority   power legitimized by respect for long-established cultural patterns

tradition-directedness   rigid conformity to time-honored ways of living

transsexuals   people who feel they are one sex even though biologically they are the other

triad   a social group with three members

underground economy   economic activity involving income not reported to the government as required by law

urban ecology   the study of the link between the physical and social dimensions of cities

urbanization   the concentration of population into cities

validity   actually measuring exactly what you intend to measure

values   culturally defined standards that people use to decide what is desireable, good, and beautiful, and that serve as broad guidelines for social living

variable   a concept whose value changes from case to case

victimless crimes   violations of law in which there are no obvious victims

war   organized, armed conflict among the people of two or more nations, directed by their governments

wealth   the total value of money and other assets, minus outstanding debts

welfare capitalism   an economic and political system that combines a mostly market-based economy with extensive social welfare programs

welfare state   government agencies and programs that provide benefits to the population

white-collar crime   crime committed by people of high social position in the course of their occupations

white-collar occupations   higher-prestige jobs that involve mostly mental activity

zero population growth   the level of reproduction that maintains population in a steady state

REFERENCES

ABBOTT, ANDREW. *The System of Professions: An Essay on the Division of Expert Labor.* Chicago: University of Chicago Press, 1988.

ABERLE, DAVID F. *The Peyote Religion among the Navaho.* Chicago: Aldine, 1966.

ADLER, JERRY. "When Harry Called Sally . . ." *Newsweek* (October 1, 1990):74.

ADORNO, T. W., et al. *The Authoritarian Personality.* New York: Harper & Brothers, 1950.

AGUIRRE, BENIGNO E., and E. L. QUARANTELLI. "Methodological, Ideological, and Conceptual-Theoretical Criticisms of Collective Behavior: A Critical Evaluation and Implications for Future Study." *Sociological Focus.* Vol. 16, No. 3 (August 1983):195–216.

AGUIRRE, BENIGNO E., E. L. QUARANTELLI, and JORGE L. MENDOZA. "The Collective Behavior of Fads: Characteristics, Effects, and Career of Streaking." *American Sociological Review.* Vol. 53, No. 4 (August 1988):569–84.

AIZCORBE, ANA M., ARTHUR B. KENNICKELL, and KEVIN B. MOORE. "Recent Changes in U.S. Family Finances: Evidence from the 1998 and 2001 Survey of Consumer Finances." *Federal Reserve Bulletin.* Vol. 89, No. 1 (January 2003):1–32. [Online] Available September 25, 2003, at http://www.federalreserve.gov/pubs/bulletin/2003/0103lead.pdf

AKERS, RONALD L., MARVIN D. KROHN, LONN LANZA-KADUCE, and MARCIA RADOSEVICH. "Social Learning and Deviant Behavior." *American Sociological Review.* Vol. 44, No. 4 (August 1979):636–55.

ALAN GUTTMACHER INSTITUTE. "Can More Progress Be Made? Teenage Sexual and Reproductive Behavior in Developed Countries." 2001. [Online] Available May 30, 2005, at http://www.guttmacher.org/pubs/summaries/euroteens_summ.pdf

———. "Teen Pregnancy: Trends and Lessons Learned." *Issues in Brief.* 2002 Series, No. 1. 2002. [Online] Available May 30, 2005, at http://www.agi-usa.org/pubs/ib_1-02.pdf

———. "U.S. Teenage Pregnancy Statistics: Overall Trends, Trends by Race and Ethnicity and State-by-State Information." Updated February 19, 2004. [Online] Available May 30, 2005, at http://www.agi-usa.org/pubs/state_pregnancy_trends.pdf

ALBON, JOAN. "Retention of Cultural Values and Differential Urban Adaptation: Samoans and American Indians in a West Coast City." *Social Forces.* Vol. 49, No. 3 (March 1971):385–93.

ALLAN, EMILIE ANDERSEN, and DARRELL J. STEFFENSMEIER. "Youth, Underemployment, and Property Crime: Differential Effects of Job Availability and Job Quality on Juvenile and Young Adult Arrest Rates." *American Sociological Review.* Vol. 54, No. 1 (February 1989):107–23.

ALLEN, THOMAS B., and CHARLES O. HYMAN. *We Americans: Celebrating a Nation, Its People, and Its Past.* Washington, D.C.: National Geographic, 1999.

ALLEN, WALTER R. "African American Family Life in Social Context: Crisis and Hope." *Sociological Forum.* Vol. 10, No. 4 (December 1995):569–92.

ALSTER, NORM. "When Gray Heads Roll, Is Age Bias at Work?" *New York Times* (January 30, 2005). [Online] Available April 15, 2005, at http://www.researchnavigator.com

ALTER, JONATHAN. "The Death Penalty on Trial." *Newsweek* (June 12, 2000):24–34.

ALTONJI, JOSEPH G., ULRICH DORASZELSKI, and LEWIS SEGAL. "Black/White Differences in Wealth." *Economic Perspectives.* Vol. 24, No. 1 (First Quarter 2000): 38–50.

AMATO, PAUL R. "What Children Learn from Divorce." *Population Today.* Vol. 29, No. 1 (January 2001):1, 4.

AMATO, PAUL R., and JULIANA M. SOBOLEWSKI. "The Effects of Divorce and Marital Discord on Adult Children's Psychological Well-Being." *American Sociological Review.* Vol. 66, No. 6 (December 2001):900–21.

AMBLER, JOHN S., and JODY NEATHERY. "Education Policy and Equality: Some Evidence from Europe." *Social Science Quarterly.* Vol. 80, No. 3 (September 1999):437–56.

AMERICAN BAR ASSOCIATION. "First-Year Enrollment in ABA-Approved Law Schools, 1947–2004 (Percentage of Women)." [Online] Available October 17, 2005, at http://www.abanet.org/legaled/statistics/femstats.html

AMERICAN CATHOLIC. "John Jay Study Reveals Extent of Abuse Problem." [Online] Available September 13, 2005, at http://www.americancatholic.org/news/clergysexabuse/johnjaycns.asp

AMERICAN DEMOGRAPHICS. "Zandi Group Survey." Vol. 20 (March 3, 1998):38.

———. (April 2002):6.

AMERICAN PSYCHOLOGICAL ASSOCIATION. *Violence and Youth: Psychology's Response.* Washington, D.C.: American Psychological Association, 1993.

AMERICAN SOCIOLOGICAL ASSOCIATION. "Code of Ethics." Washington, D.C.: American Sociological Association, 1997.

———. *Careers in Sociology.* 6th ed. Washington, D.C.: American Sociological Association, 2002.

———. *The Importance of Collecting Data and Doing Social Scientific Research on Race.* Washington, D.C.: American Sociological Association, 2003.

AMNESTY INTERNATIONAL. "Abolitionist and Retentionist Countries." [Online] Available June 4, 2005a, at http://web.amnesty.org/pages/deathpenalty-countries-eng

———. "Facts and Figures on the Death Penalty." [Online] Available June 4, 2005b, at http://web.amnesty.org/pages/deathpenalty-facts-eng

ANDERSON, ELIJAH. "The Code of the Streets." *Atlantic Monthly.* Vol. 273 (May 1994):81–94.

———. "The Ideologically Driven Critique." *American Journal of Sociology.* Vol. 197, No. 6 (May 2002):1533–50.

ANDERSON, JOHN WARD. "Early to Wed: The Child Brides of India." *Washington Post* (May 24, 1995):A27, A30.

ANDERSON, ROBERT N., and BETTY L. SMITH. "Deaths: Leading Causes for 2002." *National Vital Statistics Reports.* Vol. 53, No. 17 (March 7, 2005). Hyattsville, Md.: National Center for Health Statistics.

ANNAN, KOFI. "Astonishing Facts." *New York Times* (September 27, 1998):16.

APPLEBOME, PETER. "70 Years after Scopes Trial, Creation Debate Lives." *New York Times* (March 10, 1996):1, 10.

APUZZO, ALAN. "R.I. Official: Club Owners Not Helpful." [Online] Available February 24, 2003, at http://news.yahoo.com

ARENDT, HANNAH. *Between Past and Future: Six Exercises in Political Thought.* Cleveland, Ohio: Meridian Books, 1963.

ARIAS, ELIZABETH. "United States Life Tables, 2001." *National Vital Statistics Report.* Vol. 52, No. 14 (February 18, 2004). Hyattsville, Md.: National Center for Health Statistics.

———. "United States Life Tables, 2002." *National Vital Statistics Reports.* Vol. 53, No. 6 (November 10, 2004). Hyattsville, Md.: National Center for Health Statistics.

ARIÈS, PHILIPPE. *Centuries of Childhood: A Social History of Family Life.* New York: Vintage Books, 1965.

———. *Western Attitudes toward Death: From the Middle Ages to the Present.* Baltimore: Johns Hopkins University Press, 1974.

ARMSTRONG, ELISABETH. *The Retreat from Organization: U.S. Feminism Reconceptualized.* Albany: State University of New York Press, 2002.

ARONOWITZ, STANLEY. *The Politics of Identity: Class, Culture, and Social Movements.* New York: Routledge, 1992.

ARROW, KENNETH, SAMUEL BOWLES, and STEVEN DURLAUF. *Meritocracy and Economic Inequality.* Princeton, N.J.: Princeton University Press, 2000.

ASANTE, MOLEFI KETE. *Afrocentricity.* Trenton, N.J.: Africa World Press, 1988.

ASCH, SOLOMON. *Social Psychology.* Englewood Cliffs, N.J.: Prentice Hall, 1952.

ASHFORD, LORI S. "New Perspectives on Population: Lessons from Cairo." *Population Bulletin.* Vol. 50, No. 1 (March 1995):2–44.

———. "Young Women in Sub-Saharan Africa Face a High Risk of HIV Infection." *Population Today.* Vol. 30, No. 2 (February/March 2002):3, 6.

ASTIN, ALEXANDER W., LETICIA OSEGUERA, LINDA J. SAX, and WILLIAM S. KORN. *The American Freshman: Thirty-Five Year Trends.* Los Angeles: UCLA Higher Education Research Institute, 2002.

ATCHLEY, ROBERT C. *Aging: Continuity and Change.* Belmont, Calif.: Wadsworth, 1983.

AUSTER, CAROL J., and MINDY MACRONE. "The Classroom as a Negotiated Social Setting: An Empirical Study of the Effects of Faculty Members' Behavior on Students' Participation." *Teaching Sociology.* Vol. 22, No. 4 (October 1994): 289–300.

AXINN, WILLIAM G., and JENNIFER S. BARBER. "Mass Education and Fertility Transition." *American Sociological Review.* Vol. 66, No. 4 (August 2001):481–505.

BAINBRIDGE, JAY, MARCIA K. MEYERS, and JANE WALDFOGEL. "Childcare Reform and the Employment of Single Mothers." *Social Science Quarterly.* Vol. 84, No. 4 (December 2003):771–91.

BAKALAR, NICHOLAS. "Reactions: Go On, Laugh Your Heart Out." *New York Times* (March 8, 2005). [Online] Available March 11, 2005, at http://www.nytimes.com/2005/03/08/health/08reac.html

BAKER, MARY ANNE, et al. *Women Today: A Multidisciplinary Approach to Women's Studies.* Monterey, Calif.: Brooks/Cole, 1980.

BAKER, PATRICIA S., WILLIAM C. YOELS, JEFFREY M. CLAIR, and RICHARD M. ALLMAN. "Laughter in the Triadic Geriatric Encounters: A Transcript-Based Analysis." In REBECCA J. ERIKSON and BEVERLY CUTHBERTSON-JOHNSON, eds., *Social Perspectives on Emotion.* Vol. 4. Greenwich, Conn.: JAI Press, 1997: 179–207.

BAKER, ROSS. "Business as Usual." *American Demographics.* Vol. 19, No. 4 (April 1997):28.

BALTES, PAUL B., and K. WARNER SCHAIE. "The Myth of the Twilight Years." *Psychology Today.* Vol. 7, No. 10 (March 1974):35–39.

BALTZELL, E. DIGBY. *The Protestant Establishment: Aristocracy and Caste in America.* New York: Vintage Books, 1964.

———. "Introduction to the 1967 Edition." In W.E.B. DU BOIS, *The Philadelphia Negro: A Social Study.* New York: Schocken Books, 1967; orig. 1899.

———. *Philadelphia Gentlemen: The Making of a National Upper Class.* Philadelphia: University of Pennsylvania Press, 1979a; orig. 1958.

———. *Puritan Boston and Quaker Philadelphia.* New York: Free Press, 1979b.

———. *Sporting Gentlemen: From the Age of Honor to the Cult of the Superstar.* New York: Free Press, 1995.

BANFIELD, EDWARD C. *The Unheavenly City Revisited.* Boston: Little, Brown, 1974.

BARASH, DAVID. *The Whisperings Within.* New York: Penguin Books, 1981.

BARNES, JULIAN E. "Wanted: Readers." *U.S. News & World Report* (September 9, 2002a):44–45.

———. "War Profiteering." *U.S. News & World Report* (May 13, 2002b):20–24.

———. "Unequal Education." *U.S. News & World Report* (March 22, 2004):66–75.

BARON, JAMES N., MICHAEL T. HANNAN, and M. DIANE BURTON. "Building the Iron Cage: Determinants of Managerial Intensity in the Early Years of Organizations." *American Sociological Review.* Vol. 64, No. 4 (August 1999):527–47.

BARONE, MICHAEL. "Lessons of History." *U.S. News & World Report* (May 20, 2002):24.

BAROVICK, HARRIET. "Tongues That Go Out of Style." *Time* (June 10, 2002):22.

BARR, ROBERT. "Archbishop of Canterbury Is Enthroned." [Online] Available February 27, 2003, at http://news.yahoo.com

BARSTOW, DAVID, and C. J. CHIVERS. "A Volatile Mixture Exploded into Rampage in Central Park." *New York Times* (June 17, 2000):A1, B7.

BARTLETT, DONALD L., and JAMES B. STEELE. "Corporate Welfare." *Time* (November 9, 1998):36–54.

———. "How the Little Guy Gets Crunched." *Time* (February 7, 2000):38–41.

———. "Wheel of Misfortune." *Time* (December 16, 2002):44–58.

BASSUK, ELLEN J. "The Homelessness Problem." *Scientific American.* Vol. 251, No. 1 (July 1984):40–45.

BAUER, P. T. *Equality, the Third World, and Economic Delusion.* Cambridge, Mass.: Harvard University Press, 1981.

BAUMGARTNER, M. P. "Introduction: The Moral Voice of the Community." *Sociological Focus.* Vol. 31, No. 2 (May 1998):105–17.

BAYDAR, NAZLI, and JEANNE BROOKS-GUNN. "Effect of Maternal Employment and Child-Care Arrangements on Preschoolers' Cognitive and Behavioral Outcomes: Evidence from Children from the National Longitudinal Survey of Youth." *Developmental Psychology.* Vol. 27, No. 6 (November 1991):932–35.

BEARAK, BARRY. "Lives Held Cheap in Bangladesh Sweatshops." *New York Times* (April 15, 2001):A1, A12.

BECKER, ANNE. Paper presented at the annual meeting of the American Psychiatric Association, Washington, D.C., May 19, 1999. Reported in "Eating Disorders Jump When Fiji Gets Television." *Toledo Blade* (May 20, 1999):12.

BECKER, HOWARD S. *Outside: Studies in the Sociology of Deviance.* New York: Free Press, 1966.

BEDARD, PAUL. "Washington Whispers." *U.S. News & World Report* (March 25, 2002):2.

BEEGHLEY, LEONARD. *The Structure of Social Stratification in the United States.* Needham Heights, Mass.: Allyn & Bacon, 1989.

BEGLEY, SHARON. "Gray Matters." *Newsweek* (March 7, 1995):48–54.

———. "How to Beat the Heat." *Newsweek* (December 8, 1997):34–38.

BEINS, BARNEY, cited in "Examples of Spuriousness." *Teaching Methods.* No. 2 (Fall 1993):3.

BELL, DANIEL. *The Coming of Post-Industrial Society: A Venture in Social Forecasting.* New York: Basic Books, 1973.

BELLAH, ROBERT N. *The Broken Covenant.* New York: Seabury Press, 1975.

BELLAH, ROBERT N., RICHARD MADSEN, WILLIAM M. SULLIVAN, ANN SWIDLER, and STEVEN M. TIPTON. *Habits of the Heart: Individualism and Commitment in American Life.* New York: Harper & Row, 1985.

BELLANDI, DEANNA. "Study Finds Meal Portion Sizes Growing." [Online] Available January 3, 2003, at http://news.yahoo.com

BELLUCK, PAM. "Black Youths' Rate of Suicide Rising Sharply." *New York Times* (March 20, 1998):A1, A18.

BEM, SANDRA LIPSITZ. *The Lenses of Gender: Transforming the Debate on Sexual Inequality.* New Haven, Conn.: Yale University Press, 1993.

BENEDICT, RUTH. "Continuities and Discontinuities in Cultural Conditioning." *Psychiatry.* Vol. 1, No. 2 (May 1938):161–67.

BENJAMIN, LOIS. *The Black Elite: Facing the Color Line in the Twilight of the Twentieth Century.* Chicago: Nelson-Hall, 1991.

BENJAMIN, MATTHEW. "Suite Deals." *U.S. News & World Report* (April 29, 2002): 32–34.

BENNETT, WILLIAM J. "School Reform: What Remains to Be Done." *Wall Street Journal* (September 2, 1997):A18.

BENOKRAITIS, NIJOLE, and JOE R. FEAGIN. *Modern Sexism: Blatant, Subtle, and Overt Discrimination.* 2nd ed. Englewood Cliffs, N.J.: Prentice Hall, 1995.

BERGAMO, MONICA, and GERSON CAMAROTTI. "Brazil's Landless Millions." *World Press Review.* Vol. 43, No. 7 (July 1996):46–47.

BERGEN, RAQUEL KENNEDY. "Interviewing Survivors of Marital Rape: Doing Feminist Research on Sensitive Topics." In CLAIRE M. RENZETTI and RAYMOND M. LEE, eds., *Researching Sensitive Topics.* Thousand Oaks, Calif.: Sage, 1993.

BERGER, PETER L. *Invitation to Sociology.* New York: Anchor Books, 1963.

———. *The Sacred Canopy: Elements of a Sociological Theory of Religion.* Garden City, N.Y.: Doubleday, 1967.

———. *Facing Up to Modernity: Excursions in Society, Politics, and Religion.* New York: Basic Books, 1977.

———. *The Capitalist Revolution: Fifty Propositions about Prosperity, Equality, and Liberty.* New York: Basic Books, 1986.

———. "Sociology: A Disinvitation?" *Society.* Vol. 30, No. 1 (November/December 1992):12–18.

BERGER, PETER L., BRIGITTE BERGER, and HANSFRIED KELLNER. *The Homeless Mind: Modernization and Consciousness.* New York: Vintage Books, 1974.

BERGESEN, ALBERT, ed. *Crises in the World-System.* Beverly Hills, Calif.: Sage, 1983.

BERK, RICHARD A. *Collective Behavior.* Dubuque, Iowa: Brown, 1974.

BERNARD, JESSIE. *The Female World.* New York: Free Press, 1981.

———. *The Future of Marriage.* 2nd ed. New Haven, Conn.: Yale University Press, 1982.

BERRILL, KEVIN T. "Anti-Gay Violence and Victimization in the United States: An Overview." In GREGORY M. HEREK and KEVIN T. BERRILL, *Hate Crimes: Confronting Violence against Lesbians and Gay Men.* Newbury Park, Calif.: Sage, 1992:19–45.

BERRY, BRIAN L., and PHILIP H. REES. "The Factorial Ecology of Calcutta." *American Journal of Sociology.* Vol. 74, No. 5 (March 1969):445–91.

BERSCHEID, ELLEN, and ELAINE HATFIELD. *Interpersonal Attraction.* 2nd ed. Reading, Mass.: Addison-Wesley, 1983.

BERTEAU, CELESTE. "Disconnected Intimacy: AOL Instant Messenger Use among Kenyon College Students." Senior thesis. Kenyon College, 2005.

BESHAROV, DOUGLAS J., and PETER GERMANIS. "Welfare Reform: Four Years Later." *Public Interest.* No. 140 (Summer 2000):17–35.

BESHAROV, DOUGLAS J., and LISA A. LAUMANN. "Child Abuse Reporting." *Society.* Vol. 34, No. 4 (May/June 1996):40–46.

BEST, JOEL. "Victimization and the Victim Industry." *Society.* Vol. 34, No. 2 (May/June 1997):9–17.

BEST, RAPHAELA. *We've All Got Scars: What Boys and Girls Learn in Elementary School.* Bloomington: Indiana University Press, 1983.

BIAN, YANJIE. "Chinese Social Stratification and Social Mobility." *Annual Review of Sociology.* Vol. 28 (2002):91–116.

BIANCHI, SUZANNE M., and LYNNE M. CASPER. "American Families." *Population Bulletin.* Vol. 55, No. 4 (December 2000):3–43.

BIANCHI, SUZANNE M., and DAPHNE SPAIN. "Women, Work, and Family in America." *Population Bulletin.* Vol. 51, No. 3 (December 1996):2–48.

BLACKWOOD, EVELYN, and SASKIA WIERINGA, eds. *Female Desires: Same-Sex Relations and Transgender Practices across Cultures.* New York: Columbia University Press, 1999.

BLANK, JONAH. "The Muslim Mainstream." *U.S. News & World Report* (July 20, 1998):22–25.

BLANKENHORN, DAVID. *Fatherless America: Confronting Our Most Urgent Social Problem.* New York: HarperCollins, 1995.

BLAU, JUDITH R., and PETER M. BLAU. "The Cost of Inequality: Metropolitan Structure and Violent Crime." *American Sociological Review.* Vol. 47, No. 1 (February 1982):114–29.

BLAU, PETER M. *Exchange and Power in Social Life.* New York: Wiley, 1964.

———. *Inequality and Heterogeneity: A Primitive Theory of Social Structure.* New York: Free Press, 1977.

BLAU, PETER M., TERRY C. BLUM, and JOSEPH E. SCHWARTZ. "Heterogeneity and Intermarriage." *American Sociological Review.* Vol. 47, No. 1 (February 1982):45–62.

BLAU, PETER M., and OTIS DUDLEY DUNCAN. *The American Occupational Structure.* New York: Wiley, 1967.

BLAUSTEIN, ALBERT P., and ROBERT L. ZANGRANDO. *Civil Rights and the Black American.* New York: Washington Square Press, 1968.

BLUMBERG, PAUL. *Inequality in an Age of Decline.* New York: Oxford University Press, 1981.

BLUMER, HERBERT G. "Collective Behavior." In ALFRED MCCLUNG LEE, ed., *Principles of Sociology.* 3rd ed. New York: Barnes & Noble Books, 1969: 65–121.

BLUMSTEIN, PHILIP, and PEPPER SCHWARTZ. *American Couples.* New York: Morrow, 1983.

BOBO, LAWRENCE, and VINCENT L. HUTCHINGS. "Perceptions of Racial Group Competition: Extending Blumer's Theory of Group Position to a Multiracial Social Context." *American Sociological Review.* Vol. 61, No. 6 (December 1996):951–72.

BOERNER, CHRISTOPHER, and THOMAS LAMBERT. "Environmental Injustice." *Public Interest.* No. 124 (Winter 1995):61–82.

BOGARDUS, EMORY S. "Social Distance and Its Origins." *Sociology and Social Research.* Vol. 9 (July/August 1925):216–25.

———. *A Forty-Year Racial Distance Study.* Los Angeles: University of Southern California Press, 1967.

BOHANNAN, CECIL. "The Economic Correlates of Homelessness in Sixty Cities." *Social Science Quarterly.* Vol. 72, No. 4 (December 1991):817–25.

BOHLEN, CELESTINE. "Facing Oblivion, Rust-Belt Giants Top Russian List of Vexing Crises." *New York Times* (November 8, 1998):1, 6.

BOHON, STEPHANIE A., and CRAIG R. HUMPHREY. "Courting LULUs: Characteristics of Suitor and Objector Communities." *Rural Sociology.* Vol. 65, No. 3 (September 2000):376–95.

BONANNO, ALESSANDRO, DOUGLAS H. CONSTANCE, and HEATHER LORENZ. "Powers and Limits of Transnational Corporations: The Case of ADM." *Rural Sociology.* Vol. 65, No. 3 (September 2000):440–60.

BONNER, JANE. Research presented in the Public Broadcast System telecast *The Brain #6: The Two Brains.* Videocassette VHS 339. Newark, N.J.: WNET-13 Films, 1984.

BOOTH, ALAN, and ANN C. CROUTER, eds. *Just Living Together: Implications of Cohabitation on Families, Children, and Policy.* Mahwah, N.J.: Erlbaum, 2002.

BOOTH, ALAN, and JAMES DABBS. "Male Hormone Is Linked to Marital Problems." *Wall Street Journal* (August 19, 1992):B1.

BOOTH, WILLIAM. "By the Sweat of Their Brows: A New Economy." *Washington Post* (July 13, 1998):A1, A10–A11.

BORGMANN, ALBERT. *Crossing the Postmodern Divide.* Chicago: University of Chicago Press, 1992.

BORMANN, F. HERBERT. "The Global Environmental Deficit." *BioScience.* Vol. 40, No. 2 (1990):74.

BOSWELL, TERRY E. "A Split Labor Market Analysis of Discrimination against Chinese Immigrants, 1850–1882." *American Sociological Review.* Vol. 51, No. 3 (June 1986):352–71.

BOSWELL, TERRY E., and WILLIAM J. DIXON. "Marx's Theory of Rebellion: A Cross-National Analysis of Class Exploitation, Economic Development, and Violent Revolt." *American Sociological Review.* Vol. 58, No. 5 (October 1993):681–702.

BOTT, ELIZABETH. *Family and Social Network.* New York: Free Press, 1971; orig. 1957.

BOULDING, ELISE. *The Underside of History.* Boulder, Colo.: Westview Press, 1976.

BOWEN, WILLIAM G., and DEREK K. BOK. *The Shape of the River: Long-Term Consequences of Considering Race in College and University Admissions.* Princeton, N.J.: Princeton University Press, 1999.

BOWLES, SAMUEL, and HERBERT GINTIS. *Schooling in Capitalist America: Educational Reform and the Contradictions of Economic Life.* New York: Basic Books, 1976.

BOYER, DEBRA. "Male Prostitution and Homosexual Identity." *Journal of Homosexuality.* Vol. 17, Nos. 1–2 (1989):151–84.

BOYLE, ELIZABETH HEGER, FORTUNATA SONGORA, and GAIL FOSS. "International Discourse and Local Politics: Anti-Female-Genital-Cutting Laws in Egypt, Tanzania, and the United States." *Social Problems.* Vol. 48, No. 4 (November 2001):524–44.

BRECHIN, STEVEN R., and WILLETT KEMPTON. "Global Environmentalism: A Challenge to the Postmaterialism Thesis." *Social Science Quarterly.* Vol. 75, No. 2 (June 1994):245–69.

BRIANS, CRAIG LEONARD, and BERNARD GROFMAN. "Election Day Registration's Effect on U.S. Voter Turnout." *Social Science Quarterly.* Vol. 82, No. 1 (March 2001):170–83.

BRIGGS, TRACEY WONG. "Two Years, Changed Lives." *USA Today* (April 22, 2002): D1–D2.

BRINES, JULIE, and KARA JOYNER. "The Ties That Bind: Principles of Cohesion in Cohabitation and Marriage." *American Sociological Review.* Vol. 64, No. 3 (June 1999):333–55.

BRINK, SUSAN. "Living on the Edge." *U.S. News & World Report* (October 14, 2002):58–64.

BRINTON, MARY C. "The Social-Institutional Bases of Gender Stratification: Japan as an Illustrative Case." *American Journal of Sociology.* Vol. 94, No. 2 (September 1988):300–34.

BROCKERHOFF, MARTIN P. "An Urbanizing World." *Population Bulletin.* Vol. 55, No. 3 (September 2000):1–44.

BRODER, DAVID S. "Stock Options Belong in the Line of Fire." *Columbus Dispatch* (April 21, 2002):G3.

BRODKIN, KAREN. "How Jews Became White Folks." In PAULA S. ROTHENBERG, ed., *White Privilege.* New York: Worth, 2001.

BROOKS, DAVID. *Bobos in Paradise: The New Upper Class and How They Got There.* New York: Simon & Schuster, 2000.

BROWN, LESTER R. "Reassessing the Earth's Population." *Society.* Vol. 32, No. 4 (May/June 1995):7–10.

BROWN, LESTER R., et al., eds. *State of the World 1993: A Worldwatch Institute Report on Progress toward a Sustainable Society.* New York: Norton, 1993.

BROWNING, CHRISTOPHER R., and EDWARD O. LAUMANN. "Sexual Contact between Children and Adults: A Life Course Perspective." *American Sociological Review.* Vol. 62, No. 5 (August 1997):540–60.

BUCKLEY, STEPHEN. "A Spare and Separate Way of Life." *Washington Post* (December 18, 1996):A1, A32–A33.

BUECHLER, STEVEN M. *Social Movements in Advanced Capitalism: The Political Economy and Cultural Construction of Social Activism.* New York: Oxford University Press, 2000.

BULLETIN OF THE ATOMIC SCIENTISTS. "Current Time." [Online] Available October 19, 2005, at http://www.thebulletin.org/doomsday_clock/

BURAWAY, MICHAEL. "Review Essay: The Soviet Descent into Capitalism." *American Journal of Sociology.* Vol. 102, No. 5 (March 1997):1430–44.

BUREAU OF ALCOHOL, TOBACCO, FIREARMS, AND EXPLOSIVES. *Firearms Commerce in the United States 2001/2002.* Washington, D.C.: The Bureau, 2002.

BURKETT, ELINOR. "God Created Me to Be a Slave." *New York Times Magazine* (October 12, 1997):56–60.

BUTLER, ROBERT N. *Why Survive? Being Old in America.* New York: Harper & Row, 1975.

CALLAHAN, DANIEL. *Setting Limits: Medical Goals in an Aging Society.* New York: Simon & Schuster, 1987.

CAMARA, EVANDRO. Personal communication, 2000.

CAMERON, WILLIAM BRUCE. *Modern Social Movements: A Sociological Outline.* New York: Random House, 1966.

CAMPOLO, ANTHONY. *Partly Right: Learning from the Critics of Christianity.* Dallas: Word, 1985.

CAPEK, STELLA A. "The 'Environmental Justice' Frame: A Conceptual Discussion and an Application." *Social Problems.* Vol. 40, No. 1 (February 1993):5–24.

CAPLOW, THEODORE, HOWARD M. BAHR, JOHN MODELL, and BRUCE A. CHADWICK. *Recent Social Trends in the United States, 1960–1990.* Montreal: McGill-Queen's University Press, 1991.

CARLSON, NORMAN A. "Corrections in the United States Today: A Balance Has Been Struck." *American Criminal Law Review.* Vol. 13, No. 4 (Spring 1976):615–47.

CARMICHAEL, STOKELY, and CHARLES V. HAMILTON. *Black Power: The Politics of Liberation in America.* New York: Vintage Books, 1967.

CARMONA, RICHARD H. "The Obesity Crisis in America." Testimony before the Subcommittee on Education Reform, Committee on Education and the Workforce, United States House of Representatives. July 16, 2003. [Online] Available September 25, 2005, at http://www.surgeongeneral.gov/news/testimony/obesity07162003.htm

CARROLL, JAMES R. "Congress Is Told of Coal-Dust Fraud UMW; Senator from Minnesota Rebukes Industry." *Louisville Courier Journal* (May 27, 1999):1A.

CARUSO, DAVID B. "42 Philadelphia Schools Privatized." [Online] Available April 18, 2002, at http://news.yahoo.com

CARYL, CHRISTIAN. "Iraqi Vice." *Newsweek* (December 22, 2003):38–39.

CASTELLS, MANUEL. *The Urban Question.* Cambridge, Mass.: MIT Press, 1977.

———. *The City and the Grass Roots.* Berkeley: University of California Press, 1983.

CATALYST. *Women in Business: A Snapshot.* 2004 Factsheet. [Online] Available June 23, 2005a, at http://www.catalystwomen.org/bookstore/files/fact/Snapshot%202004.pdf

———. *Women in the Fortune 500.* Press release. February 10, 2005. [Online] Available June 23, 2005b, at http://www.catalystwomen.org/pressroom/releases.shtml

CENTER FOR AMERICAN WOMEN AND POLITICS. "Women in State Legislatures, 2005." Eagleton Institute of Politics, Rutgers University. June 2005. [Online] Available June 23, 2005, at http://www.cawp.rutgers.edu/Facts/Officeholders/stleg.pdf

CENTER ON EDUCATION POLICY. "The Good News about American Education." Reported in BRIGETTE GREENBERG, "Report Finds America's Public Schools Showing Improvement." *Naples* (Fla.) *Daily News* (January 8, 2000):4a.

CENTER FOR RESPONSIVE POLITICS. 2004 Election Overview: Stats at a Glance. [Online] Available October 19, 2005, at http://www.opensecrets.org/overview/stats.asp?cycle=2004

———. 2004 Election Overview: Totals by Sector. [Online] Available October 19, 2005, at http://www.opensecrets.org/overview/sectors.asp?cycle=2004

CENTERS FOR DISEASE CONTROL AND PREVENTION. "Trends in Cigarette Smoking among High School Students—United States, 1991–2001." *Morbidity and Mortality Weekly Report.* Vol. 51, No. 19 (May 17, 2002):409–12.

———. *HIV/AIDS Surveillance Report 2003.* Vol. 15. Atlanta, Ga.: U.S. Department of Health and Human Services, 2004. [Online] Available September 25, 2005, at http://www.cdc.gov/hiv/stats/2003SurveillanceReport.htm

———. *Sexually Transmitted Disease Surveillance, 2003.* Atlanta, Ga.: U.S. Department of Health and Human Services, September 2004. [Online] Available September 25, 2005, at http://www.cdc.gov/std/stats/toc2003.htm

———. "Annual Smoking-Attributable Mortality, Years." *Morbidity and Mortality Weekly Report.* Vol. 54, No. 25 (July 1, 2005):625–28.

———. "Cigarette Smoking among Adults—United States, 2003." *Morbidity and Mortality Weekly Report.* Vol. 54, No. 20 (May 27, 2005):509–13.

CERE, DANIEL. "Courtship Today: The View from Academia." *Public Interest.* No. 143 (Spring 2001):53–71.

CHAGNON, NAPOLEON A. *Yqnomamö: The Fierce People.* 4th ed. Austin, Tex.: Holt, Rinehart and Winston, 1992.

CHANDLER, TERTIUS, and GERALD FOX. *3000 Years of Urban History.* New York: Academic Press, 1974.

CHAVES, MARK. *Ordaining Women: Culture and Conflict in Religious Organizations.* Cambridge, Mass.: Harvard University Press, 1997.

CHAVEZ, LINDA. "Promoting Racial Harmony." In GEORGE E. CURRY, ed., *The Affirmative Action Debate.* Reading, Mass.: Addison-Wesley, 1996.

CHERLIN, ANDREW J., LINDA M. BURTON, TERA R. HART, and DIANE M. PURVIN. "The Influence of Physical and Sexual Abuse on Marriage and Cohabitation." *American Sociological Review.* Vol. 69, No. 6 (December 2004):768–89.

"China Faces Water Shortage." *Popline* (December 2001):1–4.

CHIRICOS, TED, RANEE MCENTIRE, and MARC GERTZ. "Perceived Racial and Ethnic Composition of Neighborhood and Perceived Risk of Crime." *Social Problems.* Vol. 48, No. 3 (August 2001):322–40.

CHOLDIN, HARVEY M. "Show Sampling Will Help Defeat the Undercount." *Society.* Vol. 34, No. 3 (March/April 1997):27–30.

CHRONICLE OF HIGHER EDUCATION. *Almanac 2005–06.* 2005.[Online] Available September 19, 2005, at http://chronicle.com/free/almanac/2005

CHUA-EOAN, HOWARD. "Profiles in Outrage." *Time* (September 25, 2000):38–39.

CIMINO, RICHARD, and DON LATTIN. "Choosing My Religion." *American Demographics.* Vol. 21, No. 4 (April 1999):60–65.

CLARK, J. R., and DWIGHT R. LEE. "Sentencing Laffer Curves, Political Myopia, and Prison Space." *Social Science Quarterly.* Vol. 77, No. 2 (June 1996):245–72.

CLARK, KIM. "Bankrupt Lives." *U.S. News & World Report* (September 16, 2002):52–54.

CLARK, MARGARET S., ed. *Prosocial Behavior.* Newbury Park, Calif.: Sage, 1991.

CLAWSON, DAN, and MARY ANN CLAWSON. "What Has Happened to the U.S. Labor Movement? Union Decline and Renewal." *Annual Review of Sociology.* Vol. 25 (1999):95–119.

CLEMETSON, LYNETTE. "Grandma Knows Best." *Newsweek* (June 12, 2000):60–61.

CLOUD, JOHN. "What Can the Schools Do?" *Time* (May 3, 1999):38–40.

CLOUD, JOHN, and JODIE MORSE. "Home Sweet School." *Time* (August 27, 2001):46–54.

CLOWARD, RICHARD A., and LLOYD E. OHLIN. *Delinquency and Opportunity: A Theory of Delinquent Gangs.* New York: Free Press, 1966.

COHEN, ADAM. "Test-Tube Tug-of-War." *Time* (April 6, 1998):65.

———. "A First Report Card on Vouchers." *Time* (April 26, 1999):36–38.

COHEN, ALBERT K. *Delinquent Boys: The Culture of the Gang.* New York: Free Press, 1971; orig. 1955.

COHEN, ELIAS. "The Complex Nature of Ageism: What Is It? Who Does It? Who Perceives It?" *Gerontologist.* Vol. 41, No. 5 (October 2001):576–78.

COHEN, PHILIP N., and MATT L. HUFFMAN. "Individuals, Jobs, and Labor Markets: The Devaluation of Women's Work." *American Sociological Review.* Vol. 68, No. 3 (June 2003):443–63.

COLE, GEORGE F., and CHRISTOPHER E. SMITH. *Criminal Justice in America.* 3rd ed. Belmont, Calif.: Wadsworth, 2002.

COLEMAN, JAMES S. "The Design of Organizations and the Right to Act." *Sociological Forum.* Vol. 8, No. 4 (December 1993):527–46.

COLEMAN, JAMES S., et al. *Equality of Educational Opportunity.* Washington, D.C.: U.S. Government Printing Office, 1966.

COLEMAN, JAMES S., and THOMAS HOFFER. *Public and Private High Schools: The Impact of Communities.* New York: Basic Books, 1987.

COLEMAN, JAMES S., THOMAS HOFFER, and SALLY KILGORE. *Public and Private Schools: An Analysis of Public Schools and Beyond.* Washington, D.C.: National Center for Education Statistics, 1981.

COLEMAN, RICHARD P., and BERNICE L. NEUGARTEN. *Social Status in the City.* San Francisco: Jossey-Bass, 1971.

COLLEGE BOARD. *2005 College-Bound Seniors Total Group Profile Report.* [Online] Available October 19, 2005, at http://www.collegeboard.com/prod_downloads/about/news_info/cbsenior/yr2005/2005-college-bound-seniors. pdf

COLLINS, RANDALL. *The Credential Society: A Historical Sociology of Education and Stratification.* New York: Academic Press, 1979.

COLLYMORE, YVETTE. "Migrant Street Children on the Rise in Central America." *Population Today.* Vol. 30, No. 2 (February/March 2002):1, 4.

COLTON, HELEN. *The Gift of Touch: How Physical Contact Improves Communication, Pleasure, and Health.* New York: Seaview/Putnam, 1983.

COMMISSION FOR RACIAL JUSTICE. *CRJ Reporter.* New York: United Church of Christ, 1994.

COMTE, AUGUSTE. *Auguste Comte and Positivism: The Essential Writings.* GERTRUD LENZER, ed. New York: Harper Torchbooks, 1975; orig. 1851–54.

CONNETT, PAUL H. "The Disposable Society." In F. HERBERT BORMANN and STEPHEN R. KELLERT, eds., *Ecology, Economics, and Ethics: The Broken Circle.* New Haven, Conn.: Yale University Press, 1991:99–122.

COOK, RHODES. "House Republicans Scored a Quiet Victory in '92." *Congressional Quarterly Weekly Report.* Vol. 51, No. 16 (April 17, 1993):965–68.

COOLEY, CHARLES HORTON. *Social Organization.* New York: Schocken Books, 1962; orig. 1909.

———. *Human Nature and the Social Order.* New York: Schocken Books, 1964; orig. 1902.

CORCORAN, MARY, SANDRA K. DANZIGER, ARIEL KALIL, and KRISTIN S. SEEFELDT. "How Welfare Reform Is Affecting Women's Work." *Annual Review of Sociology.* Vol. 26 (2000):241–69.

CORNELL, BARBARA. "Pulling the Plug on TV." *Time* (October 16, 2000):F16.

CORRELL, SHELLEY J. "Gender and the Career Choice Process: The Role of Biased Self-Assessment." *American Journal of Sociology.* Vol. 106, No. 6 (May 2001):1691–1730.

CORTESE, ANTHONY J. *Provocateur: Images of Women and Minorities in Advertising.* Lanham, Md.: Rowman & Littlefield, 1999.

COSER, LEWIS. *The Functions of Social Conflict.* New York: Free Press, 1956.

———. *Masters of Sociological Thought: Ideas in Historical and Social Context.* 2nd ed. New York: Harcourt Brace Jovanovich, 1977.

COURTWRIGHT, DAVID T. *Violent Land: Single Men and Social Disorder from the Frontier to the Inner City.* Cambridge, Mass.: Harvard University Press, 1996.

"Cousin Couples." [Online] Available May 29, 2005, at http://www.CousinCouples.com

COWLEY, GEOFFREY. "The Prescription That Kills." *Newsweek* (July 17, 1995):54.

COX, HARVEY. *The Secular City.* Rev. ed. New York: Macmillan, 1971.

COYOTE (Call Off Your Old Tired Ethics). "What Is COYOTE?" 2004. [Online] Available October 11, 2005, at http://www.coyotela/what-is.html

CRANE, DIANA. *Fashion and Its Social Agenda: Class, Gender, and Identity in Clothing.* Chicago: University of Chicago Press, 2000.

CRISPELL, DIANE. "Lucky to Be Alive." *American Demographics.* Vol. 19, No. 4 (April 1997):25.

CROSSETTE, BARBARA. "Female Genital Mutilation by Immigrants Is Becoming Cause for Concern in the U.S." *New York Times International* (December 10, 1995):11.

CROUSE, JAMES, and DALE TRUSHEIM. *The Case against the SAT.* Chicago: University of Chicago Press, 1988.

CRUTSINGER, MARTIN. "Trade Deficit Hits $665.9 Billion in 2004." [Online] Available March 16, 2005, at http://news.yahoo.com

CULLEN, LISA TAKEUCHI. "Will Manage for Food." *Time* (October 14, 2002):52–56.

———. "A New Battle of the Bulge." *Time* (February 24, 2003):14.

CUMMING, ELAINE, and WILLIAM E. HENRY. *Growing Old: The Process of Disengagement.* New York: Basic Books, 1961.

CUMMINGS, SCOTT, and THOMAS LAMBERT. "Anti-Hispanic and Anti-Asian Sentiments among African Americans." *Social Science Quarterly.* Vol. 78, No. 2 (June 1997):338–53.

CURRIE, ELLIOTT. *Confronting Crime: An American Challenge.* New York: Pantheon Books, 1985.

CURRY, ANDREW. "The Gullahs' Last Stand?" *U.S. News & World Report* (June 18, 2001):40–41.

CURTIS, JAMES E., DOUGLAS E. BAER, and EDWARD G. GRABB. "Nations of Joiners: Explaining Voluntary Association Membership in Democratic Societies." *American Sociological Review.* Vol. 66, No. 6 (December 2001):783–805.

CURTISS, SUSAN. *Genie: A Psycholinguistic Study of a Modern-Day "Wild Child."* New York: Academic Press, 1977.

CUTCLIFFE, JOHN R. "Hope, Counseling, and Complicated Bereavement Reactions." *Journal of Advanced Nursing.* Vol. 28, No. 4 (October 1998):754–62.

DAHL, ROBERT A. *Who Governs?* New Haven, Conn.: Yale University Press, 1961.

———. *Dilemmas of Pluralist Democracy: Autonomy vs. Control.* New Haven, Conn.: Yale University Press, 1982.

DAHRENDORF, RALF. *Class and Class Conflict in Industrial Society.* Stanford, Calif.: Stanford University Press, 1959.

DANFORTH, MARION M., and J. CONRAD GLASS JR. "Listen to My Words, Give Meaning to My Sorrow: A Study in Cognitive Constructs in Middle-Aged Bereaved Widows." *Death Studies.* Vol. 25, No. 6 (September 2001):413–30.

DARROCH, JACQUELINE E., et al. "Teenage Sexual and Reproductive Behavior in Developed Countries: Can More Progress Be Made?" 2001. [Online] Available May 30, 2005, at http://www.guttmacher.org/pubs/eurosynth_rpt.pdf

DAVIDSON, JAMES D., RALPH E. PYLE, and DAVID V. REYES. "Persistence and Change in the Protestant Establishment, 1930–1992." *Social Forces.* Vol. 74, No. 1 (September 1995):157–75.

DAVIDSON, JULIA O'CONNELL. *Prostitution, Power, and Freedom.* Ann Arbor: University of Michigan Press, 1998.

DAVIES, CHRISTIE. *Ethnic Humor around the World: A Comparative Analysis.* Bloomington: Indiana University Press, 1990.

DAVIES, MARK, and DENISE B. KANDEL. "Parental and Peer Influences on Adolescents' Educational Plans: Some Further Evidence." *American Journal of Sociology.* Vol. 87, No. 2 (September 1981):363–87.

DAVIS, BYRON BRADLEY. "Sports World." *Christian Science Monitor* (September 9, 1997):11.

DAVIS, DONALD M., cited in "TV Is a Blonde, Blonde World." *American Demographics,* special issue: *Women Change Places.* 1993.

DAVIS, KINGSLEY. "Extreme Social Isolation of a Child." *American Journal of Sociology.* Vol. 45, No. 4 (January 1940):554–65.

———. "Final Note on a Case of Extreme Isolation." *American Journal of Sociology.* Vol. 52, No. 5 (March 1947):432–37.

———. "The Myth of Functional Analysis as a Special Method in Sociology and Anthropology." *American Sociological Review.* Vol. 24, No. 1 (February 1959):75ff.

———. "Sexual Behavior." In ROBERT K. MERTON and ROBERT NISBET, eds., *Contemporary Social Problems.* 3rd ed. New York: Harcourt Brace Jovanovich, 1971:313–60.

DAVIS, KINGSLEY, and WILBERT MOORE. "Some Principles of Stratification." *American Sociological Review.* Vol. 10, No. 2 (April 1945):242–49.

DEDRICK, DENNIS K., and RICHARD E. YINGER. "MAD, SDI, and the Nuclear Arms Race." Unpublished manuscript. Georgetown, Ky.: Georgetown College, 1990.

DEFINA, ROBERT H., and THOMAS M. ARVANITES. "The Weak Effect of Imprisonment on Crime, 1971–1998." *Social Science Quarterly.* Vol. 83, No. 3 (September 2002):635–53.

DEFRANCIS, MARC. "A Spiraling Shortage of Nurses." *Population Today.* Vol. 30, No. 2 (February/March 2002a):8–9.

———. "U.S. Elder Care Is in a Fragile State." *Population Today.* Vol. 30, No. 1 (January 2002b):1–3.

DELACROIX, JACQUES, and CHARLES C. RAGIN. "Structural Blockage: A Cross-National Study of Economic Dependency, State Efficacy, and Underdevelopment." *American Journal of Sociology.* Vol. 86, No. 6 (May 1981):1311–47.

DELLA CAVA, MARCO R. "For Dutch, It's as Easy as Asking a Doctor." *USA Today* (January 7, 1997):4A.

DE MENTE, BOYE. *Japanese Etiquette and Ethics in Business.* 5th ed. Lincolnwood, Ill.: NTC Business Books, 1987.

DEMUTH, STEPHEN, and DARRELL STEFFENSMEIER. "The Impact of Gender and Race-Ethnicity in the Pretrial Release Process." *Social Problems.* Vol. 51, No. 2 (May 2004):222–42.

DENT, DAVID J. "African-Americans Turning to Christian Academies." *New York Times,* Education Life supplement (August 4, 1996):26–29.

DERBER, CHARLES. *The Wilding of America: Money, Mayhem, and the New American Dream.* 3rd ed. New York: Worth, 2004.

DERSHOWITZ, ALAN. *The Vanishing American Jew.* Boston: Little, Brown, 1997.

DERVARICS, CHARLES. "The Coming Age of Older Women." *Population Today.* Vol. 27, No. 2 (February 1999):2–3.

DEUTSCHER, IRWIN. *Making a Difference: The Practice of Sociology.* New Brunswick, N.J.: Transaction, 1999.

DICKINSON, AMY. "When Dating Is Dangerous." *Time* (August 27, 2001):76.

DIXON, WILLIAM J., and TERRY BOSWELL. "Dependency, Disarticulation, and Denominator Effects: Another Look at Foreign Capital Penetration." *American Journal of Sociology.* Vol. 102, No. 2 (September 1996):543–62.

DOBYNS, HENRY F. "An Appraisal of Techniques with a New Hemispheric Estimate." *Current Anthropology.* Vol. 7, No. 4 (October 1966):395–446.

DOLLARD, JOHN, et al. *Frustration and Aggression.* New Haven, Conn.: Yale University Press, 1939.

DOMHOFF, G. WILLIAM. *Who Rules America Now? A View of the '80s.* Englewood Cliffs, N.J.: Prentice Hall, 1983.

DONAHUE, JOHN J., III, and STEVEN D. LEAVITT. Research cited in "New Study Claims Abortion Is Behind Decrease in Crime." *Population Today.* Vol. 28, No. 1 (January 2000):1, 4.

DONNELLY, PATRICK G., and THEO J. MAJKA. "Residents' Efforts at Neighborhood Stabilization: Facing the Challenges of Inner-City Neighborhoods." *Sociological Forum.* Vol. 13, No. 2 (June 1998):189–213.

DONOVAN, VIRGINIA K., and RONNIE LITTENBERG. "Psychology of Women: Feminist Therapy." In BARBARA HABER, ed., *The Women's Annual, 1981: The Year in Review.* Boston: Hall, 1982:211–35.

DOWNEY, DOUGLAS B., PAUL T. VON HIPPEL, and BECKETT A. BROH. "Are Schools the Great Equalizer? Cognitive Inequality during the Summer Months and School Year." *American Sociological Review.* Vol. 69, No. 5 (October 2004):613–35.

DOYLE, JAMES A. *The Male Experience.* Dubuque, Iowa: Brown, 1983.

D'SOUZA, DINESH. "The Billionaire Next Door." *Forbes* (October 11, 1999): 50–62.

DU BOIS, W.E.B. *The Philadelphia Negro: A Social Study.* New York: Schocken Books, 1967; orig. 1899.

DUBOS, RENÉ. *Man Adapting.* Enlarged ed. New Haven, Conn.: Yale University Press, 1980.

DUDLEY, KATHRYN MARIE. *Debt and Dispossession: Farm Loss in America's Heartland.* Chicago: University of Chicago Press, 2000.

DUNBAR, LESLIE. *The Common Interest: How Our Social Welfare Policies Don't Work and What We Can Do about Them.* New York: Pantheon, 1988.

DUNCAN, CYNTHIA M. *Worlds Apart: Why Poverty Persists in Rural America.* New Haven, Conn.: Yale University Press, 1999.

DUNCAN, GREG J., W. JEAN YEUNG, JEANNE BROOKS-GUNN, and JUDITH R. SMITH. "How Much Does Childhood Poverty Affect the Life Chances of Children?" *American Sociological Review.* Vol. 63, No. 3 (June 1998):406–23.

DUNN, LUCIA F. "Is Combat Pay Effective? Evidence from Operation Desert Storm." *Social Science Quarterly.* Vol. 84, No. 2 (June 2003):344–58.

DUREX GLOBAL SEX SURVEY. Reported in *Time* (October 30, 2000):31.

DURKHEIM, EMILE. *The Division of Labor in Society.* New York: Free Press, 1964a; orig. 1893.

———. *The Rules of Sociological Method.* New York: Free Press, 1964b; orig. 1895.

———. *The Elementary Forms of Religious Life.* New York: Free Press, 1965; orig. 1915.

———. *Suicide.* New York: Free Press, 1966; orig. 1897.

———. *Sociology and Philosophy.* New York: Free Press, 1974; orig. 1924.

DWORKIN, ANDREA. *Intercourse.* New York: Free Press, 1987.

DWORKIN, RONALD W. "Where Have All the Nurses Gone?" *Public Interest.* No. 148 (Summer 2002):23–36.

EBAUGH, HELEN ROSE FUCHS. *Becoming an Ex: The Process of Role Exit.* Chicago: University of Chicago Press, 1988.

EBOH, CAMILLUS. "Nigerian Woman Loses Appeal against Stoning Death." [Online] Available August 19, 2002, at http://news.yahoo.com

ECK, DIANA L. A New Religious America: How a "Christian Country" Has Become the World's Most Religiously Diverse Nation. San Francisco: HarperSan Francisco, 2001.

EDWARDS, TAMALA M. "Flying Solo." Time (August 28, 2000):47–55.

EHRENREICH, BARBARA. The Hearts of Men: American Dreams and the Flight from Commitment. Garden City, N.Y.: Anchor Books, 1983.

———. "The Real Truth about the Female Body." Time (March 15, 1999):56–65.

———. Nickel and Dimed: On (Not) Getting By in America. New York: Henry Holt, 2001.

EICHLER, MARGRIT. Nonsexist Research Methods: A Practical Guide. Winchester, Mass.: Unwin Hyman, 1988.

EISEN, ARNOLD M. The Chosen People in America: A Study of Jewish Religious Ideology. Bloomington: Indiana University Press, 1983.

EISENBERG, DANIEL. "Paying to Keep Your Job." Time (October 15, 2001):80–83.

EISENSTADT, JILL. "The Maid's Tale." New York Times (July 25, 2004). [Online] Available March 22, 2005, at http://www.researchnavigator.com

EISLER, BENITA. The Lowell Offering: Writings by New England Mill Women, 1840–1845. Philadelphia: Lippincott, 1977.

EKMAN, PAUL. "Biological and Cultural Contributions to Body and Facial Movements in the Expression of Emotions." In A. RORTY, ed., Explaining Emotions. Berkeley: University of California Press, 1980a:73–101.

———. Face of Man: Universal Expression in a New Guinea Village. New York: Garland Press, 1980b.

———. Telling Lies: Clues to Deceit in the Marketplace, Politics, and Marriage. New York: Norton, 1985.

EL-ATTAR, MOHAMED. Personal communication, 1991.

ELIAS, ROBERT. The Politics of Victimization: Victims, Victimology, and Human Rights. New York: Oxford University Press, 1986.

ELLIOT, DELBERT S., and SUZANNE S. AGETON. "Reconciling Race and Class Differences in Self-Reported and Official Estimates of Delinquency." American Sociological Review. Vol. 45, No. 1 (February 1980):95–110.

ELLISON, CHRISTOPHER G., JOHN P. BARTKOWSKI, and MICHELLE L. SEGAL. "Do Conservative Protestant Parents Spank More Often? Further Evidence from the National Survey of Families and Households." Social Science Quarterly. Vol. 77, No. 3 (September 1996):663–73.

ELLWOOD, ROBERT S. "East Asian Religions in Today's America." In JACOB NEUSNER, ed. World Religions in America: An Introduction. Louisville, Ky.: Westminster John Knox Press, 2000:154–71.

ELMER-DEWITT, PHILIP. "Now for the Truth about Americans and Sex." Time (October 17, 1994):62–70.

EMBER, MELVIN, and CAROL R. EMBER. "The Conditions Favoring Matrilocal versus Patrilocal Residence." American Anthropologist. Vol. 73, No. 3 (June 1971):571–94.

———. Anthropology. 6th ed. Englewood Cliffs, N.J.: Prentice Hall, 1991.

EMERSON, JOAN P. "Behavior in Private Places: Sustaining Definitions of Reality in Gynecological Examinations." In H. P. DREITZEL, ed., Recent Sociology. Vol. 2. New York: Collier, 1970:74–97.

EMERSON, MICHAEL O., GEORGE YANCEY, and KAREN J. CHAI. "Does Race Matter in Residential Segregation? Exploring the Preferences of White Americans." American Sociological Review. Vol. 66, No. 6 (December 2001):922–35.

ENDICOTT, KAREN. "Fathering in an Egalitarian Society." In Barry S. Hewlett, ed., Father-Child Relations: Cultural and Bio-Social Contexts. New York: Aldine, 1992:281–96.

ENGELS, FRIEDRICH. The Origin of the Family. Chicago: Kerr, 1902; orig. 1884.

ENGLAND, PAULA. "Three Reviews on Marriage." Contemporary Sociology. Vol. 30, No. 6 (November 2001):564–65.

ENGLAND, PAULA, JOAN M. HERMSEN, and DAVID A. COTTER. "The Devaluation of Women's Work: A Comment on Tam." American Journal of Sociology. Vol. 105, No. 6 (May 2000):1741–60.

ERIKSON, ERIK H. Childhood and Society. New York: Norton, 1963; orig. 1950.

———. Identity and the Life Cycle. New York: Norton, 1980.

ERIKSON, KAI T. Everything in Its Path: Destruction of Community in the Buffalo Creek Flood. New York: Simon & Schuster, 1976.

———. A New Species of Trouble: Explorations in Disaster, Trauma, and Community. New York: Norton, 1994.

———. Lecture delivered at Kenyon College, Gambier, Ohio, February 7, 2005a.

———. Wayward Puritans: A Study in the Sociology of Deviance. New York: Wiley, 2005b; orig. 1966.

ERIKSON, ROBERT S., NORMAN R. LUTTBEG, and KENT L. TEDIN. American Public Opinion: Its Origins, Content, and Impact. 2nd ed. New York: Wiley, 1980.

ESTES, RICHARD J. "The Commercial Sexual Exploitation of Children in the U.S., Canada, and Mexico." Reported in "Study Explores Sexual Exploitation." [Online] Available September 10, 2001, at http://news.yahoo.com

ETZIONI, AMITAI. A Comparative Analysis of Complex Organization: On Power, Involvement, and Their Correlates. Revised and enlarged ed. New York: Free Press, 1975.

———. "Too Many Rights, Too Few Responsibilities." Society. Vol. 28, No. 2 (January/February 1991):41–48.

———. "How to Make Marriage Matter." Time (September 6, 1993):76.

———. "The Responsive Community: A Communitarian Perspective." American Sociological Review. Vol. 61, No. 1 (February 1996):1–11.

———. My Brother's Keeper: A Memoir and a Message. Lanham, Md.: Rowman & Littlefield, 2003.

EVELYN, JAMILAH. "Community Colleges Play Too Small a Role in Teacher Education, Report Concludes." Chronicle of Higher Education Online. [Online] Available October 24, 2002, at http://chronicle.com/daily/2002/10/2002102403n.htm

FAGAN, JEFFREY, FRANKLIN E. ZIMRING, and JUNE KIM. "Declining Homicide in New York City: A Tale of Two Trends." National Institute of Justice Journal. No. 237 (October 1998):12–13.

FALK, GERHARD. Personal communication, 1987.

FALLON, A. E., and P. ROZIN. "Sex Differences in Perception of Desirable Body Shape." Journal of Abnormal Psychology. Vol. 94, No. 1 (1985):100–105.

FARLEY, CHRISTOPHER JOHN. "Winning the Right to Fly." Time (August 28, 1995):62–64.

FATTAH, HASSAN. "A More Diverse Community." American Demographics. Vol. 24, No. 7 (July/August 2002):39–43.

FEAGIN, JOE R. The Urban Real Estate Game. Englewood Cliffs, N.J.: Prentice Hall, 1983.

———. "Death by Discrimination?" Newsletter of the Society for the Study of Social Problems. Vol. 28, No. 1 (Winter 1997):15–16.

FEAGIN, JOE R., and VERA HERNÁN. Liberation Sociology. Boulder, Colo.: Westview Press, 2001.

FEATHERMAN, DAVID L., and ROBERT M. HAUSER. Opportunity and Change. New York: Academic Press, 1978.

FEATHERSTONE, MIKE, ed. Global Culture: Nationalism, Globalization, and Modernity. Newbury Park, Calif.: Sage, 1990.

FEDARKO, KEVIN. "Land Mines: Cheap, Deadly, and Cruel." Time (May 13, 1996):54–55.

FEDERAL BUREAU OF INVESTIGATION. Crime in the United States, 2003. Washington, D.C.: Federal Bureau of Investigation, 2004. [Online] Available September 13, 2005, at http://www.fbi.gov

FEDERAL ELECTION COMMISSION. "PAC Activity Increases for 2004 Elections." Washington, D.C.: The Commission, 2005. [Online] Available July 29, 2005, at http://www.fec.gov/press/press2005/20050412pac/PACFinal2004.html

FELLMAN, BRUCE. "Taking the Measure of Children's TV." Yale Alumni Magazine (April 1995):46–51.

"Female Opinion and Defense since September 11th." Society. Vol. 39, No. 3 (March/April 2002):2.

FENYVESI, CHARLES. "Walled Streets." U.S. News & World Report (March 25, 2002):57.

FERNANDEZ, ROBERTO M., and NANCY WEINBERG. "Sifting and Sorting: Personal Contacts and Hiring in a Retail Bank." American Sociological Review. Vol. 62, No. 6 (December 1997):883–902.

FERRARO, KENNETH F., and JESSICA A. KELLEY-MOORE. "Cumulative Disadvantage and Health: Long-Term Consequences of Obesity?" American Sociological Review. Vol. 68, No. 5 (October 2003):707–29.

FERREE, MYRA MARX, and BETH B. HESS. Controversy and Coalition: The New Feminist Movement across Four Decades of Change. 3rd ed. New York: Routledge, 1995.

FETTO, JOHN. "Lean on Me." American Demographics. Vol. 22, No. 12 (December 2000):16–17.

———. "Gay Friendly?" American Demographics. Vol. 24, No. 5 (May 2002a):16.

———. "Roomier Rentals." American Demographics. Vol. 24, No. 5 (May 2002b):17.

———. "A View from the Top?" American Demographics. Vol. 24, No. 7 (July/August 2002c):14.

———. "Drug Money." *American Demographics.* Vol. 25, No. 2 (March 2003a):48.

———. "Me Gusta TV." *American Demographics.* Vol. 24, No. 11 (January 2003b):14–15.

FINE, GARY ALAN. "Nature and the Taming of the Wild: The Problem of 'Overpick' in the Culture of Mushroomers." *Social Problems.* Vol. 44, No. 1 (February 1997):68–88.

FINKELSTEIN, NEAL W., and RON HASKINS. "Kindergarten Children Prefer Same-Color Peers." *Child Development.* Vol. 54, No. 2 (April 1983):502–08.

FINN, CHESTER E., JR., and HERBERT J. WALBERG. "The World's Least Efficient Schools." *Wall Street Journal* (June 22, 1998):A22.

FIREBAUGH, GLENN. "Growth Effects of Foreign and Domestic Investment." *American Journal of Sociology.* Vol. 98, No. 1 (July 1992):105–30.

———. "Does Foreign Capital Harm Poor Nations? New Estimates Based on Dixon and Boswell's Measures of Capital Penetration." *American Journal of Sociology.* Vol. 102, No. 2 (September 1996):563–75.

———. "Empirics of World Income Inequality." *American Journal of Sociology.* Vol. 104, No. 6 (May 1999):1597–1630.

———. "The Trend in Between-Nation Income Inequality." *Annual Review of Sociology.* Vol. 26 (2000):323–39.

FIREBAUGH, GLENN, and FRANK D. BECK. "Does Economic Growth Benefit the Masses? Growth, Dependence, and Welfare in the Third World." *American Sociological Review.* Vol. 59, No. 5 (October 1994):631–53.

FIREBAUGH, GLENN, and KENNETH E. DAVIS. "Trends in Antiblack Prejudice, 1972–1984: Region and Cohort Effects." *American Journal of Sociology.* Vol. 94, No. 2 (September 1988):251–72.

FIREBAUGH, GLENN, and DUMITRU SANDU. "Who Supports Marketization and Democratization in Post-Communist Romania?" *Sociological Forum.* Vol. 13, No. 3 (September 1998):521–41.

FISCHER, CLAUDE W. *The Urban Experience.* 2nd ed. New York: Harcourt Brace Jovanovich, 1984.

FISHER, ELIZABETH. *Woman's Creation: Sexual Evolution and the Shaping of Society.* Garden City, N.Y.: Anchor/Doubleday, 1979.

FISHER, ROGER, and WILLIAM URY. "Getting to Yes." In WILLIAM M. EVAN and STEPHEN HILGARTNER, eds., *The Arms Race and Nuclear War.* Englewood Cliffs, N.J.: Prentice Hall, 1988:261–68.

FISKE, ALAN PAIGE. "The Cultural Relativity of Selfish Individualism: Anthropological Evidence That Humans Are Inherently Sociable." In MARGARET S. CLARK, ed., *Prosocial Behavior.* Newbury Park, Calif.: Sage, 1991:176–214.

FITZGERALD, JIM. "Martha Stewart Enjoys Comforts of Home." [Online] Available March 6, 2005, at http://news.yahoo.com

FITZGERALD, JOAN, and LOUISE SIMMONS. "From Consumption to Production: Labor Participation in Grass-Roots Movements in Pittsburgh and Hartford." *Urban Affairs Quarterly.* Vol. 26, No. 4 (June 1991):512–31.

FITZPATRICK, MARY ANNE. *Between Husbands and Wives: Communication in Marriage.* Newbury Park, Calif.: Sage, 1988.

FLAHERTY, MICHAEL G. "A Formal Approach to the Study of Amusement in Social Interaction." *Studies in Symbolic Interaction.* Vol. 5. New York: JAI Press, 1984:71–82.

———. "Two Conceptions of the Social Situation: Some Implications of Humor." *Sociological Quarterly.* Vol. 31, No. 1 (Spring 1990).

FOBES, RICHARD. "Creative Problem Solving." *Futurist.* Vol. 30, No. 1 (January/February 1996):19–22.

FOLIART, DONNE E., and MARGARET CLAUSEN. "Bereavement Practices among California Hospices: Results of a Statewide Survey." *Death Studies.* Vol. 25, No. 5 (July 2001):461–68.

FONDA, DAREN. "The Male Minority." *Time* (December 11, 2000):58–60.

———. "Selling in Tongues." *Time,* Global Business ed. (November 2001):B12–B16.

FORD, CLELLAN S., and FRANK A. BEACH. *Patterns of Sexual Behavior.* New York: Harper Bros., 1951.

FORLITI, AMY. "R.I. Nightclub Fire Kills at Least 39." [Online] Available February 21, 2003, at http://news.yahoo.com

FOUCAULT, MICHEL. *The History of Sexuality: An Introduction.* Vol. 1. ROBERT HURLEY, trans. New York: Vintage, 1990; orig. 1978.

FRANK, ANDRÉ GUNDER. *On Capitalist Underdevelopment.* Bombay: Oxford University Press, 1975.

———. *Crisis: In the World Economy.* New York: Holmes & Meier, 1980.

———. *Reflections on the World Economic Crisis.* New York: Monthly Review Press, 1981.

FRANKLIN, JOHN HOPE. *From Slavery to Freedom: A History of Negro Americans.* 3rd ed. New York: Vintage Books, 1967.

FRAZIER, E. FRANKLIN. *Black Bourgeoisie: The Rise of a New Middle Class.* New York: Free Press, 1965.

FREDRICKSON, GEORGE M. *White Supremacy: A Comparative Study in American and South African History.* New York: Oxford University Press, 1981.

FREEDMAN, ESTELLE B. *No Turning Back: The History of Feminism and the Future of Women.* New York: Ballantine Books, 2002.

FREEDOM HOUSE. *Freedom in the World 2005.* [Online] Available July 11, 2005, at http://www.freedomhouse.org

FRENCH, HOWARD W. "Teaching Japan's Salarymen to Be Their Own Men." *New York Times* (November 27, 2002):A4.

FRENCH, MARILYN. *Beyond Power: On Women, Men, and Morals.* New York: Summit Books, 1985.

FRIEDAN, BETTY. *The Fountain of Age.* New York: Simon & Schuster, 1993.

FRIEDMAN, MEYER, and RAY H. ROSENMAN. *Type A Behavior and Your Heart.* New York: Fawcett Crest, 1974.

FRIEDMAN, MILTON, and ROSE FRIEDMAN. *Free to Choose: A Personal Statement.* New York: Harcourt Brace Jovanovich, 1980.

FUGITA, STEPHEN S., and DAVID J. O'BRIEN. "Structural Assimilation, Ethnic Group Membership, and Political Participation among Japanese Americans: A Research Note." *Social Forces.* Vol. 63, No. 4 (June 1985):986–95.

FULLER, REX, and RICHARD SCHOENBERGER. "The Gender Salary Gap: Do Academic Achievement, Intern Experience, and College Major Make a Difference?" *Social Science Quarterly.* Vol. 72, No. 4 (December 1991):715–26.

FUREDI, FRANK. "New Britain: A Nation of Victims." *Society.* Vol. 35, No. 3 (April 1998):80–84.

FURSTENBERG, FRANK F., JR., and ANDREW J. CHERLIN. *Divided Families: What Happens to Children When Parents Part.* Cambridge, Mass.: Harvard University Press, 1991.

———. "Children's Adjustment to Divorce." In BONNIE J. FOX, ed., *Family Patterns, Gender Relations.* 2nd ed. New York: Oxford University Press, 2001.

GAGNÉ, PATRICIA, and RICHARD TEWKSBURY. "Conformity Pressures and Gender Resistance among Transgendered Individuals." *Social Problems.* Vol. 45, No. 1 (February 1998):81–101.

GAGNÉ, PATRICIA, RICHARD TEWKSBURY, and DEANNA McGAUGHEY. "Coming Out and Crossing Over: Identity Formation and Proclamation in a Transgender Community." *Gender and Society.* Vol. 11, No. 4 (August 1997): 478–508.

GALLAGHER, CHARLES A. "Miscounting Race: Explaining Whites' Misperceptions of Racial Group Size." *Sociological Perspectives.* Vol. 46, No. 3 (2003):381–96.

GALLAGHER, MAGGIE. "Does Bradley Know What Poverty Is?" *New York Post* (October 28, 1999):37.

GALLUP ORGANIZATION. Data reported in "Americans and Homosexual Civil Unions." *Society.* Vol. 40, No. 1 (December 2002):2.

GALSTER, GEORGE. "Black Suburbanization: Has It Changed the Relative Location of Races?" *Urban Affairs Quarterly.* Vol. 26, No. 4 (June 1991): 621–28.

GAMBLE, ANDREW, STEVE LUDLAM, and DAVID BAKER. "Britain's Ruling Class." *Economist.* Vol. 326, No. 7795 (January 23, 1993):10.

GAMSON, WILLIAM A. "Beyond the Science-versus-Advocacy Distinction." *Contemporary Sociology.* Vol. 28, No. 1 (January 1999):23–26.

GANLEY, ELAINE. "Among Islamic Countries, Women's Roles Vary Greatly." *Washington Times* (April 15, 1998):A13.

GANS, HERBERT J. *People and Plans: Essays on Urban Problems and Solutions.* New York: Basic Books, 1968.

GARDNER, MARILYN. "At-Home Dads Give Their New Career High Marks." *Christian Science Monitor* (May 30, 1996):1, 12.

GARDYN, REBECCA. "Retirement Redefined." *American Demographics.* Vol. 22, No. 11 (November 2000):52–57.

———. "The Mating Game." *American Demographics.* Vol. 24, No. 7 (July/August 2002):33–37.

GARFINKEL, HAROLD. "Conditions of Successful Degradation Ceremonies." *American Journal of Sociology.* Vol. 61, No. 2 (March 1956):420–24.

———. *Studies in Ethnomethodology.* Cambridge, Mass.: Polity Press, 1967.

GARREAU, JOEL. *Edge City.* New York: Doubleday, 1991.

GEERTZ, CLIFFORD. "Common Sense as a Cultural System." *Antioch Review.* Vol. 33, No. 1 (Spring 1975):5–26.

GELLES, RICHARD J., and CLAIRE PEDRICK CORNELL. *Intimate Violence in Families.* 2nd ed. Newbury Park, Calif.: Sage, 1990.

GEOHIVE. "Agglomerations." [Online] Available October 3, 2005, at http://www.geohive.com/charts/city_million.php

GERBER, THEODORE P., and MICHAEL HOUT. "More Shock than Therapy: Market Transition, Employment, and Income in Russia, 1991–1995." *American Journal of Sociology*. Vol. 104, No. 1 (July 1998):1–50.

GERGEN, DAVID. "King of the World." *U.S. News & World Report* (February 25, 2002):84.

GERLACH, MICHAEL L. *The Social Organization of Japanese Business*. Berkeley: University of California Press, 1992.

GERTH, H. H., and C. WRIGHT MILLS, eds. *From Max Weber: Essays in Sociology*. New York: Oxford University Press, 1946.

GESCHWENDER, JAMES A. *Racial Stratification in America*. Dubuque, Iowa: Brown, 1978.

GEWERTZ, DEBORAH. "A Historical Reconsideration of Female Dominance among the Chambri of Papua New Guinea." *American Ethnologist*. Vol. 8, No. 1 (1981):94–106.

GIBBS, NANCY. "The Pulse of America along the River." *Time* (July 10, 2000):42–46.

———. "What Kids (Really) Need." *Time* (April 30, 2001):48–49.

GIDDENS, ANTHONY. *The Transformation of Intimacy*. Cambridge: Polity Press, 1992.

GILBERTSON, GRETA A., and DOUGLAS T. GURAK. "Broadening the Enclave Debate: The Dual Labor Market Experiences of Dominican and Colombian Men in New York City." *Sociological Forum*. Vol. 8, No. 2 (June 1993):205–20.

GILL, RICHARD T. "What Happened to the American Way of Death?" *Public Interest*. No. 127 (Spring 1996):105–17.

GILLIGAN, CAROL. *In a Different Voice: Psychological Theory and Women's Development*. Cambridge, Mass.: Harvard University Press, 1982.

———. *Making Connections: The Relational Worlds of Adolescent Girls at Emma Willard School*. Cambridge, Mass.: Harvard University Press, 1990.

GILLON, RAANAN. "Euthanasia in the Netherlands: Down the Slippery Slope?" *Journal of Medical Ethics*. Vol. 25, No. 1 (February 1999):3–4.

GIOVANNINI, MAUREEN. "Female Anthropologist and Male Informant: Gender Conflict in a Sicilian Town." In JOHN J. MACIONIS and NIJOLE V. BENOKRAITIS, eds., *Seeing Ourselves: Classic, Contemporary, and Cross-Cultural Readings in Sociology*. 2nd ed. Englewood Cliffs, N.J.: Prentice Hall, 1992:27–32.

GLEICK, ELIZABETH. "The Marker We've Been Waiting For." *Time* (April 7, 1997):28–42.

GLENMARY RESEARCH CENTER. "Major Religious Families by Counties of the United States, 2000" (map). Nashville, Tenn.: Glenmary Research Center, 2002.

GLENN, NORVAL D., and BETH ANN SHELTON. "Regional Differences in Divorce in the United States." *Journal of Marriage and the Family*. Vol. 47, No. 3 (August 1985):641–52.

GLUECK, SHELDON, and ELEANOR GLUECK. *Unraveling Juvenile Delinquency*. New York: Commonwealth Fund, 1950.

GOESLING, BRIAN. "Changing Income Inequalities within and between Nations: New Evidence." *American Sociological Review*. Vol. 66, No. 5 (October 2001):745–61.

GOETTING, ANN. *Getting Out: Life Stories of Women Who Left Abusive Men*. New York: Columbia University Press, 1999.

GOFFMAN, ERVING. *The Presentation of Self in Everyday Life*. Garden City, N.Y.: Anchor Books, 1959.

———. *Asylums: Essays on the Social Situation of Mental Patients and Other Inmates*. Garden City, N.Y.: Anchor Books, 1961.

———. *Stigma: Notes on the Management of Spoiled Identity*. Englewood Cliffs, N.J.: Prentice Hall, 1963.

———. *Interactional Ritual: Essays on Face to Face Behavior*. Garden City, N.Y.: Anchor Books, 1967.

———. *Gender Advertisements*. New York: Harper Colophon, 1979.

GOLDBERG, BERNARD. *Bias: A CBS Insider Exposes How the Media Distort the News*. Washington, D.C.: Regnery, 2002.

GOLDBERG, STEVEN. *The Inevitability of Patriarchy*. New York: Morrow, 1974.

GOLDBERGER, PAUL. Lecture delivered at Kenyon College, Gambier, Ohio, September 22, 2002.

GOLDEN, DANIEL. "Some Community Colleges Fudge the Facts to Attract Foreign Students." *Wall Street Journal* (April 2, 2002):B1, B4.

GOLDEN, FREDERIC. "Lying Faces Unmasked." *Time* (April 5, 1999):52.

GOLDEN, FREDERIC, and MICHAEL D. LEMONICK. "The Race Is Over." *Time* (July 3, 2000):18–23.

GOLDFIELD, MICHAEL. "Rebounding Unions Target Service Sector." *Population Today*. Vol. 28, No. 7 (October 2000):3, 10.

GOLDSMITH, H. H. "Genetic Influences on Personality from Infancy." *Child Development*. Vol. 54, No. 2 (April 1983):331–35.

GOLDSTEIN, JOSHUA R., and CATHERINE T. KENNEY. "Marriage Delayed or Marriage Forgone? New Cohort Forecasts of First Marriage for U.S. Women." *American Sociological Review*. Vol. 66, No. 4 (August 2001):506–19.

GOODE, ERICH. "No Need to Panic? A Bumper Crop of Books on Moral Panics." *Sociological Forum*. Vol. 15, No. 3 (September 2000):543–52.

GOODE, WILLIAM J. "The Theoretical Importance of Love." *American Sociological Review*. Vol. 24, No. 1 (February 1959):38–47.

———. "Encroachment, Charlatanism, and the Emerging Profession: Psychology, Sociology, and Medicine." *American Sociological Review*. Vol. 25, No. 6 (December 1960):902–14.

GORDON, JAMES S. "The Paradigm of Holistic Medicine." In ARTHUR C. HASTINGS et al., eds., *Health for the Whole Person: The Complete Guide to Holistic Medicine*. Boulder, Colo.: Westview Press, 1980:3–27.

GORMAN, CHRISTINE. "Stressed-Out Kids." *Time* (December 25, 2000):168.

GORSKI, PHILIP S. "Historicizing the Secularization Debate: Church, State, and Society in Late Medieval and Early Modern Europe, ca. 1300 to 1700." *American Sociological Review*. Vol. 65, No. 1 (February 2000):138–67.

GOTHAM, KEVIN FOX. "Race, Mortgage Lending, and Loan Rejections in a U.S. City." *Sociological Focus*. Vol. 31, No. 4 (October 1998):391–405.

GOTTFREDSON, MICHAEL R., and TRAVIS HIRSCHI. "National Crime Control Policies." *Society*. Vol. 32, No. 2 (January/February 1995):30–36.

GOTTMANN, JEAN. *Megalopolis*. New York: Twentieth Century Fund, 1961.

GOUGH, KATHLEEN. "The Origin of the Family." In JOHN J. MACIONIS and NIJOLE V. BENOKRAITIS, eds., *Seeing Ourselves: Classic, Contemporary, and Cross-Cultural Readings in Sociology*. Englewood Cliffs, N.J.: Prentice Hall, 1989.

GOULD, STEPHEN J. "Evolution as Fact and Theory." *Discover* (May 1981):35–37.

GOULDNER, ALVIN. *The Coming Crisis of Western Sociology*. New York: Avon Books, 1970.

GRANT, DON SHERMAN II, and MICHAEL WALLACE. "Why Do Strikes Turn Violent?" *American Journal of Sociology*. Vol. 96, No. 5 (March 1991):1117–50.

GRANT, DONALD L. *The Anti-Lynching Movement*. San Francisco: R&E Research Associates, 1975.

GRATTET, RYKEN. "Hate Crimes: Better Data or Increasing Frequency?" *Population Today*. Vol. 28, No. 5 (July 2000):1, 4.

GREELEY, ANDREW M. *Religious Change in America*. Cambridge, Mass.: Harvard University Press, 1989.

———. "Religious Revival in Eastern Europe." *Society*. Vol. 39, No. 2 (January/February 2002):76–77.

GREEN, GARY PAUL, LEANN M. TIGGES, and DANIEL DIAZ. "Racial and Ethnic Differences in Job-Search Strategies in Atlanta, Boston, and Los Angeles." *Social Science Quarterly*. Vol. 80, No. 2 (June 1999):263–90.

GREENBERG, DAVID F. *The Construction of Homosexuality*. Chicago: University of Chicago Press, 1988.

GREENE, BOB. "Empty House on the Prairie." *New York Times* (March 2, 2005). [Online] Available May 24, 2005, at http://www.researchnavigator.com

GREENFIELD, LAWRENCE A. *Child Victimizers: Violent Offenders and Their Victims*. Washington, D.C.: U.S. Bureau of Justice Statistics, 1996.

GREENHOUSE, STEVEN. "Despite Defeat on China Bill, Labor Is on the Rise." *New York Times* (May 20, 2000): A1, A18.

GREENSPAN, STANLEY I. *The Four-Thirds Solution: Solving the Child-Care Crisis in America*. Cambridge, Mass.: Perseus, 2001.

GURAK, DOUGLAS T., and JOSEPH P. FITZPATRICK. "Intermarriage among Hispanic Ethnic Groups in New York City." *American Journal of Sociology*. Vol. 87, No. 4 (January 1982):921–34.

GURNETT, KATE. "On the Forefront of Feminism." *Albany Times Union* (July 5, 1998):G-1, G-6.

GWYNNE, S. C., and JOHN F. DICKERSON. "Lost in the E-Mail." *Time* (April 21, 1997):88–90.

HABERMAS, JÜRGEN. *Toward a Rational Society: Student Protest, Science, and Politics*. JEREMY J. SHAPIRO, trans. Boston: Beacon Press, 1970.

HADAWAY, C. KIRK, PENNY LONG MARLER, and MARK CHAVES. "What the Polls Don't Show: A Closer Look at U.S. Church Attendance." *American Sociological Review*. Vol. 58, No. 6 (December 1993):741–52.

HADDEN, JEFFREY K., and CHARLES E. SWAIN. *Prime-Time Preachers: The Rising Power of Televangelism*. Reading, Mass.: Addison-Wesley, 1981.

HAFNER, KATIE. "Making Sense of the Internet." *Newsweek* (October 24, 1994): 46–48.

HAGAN, JACQUELINE MARIA. "Social Networks, Gender, and Immigrant Incorporation: Resources and Restraints." *American Sociological Review*. Vol. 63, No. 1 (February 1998):55–67.

HAIG, ROBIN ANDREW. *The Anatomy of Humor: Biopsychosocial and Therapeutic Perspectives*. Springfield, Ill.: Thomas, 1988.

HALBERSTAM, DAVID. *The Reckoning.* New York: Avon Books, 1986.

HALBFINGER, DAVID M., and STEVEN A. HOLMES. "Military Mirrors Working-Class America." *New York Times* (March 20, 2003). [Online] Available April 28, 2005, at http://www.researchnavigator.com

HALEDJIAN, DEAN. "How to Tell a Businessman from a Businesswoman." Annandale: Northern Virginia Community College, 1997.

HALL, JOHN R., and MARY JO NEITZ. *Culture: Sociological Perspectives.* Englewood Cliffs, N.J.: Prentice Hall, 1993.

HALL, KELLEY J., and BETSY LUCAL. "Tapping in Parallel Universes: Using Superhero Comic Books in Sociology Courses." *Teaching Sociology.* Vol. 27, No. 1 (January 1999):60–66.

HALLINAN, MAUREEN T. "The Sociological Study of Social Change." *American Sociological Review.* Vol. 62, No. 1 (February 1997):1–11.

HAMER, DEAN, and PETER COPELAND. *The Science of Desire: The Search for the Gay Gene and the Biology of Behavior.* New York: Simon & Schuster, 1994.

HAMILTON, ANITA. "Speeders, Say Cheese." *Time* (September 17, 2001):32.

HAMILTON, RICHARD F. "*The Communist Manifesto* at 150." *Society.* Vol. 38, No. 2 (January/February 2001):75–80.

HAMRICK, MICHAEL H., DAVID J. ANSPAUGH, and GENE EZELL. *Health.* Columbus, Ohio: Merrill, 1986.

HAN, WENJUI, and JANE WALDFOGEL. "Child Care Costs and Women's Employment: A Comparison of Single and Married Mothers with Preschool-Aged Children." *Social Science Quarterly.* Vol. 83, No. 5 (September 2001):552–68.

HANDLIN, OSCAR. *Boston's Immigrants, 1790–1865: A Study in Acculturation.* Cambridge, Mass.: Harvard University Press, 1941.

HANEY, CRAIG, W. CURTIS BANKS, and PHILIP G. ZIMBARDO. "Interpersonal Dynamics in a Simulated Prison." *International Journal of Criminology and Penology.* Vol. 1 (1973):69–97.

HANEY, LYNNE. "After the Fall: East European Women since the Collapse of State Socialism." *Contexts.* Vol. 1, No. 3 (Fall 2002):27–36.

HARKNETT, KRISTEN, and SARA S. MCLANAHAN. "Racial and Ethnic Differences in Marriage after the Birth of a Child." *American Sociological Review.* Vol. 69, No. 6 (December 2004):790–811.

HARLOW, HARRY F., and MARGARET KUENNE HARLOW. "Social Deprivation in Monkeys." *Scientific American* (November 1962):137–46.

HARPSTER, PAULA, and ELIZABETH MONK-TURNER. "Why Men Do Housework: A Test of Gender Production and the Relative Resources Model." *Sociological Focus.* Vol. 31, No. 1 (February 1998):45–59.

HARRIES, KEITH D. *Serious Violence: Patterns of Homicide and Assault in America.* Springfield, Ill.: Thomas, 1990.

HARRINGTON, MICHAEL. *The New American Poverty.* New York: Penguin Books, 1984.

HARRIS, CHAUNCY D., and EDWARD L. ULLMAN. "The Nature of Cities." *Annals of the American Academy of Political and Social Sciences.* Vol. 242, No. 1 (November 1945):7–17.

HARRIS, DAVID R., and JEREMIAH JOSEPH SIM. "Who Is Multiracial? Assessing the Complexity of Lived Race." Vol. 67, No. 4 (August 2002):614–27.

HARRIS, MARVIN. *Cultural Anthropology.* 2nd ed. New York: Harper & Row, 1987.

HARRISON, C. KEITH. "Black Athletes at the Millennium." *Society.* Vol. 37, No. 3 (March/April 2000):35–39.

HAUB, CARL. "How Many People Have Ever Lived on Earth?" *Population Today.* Vol. 30, No. 8 (November/December 2002):3–4.

HAWTHORNE, PETER. "South Africa's Makeover." *Time* (July 12, 1999).

HAYDEN, THOMAS. "Losing Our Voices." *U.S. News & World Report* (May 26, 2003):42.

HAYWARD, MARK D., EILEEN M. CRIMMINS, TONI P. MILES, and YU YANG. "The Significance of Socioeconomic Status in Explaining the Racial Gap in Chronic Health Conditions." *American Sociological Review.* Vol. 65, No. 6 (December 2000):910–30.

HEATH, JULIA A., and W. DAVID BOURNE. "Husbands and Housework: Parity or Parody?" *Social Science Quarterly.* Vol. 76, No. 1 (March 1995):195–202.

HELGESEN, SALLY. *The Female Advantage: Women's Ways of Leadership.* New York: Doubleday, 1990.

HELIN, DAVID W. "When Slogans Go Wrong." *American Demographics.* Vol. 14, No. 2 (February 1992):14.

HELLMICH, NANCI. "Environment, Economics Partly to Blame." *USA Today* (October 9, 2002):9D.

HENLEY, NANCY, MYKOL HAMILTON, and BARRIE THORNE. "Womanspeak and Manspeak: Sex Differences in Communication, Verbal and Nonverbal." In JOHN J. MACIONIS and NIJOLE V. BENOKRAITIS, eds., *Seeing Ourselves: Classic,*

Contemporary, and Cross-Cultural Readings in Sociology. 2nd ed. Englewood Cliffs, N.J.: Prentice Hall, 1992:10–15.

HERDA-RAPP, ANN. "The Power of Informal Leadership: Women Leaders in the Civil Rights Movement." *Sociological Focus.* Vol. 31, No. 4 (October 1998): 341–55.

HEREK, GREGORY M. "Myths about Sexual Orientation: A Lawyer's Guide to Social Science Research." *Law and Sexuality.* No. 1 (1991):133–72.

HERMAN, DIANNE. "The Rape Culture." In JOHN J. MACIONIS and NIJOLE V. BENOKRAITIS, eds., *Seeing Ourselves: Classic, Contemporary, and Cross-Cultural Readings in Sociology.* 5th ed. Upper Saddle River, N.J.: Prentice Hall, 2001.

HERPERTZ, SABINE C., and HENNING SASS. "Emotional Deficiency and Psychopathy." *Behavioral Sciences and the Law.* Vol. 18, No. 5 (September/October 2000):567–80.

HERRING, HUBERT B. "An Aging Nation Is Choosing Younger Bosses." *New York Times* (February 20, 2005). [Online] Available April 12, 2005, at http://www.researchnavigator.com

HERRNSTEIN, RICHARD J., and CHARLES MURRAY. *The Bell Curve: Intelligence and Class Structure in American Life.* New York: Free Press, 1994.

HERZOG, BRAD. "A Man of His Words." *Cornell Alumni Magazine.* Vol. 106, No. 4 (January/February 2004):58–63.

HESS, BETH B. "Breaking and Entering the Establishment: Committing Social Change and Confronting the Backlash." *Social Problems.* Vol. 46, No. 1 (February 1999):1–12.

HEWLETT, BARRY S. "Husband-Wife Reciprocity and the Father-Infant Relationship among Aka Pygmies." In BARRY S. HEWLETT, ed., *Father-Child Relations: Cultural and Bio-Social Contexts.* New York: Aldine, 1992:153–76.

HEYMANN, PHILIP B. "Civil Liberties and Human Rights in the Aftermath of September 11." *Harvard Journal of Law and Public Policy.* Vol. 25, No. 2 (Spring 2002):441–57.

HIGHTOWER, JIM. *Eat Your Heart Out: Food Profiteering in America.* New York: Crown, 1975.

HILL, MARK E. "Race of the Interviewer and Perception of Skin Color: Evidence from the Multi-City Study of Urban Inequality." *American Sociological Review.* Vol. 67, No. 1 (February 2002):99–108.

HIMES, CHRISTINE L. "Elderly Americans." *Population Bulletin.* Vol. 56, No. 4 (December 2001):3–40.

HIRSCHI, TRAVIS. *Causes of Delinquency.* Berkeley: University of California Press, 1969.

HOBERMAN, JOHN. *Darwin's Athletes: How Sport Has Damaged Black America and Preserved the Myth of Race.* Boston: Houghton Mifflin, 1997.

——— "Response to Three Reviews of *Darwin's Athletes.*" *Social Science Quarterly.* Vol. 79, No. 4 (December 1998):898–903.

HOBSON, KATHERINE. "Kissing Cousins." *U.S. News & World Report* (April 15, 2002):77.

HOCHSCHILD, ARLIE RUSSELL. "Emotion Work, Feeling Rules, and Social Structure." *American Journal of Sociology.* Vol. 85, No. 3 (November 1979): 551–75.

———. *The Managed Heart.* Berkeley: University of California Press, 1983.

HOFFERTH, SANDRA. "Did Welfare Reform Work? Implications for 2002 and Beyond." *Contexts.* Vol. 1, No. 1 (Spring 2002):45–51.

HOGAN, RICHARD, and CAROLYN C. PERRUCCI. "Producing and Reproducing the Class and Status Differences: Racial and Gender Gaps in U.S. Employment and Retirement Income." *Social Problems.* Vol. 45, No. 4 (November 1998): 528–49.

HOLMES, THOMAS H., and RICHARD H. RAHE. "The Social Readjustment Rating Scale." *Journal of Psychosomatic Research.* Vol. 11 (1967):213-18.

HOLMSTROM, DAVID. "Abuse of Elderly, Even by Adult Children, Gets More Attention and Official Concern." *Christian Science Monitor* (July 28, 1994):1.

HONEYWELL, ROY J. *The Educational Work of Thomas Jefferson.* Cambridge, Mass.: Harvard University Press, 1931.

HOPE, TRINA L., HAROLD G. GRASMICK, and LAURA J. POINTON. "The Family in Gottfredson and Hrischi's General Theory of Crime: Structure, Parenting, and Self-Control." *Sociological Focus.* Vol. 36, No. 4 (November 2003): 291–311.

HORN, WADE F., and DOUGLAS TYNAN. "Revamping Special Education." *Public Interest.* No. 144 (Summer 2001):36–53.

HOROWITZ, IRVING LOUIS. *The Decomposition of Sociology.* New York: Oxford University Press, 1993.

HORTON, HAYWARD DERRICK. "Critical Demography: The Paradigm of the Future?" *Sociological Forum.* Vol. 14, No. 3 (September 1999):363–67.

HOSTETLER, JOHN A. *Amish Society.* 3rd ed. Baltimore: Johns Hopkins University Press, 1980.

HOUT, MICHAEL. "More Universalism, Less Structural Mobility: The American Occupational Structure in the 1980s." *American Journal of Sociology*. Vol. 95, No. 6 (May 1998):1358–1400.

HOUT, MICHAEL, CLEM BROOKS, and JEFF MANZA. "The Persistence of Classes in Post-Industrial Societies." *International Sociology*. Vol. 8, No. 3 (September 1993):259–77.

HOUT, MICHAEL, and CLAUDE S. FISHER. "Why More Americans Have No Religious Preference: Politics and Generations." *American Sociological Review*. Vol. 67, No. 2 (April 2002):165–90.

HOUT, MICHAEL, ANDREW M. GREELEY, and MELISSA J. WILDE. "The Demographic Imperative in Religious Change in the United States." *American Journal of Sociology*. Vol. 107, No. 2 (September 2001):468–500.

HOYERT, DONNA L., HSIANG-CHING KUNG, and BETTY L. SMITH. "Deaths: Preliminary Data for 2003." *National Vital Statistics Report*. Vol. 53, No. 15 (February 28, 2005).

HOYT, HOMER. *The Structure and Growth of Residential Neighborhoods in American Cities*. Washington, D.C.: Federal Housing Administration, 1939.

HSU, FRANCIS L. K. *The Challenge of the American Dream: The Chinese in the United States*. Belmont, Calif.: Wadsworth, 1971.

HUCHINGSON, JAMES E. "Science and Religion." *Miami* (Fla.) *Herald* (December 25, 1994):1M, 6M.

HUFFMAN, KAREN. *Psychology in Action*. New York: Wiley, 2000.

HUGHES, MICHAEL, and MELVIN E. THOMAS. "The Continuing Significance of Race Revisited: A Study of Race, Class, and Quality of Life in America, 1972 to 1996." *American Sociological Review*. Vol. 63, No. 6 (December 1998): 785–95.

HUMAN RIGHTS WATCH. "Children's Rights: Child Labor." 2004. [Online] Available August 29, 2005, at http://www.hrw.org/children/labor.htm

HUMMER, ROBERT A., RICHARD G. ROGERS, CHARLES B. NAM, and FELICIA B. LE CLERE. "Race/Ethnicity, Nativity, and U.S. Adult Mortality." *Social Science Quarterly*. Vol. 80, No. 1 (March 1999):136–53.

HUNTER, JAMES DAVISON. *American Evangelicalism: Conservative Religion and the Quandary of Modernity*. New Brunswick, N.J.: Rutgers University Press, 1983.

———. "Conservative Protestantism." In PHILIP E. HAMMOND, ed., *The Sacred in a Secular Age*. Berkeley: University of California Press, 1985:50–66.

———. *Evangelicalism: The Coming Generation*. Chicago: University of Chicago Press, 1987.

HYMOWITZ, CAROL. "World's Poorest Women Advance by Entrepreneurship." *Wall Street Journal* (September 9, 1995):B1.

HYMOWITZ, KAY S. "Kids Today Are Growing Up Way Too Fast." *Wall Street Journal* (October 28, 1998):A22.

———. "What to Tell the Kids about Sex." *Public Interest*. No. 153 (Fall 2003): 3–18.

IANNACCONE, LAURENCE R. "Why Strict Churches Are Strong." *American Journal of Sociology*. Vol. 99, No. 5 (March 1994):1180–1211.

IDE, THOMAS R., and ARTHUR J. CORDELL. "Automating Work." *Society*. Vol. 31, No. 6 (September/October 1994):65–71.

INCIARDI, JAMES A. *Elements of Criminal Justice*. 2nd ed. New York: Oxford University Press, 2000.

INCIARDI, JAMES A., HILARY L. SURRATT, and PAULO R. TELLES. *Sex, Drugs, and HIV/AIDS in Brazil*. Boulder, Colo.: Westview Press, 2000.

INGLEHART, RONALD. *Modernization and Postmodernization: Cultural, Economic, and Political Change in 43 Societies*. Princeton, N.J.: Princeton University Press, 1997.

INGLEHART, RONALD, et al. *World Values Surveys and European Values Surveys, 1981–1984, 1990–1993, and 1995–1997*. Computer file. Ann Arbor, Mich.: Interuniversity Consortium for Political and Social Research, 2000.

INGLEHART, RONALD, and WAYNE E. BAKER. "Modernization, Cultural Change, and the Persistence of Traditional Values." *American Sociological Review*. Vol. 65, No. 1 (February 2000):19–51.

INTERNAL REVENUE SERVICE. "Personal Wealth, 1998." *Statistics of Income Bulletin* (April 2003):88.

———. "Corporation Income Tax Returns, 2001." *Statistics of Income Bulletin* (September 2004). [Online] Available November 3, 2004, at http://www.irs.gov/pub/irs-soi/01corart.pdf

INTERNATIONAL LABOUR ORGANISATION. *World Labour Report, 1997–98*. "Table 1.2. Trade Union Density." Rev. November 1, 2002. [Online] Available October 9, 2004, at http://www.ilo.org/public/english/dialogue/ifpdial/publ/wlr97/annex/tab12.htm

INTERNATIONAL MONETARY FUND. *World Economic Outlook*. April 2000. [Online] Available http://www.imf.org/external/pubs/ft/weo/2000/01/index.htm

INTERNATIONAL TELECOMMUNICATION UNION. *World Telecommunication Development Report*. Data cited in WORLD BANK, *2005 World Development Indicators*. Washington, D.C.: World Bank, 2005.

INTER-PARLIAMENTARY UNION. "Women in National Parliaments." 2005. [Online] Available June 25, 2005, at http://www.ipu.org/wmn-e/classif.htm and http://www.ipu.org/wmn-e/world.htm

ISRAEL, GLENN D., LIONEL J. BEAULIEU, and GLEN HARTLESS. "The Influence of Family and Community Social Capital on Educational Achievement." *Rural Sociology*. Vol. 66, No. 1 (March 2001):43–68.

ISRAELY, JEFF. "Something in the Air." *Time* (December 9, 2002):16.

JACOBS, DAVID, and JASON T. CARMICHAEL. "The Political Sociology of the Death Penalty: A Pooled Time-Series Analysis." *American Sociological Review*. Vol. 67, No. 1 (February 2002):109–31.

JACOBS, DAVID, and RONALD E. HELMS. "Toward a Political Model of Incarceration: A Time-Series Examination of Multiple Explanations for Prison Admission Rates." *American Journal of Sociology*. Vol. 102, No. 2 (September 1996):323–57.

JACOBSON, JENNIFER. "Professors Are Finding Better Pay and More Freedom at Community Colleges." *Chronicle of Higher Education Online*. 2003. [Online] Available March 7, 2003, at http://chronicle.com

JACOBY, RUSSELL, and NAOMI GLAUBERMAN, eds. *The Bell Curve Debate*. New York: Random House, 1995.

JACQUET, CONSTANT H., and ALICE M. JONES. *Yearbook of American and Canadian Churches, 1991*. Nashville, Tenn.: Abingdon Press, 1991.

JAMES, DAVID R. "City Limits on Racial Equality: The Effects of City-Suburb Boundaries on Public School Desegregation, 1968–1976." *American Sociological Review*. Vol. 54, No. 6 (December 1989):963–85.

JANIS, IRVING L. *Victims of Groupthink*. Boston: Houghton Mifflin, 1972.

———. *Crucial Decisions: Leadership in Policymaking and Crisis Management*. New York: Free Press, 1989.

JAPANESE MINISTRY OF HEALTH, LABOUR, AND WELFARE. STATISTICS AND INFORMATION DEPARTMENT. *International Comparisons of Divorce Rates*. [Online] Available July 18, 2005, at http://web-jpn.org/stat/stats/02VIT33.html

JASPER, JAMES M. "The Emotions of Protest: Affective and Reactive Emotions in and around Social Movements." *Sociological Forum*. Vol. 13, No. 3 (September 1998):397–424.

JENKINS, J. CRAIG. *Images of Terror: What We Can and Can't Know about Terrorism*. Hawthorne, N.Y.: Aldine de Gruyter, 2003.

JENKINS, J. CRAIG, DAVID JACOBS, and JON AGONE. "Political Opportunities and African-American Protest, 1948–1997." *American Journal of Sociology*. Vol. 109, No. 2 (September 2003):277–303.

JENKINS, J. CRAIG, and CHARLES PERROW. "Insurgency of the Powerless: Farm Worker Movements, 1946–1972." *American Sociological Review*. Vol. 42, No. 2 (April 1977):249–68.

JENKINS, J. CRAIG, and MICHAEL WALLACE. "The Generalized Action Potential of Protest Movements: The New Class, Social Trends, and Political Exclusion Explanations." *Sociological Forum*. Vol. 11, No. 2 (June 1996):183–207.

JENNESS, VALERIE, and RYKEN GRATTET. *Making a Hate Crime: From Movement to Law Enforcement*. New York: Russell Sage Foundation, 2001.

JOHNSON, CATHRYN. "Gender, Legitimate Authority, and Leader-Subordinate Conversations." *American Sociological Review*. Vol. 59, No. 1 (February 1994):122–35.

JOHNSON, DIRK. "Death of a Small Town." *Newsweek* (September 10, 2001): 30–31.

JOHNSON, KENNETH M. "The Rural Rebound." *Population Reference Bureau Reports on America*. Vol. 1, No. 3 (September 1999). [Online] Available October 9, 2004, at http://www.prb.org/Content/NavigationMenu/PRB/About PRB/Reports_on_America/ReportonAmericaRuralRebound.pdf

JOHNSON, KENNETH M., and GLENN V. FUGUITT. "Continuity and Change in Rural Migration Patterns, 1950–1995." *Rural Sociology*. Vol. 65, No. 1 (March 2000):27–49.

JOHNSON, PAUL. "The Seven Deadly Sins of Terrorism." In BENJAMIN NETANYAHU, ed., *International Terrorism*. New Brunswick, N.J.: Transaction Books, 1981:12–22.

JOHNSTON, DAVID CAY. "Voting, America's Not Keen On. Coffee Is Another Matter." *New York Times* (November 10, 1996):sec. 4, p. 2.

JOHNSTON, R. J. "Residential Area Characteristics." In D. T. HERBERT and R. J. JOHNSTON, eds., *Social Areas in Cities. Vol. 1: Spatial Processes and Form*. New York: Wiley, 1976:193–235.

JONES, ANDREW E. G., and DAVID WILSON. *The Urban Growth Machine: Critical Perspectives*. Albany: State University of New York Press, 1999.

JONES, D. GARETH. "Brain Death." *Journal of Medical Ethics*. Vol. 24, No. 4 (August 1998):237–43.

JONES, JUDY. "More Miners Will Be Offered Free X-Rays; Federal Agency Wants to Monitor Black-Lung Cases." *Louisville Courier Journal* (May 13, 1999):1A.

JONES, KATHARINE W. *Accent on Privilege: English Identities and Anglophilia in the U.S.* Philadelphia: Temple University Press, 2001.

JORDAN, ELLEN, and ANGELA COWAN. "Warrior Narratives in the Kindergarten Classroom: Renegotiating the Social Contract?" *Gender and Society.* Vol. 9, No. 6 (December 1995):727–43.

JORDAN, MARY. "New Factors Sustain Age-Old Ritual." *Washington Post* (March 31, 1998):A12.

JOSEPHY, ALVIN M., JR. *Now That the Buffalo's Gone: A Study of Today's American Indians.* New York: Knopf, 1982.

JOYNSON, ROBERT B. "Fallible Judgments." *Society.* Vol. 31, No. 3 (March/April 1994):45–52.

KADLEC, DANIEL. "Everyone, Back in the (Labor) Pool." *Time* (July 29, 2002):22–31.

KAIN, EDWARD L. "A Note on the Integration of AIDS into the Sociology of Human Sexuality." *Teaching Sociology.* Vol. 15, No. 4 (July 1987):320–23.

———. *The Myth of Family Decline: Understanding Families in a World of Rapid Social Change.* Lexington, Mass.: Lexington Books, 1990.

KALLEBERG, ARNE L., BARBARA F. RESKIN, and KEN HUDSON. "Bad Jobs in America: Standard and Nonstandard Employment Relations and Job Quality in the United States." *American Sociological Review.* Vol. 65, No 2 (April 2000): 256–78.

KALLEBERG, ARNE L., and MARK E. VAN BUREN. "Is Bigger Better? Explaining the Relationship between Organization Size and Job Rewards." *American Sociological Review.* Vol. 61, No. 1 (February 1996):47–66.

KAMINER, WENDY. "Volunteers: Who Knows What's in It for Them?" *Ms.* (December 1984):93–96, 126–28.

———. "Demasculinizing the Army." *New York Times Review of Books* (June 15, 1997):7.

KANE, EMILY W. "Racial and Ethnic Variations in Gender-Related Attitudes." *Annual Review of Sociology.* Vol. 26 (2000):419–39.

KANTER, ROSABETH MOSS. *Men and Women of the Corporation.* New York: Basic Books, 1977.

KANTER, ROSABETH MOSS, and BARRY A. STEIN. "The Gender Pioneers: Women in an Industrial Sales Force." In ROSABETH MOSS KANTER and BARRY A. STEIN, eds., *Life in Organizations.* New York: Basic Books, 1979:134–60.

KANTROWITZ, BARBARA, and PAT WINGERT. "Unmarried with Children." *Newsweek* (May 28, 2001):46–52.

———. "What's at Stake." *Newsweek* (January 27, 2003):30–37.

KAO, GRACE. "Group Images and Possible Selves among Adolescents: Linking Stereotypes to Expectations by Race and Ethnicity." *Sociological Forum.* Vol. 15, No. 3 (September 2000):407–30.

KAPFERER, JEAN-NOEL. "How Rumors Are Born." *Society.* Vol. 29, No. 5 (July/August 1992):53–60.

KAPLAN, DAVID E., and MICHAEL SCHAFFER. "Losing the Psywar." *U.S. News & World Report* (October 8, 2001):46.

KAPTCHUK, TED. "The Holistic Logic of Chinese Medicine." In BERKELEY HOLISTIC HEALTH CENTER, *The New Holistic Health Handbook: Living Well in a New Age.* SHEPARD BLISS et al., eds. Lexington, Mass.: Steven Greene Press, 1985:41.

KARATNYCKY, ADRIAN. "The 2001–2002 Freedom House Survey of Freedom: The Democracy Gap." In *Freedom in the World: The Annual Survey of Political Rights and Civil Liberties, 2001–2002.* New York: Freedom House, 2002: 7–18.

KARP, DAVID A., and WILLIAM C. YOELS. "The College Classroom: Some Observations on the Meaning of Student Participation." *Sociology and Social Research.* Vol. 60, No. 4 (July 1976):421–39.

KARRFALT, WAYNE. "A Multicultural Mecca." *American Demographics.* Vol. 25, No. 4 (May 2003):54–55.

KATES, ROBERT W. "Ending Hunger: Current Status and Future Prospects." *Consequences.* Vol. 2, No. 2 (Summer 1996):3–11.

KAUFMAN, LESLIE. "Surge in Homeless Families Sets Off Debate on Cause." *New York Times* (July 29, 2004). [Online] Available March 24, 2005, at http://www.researchnavigator.com

KAUFMAN, MICHAEL T. "Face It: Your Looks Are Revealing." *New York Times* (2002).

KAUFMAN, ROBERT L. "Assessing Alternative Perspectives on Race and Sex Employment Segregation." *American Sociological Review.* Vol. 67, No. 4 (August 2002):547–72.

KAUFMAN, WALTER. *Religions in Four Dimensions: Existential, Aesthetic, Historical, and Comparative.* New York: Reader's Digest Press, 1976.

KAY, PAUL, and WILLETT KEMPTON. "What Is the Sapir-Whorf Hypothesis?" *American Anthropologist.* Vol. 86, No. 1 (March 1984):65–79.

KEISTER, LISA A. *Wealth in America: Trends in Wealth Inequality.* Cambridge: Cambridge University Press, 2000.

———. "Religion and Wealth: The Role of Religious Affiliation and Participation in Early Adult Asset Accumulation." *Social Forces.* Vol. 82, No. 1 (September 2003):175–207.

KEISTER, LISA A., and STEPHANIE MOLLER. "Wealth Inequality in the United States." *Annual Review of Sociology.* Vol. 26 (2000):63–81.

KELLER, HELEN. *The Story of My Life.* New York: Doubleday Page, 1903.

KELLERT, STEPHEN R., and F. HERBERT BORMANN. "Closing the Circle: Weaving Strands among Ecology, Economics, and Ethics." In F. HERBERT BORMANN and STEPHEN R. KELLERT, eds., *Ecology, Economics, and Ethics: The Broken Circle.* New Haven, Conn.: Yale University Press, 1991:205–10.

KENT, MARY M., and MARK MATHER. "What Drives U.S. Population Growth?" *Population Bulletin.* Vol. 57, No. 4 (December 2002):3–40.

KENTOR, JEFFREY. "The Long-Term Effects of Foreign Investment Dependence on Economic Growth, 1940–1990." *American Journal of Sociology.* Vol. 103, No. 4 (January 1998):1024–46.

———. "The Long-Term Effects of Globalization on Income Inequality, Population Growth, and Economic Development." *Social Problems.* Vol. 48, No. 4 (November 2001):435–55.

KERCKHOFF, ALAN C., RICHARD T. CAMPBELL, and IDEE WINFIELD-LAIRD. "Social Mobility in Great Britain and the United States." *American Journal of Sociology.* Vol. 91, No. 2 (September 1985):281–308.

KERR, RICHARD A. "Climate Models Heat Up." *Science Now* (January 26, 2005):1–3.

KEYS, JENNIFER. "Feeling Rules That Script the Abortion Experience." Paper presented at the annual meeting of the American Sociological Association, Chicago, August 2002.

KIDRON, MICHAEL, and RONALD SEGAL. *The New State of the World Atlas.* New York: Simon & Schuster, 1991.

KILBOURNE, BROCK K. "The Conway and Siegelman Claims against Religious Cults: An Assessment of Their Data." *Journal for the Scientific Study of Religion.* Vol. 22, No. 4 (December 1983):380–85.

KILGORE, SALLY B. "The Organizational Context of Tracking in Schools." *American Sociological Review.* Vol. 56, No. 2 (April 1991):189–203.

KING, KATHLEEN PIKER, and DENNIS E. CLAYSON. "The Differential Perceptions of Male and Female Deviants." *Sociological Focus.* Vol. 21, No. 2 (April 1988): 153–64.

KINKEAD, GWEN. *Chinatown: A Portrait of a Closed Society.* New York: Harper-Collins, 1992.

KINSEY, ALFRED, WARDELL BAXTER POMEROY, and CLYDE E. MARTIN. *Sexual Behavior in the Human Male.* Philadelphia: Saunders, 1948.

KINSEY, ALFRED, WARDELL BAXTER POMEROY, CLYDE E. MARTIN, and PAUL H. GEBHARD. *Sexual Behavior in the Human Female.* Philadelphia: Saunders, 1953.

KITTRIE, NICHOLAS N. *The Right to Be Different: Deviance and Enforced Therapy.* Baltimore: Johns Hopkins University Press, 1971.

KLEIN, DANIEL B., and CHARLOTTA STERN. "How Politically Diverse Are the Social Sciences and Humanities? Survey Evidence from Six Fields." National Association of Scholars. 2004. [Online] Available January 13, 2005, at http://www.nas.org/aa/klein_launch.htm

KLUCKHOHN, CLYDE. "As an Anthropologist Views It." In ALBERT DEUTH, ed., *Sex Habits of American Men.* New York: Prentice Hall, 1948.

KNOX, NOELLE. "European Gay Union Trends Influence U.S. Debate." *USA Today* (July 14, 2004):5A.

KOCHANEK, KENNETH D., et al. "Deaths: Final Data for 2002." *National Vital Statistics Report.* Vol. 53, No. 5 (October 12, 2004). Hyattsville, Md.: National Center for Health Statistics.

KOELLN, KENNETH, ROSE M. RUBIN, and MARION SMITH PICARD. "Vulnerable Elderly Households: Expenditures on Necessities by Older Americans." *Social Science Quarterly.* Vol. 76, No. 3 (September 1995):619–33.

KOHLBERG, LAWRENCE. *The Psychology of Moral Development: The Nature and Validity of Moral Stages.* New York: Harper & Row, 1981.

KOHLBERG, LAWRENCE, and CAROL GILLIGAN. "The Adolescent as Philosopher: The Discovery of Self in a Postconventional World." *Daedalus.* No. 100 (Fall 1971):1051–86.

KOHN, MELVIN L. *Class and Conformity: A Study in Values.* 2nd ed. Homewood, Ill.: Dorsey Press, 1977.

———. "The 'Bell Curve' from the Perspective of Research on Social Structure and Personality." *Sociological Forum.* Vol. 11, No. 2 (1996):395.

KOLATA, GINA. "When Grandmother Is the Mother, Until Birth." *New York Times* (August 5, 1991):1, 11.

KONO, CLIFFORD, DONALD PALMER, ROGER FRIEDLAND, and MATTHEW ZAFONTE. "Lost in Space: The Geography of Corporate Interlocking Directorates." *American Journal of Sociology*. Vol. 103, No. 4 (January 1998):863–911.

KOONTZ, STEPHANIE. *The Way We Never Were: American Families and the Nostalgia Trap*. New York: Basic Books, 1992.

KORNHAUSER, WILLIAM. *The Politics of Mass Society*. New York: Free Press, 1959.

KORZENIEWICZ, ROBERTO P., and KIMBERLY AWBREY. "Democratic Transitions and the Semiperiphery of the World Economy." *Sociological Forum*. Vol. 7, No. 4 (December 1992):609–40.

KOSTERS, MARVIN. "Looking for Jobs in All the Wrong Places." *Public Interest*. No. 125 (Fall 1996):125–31.

KOZOL, JONATHAN. *Rachel and Her Children: Homeless Families in America*. New York: Crown, 1988.

———. *Savage Inequalities: Children in America's Schools*. New York: Harper Perennial, 1992.

KRAL, BRIGITTA. "The Eyes of Jane Elliott." *Horizon Magazine*. 2000. [Online] Available June 8, 2005, at http://www.horizonmag.com/4/jane-elliott.asp

KRAYBILL, DONALD B. *The Riddle of Amish Culture*. Baltimore: Johns Hopkins University Press, 1989.

———. "The Amish Encounter with Modernity." In DONALD B. KRAYBILL and MARC A. OLSHAN, eds., *The Amish Struggle with Modernity*. Hanover, N.H.: University Press of New England, 1994:21–33.

KRAYBILL, DONALD B., and MARC A. OLSHAN, eds. *The Amish Struggle with Modernity*. Hanover, N.H.: University Press of New England, 1994.

KRUEGER, PATRICK M., RICHARD G. ROGERS, ROBERT A. HUMMER, FELICIA B. LECLERE, and STEPHANIE A. BOND HUIE. "Socioeconomic Status and Age: The Effect of Income Sources and Portfolios on U.S. Adult Maturity." *Sociological Forum*. Vol. 18, No. 3 (September 2003):465–82.

KRUGMAN, PAUL. "For Richer: How the Permissive Capitalism of the Boom Destroyed American Equality." *New York Times Magazine* (September 20, 2002):62–67, 76–77, 141–42.

KRUKS, GABRIEL N. "Gay and Lesbian Homeless/Street Youth: Special Issues and Concerns." *Journal of Adolescent Health*. Special Issue. No. 12 (1991): 515–18.

KRYSAN, MARIA. "Community Undesirability in Black and White: Examining Racial Residential Preferences through Community Perceptions." *Social Problems*. Vol. 49, No. 4 (November 2002):521–43.

KÜBLER-ROSS, ELISABETH. *On Death and Dying*. New York: Macmillan, 1969.

KUTTNER, ROBERT. "Targeting Cheats." *American Prospect Online* (March 26, 2004). [Online] Available April 23, 2005, at http://www.prospect.org/webfeatures/2004

KUUMBA, M. BAHATI. "A Cross-Cultural Race/Class/Gender Critique of Contemporary Population Policy: The Impact of Globalization." *Sociological Forum*. Vol. 14, No. 3 (March 1999):447–63.

KUZNETS, SIMON. "Economic Growth and Income Inequality." *American Economic Review*. Vol. 14, No. 1 (March 1955):1–28.

———. *Modern Economic Growth: Rate, Structure, and Spread*. New Haven, Conn.: Yale University Press, 1966.

LACAYO, RICHARD. "The Brawl over Sprawl." *Time* (March 22, 1999):44–48.

———. "Blood at the Root." *Time* (April 10, 2000):122–23.

LACH, JENNIFER. "The Color of Money." *American Demographics*. Vol. 21, No. 2 (February 1999):59–60.

LADD, JOHN. "The Definition of Death and the Right to Die." In JOHN LADD, ed., *Ethical Issues Relating to Life and Death*. New York: Oxford University Press, 1979:118–45.

LAI, H. M. "Chinese." In *Harvard Encyclopedia of American Ethnic Groups*. Cambridge, Mass.: Harvard University Press, 1980:217–33.

LANDSBERG, MITCHELL. "Health Disaster Brings Early Death in Russia." *Washington Times* (March 15, 1998):A8.

LANGBEIN, LAURA I., and ROSEANA BESS. "Sports in School: Source of Amity or Antipathy?" *Social Science Quarterly*. Vol. 83, No. 2 (June 2002):436–54.

LAPCHICK, RICHARD. *The 2004 Racial and Gender Report Cards*. Institute for Diversity and Ethics in Sport, University of Central Florida. 2005. [Online] Available July 6, 2005, at http://www.bus.ucf.edu/sport/cgi-bin/site/sitew.cgi?page=/news/index.htx

LAPPÉ, FRANCES MOORE, and JOSEPH COLLINS. *World Hunger: Twelve Myths*. New York: Grove Press/Food First Books, 1986.

LAPPÉ, FRANCES MOORE, JOSEPH COLLINS, and PETER ROSSET. *World Hunger: Twelve Myths*. 2nd ed. New York: Grove Press, 1998.

LAREAU, ANNETTE. "Invisible Inequality: Social Class and Childrearing in Black Families and White Families." *American Sociological Review*. Vol. 67, No. 5 (October 2002):747–76.

LAROSSA, RALPH, and DONALD C. REITZES. "Two? Two and One-Half? Thirty Months? Chronometrical Childhood in Early Twentieth-Century America." *Sociological Forum*. Vol. 166, No. 3 (September 2001):385–407.

LARSON, GERALD JAMES. "Hinduism in India and in America." In JACOB NEUSNER, ed., *World Religions in America: An Introduction*. Louisville, Ky.: Westminster John Knox Press, 2000:124–41.

LASLETT, BARBARA. "Family Membership, Past and Present." *Social Problems*. Vol. 25, No. 5 (June 1978):476–90.

LASLETT, PETER. *The World We Have Lost: England before the Industrial Age*. 3rd ed. New York: Scribner, 1984.

LASSWELL, MARK. "A Tribe at War: Not the Yanomami, the Anthropologists." *Wall Street Journal* (November 17, 2000):A17.

LAUMANN, EDWARD O., JOHN H. GAGNON, ROBERT T. MICHAEL, and STUART MICHAELS. *The Social Organization of Sexuality: Sexual Practices in the United States*. Chicago: University of Chicago Press, 1994.

LAVELLE, MARIANNE. "Payback Time." *U.S. News & World Report* (March 11, 2002):36–40.

LAVIN, DANIELLE, and DOUGLAS W. MAYNARD. "Standardization vs. Rapport: Respondent Laughter and Interviewer Reaction during Telephone Surveys." *American Sociological Review*. Vol. 66, No. 3 (June 2001):453–79.

LEACH, COLIN WAYNE. "Democracy's Dilemma: Explaining Racial Inequality in Egalitarian Societies." *Sociological Forum*. Vol. 17, No. 4 (December 2002): 681–96.

LEACOCK, ELEANOR. "Women's Status in Egalitarian Societies: Implications for Social Evolution." *Current Anthropology*. Vol. 19, No. 2 (June 1978):247–75.

LEAVITT, JUDITH WALZER. "Women and Health in America: An Overview." In JUDITH WALZER LEAVITT, ed., *Women and Health in America*. Madison: University of Wisconsin Press, 1984:3–7.

LE BON, GUSTAVE. *The Crowd: A Study of the Popular Mind*. New York: Viking Press, 1960; orig. 1895.

LEE, FELICIA R. "Long Buried, Death Goes Public Again." *New York Times* (2002). [Online] Available November 2, 2002, at http://www.researchnavigator.com

LEE, SHARON M., and BARRY EDMONSTON. "New Marriages, New Families: U.S. Racial and Hispanic Intermarriage." *Population Bulletin*. Vol. 60, No. 2 (June 2005):3–36

LEFEBVRE, HENRI. *The Production of Space*. Oxford: Blackwell, 1991.

LELAND, JOHN. "Bisexuality." *Newsweek* (July 17, 1995):44–49.

LEMERT, EDWIN M. *Social Pathology*. New York: McGraw-Hill, 1951.

———. *Human Deviance, Social Problems, and Social Control*. 2nd ed. Englewood Cliffs, N.J.: Prentice Hall, 1972.

LEMONICK, MICHAEL D. "The Search for a Murder Gene." *Time* (January 20, 2003):100.

LENGERMANN, PATRICIA MADOO, and JILL NIEBRUGGE-BRANTLEY. *The Women Founders: Sociology and Social Theory, 1830–1930*. New York: McGraw-Hill, 1998.

LENGERMANN, PATRICIA MADOO, and RUTH A. WALLACE. *Gender in America: Social Control and Social Change*. Englewood Cliffs, N.J.: Prentice Hall, 1985.

LENSKI, GERHARD E. *Power and Privilege: A Theory of Social Stratification*. New York: McGraw-Hill, 1966.

LENSKI, GERHARD E., PATRICK NOLAN, and JEAN LENSKI. *Human Societies: An Introduction to Macrosociology*. 7th ed. New York: McGraw-Hill, 1995.

LEONARD, EILEEN B. *Women, Crime, and Society: A Critique of Theoretical Criminology*. White Plains, N.Y.: Longman, 1982.

LETHBRIDGE-ÇEJKU, MARGARET, and JACKLINE VICKERIE. *Summary Health Statistics for U.S. Adults: National Health Interview Survey, 2003*. Vital and Health Statistics, Series 10, No. 225. Hyattsville, Md.: National Center for Health Statistics, 2005.

LETSCHER, MARTIN. "Tell Fads from Trends." *American Demographics*. Vol. 16, No. 12 (December 1994):38–45.

LEVAY, SIMON. *The Sexual Brain*. Cambridge, Mass.: MIT Press, 1993.

LEVER, JANET. "Sex Differences in the Complexity of Children's Play and Games." *American Sociological Review*. Vol. 43, No. 4 (August 1978):471–83.

LEVIN, JACK, and ARNOLD ARLUKE. *Gossip: The Inside Scoop*. New York: Plenum, 1987.

———. *Student Eating Disorders: Anorexia Nervosa and Bulimia*. Washington, D.C.: National Educational Association, 1987.

LEVINE, MICHAEL P. "Reducing Hostility Can Prevent Heart Disease." *Mount Vernon (Ohio) News* (August 7, 1990):4A.

LEVINE, SAMANTHA. "The Price of Child Abuse." *U.S. News & World Report* (April 9, 2001):58.

————. "Playing God in Illinois." *U.S. News & World Report* (January 13, 2003):13.

LEWIS, OSCAR. *The Children of Sachez.* New York: Random House, 1961.

LIAZOS, ALEXANDER. "The Poverty of the Sociology of Deviance: Nuts, Sluts, and Preverts." *Social Problems.* Vol. 20, No. 1 (Summer 1972):103–20.

————. *People First: An Introduction to Social Problems.* Needham Heights, Mass.: Allyn & Bacon, 1982.

LICHTER, DANIEL T., and MARTHA L. CROWLEY. "Poverty in America: Beyond Welfare Reform." *Population Bulletin.* Vol. 57, No. 2 (June 2002):3–34.

LICHTER, DANIEL T., and RUKMALIE JAYAKODY. "Welfare Reform: How Do We Measure Success?" *Annual Review of Sociology.* Vol. 28 (2002):117–41.

LICHTER, S. ROBERT, and DANIEL R. AMUNDSON. "Distorted Reality: Hispanic Characters in TV Entertainment." In CLARA E. RODRIGUEZ, ed., *Latin Looks: Images of Latinas and Latinos in the U.S. Media.* Boulder, Colo.: Westview Press, 1997:57–79.

LICHTER, S. ROBERT, STANLEY ROTHMAN, and LINDA S. LICHTER. *The Media Elite: America's New Powerbrokers.* New York: Hastings House, 1990.

LIN, GE, and PETER ROGERSON. Research reported in DIANE CRISPELL, "Sons and Daughters Who Keep in Touch." *American Demographics.* Vol. 16, No. 8 (August 1994):15–16.

LIN, NAN, KAREN COOK, and RONALD S. BURT, eds. *Social Capital: Theory and Research.* Hawthorne, N.Y.: Aldine de Gruyter, 2001.

LIN, NAN, and WEN XIE. "Occupational Prestige in Urban China." *American Journal of Sociology.* Vol. 93, No. 4 (January 1988):793–832.

LINDAUER, DAVID L., and AKILA WEERAPANA. "Relief for Poor Nations." *Society.* Vol. 39, No. 3 (March/April 2002):54–58.

LINDLAW, SCOTT. "President Signs Education Bill." 2002. [Online] Available January 8, 2002, at http://news.yahoo.com

LINDSTROM, BONNIE. "Chicago's Post-Industrial Suburbs." *Sociological Focus.* Vol. 28, No. 4 (October 1995):399–412.

LING, PYAU. "Causes of Chinese Emigration." In AMY TACHIKI et al., eds., *Roots: An Asian American Reader.* Los Angeles: UCLA Asian American Studies Center, 1971:134–38.

LINN, MICHAEL. "Class Notes 1970." *Cornell Alumni News.* Vol. 99, No. 2 (September 1996):25.

LINO, MARK. *Expenditures on Children by Families, 2004.* U.S. Department of Agriculture, Center for Nutrition Policy and Promotion. Miscellaneous Publication No. 1528–2004. Washington, D.C.: U.S. Government Printing Office, 2005.

LINTON, RALPH. "One Hundred Percent American." *American Mercury.* Vol. 40, No. 160 (April 1937a):427–29.

————. *The Study of Man.* New York: Appleton-Century, 1937b.

LIPSET, SEYMOUR MARTIN. *Political Man: The Social Bases of Politics.* Garden City, N.Y.: Anchor/Doubleday, 1963.

————. "Canada and the United States." CHARLES F. DONAN and JOHN H. SIGLER, eds. Englewood Cliffs, N.J.: Prentice Hall, 1985.

LISKA, ALLEN E., and BARBARA D. WARNER. "Functions of Crime: A Paradoxical Process." *American Journal of Sociology.* Vol. 96, No. 6 (May 1991):1441–63.

LITTLE, CRAIG, and ANDREA RANKIN. "Why Do They Start It? Explaining Reported Early-Teen Sexual Activity." *Sociological Forum.* Vol. 16, No. 4 (December 2001):703–29.

LIVINGSTON, KEN. "Politics and Mental Illness." *Public Interest.* No. 143 (Winter, 1999):105–9.

LOBO, SUSAN. "Census-Taking and the Invisibility of Urban American Indians." *Population Today.* Vol. 30, No. 4 (May/June 2002):3–4.

LOFLAND, LYN. *A World of Strangers.* New York: Basic Books, 1973.

LOGAN, JOHN R., RICHARD D. ALBA, and WENQUAN ZHANG. "Immigrant Enclaves and Ethnic Communities in New York and Los Angeles." *American Sociological Review.* Vol. 67, No. 2 (April 2002):299–322.

LONGINO, CHARLES F., JR. "Myths of an Aging America." *American Demographics.* Vol. 16, No. 8 (August 1994):36–42.

LORD, MARY. "Good Teachers the Newest Imports." *U.S. News & World Report* (April 9, 2001):54.

————. "A Battle for Children's Futures." *U.S. News & World Report* (March 4, 2002):35–36.

LORD, WALTER. *A Night to Remember.* Rev. ed. New York: Holt, Rinehart and Winston, 1976.

LORENZ, FREDERICK O., and BRENT T. BRUTON. "Experiments in Surveys: Linking Mass Class Questionnaires to Introductory Research Methods." *Teaching Sociology.* Vol. 24, No. 3 (July 1996):264–71.

LOVEMAN, MARA. "Is 'Race' Essential?" *American Sociological Review.* Vol. 64, No. 6 (December 1999):890–98.

LOVGREN, STEFEN. "Will All the Blue Men End Up in Timbuktu?" *U.S. News & World Report* (December 7, 1998):40.

LUND, DALE A. "Conclusions about Bereavement in Later Life and Implications for Interventions and Future Research." In DALE A. LUND, ed., *Older Bereaved Spouses: Research with Practical Applications.* London: Taylor-Francis-Hemisphere, 1989:217–31.

————. "Caregiving." *Encyclopedia of Adult Development.* Phoenix, Ariz.: Oryx Press, 1993:57–63.

LUND, DALE A., MICHAEL S. CASERTA, and MARGARET F. DIMOND. "Gender Differences through Two Years of Bereavement among the Elderly." *Gerontologist.* Vol. 26, No. 3 (1986):314–20.

LUNDMAN, RICHARD L. Personal communication, 1999.

LYNCH, MICHAEL, and DAVID BOGEN. "Sociology's Asociological 'Core': An Examination of Textbook Sociology in Light of the Sociology of Scientific Knowledge." *American Sociological Review.* Vol. 62, No. 3 (June 1997):481–93.

LYND, ROBERT S., and HELEN MERRELL LYND. *Middletown in Transition.* New York: Harcourt, Brace & World, 1937.

LYNOTT, PATRICIA PASSUTH, and BARBARA J. LOGUE. "The 'Hurried Child': The Myth of Lost Childhood on Contemporary American Society." *Sociological Forum.* Vol. 8, No. 3 (September 1993):471–91.

MABRY, MARCUS, and TOM MASLAND. "The Man after Mandela." *Newsweek* (June 7, 1999):54–55.

MACCOBY, ELEANOR EMMONS, and CAROL NAGY JACKLIN. *The Psychology of Sex Differences.* Stanford, Calif.: Stanford University Press, 1974.

MACE, DAVID, and VERA MACE. *Marriage East and West.* Garden City, N.Y.: Doubleday/Dolphin, 1960.

MACIONIS, JOHN J. "Intimacy: Structure and Process in Interpersonal Relationships." *Alternative Lifestyles.* Vol. 1, No. 1 (February 1978):113–30.

————. "A Sociological Analysis of Humor." Presentation to the Texas Junior College Teachers Association, Houston, 1987.

————. *Social Problems.* 2nd ed. Upper Saddle River, N.J.: Prentice Hall, 2005.

MACIONIS, JOHN J., and LINDA GERBER. *Sociology* (5th Canadian ed.). Scarborough, Ontario: Prentice Hall Allyn & Bacon Canada, 2005.

MACIONIS, JOHN J., and VINCENT R. PARRILLO. *Cities and Urban Life.* 3rd ed. Upper Saddle River, N.J.: Prentice Hall, 2004.

MACKAY, JUDITH. *The Penguin Atlas of Human Sexual Behavior.* New York: Penguin, 2000.

MACPHERSON, KAREN. "Children Have a Full-Time Media Habit, Study Says." *Toledo Blade* (November 18, 1999):3.

MADDOX, SETMA. "Organizational Culture and Leadership Style: Factors Affecting Self-Managed Work Team Performance." Paper presented at the annual meeting of the Southwest Social Science Association, Dallas, February 1994.

MALTHUS, THOMAS ROBERT. *First Essay on Population 1798.* London: Macmillan, 1926; orig. 1798.

MANZA, JEFF, and CLEM BROOKS. "The Religious Factor in U.S. Presidential Elections, 1960–1992." *American Journal of Sociology.* Vol. 103, No. 1 (July 1997): 38–81.

MARATHONGUIDE. "Marathon Records." 2005. [Online] Available June 22, 2005, at http://www.marathonguide.com/#Records

MARCUSE, HERBERT. *One-Dimensional Man.* Boston: Beacon Press, 1964.

MARÍN, GERARDO, and BARBARA VAN OSS MARÍN. *Research with Hispanic Populations.* Newbury Park, Calif.: Sage, 1991.

MARKLEIN, MARY BETH. "Optimism Rises as SAT Math Scores Hit 30-Year High." *USA Today* (August 30, 2000):1A.

MARKOFF, JOHN. "Remember Big Brother? Now He's a Company Man." *New York Times* (March 31, 1991):7.

MARKS, ALEXANDRA. "U.S. Shelters Swell—with Families." *Christian Science Monitor* (2001). [Online] Available December 4, 2001, at http://www.csmonitor.com

MARQUAND, ROBERT. "Worship Shift: Americans Seek Feeling of 'Awe.'" *Christian Science Monitor* (May 28, 1997):1, 8.

MARQUAND, ROBERT, and DANIEL B. WOOD. "Rise in Cults as Millennium Approaches." *Christian Science Monitor* (March 28, 1997):1, 18.

MARQUARDT, ELIZABETH, and NORVAL GLENN. *Hooking Up, Hanging Out, and Hoping for Mr. Right.* New York: Institute for American Values, 2001.

MARSHALL, SUSAN E. "Ladies against Women: Mobilization Dilemmas of Antifeminist Movements." *Social Problems.* Vol. 32, No. 4 (April 1985):348–62.

MARTIN, CAROL LYNN, and RICHARD A. FABES. Research cited in MARIANNE SZEGEDY-MASZAK, "The Power of Gender." *U.S. News & World Report* (June 4, 2001):52.

MARTIN, JOHN M., and ANNE T. ROMANO. *Multinational Crime: Terrorism, Espionage, Drug and Arms Trafficking.* Newbury Park, Calif.: Sage, 1992.

MARTIN, JOYCE A., et al. "Births: Final Data for 2003." *National Vital Statistics Report.* Vol. 54, No. 2 (September 8, 2005). Hyattsville, Md.: National Center for Health Statistics.

MARTINEZ, RAMIRO, JR. "Latinos and Lethal Violence: The Impact of Poverty and Inequality." *Social Problems.* Vol. 43, No. 2 (May 1996):131–46.

MARULLO, SAM. "The Functions and Dysfunctions of Preparations for Fighting Nuclear War." *Sociological Focus.* Vol. 20, No. 2 (April 1987):135–53.

MARX, KARL. Excerpt from "A Contribution to the Critique of Political Economy." In KARL MARX and FRIEDRICH ENGELS, *Marx and Engels: Basic Writings on Politics and Philosophy.* LEWIS S. FEURER, ed. Garden City, N.Y.: Anchor Books, 1959:42–46.

———. *Karl Marx: Early Writings.* T. B. BOTTOMORE, ed. New York: McGraw-Hill, 1964.

———. *Capital.* FRIEDRICH ENGELS, ed. New York: International Publishers, 1967; orig. 1867.

MARX, KARL, and FRIEDRICH ENGELS. "Manifesto of the Communist Party." In ROBERT C. TUCKER, ed., *The Marx-Engels Reader.* New York: Norton, 1972:331–62; orig. 1848.

———. *The Marx-Engels Reader.* 2nd ed. ROBERT C. TUCKER, ed. New York: Norton, 1978; orig. 1859.

MARX, LEO. "The Environment and the 'Two Cultures' Divide." In JAMES RODGER FLEMING and HENRY A. GEMERY, eds., *Science, Technology, and the Environment: Multidisciplinary Perspectives.* Akron, Ohio: University of Akron Press, 1994:3–21.

MASSEY, DOUGLAS S. "Housing Discrimination 101." *Population Today.* Vol. 28, No. 6 (August/September 2000):1, 4.

MASSEY, DOUGLAS S., and NANCY A. DENTON. "Hypersegregation in U.S. Metropolitan Areas: Black and Hispanic Segregation along Five Dimensions." *Demography.* Vol. 26, No. 3 (August 1989):373–91.

MATHEWS, T. J., and BRADY E. HAMILTON. "Trend Analysis of the Sex Ratio at Birth in the United States." *National Vital Statistics Reports.* Vol. 53, No. 20 (June 14, 2005). Hyattsville, Md.: National Center for Health Statistics.

MATLOFF, JUDITH. "Nomadic 'Blue Men' of the Desert Try to Go Roam Again." *Christian Science Monitor* (September 9, 1997):7.

MATTHIESSEN, PETER. *Indian Country.* New York: Viking Press, 1984.

MAUER, MARC. *The Crisis of the Young African American Male and the Criminal Justice System.* Report prepared for U.S. Commission on Civil Rights. Washington, D.C., April 15–16, 1999. [Online] Available June 5, 2005, at http://www.sentencingproject.org/pdfs/5022.pdf

MAURO, TONY. "Ruling Likely Will Add Fuel to Already Divisive Debate." *USA Today* (January 7, 1997):1A, 2A.

MAUSS, ARMAND L. *Social Problems of Social Movements.* Philadelphia: Lippincott, 1975.

MAYO, KATHERINE. *Mother India.* New York: Harcourt, Brace, 1927.

MCADAM, DOUG. *Political Process and the Development of Black Insurgency, 1930–1970.* Chicago: University of Chicago Press, 1982.

———. "Tactical Innovation and the Pace of Insurgency." *American Sociological Review.* Vol. 48, No. 6 (December 1983):735–54.

———. *Freedom Summer.* New York: Oxford University Press, 1988.

———. "The Biographical Consequences of Activism." *American Sociological Review.* Vol. 54, No. 5 (October 1989):744–60.

———. "Gender as a Mediator of the Activist Experience: The Case of Freedom Summer." *American Journal of Sociology.* Vol. 97, No. 5 (March 1992):1211–40.

MCADAM, DOUG, JOHN D. MCCARTHY, and MAYER N. ZALD. "Social Movements." In NEIL J. SMELSER, ed., *Handbook of Sociology.* Newbury Park, Calif.: Sage, 1988: 695–737.

———, eds. *Comparative Perspectives on Social Movements: Political Opportunities, Mobilizing Structures, and Cultural Framings.* New York: Cambridge University Press, 1996.

MCBROOM, WILLIAM H., and FRED W. REED. "Recent Trends in Conservatism: Evidence of Non-Unitary Patterns." *Sociological Focus.* Vol. 23, No. 4 (October 1990):355–65.

MCCAFFREY, DAWN, and JENNIFER KEYS. "Competitive Framing Processes in the Abortion Debate: Polarization-Vilification, Frame Saving, and Frame Debunking." *Sociological Quarterly.* Vol. 41, No. 1 (Winter 2000):41–61.

MCCALL, WILLIAM. "Oregon Suicides More than Double." [Online] Available March 4, 2003, at http://news.yahoo.com

MCCARTHY, JOHN D., and MAYER N. ZALD. "Resource Mobilization and Social Movements: A Partial Theory." *American Journal of Sociology.* Vol. 82, No. 6 (May 1977):1212–41.

MCCARTNEY, SCOTT. "U.S. Mulls Raising Pilot Retirement Age." *Baltimore Sun* (February 28, 2005). [Online] Available April 16, 2005, at http://www.Baltimoresun.com

MCCOLM, R. BRUCE, et al. *Freedom in the World: Political Rights and Civil Liberties, 1990–1991.* New York: Freedom House, 1991.

MCDONALD, KIM A. "Debate over How to Gauge Global Warming Heats Up Meeting of Climatologists." *Chronicle of Higher Education.* Vol. 45, No. 22 (February 5, 1999):A17.

MCDONALD, PETER. "Low Fertility Not Politically Sustainable." *Population Today.* Vol. 29, No. 6 (August/September 2001):3, 8.

MCGUIRE, MEREDITH B. *Religion: The Social Context.* 2nd ed. Belmont, Calif.: Wadsworth, 1987.

MCGURN, WILLIAM. "Philadelphia Dims Edison's Light." *Wall Street Journal* (March 20, 2002):A22.

MCKEE, VICTORIA. "Blue Blood and the Color of Money." *New York Times* (June 9, 1996):49–50.

MCLANAHAN, SARA. "Life without Father: What Happens to the Children?" *Contexts.* Vol. 1, No. 1 (Spring 2002):35–44.

MCLEOD, JANE D., and MICHAEL J. SHANAHAN. "Poverty, Parenting, and Children's Mental Health." *American Sociological Review.* Vol. 58, No. 3 (June 1993):351–66.

MCLEOD, JAY. *Ain't No Makin' It: Aspirations and Attainment in a Low-Income Neighborhood.* Boulder, Colo.: Westview Press, 1995.

MCPHAIL, CLARK. *The Myth of the Maddening Crowd.* New York: Aldine, 1991.

MCPHAIL, CLARK, and RONALD T. WOHLSTEIN. "Individual and Collective Behaviors within Gatherings, Demonstrations, and Riots." *Annual Review of Sociology.* Vol. 9. Palo Alto, Calif.: Annual Reviews, 1983:579–600.

MEAD, GEORGE HERBERT. *Mind, Self, and Society.* CHARLES W. MORRIS, ed. Chicago: University of Chicago Press, 1962; orig. 1934.

MEAD, MARGARET. *Sex and Temperament in Three Primitive Societies.* New York: Morrow, 1963; orig. 1935.

MEADOWS, DONELLA H., DENNIS L. MEADOWS, JORGAN RANDERS, and WILLIAM W. BEHRENS III. *The Limits to Growth: A Report on the Club of Rome's Project on the Predicament of Mankind.* New York: Universe, 1972.

MELTZER, BERNARD N. "Mead's Social Psychology." In JEROME G. MANIS and BERNARD N. MELTZER, eds., *Symbolic Interaction: A Reader in Social Psychology.* 3rd ed. Needham Heights, Mass.: Allyn & Bacon, 1978.

MELUCCI, ALBERTO. *Nomads of the Present: Social Movements and Individual Needs in Contemporary Society.* Philadelphia: Temple University Press, 1989.

MENJIVAR, CECILIA. "Immigrant Kinship Networks and the Impact of the Receiving Context: Salvadorans in San Francisco in the Early 1990s." *Social Problems.* Vol. 44, No. 1 (February 1997):104–23.

MERTON, ROBERT K. "Social Structure and Anomie." *American Sociological Review.* Vol. 3, No. 6 (October 1938):672–82.

———. *Social Theory and Social Structure.* New York: Free Press, 1968.

METZ, MICHAEL E., and MICHAEL H. MINER. "Psychosexual and Psychosocial Aspects of Male Aging and Sexual Health." *Canadian Journal of Human Sexuality.* Vol. 7, No. 3 (Summer 1998):245–60.

METZGER, KURT. Data presented in "Cities and Race." *Society.* Vol. 39, No. 1 (December 2001):2.

MICHELS, ROBERT. *Political Parties.* Glencoe, Ill.: Free Press, 1949; orig. 1911.

MILBRATH, LESTER W. *Envisioning a Sustainable Society: Learning Our Way Out.* Albany: State University of New York Press, 1989.

MILGRAM, STANLEY. "Behavioral Study of Obedience." *Journal of Abnormal and Social Psychology.* Vol. 67, No. 4 (1963):371–78.

———. "Group Pressure and Action against a Person." *Journal of Abnormal and Social Psychology.* Vol. 69, No. 2 (August 1964):137–43.

———. "Some Conditions of Obedience and Disobedience to Authority." *Human Relations.* Vol. 18, No. 1 (February 1965):57–76.

———. "The Small World Problem." *Psychology Today* (May 1967):60–67.

MILLER, ALAN S., and RODNEY STARK. "Gender and Religiousness: Can Socialization Explanations Be Saved?" *American Journal of Sociology.* Vol. 107, No. 6 (May 2002):1399–1423.

MILLER, ARTHUR G. *The Obedience Experiments: A Case of Controversy in Social Science.* New York: Praeger, 1986.

MILLER, DAVID L. *Introduction to Collective Behavior.* Belmont, Calif.: Wadsworth, 1985.

MILLER, FREDERICK D. "The End of SDS and the Emergence of Weatherman: Demise through Success." In JO FREEMAN, ed., *Social Movements of the Sixties and Seventies.* White Plains, N.Y.: Longman, 1983:279–97.

MILLER, G. TYLER JR. *Living in the Environment: An Introduction to Environmental Science.* Belmont, Calif.: Wadsworth, 1992.

MILLER, MATTHEW, and PETER NEWCOMB, eds. "The Forbes 400." *Forbes* (Special issue, October 10, 2005).

MILLER, WALTER B. "Lower-Class Culture as a Generating Milieu of Gang Delinquency." In MARVIN E. WOLFGANG, LEONARD SAVITZ, and NORMAN JOHNSTON, eds., *The Sociology of Crime and Delinquency.* 2nd ed. New York: Wiley, 1970:351–63.

MILLER, WILLIAM J., and RICK A. MATTHEWS. "Youth Employment, Differential Association, and Juvenile Delinquency." *Sociological Focus.* Vol. 34, No. 3 (August 2001):251–68.

MILLS, C. WRIGHT. *The Power Elite.* New York: Oxford University Press, 1956.
———. *The Sociological Imagination.* New York: Oxford University Press, 1959.

MIRACLE, TINA S., ANDREW W. MIRACLE, and ROY F. BAUMEISTER. *Human Sexuality: Meeting Your Basic Needs.* Upper Saddle River, N.J.: Prentice Hall, 2003.

MIRINGOFF, MARC, and MARQUE-LUISA MIRINGOFF. "The Social Health of the Nation." *Economist.* Vol. 352, No. 8128 (July 17, 1999):suppl. 6–7.

MITCHELL, ALISON. "Give Me a Home Where the Buffalo Roam Less." *New York Times* (January 20, 2002):sec. 4, p. 5.

MOEN, PHYLLIS, DONNA DEMPSTER-McCLAIN, and ROBIN M. WILLIAMS. "Successful Aging: A Life-Course Perspective on Women's Multiple Roles and Health." *American Journal of Sociology.* Vol. 97, No. 6 (May 1992):1612–38.

MOLOTCH, HARVEY. "The City as a Growth Machine." *American Journal of Sociology.* Vol. 82, No. 2 (September 1976):309–33.

MONTAIGNE, FEN. "Russia Rising." *National Geographic.* Vol. 200, No. 5 (September 2001):2–31.

MOORE, GWEN, et al. "Elite Interlocks in Three U.S. Sectors: Nonprofit, Corporate, and Government." *Social Science Quarterly.* Vol. 83, No. 3 (September 2002):726–44.

MOORE, WILBERT E. "Modernization as Rationalization: Processes and Restraints." In MANNING NASH, ed., *Essays on Economic Development and Cultural Change in Honor of Bert F. Hoselitz.* Chicago: University of Chicago Press, 1977:29–42.
———. *World Modernization: The Limits of Convergence.* New York: Elsevier, 1979.

MORRIS, ALDON. "Black Southern Sit-In Movement: An Analysis of Internal Organization." *American Sociological Review.* Vol. 46, No. 6 (December 1981):744–67.

MORRISON, DENTON E. "Some Notes toward Theory on Relative Deprivation, Social Movements, and Social Change." In LOUIS E. GENEVIE, ed., *Collective Behavior and Social Movements.* Itasca, Ill.: Peacock, 1978:202–9.

MORSE, JODIE. "A Victory for Vouchers." *Time* (July 8, 2002):32–34.

MOUW, TED. "Job Relocation and the Racial Gap in Unemployment in Detroit and Chicago, 1980 to 1990." *American Sociological Review.* Vol. 65, No. 5 (October 2000):730–53.

MUMFORD, LEWIS. *The City in History: Its Origins, Its Transformations, and Its Prospects.* New York: Harcourt, Brace & World, 1961.

MUNSON, MARTHA L., and PAUL D. SUTTON. "Births, Marriages, Divorces, and Deaths: Provisional Data for 2004." *National Vital Statistics Report.* Vol. 53, No. 21 (June 28, 2005). Hyattsville, Md.: National Center for Health Statistics.

MURDOCK, GEORGE PETER. "Comparative Data on the Division of Labor by Sex." *Social Forces.* Vol. 15, No. 4 (May 1937):551–53.
———. "The Common Denominator of Cultures." In RALPH LINTON, ed., *The Science of Man in World Crisis.* New York: Columbia University Press, 1945:123–42.
———. *Social Structure.* New York: Free Press, 1965; orig. 1949.

MURPHY, SHERRY L. "Deaths: Final Data for 1998." *National Vital Statistics Report.* Vol. 48, No. 11 (November 2000):1–105. Hyattsville, Md.: National Center for Health Statistics.

MURRAY, STEPHEN O., and WILL ROSCOE, eds. *Boy-Wives and Female-Husbands: Studies of African Homosexualities.* New York: St. Martin's Press, 1998.

MYERS, DAVID G. *The American Paradox: Spiritual Hunger in an Age of Plenty.* New Haven, Conn.: Yale University Press, 2000.

MYERS, NORMAN. "Humanity's Growth." In SIR EDMUND HILLARY, ed., *Ecology 2000: The Changing Face of the Earth.* New York: Beaufort Books, 1984a: 16–35.
———. "The Mega-Extinction of Animals and Plants." In SIR EDMUND HILLARY, ed., *Ecology 2000: The Changing Face of the Earth.* New York: Beaufort Books, 1984b:82–107.
———. "Biological Diversity and Global Security." In F. HERBERT BORMANN and STEPHEN R. KELLERT, eds., *Ecology, Economics, and Ethics: The Broken Circle.* New Haven, Conn.: Yale University Press, 1991:11–25.

MYERS, SHEILA, and HAROLD G. GRASMICK. "The Social Rights and Responsibilities of Pregnant Women: An Application of Parsons' Sick Role Model."

Paper presented to the Southwestern Sociological Association, Little Rock, Ark., March 1989.

MYRDAL, GUNNAR. *An American Dilemma: The Negro Problem and Modern Democracy.* New York: Harper Bros., 1944.

NATIONAL ASSESSMENT OF EDUCATIONAL PROGRESS. "Achievement-Level Trends in Mathematics 1990–2005." *The Nation's Report Card.* [Online] Available October 21, 2005, at http://nces.ed.gov/nationsreportcard

NATIONAL CENTER FOR EDUCATION STATISTICS. *Digest of Education Statistics, 2003.* Washington, D.C.: U.S. Government Printing Office, 2004.
———. *Dropout Rates in the United States, 2001.* Washington, D.C.: U.S. Government Printing Office, 2004. [Online] Available November 6, 2004, at http:// www.nces.ed.gov/pubs2005/2005046.pdf

NATIONAL CENTER ON ELDER ABUSE. *Elder Abuse Prevalence and Incidence.* Washington, D.C.: U.S. Government Printing Office, 2005. [Online] Available July 24, 2005, at http://www.elderabusecenter.org/pdf/publication/ FinalStatistics050331.pdf

NATIONAL CLEARINGHOUSE ON CHILD ABUSE AND NEGLECT INFORMATION. "Child Maltreatment, 2003: Summary of Key Findings." 2005. [Online] Available July 18, 2005, at http://nccanch.acf.hhs.gov/pubs/factsheets/ canstats.pdf

NATIONAL COMMISSION ON EXCELLENCE IN EDUCATION. *A Nation at Risk.* Washington, D.C.: U.S. Government Printing Office, 1983.

NAVARRO, MIREYA. "Puerto Rican Presence Wanes in New York." *New York Times* (February 28, 2000):A1, A20.
———. "For Younger Latinas, a Shift to Smaller Families." *New York Times* (December 5, 2004). [Online] Available April 30, 2005, at http://www. researchnavigator.com

NELSON, AMY L. "The Effect of Economic Restructuring on Family Poverty in the Industrial Heartland, 1970–1990." *Sociological Focus.* Vol. 31, No. 2 (May 1998):201–16.

NELSON, JOEL I. "Work and Benefits: The Multiple Problems of Service Sector Employment." *Social Problems.* Vol. 42, No. 2 (May 1994):240–55.

NESBITT, PAULA D. *Feminization of the Clergy in America: Occupational and Organizational Perspectives.* New York: Oxford University Press, 1997.

NESSMAN, RAVI. "Stampede at Soccer Match Kills 47." [Online]. Available April 11, 2001, at http://news.yahoo.com

NEUGARTEN, BERNICE L. "Grow Old with Me. The Best Is Yet to Be." *Psychology Today* (December 1971):45–48, 79, 81.
———. "Personality and Aging." In JAMES E. BIRREN and K. WARNER SCHAIE, eds., *Handbook of the Psychology of Aging.* New York: Van Nostrand Reinhold, 1977:626–49.

NEUHOUSER, KEVIN. "The Radicalization of the Brazilian Catholic Church in Comparative Perspective." *American Sociological Review.* Vol. 54, No. 2 (April 1989):233–44.

NEUMAN, W. LAURENCE. *Social Research Methods: Qualitative and Quantitative Approaches.* 4th ed. Boston: Allyn & Bacon, 2000.

NEWMAN, KATHERINE S. *Declining Fortunes: The Withering of the American Dream.* New York: Basic Books, 1993.

NEWMAN, WILLIAM M. *American Pluralism: A Study of Minority Groups and Social Theory.* New York: Harper & Row, 1973.

NICHOLSON, NIGEL. "Evolved to Chat: The New Word on Gossip." *Psychology Today* (May/June 2001):41–45.

NIELSEN, FRANCOIS, and ARTHUR S. ALDERSON. "The Kuznets Curve: The Great U-Turn: Income Inequality in U.S. Counties, 1970 to 1990." *American Sociological Review.* Vol. 62, No. 1 (February 1997):12–33.

NISBET, ROBERT A. *The Sociological Tradition.* New York: Basic Books, 1966.
———. *The Quest for Community.* New York: Oxford University Press, 1969.

NOCK, STEVEN L., JAMES D. WRIGHT, and LAURA SANCHEZ. "America's Divorce Problem." *Society.* Vol. 36, No. 4 (May/June 1999):43–52.

NOLAN, PATRICK, and GERHARD LENSKI. *Human Societies: An Introduction to Macrosociology.* 8th ed. New York: McGraw-Hill, 1999.
———. *Human Societies: An Introduction to Macrosociology.* 9th ed. Boulder, Colo.: Paradigm, 2004.

NORBECK, EDWARD. "Class Structure." In *Kodansha Encyclopedia of Japan.* Tokyo: Kodansha, 1983:322–25.

NORC. *General Social Surveys, 1972–1991: Cumulative Codebook.* Chicago: National Opinion Research Center, 1991.
———. *General Social Surveys, 1972–2002: Cumulative Codebook.* Chicago: National Opinion Research Center, 2003.

NORD, MARK. "Does It Cost Less to Live in Rural Areas? Evidence from New Data on Food Scarcity and Hunger." *Rural Sociology.* Vol. 65, No. 1 (March 2000):104–25.

NOVAK, VIVECA. "The Cost of Poor Advice." *Time* (July 5, 1999):38.

NULAND, SHERWIN B. "The Hazards of Hospitalization." *Wall Street Journal* (December 2, 1999):A22.

OAKES, JEANNIE. "Classroom Social Relationships: Exploring the Bowles and Gintis Hypothesis." *Sociology of Education.* Vol. 55, No. 4 (October 1982):197–212.

———. *Keeping Track: How High Schools Structure Inequality.* New Haven, Conn.: Yale University Press, 1985.

OBERSCHALL, ANTHONY. *Social Conflict and Social Movements.* Englewood Cliffs, N.J.: Prentice Hall, 1973.

O'CONNOR, RORY J. "Internet Declared Protected Speech." *Glens Falls* (N.Y.) *Post-Star* (June 27, 1997):A1–A2.

OGAWA, NAOHIRO, and ROBERT D. RETHERFORD. "Shifting Costs of Caring for the Elderly Back to Families in Japan: Will It Work?" *Population and Development Review.* Vol. 23, No. 1 (March 1997):59–95.

OGBURN, WILLIAM F. *On Culture and Social Change.* Chicago: University of Chicago Press, 1964.

OGDEN, RUSSEL D. "Nonphysician-Assisted Suicide: The Technological Imperative of the Deathing Counterculture." *Death Studies.* Vol. 25, No. 5 (July 2001):387–402.

O'HARE, WILLIAM P. "The Rise of Hispanic Affluence." *American Demographics.* Vol. 12, No. 8 (August 1990):40–43.

———. "Tracking the Trends in Low-Income Working Families." *Population Today.* Vol. 30, No. 6 (August/September 2002):1–3.

O'HARE, WILLIAM P., WILLIAM H. FREY, and DAN FOST. "Asians in the Suburbs." *American Demographics.* Vol. 16, No. 9 (May 1994):32–38.

O'HARROW, ROBERT, JR. "ID Theft Scam Hits D.C. Area Residents." [Online] Available February 21, 2005, at http://news.yahoo.com

OLSEN, GREGG M. "Remodeling Sweden: The Rise and Demise of the Compromise in a Global Economy." *Social Problems.* Vol. 43, No. 1 (February 1996):1–20.

OLZAK, SUSAN. "Labor Unrest, Immigration, and Ethnic Conflict in Urban America, 1880–1914." *American Journal of Sociology.* Vol. 94, No. 6 (May 1989):1303–33.

OLZAK, SUSAN, and ELIZABETH WEST. "Ethnic Conflict and the Rise and Fall of Ethnic Newspapers." *American Sociological Review.* Vol. 56, No. 4 (August 1991):458–74.

OMESTAD, THOMAS. "A Balance of Terror." *U.S. News & World Report* (February 3, 2003):33–35.

O'NEILL, BRIAN, and DEBORAH BALK. "World Population Futures." *Population Bulletin.* Vol. 56, No. 3 (September 2001):3–40.

"Online Privacy: It's Time for Rules in Wonderland." *Business Week* (March 20, 2000):82–96.

ORECKLIN, MICHELLE. "Earnings Report: J.K. and Judy." *Time* (January 13, 2003):72.

ORHANT, MELANIE. "Human Trafficking Exposed." *Population Today.* Vol. 30, No. 1 (January 2002):1, 4.

ORLANSKY, MICHAEL D., and WILLIAM L. HEWARD. *Voices: Interviews with Handicapped People.* Columbus, Ohio: Merrill, 1981.

ORWIN, CLIFFORD. "All Quiet on the Western Front?" *Public Interest.* No. 123 (Spring 1996):3–9.

OSTRANDER, SUSAN A. "Upper-Class Women: The Feminine Side of Privilege." *Qualitative Sociology.* Vol. 3, No. 1 (Spring 1980):23–44.

———. *Women of the Upper Class.* Philadelphia: Temple University Press, 1984.

OUCHI, WILLIAM. *Theory Z: How American Business Can Meet the Japanese Challenge.* Reading, Mass.: Addison-Wesley, 1981.

"Our Cheating Hearts." Editorial. *U.S. News & World Report* (May 6, 2002):4.

OVADIA, SETH. "Race, Class, and Gender Differences in High School Seniors' Values: Applying Intersection Theory in Empirical Analysis." *Social Science Quarterly.* Vol. 82, No. 2 (June 2001):341–56.

OWEN, CAROLYN A., HOWARD C. ELSNER, and THOMAS R. MCFAUL. "A Half-Century of Social Distance Research: National Replication of the Bogardus Studies." *Sociology and Social Research.* Vol. 66, No. 1 (1977):80–98.

PACKARD, MARK. Personal communication, 2002.

PACKER, GEORGE. "Smart-Mobbing the War." *New York Times Magazine* (March 9, 2003):46–49.

PAGER, DEVAH. "The Mark of a Criminal Record." *American Journal of Sociology.* Vol. 108, No. 5 (March 2003):937–75.

PAKULSKI, JAN. "Mass Social Movements and Social Class." *International Sociology.* Vol. 8, No. 2 (June 1993):131–58.

PALMORE, ERDMAN. "Predictors of Successful Aging." *Gerontologist.* Vol. 19, No. 5 (October 1979):427–31.

PARINI, JAY. "The Meaning of Emeritus." *Dartmouth Alumni Magazine* (July/August 2001):40–43.

PARIS, PETER J. "The Religious World of African Americans." In JACOB NEUSNER, ed., *World Religions in America: An Introduction.* Revised and expanded ed. Louisville, Ky.: Westminster John Knox Press, 2000:48–65.

PARK, ROBERT E. *Race and Culture.* Glencoe, Ill.: Free Press, 1950.

PARRILLO, VINCENT N. "Diversity in America: A Sociohistorical Analysis." *Sociological Forum.* Vol. 9, No. 4 (December 1994):42–45.

———. *Strangers to These Shores.* 7th ed. Boston: Allyn & Bacon, 2003a.

———. "Updating the Bogardus Social Distance Studies: A New National Survey." Revised version of a paper presented at the annual meeting of the American Sociological Association (August 17, 2002). Provided by the author, 2003b.

PARSONS, TALCOTT. "Age and Sex in the Social Structure of the United States." *American Sociological Review.* Vol. 7, No. 4 (August 1942):604–16.

———. *Essays in Sociological Theory.* New York: Free Press, 1954.

———. *The Social System.* New York: Free Press, 1964; orig. 1951.

———. *Societies: Evolutionary and Comparative Perspectives.* Englewood Cliffs, N.J.: Prentice Hall, 1966.

PARSONS, TALCOTT, and ROBERT F. BALES, eds. *Family, Socialization, and Interaction Process.* New York: Free Press, 1955.

PASSY, FLORENCE, and MARCO GIUGNI. "Social Networks and Individual Perceptions: Explaining Differential Participation in Social Movements." *Sociological Forum.* Vol. 16, No. 1 (March 2001):123–53.

PATTERSON, ELISSA F. "The Philosophy and Physics of Holistic Health Care: Spiritual Healing as a Workable Interpretation." *Journal of Advanced Nursing.* Vol. 27, No. 2 (February 1998):287–93.

PATTILLO-MCCOY, MARY. "Church Culture as a Strategy of Action in the Black Community." *American Sociological Review.* Vol. 63, No. 6 (December 1998): 767–84.

PAUL, PAMELA. "News, Noticias, Nouvelles." *American Demographics.* Vol. 23, No. 11 (November, 2001):26–31.

PEAR, ROBERT, and ERIK ECKHOLM. "When Healers Are Entrepreneurs: A Debate over Costs and Ethics." *New York Times* (June 2, 1991):1, 17.

PEARSON, DAVID E. "Post-Mass Culture." *Society.* Vol. 30, No. 5 (July/August 1993):17–22.

———. "Community and Sociology." *Society.* Vol. 32, No. 5 (July/August 1995): 44–50.

PEASE, JOHN, and LEE MARTIN. "Want Ads and Jobs for the Poor: A Glaring Mismatch." *Sociological Forum.* Vol. 12, No. 4 (December 1997):545–64.

PEDERSON, DANIEL, VERN E. SMITH, and JERRY ADLER. "Sprawling, Sprawling . . ." *Newsweek* (July 19, 1999):23–27.

PERLMUTTER, PHILIP. "Minority Group Prejudice." *Society.* Vol. 39, No. 3 (March/April 2002):59–65.

PERRUCCI, ROBERT. "Inventing Social Justice: SSSP and the Twenty-First Century." *Social Problems.* Vol. 48, No. 2 (May 2001):159–67.

PESSEN, EDWARD. *Riches, Class, and Power: America before the Civil War.* New Brunswick, N.J.: Transaction, 1990.

Peters Atlas of the World. New York: Harper & Row, 1990.

PETERSEN, TROND, ISHAK SAPORTA, and MARC-DAVID L. SEIDEL. "Offering a Job: Meritocracy and Social Networks." *American Journal of Sociology.* Vol. 106, No. 3 (November 2000):763–816.

PETERSILIA, JOAN. "Probation in the United States: Practices and Challenges." *National Institute of Justice Journal.* No. 233 (September 1997):4.

PETERSON, SCOTT. "Women Live on Own Terms behind the Veil." *Christian Science Monitor* (July 31, 1996):1, 10.

PHILADELPHIA, DESA. "Rookie Teacher, Age 50." *Time* (April 9, 2001):66–68.

———. "Tastier, Plusher—and Fast." *Time* (September 30, 2002):57.

PHILLIPS, MELANIE. "What about the Overclass?" *Public Interest.* No. 145 (Fall 2001):38–43.

PICHARDO, NELSON A. "The Power Elite and Elite-Driven Countermovements: The Associated Farmers of California during the 1930s." *Sociological Forum.* Vol. 10, No. 1 (March 1995):21–49.

PINCHOT, GIFFORD, and ELIZABETH PINCHOT. *The End of Bureaucracy and the Rise of the Intelligent Organization.* San Francisco: Berrett-Koehler, 1993.

PINHEY, THOMAS K., DONALD H. RUBINSTEIN, and RICHARD S. COLFAX. "Overweight and Happiness: The Reflected Self-Appraisal Hypothesis Reconsidered." *Social Science Quarterly.* Vol. 78, No. 3 (September 1997): 747–55.

PINKER, STEVEN. *The Language Instinct.* New York: Morrow, 1994.

———. "Are Your Genes to Blame?" *Time* (January 20, 2003):98–100.

PIRANDELLO, LUIGI. "The Pleasure of Honesty" (1917). In *To Clothe the Naked and Two Other Plays.* New York: Dutton, 1962:143–98.

PITTS, LEONARD, JR. "When a Win Sparks a Riot." *Philadelphia Inquirer* (June 26, 2000):A11.

PIVEN, FRANCES FOX, and RICHARD A. CLOWARD. *Poor People's Movements: Why They Succeed, How They Fail.* New York: Pantheon Books, 1977.

PODOLNY, JOEL M., and JAMES N. BARON. "Resources and Relationships: Social Networks and Mobility in the Workplace." *American Sociological Review.* Vol. 62, No. 5 (October 1997):673–93.

POLENBERG, RICHARD. *One Nation Divisible: Class, Race, and Ethnicity in the United States since 1938.* New York: Pelican, 1980.

POLLARD, KEVIN. "Play Ball! Demographics and Major League Baseball." *Population Today.* Vol. 24, No. 4 (April 1996):3.

POLSBY, NELSON W. "Three Problems in the Analysis of Community Power." *American Sociological Review.* Vol. 24, No. 6 (December 1959):796–803.

POMER, MARSHALL I. "Labor Market Structure, Intragenerational Mobility, and Discrimination: Black Male Advancement out of Low-Paying Occupations, 1962–1973." *American Sociological Review.* Vol. 51, No. 5 (October 1986): 650–59.

POPENOE, DAVID. "Family Decline in the Swedish Welfare State." *Public Interest.* No. 102 (Winter 1991):65–77.

———. "American Family Decline, 1960–1990: A Review and Appraisal." *Journal of Marriage and the Family.* Vol. 55, No. 3 (August 1993a):527–55.

———. "Parental Androgyny." *Society.* Vol. 30, No. 6 (September/October 1993b):5–11.

———. "Scandinavian Welfare." *Society.* Vol. 31, No. 6 (September/October, 1994):78–81.

———. "Can the Nuclear Family Be Revived?" *Society.* Vol. 36, No. 5 (July/August 1999):28–30.

POPENOE, DAVID, and BARBARA DAFOE WHITEHEAD. *Should We Live Together? What Young Adults Need to Know about Cohabitation before Marriage.* New Brunswick, N.J.: National Marriage Project, 1999.

POPULATION ACTION INTERNATIONAL. *People in the Balance: Population and Resources at the Turn of the Millennium.* Washington, D.C.: Population Action International, 2000.

POPULATION REFERENCE BUREAU. *1999 World Population Data Sheet.* Washington, D.C.: Population Reference Bureau, 1999.

———. *2003 World Population Data Sheet.* Washington, D.C.: Population Reference Bureau, 2003.

———. *2005 World Population Data Sheet.* Washington, D.C.: Population Reference Bureau, 2005.

Population Today. "Majority of Children in Poverty Live with Parents Who Work." Vol. 23, No. 4 (April 1995):6.

PORTER, EDUARDO. "Even 126 Sizes Do Not Fit All." *Wall Street Journal* (March 2, 2001):B1.

———. "Old, in the Way, and Hard at Work." *New York Times* (August 29, 2004). [Online] Available April 15, 2005, at http://www.researchnavigator.com

PORTES, ALEJANDRO, and LEIF JENSEN. "The Enclave and the Entrants: Patterns of Ethnic Enterprise in Miami before and after Mariel." *American Sociological Review.* Vol. 54, No. 6 (December 1989):929–49.

POSTEL, SANDRA. "Facing Water Scarcity." In LESTER R. BROWN et al., eds., *State of the World, 1993: A Worldwatch Institute Report on Progress toward a Sustainable Society.* New York: Norton, 1993:22–41.

POWELL, CHRIS, and GEORGE E. C. PATON, eds. *Humor in Society: Resistance and Control.* New York: St. Martin's Press, 1988.

PRIMEGGIA, SALVATORE, and JOSEPH A. VARACALLI. "Southern Italian Comedy: Old to New World." In JOSEPH V. SCELSA, SALVATORE J. LA GUMINA, and LYDIO TOMASI, eds., *Italian Americans in Transition.* New York: American Italian Historical Association, 1990:241–52.

PUTKA, GARY. "SAT to Become a Better Gauge." *Wall Street Journal* (November 1, 1990):B1.

PYLE, RALPH E., and JEROME R. KOCH. "The Religious Affiliation of American Elites, 1930s to 1990s: A Note on the Pace of Disestablishment." *Sociological Focus.* Vol. 34, No. 2 (May 2001):125–37.

QUILLIAN, LINCOLN, and DEVAH PAGER. "Black Neighbors, Higher Crime? The Role of Racial Stereotypes in Evaluations of Neighborhood Crime." *American Journal of Sociology.* Vol. 107, No. 3 (November 2001):717–67.

QUINNEY, RICHARD. *Class, State and Crime: On the Theory and Practice of Criminal Justice.* New York: McKay, 1977.

RABKIN, JEREMY. "The Supreme Court in the Culture Wars." *Public Interest.* No. 125 (Fall 1996):3–26.

RANK, MARK R., and THOMAS A. HIRSCHL. "Rags or Riches? Estimating the Probabilities of Poverty and Affluence across the Adult American Life Span." *Social Science Quarterly.* Vol. 82, No. 4 (December 2001):651–69.

RAPHAEL, RAY. *The Men from the Boys: Rites of Passage in Male America.* Lincoln: University of Nebraska Press, 1988.

RATNESAR, ROMESH. "Not Gone, but Forgotten?" *Time* (February 8, 1998): 30–31.

RAYMOND, JOAN. "The Multicultural Report." *American Demographics.* Vol. 23, No. 11 (November 2001):S1–S6.

RECKLESS, WALTER C., and SIMON DINITZ. "Pioneering with Self-Concept as a Vulnerability Factor in Delinquency." *Journal of Criminal Law, Criminology, and Police Science.* Vol. 58, No. 4 (December 1967):515–23.

RECTOR, ROBERT. "America Has the World's Richest Poor People." *Wall Street Journal* (September 24, 1998):A18.

REMOFF, HEATHER TREXLER. *Sexual Choice: A Woman's Decision.* New York: Dutton/ Lewis, 1984.

RESKIN, BARBARA F., and DEBRA BRANCH MCBRIER. "Why Not Ascription? Organizations' Employment of Male and Female Managers." *American Sociological Review.* Vol. 65, No. 2 (April 2000):210–33.

REVKIN, ANDREW C. "Can Global Warming Be Studied Too Much?" *New York Times* (December 3, 2002):D1, D4.

RHODES, STEVE. "The Luck of the Draw." *Newsweek* (April 26, 1999):41.

RIDDLE, JOHN M., J. WORTH ESTES, and JOSIAH C. RUSSELL. "Ever since Eve: Birth Control in the Ancient World." *Archaeology.* Vol. 47, No. 2 (March/April 1994):29–35.

RIDGEWAY, CECILIA L. *The Dynamics of Small Groups.* New York: St. Martin's Press, 1983.

RIESMAN, DAVID. *The Lonely Crowd: A Study of the Changing American Character.* New Haven, Conn.: Yale University Press, 1970; orig. 1950.

RIMER, SARA. "Blacks Carry Load of Care for Their Elderly." *New York Times* (March 15, 1998):1, 22.

RISMAN, BARBARA, and PEPPER SCHWARTZ. "After the Sexual Revolution: Gender Politics in Teen Dating." *Contexts.* Vol. 1, No. 1 (Spring 2002):16–24.

RITZER, GEORGE. *The McDonaldization of Society: An Investigation into the Changing Character of Contemporary Social Life.* Thousand Oaks, Calif.: Pine Forge Press, 1993.

———. *The McDonaldization of Society.* Rev. ed. Thousand Oaks, Calif.: Sage, 1996.

———. *The McDonaldization Thesis: Explorations and Extensions.* Thousand Oaks, Calif.: Sage, 1998.

———. "The Globalization of McDonaldization." *Spark* (February 2000): 8–9.

RITZER, GEORGE, and DAVID WALCZAK. *Working: Conflict and Change.* 4th ed. Englewood Cliffs, N.J.: Prentice Hall, 1990.

ROBERTS, J. DEOTIS. *Roots of a Black Future: Family and Church.* Philadelphia: Westminster Press, 1980.

ROBINSON, LINDA. "A Timeworn Terrorism List." *U.S. News & World Report* (May 20, 2002):18, 21.

ROBINSON, THOMAS N., et al. "Effects of Reducing Children's Television and Video Game Use on Aggressive Behavior." *Archives of Pediatrics and Adolescent Medicine.* Vol. 155, No. 1 (January 2001):17–23.

ROESCH, ROBERTA. "Violent Families." *Parents.* Vol. 59, No. 9 (September 1984): 74–76, 150–52.

ROETHLISBERGER, F. J., and WILLIAM J. DICKSON. *Management and the Worker.* Cambridge, Mass.: Harvard University Press, 1939.

ROGERS, RICHARD G., REBECCA ROSENBLATT, ROBERT A. HUMMER, and PATRICK M. KRUEGER. "Black-White Differentials in Adult Homicide Mortality in the United States." *Social Science Quarterly.* Vol. 82, No. 3 (September 2001): 435–52.

ROGERS-DILLON, ROBIN H. "What Do We Really Know about Welfare Reform?" *Society.* Vol. 38, No. 2 (January/February 2001):7–15.

ROMERO, FRANCINE SANDERS, and ADRIAN LISERIO. "Saving Open Spaces: Determinants of 1998 and 1999 'Antisprawl' Ballot Measures." *Social Science Quarterly.* Vol. 83, No. 1 (March 2002):341–52.

ROSE, FRED. "Toward a Class-Cultural Theory of Social Movements: Reinterpreting New Social Movements." *Sociological Forum.* Vol. 12, No. 3 (September 1997):461–94.

ROSE, JERRY D. *Outbreaks.* New York: Free Press, 1982.

ROSE, LOWELL C., and ALEC M. GALLUP. *The 37th Annual Phi Delta Kappa/Gallup Poll of the Public's Attitudes toward the Public Schools.* 2005. [Online] Available September 27, 2005, at http://www.pdkintl.org/kappan/k0509pol.pdf

ROSEN, ELLEN ISRAEL. *Bitter Choices: Blue-Collar Women in and out of Work.* Chicago: University of Chicago Press, 1987.

ROSENBAUM, DAVID E. "Americans Want a Right to Die. Or So They Think." *New York Times* (June 8, 1997):E3.

ROSENBAUM, MARC. "Americans' Views on Taxes." Report of an NPR/Kaiser Family Foundation/Kennedy School of Government poll. Lecture delivered at Kenyon College, Gambier, Ohio, April 23, 2003.

ROSENDAHL, MONA. *Inside the Revolution: Everyday Life in Socialist Cuba.* Ithaca, N.Y.: Cornell University Press, 1997.

ROSENFELD, RICHARD. "Crime Decline in Context." *Contexts.* Vol. 1, No. 1 (Spring 2002):20–34.

ROSENTHAL, ELIZABETH. "Canada's National Health Plan Gives Care to All, with Limits." *New York Times* (April 30, 1991):A1, A16.

ROSNOW, RALPH L., and GARY ALAN FINE. *Rumor and Gossip: The Social Psychology of Hearsay.* New York: Elsevier, 1976.

ROSS, JOHN. "To Die in the Street: Mexico City's Homeless Population Boom as Economic Crisis Shakes Social Protections." *SSSP Newsletter.* Vol. 27, No. 2 (Summer 1996):14–15.

ROSSI, ALICE S. "Gender and Parenthood." In ALICE S. ROSSI, ed., *Gender and the Life Course.* New York: Aldine, 1985:161–91.

ROSTOW, WALT W. *The Stages of Economic Growth: A Non-Communist Manifesto.* Cambridge: Cambridge University Press, 1960.

———. *The World Economy: History and Prospect.* Austin: University of Texas Press, 1978.

ROTHMAN, BARBARA KATZ. "Of Maps and Imaginations: Sociology Confronts the Genome." *Social Problems.* Vol. 42, No. 1 (February 1995):1–10.

ROTHMAN, STANLEY, and AMY E. BLACK. "Who Rules Now? American Elites in the 1990s." *Society.* Vol. 35, No. 6 (September/October 1998):17–20.

ROTHMAN, STANLEY, STEPHEN POWERS, and DAVID ROTHMAN. "Feminism in Films." *Society.* Vol. 30, No. 3 (March/April 1993):66–72.

ROUSSEAU, CARYN. "Unions Rally at Wal-Mart Stores." [Online] Available November 22, 2002, at http://news.yahoo.com

ROZELL, MARK J., CLYDE WILCOX, and JOHN C. GREEN. "Religious Constituencies and Support for the Christian Right in the 1990s." *Social Science Quarterly.* Vol. 79, No. 4 (December 1998):815–27.

RUBENSTEIN, ELI A. "The Not So Golden Years." *Newsweek* (October 7, 1991):13.

RUBIN, JOEL. "E-Mail Too Formal? Try a Text Message." Columbia News Service, March 7, 2003. [Online] Available April 25, 2005, at http://www.jrn.columbia.edu/studentwork/cns/2003-03-07/85.asp

RUBIN, LILLIAN BRESLOW. *Worlds of Pain: Life in the Working-Class Family.* New York: Basic Books, 1976.

RUDEL, THOMAS K., and JUDITH M. GERSON. "Postmodernism, Institutional Change, and Academic Workers: A Sociology of Knowledge." *Social Science Quarterly.* Vol. 80, No. 2 (June 1999):213–28.

RUDOLPH, ELLEN. "Women's Talk: Japanese Women." *New York Times Magazine* (September 1, 1991).

RULE, JAMES, and PETER BRANTLEY. "Computerized Surveillance in the Workplace: Forms and Delusions." *Sociological Forum.* Vol. 7, No. 3 (September 1992):405–23.

RUSSELL, CHERYL. "Are We in the Dumps?" *American Demographics.* Vol. 17, No. 1 (January 1995a):6.

———. "True Crime." *American Demographics.* Vol. 17, No. 8 (August 1995b):22–31.

RUSSELL, CHERYL, and MARCIA MOGELONSKY. "Riding High on the Market." *American Demographics.* Vol. 22, No. 4 (April 2000):44–54.

RUTHERFORD, MEGAN. "Women Run the World." *Time* (June 28, 1999):72.

RYAN, PATRICK J. "The Roots of Muslim Anger." *America* (November 26, 2001):8–16.

RYMER, RUSS. *Genie.* New York: HarperPerennial, 1994.

SACHS, JEFFREY. "The Real Causes of Famine." *Time* (October 26, 1998):69.

SAINT JEAN, YANICK, and JOE R. FEAGIN. *Double Burden: Black Women and Everyday Racism.* Armonk, N.Y.: Sharpe, 1998.

SALA-I-MARTIN, XAVIER. "The World Distribution of Income." Working Paper No. 8933. Cambridge, Mass.: National Bureau of Economic Research, 2002.

SALE, KIRKPATRICK. *The Conquest of Paradise: Christopher Columbus and the Columbian Legacy.* New York: Knopf, 1990.

SAMPSON, ANTHONY. *The Changing Anatomy of Britain.* New York: Random House, 1982.

SAMUELSON, ROBERT J. "The Rich and Everyone Else." *Newsweek* (January 27, 2003):57.

SANSOM, WILLIAM. *A Contest of Ladies.* London: Hogarth, 1956.

SAPIR, EDWARD. "The Status of Linguistics as a Science." *Language.* Vol. 5, No. 4 (1929):207–14.

———. *Selected Writings of Edward Sapir in Language, Culture, and Personality.* DAVID G. MANDELBAUM, ed. Berkeley: University of California Press, 1949.

SAPORITO, BILL. "Can Wal-Mart Get Any Bigger?" *Time* (January 13, 2003):38–43.

SAVISHINSKY, JOEL S. *Breaking the Watch: The Meanings of Retirement in America.* Ithaca, N.Y.: Cornell University Press, 2000.

SAX, LINDA J., et al. *The American Freshman: National Norms for Fall 2003.* Los Angeles: UCLA Higher Education Research Institute, 2003.

———. *The American Freshman: National Norms for Fall 2004.* Los Angeles: UCLA Higher Education Research Institute, 2004.

SCANLON, STEPHAN J. "Food Availability and Access in Less Industrialized Societies: A Test and Interpretation of Neo-Malthusian and Technoecological Theories." *Sociological Forum.* Vol. 16, No. 2 (June 2001):231–62.

SCHAFFER, MICHAEL. "American Dreamers." *U.S. News & World Report* (August 26, 2002):12–16.

SCHAUB, DIANA. "From Boys to Men." *Public Interest.* No. 127 (Spring 1997):108–14.

SCHEFF, THOMAS J. *Being Mentally Ill: A Sociological Theory.* 2nd ed. New York: Aldine, 1984.

SCHLESINGER, ARTHUR. "The City in American Civilization." In A. B. CALLOW JR., ed., *American Urban History.* New York: Oxford University Press, 1969:25–41.

SCHLESINGER, ARTHUR, JR. "The Cult of Ethnicity: Good and Bad." *Time* (July 8, 1991):21.

SCHLESINGER, JACOB M. "Finally, U.S. Median Income Approaches Old Heights." *Wall Street Journal* (September 25, 1998):B1.

SCHLOSSER, ERIC. *Fast-Food Nation: The Dark Side of the All-American Meal.* New York: Perennial, 2002.

SCHMIDT, ROGER. *Exploring Religion.* Belmont, Calif.: Wadsworth, 1980.

SCHMITT, ERIC. "Whites in Minority in Largest Cities, the Census Shows." *New York Times* (April 30, 2001):A1, A12.

SCHNAIBERG, ALLAN, and KENNETH ALAN GOULD. *Environment and Society: The Enduring Conflict.* New York: St. Martin's Press, 1994.

SCHNEIDER, MARK, MELISSA MARSCHALL, PAUL TESKE, and CHRISTINE ROCH. "School Choice and Culture Wars in the Classroom: What Different Parents Seek from Education." *Social Science Quarterly.* Vol. 79, No. 3 (September 1998):489–501.

SCHOFER, EVAN, and MARION FOURCADE-GOURINCHAS. "The Structural Contexts of Civil Engagement: Voluntary Association Membership in Comparative Perspective." *American Sociological Review.* Vol. 66, No. 6 (December 2001):806–28.

SCHULTZ, T. PAUL. "Inequality in the Distribution of Personal Income in the World: How It Is Changing and Why." *Journal of Population Economics.* Vol. 11, No. 2 (1998):307–44.

SCHUMAN, HOWARD, and MARIA KRYSAN. "A Historical Note on Whites' Beliefs about Racial Inequality." *American Sociological Review.* Vol. 64, No. 6 (December 1999):847–55.

SCHUR, LISA A., and DOUGLAS L. KRUSE. "What Determines Voter Turnout? Lessons from Citizens with Disabilities." *Social Science Quarterly.* Vol. 81, No. 2 (June 2000):571–87.

SCHWARTZ, BARRY. "Memory as a Cultural System: Abraham Lincoln in World War II." *American Sociological Review.* Vol. 61, No. 5 (October 1996): 908–27.

SCHWARTZ, FELICE N. "Management, Women, and the New Facts of Life." *Harvard Business Review.* Vol. 89, No. 1 (January/February 1989):65–76.

SCOMMEGNA, PAOLA. "Increased Cohabitation Changing Children's Family Settings." *Population Today.* Vol. 30, No. 7 (July 2002):3, 6.

SEAGER, JONI. *The Penguin Atlas of Women in the World.* 3rd ed. New York: Penguin Putnam, 2003.

SEARS, DAVID O., and JOHN B. McCONAHAY. *The Politics of Violence: The New Urban Blacks and the Watts Riot.* Boston: Houghton Mifflin, 1973.

SEGAL, MADY WECHSLER, and AMANDA FAITH HANSEN. "Value Rationales in Policy Debates on Women in the Military: A Content Analysis of Congressional Testimony, 1941–1985." *Social Science Quarterly.* Vol. 73, No. 2 (June 1992):296–309.

SEIDMAN, STEVEN, ed. *Queer Theory/Sociology.* Cambridge, Mass.: Blackwell, 1996.

SEKULIC, DUSKO, GARTH MASSEY, and RANDY HODSON. "Who Were the Yugoslavs? Failed Sources of Common Identity in the Former Yugoslavia." *American Sociological Review.* Vol. 59, No. 1 (February 1994):83–97.

SENNETT, RICHARD. *The Corrosion of Character: The Personal Consequences of Work in the New Capitalism.* New York: Norton, 1998.

SENNETT, RICHARD, and JONATHAN COBB. *The Hidden Injuries of Class.* New York: Vintage Books, 1973.

SENTENCING PROJECT. "Facts about Prisons and Prisoners." May 2005. [Online] Available June 5, 2005, at http://www.sentencingproject.org/pdfs/1035.pdf

SHAPIRO, JOSEPH P. "Back to Work, on Mission." *U.S. News & World Report* (June 4, 2001).

SHARPE, ANITA. "The Rich Aren't So Different After All." *Wall Street Journal* (November 12, 1996):B1, B10.

SHAWCROSS, WILLIAM. *Sideshow: Kissinger, Nixon and the Destruction of Cambodia.* New York: Pocket Books, 1979.

SHEA, RACHEL HARTIGAN. "The New Insecurity." *U.S. News & World Report* (March 25, 2002):40.

SHEEHAN, TOM. "Senior Esteem as a Factor in Socioeconomic Complexity." *Gerontologist.* Vol. 16, No. 5 (October 1976):433–40.

SHELDON, WILLIAM H., EMIL M. HARTL, and EUGENE MCDERMOTT. *Varieties of Delinquent Youth.* New York: Harper Bros., 1949.

SHELER, JEFFREY L. "Faith in America." *U.S. News & World Report* (May 6, 2002): 40–44.

SHERKAT, DARREN E., and CHRISTOPHER G. ELLISON. "Recent Developments and Current Controversies in the Sociology of Religion." *Annual Review of Sociology.* Vol. 25 (1999):363–94.

SHERMAN, LAWRENCE W., and DOUGLAS A. SMITH. "Crime, Punishment, and Stake in Conformity: Legal and Informal Control of Domestic Violence." *American Sociological Review.* Vol. 57, No. 5 (October 1992):680–90.

SHEVKY, ESHREF, and WENDELL BELL. *Social Area Analysis.* Stanford, Calif.: Stanford University Press, 1955.

SHIPLEY, JOSEPH T. *Dictionary of Word Origins.* Totowa, N.J.: Roman & Allanheld, 1985.

SHIVELY, JOELLEN. "Cowboys and Indians: Perceptions of Western Films among American Indians and Anglos." *American Sociological Review.* Vol. 57, No. 6 (December 1992):725–34.

SHUPE, ANSON. *In the Name of All That's Holy: A Theory of Clergy Malfeasance.* Westport, Conn.: Praeger, 1995.

SHUPE, ANSON, WILLIAM A. STACEY, and LONNIE R. HAZLEWOOD. *Violent Men, Violent Couples: The Dynamics of Domestic Violence.* Lexington, Mass.: Lexington Books, 1987.

SIMMEL, GEORG. *The Sociology of Georg Simmel.* KURT WOLFF, ed. New York: Free Press, 1950:118–69; orig. 1902.

———. "Fashion." In DONALD N. LEVINE, ed., *Georg Simmel: On Individuality and Social Forms.* Chicago: University of Chicago Press, 1971; orig. 1904.

SIMON, JULIAN. *The Ultimate Resource.* Princeton, N.J.: Princeton University Press, 1981.

———. "More People, Greater Wealth, More Resources, Healthier Environment." In THEODORE D. GOLDFARB, ed., *Taking Sides: Clashing Views on Controversial Environmental Issues.* 6th ed. Guilford, Conn.: Dushkin, 1995.

SIMON, ROGER, and ANGIE CANNON. "An Amazing Journey." *U.S. News & World Report* (August 6, 2001):10–19.

SIMONS, MARLISE. "The Price of Modernization: The Case of Brazil's Kaiapo Indians." In JOHN J. MACIONIS and NIJOLE V. BENOKRAITIS, eds., *Seeing Ourselves: Classic, Contemporary, and Cross-Cultural Readings in Sociology.* 7th ed. Upper Saddle River, N.J.: Prentice Hall, 2007.

SIMPSON, GEORGE EATON, and J. MILTON YINGER. *Racial and Cultural Minorities: An Analysis of Prejudice and Discrimination.* 4th ed. New York: Harper & Row, 1972.

SIPES, RICHARD G. "War, Sports, and Aggression: An Empirical Test of Two Rival Theories." *American Anthropologist.* Vol. 75, No. 1 (January 1973):64–86.

SIVARD, RUTH LEGER. *World Military and Social Expenditures, 1987–88.* 12th ed. Washington, D.C.: World Priorities, 1988.

———. *World Military and Social Expenditures, 1992–93.* 17th ed. Washington, D.C.: World Priorities, 1993.

SIZER, THEODORE R. *Horace's Compromise: The Dilemma of the American High School.* Boston: Houghton Mifflin, 1984.

SKOCPOL, THEDA. *States and Social Revolutions: A Comparative Analysis of France, Russia, and China.* Cambridge: Cambridge University Press, 1979.

SMAIL, J. KENNETH. "Let's *Reduce* Global Population!" In JOHN J. MACIONIS and NIJOLE V. BENOKRAITIS, eds., *Seeing Ourselves: Classic, Contemporary, and Cross-Cultural Readings in Sociology.* 7th ed. Upper Saddle River, N.J.: Prentice Hall, 2007.

SMART, TIM. "Not Acting Their Age." *U.S. News & World Report* (June 4, 2001): 54–60.

SMELSER, NEIL J. *Theory of Collective Behavior.* New York: Free Press, 1962.

SMITH, ADAM. *An Inquiry into the Nature and Causes of the Wealth of Nations.* New York: Modern Library, 1937; orig. 1776.

SMITH, CRAIG S. "Authorities Took Victim's Organs, His Brother Says." *Columbus (Ohio) Dispatch* (March 11, 2001):A3.

SMITH, DOUGLAS A. "Police Response to Interpersonal Violence: Defining the Parameters of Legal Control." *Social Forces.* Vol. 65, No. 3 (March 1987):767–82.

SMITH, DOUGLAS A., and PATRICK R. GARTIN. "Specifying Specific Deterrence: The Influence of Arrest on Future Criminal Activity." *American Sociological Review.* Vol. 54, No. 1 (February 1989):94–105.

SMITH, DOUGLAS A., and CHRISTY A. VISHER. "Street-Level Justice: Situational Determinants of Police Arrest Decisions." *Social Problems.* Vol. 29, No. 2 (December 1981):167–77.

SMITH, RYAN A. "Race, Gender, and Authority in the Workplace: Theory and Research." *Annual Review of Sociology.* Vol. 28 (2002):509–42.

SMITH, TOM W. "Anti-Semitism Decreases but Persists." *Society.* Vol. 33, No. 3 (March/April 1996):2.

———. "Are We Grown Up Yet? U.S. Study Says Not 'til 26." [Online] Available May 23, 2003, at http://news.yahoo.com

SMITH-LOVIN, LYNN, and CHARLES BRODY. "Interruptions in Group Discussions: The Effects of Gender and Group Composition." *American Journal of Sociology.* Vol. 54, No. 3 (June 1989):424–35.

SMOLOWE, JILL. "When Violence Hits Home." *Time* (July 4, 1994):18–25.

SNELL, MARILYN BERLIN. "The Purge of Nurture." *New Perspectives Quarterly.* Vol. 7, No. 1 (Winter 1990):1–2.

SOBEL, RACHEL K. "Herpes Tests Give Answers You Might Need to Know." *U.S. News & World Report* (June 18, 2001):53.

Society. "Female Opinion and Defense since September 11th." Vol. 39, No. 3 (March/April 2002):2.

SOUTH, SCOTT J., and KIM L. LLOYD. "Spousal Alternatives and Marital Dissolution." *American Sociological Review.* Vol. 60, No. 1 (February 1995):21–35.

SOUTH, SCOTT J., and STEVEN F. MESSNER. "Structural Determinants of Intergroup Association: Interracial Marriage and Crime." *American Journal of Sociology.* Vol. 91, No. 6 (May 1986):1409–30.

SOWELL, THOMAS. *Ethnic America.* New York: Basic Books, 1981.

———. *Compassion versus Guilt, and Other Essays.* New York: Morrow, 1987.

———. *Race and Culture.* New York: Basic Books, 1994.

———. "Ethnicity and IQ." In STEVEN FRASER, ed., *The Bell Curve Wars: Race, Intelligence, and the Future of America.* New York: Basic Books, 1995: 70–79.

SPECTER, MICHAEL. "Plunging Life Expectancy Puzzles Russia." *New York Times* (August 2, 1995):A1, A2.

———. "Yogurt? Caucasus Centenarians 'Never Eat It.'" *New York Times* (March 14, 1998):A1, A4.

SPEIER, HANS. "Wit and Politics: An Essay on Laughter and Power." ROBERT JACKALL, ed. and trans. *American Journal of Sociology.* Vol. 103, No. 5 (March 1998):1352–1401.

SPITZER, STEVEN. "Toward a Marxian Theory of Deviance." In DELOS H. KELLY, ed., *Criminal Behavior: Readings in Criminology.* New York: St. Martin's Press, 1980:175–91.

STACEY, JUDITH. *Patriarchy and Socialist Revolution in China.* Berkeley: University of California Press, 1983.

———. *Brave New Families: Stories of Domestic Upheaval in Late Twentieth-Century America.* New York: Basic Books, 1990.

———. "'Good Riddance to 'The Family': A Response to David Popenoe." *Journal of Marriage and the Family.* Vol. 55, No. 3 (August 1993):545–47.

STACK, CAROL B. *All Our Kin: Strategies for Survival in a Black Community.* New York: Harper & Row, 1975.

STACK, STEVEN. "Occupation and Suicide." *Social Science Quarterly.* Vol. 82, No. 2 (June 2001):384–96.

STACK, STEVEN, IRA WASSERMAN, and ROGER KERN. "Adult Social Bonds and the Use of Internet Pornography." *Social Science Quarterly.* Vol. 85, No. 1 (March 2004):75–88.

STAHURA, JOHN M. "Suburban Development, Black Suburbanization, and the Black Civil Rights Movement since World War II." *American Sociological Review.* Vol. 51, No. 1 (February 1986):131–44.

STAPINSKI, HELENE. "Let's Talk Dirty." *American Demographics.* Vol. 20, No. 11 (November 1998):50–56.

STARK, RODNEY. *Sociology.* Belmont, Calif.: Wadsworth, 1985.

STARK, RODNEY, and WILLIAM SIMS BAINBRIDGE. "Of Churches, Sects, and Cults: Preliminary Concepts for a Theory of Religious Movements." *Journal for the Scientific Study of Religion.* Vol. 18, No. 2 (June 1979):117–31.

———. "Secularization and Cult Formation in the Jazz Age." *Journal for the Scientific Study of Religion.* Vol. 20, No. 4 (December 1981):360–73.

STARK, RODNEY, and ROGER FINKE. *Acts of Faith: Explaining the Human Side of Religion.* Berkeley: University of California Press, 2000.

STARR, PAUL. *The Social Transformation of American Medicine.* New York: Basic Books, 1982.

STEELE, RANDY. "Awful but Lawful." *Boating* (June 2000):36.

STEELE, SHELBY. *The Content of Our Character: A New Vision of Race in America.* New York: St. Martin's Press, 1990.

STEINBERG, LAURENCE. "Failure outside the Classroom." *Wall Street Journal* (July 11, 1996):A14.

STEPHENS, JOHN D. *The Transition from Capitalism to Socialism.* Urbana: University of Illinois Press, 1986.

STERKE, CLAIRE E. *Tricking and Tripping: Prostitution in the Era of AIDS.* Putnam Valley, N.Y.: Social Change Press, 2000.

STEVENS, GILLIAN, and GRAY SWICEGOOD. "The Linguistic Context of Ethnic Endogamy." *American Sociological Review.* Vol. 52, No. 1 (February 1987):73–82.

STIER, HAYA. "Continuity and Change in Women's Occupations following First Childbirth." *Social Science Quarterly.* Vol. 77, No. 1 (March 1996):60–75.

STOFFERAHN, CURTIS W. "Underemployment: Social Fact or Socially Constructed Reality?" *Rural Sociology.* Vol. 65, No. 2 (June 2000):311–30.

STONE, LAWRENCE. *The Family, Sex, and Marriage in England, 1500–1800.* New York: Harper & Row, 1977.

STONE, PAMELA. "Ghettoized and Marginalized: The Coverage of Racial and Ethnic Groups in Introductory Sociology Texts." *Teaching Sociology.* Vol. 24, No. 4 (October 1996):356–63.

STORMS, MICHAEL D. "Theories of Sexual Orientation." *Journal of Personality and Social Psychology.* Vol. 38, No. 5 (May 1980):783–92.

STOUFFER, SAMUEL A., et al. *The American Soldier: Adjustment during Army Life.* Princeton, N.J.: Princeton University Press, 1949.

STOUT, DAVID. "Supreme Court Splits on Diversity Efforts at University of Michigan." [Online] Available June 23, 2003, at http://news.yahoo.com

STRATTON, LESLIE S. "Why Does More Housework Lower Women's Wages? Testing Hypotheses Involving Job Effort and Hours Flexibility." *Social Sciences Quarterly.* Vol. 82, No. 1 (March 2001):67–76.

STREIB, GORDON F. "Are the Aged a Minority Group?" In BERNICE L. NEUGARTEN, ed., *Middle Age and Aging: A Reader in Social Psychology.* Chicago: University of Chicago Press, 1968:35–46.

STROSS, RANDALL E. "The McPeace Dividend." *U.S. News & World Report* (April 1, 2002):36.

SULLIVAN, ANDREW. Lecture delivered at Kenyon College, Gambier, Ohio, April 4, 2002.

SULLIVAN, BARBARA. "McDonald's Sees India as Golden Opportunity." *Chicago Tribune* (April 5, 1995):B1.

SUMNER, WILLIAM GRAHAM. *Folkways.* New York: Dover, 1959; orig. 1906.

SUN, LENA H. "WWII's Forgotten Internees Await Apology." *Washington Post* (March 9, 1998):A1, A5, A6.

SUTHERLAND, EDWIN H. "White Collar Criminality." *American Sociological Review.* Vol. 5, No. 1 (February 1940):1–12.

SWARTZ, STEVE. "Why Michael Milken Stands to Qualify for Guinness Book." *Wall Street Journal* (March 31, 1989):1, 4.

SZASZ, THOMAS S. "Idleness and Lawlessness in the Therapeutic State." *Society.* Vol. 32, No. 4 (May/June 1995):30–35.

———. "Cleansing the Modern Heart." *Society.* Vol. 40, No. 4 (May/June 2003):52–59.

———. "Protecting Patients against Psychiatric Intervention." *Society.* Vol. 41, No. 3 (March/April 2004):7–10.

TAJFEL, HENRI. "Social Psychology of Intergroup Relations." *Annual Review of Psychology.* Palo Alto, Calif.: Annual Reviews, 1982:1–39.

TAKAKI, RONALD. *Strangers from a Different Shore.* Boston: Back Bay Books, 1998.

TALLICHET, SUZANNE E. "Barriers to Women's Advancement in Underground Coal Mining." *Rural Sociology.* Vol. 65, No. 2 (June 2000):234–52.

TANNEN, DEBORAH. *You Just Don't Understand: Women and Men in Conversation.* New York: Morrow, 1990.

———. *Talking from 9 to 5: How Women's and Men's Conversational Styles Affect Who Gets Heard, Who Gets Credit, and What Gets Done at Work.* New York: Morrow, 1994.

TAX FOUNDATION. *America Celebrates Tax Freedom Day.* Special report. No. 134 (April 2005). [Online] Available October 19, 2005, at http://www.taxfoundation.org/publications/showtype/27.html

TAVRIS, CAROL, and CAROL WADE. *Psychology in Perspective.* 3rd ed. Upper Saddle River, N.J.: Prentice Hall, 2001.

TAYLOR, FREDERICK WINSLOW. *The Principles of Scientific Management.* New York: Harper Bros., 1911.

TERKEL, STUDS. *Working.* New York: Pantheon Books, 1974.

"Terrorist Attacks Spur Unseen Human Toll." *Popline* (December 2001):1–2.

TERRY, DON. "In Crackdown on Bias, a New Tool." *New York Times* (June 12, 1993):8.

TEWKSBURY, RICHARD, and PATRICIA GAGNÉ. "Transgenderists: Products of Nonnormative Intersections of Sex, Gender, and Sexuality." *Journal of Men's Studies.* Vol. 5, No. 2 (November 1996):105–29.

THERNSTROM, ABIGAIL, and STEPHAN THERNSTROM. "American Apartheid? Don't Believe It." *Wall Street Journal* (March 2, 1998):A18.

THOMAS, EDWARD J. *The Life of Buddha as Legend and History.* London: Routledge & Kegan Paul, 1975.

THOMAS, PAULETTE. "Success at a Huge Personal Cost." *Wall Street Journal* (July 26, 1995):B1, B6.

THOMAS, PIRI. *Down These Mean Streets.* New York: Signet, 1967.

THOMAS, W. I. "The Relation of Research to the Social Process." In MORRIS JANOWITZ, ed., *W. I. Thomas on Social Organization and Social Personality.* Chicago: University of Chicago Press, 1966:289–305; orig. 1931.

THOMMA, STEVEN. "Christian Coalition Demands Action from GOP." *Philadelphia Inquirer* (September 14, 1997):A2.

THOMPSON, DICK. "Gene Maverick." *Time* (January 11, 1999):54–55.

THOMPSON, MARK. "Fatal Neglect." *Time* (October 27, 1997):34–38.

———. "Shining a Light on Abuse." *Time* (August 3, 1998):42–43.

THOMPSON, MARK, and DOUGLAS WALLER. "Shield of Dreams." *Time* (May 8, 2001):45–47.

THORLINDSSON, THOROLFUR, and THORODDUR BJARNASON. "Modeling Durkheim on the Micro Level: A Study of Youth Suicidality." *American Sociological Review.* Vol. 63, No. 1 (February 1998):94–110.

THORNBERRY, TERRANCE, and MARGARET FARNSWORTH. "Social Correlates of Criminal Involvement: Further Evidence on the Relationship between Social Status and Criminal Behavior." *American Sociological Review.* Vol. 47, No. 4 (August 1982):505–18.

THORNE, BARRIE, CHERIS KRAMARAE, and NANCY HENLEY, eds. *Language, Gender, and Society.* Rowley, Mass.: Newbury House, 1983.

TILLY, CHARLES. *From Mobilization to Revolution.* Reading, Mass.: Addison-Wesley, 1978.

———. "Does Modernization Breed Revolution?" In JACK A. GOLDSTONE, ed., *Revolutions: Theoretical, Comparative, and Historical Studies.* New York: Harcourt Brace Jovanovich, 1986:47–57.

TIRYAKIAN, EDWARD A. "Revisiting Sociology's First Classic: The Division of Labor in Society and Its Actuality." *Sociological Forum.* Vol. 9, No. 1 (March 1994):3–16.

TITTLE, CHARLES R., WAYNE J. VILLEMEZ, and DOUGLAS A. SMITH. "The Myth of Social Class and Criminality: An Empirical Assessment of the Empirical Evidence." *American Sociological Review.* Vol. 43, No. 5 (October 1978):643–56.

TOCQUEVILLE, ALEXIS DE. *The Old Regime and the French Revolution.* STUART GILBERT, trans. Garden City, N.Y.: Anchor/Doubleday, 1955; orig. 1856.

TOLSON, JAY. "The Trouble with Elites." *Wilson Quarterly.* Vol. 19, No. 1 (Winter 1995):6–8.

TÖNNIES, FERDINAND. *Community and Society (Gemeinschaft und Gesellschaft).* New York: Harper & Row, 1963; orig. 1887.

TOOSSI, MITRA. "Labor Force Projections to 2012: The Graying of the U.S. Workforce." *Monthly Labor Review.* Vol. 127, No. 2 (February 2004):37–57. [Online] Available July 30, 2004, at http://www.bls.gov/opub/mlr/2004/02/art3full.pdf

TOPPO, GREG, and ANTHONY DE BARROS. "Reality Weighs Down Dreams of College." *USA Today* (February 2, 2005):A1.

TORRES, LISA, and MATT L. HUFFMAN. "Social Networks and Job Search Outcomes among Male and Female Professional, Technical, and Managerial Workers." *Sociological Focus.* Vol. 35, No. 1 (February 2002):25–42.

TREAS, JUDITH. "Older Americans in the 1990s and Beyond." *Population Bulletin.* Vol. 50, No. 2 (May 1995):2–46.

TRENT, KATHERINE. "Family Context and Adolescents' Expectations about Marriage, Fertility, and Nonmarital Childbearing." *Social Science Quarterly.* Vol. 75, No. 2 (June 1994):319–39.

TROELTSCH, ERNST. *The Social Teaching of the Christian Churches*. New York: Macmillan, 1931.

TUCKER, JAMES. "New Age Religion and the Cult of the Self." *Society*. Vol. 39, No. 2 (February 2002):46–51.

TUMIN, MELVIN M. "Some Principles of Stratification: A Critical Analysis." *American Sociological Review*. Vol. 18, No. 4 (August 1953):387–94.

———. *Social Stratification: The Forms and Functions of Inequality*. 2nd ed. Englewood Cliffs, N.J.: Prentice Hall, 1985.

TURNER, JONATHAN. *On the Origins of Human Emotions: A Sociological Inquiry into the Evolution of Human Emotions*. Stanford, Calif.: Stanford University Press, 2000.

TURNER, RALPH H., and LEWIS M. KILLIAN. *Collective Behavior*. 3rd ed. Englewood Cliffs, N.J.: Prentice Hall, 1987

———. *Collective Behavior*. 4th ed. Englewood Cliffs, N.J.: Prentice Hall, 1993.

TYLER, S. LYMAN. *A History of Indian Policy*. Washington, D.C.: U.S. Department of the Interior, Bureau of Indian Affairs, 1973.

UDRY, J. RICHARD. "Biological Limitations of Gender Construction." *American Sociological Review*. Vol. 65, No. 3 (June 2000):443–57.

UGGEN, CHRISTOPHER. "Ex-Offenders and the Conformist Alternative: A Job-Quality Model of Work and Crime." *Social Problems*. Vol. 46, No. 1 (February 1999):127–51.

UGGEN, CHRISTOPHER, and JEFF MANZA. "Democratic Contraction? Political Consequences of Felon Disenfranchisement in the United States." *American Sociological Review*. Vol. 67, No. 6 (December 2002):777–803.

UNESCO. Data reported in "Tower of Babel Is Tumbling Down—Slowly." *U.S. News & World Report* (July 2, 2001):9.

UNITED NATIONS. *The World's Women, 2000: Trends and Statistics*. New York: United Nations, 2000.

UNITED NATIONS. "Executive Summary." *World Population Ageing 1950–2050*. New York: United Nations, 2002. [Online] Available October 20, 2005, at http://www.un.org/esa/population/publications/worldageing19502050/index.htm

UNITED NATIONS. *AIDS Epidemic Update*. December 2004. [Online] Available September 28, 2005, at http://www.unaids.org/

UNITED NATIONS DEVELOPMENT PROGRAMME. *Human Development Report 1990*. New York: Oxford University Press, 1990.

———. *Human Development Report 1995*. New York: Oxford University Press, 1995.

———. *Human Development Report 1996*. New York: Oxford University Press, 1996.

———. *Human Development Report 2000*. New York: Oxford University Press, 2000.

———. *Human Development Report 2001*. New York: Oxford University Press, 2001.

———. *Human Development Report 2004*. New York: Oxford University Press, 2004.

———. *Human Development Report 2005*. New York: Oxford University Press, 2005.

UPTHEGROVE, TAYNA R., VINCENT J. ROSCIGNO, and CAMILLE ZUBRINSKY CHARLES. "Big Money Collegiate Sports: Racial Concentration, Contradictory Pressures, and Academic Performance." *Social Science Quarterly*. Vol. 80, No. 4 (December 1999):718–37.

URBAN INSTITUTE. "Nearly 3 out of 4 Young Children with Employed Mothers Are Regularly in Child Care." *Fast Facts on Welfare Policy*. April 28, 2004. [Online] Available July 18, 2005, at http://www.urban.org/UploadedPDF/900706.pdf

U.S. BUREAU OF ECONOMIC ANALYSIS. "Foreign Direct Investment in the United States: Selected Items by Detailed Country." [Online] Available October 18, 2005, at http://www.bea.doc.gov/bea/di/fdilongcty.htm

U.S. BUREAU OF JUSTICE STATISTICS. *Capital Punishment, 2003*. Washington, D.C.: U.S. Government Printing Office, 2004. [Online] Available June 5, 2005, at http://www.ojp.usdoj.gov/bjs/pub/pdf/cp03.pdf

———. *Criminal Victimization, 2003*. Washington, D.C.: U.S. Government Printing Office, 2004. [Online] Available October 14, 2005, at http://www.ojp.usdoj.gov/bjs/pub/pdf/cv03.pdf

———. *Criminal Victimization, 2004*. Washington, D.C.: U.S. Government Printing Office, 2005. [Online] Available October 13, 2005, at http://www.ojp.usdoj.gov/bjs/pub/pdf/cv04.pdf

———. "Family Violence Statistics: Including Statistics on Strangers and Acquaintances." Washington, D.C.: U.S. Government Printing Office, 2005.

———. *Prison and Jail Inmates at Midyear 2004*. April 2005. [Online] Available October 14, 2005, at http://www.ojp.usdoj.gov/bjs/pub/pdf/pjim04.pdf

———. *Sourcebook of Criminal Justice Statistics Online*. [Online] Available September 13, 2005, at http://www.albany.edu/sourcebook/

U.S. CENSUS BUREAU. *65+ in the United States*. Washington, D.C.: U.S. Government Printing Office, 1996.

———. "Census Bureau Counts 170,000 at Homeless Shelters." News release, October 31, 2000.

———. *Educational Attainment in the United States: March 2000* (Update). Current Population Reports, P20–536. Washington, D.C.: U.S. Government Printing Office, 2000.

———. *America's Families and Living Arrangements: 2000*. Current Population Reports, P20–537. Washington, D.C.: U.S. Government Printing Office, 2001. [Online] Available October 28, 2005, at http://www.census.gov/population/www/socdemo/hh-fam.htm/

———. *The Black Population: 2000*. Census 2000 Brief, C2KBR/01–5. Washington, D.C.: U.S. Government Printing Office, 2001. [Online] Available October 24, 2002, at http://www.census.gov/population/www/cen2000/briefs.html

———. *The Hispanic Population: 2000*. Census 2000 Brief, C2KBR/01–3. Washington, D.C.: U.S. Government Printing Office, 2001. [Online] Available October 24, 2002, at http://www.census.gov/population/www/cen2000/briefs.html

———. *Mapping Census 2000: The Geography of U.S. Diversity*. Census Special Reports, Series CENSR/01–1. Washington, D.C.: U.S. Government Printing Office, 2001.

———. *Money Income in the United States: 2000*. Current Population Reports, P60–213. Washington, D.C.: U.S. Government Printing Office, 2001.

———. *The Native Hawaiian and Other Pacific Islander Population: 2000*. Census 2000 Brief, C2KBR/01–14. Washington, D.C.: U.S. Government Printing Office, 2001. [Online] Available October 24, 2002, at http://www.census.gov/ population/www/cen2000/briefs.html

———. *Overview of Race and Hispanic Origin: 2000*. Census 2000 Brief, C2KBR/01–1. Washington, D.C.: U.S. Government Printing Office, 2001. [Online] Available October 24, 2002, at http://www.census.gov/population/www/ cen2000/briefs.html

———. *Population Change and Distribution: 1990 to 2000*. Census 2000 Brief, C2KBR/01–2. [Online] Available April 2001 at http://www.census.gov/population/www/cen2000/briefs.html

———. *Poverty in the United States: 2000*. Current Population Reports, P60–214. Washington, D.C.: U.S. Government Printing Office, 2001.

———. *The 65 Years and Over Population: 2000*. Census 2000 Brief, C2KBR/01–10. Washington, D.C.: U.S. Government Printing Office, 2001. [Online] Available October 24, 2002, at http://www.census.gov/population/www/cen2000/briefs.html

———. *The Two or More Races Population: 2000*. Census 2000 Brief, C2KBR/01–6. Washington, D.C.: U.S. Government Printing Office, 2001. [Online] Available October 24, 2002, at http://www.census.gov/population/www/cen2000/ briefs.html

———. *The White Population: 2000*. Census 2000 Brief, C2KBR/01–4. Washington, D.C.: U.S. Government Printing Office, 2001. [Online] Available October 24, 2002, at http://www.census.gov/population/www/cen2000/briefs.html

———. *The American Indian and Alaska Native Population: 2000*. Census 2000 Brief, C2KBR/01–15. Washington, D.C.: U.S. Government Printing Office, 2002. [Online] Available October 24, 2002, at http://www.census.gov/population/www/cen2000/briefs.html

———. *The Asian Population: 2000*. Census 2000 Brief, C2KBR/01–16. Washington, D.C.: U.S. Government Printing Office, 2002. [Online] Available October 24, 2002, at http://www.census.gov/population/www/cen2000/briefs.html

———. Historical Income Tables—People. Tables P-10, P-36. [Online] Available September 26, 2002, at http://www.census.gov/hhes/income/histinc/histinctb.html

———. *Custodial Mothers and Fathers and Their Child Support: 2001*. Current Population Reports, P60-225. October, 2003. [Online] Available October 28, 2005, at http://www.census.gov/hhes/www/childsupport/childsupport.html

———. *Fertility of American Women: June 2002*. Current Population Reports, P20-548. Washington, D.C.: U.S. Government Printing Office, 2003.

———. *Grandparents Living with Grandchildren: 2000*. Census 2000 Brief, C2KBR-31. Washington, D.C.: U.S. Government Printing Office, 2003.

———. *The Hispanic Population in the United States: March 2002*. Current Population Reports (P20–545). Washington, D.C.: U.S. Government Printing Office, 2003.

———. *Language Use and English-Speaking Ability: 2000.* Census 2000 Brief, C2KBR-29. Washington, D.C.: U.S. Government Printing Office, 2003.

———. *Married-Couple and Unmarried-Partner Households: 2000.* Washington, D.C.: U.S. Government Printing Office, 2003.

———. *America's Families and Living Arrangements: 2003.* Current Population Survey (P20-553). Washington, D.C.: U.S. Government Printing Office, 2004.

———. Census 2000 American Indian and Alaska Native Summary File (AIANSF). "(Table) DP-3. Profile of Selected Economic Characteristics, 2000." [Online] Available October 8, 2004, at http://factfinder.census.gov/

———. Census 2000 Summary File 3. "(Table) QT-P13. Ancestry, 2000." [Online] Available October 7, 2004, at http://factfinder.census.gov/

———. *Income, Poverty, and Health Insurance Coverage in the United States, 2003.* Current Population Reports (P60-226). Washington, D.C.: U.S. Government Printing Office, 2004.

———. *School Enrollment—Social and Economic Characteristics of Students: October 2002.* "(Table) 15." Rev. January 8, 2004. [Online] Available August 16, 2004, at http://www.census.gov/population/socdemo/school/cps2002.html

———. *Statistical Abstract of the United States: 2004–2005.* Washington, D.C.: U.S. Government Printing Office, 2004.

———. "(Table) 2a. Projected Population of the United States, by Age and Sex: 2000 to 2050." Rev. March 18, 2004. [Online] Available July 24, 2005, at http://www.census.gov/ipc/www/usinterimproj/natprojtab02a.pdf

———. "About Metropolitan and Micropolitan Statistical Areas." Rev. June 7, 2005. [Online] Available October 23, 2005, at http://www.census.gov/population/www/estimates/aboutmetro.html

———. *America's Families and Living Arrangements: 2004.* Detailed tables. Rev. June 29, 2005. [Online] Available October 21, 2005, at http://www.census.gov/population/www/socdemo/hh-fam/cps2004.html

———. Current Population Survey, 2005 Annual Social and Economic Supplement. "(Tables) FINC-01, FINC-02." Rev. June 24, 2005. [Online] Available October 14, 2005, at http://pubdb3.census.gov/macro/032005/faminc/toc.htm

———. Current Population Survey, 2005 Annual Social and Economic Supplement. "(Table) H101." Rev. July 19, 2005. [Online] Available October 23, 2005, at http://pubdb3.census.gov/macro/032005/health/toc.htm

———. Current Population Survey, 2005 Annual Social and Economic Supplement. "(Tables) PINC-01, PINC-03, PINC-05." Rev. May 5, 2005. [Online] Available September 13, 2005, at http://pubdb3.census.gov/macro/032005/perinc/toc.htm

———. Current Population Survey, 2005 Annual Social and Economic Supplement. "(Tables) POV01, POV06, POV14." Rev. June 10, 2005. [Online] Available September 15, 2005, at http://pubdb3.census.gov/macro/032005/pov/toc.htm

———. *Educational Attainment in the United States: 2004.* Detailed tables. Rev. March 27, 2005. [Online] Available October 21, 2005, at http://www.census.gov/population/www/socdemo/education/cps2004.html

———. Historical Income Tables—Families. "(Tables) F-1, F-2, F-3, F-6, F-23." Rev. June 22, 2005. [Online] Available September 14, 2005, at http://www.census.gov/hhes/www/income/histinc/incfamdet.html

———. Historical Income Tables—People. "(Tables) P-10, P-54." Rev. May 18, 2005. [Online] Available October 14, 2005, at http://www.census.gov/hhes/www/income/histinc/incpertoc.html

———. Historical Poverty Tables—Families. "(Table) 4." Rev. August 30, 2005. [Online] Available October 14, 2005, at http://www.census.gov/hhes/www/poverty/histpov/famindex.html

———. Historical Tables—Educational Attainment. "(Table) A-2." March 2005. [Online] Available October 27, 2005, at http://www.census.gov/population/socdemo/educ-attn.html

———. *Housing Vacancies and Homeownership.* (CPS/HVS). Annual Statistics: 2004. Table 20. Homeownership Rates by Race and Ethnicity of Householder: 1994 to 2004. Washington, D.C.: U.S. Government Printing Office, 2005.

———. *Income, Poverty, and Health Insurance Coverage in the United States: 2004.* Current Population Reports (P60-229). Washington, D.C.: U.S. Government Printing Office, 2005.

———. International Database. IDB Population Pyramids. April 26, 2005. [Online] Available October 23, 2005, at http://www.census.gov/ipc/www/idbpyr.html

———. National Population Estimates tables. Rev. January 28, 2005. [Online] Available October 27, 2005 at http://www.census.gov/popest/estimates.php,

http://www.census.gov/popest/national/asrh, and http://www.census.gov/popest/national/index.html

———. "Port St. Lucie, Florida, Is Fastest-Growing City, Census Bureau Says." Press release, June 30, 2005. [Online] Available October 23, 2005, at http://www.census.gov/Press-Release/www/releases/archives/population/005268.html

———. Voting and Registration in the Election of November 2004. "(Tables) 1, 2, 8." Rev. May 25, 2005. [Online] Available October 19, 2005, at http://www.census.gov/population/socdemo/voting/cps2004.html

U.S. CHARTER SCHOOLS. "About the Charter School Movement." [Online] Available October 21, 2005, at http://www.uscharterschools.org/pub/uscs_docs/o/movement.htm

U.S. CITIZENSHIP AND IMMIGRATION SERVICES. *2003 Yearbook of Immigration Statistics.* September 2004. [Online] Available October 19, 2005, at http://uscis.gov/graphics/shared/statistics/yearbook/2003/2003Yearbook.pdf

U.S. DEPARTMENT OF EDUCATION. *Evaluation of the Public Charter Schools Program: Final Report. 2004.* [Online] Available October 21, 2005, at http://www.ed.gov/rschstat/eval/choice/pcsp-final/finalreport.pdf

U.S. DEPARTMENT OF HEALTH AND HUMAN SERVICES. *Administration for Children and Families. Temporary Assistance for Needy Families (TANF) Program; Third Annual Report to Congress, August 2000.* Washington, D.C.: The Administration, 2000.

U.S. DEPARTMENT OF HOMELAND SECURITY. *2004 Yearbook of Immigration Statistics.* Rev. June 24, 2005. [Online] Available July 23, 2005, at http://uscis.gov/graphics/shared/statistics/yearbook/YrBk04Im.htm

U.S. DEPARTMENT OF HOUSING AND URBAN DEVELOPMENT. "The Forgotten Americans: Homelessness—Programs and the People They Serve." December 1999. [Online] Available October 4, 2004, at http://www.huduser.org/publications/homeless/homelessness/contents.html

U.S. DEPARTMENT OF JUSTICE. *The Sexual Victimization of College Women.* December 2000. [Online] Available October 17, 2005, at http://www.ncjrs.org/pdffiles1/nij/182369.pdf

U.S. DEPARTMENT OF LABOR. Bureau of Labor Statistics. *Employment and Earnings.* Vol. 52, No. 1 (January 2005). [Online] Available October 17, 2005, at http://www.bls.gov/cps

———. Bureau of Labor Statistics. *Women in the Labor Force: A Databook.* Report 985. Washington, D.C.: U.S. Government Printing Office, 2005.

U.S. DEPARTMENT OF STATE. "Remarks on Release of 'Country Reports on Terrorism' for 2004." Washington, D.C. (April 27, 2005). [Online] Available September 26, 2005, at http://www.state.gov/s/ct/rls/rm/45279.htm

U.S. ENVIRONMENTAL PROTECTION AGENCY. "Municipal Solid Waste." May 17, 2005. [Online] Available October 3, 2005, at http://www.epa.gov/msw/facts.htm

U.S. EQUAL EMPLOYMENT OPPORTUNITY COMMISSION. "Occupational Employment in Private Industry by Race/Ethnic Group/Sex, and by Industry, United States, 2003." Rev. May 9, 2005. [Online] Available July 7, 2005, at http://www.eeoc.gov/stats/jobpat/2003/national.html

U.S. FEDERAL INTERAGENCY FORUM ON AGING-RELATED STATISTICS. *Older Americans 2004: Key Indicators of Well Being.* Rev. July 13, 2005. [Online] Available October 1, 2005, at http://www.agingstats.gov/chartbook2004/healthstatus.html

U.S. SMALL BUSINESS ADMINISTRATION. *Minorities in Business, 2001.* 2001. [Online] Available October 28, 2005, at http://www.sba.gov/advo/research/minority.html

———. *Women in Business, 2001.* October 2001. [Online] Available October 28, 2005, at http://www.sba.gov/advo/research/women.html

VALDEZ, A. "In the Hood: Street Gangs Discover White-Collar Crime." *Police.* Vol. 21, No. 5 (May 1997):49–50, 56.

VALLAS, STEPHEN P., and JOHN P. BECK. "The Transformation of Work Revisited: The Limits of Flexibility in American Manufacturing." *Social Problems.* Vol. 43, No. 3 (August 1996):339–61.

VALOCCHI, STEVE. "The Emergence of the Integrationist Ideology in the Civil Rights Movement." *Social Problems.* Vol. 43, No. 1 (February 1996):116–30.

VAN BIEMA, DAVID. "Buddhism in America." *Time* (October 13, 1997):71–81.

———. "Spiriting Prayer into School." *Time* (April 27, 1998):38–41.

———. "A Surge of Teen Spirit." *Time* (May 31, 1999):58–59.

VANDIVERE, SHARON, et al. *Unsupervised Time: Factors Associated with Self-Care.* Washington, D.C.: Urban Institute, 2003. [Online] Available July 18, 2005, at http://www.urban.org/UploadedPDF/310894_OP71.pdf

VAN DYKE, NELLA, and SARAH A. SOULE. "Structural Social Change and the Mobilizing Effect of Threat: Explaining Levels of Patriot and Militia Organizing in the United States." *Social Problems.* Vol. 49, No. 4 (November 2002):497–520.

VEBLEN, THORSTEIN. *The Theory of the Leisure Class.* New York: New American Library, 1953; orig. 1899.

VEDDER, RICHARD, and LOWELL GALLAWAY. "Declining Black Employment." *Society.* Vol. 30, No. 5 (July/August 1993):56–63.

VINOVSKIS, MARIS A. "Have Social Historians Lost the Civil War? Some Preliminary Demographic Speculations." *Journal of American History.* Vol. 76, No. 1 (June 1989):34–58.

VOGEL, EZRA F. *The Four Little Dragons: The Spread of Industrialization in East Asia.* Cambridge, Mass.: Harvard University Press, 1991.

VOGEL, LISE. *Marxism and the Oppression of Women: Toward a Unitary Theory.* New Brunswick, N.J.: Rutgers University Press, 1983.

VOLD, GEORGE B., and THOMAS J. BERNARD. *Theoretical Criminology.* 3rd ed. New York: Oxford University Press, 1986.

VONNEGUT, KURT, JR. "Harrison Bergeron." In *Welcome to the Monkey House.* New York: Delacorte Press, 1968:7–13.

WAHL, JENNY B. "From Riches to Riches: Intergenerational Transfers and the Evidence from Estate Tax Returns." *Social Science Quarterly.* Vol. 84, No. 2 (June 2003):278–96.

WALDER, ANDREW G. "Career Mobility and the Communist Political Order." *American Sociological Review.* Vol. 60, No. 3 (June 1995):309–28.

WALDFOGEL, JANE. "The Effect of Children on Women's Wages." *American Sociological Review.* Vol. 62, No. 2 (April 1997):209–17.

WALDROP, JUDITH. "Live Long and Prosper." *American Demographics.* Vol. 14, No. 10 (October 1992):40–45.

WALKER, KAREN. "'Always There for Me': Friendship Patterns and Expectations among Middle- and Working-Class Men and Women." *Sociological Forum.* Vol. 10, No. 2 (June 1995):273–96.

WALL, THOMAS F. *Medical Ethics: Basic Moral Issues.* Washington, D.C.: University Press of America, 1980.

WALLERSTEIN, IMMANUEL. *The Modern World-System: Capitalist Agriculture and the Origins of the European World-Economy in the Sixteenth Century.* New York: Academic Press, 1974.

———. *The Capitalist World-Economy.* New York: Cambridge University Press, 1979.

———. "Crises: The World Economy, the Movements, and the Ideologies." In ALBERT BERGESEN, ed., *Crises in the World-System.* Beverly Hills, Calif.: Sage, 1983:21–36.

———. *The Politics of the World Economy: The States, the Movements, and the Civilizations.* Cambridge: Cambridge University Press, 1984.

WALLERSTEIN, JUDITH S., and SANDRA BLAKESLEE. *Second Chances: Men, Women, and Children a Decade after Divorce.* New York: Ticknor & Fields, 1989.

WALSH, MARY WILLIAMS. "No To Put Your Feet Up as Retirement Comes in Stages." *New York Times* (April 15, 2001):1, 18.

WALTON, JOHN, and CHARLES RAGIN. "Global and National Sources of Political Protest: Third World Responses to the Debt Crisis." *American Sociological Review.* Vol. 55, No. 6 (December 1990):876–90.

WARNER, W. LLOYD, and PAUL S. LUNT. *The Social Life of a Modern Community.* New Haven, Conn.: Yale University Press, 1941.

WARR, MARK, and CHRISTOPHER G. ELLISON. "Rethinking Social Reactions to Crime: Personal and Altruistic Fear in Family Households." *American Journal of Sociology.* Vol. 106, No. 3 (November 2000):551–78.

WATERS, MELISSA S., WILL CARRINGTON HEATH, and JOHN KEITH WATSON. "A Positive Model of the Determination of Religious Affiliation." *Social Science Quarterly.* Vol. 76, No. 1 (March 1995):105–23.

WATTS, DUNCAN J. "Networks, Dynamics, and the Small-World Phenomenon." *American Journal of Sociology.* Vol. 105, No. 2 (September 1999):493–527.

WEBER, ADNA FERRIN. *The Growth of Cities.* New York: Columbia University Press, 1963; orig. 1899.

WEBER, MAX. *The Protestant Ethic and the Spirit of Capitalism.* New York: Scribner, 1958; orig. 1904–05.

———. *Economy and Society: An Outline of Interpretive Sociology.* GUENTHER ROTH and CLAUS WITTICH, eds. Berkeley: University of California Press, 1978; orig. 1921.

WEBSTER, ANDREW. *Introduction to the Sociology of Development.* London: Macmillan, 1984.

WEEKS, JOHN R. "The Demography of Islamic Nations." *Population Bulletin.* Vol. 43, No. 4 (December 1988).

WEIDENBAUM, MURRAY. "The Evolving Corporate Board." *Society.* Vol. 32, No. 3 (March/April 1995):9–20.

WEINBERG, GEORGE. *Society and the Healthy Homosexual.* Garden City, N.Y.: Anchor Books, 1973.

WEISBERG, D. KELLY. *Children of the Night: A Study of Adolescent Prostitution.* Lexington, Mass.: Heath, 1985.

WEITZMAN, LENORE J. *The Divorce Revolution: The Unexpected Social and Economic Consequences for Women and Children in America.* New York: Free Press, 1985.

———. "The Economic Consequences of Divorce Are Still Unequal: Comment on Peterson." *American Sociological Review.* Vol. 61, No. 3 (June 1996):537–38.

WELLER, JACK M., and E. L. QUARANTELLI. "Neglected Characteristics of Collective Behavior." *American Journal of Sociology.* Vol. 79, No. 3 (November 1973):665–85.

WELLNER, ALISON STEIN. "Discovering Native America." *American Demographics.* Vol. 23, No. 8 (August 2001):21.

———. "The Power of the Purse." *American Demographics.* Vol. 24, No. 7 (January/February 2002):S3–S10.

WERTHEIMER, BARBARA MAYER. "The Factory Bell." In LINDA K. KERBER and JANE DE HART MATHEWS, eds., *Women's America: Refocusing the Past.* New York: Oxford University Press, 1982:130–40.

WESSELMAN, HANK. *Visionseeker: Shared Wisdom from the Place of Refuge.* Carlsbad, Calif.: Hay House, 2001.

WESTERN, BRUCE. "The Impact of Incarceration on Wage Mobility and Inequality." *American Sociological Review.* Vol. 67, No. 4 (August 2002):526–46.

WHALEN, JACK, and RICHARD FLACKS. *Beyond the Barricades: The Sixties Generation Grows Up.* Philadelphia: Temple University Press, 1989.

WHEELIS, ALLEN. *The Quest for Identity.* New York: Norton, 1958.

WHITAKER, MARK. "Ten Ways to Fight Terrorism." *Newsweek* (July 1, 1985): 26–29.

WHITE, JACK E. "I'm Just Who I Am." *Time* (May 5, 1997):32–36.

WHITE, RALPH, and RONALD LIPPITT. "Leader Behavior and Member Reaction in Three 'Social Climates.'" In DORWIN CARTWRIGHT and ALVIN ZANDER, eds., *Group Dynamics.* Evanston, Ill.: Row & Peterson, 1953:586–611.

WHITE, WALTER. *Rope and Faggot.* New York: Arno Press/New York Times, 1969; orig. 1929.

WHITMAN, DAVID. "Shattering Myths about the Homeless." *U.S. News & World Report* (March 20, 1989):26, 28.

WHORF, BENJAMIN LEE. "The Relation of Habitual Thought and Behavior to Language." In *Language, Thought, and Reality.* Cambridge, Mass.: Technology Press of MIT; New York: Wiley, 1956:134–59; orig. 1941.

WHYTE, WILLIAM FOOTE. *Street Corner Society.* 3rd ed. Chicago: University of Chicago Press, 1981; orig. 1943.

WICKHAM, DEWAYNE. "Homeless Receive Little Attention from Candidates." [Online] Accessed October 24, 2000, at http://www.usatoday.com/usatonline

WILCOX, CLYDE. "Race, Gender, and Support for Women in the Military." *Social Science Quarterly.* Vol. 73, No. 2 (June 1992):310–23.

WILDAVSKY, BEN. "Small World, Isn't It?" *U.S. News & World Report* (April 1, 2002):68.

WILES, P. J. D. *Economic Institutions Compared.* New York: Halsted Press, 1977.

WILKINSON, DORIS. "Transforming the Social Order: The Role of the University in Social Change." *Sociological Forum.* Vol. 9, No. 3 (September 1994): 325–41.

WILLIAMS, JOHNNY E. "Linking Beliefs to Collective Action: Politicized Religious Beliefs and the Civil Rights Movement." *Sociological Forum.* Vol. 17, No. 2 (June 2002):203–22.

WILLIAMS, PETER W. *America's Religions: From Their Origins to the Twenty-First Century.* Urbana: University of Illinois Press, 2002.

WILLIAMS, RHYS H., and N. J. DEMERATH III. "Religion and Political Process in an American City." *American Sociological Review.* Vol. 56, No. 4 (August 1991):417–31.

WILLIAMS, ROBIN M., JR. *American Society: A Sociological Interpretation.* 3rd ed. New York: Knopf, 1970.

WILLIAMSON, JEFFREY G., and PETER H. LINDERT. *American Inequality: A Macroeconomic History.* New York: Academic Press, 1980.

WILSON, BARBARA. "National Television Violence Study." Reported in JULIA DUIN, "Study Finds Cartoon Heroes Initiate Too Much Violence." *Washington Times* (April 17, 1998):A4.

WILSON, EDWARD O. "Biodiversity, Prosperity, and Value." In F. HERBERT BORMANN and STEPHEN R. KELLERT, eds., *Ecology, Economics, and Ethics: The Broken Circle.* New Haven, Conn.: Yale University Press, 1991:3–10.

WILSON, JAMES Q. "Crime, Race, and Values." *Society.* Vol. 30, No. 1 (November/December 1992):90–93.

WILSON, THOMAS C. "Urbanism and Tolerance: A Test of Some Hypotheses Drawn from Wirth and Stouffer." *American Sociological Review.* Vol. 50, No. 1 (February 1985):117–23.

———. "Urbanism and Unconventionality: The Case of Sexual Behavior." *Social Science Quarterly.* Vol. 76, No. 2 (June 1995):346–63.

WILSON, WILLIAM JULIUS. *The Declining Significance of Race.* Chicago: University of Chicago Press, 1978.

———. *When Work Disappears: The World of the New Urban Poor.* New York: Knopf, 1996a.

———. "Work." *New York Times Magazine* (August 18, 1996b):26 ff.

WINES, MICHAEL. "Democracy Has to Start Somewhere." *New York Times* (February 6, 2005). [Online] Available April 24, 2005, at http://www.research navigator.com

WINNICK, LOUIS. "America's 'Model Minority'." *Commentary.* Vol. 90, No. 2 (August 1990):22–29.

WINSHIP, CHRISTOPHER, and JENNY BERRIEN. "Boston Cops and Black Churches." *Public Interest.* No. 136 (Summer 1999):52–68.

WINTER, GREG. "Wider Gap Found between Wealthy and Poor Schools." *New York Times* (October 6, 2004). [Online] Available June 8, 2005, at http://www.researchnavigator.com

WINTERS, REBECCA. "Trouble for School Inc." *Time* (May 27, 2002):53.

WIRTH, LOUIS. "Urbanism as a Way of Life." *American Journal of Sociology.* Vol. 44, No. 1 (July 1938):1–24.

WITKIN, GORDON. "The Crime Bust." *U.S. News & World Report* (May 25, 1998):28–40.

WITT, G. EVANS. "Say What You Mean." *American Demographics.* Vol. 21, No. 2 (February 1999):23.

WITT, LOUISE. "Why We're Losing the War against Obesity." *American Demographics.* Vol. 25, No. 10 (January 2004):27–31.

WOLF, NAOMI. *The Beauty Myth: How Images of Beauty Are Used against Women.* New York: Morrow, 1990.

WOLFE, DAVID B. "Targeting the Mature Mind." *American Demographics.* Vol. 16, No. 3 (March 1994):32–36.

WOLFGANG, MARVIN E., ROBERT M. FIGLIO, and THORSTEN SELLIN. *Delinquency in a Birth Cohort.* Chicago: University of Chicago Press, 1972.

WOLFGANG, MARVIN E., TERRENCE P. THORNBERRY, and ROBERT M. FIGLIO. *From Boy to Man, from Delinquency to Crime.* Chicago: University of Chicago Press, 1987.

WONDERS, NANCY A., and RAYMOND MICHALOWSKI. "Bodies, Borders, and Sex Tourism in a Globalized World: A Tale of Two Cities—Amsterdam and Havana." *Social Problems.* Vol. 48, No. 4 (November 2001):545–71.

WONG, BUCK. "Need for Awareness: An Essay on Chinatown, San Francisco." In AMY TACHIKI et al., eds., *Roots: An Asian American Reader.* Los Angeles: UCLA Asian American Studies Center, 1971:265–73.

WOODWARD, KENNETH L. "Feminism and the Churches." *Newsweek* (February 13, 1989):58–61.

———. "Talking to God." *Newsweek* (January 6, 1992a):38–44.

———. "The Elite, and How to Avoid It." *Newsweek* (July 20, 1992b):55.

WORLD BANK. *World Development Report 1993.* New York: Oxford University Press, 1993.

———. *Entering the 21st Century: World Development Report 1999/2000.* New York: Oxford University Press, 2000.

———. *World Development Report 2000/2001.* Washington, D.C.: World Bank, 2001.

———. *2004 World Development Indicators.* Washington, D.C.: World Bank, 2004.

———. *2005 World Development Indicators.* Washington, D.C.: World Bank, 2005.

"WORLD DIVORCE RATES." [Online] Available October 21, 2005, at http://www.divorcereform.org/gul.html

WORLD VALUES SURVEY. "Latest Publications: Predict 2005—FIGURE." 2004. [Online] Available April 25, 2005, at http://www.worldvaluessurvey.com/library/index.html

WORSLEY, PETER. "Models of the World System." In MIKE FEATHERSTONE, ed., *Global Culture: Nationalism, Globalization, and Modernity.* Newbury Park, Calif.: Sage, 1990:83–95.

WREN, CHRISTOPHER S. "In Soweto-by-the-Sea, Misery Lives on as Apartheid Fades." *New York Times* (June 9, 1991):1, 7.

WRIGHT, JAMES D. "Address Unknown: Homelessness in Contemporary America." *Society.* Vol. 26, No. 6 (September/October 1989):45–53.

———. "Ten Essential Observations on Guns in America." *Society.* Vol. 32, No. 3 (March/April 1995):63–68.

WRIGHT, QUINCY. "Causes of War in the Atomic Age." In WILLIAM M. EVAN and STEPHEN HILGARTNER, eds., *The Arms Race and Nuclear War.* Englewood Cliffs, N.J.: Prentice Hall, 1987:7–10.

WRIGHT, RICHARD A. *In Defense of Prisons.* Westport, Conn.: Greenwood Press, 1994.

WRIGHT, ROBERT. "Sin in the Global Village." *Time* (October 19, 1998):130.

WRIGHT, STUART A., and ELIZABETH S. PIPER. "Families and Cults: Familial Factors Related to Youth Leaving or Remaining in Deviant Religious Groups." *Journal of Marriage and the Family.* Vol. 48, No. 1 (February 1986):15–25.

WU, LAWRENCE L. "Effects of Family Instability, Income, and Income Instability on the Risk of a Premarital Birth." *American Sociological Review.* Vol. 61, No. 3 (June 1996):386–406.

YANG, FENGGANG, and HELEN ROSE FUCHS EBAUGH. "Transformations in New Immigrant Religions and Their Global Implications." *American Sociological Review.* Vol. 66, No. 2 (April 2001):269–88.

YANKELOVICH, DANIEL. "How Changes in the Economy Are Reshaping American Values." In HENRY J. AARON, THOMAS E. MANN, and TIMOTHY TAYLOR, eds., *Values and Public Policy.* Washington, D.C.: Brookings Institution, 1994:20.

YATES, RONALD E. "Growing Old in Japan: They Ask Gods for a Way Out." *Philadelphia Inquirer* (August 14, 1986):3A.

YEATTS, DALE E. "Creating the High Performance Self-Managed Work Team: A Review of Theoretical Perspectives." Paper presented at the annual meeting of the Southwest Social Science Association, Dallas, February 1994.

YIN, SANDRA. "Wanted: One Million Nurses." *American Demographics.* Vol. 24, No. 8 (September 2002):63–65.

YOELS, WILLIAM C., and JEFFREY MICHAEL CLAIR. "Laughter in the Clinic: Humor in Social Organization." *Symbolic Interaction.* Vol. 18, No. 1 (1995):39–58.

YORK, RICHARD, EUGENE A. ROSA, and THOMAS DEITZ. "Bridging Environmental Science with Environmental Policy: Plasticity of Population, Affluence, and Technology." *Social Science Quarterly.* Vol. 83, No. 1 (March 2002):18–34.

YUDELMAN, MONTAGUE, and LAURA J. M. KEALY. "The Graying of Farmers." *Population Today.* Vol. 28, No. 4 (May/June, 2000):6.

ZAKARIA, FAREED. "How to Wage the Peace." *Newsweek* (April 21, 2003):38, 48.

ZALMAN, MARVIN, and STEVEN STACK. "The Relationship between Euthanasia and Suicide in the Netherlands: A Time-Series Analysis, 1950–1990." *Social Science Quarterly.* Vol. 77, No. 3 (September 1996):576–93.

ZHAO, DINGXIN. "Ecologies of Social Movements: Student Mobilization during the 1989 Prodemocracy Movement in Beijing." *American Journal of Sociology.* Vol. 103, No. 6 (May 1998):1493–1529.

ZHOU, XUEGUANG, and LIREN HOU. "Children of the Cultural Revolution: The State and the Life Course in the People's Republic of China." *American Sociological Review.* Vol. 64, No. 1 (February 1999):12–36.

ZICKLIN, G. "Rebiologizing Sexual Orientation: A Critique." Paper presented at the annual meeting of the Society for the Study of Social Problems, Pittsburgh, 1992.

ZIMBARDO, PHILIP G. "Pathology of Imprisonment." *Society.* Vol. 9, No. 1 (April 1972):4–8.

ZIPP, JOHN F. "The Impact of Social Structure on Mate Selection: An Empirical Evaluation of an Active-Learning Exercise." *Teaching Sociology.* Vol. 30, No. 2 (April 2002):174–84.

ZOGBY INTERNATIONAL. Poll reported in SANDRA YIN, "Race and Politics." *American Demographics.* Vol. 23, No. 8 (August 2001):11–13.

ZURCHER, LOUIS A., and DAVID A. SNOW. "Collective Behavior and Social Movements." In MORRIS ROSENBERG and RALPH H. TURNER, eds., *Social Psychology: Sociological Perspectives.* New York: Basic Books, 1981:447–82.

PHOTO CREDITS

Bettmann, 321 (left); Robert van der Hilst/Corbis/Bettmann, 321 (center); Robert van der Hilst/ Corbis/Bettmann, 321 (right); Robert van der Hilst/The Image Works, 322; Mark Edwards/Still Pictures/Peter Arnold, Inc., 325.

CHAPTER 13: Bob Daemmrich/The Image Works; 332 (left); Corbis Royalty Free, 332 (center); Joe Bator/Corbis/Bettmann, 332 (right); Gideon Mendel/Corbis/Bettmann, 333; Corbis/Bettmann, 334; Nancy Richmond/ The Image Works, 336; Angela Fisher/Carol Beckwith/Robert Estall Photo Agency, 337; CBS TV/Picture Desk, Inc./Kobal Collection, 340; Topham/The Image Works, 341; AP Wide World Photos, 344; David Grossman/The Image Works, 347; Kuenzig/laif/Aurora Photos, 349; Willinger/Hulton Archive/ Getty Images Inc.—Hulton Archive Photos, 351; HBO/Picture Desk, Inc./ Kobal Collection, 352.

CHAPTER 14: Marcia Keegan, Corbis/Bettmann, 360 (left); Carole Bellaiche/Corbis/Sygma 360 (center), Kevin Fleming/Corbis/Bettmann, 360 (right); David R. Frazier Photolibrary, Inc., 361; Bryant Mason, College Relations, Bronx Community College, 362; Joel Gordon/Joel Gordon Photography, 363 (top left); Leong Ka Tai, 363 (top center); Owen Franken/Corbis/ Bettmann, 363 (top right); Charles O'Rear/Corbis/Bettmann, 363 (bottom left); Paul W. Liebhardt, 363 (bottom center); Lisi Dennis/Lisl Dennis, 363 (bottom right); AP Wide World Photos, 364; Bob Daemmrich Photography, Inc., 367; Paul Conklin/PhotoEdit, 369; Western History Collections, University of Oklahoma Libraries, 373; Corbis/Bettmann, 378 (left); Culver Pictures, Inc., 378 (left center); Photographs and Prints Division, Schomburg Center for Research in Black Culture/The New York Public Library/Astor, Lenox and Tilden Foundations, 378 (right center); UPI/Corbis/Bettmann, 378 (right); A. Ramey/Woodfin Camp & Associates, 380; Warner Bros. TV/Amblin TV/ Picture Desk, Inc./Kobal Collection, 382; M. Lee Fatherree/Carmen Lomas Garza, 383; Carl D. Walsh/Aurora & Quanta Productions Inc., 386.

CHAPTER 15: Karen Kasmauski/Corbis/Bettmann, 392 (left); UN/DPI, 392 (center); AP Wide World Photos, 392 (right); Ariel Skelley/Corbis/ Bettmann, 393; David Young-Wolff/PhotoEdit, 394; Tom Wagner/Corbis/ SABA Press Photos, Inc., 396; Michael Newman/PhotoEdit, 398 (left); © John Garrett/Corbis, 398 (right); Laima Druskis/Pearson Education/PH College, 407; Chris Rainier/Corbis/Bettmann, 409; Spencer Grant/Stock Boston, 411; Merie W. Wallace/Warner Bros/Bureau L.A. Collections/Corbis/ Bettmann, 412.

CHAPTER 16: Jonathan Blair/Corbis/Bettmann, 416 (left); Beawiharta/ Reuters/Corbis/Bettmann, 416 (center); Jim Pickerell/The Stock Connection, 416 (right); Mark Wilson/Getty Images, Inc.—Liaison, 417; AP Wide World Photos, 418, AP Wide World Photos, 419; Underwood & Underwood/Library of Congress, 420; Sven-Olof Lindblad/Photo Researchers, Inc., 422; Bellavia/ REA/Corbis/SABA Press Photos, Inc., 425 (left); John Bryson/Corbis/Sygma, 425 (right); Alamy Images, 426; Gamma Press USA, Inc., 427; Chien-Chi Chang/Magnum Photos, Inc., 431; Matthew Borkoski/Index Stock Imagery, Inc., 433.

CHAPTER 17: Paul Fusco/Magnum Photos, Inc, 442 (left); Toby Talbot/AP Wide World Photos, 442 (center); Jason Reed/Reuters/Corbis/Reuters America LLC, 442 (right); William Thomas/Getty Images, 443; AP Wide World Photos, 444; Durand/SIPA Press, 446; David Ball/Index Stock Imagery, Inc., 449; Ramin Talaie/Corbis/Bettmann, 451 (left); Joel Gordon Photography, 451 (right); AP Wide World Photos, 457; AP Wide World Photos, 459; Joe McNally, Life Magazine © TimePix.

CHAPTER 18: Corbis Royalty Free, 468 (left, center); Owen Franken/ Corbis/Bettmann, 468 (right); TO COME, 469; Michael Newman/PhotoEdit, 470; Getty Images, 471 (left); AP Wide World Photos, 471 (right); John Terence Turner/Getty Images, Inc.—Taxi, 472; The Bridgeman Art Library International, 475; Paul Marcus/Studio SPM, Inc., 476; AP Wide World Photos, 478; The Cartoon Bank, 479; Mark J. Barrett/Creative Eye/MIRA.com, 486; Bill Bachmann/The Image Works, 488.

CHAPTER 19: Bojan Brecelj/Corbis/Bettmann, 496 (left); Mashkov Yuri/ITAR-TASS/Corbis/Bettmann, 496 (center) Friedrich Stark/Das Fotoarchiv/Peter Arnold, Inc., 496 (right); Jason Reed/Reuters/Corbis/ Reuters America LLC, 497; Michael Newman/PhotoEdit, 499; Galen Rowell/ Peter Arnold, Inc., 500; © David Rubinger/Bettmann/CORBIS All Rights Reserved, 502; © Doranne Jacobson/International Images, 504; Ian Berry/ Magnum Photos, Inc., 505; Annie Griffiths Belt/NGS Image Collection, 508;

AP Wide World Photos, 511; © Bettmann/CORBIS All rights reserved, 516; Philip North-Coombes/Getty Images Inc.—Stone Allstock, 517; © Gary Braasch/Bettmann/CORBIS All rights reserved, 521.

CHAPTER 20: Lynsey Addario/Corbis/Bettmann, 524 (left); UN/DPI, 524 (center); Louise Gubb/Corbis/SABA Press Photos, Inc., 524 (right); Paul Barton/Corbis/Bettmann, 525; © Andrew Holbrooke/Bettmann/CORBIS All rights reserved, 526; AP Wide World Photos, 527; Bob Daemmrich Photography, Inc., 531; Michael Newman/PhotoEdit, 532 (left); Getty Images, Inc., 532 (right); Lawrence Migdale/Pix, 539; AP Wide World Photos, 543; Bob Daemmrich Photography, Inc., 544; Kevin Virobik-Adams, Progressive Photo, 546.

CHAPTER 21: Gregory Primo Gottman, 550 (left); Richard T. Nowitz/Corbis/Bettmann (550 (center); Gideon Mendel/Corbis/Bettmann, 550 (right); AP Wide World Photos, 551; Martin Parr/Magnum Photos, Inc., 552; Steve Prezant/Corbis/Stock Market, 555; © Lucy Nicholson/Bettmann/CORBIS All Rights Reserved, 557; George Mulala/Peter Arnold, Inc., 560; Adalbert Franz Seligmann, *Allgemeines Krankenhaus* (General Hospital), 19th Century Painting, canvas. *Professor Theodor Billroth lectures at the General Hospital, Vienna. 1880.* Erich Lessing/Art Resource, NY, 563; Galen Rowell/Mountain Light Photography, Inc., 566; John Cancalosi/Stock Boston, 567; Billy E. Barnes/ PhotoEdit, 569; Al Diaz, 572; Steve Murez/Black Star, 574.

CHAPTER 22: Dinodia/The Image Works, 578 (left); Lester Lefkowitz/ Corbis/Bettmann, 578 (center); David Austen/Woodfin Camp & Associates, 578 (right); Wilfried Krecichwost/Zefa/Corbis Zefa Collection, 579; © Annie Griffiths/Bettmann/CORBIS All Rights Reserved, 580; AP Wide World Photos, 585; David and Peter Turnley/Corbis/Bettmann, 587; Lauren Goodsmith/ The Image Works, 588; Mario Tursi /Miramax /Dimension Films /The Kobal Collection, 590; Steve C. Wilson/Online USA, Inc./Getty Images Inc.— Hulton Archive Photos, 592; Christie's Images Inc., 593 (left); SuperStock, Inc., 593 (right); James King-Holmes/Science Photo Library/Photo Researchers, Inc., 597; Culver Pictures, Inc., 600; Dave Amit/Reuters/Landov LLC, 601; Eric Pasquier/Corbis/Sygma, 604.

CHAPTER 23: Bobby Yip/Retuers/Corbis/Reuters America LLC, 610 (left); A. Ramey/PhotoEdit, 610 (center); Fabrizio Bensch/Reuters/Corbis/Reuters America LLC, 610 (right); AP Wide World Photos, 611, 612, 613; © David Butow/Corbis SABA, 615; Sabina Dowell, 617; © Joel Gordon 2005—All rights reserved, 619; Rick Wilking/Reuters/Corbis/Bettmann, 620 (left); Al Grillo/Peter Arnold, Inc., 620 (center); AP Wide World Photos, 620 (right); CORBIS–NY, 621; AP Wide World Photos, 625; Corbis/Bettmann, 627 (left); Huynh Cong "Nick" Ut/AP Wide World Photos, 627 (right).

CHAPTER 24: Joe McDonald/Joe McDonald, 636 (left); Ed Kashi/Corbis/ Bettmann, 636 (center); B.S.P.I./Corbis/Bettmann, 636 (right); Robert Essel NYC/Corbis/Bettmann, 637; Culver Pictures, Inc., 638; China Images/Getty Images, Inc., 640; The Bridgeman Art Library International, 643; Whitney Museum of American Art, 644; Eric Draper/AP Wide World Photos, 648; Ed Pritchard/Getty Images Inc.—Stone Allstock, 651 (left); Mark Richards/ PhotoEdit, 651 (right); Mauri Rautkari/WWF UK (World Wide Fund For Nature), 652; Kelly-Mooney Photography/Corbis/Bettmann, 653; Paul Howell/Getty Images, Inc.—Liaison, 658.

Timeline: 1807: Getty Images Inc.—Hulton Archive Photos; 1829: Association of American Railroads; 1848: North Carolina Museum of History; 1876: Property of AT&T Archives, reprinted with permission of AT&T; 1886 (top): Irene Springer/Pearson Education/PH College; 1886 (bottom): "Coca-Cola" is a registered trademark of The Coca-Cola Company and is reproduced with kind permission from The Coca-Cola Company; 1893: Library of Congress; 1910: Tim Ridley © Dorling Kindersley; 1912: Wilton, Chris Alan/Getty Images Inc.—Image Bank; 1913: Library of Congress; 1921: Getty Images Inc.— Hulton Archive Photos; 1927: Corbis/Bettmann; 1931: Texas State Library and Archives Commission; 1945: U.S. Air Force; 1946: Photo courtesy of Unisys Corporation; 1947: © CORBIS/Bettmann; 1950: Corbis/Bettmann; 1952: © Dorling Kindersley; 1955: AP Wide World Photos; 1964: Getty Images Inc.—Hulton Archive Photos; 1969 (top): AP Wide World Photos; 1969 (bottom): NASA/Johnson Space Center; 1970: Jason Laure/Woodfin Camp & Associates; 1980: Laima Druskis/Pearson Education/PH College; 1981: Jan Butchofsky-Houser/AP Wide World Photos; 1987: John Serafin; 1990s: Gerald Lopez © Dorling Kindersley; 2000: Brady/Pearson Education/PH College.

NAME INDEX

SUBJECT INDEX

Affluence (*see* Wealth)
Africa (*see also* name of country)
  age at death, global median, 314, 315
  Aka, 93
  Bushmen, 93
  childbearing, 4
  child labor, 132, 133
  colonialism, 323–24
  family size, 4, 480
  female circumcision, 213, 348
  female genital mutilation, 348, 349
  genocide, 374
  high-income countries in, 308, 309
  HIV/AIDS in, 560, 561
  housework performed by women, 148
  income inequality, 273
  life expectancy in, 553, 582
  low-income countries in, 309, 310–12, 313
  marriage in, 473
  Masai, 65
  middle-income countries in, 309, 310, 313
  Pokot, 196
  population growth, 584
  Pygmies, 93
  servile forms of marriage, 317
  slavery, 317, 318
  Tuareg, 92, 94, 105
  water supply problems, 581, 601
  women, social status of, 337, 338
African Americans (*see also* Race; Racial discrimination; Racial segregation; Racism)
  affirmative action, 386–87
  affluent, 285
  arrest rates, 240
  civil rights movement, 379, 614, 624–25
  crime rates, 239–40
  demographics map, 384
  divorce and, 485
  education and, 372, 373, 379, 534–35
  family life, 483–84
  family size, 480n
  feminism and, 354–55
  Gullah community, 651, 652–53
  health and, 556
  HIV/AIDS and, 560
  income/income inequality and, 283–84, 285, 290–91, 346, 379, 483–84
  infant mortality rates, 582
  intelligence and racism, 370
  interracial marriage, 484–85
  Jim Crow laws, 379
  life expectancy and, 556
  lynching, 379, 614
  parenting, single, 484, 488
  parenting and role of grandmothers, 480
  political party identification and, 452
  poverty and, 294–95, 405, 556
  religion and, 513
  riots and, 614, 624–25
  self development in adolescents, 136
  sexually transmitted diseases and, 559
  slavery, 378–79
  social class and, 283–84
  in sports, 22–23
  stereotypes, 366

  suicide rates, 5
  unemployment and, 430
  voting participation and, 454
  voting rights, 379
  women, as head of household, 484
  women, working, 346, 427, 432
  women leaders, accomplished, 378
  work and, 427, 432
African American women *See* Women, African American
Afrocentrism, 78
Age
  bias and old, 135
  crime rates according to, 238
  at death, global median, 314, 315
  discrimination, 394
  life course stages, 133–37
  poverty and, 294
  stratification, 399
Ageism, 406
Age-sex pyramid, 583–84
Aggression. *See* Violence
Aging (*see also* Elderly)
  biological changes, 397–98
  cultural differences, 398–99
  death and dying, 135–37, 408–12
  psychological changes, 398
  social-conflict analysis, 408
  structural-functional analysis, 407
  symbolic-interaction analysis, 408
  transitions and challenges of, 401–6
Agrarian societies
  caste system, 256, 264
  descent patterns, 473
  description of, 95–96
  elderly in, 399
  employment, map, 423
  gender differences/roles, 336
  health in, 553
  population growth, 586
  religion and, 505
  social stratification and, 271
  status, 269
Agricultural revolution, 418–19
Agriculture
  corporate, 428
  decline of work in, 428
  defined, 95
  development of, 95–96
  employment, map of global, 423
  Green Revolution, 322
  modernization theory, 322
Aid for Dependent Children (AFDC), 299
AIDS (acquired immune deficiency syndrome) (*see* HIV/AIDS)
Air pollution, 602–3
Aka, 93
Albania, public display of religion, 224
Alcoholics Anonymous, 623
Alcoholism, deviance and medicalization of, 230
Algeria
  gross domestic product, 313
  as a middle-income country, 313
  quality of life, 313
Alienation
  bureaucratic, 179–80
  Marxist views on, 103
  rationality and, 108
  voter, 455
  Weber's views on, 108
  of workers, 103
Al-Jazeera, 461
Alterative social movements, 622, 624

American dream
  las colonias and, 311
  myth versus reality, 291–92
American Medical Association (AMA)
  formation of, 563
  television violence and, 131
American Psychiatric Association, homosexuality and, 206
American Revolution, 457
American Sociological Association, 12
  ethical guidelines, 40
Amish
  birth rates/family size, 581, 587
  identity and purpose, 74
  sects, 504
  self segregation, 373
  social experiences and, 650
  structural-functional analysis, 82, 83
  technology and, 105
  traditional work, 110
Amnesty International, 241, 450
Anal sex, HIV/AIDS and, 560
Ancestry, social class and, 283
Ancient era, early cities in Greece and Roman Empire, 589
Androcentricity, 39
Anglican Church, 503
Anglicans, 377
Animals, domestication of, 94–95
Animism, 505
Anomie, 110, 644
Anorexia nervosa, 557, 558
Anticipatory socialization, 130
Anti-Semitism, 509
Anti-Slavery International (ASI), 317
Apartheid, 256–57, 264
Apathy, voting, 454–55
Arabs (*see also* Islamic societies; Middle East)
  social distance and, 369
Arapesh, New Guinea, Mead's gender studies, 335–36
Argentina, as a high-income country, 308, 309
Arithmetic progression, 585
Arms race
  nuclear weapons, 461
  rationale for, 460–61
Arranged marriages, 256, 477, 478
Arrest, process of, 242–43
Artifacts, 73
Ascribed status, 145
Asexuality, 203
Asia (*see also* under name of country)
  age at death, global median, 314, 315
  agricultural employment, map of global, 423
  childbearing, 4
  child labor, 132, 133
  family size, 4, 480
  female genital mutilation, 348
  high-income countries in, 308, 309, 313
  HIV/AIDS in, 561
  housework performed by women, 148
  low-income countries in, 309, 310–12, 313
  middle-income countries in, 309, 310, 313
  population growth, 584
  service-sector employment, 423
  slavery in, 317

  smoking in, 557
  water supply problems, 581, 601
Asian Americans (*see also* Race; Racial discrimination; Racial segregation; Racism)
  achievements of, 380
  arrest rates, 240
  Chinese Americans, 380–81
  crime rates, 240
  demographics map, 384
  education and, 381
  fertility and, 581
  Filipinos, 383
  HIV/AIDS and, 560
  income of, 381
  intelligence and racism, 370
  interracial marriages, 484–85
  Japanese Americans, 381–82
  Korean Americans, 382–83
  model minority image, 380
  parental discipline and cultural differences, 76–77
  parenting, single, 484, 488–89
  political party identification and, 452
  poverty and, 294, 381
  self development in adolescents, 136
  sexually transmitted diseases and, 559
  social standing of, 381
  statistics on, 380
  stereotypes, 366
  women, as head of household, 484
  women, working, 432
  work and, 427, 432
Asian American women (*see* Women, Asian American)
Assemblies of God, 519
Assimilation
  defined, 373
  interracial marriages, 484–85
  Native Americans and, 373, 375
Athletes (*see* Sports)
Australia
  Aborigines, 93
  comparable worth, 343
  gross domestic product, 313
  as a high-income country, 308, 309, 313
  quality of life index, 313
  women, social status of, 337, 338
Authoritarianism, 448, 449
Authoritarian leadership, 170–71
Authoritarian personality theory, 371
Authority
  bureaucratic, 445
  charismatic, 445
  defined, 444
  patterns of, 473
  rational-legal, 445
  traditional, 444–45
Automobiles, modernization and, 643
Autonomy
  creative, 185
  Erikson's stage, 126
Average middle class, 286–87

Baby boomers
  as caregivers, 480
  premarital sex and, 201
  sandwich generation, 480
  sexual revolution and, 199
  time span of, 199, 583
Baby bust, 583
Bahrain, monarchy in, 446n, 448

Balkans, genocide, 374
Bangladesh
  education in, 527
  garment industry in, 306, 316
  gross domestic product, 313
  as a low-income country, 309, 311, 313
  modernization theory, 321
  quality of life, 313
Baptists, 506, 512
  social class and, 513
Barter system, 95
Batek, 93
Bay of Pigs, groupthink and, 172
B.C.E. (before common era), use of term, 13n
Beauty
  cultural differences, 73, 195
  eating disorders and, 557, 558
  myth and advertising, 341
Behavior (*see* Collective behavior; Mass behavior)
Behaviorism, 119
Belgium
  affection, display of, 196
  homosexual marriages, 489
Beliefs
  defined, 68
  deviance and, 231
  social control and, 231
  values and, 68–71
Bell cure, 274, 370
Bell Curve: Intelligence and Class Structure in American Life, The (Herrnstein and Murray), 274
Bias
  old age and, 135
  standardized testing and, 532
  television and, 131
Bible, 498
  fundamentalist view, 518
  portrayal of women, 502–3
Bilateral descent, 473
Bill of Rights, U.S.
  due process, 242
  individualism and, 450
Biodiversity, declining, 604–5
Biology
  aging and, 397–98
  deviance and, 223
  emotions and, 157
  human development and, 118–19
  sex determination, 194–95
  sexual orientation and, 204–5
Birth control
  map of global use of, 202
  oral contraceptives, 200
  statistics (global) on, 353
Birth rates
  childbearing, globally, 4
  crude, 580–81
  decline in U.S., 394, 470
Bisexuality, 203
  HIV/AIDS and, 560
Black Americans (*see* African Americans)
Black church, 513
Black Power, 379
Blasé urbanite, 594
Blended families, 487
Blue-collar occupations
  defined, 267
  self-employment, 430
Body language, 153, 154–55
Body mass index (BMI), calculating, 558

Bolivia
  gross domestic product, 313
  as a low-income country, 313
  quality of life, 313
Bosnia, genocide, 374
Botswana
  gross domestic product, 313
  HIV/AIDS in, 561
  as a middle-income country, 309, 310, 313
  quality of life, 313
Bourgeoisie, 589
Brazil
  crime in, 240
  economic inequality, 262
  gross domestic product, 313
  income inequality, 273
  Kaiapo, 651, 652–53
  as a middle-income country, 309, 310, 313
  quality of life, 313
  street children, 315
  Yąnomamö, 61, 63, 73, 74, 459
Britain
  class system, 258–60
  colonialism, 323
  comparable worth, 343
  economic inequality, 262
  education in, 529
  estate system, 258–59
  gross domestic product, 313
  high-income countries in, 313
  medicine in, 567, 568
  meritocracy, 258–60
  monarchy in, 446n
  quality of life, 313
  religion in, 503
  slavery issues, 317
Brown v. Board of Education of Topeka, 372
Buddhism, 509–10
Bulgaria
  market reforms, 427
  socialism, decline of, 427
Bulimia, 557, 558
Bureaucracy (*see also* Formal organizations; Organizations)
  alienation, 179–80
  authority, 445
  characteristics of, 107, 177–78
  defined, 108, 177
  democracy and, 446, 448
  inefficiency, 180
  inertia, 181
  informality of, 178–79
  organization environment, 178
  privacy issues, 186–87
  problems with, 179–81
  ritualism, 180
  in schools, 129, 538–39
  social movements and, 630
Bureau of Indian Affairs, 373
Burkina Faso, social status of women, 337, 338
Burundi, social status of women, 337, 338
Bushmen, 93
Busing, school, 534

Call girls, 208
Calvinism, capitalism and, 105–7, 501–2
Cambodia
  genocide, 374
  HIV/AIDS in, 561

Canada
  culture in, compared with the U.S., 86
  gross domestic product, 313
  as a high-income country, 308, 309, 313
  homosexual marriages, 489
  Kaska Indians, 93
  medicine in, 567, 568
  population growth, 584
  quality of life index, 313
  union membership, decline in, 429
Capitalism
  alienation of workers and, 103
  Calvinism and, 105–7, 501–2
  class conflict and, 102–3, 265–68
  compared to socialism, 426–27
  defined, 424
  democracy and freedom and, 448
  deviance and, 232
  features of, 424
  gender and, 352
  invisible hand, 424, 438
  Marx, views of, 101, 102–3, 265–68, 645–46
  medicine and, 566–68
  modernization and, 645–463
  Protestantism and, 105–7, 501–2
  rationality and, 105
  reasons there has been no overthrow, 267–68
  state, 426
  welfare, 425–26
Capitalists
  defined, 101
  Marxist definition, 284
  revolution, 645
Capital punishment
  global map, 241
  pros and cons of, 246–47
Career deviance, corporate crime, 233
Careers, in sociology, 11–12
Caregiving, 405–6, 480
Case studies, 47
Caste system, 255–57
Catholicism (Catholics)
  capitalism and, 107
  ethnicity and, 513
  Kennedy as first Irish Catholic president, 377
  practice of, 511–12
  Roman Empire and, 506
  social standing and, 513
Caucasoid, racial type, 363
Cause and effect, 34–35, 36
C.E. (common era), use of term, 13n
Central African Republic, income inequality, 273
Chad, as a low-income country, 309, 311
Change
  cultural, 79–81
  importance of, 39
Charisma, defined, 504
Charismatic authority, 445
Charter schools, 543
Chattel slavery, 317
Cheating, acceptance of, 228
Chicago School, urbanization and, 594
Chicanos (*see* Hispanic Americans)
Chief executive officers (CEOs), wealth of, 293
Child abuse, 488
Childbearing
  fertility, 580–81

global view of, 5
map on, 4
Childhood (*see* Children)
Child labor
  cultural differences, 80
  global, 132, 133, 321
  in India, 527
  map, 132
Children
  Aid for Dependent Children (AFDC), 299
  case studies of isolated, 120
  cognitive development, 122
  divorce and, 486–87
  effects of social class on, 289
  HIV/AIDS and, 560
  latchkey, 480
  life expectancy of U.S., 556
  moral development, 123
  mortality rates, 479, 581
  personality development, 121–22
  poverty and, 294, 295, 315, 484
  raising, 479–80, 481
  self development, 125–26
  sex education, 213
  slavery, 317
  socialization, 127–30, 133
  street, 315
  violence and, 488
  war and effects on, 121
  weddings in India, 478
Chile, as a middle-income country, 309, 310
China
  affection, display of, 196
  capital punishment in, 241
  communism in, 262
  Confucianism, 510–11
  cultural differences in, 66
  economic inequality, 263
  economy in, 263, 425
  gender equality in, 208
  Great Wall of China, 96
  gross domestic product, 313
  languages in, 67
  medicine in, 566
  as a middle-income country, 309, 310, 313
  modernity, 653
  quality of life, 313
  sex, regulation of, 197
  social stratification in, 263
  water supply problems, 601
Chinese Americans
  discrimination against, 380–81
  education and, 381
  ethnic villages, 373
  income of, 381
  parental discipline and cultural differences, 76–77
  poverty and, 294, 381
  social standing of, 381
Chinese language, 67
Christianity
  African Americans and, 513
  denominations, 503–4
  description of, 506
  global map, 507
  patriarchy, 502–3
Church (es)
  black, 513
  defined, 503
  electronic, 520
  state, 503
Church of England, 501, 503

Mexico
  age-sex pyramid, 583–84
  gross domestic product, 313
  as a middle-income country, 313
  modernization theory, 322, 652
  quality of life, 313
  water supply problems, 601
Micro-level orientation, 20
Microsoft Corp., 179
Middle Ages, 14
  absolute monarchs, 446
  children in, 133
  cities in, 589
  crime, as a sin, 244
  estate system, 258–59
  sexuality, control of, 213
Middle class, 286–87, 589
Middle East (*see also* under name of
    country)
  agrarian societies, 95–96
  female genital mutilation, 213
  high-income countries in, 308, 309
  HIV/AIDS in, 561
  income inequality, 273
  marriage in, 473
  middle-income countries in, 309,
    310, 313
  personal space, 155
  slavery, 317
  water supply problems, 601
Middle-income countries (*see also*
    name of country)
  age at death, global median, 314,
    315
  childbearing, map on, 4
  countries considered, 8, 309, 310
  defined, 7, 307, 310
  economic sectors, 421
  gross domestic product (GDP),
    309n, 313
  map of, 309
  per capital income, 310
  population figures, 310
  productivity of, 310
  quality of life index, 313
Middletown, 456
Midlife (*see* Adulthood)
Migration
  defined, 582
  forced/slavery, 582
  global, 82
  Great, in the U.S., 379
  internal, 582
  social change and, 641
Military
  -industrial complex, 461
  social class, 459–60
  women in, 345–46
Minorities (*see also* Ethnicity; Race)
  assimilation, 373, 375
  characteristics of, 365
  in cities, 595
  defined, 346, 365
  elderly as, 406–7
  genocide, 374, 629
  HIV/AIDS and, 560
  intersection theory, 346
  model minority image, 380
  national map of, 366
  pluralism, 372–73
  segregation, 373–74
  stereotypes, 366
  women as, 346
  workplace discrimination, 183
Miscegenation, 373
Mixed (interracial) marriages, 484–85

Mobility (*see* Social mobility)
Mobs, 614
Mode, 34
Model minority image, 380
Modernity
  affects on society, 110
  capitalism, Marx, 645–46, 648
  class society, 650–51
  defined, 641
  division of labor, Durkheim,
    643–44
  future for, 656–58
  globally, 652–55
  individualism and, 649–51
  loss of community, Tönnies,
    642–43
  mass society and, 646–48, 649–50
  post-, 654–56
  progress and, 651–52
  rationalization, Weber, 644–45
  social-conflict analysis, 648–49
  structural-functional analysis,
    646–48
  traditional societies versus, 647
Modernization
  characteristics of, 641–42
  defined, 641
  stages of, 320–22
Modernization theory
  compared to dependency theory,
    326
  culture and, 320–21
  defined, 319
  evaluation of, 323
  high-income countries and, 322–23
  historical, 319–20
  stages of, 320–22
Modesty, cultural differences, 197
Monarchy (monarchies)
  absolute, 446
  constitutional, 446
  countries that have, 446n
  defined, 446
Money (*see* Economy; Income)
Mongoloid, racial type, 363
Monogamy, 471
Monopolies, 435
Monotheism, 506
Moral development
  gender differences, 123–24
  Gilligan's theory, 123–24
  Kohlberg's theory, 123
Moral panic, 619
Moral reasoning, 123
Mores, 72
Mormons, 512, 517
Morocco
  beauty in, 195
  as a middle-income country, 309,
    310
  state religion, 503
Mortality rates
  children and, 479, 556, 581
  gender differences, 5
  infant, 556, 581, 582
  measuring, 581
  racial differences, 5
Multiculturalism
  assimilation, 373
  controversies over, 77–78
  defined, 64, 76–77
  in the U.S., 64
Multinational corporations (*see also*
    Corporations)
  defined, 319
  growth and control by, 422

neocolonialism and, 319
Mundugumor, New Guinea, Mead's
    gender studies, 335–36
Muslims (*see also* Arabs; Islam;
    Islamic societies)
  defined, 506
  social distance and, 369
Muslim women (*see* Women, Islamic)
Mutual assured destruction (MAD),
    461
Myanmar (Burma), beauty in, 195

NAACP (National Association for the
    Advancement of Colored People),
    19, 20
Namibia, as a middle-income country,
    309, 310
Nankani, 73
Nation
  defined, 64
  states, 446
National Rifle Association, 453
Nation at Risk, A (NCEE), 540–42
Native Americans
  animism and, 505
  assimilation, 373, 375
  citizenship for, 375
  cultural revival, 376
  descent patterns, 473
  education of, 375
  family life, 482–83
  gambling, 376
  gender differences/roles, 337
  genocide, 375
  HIV/AIDS and, 560
  incest taboo, 197
  income of, 375
  Indians, use of term, 375
  intersexual people and, 196
  land controlled by, map of, 374
  migration to North America, 375
  norms and, 71
  on reservations, 375, 482
  sexually transmitted diseases and,
    559
  use of term, 375
Natural disasters, 619
Natural environment (*see also*
    Environment)
  defined, 597
Natural selection, 84
Nature versus nurture, 118–19
Navajo
  incest taboo, 197, 475
  intersexual people and, 196
Nazis
  Holocaust, 374, 509
  mass-society theory, 625–26
Negroid, racial type, 363
Neocolonialism
  defined, 319
  poverty and, 319
Neolocality, 473
Netherlands
  euthanasia in, 410
  homosexual marriages, 489
Networks
  defined, 174
  gender differences, 175
  grapevines, 179
  Internet, 175, 176
  social groups and, 174–75
New Age religion, 515–17
New Guinea, Mead's gender studies,
    335–36

New social movements theory,
    628–29
New York City, changing
    neighborhoods, 376–77
New Zealand, as a high-income
    country, 308, 309
Nicaragua
  education in, 527
  quality of life, 323
Niger
  modernization theory, 321
  women, social status of, 337, 338
Nigeria
  affection, display of, 196
  beauty in, 195
  constraints put on women, 236
  female genital mutilation, 349
Nike Corp., 133
Nongovernmental organizations
    (NGOs), 450
Nonmaterial culture, 60
Nonverbal communication
  body language, 153, 154–55
  deception, spotting, 154
  defined, 153
  demeanor, 155
  eye contact, 153–54, 155–56
  facial expressions, 153, 154, 155,
    156
  gender differences, 155–56
  hand gestures, 154, 155
  personal space, 155
  social interaction and, 153–56
Normative organizations, 177
Norms
  defined, 71–72
  folkways and mores, 72
  social control and, 73
  superego, 121
  totalitarianism, 449
North American Free Trade
    Agreement (NAFTA), 327
North Korea
  nuclear weapons in, 461
  totalitarianism in, 449, 450
Norway
  gross domestic product, 313
  as a high-income country, 313
  quality of life index, 313
  women, social status of, 337, 338
Nuclear family, 471
Nuclear proliferation, 461
Nuclear weapons, 461
Nursing shortage, in U.S., 569–70
Nurture, nature versus, 118–19

Obesity
  causes of, 558
  defined, 557
  health effects, 558
  in the U.S., map of, 559
Objectivity
  defined, 36
  scientific, 36–37
Observation, participant, 47–49
Occupations (*see also*
    Work/workplace)
  prestige, 282, 283
  versus professions, 429
Old age (*see also* Elderly)
  dependency ratio, 395
Oligarchy, 181–82
Oligopoly, 435
One-parent families, 483, 484,
    488–89, 491

social class and, 512
Presentation of self, 151
Presidential election of 2004
　popular vote by county, map, 454
　rural-urban division, 453
Prestige, occupational, 282, 283
Pretesting, 44
Primary deviance, 229
Primary economic sectors, 421
Primary groups, 169–70
Primary labor market, 428
Primary sex characteristics, 195
Primates, Rhesus monkeys social
　isolation experiment, 120
Primogeniture, 259
Prisons
　community-based corrections
　　versus, 247
　increase in inmates, 244–45
　justification for, 243–46
　resocialization, 137–38
　Stanford County prison
　　experiment, 43, 52
　statistics on number of inmates, 245
　voting and criminals, 455
Privacy
　laws related to, 187
　surveillance methods, 186
　technology and erosion of, 186–87
Private schools, in the U.S., 533
Probation, 247
Profane, defined, 498
Professions
　characteristics of, 429
　defined, 429
　para-, 430
Profit
　capitalism and personal, 424
　medicine and, 572
　schooling for, 543–44
Progress
　modernity/social change and,
　　651–52
　U.S. value, 69
Progressive education, 530
Prohibition, 234
Projective labeling, 229
Proletarians, 101
Promise Keepers, 519
Propaganda, 618
Property crimes, 237
Property ownership
　capitalism and, 424
　collective, 424
　estate system, 258–59
　inheritance rules, 476
　socialism and, 424
Proselytizing, religious, 504
Prostitution
　defined, 207
　global, 207–8
　human trafficking, 318
　latent functions, 212
　legalized, 209
　types of, 208–9
　as a victimless crime, 209
Protestantism
　capitalism and, 105–7, 501–2
　denominations, 503
　fundamentalism, 517–19
　social class and, 512
　white Anglo-Saxon, 376–77
　women and, 503
　work ethic, 377
Protestant Reformation, 506
Psychoanalysis, 121

Psychological changes, aging and, 398
Psychosomatic disorders, 571
Public opinion, 618
Public policy, sociology and, 10–11
Public schools, in the U.S., 533
Puerto Ricans
　education and, 385
　income of, 385, 386
　poverty and, 385
　revolving door policy, 386
　social standing of, 385
　Spanish language, use of, 386
Puerto Rico, modernization theory,
　322
Punishment, for criminals, 243–47
*Puritan Boston and Quaker
　Philadelphia* (Baltzell), 49–51
Puritans, 225–26
Pygmies, 93
Pyramids of Giza, Egypt, 95, 96

Qualitative data, 38
Quality circles, work in Japan, 183–84
Quality of life
　elderly and, 399
　globally, 313
Quantitative data, 38
Queer theory, 214–15
Questionnaires, research, 44
Quid pro quo, sexual harassment and,
　350
Qur'an (Koran), 498, 502, 506–7

Race (*see also* Ethnicity)
　assimilation, 373
　categories/types, 363, 365
　-conflict approach, 19–20
　consciousness, 371
　crime and, 239–40
　defined, 362–63
　diversity map for the U.S., 128
　future issues, 388
　group dynamics and, 174
　hate crimes, 235
　income inequality and, 283–84, 285
　intelligence and, 370
　majority/minority patterns of
　　interaction, 372–74
　pluralism, 372–73
　poverty and, 294–95
　prejudice, 366–69
　religion and, 513
　riots, 614, 624–25
　social class and, 283–84
　socialization and, 128
　socially constructed, 362
　stereotypes, 366
　U.S. Census Bureau definition of, 33
Racial blends, 364
Racial differences
　feminism and, 354–55
　health and, 556
　physical traits and, 362–63
　political party identification and,
　　452
　suicide rates, 5
　television and, 340
　unemployment and, 430
　work and, 427, 432
Racial discrimination
　affirmative action, 386–87
　African Americans and, 378–80
　anti-Semitism, 509
　apartheid, 256–57

arrests and, 239
Asian Americans and, 380–83
civil rights movement, 379, 624–25
Dred Scott case, 378–79
Du Bois, work of, 19–20, 30n, 380
institutional, 372
Japanese Americans and, 381–82
Jim Crow laws, 379, 624
lynching, 379, 614
Native Americans and, 375–76
prejudice, 366–69
sports and, 22–23
successful African Americans and,
　45–47
in the U.S., 69, 183, 378–79
voting rights, 379
in the workplace, 183
Racial segregation
　apartheid, 256–57
　*Brown v. Board of Education of
　　Topeka*, 372
　civil rights movement, 379, 624–25
　de jure and *de facto*, 373
　history of, in the U.S., 373
　hyper-, 374
　Japanese American internment,
　　381–82
　in schools, 372, 534–35
　in U.S. cities, 373
Racism
　defined, 369, 371
　environmental, 605
　future issues, 388
　hate crimes, 235
　intelligence and, 370
　lynching, 379, 614
Radical feminism, 354
Rain forests, 603
Random sampling, 44
Rape
　date, 210
　defined, 210
　marital, 487–88
　of men, 210
　pornography and, 207
　statistics on, 209, 347
Rationality
　alienation and, 108
　bureaucracy and science and, 108
　defined, 105
　McDonaldization concept, 188
　modernization and, 644–45
　Weber and, 644–45
Rationalization of society, 104–8
Rational-legal authority, 445
Raves, 48
Real culture, 73
Reality
　language and, 68
　social construction of, 149–51
Recidivism, criminal, 246
Recycling, 600
Redemptive social movements,
　622–23, 624
Red tape, bureaucratic, 180
Reference groups, 172
Reformative social movements, 623,
　624
Reformatories, 245
Rehabilitation, of criminals, 244–45,
　246
Relative deprivation, 624
Relative opportunity, 226
Relative poverty, 294, 314–15
Reliability, 33–34
Religion (*see also* name of)

in agrarian societies, 96
basic concepts, 498–99
capitalism and, 105–7
civil, 515
in colonial America, 377
defined, 498
diversity across U.S., map, 514
East versus West, 511
electronic church, 520
ethnicity and, 513
functions of, 499–500
fundamentalism, 517–19
future for, 520
gender issues, 502–3
in history, 505–6
in horticultural societies, 95
in hunting and gathering societies,
　94, 95, 505
in industrial societies, 505–6
membership across U.S., map, 514
militants in the U.S., 79
New Age, 515–17
in pastoral societies, 95
patriarchy and, 502–3
postdenomination society, 515–16
in preindustrial societies, 505
race and, 513
science and, 521
secularization, 513–15
social change and, 501–2
social class and, 512–13
social-conflict analysis, 500
sociology and, 499
structural-functional analysis,
　499–500
symbolic-interaction analysis, 500
in the U.S., 511–13
Religiosity
　defined, 512
　globally, 512
　importance of, 512
Religious affiliation
　college students and, 515
　diversity across U.S., map, 514
　membership across U.S., map, 514
　racial/ethnic, 513
　social class and, 512–13
Religious organization, types of
　churches, 503–4
　cults, 504–5
　denominations, 503–4
　electronic church, 520
　sects, 504
　state church, 503
Remarriage, 487
Renaissance, 14
Replication, 37
Reproduction
　family and new technology, 492
　in vitro fertilization, 492
　sex determination, 194–95
　test tube babies, 492
Republican party, 452
Research (*see* Sociological
　investigation)
Research methods
　data, using existing, 49–51
　defined, 41
　experiments, 41–43
　participant observation, 47–49
　surveys, 43–47
Reservations, Native Americans
　on, 375
Residential patterns
　industrial societies and, 473
　preindustrial societies and, 473

scientific sociology, 33–38
statistics, use of, 34, 54–55
surveys, 43–47
tables, use of, 46
ten steps in, 53
Sociological perspective, 2–12
applications of, 10–12
crisis, 6
defined, 2
importance of, 6–9
marginality, 6
role of, 2–6
Sociological research (*see* Sociological
investigation)
Sociological theories (*see* Social-
conflict approach; Structural-
functional approach;
Symbolic-interaction approach)
Sociology
careers in, 11–12
critical, 39
defined, 2
first use of term, 13
interpretive, 38–39
origins of, 12–14
personal growth and, 11
public policy and, 10–11
religion and, 499
science and, 13–14
scientific, 33–38
social change and, 12–13
theory, 14–15
Solidarity
mechanical, 110, 593–94, 643
movement in Poland, 626
organic, 110–11, 593–94, 644
Solid waste, 599–600
Somalia
female genital mutilation, 348, 349
modernization theory, 321
South Africa
apartheid, 256–57, 264
beauty in, 195
caste system, 257
economic inequality, 262
as a high-income country, 308, 309
licensing of physicians, 564–65
South Korea
gross domestic product, 313
as a high-income country, 308, 309,
313
modernization theory, 322, 323
quality of life, 313
state capitalism, in, 426
Soviet Union (*see also* Russia)
collapse of communism, 262
genocide, 374
perestroika, 262, 626
socialism, decline of, 427
social stratification in, 261–63
Space, social interaction and personal,
155
Spain, homosexual marriages, 489
Spanish language, 67
Special-interest groups, 453–54, 618
Spiritual beliefs (*see* Religion)
Sports
conflict and, 22–23
functions of, 21
gender differences, 22, 334, 335, 339
interaction and, 23
racial discrimination and, 22–23
sociological approaches applied to,
21–23
Spurious correlation, 35
Sri Lanka, arranged marriages, 477

Stalking laws, 488
Standardized testing
bias in, 532
SAT scores, 541
Stanford County prison experiment,
43, 52
Staring, social interaction and,
155–56
Starvation
food as a weapon, 326
high-income nations, role of,
325–27
State capitalism, 426
State church, 503
Statistical measurements, 34
truth and, 54–55
Statue of Liberty, 375, 377
Status
ascribed and achieved, 145
consistency, 258
defined, 145
master, 145–46, 365
set, 145
STDs (*see* Sexually transmitted
diseases)
Steam engine, 419
Stereotypes, 24
defined, 366
minorities, 366
racial, 366
television and, 131
Stigma
defined, 229
labeling theory and, 229
Strain
role, 147
theory on deviance, Merton's, 226
Strategic defense initiative (SDI), 461
Stratification (*see* Social stratification)
Street children, 315
Street Corner Society (Whyte), 48–49
Street criminal, profile of, 237–40
Street gangs, 227
Street smarts, 149–50
Streetwalkers, 209
Stress, Type A personality, 337, 555
Structural-functional approach,
15–17, 22
aging and, 407
culture and, 82–83, 85
deviance and, 224–27, 234
education and, 538
family and, 474–75, 477
gender stratification and, 350,
351–52
health/medicine and, 570, 573
modernity and, 646–48
religion and, 499–500, 501
sexuality and, 211–12
social stratification and, 271
Structural social mobility, 262, 289
Structural-strain theory, 626, 629
Students (*see also* College students)
passivity, 538–39
Subcultures
conflict, 226–27
defined, 75–76
deviant, 226–28
retreatist, 227
Sublimation, 122
Sub-Saharan Africa, HIV/AIDS in,
561
Substance abuse (*see* Alcoholism;
Drug abuse)
Suburbs
defined, 591

growth and decline of, 591
Sudan
female genital mutilation, 348
quality of life, 323
Suicide rates
causes of, 109–10
Durkheim's study on, 5, 109–10,
644
map of, across the U.S., 14
modernization and, 644
racial and gender differences, 5
social isolation and, 16–17
Sunbelt cities, 591
Superego, 121
Supply and demand, capitalism and,
424
Surveys
defined, 43
of elite African Americans, 45
focus groups, 45
interviews, conducting, 45
population, 44
questionnaires, use of, 44
sampling, 44
self-administered, 44
victimization, 237
Survival of the fittest, 264
Sustainable culture, ecologically, 605
Swaziland, HIV/AIDS in, 561
Sweatshops, 306, 316, 317
Sweden
cohabitation, 489
economic inequality, 262
family life in, 472
gross domestic product, 313
as a high-income country, 313
medicine in, 566, 568
quality of life, 313
television ownership, 131
union membership, decline in,
429
welfare capitalism in, 425–26
women, social status of, 337, 338
Symbolic-interaction approach,
20–21, 22
aging and, 408
deviance and, 228–31, 234
education and, 538
family and, 476, 477
health/medicine and, 570–71, 573
religion and, 500, 501
sexuality and, 212–13
social stratification and, 271
Symbols
cultural differences, 65–66
cyber, 64, 65
defined, 64
language as, 66
Syphilis, 559
Syria
gross domestic product, 313
as a middle-income country, 313
quality of life, 313

Tables, use of research, 46
Taboos, 72
Tact, social interaction and, 156–57
Taiwan
languages in, 67
modernization theory, 323
Tchambuli, New Guinea, Mead's
gender studies, 336
Teachers
salaries across U.S., map, 533
shortage of, 545

Technology (*see also* Information
technology)
agrarian societies and, 95
culture and, 73–74
defined, 73
environment and effects of, 597–98
in industrial societies, 96–98
limitations of, 99–100
map of high, 106
modernization and, 643
poverty and, 318–19
privacy issues, 186–87
sexual revolution and, 200
social stratification and, 271–72
society and, 92–100
Teenagers (*see* Adolescence)
Telephone interviews, conducting, 45
Telephones, modernization and, 643
Television
bias and, 131, 340
gender differences on, 340
modernization and, 643
racial differences on, 340
statistics on, 131
violence and, 131–33
Temporary Assistance for Needy
Families (TANF), 299
Terminal illness, right-to-die debate,
410–11, 562
Terrorism (*see also* September 11,
2001 attacks)
characteristics of, 458
compared to conventional war, 460
defined, 458
effects of, on education in U.S., 530
religion and, 500
state, 458
as a type of war, 460
Tertiary economic sector, 422
Tests, standardized
bias in, 532
SAT scores, 541
Test tube babies, 492
Thailand
gross domestic product, 313
HIV/AIDS in, 561
as a middle-income country, 313,
321
modernization theory, 321
prostitution, 209
quality of life, 313
servile forms of marriage, 317
Thanatos (death instinct), 121
Theological stage, 14
Theoretical approach, 15
Theory
defined, 14
social-conflict approach, 17–20, 22
sociological, 14–15
structural-functional approach,
15–17, 22
symbolic-interaction approach,
20–21, 22
Third world countries (*see* Low-
income countries)
Thirteenth Amendment, 379
Thomas theorem, 150, 372, 531
Three worlds model, 307
Tibet
marriage in, 473
modernity, 653–55
Titanic, 254
Tobacco industry (*see* Smoking)
Togo, female genital mutilation, 349
Torah, 498, 508
Total institutions, 137, 245

in hunting and gathering societies, 93
matrilineal descent, 473
in the military, 345–36
as minorities, 346
political party identification and, 452
politics and, 344–45
population growth and role of, 588
poverty and, 295, 316
premarital sex, 201
prostitution, 207–9
religion and, 502–3
sexual revolution, 199–200
single-parenthood, 483, 484, 488–89, 491
as slaves, 317–18
social mobility and, 291
social movements and, 629
status of, globally, 336, 337
upper-upper class, 286
Women, African American
as head of household, 484
as leaders, 378
life expectancy and, 556
parenting and role of grandmothers, 480
work and, 346, 427, 432
Women, Asian American
as head of household, 484
work and, 261, 383, 427, 432
Women, Hispanic American/Latinos
as head of household, 483, 484
work and, 346, 427, 432
Women, Islamic
constraints put on, 235–36
female genital mutilation, 213
modesty, 197
Qur'an and portrayal of, 502
social standing of, 508
wearing of makeup banned, 224

Women, violence against
assaults, 347
date rape, 210
domestic violence, 487–88
elder abuse, 406
female genital mutilation, 213, 347, 348, 349
pornography as a cause, 207, 350
prostitution and, 209
rape, 209–10
rape, marital, 487–88
sexual harassment, 348, 350
Women, in the workplace
African American, 346, 427, 432
Asian American, 427, 432
discrimination, 183
earnings gap, 291
as entrepreneurs, 342
female advantage, 183
Filipino Americans, 383
gender inequality, 340–43
glass ceiling, 342
Hispanic American, 346, 427, 432
income inequality, 291, 342–44
Japanese, 261
in managerial positions, 183
mills, 420
occupations, 340–41
pink-collar jobs, 341
racial differences, 427
in secondary labor market, 428
self-employed, 430
statistics on, 340
whites, 427, 432
Women's movement, feminism, 353–55
Work/workplace (see also Women, in the workplace)
blue-collar, 267
changes in the nature of, 184–85, 427–28

child labor, 80, 132, 133, 321, 527
computers, effects of, 433, 434–35
debt bondage, 317
discrimination, 182–83, 291
diversity, 431, 432
division of labor, 111, 643–44
elderly and, 399
ethic, Protestant, 377
expressing emotions at, 158
factories, 419, 422
garment industry, in Bangladesh, 306
gender differences, 340–44, 431, 432, 427, 432
global economy and effects on U.S., 292–94
housework and, 147, 148, 342, 343
immigrants and, 367
income inequality, 291, 342–44
Industrial Revolution, 419–20
in industrial societies, 97–98
Information Revolution and, 432–33
Japanese, 183–84
job projections to 2010, 437
jobs with the highest concentrations of women, 342
lack of, and poverty, 296, 297
legal protections, 268
managerial positions in the U.S., 183
mills, 420
pink-collar jobs, 341
in postindustrial economy, 421, 427–37
professions, 429–30
projections of, to 2010, map of, 437
prostitution as, 208–9
Protestant work ethic, 377
racial differences, 427, 432
scientific management, 182

self-employment, 430
service, 428
social class and, 282, 283
teams, 185
technology and, 432–33
unemployment, 430
unions, 268, 428
U.S. value, 69
white-collar, 267
Workforce
capitalism and alienation of, 103
diversity, 431, 432
Working class
blue-collar, 267
defined, 287
marriages, 289
Working poor, 287, 296, 298
WorldCom, 431
World economy, Wallerstein's capitalist, 324–25
World Trade Center (see September 11, 2001 attacks)
World War II
Japanese American internment, 382
reference group study, 172

Xenophobia, 388

Yąnomamö, 61, 63, 73, 74, 459
Yugoslavia
cultural conflict in, 75–76
genocide, 620

Zambia, economic inequality, 262
Zero population growth, 587
Zimbabwe, education in, 527

Want to get a better grade?

"Making the Grade" End-of-Chapter Review

The end-of-chapter material will help you make the best use of your textbook as a study tool and help you to be more successful in your course. The review material at the end of every chapter will help you focus on important concepts. It also gives you actual practice with sample test questions and applications and exercises, all written by John Macionis, to help test your knowledge.

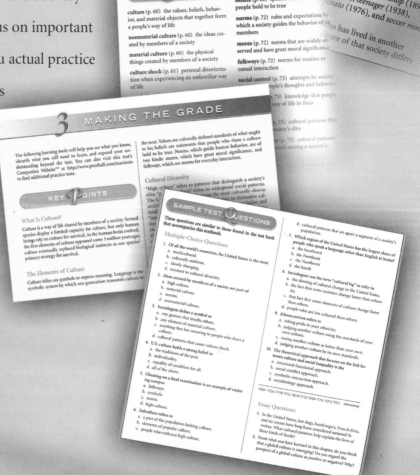